W9-AFC-057

The Presidents Fact Book

The Presidents Fact Book

The Achievements, Campaigns, Events, Triumphs, and
Legacies of Every President

Roger Matuz
Revised and Updated by Bill Harris &
Thomas J. Craughwell

BLACK DOG
& LEVENTHAL
PUBLISHERS
NEW YORK

Copyright © 2004, 2009, 2017, 2021 by Black Dog & Leventhal Publishers, Inc.
Adapted by permission from *Complete American Presidents Sourcebook, Volumes 1–5,* Copyright © 2001 by U•X•L, an imprint of The Gale Group.

Cover design by Carlos Esparza
Cover photograph © The Granger Collection (left) and
Official White House / David Lienemann (right)
Cover copyright © 2021 by Hachette Book Group, Inc.

Hachette Book Group supports the right to free expression and the value of copyright. The purpose of copyright is to encourage writers and artists to produce the creative works that enrich our culture.

The scanning, uploading, and distribution of this book without permission is a theft of the author's intellectual property. If you would like permission to use material from the book (other than for review purposes), please contact permissions@hbgusa.com. Thank you for your support of the author's rights.

Black Dog & Leventhal Publishers
Hachette Book Group
1290 Avenue of the Americas
New York, NY 10104

www.hachettebookgroup.com
www.blackdogandleventhal.com

First Revised Paperback Edition: January 2017
Second Revised Paperback Edition: September 2021

Black Dog & Leventhal Publishers is an imprint of Perseus Books, LLC, a division of Hachette Book Group. The Black Dog & Leventhal Publishers name and logo are trademarks of Hachette Book Group, Inc.

The Hachette Speakers Bureau provides a wide range of authors for speaking events. To find out more, go to www.HachetteSpeakersBureau.com or call (866) 376-6591.

Additional photo credits information is on page 835.

Print book interior design by Scot Covey

Library of Congress Control Number: 2021933993

ISBNs: 978-0-7624-7844-6 (paperback); 978-0-7624-7845-3 (e-book)

Printed in United States of America

LSC

Printing 1, 2021

Table of Contents

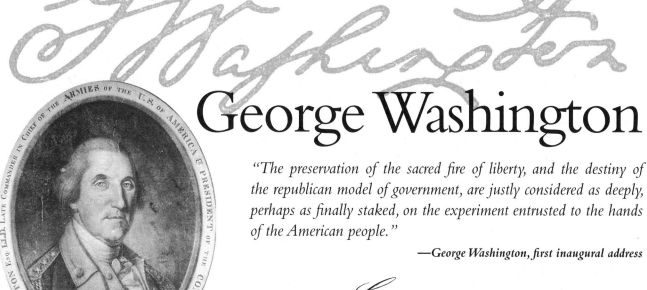

George Washington

"The preservation of the sacred fire of liberty, and the destiny of the republican model of government, are justly considered as deeply, perhaps as finally staked, on the experiment entrusted to the hands of the American people."

—*George Washington, first inaugural address*

First president of the United States, 1789–1797

Full name: *George Washington*

Born: *February 22, 1732, Westmoreland County, Virginia*

Died: *December 14, 1799, Mount Vernon, Virginia*

Burial site: *Washington burial vault, Mount Vernon, Virginia*

Parents: *Augustine and Mary Ball Washington*

Spouse: *Martha Dandridge Custis (1732–1802; m. 1759)*

Children: *John Custis (1754–81), Martha Custis (1755–73) (stepchildren)*

Religion: *Episcopalian*

Education: *Home-schooled*

Occupation: *Surveyor, planter, general*

Government positions: *Virginia House of Burgesses, member; Continental Congress, representative; Constitutional Convention, chairman*

Political party: *Federalist*

Dates as president: *April 30, 1789–March 4, 1793 (first term); March 4, 1793–March 4, 1797 (second term)*

Age upon taking office: *57*

George Washington is called "the father of his country" for several reasons. He was an outspoken early proponent of American independence from Great Britain. He commanded the American Continental Army in its long and ultimately successful struggle in the Revolutionary War (1775-83), and after the war, Washington presided over the Constitutional Convention (1787), which established the country's representative form of government. As the first president of the United States, Washington proved by example that the American system could work by creating a model of how the presidency should function.

The young nation's unity was threatened by political differences, and Washington served a second term as president to keep the increasingly divided nation together. During that second term, he avoided a war with Great Britain that could have slowed the nation's progress, and when he left office, the peaceful transition to another elected president proved that the American system of government was sound.

Many myths about him suggest that George Washington was a man with almost superhuman virtues, but among the realities, according to some historians, was that he had a quick temper, which they claim led to several questionable decisions as a military leader.

Some also say that his dealings with Great Britain as America's chief executive were often too lenient. His contemporaries also mistook his dignified reserve as a sign of pomposity.

However, these human flaws are balanced by Washington's positive qualities, which included sound decision-making. He understood the concerns of the American people, and he held firm to his beliefs, both as a general and as president. These qualities led his fellow Virginian, Henry Lee, to remark at the time of the president's death that George Washington had been "first in war, first in peace, and first in the hearts of his countrymen." Washington was first in the hearts of other as well. England's King William IV, the son of Washington's old adversary, George III, called him "the greatest man who ever lived."

Close to the Land

George Washington was born on February 22, 1732, in Westmoreland County, Virginia, on his father Augustine's farm, Wakefield. Augustine had two sons and a daughter before becoming a widower; his second wife, Mary Ball Washington, gave birth to six more children, including George. The family moved to nearby Ferry Farm in 1738, where Augustine Washington died five years later, when George was eleven.

Birthday Celebrations

Although we mark Washington's birthday with President's Day, a Monday in February, for many years the celebration took place on February 22, and Washington himself celebrated on February 11. Washington was born on the eleventh under the "Old Style," or Julian, calendar, which was replaced by royal decree in England and her colonies with the Gregorian, or "New Style" calendar on April 5, 1751, when Washington was twenty years old. In order to convert from the Julian to the Gregorian, ten days were dropped from September 1752. (So a person going to bed on September 2, say at 11:00 P.M., and sleeping eight hours would wake up at 7:00 A.M. to find it was September 13, not September 3.) Dropping those ten days from a year moved everybody's birthday, including Washington's—why his birthday was celebrated on February 22 instead of February 11. But Washington was an old-fashioned guy, and he stuck with the old date all his life.

Timeline

1732: Born in Virginia
1759–74: Serves as member of the Virginia House of Burgesses
1775: Unanimously elected by the Continental Congress to command the Continental Army
1787: Serves as chairman of the Constitutional Convention
1789–97: Serves as first U.S. president
1793: Declares American neutrality when war breaks out between Britain and France
1794: Calls federal troops to suppress armed insurgence in Western Pennsylvania, the Whiskey Rebellion
1799: Dies in Virginia

Young George was schooled primarily at home because his mother didn't want to send him to England for his education, as was customary at the time. He was especially interested in mathematics, and that prompted him to learn the art of land surveying.

Washington was close to his older half-brother, Lawrence, who was married to Anne Fairfax, a daughter of a wealthy and distinguished Virginia family. When he was sixteen, George accompanied Anne's brother, George Fairfax, to measure and map the family's land holdings in western Virginia, across the Blue Ridge Mountains and into the Shenandoah Valley. A year later, because of

Below: Washington's survey of the Fairfax holdings.

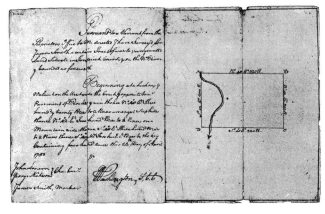

his success with that assignment, he became the official surveyor of Culpeper County, Virginia.

By then, at the age of seventeen, Washington was growing into a large man, eventually weighing 175 pounds in his prime. As an adult he stood six-foot-two and wore size thirteen shoes. Always fashionably dressed, he was erect in bearing, muscular, and broad-shouldered. He had a long, high-cheekboned face with a large straight nose and a determined chin. His blue-gray eyes were set under heavy brows, and he frequently powdered his dark brown hair, tying it back in a queue. He lost all but one of his teeth, and wore dentures, which were frequently replaced. They were generally made of human teeth or those of animals, sometimes of ivory and sometimes lead, but never did George Washington wear wooden false teeth, as is popularly believed.

In 1751, Washington accompanied Lawrence to the Caribbean island of Barbados. Lawrence was suffering from tuberculosis and hoped that the warmer climate would help improve his health, although he died the following year. In the meantime, Washington contracted a mild case of smallpox, which left him with permanent scars on his face. However, his bout with smallpox gave him immunity to the disease—likely saving him later during the Revolutionary War, when many of his men were afflicted with smallpox under rough conditions.

After he returned to Virginia from Barbados, Washington inherited the family estate of Mount Vernon from his late half-brother. It would be his home for the rest of his life. He was also appointed to Lawrence's former post as an officer in the Virginia militia, which made him responsible for enlisting, inspecting, and commanding troops.

In 1753, Virginia's royal governor, Robert Dinwiddie, dispatched Washington on a 300-mile journey to the Ohio River Valley to present demands from King George II of England to the French authorities. The king ordered the French soldiers to stop building a fort (Fort La Boeuf) in English territory. But the French officers rejected it, and Washington trudged back home through miserable winter conditions, memorizing details of the landscape along the way. When he got back to Virginia, he delivered a map pointing to a strategic location where the British might build a fort of their own.

Military Ambitions Thwarted

Washington was commissioned as a lieutenant colonel in 1754. His idea for a new fort was approved, and he followed the builders to the site, which is where Pittsburgh's Three Rivers Stadium stands today. When he arrived, Washington found the builders scattered. Instead, the French were at work constructing a stronghold of their own, which they called Fort Duquesne. Washington led an attack on it, killing ten French soldiers and their commander, Ensign Joseph Coulon de Villiers.

Washington built a stockade nearby, which he called Fort Necessity, and waited for reinforcements. Before they arrived, though, his own troops were overcome, and Colonel Washington was forced to surrender. The terms were lenient, but the document that made the surrender official was written in French. Washington, who didn't speak the language, had no idea that by signing it he was confessing to the assassination of Ensign Coulon.

Left: The taking of Fort Necessity was a setback in Washington's early military career.

The skirmish, which seemed insignificant, coupled with Washington's "confession," which wasn't, gave the French an excuse to brand Washington and the British troops he led as aggressors. This, in turn, contributed to the start of the French and Indian War, which raged on the frontier from 1754 to 1763 between British and French forces and their respective Native American allies.

Washington received a hero's welcome when he got back to Williamsburg, the capital of Virginia. He expected that his performance would earn him a command position, but the British military had a policy that only men born in Great Britain could lead their troops. This, Washington decided, was another example of British arrogance toward the colonists, and it kindled his passion for American independence.

In 1755, Washington was appointed aide to the British general Edward Braddock, who was to lead thirteen hundred men in an attack on Fort Duquesne. The attack was a failure: British soldiers fought in their conventional manner—in the open and in succeeding lines—while the French and Indian fighters were scattered and used the dense woods to their advantage. Washington and a group of colonial soldiers held their ground, but they were forced to join the British retreat. The French and Indian tactics of using the natural environment would later serve Washington well in the Revolutionary War.

After Braddock's defeat, Washington was made a colonel of the colonial troops, and for the next few years, his assignment was to guard Virginia's three-hundred-mile frontier from attack by the French. The attacks never came, but in 1758 he joined the British regiment that recaptured Fort Duquesne, after which he resigned his commission.

Gentleman Farmer

On January 6, 1759, Washington married Martha Dandridge Custis, a wealthy widow with two children, whom he affectionately called "Patsy." Martha had a home in Williamsburg and seventeen thousand acres of farmland to add to his five thousand adjacent acres at Mount Vernon. Washington's expanded holdings allowed him to become a substantial planter, and the "Old Man," as Patsy called him (although she was a year older), settled into the life of a gentleman farmer, experimenting with new agricultural methods and equipment. He lost money growing tobacco, and he was convinced that it was because British sales agents were cheating him. He

Parlez-vous . . .

Because he didn't have a university education, Washington was one of the very few "founding fathers" who didn't speak French, which was considered to be the language of diplomacy in the eighteenth century.

Right: The French and Indian War gave young Washington valuable experience in military tactics.

Above: As a gentleman farmer, Washington branched out with other activities, including a profitable mill.

turned to other crops, particularly wheat, and built a mill, fisheries, ironworks, and even a brewery.

Washington's anti-British sentiments deepened in the years between 1759 and 1774, when he was a member of the Virginia legislature, the House of Burgesses. Other colonists were joining with him, especially in protesting what they regarded as unfair taxation, beginning with the 1765 Stamp Act, which required the purchase of stamps to make documents legal. The taxes on imported goods included one on tea, which led Massachusetts patriots to dump cargoes of it into Boston harbor in 1773 (an act that came to be known as the "Boston Tea Party").

When Virginia's House of Burgesses seemed to be growing increasingly rebellious, the British authorities dissolved it. Washington made his burgeoning anti-British activism clear in a secret meeting of former burgesses at Williamsburg's Raleigh Tavern. The former legislators, including Washington and Thomas Jefferson, voted to express sympathy for Massachusetts in its refusal to pay the onerous taxes imposed by the British. Washington was later chosen as Virginia's representative to the First Continental Congress when it convened with delegates from all thirteen colonies at Philadelphia in 1774.

A year later, after assuming command of five Virginia militia units, Washington was chosen as a delegate to the Second Continental Congress, and he arrived in Philadelphia in full military dress. The colors of the Fairfax Militia, blue and beige, were adopted for the Continental Army, and in June 1775, George Washington was appointed its commander in chief.

The Long Fight for Independence

The Continental Army was made up of all the local and state militias representing the solidarity of all the colonies against Great Britain. It was also augmented by volunteers eager to join the American cause.

The Revolutionary War had already begun when Washington assumed command. On April 18, 1775, a unit of the Massachusetts militia—who called themselves "Minutemen," because they could be ready to fight at a moment's notice—routed a 700-man British force at Concord Bridge, about twenty miles west of Boston. The British had hoped to seize a cache of guns and ammunition, but went back to Boston empty-handed. The British were met there by more Minutemen, who kept them under siege.

General Washington took command of the American forces at Cambridge, Massachusetts, on July 2. While continuing to lay siege to Boston, he concentrated

Right: The Boston Tea Party was one of the first anti-British demonstrations that led to a full rebellion.

on training and organizing his army of about thirteen thousand men. Armed with cannons captured from a British fort at Ticonderoga on Lake Champlain, Washington's forces occupied a hill outside of Boston and threatened to attack the city itself. In March 1776, 11,000 British troops under General William Howe evacuated Boston by ship, and sailed to Halifax, Nova Scotia.

As Washington continued to organize his troops, Howe's army landed in New York at the end of June to begin fighting in earnest. Howe's well-equipped force consisted of 32,000 soldiers, including 8,000 German mercenaries, professional soldiers known as Hessians because most of them came from the Hesse-Kassel and Hesse-Hanau regions of Germany. In the battles that followed, Washington's men were forced into a series of demoralizing defeats—from Brooklyn to Manhattan and then across New Jersey. Washington led his forces across into Pennsylvania in early December and appeared to be settling in for the winter. The enemy retreated to Manhattan, leaving several outposts in New Jersey, which were manned by some 12,000 Hessians.

The war hadn't been going well for the Continental Army, and Washington himself said, "I think the game is pretty much up." But he made a bold move that not only won back some ground but cheered his weary troops. On Christmas night in 1776, Washington led his men back across the icy Delaware River, where they overwhelmed

Below: In a bold move, Washington crossed the Delaware River to attack the enemy at Trenton on Christmas night in 1776.

the surprised Hessian garrison at Trenton, New Jersey. Moving north, Washington's army routed three enemy units at Princeton on January 3. Then Washington established a camp at Morristown, New Jersey, and began rebuilding his forces.

Washington had made it a point to avoid any all-out battles with the British. He preferred smaller engagements, all the while looking for an edge that would give the Americans the advantage, but gaining such an edge would take time. In August 1777, Washington's army failed to stop a British advance on Philadelphia at the Battle of Brandywine Creek; two months later it was forced to withdraw again after attacking Howe's forces at Germantown. With those bitter defeats haunting them, Washington's 11,000 men retreated to Valley Forge, Pennsylvania, where they barely survived the frigid winter of 1777-78.

Meanwhile, the performance of the Continental Army had made an impression on Great Britain's other enemies. Early in 1778, Washington received secret messages from Benjamin Franklin, the American minister

Fruits of Defeat

After the British took Philadelphia, Congress was forced to relocate, and many Congressmen blamed it all on Washington. A bill was introduced to have the general replaced by what they considered a better candidate for commander in chief in the person of General Horatio Gates, who had defeated the British under General John Burgoyne at the Battle of Saratoga that fall. However, Washington had more friends than enemies in the Congress, and this saved his job.

to France, informing him that the French were ready to recognize the independence of the colonies; to sign a treaty of commerce and alliance; and to supply arms, clothing, money, and a French fleet.

Washington also learned from British sources that London was growing tired of the war, and he began to hope for a major triumph that might break the weakened British resolve. Still, the battles dragged on into 1781 before he finally found the opportunity for which he had been looking.

Twenty-nine French ships were sailing toward Chesapeake Bay, and with the prospect of their help, Washington decided to attack the forces of British general Charles Cornwallis, which were camped at Yorktown, Virginia. Washington's forces and those of French general Jean-Baptiste Rochambeau—a total of about 16,000 men—advanced on land while the French also attacked by water. The French ships drove off a British fleet and cut off their access from Yorktown to the sea, thereby making retreat impossible. After several unsuccessful attempts to break through Washington's siege, Cornwallis surrendered on October 19, 1781.

Although several minor skirmishes erupted after that, Yorktown proved to be the decisive battle of the war. In March 1782, the British House of Commons declared its unwillingness to continue supporting the war in America. Peace was declared in April of 1783, and The Treaty of Paris, which officially ended the war, was signed in September. On December 4, 1783, Washington took leave of his officers at Fraunces Tavern in New York City, and nineteen days later, resigned his commission at Annapolis, Maryland.

Top left: The Continental Army spent the brutal winter of 1777–78 encamped at Valley Forge, Pennsylvania.

Center left: The Revolutionary War came to an end at Yorktown, Virginia, more than five years after it began.

Bottom left: Washington resigned his command in New York and headed back to Mount Vernon and retirement as a farmer.

The Constitution

After the war, Washington went home to Mount Vernon with empty pockets. He had used some of his own resources during the war and had refused to accept pay for his services. He began to repair his farm, and in 1784, crossed the Blue Ridge Mountains to survey 30,000 acres of land he owned in the Ohio Valley. Parts of the land had been claimed by squatters, however, and he found other areas guarded by Native Americans.

The difficulty of crossing over the mountains to the frontier led Washington to consider an alternate route. He worked out a plan for a system of canals that could be extended from the Potomac River, and he formed the Potomac Company to make it a reality. In March of 1785, Washington presented his idea to members of the Virginia and Maryland legislatures, whose borders were formed by the river—it was the first such gesture extended to them as free and independent states.

The meetings of state representatives were so successful that Virginian James Madison proposed a convention of representatives from all states to discuss issues of mutual interest, such as the Potomac Canal. The convention was held the following year in Annapolis, Maryland, but only five of the thirteen states sent delegates. Still, those present decided to hold yet another convention in May 1787 at Philadelphia. Washington's canal idea never materialized, but once again he displayed his ability to bring Americans together.

Meanwhile, with little power to raise taxes or make binding decisions, the post-revolutionary colonial government was failing. The British government enacted commercial sanctions meant to intimidate the new country, and the individual states responded differently to them. The growing presence of British forces on the frontier beyond the borders of the new United States,

The Man Who Wouldn't Be King

By the time Washington became president, he was already the object of much love and respect from his fellow Americans. He was widely known as "the father of his country," a mark of affection that had formerly been reserved for England's kings, and his birthday was celebrated as a national holiday, like the birthdays of royalty in Britain. But Washington himself had led discussions at the Constitutional Convention on limiting presidential powers and prohibiting titles of nobility. It must have surprised him when his vice president, John Adams, suggested that he be addressed as "Your Highness." Washington quietly rejected the idea with the suggestion that he and his successors be called, simply, "Mr. President."

as well as on the Great Lakes, was a looming threat. A 1786 uprising of debt-ridden farmers in Massachusetts—known as Shay's Rebellion—further exposed the weakness of the central government.

The 1787 convention at Philadelphia was intended to firm up the Articles of Confederation that united the thirteen former colonies, and to strengthen the government. Washington was elected to preside over what would later become known as the Constitutional Convention.

Representatives from the states argued over many issues all summer long, including whether or not it was a good idea to establish a strong central government. They came together in the end, and adopted the Constitution of the United States. It wouldn't become binding until nine of the thirteen former colonies had approved it, and in June of 1788, New Hampshire became the ninth state to do so. Among its many provisions, the new Constitution called for the election of a president.

Below: America was farm country in the 1790s, which was very much to the president's liking.

Each of the thirteen states was represented by electors for the first presidential election, with the number of electors in each state based on its population. Each of these electors voted for two men, and the man receiving the most votes would become president; the man with the second-highest number became vice president. George Washington was elected unanimously to serve as the nation's first president, and John Adams became the first vice president.

Not Quite All

Washington was the only president elected by a unanimous electoral vote—none of the sixty-nine electors voted against him. But he actually carried only ten of the thirteen states. North Carolina and Rhode Island hadn't ratified the Constitution in time, and New York couldn't agree on whom should be given the honor of casting their vote. For his second term Washington was nominated unanimously again. There were 15 states by then, and 132 electors.

Election Results

1789

Presidential/Vice Presidential Candidates	Popular Vote	Electoral vote
George Washington	—	69
John Adams	—	34
John Jay	—	9
Others	—	15

1792

Presidential/Vice Presidential Candidates	Popular Vote	Electoral vote
George Washington	—	132
John Adams	—	77
George Clinton	—	50
Others	—	5

Popular votes were not yet part of these presidential elections. Washington received all 69 electoral votes in 1789, and all 132 in 1792. Under the system, the person with the second-highest number of electoral votes—John Adams in these elections—became the vice president.

Mother's Day

George Washington may have been part of Virginia's landed gentry, but he was land-poor. Still, he had an obligation to support his mother, Mary Ball Washington, who found his efforts unsatisfactory. She berated him for going off to war instead of staying home to take care of her, and she refused to go to New York to see him inaugurated as president. At one point, Mary Washington petitioned the Virginia House of Burgesses for a financial grant, and when Washington heard what she had done, he wrote to her that, "I am viewed as a delinquent, and am considered by the world as an unjust and undutiful son."

At the time of the election, Washington was at Mount Vernon trying to deal with his debts. He had to borrow $600 to make the trip from Virginia to New York City, where the seat of government had been established. Washington took the oath of office on April 30, 1789, in a ceremony on Wall Street that was attended by Adams, congressmen elected to serve in the first Congress, and a lively crowd. A few years later, the site of the swearing-in, the former New York City Hall, was torn down and sold for scrap. It was replaced by the building now known as Federal Hall Memorial, at the corner of Wall and Broad streets in Manhattan.

Above: Washington took the oath of office as the first president on a balcony of New York's Federal Hall.

Center: The first "White House" was a rented mansion on New York's Cherry Street, which was demolished to make way for the Brooklyn Bridge.

Bottom: The president and members of his cabinet

The President of Precedents

Washington was extremely careful to establish precedents for the behavior of future presidents. In most instances, he acted with authority as the highest elected official of the land, but he did not attempt to influence Congress. Having presided over the Constitutional Convention, he was well aware of various opinions about the presidency. He was also conscious of different views about the relationship between the states and the federal government. In a gesture of goodwill, he went out to meet the people on two tours of New England in 1789, and through the South two years later.

It was around this time that Congress began discussing the Bill of Rights, which became the first ten amendments to the Constitution in 1789. In the meantime, although the idea hadn't been addressed by the Constitution, Washington hoped to form a cabinet of advisors to assist him in his presidential duties. Congress agreed on five such posts: an attorney general to serve as the federal prosecutor; a secretary of war to run day-to-day operations of the military; a secretary of state to pursue the president's foreign policy; a secretary of the treasury to oversee the nation's finances; and a postmaster general to run the mail system. Washington carefully chose men with varying views of government for these positions.

Treasury Secretary Alexander Hamilton and War Secretary Henry Knox had a Federalist viewpoint, favoring a strong central authority. Conversely, Secretary of State Thomas Jefferson and Attorney General Edmund Randolph favored limiting the powers of the federal government. (Postmaster General Samuel Osgood did not contribute to discussions of policy.)

Congress established the nation's court system in 1789 with the Judiciary Act. The Supreme Court was instituted with a chief justice, John Jay, and five associate justices. The First Congress also passed the first tax, a tariff that would make imported goods more expensive. The import tax was intended to protect American manufacturers while bringing much needed income to run the federal government.

The Washington Administration

Administration Dates: April 30, 1789–March 4, 1797
Vice President: John Adams (1789–97)
Cabinet:

Secretary of State	Thomas Jefferson (1790–93)
	Edmund J. Randolph (1794–95)
	Timothy Pickering (1795–97)
Secretary of the Treasury	Alexander Hamilton (1789–95)
	Timothy Pickering (1795–97)
Secretary of War	Henry Knox (1789–94)
	Timothy Pickering (1795)
	James McHenry (1796–97)
Attorney General	Edmund J. Randolph (1789–94)
	William Bradford (1794–95)
	Charles Lee (1795–97)
Postmaster General	Samuel Osgood (1789–91)
	Timothy Pickering (1791–95)
	Joseph Habersham (1795–97)

On the Move

New York was the nation's capital when Washington first took office in 1789. The capital was moved to Philadelphia the following year, and it was there that Washington was sworn into his second term. The District of Columbia was still under construction, and work on the Capitol building began in 1793. Washington was the only president who did not live in Washington, D.C.

Washington looked to Hamilton to establish a financial system for the United States, and the Treasury Secretary introduced part of his plan to Congress in January 1790. It was challenged immediately. Those who believed in limiting the powers of the federal government, led by Thomas Jefferson in the administration, and James Madison in Congress, angrily denounced Hamilton's Federalist plans; in spite of the heated debate, Congress approved most elements of the financial plan, which became law.

Jefferson and Hamilton were at odds over taxes, but Jefferson cooled his opposition when Hamilton agreed to support his plan to move the nation's capital from New York to land donated by the states of Virginia and Maryland. Jefferson's plan passed in July of 1790. The District of Columbia became America's seat of government in 1800. Construction began almost as soon as the legislation was passed, and Washington himself laid the cornerstone of the White House, then called the President's House, in 1793.

Hamilton introduced the rest of his financial plan in December 1790. It called for the creation of a national bank, which Jefferson attacked as unconstitutional, arguing that Congress didn't have the authority to charter a bank. But in his counterargument, Hamilton noted that the Constitution gave Congress the right to levy taxes, to coin money, and to pay the nation's debts—all of which would be functions of a national bank. After a great deal of debate, Congress approved a charter for the First Bank of the United States, and President Washington signed it into law in February 1791.

The controversy over taxes continued to divide the lawmakers, and the 1791 Excise Tax on production and sale of whiskey proved to be the most unpopular of Hamilton's proposed levies. This tax, intended to pay off interest on the national debt, was especially hard on small farmers, many of whom distilled part of their corn crop into whiskey, which they could store easily and sell locally, to avoid the high cost of shipping corn to market.

Disagreements among different factions over interpretations of the Constitution, taxes, federal authority,

Left: Manhattan's Wall Street became America's financial center largely thanks to Alexander Hamilton.

Alexander Hamilton

Alexander Hamilton was born on the small West Indies island of Nevis in 1755 and moved to Boston, Massachusetts, in 1773. Hamilton joined the New York infantry as a captain in the Revolutionary War (1775-83) and later distinguished himself in the famous battle at Yorktown.

Hamilton served in the Continental Congress from November 1782 through July 1783, and from 1783 to 1789, practiced law while advocating a stronger federal government. He favored reform of the Articles of Confederation and called for and attended the Constitutional Convention. His idea of the ideal government was one in which only property owners should be allowed to vote, a president should be chosen by landholders to hold the office for life, and the president would have power over a popularly elected assembly that would have little voice in government. A second legislature would consist of propertied men elected for life by electors chosen by the people. The federal government would appoint a governor for each state, also for life, who would preside over a legislature and have absolute veto power. Hamilton viewed the Constitution, drawn up in 1787, as being frail, but he supported its experiment with a republican form of government. He contributed to a series of articles called the Federalist Papers that supported the new Constitution.

As the first secretary of the treasury, Hamilton established a credit rating for the federal government by pledging to pay off all foreign debts incurred during the war. He also agreed to pay all debts incurred by individual states, as a way to unite the states.

Hamilton urged the formation of a national bank that would develop a system of notes to serve as money and make the payment of taxes easier. It could also loan money to help build American businesses. As a control, the Treasury Department would supervise the bank's bookkeeping. Even before the bank proposal was made, however, some politicians—such as Secretary of State Thomas Jefferson—were against it. Some states already had their own banks and currency. Hamilton contended the Constitution demanded that the government regulate trade, collect taxes, provide for a common defense, and promote the general welfare. He believed that some powers must be implied by these sweeping demands, and one of these powers must be the ability to raise funds to meet such lofty goals. Establishing a national bank would allow the government to meet those financial demands. The Bank of the United States was chartered in February 1791. But more important, Hamilton had succeeded in permitting the Constitution to be open for interpretation.

Hamilton left his treasury post in 1795 and retired to law and politics in New York. In 1804, he spoke out against Burr in his candidacy for governor of New York, calling him "a man of irregular and unsatiable ambition who ought not to be trusted with the reins of government," a comment which cost him his life. Burr took offense, and a duel followed on July 12, 1804. Hamilton fired in the air, obviously intending to miss his mark, but Burr shot and wounded Hamilton. He died the next day at age forty-nine.

and the bank became so heated that it seemed to be endangering the unity of the young nation. Washington had been planning to retire to his Virginia plantation following a single term as president, but he was persuaded for the sake of the country to run again in 1792. He won unanimous approval from the electors once again—he was named on all 132 ballots—and John Adams remained his vice president.

Staying the Course

Soon after Washington's second term began in March 1793, French king Louis XVI was executed in the French Revolution, and the new French government immediately declared war on England.

Recognizing that the United States couldn't afford to become embroiled in the war or lose revenue from discontinued trade with Great Britain, President

Washington proclaimed American neutrality. The French and their American supporters, including Jefferson, were outraged and felt betrayed because the alliance treaty signed by America and France during the American Revolution was still in effect.

Washington responded by asserting his authority as president. The Constitution gave Congress the power to declare war, but it did not address the issue of declaring neutrality. To help ease tensions with France, Washington released an official statement that did not use the word neutral, but agreed to a cautious interpretation of the terms of the Franco-American treaty and accepted the new French government's American diplomatic mission.

Many Americans resented the British, and Washington's stand proved to be an unpopular one. Their resentment was further inflamed when Britain began stopping American ships at sea, claiming to search for British citizens who had deserted from the army. Then the situation worsened when the British also began seizing all cargoes not bound for Great Britain on the suspicion that they were intended for enemies. The situation grew worse in early 1794 when Britain closed off trade between the United States and their West Indian colonies. In response to calls for war from America's citizens, Washington sent John Jay to England to negotiate a peaceful settlement.

Meanwhile, there was more unrest on the home front. Rioting occurred in western Pennsylvania primarily over the Excise Tax. The Whiskey Rebellion, as it was called, ended after Washington directed 15,000 troops—the

Above: John Jay drafted a treaty with Britain that headed off a war, but cut into Washington's legendary popularity.

Below: The Whiskey Rebellion was Washington's first major domestic challenge.

militias of New Jersey, Virginia, and Maryland—to restore order, and personally went along to inspect them. At the same time, further west on the Ohio Valley frontier and around the Great Lakes, settlers were being threatened by a series of Indian uprisings. The situation was eased when a coalition of tribes was defeated on August 20, 1794, near present-day Toledo, Ohio, by the forces of General "Mad Anthony" Wayne. The alliance of tribes had apparently received aid from the British, who continued to operate several forts on the Great Lakes. Wayne concluded a treaty with the tribal coalition that effectively ended their claims on the Ohio River Valley and reopened the frontier to European settlement.

The treaty John Jay negotiated with Great Britain did not address British aggression at sea, and it didn't allow the United States to restrict British imports or open up the British-controlled West Indies to American trade. Although unpopular with the American people, the treaty's terms were agreed to by Washington, who called a special session of Congress to debate them. In Washington's view, the treaty achieved two basic purposes: First, it avoided war, which the president believed would devastate the young nation. Second, Great Britain agreed to evacuate its forts on the Great Lakes by June 1, 1796. Coupled with Wayne's victory, the United States would become the major power in the northwest territory that stretched to the Mississippi River and encompassed the Great Lakes and the Ohio River Valley. After two weeks of debate, the Senate approved the treaty by the necessary two-thirds majority, twenty votes to ten.

Washington's term ended with the passage of two other treaties. The Treaty of San Lorenzo between the United States and Spain granted U.S. citizens free and unlimited access to the Mississippi River all the way to New Orleans, which at that time was controlled by Spanish authorities. The treaty also settled the western boundary of Spanish Florida.

A treaty with the nation of Algiers freed ten American sailors who had been held in captivity since 1785. They had been captured by Barbary Coast pirates, various factions of which had been operating off the Algerian coast of the Mediterranean since the 1400s. Among Algiers's terms was the payment of ransom, which many members of Congress opposed. They moved to halt appropriations for six frigates that Washington had ordered for the U.S. Navy, but Washington countered that such warships were needed to more forcefully address lawlessness at sea.

As Washington's second term neared its end, he insisted on retiring. The precedent he set of serving a maximum of two terms was broken only once—by Franklin D. Roosevelt, who was elected president four times. Washington had held together the young nation through the difficult early stages. Some of his decisions were unpopular, but all of them were made with the judgment that they would be in the best interest of the nation.

Washington returned to Mount Vernon to enjoy retirement with Martha, but their peace together did not last long. The former president was asked by his successor, John Adams, to lead American troops in case of war with France during a period of tense relations with that nation. Washington died in 1799. He had caught cold and, as was customary in those days, doctors took large amounts of his blood, which was believed an effective cure for illness. Instead, the loss of blood weakened him further, and brought about his death.

Right: The Washington plantation at Mount Vernon, Virginia, was his pride and joy.

Left: The first president died at Mount Vernon of a condition easily curable today, but instead the medical practices common in 1799 actually contributed to his death.

Family Man

George and Martha had no children, but he adopted her two children from her previous marriage, John Parke Custis and Martha Parke Custis. John's granddaughter, Mary Custis, married the Confederate general Robert E. Lee, who was George Washington's third cousin, twice removed.

Legacy

George Washington's legacy is enormous. His leadership as citizen, general, and president kept the young and inexperienced country on course through difficult times. As president, he set the example for using the authority of the nation's highest elected official while respecting the equal and balancing legislative powers of Congress and judicial powers of the Supreme Court. Among his many precedents for presidential action, Washington established three patterns in the areas of treaty negotiation.

First, after enduring exhaustive debate with Congress over an early treaty with the Creek Nation of Native Americans, Washington did not consult with Congress on later treaties. The Constitution mandates that all treaties must be ratified by a two-thirds majority of the Senate, but Washington recognized that the president alone had the power to negotiate treaties, while Congress had the power to accept or reject them.

Second, Washington assigned aides to negotiate treaties, creating a model for presidential appointments that do not have to be approved by Congress.

Third, during the debate over appropriating funds for Jay's Treaty, the House of Representatives demanded that Washington turn over all documents, including instructions and correspondence, between the president and his negotiator regarding the treaty. Washington refused. The Constitution did not require him to do so, and he felt such an action could undermine the power of the presidency. That power of the presidency is called "executive privilege."

While maintaining progress among opposing factions, Washington's administration established national financial institutions. He used the authority of the federal government to stop a rebellion and to avoid what could have been a devastating war with England. He filled his administration with men representing various viewpoints. As he had done in the Revolutionary War, Washington helped hold together a group of inexperienced and idealistic revolutionaries through tough battles to progress toward a stronger union.

Martha Washington

Born: *June 2, 1731, near Williamsburg, Virginia*
Died: *March 22, 1802, Mount Vernon, Virginia*

Martha Washington was a gracious and unassuming woman who enjoyed private life. For the first fifteen years of her marriage to George Washington, the couple lived quietly on his Virginia estate, Mount Vernon, as Washington settled into life as a planter. They often traveled to Williamsburg, the capital of Virginia at the time. She owned a home there, and her husband was a member of Virginia's House of Burgesses, which met there.

The Washingtons were both in their early forties when their calm lives suddenly changed. George Washington would spend more than seven years commanding American forces in the Revolutionary War, and after settling back into life in Virginia, the Washingtons spent eight years in New York and Philadelphia when he served as president of the United States. Even after he left office, at the age of sixty-five, Washington was asked to hold himself in readiness to command American forces if a threatened war broke out with France.

Martha Washington preferred a quiet life, but she adapted to changing circumstances. She acted with the same tactfulness and cheerful spirit wherever the couple's adventures led.

When she was eighteen, she married Daniel Park Custis, a wealthy planter, and moved into his mansion, which (oddly enough) he called the White House. During the next seven years, Martha bore four children, two of whom died in infancy. She became a widow when her husband died in 1757. Martha was consoled by friends, and in May 1758, she was invited to stay with a neighboring family, the Chamberlaynes. During her stay, Colonel Richard Chamberlayne was out walking when he met George Washington on the banks of the Pamunkey River, where he had stopped to rest on his way to Williamsburg. Washington, then twenty-six, had spent most of the previous six years as a military officer and was looking forward to returning to civilian life.

A Young Widow

Born Martha Dandridge on June 2, 1731, on a plantation near Williamsburg, she was the oldest daughter of wealthy planters John and Frances Dandridge. She had a modest amount of schooling—typical for an eighteenth-century girl. Martha enjoyed riding horses and embroidering while growing up and learning how to manage a household.

Right: After the capital was moved to Philadelphia, this elegant house became the couple's home.

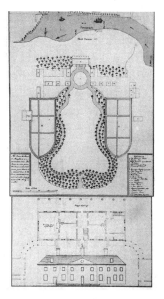

Left: The original plan for Mount Vernon came together in stages.

Right: George and Martha Washington and her two children, whom George adopted.

Chamberlayne invited him to dinner, but Washington declined, wanting to continue on to Williamsburg. But Chamberlayne persisted, promising to introduce him to "the prettiest and wealthiest widow in Virginia." Washington eventually accepted the invitation. The Old Man and Patsy (as they later called each other) hit it off that evening. Washington followed up by sending letters to Martha as he completed his military service and returned to live on his estate, Mount Vernon. The couple married in January of 1759.

Secret Love

Although he was devoted to Martha, young George Washington had been smitten by Sarah Cary "Sally" Fairfax, who he first met when she was the eighteen-year-old bride of his neighbor, George William Fairfax. They corresponded with one another for many years, and on one occasion he wrote, "… the world has no business to know the object of my love, declared in this manner to you." Fortunately, he had met her too late. Sally and George turned out to be Tories, supporters of the English king, and they moved to England after news of the Boston Tea Party reached them.

From Mount Vernon to Valley Forge

The next fifteen years were happy ones for the couple, except that Washington was growing increasingly frustrated with British rule in America. In addition to ever increasing taxes, he felt that American goods were being undersold by British agents. As rebellion began to spread throughout the colonies, Washington became commander of Virginia militia outfits in 1774, and the following year he was elected commander of the Continental Army when the American Revolution was underway.

Right: The French Revolution had a profound effect on America's history, although Americans held their peace at the time.

During the war, Martha joined her husband whenever it was safe. She traveled to Cambridge, Massachusetts, after Washington assumed command of the army and held British forces under siege in nearby Boston. She was also at his side during the dreadful winter of 1777-78 when some twelve thousand American soldiers suffered under terrible conditions at Valley Forge, Pennsylvania, about twenty miles northwest of Philadelphia.

Discouraged by defeats outside Philadelphia, which was held by British forces, the troops wintered at Valley Forge to protect Congress, in session at nearby York, Pennsylvania, from sudden British attack. Lacking supplies, food, and clothing, and sheltered in small huts they had built, many soldiers died of starvation and cold. Doing whatever she could to help, Martha remained constantly busy—mending clothes, stitching blankets, nursing solders, and attempting to keep up everyone's morale.

After the hardships of Valley Forge, the Continental Army began having more success, but the war dragged on into 1782. With a climactic victory at Yorktown, Virginia, Washington received the surrender of British general Charles Cornwallis not far from the estate where he had first met Martha.

Not until the end of 1784 did Washington officially end his service with the Continental Army and go home to Mount Vernon. However, he and Martha were not able to resume their quiet lives. The weak, post-Revolution American government needed to be changed, and Washington traveled to Philadelphia in 1787 to preside over the necessary debate. The Convention succeeded in drawing up the American Constitution. It called for the creation of an executive branch of government that would be led by the nation's highest elected official, the president. Washington was elected president in 1789, and reelected in 1792.

Busy in Their Sixties

The Washingtons lived in New York, the seat of government in 1789, and then in Philadelphia, the temporary capital from 1790 to 1799. Though she didn't enjoy her social role as first lady, Martha made the best of it. She helped "the general" (as she now called her husband) establish formal and respectful social occasions. She helped keep a sense of ease at such gatherings to ensure that the presidency did not take on airs of royalty. "I am fond of only what comes from the heart," she said while receiving guests politely and without fanfare. Whenever political topics were being discussed, she worked to change the subject to other things, separating business and pleasure. She held her own weekly Friday receptions that Washington would occasionally attend.

As conflicts between political factions began to grow during Washington's presidency, Martha turned cool toward those who were critical of her husband's policies, including Secretary of State Thomas Jefferson. Nevertheless, there was never a loss of dignity in the social circles that surrounded the president.

In 1797, the Washingtons, then in their mid-sixties, were finally able to return to Mount Vernon. Their happy time there included entertaining many visitors, but it was interrupted. Washington was asked by President John Adams in 1798 to prepare to command American forces in case tensions between America and France escalated into war. In 1799, Washington caught a nasty cold from which he never recovered. He died on December 14, 1799. Martha Washington lived on until May 22, 1802. The Washingtons are both buried in a modest tomb at Mount Vernon.

The Articles of Confederation

Adopted March 1, 1781

The document that was the nation's first attempt at establishing a federal government grew from a suggestion by John Dickenson to his fellow members of the Second Continental Congress in 1776. It was not approved until five years later. The articles ultimately failed because Americans—after their experience under the English monarchy—were reluctant to approve a strong central government or a single powerful leader.

Under the Articles, Congress was the only branch of the central government. Each state had one vote in Congress, and Congressional delegates were selected by state legislatures. A simple majority decided issues, except for some that required approval of nine of thirteen states. Each state could impose its own taxes on citizens, but there was no national tax. The authority of Congress included military matters, negotiating treaties and alliances, Indian relations, managing postal affairs, coining money, and settling disputes between states.

The Articles created a loose confederation of independent states and gave limited powers to the central government. There was no independent executive. The federal government had no judicial branch, and the only judicial authority it had was the power to arbitrate disputes between states. Judicial proceedings in each state were to be honored by all other states.

The Articles of Confederation was ultimately superceded by the Constitution of the United States.

Excerpt from the Articles of Confederation

ARTICLE I

The Stile of this confederacy shall be "The United States of America."

ARTICLE II

Each state retains its sovereignty, freedom and independence, and every Power, Jurisdiction and right, which is not by this confederation expressly delegated to the United States, in Congress assembled.

ARTICLE III

The said states hereby severally enter into a firm league of friendship with each other, for their common defence, the security of their Liberties, and their mutual and general welfare, binding themselves to assist each other, against all force offered to, or attacks made upon them, or any of them, on account of religion, sovereignty, trade, or any other pretence whatever.

ARTICLE IV

The better to secure and perpetuate mutual friendship and intercourse among the people of the different states in this union, the free inhabitants of each of these states, paupers, vagabonds and fugitives from Justice excepted, shall be entitled to all privileges and immunities of free citizens in the several states; and the people of each state shall have free ingress and regress to and from any other state, and shall enjoy therein all the privileges of trade and commerce, subject to the same duties, impositions and restrictions as the inhabitants thereof respectively, provided that such restriction shall not extend so far as to prevent the removal of property imported into any state, to any other state of which the Owner is an inhabitant; provided also that no imposition, duties or restriction shall be laid by any state, on the property of the United States, or either of them.

If any Person guilty of, or charged with treason, felony, or other high misdemeanor in any state, shall flee from Justice, and be found in any of the united states [*sic*], he shall upon demand of the Governor or executive power, of the state from which he fled, be delivered up and removed to the state having jurisdiction of his offence.

Full faith and credit shall be given in each of these states to the records, acts and judicial proceedings of the courts and magistrates of every other state.

ARTICLE V

For the more convenient management of the general interests of the United States, delegates shall be annually appointed in such manner as the legislature of each state shall direct, to meet in Congress on the first Monday in November, in every year, with a power reserved to each state, to recall its delegates, or any of them, at any time within the year, and to send others in their stead, for the remainder of the Year.

No state shall be represented in Congress by less than two, nor by more than seven Members; and no person shall be capable of being a delegate for more than three years in any term of six years; nor shall any person, being a delegate, be capable of holding any office under the united states, for which he, or another for his benefit receives any salary, fees or emolument of any kind.

Each state shall maintain its own delegates in a meeting of the states, and while they act as members of the committee of the states.

In determining questions in the United States, in Congress assembled, each state shall have one vote.

Freedom of speech and debate in Congress shall not be impeached or questioned in any Court, or place out of Congress, and the members of Congress shall be protected in their persons from arrests and imprisonments, during the time of their going to and from, and attendance on Congress, except for treason, felony, or breach of the peace.

ARTICLE VI

No state without the Consent of the United States in Congress assembled, shall send any embassy to, or receive any embassy from, or enter into any conference, agreement, or alliance or treaty with any King, prince or state; nor shall any person holding any office of profit or trust under the United States, or any of them, accept of any present, emolument, office or title of any kind whatever from any king, prince or foreign state; nor shall the United States in Congress assembled, or any of them, grant any title of nobility.

No two or more states shall enter into any treaty, confederation or alliance whatever between them, without the consent of the united states in Congress assembled, specifying accurately the purposes for which the same is to be entered into, and how long it shall continue.

No state shall lay any imposts or duties, which may interfere with any stipulations in treaties, entered into by the United States in Congress assembled, with any king, prince or state, in pursuance of any treaties already proposed by congress, to the courts of France and Spain.

No vessel of war shall be kept up in time of peace by any State, except such number only, as shall be deemed necessary by the United States in Congress assembled, for the defense of such State, or its trade; nor shall any body of forces be kept up by any State in time of peace, except such number only, as in the judgement [sic] of the United States in Congress assembled, shall be deemed requisite to garrison the forts necessary for the defense of such State; but every State shall always keep up a well-regulated and disciplined militia, sufficiently armed and accoutered, and shall provide and constantly have ready for use, in public stores, a due number of filed pieces and tents, and a proper quantity of arms, ammunition and camp equipage.

No State shall engage in any war without the consent of the United States in Congress assembled, unless such State be actually invaded by enemies, or shall have received certain advice of a resolution being formed by some nation of Indians to invade such State, and the danger is so imminent as not to admit of a delay till the United States in Congress assembled can be consulted; nor shall any State grant commissions to any ships or vessels of war, nor letters of marque or reprisal, except it be after a declaration of war by the United States in Congress assembled, and then only against the Kingdom or State and the subjects thereof, against which war has been so declared, and under such regulations as shall be established by the United States in Congress assembled, unless such State be infested by pirates, in which case vessels of war may be fitted out for that occasion, and kept so long as the danger shall continue, or until the United States in Congress assembled shall determine otherwise.

ARTICLE VII

When land-forces are raised by any state for the common defence, all officers of or under the rank of colonel, shall be appointed by the legislature of each state respectively by whom such forces shall be raised, or in such manner as such state shall direct, and all vacancies shall be filled up by the state which first made the appointment.

ARTICLE VIII

All charges of war, and all other expenses that shall be incurred for the common defence or general welfare, and allowed by the United States in Congress assembled, shall be defrayed out of a common treasury, which shall be supplied by the several states, in proportion to the value of all land within each state, granted to or surveyed for any Person, as such land and the buildings and improvements thereon shall be estimated according to such mode

as the united states in congress assembled, shall from time to time direct and appoint. The taxes for paying that proportion shall be laid and levied by the authority and direction of the legislatures of the several states within the time agreed upon by the United States in Congress assembled.

ARTICLE IX

The United States in congress assembled, shall have the sole and exclusive right and power of determining on peace and war, except in the cases mentioned in the sixth article—of sending and receiving ambassadors—entering into treaties and alliances, provided that no treaty of commerce shall be made whereby the legislative power of the respective states shall be restrained from imposing such imposts and duties on foreigners, as their own people are subjected to, or from prohibiting the exportation or importation of any species of goods or commodities whatsoever—of establishing rules for deciding in all cases, what captures on land or water shall be legal, and in what manner prizes taken by land or naval forces in the service of the United States shall be divided or appropriated—of granting letters of marque and reprisal in times of peace—appointing courts for the trial of piracies and felonies committed on the high seas and establishing courts for receiving and determining finally appeals in all cases of captures, provided that no member of Congress shall be appointed a judge of any of the said courts.

[...]

ARTICLE X

The committee of the states, or any nine of them, shall be authorized to execute, in the recess of Congress, such of the powers of Congress as the United States in Congress assembled, by the consent of nine states, shall from time to time think expedient to vest them with; provided that no power be delegated to the said committee, for the exercise of which, by the articles of confederation, the voice of nine states in the Congress of the United States assembled is requisite.

ARTICLE XI

Canada acceding to this confederation, and joining in the measures of the United States, shall be admitted into, and entitled to all the advantages of this union: but no other colony shall be admitted into the same, unless such admission be agreed to by nine states.

ARTICLE XII

All bills of credit emitted, monies borrowed and debts contracted by, or under the authority of Congress, before the assembling of the United States, in pursuance of the present confederation, shall be deemed and considered as a charge against the United States, for payment and satisfaction whereof the said United States, and the public faith are hereby solemnly pledged.

ARTICLE XIII

Every state shall abide by the determinations of the United States in Congress assembled, on all questions which by this confederation are submitted to them. And the Articles of this confederation shall be inviolably observed by every state, and the union shall be perpetual; nor shall any alteration at any time hereafter be made in any of them; unless such alteration be agreed to in a Congress of the United States, and be afterwards confirmed by the legislatures of every state.

President Washington's Farewell Address

Delivered on September 17, 1796

Washington used the occasion of his farewell address to express his pride in America and to warn about divisions that could break it apart. The address remains important today as a plea for unity over special interests.

Excerpt from President Washington's Farewell Address

The unity of Government, which constitutes you one people, is also now dear to you. It is justly so; for it is a main pillar in the edifice of your real independence, the support of your tranquillity [sic] at home, your peace abroad; of your safety; of your prosperity; of that very Liberty, which you so highly prize. But as it is easy to foresee, that, from different causes and from different quarters, much pains will be taken, many Artifices employed, to weaken in your minds the conviction of this truth; as this is the point in your political fortress against which the batteries of internal and external enemies will be most constantly and actively (though often covertly and insidiously) directed, it is of infinite moment, that you should properly estimate the immense value of your national Union to your collective and individual happiness; that you should cherish a cordial, habitual, and immovable attachment to it; accustoming yourselves to think and speak of it as of the Palladium of your political safety and prosperity; watching for its preservation with jealous anxiety; discountenancing whatever may suggest even a suspicion that it can in any event be abandoned, and indignantly frowning upon the first dawning of every attempt to alienate any portion of our country from the rest or to enfeeble the sacred ties which now link together the various parts.

[…]

For this you have every inducement of sympathy and interest. Citizens, by birth or choice, of a common country, that country has a right to concentrate your affections. The name of American, which belongs to you, in your national capacity, must always exalt the just pride of Patriotism, more than any appellation derived from local discriminations. With slight shades of difference, you have the same religion, manners, habits, and political principles. You have in a common cause fought and triumphed together; the Independence and Liberty you possess are the work of joint counsels, and joint efforts, of common dangers, sufferings, and successes.

[…]

In contemplating the causes, which may disturb our Union, it occurs as matter of serious concern, that any ground should have been furnished for characterizing parties by Geographical discriminations, Northern and Southern, Atlantic and Western; whence designing men may endeavour to excite a belief, that there is a real difference of local interests and views. One of the expedients of party to acquire influence, within particular districts, is to misrepresent the opinions and aims of other districts. You cannot shield yourselves too much against the jealousies and heart-burnings, which spring from these misrepresentations; they tend to render alien to each other those, who ought to be bound together by fraternal affection. The inhabitants of our western country have lately had a useful lesson on this head; they have seen, in the negotiation by the Executive, and in the unanimous ratification by the Senate, of the treaty with Spain, and in the universal satisfaction at that event, throughout the United States, a decisive proof how unfounded were the suspicions propagated among them of a policy in the General Government and in the Atlantic States unfriendly to their interests in regard to the Mississippi; they have been witnesses to the formation of two treaties, that with Great Britain, and that with Spain, which secure to them every thing they could desire, in respect to our foreign relations, towards confirming their prosperity. Will it not be their wisdom to rely for the preservation of these advantages on the union by which they were procured? Will they not henceforth be deaf to those advisers, if such there are, who would sever them from their brethren, and connect them with aliens?

To the efficacy and permanency of your Union, a Government for the whole is indispensable. No alliances, however strict, between the parts can be an adequate substitute; they must inevitably experience the infractions and interruptions, which all alliances in all times have experienced. Sensible of this momentous truth, you have improved upon your first essay, by the adoption of a Constitution of Government better calculated than your former for an intimate Union, and for the efficacious management of your common concerns. This Government, the offspring of our own choice, uninfluenced and unawed, adopted upon full investigation and mature deliberation, completely free in its principles, in the distribution of its powers, uniting security with energy, and containing within itself a provision for its own amendment, has a just claim to your confidence and your support. Respect for its authority, compliance with its laws, acquiescence in its measures, are duties enjoined by the fundamental maxims of true Liberty. The basis of our political systems is the right of the people to make and to alter their Constitutions of Government. But the Constitution which at any time exists, till changed by an explicit and authentic act of the whole people, is sacredly obligatory upon all. The very idea of the power and the right of the people to establish Government presupposes the duty of every individual to obey the established Government.

All obstructions to the execution of the Laws, all combinations and associations, under whatever plausible character, with the real design to direct, control, counteract, or awe the regular deliberation and action of the constituted authorities, are destructive of this fundamental principle, and of fatal tendency. They serve to organize faction, to give it an artificial and extraordinary force; to put, in the place of the delegated will of the nation, the will of a party, often a small but artful and enterprising minority of the community; and, according to the alternate triumphs of different parties, to make the public administration the mirror of the ill-concerted and incongruous projects of faction, rather than the organ of consistent and wholesome plans digested by common counsels, and modified by mutual interests.

However combinations or associations of the above description may now and then answer popular ends, they are likely, in the course of time and things, to become potent engines, by which cunning, ambitious, and unprincipled men will be enabled to subvert the power of the people, and to usurp for themselves the reins of government; destroying afterwards the very engines, which have lifted them to unjust dominion.

Towards the preservation of your government, and the permanency of your present happy state, it is requisite, not only that you steadily discountenance irregular oppositions to its acknowledged authority, but also that you resist with care the spirit of innovation upon its principles, however specious the pretexts. One method of assault may be to effect, in the forms of the constitution, alterations, which will impair the energy of the system, and thus to undermine what cannot be directly overthrown. In all the changes to which you may be invited, remember that time and habit are at least as necessary to fix the true character of governments, as of other human institutions; that experience is the surest standard, by which to test the real tendency of the existing constitution of a country; that facility in changes, upon the credit of mere hypothesis and opinion, exposes to perpetual change, from the endless variety of hypothesis and opinion; and remember, especially, that, for the efficient management of your common interests in a country so extensive as ours a government of as much vigor as is consistent with the perfect security of liberty is indispensable.

[…]

I have already intimated to you the danger of parties in the state, with particular reference to the founding of them on geographical discriminations. Let me now take a more comprehensive view, and warn you in the most solemn manner against the baneful effects of the spirit of party, generally.

This spirit, unfortunately, is inseparable from our nature, having its root in the strongest passions of the human mind. It exists under different shapes in all governments, more or less stifled, controlled, or repressed; but, in those of the popular form, it is seen in its greatest rankness, and is truly their worst enemy.

The alternate domination of one faction over another, sharpened by the spirit of revenge, natural to party dissension, which in different ages and countries has perpetrated the most horrid enormities, is itself a frightful despotism. But this leads at length to a more formal and permanent despotism. The disorders and miseries, which result, gradually incline the minds of men to seek security and repose in the absolute power of an individual; and sooner or later the chief of some prevailing faction, more able or more fortunate than his competitors, turns this disposition to the purposes of his own elevation, on the ruins of Public Liberty.

Without looking forward to an extremity of this kind, (which nevertheless ought not to be entirely out of sight,) the common and continual mischiefs of the spirit of party are sufficient to make it the interest and duty of a wise people to discourage and restrain it.

[…]

In offering to you, my countrymen, these counsels of an old and affectionate friend, I dare not hope they will make the strong and lasting impression I could wish; that they will control the usual current of the passions, or prevent our nation from running the course, which has hitherto marked the destiny of nations. But, if I may even flatter myself, that they may be productive of some partial benefit, some occasional good; that they may now and then recur to moderate the fury of party spirit, to warn against the mischiefs of foreign intrigue, to guard against the impostures of pretended patriotism; this hope will be a full recompense for the solicitude for your welfare, by which they have been dictated. […]

What Happened Next

Washington's warnings about the dangers of factions were soon borne out. In the election that same year, the Federalist party, under Alexander Hamilton, convinced some electors to support candidates other than John Adams, with the result that with several candidates receiving votes, Thomas Jefferson, Hamilton's arch-rival, representing the Democratic-Republicans, finished second to Adams and became vice president.

Washington's warning against promoting one's region over the concerns of the nation were also ignored. Northern politicians consistently lobbied for favorable business policies, and Southerners rallied against them with the promotion of states' rights. These differences ultimately contributed to the American Civil War.

The first president's concern over the influence of special interests and partisan politics was another part of his address that has been consistently ignored even though he cautioned that party and other loyalties were not in the country's best interest.

John Adams

Independence Day "ought to be solemnized with pomp and parade, with shows, games, sports, guns, bells, bonfires, and illuminations, from one end of this continent to the other, from this time forward for evermore."

—*John Adams*

Second president of the United States, 1797–1801

Full name: *John Adams*
Born: *October 30, 1735, Braintree, Massachusetts*
Died: *July 4, 1826, Quincy, Massachusetts*
Burial site: *First Unitarian Church, Quincy, Massachusetts*
Parents: *John and Susanna Boylston Adams*
Spouse: *Abigail Smith (1744–1818; m. 1764)*
Children: *Abigail Amelia (1765–1813); John Quincy (1767–1848); Susanna (1768–1770); Charles (1770–1800); Thomas Boylston (1772–1832)*
Religion: *Unitarian*
Education: *Harvard College (B.A., 1755)*
Occupations: *Farmer; teacher; attorney*
Government positions: *Continental congressman; minister to France, the Netherlands, and England; vice president under George Washington*
Political party: *Federalist*
Dates as president: *March 4, 1797–March 4, 1801*
Age upon taking office: *61*

As one of the nation's Founding Fathers, John Adams enjoyed a long and distinguished career as a public servant. He was a Massachusetts delegate to the Continental Congress and was a member of the team that drafted the Declaration of Independence in 1776. Adams served as a diplomat in England, the Netherlands, and France. He also lead the Massachusetts State Constitutional Convention in 1779, and served eight years as the first vice president of the United States.

Adams wasn't able to forge a coalition of support during his own presidency, even though he had worked with America's leaders for decades. He faced bickering within his own Federalist party and dissension among the sixteen states of the Union as well. He was the first sitting president to lose reelection, but still Adams remains a significant figure among the nation's Founding Fathers. He left behind a large body of writings that show a great deal of insight into the exciting times he lived through. His writing also reveals a warm, witty, and sometimes cranky personality.

A Puritan Legacy

John Adams was born on October 30, 1736 and raised in Braintree, Massachusetts, which later became known as Quincy, where his father's family had settled about a century before. He grew up in a Puritan household, following simple ceremonies and strict religious discipline. The Adams family belonged to the Unitarian branch of the Congregational church, which has a form of organization used by the Puritans, with self-governing local congregations. Both his mother, Susanna, and his father, John—a church deacon, farmer, and local elected official—had forceful personalities.

A talkative boy who loved the outdoors, young Adams despised school. When he wasn't cutting class to hunt and fish in the nearby woods and skate on frozen ponds, Adams studied classical languages, logic, and rhetoric. He informed his father that all this was an unnecessary expense, because he planned to become a farmer, and wouldn't need this learning. The elder

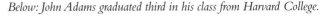

Adams responded by forcing the boy to spend an entire day, sunrise to sunset, alongside him at work. Exhausted but still prideful, Adams refused to admit that farming involved backbreaking work, but his father settled the question by sending him back to class the next day.

Adams entered Harvard College at the age of fifteen in the fall of 1751, following in the footsteps of his uncle, who had studied there to become a minister. Although he excelled as a student, Adams began to have doubts about his suitability for the life of cleric, and after graduating third in the class of 1755, he decided to become a teacher to give him time to think about his future goals.

Below: The Adams home in Quincy, Massachusetts, was considered quite grand when John was growing up there.

Below: John Adams graduated third in his class from Harvard College.

Prominent Boston Attorney

Adams decided that he had a future as a lawyer, and he studied with a Worcester attorney for two years before he was admitted to the Massachusetts bar in 1758. Beginning his practice in Braintree, he rose to a position of local importance within a few years, and he spread his influence by traveling frequently to Boston to argue cases. Once he was financially secure, he began courting Abigail Smith, the seventeen-year-old daughter of a well-to-do minister in nearby Weymouth. They were married on October 25, 1764, after a three-year courtship, and over the next decade, they had five children.

Adams grew increasingly involved in colonial politics, forging ties with a number of emerging patriots who were rallying to protest the English Parliament's Stamp Act of 1765, which required the payment of a tax on papers and documents produced in the colonies. The tax caused considerable public outcry and even riots. Adams wrote Braintree's official protest letter, and wrote angry columns against the tax for the Boston Gazette. The rights of Englishmen, he declared, came from God, not the Crown or the British Parliament. The colonists were the equals of English citizens, he added, and shouldn't be forced to accept unfair laws.

Timeline

1735: Born in Massachusetts
1755–1758: Teaches grammar school
1756: Begins studying law
1758: Admitted to the bar of the State of Massachusetts
1773: Serves in Massachusetts state legislature
1774: Serves as delegate to First Continental Congress and to Second Continental Congress (1775)
1779: Elected to Massachusetts Constitutional Convention and writes the state constitution
1780–85: Serves as U.S. envoy in France and the Netherlands; member of negotiation committee for the Treaty of Paris, 1783
1785–88: Serves as U.S. minister to Britain
1789–97: Serves as vice president under George Washington
1796–1801: Serves as second U.S. president
1826: Dies in Massachusetts

To Your Health

John Adams once said, "My constitution is a glass bubble." He seemed to be always suffering from colds, and he had frequent chest pains, heartburn and headaches. He fell into a coma with what he called "the Dutch disease," while he was serving in Amsterdam, and later in life he contracted palsy. Yet he lived to the ripe old age of ninety.

Left: As a young woman, Abigail Adams was regarded as a person of uncommon learning, although she didn't have a formal education.

Right: A tax stamp required for documents rallied the Colonials to the edge of rebellion.

Left: In the aftermath of the
Boston Massacre, Adams took on
the unpopular job of defending
the British officers in court.

Right: Rioting in the streets to
protest the Stamp Act.

A Revolutionary Spirit

Adams was elected to the Massachusetts legislature, the General Court, in 1770, and soon became firmly convinced that the colonies could benefit by breaking their ties with England. He was selected as a delegate to the First Continental Congress, held in Philadelphia, Pennsylvania, in 1774. When war broke out the following year, the Second Continental Congress met and created a Continental Army combining the individual state militias and enlisting new recruits, and Adams nominated George Washington of Virginia as its commander in chief. Recognizing the need, should independence be achieved, for some type of a uniting framework for the colonies,

Taking Sides

In 1770, a Boston mob taunted some British soldiers and goaded them into firing on them, killing three, including a black man, Crispus Attucks. Called "the Boston Massacre," these were the first deaths in what would become a bloody revolution, and Boston patriots called for quick justice. The British government arrested the soldiers and promised a fair trial, but no local lawyer was willing to defend them until John Adams and Josiah Quincy stepped forward, knowing very well that their friends and neighbors were ready to lynch the offenders. But Adams believed in the soldiers' innocence, and he managed to get an acquittal for their leader, Captain Thomas Preston, and six of his men from a hostile jury. Two others were found guilty of manslaughter and sentenced to having their thumbs branded.

Right: Adams led the congressional debate on appointing George Washington commander of the Continental Army.

Adams wrote an essay, "Thoughts on Government," presenting a detailed plan for a government with three branches—executive, legislative, and judicial.

Adams was part of the Continental Congress of 1776, which ratified the Declaration of Independence. With war and American independence declared, Adams was finally able to go home to his family in Braintree. Late the following year, however, he sailed for France with his ten-year-old son, John Quincy Adams, in hopes of negotiating a treaty of alliance. The senior Adams stayed there for two years as a diplomat, and when he returned home, he became a delegate to the Massachusetts Constitutional Convention, where he wrote the document supporting statehood. Adams returned to France when the end to the Revolutionary War seemed close at hand, and he signed the Treaty of Paris in 1783, formally ending the war.

The Ambassador from Where?

When John Adams went to London as America's first Ambassador to the Court of Saint James, a newspaper there noted his arrival with the headline, "An Ambassador From America! Good Heavens—What a Sound!" The British were not amused that the upstarts from across the Atlantic were beginning to act like their equals. They even charged the Adamses an import duty on the wine they had brought with them. But John Adams was too busy to notice the snubs. He used his spare time there to collect and digest books on history and political science and became the world's leading authority on the art of government.

Right: As minister to Great Britain, Adams was the first of the rebels to meet the former archenemy King George III.

Left: The first reading of the Declaration of Independence, Philadelphia, July 4, 1776.

He was named minister to Britain in 1785, and lived in London for the next three years, forging a close friendship with Thomas Jefferson, who was minister to France. During this time, Adams wrote "Defence of the Constitutions of Government of the United States of America," which urged the formation of an American government with three branches that could review and dismiss acts passed by one of the other branches, thus creating a system of checks and balances. Adams's theory of government included an upper legislative chamber made up of "the rich, the well-born and the able," an aristocratic pretension that caused some members of the Constitutional Convention to dismiss Adams as a potential leader of the new nation.

First Vice President

When the time came to elect the nation's first president in 1789, electors unanimously favored George Washington, and under the Constitution's terms, Adams became vice president by finishing second in the voting.

Above: As Washington's vice president Adams served as president of the Senate.

Alexander Hamilton, a younger political figure, didn't like Adams and had lobbied against him during the balloting. It was the beginning of a long feud between the two men, especially as Hamilton—as secretary of the treasury—became the most trusted of Washington's cabinet officials.

As Washington's vice president for two terms, Adams began to despise the job. He had very few duties or official roles, other than to serve as the tiebreaking vote for the Senate. He called the vice presidency "the most insignificant office that ever the invention of man contrived or his imagination conceived." His frustration was compounded by growing political unrest among the patriots of 1776.

Those who favored a strong central government, life terms for senators, and a political system that encouraged trade and commerce, became known as Federalists, and Hamilton became their unofficial leader. The Federalists were countered by a group called anti-Federalists, led by Thomas Jefferson, who believed that a strong federal government would lead to a corrupt ruling class. They were distrustful of the advantages that a Federalist agenda seemed to give New England merchant and the industrial class over the nation's farmers.

Adams, widely viewed as Washington's successor, did not wholeheartedly support the Federalist concept. He disagreed with Hamilton's arguments for the creation of a national bank and a large standing army. Moreover, he was wary about the large number of Americans formerly loyal to Britain among the Federalist ranks. Opposition to Federalists centered around Jefferson and the newly emerging Democratic-Republican Party, which championed states' rights and limited terms for elected officials.

The election of 1796 marked the first true contest between these political ideologies. Adams ran as the Federalist candidate after Washington announced his

1796 Election Results

Presidential / Vice Presidential Candidates	Popular Votes	Electoral Votes
John Adams (Federalist)	—	71
Thomas Jefferson (Democratic-Republican)	—	68
Thomas Pinckney (Federalist)	—	59
Aaron Burr (Democratic-Republican)	—	30
Others	—	48

The public at large did not vote in the 1796 presidential election. Adams received a majority of the total electoral votes, making him the president. Under the system then in place, the person with the second highest number of electoral votes became the vice president.

Left: George Washington offers a farewell toast to Adams as his presidency comes to an end.

retirement from politics. The campaign was largely carried out as a press war fought in opinionated broadsheet newspapers loyal to one side or another.

In the first few presidential elections, each state was represented by a number of electors determined by its population who actually cast the votes. Each elector voted for two candidates, and the one who received the most votes became president, with the runner-up becoming vice president. Hamilton took advantage of the system to work behind the scenes against Adams by convincing some Federalist electors to vote, not for Adams himself but for his chosen vice presidential candidate, Thomas Pinckney.

As it turned out, Hamilton's scheme backfired. Enough delegates withheld votes from Pinckney to cause Thomas Jefferson to finish second and become Adams's vice president. It was the only time in American history that the two offices were held by members of opposing parties. (In the 1864 election, Republican incumbent president Abraham Lincoln chose Democrat Andrew Johnson as his running mate, but in the spirit of "national union" in the Civil War era, the Republican Party temporarily changed its name to the National Union Party. Thus, in this case—unlike the Adams-Jefferson situation—opposing party members willingly ran on a national ticket and won.)

Elected by a margin of just three votes, Adams was inaugurated as president on March 4, 1797, at Congress Hall in Philadelphia. He called for national unity and an end to domestic disagreements in his first presidential speech, and he stressed the need to maintain peace with all nations and to keep free of any difficult situations with foreign powers.

The Nation's Second President

Adams was the first president elected to succeed another, and there was no precedent for him to follow. His fatal error, which he himself admitted and later political analysts confirmed, was to keep Washington's cabinet, which was dominated by men faithful to Hamilton. Another mistake was Adams's habit of spending too much time back home in Braintree. He wasn't able to see firsthand how slowly or incorrectly his directives were being carried out by Hamilton's people.

The Adams administration was dominated by a threat of war with France, whose monarchy had been overthrown in the Revolution of 1789. France's new leaders were eagerly exploiting political unrest across Europe, and sought to spread their revolutionary spirit through armed conflict. Under President Washington, the United States declared itself neutral in France's war with England, but both nations were stopping American ships at sea to seize cargoes they believed were destined for their enemies. France had seized nearly 300 American merchant vessels by the time Adams took office.

Right: The official portrait of John Adams as the nation's second president.

John Marshall

John Marshall was a key adviser to the nation's first two presidents and the chief justice of the Supreme Court for thirty-five years. After a strong career in the military during the Revolutionary War, Marshall became a lawyer. His ability to gather bits of evidence into a logical and convincing argument soon earned him a place among the great lawyers of the day and a position in the Virginia legislature. Marshall was among many dissatisfied with the government established in 1781 by the Articles of Confederation. He supported adoption of the Constitution as a protection of human rights and as a base for a strong federal government.

Almost immediately after the Constitution was ratified in 1789, Marshall helped define the roles of various government officers. In 1796 and 1799, he supported the president's right to negotiate with foreign countries. President Washington offered Marshall the position of attorney general, but he declined. He also turned down the offer from John Adams to become either secretary of war or minister to France. Though he supported Adams and served as Adams's secretary of state in 1800–1801, Marshall opposed the Alien and Sedition Acts (1798). Adams's sound defeat by Thomas Jefferson in the presidential election of 1800 indicated the decline of the Federalist Party (of which Adams and Marshall were leaders). Hoping to salvage some power, Adams appointed numerous Federalists as judges before he left office. In one of his last acts as president, Adams nominated Marshall for chief justice of the Supreme Court.

As chief justice, Marshall quickly won the respect of the other justices. His first major case was Marbury v. Madison (1803). Just before Adams left office, he had nominated William Marbury to be justice of the peace of Washington, D.C. His appointment had been confirmed by the Senate, but Adams had left office before the official papers could be delivered to Marbury. President Jefferson ordered Secretary of State James Madison not to deliver the appointment. Marbury petitioned the Supreme Court for a writ of mandamus (a command placed on an official to perform his duty). Jefferson, a supporter of states' rights, favored a weak Supreme Court. Marshall, on the other hand, favored a strong central government. If the judgment were based on politics, Marshall would have ruled in favor of Marbury.

Marshall, however, was committed to making the Constitution serve as a guide for the United States. Ruling that Congress had no authority to pass the part of a law in 1789 upon which Marbury based his claim, Marshall declared the act unconstitutional because it gave the Supreme Court powers that the Constitution had not intended. The Court refused to hear Marbury v. Madison. It was a brilliant decision for the Court. Marshall had established an important pattern. All federal laws had to be in keeping with the Constitution, and the Court would serve to judge them.

Three years later, in the trial of U.S. senator Aaron Burr, Marshall again showed sound judgment. Burr had embarked on a mysterious trip down the Ohio and Mississippi rivers, gathering followers and arming them for some unspecified reason. Pursued by the military, Burr was arrested for treason, accused of attempting to establish a new country in the Louisiana Territory and Mexico. An angry Jefferson called for Burr's prosecution. But in the trial, Marshall insisted on the principle of "innocent until proven guilty," stating that talking about rebellion and carrying out a rebellion were two different issues. He ruled that it was necessary to prove an act of treason by the testimony of at least two witnesses. Since Burr had not engaged in an act of war witnessed by at least two people, Marshall refused to try him on the charge of treason. Instead, Burr was tried on a lesser charge, and he was found not guilty. Marshall had again identified the Supreme Court as interpreter of the Constitution and limited in its powers by that document.

Through the years, Marshall went on to write forty-four decisions, many of them laying the groundwork for the form of government still in operation in the United States. Marshall died in 1835.

In the summer of 1797, Adams sent a team of diplomats—Massachusetts politician Elbridge Gerry, Virginia Federalist leader John Marshall, and Charles C. Pinckney, the former minister to France—to negotiate with French foreign minister Charles-Maurice de Talleyrand-Périgord, but the minister refused to meet with them and sent three aides instead. They opened the meeting asking for a bribe of $250,000 for Talleyrand-Périgord, a loan for France, and an apology from Adams. Because overseas communication took so long in those days, Adams did not learn of these demands until a dispatch arrived on his desk in March of 1798. Some members of his cabinet urged a declaration of war with France, while others called for an alliance with England. Adams decided to continue negotiating for peace but to prepare for war. Congress demanded that the details be made public, and Adams complied, but he kept the names of the French envoys secret and referred to them only as X, Y, and Z. The incident became known as the XYZ Affair.

The public was outraged, and war fever immediately swept the country. But Adams, like Washington before him, felt that the United States was not prepared to do

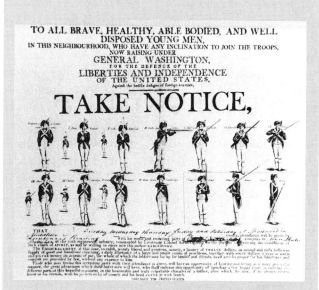

Insulting demands by the French roused Americans to call for war.

The Alien and Sedition Acts

These four laws were passed in the wake of the XYZ Affair, in which President Adams bowed to pressure to release documents proving that French Foreign Minister Talleyrand had demanded a $25,000 bribe through his representatives, M. Bellamy, M. Hauteval, and M. Hottinguer. Rather than implicating the French agents, he substituted the letters X, Y, and Z for their names.

The XYZ Affair raised a storm of anti-Democratic-Republican sentiment, and Adams signed the four bills to crush the opposition. The Naturalization Act made it more difficult for immigrants, most of whom were Jeffersonians, to become citizens. The Alien Act was intended to rid the country of vocal pro-republican immigrants by giving the president the authority to deport them. The Alien Enemies Act was written with French aliens in mind, and authorized the president to deport them if war should break out, as many thought it would. The Sedition Act was a direct attack on Republican-leaning newspapers.

The Naturalization Act was repealed by Congress in 1802, and the other three acts, which had been enacted with two-year expiration dates, were allowed to lapse in 1800.

Left: The French foreign minister Charles-Maurice de Talleyrand-Périgord.

battle against one of Europe's mightiest powers. He acted with restraint. Throughout 1798 and into the next year, an unofficial war, known as the Quasi-War, was waged by American and French ships on the Atlantic. Adams won funds from Congress to enlarge the army and to create a separate naval force that would be administered by a new cabinet post, secretary of the navy. Adams asked George Washington to head the army and Benjamin Stoddert to be the secretary of the navy. While Adams was away in Massachusetts, his cabinet voted to make Hamilton second in command to Washington. Hamilton was what we would call a "hawk" today, and immediately called for war with both France and Spanish America, which worried President Adams, who felt that a seditious government takeover by the army, under Hamilton's leadership, was entirely possible.

Alien and Sedition Acts

The country was split into two camps, pro-French and pro-British, with Federalists foursquare against the French. They believed that there were too many French spies among the country's rapidly increasing immigrant population. The Federalists were also concerned about Irish Americans, many of whom were longtime enemies of the British. Jefferson's anti-British Democratic-Republicans were concerned that Adams was planning to establish a monarchy. Sympathetic newspapers of the day, especially the Philadelphia *Aurora*, referred to Adams as the "Duke of Braintree," and the president was criticized for appointing his son, John Quincy Adams, as minister to Prussia, while rumors were spread that the family was enriching its fortunes at the public's expense. Meanwhile, Hamilton and the Federalists won a Congressional majority in the 1798 midterm elections, which they saw an opportunity to forcibly eliminate their opposition.

Congress quickly passed four bills in the tense summer of 1798, and—against his better judgment—President Adams signed them. The Naturalization Act, the Alien Act, the Alien Enemies Act, and the Sedition Act aroused a tremendous public outcry. The Naturalization

Act extended the waiting period for citizenship, and with it an immigrant's right to vote, from five to fourteen years. The alien acts gave the president the right to deport or jail any foreign citizens he judged to be a threat to the nation's stability, especially during wartime. The Sedition Act criminalized criticism of the government. To write or publish views ridiculing the administration was punishable by harsh fines and jail terms. In all, twenty-five people were arrested and ten convicted under the sedition law. All of them were journalists, including Benjamin Franklin Bache, publisher of the Philadelphia *Aurora* and grandson of Benjamin Franklin.

Vice President Thomas Jefferson vehemently opposed the Alien and Sedition Acts, as the four acts were called, and he argued that they were unconstitutional. He saw the Sedition Act, in particular, as a violation of the First Amendment guarantee of the right to free speech. With the help of former U.S. representative James Madison, Jefferson wrote the Kentucky and Virginia Resolutions, which were passed by the legislatures of those states. They challenged federal authority to enact such laws, and the Kentucky Resolution went a step further by asserting that states had the right to reject federal laws. This was the first challenge to the Constitution in American history.

Move to Washington

It was not surprising that John Adams was miserable in his single term as president. The outcry against the Alien and Sedition Acts was widespread, but he was forced to defend them. The undeclared war with France

Right: Adams was the first president to move into the presidential mansion in Washington, but it was far from mansion-like at the time.

Cleaning House

Thomas Pickering of Massachusetts, who served as Adams's first secretary of state, had been a member of George Washington's cabinet, first as war secretary and then as secretary of state. His loyalties, though, were to Alexander Hamilton, and when Adams found out that Pickering was undermining his administration, he asked him to resign. But Pickering refused, and the president fired him. It was the only time in American history that a secretary of state has been forced out by a direct presidential order.

still dragged on, but much of Europe was now uniting against France, and Adams felt that the prospects for a new peace accord were promising. Early in 1799, he sent a new minister to France to renew the negotiations, a move that caused a furor in the Senate, which was packed with pro-war Federalists, and pro-Hamilton cabinet members attempted to delay the mission by slowing correspondence and instructions. Despite these obstacles, when the Convention of 1800 was concluded, Adams took credit and was justly proud of his avoidance of full-scale battle. He would write later, "I desire no other inscription over my gravestone than: 'Here lies John Adams, who took upon himself the responsibility of the peace with France in the year 1800'."

The Adams Administration

Administration Dates: March 4, 1797–March 4, 1801
Vice President: Thomas Jefferson (1797–1801)
Cabinet:

Secretary of State	Timothy Pickering (1797–1800)
	John Marshall (1800–1801)
Secretary of the Treasury	Oliver Wolcott Jr. (1797–1801)
	Samuel Dexter (1801)
Secretary of War	James McHenry (1797–1800)
	Samuel Dexter (1800–1801)
Attorney General	Charles Lee (1797–1801)
Secretary of the Navy (created in 1798)	Benjamin Stoddert (1798–1801)
Postmaster General	Joseph Habersham (1797–1801)

When the seat of government moved to Washington, D.C., in 1800, Adams made the journey to what New Englanders like him viewed as a muddy, malarial swamp

in the middle of nowhere. A carriage carrying Abigail Adams there for the first time became lost in the woods. The White House, then called the President's House, was still unfinished, and the damp draftiness permanently aggravated the First lady's chronic rheumatism. Their son Charles, an alcoholic, died that year, but Adams somewhat halfheartedly agreed to run for a second term.

As the election of 1800 neared, the power of the Federalists was rapidly disintegrating, and Congressional debate over ratification of the treaty with France split them further. Hamilton attacked Adams in a harsh fifty-page document that called him unfit to hold the presidency and characterized him as a leader who had humiliated the nation. Meanwhile, Democratic-Republicans were gaining political strength in several states, and Adams and his running mate Pinckney were beaten by fewer than a dozen electoral votes apiece by Jefferson and Aaron Burr. Responding to his loss, Adams created over two hundred new judicial positions during the final days of his term, filling them with Federalists in what became known as the Midnight Appointments.

Quote, Unquote

"The people, when they have been unchecked, have been as unjust, tyrannical, brutal, barbarous, and cruel, as any king or senate possessed of uncontrollable power. The majority has eternally, and without one exception, usurped over the rights of the minority."
—*John Adams*

Retirement

When Jefferson was inaugurated, Adams refused to formally greet him at the ceremony. He left early that morning for his family estate in Massachusetts, where he spent the next quarter-century roaming its lands once again. He spent his time reading and writing, and when his eyesight failed, listening to his grandchildren read aloud to him. He and his longtime enemy, Jefferson, eventually made peace in 1812, and corresponded regularly after that. Widowed in 1818, Adams had the honor of watching his son, John Quincy Adams, sworn in as the sixth president in 1825.

Left: Thomas Jefferson, Adams's successor in the presidency, had different views on running the new nation.

Adams lived to be ninety years old. He died in Quincy on July 4, 1826, the same day the nation was celebrating the fiftieth anniversary of the Declaration of Independence. His famous last words were, "Jefferson still survives." But John Adams was unaware that Thomas Jefferson had died in Virginia earlier that same day.

Legacy

John Adams was a major influence during the period when the colonies were transformed into the United States of America. His political views, combined with his sense of public service, helped shape the nation's early history and affirm America's sovereignty. His contributions to the Declaration of Independence and the Constitution were especially important.

As president, Adams was justly proud of his major accomplishment—avoiding full-scale conflict with France. Despite the excited public cries for war and the determined militarism of his own Federalist party, he

kept the new, unsteady nation out of battle against a far more powerful foe. He was the first president to achieve a major, lasting peace agreement with a foreign power. Yet the pro-war attitude of many Americans had made him fearful. Some Federalists cautioned him that an unruly mob might execute the first family, in the style of the French Revolution. Adams was outraged by attacks in the press on him, his administration, and his family. As a result, he signed into law the repressive Sedition Act, which borrowed its harsh measures from the restrictive decrees common to the European monarchies.

The Sedition Act was scheduled to expire on the day that Adams left office, but in the meantime, his own vice president, Thomas Jefferson, issued a resolution condemning it. Jefferson's challenge asserted that the federal government did not have the right to exercise powers that weren't entrusted to it by the Constitution. The Kentucky Resolution, furthermore, declared that states had the right to nullify objectionable federal laws. Debate over that question become more pronounced during the next six decades of American politics and history.

Adams's midnight appointments were challenged by the new President Jefferson, who refused to honor them when he took office. The debate over this issue eventually led to the 1803 Supreme Court decision *Marbury v. Madison*, which marked the high court's first invalidation of a law passed in Congress. John Marshall, the chief justice of the Supreme Court at the time, had been reappointed by Adams. He went on to a distinguished tenure on the Court that helped define its place in American government. His lifetime appointment made him the last important Federalist to stay in power.

The awkwardness of having a vice president from a different political party that existed throughout Adams's term never occurred again after 1804, with the passage of the Constitution's Twelfth Amendment, which revised the electoral process and separated the election of president and vice president.

Abigail Adams

Born: *November 1744, Weymouth, Massachusetts*
Died October 28, 1818, Quincy, Massachusetts

"Patriotism in the female sex is the most disinterested of all virtues. Excluded from honors and from offices, we cannot attach ourselves to the State or Government from having held a place of eminence."
—*Abigail Adams*

The wife of one president and mother of another, Abigail Adams was an intelligent, and very independent, woman. For several years, while her husband, John Adams, traveled on diplomatic assignments, she was left to fend for herself and her young children. She corresponded with him frequently, and the ideas and impressions she expressed have been published and add greatly to official sources from this era.

An early champion of equal rights for women, Abigail urged her husband to put his fair-minded practices into law. "I desire you would remember the ladies and be more generous and favorable to them than your ancestors," she wrote to him. "Do not put such power into the hands of the Husbands," She added, "Remember [that] all men would be tyrants if they could."

Left: Boston in the 1760s, when John and Abigail Adams were married.

Parson's Daughter

Abigail Smith Adams was born in November of 1744, in Weymouth, Massachusetts, a seaport fourteen miles outside Boston. Her mother, Elizabeth Quincy, was descended from one of the colony's oldest and most prominent families. Her father, William Smith, was a Harvard-trained Congregationalist minister who taught Abigail and her two sisters to read. Though she had no formal schooling, Abigail read avidly as a young girl, and it gave her a sharp, independent cast of mind.

Abigail met her future husband through an introduction by her older sister's fiancé. Eleven years older than she, John Adams was a Harvard graduate working as a lawyer in Braintree, Massachusetts. He was clearly enchanted both by her intelligence and her opinions. In letters from this period, he called her "Miss Jemima," and he once wrote a "Catalogue of your Faults," pointing out in endearing terms that she was bad at cards, couldn't sing, and walked pigeon-toed. He often noted that she kept her head downcast—a habit that stemmed, he said, from her frequent reading.

They were married by her father in 1764 and moved to property that he owned in Braintree. Their first child, a daughter named after her mother but called "Nabby," was born in 1765, and a son, John Quincy Adams, arrived two years later. By the time their fifth child, Thomas, was born in 1772, the political climate in New England was increasingly tense, and John Adams was one of a number of young, educated colonial lawyers and activists who were advocating independence from England. To protest a tax on tea, angry colonists disguised as Native Americans dumped the unloaded tea from three ships in Boston Harbor in 1773, an event that became known as the Boston Tea Party. Not long afterward, John Adams left for Philadelphia as a delegate to the Continental Congress.

Abigail was left to run the family estate and to care for four children (a fifth child had died in 1770) in an atmosphere of uncertainty and political violence. Her husband came home occasionally, but when war broke out in April 1775, John Adams left again for Philadelphia. The letters she wrote him reveal a lot about the fears faced by ordinary New Englanders during this period. Enemy soldiers were often perilously near, and outbreaks of diseases like smallpox and dysentery left many dead, including her mother. Cannons sometimes boomed all night long. With her son John Quincy, then just seven years old, she watched the battle of Bunker Hill from a far hilltop. Like other homeowners, Abigail was expected to occasionally house militiamen. On one occasion, she melted pewter spoons in a kettle to make bullets for her husband's brother Elihu, a Minuteman.

Reunited

Boston was liberated from the British in March of 1776, and the thirteen colonies signed the Declaration of Independence four months later. Beginning in early 1778, John Adams went to England as a diplomat, and Abigail and their daughter Nabby sailed for London to join him in the summer of 1784. It was the first time Abigail had seen her husband in nearly five years. The family went to Paris from there as John began his duties as the U.S. minister to France. Abigail was shocked by what she felt were rather indecent manners of the French, but she was delighted to attend the theater and ballet, both nonexistent in New England. From 1785 to 1787, Abigail lived in London again after her husband was made the first U.S. minister to the Court of St. James. Irritated by the complexities of running a diplomatic residence with its customary dinner parties—Congress didn't provide funds for their official household—she was worried that she and her husband would be financially ruined, which prompted her to economize. London newspapers poked fun at her thrifty ways.

Abigail was happy to return to Massachusetts in 1788. Shortly afterward, her husband was elected to the office of vice president under George Washington, but she couldn't attend the New York City inauguration because of the late-winter road conditions. John Adams urged his wife to join him rather than face another long separation, and they rented an estate called Richmond Hill, which was considered far removed from town, in what is now Greenwich Village. After accompanying him to Philadelphia when the capital was moved there in 1790, she hosted an open house every Monday and a formal dinner each Wednesday. She also became a close friend of First Lady Martha Washington.

As she approached her fiftieth birthday, Abigail's health began to decline. She returned to Braintree and corresponded steadily with her husband, who wrote back extensively on political matters, such as debates in Congress. In turn, she provided him with her accounts of the local political mood in Massachusetts. Both were delighted when they expressed the same opinion in letters that crossed in the mail. Their children were marrying and beginning families of their own. At various times, they lived with her or sent grandchildren to stay for extended periods.

White House Legacy

After his first night alone in the new presidential home, John Adams wrote in a letter to Abigail back in Philadelphia, "I pray heaven to bestow the best of blessings on this house and all that shall hereafter live in it. May none but honest and wise men ever rule under this roof." A later president, Franklin D. Roosevelt, had the statement engraved over the fireplace in the state dining room.

America's Second First Lady

When John Adams became the second president of the United States in 1797, Abigail again missed the inauguration ceremony because of the difficult winter trek. Soon the chief executive was pleading in letters for her to join him. "The times are critical and dangerous, and I must have you here to assist me," he wrote. "I can do nothing without you." Abigail arrived in Philadelphia in the spring and took over her duties as wife of the president, which involved supervising a staff, planning menus for official dinners, and receiving callers. She also assisted her husband in other matters: She offered her opinions on policy issues, helped him draft correspondence, and relayed discussions she had with members of Congress and other officials. Abigail was sometimes called a "minister without portfolio," or a cabinet secretary without a department.

When her husband's popularity declined as he refused to go to war with France, Abigail grew irritated by newspaper attacks on him. Although she supported the idea of a free press, she was strongly opposed to its penchant for making libelous statements and attacks upon her family. In a letter to her sister, she confirmed her support for a sedition bill pending in Congress, which eventually passed. Several newspaper editors were jailed under its harsh terms, and the resulting uproar contributed to the downfall of her husband's administration.

The "President's House"

When the nation's capital was moved to the District of Columbia in 1800, President Adams left for the new Federal City without his wife. On her way back to Braintree from Philadelphia, she stopped in New York to visit her ailing son Charles, whose alcoholism and gambling had long grieved his parents. She was at his side when he died.

When the "President's House" (the new building was not yet called the White House) was ready for occupancy, Abigail made the trip south. Washington, D.C., was still an isolated, unpopulated swamp tending to promote outbreaks of yellow fever. She found the palace unfinished, damp, and drafty, which aggravated her rheumatism. With little space available, she ordered the family's laundry to be hung in what became known as the East Room. Nevertheless, she entertained as was expected, hosting the first reception on New Year's Day, 1801, in what would become the Oval Room of the White House.

Together at Last

John Adams lost his bid for reelection to Thomas Jefferson in 1800 and he went back to Massachusetts and to his wife, who had left the capital, a month earlier. Their home was now located in Quincy, renamed from Braintree in 1792 in honor of her grandfather, John Quincy. The ex-president and former first lady spent the next seventeen years together, the longest continuous period of each other's company in their marriage. The retirement, however, was marked by more family tragedy as Nabby was diagnosed with breast cancer. Medical treatment for cancer was very primitive in those days, and she underwent a mastectomy without anesthesia in her parents' home. She suffered terribly, but went into remission for another two years. Sadly, she had married an undependable man who left her for long periods of time and often with no funds. Nabby became ill once again and returned to Quincy with her two children so that she could die at the family home.

Abigail Adams outlived three of her own children and her younger and older sisters as well. She contracted typhoid fever a few weeks before her seventy-fourth birthday, and died at home on October 28, 1818. The entire town of Quincy mourned her passing, and both the governor of Massachusetts and the president of Harvard College were among her pallbearers. Her husband remarked that a part of him died with her. Son John Quincy wrote to his brother Thomas that their mother's life "gave the lie to every libel on her sex that was ever written."

John Adams Inaugural Address

Delivered before a Joint Session of Congress, March 4, 1797

When it was first perceived, in early times, that no middle course for America remained between unlimited submission to a foreign legislature and a total independence of its claims, men of reflection were less apprehensive of danger from the formidable power of fleets and armies they must determine to resist than from those contests and dissensions which would certainly arise concerning the forms of government to be instituted over the whole and over the parts of this extensive country. Relying, however, on the purity of their intentions, the justice of their cause, and the integrity and intelligence of the people, under an overruling Providence which had so signally protected this country from the first, the representatives of this nation, then consisting of little more than half its present number, not only broke to pieces the chains which were forging and the rod of iron that was lifted up, but frankly cut asunder the ties which had bound them, and launched into an ocean of uncertainty.

The zeal and ardor of the people during the Revolutionary war, supplying the place of government, commanded a degree of order sufficient at least for the temporary preservation of society. The Confederation which was early felt to be necessary was prepared from the models of the Batavian and Helvetic confederacies, the only examples which remain with any detail and precision in history, and certainly the only ones which the people at large had ever considered. But reflecting on the striking difference in so many particulars between this country and those where a courier may go from the seat of government to the frontier in a single day, it was then certainly foreseen by some who assisted in Congress at the formation of it that it could not be durable.

Negligence of its regulations, inattention to its recommendations, if not disobedience to its authority, not only in individuals but in States, soon appeared with their melancholy consequences—universal languor, jealousies and rivalries of States, decline of navigation and commerce, discouragement of necessary manufactures, universal fall in the value of lands and their produce, contempt of public and private faith, loss of consideration and credit with foreign nations, and at length in discontents, animosities, combinations, partial conventions, and insurrection, threatening some great national calamity.

In this dangerous crisis the people of America were not abandoned by their usual good sense, presence of mind, resolution, or integrity. Measures were pursued to concert a plan to form a more perfect union, establish justice, insure domestic tranquility, provide for the common defense, promote the general welfare, and secure the blessings of liberty. The public disquisitions, discussions, and deliberations issued in the present happy Constitution of Government.

Employed in the service of my country abroad during the whole course of these transactions, I first saw the Constitution of the United States in a foreign country. Irritated by no literary altercation, animated by no public debate, heated by no party animosity, I read it with great satisfaction, as the result of good heads prompted by good hearts, as an experiment better adapted to the genius, character, situation, and relations of this nation and country than any which had ever been proposed or suggested. In its general principles and great outlines it was conformable to such a system of government as I had ever most esteemed, and in some States, my own native State in particular, had contributed to establish. Claiming a right of suffrage, in common with my fellow-citizens, in the adoption or rejection of a constitution which was to rule me and my posterity, as well as them and theirs, I did not hesitate to express my approbation of it on all occasions, in public and in private. It was not then, nor has been since, any objection to it in my mind that the Executive and Senate were not more permanent. Nor have I ever entertained a thought of promoting any alteration in it but such as the people themselves, in the course of their experience, should see and feel to be necessary or expedient, and by their representatives in Congress and the State legislatures, according to the Constitution itself, adopt and ordain.

Returning to the bosom of my country after a painful separation from it for ten years, I had the honor to be elected to a station under the new order of things, and I have repeatedly laid myself under the most serious obligations to support the Constitution. The operation of it has equaled the most sanguine expectations of its friends, and from an habitual attention to it, satisfaction in its administration, and delight in its effects upon the peace, order, prosperity, and happiness of the nation I have acquired an habitual attachment to it and veneration for it. What other form of government, indeed, can so well deserve our esteem and love?

There may be little solidity in an ancient idea that congregations of men into cities and nations are the most pleasing objects in the sight of superior intelligences, but this is very certain, that to a benevolent human mind there can be no spectacle presented by any nation more pleasing, more noble, majestic, or august, than an assembly like that which has so often been seen in this and the other Chamber of Congress, of a Government in which the Executive authority, as well as that of all the branches of the Legislature, are exercised by citizens selected at regular periods by their neighbors to make and execute laws for the general good. Can anything essential, anything more than mere ornament and decoration, be added to this by robes and diamonds? Can authority be more amiable and respectable when it descends from accidents or institutions established in remote antiquity than when it springs fresh from the hearts and judgments of an honest and enlightened people? For it is the people only that are represented. It is their power and majesty that is reflected, and only for their good, in every legitimate government, under whatever form it may appear. The existence of such a government as ours for any length of time is a full proof of a general dissemination of knowledge and virtue throughout the whole body of the people. And what object or consideration more pleasing than this can be presented to the human mind? If national pride is ever justifiable or excusable it is when it springs, not from power or riches, grandeur or glory, but from conviction of national innocence, information, and benevolence.

In the midst of these pleasing ideas we should be unfaithful to ourselves if we should ever lose sight of the danger to our liberties if anything partial or extraneous should infect the purity of our free, fair, virtuous, and independent elections. If an election is to be determined by a majority of a single vote, and that can be procured by a party through artifice or corruption, the Government may be the choice of a party for its own ends, not of the nation for the national good. If that solitary suffrage can be obtained by foreign nations by flattery or menaces, by fraud or violence, by terror, intrigue, or venality, the Government may not be the choice of the American people, but of foreign nations. It may be foreign nations who govern us, and not we, the people, who govern ourselves; and candid men will acknowledge that in such cases choice would have little advantage to boast of over lot or chance.

Such is the amiable and interesting system of government (and such are some of the abuses to which it may be exposed) which the people of America have exhibited to the admiration and anxiety of the wise and virtuous of all nations for eight years under the administration of a citizen who, by a long course of great actions, regulated by prudence, justice, temperance, and fortitude, conducting a people inspired with the same virtues and animated with the same ardent patriotism and love of liberty to independence and peace, to increasing wealth and unexampled prosperity, has merited the gratitude of his fellow-citizens, commanded the highest praises of foreign nations, and secured immortal glory with posterity.

In that retirement which is his voluntary choice may he long live to enjoy the delicious recollection of his services, the gratitude of mankind, the happy fruits of them to himself and the world, which are daily increasing, and that splendid prospect of the future fortunes of this country which is opening from year to year. His name may be still a rampart, and the knowledge that he lives a bulwark, against all open or secret enemies of his country's peace. This example has been recommended to the imitation of his successors by both Houses of Congress and by the voice of the legislatures and the people throughout the nation.

On this subject it might become me better to be silent or to speak with diffidence; but as something may be expected, the occasion, I hope, will be admitted as an apology if I venture to say that if a preference, upon principle, of a free republican government, formed upon long and serious reflection, after a diligent and impartial inquiry after truth; if an attachment to the Constitution of the United States, and a conscientious determination to support it until it shall be altered by the judgments and wishes of the people, expressed in the mode prescribed in it; if a respectful attention to the constitutions of the individual States and a constant caution and delicacy toward the State governments; if an equal and impartial regard to the rights, interest, honor, and happiness of all the States in the Union, without preference or regard to a northern or southern, an eastern or western, position, their various political opinions on unessential points or their personal attachments; if a love of virtuous men of all parties and denominations; if a love of science and letters and a wish to patronize every rational effort to encourage schools, colleges, universities, academies, and every institution for propagating knowledge, virtue, and religion among all classes of the people, not only for their benign influence on the happiness of life in all its stages and classes, and of society in all its forms, but as the only means of preserving our Constitution from its natural enemies, the spirit of sophistry, the spirit of party, the spirit of intrigue, the profligacy of corruption, and the pestilence of foreign influence, which is the angel of destruction to elective governments; if a love of equal laws, of justice, and humanity in the interior administration; if an inclination to improve agriculture, commerce, and manufacturers for necessity, convenience, and defense; if a spirit of equity and humanity toward the aboriginal nations of America, and a disposition to meliorate their condition by inclining them to be more friendly to us, and our citizens to be more friendly to them; if an inflexible determination to maintain peace and inviolable faith with all nations, and that system of neutrality and impartiality among the belligerent powers of Europe which has been adopted by this Government and so solemnly sanctioned by both Houses of Congress and applauded by the legislatures of the States and the public opinion, until it shall be otherwise ordained by Congress; if a personal esteem for the French nation, formed in a residence of seven years chiefly among them, and a sincere desire to preserve the friendship which has been so much for the honor and interest of both nations; if, while the conscious honor and integrity of the people of America and the internal sentiment of their own power and energies must be preserved, an earnest endeavor to investigate every just cause and remove every colorable pretense of complaint; if an intention to pursue by amicable negotiation a reparation for the injuries that have been committed on the commerce of our fellow-citizens by whatever nation, and if success can not be obtained, to lay the facts before the Legislature, that they may consider what further measures the honor and interest of the Government and its constituents demand; if a resolution to do justice as far as may depend upon me, at all times and to all nations, and maintain peace, friendship, and benevolence with all the world; if an unshaken confidence in the honor, spirit, and resources of the American people, on which I have so often hazarded my all and never been deceived; if elevated ideas of the high destinies of this country and of my own duties toward it, founded on a knowledge of the moral principles and intellectual improvements of the people deeply engraven on my mind in early life, and not obscured but exalted by experience and age; and, with humble reverence, I feel it to be my duty to add, if a veneration for the religion of a people who profess and call themselves Christians, and a fixed resolution to consider a decent respect for Christianity among the best recommendations for the public service, can enable me in any degree to comply with your wishes, it shall be my strenuous endeavor that this sagacious injunction of the two Houses shall not be without effect.

With this great example before me, with the sense and spirit, the faith and honor, the duty and interest, of the same American people pledged to support the Constitution of the United States, I entertain no doubt of its continuance in all its energy, and my mind is prepared without hesitation to lay myself under the most solemn obligations to support it to the utmost of my power.

And may that Being who is supreme over all, the Patron of Order, the Fountain of Justice, and the Protector in all ages of the world of virtuous liberty, continue His blessing upon this nation and its Government and give it all possible success and duration consistent with the ends of His providence.

Adams's "Thoughts on Government"

Written in January 1776

John Adams made contributions to the Declaration of Independence and the American Constitution. His ideas influenced the kind of government that was adopted by the state of Massachusetts. Adams and several other American leaders formed similar ideas about how government can operate. The unique American system was developed by a group that drew on personal experiences as well as examples of past political structures.

With the beginning of the American Revolution in 1775, the prospect of American independence became possible. Having rallied against what they viewed as excessive authority of the British government, Americans faced the issue of what kind of government would best serve such ideals as individual liberty and representation, and what kind of government would foster the pursuit of happiness.

George Wythe, a patriot and Virginia judge, who had signed the Declaration of Independence, put these questions to John Adams, who responded with his "Thoughts on Government," which became a blueprint for individual state governments as well as the Constitution of the United States.

Excerpt from "Thoughts on Government"

We ought to consider what is the end of government, before we determine which is the best form. Upon this point all speculative politicians will agree, that the happiness of society is the end of government, as all divines and moral philosophers will agree that the happiness of the individual is the end of man. From this principle it will follow, that the form of government which communicates ease, comfort, security, or, in one word, happiness, to the greatest number of persons, and in the greatest degree, is the best.

All sober inquirers after truth, ancient and modern, pagan and Christian, have declared that the happiness of man, as well as his dignity, consists in virtue. Confucius, Zoroaster, Socrates, Mahomet, not to mention authorities really sacred, have agreed in this.

If there is a form of government, then, whose principle and foundation is virtue, will not every sober man acknowledge it better calculated to promote the general happiness than any other form?

Fear is the foundation of most governments; but it is so sordid and brutal a passion, and renders men in whose breasts it predominates so stupid and miserable, that Americans will not be likely to approve of any political institution which is founded on it.

Honor is truly sacred, but holds a lower rank in the scale of moral excellence than virtue. Indeed, the former is but a part of the latter, and consequently has not equal pretensions to support a frame of government productive of human happiness.

The foundation of every government is some principle or passion in the minds of the people. The noblest principles and most generous affections in our nature, then, have the fairest chance to support the noblest and most generous models of government.

A man must be indifferent to the sneers of modern English men, to mention in their company the names of Sidney, Harrington, Locke, Milton, Nedham, Neville, Burnet, and Hoadly. No small fortitude is necessary to confess that one has read them. The wretched condition of this country, however, for ten or fifteen years past, has frequently reminded me of their principles and reasonings. They will convince any candid mind, that there is no good government but what is republican. That the only valuable part of the British constitution is so; because the very definition of a republic is "an empire of laws, and not of men." That, as a republic is the best of governments, so that particular arrangement of the powers of society, or, in other words, that form of government which is best contrived to secure an impartial and exact execution of the laws, is the best of republics.

Of republics there is an inexhaustible variety, because the possible combinations of the powers of society are capable of innumerable variations.

As good government is an empire of laws, how shall your laws be made? In a large society, inhabiting an extensive country, it is impossible that the whole should assemble to make laws. The first necessary step, then, is to depute power from the many to a few of the most wise and good. But by what rules shall you choose your representatives? Agree upon the number and qualifications of persons who shall have the benefit of choosing, or annex this privilege to the inhabitants of a certain extent of ground.

The principal difficulty lies, and the greatest care should be employed, in constituting this representative assembly. It should be in miniature an exact portrait of the people at large. It should think, feel, reason, and act like them. That it may be the interest of this assembly to do strict justice at all times, it should be an equal representation, or, in other words, equal interests among the people should have equal interests in it. Great care should be taken to effect this, and to prevent unfair, partial, and corrupt elections. Such regulations, however, may be better made in times of greater tranquillity than the present; and they will spring up themselves naturally, when all the powers of government come to be in the hands of the people's friends. At present, it will be safest to proceed in all established modes, to which the people have been familiarized by habit.

A representation of the people in one assembly being obtained, a question arises, whether all the powers of government, legislative, executive, and judicial, shall be left in this body? I think a people cannot be long free, nor ever happy, whose government is in one assembly. My reasons for this opinion are as follow:

1. A single assembly is liable to all the vices, follies, and frailties of an individual; subject to fits of humor, starts of passion, flights of enthusiasm, partialities, or prejudice, and consequently productive of hasty results and absurd judgments. And all these errors ought to be corrected and defects supplied by some controlling power.

2. A single assembly is apt to be avaricious, and in time will not scruple to exempt itself from burden which it will lay, without compunction, on to its constituents.

3. A single assembly is apt to grow ambitious, and after a time will not hesitate to vote itself perpetual.[. . .]

4. A representative assembly, although extremely well qualified, and absolutely necessary, as a branch of the legislative, is unfit to exercise the executive power, for want of two essential properties, secrecy and despatch.

5. A representative assembly is still less qualified for the judicial power, because it is too numerous, too slow, and too little skilled in the laws.

6. Because a single assembly, possessed of all the powers of government, would make arbitrary laws for their own interest, execute all laws arbitrarily for their own interest, and adjudge all controversies in their own favor.

But shall the whole power of legislation rest in one assembly? Most of the foregoing reasons apply equally to prove that the legislative power ought to be more complex; to which we may add, that if the legislative power is wholly in one assembly, and the executive in another, or in a single person, these two powers will oppose and encroach upon each other, until the contest shall end in war, and the whole power, legislative and executive, be usurped by the strongest.

The judicial power, in such case, could not mediate, or hold the balance between the two contending powers, because the legislative would undermine it. And this shows the necessity, too, of giving the executive power a negative upon the legislative, otherwise this will be continually encroaching upon that.

To avoid these dangers, let a distinct assembly be constituted, as a mediator between the two extreme branches of the legislature, that which represents the people, and that which is vested with the executive power.

Let the representative assembly then elect by ballot, from among themselves or their constituents, or both, a distinct assembly, which, for the sake of perspicuity, we will call a council. It may consist of any number you please, say twenty or thirty, and should have a free and independent exercise of its judgment, and consequently a negative voice in the legislature.

These two bodies, thus constituted, and made integral parts of the legislature, let them unite, and by joint ballot choose a governor, who, after being stripped of most of those badges of domination, called prerogatives, should have a free and independent exercise of his judgment, and be made also an integral part of the legislature. This, I know, is liable to objections; and, if you please, you may make him only president of the council, as in Connecticut. But as the governor is to be invested with the executive power, with consent of council, I think he ought to have a negative upon the legislative. If he is annually elective, as he ought to be, he will always have so much reverence and affection for the people, their representatives and counsellors, that, although you give him an independent exercise of his judgment, he will seldom use it in opposition to the two houses, except in cases the public utility of which would be conspicuous; and some such cases would happen.

In the present exigency of American affairs, when, by an act of Parliament, we are put out of the royal protection, and consequently discharged from our allegiance, and it has become necessary to assume government for our immediate security, the governor, lieutenant-governor, secretary, treasurer, commissary, attorney-general, should be chosen by joint ballot of both houses. And these and all other elections, especially of representatives and counsellors, should be annual, there not being in the whole circle of the sciences a maxim more infallible than this, "where annual elections end, there slavery begins."

[. . .]

The dignity and stability of government in all its branches, the morals of the people, and every blessing of society depend so much upon an upright and skillful administration of justice, that the judicial power ought to be distinct from both the legislative and executive, and independent upon both, that so it may be a check upon both, as both should be checks upon that. The judges, therefore, should be always men of learning and experience in the laws, of exemplary morals, great patience, calmness, coolness, and attention. Their minds should not be distracted with jarring interests; they should not be dependent upon any man, or body of men. To these ends, they should hold estates for life in their offices; or, in other words, their commissions should be during good behavior, and their salaries ascertained and established by law. For misbehavior, the grand inquest of the colony, the house of representatives, should impeach them before the governor and council, where they should have time and opportunity to make their defence; but, if convicted, should be removed from their offices, and subjected to such other punishment as shall be thought proper.

[. . .]

If the colonies should assume governments separately, they should be left entirely to their own choice of the forms; and if a continental constitution should be formed, it should be a congress, containing a fair and adequate representation of the colonies, and its authority should sacredly be confined to these cases, namely, war, trade, disputes between colony and colony, the post office, and the unappropriated lands of the crown, as they used to be called. These colonies, under such forms of government, and in such a union, would be unconquerable by all the monarchies of Europe. You and I, my dear friend, have been sent into life at a time when the greatest lawgivers of antiquity would have wished to live. How few of the human race have ever enjoyed an opportunity of making an election of government, more than of air, soil, or climate, for themselves or their children! When, before the present epoch, had three millions of people full power and a fair opportunity to form and establish the wisest and happiest government that human wisdom can contrive? I hope you will avail yourself and your country of that extensive learning and indefatigable industry which you possess, to assist her in the formation of the happiest governments and the best character of a great people. For myself, I must beg you to keep my name out of sight; for this feeble attempt, if it should be known to be mine, would oblige me to apply to myself those lines of the immortal John Milton, in one of his sonnets:

I did but prompt the age to quit their clogs
By the known rules of ancient liberty,
When straight a barbarous noise environs me
Of owls and cuckoos, asses, apes, and dogs . . .

Thomas Jefferson

"The God who gave us life, gave us liberty at the same time."
—*Thomas Jefferson*

homas Jefferson was an accomplished writer, architect, naturalist, inventor, diplomat, and educator, among his many talents. He was of great service to his home state of Virginia, as well as his country. Jefferson helped draft the original documents when Virginia established its postcolonial government in 1781. He wrote an internationally acclaimed book, *Notes on the State of Virginia*, and his Virginia Act for Establishing Religious Freedom was adopted by the state in 1786, and he founded the University of Virginia. In service to his country, Jefferson wrote the Declaration of Independence and he served as a diplomat, secretary of state, vice president, and president. He continually fought for America's most cherished ideals of liberty, asserting that human beings are born with natural rights, rather than having rights bestowed upon them by a government, and that governments govern by consent of the people, rather than by forcing their will upon the people.

Third president of the United States, 1801–1809

Full name: *Thomas Jefferson*

Born: *April 13, 1743, Goochland (now Albemarle) County, Virginia*

Died: *July 4, 1826, Charlottesville, Virginia*

Burial site: *Monticello, Charlottesville, Virginia*

Parents: *Peter and Jane Randolph Jefferson*

Spouse: *Martha Wayles Skelton (1748–82; m. 1772)*

Children: *Martha Washington (1772–1836); Jane Randolph (1774–75); infant son (1777–77); Mary (1778–1804); Lucy Elizabeth (1780–81); Lucy Elizabeth (1782–84); in addition, scientific evidence strongly suggests that Jefferson fathered at least one and as many as six children by slave Sally Hemings*

Religion: *Deism*

Education: *Attended College of William and Mary*

Occupations: *Farmer; lawyer*

Government positions: *Virginia House of Burgesses delegate; Continental Congress member; Virginia governor; minister to France; secretary of state under George Washington; vice president under John Adams*

Political party: *Democratic-Republican*

Dates as president: *March 4, 1801–March 4, 1805 (first term); March 4, 1805–March 4, 1809 (second term)*

Age upon taking office: *57*

Genius of Historic Proportions

President John F. Kennedy once hosted a White House dinner attended by many Nobel Prize winners. Looking out on the gathering of famous scientists, physicians, and writers, he remarked that it was "the most extraordinary collection of talent" that had "ever been gathered together at the White House, with the possible exception of when Thomas Jefferson dined alone."

Always Doing Something

Thomas Jefferson was born in a log cabin in Goochland (now Albemarle) County, Virginia, on April 13, 1743. His father, Peter, had recently acquired 400 acres in an undeveloped area, and the cabin was the beginning of an estate called Shadwell that Peter was building. Jefferson's mother, Jane Randolph Jefferson, was a descendant of original English settlers in Virginia.

A farmer and a surveyor, Peter became a justice of the peace, a judge, and a militia leader as the area around him formed into Albemarle County in 1744. The following year, he took on additional responsibilities upon the death of his friend and his wife's cousin, William Randolph. The Jefferson family moved to Randolph's home, Tuckahoe, for a short time while Peter managed the estate and supervised the education of the four Randolph children as well as his own. Jefferson had two older sisters at the time, and he would soon have three younger sisters and a brother.

Jefferson began receiving private tutoring when he was five years old, and he developed into an excellent student, learning Latin and Greek, reading classical texts and modern literature, and studying geography and the natural sciences. Red-haired and tall (he would eventually be well over six feet), Jefferson played the violin and enjoyed riding and dancing. He entered the College of William and Mary in 1760 and, after graduation, studied law and continued to read widely.

In 1767, Jefferson was certified as a lawyer in Virginia, but by then he was more interested in improving the Shadwell estate. He began planning his own estate based on classical styles of architecture. Always busy, he observed and wrote about wildlife and plants. He practiced crop rotation, the farming technique of switching back and forth between crops for the purpose of improving the soil, and he pursued an interest in new medicines, even traveling to Philadelphia for a newly developed smallpox vaccination. He applied scientific methods to every aspect of his life, keeping detailed records of everything from the daily temperature and weather to expenses and recipes.

Writer and Politician

Jefferson was elected to Virginia's legislature, the House of Burgesses, in 1768 at the age of twenty-five, and two of his lasting political traits surfaced immediately. First, he challenged the influence of wealthy landowners, in favor of the cause of more modest, self-made men. Second, although he was not a skilled speaker, he was an excellent writer, and others turned to him to express their ideas.

In 1769, Jefferson began construction on the estate he designed, calling it Monticello (Italian for

Timeline

1743: Born in Virginia
1762: Graduates from College of William and Mary
1769–74: Serves in Virginia House of Burgesses
1776: Writes the Declaration of Independence
1779–81: Serves as governor of Virginia
1785–89: Serves as minister to France
1790–93: Serves as secretary of state
1797–1801: Serves as vice president
1801–9: Serves as third U.S. president
1803: Louisiana Territory is purchased from France for
$15 million dollars
1804: Lewis and Clark expedition begins
1807: Embargo Act forbids American ships from
leaving American waters
1819: University of Virginia is founded
1826: Dies in Virginia

Left: The Virginia House of Burgesses is the centerpiece of today's Williamsburg restoration.

Right: Richard Henry Lee was an early and vocal supporter of the revolution.

"small mountain"). Two years later, he married Martha Wayles Skelton, a twenty-four-year-old widow who he called "Patsy," who shared his love of music, and played harpsichord and organ. They had six children, but only two of their daughters survived into adulthood.

Jefferson was swept into growing rebellious fervor, especially from Massachusetts, against a series of taxes imposed on the colonies by British authority. The growing rebelliousness of the House of Burgesses led the British to dissolve it. In response, Jefferson and other former House of Burgesses delegates, including George Washington, met secretly in the Raleigh Tavern at Williamsburg, Virginia's capital, and voted to express sympathy toward Massachusetts in its boycott of British goods. Patrick Henry and Richard Henry Lee joined their fellow Virginians in supporting the resistance and, along with Jefferson, organized a protest against British plans to deport colonists to England for trial and execution on charges of burning a British ship off the coast of Rhode Island.

Jefferson was elected delegate to a Virginia convention called to establish a plan of action for the colony, during which he wrote "A Summary of the Rights of British America," a position paper declaring that the English parliament had no authority over the colonies and that its acts were bald attempts to smother basic colonial freedoms. He accused the British of rejecting colonial laws and of preventing the colonies from outlawing slavery. A major theme in the Summary, which became central to the American cause, was an assertion that human rights are derived from the laws of nature, not granted as gifts from monarchs.

Below: Williamsburg's Raleigh Tavern, where Virginians met secretly to decide on whether to support the coming revolution.

Country Boy

To look at him, no one would have guessed Thomas Jefferson's greatness. He was tall (six feet, two inches) and thin. His hazel eyes were small, his nose angular, his lips thin, and his chin pointed. He had red hair and, as a youngster, masses of freckles. His posture was terrible, and he dressed in whatever pleased him, with no sense of fashion at all, even after his sojourn in Paris. Although he was a brilliant conversationalist, Jefferson slipped into a nearly incoherent mumble when he spoke to large groups.

Jefferson fell ill and could not attend the Virginia convention but his Summary was read and applauded by the delegates, although many of its statements were rewritten to avoid offending British authorities. Another Virginia convention met in 1775 to discuss resolutions of the First Continental Congress, a group of representatives from each of the colonies who had met in Philadelphia that had resolved to unite against British authority. Patrick Henry best represented the Virginia convention's support for the Congress by stating, "Give me liberty, or give me death!"

The Declaration of Independence

In 1775, Jefferson spoke before the Second Continental Congress, made up of representatives of all the colonies and who met and served as the American government until the Constitutional Convention twelve years later. The delegates pressed Jefferson to write a summary of his views, but once again his statements were edited and watered down.

The Revolutionary War was well underway when the Congress met again the following year. The delegates wanted to issue a proclamation ending the colonies' allegiance to Britain, and Jefferson was asked to write it. "I will do as well as I can," he replied. His draft was appraised by John Adams, the Massachusetts delegate, and Pennsylvania statesman Benjamin Franklin, who suggested only minor changes, and the document was approved on July 2, 1776. After a few more changes, including the removal of a paragraph denouncing slavery, the Declaration of Independence was officially issued on July 4, 1776. A justification for American independence, its major themes—that humans enjoy natural rights provided by a creator, not by monarchs, and that governments govern by consent of the people, not by forcing government on the people—were familiar Jeffersonian ideals, influenced by British philosopher John Locke. Copies of the new declaration spread throughout the colonies and were received with great enthusiasm.

Patrick Henry

Born in Hanover County, Virginia, in 1736, Patrick Henry was self-educated. After failing as a storekeeper and a farmer, Henry studied law and became a lawyer in 1760.

In 1765, he became a member of the House of Burgesses, the colonial legislature of Virginia. Fiercely rebellious, he led protests against British taxes imposed on the colonies. In 1769, he urged a break from Great Britain. Henry was chairman of a committee that prepared a defense plan for Virginia during the American Revolution (1775–83) and helped draft the Virginia Constitution. He was governor of Virginia (1776–79, 1784–86) and a delegate to the Virginia convention (1788) for the ratification of the U.S. Constitution. Believing the Constitution did not safeguard the rights of states and of individuals, he led support for the Bill of Rights—the first ten amendments to the Constitution. After declining several government positions, he was elected to the Virginia legislature in 1799, but died before his term began.

John Locke

John Locke was an English philosopher who emphasized empiricism, the importance of experience of the senses in pursuit of knowledge rather than instinctive speculation or deduction. Locke's doctrine was expressed in his Essay Concerning Human Understanding (1690). He regarded the mind of a person at birth as a tabula rasa (a blank slate) upon which experience created and stored knowledge, just as a person can write facts on a chalkboard. Locke held that all persons are born good, independent, and equal.

In his Two Treatises of Government (1690), Locke attacked the theory of divine right of kings. He argued that sovereignty (supreme authority) resided with the people. He further stated that the state is bound by civil law and natural law. Locke argued that revolution was not only a right, but often an obligation whenever natural rights are threatened. "Property" is defined as a person's body and all things that the person legally possesses under civil law.

Locke died in 1704, but his works were highly influential during the eighteenth century. His impact on Jefferson and other American leaders is reflected in both the Declaration of Independence and the Constitution. The Declaration of Independence is a justification for American rebellion: natural rights, life, and liberty had been violated by Great Britain (the violations are listed in the document), and after attempts to address those wrongs had failed, Americans felt impelled to declare independence. Locke's belief that governments should follow majority rule is reflected in the Constitution. Locke had proposed a government consisting of three branches, each of which could check and balance the actions of the other branches (but Locke's system called for a more powerful legislative branch than the Constitution outlines). Locke's writings helped American leaders to form their ideas on human rights and to establish a system of government that reflected the will of the people.

Above: New Yorkers toppled a statue of King George III and melted it down for bullets to use against his troops.

Representing His State

Jefferson resigned from the Continental Congress to return to Virginia to take part in drafting a form of republican government for the colony, putting power into the hands of the citizens, who choose their leaders in elections. His ideas for placing few restrictions on individuals and expanding voting rights to include small landowners were adopted, and a milder form of his stand on religious freedom and separation of church and state was accepted. His provision to guarantee public education for all children, regardless of economic background, was rejected.

Jefferson occupied himself through 1779 building and refining his estate at Monticello. During his years there, he introduced olive trees to North America, and he experimented with introducing other tree species not native to Virginia, including orange trees. He perfected an improved plow that won a gold medal from the French Agricultural Society. He also invented such conveniences as a swivel chair and a dumbwaiter to get food up from the basement kitchen to the ground-floor dining room, and even a kind of duplicating machine that connected the motion of one handheld pen with another, creating a

Right: An early draft of the Declaration of Independence hangs in Jefferson's home at Monticello.

Credit Where It Is Due

Jefferson didn't think he was qualified to write the Declaration of Independence, and suggested that John Adams was the right person to do it. Adams didn't agree, responding: "Reason first: you are a Virginian, and Virginia ought to be at the head of this business. Reason second: I am obnoxious, suspected and unpopular; you are very much otherwise. Reason third: you can write ten times better than I can."

copy when the writer moved the first pen. Jefferson also tinkered with clocks, steam engines, and central heating; drew plans for cities; and read and collected books on every subject imaginable.

When Jefferson was elected governor of Virginia in 1779, fighting in the Revolution had spread from New England to the southern states. Georgia and the Carolinas fell under British control, and British troops moved into Virginia, setting up headquarters in Yorktown. Military shrewdness was not among Jefferson's talents, and Virginia fell when he responded too slowly to the enemy advance. He barely escaped an attack on Monticello. He declined reelection in 1781 in favor of someone with a military background. His conduct during the war was investigated by the Virginia legislature in 1781, but a newly elected legislature cleared him of all charges the following year.

Jefferson continued to study, tinker, and write. In 1785, he wrote an internationally acclaimed book,

Notes on the State of Virginia, containing observations on the natural history, geography, climate, agriculture, and economy of the state. The book also included insights on Native Americans of the region, as well as Jefferson's views on balance of powers in government, and an essay denouncing slavery. The essay led to his Act for Establishing Religious Freedom, which was adopted in Virginia in 1786.

However, that period was also a sad time for Jefferson. Patsy, his wife for ten years, died on September 6, 1782, and two of their daughters and a son had died as infants. Another daughter, Elizabeth, born shortly before Patsy's death, died in 1784. Jefferson remained in seclusion for several months following his wife's death, reemerging in 1783 when he was elected to the Congress established by the Articles of Confederation to set the course of the new country's government. He issued several papers expressing his ideas, one of which recommended that American currency should be based on the decimal system, based on the number ten, which led to the establishment of the penny and the dime.

Jefferson was appointed Minister to France in 1784, and joined his friends John Adams and Benjamin Franklin in Paris. Franklin retired the following year, and Adams returned to England to represent America there while Jefferson stayed behind and helped negotiate treaties with European nations. He became a great favorite among the French and was charmed by their country as well. The widower Jefferson apparently began a romance with Sally

Religious Freedom

Thomas Jefferson was a strong believer in the separation of church and state, and he practiced what he preached. He didn't belong to any church. He was a strong believer in Christian ideas, though. He wrote that, "I am a real Christian, that is to say, a disciple of the doctrines of Jesus." But he added that these doctrines, while they were "the most perfect and sublime that has ever been taught by man … [had been] adulterated and sophisticated" by priests and ministers. Jefferson was a reader of the Bible, but he approached it with the same analytical frame of mind as with all the other books he read.

Hemings, one of his slaves, who traveled with him during this time.

As political struggles developed in France late in the 1780s, Jefferson hoped for a peaceful revolution that would transform it from a monarchy to a representative government, but the extremely violent French Revolution (1789-1803) occurred instead. While he was in France, Jefferson was sent a copy of the Constitution that had been accepted by a 1787 convention in

Sally Hemings

In colonial America, the status of the mother—free or slave—determined the status of the child. Sally Hemings's father, John Wayles, was white, but her mother, Elizabeth Hemings, was a mulatto slave—the child of a white father and an African mother. Elizabeth was Wayles' slave from birth, and after the death of his wife, she became his mistress. Together they had six children.

Wayles died in 1773, the same year Sally was born. Sally, her mother, and her five siblings (along with about 125 other slaves and 11,000 acres of land), were inherited by Martha Wayles Jefferson, wife of Thomas Jefferson. Sally Hemings was Martha's half-sister, sharing the same father. Since Martha was born in wedlock, she had rights to the family estate. The Hemings children were taken to Monticello, Jefferson's Virginia estate, and made house slaves.

Martha Jefferson died in September of 1782, leaving Thomas Jefferson a widower and the father of two girls. He was sent as a diplomat to France two years later. Jefferson's eldest daughter, Martha, joined him in Paris to attend school, and in 1787, he sent for his other daughter, Maria, who brought Sally with her.

Historians are not certain exactly what happened in Paris between Thomas Jefferson and Sally Hemings. Legally, she was a free person in Paris, as slavery had been abolished there. In the fall of 1789, Jefferson returned to America with his two daughters, as well as Sally and her brother James, who had been in Paris working for Jefferson and apprenticing as a chef.

By all accounts, Sally was visibly pregnant when she arrived back at Monticello. Many years later, in 1873, Madison Hemings, Sally's sixth child, spoke of his mother's return from Paris in an Ohio newspaper, the Pike County Republican. During her time in Paris, he said, "My mother became Mr. Jefferson's concubine, and when he was called back home she was [pregnant] by him." He went

on to say that his mother balked at returning to America, because "in France she was free, while [in] Virginia she would be re-enslaved." Madison Hemings said that Jefferson "promised her extraordinary privileges, and made a solemn pledge that her children should be freed at the age of twenty-one years" if Sally left Paris. "Soon after their arrival, [my mother] gave birth to a child, of whom Thomas Jefferson was the father."

Between 1790 and 1808, Sally Hemings gave birth to seven children while residing at Monticello. Two children were listed as "runaways" in Jefferson's personal records, but the reality was that they were allowed to walk away, and were able to blend into the free white world of Washington, D.C., because of their light-colored skin. Two other children were freed in Jefferson's will when he died in 1826, and his daughter, Martha, freed Sally Hemings, who died in 1835.

The public first learned of Sally Hemings in 1802, during the second year of Jefferson's presidency, when the Richmond Recorder published an article that speculated on a relationship between Hemings and the president. The possibility that Jefferson had fathered Sally's children caused great controversy. At the time, the charge was proven neither true nor false; the president himself never denied or confirmed the relationship.

Historians argued about the Jefferson-Hemings relationship for years, but the results of a 1998 DNA test on known descendants of both Jefferson and Hemings added great weight to the historical evidence for a connection. The complex test results showed a definite genetic link between the two families, but could only confirm that a Jefferson family member, and not necessarily Thomas Jefferson, fathered Sally Hemings's children. The president's brother, Randolph, and his two sons, spent some time at Monticello. More tests will be needed before any definitive scientific findings can prove Jefferson's paternity one way or another.

Left: French privateers routinely attacked American ships and kidnapped American seamen.

Philadelphia. Jefferson wrote to fellow Virginian James Madison, a delegate of the Convention, that he approved of the document, but recommended that a bill of rights for citizens be added. He also expressed fear that there was no provision that could stop a president from being continually reelected. As a congressman in the newly formed United States, Madison fought for Jefferson's idea of a Bill of Rights, which became the first ten amendments to the U.S. Constitution in 1791. Jefferson, meanwhile, had been called back to the United States in 1789 to serve as secretary of state for the nation's first president, George Washington.

Jefferson and Hamilton

During Washington's administration, Thomas Jefferson and Alexander Hamilton, the secretary of the treasury, led different approaches to the federal government. Favoring few federal laws and a farm-based economy that valued small landowners, Jefferson clashed with Hamilton's Federalist plans for a strong central government and an economy led by commerce and industry. Washington often sided with Hamilton, though he encouraged and respected their varying views.

"Those who labor in the earth are the chosen people of God, if ever He had a chosen people, whose breasts He has made His peculiar deposit for substantial and genuine virtue."

—*Thomas Jefferson*

Jefferson's views were represented in Congress by Madison and others who became known as Anti-Federalists. They opposed a strong central government as well as the Federalist plan for introducing taxes and creating a national bank. Hamilton argued that taxes were needed for such things as paying off the nation's debt and funding federal programs, but the anti-Federalists countered that tax revenues would fuel a large-scale federal government that would dilute the powers of the individual states. They also believed that the creation of a national bank system would create an economy that rewarded lenders and merchants at the expense of producers of goods, like farmers and craftsmen.

Jefferson called the Federalists' bank measure unconstitutional, arguing that Congress was not authorized to charter a national bank, but Hamilton countered that Congress was granted by the Constitution the right to levy taxes, coin money, and pay the nation's debts—all of which were functions of a national bank.

The dispute between the Federalists and anti-Federalists widened when Great Britain and France went to war in 1793. President Washington wanted to stay out

Right: The French ambassador, Edmond Charles Genet.

of the conflict to protect the young nation, but Hamilton favored maintaining ties with Great Britain to continue receiving its trade revenue. On the other hand, Jefferson and his followers sided with France, noting that the French had formed an alliance with America that made independence possible. Washington sided with Hamilton and the Federalists.

The disputes between Hamilton and Jefferson led to the formation of opposing political parties, the Federalists and the Democratic-Republicans. These parties were much less organized than the modern-day ones that emerged in the 1830s. Federalists generally included those who favored a strong central government, Hamilton's economic system, and flexible interpretation of the Constitution. Democratic-Republicans, on the other hand, wanted to limit national government to emphasize states' rights. Called "constructionists," they argued that if the Constitution was to remain meaningful, it must be followed to the letter, while others, like Hamilton, contended that the document served as a framework and guide. They agreed that its basic principles must be followed, but they believed that the Constitution was open to interpretation.

Jefferson grew increasingly frustrated by Washington's administration. Washington had planned to serve only one term, but the nation was growing apart, and for the sake of maintaining unity, he ran for a second term. He asked Jefferson to continue on as secretary of state, and he remained in the administration until 1794. He returned to Monticello, but he stayed politically active by writing commentary in various journals, and he became president of the American Philosophical Society in 1797.

Jefferson and Adams

As Washington's second term approached its end, Jefferson announced his own candidacy for president. In the first few presidential elections, each state government appointed electors based on their populations. Each elector voted for two candidates, and the candidate with the most votes became president, while the runner-up became vice president. John Adams edged Jefferson by three electoral votes to claim the presidency in 1796, and as vice president, Jefferson was back in Philadelphia serving an administration whose policies countered his beliefs.

Shortly after he became president, Adams sent diplomats to France, but three French agents informed them that a bribe was expected to be paid before negotiations could begin. Adams made the French demands public in 1798, identifying the three French agents as simply X, Y, and Z. The American public was outraged toward France over what they called the XYZ Affair, and former president Washington was alerted to be ready to command American troops in a possible war with France, which seemed quite likely.

The American army and navy were expanded to prepare for war, and the Department of the Navy was created. Those actions increased the federal government's powers, which Jefferson found objectionable, and he became further incensed when Federalists passed the Alien and Sedition Acts, four bills passed by Congress and signed into law by President Adams in 1798. The Naturalization Act extended the waiting period for immigrant citizenship, and their right to vote, from five to fourteen years. The Alien Acts gave the president the right to deport or jail foreign citizens he thought were a threat to the nation's stability, especially during wartime. The Sedition Act, intended to stifle criticism of the government, made it a criminal offense to print or publish false, malicious, or scandalous statements directed against the U.S. government, the president, or Congress. Writing or publishing views that disparaged the administration was punishable by harsh fines and jail terms. It was an attempt by Federalists to silence newspapers supporting the Democratic-Republican Party.

Jefferson and Madison were the most outspoken opponents of these laws. To protest Federalist violations of civil liberties and the freedom of the press, Jefferson worked through the Kentucky legislature and Madison through Virginia's legislature. Both states passed resolutions declaring that states had a right to nullify federal laws they considered excessive. Although the resolutions accomplished little at the time, they were part of a larger, negative response to the Federalist-dominated government. Adams became hugely unpopular after the acts went into effect, and he backlash against the Federalists was the beginning of the party's downfall.

Actions vs. Ideology

Political power in the United States moved from the Federalists to the Democratic-Republicans with the election of 1800. Jefferson and Aaron Burr another Democratic-Republican, both finished ahead of Adams in electoral votes, but there was a problem. Jefferson and Burr tied with 73 electoral votes. Each elector voted for two candidates, but they weren't required to specifically name which one they favored for president. It was assumed all along that Jefferson was the presidential candidate, but the Constitution mandates that if no candidate receives a majority of votes, the election is to be decided in the House of Representatives, with each state having one vote.

Election Results

1800

Presidential / Vice Presidential Candidates	Popular votes	Electoral votes
Thomas Jefferson (Democratic-Republican)	—	73
Aaron Burr (Democratic-Republican)	—	73
John Adams (Federalist)	—	65
Charles C. Pinckney (Federalist)	—	64
John Jay (Federalist)	—	1

Popular votes were not yet part of the presidential election of 1800. (The general public did not vote.) Under the system then in place, the person with the highest number of electoral votes became president; the person in second place became the vice president. Because both Jefferson and Burr received 73 votes, the vote went to the U.S. House of Representatives, where each state had a single vote. On the thirty-sixth ballot, Jefferson received ten votes, Burr received four, and two states abstained. Thus, Jefferson became president and Burr became vice president.

1804

Presidential / Vice Presidential Candidates	Popular votes	Electoral votes
Thomas Jefferson/George Clinton (Democratic-Republican)	—	162
Charles C. Pinckney/Rufus King (Federalist)	—	14

Popular votes were not yet part of the presidential election of 1804. (The general public did not vote.) The 1804 election was the first election held under the Twelfth Amendment to the U.S. Constitution, which requires electors to cast separate ballots for president and vice president during the nomination process.

The House voted thirty-six times without resolving the election, with Federalists doing all they could to block Jefferson's election. Jefferson finally prevailed on the thirty-seventh ballot, 10 votes to 4, with two states voting for other candidates, and he became the first president to be inaugurated in the nation's new capital, the District of Columbia. He regarded his victory as a "revolution" representing the will of common people. However, he made an attempt to bring the nation together with a calming and modest inaugural address. "We are all Federalists, we are all Republicans," he said.

Differences between Adams and Jefferson were so strained that Adams did not attend the inauguration. The two men, who had worked together on the Declaration of Independence and as diplomats in France, did not speak

Shake on It

During a Fourth of July reception in 1801, Jefferson shook hands with his diplomat guests, beginning a custom that presidents have followed ever since. The first two presidents, Washington and Adams, bowed to their guests.

again for many years. After the election, while serving out his term, Adams and lame duck Federalists in Congress created some 200 new judicial posts and filled them with Federalist sympathizers. With their influence in the presidency and Congress lost, the Federalists intended to maintain power through the federal court system.

Upon taking office, Jefferson immediately instructed his secretary of state, James Madison, to withhold all judicial appointments that had not yet been commissioned. Judge William Marbury, one of those affected by Jefferson's actions, sued to have the Supreme Court to intervene, and in the historic *Marbury v. Madison* ruling of 1803, Chief Justice John Marshall, himself a Federalist, ruled that the law passed by Congress allowing Marbury to sue was unconstitutional. At the same time, he took the opportunity to severely criticize the actions of Jefferson and Madison. The case set a precedent for judicial review—meaning that the Supreme Court, if petitioned, could determine the constitutionality of actions undertaken by the other two branches of the federal government.

Jefferson faced war soon after taking office. Barbary pirates, who controlled parts of the Mediterranean Sea from ports on the Barbary coast, present-day Algeria, Libya, and Tunisia, demanded payment of "tributes" to keep them from attacking vessels passing their territory. Jefferson refused to pay these bribes, and the conflict eventually led to a series of naval battles, which the United States won, in 1805.

The Jefferson Administration

Administration Dates:	March 4, 1801–March 4, 1805
	March 4, 1805–March 4, 1809
Vice President:	Aaron Burr (1801–5)
	George Clinton (1805–9)
Cabinet:	
Secretary of State	James Madison (1801–9)
Secretary of the Treasury	Samuel Dexter (1801)
	Albert Gallatin (1801–9)
Secretary of War	Henry Dearborn (1801–9)
Attorney General	Levi Lincoln (1801–5)
	John Breckinridge (1805–6)
	Caesar A. Rodney (1807–9)
Secretary of the Navy	Benjamin Stoddert (1801)
	Robert Smith (1801–9)
Postmaster General	Joseph Habersham (1801)
	Gideon Granger (1801–9)

Meanwhile, American diplomats were negotiating with the French Emperor Napoleon to purchase the port city of New Orleans, which was soon to return from Spanish to French control. In 1803, Napoleon expanded his offer to include the entire French colony of Louisiana—an area of more than 800,000 square miles west of the Mississippi River.

Ideologically, Jefferson was a strict constructionist of the Constitution, which is silent on land acquisitions. He considered proposing a constitutional amendment in order to make the purchase, but when Napoleon began indicating that he was having second thoughts about

The Shores of Tripoli

The pirates along North Africa's Barbary coast had been the scourge of the Mediterranean for generations, attacking the ships of countries that didn't pay tribute for protection. The United States and other countries went along on the theory that tribute was cheaper than war. But when the pirates raised the ante in 1801, President Jefferson sent in a naval fleet to put them out of business. When the pirates captured the S.S. Philadelphia in 1803 after a long game of cat and mouse, Lieutenant Stephen Decatur attacked their capital at Tripoli. In the wake of Decatur's victory, Jefferson ordered the entire navy into the region. The pirates ended their demands for tribute, but they still had the Philadelphia's crew in custody, and collected a $60,000 ransom for them.

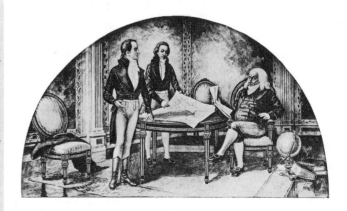

Above: James Monroe and Robert R. Livingston negotiated the Louisiana Purchase with French Emperor Napoleon I.

LOUISIANA PURCHASE

Left: The Louisiana Purchase added more than 800,000 square miles to U.S. territory.

officials in the capital began a kind of social war with American diplomats; each side began to slight the other, disregarding the conventional manners of the time.

During his first term, Jefferson established the Lewis and Clark expedition to explore and report on western North America. He charged Meriwether Lewis and William Clark with reporting on the West's physical features, climate, wildlife, and Native American customs and languages. They began their journey at the headwaters of the Missouri River near St. Louis, Missouri, on May 4, 1804, and reached the Pacific Ocean in January 1807. In addition to bringing back invaluable information on the frontier, the expedition allowed the United States to make a claim on western area beyond the Louisiana Purchase, which was called the Oregon Territory.

Jefferson also authorized several other expeditions. An 1804 trek traced the Red River, the southernmost of the larger Mississippi River tributaries to its source in present-day Oklahoma. And he sent adventurer Zebulon Pike on an 1805 journey to the source of the Mississippi River. A year later, Pike traced the Arkansas River from its headwaters at the Mississippi River into present-day Colorado.

his offer, Jefferson approached Congress and asked for immediate approval by considering the purchase a treaty, which only needed ratification by a two-thirds majority of the Senate for ratification. The Louisiana Purchase— the largest real estate transaction in history—became official on October 20, 1803. The $15 million deal doubled American territory.

But it was still not a done deal. Spain indicated that it was still considering whether or not to give up New Orleans. Jefferson responded by sending military troops to the city and Spain made its decision. The American flag was raised for the first time in New Orleans on December 20, 1803.

The Louisiana Purchase, Jefferson's anti-Federalist actions, and his shows of military strength made him a popular president. His personal style was also well received. He refused all examples of pomp and formality. Even state dinners were casual. Instead of preassigned seating, guests could expect a first-come, first-served arrangement. Foreign diplomats were not officially greeted or announced, and Jefferson often received them dressed casually and wearing slippers. British and Spanish

Quarrelsome Second Term

Jefferson was at the height of his national popularity around election time in 1804. The Twelfth Amendment

Right: Meriwether Lewis and William Clark wrote detailed journals describing everything they saw and did.

Lewis and Clark Expedition

Meriwether Lewis was born in Albemarle County, Virginia—the same county where Thomas Jefferson was born. He seemed destined for the life of a Virginia gentleman farmer, but in 1794, when Pennsylvania insurgents brought on the Whiskey Rebellion, Lewis answered President George Washington's call for militia volunteers. The campaign was bloodless, but Lewis enjoyed himself. He wrote his mother, "I am quite delighted with a soldier's life."

While on frontier duty, Lewis met William Clark, the commander of a special company of sharpshooters into which Lewis was transferred. After service on the Mississippi River, Lewis was asked by his old Virginia friend Thomas Jefferson, then the president of the United States, to become his confidential White House secretary. While Lewis served in that capacity from 1801 until 1803, the president discussed with him his dream of sending an exploring expedition to the Pacific via the Missouri River. When Jefferson offered him leadership of the expedition, Lewis accepted, choosing Clark as his associate. He took a "crash course" in science from scholars of the American Philosophical Society, since he was to make scientific reports on the West.

William Clark was born in Caroline County, Virginia. He joined militia companies fighting local tribes in the Ohio country in 1789, and was commissioned an infantry lieutenant three years later. He served in the campaign of General "Mad Anthony" Wayne that ended with victory over the Native Americans in the 1794 Battle of Fallen Timbers.

Clark led the expedition's fleet of boats up the Missouri River on May 14, 1804, and Lewis joined him to begin leading their men to the territory of the Mandan Indian tribe, in what is now North Dakota. They wintered there before continuing in the spring of 1805.

By August, the Missouri River had dwindled to a series of shallow tributaries that canoes could not negotiate. Luckily, Lewis had hired Toussaint Charbonneau as an interpreter-guide. He turned out to be nearly worthless but his wife, Sacajawea, the sister of the chief of the Shoshone tribe, was an outstanding guide. It was through her that Lewis got the horses he needed to cross the Rocky Mountains. Once across, the explorers drifted in new canoes down the Clearwater and Snake rivers and continued down the Columbia River to the Pacific Ocean. Winter quarters were built at Fort Clatsop, on the Oregon coast south of the Columbia's mouth.

Lewis decided to split the party for its return to Missouri, sending Clark to explore the Yellowstone River while he made a first exploration of the Marias River. Clark's wilderness and leadership skills contributed to the success of the expedition. He got along better with the men than his co-leader, and he was a fine mapmaker. Both men kept detailed diaries of the journey.

Much later, Sacajawea was honored by the U.S. Mint when her likeness was selected to appear on the new dollar coin that went into circulation in 2000.

Above: Meriwether Lewis, a former soldier, was Jefferson's confidential secretary before the president turned him into an explorer.

Below: Sacajawea, a sister of the chief of the Shoshones, was the most valuable member of the Lewis and Clark expedition.

to the Constitution, providing for separate elections for president and vice president, had been adopted after the contested election of 1800. Jefferson won in a landslide, 162 electoral votes to 14 for the Federalist candidate Charles C. Pinckney. George Clinton, a six-term governor of New York, replaced Aaron Burr as vice president. Jefferson had won the electoral votes of every state except Connecticut and Delaware. With the exception of James Monroe, no other president would score such an overwhelming victory for 130 years.

Burr remained in the public eye, however. After losing his bid to succeed Clinton as governor of New York in 1804, he challenged Alexander Hamilton to a duel and killed him. Hamilton had spoken out vigorously against him during the campaign. Shortly after, Burr became involved in a conspiracy on the frontier. With a small military force, he planned either to take possession of part of the Louisiana territory or to invade Mexico, but he was captured and brought to trial on charges of treason in 1807.

Jefferson was so outraged by Burr's action that he overstepped his authority as president as well as his own ideals. He demanded that Burr be found guilty even before the trial began. Chief Justice John Marshall presided over the case, and despite Jefferson's protests, he disallowed many pieces of evidence the government presented. The remaining evidence was insufficient for a guilty verdict, and Burr was set free largely because Jefferson's impulsiveness helped weaken the case against him.

"We lament the mistakes of a good man, and do not begin to detest him until he affects to renounce his principles."

—*Thomas Jefferson*

Meanwhile, Great Britain and France were at war again. Each side forbade any nation to trade with its opponent, and Jefferson replied by pushing the Embargo Act through Congress. In an attempt to have them respect America's neutral rights and to show the importance of trade with the United States, it banned trade with both nations. The embargo was an effort to punish both nations, but it had the opposite effect. With the absence of American trade competition, both nations prospered in international markets. The loss of tariff income was costly to the federal treasury and to those who depended on

Below: Burr is best remembered as the man who killed Alexander Hamilton in a duel.

Below right: Aaron Burr, a former vice president, was a thorn in President Jefferson's side.

trade from Northern industrialists to Southern farmers. Smuggling increased dramatically.

The embargo was extremely unpopular and even considered unconstitutional, but Jefferson maintained it until just before he left office in 1809. He had lost the great support he enjoyed when he was elected to his second term by then, but he was still invited by Democratic-Republicans to run again. He would have likely won the election of 1808, but following the two-term precedent set by George Washington, Jefferson declined to run. James Madison, his longtime friend and political ally, succeeded him as president.

The Sage of Monticello

When Jefferson retired to Monticello after leaving the presidency, he restored the gardens and refurbished the interior of his home with new furniture and his own inventions. Known as the Sage of Monticello, Jefferson frequently received guests, many of whom stayed overnight and for several days. He doted on his grandchildren. After the Library of Congress was burned in the British invasion of Washington, D.C. during the War of 1812, Jefferson sold 6,500 books to the library to begin a new national collection.

Jefferson founded the University of Virginia and became its rector in 1819. He designed the campus and watched the progress of construction through a telescope perched on his "little mountain" overlooking the campus. He helped select professors and the school's curriculum, and he instituted another of his cherished ideals: The university was founded to accept students based on merit, rather than wealth.

Jefferson renewed his friendship with John Adams during the last decade of his life. The two men, who had worked together on the Declaration of Independence, both died on July 4, 1826—fifty years to the day since the declaration was made public. Approaching death, Jefferson wrote his own epitaph, revealing what he considered his three greatest accomplishments:

HERE WAS BURIED
THOMAS JEFFERSON
AUTHOR OF THE DECLARATION OF AMERICAN INDEPENDENCE
OF THE STATUTE OF VIRGINIA FOR RELIGIOUS FREEDOM
AND FATHER OF THE UNIVERSITY OF VIRGINIA.

He neglected to mention that he had also been president of the United States.

The Jefferson Lottery

Although he enriched the country, the country didn't return the favor, and Jefferson retired from the presidency deep in debt. Some of his supporters got together and established a lottery to raise funds for him, but it was never actually held. Instead, a group of his close friends raised enough cash to pay off most of his debt, estimated at well over $100,000, allowing him to live out his days in peace at his beloved Monticello.

Legacy

As a man of many achievements, Thomas Jefferson was both versatile and resourceful. He was able to learn and achieve almost everything he set his mind to, which served him well as president. Although he favored limited power for the federal government and was a constructionist regarding the Constitution, some of his most noteworthy actions as president came when he showed flexibility or used his presidential power. The timing of the Louisiana Purchase, for example, made it important for him to act quickly, decisively, and forcefully—even if his actions were constitutionally questionable. His use of the military—to confront pirates in the Mediterranean and to ensure that Spain would hand over New Orleans as promised—were successful.

However, Jefferson's quick actions in some other areas proved unsuccessful. His challenge to his predecessors' judicial appointments led to the *Marbury v. Madison* case. The decision brought a needed balance of powers—but less presidential power—by establishing the Supreme Court's right to decide the constitutionality of acts of Congress and the executive branch. Jefferson's insistence that his former vice president, Aaron Burr, be found guilty of treason went against his own principles of justice and fair trial. His 1807 Embargo also ended up hurting America, although it was meant to punish Great Britain and France.

Left: Jefferson's beloved home, Monticello.

Martha Jefferson

Born October 19, 1748, Charles City County, Virginia
Died September 6, 1782, Charlottesville, Virginia

"[Martha was] the cherished companion of my life, in whose affections ... I have lived ... the last ten years of my life in unchequered happiness."

—*Thomas Jefferson*

When Thomas Jefferson became president in 1801, he had been a widower for nearly twenty years. His daughter, Patsy, teamed with future First Lady Dolley Madison, the spirited wife of Jefferson's secretary of state, James Madison, to host official social occasions.

Festivities at the Presidential Palace (as the White House was then called) under Jefferson did not demand much effort from the host and hostesses since Jefferson was quite informal.

Things probably would have been different had Martha Wayles Skelton Jefferson lived to see her husband become president. The Presidential Palace would certainly have been filled with music. Thomas and Martha, who he called "Patsy," first found romantic harmony by playing music together—he the violin, and she the harpsichord.

A Duet

Not much is known about Patsy. Jefferson was deeply grieved by her death and rarely wrote or spoke about her afterward. Upon her death, he mourned the loss of "the cherished companion of my life, in whose affections, unabated on both sides, I have lived the last ten years of my life in unchequered happiness."

She was born Martha Wayles on October 19, 1748, in Charles City County, Virginia. At the age of eighteen, she married Bathurst Skelton, a young attorney who died two years later. As a pretty and lively young widow, Martha soon had a few suitors including Thomas Jeffer-

son. He was an attorney, but most of his attention was concentrated on constructing an estate he had designed called Monticello.

Jefferson met Patsy when he was at Williamsburg, the capital of Virginia, serving in the House of Burgesses—the colony's legislative assembly. She lived nearby on the estate called "The Forest," which she had inherited from Skelton.

When Jefferson became interested in Patsy, he wooed her with music. According to some accounts, she was being courted by two other gentleman who showed up at her home one day to find Jefferson already there. He was playing violin, she was playing harpsichord, and they both were singing merrily. The two suitors gave up. Jefferson presented Patsy with a piano during their courtship. The two enjoyed dancing as well.

They were a happy couple. Their wedding was held at The Forest on January 1, 1772. Several days of festivities followed, and then they made the 100-mile ride to Monticello by carriage through increasingly wintry conditions. At the foot of Monticello, they discovered that the roads were impassable for the carriage. Not discouraged, the newlyweds mounted horses and slowly wound their way up to their new home. Because of the storm, there was no one there to greet them, and the house was cold, empty, and dark. But they got a fire going and found a bottle of wine to toast their new life together.

"Time wastes too fast..."

An evening alone together would be rare over the next ten years. Jefferson was increasingly involved in the American Revolution and in the establishment of the postcolonial state of Virginia. Patsy bore six children during that period. Their oldest daughter, Martha, was born in September 1772. Of their six children, only two survived into adulthood—Martha, called Patsy like her mother, and Mary, who was more often called Maria or Polly.

Meanwhile, Jefferson continued to serve in the increasingly rebellious House of Burgesses, which was dissolved by British authorities in 1774. He wrote books and served as a delegate to the Continental Congress. In 1776, he wrote the Declaration of Independence, and from 1777 to 1779, he continually improved Monticello. The work was put on hold when he was elected governor of Virginia in 1779.

Patsy grew frail from her frequent pregnancies. Jefferson turned down an appointment to serve as a diplomat in France, wanting to stay near his invalid wife. In the meantime, the Revolutionary War spread to Virginia. Patsy was in Richmond, Virginia, with her newborn daughter, Lucy Elizabeth, in January 1781, and had to flee an oncoming British attack. Lucy died in April. In June, the family barely escaped when British soldiers stormed Monticello.

The strain of bearing another child in 1782 weakened Patsy further, and she never recovered. She died on September 6, 1782. Jefferson was at her side during her illness. Near her death, Patsy was reading a book by one of her (and Jefferson's) favorite contemporary authors, Laurence Stern. Patsy began copying a passage from his novel *Tristram Shandy* that began, "Time wastes too fast…" When she grew too tired to continue, Jefferson finished the passage for her: "Every time I kiss thy hand to bid adieu, every absence which follows it, are preludes to that eternal separation we are shortly to make."

White House Baby

When Jefferson became president, his daughter Patsy (Mrs. Thomas Mann Randolph Jr.) was the lady of the house in the winter of 1802-03 and again in 1805-06. She gave birth to a son—the first child born in the presidential mansion—and named him James, honoring family friend and Secretary of State James Madison. After Jefferson's presidency ended in 1809, he retired to Monticello, where he lived happily for seventeen more years. Daughter Patsy and her family lived there as well, allowing Jefferson—now called the Sage of Monticello—to dote on his grandchildren while attending to his estate. He received many visitors there until his death in 1826. Both he and his beloved wife are buried at Monticello.

The Declaration of Independence

Issued on July 4, 1776

When the First Continental Congress met in 1774, it sent a list of grievances against British authority in the colonies to England's King George III. But when the Second Continental Congress met, the following year, the King had not responded, and the first battles of the American Revolution had broken out.

By the summer of 1776, colonial sentiment clearly favored independence from Great Britain. England had already declared that American colonists were engaging in "open and avowed rebellion," and had hired German mercenaries to fight in America. On June 7, 1776,

Richard Henry Lee, a Virginia delegate, proposed a resolution to the Congress: "Resolved: That these United Colonies are, and of right ought to be, free and independent states, that they are absolved from all allegiance to the British crown."

A group of men—called the Committee of Five—was appointed to draft an official statement that would present to the world the case for the colonies' independence. It consisted of John Adams of Massachusetts, Roger Sherman of Connecticut, Benjamin Franklin of Pennsylvania, Robert Livingston of New York, and Thomas Jefferson of Virginia.

They voted unanimously to have Jefferson write the statement. He showed the completed text to Adams and Franklin, who suggested only minor changes, and the Committee presented the document—the Declaration of Independence—to Congress, which approved it on July 2. After a few more changes were made, it was printed and made public on July 4, 1776.

Jefferson explained later that the purpose of the Declaration was "not to find out new principles, or new arguments, never before thought of . . . but to place before mankind the common sense of the subject, in terms so plain and firm as to command their assent, and to justify ourselves in the independent stand we are compelled to take."

Below: King George III, "A history of repeated injuries and usurpations ..."

The Declaration of Independence

IN CONGRESS, July 4, 1776.

The unanimous Declaration of the thirteen united States of America,

When in the Course of human events, it becomes necessary for one people to dissolve the political bands which have connected them with another, and to assume among the powers of the earth, the separate and equal station to which the Laws of Nature and of Nature's God entitle them, a decent respect to the opinions of mankind requires that they should declare the causes which impel them to the separation.

We hold these truths to be self-evident, that all men are created equal, that they are endowed by their Creator with certain unalienable Rights, that among these are Life, Liberty and the pursuit of Happiness.—That to secure these rights, Governments are instituted among Men, deriving their just powers from the consent of the governed,—That whenever any Form of Government becomes destructive of these ends, it is the Right of the People to alter or to abolish it, and to institute new Government, laying its foundation on such principles and organizing its powers in such form, as to them shall seem most likely to effect their Safety and Happiness. Prudence, indeed, will dictate that Governments long established should not be changed for light and transient causes; and accordingly all experience hath shewn, that mankind are more disposed to suffer, while evils are sufferable, than to right themselves by abolishing the forms to which they are accustomed. But when a long train of abuses and usurpations, pursuing invariably the same Object evinces a design to reduce them under absolute Despotism, it is their right, it is their duty, to throw off such Government, and to provide new Guards for their future security.—Such has been the patient sufferance of these Colonies; and such is now the necessity which constrains them to alter their former Systems of Government. The history of the present King of Great Britain is a history of repeated injuries and usurpations, all having in direct object the establishment of an absolute Tyranny over these States. To prove this, let Facts be submitted to a candid world.

He has refused his Assent to Laws, the most wholesome and necessary for the public good.

He has forbidden his Governors to pass Laws of immediate and pressing importance, unless suspended in their operation till his Assent should be obtained; and when so suspended, he has utterly neglected to attend to them.

He has refused to pass other Laws for the accommodation of large districts of people, unless those people would relinquish the right of Representation in the Legislature, a right inestimable to them and formidable to tyrants only.

He has called together legislative bodies at places unusual, uncomfortable, and distant from the depository of their public Records, for the sole purpose of fatiguing them into compliance with his measures.

He has dissolved Representative Houses repeatedly, for opposing with manly firmness his invasions on the rights of the people.

He has refused for a long time, after such dissolutions, to cause others to be elected; whereby the Legislative powers, incapable of Annihilation, have returned to the People at large for their exercise; the State remaining in the mean time exposed to all the dangers of invasion from without, and convulsions within.

He has endeavoured to prevent the population of these States; for that purpose obstructing the Laws for Naturalization of Foreigners; refusing to pass others to encourage their migrations hither, and raising the conditions of new Appropriations of Lands.

He has obstructed the Administration of Justice, by refusing his Assent to Laws for establishing Judiciary powers.

He has made Judges dependent on his Will alone, for the tenure of their offices, and the amount and payment of their salaries.

He has erected a multitude of New Offices, and sent hither swarms of Officers to harrass our people, and eat out their substance.

He has kept among us, in times of peace, Standing Armies without the Consent of our legislatures.

He has affected to render the Military independent of and superior to the Civil power.

He has combined with others to subject us to a jurisdiction foreign to our constitution, and unacknowledged by our laws; giving his Assent to their Acts of pretended Legislation:

For Quartering large bodies of armed troops among us:

For protecting them, by a mock Trial, from punishment for any Murders which they should commit on the Inhabitants of these States:

For cutting off our Trade with all parts of the world:

For imposing Taxes on us without our Consent:

For depriving us in many cases, of the benefits of Trial by Jury:

For transporting us beyond Seas to be tried for pretended offences[:]

For abolishing the free System of English Laws in a neighbouring Province, establishing therein an Arbitrary government, and enlarging its Boundaries so as to render it at once an example and fit instrument for introducing the same absolute rule into these Colonies:

For taking away our Charters, abolishing our most valuable Laws, and altering fundamentally the Forms of our Governments:

For suspending our own Legislatures, and declaring themselves invested with power to legislate for us in all cases whatsoever.

He has abdicated Government here, by declaring us out of his Protection and waging War against us.

He has plundered our seas, ravaged our Coasts, burnt our towns, and destroyed the lives of our people.

He is at this time transporting large Armies of foreign Mercenaries to compleat the works of death, desolation and tyranny, already begun with circumstances of Cruelty & perfidy scarcely paralleled in the most barbarous ages, and totally unworthy the Head of a civilized nation.

He has constrained our fellow Citizens taken Captive on the high Seas to bear Arms against their Country, to become the executioners of their friends and Brethren, or to fall themselves by their Hands.

He has excited domestic insurrections amongst us, and has endeavoured to bring on the inhabitants of our frontiers, the merciless Indian Savages, whose known rule of warfare, is an undistinguished destruction of all ages, sexes and conditions.

In every stage of these Oppressions We have Petitioned for Redress in the most humble terms: Our repeated Petitions have been answered only by repeated injury. A Prince whose character is thus marked by every act which may define a Tyrant, is unfit to be the ruler of a free people.

Nor have We been wanting in attentions to our British brethren. We have warned them from time to time of attempts by their legislature to extend an unwarrantable jurisdiction over us. We have reminded them of the circumstances of our emigration and settlement here. We have appealed to their native justice and magnanimity, and we have conjured them by the ties of our common kindred to disavow these usurpations, which, would inevitably interrupt our connections and correspondence. They too have been deaf to the voice of justice and of consanguinity. We must, therefore, acquiesce in the necessity, which denounces our Separation, and hold them, as we hold the rest of mankind, Enemies in War, in Peace Friends.

We, therefore, the Representatives of the united States of America, in General Congress, Assembled, appealing to the Supreme Judge of the world for the rectitude of our intentions, do, in the Name, and by Authority of the good People of these Colonies, solemnly publish and declare, That these United Colonies are, and of Right ought to be Free and Independent States; that they are Absolved from all Allegiance to the British Crown, and that all political connection between them and the State of Great Britain, is and ought to be totally dissolved; and that as Free and Independent States, they have full Power to levy War, conclude Peace, contract Alliances, establish Commerce, and to do all other Acts and Things which Independent States may of right do. And for the support of this Declaration, with a firm reliance on the protection of divine Providence, we mutually pledge to each other our Lives, our Fortunes and our sacred Honor.

The Declaration of Independence was signed by fifty-six representatives of the thirteen colonies. In alphabetical order by state, they were:

Connecticut: Samuel Huntington, Roger Sherman, William Williams, and Oliver Wolcott; Delaware: Thomas McKean, George Read, and Caesar Rodney; Georgia: Button Gwinnett, Lyman Hall, and George Walton; Maryland: Charles Carroll, Samuel Chase, William Paca, and Thomas Stone; Massachusetts: John Adams, Samuel Adams, Elbridge Gerry, John Hancock, and Robert Treat Paine; New Hampshire: Josiah Bartlett, Matthew Thornton, and William Whipple; New Jersey: Abraham Clark, John Hart, Francis Hopkinson, Richard Stockton, and John Witherspoon; New York: William Floyd, Francis Lewis, Philip Livingston, and Lewis Morris; North Carolina: Joseph Hewes, William Hooper, and John Penn; Pennsylvania: George Clymer, Benjamin Franklin, Robert Morris, John Morton, George Ross, Benjamin Rush, James Smith, George Taylor, and James Wilson; Rhode Island: William Ellery and Stephen Hopkins; South Carolina: Thomas Heyward Jr., Thomas Lynch Jr., Arthur Middleton, and Edward Rutledge; and Virginia: Carter Braxton, Benjamin Harrison, Thomas Jefferson, Francis Lightfoot Lee, Richard Henry Lee, Thomas Nelson Jr., and George Wythe.

What Happened Next

Church bells rang throughout Philadelphia, Pennsylvania, on the afternoon of July 4, 1776, to signal that the Declaration of Independence had been ratified by the Continental Congress. Copies were published the following day for distribution, while the actual original document remained with the Congress. The Declaration was cheered throughout the colonies, where the Revolutionary War had been going on for over a year.

Many of the charges against King George were challenged or refuted by John Lind, on behalf of the English government. He wrote a 118-page response to the one-page Declaration. Nevertheless, the Declaration of Independence was regarded then, as it is now, as a well-reasoned and impassioned expression of liberty and the right to overthrow tyranny.

Jefferson's Second Inaugural Address

Monday, March 4, 1805

The oath of office for Thomas Jefferson's second term was administered by Chief Justice John Marshall in the Senate Chamber of the Capitol Building in Washington, D.C. In his address, Jefferson looked back at the accomplishments of his first four years in office, and forward to the country's future.

Proceeding, fellow-citizens, to that qualification which the Constitution requires before my entrance on the charge again conferred on me, it is my duty to express the deep sense I entertain of this new proof of confidence from my fellow-citizens at large, and the zeal with which it inspires me so to conduct myself as may best satisfy their just expectations.

On taking this station on a former occasion I declared the principles on which I believed it my duty to administer the affairs of our Commonwealth. My conscience tells me I have on every occasion acted up to that declaration according to its obvious import and to the understanding of every candid mind.

In the transaction of your foreign affairs we have endeavored to cultivate the friendship of all nations, and especially of those with which we have the most important relations. We have done them justice on all occasions, favored where favor was lawful, and cherished mutual interests and intercourse on fair and equal terms. We are firmly convinced, and we act on that conviction, that with nations as with individuals our interests soundly calculated will ever be found inseparable from our moral duties, and history bears witness to the fact that a just nation is trusted on its word when recourse is had to armaments and wars to bridle others.

At home, fellow-citizens, you best know whether we have done well or ill. The suppression of unnecessary offices, of useless establishments and expenses, enabled us to discontinue our internal taxes. These, covering our land with officers and opening our doors to their intrusions, had already begun that process of domiciliary vexation which once entered is scarcely to be restrained from reaching successively every article of property and produce. If among these taxes some minor ones fell which had not been inconvenient, it was because their amount would not have paid the officers who collected them, and because, if they had any merit, the State authorities might adopt them instead of others less approved.

The remaining revenue on the consumption of foreign articles is paid chiefly by those who can afford to add foreign luxuries to domestic comforts, being collected on our seaboard and frontiers only, and incorporated with the transactions of our mercantile citizens, it may be the pleasure and the pride of an American to ask, What farmer, what mechanic, what laborer ever sees a taxgatherer of the United States? These contributions enable us to support the current expenses of the Government, to fulfill contracts with foreign nations, to extinguish the native right of soil within our limits, to extend those limits, and to apply such a surplus to our public debts as places at a short day their final redemption, and that redemption once effected the revenue thereby liberated may, by a just repartition of it among the States and a corresponding amendment of the Constitution, be applied *in time of peace* to rivers, canals, roads, arts, manufactures, education, and other great objects within each State. *In time of war,* if injustice by ourselves or others must sometimes produce war, increased as the same revenue will be by increased population and consumption, and aided by other resources reserved for that crisis, it may meet within the year all the expenses of the year without encroaching on the rights of future generations by burthening them with the debts of the past. War will then be but a suspension of useful works, and a return to a state of peace, a return to the progress of improvement.

I have said, fellow-citizens, that the income reserved had enabled us to extend our limits, but that extension may possibly pay for itself before we are called on, and in the meantime may keep down the accruing interest; in all events, it will replace the advances we shall have made. I know that the acquisition of Louisiana had been disapproved by some from a candid apprehension that the enlargement of our territory would endanger its union. But who can limit the extent to which the federative principle may operate effectively? The larger our association the less will it be shaken by local passions; and in any view is it not better that the opposite bank of the Mississippi should be settled by our own brethren and children than by strangers of another family? With which should we be most likely to live in harmony and friendly intercourse?

In matters of religion I have considered that its free exercise is placed by the Constitution independent of the powers of the General Government. I have therefore undertaken on no occasion to prescribe the religious exercises suited to it, but have left them, as the Constitution found them, under the direction and discipline of the church or state authorities acknowledged by the several religious societies.

The aboriginal inhabitants of these countries I have regarded with the commiseration their history inspires. Endowed with the faculties and the rights of men, breathing an ardent love of liberty and independence, and occupying a country which left them no desire but to be undisturbed, the stream of overflowing population from other regions directed itself on these shores; without power to divert or habits to contend against it, they have been overwhelmed by the current or driven before it; now reduced within limits too narrow for the hunter's state, humanity enjoins us to teach them agriculture and the domestic arts; to encourage them to that industry which alone can enable them to maintain their place in existence and to prepare them in time for that state of society which to bodily comforts adds the improvement of the mind and morals. We have therefore liberally furnished them with the implements of husbandry and household use; we have placed among them instructors in the arts of first necessity, and they are covered with the aegis of the law against aggressors from among ourselves.

But the endeavors to enlighten them on the fate which awaits their present course of life, to induce them to exercise their reason, follow its dictates, and change their pursuits with the change of circumstances have powerful obstacles to encounter; they are combated by the habits of their bodies, prejudices of their minds, ignorance, pride, and the influence of interested and crafty individuals among them who feel themselves something in the present order of things and fear to become nothing in any other. These persons inculcate a sanctimonious reverence for the customs of their ancestors; that whatsoever they did must be done through all time; that reason is a false guide, and to advance under its counsel in their physical, moral, or political condition is perilous innovation; that their duty is to remain as their Creator made them, ignorance being safety and knowledge full of danger; in short, my friends, among them also is seen the action and counteraction of good sense and of bigotry; they too have their antiphilosophists who find an interest in keeping things in their present state, who dread reformation, and exert all their faculties to maintain the ascendancy of habit over the duty of improving our reason and obeying its mandates.

In giving these outlines I do not mean, fellow-citizens, to arrogate to myself the merit of the measures. That is due, in the first place, to the reflecting character of our citizens at large, who, by the weight of public opinion, influence and strengthen the public measures. It is due to the sound discretion with which they select from among themselves those to whom they confide the legislative duties. It is due to the zeal and wisdom of the characters thus selected, who lay the foundations of public happiness in wholesome laws, the execution of which alone remains for others, and it is due to the able and faithful auxiliaries, whose patriotism has associated them with me in the executive functions.

During this course of administration, and in order to disturb it, the artillery of the press has been leveled against us, charged with whatsoever its licentiousness could devise or dare. These abuses of an institution so important to freedom and science are deeply to be regretted, inasmuch as they tend to lessen its usefulness and to sap its safety. They might, indeed, have been corrected by the wholesome punishments reserved to and provided by the laws of the several States against falsehood and defamation, but public duties more urgent press on the time of public servants, and the offenders have therefore been left to find their punishment in the public indignation.

Nor was it uninteresting to the world that an experiment should be fairly and fully made, whether freedom of discussion, unaided by power, is not sufficient for the propagation and protection of truth—whether a government conducting itself in the true spirit of its constitution, with zeal and purity, and doing no act which it would be unwilling the whole world should witness, can be written down by falsehood and defamation. The experiment has been tried; you have witnessed the scene; our fellow-citizens looked on, cool and collected; they saw the latent source from which these outrages proceeded; they gathered around their public functionaries, and when the Constitution called them to the decision by suffrage, they pronounced their verdict, honorable to those who had served them and consolatory to the friend of man who believes that he may be trusted with the control of his own affairs.

No inference is here intended that the laws provided by the States against false and defamatory publications should not be enforced; he who has time renders a service to public morals and public tranquillity in reforming these abuses by the salutary coercions of the law; but the experiment is noted to prove that, since truth and reason have maintained their ground against false opinions in league with false facts, the press, confined to truth, needs no other legal restraint; the public judgment will correct false reasoning and opinions on a full hearing of all parties; and no other definite line can be drawn between the inestimable liberty of the press and its demoralizing licentiousness. If there be still improprieties which this rule would not restrain, its supplement must be sought in the censorship of public opinion.

Contemplating the union of sentiment now manifested so generally as auguring harmony and happiness to our future course, I offer to our country sincere congratulations. With those, too, not yet rallied to the same point the disposition to do so is gaining strength; facts are piercing through the veil drawn over them, and our doubting brethren will at length see that the mass of their fellow-citizens with whom they can not yet resolve to act as to principles and measures, think as they think and desire what they desire; that our wish as well as theirs is that the public efforts may be directed honestly to the public good, that peace be cultivated, civil and religious liberty unassailed, law and order preserved, equality of rights maintained, and that state of property, equal or unequal, which results to every man from his own industry or that of his father's. When satisfied of these views it is not in human nature that they should not approve and support them. In the meantime let us cherish them with patient affection, let us do them justice,

and more than justice, in all competitions of interest; and we need not doubt that truth, reason, and their own interests will at length prevail, will gather them into the fold of their country, and will complete that entire union of opinion which gives to a nation the blessing of harmony and the benefit of all its strength.

I shall now enter on the duties to which my fellow-citizens have again called me, and shall proceed in the spirit of those principles which they have approved. I fear not that any motives of interest may lead me astray; I am sensible of no passion which could seduce me knowingly from the path of justice, but the weaknesses of human nature and the limits of my own understanding will produce errors of judgment sometimes injurious to your interests. I shall need, therefore, all the indulgence which I have heretofore experienced from my constituents; the want of it will certainly not lessen with increasing years. I shall need, too, the favor of that Being in whose hands we are, who led our fathers, as Israel of old, from their native land and planted them in a country flowing with all the necessaries and comforts of life; who has covered our infancy with His providence and our riper years with His wisdom and power, and to whose goodness I ask you to join in supplications with me that He will so enlighten the minds of your servants, guide their councils, and prosper their measures that whatsoever they do shall result in your good, and shall secure to you the peace, friendship, and approbation of all nations.

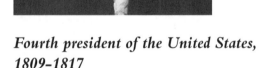

James Madison

"Every word of the Constitution decides a question between power and liberty."

—*James Madison*

Fourth president of the United States, 1809–1817

Full name: *James Madison*
Born: *March 16, 1751, Port Conway, Virginia*
Died: *June 28, 1836, Montpelier, Virginia*
Burial site: *Family cemetery, Montpelier, Virginia*
Parents: *James and Eleanor Rose Conway Madison*
Spouse: *Dolley Dandridge Payne Todd (1768–1849; m. 1794)*
Children: *One stepson*
Religion: *Episcopalian*
Education: *College of New Jersey (now Princeton University; B.A., 1771)*
Occupations: *Politician; farmer*
Government positions: *U.S. Virginia Constitutional Convention member; Continental congressman; Virginia state delegate; U.S. Constitutional representative from Virginia; secretary of state under Thomas Jefferson*
Political party: *Democratic-Republican*
Dates as president: *March 4, 1809–March 4, 1813 (first term); March 4, 1813–March 4, 1817 (second term)*
Age upon taking office: *57*

James Madison helped arrange the convention of 1787 at which the Constitution was written, and he was a leading promoter and defender of the document during the ratification process. He later championed its first ten amendments, the Bill of Rights.

Madison's efforts with the Constitution reflected his particular strengths. Skillful in debate and levelheaded, he was able to balance ideals and realities, conviction and compromise. Standing just five feet, four inches tall and weighing about 100 pounds, he was the smallest of all U.S. presidents. But if he was small in stature, he was large in character, and helped find practical ways to establish a republican form of government representing the will of the people and able to improve on its own imperfections.

Madison was elected president in 1808 during troubling times. Great Britain and France were at war, and neither side respected America's shipping rights. Both countries ignored the young nation's attempts to assert its rights through diplomacy. Madison steered America into the War of 1812 (1812-15) with Great Britain, although the country was ill prepared. The war ended without victory for either side, but American spirits were bolstered by having simply survived it. They also benefited by land and naval victories in the Great Lakes region that secured the frontier north of the Ohio River and west to the Mississippi River for settlement. When Madison left office, the United States was emerging as an equal among the most powerful nations.

Political and Other Fevers

James Madison was born on March 16, 1751, in the home of his maternal grandparents along the Rappahannock River in Port Conway, Virginia. He grew up on a five-thousand-acre estate called Montpelier, which he eventually inherited from his father, also named James, a tobacco grower.

Madison was schooled primarily at home and later studied history, government, and law at the College of New Jersey (later Princeton University), graduating in 1771, a time when American colonists were growing increasingly rebellious against British rule. Madison remained awhile in New Jersey, trying to decide between a career as a clergyman or as a lawyer. Meanwhile, he caught political fever during meetings with a local group that debated issues of the day, like the future course of America.

Six months after graduation, Madison returned to Montpelier in ill health and spent over a year recuperating. Historians generally agree that Madison was a hypochondriac as a young man, claiming repeated illnesses but showing few real symptoms. He spent much of his recuperation period reading and forming ideas for a republican form of government. By 1774, he was determined to participate in pro-independence movements, and he was appointed to the Committee of Safety, a local Virginia defense organization.

Madison was a member of the Virginia Convention, which formed the state's constitution in 1776. He worked to promote religious freedom with another Virginia delegate, Thomas Jefferson, who had recently returned from Philadelphia, Pennsylvania, where he had written

Timeline

1751: Born in Virginia
1771: Graduates from the College of New Jersey (now Princeton University)
1776: Serves as member of Virginia Constitutional Convention
1780–83: Serves as member of Continental Congress
1787: Serves as member of Constitutional Convention
1789–97: Serves in U.S. House of Representatives
1801–9: Serves as secretary of state under Thomas Jefferson
1809–17: Serves as fourth U.S. president
1812: War of 1812 begins
1814: Washington, D.C., captured and burned by British; Francis Scott Key writes "The Star-Spangled Banner"
1836: Dies in Virginia

the Declaration of Independence. Madison served on the state executive council from 1777 to 1778 under Virginia governor Patrick Henry. In 1779, he was elected to the Continental Congress, where, at age twenty-nine, he was the youngest congressman.

"I believe there are more instances of the abridgement of the freedom of the people by gradual and silent encroachements of those in power than by violent and sudden usurpations."

—*James Madison*

Reserved at first, Madison gradually began to participate in the proceedings and became an effective debater and legislator. Like fellow Virginian George Washington, who was then commanding the Continental Army, Madison consistently argued for a stronger central government than the one that had been established by the Articles of Confederation.

Madison returned to Montpelier in 1783. His engagement to a young woman had broken off and he was feeling sad, but he emerged again in 1784, when he was elected to the Virginia legislature. During his time in office, he strongly supported Jefferson's Act for Establishing Religious Freedom, which was passed in 1786. When commerce issues arose between the states of Virginia and Maryland, Madison invited representatives

First Mother

James Madison's mother, Rose Conway Madison, also known as "Nelly," lived to be ninety-eight years old and was of sound mind and body all the way to the end. Her mind was sharp, she didn't need glasses, and it was noted that in her last years, her skin was less wrinkled than her son's. The former president was in his seventies at the time. He would live to eighty-five.

Bookworms

After a postgraduate study of Hebrew and philosophy, Madison went home from Princeton determined to build the most impressive library in Virginia. Thomas Jefferson had beaten him to it, but after the two met in 1776, they set up a kind of interlibrary loan system. Individually, these men ranked as two of America's greatest intellects. Together, they were formidable.

from all the states to a meeting he helped arrange between them. Only five states sent delegates to that Annapolis convention, but they discovered many areas of mutual concern and cooperation. Alexander Hamilton of New York was there, and he and Madison became powerful allies before they eventually parted as leaders of opposing political parties. A second convention was scheduled for the following May in Philadelphia, and Madison's long-held hope of strengthening the central government was on the agenda.

Father of the Constitution

Madison arrived early and well prepared for the convention. He had researched and written a paper on ancient and modern confederacies, and prepared another detailing his observations on the strengths and weaknesses of the Articles of Confederation. He immediately introduced resolutions calling for a new central American government with stronger powers, a plan including an elected chief executive with veto power over legislation, a federal judiciary branch, and a two-chambered legislature. These various branches of government would have specific responsibilities, but they would also have the ability to take part in checks and balances with each other, by approving or disapproving

actions taken by the others. All of these ideas, which had been proposed and favored by several Americans for some time, were adopted into the new Constitution, which replaced the Articles of Confederation.

Madison's Virginia Plan for a bicameral legislature called for a House of Representatives and a Senate. In the House, the number of representatives from each state was determined by its population, and the Senate would be elected by the House of Representatives. A different approach, called the New Jersey Plan, suggested equal representation from each state in a single legislature. Finally, a compromise—called the Connecticut Plan—established a House of Representatives under the Virginia Plan model, but the Senate would have equal representation for each of the states.

Madison attended every convention session, and he was present for every major debate, speech, and vote. His detailed notes on the gathering were collected and published in 1840 as "Journal of the Federal Convention."

Right: Madison was on hand for every session of the Constitutional Convention and published detailed notes on what happened there.

Left: Madison was an influential member of the Continental Congress.

The United States Begins

In order for the Constitution to have legal authority, at least nine of the thirteen states had to ratify it. Madison worked tirelessly for passage. Along with Hamilton and foreign affairs secretary, John Jay, had published a series of essays called "The Federalist Papers," which carefully explained the Constitution's philosophy and countered criticisms of it. In all, eighty-five Federalist papers were issued under the pseudonyms, "A Citizen of New York," or "Publius," and Madison is generally credited with having written twenty-six of them. He consistently argued for the federal government plan and stressed that government in a democratic society can allow for conflicting views.

Meanwhile, Virginia's convention to ratify the Constitution proved challenging. Madison found himself debating against Patrick Henry, James Monroe, and George Mason, all of whom felt that individual states would be dominated by the new national government and that individual rights weren't guaranteed in the document. Madison convinced enough delegates otherwise though, and the Constitution was ratified in Virginia by a slim margin—89 votes to 79. Addressing concerns about federal power, Madison pointed out that a national government would be a more forceful power for negotiating treaties than would individual states.

George Mason

Born in Fairfax County, Virginia, in 1725, George Mason was the son of a wealthy planter who died when Mason was nine years old. He never aspired for high public office, but he proved influential in pursuing ideals that form the basis of American government. Mason served at the Virginia Convention (July 1775), where the colony prepared for armed struggle with Great Britain. At Virginia's constitutional convention in 1776, he introduced the Virginia Declaration of Rights, which protects individual liberties and was a forerunner to the Bill of Rights in the Constitution. Mason's drafts of the Declaration of Rights and the constitution emerged as models for other colonies. Mason was a force for religious tolerance, helping make Virginia an attractive destination for immigrants of various faiths. An expert in land laws, he outlined a plan in 1780 that was later used to form the Northwest Territory as settlers moved into present-day Ohio, Indiana, and Michigan.

Mason was a delegate to the 1787 Constitutional Convention in Philadelphia, Pennsylvania. He was unhappy with the extent of federal power outlined by the Constitution, its failure to limit slavery, and the lack of a bill of rights. On those grounds, he opposed its ratification. After the Bill of Rights was adopted in 1791, Mason conceded that with a few more alterations "I could chearfully [sic] put my hand and heart to the new government." He died at his Virginia plantation home, Gunston Hall, on October 7, 1792.

Right: A New York parade that was one of many to rally support for ratification of the Constitution.

Elected to the U.S. House of Representatives in 1788, Madison became one of its first great legislators. He was instrumental in passage of the Constitution' first ten amendments, the Bill of Rights, and while serving in Congress, he worked closely with President George Washington in establishing his cabinet.

But Madison was soon at odds with the Washington administration, especially with Secretary of the Treasury, Alexander Hamilton. Hamilton had proposed financial plans for the federal government favoring commercial development, along with a national banking system. Both policies were generally more favorable to northern states, and Madison, like Jefferson, wanted a government that supported self-reliant farmers and artisans over those engaged in banking and selling. Hamilton's plan also called for the federal government to assume all state debts, which would require taxes to reduce the revenue that would be needed. Madison represented Virginia, a large and prosperous state that had no debts.

Hamilton's Federalist plan passed through Congress, with Washington's strong support. By election time in 1792, Madison had aligned with Thomas Jefferson against the administration, a faction that became known as Anti-Federalists. The split widened when Great Britain and France went to war in 1793. Federalists favored keeping ties with England to maintain high trade revenue, but the Anti-Federalists favored France. The United States had an alliance with the French dating back to the Revolutionary War, and France had also adopted a more republican form of government. The Federalist candidate, John Adams won the presidential election of 1796. Madison continued to fight the emphasis on commercial development, but he retired from Congress the following year.

Resurgence

Madison was not despairing during those disappointing times. His personal life had changed significantly at the age of forty-three when he married Dolley Payne Todd, a vivacious twenty-six-year-old widow, in 1794. They'd had a passing acquaintance through social circles

in Philadelphia, the seat of the government at the time. After he retired from Congress, three years later, they moved to Montpelier and settled in to an extremely happy domestic life.

Madison jumped back into a political life following the 1798 passage of the Alien and Sedition Acts which, among other things, limited freedom of the press. Working through the Virginia legislature, Madison sponsored the Virginia Resolution, and a similar resolution was passed by the Kentucky legislature through the efforts of Vice President Jefferson. These resolutions, which insisted that states have the right to protest unconstitutional federal laws, were more significant as ideals than for their results. Still, they helped to solidify anti-Federalist support that turned the Jefferson's Democratic-Republican party into the nation's dominant political group. When Jefferson was elected president over Adams in 1800, he appointed Madison, his long-time friend and ally, to the post of secretary of state.

The Virginia Dynasty

As Jefferson's closest advisor, Madison supported and shared in the president's first-term successes—the Louisiana Purchase, a huge area of land bought from France for $15 million, and victory at sea over Barbary pirates, who controlled trade routes in parts of the Mediterranean Sea and who demanded payments from ships using those routes. Jefferson's second term was made difficult by war between England and France. Both nations seized cargoes from American ships and sealed off areas around the world from American trade, and Jefferson countered with the Embargo Act of 1807, intended to teach those nations a lesson about the importance of American trade and to have them respect the nation's neutrality. But the Act proved disastrous when England and France both benefited by the lack of American trade competition. The embargo also hurt Americans at home—from thriving industries in the North to farmers in the agricultural South, who relied on foreign trade. Jefferson repealed the embargo shortly before leaving office.

Even with the vastly unpopular embargo, Democratic-Republicans remained powerful nationally, and in 1808, Jefferson was succeeded by Madison. The new president was still confronted with disrespect toward the United States from England and France—the world's two most powerful nations.

Madison's inauguration was impressive, and his administration began with great fanfare—the first-ever inaugural ball followed his spirited inaugural address. He announced in the speech that the United States would not tolerate foreign interference, but still, England and France continued to frustrate American shipping. England impressed some American sailors into war service in its confidence that the United States was weak militarily and growing disunited.

Madison surrounded himself with ineffective cabinet officials. As attempts at diplomacy with England and France were ignored, New England Federalists were

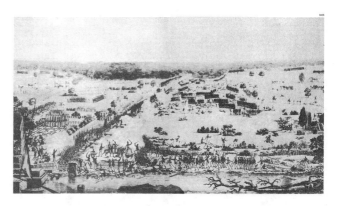

Above: The Battle of New Orleans saw the final shot in the War of 1812.

Below: English ships that pressed American sailors into their service put the nation in a mood for war.

Election Results

1808

Presidential / Vice Presidential Candidates	Popular Votes	Electoral Votes
James Madison / George Clinton (Democratic-Republican)	—	122
George C. Pinckney / Rufus King (Federalist)	—	47

1812

James Madison / Elbridge Gerry (Democratic-Republican)	—	128
DeWitt Clinton / Jared Ingersoll (Federalist)	—	89

Popular votes were not yet part of the presidential elections of 1808 and 1812. (The general public did not vote.) In the 1812 election, New Hampshire governor John Langdon was originally nominated as Democratic-Republican vice president, but he declined.

Above: Battles at sea and on the Great Lakes were a large part of the War of 1812.

Below: The attack on Fort McHenry in Baltimore inspired Francis Scott Key to write the "Star Spangled Banner."

growing rebellious. Southern Congressional hawks led by Henry Clay of Kentucky and John C. Calhoun of South Carolina clamored for war. After Madison exhausted all diplomatic options, war was declared against Great Britain in June of 1812. Reflecting growing national divisions, the war declaration narrowly passed both houses of Congress, and Madison's opponents began calling the War of 1812 "Mr. Madison's War." In spite of the war, Madison was reelected in a close contest in 1812 over New York lieutenant governor DeWitt Clinton, and Massachusetts statesman Elbridge Gerry was elected vice president. His predecessor, George Clinton, had died during Madison's first term, and in 1814, Gerry, too, would die in office.

The Madison Administration

Administration Dates:	March 4, 1809–March 4, 1813
	March 4, 1813–March 4, 1817
Vice President:	George Clinton (1809–12)
	None (1812–13)
	Elbridge Gerry (1813–14)
	None (1814–17)
Cabinet:	
Secretary of State	Robert Smith (1809–11)
	James Monroe (1811–17)★
Secretary of the Treasury	Albert Gallatin (1809–14)
	George W. Campbell (1814)
	Alexander J. Dallas (1814–16)
	William H. Crawford (1816–17)
Secretary of War	William Eustis (1809–13)
	John Armstrong (1813–14)
	James Monroe (1814–15)★
	William H. Crawford (1815–16)
Attorney General	Caesar A. Rodney (1809–11)
	William Pinkney (1811–14)
	Richard Rush (1814–17)
Secretary of the Navy	Robert Smith (1809)
	Paul Hamilton (1809–12)
	William Jones (1813–14)
	Benjamin W. Crowninshield (1815–17)
Postmaster General	Gideon Granger (1809–14)
	R. Jonathan Meigs Jr. (1814–17)

★*Monroe was appointed secretary of war in 1814 and served in that role until 1815, while also serving as secretary of state.*

The Rocket's Red Glare

The weakness of the American military was exposed early. War hawks had hoped that the United States could expand its territory by winning British Canada and Spanish Florida. Instead, the country was in for a serious struggle. It had started out the war with a bankrupt national treasury, a poorly equipped and poorly led army, and an increasingly hostile Congress. Some New England congressmen threatened that their states would secede from the union over the war.

The War of 1812 proved futile. By its end in 1814, little had been accomplished. The United States did not win any new territory and was unable to persuade Great Britain to respect American rights at sea, and both nations were exhausted by the effort. A British force invaded and burned Washington, D.C., in 1814, but failed to advance further, and became stalled in nearby Chesapeake Bay. These battles near Fort McHenry were watched by poet Francis Scott Key, who was inspired to write what would later be called "The Star-Spangled Banner." It eventually became the national anthem.

Above: Francis Scott Key

There were some highlights for the United States in the War of 1812. Power on the Great Lakes was secured with victories on Lake Erie by commander Admiral Oliver Hazard Perry, and an army commanded by future president William Henry Harrison freed Fort Detroit from British occupation and pursued an alliance of British and Indian forces into Canada, scoring a victory in the Battle of the Thames in present-day Ontario. With these victories, the frontier from the Ohio River north to the Great Lakes was made secure for further American expansion and settlement.

After a peace settlement was reached in December 1814, General Andrew Jackson, another future president, led American forces to an overwhelming victory in the

A Historic Anthem

Francis Scott Key was born on his family's 2,800-acre estate, Terra Rubra, near Frederick County, Maryland, on August 1, 1779. In 1803, Key and his family moved to Georgetown, in the District of Columbia, where he was an active member of St. John's Episcopal Church. His faith led him to maintain a pacifist stance as relations between England and the United States grew increasingly tense and culminated with the War of 1812 (1812–15). When England defeated France in 1814 and turned its full attention to fighting the United States, Key reversed his position and enlisted in the District of Columbia's militia. American forces clustered around Baltimore, anticipating that it would be the main target of British attacks. Instead, the British landed near Washington, D.C., and in August 1814 they managed to capture the city and burn the Capitol building and the White House.

Key embarked on a mission on September 3, 1814, to help secure the release of an American physician, William Beanes, taken prisoner by the British. At first, the captors refused to release Beanes, but they eventually agreed after reading the testimonials Key had secured. The two men's departure was delayed, however, to prevent them from revealing British plans to launch a full-scale attack on Baltimore. Their boat was put in tow behind the British fleet as it approached Fort McHenry. As sixteen British warships formed a semicircle around the fort, Key noticed a thirty-by-forty-two-foot American flag flying over it. The ships commenced bombing on September 13 and continued for the next twenty-four hours. When the shelling finally stopped, it was still dark, and Key waited impatiently to learn how the fort had fared. At dawn, he saw the American flag still flying defiantly over Fort McHenry. In the early morning hours of September 14, 1814, Key wrote a poem conveying his patriotic feelings about the battle. Key's poem, "The Defense of Fort McHenry," was published in a newspaper. The verse quickly gained popularity as it was reprinted in newspapers across the country and set to the tune of a popular song, "To Anacreon in Heaven." Key's song, renamed "The Star-Spangled Banner" in 1815, was adopted by the Union Army during the Civil War (1861–65) and was declared the anthem of the American military during World War I (1914–18). It was recognized by Congress as the national anthem of the United States in 1931.

Battle of New Orleans in January 1815. Although the war had already ended, news of the peace agreement had not yet reached that far south. By the time the treaty was signed in 1815, a stronger sense of national spirit had arisen. Though it hadn't emerged victorious, the United States had proved that it could defend its rights against international powers.

Madison and the nation showed new confidence and began thinking more in national terms. He supported the formation of the Second National Bank to handle federal finances, he backed a moderate tax on imports to protect American commerce, and he promoted plans for road and canal improvements. All these efforts were similar to Federalist policies Madison had previously opposed, but times had changed and the imperfections of the American system demanded attention. Involving the federal government in national improvements of finance and transportation, enhanced by national pride at having stood up against the British Empire, made Madison popular. His last two years in office were his most effective, and Madison left office on a positive note in 1817, while the country was enjoying prosperity and expansion.

"I can conscientiously say that I do not know in the world a man of purer integrity, more dispassionate, disinterested and devoted to genuine republicanism; nor could I in the whole scope of America and Europe point out an abler head."

—*Thomas Jefferson*

Farmer Again

The Madisons retired to Montpelier, Virginia, where he took up the life of a gentleman farmer. He served as an advisor to his successor, James Monroe, and became rector of the University of Virginia after Thomas Jefferson's death in 1826. He wrote and revised papers ranging from his days as a young politician to his position as a leader of the Constitutional Convention, and through his time as president.

At the 1829 Virginia Convention to revise the state's constitution, Madison argued for expanding voting rights and attempting to limit slavery in the state. He spoke against the theory of nullification during President Andrew Jackson's administration, when the state of South Carolina attempted to dismiss a federal tariff it opposed. By the time of his death on June 28, 1836, James Madison was the last of the Founding Fathers who had steered the nation to independence.

Legacy

Madison's legacy rests with his tireless actions in forging the Constitution. He was always well informed, well reasoned, and able to express his convictions without flamboyance, and he was willing to compromise for the greater good.

Madison had the distinction of presiding during an unpopular war that accomplished little but strengthened Americans' national identity. Madison always recognized the necessity of a strong federal government, and expanded upon his own ideas to begin programs that would further strengthen the nation. Appropriately, before beginning federal programs he encouraged debate about the constitutionality of such actions. He expanded the power of the presidency, putting the nation's concerns above the interests of individual states.

Left: The Liberty Bell became an American icon after it was rung during sessions of the Second Continental Congress.

Dolley Madison

Born May 20, 1768, Guilford County, North Carolina
Died July 12, 1849, Washington, D.C.

"The profusion of my table is the result of the prosperity of my country, and I shall continue to prefer Virginia liberality to European elegance."

—Dolley Madison

Charming and fashionable, Dolley Madison was an energetic first lady with a flair for entertaining. Her service as first lady extended beyond the eight years of her husband, James Madison's presidency. She also helped host official social functions for three other presidents: Thomas Jefferson, Martin Van Buren, and John Tyler.

Modest Beginnings

Dolley Dandridge Payne was born in Guilford County, North Carolina, on May 20, 1768, to John and Mary Payne, settlers from Virginia. Raised in a devout Quaker household, she was taught to dress plainly and behave humbly. Though sometimes referred to in biographies as Dorothy or Dorothea, Dolley was the name she always used. It was recorded in her birth record by the Quaker community in Piedmont, North Carolina.

In 1769, the Payne family moved to Virginia in 1769, and to Philadelphia fourteen years later, when Dolley was fifteen years old. By that time, she had received private tutoring and had attended Quaker schools. She also learned to cook and sew. Although she continued to dress plainly, Dolley learned more colorful social customs from her maternal grandmother, who she would later call her greatest influence. Her grandmother, who introduced her to fine food, clothing, and jewelry, gave her a gold brooch, which Dolley wore under her drab clothing.

After her father's Philadelphia laundry business failed, the family ran a boardinghouse, with Dolley serving as the cook. Anxious to begin her own life and to assert her identity as a lively young woman, she married Philadelphia lawyer John Todd in 1790. They had two children, but her husband and one of their children died in a yellow fever epidemic in 1792, leaving Dolley to carry on as a widow with a young boy.

The "Great Little Madison"

As a personable and attractive young widow, Dolley had several suitors. She moved in a social circle that included national politicians in Philadelphia, which was the country's capital from 1790 to 1799. In May of 1794, New York senator Aaron Burr, who had stayed in the Payne boardinghouse, informed Dolley that Virginia representative James Madison was interested in being introduced to her. Excited at the prospect of meeting him, she sent a note to a friend of hers, stating, "Aaron Burr says that the great little Madison has asked to be brought to see me this evening." Famous as an influential congressman and for his contributions to the U.S. Constitution, Madison was great, indeed, even though he was physically small. He was also eighteen years older than she was.

Dolley and "Little Jemmy," as she called Madison, hit it off, and their romance was encouraged by others. At a state dinner, for example, President George Washington and First Lady Martha Washington each on separate occasions spoke to Dolley in glowing terms about Madison.

Dolley, meanwhile, delighted political social circles with her friendliness, fashionable dress, and love of dancing. Madison, who had always been reserved and somewhat formal, became more sociable under her influence, proving to be a lively conversationalist and a graceful dancer. The couple was married on September 15, 1794.

Dolley Madison was soon the toast of Philadelphia. She wore elegant gowns, modeled the newest fashions in clothes and shoes, and was a spirited entertainer. After Madison retired from Congress in 1797, they moved to his Virginia plantation, Montpelier, where they continued to entertain regularly.

The Madisons moved to the new capital, Washington, D.C., in 1801. He served as secretary of state under Thomas Jefferson, and Dolley occasionally served as hostess for official functions, since Jefferson's wife, Martha, had died nineteen years earlier. She helped instill Jefferson's preference for informal and simple social occasions, and collected recipes from throughout the United States to establish a distinctly American cuisine. In addition to dressing in the latest fashions, she often started trends. Her distinctive headdress of scarves wrapped around her head became known as the "Dolley turban." She was probably the best known and most popular woman in America by 1808, when her husband ran for president; at least, Madison's opponent, Charles C. Pinckney, thought so. After losing the election, he remarked, "I might have had a better chance had I faced Mr. Madison alone."

"Lady Presidentess"

As first lady, Dolley introduced a more elegant style to presidential social occasions. There was a first-ever White House inaugural ball when President Madison took office. Soon after, she successfully lobbied congress for funds to improve the executive mansion. She hired a chef and expanded guest lists for parties beyond the usual political crowd, inviting writers, artists, and other newsmakers. Her regular Wednesday drawing room parties and special events were all spirited occasions and earned her the nickname "Lady Presidentess."

During the War of 1812, Dolley toned down social occasions, except to celebrate American successes. When British forces marched toward Washington in 1814, President Madison abandoned the city with retreating soldiers, while Dolley planned to move in with friends in Virginia for safety. Instead, she remained at the White House until the last possible moment, supervising the removal of precious items, including a famous painting of George Washington, for safekeeping. The items were placed in carriages and moved from the mansion just ahead of British troops who set fire to the building. The British occupied the capital for a few days, long enough to set fire to other government buildings, including the capital and the Library of Congress.

When she returned to Washington, Dolley was cheered by people in the streets and promised them that the capital would be rebuilt. It was, and the new Presidential Palace was restocked with the items that she had helped to save.

Making It Official

For much of American history, the "White House" was simply a nickname used to describe the presidential mansion. It was not considered the proper name of the property until September 1901, when President Theodore Roosevelt made it the official moniker.

Left: Dolley Madison's gift to American fashion was her famous turban.

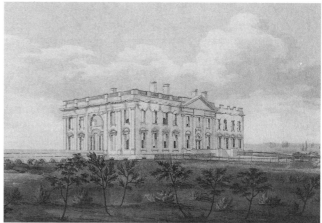

Above: After being burned, the presidential mansion was reduced to a charred shell.

Left: Lucky to escape with her life, Dolley paused long enough to save George Washington's portrait from the flames of the White House fire.

Buy American

James Madison was always careful to wear clothes (always a black suit) that were made in America, But Dolley, who didn't object to Paris fashions, made the mistake of buying an imported mirror for the executive mansion. A Senate committee, objecting to its $40 price tag, spent $2,000 investigating it.

Afterglow

The couple retired to Montpelier when Madison's presidency ended in 1817, and Dolley continued her habit of hosting elegant parties. The former president and first lady enjoyed festive and quiet times together until Madison died nineteen years later. Dolley nursed her husband during his long fatal illness, taking dictation as he expressed his final thoughts on government.

A widow again, Dolley returned to Washington, D.C., in 1837. She was short of money and had to sell Montpelier to settle debts incurred by her son. She was still known and celebrated as the grand dame of Washington society, and. she remained as likable and demonstrative as ever, greeting fellow guests with hugs and always knowing everyone by name.

In 1838, Dolley served as adviser to White House hostess Angelica Van Buren, daughter-in-law of President Martin Van Buren. In the early 1840s, she assisted first lady Letitia Tyler and her daughters during the early part of John Tyler's presidency. And in the mid 1840s, she also counseled first lady Sarah Polk, who was not accustomed to large social functions. Even in her eighties, Dolley Madison was still active and vibrant. When she died in 1849, President Zachary Taylor noted that, "She will never be forgotten because she was truly our first lady for half a century."

Madison's Bill of Rights Proposal

Delivered on June 8, 1789

Beginning on May 25, 1787, fifty-five delegates representing twelve of the thirteen states united by the Articles of Confederation met in Philadelphia, Pennsylvania. Many felt that the national government created by the Articles was too weak to be effective. Virginia delegate George Washington, who presided over the convention, was among those calling for strengthening central government.

After a long debate, the new U.S. Constitution was completed on September 17, 1787, and submitted to individual states, nine of which had to ratify it in order to put it into effect. Delaware's representatives voted for ratification on December 7, making it the first state in the union. New Hampshire became the ninth state to approve the Constitution on June 21, 1788, and the U.S. government became official.

There had been lively debates in each of the states. Virginia was typical: Such leaders as Patrick Henry, James Monroe, and George Mason were against the Constitution, fearing that it would make the federal government too powerful. They also objected to a lack of guarantees for individual liberty. James Madison was able to argue convincingly enough for Virginia's ratification by a slim margin, 89–79. Madison didn't believe that a bill of rights was necessary, but he vigorously pursued amendments to guarantee liberties, to honor those who wanted it and to calm those who were unhappy with the Constitution and were calling for another constitutional convention.

Madison was elected to the House of Representatives, which met on March 4, 1789. During this session, a series of amendments were proposed that would become known as the Bill of Rights—the first ten amendments to the Constitution.

James Madison's Bill of Rights Proposal

It appears to me that this house is bound by every motive of prudence, not to let the first session pass over without proposing to the state legislatures some things to be incorporated into the constitution, as will render it as acceptable to the whole people of the United States, as it has been found acceptable to a majority of them.

I wish, among other reasons why something should be done, that those who have been friendly to the adoption of this constitution, may have the opportunity of proving to those who were opposed to it, that they were as sincerely devoted to liberty and a republican government, as those who charged them with wishing the adoption of this constitution in order to

lay the foundation of an aristocracy or despotism. It will be a desirable thing to extinguish from the bosom of every member of the community any apprehensions, that there are those among his countrymen who wish to deprive them of the liberty for which they valiantly fought and honorably bled. And if there are amendments desired, of such a nature as will not injure the constitution, and they can be engrafted so as to give satisfaction to the doubting part of our fellow citizens; the friends of the federal government will evince that spirit of deference and concession for which they have hitherto been distinguished.

It cannot be a secret to the gentlemen in this house, that, notwithstanding the ratification of this system of government by eleven of the thirteen United States [North Carolina and Rhode Island had not yet ratified the Constitution] in some cases unanimously, in others by large majorities; yet still there is a great number of our constituents who are dissatisfied with it; among whom are many respectable for their talents, their patriotism, and respectable for the jealousy they have for their liberty, which, though mistaken in its object, is laudable in its motive. There is a great body of the people falling under this description, who as present feel much inclined to join their support to the cause of federalism, if they were satisfied in this one point: We ought not to disregard their inclination, but, on principles of amity and moderation, conform to their wishes, and expressly declare the great rights of mankind secured under this constitution.

The acquiescence which our fellow citizens show under the government, calls upon us for a like return of moderation. But perhaps there is a stronger motive than this for our going into a consideration of the subject; it is to provide those securities for liberty which are required by a part of the community. I allude in a particular manner to those two states who have not thought fit to throw themselves into the bosom of the confederacy: it is a desirable thing, on our part as well as theirs, that a re-union should take place as soon as possible. I have no doubt, if we proceed to take those steps which would be prudent and requisite at this juncture, that in a short time we should see that disposition prevailing in those states that are not come in, that we have seen prevailing [in] those states which are.

But I will candidly acknowledge, that, over and above all these considerations, I do conceive that the constitution may be amended; that is to say, if all power is subject to abuse, that then it is possible the abuse of the powers of the general government may be guarded against in a more secure manner than is now done, while no one advantage, arising from the exercise of that power, shall be damaged or endangered by it. We have in this way something to gain, and, if we proceed with caution, nothing to lose; and in this case it is necessary to proceed with caution; for while we feel all these inducements to go into a revisal of the constitution, we must feel for the constitution itself, and make that revisal a moderate one. I should be unwilling to see a door opened for a re-consideration of the whole structure of the government, for a re-consideration of the principles and the substance of the powers given; because I doubt, if such a door was opened, if we should be very likely to stop at that point which would be safe to the government itself: But I do wish to see a door opened to consider, so far as to incorporate those provisions for the security of rights, against which I believe no serious objection has been made by any class of our constituents, such as would be likely to meet with the concurrence of two-thirds of both houses, and the approbation of three-fourths of the state legislatures. I will not propose a single alteration which I do not wish to see take place, as intrinsically proper in itself, or proper because it is wished for by a respectable number of my fellow citizens; and therefore I shall not propose a single alteration but is likely to meet the concurrence required by the constitution.

There have been objections of various kinds made against the constitution: Some were leveled against its structure, because the president was without a council; because the senate, which is a legislative body, had judicial powers in trials on impeachments; and because the powers of that body were compounded in other respects, in a manner that did not correspond with a particular theory; because it grants more power than is supposed to be necessary for every good purpose; and controls the ordinary powers of the state governments. I know some respectable characters who opposed this government on these grounds; but I believe that the great mass of the people who opposed it, disliked it because it did not contain effectual provision against encroachments on particular rights, and those safeguards which they have been long accustomed to have interposed between them and the magistrate who exercised the sovereign power: nor ought we to consider them safe, while a great number of our fellow citizens think these securities necessary.

It has been a fortunate thing that the objection to the government has been made on the ground I stated; because it will be practicable on that ground to obviate the objection, so far as to satisfy the public mind that their liberties will be perpetual, and this without endangering any part of the constitution, which is considered as essential to the existence of the government by those who promoted its adoption.

The amendments which have occurred to me, proper to be recommended by congress to the state legislatures are these:

First.

That there be prefixed to the constitution a declaration—That all power is originally vested in, and consequently derived from the people. That government is instituted, and ought to be exercised for the benefit of the people; which consists in the enjoyment of life and liberty, with the right of acquiring and using property, and generally of pursuing and obtaining happiness and safety. That the people have an indubitable, unalienable, and indefeasible right to reform or change their government, whenever it be found adverse or inadequate to the purposes of its institution.

[. . .]

Fourthly.

That in article 2nd, section 9, between clauses 3 and 4 [1:9:3], be inserted these clauses, to wit,

The civil rights of none shall be abridged on account of religious belief or worship, nor shall any national religion be established, nor shall the full and equal rights of conscience by in any manner, or on any pretext infringed. The people shall not be deprived or abridged of their right to speak, to write, or to publish their sentiments; and the freedom of the press, as one of the great bulwarks of liberty, shall be inviolable.

The people shall not be restrained from peaceably assembling and consulting for their common good, nor from applying to the legislature by petitions, or remonstrances for redress of their grievances.

The right of the people to keep and bear arms shall not be infringed; a well armed, and well regulated militia being the best security of a free country: but no person religiously scrupulous of bearing arms, shall be compelled to render military service in person.

No soldier shall in time of peace be quartered in any house without the consent of the owner; nor at any time, but in a manner warranted by law.

No person shall be subject, except in cases of impeachment, to more than one punishment, or one trial for the same offence; nor shall be compelled to be a witness against himself; nor be deprived of life, liberty, or property without due process of law; nor be obliged to relinquish his property, where it may be necessary for public use, without a just compensation.

Excessive bail shall not be required, nor excessive fines imposed, nor cruel and unusual punishments inflicted.

The rights of the people to be secured in their persons, their houses, their papers, and their other property from all unreasonable searches and seizures, shall not be violated by warrants issued without probable cause, supported by oath or affirmation, or not particularly describing the places to be searched, or the persons or things to be seized.

In all criminal prosecutions, the accused shall enjoy the right to a speedy and public trial, to be informed of the cause and nature of the accusation, to be confronted with his accusers, and the witnesses against him; to have a compulsory process for obtaining witnesses in his favor; and to have the assistance of counsel for his defense.

The exceptions here or elsewhere in the constitution, made in favor of particular rights, shall not be so construed as to diminish the just importance of other rights retained by the people; or as to enlarge the powers delegated by the constitution; but either as actual limitations of such powers, or as inserted merely for greater caution.

Fifthly.

That in article 2nd, section 10, between clauses 1 and 2, be inserted this clause, to wit: No state shall violate the equal rights of conscience, or the freedom of the press, or the trial by jury in criminal cases.

[. . .]

It has been said by way of objection to a bill of rights, by many respectable gentlemen out of doors, and I find opposition on the same principles likely to be made by gentlemen on this floor, that they are unnecessary articles of a republican government, upon the presumption that the people have those rights in their own hands, and that is the proper place for them to rest. It would be a sufficient answer to say that this objection lies against such provisions under the state governments as well as under the general government; and there are, I believe, but few gentlemen who are inclined to push their theory so far as to say that a declaration of rights in those cases is either ineffectual or improper.

It has been said that in the federal government they are unnecessary, because the powers are enumerated, and it follows that all that are not granted by the constitution are retained: that the constitution is a bill of powers, the great residuum being the rights of the people; and therefore a bill of rights cannot be so necessary as if the residuum was thrown into the hands of the government. I admit that these arguments are not entirely without foundation; but they are not conclusive to the extent which has been supposed. It is true the powers of the general government are circumscribed; they are directed to particular objects; but even if government keeps within those limits, it has certain discretionary powers with respect to the means, which may admit of abuse to a certain extent, in the same manner as the powers of the state governments under their constitutions may to an indefinite extent; because in the constitution of the United States there is a clause granting to Congress the power to make all laws which shall be necessary and proper for carrying into execution all the powers vested in the government of the United States, or in any department or officer thereof; this enables them to fulfil every purpose for which the government was established. Now, may not laws be considered necessary and proper by Congress, for it is them who are to judge of the necessity and propriety to accomplish those special purposes which they may have in contemplation, which laws in themselves are neither necessary or proper; as well as improper laws could be enacted by the state legislatures, for fulfilling the more extended objects of those governments. I will state an instance which I think in point, and proves that this might be the case. The general government has a right to pass all laws which shall be necessary to collect its revenue; the means for enforcing the collection are within the direction of the legislature: may not general warrants be considered necessary for this purpose, as well as for some purposes which it was supposed at the framing of their constitutions the state governments had

in view. If there was reason for restraining the state governments from exercising this power, there is like reason for restraining the federal government.

[. . .]

Having done what I conceived was my duty, in bringing before this house the subject of amendments, and also stated such as wish for and approve, and offered the reasons which occurred to me in their support; I shall content myself for the present with moving, that a committee be appointed to consider of and report such amendments as ought to be proposed by congress to the legislatures of the states, to become, if ratified by three-fourths thereof, part of the constitution of the United States. By agreeing to this motion, the subject may be going on in the committee, while other important business is proceeding to a conclusion in the house. I should advocate greater dispatch in the business of amendments, if I was not convinced of the absolute necessity there is of pursuing the organization of the government; because I think we should obtain the confidence of our fellow citizens, in proportion as we fortify the rights of the people against the encroachments of the government.

What Happened Next

After debate, the amendments Madison suggested for granting individual liberties were formed into twelve amendments that were sent to states for ratification. Ten amendments—collectively called the Bill of Rights— were added to the Constitution after being ratified by three-fourths of the states in the union. The first nine amendments are similar to Madison's original proposals. The tenth—"The powers not delegated to the United States by the Constitution, nor prohibited by it to the States, are reserved to the States respectively, or to the people"—was added by those who insisted that the powers of states needed to be recognized.

The Constitution's first ten amendments—the Bill of Rights—were ratified December 15, 1791.

The Bill of Rights

AMENDMENT 1: Congress shall make no law respecting an establishment of religion, or prohibiting the free exercise thereof; or abridging the freedom of speech, or of the press, or the right of the people peaceably to assemble, and to petition the Government for a redress of grievances.

AMENDMENT 2: A well regulated Militia, being necessary to the security of a free State, the right of the people to keep and bear Arms, shall not be infringed.

AMENDMENT 3: No Soldier shall, in time of peace be quartered in any house, without the consent of the Owner, nor in time of war, but in a manner to be prescribed by law.

AMENDMENT 4: The right of the people to be secure in their persons, houses, papers, and effects, against unreasonable searches and seizures, shall not be violated, and no Warrants shall issue, but upon probable cause, supported by Oath or affirmation, and particularly describing the place to be searched, and the persons or things to be seized.

AMENDMENT 5: No person shall be held to answer for a capital, or otherwise infamous crime, unless on a presentment or indictment of a Grand Jury, except in cases arising in the land or naval forces, or in the Militia, when in actual service in time of War or public danger; nor shall any person be subject for the same offence to be twice put in jeopardy of life or limb; nor shall be compelled in any criminal case to be a witness against himself, nor be deprived of life, liberty, or property, without due process of law; nor shall private property be taken for public use without just compensation.

AMENDMENT 6: In all criminal prosecutions, the accused shall enjoy the right to a speedy and public trial, by an impartial jury of the State and district wherein the crime shall have been committed, which district shall have been previously ascertained by law, and to be informed of the nature and cause of the accusation; to be confronted with the witnesses against him; to have compulsory process for obtaining witnesses in his favor, and to have the Assistance of Counsel for his defence.

AMENDMENT 7: In Suits at common law, where the value in controversy shall exceed twenty dollars, the right of trial by jury shall be preserved, and no fact tried by a jury, shall be otherwise re-examined in any Court of the United States, than according to the rules of the common law.

AMENDMENT 8: Excessive bail shall not be required nor excessive fines imposed, nor cruel and unusual punishments inflicted.

AMENDMENT 9: The enumeration in the Constitution, of certain rights, shall not be construed to deny or disparage others retained by the people.

AMENDMENT 10: The powers not delegated to the United States by the Constitution, nor prohibited by it to the States, are reserved to the States respectively, or to the people.

Madison's First Inaugural Address

Saturday, March 4, 1809

Chief Justice John Marshall administered the oath of office in the Hall of the House or Representatives, now National Statuary Hall, in the Capitol Building at Washington, D.C. Some 10,000 people were on hand to hear the inaugural address, which was followed that evening by the first inaugural ball.

Unwilling to depart from examples of the most revered authority, I avail myself of the occasion now presented to express the profound impression made on me by the call of my country to the station to the duties of which I am about to pledge myself by the most solemn of sanctions. So distinguished a mark of confidence, proceeding from the deliberate and tranquil suffrage of a free and virtuous nation, would under any circumstances have commanded my gratitude and devotion, as well as filled me with an awful sense of the trust to be assumed. Under the various circumstances which give peculiar solemnity to the existing period, I feel that both the honor and the responsibility allotted to me are inexpressibly enhanced.

The present situation of the world is indeed without a parallel and that of our own country full of difficulties. The pressure of these, too, is the more severely felt because they have fallen upon us at a moment when the national prosperity being at a height not before attained, the contrast resulting from the change has been rendered the more striking. Under the benign influence of our republican institutions, and the maintenance of peace with all nations whilst so many of them were engaged in bloody and wasteful wars, the fruits of a just policy were enjoyed in an unrivaled growth of our faculties and resources. Proofs of this were seen in the improvements of agriculture, in the successful enterprises of commerce, in the progress of manufacturers and useful arts, in the increase of the public revenue and the use made of it in reducing the public debt, and in the valuable works and establishments everywhere multiplying over the face of our land.

It is a precious reflection that the transition from this prosperous condition of our country to the scene which has for some time been distressing us is not chargeable on any unwarrantable views, nor, as I trust, on any involuntary errors in the public councils.

Indulging no passions which trespass on the rights or the repose of other nations, it has been the true glory of the United States to cultivate peace by observing justice, and to entitle themselves to the respect of the nations at war by fulfilling their neutral obligations with the most scrupulous impartiality. If there be candor in the world, the truth of these assertions will not be questioned; posterity at least will do justice to them.

This unexceptionable course could not avail against the injustice and violence of the belligerent powers. In their rage against each other, or impelled by more direct motives, principles of retaliation have been introduced equally contrary to universal reason and acknowledged law. How long their arbitrary edicts will be continued in spite of the demonstrations that not even a pretext for them has been given by the United States, and of the fair and liberal attempt to induce a revocation of them, can not be anticipated. Assuring myself that under every vicissitude the determined spirit and united councils of the nation will be safeguards to its honor and its essential interests, I repair to the post assigned me with no other discouragement than what springs from my own inadequacy to its high duties. If I do not sink under the weight of this deep conviction it is because I find some support in a consciousness of the purposes and a confidence in the principles which I bring with me into this arduous service.

To cherish peace and friendly intercourse with all nations having correspondent dispositions; to maintain sincere neutrality toward belligerent nations; to prefer in all cases amicable discussion and reasonable accommodation of differences to a decision of them by an appeal to arms; to exclude foreign intrigues and foreign partialities, so degrading to all countries and so baneful to free ones; to foster a spirit of independence too just to invade the rights of others, too proud to surrender our own, too liberal to indulge unworthy prejudices ourselves and too elevated not to look down upon them in others; to hold the union of the States as the basis of their peace and happiness; to support the Constitution, which is the cement of the Union, as well in its limitations as in its authorities; to respect the rights and authorities reserved to the States and to the people as equally incorporated with and essential to the success of the general system; to avoid the slightest interference with the right of conscience or the functions of religion, so wisely exempted from civil jurisdiction; to preserve in their full energy the other salutary provisions in behalf of private and personal rights, and of the freedom of the press; to observe economy in public expenditures; to liberate the public resources by an honorable discharge of the public debts; to keep within the requisite limits a standing military force, always remembering that an armed and trained militia is the firmest bulwark of republics—that without standing armies their liberty can never be in danger, nor with large ones safe; to promote by authorized means improvements friendly to agriculture, to manufactures, and to external as well as internal commerce; to favor in like manner the advancement of science and the diffusion of information as the best aliment to true liberty; to carry on the benevolent plans which have been so meritoriously applied to the conversion of our aboriginal neighbors from the degradation and wretchedness of savage life to a participation of the improvements of which the human mind and manners are susceptible in a civilized state—as far as sentiments and intentions such as these can aid the fulfillment of my duty, they will be a resource which can not fail me.

It is my good fortune, moreover, to have the path in which I am to tread lighted by examples of illustrious services successfully rendered in the most trying difficulties by those who have marched before me. Of those of my immediate predecessor it might least become me here to speak. I may, however, be pardoned for not suppressing the sympathy with which my heart is full in the rich reward he enjoys in the benedictions of a beloved country, gratefully bestowed or exalted talents zealously devoted through a long career to the advancement of its highest interest and happiness.

But the source to which I look or the aids which alone can supply my deficiencies is in the well-tried intelligence and virtue of my fellow-citizens, and in the counsels of those representing them in the other departments associated in the care of the national interests. In these my confidence will under every difficulty be best placed, next to that which we have all been encouraged to feel in the guardianship and guidance of that Almighty Being whose power regulates the destiny of nations, whose blessings have been so conspicuously dispensed to this rising Republic, and to whom we are bound to address our devout gratitude for the past, as well as our fervent supplications and best hopes for the future.

Federalist No. 46

The Influence of the State and Federal Governments Compared

Excerpted From the New York Packet, *Tuesday, January 29, 1788.*

The Federalist Papers, written to encourage support for ratification of the Constitution, were variously the work of Alexander Hamilton, John Jay, and James Madison, and were usually signed with the pseudonym, "Publius." There were 85 such appeals, which appeared in local newspapers in space we would call an Op-Ed Page today, and Madison wrote 29 of them. The following excerpts from Federalist No. 46 were Madison's work.

To the People of the State of New York:

RESUMING the subject of the last paper, I proceed to inquire whether the federal government or the State governments will have the advantage with regard to the predilection and support of the people. Notwithstanding the different modes in which they are appointed, we must consider both of them as substantially dependent on the great body of the citizens of the United States. I assume this position here as it respects the first, reserving the proofs for another place. The federal and State governments are in fact but different agents and trustees of the people, constituted with different powers, and designed for different purposes. The adversaries of the Constitution seem to have lost sight of the people altogether in their reasonings on this subject; and to have viewed these different establishments, not only as mutual rivals and enemies, but as uncontrolled by any common superior in their efforts to usurp the authorities of each other. These gentlemen must here be reminded of their error. They must be told that the ultimate authority, wherever the derivative may be found, resides in the people alone, and that it will not depend merely on the comparative ambition or address of the different governments, whether either, or which of them, will be able to enlarge its sphere of jurisdiction at the expense of the other. Truth, no less than decency, requires that the event in every case should be supposed to depend on the sentiments and sanction of their common constituents.

Many considerations, besides those suggested on a former occasion, seem to place it beyond doubt that the first and most natural attachment of the people will be to the governments of their respective States.

…Experience speaks the same language in this case. The federal administration, though hitherto very defective in comparison with what may be hoped under a better system, had, during the war, and particularly whilst the independent fund of paper emissions was in credit, an activity and importance as great as it can well have in any future circumstances whatever. It was engaged, too, in a course of measures which had for their object the protection of everything that was dear, and the acquisition of everything that could be desirable to the people at large. It was, nevertheless, invariably found, after the transient enthusiasm for the early Congresses was over, that the attention and attachment of the people were turned anew to their own particular governments; that the federal council was at no time the idol of popular favor; and that opposition to proposed enlargements of its powers and importance was the side usually taken by the men who wished to build their political consequence on the prepossessions of their fellow-citizens.

If, therefore, as has been elsewhere remarked, the people should in future become more partial to the federal than to the State governments, the change can only result from such manifest and irresistible proofs of a better administration, as will overcome all their antecedent propensities. And in that case, the people ought not surely to be precluded from giving most of their confidence where they may discover it to be most due; but even in that case the State governments could have little to apprehend, because it is only within a certain sphere that the federal power can, in the nature of things, be advantageously administered.

…It has been already proved that the members of the federal will be more dependent on the members of the State governments, than the latter will be on the former. It has appeared also, that the prepossessions of the people, on whom both will depend, will be more on the side of the State governments, than of the federal government. So far as the disposition of each towards the other may be influenced by these causes, the State governments must clearly have the advantage. But in a distinct and very important point of view, the advantage will lie on the same side. The prepossessions, which the members themselves will carry into the federal government, will generally be favorable to the States; whilst it will rarely happen, that the members of the State governments will carry into the public councils a bias in favor of the general government. A local spirit will infallibly prevail much more in the members of Congress, than a national spirit will prevail in the legislatures of the particular States. Every one knows that a great proportion of the errors committed by the State legislatures proceeds from the disposition of the members to sacrifice the comprehensive and permanent interest of the State, to the particular and separate views of the counties or districts in which they reside. And if they do not sufficiently enlarge their policy to embrace the collective welfare of their particular State, how can it be imagined that they will make the aggregate prosperity of the Union, and the dignity and respectability of its government, the objects of their affections and consultations? For the same reason that the members of the State legislatures will be unlikely to attach themselves sufficiently to national objects, the members of the federal legislature will be likely to attach themselves too much to local objects. The States will be to the latter what counties and towns are to the former. ...Were it admitted, however, that the Federal government may feel an equal disposition with the State governments to extend its power beyond the due limits, the latter would still have the advantage in the means of defeating such encroachments. If an act of a particular State, though unfriendly to the national government, be generally popular in that State and should not too grossly violate the oaths of the State officers, it is executed immediately and, of course, by means on the spot and depending on the State alone. The opposition of the federal government, or the interposition of federal officers, would but inflame the zeal of all parties on the side of the State, and the evil could not be prevented or repaired, if at all, without the employment of means which must always be resorted to with reluctance and difficulty.

...But ambitious encroachments of the federal government, on the authority of the State governments, would not excite the opposition of a single State, or of a few States only. They would be signals of general alarm. Every government would espouse the common cause. A correspondence would be opened. Plans of resistance would be concerted. One spirit would animate and conduct the whole. The same combinations, in short, would result from an apprehension of the federal, as was produced by the dread of a foreign, yoke; and unless the projected innovations should be voluntarily renounced, the same appeal to a trial of force would be made in the one case as was made in the other. But what degree of madness could ever drive the federal government to such an extremity. In the contest with Great Britain, one part of the empire was employed against the other. The more numerous part invaded the rights of the less numerous part. The attempt was unjust and unwise; but it was not in speculation absolutely chimerical. But what would be the contest in the case we are supposing? Who would be the parties? A few representatives of the people would be opposed to the people themselves; or rather one set of representatives would be contending against thirteen sets of representatives, with the whole body of their common constituents on the side of the latter.

...On summing up the considerations stated in this and the last paper, they seem to amount to the most convincing evidence, that the powers proposed to be lodged in the federal government are as little formidable to those reserved to the individual States, as they are indispensably necessary to accomplish the purposes of the Union; and that all those alarms which have been sounded, of a meditated and consequential annihilation of the State governments, must, on the most favorable interpretation, be ascribed to the chimerical fears of the authors of them.

PUBLIUS.

James Monroe

"National honor is national property of the highest value."

— *James Monroe*

Fifth president of the United States (1817–1825)

Full name: *James Monroe*

Born: *April 28, 1758, Westmoreland County, Virginia*

Died: *July 4, 1831, New York, New York*

Burial site: *Gouverneur Vault, Second Street Cemetery, New York, New York; moved in 1858 to Hollywood Cemetery, Richmond, Virginia*

Parents: *Spence and Elizabeth Jones Monroe*

Spouse: *Elizabeth Kortright (1768–1830; m. 1786)*

Children: *Eliza Kortright (1787–1840); James Spence (1799–1800); Maria Hester (1803–1850)*

Religion: *Episcopalian*

Education: *Attended College of William and Mary*

Occupations: *Farmer; lawyer; military man*

Government positions: *Virginia state assemblyman; Continental congressman; U.S. senator; minister to France and England; Virginia governor; envoy to Spain; secretary of state and secretary of war under James Madison*

Political party: *Democratic-Republican*

Dates as president: *March 4, 1817–March 4, 1821 (first term); March 4, 1821–March 4, 1825 (second term)*

Age upon taking office: *58*

ames Monroe, elected in 1816, presided during the "Era of Good Feelings." The young United States was establishing its national identity in exciting times. The War of 1812 was over, the nation was expanding beyond the original thirteen colonies as people were moving west for new opportunities, and the Democratic-Republicans were enjoying widespread support and influence. Monroe won the electoral votes of all but three states in 1816, and four years later, he won all of them.

The United States began its development as a major international power with the Monroe Doctrine, announced in December of 1823. The young nation had been involved in a series of international disputes in the Americas involving Great Britain, France, Spain, and Russia, and the doctrine declared that it would not tolerate any further acts of European intervention in the western hemisphere.

The Era of Good Feelings was gradually fading by the time Monroe's second term began. An economic downturn occurred in 1819, and the issue of slavery continued to divide the nation. Still, Monroe remained very popular, and many historians regard him as one of our most effective presidents. He was the last of the "Virginia dynasty" that included his predecessors, Thomas Jefferson and James Madison. Combined, the three Virginians held the office of president for twenty-four years.

Timeline

Modest Beginnings

The oldest of five children, James Monroe was born on April 28, 1758, on his family's small farm in Westmoreland County, Virginia. His father, Spence Monroe, was a carpenter. Because he lived in an isolated area, Monroe had to travel several miles to school, at times to study with John Marshall, who later became chief justice of the U.S. Supreme Court.

"[Monroe] had a rare ability of putting men at ease by his courtesy, his lack of condescension, his frankness, and by what his contemporaries looked upon as his essential goodness and kindness of heart."
—Monroe biographer Harry Ammon

Monroe went on to the College of William and Mary at Williamsburg, Virginia, in 1774. When the American Revolution broke out the following year, he began training with student military companies, and was assigned to the Third Virginia Regiment of the Continental Army. In August 1776, the regiment moved north to help support the army in a battle at Harlem Heights, New York. They arrived as the army was retreating, and moved west with them through New Jersey, eventually crossing the Delaware River into Pennsylvania. Lieutenant Monroe led a charge on Hessian cannons during the Battle of Trenton, and nearly bled to death from his wounds. He survived the terrible winter at Valley Forge, and went on to become adjutant general under Lord Stirling. At the end of the war, General Washington wrote of him that, "He has in every instance, maintained the reputation of a brave, active, and sensible officer."

Many militia groups were formed during the American Revolution. They weren't ordinarily part of a regular army, but citizens organized themselves for military service during emergencies. With a letter of recommendation from General George Washington, Monroe was commissioned a lieutenant colonel and military commissioner of Virginia. However, his regiment never actually came together because of a lack of funds,

Left: The Marquis de Lafayette, a hero of the American Revolution.

and instead, Monroe became an aide to Virginia's governor Thomas Jefferson, and the two became close friends. Monroe decided to go into politics while he was studying law with Jefferson, and he was elected to the Virginia legislature in 1782 at the age of twenty-four.

A federal government had been created by the Articles of Confederation in 1781. The Articles, which preceded the U.S. Constitution, were the first attempt at defining the powers and the duties of the new government, and they also addressed the rights of the people. Monroe was elected to the Congress of the Confederation in 1783.

Monroe was greatly interested in the potential for American expansion beyond the thirteen colonies, and one of his first acts as a congressman was to take a trip to the Northwest, which in those days included the lands west of the Allegheny Mountains to the Mississippi River, with the Ohio River forming its southern boundary, and the Great Lakes defining the northern edge. Monroe traveled north from New York City up the Hudson River and other waterways to the Great Lakes and then he headed west, making several stops to tour inland areas.

The trip made a great impression on him. When he got back to New York, where the Congress of the Confederation met, he began contributing to a plan that became the Northwest Ordinance of 1787, forming a territorial government in the region bordered by the Ohio River to the south and the Mississippi to the west.

While he was serving in New York, Monroe met Elizabeth Kortright, the raven-haired, blue-eyed daughter of a wealthy local merchant, and he married her in 1786. They would have three children—two daughters and a son who died in early childhood.

Monroe had hoped to attend the Constitutional Convention when it met in Philadelphia, in 1787 to strengthen the Articles of Confederation. However, he was passed over as a Virginia's representative in favor of James Madison. The convention replaced the Articles of Confederation with a new document called the Constitution that established a stronger federal government. It was largely the work of James Madison, who became known as "the Father of the Constitution."

The Constitution had to be approved by representatives from the individual states, and Monroe represented Virginia during the process. He was opposed to the new document, believing that the federal authority it outlined gave too much power to the national government, and didn't guarantee protection of individual liberties. He voted against the Constitution, but he welcomed the new government when the document was eventually ratified.

Monroe lost his bid for a seat in the House of Representatives to James Madison in 1788. The relationship between the two men was strained, but they were able to patch up their differences. In the meantime, the Monroes established a Virginia estate they called Ash Lawn, near Thomas Jefferson's home at Monticello.

Monroe was elected to the U.S. Senate in 1790, a time when there were no formal political parties. Politicians generally divided themselves into small factions, and in those days there were two. Those who favored a strong central government were called Federalists, and those wanted to limit federal power in favor of states' rights were known as Anti-Federalists. Monroe, Madison, and

Father of the Bride

Maria Hester Monroe, James's daughter, was still at school in Philadelphia when Monroe became president. She moved to the executive mansion in 1819, and was married there a year later. The first marriage in the Presidential Palace was closed to all except family and close friends. Maria and her husband, Samuel Gouverneur, settled in New York City, and former president Monroe went there to live with them when he retired.

Thomas Paine

Thomas Paine was born in Thetford, Norfolk, England, on January 29, 1737. After seven years of school, he apprenticed to his father, a corset maker. Paine ran away to sea at the age of sixteen, but soon returned, finished his apprenticeship, and worked in several towns before starting his own shop. In 1759, he married Mary Lambert. When she died suddenly the following year, Paine abandoned his trade to become an exciseman (collector of taxes on goods produced and sold in a country). He remarried in 1768 and continued his education by reading books, attending lectures, and conducting scientific experiments.

In 1772, Payne wrote a pamphlet calling for pay increases for excisemen. The new salaries were denied, and Paine was fired from his job. He went bankrupt and was divorced from his second wife, but his career of fighting for reform had begun. His work caught the attention of Benjamin Franklin (1706–90), who was in London at the time. Franklin encouraged Paine to sail to America and gave him a letter of recommendation. Paine arrived in Philadelphia in 1774 and found work with the new Pennsylvania magazine. Inspired by the revolutionary spirit growing around him, Payne published the pamphlet "Common Sense," in which he presented arguments for America's independence from England. Written in clear and common language, the pamphlet proved popular, with twenty-five editions published during 1776.

Paine served as a military aide during the Revolutionary War (1775–83), but he continued to raise support for the American war effort through his writings. In December 1776, he began publishing The Crisis, a set of sixteen inspiring essays, the first of which began with the famous line, "These are the times that try men's souls." General George Washington often had the essays read to his soldiers.

A few years after the war ended and America gained independence, Paine sailed back to England to work on the design of an iron bridge. With the outbreak of the French Revolution in 1789, however, he was drawn back into political conflict. Many people criticized the Revolution for trying to overthrow the monarchy. Paine, on the other hand, supported it and responded to this criticism in 1791 by writing a two-part work, The Rights of Man.

Paine was influenced by the Enlightenment, a philosophical movement that held that natural laws existed for all people, and governments were only formed to protect them. Paine argued that if people were fighting for a truly representative government, then their fight was just. He further argued that it was the duty of governments to provide universal education, unemployment relief, and

assistance for the poor. Because he criticized the English monarchy in this work, Paine was threatened with imprisonment for treason. In 1792, he fled to France where he was welcomed as a hero and was elected to the National Convention, the country's new body of representatives. Paine, however, soon opposed the mob violence of the French Revolution and the execution of French king Louis XVI (1774–93). Branded a traitor, Paine was jailed from December of 1793 to November of 1794.

While he was imprisoned, Paine wrote The Age of Reason, in which he attempted to define his belief in the religious philosophy called Deism. Deists did not reject God, but thought God set up the universe like an intricate clock and left it running, never to interfere with it. They believed the Bible was only a moral guide, and that the natural laws of the universe (and God's perfection) could be discovered through education and reason. Paine urged people to abandon Christianity, which he called absurd and contradictory, and to follow a natural religion of good deeds and humanitarianism.

Paine's work on Deism proved to be his undoing. Upon his return to America in 1802, he faced great hostility. Many people saw The Age of Reason as an attack on society and labeled him an atheist. Even those people who had supported his earlier writings turned against him. His great accomplishments as a champion of liberty soon faded from their memories. Paine, who had argued on behalf of the poor throughout his life, lived his last seven years in poverty. He died alone in New York on June 8, 1809.

A Matter of Honor

Monroe spent the summer of 1797 in a war of words with his rival Alexander Hamilton that resulted in a challenge to a duel between them. Ironically, Monroe named Aaron Burr, who would eventually kill Hamilton in another duel, as his second, and instructed him to postpone the encounter for a few weeks; Monroe wanted time to vindicate himself over his recall from France. The rivalry cooled as Federalist power slipped away, and the Monroe-Hamilton duel was cancelled.

Jefferson were among the most powerful of the Anti-Federalists.

Mixed Results in Europe

Monroe resigned from his senate seat in 1794 to accept a ministry post in France (a minister ranks below an ambassador). President George Washington wanted him to maintain friendly relations with France while the United States worked more closely with Great Britain, France's enemy at the time. Monroe became a great favorite in France, and while he was there, he helped secure the release of the writer Thomas Paine, who had been imprisoned for opposing the execution of King Louis XVI during the French Revolution.

President Washington recalled Monroe in 1796 out of fear that relations between America and France might upset Great Britain. This development resulted in the end of Washington and Monroe's friendship. Monroe had served under Washington during the Revolutionary War, and Washington had helped him start his political career. But he joined such politicians as Jefferson and Madison in criticizing the president for not being more aggressive toward Britain.

Monroe was elected Governor of Virginia in 1798, as the divide between Federalists and Anti-Federalists was growing larger. In his 1797 farewell address, Washington urged the nation to avoid splitting into political parties, but it was already too late. During the 1800 presidential election, Anti-Federalists transformed into the Democratic-Republican Party, and its leader, Thomas Jefferson, was elected president.

In 1803, President Jefferson appointed Monroe as a special envoy to France as part of a delegation negotiating the purchase of the city of New Orleans in the Louisiana Territory. Monroe and chief negotiator Robert R. Livingston showed strong interest when the French Emperor Napoleon I suggested that France might be interested in selling the entire Louisiana colony to the United States. The negotiations concluded with the largest real estate acquisition ever—the Louisiana Purchase.

Monroe stayed on in Europe after the Louisiana

Left: As governor of Virginia, Monroe quashed Gabriel's Uprising, a revolt of more than 1,000 slaves.

Right: Napoleon Bonaparte's subjects in Louisiana reacted to news of the Purchase with much concern.

Above: Napoleon I.

Below: The streets of London as Monroe knew them.

Purchase, but he failed in two missions. He wasn't successful in convincing Great Britain to stop seizing the cargoes of American ships bound for France, England's enemy. As a neutral nation, not allied with either side, America claimed the right to trade with all countries. After diplomacy failed, President Jefferson issued the Embargo Act of 1807, cutting off U.S. trade with all nations in an attempt to punish Britain. This move did not work, however. Without American competition, England increased its trade with other countries.

Between diplomatic sessions with Great Britain, Monroe traveled to Spain to try to convince that nation to sell its Florida colony. Spain refused, and Monroe returned empty-handed to the United States as Jefferson's presidency was ending.

When James Madison won the 1808 presidential election, Monroe expected to be offered a cabinet post, but relations between the two men hadn't been good since Monroe's loss of his seat in the House of Representatives to Madison. Their relationship became further strained when Madison's cabinet offer wasn't forthcoming. While serving again in the Virginia legislature and then as the state's governor, Monroe found opportunities to settle their differences, and in 1811, Madison appointed him to the post of secretary of state.

Great Britain and France were at war again, and each of them was seizing American cargoes bound for the other. France relented to American demands to stop the practice, but England refused to recognize the United States as a neutral nation. Monroe opposed going to war over the matter, but once the War of 1812 broke out, he supported the conflict against Great Britain.

Tough Talk

When Monroe and the others went to Paris to negotiate for the sale of New Orleans, they weren't expecting a love fest. They opened their discussions with a strong threat that the Americans were prepared to send troops down the Mississippi to take the city by force if the negotiations didn't work out. Then, they said, their country intended to join forces with the British to prevent the western part of the continent from developing a French accent. Napoleon surprised them by offering to sell the whole thing to the American government. All that remained was to establish a price, and that job fell to Monroe and the American minister, Robert Livingston.

Emerges as National Leader

Monroe took an active military role in his support for the war, helping the Maryland militia in its failed defense of Fort Bradenburg against a British assault. When British forces moved on Washington, DC, and burned the nation's capital, President Madison fired his secretary of war, John Armstrong, and placed Monroe in a dual role of secretary of state and secretary of war. Monroe faced tremendous challenges with a bankrupt national treasury, and a poorly equipped and poorly led army. He also had to deal with an increasingly unfriendly Congress that included some New Englanders who threatened that their states would secede from the union over the war.

Monroe acted quickly and decisively, first securing loans to finance the war effort. To lift soldiers' morale and to attract additional men, he increased the amount of land that war veterans could claim after their military service, and then he merged state militias into the federal army to create a larger, stronger, united force.

The War of 1812 officially ended early in 1815. Americans could take heart that although the nation did not emerge victorious, it wasn't defeated either. The national mood brightened when news of the dramatic victory in the 1815 Battle of New Orleans spread. A resounding victory for the United States, the battle had

Above: Rufus King, the losing Federalist candidate in the 1816 election.

actually been fought after both sides had agreed on a cease-fire and a peace treaty: News traveled slowly in those days, and word of the truce hadn't reached the winning commander, Andrew Jackson, who became a national hero.

Madison decided not to run for a third term in 1816, and Monroe defeated U.S. senator Rufus King of New York to become the nation's fifth president. Monroe's old classmate, Chief Justice John Marshall, administered the oath of office at his inauguration. As one of his first

Election Results

1816

Presidential / Vice Presidential Candidates	Popular votes	Presidential electoral votes
James Monroe / Daniel D. Tompkins (Democratic-Republican)	—	183
Rufus King / John E. Howard (Federalist)	—	34

1820

Presidential / Vice Presidential Candidates	Popular votes	Presidential electoral votes
James Monroe / Daniel D. Tompkins (Democratic-Republican)	—	231
John Quincy Adams / Richard Stockton (Democratic-Republican)	—	1

Popular votes were not yet part of these presidential elections. (The general public did not vote.) Due to the demise of the Federalist Party, candidates in the 1820 election represented different factions of the same party. For all intents and purposes, however, due to Monroe's popularity, he ran unopposed. One elector voted for Adams to ensure that George Washington remained the only president to be elected unanimously.

Also-Ran

Monroe's opponent in the 1816 election was Rufus King of New York, who hadn't been officially nominated, but was supported by the dying Federalists. Some of them tried to oppose Monroe for his failures in Europe, but King had little to say one way or the other. Since his nomination was the same as being elected, Monroe and his supporters did little campaigning, either, preferring to let sleeping dogs lie. Monroe carried all twenty-four states.

presidential acts, Monroe toured New England, hoping to smooth over differences that had made some of the states threaten secession from the union over the war. The tour was so successful that a Boston newspaper, the *Columbian Centinel,* reported that the new president had ushered in an "Era of Good Feelings.."

The Era of Good Feelings

Along with a sense of increased national pride, this Era of Good Feelings was highlighted by several developments. American territory continued to expand as settlers were finding new opportunities in former frontier land; Atlantic coast ports along the Atlantic Ocean were fortified to provide better defense; and the nation's political divisions seemed to have disappeared.

Still, the country was not without problems. When a patrol crossed the border from Georgia into Spanish Florida looking for runaway slaves, Seminole Indians from there retaliated by making raids into Georgia. General Andrew Jackson, the hero of the Battle of New Orleans, was called in to help drive them out, and followed the retreating Seminoles into Spanish Florida. Jackson captured two forts there, and he executed two British citizens for encouraging the Seminoles to mount surprise ambushes.

This action became a major international incident and the possibility of war with England loomed again, while Spain demanded the return of its forts. Many in Congress wanted to censure Jackson, but Monroe, who surrounded himself with excellent cabinet officials and consulted regularly with ex-presidents Jefferson and Madison, was urged to apologize to Great Britain and Spain. Instead, he followed the advice of his secretary of state, John Quincy Adams, returning the forts, and offering a simple explanation of Jackson's action—but not an apology—to Britain. Monroe used the incident to show the European nations how difficult it could be to maintain order in lands across the ocean. Adams took the opportunity to negotiate with Spain to purchase Florida.

The Florida Purchase was made during Monroe's first term, and Adams negotiated with England over western lands beyond the territory the United States had acquired in the Louisiana Purchase. The two nations agreed to joint control of the Oregon Territory and established a border at the 49th parallel latitude. This border, running

Right: Landing troops in Florida to fight the Seminole War.

The Missouri Compromise

The Missouri territory applied for admission to the union as a slave state early in 1819, spurring a full-fledged congressional debate on the nature of slavery and the expansion of the institution into new territories. In February 1819, Representative James Tallmadge of New York offered an amendment to the Missouri Enabling Bill to prohibit further introduction of slavery into the territory and provide for the gradual emancipation of slaves already in Missouri. The amendment was passed by the Northern-dominated House of Representatives and was sent to the Senate, where the amendment was eliminated from the bill. The House refused to follow the Senate action, but Congress soon adjourned. Thus, the slavery issue awaited the organization of the Sixteenth Congress, which hammered out the Missouri Compromise.

The Tallmadge Amendment stirred up the South, which was entering an era of great expansion westward, and the plantation system was advancing beyond the Mississippi River. The Tallmadge Amendment challenged the doctrine of states' rights, which had become accepted as a defense of slavery throughout much of the South. The Sixteenth Congress debated all aspects of the question from December of 1819 through March of 1820.

A compromise was proposed by Senator Jesse B. Thomas of Illinois. The Thomas Amendment coupled the admission of Missouri as a slave state with that of Maine, which was also applying for statehood, as a free state and prohibited the introduction of slavery into the remaining areas acquired through the Louisiana Purchase. The bill was passed by both Houses with this amendment. However, Congress and the nation were not quite finished with Missouri. A second, if less dramatic, debate occurred with the submission of Missouri's proposed constitution to Congress.

In the proposed constitution, the Missouri Assembly was ordered to pass laws prohibiting free blacks or mulattoes from entering the state. This went against the U.S. Constitution's guarantee that "the citizens of each State shall be entitled to all of the privileges and immunities of citizens of the several States." The status of free blacks in the North was at stake. For instance, free blacks in Massachusetts were considered citizens. Were their rights to be denied? Under the leadership of Speaker of the House Henry Clay, Congress passed a resolution admitting Missouri on the condition that its legislature refuse to pass any laws denying privileges of citizenship. Later, in 1825 and 1847, Missouri passed acts designed to prohibit the immigration of free Negroes and mulattoes into the state.

The Missouri Compromise debate of 1820 was the start of great discussions over the nature of the Union and the expansion of slavery, which dominated the nation's political life during the 1840s and 1850s. The Compromise of 1850 was yet another attempt to address the sectional dispute over slavery.

from Lake of the Woods in present-day Minnesota to the Pacific Ocean, forms the present-day boundary between the United States and Canada west of the Great Lakes.

The Monroe Administration

Administration Dates:	March 4, 1817–March 4, 1821
	March 4, 1821–March 4, 1825
Vice President:	Daniel D. Tompkins (1817–25)
Cabinet:	
Secretary of State	John Quincy Adams (1817–25)
Secretary of the Treasury	William H. Crawford (1817–25)
Secretary of War	John C. Calhoun (1817–25)
Attorney General	Richard Rush (1817)
	William Wirt (1817–25)
Secretary of the Navy	Benjamin W. Crowninshield (1817–18)
	Smith Thompson (1819–23)
	Samuel L. Southard (1823–25)
Postmaster General	R. Jonathan Meigs Jr. (1817–23)
	John McLean (1823–25)

Meanwhile, 1819 turned out to be an era of bad feelings. An economic slump led to financial problems for many citizens and brought a halt to road and canal projects that were improving the nation's infrastructure. Then, when Maine and Missouri petitioned to join the Union as states, the issue of slavery sharply divided Congress. Slavery was outlawed in much of the North, and Maine proposed to enter as a free state. Missouri, however, petitioned to enter as a slave state, and a great heated debate on the slavery issue followed. Their differences were eased with the Missouri Compromise of 1820.

The Missouri Compromise was intended to maintain a balance of slave and free states in the Union. Addressing the fear that slavery might expand to new states formed in the area acquired in the Louisiana Purchase, the Compromise set a dividing line at the southern border of Missouri. All states formed south of it could enter as slave states, if it was the will of the people; and all states formed north of the line would be free states.

Monroe easily won reelection in 1820, and the nation continued to grow and prosper during his second term, but he faced three difficult issues during his second

Above: Native Americans in the early 19th century.

Left: The beginnings of the city of Monrovia in Liberia.

four years. In an effort to assert America's international influence and to restrict European nations from controlling parts of North and South America, he issued what came to be known as the "Monroe Doctrine" in 1823. He was personally against slavery, but he had signed the Missouri Compromise because it offered the best alternative to dividing the nation at that time. Both Monroe and his secretary of state, John Quincy Adams, believed that great debates and battles over slavery would follow. Like the issue of slavery, Monroe questioned whether Congress had the authority to enact laws for federally led improvements of roads and canals, and he vetoed an improvements bill on that ground. Debates on slavery and the powers of the federal government heated up considerably after he left office.

Monroe called slavery the "most menacing" issue confronting the nation, and he supported a law that returned illegally captured African slaves to their home continent. A group called the American Colonization Society had purchased land on the West Coast of Africa and formed the nation of Liberia there, intending it to be a colony where returned slaves could live. To honor the

president's support for the cause, the Liberian capital was named Monrovia.

Monroe also wanted to protect the rights of Native Americans, especially as white settlers moved into the frontier. He supported a policy that set aside certain areas as Indian Territory for "as long as grass shall grow and rivers run." In spite of his best intentions, however, within a decade the United States would adopt policies that forcefully removed Native Americans from their lands.

Congratulations, But...

When Monroe retired from the presidency, he received the acclaim of the people, but not their financial blessing. He was deep in debt, and Congress turned a deaf ear to his pleas for reimbursement for his various missions to Europe or even for his army service. Among the congratulatory letters he received was one from John Jacob Astor, the richest man in the United States at the time, wishing him a long life "...to witness the prosperity of the country to which you have so generously contributed." The letter ended with a demand for repayment of a loan the great man had made to him.

End of an Era

Monroe's policies toward Native Americans and African Americans did not last beyond his presidency. On the other hand, the most noted historical event of his second term—the introduction of the Monroe Doctrine—would have much greater impact in later years than it had at the time. A series of revolutions in Latin America and continuing disputes between the United States and Russia over lands in the far west in North America created international tension. In the early 1820s, an alliance of Russia, Austria, France, and Prussia helped restore the fallen Spanish monarchy, and with revolutions brewing in Spain's American colonies, the United States and Britain both feared that this coalition would help Spain maintain those colonies.

Great Britain and the United States agreed to withstand any such interference, and they planned to issue a joint statement of cooperation. Monroe, as usual, took his time to carefully examine the issue from several angles, consulting with his cabinet, congressmen, and ex-presidents Jefferson and Madison. Most of them were in favor of the joint policy, but Secretary of State Adams wanted the United States to make its own individual statement on the matter, and Monroe agreed. In his 1823 annual address to Congress, the president announced the policy that would become the Monroe Doctrine.

The Monroe Doctrine was applauded at home as another sign of the emergence of the United States as a major nation, but it went largely unnoticed in the international community. Britain had planned to fight any attempt by other European nations to protect or expand their influence in the America, and other European nations couldn't afford to maintain their vast colonial empires any longer. Still, the Monroe Doctrine was a major statement. It would be used and expanded by U.S. presidents several times through the years to challenge European intervention in the affairs of the Americas.

Meanwhile, the political unity that Monroe had enjoyed gradually began to dissolve. The Federalist Party had disappeared, and the Democratic-Republican Party was splitting into factions around potential candidates for the 1824 presidential election. Slavery continued to divide the nation, and regional difficulties grew larger over the introduction of a new tax on imports in 1824 that was more favorable to northern states.

Following the precedents set by George Washington and his Virginia Dynasty predecessors, Monroe limited his presidential tenure to two terms. When he left office in 1825, he found himself deeply in debt. All his years of public service had brought him only a small part of the financial stability he could have built as a private citizen. After Elizabeth Monroe died in 1830, James sold his estate, Ash Lawn, and moved to New York City to live in the home of his youngest daughter, Maria. It wasn't until several years after he left office that Monroe received any form of reimbursement and a pension from the government he had served so well.

James Monroe died on July 4, 1831, five years to the day after the deaths of two previous presidents, John Adams and Thomas Jefferson. He was buried in New York, but in 1858 his remains were moved to Richmond, the capital of Virginia.

Kind Words

When Monroe retired from the presidency, his successor, John Quincy Adams, summed up his incredible success at shoring up the Union by saying, "He is entitled to say, like Augustus Caesar of his imperial city, that he found her built of brick and left her constructed of marble."

Right: A cartoon showing European leaders observing America's new foreign policy.

Legacy

James Monroe was the last president to govern with nearly full political support. The election of 1824 bitterly divided Democratic-Republicans, and the political landscape in America was forever altered soon after by the establishment of modern-day political parties. Like Washington, Monroe had warned against such a development, which he believed would place the interests of politics above those of the nation.

The Monroe Doctrine became perhaps the most significant foreign policy statement in American history. Several U.S. presidents invoked it through the years to challenge European intervention in the affairs of the Americas, and later to protect island nations of the Pacific.

The Missouri Compromise of 1820 brought a temporary calm to divisiveness on the issue of slavery and it served as a guide into the 1850s. Monroe, following his principles that Congress should act independent of the president, did not engage in the debate. The issue of slavery continued to be a threat to the nation, though, and harsher government policies toward Native Americans followed soon after Monroe's presidency.

Plantation for Sale

After his retirement, Madison sold his beloved "cabin castle," the Virginia plantation he had called Highland. The new owner, who paid $75,000 for the place, was a Baptist minister named John Massey. He renamed it Ash Lawn, and added a Victorian wing that served as a school for educating newly freed slaves. It was bought in 1930 by Jay Winston Johns, a Pennsylvania businessman who began restoring it as a presidential landmark. He willed the house and its furnishings to the College of William and Mary, which is still at work bringing it back to the working farm of Madison's day.

Monroe's personal legacy rests with his ability to unite the nation and to help instill a sense of national identity. The young nation matured during his presidency. John Quincy Adams, who had served with distinction as an American diplomat and as secretary of state, followed Monroe as president, but he was rendered ineffective because of political differences with Congress. Adams, who later would redistinguish himself as a congressman, wrote that the Monroe years would be remembered as "the Golden Age of this Republic."

Elizabeth Monroe

Born June 30, 1768, New York, New York
Died September 23, 1830, Loudoun County, Virginia

"Elizabeth Monroe had a complete absorption in the affairs of her family and a total detachment from the world of politics and business."

—Historian Harry Ammon

Elizabeth Monroe was a woman of calm dignity who disliked fanfare and social activity. However, her quiet personality did not stop her from helping to free Madame Adrienne de Noailles Lafayette, Marquise de Lafayette, from execution in 1795.

Elizabeth Kortright was born on June 30, 1768, into a wealthy family that moved within a small social circle

in New York City. Her father, Lawrence, supported the Tory party of Great Britain and wanted the American colonies to remain under British rule. By the time of the American Revolution, he was established as a wealthy merchant, following an earlier success as a privateer, a private trader and merchant licensed to carry arms and provide military support for his nation. Kortright traded with American, Native American, British, and French settlers in North America and, if needed, he could serve the British military as a civilian. By the time the American Revolution began, however, Kortright was not involved in fighting for the British cause.

Meanwhile, James Monroe had served valiantly on the American side in the war. He met Elizabeth while he was serving in the Congress of the Confederation, which met in New York. In spite of their different family backgrounds—he came from a modest family and fought for American independence—they started a romance and were married in 1786.

They had a daughter, Elizabeth Kortright Monroe, in 1787, and moved to Fredericksburg, Virginia, in Monroe's native state. The couple had two other children: James Spence, who was born in 1799 but died a year later, and Maria Hester Monroe, who was born in 1803.

Major General Lafayette

Marie-Joseph-Paul-Yves-Roch-Gilbert du Motier de Lafayette was born on September 6, 1757, to the Motier family—better known by their noble title of La Fayette ("Lafayette" is an American spelling). After three years of study in the Collège du Plessis, a distinguished secondary school in Paris, France, Lafayette joined the French army in 1771. In 1773, Lafayette married Adrienne de Noailles (1759–1807), daughter of the Duc d'Ayen. After the outbreak of the American Revolution in 1775, Lafayette decided to put his military training to use by assisting America against France's historic enemy, England. Refused the king's permission to go to America, Lafayette sailed anyway, after buying and equipping a ship with his own money.

On June 13, 1777, he landed in North Carolina. The Continental Congress had given the distinguished volunteer an honorary commission as a major-general, but his actual duties were as aide-de-camp to General George Washington. After performing well in battles against the British in Pennsylvania and New Jersey, Lafayette was given command of a division of American troops. He became friends with future president James Monroe during battles in Pennsylvania. The next year, Lafayette was sent back to France with the mission of obtaining greater French support for the Americans. Upon landing in his homeland early in 1779, Lafayette was arrested for having disobeyed the royal command in going to America. But he was soon summoned by the king, who wanted a firsthand report on how things stood in America.

Lafayette returned to America in April 1780 in command of French auxiliary forces. His maneuverings in 1781 in Virginia eventually drew English commander Charles Cornwallis (1738–1805) into the trap at Yorktown. Cornwallis's surrender on October 19 brought the American war of independence to its military conclusion and was the culmination of Lafayette's career as a soldier. When Lafayette returned to France in 1782, it was as a hero—Washington's friend—and he was made a brigadier general in the French army.

Lafayette was influential in the first months of the French Revolution, which began in 1789. The Declaration of the Rights of Man and the Citizen was adopted at his initiative, and his military fame and political reputation combined to win for him, on the day after the Bastille fell (July 14), the command of the Parisian national guard, the force of citizen-soldiers created to defend the new regime. Lafayette favored a parliamentary monarchy like England's but one based on a formal written constitution, like that just adopted in America. However, he had to cope with radical mob violence. His efforts to hold the Revolution to a moderate course proved unpopular, and his command to his troops to fire on a mob in July 1791 led to his retirement in September from command of the national guard.

However, the onset of war against Austria and Prussia in 1792 brought Lafayette's return to military life as the commander of the Army of the Ardennes. He invaded the Austrian Netherlands (Belgium) and then withdrew for lack of support. He was treated as a prisoner of war until 1797, when the victorious Napoleon obtained his release from jail. He was not allowed to return to France until 1799, when he was given a military pension as a retired general and allowed to live quietly on his country estate.

Lafayette did not engage in political activity again until 1814, when he was elected to the legislative chamber. From 1818 to 1824, he sat in the Chamber of Deputies as a leading member of the second most powerful political group in France. In 1824, Lafayette was invited by the U.S. government during the administration of President Monroe to visit America as its guest, and his triumphant tour of the country lasted fifteen months. Congress gave him a gift of $200,000 and a sizable tract of land, and Lafayette returned to France in 1825 to great acclaim as the "hero of two worlds."

Lafayette did not regain political prominence until the outbreak of revolution in 1830, when he became the symbol of moderate republicanism (a form of government in which citizens elect their leaders). However, when Lafayette died in Paris on May 20, 1834, he had few followers left.

Madame Lafayette's Life Is Spared

James Monroe served as a diplomat in France from 1794 to 1796, and it was during that period that Elizabeth Monroe helped secure Madame Lafayette's release from prison. Monroe had been a friend of Major General Lafayette since helping to tend the general's wounds during the American Revolution. Lafayette was a French citizen who fought for the American cause and was made a major-general in the Continental Army. Lafayette returned to France after the war ended, and played an important role in the French Revolution, eventually serving in the new government that emerged from it. He was commanding the French army in a war against Austria when the French political power shifted to his opponents. Lafayette was branded a traitor, and was captured and held in prisons in Prussia and Austria from 1792 to 1798. His wife, meanwhile, became a political prisoner in Paris.

Elizabeth Monroe visited Madame Lafayette and her two children in the French jail. At that time, carriages were banned from the streets of Paris because they represented a status symbol of wealth. Nevertheless, Elizabeth Monroe hired a carriage to take her to the prison, and her ride to the jail and her arrival there drew a crowd of onlookers. The prison gatekeeper was surprised by her arrival, but he allowed her to enter and led her to a waiting room. When Madame Lafayette was brought in, she burst into tears when saw her friend. She had been waiting in her cell for a summons to her execution, which had been scheduled for that very afternoon.

Elizabeth Monroe spoke briefly with Madame Lafayette, and as she rose to leave, she announced loudly that she would return for another visit the next morning. In the meantime, French officials had received word of her prison visit, and eager to promote goodwill between France and America, they freed Madame Lafayette that afternoon.

As Monroe's political career blossomed with his election to governor of Virginia in 1798, Elizabeth concentrated on raising her daughters. When President Thomas Jefferson appointed him as a special envoy to France in 1803, he was included in a delegation that was negotiating the land sale that eventually became the Louisiana Purchase. Eliza, as she was called, accompanied her husband. She was well liked in Paris society, where she was affectionately called *la belle americaine*, "the beautiful American." The Monroes enjoyed attending theaters in Paris, and whenever they entered a playhouse, the orchestra would play the unofficial American anthem, "Yankee Doodle," in their honor.

The Monroes remained in Europe until 1807, often traveling between Great Britain, France, and Spain while Mr. Monroe represented various foreign policy interests of President Jefferson. After returning home, Monroe served in the Virginia legislature and then, again, briefly, as the state's governor. During this period, Elizabeth and her daughters lived at Ash Lawn, the Monroe estate at Charlottesville, Virginia. They went back to Washington after President James Madison appointed Monroe as secretary of state in 1811.

The Era of Good Feelings

After serving Madison as secretary of state and secretary of war, James Monroe was elected president in 1816. He served two terms during which the young United States became a stronger and more prosperous nation, a period has been called the "Era of Good Feelings."

Those good feelings did not always extend to Elizabeth Monroe. She did not compare well to her more outgoing predecessor, Dolley Madison. Mrs. Madison often visited the wives of political officials and dignitaries, and she entertained frequently. However, Elizabeth soon developed a style of her own, preferring a much less active social role. Social events were fewer and more formal during the Monroe administration, and Elizabeth didn't always attend dinner parties at the executive mansion. Rather than making the rounds in Washington, D.C., Elizabeth expected the wives of political officials and dignitaries to make appointments to visit her. She and her two daughters, however, served as hostesses for weekly receptions that were open to the public.

The Monroes retired to Ash Lawn at the end of President Monroe's second term in 1825. However, Monroe had fallen deeply into debt. He had not received sufficient compensation for all his years of public service. The couple eventually benefited from a pension and lived reasonably well. Elizabeth Monroe died in September of 1830. Her husband died less than a year later.

Right: James Monroe's inauguration.

Monroe's First Inaugural Address

Tuesday, March 4, 1817

The Capitol was still being rebuilt after its burning by the British invasion in 1814, and President-elect Monroe offered to take his oath of office in the second-floor House Chamber of the temporary "Brick Capitol," on the site of the future Supreme Court building. Speaker of the House Henry Clay refused to allow the hall to be used, and suggested instead that the ceremony should be held outdoors instead. The President's speech to the crowd from a platform adjacent to the brick building was the first outdoor inaugural address. Chief Justice John Marshall administered the oath of office.

I should be destitute of feeling if I was not deeply affected by the strong proof which my fellow-citizens have given me of their confidence in calling me to the high office whose functions I am about to assume. As the expression of their good opinion of my conduct in the public service, I derive from it a gratification which those who are conscious of having done all that they could to merit it can alone feel. MY [*sic*] sensibility is increased by a just estimate of the importance of the trust and of the nature and extent of its duties, with the proper discharge of which the highest interests of a great and free people are intimately connected. Conscious of my own deficiency, I cannot enter on these duties without great anxiety for the result. From a just responsibility I will never shrink, calculating with confidence that in my best efforts to promote the public welfare my motives will always be duly appreciated and my conduct be viewed with that candor and indulgence which I have experienced in other stations.

In commencing the duties of the chief executive office it has been the practice of the distinguished men who have gone before me to explain the principles which would govern them in their respective Administrations. In following their venerated example my attention is naturally drawn to the great causes which have contributed in a principal degree to produce the present happy condition of the United States. They will best explain the nature of our duties and shed much light on the policy which ought to be pursued in future.

From the commencement of our Revolution to the present day almost forty years have elapsed, and from the establishment of this Constitution twenty-eight. Through this whole term the Government has been what may emphatically be called self-government. And what has been the effect? To whatever object we turn our attention, whether it relates to our foreign or domestic concerns, we find abundant cause to felicitate ourselves in the excellence of our institutions. During a period fraught with difficulties and marked by very extraordinary events the United States have flourished beyond example. Their citizens individually have been happy and the nation prosperous.

Under this Constitution our commerce has been wisely regulated with foreign nations and between the States; new States have been admitted into our Union; our territory has been enlarged by fair and honorable treaty, and with great advantage to the original States; the States, respectively protected by the National Government under a mild, parental system against foreign dangers, and enjoying within their separate spheres, by a wise partition of power, a just proportion of the sovereignty, have improved their police, extended their settlements, and attained a strength and maturity which are the best proofs of wholesome laws well administered. And if we look to the condition of individuals what a proud spectacle does it exhibit! On whom has oppression fallen in any quarter of our Union? Who has been deprived of any right of person or property? Who restrained from offering his vows in the mode which he prefers to the Divine Author of his being? It is well known that all these blessings have been enjoyed in their fullest extent; and I add with peculiar satisfaction that there has been no example of a capital punishment being inflicted on anyone for the crime of high treason.

Some who might admit the competency of our Government to these beneficent duties might doubt it in trials which put to the test its strength and efficiency as a member of the great community of nations. Here too experience has afforded us the most satisfactory proof in its favor. Just as this Constitution was put into action several of the principal States of Europe had become much agitated and some of them seriously convulsed. Destructive wars ensued, which have of late only been terminated. In the course of these conflicts the United States received great injury from several of the parties. It was their interest to stand aloof from the contest, to demand justice from the party committing the injury, and to cultivate by a fair and honorable conduct the friendship of all. War became at length inevitable, and the result has shown that our Government is equal to that, the greatest of trials, under the most unfavorable circumstances. Of the virtue of the people and of the heroic exploits of the Army, the Navy, and the militia I need not speak.

Such, then, is the happy Government under which we live—a Government adequate to every purpose for which the social compact is formed; a Government elective in all its branches, under which every citizen may by his merit obtain the highest trust recognized by the Constitution; which contains within it no cause of discord, none to put at variance one portion of the community with another; a Government which protects every citizen in the full enjoyment of his rights, and is able to protect the nation against injustice from foreign powers.

Other considerations of the highest importance admonish us to cherish our Union and to cling to the Government which supports it. Fortunate as we are in our political institutions, we have not been less so in other circumstances on which our prosperity and happiness essentially depend. Situated within the temperate zone, and extending through many degrees of latitude along the Atlantic, the United States enjoy all the varieties of climate, and every production incident to that portion of the globe. Penetrating internally to the Great Lakes and beyond the sources of the great rivers which communicate through our whole interior, no country was ever happier with respect to its domain. Blessed, too, with a fertile soil, our produce has always been very abundant, leaving, even in years the least favorable, a surplus for the wants of our

fellow-men in other countries. Such is our peculiar felicity that there is not a part of our Union that is not particularly interested in preserving it. The great agricultural interest of the nation prospers under its protection. Local interests are not less fostered by it. Our fellow-citizens of the North engaged in navigation find great encouragement in being made the favored carriers of the vast productions of the other portions of the United States, while the inhabitants of these are amply recompensed, in their turn, by the nursery for seamen and naval force thus formed and reared up for the support of our common rights. Our manufactures find a generous encouragement by the policy which patronizes domestic industry, and the surplus of our produce a steady and profitable market by local wants in less-favored parts at home.

Such, then, being the highly favored condition of our country, it is the interest of every citizen to maintain it. What are the dangers which menace us? If any exist they ought to be ascertained and guarded against.

In explaining my sentiments on this subject it may be asked, What raised us to the present happy state? How did we accomplish the Revolution? How remedy the defects of the first instrument of our Union, by infusing into the National Government sufficient power for national purposes, without impairing the just rights of the States or affecting those of individuals? How sustain and pass with glory through the late war? The Government has been in the hands of the people. To the people, therefore, and to the faithful and able depositaries of their trust is the credit due. Had the people of the United States been educated in different principles had they been less intelligent, less independent, or less virtuous can it be believed that we should have maintained the same steady and consistent career or been blessed with the same success? While, then, the constituent body retains its present sound and healthful state everything will be safe. They will choose competent and faithful representatives for every department. It is only when the people become ignorant and corrupt, when they degenerate into a populace, that they are incapable of exercising the sovereignty. Usurpation is then an easy attainment, and an usurper soon found. The people themselves become the willing instruments of their own debasement and ruin. Let us, then, look to the great cause, and endeavor to preserve it in full force. Let us by all wise and constitutional measures promote intelligence among the people as the best means of preserving our liberties.

Dangers from abroad are not less deserving of attention. Experiencing the fortune of other nations, the United States may be again involved in war, and it may in that event be the object of the adverse party to overset our Government, to break our Union, and demolish us as a nation. Our distance from Europe and the just, moderate, and pacific policy of our Government may form some security against these dangers, but they ought to be anticipated and guarded against. Many of our citizens are engaged in commerce and navigation, and all of them are in a certain degree dependent on their prosperous state. Many are engaged in the fisheries. These interests are exposed to invasion in the wars between other powers, and we should disregard the faithful admonition of experience if we did not expect it. We must support our rights or lose our character, and with it, perhaps, our liberties. A people who fail to do it can scarcely be said to hold a place among independent nations. National honor is national property of the highest value. The sentiment in the mind of every citizen is national strength. It ought therefore to be cherished.

To secure us against these dangers our coast and inland frontiers should be fortified, our Army and Navy, regulated upon just principles as to the force of each, be kept in perfect order, and our militia be placed on the best practicable footing. To put our extensive coast in such a state of defense as to secure our cities and interior from invasion will be attended with expense, but the work when finished will be permanent, and it is fair to presume that a single campaign of invasion by a naval force superior to our own, aided by a few thousand land troops, would expose us to greater expense, without taking into the estimate the loss of property and distress of our citizens, than would be sufficient for this great work. Our land and naval forces should be moderate, but adequate to the necessary purposes—the former to garrison and preserve our fortifications and to meet the first invasions of a foreign foe, and, while constituting the elements of a greater force, to preserve the science as well as all the necessary implements of war in a state to be brought into activity in the event of war; the latter, retained within the limits proper in a state of peace, might aid in maintaining the neutrality of the United States with dignity in the wars of other powers and in saving the property of their citizens from spoliation. In time of war, with the enlargement of which the great naval resources of the country render it susceptible, and which should be duly fostered in time of peace, it would contribute essentially, both as an auxiliary of defense and as a powerful engine of annoyance, to diminish the calamities of war and to bring the war to a speedy and honorable termination.

But it ought always to be held prominently in view that the safety of these States and of everything dear to a free people must depend in an eminent degree on the militia. Invasions may be made too formidable to be resisted by any land and naval force which it would comport either with the principles of our Government or the circumstances of the United States to maintain. In such cases recourse must be had to the great body of the people, and in a manner to produce the best effect. It is of the highest importance, therefore, that they be so organized and trained as to be prepared for any emergency. The arrangement should be such as to put at the command of the Government the ardent patriotism and youthful vigor of the country. If formed on equal and just principles, it can not be oppressive. It is the crisis which makes the pressure, and not the laws which provide a remedy for it. This arrangement should be formed, too, in time of peace, to be the better prepared for war. With such an organization of such a people the United States have nothing to dread from foreign invasion. At its approach an overwhelming force of gallant men might always be put in motion.

Other interests of high importance will claim attention, among which the improvement of our country by roads and canals, proceeding always with a constitutional sanction, holds a distinguished place. By thus facilitating the intercourse between the States we shall add much to the convenience and comfort of our fellow-citizens, much to the ornament of the country, and, what is of greater importance, we shall shorten distances, and, by making each part more accessible to and dependent on the other, we shall bind the Union more closely together. Nature has done so much for us by intersecting the country with so many great rivers, bays, and lakes, approaching from distant points so near to each other, that the inducement to complete the work seems to be peculiarly strong. A more interesting spectacle was perhaps never seen than is exhibited within the limits of the United States—a territory so vast and advantageously situated, containing objects so grand, so useful, so happily connected in all their parts!

Our manufacturers will likewise require the systematic and fostering care of the Government. Possessing as we do all the raw materials, the fruit of our own soil and industry, we ought not to depend in the degree we have done on supplies from other countries. While we are thus dependent the sudden event of war, unsought and unexpected, can not fail to plunge us into the most serious difficulties. It is important, too, that the capital which nourishes our manufacturers should be domestic, as its influence in that case instead of exhausting, as it may do in foreign hands, would be felt advantageously on agriculture and every other branch of industry Equally important is it to provide at home a market for our raw materials, as by extending the competition it will enhance the price and protect the cultivator against the casualties incident to foreign markets.

With the Indian tribes it is our duty to cultivate friendly relations and to act with kindness and liberality in all our transactions. Equally proper is it to persevere in our efforts to extend to them the advantages of civilization.

The great amount of our revenue and the flourishing state of the Treasury are a full proof of the competency of the national resources for any emergency, as they are of the willingness of our fellow-citizens to bear the burdens which the public necessities require. The vast amount of vacant lands, the value of which daily augments, forms an additional resource of great extent and duration. These resources, besides accomplishing every other necessary purpose, put it completely in the power of the United States to discharge the national debt at an early period. Peace is the best time for improvement and preparation of every kind; it is in peace that our commerce flourishes most, that taxes are most easily paid, and that the revenue is most productive.

The Executive is charged officially in the Departments under it with the disbursement of the public money, and is responsible for the faithful application of it to the purposes for which it is raised. The Legislature is the watchful guardian over the public purse. It is its duty to see that the disbursement has been honestly made. To meet the requisite responsibility every facility should be afforded to the Executive to enable it to bring the public agents intrusted with the public money strictly and promptly to account. Nothing should be presumed against them; but if, with the requisite facilities, the public money is suffered to lie long and uselessly in their hands, they will not be the only defaulters, nor will the demoralizing effect be confined to them. It will evince a relaxation and want of tone in the Administration which will be felt by the whole community. I shall do all I can to secure economy and fidelity in this important branch of the Administration, and I doubt not that the Legislature will perform its duty with equal zeal. A thorough examination should be regularly made, and I will promote it.

It is particularly gratifying to me to enter on the discharge of these duties at a time when the United States are blessed with peace. It is a state most consistent with their prosperity and happiness. It will be my sincere desire to preserve it, so far as depends on the Executive, on just principles with all nations, claiming nothing unreasonable of any and rendering to each what is its due.

Equally gratifying is it to witness the increased harmony of opinion which pervades our Union. Discord does not belong to our system. Union is recommended as well by the free and benign principles of our Government, extending its blessings to every individual, as by the other eminent advantages attending it. The American people have encountered together great dangers and sustained severe trials with success. They constitute one great family with a common interest. Experience has enlightened us on some questions of essential importance to the country. The progress has been slow, dictated by a just reflection and a faithful regard to every interest connected with it. To promote this harmony in accord with the principles of our republican Government and in a manner to give them the most complete effect, and to advance in all other respects the best interests of our Union, will be the object of my constant and zealous exertions.

Never did a government commence under auspices so favorable, nor ever was success so complete. If we look to the history of other nations, ancient or modern, we find no example of a growth so rapid, so gigantic, of a people so prosperous and happy. In contemplating what we have still to perform, the heart of every citizen must expand with joy when he reflects how near our Government has approached to perfection; that in respect to it we have no essential improvement to make; that the great object is to preserve it in the essential principles and features which characterize it, and that is to be done by preserving the virtue and enlightening the minds of the people; and as a security against foreign dangers to adopt such arrangements as are indispensable to the support of our independence, our rights and liberties. If we persevere in the career in which we have advanced so far and in the path already traced, we can not fail, under the favor of a gracious Providence, to attain the high destiny which seems to await us.

In the Administrations of the illustrious men who have preceded me in this high station, with some of whom I have been connected by the closest ties from early life, examples are presented which will always be found highly instructive and useful to their successors. From these I shall endeavor to derive all the advantages which they may afford. Of my immediate predecessor, under whom so important a portion of this great and successful experiment has been made, I shall be pardoned for expressing my earnest wishes that he may long enjoy in his retirement the affections of a grateful country, the best reward of exalted talents and the most faithful and meritorious service. Relying on the aid to be derived from the other departments of the Government, I enter on the trust to which I have been called by the suffrages of my fellow-citizens with my fervent prayers to the Almighty that He will be graciously pleased to continue to us that protection which He has already so conspicuously displayed in our favor.

The Monroe Doctrine

Delivered as part of Monroe's Seventh Annual Address to Congress, December 2, 1823

During James Monroe's presidency, there were continuing disputes between the United States and Russia over lands in the far west of North America. In addition, a series of revolutions occurred against authorities in Spain and Portugal's Latin American colonies. When an alliance of Russia, Austria, France, and Prussia helped restore the fallen monarchy of Spain in the early 1820s, the United States and Great Britain grew concerned that the alliance would provide assistance to Spain to help it maintain its colonies in the Americas.

Great Britain and the United States agreed to withstand any such interference. The two nations were planning to issue a joint policy, but Secretary of State John Quincy Adams convinced Monroe that the United States should make its own statement on the matter. In his annual address to Congress in December 1823, Monroe announced the policy that would become known as the Monroe Doctrine.

Excerpt from the Monroe Doctrine

A precise knowledge of our relations with foreign powers as respects our negotiations and transactions with each is thought to be particularly necessary. Equally necessary is it that we should for a just estimate of our resources, revenue, and progress in every kind of improvement connected with the national prosperity and public defense. It is by rendering justice to other nations that we may expect it from them. It is by our ability to resent injuries and redress wrongs that we may avoid them.

[…]

At the proposal of the Russian Imperial Government, made through the minister of the Emperor residing here, a full power and instructions have been transmitted to the minister of the United States at St. Petersburg to arrange by amicable negotiation the respective rights and interests of the two nations on the North West coast of this continent. A similar proposal had been made by His Imperial Majesty to the Government of Great Britain, which has likewise been acceded to. The Government of the United States has been desirous by this friendly proceeding of manifesting the great value which they have invariably attached to the friendship of the Emperor and their solicitude to cultivate the best understanding with his Government. In the discussions to which this interest has given rise and in the arrangements by which they may terminate the occasion has been judged proper for asserting, as a principle in which the rights and interests of the United States are involved, that the American continents, by the free and independent condition which they have assumed and maintain, are henceforth not to be considered as subjects for future colonization by any European powers.

[…]

The citizens of the United States cherish sentiments the most friendly in favor of the liberty and happiness of their fellow men on that side of the Atlantic. In the wars of the European powers in matters relating to themselves we have never taken any part, nor does it comport with our policy so to do.

It is only when our rights are invaded or seriously menaced that we resent injuries or make preparation for our defense. With the movements in this hemisphere we are of necessity more immediately connected, and by causes which must be obvious to all enlightened and impartial observers.

The political system of the allied powers is essentially different in this respect from that of America. This difference proceeds from that which exists in their respective Governments; and to the defense of our own, which has been achieved by the loss of so much blood and treasure, and matured by the wisdom of their most enlightened citizens, and under which we have enjoyed unexampled felicity, this whole nation is devoted.

We owe it, therefore, to candor and to the amicable relations existing between the United States and those powers to declare that we should consider any attempt on their part to extend their system to any portion of this hemisphere as dangerous to our peace and safety. With the existing colonies or dependencies of any European power we have not interfered and shall not interfere, but with the Governments who have declared their independence and maintained it, and whose independence we have, on great consideration and on just principles, acknowledged, we could not view any interposition for the purpose of oppressing them, or controlling in any other manner their destiny, by any European power in any other light than as the manifestation of an unfriendly disposition toward the United States.

In the war between those new Governments and Spain we declared our neutrality at the time of their recognition, and to this we have adhered, and shall continue to adhere, provided no change shall occur which, in the judgment of the competent authorities of this Government, shall make a corresponding change on the part of the United States indispensable to their security.

The late events in Spain and Portugal shew that Europe is still unsettled. Of this important fact no stronger proof can be adduced than that the allied powers should have thought it proper, on any principle satisfactory to themselves, to have interposed by force in the internal concerns of Spain. To what extent such interposition may be carried, on the same principle, is a question in which all independent powers whose governments differ from theirs are interested, even those most remote, and surely none more so than the United States.

Our policy in regard to Europe, which was adopted at an early stage of the wars which have so long agitated that quarter of the globe, nevertheless remains the same, which is, not to interfere in the internal concerns of any of its powers; to consider the government de facto as the legitimate government for us; to cultivate friendly relations with it, and to preserve those relations by a frank, firm, and manly policy, meeting in all instances the just claims of every power, submitting to injuries from none.

But in regard to those continents circumstances are eminently and conspicuously different. It is impossible that the allied powers should extend their political system to any portion of either continent without endangering our peace and happiness; nor can anyone believe that our southern brethren, if left to themselves, would adopt it of their own accord. It is equally impossible, therefore, that we should behold such interposition in any form with indifference. If we look to the comparative strength and resources of Spain and those new Governments, and their distance from each other, it must be obvious that she can never subdue them. It is still the true policy of the United States to leave the parties to themselves, in the hope that other powers will pursue the same course.

What Happened Next

The Monroe Doctrine was a sign of the emergence of the United States as a major international power, but it went largely unnoticed in the international community. European nations could no longer afford to maintain their vast colonial empires, and Great Britain was prepared to fight any attempt by other European powers to protect or expand influence in the Americas.

The Monroe Doctrine proved to be one of the most important policies in American history. Several presidents, including James K. Polk, William McKinley, and Theodore Roosevelt, invoked it to protect U.S. interests, and the doctrine was eventually expanded into the Pacific to include the Hawaiian Islands. President John F. Kennedy referred to the doctrine in 1961 during the Cuban missile crisis between the United States and the Soviet Union.

Below: Monroe discusses the Monroe Doctrine with members of his administration: (L-R) John Quincy Adams, William H. Crawford, William Wirt, John C. Calhoun, Daniel D. Tompkins, and John McLean.

John Quincy Adams

"In charity to all mankind, bearing no malice or ill will to any human being, and even compassionating those who hold in bondage their fellow men, not knowing what they do."

—*John Quincy Adams*

Sixth president of the United States, 1825–1829

Full name: *John Quincy Adams*
Born: *July 11, 1767, Braintree, Massachusetts*
Died: *February 23, 1848, Washington, D.C.*
Burial site: *First Unitarian Church, Quincy, Massachusetts*
Parents: *John and Abigail Smith Adams*
Spouse: *Louisa Catherine Johnson (1775–1852; m. 1797)*
Children: *George Washington (1801–1829); John II (1803–1834); Charles Francis (1807–1886); Louisa Catherine (1811–1812)*
Religion: *Unitarian*
Education: *Harvard College (B.A., 1787)*
Occupation: *Lawyer*
Government positions: *Minister to the Netherlands, Prussia, and Russia; U.S. senator and representative (Mass.); peace commissioner at the Treaty of Ghent; secretary of state under James Monroe*
Political party: *Democratic-Republican*
Dates as president: *March 4, 1825–March 4, 1829*
Age upon taking office: *57*

A member of an influential family that contributed greatly to the early years of the United States, John Quincy Adams was the first son of a former chief executive to also be elected president. Like John Adams, his father and the second U.S. president, John Quincy Adams served only one term and was neither a popular nor an effective chief executive. He won a disputed election. No candidate in the 1824 presidential race received enough electoral votes, so the election was decided by the House of Representatives, as required by the Constitution. Because of the resulting controversy, nearly every piece of legislation Adams or his allies in the Democratic-Republican Party attempted to pass was blocked by their political rivals.

Indeed, shortly after Adams's election, war hero Andrew Jackson, who had received more popular votes than Adams, resigned his seat in Congress to begin campaigning for the 1828 presidential election. He was able to drum up tremendous opposition against Adams, both on Capitol Hill and with the general public. The power struggle between them represented a contest between the entrenched New England political and economic order, which Adams represented, and the independent-minded new Southern and Western states that had more recently entered the Union.

Timeline

1767: Born in Massachusetts
1775: American Revolutionary War begins
1787: Earns degree from Harvard College
1790–94: Works as attorney in private practice in Boston
1794–97: Serves as minister to Holland
1796: Father John Adams elected president
1797–1801: Serves as minister to the Court of Prussia
1803–8: Serves in the U.S. Senate as a Federalist from Massachusetts; recalled by special election in 1808
1809–15: Serves as minister to Russia during presidency of James Madison
1812: War of 1812 begins
1815–17: Serves as minister to Great Britain; negotiator of Treaty of Ghent, which ended the War of 1812
1817–24: Serves as U.S. secretary of state; writes the Monroe Doctrine
1825–29: Serves as sixth U.S. president
1831–49: Serves in the U.S. House of Representatives from Plymouth District, Massachusetts
1841: Serves as co-counsel on the Amistad case argued before the U.S. Supreme Court, delivering the closing argument
1844: Successful in rescinding a Congressional gag rule on slavery
1846: Opposes U.S. conflict with Mexico
1848: Dies in Washington, D.C.

Prior to becoming president, Adams enjoyed a prominent career as a diplomat. He was instrumental in the drafting or signing of several important pacts that helped establish American foreign policy in the early decades of the new nation's history. As secretary of state under James Monroe, for example, he wrote the speech that became known as the Monroe Doctrine, firmly stating American intentions to oppose further European colonization in the Americas.

After he failed to be reelected as president in 1828, Adams became the only former president to be elected to the House of Representatives, and he was far more effective as a congressman than he had been as president. An outspoken opponent of slavery, Adams spent seventeen years battling—and sometimes belittling—colleagues who fought to maintain the institution, and he earned

No Entry

Adams was stopped from entering through the gates of Berlin in 1797 when he arrived to serve as a diplomat. An officer refused to allow him to pass into the royal court because he had never heard of the country—"the United States"—that Adams was supposed to represent.

the nickname "Old Man Eloquent" for his impassioned speeches.

Though he was a talented and highly regarded foreign diplomat, John Quincy Adams probably would have been much happier had he never entered American politics. A skilled speaker and linguist, he wrote poetry, kept a journal from the age of eleven, and translated *Oberon*, a famous German work by Christoph Martin Wieland, into English. Adams was also an avid collector of books, and he worked hard to secure a place in American libraries for many of his foreign editions. Later in his career as a legislator, Adams helped direct a large bequest from an English chemist, James Smithson, to form the Smithsonian Institution, which runs a number of important museums and historical collections in Washington, D.C.

An Auspicious Beginning

John Quincy Adams was born at his family's home in Braintree, Massachusetts, on July 11, 1767. His family ancestry stretched back several generations in New England. An Adams forebear arrived from England in 1632, and one of his descendants married the granddaughter of *Mayflower* pilgrims John Alden and Priscilla Mullins Alden. The couple's romance was a legendary tale in Plymouth Colony history and was the subject of Henry Wadsworth Longfellow's "The Courtship of Miles Standish."

The Smith and Quincy family line of his mother, Abigail Adams, was equally deep-rooted. The Smiths had been involved in the shipping business for generations, and her first Quincy ancestor had arrived in America in 1633, establishing a long line of prominent Quincy figures in early New England history.

Adams was the second child born to John Adams, a prominent Boston lawyer, and Abigail Smith Adams, a parson's daughter, who were married in 1764. Abigail Adams was a learned, progressive woman. Although not formally schooled, she was an avid reader, writer, and debater. The 2,000 letters she left behind reveal a woman of intelligence, with a passion for English literature and a dedication to democratic ideals and the American cause. Her son was named John Quincy after her great-grandfather, who died two days after the boy was born. His siblings included an older sister Abigail, whom the family called "Nabby," and two younger brothers, Charles and Thomas Boylston Adams. Their younger sister, Susanna, died as a toddler.

Adams's early childhood was spent between homes in Boston and Braintree, where the Quincy clan owned a large seaside estate called Mount Wollaston, which he later inherited. The parcel, in the family since 1633, had originally been known as Merrie Mount and was settled by fun-loving dissidents who were a thorn in the side of the Puritan establishment. The colonial city of Boston, where John Adams practiced law, was a thriving and increasingly rebellious port town at the start of the American Revolution in 1775, when John Quincy Adams was seven.

War brought abrupt changes to his early life. His village school in Braintree closed when its headmaster

Below: Boston's Fanueil Hall, where the Adams name was associated with many historic moments.

departed to serve in the Continental Army, and his father left for Philadelphia to take part in the Continental Congress, where he served as a delegate for three years and was a member of the committee that helped Thomas Jefferson write the Declaration of Independence. Closer to home, the war's violence came very near to the Adams residence when, in 1775, young John Quincy Adams watched the Battle of Bunker Hill with his mother from a nearby hilltop.

First of Many European Sojourns

In 1778, when Adams was eleven years old, his father was named the U.S. minister to France, and took his son along with him to Paris. On a return trip to Europe, the elder Adams again served as a diplomat and again took his son. During this time, John Quincy studied at Holland's University of Leyden, although he was not yet fourteen. Later that year, Francis Dana, the first American envoy to Russia, requested that the teenager serve as his secretary, and he spent the next fourteen months at St. Petersburg.

When Adams returned to the United States in 1785, his impressive work as a junior diplomat had made him a young celebrity. He suffered an embarrassing setback, however, when he failed his first oral entrance examination to Harvard College. But when he graduated from Harvard in 1787, second in his class, he was class orator—the most skilled public speaker among his fellow graduates.

Adams seemed destined to enter a career in law, and after being admitted to the Massachusetts bar, he began practicing in Boston. But he didn't like the daily grind of a lawyer's life, much preferring to write on political matters for New England newspapers. He became one of the country's leading political commentators between 1790 and 1794. He had inherited his mother's love of literature and learning, and spent much of his time in intellectual pursuits, including becoming a devoted book collector.

In 1794, President George Washington named young Adams minister to the Netherlands, a job he accepted with some hesitation, fearing he was not quite qualified.

Boy Wonder

After his time in Russia, the fifteen-year-old John Quincy Adams made a five-month tour of the Scandinavian countries on his own. He was educated in Paris and Amsterdam, studying fencing, music, dance, and art, along with the classics, and by the time he went to back to America at the age of eighteen, he spoke French, Latin, Greek, and Dutch fluently, and he could carry on a conversation in Spanish as well. As a student at Harvard College, he was a member of the Phi Beta Kappa Society.

In 1795, Adams was sent to London for the ratification of Jay's Treaty, which helped soothe increasing tensions between Great Britain and the United States, and while he was there, he met Louisa Johnson, the daughter of the American consul, Joshua Johnson. After a long engagement, the couple was married in London in July 1797. The event was a major story for the London newspapers, because the bridegroom's father, John Adams, had recently become the second U.S. president. John Quincy Adams was called the "American Prince of Wales." Meanwhile, Louisa Adams, who was half-British by birth, was a topic of some nasty remarks back in America because of her heritage.

"Mr. Adams is the most valuable public character we have abroad … There remains no doubt in my mind that he will prove himself to be the ablest of all our diplomatic corps."

—*President George Washington*

Above: John Quincy Adams as a young man.

Elected to the U.S. Senate

Soon after his marriage, John Quincy Adams was named envoy to the Court of Prussia by his father, President Adams. The younger Adams and Louisa enjoyed their time in Berlin, where their first child, George, was born, but they returned to the United States in 1801 when Thomas Jefferson succeeded the elder Adams to the presidency. Back in Boston with Louisa and George, Adams resumed his law practice, but he quickly abandoned it in 1803 when the Massachusetts legislature appointed him to a vacant seat in the United States Senate as a member of the Federalist Party.

Adams had a falling-out with his party while serving in the Senate, however. He supported the rival Democratic-Republican president, Thomas Jefferson, on two major issues—the Louisiana Purchase and the Embargo Act of 1807. Because he sided with a Democratic-Republican, he was recalled from his seat by the Massachu-

Left: John Quincy Adams went to the Netherlands as the country's first foreign minister.

setts legislature, which, at that time, elected the state's U.S. senators. The legislators instead chose a Federalist, James Lloyd, who could be counted on to support the party's interests. Partisan politics taught Adams an especially bitter lesson, but he remained loyal to his own beliefs rather than to those of his political party.

Beginning in 1806, Adams taught at Harvard and soon became an active member of the Democratic-Republican party organization, the rival of the Federalist Party of his father and George Washington. When fellow Democratic-Republican James Madison was elected president, Adams was named U.S. minister to Russia. He and Louisa left for St. Petersburg in 1809, leaving two older sons behind with relatives but taking two-year-old Charles with them for the six-thousand-mile voyage.

By this time, the forty-two-year-old Adams was a respected senior member of the American diplomatic corps. He was part of the team that negotiated the Treaty of Ghent in 1814, ending the War of 1812, between the United States and England. Then he was given the very desirable assignment of minister to Great Britain in 1815. President Madison subsequently appointed him to the U.S. Supreme Court, but he turned down the offer.

Another Democratic-Republican president, James Monroe, chose Adams to be his secretary of state when he named his cabinet in early 1817. At fifty years of age, Adams had attained a post that was viewed as the stepping-stone to the presidency. His term as secretary of state was marked by several notable achievements that shaped American history and geography in the

Below: Adams served as secretary to the U.S. envoy in Russia when he was still a teenager.

nineteenth century, among them the Monroe Doctrine. Adams wrote the speech that Monroe delivered to Congress explaining the doctrine.

A Contested Election

Adams ran for president in 1824 against three other men. General Andrew Jackson, a popular hero from the War of 1812 who had support from the new "Western" states of Kentucky and Tennessee, received 43.1 percent of the popular vote, a plurality of the popular vote—more votes than any other candidate but less than half of the number cast. However, none of the four contenders—all Democratic-Republicans—won a majority of electoral votes. Thus, the decision went to the House of Representatives, as dictated by the Constitution. The House elected Adams by a narrow margin on February 9, 1825, and he became the first president to take office without a majority of electoral votes.

The narrow margin would spell political doom for Adams, however. Among his three rivals for the top office had been Henry Clay, the Speaker of the House of Representatives. When neither Adams nor Clay

Setting a Precedent?

John Quincy Adams was the first president to assume the office without a majority of the popular vote, but he was by no means the last. It happened five times. Others who didn't have a clear mandate were Rutherford B. Hayes, Benjamin Harrison, George W. Bush, and Donald Trump.

1824 Election Results

Presidential / Vice Presidential Candidates	Popular Votes	Electoral Votes
John Quincy Adams (Democratic-Republican)	108,740	84
Andrew Jackson (Democratic-Republican)	153,544	99
William H. Crawford (Democratic-Republican)	47,136	41
Henry Clay (Democratic-Republican)	46,618	37

Only the Democratic-Republican Party was represented in this election; different factions of that party nominated different candidates. When no candidate received a majority of electoral votes, it became the responsibility of the House of Representatives to elect a president. Clay's supporters largely threw their support to Adams, which helped elect Adams president. John C. Calhoun received the most votes as a vice presidential nominee. This was also the first election where popular votes were counted.

received a majority of electoral votes in the election, Clay allied with Adams and instructed his legislative colleagues to throw their votes to him. When Adams later named Clay to the post of secretary of state, Jackson's supporters—especially Southern politicians—denounced the appointment as unfair.

Clay's acceptance of the important cabinet post was a disastrous move. Jackson and his supporters accused Adams of engaging in a "corrupt bargain" when he made the appointment. Although Adams and Clay were neither friends nor political allies, it caused such an uproar that Clay later said it had permanently stained his political career. Adams also wanted to name Jackson as his secretary of war, but the war hero declined.

An Ineffective Administration

Adams's journals indicate that the four years between 1825 and 1829 were the most difficult and painful years of his otherwise distinguished career. The press criticized him unmercifully. He was accused of having European intellectual tendencies and was called a Yankee elitist. Although Adams was president during a period of American prosperity, there were no major achievements during his administration.

In his first Annual Message to Congress, Adams called for such public improvement projects as a national university and an astronomical observatory. He noted that Europe already had 130 such scientific stations, while America had none. The anti-Adams press made great

fun of his proposal, explaining to a skeptical American public that Adams wanted to spend federal money on scientific explorations of the heavens, and the proposal went nowhere. Nearly two decades later, however, he attended the opening of the first American astronomical observatory, built in 1843 on a hill named Mount Adams near Cincinnati, Ohio.

"It is said [John Quincy Adams] is a disgusting man. … Coarse, dirty and clownish in his address and stiff and abstracted in his opinions, which are drawn from books exclusively."

—*William Henry Harrison*

Adams tried to push forward legislation that would expand the American road and canal system, in the belief that westward expansion would secure the nation's power and economic strength, but his enemies in Congress blocked every piece of legislation he introduced. After the midterm Congressional elections of 1826, which brought a new group of anti-Adams opposition to

The Adams Administration

Administration Dates: March 4, 1825–March 4, 1829
Vice President: John C. Calhoun (1825–29)
Cabinet:

Secretary of State	Henry Clay (1825–29)
Secretary of the Treasury	Richard Rush (1825–29)
Secretary of War	James Barbour (1825–28)
	Peter B. Porter (1828–29)
Attorney General	William Wirt (1825–29)
Secretary of the Navy	Samuel L. Southard (1825–29)
Postmaster General	John McLean (1825–29)

Congress, he wrote in his journal that, "days of trial are coming again." He noted that Washington seemed populated by "thousands of persons occupied with little else than to work up the passions of the people." Even his vice president, John C. Calhoun, had switched his allegiance to Jackson by then.

Ironically, Adams's belief that the federal government should play an active role in creating an infrastructure to benefit and strengthen all regions became another of his political liabilities. Henry Clay had earlier proposed what he termed the "American system," a strategic plan that would impose tariffs on imported goods to pay for an infrastructure that would encourage greater trade between the factories of the North and the farm-based economies of the South and the West. But opponents in Congress believed that such a plan would benefit the North at the expense of the South. Debate continued about the power of the federal government to implement such programs against the wishes of individual states. The Adams administration managed to pass an act that allowed the Cumberland Road—the first federal road in the United States—to extend into Ohio, and he also succeeded in pushing through legislation to fund a canal linking the Chesapeake Bay with the Ohio River.

Land rights for Native Americans also caused a great deal of disagreement during this era. Adams fought for fairness in dealing with the Native Americans—in fact, his

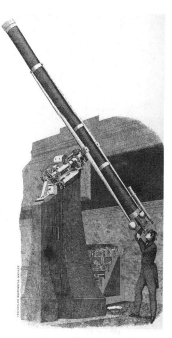

Right: Adams proposed establishing a national astronomical observatory, but he was twenty years into retirement before one was built near Cincinnati, Ohio, on a hill named for him.

opponents used that against him in the 1828 presidential campaign, calling him "pro-Indian." Not surprisingly, Adams wasn't successful with his Indian policy. Georgia landowners produced an agreement, which they said had been signed by Cherokee chiefs, that would force several thousand Creeks and Cherokees from their richly fertile ancestral lands. Adams reluctantly signed the treaty, which was later revealed to be a fake. The fairer treaty that replaced it was opposed by the Georgia legislature, and Adams contemplated sending in federal troops to enforce it, but he decided against the show of force. Possibly taking this as a sign of weakness, two other southern states, Mississippi and Alabama, followed Georgia's lead in taking a strong position against federal intervention in matters regarding Native Americans.

Although he was often overworked and depressed, Adams still rose at 5:00 every morning for a long, vigorous walk or a swim in the Potomac River. (In fact, he often skinny-dipped in the river during the summer, a practice he followed as a congressman and continued until he was seventy-nine years old.) There was little security in the executive mansion at the time, and a constant stream of visitors and tourists frequently interrupted him. For instance, one day, Adams was greatly entertained by his conversations with a man who sat down with him on a park bench, claiming to be the Messiah.

Below: The Erie Canal opened trade between the Atlantic seaboard and the Great Lakes.

Henry Clay

Known as "The Great Compromiser" for his ability to convince diverse factions in Congress to agree on legislation that would preserve the union, Clay helped avert—or delay—a national crisis over slavery. He was a forceful proponent of a strong federal government building interstate roads and canals and making other national improvements during a period when the constitutionality of such actions was debated.

Clay was elected to the Kentucky legislature in 1803. In 1806 and again in 1810, he finished the terms of U.S. senators who left office. In 1811, he was elected to the House of Representatives. He was immediately chosen Speaker and was reelected five times to that position. Clay was a "war hawk"—one who favored armed conflict against Great Britain, with whom the United States had been feuding for several years. The ensuing War of 1812 (1812–15) accomplished little, but the nation emerged stronger.

Beginning in 1815, Clay pushed for his "American System," a program intended to protect American industries against foreign competition, provide federal financing for improvements of highways and canals, and bolster the United States Bank to provide centralized financial control. Clay succeeded for a time: The Federal Bank was strong from 1815 to 1832 and tariffs were enacted, but the internal improvements, opposed by those who believed they infringed on the powers of individual states, were not carried out.

Missouri's application for statehood in 1819 shocked the North. If accepted, Missouri would be the first new state to permit slavery. Clay had advocated gradual emancipation of slaves in Kentucky in 1798, but by 1819 he was a slave owner. In the Missouri debate, he resolved a crisis caused by the Missouri constitutional provision that free blacks could not enter the state. The Missouri legislature assured Clay that it would pass no law abridging the privileges and immunities of U.S. citizens of whatever race.

Clay was a candidate for the presidency in 1824, but three others received more votes, so he was not a candidate when the election was decided in the House of Representatives. He defied Kentucky's instruction to cast the state's votes for Jackson, saying he could not support a "military chieftain;" instead, he supported eventual victor John Quincy Adams. When Adams named Clay secretary of state, opponents accused the pair of devising a "corrupt bargain." Clay had merely supported the man whose views were closest to his own, but the charge lingered for the rest of his life.

When Adams lost in his reelection bid in 1828, he offered to appoint Clay to the Supreme Court, but he declined and returned to Kentucky. In 1831, he was elected to the Senate and served until 1842. In the mid-1830s, anti-Jacksonians formed the Whig Party. Clay expected the Whig nomination for president in 1840, but aging military hero William Henry Harrison won it instead. When Harrison, who lacked political savvy, won the election, Clay anticipated that he would be the actual leader of the administration. But Harrison died after only a month in office, and his successor, John Tyler, a states' rights advocate, opposed the principles of Clay's program. Clay resigned from the Senate in disgust.

Clay was the Whig presidential candidate in 1844, but his unwillingness to take a firm stand on the annexation of Texas cost him the election. He made another effort for the 1848 nomination, but that went to General Zachary Taylor, a Mexican War (1846–48) hero. American victory in the war brought on another sectional crisis, with threats to dissolve the Union over the expansion of slavery into new territories. Clay returned to the Senate in poor health and led in working out the Compromise of 1850. This series of measures admitted California as a free state, organized new territories, and enacted a fugitive slave law that denied protection of the laws to African Americans who escaped from slavery and fled to the North. The Compromise helped preserve the Union, but merely delayed the inevitable conflict that erupted into the Civil War in 1861. Clay died in Washington on June 29, 1852, confident that armed conflict had been averted.

The Tariff of Abominations

One of the more infamous acts passed by Congress during Adams's tenure was the so-called Tariff of Abominations, formally known as the Tariff of 1828. Adams had been a strong advocate for a higher tariff, but Andrew Jackson's supporters in Congress amended his original tariff bill to include much higher taxes on imported raw materials as well. They believed that northern legislators and Adams supporters would never vote for such a thing, because it would mean that New England manufacturers would pay much higher prices for their raw materials. However, the bill passed, and consumer prices for many things jumped considerably. Needless to say, it was an extremely unpopular piece of legislation with the general public.

In spite of his disappointments and a growing distaste for the job, Adams ran for reelection in 1828, but he took part only halfheartedly in a campaign that was one of the ugliest in American history, with both sides continually on the attack. Andrew Jackson won 56 percent of the popular vote, and Adams lost the election by a wide margin in the Electoral College, becoming the second president in American history to serve only one term. His father had been the first.

Old Man Eloquent

After he left office, Adams's health and outlook brightened considerably, and he regained most of the energy and spirit that his recent job had drained from him. Nevertheless, a series of personal setbacks struck the family after his defeat, including the death of the two elder sons, George and John, while they were still relatively young men. Both of them had been heavy drinkers and gamblers.

Over his wife's strong objections, Adams ran for and won a seat from Massachusetts in the U.S. House of Representatives in 1830, making him the only former president to serve in the lower chamber of Congress. He was reelected eight more times and enjoyed a legislative career marked by great bitterness among his opponents,

but also by well-earned respect as an elder statesperson. He became a member of the newly formed Whig Party, which opposed the policies of President Jackson and his new Democratic Party. Adams especially relished the opportunity to tangle with his political enemies from the South in floor debates, expressing passionate opposition to slavery. Although he had made only two public speeches as president, including the obligatory inaugural address, the power of his oratory on the floor of the House earned him the nickname, "Old Man Eloquent." As the leader of the House's antislavery wing, he coined the term "slavocracy" to describe the powerful faction that represented southern landowners and supporters of slavery, whom he believed ran directly counter to the nation's sacred democratic principles.

Adams's abolitionist leanings were part of the reason that he was asked to serve as co-counsel on the 1841 *Amistad* case when it was argued before the U.S. Supreme Court. Roger S. Baldwin, a prominent lawyer, requested Adams's help in defending Africans who had mutinied on a Spanish slave ship, and had been tricked into sailing to Long Island, New York, where they were capture by the U.S. Navy, instead of back to Africa as they had been promised. Adams delivered an eloquent closing argument against returning them to Spanish jurisdiction and a life of slavery, and the high court declared that they should be set free.

One of Adams's greatest achievements as a Congressman was his success in repealing a congressional gag rule limiting debate on slavery. This rule, which was in place from 1836 to 1844, had been pushed through by southern politicians to bar discussion of the slavery issue in both the Senate and the House. Adams never stinted in annoying his colleagues during those years by reading aloud petitions from his constituents calling for a repeal of the rule under the First Amendment's guarantee of free speech. When he read one petition that called for a breaking up of the Union, on grounds that federal money was being used to support the enslavement of human beings, there was an outcry in the House. Southern legislators voted to eject him from Congress for high treason. Defending himself before a House judicial

Left: The Tariff of Abominations gave political cartoonists plenty of grist for their mills.

Above: Andrew Jackson easily won the presidency and made Adams a one-term chief executive.

Above: John Quincy Adams was a dedicated statesman until the end: He fell ill while at work at the House of Representatives and later died within its chambers.

committee, Adams also argued successfully for the repeal of the gag rule, and his acquittal was seen as a significant early victory in the battle to end slavery.

As a congressman, Adams was passionately opposed to the U.S. war with Mexico in 1846, which he bluntly called unfair. In February 1848—well into his eighties—he rose to express his opposition to a proposal to award swords of honor to some of the American generals who had fought in the war. He collapsed from what was probably a stroke in the middle of his speech, and he died two days later. Adams's body laid in state in the Capitol building, where thousands came to pay their respects, and thirty members of Congress accompanied his funeral procession to Boston. He was buried in the Adams family vault in Quincy, Massachusetts, which is now part of the Adams National Historical Site.

Legacy

John Quincy Adams's term as president was the most difficult period of his long career. He achieved little as president, but the foresight behind many of his ideas to invest in the national infrastructure would be borne out later by successors. Ironically, Adams was portrayed as an elitist, while his opponent, Andrew Jackson, was considered a champion of the common man. Adams, however, wanted the federal government to take an active part in improving roads and education, which would have benefited poorer areas of the nation.

The detested Tariff of Abominations would grow into an even larger political problem during his successor's administration. Jackson's vice president, John Calhoun, firmly believed that it violated states' rights as set forth by Thomas Jefferson. He argued the Theory of Nullification, suggesting that individual states could choose to willfully disobey such federal laws. Congress passed a law in 1832 that reduced some of the tariff rates, but South Carolina still objected. The possibility of using federal troops to enforce federal acts loomed as a harbinger of the American Civil War.

During his nine terms in Congress, Adams was vocally opposed to the South's threat of nullification. The debate over state-versus-federal power would eventually cause the issue of slavery to boil over and ultimately lead to the Civil War.

Adams's entire presidential administration was a battleground between fiercely opposed political forces. On his side were the federalist lawmakers who believed that a strong central government would lead America to economic prosperity and international power. On the other side stood forceful newcomers from the South and West, encouraged by regional economic success, and standing foursquare on the side of giving power to the individual states.

A Dynasty of Historians

Later generations of the Adams family distinguished themselves in many ways, but most importantly as historians. Charles Francis Adams II, John Quincy Adams's grandson, wrote a biography of his father and his own autobiography, detailing his career as a railroad executive and exposing its corrupt practices. Another grandson, Henry Adams, was a professor of history at Harvard University and wrote a nine-volume history of the Jefferson and Madison presidencies, as well as the prize-winning autobiography The Education of Henry Adams.

Adams's archrival, Andrew Jackson, united some of the groups opposing him, forming an alliance that would eventually cause the Democratic-Republican Party to dissolve. Jackson's followers would become the Democratic Party in 1832, and his opponents formed the Whig Party a few years later.

Born February 12, 1775, London, England
Died May 15, 1852, Washington, D.C.

"Try as she might, the Madam could never be a Bostonian, and it was her cross in life."
—Henry Adams, in reference to his grandmother, Louisa Adams

Louisa Adams was much beloved by her husband, John Quincy Adams, for her intelligence, temperament, and sense of daring, but she was often the target of sarcastic political gibes from his opponents because of her heritage: Her mother was British, and Louisa remains the only first lady who was born outside the United States.

Louisa Adams also had an uneasy relationship with her famous mother-in-law, Abigail Adams, who thought that Louisa had extravagant "foreign" tendencies. Indeed, John Quincy Adams had been fearful that his mother might try to arrange a marriage for him with an American woman if she found out that he was courting Louisa. He romanced Louisa for some time in England, where he was a diplomat, before revealing his intention

to marry her in a letter to his family. He sent the letter knowing it would arrive too late for his mother to do anything about the marriage.

London Years

Born Louisa Catherine Johnson on February 12, 1775, she spent her earliest years in Nantes, France, because the outbreak of war between the colonies and Britain had forced her father, Joshua Johnson, a strong American sympathizer, to relocate his family from

England. The Maryland-born Johnson had gone to London as the American consul, but he was no longer welcome there. His English wife, Catherine Nuth, was known for maintaining a lavish household, sparing no expense for food and entertainment. Louisa and her two sisters—all close in age, attractive, and musically gifted—were popular debutantes in London at the time.

John Quincy Adams arrived in London in 1795 for the formal ratification of Jay's Treaty, which settled commercial issues between the newly created United States and the powerful British Empire. The son of America's first vice president, John Adams, he was already a well-known diplomat with several notable career achievements. The twenty-eight-year-old Adams first met Louisa when he went to the Johnson home one evening to drop off some official papers and was invited to stay for dinner.

Adams and Louisa began to date. One of the qualities that attracted them to each other was their mutual love of literature. She wrote essays, poems, and plays—though none were ever published—in addition to maintaining a journal for many years. Louisa also spoke French fluently, as did Adams.

The courtship between these two independent-minded spirits was somewhat stormy. Adams was apparently hesitant to set a wedding date until he was almost forced into it by Louisa's father. In the beginning, Adams had been led to believe the Johnsons owned a vast Georgia plantation, but as the couple's relationship developed, it became clear to him that Joshua Johnson was in deep financial trouble.

John and Louisa were married on July 26, 1797, at All Hallows Barking, a church inside the Tower of London whose origins dated back to the year 675. Adams's father had recently been elected the second American president, and had appointed John minister to the Court of Prussia. The couple left for Berlin soon after their wedding.

A Traveling Life

The Adamses spent the first years of their marriage in Berlin, where Louisa suffered four miscarriages before giving birth to a son, George Washington Adams, in 1801. The Prussian king, Frederick William III, was fond of the young couple, and in a gesture that demonstrated how well-liked they were, the king issued an order prohibiting traffic on the street where they lived so that the new baby could sleep undisturbed.

During the first few years of marriage, Adams's diaries reveal a deep appreciation of his choice of a wife. Among other qualities he found admirable, he was especially pleased that Louisa was a brilliant conversationalist, which made her a valuable companion in the round of official functions that they were required to attend. Privately, Louisa suffered the trials of travel and the miscarriages with a fortitude that surprised him. Abigail Adams, however, had called the young bride a "half-breed" and proclaimed her to be a European beauty accustomed to a lavish lifestyle that would likely bankrupt her son.

After the elder Adams's presidency ended in 1801, John Quincy, Louisa, and their son went back to the United States, settling in Boston's Hanover Square area. Louisa continued to have a strained relationship with Abigail during this time, but her father-in-law, the former president, greatly admired her and he recognized that his son's marriage was solid. During brief separations, Louisa received passionate poems from her husband.

The Adams family expanded with the arrival of two more sons, John II in 1803 and Charles Francis in 1807. Both were born in the United States while Adams was a Boston lawyer and then a member of Congress. Two years later, when Adams was named U.S. minister to Russia, he and Louisa left the two older boys behind with relatives and set out with the two-year-old Charles on the six-thousand-mile voyage to St. Petersburg.

The capital of Imperial Russia was a rough place at the time, with dreadful winters and a poor water supply. Finding a warm apartment also proved difficult. A daughter, Louisa Catherine, was born in 1811 but died a year later, a terrible tragedy for her parents. When Mrs. Adams left the city to join her husband in London four years later, the child was left behind, buried in St. Petersburg's Anglican cemetery.

"The art of making love, muffled up in furs, in the open air, with the thermometer at zero, is a Yankee invention, which requires a Yankee poet to describe."

—*John Quincy Adams*

Adams had been named minister to Great Britain, and there, he and Louisa were reunited with sons George and John. They had not seen the boys in six years. The family lived in a suburb of London from 1815 until 1817, when John and Louisa became increasingly worried over the undisciplined habits of the two older boys.

The family returned to the United States again when Adams was named secretary of state in the administration of newly elected president James Monroe. After so many years abroad, they found adjusting to life in America quite difficult. Living in the District of Columbia, a national capital with a distinct absence of grandeur at that time, proved to be the most challenging. Washington was a muddy and isolated town in those days, and even when John Quincy Adams was elected president in 1824. The Presidential Palace still hadn't begun living up to its name. Cows, horses, and sheep grazed nearby, and there was no indoor plumbing. Security was poor, if not nonexistent, and anyone could simply walk in unannounced.

Louisa worried a great deal about her husband during his term as president because of the tremendous strain she knew he was under. He was severely criticized in the press—which usually described him as a Yankee aristocrat with a foreign wife—and he was also subject to harsh attacks by the opposition party. Adams was hindered by supporters of political rival Andrew Jackson for the entire duration of his single term. They thwarted nearly every piece of legislation he introduced, regardless of its merit, with the result that he lost a great deal of weight and suffered from long bouts of depression. Louisa made the best of it all, participating in elegant receptions and showing hospitality to her guests.

Even after Adams lost the 1828 election to Jackson and his health rapidly returned, the Adamses faced personal trials that were far worse. Their eldest son, George, a heavy drinker and gambler, disappeared from a ship in the Atlantic in April of 1829. His hat and overcoat were found, and his body washed up on City Island, a part of the Bronx in Long Island Sound, a month later. Five years later, John II, also an alcoholic, went into a coma at the age of thirty-one and died debt-ridden, leaving his wife and two children to the care of his mother and father.

Louisa was depressed at first about the prospect of going back to Washington when her husband was elected

Above: The executive mansion glowed brilliantly when Louisa staged balls and receptions there.

to Congress in 1830. She would miss summers at the family estate in Quincy, Massachusetts, but after settling down in Washington, she became one of the capital's most renowned party givers, rivaling another former first lady, Dolley Madison.

John Quincy Adams suffered a stroke and died in 1848, and Louisa also died as the result of a stroke four years later. She left behind a large collection of writings, including a diary, a great deal of correspondence, poems, and plays, which ultimately became part of the vast Adams Papers archive of the Massachusetts Historical Society. Louisa was laid to rest next to her husband inside the United First Parish Church—also known as the Adams Temple—at Quincy.

Adams's Inaugural Address

Friday, March 4, 1825

John Quincy Adams was chosen president by the House of Representatives after the Electoral College failed to determine the winner of the 1824 election. The outcome was assured when the oath of office was administered by Chief Justice John Marshall inside the Hall of the House of Representatives.

Excerpt from Adams's Inaugural Address

In compliance with an usage coeval with the existence of our Federal Constitution, and sanctioned by the example of my predecessors in the career upon which I am about to enter, I appear, my fellow-citizens, in your presence and in that of Heaven to bind myself by the solemnities of religious obligation to the faithful performance of the duties allotted to me in the station to which I have been called.

In unfolding to my countrymen the principles by which I shall be governed in the fulfillment of those duties my first resort will be to that Constitution which I shall swear to the best of my ability to preserve, protect, and defend.[...]

In the compass of thirty-six years since this great national covenant was instituted a body of laws enacted under its authority and in conformity with its provisions has unfolded its powers and carried into practical operation its effective energies. Subordinate departments have distributed the executive functions in their various relations to foreign affairs, to the revenue and expenditures, and to the military force of the Union by land and sea. A coordinate department of the judiciary has expounded the Constitution and the laws, settling in harmonious coincidence with the legislative will numerous weighty questions of construction which the imperfection of human language had rendered unavoidable. The year of jubilee since the first formation of our Union has just elapsed that of the declaration of our independence is at hand.[...]

Since that period a population of four millions has multiplied to twelve. A territory bounded by the Mississippi has been extended from sea to sea. New States have been admitted to the Union in numbers nearly equal to those of the first Confederation. Treaties of peace, amity, and commerce have been concluded with the principal dominions of the earth. The people of other nations, inhabitants of regions acquired not by conquest, but by compact, have been united with us in the participation of our rights and duties, of our burdens and blessings. The forest has fallen by the ax of our woodsmen; the soil has been made to teem by the tillage of our farmers; our commerce has whitened every ocean. The dominion of man over physical nature has been extended by the invention of our artists. Liberty and law have marched hand in hand. All the purposes of human association have been accomplished as effectively as under any other government on the globe, and at a cost little exceeding in a whole generation the expenditure of other nations in a single year.

Such is the unexaggerated picture of our condition under a Constitution founded upon the republican principle of equal rights. To admit that this picture has its shades is but to say that it is still the condition of men upon earth. From evil—physical, moral, and political—it is not our claim to be exempt. We have suffered sometimes by the visitation of Heaven through disease; often by the wrongs and injustice of other nations, even to the extremities of war; and, lastly, by dissensions among ourselves— dissensions perhaps inseparable from the enjoyment of freedom, but which have more than once appeared to threaten the dissolution of the Union, and with it the overthrow of all the enjoyments of our present lot and all our earthly hopes of the future. The causes of these dissensions have been various, founded upon differences of speculation in the theory of republican government; upon conflicting views of policy in our relations with foreign nations; upon jealousies of partial and sectional interests, aggravated by prejudices and prepossessions which strangers to each other are ever apt to entertain.

It is a source of gratification and of encouragement to me to observe that the great result of this experiment upon the theory of human rights has at the close of that generation by which it was formed been crowned with success equal to the most sanguine expectations of its founders. Union, justice, tranquillity, the common defense, the general welfare, and the blessings of liberty—all have been promoted by the Government under which we have lived. Standing at this point of time, looking back to that generation which has gone by and forward to that which is advancing, we may at once indulge in grateful exultation and in cheering hope. From the experience of the past we derive instructive lessons for the future. Of the two great political parties which have divided the opinions and feelings of our country, the candid and the just will now admit that both have contributed splendid talents, spotless integrity, ardent patriotism, and disinterested sacrifices to the formation and administration of this Government, and that both have required a liberal indulgence for a portion of human infirmity and error.

[...]

Our political creed is, without a dissenting voice that can be heard, that the will of the people is the source and the happiness of the people the end of all legitimate government upon earth; that the best security for the beneficence and the best guaranty against the abuse of power consists in the freedom, the purity, and the frequency of popular elections; that the General Government of the Union and the separate governments of the States are all sovereignties of limited powers, fellow- servants of the same masters, uncontrolled within their respective spheres, uncontrollable by encroachments upon each other; that the firmest security of peace is the preparation during peace of the defenses of war; that a rigorous economy and accountability of public expenditures should guard against the aggravation and alleviate when possible the burden of taxation; that the military should be kept in strict subordination to the civil power; that the freedom of the press and of religious opinion should be inviolate; that the policy of our country is peace and the ark of our salvation union are articles of faith upon which we are all now agreed. If there have been those who doubted whether a confederated representative democracy were a government competent to the wise and orderly management of the common concerns of a mighty nation, those doubts have been dispelled; if there have been projects of partial confederacies to be erected upon the ruins of the Union, they have been scattered to the winds; if there have been dangerous attachments to one foreign nation and antipathies against another, they have been extinguished. Ten years of peace, at home and abroad, have assuaged the animosities of political contention and blended into harmony the most discordant elements of public opinion There still remains one effort of magnanimity, one sacrifice of prejudice and passion, to be made by the individuals throughout the nation who have heretofore followed the standards of political party. It is that of discarding every remnant of rancor against each other, of embracing as countrymen and friends, and of yielding to talents and virtue alone that confidence which in times of contention for principle was bestowed only upon those who bore the badge of party communion.

The collisions of party spirit which originate in speculative opinions or in different views of administrative policy are in their nature transitory. Those which are founded on geographical divisions, adverse interests of soil, climate, and modes of domestic life are more permanent, and therefore, perhaps, more dangerous. It is this which gives inestimable value to the character of our Government, at once federal and national. It holds out to us a perpetual admonition to preserve alike and with equal anxiety the rights of each individual State in its own government and the rights of the whole nation in that of the Union. Whatsoever is of domestic concernment, unconnected with the other members of the Union or with foreign lands, belongs exclusively to the administration of the State governments. Whatsoever directly involves the rights and interests of the federative fraternity or of foreign powers is of the resort of this General Government. The duties of both are obvious in the general principle, though sometimes perplexed with difficulties in the detail. To respect the rights of the State governments is the inviolable duty of that of the Union; the government of every State will feel its own obligation to respect and preserve the rights of the whole. The prejudices everywhere too commonly entertained against distant strangers are worn away, and the jealousies of jarring interests are allayed by the composition and functions of the great national councils annually assembled from all quarters of the Union at this place. Here the distinguished men from every section of our country, while meeting to deliberate upon the great interests of those by whom they are deputed, learn to estimate the talents and do justice to the virtues of each other.

[...] The Floridas have been peaceably acquired, and our boundary has been extended to the Pacific Ocean; the independence of the southern nations of this hemisphere has been recognized, and recommended by example and by counsel to the potentates of Europe; progress has been made in the defense of the country by fortifications and the increase of the Navy, toward the effectual suppression of the African traffic in slaves; in alluring the aboriginal hunters of our land to the cultivation of the soil and of the mind, in exploring the interior regions of the Union, and in preparing by scientific researches and surveys for the further application of our national resources to the internal improvement of our country.

[...] It is that from which I am convinced that the unborn millions of our posterity who are in future ages to people this continent will derive their most fervent gratitude to the founders of the Union; that in which the beneficent action of its Government will be most deeply felt and acknowledged. The magnificence and splendor of their public works are among the imperishable glories of the ancient republics. The roads and aqueducts of Rome have been the admiration of all after ages, and have survived thousands of years after all her conquests have been swallowed up in despotism or become the spoil of barbarians.[...] But nearly twenty years have passed since the construction of the first national road was commenced. The authority for its construction was then unquestioned. To how many thousands of our countrymen has it proved a benefit? To what single individual has it ever proved an injury? Repeated, liberal, and candid discussions in the Legislature have conciliated the sentiments and approximated the opinions of enlightened minds upon the question of constitutional power. I can not but hope that by the same process of friendly, patient, and persevering deliberation all constitutional objections will ultimately be removed. The extent and limitation of the powers of the General Government in relation to this transcendently important interest will be settled and acknowledged to the common satisfaction of all, and every speculative scruple will be solved by a practical public blessing.

Fellow-citizens, you are acquainted with the peculiar circumstances of the recent election, which have resulted in affording me the opportunity of addressing you at this time. You have heard the exposition of the principles which will direct me in the fulfillment of the high and solemn trust imposed upon me in this station. Less possessed of your confidence in advance than any of my predecessors, I am deeply conscious of the prospect that I shall stand more and oftener in need of your indulgence. Intentions upright and pure, a heart devoted to the welfare of our country, and the unceasing application of all the faculties allotted to me to her service are all the pledges that I can give for the faithful performance of the arduous duties I am to undertake.[...] I shall look for whatever success may attend my public service; and knowing that "except the Lord keep the city the watchman waketh but in vain," with fervent supplications for His favor, to His overruling providence I commit with humble but fearless confidence my own fate and the future destinies of my country.

Adams's Closing Argument in the Amistad Case

Delivered before the United States Supreme Court on February 24 and March 1, 1841

In 1839, fifty-three Africans sold into slavery were to be taken to Cuba, then a Spanish colony, aboard the Amistad, a Spanish vessel. The men seized control of the vessel off the coast of Cuba; killing two crew members and directing the remaining crew to sail them back to Africa. Instead, the crew piloted the ship off the American coast, where it was seized by a U.S. warship, and the Africans were jailed in the United States. President Martin Van Buren intended to surrender them to Spanish authorities in Cuba.

The Africans were defended in American courts under an international law prohibiting the slave trade. Murder charges against them were dropped, but they remained in prison while claims on them were made by the government of Spain, along with planters who had bought them as slave. A lower court ruled that claims to the Africans as property were unwarranted because they were being held illegally as slaves.

The case was eventually heard by the U.S. Supreme Court, and former president John Quincy Adams was enlisted to present closing arguments before the court in defense of thirty-six of the Africans. Adams, whose postpresidential career was as a member of the U.S. House of Representatives, was a staunch abolitionist who had become known as "Old Man Eloquent" for his impassioned speeches in Congress against slavery.

Excerpt from Adams's Closing Argument

May it please your honors—

(This) Court is a Court of JUSTICE. And in saying so very trivial a thing, I should not on any other occasion, perhaps, be warranted in asking the Court to consider what justice is. Justice, as defined in the Institutes of Justinian, nearly 2000 years ago, and as it is felt and understood by all who understand human relations and human rights, is—

Constans et perpetua voluntas, jus SUUM cuique tribuendi ("The constant and perpetual will to secure to every one HIS OWN right.")

And in a Court of Justice, where there are two parties present, justice demands that the rights of each party should be allowed to himself, as well as that each party has a right, to be secured and protected by the Court. This observation is important, because I appear here on the behalf of thirty-six individuals, the life and liberty of every one of whom depend on the decision of this Court. The Court, therefore, I trust, in deciding this case, will form no lumping judgment on these thirty-six individuals, but will act on the consideration that the life and the liberty of every one of them must be determined by its decision for himself alone.

They are here, individually, under very different circumstances, and in very different characters. Some are in one predicament, some in another. In some of the proceedings by which they have been brought into the custody and under the protection of this Court, thirty-two or three of them have been charged with the crime of murder. Three or four of them are female children, incapable, in the judgment of our laws, of the crime of murder or piracy, or, perhaps, of any other crime. Yet, from the day when the vessel was taken possession of by one of our naval officers, they have all been held as close prisoners, now for the period of eighteen long months, under custody and by authority of the Courts of the United States. I trust, therefore, that before the ultimate decision of this Court is established, its honorable members will pay due attention to the circumstances and condition of every individual concerned.

When I say I derive consolation from the consideration that I stand before a Court of Justice, I am obliged to take this ground, because, as I shall show, another Department of the Government of the United States has taken, with reference to this case, the ground of utter injustice, and these individuals for whom I appear, stand before this Court, awaiting their fate from its decision, under the array of the whole Executive power of this nation against them, in addition to that of a foreign nation. And here arises a consideration, the most painful of all others, in considering the duty I have to discharge, in which, in supporting the motion to dismiss the appeal, I shall be obliged not only to investigate and submit to the censure of this Court, the form and manner of the proceedings of the Executive in this case, but the validity, and the motive of the reasons assigned for its interference in this unusual manner in a suit between parties for their individual rights.

[. . .]

It is [. . .] peculiarly painful to me, under present circumstances, to be under the necessity of arraigning before this Court and before the civilized world, the course of the existing Administration in this case. But I must do it. That Government is still in power, and thus, subject to the control of the Court, the lives and liberties of all my clients are in its hands. And if I should pass over the course it has pursued, those who have not had an opportunity to examine the case and perhaps the Court itself, might decide that nothing improper had been done, and that the parties I represent had not been wronged by the course pursued by the Executive. In making this charge, or arraignment, as defensive of the rights of my clients, I now proceed to an examination of the correspondence of the Secretary of State with the ambassador of her Catholic Majesty, as officially communicated to Congress, and published among the national documents.

The charge I make against the present Executive administration is that in all their proceedings relating to these unfortunate men, instead of that Justice, which they were bound not less than this honorable Court itself to observe, they have substituted Sympathy!—sympathy with one of the parties in this conflict of justice, and Antipathy to the other. Sympathy with the white, antipathy to the black—and in proof of this charge I adduce the admission and avowal of the Secretary of State himself. In the letter of Mr. Forsyth to the Spanish Minister [Chevalier] d'Argaiz, of 13th of December 1839, [Document H. R. N. S. 185,] defending the course of the administration against the reproaches utterly groundless, but not the less bitter of the Spanish Envoy, he says:

The undersigned cannot conclude this communication without calling the attention of the Chevalier d'Argaiz to the fact, that with the single exception of the vexatious detention to which Messrs. Montes and Ruiz have been subjected in consequence of the civil suit instituted against them, all the proceedings in the matter, on the part both the Executive and Judicial branches of the government have had their foundation in the ASSUMPTION that these persons ALONE were the parties aggrieved; and that their claims to the surrender of the property was founded in fact and in justice.

At the date of this letter, this statement of Mr. Forsyth was strictly true. All the proceedings of the government, Executive and Judicial, in this case had been founded on the assumption that the two Spanish slave-dealers were the only parties aggrieved—that all the right was on their side, and all the wrong on the side of their surviving self-emancipated victims. I ask your honors, was this JUSTICE? No. It was not so considered by Mr. Forsyth himself. It was sympathy, and he so calls it, for in the preceding page of the same letter referring to the proceedings of this Government from the very first intervention of Lieut. Gedney, he says:

Messrs. Ruiz and Montes were first found near the coast of the United States, deprived of their property and of their freedom, suffering from lawless violence in their persons, and in imminent and constant danger of being deprived of their lives also.
They were found in this distressing and perilous situation by officers of the United States, who, moved towards them by sympathetic feeling which subsequently became, as it were national, immediately rescued them from personal danger, restored them to freedom, secured their oppressors that they might abide the consequences of the acts of violence perpetrated upon them, and placed under the safeguard of the laws all the property which they claimed as their own, to remain in safety

until the competent authority could examine their title to it, and pronounce upon the question of ownership agreeably to the provisions of the 9th article of the treaty of 1795.

This sympathy with Spanish slave-traders is declared by the Secretary to have been first felt by Lieutenant Gedney. I hope this is not correctly represented. It is imputed to him and declared to have become in a manner national. The national sympathy with the slave-traders of the barracoons is officially declared to have been the prime motive of action of the government: And this fact is given as an answer to all the claims, demands and reproaches of the Spanish minister! I cannot urge the same objection to this that was brought against the assertion in the libel—that it said the thing which is not—too unfortunately it was so, as he said. The sympathy of the Executive government, and as it were of the nation, in favor of the slave-traders, and against these poor, unfortunate, helpless, tongueless, defenseless Africans, was the cause and foundation and motive of all these proceedings, and has brought this case up for trial before your honors.

After seven years of litigation (in the case of a similar revolt aboard the ship, the Antelope) in the Courts of the United States, and, of course, of captivity to nearly all of these Africans who survived the operation; after decrees of the District Court, reversed by the Circuit Court, and three successive annual reversals by the Supreme Court of the decrees of the Circuit Court; what was the result of this most troublesome charge? The vessel was restored to certain Spanish slave-traders in the island of Cuba. Of the Africans, about fifty had perished by the benignity of their treatment in this land of liberty, during its suspended animation as to them; sixteen, drawn by lot from the whole number, (by the merciful dispensation of the Circuit Court, under the arbitrary enlargement of the tender mercies of the District Judge, which had limited the number to seven,)—sixteen had drawn the prize of liberty, to which the whole number were entitled by the letter of the law; and, of the remainder, THIRTY-NINE, upon evidence inadmissible upon the most trifling question of property in any court of justice, were, under the very peculiar circumstances of the case, surrendered! delivered up to the Spanish vice-consul—AS SLAVES! To the rest was at last extended the benefit of the laws which had foreordained their emancipation. They were delivered over to safe keeping, support, and transportation, as freemen, beyond the limits of the United States, by the Chief Magistrate of the Union.

And now, by what possible process of reasoning can any decision of the Supreme Court of the United States in the case of the Antelope, be adduced as authorizing the President of the United States to seize and deliver up to the order of the Spanish minister the captives of the Amistad? Even the judge of the District Court in Georgia, who would have enslaved all the unfortunate of the Antelope but seven, distinctly admitted, that, if they had been bought in Africa after the prohibition of the trade by Spain he would have liberated them all. In delivering the opinion of the Supreme Court, on their first decree in the case of the Antelope, Chief Justice [John] Marshall, after reviewing the decisions in the British Courts of Admiralty, says, "The principle common to these cases is, that the legality of the capture of a vessel engaged in the slave-trade depends on the law of the country to which the vessel belongs. If that law gives its sanction to the trade, restitution will be decreed: if that law prohibits it, the vessel and cargo will be condemned as good prize." It was by the application of this principle, to the fact, that, at the time when the Antelope was taken by the Arraganta, the slave-trade, in which the Antelope was engaged, had not yet been made unlawful by Spain, that the Supreme Court affirmed so much of the decree of the Circuit Court as directed restitution to the Spanish claimant of the Africans found on board the Antelope when captured by the Arraganta. But by the same identical principle, applied to the case of the Amistad, if, when captured by Lieutenant Gedney, she and her cargo had been in possession of the Spaniards, and the Africans in the condition of slaves, the vessel would have been condemned, and the slaves liberated, by the laws of the United States; because she was engaged in the slave-trade in violation of the laws of Spain. She was in possession of the Africans, self-emancipated, and not in the condition of slaves. That, surely, could not legalize the trade in which she had been engaged. By the principle asserted in the opinion of the Supreme Court, declared by Chief Justice Marshall, it would have saved the vessel, at once, from condemnation and from restitution, and would have relieved the Court from the necessity of restoring to the Africans their freedom. Thus the opinion of the Supreme Court, as declared by the Chief Justice, in the case of the Antelope, was in fact, an authority in point, against the surrender of the Amistad, and in favor of the liberation of the Africans in her, even if they had been, when taken, in the condition of slaves. How monstrous, then, is the claim upon the Courts of the United States to re-inslave them, as thralls to the Spaniards, Ruiz and Montes, or to transport them beyond the seas, at the demand of the Minister of Spain!. [. . .]

I said, when I began this plea, that my final reliance for success in this case was on this Court as a court of JUSTICE; and in the confidence this fact inspired that, in the administration of justice, in a case of no less importance than the liberty and the life of a large number of persons, this Court would not decide but on a due consideration of all the rights, both natural and social, of every one of these individuals. I have endeavored to show that they are entitled to their liberty from this Court. I have avoided, purposely avoided, and this Court will do justice to the motive for which I have avoided, a recurrence to those first principles of liberty which might well have been invoked in the argument of this cause. I have shown that Ruiz and Montes, the only parties in interest here, for whose sole benefit this suit is carried on by the Government, were acting at the time in a way that is forbidden by the laws of Great Britain, of Spain, and of the United States, and that the mere signature of the Governor General of Cuba ought not to prevail over the ample evidence in the case that these negroes were free and had a right to assert their liberty. I have shown that the papers in question are absolutely null and insufficient as passports for persons, and still more invalid to convey or prove a title to property.

What Happened Next

The Supreme Court ruled in favor of the *Amistad* defendants in March of 1841. They were set free and allowed to return to Africa. It took several months for enough money to be raised for the voyage. They arrived in Freetown, Sierra Leone, the following January.

Adams continued to serve in the House of Representatives and agitate for an end of slavery until his death in 1848. His performance during the *Amistad* trial dazzled spectators and the Supreme Court judges as well. Adams had been able to draw on fifty years of experience in negotiating treaties and fighting for human rights.

Andrew Jackson

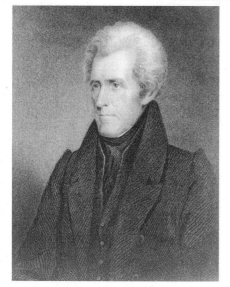

"The brave man inattentive to his duty is worth little more to his country than the coward who deserts her in the hour of danger."
—*Andrew Jackson*

Seventh president of the United States, 1829–1837

Full name: *Andrew Jackson*
Born: *March 15, 1767, Waxhaw, South Carolina*
Died: *June 8, 1845, Nashville, Tennessee*
Burial site: *The Hermitage Estate, near Nashville, Tennessee*
Parents: *Andrew and Elizabeth Hutchinson Jackson*
Spouse: *Rachel Donelson Robards (1767–1828; m. 1791 and in a second ceremony in 1794)*
Children: *Andrew Jr. (adopted; 1808–1865)*
Religion: *Presbyterian*
Education: *No formal education*
Occupations: *Attorney; soldier*
Government positions: *U.S. representative and senator from Tennessee; Tennessee state supreme court justice and senator; Florida territory governor*
Political party: *Democratic*
Dates as president: *March 4, 1829–March 4, 1833 (first term); March 4, 1833–March 4, 1837 (second term)*
Age upon taking office: *61*

*A*ndrew Jackson was nicknamed "Old Hickory" after the tough hardwood tree. He had a fiery temper and an iron will, but like the hickory tree, which produces flavorful nuts that can be used as a sweetener, he had a soft side. He was devoted to his wife, Rachel Jackson, his friends, his troops, and his extended family.

Jackson's long and colorful life included a wild boyhood on the frontier, becoming a self-made man, and serving as one of the original political leaders of the state of Tennessee. He won fame in his forties as a controversial military commander, and by the time he reached his sixties, he was at the head of a national political dynasty that lasted for twenty years, from 1828 to 1848, a period in American history often called "The Age of Jackson." Two of his key supporters—Martin Van Buren and James K. Polk—followed him as president.

Wild youth

Andrew Jackson was born in frontier country—the backwoods of the Waxhaw River community in South Carolina. His parents had emigrated there from Ireland with his two older brothers in 1765. His father, also named Andrew Jackson, died just a few days before March 15, 1767, when young Andrew was born.

Timeline

1767: Born in South Carolina a few days after his father dies

1780: American Revolution spreads to the Carolinas; Jackson's oldest brother is killed; Jackson and his surviving brother Robert are imprisoned by British soldiers; Robert and mother die of smallpox

1787: Certified to practice law

1792: Marries Rachel Donelson, whose husband, Lewis Robards, had petitioned for divorce in 1791

1793: Robards, who never completed the original divorce proceedings, sues to divorce Rachel Jackson as an adulterer; Andrew and Rachel marry again in 1794

1796: Jackson attends convention where the state of Tennessee is established

1796–97: Serves as Tennessee's first member in the U.S. House of Representatives

1797–98: Serves Tennessee as U.S. senator

1798–1804: Serves as justice on Tennessee Supreme Court

1803: Commissioned as major general of Tennessee militia

1815: Soundly defeats British forces in the Battle of New Orleans

1818: Controversy over his killing two British citizens for inciting Seminole Indians to raid nearly leads to his censure by Congress

1821: Serves as governor of the Florida Territory

1823–25: Serves as U.S. senator from Tennessee

1829–37: Serves as seventh U.S. president

1833: Removes funds from the Second National Bank of the United States and disperses them in state banks; censured by Congress and vilified by opponents as "King Andrew;" censure is later erased (1836) from the Congressional Record

1837: Retires to his home, The Hermitage

1845: Dies in Tennessee

Like the tough but flavorful hickory tree, Jackson was a man of contradictions. Sometimes he seemed to hold two opposing views at the same time. For example, he and his wife, Rachel, raised an orphaned Indian boy. But Jackson was a fierce fighter of Native Americans and played a significant role in their removal from the Southeast to the "Indian Lands," an area in and around

Disputed Birthplace

Elizabeth Hutchinson Jackson, widowed and pregnant, decided to go to her sister's home in South Carolina to deliver her child. However, some say she didn't get that far, and stopped instead at the home of another sister in North Carolina, where Andrew was ultimately born. Jackson always considered himself a native South Carolinian, but many historians disagree.

what is now Oklahoma. As a politician, he opposed federal influence on state governments, but came close to using national force when the state of South Carolina threatened to nullify federal tariffs and secede from the Union.

"Faults he had, undoubtedly; such faults as often belong to an ardent, generous, sincere nature—the weeds that grow in rich soil. Notwithstanding this, he was precisely the man for the period in which he nobly and well discharged the duties demanded of him by the times."

—*William Cullen Bryant*

The nation was changing at the time Jackson took office. The generations born after the ratification of the U.S. Constitution were coming of age. People were settling in former frontier lands. Industrialization and modern urban centers were taking hold. People were looking beyond the aristocrats of New England and Virginia for leaders who would represent their interests, and Jackson was their man. He was the first president who came from west of the Appalachian Mountains, and had a strong appeal to small farmers, laborers, and the common people. Jackson saw himself as the highest-elected representative of the common man, and he became one of the most powerful presidents in the nation's history.

Jackson learned to read and write in makeshift frontier schools where classes were held wherever it was convenient. After the American Revolution broke out in 1775, he expanded his education by becoming a public reader of newspaper articles and letters from Philadelphia and other northern towns to his illiterate neighbors in the Waxhaw River community.

The Revolution spread to the Carolinas by 1780, when Jackson was thirteen. He served as an orderly and

Above: Young Andy Jackson was severely beaten and scarred for life by a British soldier when he was a prisoner of war.

a messenger for Colonel William Richardson Davie and his troops. His oldest brother died during this time, and Andrew and his other brother, Robert, were captured and imprisoned by the British for their role in the American rebellion. Andrew was beaten by a British soldier for refusing to shine the soldier's boots. The wounds he suffered left permanent scars on his face and body.

A smallpox epidemic spread through the area where the Jackson brothers were being held, and their mother, Elizabeth Hutchinson Jackson, demanded their release, but her pleas came too late for Robert, who died from the disease. Elizabeth went on to Charleston to nurse soldiers being held on British prison ships, where she contracted cholera and died. Andrew was fourteen years old at the time.

Left an orphan, young Andrew learned the art of saddle making, and he also taught school to earn money. He began studying law with an attorney in Salisbury, North Carolina, and was certified to practice in 1787. At age twenty, he set up a law office in McLeanville, North Carolina. Meanwhile, he indulged in horse racing, cockfighting, card playing, and other forms of gambling, eventually gambling away all of a small inheritance he had received from his Irish grandfather.

Right: The Hermitage, Jackson's Nashville estate.

Teenage War Hero

Fourteen-year-old Andrew Jackson became a prisoner of the British during the Revolutionary War, and he and his brother Robert, a fellow prisoner, were force-marched forty miles to a prisoner-of-war camp at Camden, South Carolina, where they were held for two weeks before their release in a prisoner exchange. Jackson was the last president to have served in the Revolution, and the only one ever to have been a prisoner of war.

Jackson and his friend John McNairy traveled to Nashville, a frontier village in what was then called the Western District of North Carolina, where McNairy became a judge and named Jackson to the post of solicitor general. He was responsible for preparing cases on behalf of the state and for prosecuting debtors, and often accepted small parcels of land instead of money for his services. Using this land, Jackson formed an estate that would become known as The Hermitage in 1804, but he fell into debt when he was unable to make payments for loans he had received.

In 1790, Jackson rented a room from John Donelson, a former surveyor, Virginia legislator, and pioneer Tennessee settler. It was there that he met Donelson's daughter, Rachel, who traveled to the area to escape her jealous and violent husband, Lewis Robards. She was planning to join her sister in Natchez, Mississippi, a rough journey of over three hundred miles, and asked Andrew to escort her there. He did, and fell in love with Rachel along the way.

Rachel Donelson Robards and her husband had agreed to a divorce, which was rare in those days and involved petitioning the state legislature for permission. When Jackson found out that Lewis Robards had been granted legal permission to seek the divorce, leaving only minor paperwork to make it legal, he went back to Natchez to find Rachel, and they were married there in 1791.

They found out a couple of years later that her first husband had not completed the divorce proceedings, and when he heard that Rachel had married someone else, the mean-spirited Robards completed new divorce proceedings based on grounds of adultery.

Andrew and Rachel were married again in 1794. Although the incident had been the fault of Rachel's ex-husband, the fact remained that Jackson had wooed and wed a married woman, which was an issue for slander by his opponents through the years. Jackson fiercely defended his wife's honor, often with his fists, and sometimes in duels.

In 1806, Jackson dueled, either over slander or a gambling argument, with an excellent gunfighter named Charles Dickinson, who got off the first shot and hit Jackson in the chest, leaving a wound that never completely healed. In spite of the wound, Jackson maintained his position and shot back at Dickinson, killing him.

Jackson built a strong reputation for himself in the Nashville area. He was invited to attend the state constitutional convention that made Tennessee a state in 1796, and he was the first person to represent the state in Congress, where he expressed his view that President George Washington was not being tough enough in dealings with Great Britain. He was elected to the U.S. Senate the following year by Tennessee's state legislature. But he resigned after one year because he wasn't comfortable with a senator's responsibilities, and he needed to attend to his own personal responsibilities and debts back in Nashville.

Back home, he was appointed a judge of the Tennessee State Superior Court and gradually improved his plantation, The Hermitage, where he bred racehorses. He was also commissioned a major general of the Tennessee militia, and the first decade of the nineteenth century was the happiest period in the lives of Andrew and Rachel Jackson.

War Hero

Jackson spent most of that first decade of the 1800s tending to The Hermitage, training militia troops, and serving as a judge. He became a strong supporter of war against Great Britain as hostilities between the nations increased toward what became the War of 1812. He volunteered to lead a raid into British-controlled Canada, but instead, the governor of Tennessee sent him to lead his troops to help protect the vital port city of New Orleans.

Right: Major General Jackson early in his military career.

Jackson and his 2,500 men were poorly equipped for the journey, and only made it as far as Natchez, Mississippi, still over 100 miles from New Orleans, when they were ordered to disband. The order requested Jackson to leave the men and get back to Tennessee. Instead, he led the exhausted and hungry men back with him. It was during that difficult march that his men gave him the nickname "Old Hickory."

In 1813, Jackson was ordered to lead 2,000 men to fight the Upper Creek Indian nation, which had allied with the British and killed 250 settlers at Fort Mims in what is now Alabama. Despite poor equipment and supplies, Jackson's forces won a series of skirmishes that culminated with the March 1814 battle at Horseshoe Bend on the Tallapoosa River. Jackson allowed Indian women and children to cross the river, and then his forces systematically wiped out the Upper Creek warriors. The treaty Jackson wrote when the battle ended forced the Creek nation to hand over 9 million acres of land, which now forms about 20 percent of Georgia and over 60 percent of Alabama.

Jackson's victory led to his promotion to major general in the federal army with orders to defend New Orleans against British attack. As he was leading his troops south from Tennessee, Jackson made a slight detour to attack and capture a British base in present-day Pensacola, Florida. Then he led his men on to New Orleans, where he found the town virtually defenseless. In addition to his group of Tennessee and Kentucky militiamen, Jackson pressed local Creoles, blacks, and Frenchmen into service to form a force of 5,000 men to fight 9,000 British troops.

Jackson set up three lines of defense beyond a dry canal, and when the British forces began a massive attack they found themselves exposed as easy targets to the well-concealed and surprisingly large number of defenders. More than 2,000 British soldiers were killed in the assault on January 8, 1815, that became known as the Battle of New Orleans. The Americans suffered fewer than one hundred casualties: thirteen dead, thirty-nine

The Man Behind the Man

Andrew Jackson began to look very presidential in the early 1820s, and the first to notice was his friend and neighbor, William Lewis, who assembled a group of influential politicians to make it happen. Their campaign began when they engineered Jackson's election to the U.S. Senate, and they didn't stop pulling strings and engineering events until their man won his second presidential election. During all that time, they didn't make a move that wasn't calculated to bring their man closer to the presidency, but even Jackson himself never knew what they were up to. When he found out, he offered Lewis a cabinet post, but his mentor refused. All he wanted, he said, was a job that didn't require any work. Jackson found one for him as a treasury auditor.

wounded, and nineteen missing, and General Jackson was a national hero.

The Battle of New Orleans was actually fought after British and U.S. officials had called an armistice, and were negotiating the Treaty of Ghent that ended the war. But news traveled slowly in those days and word that the fighting had stopped had not yet reached New

Orleans. The Treaty of Ghent that officially ended the war was signed in February 1815, a couple of weeks after the battle. U.S. forces had been vulnerable all through the war, and their military leadership was weak, which made Jackson's dramatic victory all the sweeter, and the American people never forgot it.

More Exploits, More Controversy

Jackson's military exploits continued over the next few years, although sometimes with controversy. He was named commander of the Southern District of the U.S. Army in 1815, and he led a punitive expedition against the Seminole Indians. The tribal warriors had been staging raids in southern Georgia and slipping back to Florida, which was a still a Spanish colony. Jackson led his forces into Spanish Florida, against orders, and he himself killed two British citizens accused of having incited the Seminoles against the United States.

Jackson was formally criticized by the British and the Spanish governments for what they characterized as murder and trespass. Many in Congress also called for censure by his own government, but President James Monroe was persuaded by his secretary of state, John Quincy Adams, not to resort to such formal punishment. Ironically, Adams and Jackson would later become bitter political rivals.

After Adams negotiated the sale of Florida from Spain to the United States, Jackson was appointed its territorial governor, a job he accepted hoping it would vindicate his earlier actions there. But he went back to Tennessee after only a month to begin work on other, bigger, goals. In 1822, he became a candidate for the 1824 presidential election and the following year, the Tennessee legislature elected him to the U.S. Senate again, giving

The People's House

The name "White House" wasn't given to the president's official home until the administration of Theodore Roosevelt. It had been variously called the "Presidential Palace" and the "executive mansion," but when Andrew Jackson moved in, folks began calling it the "people's house." They established their lease with an incredible party on inauguration day when the biggest crowd yet assembled showed up to wish him well. Jackson himself had trouble getting into the house through the sea of humanity, and when he finally did, he was crushed against a wall gasping for air. Aides managed to evacuate him through a window and into a waiting carriage that sped him away. It was said that nobody noticed that the president wasn't on hand for his own reception. In an attempt to get the well-wishers out of the house, refreshments were set up out on the lawn, but it was too little, too late. In the rush, the mob broke thousands of dollars worth of crockery and glassware, tracked mud onto the carpets, and destroyed a great deal of furniture—but these mishaps were the result of overcrowding, and not malicious acts of vandalism.

Right: An early example of political attack advertising as "Old Hickory" Jackson takes on John Quincy Adams.

him more national exposure to build on his impressive base of popular support.

Jackson was popular indeed. In the 1824 election, he easily outpolled three other candidates in both popular and electoral vote: secretary of state John Quincy Adams; William H. Crawford, a Georgian who had been secretary of the treasury; and Henry Clay, a Kentuckian who was Speaker of the House of Representatives. However, none of them had won the required majority of electoral votes. The Constitution mandated that in such an event, the election was to be decided in the House of Representatives, with each state casting one vote for one of the top three finishers in the election.

"[Jackson] spent the prime of his life in gambling, in cock-fighting, in horseracing ... and to cap it all, tore from a husband the wife of his bosom."

—*Thomas Arnold, a Tennessee political opponent*

Henry Clay, who was out of the running, threw his support to Adams, which made Adams the winner of the House vote and gave him the presidency. Later, when he named Clay his secretary of state, Jackson followers were up in arms, accusing the two men of having made "a corrupt bargain." Jackson immediately began campaigning for the 1828 presidential election. and the accusation of corruption against Adams became a key issue in his long campaign for democratic reform.

With Jackson in the background, Adams's presidency was largely ineffective. Jackson had many political allies in Congress, including future presidents Martin Van Buren and James K. Polk, both of whom were on a fast track building their young national political careers. New Yorker Van Buren helped Jackson carry the Empire State in Jackson's sweeping victory in the 1828 election, which ended with no electoral dispute: Jackson won it with 178 electoral votes to 83 for Adams.

The 1828 presidential election campaign was one of the ugliest in American history. Slanders against Jackson and his wife were common, and Adams endured charges that he was an elitist and a grafter. The factions supporting both men were willing to use any means to defame their opponents.

The Age of Jackson

Jackson's triumph came during a difficult period for him. Rachel died of a heart attack shortly after the election, and he blamed her death on the insults his enemies routinely made about her, especially regarding her first marriage. Jackson was sixty years old when he took office, and he was enduring almost constant pain from his old war wounds and other ailments. He was tall and extremely thin, with a scar on his face and two bullets from old duels still in his body. He had trouble breathing, he had frequent headaches, and a chronic hacking cough, and by the time he became president, he needed a cane to walk.

Election Results

1828

Presidential / Vice Presidential Candidates	Popular votes	Electoral votes
Andrew Jackson / John C. Calhoun (Democratic)	647,231	178
John Quincy Adams / Richard Rush (National Republican)	509,097	83

1832

Presidential / Vice Presidential Candidates	Popular votes	Electoral votes
Andrew Jackson / Martin Van Buren (Democratic)	687,507	219
Henry Clay / John Sergeant (National Republican)	530,189	49
Others	unknown	18

John C. Calhoun

John Caldwell Calhoun was born on March 18, 1782, in rural South Carolina (near present-day Abbeville). He grew up to become a country lawyer, with a successful practice in his hometown.

In the summer of 1807, Calhoun led the small community in protest against the British attack on the American frigate Chesapeake, and drafted a set of resolutions denouncing the outrage. The resolutions brought him to public attention as a champion of national honor. He was elected to the state legislature in 1808. He won election to the U.S. Congress in 1810 as part of the "War Hawks," a group of youthful southerners and westerners who demanded territorial expansion and war against Britain. Right after the election, Calhoun purchased a plantation above the Savannah River and married a distant cousin, Floride Bonneau Calhoun.

Calhoun quickly established himself as a strong supporter of the War of 1812 (1812–15) between the United States and Great Britain. By the war's end, Calhoun dominated congressional debate in favor of a national bank and a protective tariff (tax on imports). He also championed an ambitious scheme of federally sponsored improvements to roads and canals. In December 1817, Calhoun accepted the post of secretary of war under James Monroe. Calhoun ran for president in 1824, but settled for the vice presidency under John Quincy Adams when it became apparent that he could not win. With his eyes still on the presidency, Calhoun supported Andrew Jackson against Adams in 1828 and was elected for a second term to the vice presidency. The next four years brought events and issues that had a profound impact upon Calhoun's future.

Declining cotton prices and a steady departure of people from his native state had led South Carolinians to denounce protective tariffs as instruments of Northern domination. Calhoun sought to balance his position at home and his presidential ambitions in the nation by writing a doctrine on nullification. In essence, he believed that a state could not be bound by a law the state considered unconstitutional. In such a case, a state could nullify the law, declaring it void in that state. When an even higher protective tariff was passed into law in 1832, Calhoun quickly returned to South Carolina, where the state legislature initiated the nullification procedure. A subsequent state convention voted to nullify the tariffs of 1828 and 1832. Calhoun resigned his post as vice president in December 1832 after being elected as a U.S. senator from South Carolina.

Attention focused on Calhoun—called the Great Nullifier—when he took his Senate seat and defended a policy he believed was constitutional. In 1833, Calhoun worked with U.S. senator Henry Clay of Kentucky to produce a compromise tariff. Some in South Carolina called for the state to secede from the Union; President Jackson, in turn, threatened to use force to keep the Union together.

In February 1844, President John Tyler appointed Calhoun secretary of state after Daniel Webster resigned from the position. In his brief tenure (1844–45), Calhoun completed negotiations for a treaty that eventually admitted the Republic of Texas into the Union as a slave state in 1845. Calhoun returned to manage his plantation after James K. Polk replaced Tyler as president in 1845, but he returned to the Senate later that year to oppose war with Mexico over the boundary of Texas. Calhoun was against the Polk administration's conduct in the Mexican War (1846–48) to such an extent that Polk declared him the most mischievous man in the Senate. Calhoun believed the war was a pretense for invading and taking over Mexican territory stretching west from Texas to the Pacific Ocean.

When the war ended, Calhoun focused his attention against the growing Northern demand to exclude slavery in the territories (much of present-day New Mexico, Arizona, and California) acquired in the war. When California sought admission to the Union as a free state, a gravely ill Calhoun entered the Senate chamber on March 4, 1850, to vehemently oppose it. Too weak to speak, Calhoun listened as Senator James Mason read Calhoun's warning that the balance between North and South would forever be destroyed if California entered the Union. It would be Calhoun's last major speech. He died on March 31, 1850.

Still, his triumph at the polls gave him strength. After his first inauguration, wild festivities attracted huge crowds that spilled onto the executive mansion's grounds. Showing the same iron will and fighting spirit he displayed in battle, Jackson proved to be among the most powerful of all the American presidents. Reflecting his view that the president is the nation's highest elected leader, he set out a course to promote the interests of the common man and to protect the rights of states from undue federal influence.

Several issues challenged Jackson's views. Before he took office, Congress had passed a tariff that Southern states felt was unfair to their part of the country. John C. Calhoun, who had served as Adams's vice president, was elected Jackson's vice president as well, and announced his Theory of Nullification. He believed that a state had the right to disobey federal laws that it considered harmful to its interests; although Jackson was a champion of states' rights, he was opposed to the idea of nullification because it threatened to undermine the federal government's supreme power.

Southerners naturally expected Jackson to support their cause, which was led by South Carolinian Calhoun, but the president sided with federal powers instead. His stand, and Calhoun's dissenting opinion, were made clear at a ceremonial dinner on the occasion of the late Thomas Jefferson's birthday. President Jackson rose to make a toast, and looking directly at Calhoun, said, "Our federal union! It must be preserved." Calhoun responded, "The Union, next to our liberty, most dear."

The nullification issue heated up again around election time in 1832. South Carolina not only planned to nullify a new tariff, but threatened to secede from the Union over it. Jackson's response was swift. He rallied the support of the people and threatened to send federal

Above: Jackson's inaugural reception was the wildest party ever seen at the Executive Mansion, which became known as "The People's House."

The Jackson Administration

Administration Dates:	March 4, 1829–March 4, 1833
	March 4, 1833–March 4, 1837
Vice President:	John Caldwell Calhoun
	(1829–32)
	none (1832–33)
	Martin Van Buren (1833–37)
Cabinet:	
Secretary of State	Martin Van Buren (1829–31)
	Edward Livingston (1831–33)
	Louis McLane (1833–34)
	John Forsyth (1834–37)
Secretary of the Treasury	Samuel D. Ingham (1829–31)
	Louis McLane (1831–33)
	William J. Duane (1833)
	Roger B. Taney (1833–34)
	Levi Woodbury (1834–37)
Secretary of War	John H. Eaton (1829–31)
	Lewis Cass (1831–36)
Attorney General	John M. Berrien (1829–31)
	Roger B. Taney (1831–33)
	Benjamin F. Butler (1833–37)
Secretary of the Navy	John Branch (1829–31)
	Levi Woodbury (1831–34)
	Mahlon Dickerson (1834–37)
Postmaster General	John McLean (1823–29)
	William T. Barry (1829–35)
	Amos Kendall (1835–37)

The "Kitchen Cabinet"

Unhappy with the members of his cabinet, Jackson stopped holding meetings with his official advisors and substituted them with gatherings of trusted cronies, a group he called his "Kitchen Cabinet." Among them were Secretary of War John Eaton and Vice President Martin Van Buren, along with two journalists and Jackson's nephew, Andrew Jackson Donelson, who was the president's secretary.

troops to South Carolina to enforce federal law. In the meantime, a compromise was worked out; when a lower tariff passed in Congress the following year, force became unnecessary.

" … To make the rich richer and the potent more powerful, the humble members of society—the farmers, mechanics and laborers—who have neither the time nor the means of securing like favors to themselves, have a right to complain of the injustice of their Government."
—*Andrew Jackson*

Another major issue revolved around the charter for the Second National Bank, the federal bank. It was empowered to regulate the flow of currency and to perform functions for the Department of Treasury. Jackson felt that the federal bank was dominated by wealthy, private interests that did not represent the majority of the people. When he vetoed a bill to recharter the bank, many in Congress were outraged and planned to make the veto a major campaign issue for the election of 1832.

Meanwhile, Jackson and Vice President Calhoun were at odds with one another. In addition to clashing over the nullification issue, they had a difference of opinion on how to deal with a scandal involving Secretary of War John Eaton, a Jackson ally. Eaton had married the recently widowed Margaret (Peggy) Timberlake, and rumors swirled around Washington that he had been carrying on an affair with her before her husband's death. Jackson, who himself had been a victim of malicious gossip, supported his friend, but all other administration officials and their wives, except for Secretary of State Martin Van Buren, snubbed Eaton, and in spite of the president's demands, they continued to ostracize Eaton and his wife until he resigned three years later. Van Buren soon became the head power broker in Jackson's administration. Calhoun's fall from power was sealed when Jackson learned that he had been among the congressmen who had wanted Jackson censured back in 1818 after he killed two British citizens in Florida.

Jackson wanted to change members of his cabinet near the end of his first term, but he knew that a clash with Calhoun would give him problems in the upcoming election. Van Buren helped solve the issue by resigning from his post as secretary of state, after which Jackson asked all his cabinet members to resign to give him a

Lost Kingdom

The first-ever assassination attempt on an American president was made against Andrew Jackson in 1835. The would-be assassin, Richard Lawrence, attacked him with a pair of pistols because he believed that Jackson was depriving him of his birthright to become king of America. Both guns misfired, a lucky break for Jackson, who was already carrying two bullets in his body, one close to his heart, and another in his arm. These were souvenirs of duels he had fought defending his wife's honor.

Left: In this cartoon a multi-headed snake representing individual states threatens Jackson and his vice president Martin Van Buren as they attempt to destroy the federal banking system.

Right: Peggy Eaton, the wife of Jackson's secretary of war, sparked a scandal that tore Jackson's administration apart.

clean slate should he win a second term. Calhoun wound up resigning anyway after he was elected to the U.S. Senate.

The 1832 election was a landmark in American political history. Following the quarrelsome election of 1824, the Democratic-Republican Party became split among supporters of Adams, who were called the National Republican Party, and Jackson supporters, who called themselves Jacksonian Democrats. Martin Van Buren helped to solidify Jackson's group of Northern and Southern supporters who were for states' rights and the common people. They held their own convention in 1832 and emerged as the Democratic Party, with Jackson as their nominee. Jackson was opposed in the national election by Henry Clay, the leader of the short-lived National Republican Party, which strongly supported a national bank. Jackson easily won reelection.

"King Andrew"

Jackson regarded his second victory as a mandate to dismantle the federal banking system. He withdrew funds from the national bank and deposited them among various state banks. This action, following on the heels of his threat to use federal force in South Carolina, didn't sit at all well with Congress Jackson was formally censured through a joint resolution of both the Senate and the House of Representatives—the only time in history that Congress has voted to go on record to criticize a president. He was ridiculed by his political and journalistic opponents as "King Andrew."

Jackson, however, continued to be so popular with the people that his political allies were able to have the censure erased from the Congressional Record. Jackson's victory was complete when the charter for the Second National Bank expired in 1836.

Meanwhile, Jackson had promised to pay off the national debt, and in keeping with this goal and maintaining his states' rights principles, he vetoed a bill that would have provided federal funds to build a road in Kentucky between the towns of Maysville and Lexington.

Right: Jackson's banking ideas prompted his enemies to characterize him as "King Andrew."

Above: Jackson had been involved in several duels in his life, and an unsuccessful assassination attempt in 1835 must have seemed unthreatening to him.

Big Cheese

Near the end of his presidency, the dairy farmers of New York State sent Jackson a gift of a 1,400-pound wheel of cheese. It gave him the inspiration to have a party, which turned out be nearly as well-attended as the impromptu affair on inauguration day. But there was a problem The cheese stunk to high heaven, so the revelers carried it indoors. It took weeks to get rid of the smell, but only an afternoon to devour the cheese.

The veto was sustained and established a trend that made states responsible for the building and improving of roads and canals within their borders.

Jackson successfully paid off the country's debt, and there were other triumphs, too. A trade agreement with Britain opened up the West Indies as a market for American goods. His administration convinced France to make reparation payments for ships destroyed in the Napoleonic wars more than fifteen years earlier. Finally, Jackson had the opportunity during his two terms to fill five vacancies on the Supreme Court, stacking it with his supporters, and ensuring that Jacksonian politics would be carried on through the government's judicial system.

Jacksonian policies caused lasting problems in several other areas, though. His decision to place federal funds in state banks led to a deregulation of the currency supply as well as an overextension of credit. The dollar lost value. Previously, the value of currency matched the nation's gold supply at one dollar for each dollar's worth of gold, but the increased amount of currency inflated the ratio to $12 for each dollar of the gold. Money lost value, and individuals were unable to pay off their debts on credit that had largely been extended for land speculation. Jackson helped ease the problem by declaring that land could be bought only with gold or silver, but the economy had already taken a downturn near the end of his second term.

Jackson's Native American policy was harsh. When the state of Georgia began confiscating Cherokee lands, he saw it as a states' rights issue, and even after the Supreme Court ruled that the dispute was a federal matter, he didn't enforce treaties honoring Cherokee claims to the land. In 1834, a large area of the frontier, mostly in present-day Oklahoma, was set aside as "Indian territory," and Native Americans of the Southeast were forcibly moved there. Last stands among Indian warriors, such as the Black Hawk War of 1832 and the Seminole War of 1835, failed to stop the flow of broken treaties and forced removal.

Troubles Back Home

Like most of his predecessors, Andrew Jackson faced huge financial problems in his retirement. But unlike them, his troubles were unexpected. Jackson's plantation, The Hermitage, had been productive. But the strong economic downturn that took place in 1837, the year Jackson returned home, took all the profit out of cotton farming, and he had to borrow heavily to keep his property. Ironically, the banking panic was a direct result of his own presidential battle against rechartering the second Bank of the United States.

Settlers on the frontier supported Jackson's policies, and he continued to be a popular president through the end of his tenure. He handpicked his replacement, Martin Van Buren, who went on to win the election of 1836. After a raucous farewell party in Washington, D.C., attended by thousands of well-wishers, Jackson retired to The Hermitage, his plantation in Nashville, Tennessee. He remained politically active, vigorously supporting states' rights, the annexation of Texas, and, above all, preservation of the Union. Jackson died at The Hermitage in 1844 shortly after the election of his longtime ally, James K. Polk, to the presidency. Polk defeated Jackson's longtime adversary, Henry Clay.

Legacy

Andrew Jackson was among the most powerful of all the American presidents. His predecessors often left it up to Congress to guide national policies and pledged to remain above party concerns. Jackson, however, was unabashedly the head of his political party, and he intended to lead the course of the nation himself. The six presidents who preceded him had vetoed Congressional legislation a combined total of nine times. Jackson used the presidential veto twelve times to enforce his views.

Jacksonian politicians continued to dominate American government for the next dozen years after his presidency ended. His close associates Martin Van Buren and James K. Polk each won a presidential election, and between their respective administrations, Whig party president John Tyler—who finished William Henry Harrison's term—was largely ineffective. Although

Tyler had deep anti-Jackson sentiments, he too vetoed the rechartering of the Second National Bank and maintained a strongly Jackson-like pro-states policy.

Ironically, the Second National Bank issue was revived twice—first by Van Buren, and then by Polk. Polk's rechartering was sustained through 1913, when the Federal Reserve System replaced the national bank. Jackson's removal of funds to states had negative repercussions shortly after he left office, including the Panic of 1837, which caused banks to fail and forced businesses and individuals into bankruptcy. The prosperity of the Jackson presidency vanished quickly.

Jackson's Native American policy left a bitter and tragic mark on American history. He supported the right of each state to decide on the institution of slavery, but this did nothing to improve national disagreement on the issue. His threat of using federal force against South Carolina in order to preserve the Union was played out on a much larger scale three decades later, with the outbreak of the Civil War in 1861.

Jackson's presidency reflected a shift to a new America, led by individuals born after the nation was founded. His successor, Martin Van Buren, was the first president born after the Declaration of Independence. Jackson himself was the first president from west of the Appalachians, and his presidency represented a majority—consisting of the common people—who looked to him as their national leader.

Last Words

Near the end of Jackson's life, a host of ailments came back to haunt him. By early June 1845, he needed to be propped up in bed because it was impossible for him to lie flat. He fell unconscious on June 8, but was revived with a shot of brandy, which allowed him to hear the wailing of his slaves gathered under the window. "Oh, do not cry," he murmured, "Be good children and we shall all meet in heaven." Moments later, Old Hickory was dead.

Rachel Jackson

Born June 15, 1767, Halifax County, Virginia
Died December 22, 1828, Nashville, Tennessee

"In the presence of this dear saint, I can and do forgive all my enemies but those vile wretches who slandered her must look to God for mercy."

—Andrew Jackson

Rachel Jackson was raised on the frontier. Her early life took place in a backwoods environment, where there were few comforts or opportunities to be educated. Yet this life proved more hospitable and dignified than did her later life as the wife of a military hero and politician, when she was often the object of gossip and slander.

Rachel and Andrew Jackson were married in Tennessee in 1791 after learning that Rachel's first husband, Lewis Robards, had divorced her. Two years later, though, they found out that Robards had filed for divorce in Kentucky but hadn't followed through on minor legal proceedings. Robards promptly renewed his divorce claim when he learned that Rachel had remarried, claiming that she had committed adultery, and the divorce was granted on those grounds.

The mistake of believing Rachel had been divorced when she and Andrew first married was in all likelihood an honest one. Legal proceedings on the frontier were often complicated, news traveled slowly, and Robards had done little to distinguish himself as an honest gentleman. However, the legal technicality of Jackson being branded an adulterer gave enemies a way to attack him and to undermine his political fortunes. Jackson often responded with his fists, and he even dueled over the matter. Rachel bore the insults with quiet dignity, but the strain eventually affected her health.

Girl of the Wild Frontier

Rachel Donelson Robards Jackson was born in Halifax County, Virginia, on June 15, 1767, the eighth of eleven children of John and Rachel Stockley Donelson. Her father was a surveyor, a member of the Virginia legislature, and a militia leader. As a young girl Rachel occasionally accompanied her father on politically related trips, and met fellow Virginians and future U.S. presidents George Washington and Thomas Jefferson.

When Rachel was twelve, her family moved as part of an expedition to help settle a remote area of modern-day eastern Tennessee. She had little schooling, but she learned to read and write and played the harpsichord. She spent most of her time helping with the chores necessary to establish a backwoods community.

The family moved to Kentucky when she was seventeen, and it was there that she met Lewis Robards, who came from a prominent local family. They were married in 1785 in Harrodsburg, Kentucky. Robards proved to be an abusive and extremely jealous man, and the couple separated and reconciled on three different occasions. In 1790, Rachel ran off to what was then the Western District of North Carolina (now Tennessee), fearing for her safety, and Robards responded by starting legal proceedings for divorce on the grounds of desertion.

Andrew Jackson, a young lawyer in the Nashville area, was a boarder at a home owned by Rachel's father, who asked him to help her relocate to Natchez, Mississippi, where one of her sisters lived. It was during that long, three-hundred-mile journey that Jackson fell in love with Rachel.

After returning to Nashville, Jackson learned that Robards had followed the proper legal procedure for a divorce, which was very rare in those days, and he assumed that the divorce had been finalized. As a lawyer, Jackson knew that once the party seeking a divorce received permission from the legislature, only minor details were left to be completed by the petitioner to make it final.

Jackson immediately headed to Natchez and asked Rachel to marry him. They were married, probably in a civil ceremony, in 1791. They shared a happy life together, but Robards came back into the picture two years later, in 1793, bringing what would be a lasting sense of grief to the new couple. Robards hadn't bothered to sign the divorce papers, and he renewed the proceedings, claiming adultery against Rachel in the decree that was finalized in September 1793.

Rachel and Andrew were married again in 1794. They were devoted to each other and to her extended family, the child they adopted, and other children they helped raise, but people would make judgments about their relationship throughout the rest of their lives.

The Hermitage

Jackson gradually became a major figure in Nashville, and their early years there were happy times. In 1796, he was involved in the actions that led Tennessee to statehood, and he became its first representative in Congress. In the early 1800s, he was able to transform land he had gradually acquired into an estate he called The Hermitage. He served as a judge and was named head of the Tennessee state militia.

Still, the Jacksons frequently faced insults over events surrounding their marriage. Jackson had grown up in rough circumstances on the frontier, and he knew how to fight, often replying to insults with his fists or with dueling challenges.

Jackson's life became even more adventurous beginning in 1812. He led American forces from Tennessee into Mississippi, Florida, and Louisiana during the War of 1812. He fought in Florida against Seminole Indians, and he was named governor of the newly acquired Florida territory, which the United States purchased from Spain in 1821. Jackson was a celebrated war hero after winning the Battle of New Orleans, but he was accused of overstepping his bounds as a military leader in 1818, when he allegedly killed two British citizens in Florida for encouraging Seminole raids on American settlements.

Throughout his stormy military career, Rachel and Andrew remained a devoted couple. She maintained The Hermitage during his frequent absences and occasionally joined him at outposts in New Orleans and Florida. Rachel Jackson preferred a quiet, domestic life, and helped raise thirteen children—nieces, nephews, the couple's own adopted child, and other children who needed their love. She provided guidance and tools for new settlers in the region, and she often put in a full day of domestic and farm work before resting in the evening, when she could smoke her pipe.

Andrew Jackson began serving in Congress in 1823 as he prepared for a run for the presidency. He won a majority of the popular vote in the 1824 election, but not enough electoral votes to secure the presidency. Since none of the candidates had received the required majority of electoral votes, the election was decided by Congress. When John Quincy Adams was chosen, Jackson immediately began campaigning for the 1828 election.

Although Rachel supported her husband's political ambitions, she could not have been delighted by the prospect of becoming first lady. In both the 1824 and 1828 campaigns, opponents used the controversy surrounding the Jacksons' marriage in an attempt to discredit Andrew with voters. In addition, Rachel was a simple woman, not accustomed to the formal parties and conversations of Washington's political social circles. Both Rachel and Andrew had celebrated their sixtieth birthdays, and both were in frail health when Andrew Jackson was elected president in 1828.

Rachel became ill not long after the election. Perhaps feeling that her death near, she made arrangements for her

niece, Emily Donelson, to learn the intricacies of hosting large gatherings. Rachel didn't look forward to going back to Washington to be among "cave dwellers" and face the persistent gossip and slander. Jackson's friend and political ally John Eaton, who himself would face accusations of improper behavior when he married a recently widowed woman, urged her to go to Washington. Otherwise, he told her, her persecutors would laugh at her and say that they managed to keep her away.

Rachel Jackson didn't go to Washington. She died in 1828 before her husband was inaugurated. He remained convinced that the continuous slander and accusations had been the strain that led to the heart attack that killed her. He buried her at The Hermitage with an inscription on her tombstone that reads, "A being so gentle and so virtuous slander might wound, but could not dishonor."

Jackson's Veto Message Regarding the Bank of the United States

Sent to Congress on July 10, 1832

The creation of the First National Bank in 1791 during George Washington's administration was one of the most controversial issues facing the young nation. Opponents argued that the bank was an expansion of federal power not authorized by the Constitution and an intrusion on the rights of states. Debate over the bank, which controlled the nation's money supply, continued for more than fifty years.

The charter for the federal bank was authorized in 1791 and renewed for twenty years in 1816, when the second national bank was formed. Congress moved early to renew it again four years before it was due to expire. It was an election year, and Henry Clay, who led support for the national bank, was the leading candidate against incumbent president Andrew Jackson. The bill to renew the national bank was approved by the Senate on June 11, 1832, and by the House less than a month later. President Jackson, suspicious of the wealthy group of bank leaders who weren't elected officials, vetoed the bill and sent a strongly worded message to the Senate explaining why.

Jackson's veto started a serious "bank war" with Massachusetts senator Daniel Webster, who accused the president of overstepping his authority. It was one of several incidents that led Jackson's detractors to call him "King Andrew."

Excerpts from President Jackson's Veto Message to the Senate

[...] A bank of the United States is in many respects convenient for the Government and useful to the people. Entertaining this opinion, and deeply impressed with the belief that some of the powers and privileges possessed by the existing bank are unauthorized by the Constitution, subversive of the rights of the States, and dangerous to the liberties of the people, I felt it my duty at an early period of my Administration to call the attention of Congress to the practicability of organizing an institution combining all its advantages and obviating these objections. I sincerely regret that in the act before me I can perceive none of those modifications of the bank charter which are necessary, in my opinion, to make it compatible with justice, with sound policy, or with the Constitution of our country.

The present; corporate body, denominated the president, directors, and company of the Bank of the United States, will have existed at the time this act is intended to take effect twenty years. It enjoys an exclusive privilege of banking under the authority of the General Government, a monopoly of its favor and support, and, as a necessary consequence, almost a monopoly of the foreign and domestic exchange. The powers, privileges, and favors bestowed upon it in the original charter, by increasing the value of the stock far above its par value, operated as a gratuity of many millions to the stockholders.

An apology may be found for the failure to guard against this result in the consideration that the effect of the original act of incorporation could not be certainly foreseen at the time of its passage. The act before me proposes another gratuity to the holders of the same stock, and in many cases to the same men, of at least seven millions more. This donation finds no apology in any uncertainty as to the effect of the act. On all hands it is conceded that its passage will increase at least so or 30 per cent more the market price of the stock, subject to the payment of the annuity of $200,000 per year secured by the act, thus adding in a moment one-fourth to its par value. It is not our own citizens only who are to receive the bounty of our Government. More than eight millions of the stock of this bank are held by foreigners. By this act the American Republic proposes virtually to make them a present of some millions of dollars. For these gratuities to foreigners and to some of our own opulent citizens the act secures no equivalent whatever. They are the certain gains of the present stockholders under the operation of this act, after making full allowance for the payment of the bonus.

Every monopoly and all exclusive privileges are granted at the expense of the public, which ought to receive a fair equivalent. The many millions which this act proposes to bestow on the stockholders of the existing bank must come directly or indirectly out of the earnings of the American people. It is due to them, therefore, if their Government sell monopolies and exclusive privileges, that they should at least exact for them as much as they are worth in open market. [. . .]

It is not conceivable how the present stockholders can have any claim to the special favor of the Government. The present corporation has enjoyed its monopoly during the period stipulated in the original contract. If we must have such a corporation, why should not the Government sell out the whole stock and thus secure to the people the full market value of the privileges granted? Why should not Congress create and sell twenty-eight millions of stock, incorporating the purchasers with all the powers

and privileges secured in this act and putting the premium upon the sales into the Treasury?

But this act does not permit competition in the purchase of this monopoly. It seems to be predicated on the erroneous idea that the present stockholders have a prescriptive right not only to the favor but to the bounty of Government. It appears that more than a fourth part of the stock is held by foreigners and the residue is held by a few hundred of our own citizens, chiefly of the richest class. For their benefit does this act exclude the whole American people from competition in the purchase of this monopoly and dispose of it for many millions less than it is worth. This seems the less excusable because some of our citizens not now stockholders petitioned that the door of competition might be opened, and offered to take a charter on terms much more favorable to the Government and country.

What Happened Next

Jackson's veto of the second national bank charter set off "the Bank War," a battle against the bank's supporters, which Jackson won: His veto was sustained, and he was reelected president in 1832. During his second term, Jackson weakened the national bank by authorizing government funds to be deposited in various state banks, rather than the national treasury, outraging many in Congress. But they weren't able to successfully challenge the popular president.

The "pet banks," as the state banks Jackson used were called, were not as stable as the national bank. A severe financial crisis occurred when many people who were loaned money by them were unable to pay back the money. Thousands of citizens lost their savings, and a financial panic swept the nation in 1836, and by the following year, when Jackson left office, the crisis had ruined the American economy, and it wouldn't recover for many years. Twenty-eight thousand Americans declared bankruptcy as late as 1841.

Jackson signed a bill into law that modified the more objectionable "Tariff of Abominations," that had been passed three years earlier. It failed to satisfy South Carolina, though, and its legislature enacted a law declaring the import duties null and void within its borders, and some of the state legislators threatened to secede from the Union. Jackson responded with a strong proclamation, written by his secretary of state, Edward Livingston of Louisiana.

Excerpt from the Proclamation Regarding Nullification, December 10, 1832

[. . .] The said ordinance prescribes to the people of South Carolina a course of conduct in direct violation of their duty as citizens of the United States, contrary to the laws of their country, subversive of its Constitution, and having for its object the instruction of the Union—that Union, which, coeval with our political existence, led our fathers, without any other ties to unite them than those of patriotism and common cause, through the sanguinary struggle to a glorious independence—that sacred Union, hitherto inviolate, which, perfected by our happy Constitution, has brought us, by the favor of Heaven, to a state of prosperity at home, and high consideration abroad, rarely, if ever, equaled in the history of nations; to preserve this bond of our political existence from destruction, to maintain inviolate this state of national honor and prosperity, and to justify the confidence my fellow-citizens have reposed in me, I, Andrew Jackson, President of the United States, have thought proper to issue this my Proclamation, stating my views of the Constitution and laws applicable to the measures adopted by the Convention of South Carolina.

[. . .]

[Our Constitution] was formed for important objects that are announced in the preamble made in the name and by the authority of the people of the United States, whose delegates framed, and whose conventions approved it. The most important among these objects, that which is placed first in rank, on which all the others rest, is "to form a more perfect Union."[. . .]

I consider, then, the power to annul a law of the United States, assumed by one State, incompatible with the existence of the Union, contradicted expressly by the letter of the Constitution, unauthorized by its spirit, inconsistent with every principle on which it was founded, and destructive of the great object for which it was formed.[. . .]

The preamble rests its justification on these grounds: It assumes as a fact, that the obnoxious laws, although they purport to be laws for raising revenue, were in reality intended for the protection of manufactures, which purpose it asserts to be unconstitutional; that the operation of these laws is unequal, that the amount raised by them is greater than is required by the wants of the Government; and, finally, that the proceeds are to be applied to objects unauthorized by the Constitution. These are the only causes alleged to justify an open opposition to the laws of the country, and a threat of seceding from the Union, if any attempt should be made to enforce them.

[. . .]

The next objection is, that the laws in question operate unequally. This objection may be made with truth to every law that has been or can be passed. The wisdom of man never yet contrived a system of taxation that would operate with perfect equality. If the unequal operation of a law makes it unconstitutional and if all laws of that description may be abrogated by any State for that cause, then, indeed, is the federal Constitution unworthy of the slightest effort for its preservation. We have hitherto relied on it as the perpetual bond of our Union.[. . .] Were we mistaken, my countrymen, in attaching this importance to the Constitution of our country? Was our devotion paid to the wretched, inefficient, clumsy contrivance, which this new doctrine would make it? Did we pledge ourselves to the support of an airy nothing—a bubble that must be blown away by the first breath of disaffection? Was this self-destroying, visionary theory the work of the profound statesmen, the exalted patriots, to whom the task of constitutional reform was intrusted? Did the name of Washington sanction, did the States deliberately ratify, such an anomaly in the history of fundamental legislation? No. We were not mistaken. The letter of this great instrument is free from this radical fault; its language directly contradicts the imputation, its spirit, its evident intent, contradicts it. No, we did not err. Our Constitution does not contain the absurdity of giving power to make laws, and another power to resist them. The sages, whose memory will always be reverenced, have given us a practical, and, as they hoped, a permanent constitutional compact. The Father of his Country did not affix his revered name to so palpable an absurdity. Nor did the States, when they severally ratified it, do so under the impression that a veto on the laws of the United States was reserved to them, or that they could exercise it by application.[. . .] No, we have not erred! The Constitution is still the object of our reverence, the bond of our Union, our defense in danger, the source of our prosperity in peace. It shall descend, as we have received it, uncorrupted by sophistical construction to our posterity; and the sacrifices of local interest, of State prejudices, of personal animosities, that were made to bring it into existence, will again be patriotically offered for its support.

The two remaining objections made by the ordinance to these laws are, that the sums intended to be raised by them are greater than are required, and that the proceeds will be unconstitutionally employed. The Constitution has given expressly to Congress the right of raising revenue, and of determining the sum the public exigencies will require. The States have no control over the exercise of this right other than that which results from the power of changing the representatives who abuse it, and thus procure redress. Congress may undoubtedly abuse this discretionary power, but the same may be said of others with which they are vested. Yet the discretion must exist somewhere. The Constitution has given it to the representatives of all the people, checked by the representatives of the States, and by the executive power. The South Carolina construction gives it to the legislature, or the convention of a single State, where neither the people of the different States, nor the States in their separate capacity, nor the chief magistrate elected by the people, have any representation. Which is the most discreet disposition of the power? I do not ask you, fellow-citizens, which is the constitutional disposition-that instrument speaks a language not to be misunderstood. But if you were assembled in general convention, which would you think the safest depository of this discretionary power in the last resort? Would you add a clause giving it to each of the States, or would you sanction the wise provisions already made by your Constitution? If this should be the result of your deliberations when providing for the future, are you—can you—be ready to risk all that we hold dear, to establish, for a temporary and a local purpose, that which you must acknowledge to be destructive, and even absurd, as a general provision? Carry out the consequences of this right vested in the different States, and you must perceive that the crisis your conduct presents at this day would recur whenever any law of the United States displeased any of the States, and that we should soon cease to be a nation. [...]

Martin Van Buren

"There is a power in public opinion in this country—and I thank God for it; for it is the most honest and best of all powers."
—*Martin Van Buren*

Eighth president of the United States, 1837–1841

Full name: *Martin Van Buren*
Born: *December 5, 1782, Kinderhook, New York*
Died: *July 24, 1862, Kinderhook, New York*
Burial site: *Kinderhook Cemetery, Kinderhook, New York*
Parents: *Abraham and Maria Hoes Van Alen Van Buren*
Spouse: *Hannah Hoes (1783–1819; m. 1807)*
Children: *Abraham (1807–1873); John (1810–1866); Martin (1812–1855); Winfield Scott (1814–1814); Smith Thompson (1817–1876)*
Religion: *Dutch Reformed*
Education: *No formal education*
Occupations: *Attorney*
Government positions: *New York state senator; U.S. senator and governor of New York; secretary of state and vice president under Andrew Jackson*
Political party: *Democratic*
Dates as president: *March 4, 1837–March 4, 1841*
Age upon taking office: *54*

*M*artin Van Buren was the first president born after the signing of the Declaration of Independence, and the last to be born before the ratification of the Constitution. He grew up to be a clever and resourceful politician able to anticipate and handle the most complex political trends. His almost uncanny political savvy earned him the nicknames the "Little Magician" and the "Red Fox of Kinderhook," depending on whether they were applied by his allies or his enemies. Van Buren seemed to have more of both than any other man in America. Even his best friends had to admit that he was sly as a fox, and he resembled one, too. He was a wiry man, only five-and-a-half feet tall, and he had wild sandy hair with bushy sideburns.

Van Buren's presidency was eclipsed and made unpopular by the Panic of 1837—the worst depression to hit the United States up until that time. He faced the challenge by introducing policies to counteract the cycle of boom and bust that had characterized the American economy since the nation began. Nevertheless, in the eyes of the voters, Van Buren was never able to shake the stigma of the bank panic of 1837. After serving a single term as president, he later received only 10 percent of the vote as a third-party presidential candidate.

Timeline

1782: Born in New York

1796: Graduates form Kinderhook Academy; serves as clerk for lawyer and begins studying law

1803: Passes New York bar; sets up law practice in Kinderhook

1813–20: Serves in New York senate

1815–19: Serves as New York attorney general

1821–28: Serves as U.S. senator from New York

1828: Elected governor of New York; resigns in March 1829 to join President Andrew Jackson's cabinet as secretary of state

1831: Resigns as secretary of state and is nominated by Jackson as minister to England, but the nomination is rejected by Congress

1832: Helps establish the Democratic party, which nominates Jackson for second term; Jackson wins election with Van Buren as vice president

1837–41: Serves as eighth U.S. president

1837: Banks close in Philadelphia and New York City on May 10, beginning the Panic of 1837 and a depression that lasts throughout Van Buren's term

1838: Van Buren continues Jackson's Indian policy, culminating with the Trail of Tears, when thousands of Native Americans are forced westward from the Southeast to present-day Oklahoma

1840: Loses presidential election to William Henry Harrison

1844: Despite being the favorite, Van Buren loses the Democratic party presidential nomination to dark-horse candidate James K. Polk

1848: Runs for president as a member of the Free Soil party but receives only 10 percent of the vote

1862: Dies in New York

Van Buren's lasting significance in American politics is based more on the periods before and after his presidency. He was a prime mover in establishing the first modern national political party, and later he became an uncompromising force against the expansion of slavery and remained so until his death after the advent of the Civil War.

Fugitive

Billy Van Ness, the son of Van Buren's mentor, William P. Van Ness, served as Aaron Burr's second in his fatal duel with Alexander Hamilton in 1804, and ran for his own life from the authorities when it ended. He ran all the way to Kinderhook and knocked frantically on the door of his father's house, but was captured when no one responded. When Van Buren bought the house thirty-five years later, he remodeled it almost beyond recognition as the centerpiece of the estate he called Lindenwald. But the one thing he didn't change was the front door and knocker that had frustrated young Billy Van Ness.

Raised in a Political Environment

Martin Van Buren was born on December 5, 1782, in Kinderhook, New York, to Abraham and Hannah Van Buren. His father was a farmer and innkeeper whose tavern was a popular stopping point for politicians on the road between Albany and New York City. There, young Martin overheard lively discussions on states' rights and growing anti-Federalist sentiments—conversations that later had a strong influence on his own political opinions. Coming from a modest background, he leaned away from the aristocrats who dominated American politics at the time. Van Buren became a champion of the common man. It was a personal belief, but it was a shrewd political stand as well. His successful work in New York to expand the base of eligible voters increased the number of people who were likely to vote for him.

Van Buren got his basic education in a one-room schoolhouse, and then became a clerk in the offices of a local attorney named Francis Sylvester. He ran errands, swept floors, studied law, and attended trials. According to some accounts, when he was fifteen, a judge was impressed by his rapt attention and furious note-taking during a trial and asked him to sum up the case to the jury. Whether that story is true or not, Van Buren did indeed excel in his law preparation and he went to New York City to finish his last year of studies at the firm of William P. Van Ness, a close associate of Aaron Burr.

Van Buren was admitted to the bar in 1803 and went home to Kinderhook to establish his own law practice. He quickly earned a local reputation as a skillful lawyer

What's That You Said?

Martin Van Buren was regarded as a brilliant conversationalist, but when the talk turned to politics, he was more of a listener. He kept his own opinions to himself or, as one of his friends said, he "rowed to his object with muffled oars." When he did speak, it was always with caution, and it was hard to know exactly what was in the back of his mind. It was these traits that earned him the nicknames the "Red Fox of Kinderhook," and the "Little Magician." It wasn't as though Van Buren didn't have opinions of his own—far from it. He was just careful about expressing them.

Above: New York Governor Dewitt Clinton formally opens the Erie Canal by pouring water from Lake Erie into New York City's harbor.

and branched out statewide, taking cases against Federalist attorneys representing wealthy clients. He became a rising star among Democratic-Republicans, and gradually assumed a leading role in their ranks in New York. The party represented agrarian-based ideals and had a strong appeal to the working class, in opposition to the aristocratic leanings of the Federalists.

Van Buren married Hannah Hoes, a childhood friend and a distant cousin, in February 1807. They had five children—Abraham, Martin, John, Winfield Scott (who died as an infant), and Smith Thompson before Hannah died in 1819. Van Buren never remarried.

He was elected to the New York state senate in 1812, and received some national recognition by proposing compulsory military service as a way of beefing up the army. His arguments won some approval as American forces struggled during the War of 1812. He became New York's attorney general three years later, and almost immediately took on a high-profile national case, in which he prosecuted Brigadier General William Hull, who had been charged with treason for surrendering Fort Detroit to the British. Hull was convicted and sentenced to death by firing squad, but the sentence was commuted by President James Madison before it could be carried out.

Meanwhile, Van Buren was busy organizing Democratic-Republicans. Political parties, in those days, were regional coalitions of like-minded individuals. By organizing Democratic-Republicans on key issues, including expanding the pool of eligible voters, Van Buren was able to forge a powerful political group called the Albany Regency. This group began challenging dominant "Clintonians," named after New York's governor, DeWitt Clinton, and eventually Van Buren was able to shift the power to his group and ride the new wave of influence to win election to the U.S. Senate in 1820.

Ally to Jackson

As an even-tempered but resourceful and eloquent politician, Van Buren quickly rose to chair the Senate Judiciary Committee. He became a fierce opponent of President John Quincy Adams and was a prime mover in frustrating the administration's plans for using federal money to build and improve roads, a scheme that Van Buren saw as a national intrusion on states' rights.

Van Buren gave his unqualified support to Andrew Jackson, who had received more electoral votes than Adams in the first balloting of the 1824 election, but had not received the majority required to win the presidency. Adams won when the vote was thrown into the House of Representatives, and other candidates' supporters switched

The Crime of Poverty

As a New York state senator, Van Buren was among the first politicians to call for an end to imprisonment of people who were unable to pay their debts. Van Buren felt these people were jailed "not for crimes which they [had] committed, not for frauds which they [had] practiced on the credulous and unwary ... but for the misfortune of being poor, of being unable to satisfy the all-digesting stomach of some ravenous creditor."

their votes to him. When Jackson began immediately to campaign for the 1828 election, Van Buren skillfully put together a coalition of supporters from both the North and the South to promote Jackson's candidacy. Adams and Jackson had both been Democratic-Republicans, but Jackson's faction within the party became known as Jacksonian Democrats. Van Buren helped transform a coalition of anti-aristocratic northern politicians and southern planters into the Democratic party by the 1832 election.

In the early days of the republic, presidents had regarded themselves as independent of Congress and tried to avoid influencing its decisions. By 1832, however, President Andrew Jackson ran for reelection to his second term as the head of the Democratic party, whose members in Congress doggedly followed his leadership and embraced the Democratic party platform.

"The more I see of Mr. Van Buren, the more I feel confirmed in a strong personal regard for him. He is one of the gentlest and most amiable men I have ever met with."

—*Washington Irving*

In a shrewd political move to help secure Jackson's election in 1828, Van Buren gave up his Senate seat before his term expired and ran for governor of New York. As was expected, he won the election, and his increased power within the state helped Jackson win New York's electoral votes, which was unheard of for a Southern politician. Van Buren had squeaked by in the gubernatorial election, and then promptly resigned after three months when Jackson called him to Washington as a reward for his support. Jackson named Van Buren his secretary of state. It was no coincidence that the job was a sure stepping-stone to the presidency—four of the first six presidents had held that position.

As secretary of state, Van Buren was effective in opening up the West Indies for trade through a treaty with Great Britain. He was successful in winning repayment from France for American shipping destroyed during the Napoleonic wars. And Van Buren shaped Jackson's position on states' rights when he prepared the speech explaining the president's veto of a federal appropriation bill to build a road in Kentucky that would link the towns

OK by Me

Among his many nicknames, Martin Van Buren was known as "Old Kinderhook," and he used it to describe himself in election campaigns. When he got to Washington, he usually signed memos and documents with the initials "OK," and before long they found their way into the American vocabulary.

Below: Van Buren at the beginning of his career as governor of New York.

of Maysville and Lexington. Insisting the road was not a federal matter but of concern only to the state (because it was entirely within its borders), Jackson vetoed the Maysville Road bill and established a trend that made states responsible for the building and improving of roads and canals.

Van Buren's work drew increasing respect from Jackson, but it led to some cabinet power struggles, particularly between Van Buren and Vice President John C. Calhoun, who nursed a dream to succeed Jackson as president. Relations among all of the cabinet officials became more hostile over a scandal surrounding Secretary of War John H. Eaton, who married a woman he'd been rumored to have had an affair with while she was married to another man. Both Jackson and Van Buren supported Eaton, but other cabinet members and their wives refused even to speak to him.

Another disagreement developed over the issue of nullification, the theory that a state can disregard a federal law within its borders. Jackson and Van Buren strongly supported states' rights in most matters, but when South Carolina threatened to nullify the Tariff of 1828, legislation that placed an extremely high tax on imported goods, they altered their course. This was a tax that Jackson and Van Buren had pushed for to help Western states compete in the American economy. Jackson threatened to send federal troops to South Carolina if it followed through with its nullification threat, which also included the possibility of seceding from the Union. Vice President Calhoun, a South Carolina native, sided with his state, and widened the gulf between himself and the president. Calhoun's doom was sealed when Jackson learned that he had supported the censure of Jackson in 1818. (Jackson had been an army general at the time and had led a raid into Florida's Seminole lands outside U.S. jurisdiction; it was rumored that he had killed two British citizens in Spanish Florida as well.)

As the end of his first term approached, Jackson wanted to shake up his cabinet but avoid public and political criticism while doing so. Van Buren helped Jackson tactfully handle the changes. He resigned from his cabinet position and was nominated by Jackson to become minister to Great Britain. Van Buren began serving in his new position before being confirmed by Congress and, as

it happened, the confirmation vote in the Senate ended in a tie. This meant that Van Buren's old adversary, Vice President Calhoun, who served as president of the Senate, was required to cast the deciding vote. Naturally, he voted against the Van Buren appointment, a move that just as naturally infuriated Jackson, who was more than pleased to accept his vice president's resignation when he was elected to the Senate a short time later.

Following Van Buren's resignation as secretary of state, Jackson asked all cabinet members to resign as his first term ended, allowing him to start fresh for his second. The 1832 election, which returned Jackson to office, was the first of the modern party system. Under this system—still in place in the twenty-first century—party delegates nominate their presidential candidate at a national convention. Van Buren was a leading force in helping to establish the practice, and he transformed the Jackson Democrats of the Democratic-Republican party into the Democratic party. Jackson won the party nomination easily and swept in the national election over candidates of two short-lived parties, the National Republicans and the Anti-Masonics. Van Buren was elected Jackson's new vice president.

Vice President and Heir Apparent

As vice president, Van Buren spent a great deal of time defending Jackson's first-term veto of the Maysville, Kentucky, road bill. He also defended Jackson's continued opposition to rechartering the second bank of the United States, a federal bank that controlled the nation's currency. Jackson argued that this bank was not responsive to the will of the people, and Van Buren supported him, although he was not personally convinced that the bank ought to be dismantled. Jackson caused political commotion when he boldly moved funds from the federal bank to various state banks, an act that brought him formal Congressional censure—the only time in the nation's history that Congress has censured a president. Through it all, Van Buren loyally continued to support the president.

"Van Buren is an opposite to General Jackson as dug is to a diamond… he is what the English call a dandy. When he enters the senate chamber in the morning, he struts and swaggers like a crow in the gutter. He is laced up in corsets, such as women in town wear, and, if possible, tighter than the best of them. It would be difficult to say, from his personal appearance, whether he was a man or a woman, but for his large whiskers."

—Davy Crockett

Despite the censure, Jackson remained very popular among the people, and he was firmly in charge of the Democratic party. This ensured that his most loyal supporter, Van Buren, would be his heir apparent. He was unanimously nominated as the Democratic party candidate at its national convention in Baltimore, Maryland, in 1836.

In the meantime, the National Republican party had transformed into the new Whig party, and its members were firmly united in their anti-Jacksonian sentiments, particularly against what they saw as excessive use of presidential power. The Whigs didn't hold a convention that year, instead nominating four regional candidates—General William Henry Harrison of Ohio; Congressman Willie Person Mangum of North Carolina; U.S. Senator Daniel Webster of Massachusetts; and U.S. Senator Hugh Lawson White of Tennessee. The Whigs were hoping to flood the field so that no candidate would receive the required number of electoral votes, which would throw the election to the House of Representatives, where they held an edge. The strategy failed. Van Buren won 170 electoral votes to 125 for the stable of Whig candidates.

1836 Election Results

Presidential / Vice Presidential Candidates	Popular Votes	Electoral Votes
Martin Van Buren / Richard M. Johnson (Democratic)	762,678	170
William Henry Harrison / Francis Granger (Whig)	550,816	73
Hugh Lawson White (Whig)	146,107	26
Daniel Webster (Whig)	41,201	14
Willie Person Mangum (Whig)	unknown	11

The Whig party presented four regional candidates for president. John Tyler and William Smith were also Whig vice presidential candidates. Democratic vice presidential nominee Johnson did not receive a majority of electoral votes, so his election came as a result of a vote in the U.S. Senate, the only vice president in history to be elected that way.

The Van Buren Administration

Administration Dates: March 4, 1837–March 4, 1841
Vice President: Richard Mentor Johnson (1837–41)

Cabinet:

Secretary of State	John Forsyth (1837–41)
Secretary of the Treasury	Levi Woodbury (1837–41)
Secretary of War	Joel R. Poinsett (1837–41)
Attorney General	Benjamin F. Butler (1837–38)
	Felix Grundy (1838–39)
	Henry D. Gilpin (1840–41)
Secretary of the Navy	Mahlon Dickerson (1837–38)
	James K. Paulding (1838–41)
Postmaster General	Amos Kendall (1837–40)
	John M. Niles (1840–41)

Political Specimen

Joel R. Poinsett, Van Buren's secretary of war, was responsible for introducing numerous tropical plants to the United States while he was minister to Mexico in the John Quincy Adams administration. Among them was the one that bears his name: the poinsettia.

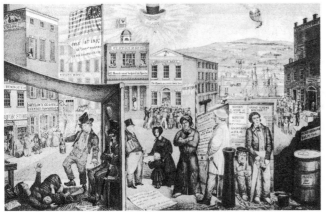

A President in the Jacksonian Mold

In his inaugural address, Van Buren announced his intention to continue Jackson's policies, and he also kept most of his predecessor's cabinet. However, a worldwide depression struck early into his presidency. The United States, which had enjoyed tremendous economic growth during the Jackson years, was severely affected, and the political repercussions for Van Buren from the Panic of 1837 were devastating. His popularity took a nose dive along with the economy, as jobs were lost, businesses went bankrupt, and banks failed.

Van Buren did have some financial skills, however. During his short term as governor of New York, for instance, he established a then-innovative "safety fund system" to insure individual bank savings. As vice president, he had been supportive, against his better judgment, of Jackson's opposition to the federal banking system and to his transfer of federal funds to state banks. He recognized too late that states had used those funds to issue unlimited credit to customers. The economic downturn escalated into a full-fledged depression as a result of this cheap credit, which ruined both the banks and their customers.

Van Buren proposed reestablishing an independent banking system that would control federal funds, and the Independent Treasury System was approved in 1840. Although it was disbanded by the next administration, the system was revived again during the 1840s, and it served as the federal banking system through 1913, when the Federal Reserve was established during the administration of President Woodrow Wilson.

Van Buren lost further popularity over his handling of a crisis with Great Britain. He managed to avoid war and helped settle the conflict, but his use of diplomacy when American passions were aroused for war lowered his political standing. The incident grew in significance

Above left: The Bank Panic of 1837 turned into a full-fledged depression and ruined thousands of lives.

Left: Van Buren at the pinnacle of his career as president of the United States.

Winfield Scott

From the War of 1812 to the Civil War and many battles in between, Winfield Scott was one of America's leading military commanders. He was so popularly known that he ran for president in 1852. His father, William Scott, had been a captain during the American Revolution.

Scott was born on June 13, 1786, on his parents' large farm near Petersburg, Virginia. His father died when Scott was six years old, leaving his mother, Ann, to raise him alone. She died when he was seventeen. After one year each of high school and college, he began to study law. He soon started his own practice, traveling around Virginia to provide legal aid where needed. In 1807, Scott watched the treason trial of former vice president Aaron Burr. Scott declared publicly that he believed Burr and his cohort, General James Wilkinson, were guilty. Scott's statement angered Wilkinson, who, along with Burr, was found not guilty.

Meanwhile, hostilities between Great Britain and the United States were growing dangerous. President Thomas Jefferson closed American harbors to international trade, beginning the Embargo of 1807. Jefferson had deliberately reduced the size of the army as part of his plan to have a weak central government. Needing troops to keep the British out, Jefferson called for a militia. Scott applied to Jefferson for a permanent position in the army. Impressed with the eager young man, Jefferson gave him the rank of captain. In 1808, Scott and his company proceeded to New Orleans.

Meanwhile, Wilkinson was now in charge of the army in the South. He and Scott disliked each other, but they held an uneasy truce for two years. In 1810, their conflict came to a head when Scott was reprimanded for remarks against his commanding officer. Scott left the army to resume his law practice.

Scott soon returned to service and was promoted to the rank of lieutenant colonel. During the War of 1812, he was given a unit positioned on a high post overlooking British forces in Queenston, Ontario, Canada. Greatly outnumbered, Scott retreated and then surrendered. In spite of the defeat, he showed courage and was promoted to the rank of colonel and, later, brevet major general.

In 1815, Scott turned down President James Madison's offer to become secretary of war. Instead, he withdrew from public life, and traveled to Europe. Upon his return, Scott vied for several years with Edmund Gaines for the highest rank in the army. In 1821, Scott was named head of the army of the East and Gaines headed the army of the West; both were given the rank of brigadier general. When the position of general of the entire army opened up in 1825, Gaines and Scott were each passed over in favor of Alexander Macomb, a major general during the War of 1812. Scott wrote to the secretary of war stating that he would not take orders from Macomb; Scott was immediately relieved of his command. With no one to command and no official army duties, Scott again headed for Europe.

Scott returned in 1830 and was given command of forces in Atlanta, Georgia. Citizens there refused to accept federal decisions to respect the land of the Cherokees. Scott's balance of military

strength and patient explanations of the government's position eased tensions and made him popular with the military and the public once again. When the Black Hawk War erupted in 1832, President Andrew Jackson turned to Scott, whom he respected. Arriving in the Illinois area as the war ended, Scott supervised the treaty at which the Sauk tribe signed away its longstanding rights to land along the eastern border of the Mississippi River.

Meanwhile, Jackson had convinced the head chief of the Seminole to leave the tribe's area and move west. After two years passed and only a few of the Seminole had left, the United States fought against the forces of the great Seminole chief Osceola. His people were eventually defeated, and nearly 4,000 of them were forced to move to Oklahoma in 1843. By then, Scott had left to command the removal of the much larger group of the Cherokee. Under Scott's orders, the troops were disposed at various points throughout Cherokee country, where forts were erected for holding the Native Americans before their removal. Scott ordered his soldiers to treat the Native Americans with respect. More than 13,000 Cherokee made the move to Oklahoma along what became known as the Trail of Tears.

In 1841, Scott became major general and commander in chief of the army. When war erupted with Mexico in 1845, he took a force of 12,000 men and seized the national palace. Scott returned home a hero. The Whig party sought to capitalize on Scott's popularity by nominating him as its presidential candidate in 1852. However, Democrat Franklin Pierce won the election. Scott was still in charge of the army when the Civil War erupted in 1861. But the seventy-five-year-old soon retired. He died on May 29, 1866.

as Americans began to help Canadians rebelling for independence from Great Britain. *The Caroline*, an American steamer stocked with supplies for Canadian rebels, was seized by Great Britain and burned, and an American named Amos Durfee was killed during the incident. Several American reprisal raids followed. The United States demanded reparations for *The Caroline*, which Britain refused to pay. Meanwhile, Van Buren called for order on the American side and sent Major General Winfield Scott to stop the raiding.

Trouble reared its head again when a Canadian was arrested on charges of having killed Durfee, which he had bragged about in a New York City tavern. This development and a renewal of skirmishes along the disputed border between Maine and Canada renewed passion for war. Major General Scott was dispatched to the area again to maintain peace while diplomatic solutions were being worked out. Van Buren eventually succeeded in winning "peace with honor," but at great political cost for the Little Magician.

Along with conflicts on the northern border, the United States continued to deal with struggles in the South. The policy of removing Native Americans from the Southeast to the Southwest had met strong resistance from Seminoles in Florida. Efforts were renewed to carry out the American policy begun by Jackson, and in addition to approving raids on the Seminoles, Van Buren supported the forcible relocation of the Cherokee nation to "Indian Territory:" in the present-day Oklahoma area. About a quarter of the Cherokee population died during the relocation, remembered as the Trail of Tears.

Losses and Changes

Van Buren was unanimously nominated by the Democratic party to run for a second term, but he was so unpopular by then that the Whig party was able to run a spirited public campaign without much mention of issues that might be significant to the voters. Their candidate, William Henry Harrison, was sixty-seven years old, which might have been an issue with some voters, and he ran without a platform. The Whigs concentrated instead on creating a mood of good feeling with songs echoing their "Tippecanoe and Tyler Too" slogan. Harrison was well known for his decisive victory over Native American forces some three decades earlier at the Battle of Tippecanoe. John Tyler, the "Tyler too" half of the slogan, was a handsome statesman with the double distinction of promoting states' rights while still being anti-Jacksonian—he had sharply criticized Jackson for transferring funds from the federal bank during his presidency. Van Buren won forty-four percent of the popular vote but was trounced in the Electoral College, where he lost 234 to 60. The election went to Old Tippecanoe (and Tyler, too).

After his defeat, the model politician Van Buren gradually transformed himself into a statesman and at the same time renewed his common-man image. One of his final acts as president was an executive order that limited federal workers to a ten-hour day, a victory for labor reform. He traveled around the United States, became involved in the Texas annexation issue, and ran for president two more times during the 1840s. When

he became the first former president to tour Europe, dignitaries weren't sure how to welcome a figure who neither held elective office nor was a member or an associate of royalty. Van Buren gladly solved their problem by asking to be treated as a common American citizen.

On the annexation issue, Van Buren was against admitting Texas into the Union. If Texas were admitted, it would be a slave state, which would upset the balance of fifteen slave states and fifteen non-slave states. Van Buren gradually moved away from recognizing states' rights on the slavery issue to openly opposing the expansion of slavery to new states. He was the leading contender for the Democratic nomination in 1844, but couldn't win the necessary number of delegates at the convention, and the nomination went to James K. Polk, who clearly supported annexing Texas.

Van Buren ran for president again in 1848 as the nominee of the Free Soil party, which was led by his son, John. The party maintained Jacksonian ideals while taking a stand against the expansion of slavery. Van Buren won only 10 percent of the national vote, but his presence on the New York ballot stole votes from the Democratic nominee Lewis Cass, and tipped the state's electoral votes, and the election, to Whig candidate Zachary Taylor.

Van Buren retired after that to Lindenwald, his estate in Kinderhook, where he wrote his memoirs and occasionally become active in national affairs. He opposed the repeal of the Missouri Compromise, which limited the expansion of slavery, and although a staunch Democrat, he supported the election of the Republican Abraham Lincoln in 1860. Van Buren died at Kinderhook two years later.

Legacy

Martin Van Buren's role in helping form the Democratic party in 1832 out of a splintered group of Democratic-Republicans remains his most lasting achievement. He had a more powerful effect on the nation's political affairs as a political power broker during the 1820s, and as secretary of state and, later, vice president to Andrew Jackson, than he did as president.

Nevertheless, Van Buren's presidential act of reinstituting the federal bank, and his avoidance of war with Great Britain were important, sound decisions. His fiscal policies helped address the problem of economic boom-and-bust cycles, although the cyclical nature of the economy would continue to plague the nation through the nineteenth century.

Van Buren carried on Andrew Jackson's policies (except for his stance on the national bank issue), and James K. Polk followed the same practices during his presidency in the mid-1840s. Van Buren supported states' rights, and his even-tempered approach saw the tradition of Jacksonian politics through a severe economic crisis. His legacy remains as a key political figure of the Jackson era, which ran from the mid-1820s through the late 1840s, interrupted only between 1841 and 1845 by the largely ineffective Harrison/Tyler administration.

Hannah Van Buren

Born March 8, 1783, Kinderhook, New York
Died February 5, 1819, Albany, New York

"She was a sincere Christian, a dutiful child, tender mother, affectionate wife."

—*Inscription on Hannah Van Buren's tombstone*

When Martin Van Buren became president in 1837, he had been a widower for eighteen years and had four bachelor sons. No one was available to serve in the official capacities of the first lady. The situation changed when his eldest son, Abraham, married Angelica Singleton at the end of 1838. She took on the responsibilities of Van Buren's first lady after she returned from honeymooning in Europe with her new husband, who served as his father's secretary.

With former first lady Dolley Madison as an advisor, Angelica became the hostess at White House gatherings and brought a feminine sensibility to the Van Buren White House. Angelica was the daughter of one of Dolley's in-laws and had traveled to Washington to visit her famous relative, who took her to a White House function soon after the Van Buren administration began. It was there that she and Abraham first met.

Hannah Van Buren died in 1818, shortly after giving birth to the couple's fifth son, Smith Thompson (another son had died in infancy). She and her future husband

had grown up together in the small Dutch immigrant community of Kinderhook, New York, and were distant cousins. Their families were close friends; Van Buren's parents had been sponsors at Hannah's baptism at the local Dutch Reformed church.

Van Buren began a law career while he was still a teenager, and he went to New York City to finish his preparation to become a lawyer. He went home to Kinderhook and established a successful practice, and he and Hannah were married in 1807, when they were both twenty-four years old. Hannah was a modest and unassuming woman, content to stay at home and raise a family. The couple's first son, Abraham, was born in Kinderhook.

Martin Van Buren was elected to the New York state senate in 1812, and three years later became the state's attorney general. The Van Burens and their three sons moved to Albany, where their home became a whirl of activity, with apprentice lawyers and clerks often working in the house, as Van Buren took on several high-profile cases.

Hannah Hoes Van Buren fell ill during her fifth pregnancy, and she never recovered after giving birth. She died in 1818 at the age of thirty-five. The cause of death was believed to have been tuberculosis. Though grief-stricken, Van Buren was consoled by the many friends he had made while organizing the Albany Regency, a strong political party in New York state. He was elected to the U.S. Senate in 1820, beginning a long and remarkable

No Melting Pot

Hannah Van Buren spoke English with a Dutch accent, and she and her husband often found it easier to converse in Dutch, which was more commonly spoken in Kinderhook than English, even though numerous families had lived there for as many as six generations. Van Buren said of the people in Kinderhook that "there has not been a single intermarriage with one of a different extraction from the time of the arrival of the first immigrant to that of the marriage of my eldest son, embracing a period of over two centuries."

political career on the federal level, which included positions as secretary of state and vice president. In 1836, he was elected president of the United States.

Van Buren had become accustomed to living in a style that combined luxury and a work environment. He and his sons began restoring a sense of elegance to the White House that his earthier predecessor, Andrew Jackson, would have found showy. Angelica Singleton's arrival as daughter-in-law helped complete the transformation. With the assistance of Dolley Madison, presidential receptions were lively and festive for the next several years.

Van Buren's Inaugural Address

Delivered on March 4, 1837

Martin Van Buren was the closest advisor to President Andrew Jackson, whom he served as secretary of state and vice president. As Jackson's handpicked successor, he won election to president in 1836. Jackson had been a strong president: His administration was enormously popular and controversial. His support for states' rights against the powers of the federal government made him especially popular among Southerners and among working people in the North and West.

Southerners were concerned about how fully Van Buren, a New Yorker, would follow the policies of Jackson, a Tennessean. Van Buren answered them in his inaugural address. After expressing optimism for the nation, which had prospered during Jackson's administration, Van Buren announced policies similar to those of his predecessor, including support for states' rights in deciding such issues as whether or not to permit slavery.

Excerpt from President Van Buren's Inaugural Address

In the early stages of the new Government, when all felt the imposing influence as they recognized the unequaled services of the first President, it was a common sentiment that the great weight of his character could alone bind the discordant materials of our Government together and save us from the violence of contending factions. Since his death nearly forty years are gone. Party exasperation has been often carried to its highest point; the virtue and fortitude of the people have sometimes been greatly tried; yet our system, purified and enhanced in value by all it has encountered, still preserves its spirit of free and fearless discussion, blended with unimpaired fraternal feeling.

The capacity of the people for self-government, and their willingness, from a high sense of duty and without those exhibitions of coercive power so generally employed in other countries, to submit to all needful restraints and exactions of municipal law, have also been favorably exemplified in the history of the American States. Occasionally, it is true, the ardor of public sentiment, outrunning the regular progress of the judicial tribunals or seeking to reach cases not denounced as criminal by the existing law, has displayed itself in a manner calculated to give pain to the friends of free government and to encourage the hopes of those who wish for its overthrow. These occurrences, however, have been far less frequent in our country than in any other of equal population on the globe, and with the diffusion of intelligence it may well be hoped that they will constantly diminish in frequency and violence. The generous patriotism and sound common sense of the great mass of our fellow-citizens will assuredly in time produce this result; for as every assumption of illegal power not only wounds the majesty of the law, but furnishes a pretext for abridging the liberties of the people, the latter have the most direct and permanent interest in preserving the landmarks of social order and maintaining on all occasions the inviolability of those constitutional and legal provisions which they themselves have made.[...]

Certain danger was foretold from the extension of our territory, the multiplication of States, and the increase of population. Our system was supposed to be adapted only to boundaries comparatively narrow. These have been widened beyond conjecture; the members of our Confederacy are already doubled, and the numbers of our people are incredibly augmented. The alleged causes of danger have long surpassed anticipation, but none of the consequences have followed. The power and influence of the Republic have arisen to a height obvious to all mankind; respect for its authority was not more apparent at its ancient than it is at its present limits; new and inexhaustible sources of general prosperity have been opened; the effects of distance have been averted by the inventive genius of our people, developed and fostered by the spirit of our institutions; and the enlarged variety and amount of interests, productions, and pursuits have strengthened the chain of mutual dependence and formed a circle of mutual benefits too apparent ever to be overlooked.

In justly balancing the powers of the Federal and State authorities difficulties nearly insurmountable arose at the outset and subsequent collisions were deemed inevitable. Amid these it was scarcely believed possible that a scheme of government so complex in construction could remain uninjured. From time to time embarrassments have certainly occurred; but how just is the confidence of future safety imparted by the knowledge that each in succession has been happily removed! Overlooking partial and temporary evils as inseparable from the practical operation of all human institutions, and looking only to the general result, every patriot has reason to be satisfied. While the Federal Government has successfully performed its appropriate functions in relation to foreign affairs and concerns evidently national, that of every State has remarkably improved in protecting and developing local interests and individual welfare; and if the vibrations of authority have occasionally tended too much toward one or the other, it is unquestionably certain that the ultimate operation of the entire system has been to strengthen all the existing institutions and to elevate our whole country in prosperity and renown.

The last, perhaps the greatest, of the prominent sources of discord and disaster supposed to lurk in our political condition was the institution of domestic slavery. Our forefathers were deeply impressed with the delicacy of this subject, and they treated it with a forbearance so evidently wise that in spite of every sinister foreboding it never until the present period disturbed the tranquillity of our common country. Such a result is sufficient evidence of the justice and the patriotism of their course; it is evidence not to be mistaken that an adherence to it can prevent all embarrassment from this as well as from every other anticipated cause of difficulty or danger. Have not recent events made it obvious to the slightest reflection that the least deviation from this spirit of forbearance is injurious to every interest, that of humanity included? Amidst the violence of excited passions this generous and fraternal feeling has been sometimes disregarded; and standing as I now do before my countrymen, in this high place of honor and of trust, I can not refrain from anxiously invoking my fellow-citizens never to be deaf to its dictates. Perceiving before my election the deep interest this subject was beginning to excite, I believed it a solemn duty fully to make known my sentiments in regard to it, and now, when every motive for misrepresentation has passed away, I trust that they will be candidly weighed and understood. At least they will be my standard of conduct in the path before me. I then declared that if the desire of those of my countrymen who were favorable to my election was gratified "I must go into the Presidential chair the inflexible and uncompromising opponent of every attempt on the part of Congress to abolish slavery in the District of Columbia against the wishes of the slaveholding States, and also with a determination equally decided to resist the slightest interference with it in the States where it exists." I submitted also to my fellow-citizens, with fullness and frankness, the reasons which led me to this determination. The result authorizes me to believe that they have been approved and are confided in by a majority of the people of the United States, including those whom they most immediately affect. It now only remains to add that no bill conflicting with these views can ever receive my constitutional sanction. These opinions have been adopted in the firm belief that they are in accordance with the spirit that actuated the venerated fathers of the Republic, and that succeeding experience has proved them to be humane, patriotic, expedient, honorable, and just. If the agitation of this subject was intended to reach the stability of our institutions, enough has occurred to show that it has signally failed, and that in this as in every other instance the apprehensions of the timid and the hopes of the wicked for the destruction of our Government are again destined to be disappointed. Here and there, indeed, scenes of dangerous excitement have occurred, terrifying instances of local violence have been witnessed, and a reckless disregard of the consequences of their conduct has exposed individuals to popular indignation; but neither masses of the people nor sections of the country have been swerved from their devotion to the bond of union and the principles it has made sacred. It will be ever thus. Such attempts at dangerous agitation may periodically return, but with each the object will be better understood. That predominating affection for our political system which prevails throughout our territorial limits, that calm and enlightened judgment which ultimately governs our people as one vast body, will always be at hand to resist and control every effort, foreign or domestic, which aims or would lead to overthrow our institutions.

What can be more gratifying than such a retrospect as this? We look back on obstacles avoided and dangers overcome, on expectations more than realized and prosperity perfectly secured. To the hopes of the hostile, the fears of the timid, and the doubts of the anxious actual experience has given the conclusive reply. We have seen time gradually dispel every unfavorable foreboding and our Constitution surmount every adverse circumstance dreaded at the outset as beyond control. Present excitement will at all times magnify present dangers, but true philosophy must teach us that none more threatening than the past can remain to be overcome; and we ought (for we have just reason) to entertain an abiding confidence in the stability of our institutions and an entire conviction that if administered in the true form, character, and spirit in which they were established they are abundantly adequate to preserve to us and our children the rich blessings already derived from them, to make our beloved land for a thousand generations that chosen spot where happiness springs from a perfect equality of political rights.

For myself, therefore, I desire to declare that the principle that will govern me in the high duty to which my country calls me is a strict adherence to the letter and spirit of the Constitution as it was designed by those who framed it. Looking back to it as a sacred instrument carefully and not easily framed; remembering that it was throughout a work of concession and compromise; viewing it as limited to national objects; regarding it as leaving to the people and the States all power not explicitly parted with, I shall endeavor to preserve, protect, and defend it by anxiously referring to its provision for direction in every action. To matters of domestic concernment which it has entrusted to the Federal Government and to such as relate to our intercourse with foreign nations I shall zealously devote myself; beyond those limits I shall never pass.

What Happened Next

The great optimism that Van Buren wanted to promote when he took office was soon overwhelmed when a financial crisis struck the United States in 1837. Van Buren struggled against the effects of a poor economy and dwindling popular support through much of his term. Meanwhile, his belief that the issue of slavery was, according to the Constitution, to be determined by individual states was severely tested by growing sentiment for abolition of the institution. A great divide between North and South was occurring over the issue.

Van Buren had helped establish the Democratic party, along with members of the Democratic-Republican party who had favored Andrew Jackson against fellow Democratic-Republican John Quincy Adams in the presidential elections of 1824 and 1828. When controversy over Jackson's use of presidential authority erupted in the early 1830s, opponents gradually formed the rival Whig party, which gained power during Van Buren's administration as the economy fell apart and the issue of slavery became more divisive. Van Buren lost reelection in 1840 to the Whig candidate William Henry Harrison.

William Henry Harrison

> "See to the government. See that the government does not acquire too much power. Keep a check on your rulers. Do this and liberty is safe."
>
> —*William Henry Harrison*

Ninth president of the United States, 1841

Full name: *William Henry Harrison*
Born: *February 9, 1773, Charles City County, Virginia*
Died: *April 4, 1841, Washington, D.C.*
Burial site: *William Henry Harrison Memorial State Park, North Bend, Ohio*
Parents: *Benjamin and Elizabeth Bassett Harrison*
Spouse: *Anna Tuthill Symmes (1775–1864; m. 1795)*
Children: *Elizabeth Bassett (1796–1846); John Cleves Symmes (1798–1830); Lucy Singleton (1800–1826); William Henry Jr. (1802–1838); John Scott (1804–1878); Benjamin (1806–1840); Mary Symmes (1809–1842); Carter Bassett (1811–1839); Anna Tuthill (1813–1865); James Findlay (1814–1819)*
Religion: *Episcopalian*
Education: *Attended Hampden-Sydney College and University of Pennsylvania Medical School*
Occupation: *Soldier*
Government positions: *secretary of the Northwest Territory; territorial delegate to U.S. Congress; territorial governor of Indiana; governor of Louisiana Territory; state senator from Ohio; U.S. congressman and senator from Ohio; minister to Colombia*
Political party: *Whig*
Dates as president: *March 4, 1841–April 4, 1841*
Age upon taking office: *68*

William Henry Harrison served as president for just one month before dying of pneumonia on April 4, 1841. There were some clues that he may have become a more independent president than anyone expected. But his inaugural address suggested that he would allow Congress to lead the nation for him, a scenario that members of his Whig party had been planning. The Whigs were a new political entity made up of different groups from within the former Democratic-Republican party who refused to join the followers of Andrew Jackson's Democrats.

Harrison is associated with a presidential campaign that introduced a manipulative element into American politics. His run for the presidency was a shrewdly managed campaign, with image counting far more than reality, with songs and slogans overwhelming discussion on issues, and with powerful figures behind the scenes holding the real power. Harrison was the Tippecanoe half of the famous political slogan, "Tippecanoe and Tyler Too," a nickname he earned for his victory over Native American warriors at the frontier Battle of Tippecanoe in 1811.

Harrison came from a wealthier background than his opponent, incumbent Martin Van Buren, but his handlers painted him in a different light to give him an image of humble beginnings. They believed this would appeal to voters who still longed for a man like Andrew

Timeline

1773: Born in Virginia

1791: Drops his studies in medicine in favor of becoming a soldier; leads group of eighty men from Philadelphia to protect settlers in the Northwest Territory (present-day Ohio)

1794: Cited for bravery in the Battle of Fallen Timbers, during which Native American forces are defeated by General Anthony Wayne

1798–1801: Serves as secretary of the Northwest Territory, and then territorial delegate to Congress

1801–12: Serves as territorial governor of Indiana

1811: Breaks Indian confederacy led by Shawnee Chief Tecumseh in the Battle of Tippecanoe in present-day Indiana

1813: After retaking Fort Detroit, which had been surrendered to the British in 1812, Brigadier General Harrison defeats an alliance of British and Native American forces in the Battle of the Thames in present-day Ontario, Canada

1816–19: Serves as U.S. congressman from Ohio

1819–21: Serves as Ohio state senator

1825–28: Serves as U.S. senator

1828: Named minister to Colombia by President John Quincy Adams; recalled in 1829 by President Andrew Jackson

1836: As one of four regional Whig candidates, Harrison wins seven states and seventy-three electoral votes in the presidential election but loses to Martin Van Buren

1841: Elected ninth U.S. president; one month later, becomes the first president to die in office

Jackson to lead them. He was portrayed during the 1840 presidential campaign as a small farmer who lived in a log cabin and preferred hard cider to Van Buren's taste for fine wines and champagne. Fermented apple juice was served by the barrel at Harrison campaign rallies, while aides handed out coonskin caps as symbols of his life as a frontiersman, and bands played noisy, high-spirited music. Harrison was urged by the Whig leaders to keep his pro-slavery and high-tariff views to himself. Meanwhile, those same leaders carefully planned legislation that would be enacted by a president who pledged to follow Congress.

The strategy of style over substance worked very well. Over 50 percent more eligible voters went to the polls in 1840 than had voted in 1836, and they favored Harrison, who won in a landslide in the Electoral College.

While he had been a man of few words during the campaign, Harrison delivered the longest inaugural address of any president on a March day that was frigid even by Washington standards. All the big plans he had promised for the Whig party were suddenly halted, however, when Harrison developed pneumonia a few days later. He died on April 4, just one month—to the day—into his presidency.

Frontiersman with an Aristocratic Past

William Henry Harrison was born on February 9, 1773, at his family estate, Berkeley Plantation, on the James River in Charles County, Virginia. Three years later, his father, Benjamin Harrison, was among the fifty-six men who signed the Declaration of Independence. Benjamin Harrison would later become governor of Virginia.

Harrison was privately tutored while he was growing up. He studied classical literature and history at Virginia's Hampden-Sydney College and, following his father's wishes, he went on to Richmond to study medicine, and he continued those studies at the University of Pennsylvania under Benjamin Rush, one of the most famous physicians of the day. When his father died in 1791, the eighteen-year-old Harrison decided to go his own way and gave up his medical studies. With the help of Senator Richard Henry Lee of Virginia, he was assigned to the First Infantry of the Regular Army.

Recruiting a group of eighty men, Harrison set out for the Northwest frontier—lands bordered by the Ohio River on the south and the Mississippi River on the west. They hiked to Fort Pitt (now Pittsburgh)

The British Are Coming

When William Henry Harrison was eight years old, a British force under General Benedict Arnold attacked the family's Virginia plantation, stealing the furniture, killing cattle, and making off with horses and slaves. The family had been warned in advance and escaped the attack themselves.

Above: Harrison attended the University of Pennsylvania medical school, but abandoned his quest of becoming a doctor to become a soldier.

from Philadelphia, and then traveled by boat to Fort Washington (now Cincinnati), where they had orders to defend settlers from Indian attack, for which they were paid two dollars a month.

Harrison and his troops came under the command of General "Mad Anthony" Wayne to take part in the Battle of Fallen Timbers near present-day Toledo, Ohio. Their victory against a coalition of Indian tribes, which earned a citation for bravery for Harrison, made it safe for more settlers to move into the region.

Harrison was named commander of Fort Washington soon afterward, and it was there that he met Anna Symmes, who would become his wife. Anna was the daughter of a judge who owned huge tracts of land in present-day Ohio and Indiana, but her father was not impressed with Harrison. He expected his daughter to marry a preacher or a farmer, and not a soldier, whose job was not only dangerous, but low-paying as well. However,

while Anna's father was away, the couple eloped and was married without his permission on November 22, 1795. Judge Symmes reluctantly accepted the inevitable a few weeks later, even if he didn't approve of his new son-in-law. The Harrisons would have ten children, and their fifth child, John Scott, would eventually become the father of Benjamin Harrison, the twenty-third U.S. president.

Harrison established a large farm he called Grouseland along the Ohio River a few miles southwest of Cincinnati, and he built a mill there. The house he built was a replica of the Virginia estate where he had been raised, and some of his neighbors worried that he might establish a plantation society, slaves and all, in the territory.

Harrison was appointed secretary of the newly created Northwest Territory in 1798, and he also represented the area as a delegate to Congress. The job required him to attend sessions of Congress as a representative of his

Below: Harrison made a name for himself as a military hero in the Northwest Territory.

The Next Generation

Harrison's oldest son, John Cleves Symmes Harrison, who had married the daughter of explorer Zebulon Pike, died leaving six children for his mother and father to raise. Another son, William Henry Harrison Jr., died at the age of thirty-five, and his children joined their grandparents' household, too. John Scott Harrison, the only man to be the son of a president and the father of another (Benjamin Harrison), lived to the age of seventy-three. His body was stolen by grave robbers and sold to the Ohio Medical College. Another of his sons, John Harrison, was in for a shocking surprise when he visited the school and found his father's body there.

Left: "The Prophet" Tenskwatawa.

Right: The battle of Tippecanoe where Harrison earned national attention.

territory, but did not afford him voting rights. He advised Congress to divide government land in the territory into small homestead lots that settlers could purchase cheaply, and Congress agreed. They also voted to split a section of the Northwest Territory to form the Indiana Territory, and Harrison became its first governor. The Indiana Territory was made up of present-day Indiana, Illinois, and Wisconsin, as well as parts of what are now Minnesota and Michigan.

As governor, Harrison was under orders from President Thomas Jefferson to acquire land from Native Americans through treaties, and to defend settlers as they passed into and through the territory.

"Indian Fighter"

Harrison followed the order and steadily acquired land for the federal government, although not always through negotiation. Sometimes he fought for it. In the Treaty of Fort Wayne, several of the tribes handed over a total of 3 million acres of land for annual payments that ranged from $200 to $5,000. Meanwhile, Harrison was not successful in negotiating with the powerful Shawnee chief Tecumseh and his brother Tenskwatawa, who was also known as "The Prophet." Tecumseh refused to give up land, but when he went away to meet with other

tribes that had allied with the Shawnees, Harrison moved in. He placed his troops at Tecumseh's stronghold at the meeting point of the Tippecanoe and Wabash rivers, and then invited the Prophet to a powwow.

Harrison's force of about a thousand men was attacked before dawn on November 7, 1811. Although they suffered losses, they managed to demolish the Indian village, known as Prophetstown, and effectively broke the confederation Tecumseh and his brother had put together. Indian raids continued after that, but reports of the Battle of Tippecanoe made Harrison a national hero and encouraged more people to settle in the region. Later in life, Harrison was nicknamed "Old Tippecanoe." But there were other battles to add to his legend.

His reputation grew even more during the War of 1812, between the United States and Britain. Harrison welcomed the war because he believed that British forces in Canada were selling guns to the Shawnees. After the surrender of Fort Detroit by General William Hull, Brigadier General Harrison led his troops to the Maumee

Tecumseh

The great Shawnee warrior Tecumseh was born around 1768. He participated in his first battle as a teenager, and throughout his life, battled to protect the Shawnee boundary on the Ohio River. He played an important role during an attack in present-day Kentucky, where the Indians killed all but one settler. Watching the lone survivor being tortured, Tecumseh denounced his tribesmen, saying that such practices dishonored a warrior. The incident led the Shawnee to abandon the practice, and Tecumseh learned that his speechmaking could be as effective as any weapon. He soon emerged as a tribal leader.

In the early 1790s, Tecumseh followed the Miami tribe's call to unite against the white men, and when the U.S. Army's general-in-chief "Mad Anthony" Wayne launched a devastating attack at Fallen Timbers on Ohio's Maumee River, Tecumseh was in the thick of the fight. The Americans lost only thirty-eight men, while Indian casualties were several hundred, including one of Tecumseh's brothers. The following spring, Wayne met with representatives from twelve different tribes who signed the Greenville Treaty, ceding to the United States the bulk of Ohio, part of Indiana, and Fort Detroit (in present-day Michigan) for a $10,000 annuity. Ironically, these tribes were relative newcomers themselves, having been driven west by colonists along the eastern seaboard.

Tecumseh had not attended the council, and he was furious with the chiefs for signing away the land. Refusing to abide by the treaty, he headed west to the Wabash River in Indiana with a group of warriors and became the leading hostile chief in the area. Tecumseh's vision for the future of the Indians began to materialize. His people had always lived without boundaries, fences, or border guards. The land had belonged to all Indians, each tribe respecting another's right to occupy it. Consequently, he reasoned, no tribe had the right to sign away another's land.

In 1805, Tecumseh's brother Laulewasika reportedly fell into a trance, during which he spoke with the supreme deity who revealed the path of action his Indian brothers must follow. Changing his name to Tenskwatawa ("the open door"), he named himself the Prophet and began preaching a return to the roots of Shawnee culture. He told his followers to renounce the white man's ways and give up the tools, clothing, weapons, and alcohol that would lead them to ruin. Tecumseh realized that his brother's preaching squared with his own ideals, and he used it as an opportunity to increase his force of warriors.

The brothers established a settlement known as Prophetstown on the west bank of the Tippecanoe River in present-day Indiana, which would become their home base, and Tecumseh began visiting tribes from Missouri to Florida, calling the local tribes to arms with his powerful oratory. Tecumseh's talk of an Indian confederacy impressed the warriors, and he gathered the support of the Sauk, Winnebago, Creek, Cherokee, and Seminole tribes. Two years after the founding of Prophetstown, 1,000 warriors were gathered there.

By the time Tecumseh returned from his journey, the governor of the Northwest Territory and superintendent of Indian Affairs, General William Henry Harrison, had persuaded the chiefs of the Delaware, Miami, and Potawatomi tribes to sign the Treaty of Fort Wayne, giving the United States 3 million acres of land. When word of The Prophet's growing influence among the previously divided tribes reached Harrison, he invited The Prophet to Vincennes, the territorial capital, to discuss the treaty.

Instead, Tecumseh pulled into Vincennes with a party of four hundred warriors, spreading terror through the settlement. On August 12, Harrison met with Tecumseh and forty of his braves. The chief explained that no Indian had the authority to sell land that had always belonged to all Indians, but Harrison's reply was dismissive. With Tecumseh's anger boiling over—and his warriors reaching for their clubs—guards were called in, and Tecumseh was sent back to his camp. Even though the meeting had gone badly, Harrison recognized the chief's impressive talents: He wrote, "The implicit obedience and respect which the followers of Tecumseh pay him is really astonishing and [. . .] bespeaks him as one of those uncommon geniuses, which spring up occasionally to produce revolutions."

Believing that war was imminent, Tecumseh set off a few months later with twenty-four warriors to organize the southern tribes for battle. Instructed to avoid contact with the enemy, Tenskwatawa was responsible for protecting Prophetstown while his brother was away. Harrison saw this as an opportunity, and taking advantage of Tecumseh's absence, he led his militia of a thousand men across the Fort Wayne Treaty line toward Prophetstown. Tenskwatawa ordered an immediate attack on Harrison's camp, but Harrison's men drove the Indians off in an historic defensive action that became known as the Battle of Tippecanoe. On November 8, 1811, the Americans reached Prophetstown, and when they found it deserted, they burned it to the ground. When Tecumseh came back, he found a discredited brother, a diminished group of followers, and charred rubble.

Tecumseh soon joined forces with the British in their fight against the Americans in the War of 1812, and he was given a regular commission as a brigadier general, an unusually high rank for a tribal leader. When he and his British allies captured Fort Detroit, they seemed to have saved Upper Canada for the British, but an American naval victory on Lake Erie opened up a passage to the fort, forcing the English troops to retreat, and leaving Tecumseh with no choice but to follow them into Canada.

Tecumseh was killed by a stray bullet just before a crucial battle along the Thames River in present-day Ontario, which Harrison's forces won. The so-called the Battle of the Thames effectively ended both Indian and British power in the Great Lakes region.

River, near the site of the Battle of Fallen Timbers, and then moved north to recapture Detroit after American naval forces took control of Lake Erie. Harrison's troops chased the retreating British soldiers and their Indian allies into Canada, and his pursuit culminated in the Battle of the Thames, named for a river in the southwestern part of present-day Ontario. There, Harrison's soldiers defeated the combined force on October 5, 1813. The defeat closed off the west to the British and effectively ended Native American power in the region. Tecumseh died in the battle.

Political Aspirations

About a year later, Harrison resigned his military commission at age forty-one and went back to his family farm at North Bend, Ohio, a town that had been established by his father-in-law. Harrison became a member of Christ Episcopal Church and a trustee of Cincinnati College, hoping it would all lead to a political career, but he achieved mixed results over the next twenty years.

He served as a congressman from 1816 to 1819 during the administration of James Monroe, whom Harrison lobbied unsuccessfully for such positions as secretary of state and minister to Russia. He was elected to Ohio's state senate in 1819, but he failed in bids for governor, representative, and senator before finally being elected to the U.S. Senate six years later.

Harrison was one of the few supporters of President John Quincy Adams, whose administration was largely ineffective because of opposition by political forces loyal to Andrew Jackson. He was named minister to Colombia in 1828, but Adams wasn't sure it was a good idea. He noted in his diary that Harrison had an "absolutely rabid" thirst for higher office.

By the time Harrison reached Colombia, however, Adams had lost the 1828 election to Andrew Jackson, and he was greeted with news that he was about to be recalled. He stayed on until the Adams administration ended, and in the meantime, he managed to make an enemy of Símon Bolívar, the popular South American revolutionary leader. Harrison had been under strict orders to remain neutral, but he openly sided with

The Prophet's Curse

When Harrison was nominated as one of the stable of Whig candidates in 1836, the Shawnee Prophet, whom he had defeated in the Battle of Tippecanoe, emerged again to put a curse on him. "Harrison will not win this year to be the Great Chief," he predicted, "but he may win next time. If he does ... he will not finish his term. He will die in office. [...] And when he does, you will remember my brother Tecumseh's death. You think that I have lost my powers. I who caused the sun to darken and red men to give up firewater. But I tell you, Harrison will die, and after him every Great Chief chosen every twenty years thereafter shall also die. When each one dies, let everyone remember the death of my people." An idle threat? Who knows? But the fact is, the twenty-year cycle of death played itself out with Harrison (1840), Lincoln (1860), Garfield (1880), McKinley (1900), Harding (1920), Franklin D. Roosevelt (1940), and Kennedy (1960). Only Ronald Reagan, elected in 1980, escaped the curse, though he was shot in an assassination attempt.

Bolívar's opponents, and his quick recall by Jackson probably saved him from being formally expelled.

Harrison went back to Indiana with little money, and he accepted a position as a courtroom clerk to support his family. Meanwhile, he started a grassroots political campaign in Indiana and Illinois, and it began to blossom when he went to an anniversary celebration of the Battle of Tippecanoe, where he was widely interviewed and praised for his heroism in the battle as well as at the Battle of the Thames. These accolades came at the time politicians were organizing themselves as the Whig party, in hopes of defeating Martin Van Buren, Andrew Jackson's handpicked successor for the presidency, in the 1836 election.

The Whigs decided to run four regional candidates, hoping that no candidate in the election—including Van Buren—would get the necessary number of electoral votes. In such an event, the Constitution mandates that the election should be decided in the House of Representatives, and the Whigs felt they had a better chance with that scenario than with a general election. Their candidates were Harrison of Ohio; U.S. representative Willie Person Mangum of North Carolina; U.S. senator Daniel Webster of Massachusetts; and U.S. senator Hugh Lawson White of Tennessee. The scheme failed. Van Buren won 170 electoral votes to 124 for all

Above: "Keep the ball rolling." A petition drive in the direction of the White House.

the Whig candidates combined (Harrison, 73; White, 26; Webster, 14; Mangum, 11). Harrison did well enough in winning seven states to impress the Whigs as a viable national candidate the next time around.

The Whig party didn't bother to draft a platform, but instead mounted a campaign featuring songs and colorful slogans, the most famous of which was "Tippecanoe and Tyler Too." In a response to a newspaper article suggesting that Harrison ought to go back to the frontier instead of to Washington, the Whigs began describing him as a small farmer who lived in a log cabin. They painted a picture of Van Buren as a drinker of champagne and fine wines, while their candidate enjoyed a glass of homemade hard

Old Tippecanoe

Harrison kept right on campaigning after the election, and he built a strong base of support among war veterans, which increased his standing in the Whig party even more, and he easily won the nomination at their 1839 convention to run against Van Buren. He was presented as a Westerner, a war hero, and an Indian fighter, and his running mate, Virginia speaker of the house John Tyler, was named to balance the ticket and appeal to Southern voters. Actually, both Harrison and Tyler had been raised in aristocratic families in the same county of Virginia.

Smile When You Say That

Right after Harrison's nomination, the Baltimore American published an editorial that said: "[...] Give him a barrel of hard cider and settle a pension of $2,000 a year on him and, my word for it, he will sit the remainder of his days in a log cabin by the side of a sea coal fire and study moral philosophy." It was intended to be a slur, but it was exactly the image the Whig bigwigs had been looking for to make their candidate the people's choice.

cider every now and then. The fermented apple juice was dispensed in teacups in the shape of log cabins at his campaign rallies, and coonskin hats, symbolic of his life on the frontier, were given to any potential voter willing to be seen wearing one. While bands played loud and long, Harrison, following the advice of Whig leaders, kept his speeches short and kept his pro-slavery views to himself. He won the election with a landslide in the Electoral College, taking 19 states and 234 votes to Van Buren's 7 states and 60 electoral votes.

"Let the use of pen and ink be wholly forbidden as though he were a mad poet in Bedlam."

—Whig campaign directive intended to ensure that their candidate wouldn't make any revealing statements

---

The Harrison Administration

Administration Dates: March 4, 1841–April 4, 1841
Vice President: John Tyler (1841)
Cabinet:

Secretary of State	Daniel Webster (1841)
Secretary of the Treasury	Thomas Ewing (1841)
Secretary of War	John Bell (1841)
Attorney General	John J. Crittenden (1841)
Secretary of the Navy	George E. Badger (1841)
Postmaster General	Francis Granger (1841)

Left: A campaign rally for Old Tippecanoe.

A Falling Off of Whigs

Harrison arranged a large party to accompany him to Washington, D.C. On the frigid day he took the oath of office, he gave the longest inauguration speech ever made, even though Henry Clay, one of the Whig power brokers, had cut it down. He bragged that he had removed most of the references to Roman history and literature. Clay and Daniel Webster had ordered Harrison to emphasize his intention to follow the lead of Congress, because they were eager to enact policies they had been fighting for with no success during the administrations of Jackson and Van Buren.

Later that March, however, Harrison fell gravely ill. When he died on April 4, 1841, he was the first president to die in office. After a hastily arranged state funeral, his body was returned for burial in North Bend, Ohio.

Legacy

William Henry Harrison's death touched off a Constitutional crisis. The Constitution had not specifically addressed any means of succession, and there was no standard method for determining who would take on the chief executive's duties if a president wasn't able to serve for any reason. It was expected that Vice President Tyler would serve as a temporary president until

Busy Month

President Harrison didn't fall ill until a couple of weeks into his administration. He insisted on doing his own grocery shopping, and on one of those trips to buy the makings of breakfast, he was caught in a sudden downpour, which led to the cold that eventually took his life. His last days were filled with fending off job-seekers following the time-honored spoils system. He managed to cut down on the number of available jobs by decreeing that no officeholder could be removed except for incompetence, but still the office-seekers kept coming. When he was delirious in a coma, he muttered over and over, "These applications, will they ever cease?"

1840 Election Results

Presidential / Vice Presidential Candidates	Popular Votes	Electoral Votes
William Henry Harrison / John Tyler (Whig)	1,275,016	234
Martin Van Buren / Richard M. Johnson (Democratic)	1,129,102	60

Above: Harrison was the first American president to die in office. His term lasted just one month.

of the country. Harrison had been nominated as a man Whig leaders believed they could easily manipulate, but he still seemed to have had some fight left in him before he died.

Congress could decide on a course of action and naming a successor. But while everyone else was debating, Tyler had himself sworn into office and began performing presidential duties as if nothing unusual had happened.

Tyler surprised the Whigs by challenging the legislation they had expected to breeze through the Harrison administration. Instead of a president who could be influenced by Clay and Webster to rubber stamp their agenda passed by Congress, they met with resistance from Tyler. The relationship between Congress and the presidency quickly deteriorated, making both Tyler and the Whigs ineffective.

The situation marked the beginning of the end of the Whig party. They would win another election with another military hero, Zachary Taylor, as their candidate in 1848. But Taylor, like Tyler, proved to be his own man. And, like Harrison, Taylor, too, died shortly after taking office. His vice president, Millard Fillmore, wasn't an effective leader either, and the Whig party dissolved shortly after he left office. Abolitionists among the Whigs turned to the Republican party, which was formed in 1854.

It is impossible to determine how Harrison might have fared as president. Shortly after his election, he indicated to Henry Clay that he was going to refuse to be dominated. Daniel Webster was named secretary of state, and other cabinet posts went to respected and independent Whig politicians representing various sections

IN MEMORY OF

PRESIDENT WM. H. HARRISON, WHO DEPARTED THIS LIFE, APRIL 4, 1841, AGED 68,

Deeply lamented by 16 Millions of people.

Left: While 16 million mourned, one man, Vice President John Tyler, swiftly engineered his own succession even though his Constitutional authority was unclear.

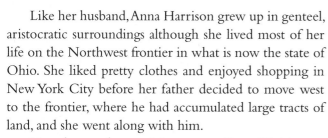

Anna Harrison

Born July 25, 1775, Flatbrook, New Jersey
Died February 25, 1864, North Bend, Ohio

"I wish that my husband's friends had left him where he is, happy and contented in retirement."

—*Anna Harrison*

Like her husband, Anna Harrison grew up in genteel, aristocratic surroundings although she lived most of her life on the Northwest frontier in what is now the state of Ohio. She liked pretty clothes and enjoyed shopping in New York City before her father decided to move west to the frontier, where he had accumulated large tracts of land, and she went along with him.

Not long after arriving near Fort Washington (present-day Cincinnati), Anna met and eloped with William Henry Harrison. She became a strong frontier woman, bearing ten children. She often served as a teacher for them and for other local children, since few teachers had made their way that far west.

Anna Harrison was sixty-five at the time her husband was elected president, and she was not pleased about his new job. "I wish that my husband's friends had left him where he is, happy and contented in retirement," she said. Anna was ill when the time came to set out to Washington, D.C., for her husband's inauguration in early March of 1841, and her doctor advised her not to make the trip. She planned instead to join her husband in May, when the weather was warmer.

Anna never made that trip. Shortly after his March 4 inauguration, William Henry Harrison fell ill with a cold that quickly turned to pneumonia, and he died on April 4, 1841. Instead of going to Washington, Anna Harrison waited at home for her husband's body to be returned for burial in the area they had called home for almost fifty years.

Snuck through Enemy Lines

Anna Tuthill Symmes was born in Flatbrook, New Jersey, in 1775. Her father, John Cleve Symmes, was a judge who served in the American Revolution as a colonel in the Continental Army. Anna was four when her mother died, and her father wanted to take her to Long Island to be cared for by her grandparents while he continued fighting. Unfortunately, they had to cross through British-occupied territory in order to reach Long Island. He disguised himself as a British redcoat and managed to pass through with his daughter in his arms to deliver her safely to her grandparents. Then he went back to war.

Anna received a fine education growing up in New York. At nineteen, just as she was getting used to the pleasures of city living, her father decided to move west. Anna went with him across the Allegheny Mountains of Pennsylvania and into the Northwest Territory, where they reached Fort Washington, and then they continued on a few more miles southwest along the Ohio River to establish an estate and a town that her father named North Bend.

Anna met William Henry Harrison not long afterward. He had recently returned to Fort Washington as commander after having left to serve with General "Mad Anthony" Wayne at the Battle of Fallen Timbers in 1794. Harrison was cited for bravery in that decisive battle, in which American forces defeated an alliance of Native

Left: General "Mad Anthony" Wayne.

American tribes. Only three years earlier, Harrison had been studying medicine in Philadelphia, but he decided on a military career on the wild frontier instead.

Anna and William Henry soon began a romance, but her father disapproved of her dating a military man. Soldiering was not only a dangerous profession, but the pay was poor. While her father was away on a November day in 1795, however, the couple ran away to be secretly married by a justice of the peace, later settling in Fort Washington before establishing a farm near her father's estate. By that time, John Symmes had resigned himself to the idea that his daughter had married a soldier instead of a farmer or a preacher.

Except for occasional trips, Anna stayed at North Bend for most of her life. She and her husband once traveled to Virginia so her husband could show her the plantation where he had been raised. It must have looked familiar to her, since Harrison modeled their home on the one he grew up in.

Often on Her Own

For the first twenty years of their marriage, Anna was frequently at home in North Bend without her husband for extended periods. He traveled to Philadelphia, where Congress met in those days, to represent the Northwest Territory from 1799 to 1801, and he was also often away on military excursions, including the ones involving his famous victories in the Battle of Tippecanoe in 1811 and the Battle of the Thames two years later.

Anna, meanwhile, was busy raising her family. Harrison resigned from the army and went back home in 1815, after which the couple often invited all the members of their church to barbecues at their farm, and a steady stream of visitors stayed at their home as well.

But Harrison left home again, this time as a politician. He served as a congressman from 1816 through 1819, and after returning home for about five years, he was elected to the U.S. Senate in 1825, an office he held for three years before he was appointed minister to Colombia. He made the long journey there only to be recalled in 1829 by the newly elected president Andrew Jackson.

Finally, when Harrison went home in 1830 at age fifty-seven, he and Anna could look forward to retiring together. Although he took a minor court job to help earn extra money, they were able to be together on their farm. Only two of their ten children, however, had lived to adulthood, and it had been a long and often difficult life on the frontier. But the Harrisons had each proved to have the hardiness they needed to survive.

Politically Active Again

Harrison had remained a popular figure in the area for his military exploits. He attended anniversaries of his famous battle at Tippecanoe and was a celebrity in the ever-growing number of small towns dotting the former frontier. The appearances he made celebrating his past gradually turned to opportunities for running for high office. He was such a beloved figure that Whig party members placed him on their ballot in Western states as a candidate for president in 1836. He finished so well that he was nominated as the national Whig candidate in 1840.

Anna supported her sixty-six-year-old husband on his last campaign, although grudgingly. She thought it would be better for him to enjoy a quiet retirement, but "Pah," as she called him, was swept into office on a wave of popularity.

When Harrison left for Washington, Anna stayed home nursing an ailment. It was the last time she saw him alive; he died from pneumonia a month after taking office. Jane Irwin Harrison, widow of the Harrisons' son William, accompanied the new president to act as hostess until Anna's scheduled arrival in May. Instead, Anna received word of his death at about the time she had started packing for her journey to the nation's capital. She waited at home for his body to arrive, then saw to his burial on the land where they had lived for almost fifty years.

Above: The inauguration of William Henry Harrison.

Anna remained at her home in North Bend until the house burned down in 1858, when she was eighty-three years old. She then moved to the nearby farm of her last surviving child, John Scott Harrison, and she helped deliver one of John's sons into the world. That boy, Benjamin Harrison, was fighting in the Civil War when she died in February of 1864 at the age of eighty-eight. He would later become president of the United States.

Harrison's Inaugural Address

Delivered on March 4, 1841

William Henry Harrison rode into the presidency on a wave of popularity stemming from his legendary military career and a colorful campaign. Aged sixty-eight at his inaugural, he was the nation's oldest president until sixty-nine-year-old Ronald Reagan took office 140 years later. Harrison gave his inaugural address—the longest of any president—outdoors on a bitter cold day. He dressed lightly for the occasion, probably to show his hardiness. Within a few days, he caught a cold that soon developed into pneumonia and killed him.

Though he had very little time to act upon what he put forward in his address, the speech remains significant as a statement on limited presidential authority. Harrison indicated that he generally planned to follow the lead of Congress. Two powerful congressmen of his Whig party—Daniel Webster and Henry Clay—edited and contributed to the speech, doubtlessly influencing the president's modest approach to office. While Harrison may well have gone on to act in a more independent and forceful manner than he indicated in the speech, his inaugural address stands as a clear call for limiting presidential authority.

Excerpt from President Harrison's Inaugural Address

When the Constitution of the United States first came from the hands of the Convention which formed it, many of the sternest republicans of the day were alarmed at the extent of the power which had been granted to the Federal Government, and more particularly of that portion which had been assigned to the executive branch. There were in it features which appeared not to be in harmony with their ideas of a simple representative democracy or republic, and knowing the tendency of power to increase itself, particularly when exercised by a single individual, predictions were made that at no very remote period the Government would terminate in virtual monarchy. It would not become me to say that the fears of these patriots have been already realized; but as I sincerely believe that the tendency of measures and of men's opinions for some years past has been in that direction, it is, I conceive, strictly proper that I should take this occasion to repeat the assurances I have heretofore given of my determination to arrest the progress of that tendency if it really exists and restore the Government to its pristine health and vigor, as far as this can be effected by any legitimate exercise of the power placed in my hands.

I proceed to state in as summary a manner as I can my opinion of the sources of the evils which have been so extensively complained of and the correctives which may be applied. Some of the former are unquestionably to be found in the defects of the Constitution; others, in my judgment, are attributable to a misconstruction of some of its provisions. Of the former is the eligibility of the same individual to a second term of the Presidency. The sagacious mind of [former president] Mr. [Thomas] Jefferson early saw and lamented this error, and attempts have been made, hitherto without success, to apply the amendatory power of the States to its correction. As, however, one mode of correction is in the power of every President, and consequently in mine, it would be useless, and perhaps invidious, to enumerate the evils of which, in the opinion of many of our fellow-citizens, this error of the sages who framed the Constitution may have been the source and the bitter fruits which we are still to gather from it if it continues to disfigure our system. It may be observed, however, as a general remark, that republics can commit no greater error than to adopt or continue any feature in their systems of government which may be calculated to create or increase the lover of power in the bosoms of those to whom necessity obliges them to commit the management of their affairs; and surely nothing is more likely to produce such a state of mind than the long continuance of an office of high trust. Nothing can be more corrupting, nothing more destructive of all those noble feelings which belong to the character of a devoted republican patriot. When this corrupting passion once takes possession of the human mind, like the love of gold it becomes insatiable. It is the never-dying worm in his bosom, grows with his growth and strengthens with the declining years of its victim. If this is true, it is the part of wisdom for a republic to limit the service of that officer at least to whom she has intrusted the management of her foreign relations, the execution of her laws, and the command of her armies and navies to a period so short as to prevent his forgetting that he is the accountable agent, not the principal; the servant, not the master. Until an amendment of the Constitution can be effected public opinion may secure the desired object. I give my aid to it by renewing the pledge heretofore given that under no circumstances will I consent to serve a second term.

[. . .]

It may be said, indeed, that the Constitution has given to the Executive the power to annul the acts of the legislative body by refusing to them his assent. So a similar power has necessarily resulted from that instrument to the judiciary, and yet the judiciary forms no part of the Legislature. There is, it is true, this difference between these grants of power: The Executive can put his negative upon the acts of the Legislature for other cause than that of want of conformity to the Constitution, whilst the judiciary can only declare void those which violate that instrument. But the decision of the judiciary is final in such a case, whereas in every instance where the veto of the Executive is applied it may be overcome by a vote of two-thirds of both Houses of Congress. The negative upon the acts of the legislative by the executive authority, and that in the hands of one individual, would seem to be an incongruity in our system. Like some others of a similar character, however, it appears to be highly expedient, and if used only with the forbearance and in the spirit which was intended by its authors it may be productive of great good and be found one of the best safeguards to the Union. At the period of the formation of the Constitution the principle does not appear to have enjoyed much favor in the State governments. It existed but in two, and in one of these there was a plural executive. If we would search for the motives which operated upon the purely patriotic and enlightened assembly which framed the Constitution for the adoption of a provision so apparently repugnant to the leading democratic principle that the majority should govern, we must reject the idea that they anticipated from it any benefit to the ordinary course of legislation. They knew too well the high degree of intelligence which existed among the people and the enlightened character of the State legislatures not to have the fullest confidence that the two bodies elected by them would be worthy representatives of such constituents, and, of course, that they would require no aid in conceiving and maturing the measures which the circumstances of the country might require. And it is preposterous to suppose that a thought could for a moment have been entertained that the President, placed at the capital, in the center of the country, could better understand the wants and wishes of the people than their own immediate representatives, who spend a part of every year among them, living with them, often laboring with them, and bound to them by the triple tie of interest, duty, and affection. To assist or control Congress, then, in its ordinary legislation could not, I conceive, have been the motive for conferring the veto power on the President. This argument acquires additional force from the fact of its never having been thus used by the first six Presidents—and two of them were members of the Convention, one presiding over its deliberations and the other bearing a larger share in consummating the labors of that august body than any other person. But if bills were never returned to Congress by either of the Presidents above referred to upon the ground of their being inexpedient or not as well adapted as they might be to the wants of the people, the veto was applied upon that of want of conformity to the Constitution or because errors had been committed from a too hasty enactment.

There is another ground for the adoption of the veto principle, which had probably more influence in recommending it to the Convention than any other. I refer to the security which it gives to the just and equitable action of the Legislature upon all parts of the Union. It could not but have occurred to the

Convention that in a country so extensive, embracing so great a variety of soil and climate, and consequently of products, and which from the same causes must ever exhibit a great difference in the amount of the population of its various sections, calling for a great diversity in the employments of the people, that the legislation of the majority might not always justly regard the rights and interests of the minority, and that acts of this character might be passed under an express grant by the words of the Constitution, and therefore not within the competency of the judiciary to declare void; that however enlightened and patriotic they might suppose from past experience the members of Congress might be, and however largely partaking, in the general, of the liberal feelings of the people, it was impossible to expect that bodies so constituted should not sometimes be controlled by local interests and sectional feelings. It was proper, therefore, to provide some umpire from whose situation and mode of appointment more independence and freedom from such influences might be expected. Such a one was afforded by the executive department constituted by the Constitution. A person elected to that high office, having his constituents in every section, State, and subdivision of the Union, must consider himself bound by the most solemn sanctions to guard, protect, and defend the rights of all and of every portion, great or small, from the injustice and oppression of the rest. I consider the veto power, therefore, given by the Constitution to the Executive of the United States solely as a conservative power, to be used only first, to protect the Constitution from violation; secondly, the people from the effects of hasty legislation where their will has been probably disregarded or not well understood, and, thirdly, to prevent the effects of combinations violative of the rights of minorities. In reference to the second of these objects I may observe that I consider it the right and privilege of the people to decide disputed points of the Constitution arising from the general grant of power to Congress to carry into effect the powers expressly given; and I believe with [former president] Mr. [James] Madison that "repeated recognitions under varied circumstances in acts of the legislative, executive, and judicial branches of the Government, accompanied by indications in different modes of the concurrence of the general will of the nation," as affording to the President sufficient authority for his considering such disputed points as settled.

What Happened Next

Harrison died within a month, becoming the first president who did not serve an entire term. Vice President John Tyler of Virginia had been chosen as his running mate primarily for regional balance, since Harrison was best known in the western part (the present-day Midwest) of the United States. Tyler proved to be a much more independent leader. Plans that Daniel Webster and Henry Clay had for running their programs quickly through the Harrison administration were soon roadblocked by Tyler. Upsetting the leaders of his own party was one of many factors that made Tyler an ineffective president. He served only the remainder of Harrison's term.

The history of the United States during the 1840s would have been different had Harrison lived. The Whig party may have come to dominate American politics in the way that Jacksonian Democrats had from 1828 to 1840. Instead, a Democrat, James K. Polk was elected president in 1844, and the Whig party faded by the early 1850s. Daniel Webster served as Tyler's secretary of state but he resigned before the end of the term, and Clay was defeated by Polk in the presidential election of 1844. With the exception of Abraham Lincoln, who served from 1861 to 1865, a series of presidents from 1852 through 1884 were generally dominated by Congress. If Andrew Jackson had been powerful to the point of being dangerous, as Harrison implied in his inaugural address, so, too, history shows, it is equally dangerous when Congress dominates the executive branch.

After getting an authorization from the war department in Washington, William Henry Harrison, the territorial governor of Indiana, led 300 regular army troops and 650 militiamen against the Indian confederation led by the Shawnee chief Tecumseh, and his brother, who was known as the Prophet. They camped along the Tippecanoe River, and were still in their tents on the morning of November 7, 1811, when more than 600 Indian warriors attacked. They had been told by the Prophet that his magic made the white men's guns unable to harm them, and they stormed the camp with unusual ferocity. Although they were completely surprised, Harrison rallied his troops, and after more than two hours of hand-to-hand fighting, they managed to push the invaders back. Casualties were less than 200 on each side. Harrison went on to destroy the Indian village, known as Prophetstown, totally demoralizing the Native Americans who survived. Before he left the battlefield, Harrison wrote the following report to the secretary of war.

Headquarters
Near the Prophets Town
Nov. 8th, 1811

Sir

I have the honor to inform you that the dawn of yesterday terminated an action between the troops under my command and the whole of the Prophet's force—their precipate retreat leaving a number of the warrior dead on the field and the subsequent abandonment of their Town (which was partially fortified) attest for us a complete and decisive victory. It has however been dearly purchased—a number of brave and valuable men have fallen victims to their zeal for their country's service.

The behavior of both regulars and militia troops was such as would have done honor to veterans. I arrived at my XX position (a mile from the Town) on the evening of the sixth instant. A correspondence was immediately opened with the Prophet and there was every appearance of a successful termination of the expedition without bloodshed. Indeed there was an agreement for a suspension of hostilities until a further communication should take place on the next day. Contrary however to this engagement he attacked me at half past four o'clock in the morning so suddenly that the Indians were in the camp before many of the men could get out of their tents. A little confusion for a short time prevailed, but aided by the great exertions of the officers I was soon enabled to form the men in order. The companies which were hard pressed were supported. Several successful charges made and about daylight the enemy were finally put to flight after having penetrated to and killed men in the very center of our camp.

Our killed and wounded amount to 179 of these 42 are now dead and seven or eight more will certainly die. I believe that the Prophet's force is so entirely routed that he will not be able to collect a sufficient number to harrass us on our return. But should this be the case it may be in his power encumbered as we are with the wounded to do us considerable injury. We are moreover XX of every article of provision excepting the corn (which we have taken) and about four days XX of flour at the short allowance of 3/4 of a pound per diem. Indeed the army have drawn no more then this for three weeks and all our beef cattle broke from us the night of the action and were dispersed and driven off by the Indians. You may rest assured Sir that I shall make every exertion in my power to conduct the Troops in safety to the settlements. I have not been able to ascertain the number of Indians in the action —it must however been considerable. The principal chief of those Potawatimies who have joined the Prophet is wounded and in our possession. I have taken care of him and shall send him back to his tribe. At a more leasure [sic] moment I shall do myself the honor to transmit a more particular account of the action and of our previous movements and am with the highest respect

Sir your
Hbl Svt

William Henry Harrison

The Honorable William Eustis
Secretary of War

John Tyler

Tenth president of the United States, 1841–1845

Full name: John Tyler
Born: March 29, 1790, Greenway, Virginia
Died: January 18, 1862, Richmond, Virginia
Burial site: Hollywood Cemetery, Richmond, Virginia
Parents: John and Mary Marot Armistead Tyler
Spouse: Letitia Christian (1790–1842; m. 1813);
    Julia Gardiner (1820–1889; m. 1844)
Children: Mary (1815–1848); Robert (1816–1877); John
    (1819–1896); Letitia (1821–1907); Elizabeth (1823–
    1850); Ann Contesse (1825–1825); Alice (1827–1854);
    Tazewell (1830–1874); David Gardiner (1846–1927);
    John Alexander (1848–1883); Julia Gardiner (1849–1871);
    Lachlan (1851–1902); Lyon Gardiner (1853–1935); Robert
    Fitzwalter (1856–1927); Pearl (1860–1947)
Religion: Episcopalian
Education: College of William and Mary (1807)
Occupation: Lawyer
Government positions: Virginia house delegate; U.S. representative
    and senator from Virginia; Virginia governor; vice president
    under William Henry Harrison; elected as Confederate States
    congressman (died before term began)
Political party: Whig
Dates as president: April 4, 1841–March 4, 1845
Age upon taking office: 51

"I represent the executive authority of the people of the United States and it is in their name ... that I protest against every attempt to break down the undoubted constitutional power of this department without a solemn amendment of that fundamental law."

—*John Tyler*

The two most notable events of John Tyler's presidency happened at the very beginning and at the very end of his term. In between, the Tyler administration was rendered largely ineffective by a hostile Congress and a lack of popular support. Indeed, during his presidency Tyler was ostracized from his own party, endured the resignation of his cabinet, and faced a vote of impeachment. But he weathered those storms with the same dignity and good humor that he displayed throughout his political career.

He had always been a strict constructionist, believing in literal interpretations of the Constitution, which is a difficult position to hold if the Constitution is not clear about an issue. Regarding the two major events of his presidency that had lasting significance, he did not respond as a constructionist. Instead, he applied his own interpretation to matters the Constitution had not specifically addressed.

The first event involved the manner in which Tyler became president. He was the first vice president to assume the nation's highest office following the death of the president. William Henry Harrison died from pneumonia just thirty-one days into his presidency. Vice President Tyler became acting president, but the Constitution wasn't clear about what should happen next. It stated only that if a president is removed from

Timeline

1790: Born in Virginia
1807: Graduates from the College of William and Mary
1811–16: Serves in Virginia House of Delegates
1817–21: Serves in U.S. House of Representatives
1823: Elected to Virginia state legislature
1825–26: Serves as governor of Virginia
1827–36: Serves in U.S. Senate
1838–40: Member of the Virginia House of Delegates as Speaker
1839: Loses Virginia gubernatorial election
1841: Serves as vice president under William Henry Harrison for thirty-one days; becomes president following Harrison's death
1841–45: Serves as tenth U.S. president
1845: Signs the Congressional Resolution annexing Texas
1861: Elected to Confederate States Congress
1862: Dies in Virginia

office, dies, resigns, or is unable to discharge his duties, the office "will devolve on the vice president." It does not specifically state whether the vice president will complete the full term of the elected president or just serve temporarily until a new election can be held.

Most legislators assumed that Congress would convene to debate the question while Tyler served as interim president. But Tyler had himself sworn in as the new president and started carrying out the duties of the office without waiting for Congress to weigh in on the matter. Many congressmen and a fair portion of the public were outraged by this act, but Tyler just ignored them. As president, he immediately followed his constructionist principles by challenging major pieces of legislation proposed and passed by his own Whig party, which made the rest of his term acrimonious as his fellow Whigs fought him at every turn.

Tyler's last official act as president was to sign a bill annexing Texas as a state. The Republic of Texas had ceded from Mexico, but many congressmen were unwilling to admit the territory because it would add another slave state to the Union.

Annexation had failed twice in Senate ratification votes, and Tyler decided to sidestep the normal treaty procedure, which calls for a two-thirds majority in the Senate. Instead of presenting the act as a treaty, he introduced the annexation of Texas as a joint resolution of Congress, which requires only a simple majority of votes in both houses to be accepted. His resolution passed the House easily and it squeaked through the Senate by the slimmest of margins—twenty-seven votes to twenty-five. Many were outraged, once again, but not having run for another term as president, the lame duck Tyler simply went about serving the final two days of his administration and then retired to his Virginia plantation.

Aristocratic Background

John Tyler was born on March 29, 1790, on his family's Greenway Plantation along the James River in the Charles City County area of Virginia where his father, John, was a judge. He attended local schools until he was twelve, when he entered the preparatory school of the College of William and Mary. He moved on to the college after completing preparatory school and graduated in 1807. Tyler went home to study law in Charles City County, first with his father, then with a cousin, Samuel Tyler. These men and Tyler's grandfather influenced his agricultural and constructionist values, as did the philosophy of fellow Virginian Thomas Jefferson, who was then president.

Tyler passed the state's bar exam in 1809, the same year his father was elected governor of Virginia. Tyler moved with his father to the state capital in Richmond and began practicing law there with Edmund Jennings Randolph, a respected statesman and a former Virginia governor, U.S. attorney general, and U.S. secretary of state. Tyler was elected to the Virginia legislature with Randolph's support, and he later joined the Virginia militia during the War of 1812, although he didn't see any action. In 1813, he married Letitia Christian, who came from a wealthy Virginia family. They would have eight children together.

John Tyler was elected to the U.S. House of Representatives three years later, but although he distinguished himself as a Constitutional constructionist, Tyler's tenure in the House couldn't be called successful. He resigned in frustration in 1821. He was associated

Presidential Succession

The original wording of the Constitution regarding who should succeed a president unable to complete his term was vague enough to spur controversy in 1841. This is an excerpt from Article II of the Constitution describing what should happen if a president is unable to fulfill his duties.

From Article II of the Constitution

In Case of the Removal of the President from Office, or of his Death, Resignation, or Inability to discharge the Powers and Duties of the said Office, the Same shall devolve on the Vice President, and the Congress may by Law provide for the Case of Removal, Death, Resignation or Inability, both of the President and Vice President, declaring what Officer shall then act as President, and such Officer shall act accordingly, until the Disability be removed, or a President shall be elected.

Excerpt from Amendment 25

Ratified February 10, 1967. The Constitution was amended to clarify the line of succession further.

SECTION 1. In case of the removal of the President from office or of his death or resignation, the Vice President shall become President.

SECTION 2. Whenever there is a vacancy in the office of the Vice President, the President shall nominate a Vice President who shall take office upon confirmation by a majority vote of both Houses of Congress.

SECTION 3. Whenever the President transmits to the President pro tempore of the Senate and the Speaker of the House of Representatives his written declaration that he is unable to discharge the powers and duties of his office, and until he transmits to them a written declaration to the contrary, such powers and duties shall be discharged by the Vice President as Acting President.

SECTION 4. Whenever the Vice President and a majority of either the principal officers of the executive departments or of such other body as Congress may by law provide, transmit to the President pro tempore of the Senate and the Speaker of the House of Representatives their written declaration that the President is unable to discharge the powers and duties of his office, the Vice President shall immediately assume the powers and duties of the office as Acting President.

Thereafter, when the President transmits to the President pro tempore of the Senate and the Speaker of the House of Representatives his written declaration that no inability exists, he shall resume the powers and duties of his office unless the Vice President and a majority of either the principal officers of the executive department or of such other body as Congress may by law provide, transmit within four days to the President pro tempore of the Senate and the Speaker of the House of Representatives their written declaration that the President is unable to discharge the powers and duties of his office. Thereupon Congress shall decide the issue, assembling within forty-eight hours for that purpose if not in session. If the Congress, within twenty-one days after receipt of the latter written declaration, or, if Congress is not in session, within twenty-one days after Congress is required to assemble, determines by two-thirds vote of both Houses that the President is unable to discharge the powers and duties of his office, the Vice President shall continue to discharge the same as Acting President; otherwise, the President shall resume the powers and duties of his office.

---

with the landed aristocracy all of his life, but times were changing toward a greater participation of the common people. The War of 1812 had helped to inspire a wave of nationalism and desire for a strong federal government. Tyler, however, still maintained his belief in limited federal power in favor of states' rights, but he wasn't successful in opposing what he felt were federal intrusions on the states, specifically in three major measures: protective tariffs; the rechartering of the federal bank; and the Missouri Compromise, which drew a geographic line between new states, allowing or forbidding slavery.

Tyler quickly restarted his political career after he went home to Virginia. He was elected to the Virginia legislature in 1823, to the governorship in 1825, and to the U.S. Senate in 1826. As a senator, he immediately became an outspoken opponent of the nationalist policies of President John Quincy Adams, actively opposing bills that mandated federal spending for improving roads and bridges and other infrastructure. He also spoke out against national laws that regulated commerce and agriculture, and he found a like-minded advocate for states' rights in Andrew Jackson, whom he backed for president in 1828.

Although Tyler shared Jackson's philosophical views, he was troubled by what he believed were his excessive uses of federal powers as president. After helping the Jackson forces deny the rechartering of the second national bank, Tyler broke his alliance with the president when Jackson removed government funds from the bank,

Above: Edmund Randolph, Tyler's political mentor.

a move Tyler believed was unconstitutional.

Another break occurred as a result of a tariff that adversely affected the economy of the South. The state of South Carolina threatened to secede from the Union because of the tax on imports. Jackson threatened to meet the threat with federal force, but Tyler stuck to his principles on states' rights and defended South Carolina's actions.

By 1836, when Jackson was reelected, Tyler had become a member of the newly formed Whig party, a diverse collection of politicians loosely linked by their support for states' rights and their opposition to Jackson. He even appeared as a vice presidential candidate on the ballots of two states in the 1836 presidential election. Tyler's dislike of Jackson ran deep. When he became the first (and only) president to be censured by Congress, a result of his seizing the funds of the second national bank, Congress began debating whether or not to erase the censure from the congressional record. Tyler was ordered by a proclamation of the Virginia legislature to vote for

removal of the censure, but he resigned his seat rather than obey it.

Tyler, Too!

Tyler again found himself at home after a frustrating time in Washington. However, not all of his problems were political. His wife, Letitia, had suffered a stroke that left her in need of constant care. Then, in 1839, he was defeated in a bid to reclaim his Senate seat.

The following year, however, he was back on the national scene again. The Whig party had nominated sixty-seven-year-old William Henry Harrison for the 1840 presidential election. He had long been popular in the North and the West, dating back thirty years. As a general, he led American troops to victory over Native Americans in the Battle of Tippecanoe. To round out national support for their candidate, the party chose Tyler, who continued to have strong political recognition in the South. The ticket inspired the famous slogan, "Tippecanoe and Tyler Too," which gave him even more name recognition.

The colorful slogan reflected the substance of the Whig campaign. Songs, slogans, parades, and other kinds of hoopla were emphasized over discussion on the issues of the day. In fact, the Whig party did not even present a political platform that might bring those issues into the daylight. Harrison was a popular, grandfatherly figure, and Tyler was handsome and statesmanlike. The candidates had rarely met before they were paired on the ticket, but they formed a solid front providing cover for Whig leaders scheming to advance their own questionable programs. Following Harrison's victory, Whig leaders Henry Clay and Daniel Webster handpicked nearly all of the members of the new cabinet. They also edited portions of the new president's first speech, his inaugural address—specifically those passages announcing his plans to follow the lead of Congress in running the country. But everything changed when Harrison died thirty-one days after taking office.

The Tyler Administration

Administration Dates: April 4, 1841–March 4, 1845
Vice President: None
Cabinet:

Secretary of State	Daniel Webster (1841–43)
	Abel P. Upshur (1843–44)
	John C. Calhoun (1844–45)
Secretary of the Treasury	Thomas Ewing (1841)
	Walter Forward (1841–43)
	John C. Spencer (1843–44)
	George M. Bibb (1844–45)
Secretary of War	John Bell (1841)
	John C. Spencer (1841–43)
	James M. Porter (1843–44)
	William Wilkins (1844–45)
Attorney General	John J. Crittenden (1841)
	Hugh S. Legaré (1841–43)
	John Nelson (1843–45)
Secretary of the Navy	George E. Badger (1841)
	Abel P. Upshur (1841–43)
	David Henshaw (1843–44)
	Thomas Walker Gilmer (1844)
	John Y. Mason (1844–45)
Postmaster General	Francis Granger (1841)
	Charles A. Wickliffe (1841–45)

The Old Plantation

The 1,600-acre estate John Tyler bought is still in the Tyler family, unusual for presidential homes, and it is still a working farm as it has been since the place he called Sherwood Forest was established in 1730. The family members who live there now share it with the ghost of a women they call the "Gray Lady," who often appears in the sitting room by way of a secret staircase and rocks the night away in a phantom rocking chair. Some say it might be the shade of Julia Tyler, but the lady isn't talking.

"His Accidency"

John Tyler was not even in Washington at the time of Harrison's death. But he arrived shortly thereafter and began to perform the duties of president even before Congress could begin serious debate on how to proceed in naming a new president. The Constitution was not clear on the exact manner of succession. On April 6, Tyler decided the issue for them, and had himself sworn into office, an action that led to a great deal of political and some public outcry. In spite of the protests, the deed was done, and it eventually set the precedent for the mode of succession through the history of the American presidency.

"I am the president and I shall be held responsible for my Administration. I shall be pleased to accept your counsel and advice. But I can never consent being dictated to. …When you think otherwise, your resignations will be accepted."

—John Tyler to his cabinet

Tyler was popular among the voters, but not with the politicians. He had been an outspoken opponent of the Democratic party through the 1830s. He joined the Whig party to oppose Democrats, even though he didn't share the party's views on the role of the federal government. Tyler favored states' rights, while Whigs generally wanted to expand the federal government. A good portion of the opposition, then, to Tyler's completing the entire term

Left: William Henry Harrison, Tyler's predecessor.

Family Secret

Before John Tyler and Julia Gardiner slipped away to New York to be married, none of his children had any idea of their plans, although John Jr. had been told at the last minute so that he could serve as his father's best man. After they learned that they had a new mother, Tyler's sons welcomed Julia into the family, but his daughters were less than pleased. The oldest, Mary, didn't know how to deal with a mother who was five years younger than she was, and Mary's younger sister, Letitia, never did get used to the idea, even though she and Julia were about the same age.

of William Henry Harrison came from within his own Whig party.

Tyler's action met with floods of disapproval from Congress, the cabinet, the press, and the people. He was called "His Accidency" and "Vice President Acting President Tyler" The situation grew worse whenever Tyler made an unpopular decision, which seemed to be often, and protest demonstrations occurred regularly around the executive mansion, frequently ending with the president burned in effigy.

The Whigs, who held a solid majority in Congress, were confident that they could push their programs through the Whig-dominated administration and they began passing major legislation. One of their first bills called for rechartering the second national bank of the United States and making it part of the federal banking system. With offices in several states, the bank would regulate the flow of currency and oversee the nation's money supply. Tyler believed that the bill trespassed on the rights of states to decide whether or not to have bank branches in their state, and he vetoed the measure. Congress was outraged and immediately passed a second similar bill on the bank, which Tyler just as immediately vetoed.

"[President Tyler's] manner was remarkably unaffected. I thought that in his whole carriage he became his station well."
—*Charles Dickens after his Washington visit in 1842*

Following the second veto, his entire cabinet, with the exception of Secretary of State Daniel Webster, resigned in protest. Tyler took fast action on that, too. He appointed their successors within two days, which led the Whigs to drum him out of their ranks. The situation grew worse when Tyler vetoed a series of tariff bills, believing that high import taxes represented federal power over self-determination by states. The House swiftly called for a resolution to impeach him, and anti-Tyler demonstrations grew larger, louder, and nastier. However, fewer than half of the Congressmen voted to impeach the president. The measure failed 127 to 83. A new tariff, more modest and carefully worded, was later passed and Tyler signed it into law.

Tyler's wife died in the midst of all this turmoil. Letitia Tyler had been ill since her stroke three years earlier. A few months after her death, Tyler met Julia Gardiner, a member of a wealthy New York family, who was some thirty years younger than he was. They were married in June of 1844, the first time that a president had married

Right: Daniel Webster, Tyler's secretary of state.

while in office. They would have seven children. Added to the eight children from his first wife this made Tyler the father of fifteen children, a record for any president (Tyler had eight children with his first wife, but one child, Ann Contesse, died within a year).

The Constitutional Sidestep

The Tyler administration wasn't without some successes. The Webster-Ashburton Treaty of 1842 ended a dispute between the United States and England over the border between the state of Maine and the Canadian province of New Brunswick. It also instituted U.S. participation in policing the coast of Africa to stop the illegal slave trade. The United States expanded its presence in the Pacific Ocean under President Tyler as well. He invoked the Monroe Doctrine to prevent the Hawaiian islands from becoming a colony of any European or Asian nation, and his administration negotiated a trade treaty with China, opening up huge new markets for both nations. Bitterness continued to linger against the president without a party, but Tyler continued to stick to his constructionist principles, particularly setting his sights on annexing Texas, which had separated from Mexico in 1836.

The United States, Great Britain, and France all recognized the Republic of Texas as an independent state, and only Mexico continued to lay claim to it. By considering the annexation of Texas, the United States was risking a war with Mexico, and beyond that, many Americans, particularly Northerners, were concerned about admitting a new—and huge—slave state into the Union.

When Tyler began pursuing annexation, Secretary of State Webster resisted because of the slave issue, and as Tyler continued to press the issue on annexation, Webster resigned from the cabinet. Tyler immediately replaced him with John C. Calhoun, a highly respected Southern politician. Calhoun was a former vice president, and had become the first man to resign from that post when Andrew Jackson showed intentions of using federal troops to enforce tariffs in Calhoun's native South Carolina. He had also engaged in a historic debate on slavery in 1833 with Daniel Webster, the man he replaced as secretary of state. Negotiations intensified between Tyler and Sam Houston, the president of the Republic of Texas, and a treaty was signed by both men in April of 1844.

All treaties negotiated by the president must be ratified by a two-thirds majority in the Senate. The slavery issue dominated Senate debate on the Texas treaty and when it proved irreconcilable, the Senate failed to ratify the treaty. Debate about annexing Texas moved from the Senate floor to the electorate as the major campaign issue in the 1844 presidential election.

"John Tyler, the poor, miserable, despised imbecile, who now goes from the presidential chair scorned of all parties, but for his profligate and disgraceful, though impotent efforts for a reelection, would have passed decently through his official course."

—*Albany (NY)* Evening Journal

Left: The Whigs parade in New York for their 1844 candidate Henry Clay, who lost his bid to James K. Polk.

Honor Denied

After he died in Richmond, John Tyler's body was buried in a flag-draped coffin next to the tomb of another former president, James Monroe. But it was a Confederate flag. Tyler had gone to Richmond to join the congress of the Confederacy. In the eyes of the North, that made him a traitor—the only president ever branded with that offense. Congress didn't authorize a memorial stone for his grave until 1915.

Tyler formed the small National Democratic party, consisting principally of officials from his administration. They met in Baltimore, Maryland, and nominated him as their presidential candidate. The Whig party nominated Henry Clay, a widely respected two-time presidential candidate known as the Great Pacifier for his ability to find winning compromises on controversial issues. The Democrats nominated James K. Polk, a former U.S. congressman and Tennessee governor strongly associated with the Jacksonian ideals that were still popular in the South.

Polk maneuvered quickly by announcing his support for the annexation of Texas. With his major issue gone, the unpopular Tyler quit the race. Clay, meanwhile, failed to take a firm stand on the Texas issue, and Tyler threw his support to Polk while continuing to press for Texas annexation in his role as president. Polk ended up winning what turned out to be a close election, and with it a mandate for annexing the Texas Republic.

Polk's victory encouraged Tyler to try one more time to have the Texas treaty passed, but when it became clear that he couldn't win the required two-thirds majority he came up with a scheme. Confident that he was carrying out the people's wishes, and putting his constructionist philosophy aside, he proposed that Congress should vote on annexation with a joint resolution that requires only a simple majority of both houses of Congress. When the measure squeaked through in the Senate by two votes,

after having passed easily in the House, Tyler signed the Texas resolution annexing the state into law, three days before leaving office.

Following his presidency, Tyler retired to his Virginia plantation, Sherwood Forest, with his new wife, Julia. The unpopular president gradually won back respect largely because through all the turmoil and resentment of his administration, he had remained calm and gracious and had gone about his job with integrity. Besides, John Tyler was a charming man who everyone found easy to like, and even forgive.

The slavery issue that had threatened his hopes for annexing Texas continued to divide the Union, and still faithful to his ideas about states' rights and limited federal powers, Tyler sided with his southern neighbors. Now over seventy years of age, he reentered the political arena in 1861, after becoming alarmed by the inaugural address of Abraham Lincoln, which stated that federal powers would be used to maintain the Union. Tyler became active in helping Virginia secede from the Union, he attended the provisional Confederate Congress, and he was elected to, the Confederate House of Representatives. However, before he could begin serving, his health failed and he died in early 1862. He was buried in Richmond next to the grave of James Monroe, another former president and fellow Virginian.

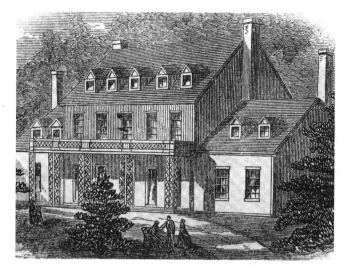

Above: The Tyler estate, Sherwood Forest, in Virginia.

Legacy

John Tyler set the precedent for succession to the presidency in cases where the elected chief executive cannot complete his term. The Constitution was later amended to clarify the exact mode of succession, which begins with the vice president.

The annexation of Texas proved to be contentious, as expected, over the slavery issue. The addition of other territories during Polk's administration, which followed Tyler's, further complicated the issue, resulting in legislation called the Compromise of 1850 that continued to support states' rights in determining whether or not to allow slavery. The issue was far from settled, however, and Tyler continued to participate in the debate. Tyler died as the issue was about to erupt into the Civil War.

Letitia Tyler

Born November 12, 1790, Cedar Grove, Virginia
Died September 10, 1842, Washington, D.C.

"[Letitia Tyler] is the most unselfish person you can imagine. … Mother attends to and regulates all the household affairs and all so quietly that you can't tell when she does it."
—Daughter-in-law Priscilla Cooper Tyler

Letitia Tyler's time as first lady was brief—from June of 1841 to September 1842—and difficult, because a stroke had left her incapacitated since 1839. She was accustomed to planning and managing events, having overseen many of the operations of the Tyler plantation and raised seven children while her husband held various elected positions. Despite her illness, she presided over her responsibilities as first lady from her second-story bedroom in the presidential mansion. She made only one public appearance as first lady—at the wedding of her daughter Elizabeth.

She was born Letitia Christian on November 12, 1790, on a plantation near Tidewater, Virginia, and she was raised to learn domestic responsibilities, from family care to plantation management. Her father was a wealthy merchant involved in Virginia politics.

John Tyler's father was elected governor of Virginia in 1809, and John accompanied his father to the state capital in Richmond, where he became acquainted with powerful men, including the well-known and respected American statesman Edmund Jennings Randolph, and Letitia's father, Robert Christian. Tyler became acquainted with Letitia through these aristocratic leaders, and they became engaged. After Tyler served briefly during the War of 1812, without seeing action, the couple was married on February 29, 1813.

Tyler's close association with Randolph helped his political career, and he pursued politics while Letitia raised their family and presided over their plantation. She bore eight children, seven of whom survived.

Tyler's political career took him back and forth between Washington and Richmond, while Letitia stayed home on the plantation. He served as a U.S. representative from 1816 to 1821, went to the Virginia legislature two years later, and was elected governor in 1825. He then became a U.S. senator, a position he held for ten years before being defeated in a bid to keep his seat in 1839. It was then that he found himself the Whig party's vice presidential candidate and the Southern counterpart to Northerner William Henry Harrison, who was nominated for president in 1840. Although the two candidates barely knew each other and had differing political views, they became linked through the famous campaign slogan, "Tippecanoe and Tyler Too!"

Letitia Tyler wasn't able to share in her husband's return to the national political scene. After her stroke in 1839, she lost much of her physical strength. Following the victory of Harrison and Tyler, her husband remained with her at the plantation. Since vice presidents traditionally had little say in presidential administrations, he decided that he could easily hold the position at home. However, Harrison died of pneumonia just thirty-one days after he was inaugurated. Tyler had himself sworn in as president and assumed full responsibilities, and his family soon followed him to Washington.

Letitia Tyler wasn't able to perform in a public role as first lady. That responsibility fell to her daughters and, especially, her daughter-in-law, Priscilla Cooper Tyler, who had married the Tylers' son Robert in 1839. She was accustomed to public events, having been an actress and the daughter of a noted actor, Thomas Cooper,

Above: The White House in the 1840s.

who was famous for his leading roles in Shakespearian tragedies. At the age of seventeen, Priscilla had played the role of Desdemona to her father's Othello in a touring production of the Shakespeare play.

Former first lady and Washington socialite Dolley Madison was still on the scene, and with her guidance, Priscilla became known as a charming and popular hostess, arranging lavish state parties and entertaining many guests, including the famous author Charles Dickens. Dolley Madison had also guided Priscilla's predecessor, surrogate first lady Angelica Singleton Van Buren, who assumed the role after marrying Martin Van Buren's son Abraham. Martin Van Buren was a longtime widower by the time he was elected president.

Priscilla and Letitia helped arrange the White House wedding of the Tyler's daughter Elizabeth, herself a spirited hostess, to William N. Waller on January 31, 1842. Letitia made her only public appearance at this executive mansion wedding, greeting guests and enjoying the festivities from her seat. She died on September 10, 1842, and was buried at the plantation where she had been raised.

Buried Treasure

Gardiner's Island, in Long Island Sound between two eastern forks of Long Island, is said to be the place where the accused pirate Captain William Kidd buried his fabulous treasure before going to London to keep a date with the hangman. It still hasn't been found, but treasure hunters are waved off whenever they approach the island, which is still privately owned by the Gardiner family.

Julia Tyler

Born May 4, 1820, Gardiner's Island, New York
Died July 10, 1889, Richmond, Virginia

Julia Tyler was among the liveliest, most spirited, and most public of all first ladies. She clearly enjoyed her role as hostess at official receptions and parties during her brief period in Washington from late June 1844, until the following March. Accustomed to the life of a debutante in New York, Julia made these social occasions formal affairs. Guests were announced and received, orchestras played, and dancing was encouraged—especially waltzes, which were considered a bit risqué in those days. She also actively defended the political positions she and her husband shared.

Julia Gardiner Tyler was born to a prominent New York family on May 4, 1820. Her father, David Gardiner, was a lawyer and state senator, and her mother, Juliana McLachlan, was an heiress to the fortune of a Scottish brewer. The Gardiners owned an island home in Long Island Sound that had been in the family since 1639, when adventurer Lion Gardiner purchased it from Native Americans of the Algonquin tribe.

Julia was raised primarily at her family's estate in East Hampton, where she received private tutoring, and later attended a private school in Manhattan. As a pretty and wealthy young debutante, she had a coming-out party and joined New York society, where she was affectionately known as "the Rose of Long Island."

Julia traveled with her parents on a European tour that included study, sightseeing, and meetings and dinners with various heads of state. Her family arranged the tour, according to some sources, after Julia had appeared as a model in a newspaper advertisement for a department store. Such public displays were considered unbecoming in upper-class New York social circles of the time.

In 1842, the twenty-two-year-old Julia's parents took her with them to Washington, where they made the social rounds in hopes of find a suitably wealthy or powerful beau for her. She was quite popular and apparently received several marriage proposals. It was during that time that she first met President Tyler, whose invalid wife, Letitia, had died two months earlier. They met again during the winter of 1843, when the Gardiners were among special guests invited to ride on a new steam frigate, the U.S.S. *Princeton*, with members of the Tyler administration. The journey turned tragic when a large navy gun exploded on the warship, resulting in several deaths, among them Julia's father and Secretary of State Abel Upshur.

While President Tyler was consoling Julia on her father's death, the two fell in love, and became secretly engaged. They were married at the Episcopal Church of the Ascension on Fifth Avenue in New York on June 26, 1844. The marriage—the first for a sitting president—was announced publicly the following day and created some controversy, especially over their thirty-year age difference.

The Peacemaker

The U.S.S. Princeton *was the pride of the U.S. Navy, one of the first steamships to be driven by screw propellers. Her pride and joy was the "Peacemaker," the largest naval gun in existence. On February 28, 1844, President Tyler invited dignitaries, including the Gardiner family, to take a cruise aboard her up and down the Potomac River. Part of the adventure was to be the firing of the gun, and it had been test-fired that morning. It was fired twice during the cruise, but the third time it exploded at the breech, killing four people on deck, including Julia's father, David Gardiner.*

Julia thoroughly enjoyed her role as first lady, giving several balls where guests were formally presented to the president and first lady, and couples waltzed the night away. She introduced the custom of having a band play "Hail to the Chief" whenever the president was introduced at formal occasions. She used her influence to obtain choice positions for friends, and she often defended her husband, whose administration was widely unpopular with the press and his political opponents. To some, her lavish parties were examples of aristocratic extravagance, but to others she represented youthful vigor during a period when American popular culture was embracing new ideas.

Julia's time in the White House, however, was brief. President Tyler dropped out of his reelection campaign in 1844 after it became obvious that he didn't have a chance of winning. After his term was over, the couple retired to his Virginia estate, Sherwood Forest, and raised seven children. The Tylers remained outspoken in defending such political issues as states' rights and slavery.

Julia disagreed with a statement signed by several prominent women from the United States and Great Britain calling for an end to slavery, and she responded with an impassioned defense of the institution that was published in the Richmond *Enquirer* and then reprinted in the popular magazine *Southern Literary Messenger*. The piece was called "A Letter to the Duchess of Sutherland and Ladies of England in Reply to Their 'Christian Address' on the Subject of Slavery in the Southern States." It argued that black slaves of the South were better off than poor laborers of the North and Great Britain, and suggested that the proabolitionist women ought to be putting their efforts into improving the downtrodden in their own parts of the world.

Former president Tyler became increasingly involved in the slavery issue as well. He supported Virginia's secession from the Union on the eve of the Civil War in 1861, and he was elected as a representative to the Confederate Congress. However, he died shortly before taking office, leaving Julia to run the huge plantation and take care of their large family. She fell on bad times when the Civil War broke out, and her Virginia home was no longer safe. She made plans to move her family to her mother's home on Staten Island, New York, but the move north required her to sign an oath of allegiance to the Union, and when she refused, the trip was called off.

Julia arranged passage on a boat that could get around the North's blockade of southern ports, and she and her family sailed from North Carolina to Bermuda and then, illegally, to New York. Later, when the boat captain who had smuggled her was arrested for avoiding the blockade, she lobbied—unsuccessfully—to have him pardoned.

While she was in New York, Julia worked as a volunteer for the Confederate cause, and by the time the South was defeated, she had run out of money. Her anti-Union activities left her at odds with her brother, which led to disputes over the family inheritance. She received some compensation through her husband's military pension from his service in the War of 1812, but it was not until 1870 that presidential widows began receiving federal pensions.

Julia went back to live in Richmond after the war, and in 1872, she converted to the Roman Catholic Church for the rest of her life. She paid a respectful visit to President Ulysses S. Grant in a gesture intended to help heal the wounds of the Civil War. She died in Richmond on July 10, 1889, and was buried in the Virginia Capital next to her husband.

Tyler's Address to Congress

During John Tyler's administration the Republic of Texas, which had been established in 1836, petitioned to become a state. It had been a province of Mexico after its independence from Spain fifteen years earlier. Texas's population expanded greatly during those years, and most of the newcomers were Americans. Tensions rose as they rebelled under the thumb of the Mexican government. Their budding revolution seemed to end with the defeat of American rebels in the battle of the Alamo in March of 1836, but a month later the Texas army, under

Sam Houston, won a major battle at San Jacinto. The army rallied under the battle cry "Remember the Alamo, remember Goliad"— references to two earlier defeats. Following the victory at San Jacinto, Americans in Texas formed an independent republic.

Faced with debts and a border dispute with Mexico, the Texans formally requested statehood. Many Northerners were against the idea, fearing that slavery would expand to the new state, but Tyler believed that Texas had real economic potential and negotiated the treaty of annexation. Under the Constitution, the president has the power to negotiate treaties, but they must be ratified by the Senate. The treaty annexing Texas failed to receive the necessary two-thirds approval in the Senate on two different occasions. Tyler used his final annual address to Congress to rally support for annexation. He suggested a sly solution: Instead of having the treaty subject to Senate ratification, Tyler proposed that Texas annexation should be handled as a joint resolution of Congress, which would only need a simple majority vote in both Houses to pass.

At the time of this speech, Tyler was a lame duck finishing his term until the recently elected James K. Polk would officially take over as president. Polk was a strong supporter of Texas annexation, and Tyler argued that his victory showed that a majority of Americans also supported it.

Excerpt from Tyler's Final Annual Address to Congress

December 3, 1844

In my last annual message I felt it to be my duty to make known to Congress, in terms both plain and emphatic, my opinion in regard to the war which has so long existed between Mexico and Texas, which since the battle of San Jacinto has consisted altogether of predatory incursions, attended by circumstances revolting to humanity. I repeat now what I then said, that after eight years of feeble and ineffectual efforts to reconquer Texas it was time that the war should have ceased. The United States have a direct interest in the question. The contiguity of the two nations to our territory was but too well calculated to involve our peace. Unjust suspicions were engendered in the mind of one or the other of the belligerents against us, and as a necessary consequence American interests were made to suffer and our peace became daily endangered; in addition to which it must have been obvious to all that the exhaustion produced by the war subjected both Mexico and Texas to the interference of other powers, which, without the interposition of this Government, might eventuate in the most serious injury to the United States. This Government from time to time exerted its friendly offices to bring about a termination of hostilities upon terms honorable alike to both the belligerents. Its efforts in this behalf proved unavailing. Mexico seemed almost without an object to persevere in the war, and no other alternative was left the Executive but to take advantage of the well-known dispositions of Texas and to invite her to enter into a treaty for annexing her territory to that of the United States.

Since your last session Mexico has threatened to renew the war, and has either made or proposes to make formidable preparations for invading Texas. She has issued decrees and proclamations, preparatory to the commencement of hostilities, full of threats revolting to humanity, and which if carried into effect would arouse the attention of all Christendom. This new demonstration of feeling, there is too much reason to believe, has been produced in consequence of the negotiation of the late treaty of annexation with Texas. The Executive, therefore, could not be indifferent to such proceedings, and it felt it to be due as well to itself as to the honor of the country that a strong representation should be made to the Mexican Government upon the subject. This was accordingly done, as will be seen by the copy of the accompanying dispatch from the Secretary of State to the United States envoy at Mexico. Mexico has no right to jeopard the peace of the world by urging any longer a useless and fruitless contest. Such a condition of things would lot be tolerated on the European continent. Why should it be on this? A war of desolation, such as is now threatened by Mexico, can not be waged without involving our peace and tranquillity. It is idle to believe that such a war could be looked upon with indifference by our own citizens inhabiting adjoining States; and our neutrality would be violated in despite of all efforts on the part of the Government to prevent it. The country is settled by emigrants; from the United States under invitations held out to them by Spain and Mexico. Those emigrants have left behind them friends and relatives, who would not fail to sympathize with them in their difficulties, and who would be led by those sympathies to participate in their struggles, however energetic the action of the Government to prevent it. Nor would the numerous and formidable bands of Indians "the most warlike to be found in any land" which occupy the extensive regions contiguous to the States of Arkansas and Missouri, and who are in possession of large tracts of country within the limits of Texas, be likely to remain passive. The inclinations of those numerous tribes lead them invariably to war whenever pretexts exist.

Mexico had no just ground of displeasure against this Government or people for negotiating the treaty. What interest of hers was affected by the treaty? She was despoiled of nothing, since Texas was forever lost to her. The independence of Texas was recognized by several of the leading powers of the earth. She was free to treat, free to adopt her own line of policy, free to take the course which she believed was best calculated to secure her happiness.

Her Government and people decided on annexation to the United States, and the Executive saw in the acquisition of such a territory the means of advancing their permanent happiness and glory. What principle of good faith, then, was violated? What rule of political morals trampled under foot? So far as Mexico herself was concerned, the measure should have been regarded by her as highly beneficial. Her inability to reconquer Texas had been exhibited, I repeat, by eight (now nine) years of fruitless and ruinous contest. In the meantime Texas has been growing in population and resources.

[. . .]

Upon the ratification of the treaty the Executive was prepared to treat with her on the most liberal basis. Hence the boundaries of Texas were left undefined by the treaty. The Executive proposed to settle these upon terms that all the world should have pronounced just and reasonable. No negotiation upon that point could have been undertaken between the United States and Mexico in advance of the ratification of the treaty. We should have tried no right, no power, no authority, to have conducted such a negotiation, and to have undertaken it would have been an assumption equally revolting to the pride of Mexico and Texas and subjecting us to the charge of arrogance, while to have proposed in advance of annexation to satisfy Mexico for any contingent interest she might have in Texas would have been to have treated Texas not as an independent power, but as a mere dependency of Mexico. This assumption could not have been acted on by the Executive without setting at defiance your own solemn declaration that that Republic was an independent State. Mexico had, it is true, threatened war against the United States in the event the treaty of annexation was ratified. The Executive could not permit itself to be influenced by this threat. It represented in this the spirit of our people, who are ready to sacrifice much for peace, but nothing to intimidation. A war under any circumstances is greatly to be deplored, and the United States is the last nation to desire it; but if, as the condition of peace, it be required of us to forego the unquestionable right of treating with an independent power of our own continent upon matters highly interesting to both, and that upon a naked and unsustained pretension of claim by a third power to control the free will of the power with whom we treat, devoted as we may be to peace and anxious to cultivate friendly relations with the whole world, the Executive does not hesitate to say that the people of the United States would be ready to brave all consequences sooner than submit to such condition. But no apprehension of war was entertained by the Executive, and I must express frankly the opinion that had the treaty been ratified by the Senate it would have been followed by a prompt settlement, to the entire satisfaction of Mexico, of every matter in difference between the two countries. Seeing, then, that new preparations for hostile invasion of Texas were about to be adopted by Mexico, and that these were brought about because Texas had adopted the suggestions of the Executive upon the subject of annexation, it could not passively have folded its arms and permitted a war, threatened to be accompanied by every act that could mark a barbarous age, to be waged against her because she had done so.

Other considerations of a controlling character influenced the course of the Executive. The treaty which had thus been negotiated had failed to receive the ratification of the Senate. One of the chief objections which was urged against it was found to consist in the fact that the question of annexation had not been submitted to the ordeal of public opinion in the United States. However untenable such an objection was esteemed to be, in view of the unquestionable power of the Executive to negotiate the treaty and the great and lasting interests involved in the question, I felt it to be my duty to submit the whole subject to Congress as the best expounders of popular sentiment. No definitive action having been taken on the subject by Congress, the question referred itself directly to the decision of the States and people. The great popular election which has just terminated afforded the best opportunity of ascertaining the will of the States and the people upon it. Pending that issue it became the imperative duty of the Executive to inform Mexico that the question of annexation was still before the American people, and that until their decision was pronounced any serious invasion of Texas would be regarded as an attempt to forestall their judgment and could not be looked upon with indifference. I am most happy to inform you that no such invasion has taken place; and I trust that whatever your action may be upon it Mexico will see the importance of deciding the matter by a resort to peaceful expedients in preference to those of arms. The decision of the people and the States on this great and interesting subject has been decisively manifested. The question of annexation has been presented nakedly to their consideration. By the treaty itself all collateral and incidental issues which were calculated to divide and distract the public councils were carefully avoided. These were left to the wisdom of the future to determine. It presented, I repeat, the isolated question of annexation, and in that form it has been submitted to the ordeal of public sentiment. A controlling majority of the people and a large majority of the States have declared in favor of immediate annexation. Instructions have thus come up to both branches of Congress from their respective constituents in terms the most emphatic. It is the will of both the people and the States that Texas shall be annexed to the Union promptly and immediately. It may be hoped that in carrying into execution the public will thus declared all collateral issues may be avoided. [. . .] Free and independent herself, she asks to be received into our Union. It is a question for our own decision whether she shall be received or not. The two Governments having already agreed through their respective organs on the terms of annexation, I would recommend their adoption by Congress in the form of a joint resolution or act to be perfected and made binding on the two countries when adopted in like manner by the Government of Texas.

What Happened Next

The joint resolution idea Tyler proposed proved successful. Just a few days before leaving office, President Tyler offered Texas statehood.

In his final annual address, Tyler noted that a dispute concerning the southern border of Texas was still not resolved. Texas claimed the Rio Grande as its border, while Mexico argued that the border was further north. In 1846, armies from both nations were camped along the Rio Grande, and when a scuffle ensued, President Polk asked Congress to declare war on Mexico. The Mexican War that followed was controversial, but an American victory settled the Texas border at the Rio Grande, and the United States negotiated a treaty to take possession of other Mexican territories, most of present-day New Mexico, Arizona, and California.

The issue of slavery expanding into Texas was another problem, and a compromise was reached admitting Texas as a slave state and California as a free state. Nevertheless, the expansion of slavery proved to be an issue that could be resolved only by war. Texas was among the states that seceded from the Union to form the Confederate States of America in 1861, and it fought on the side of the South in the Civil War.

James K. Polk

"Though I occupy a very high position, I am the hardest-working man in this country."

—*James K. Polk*

In his inaugural address, James K. Polk outlined four major economic and geographic goals for his administration. He achieved those goals by stabilizing the economy and overseeing the largest expansion of U.S. territory of any president. Those accomplishments alone should rank him among the most successful of America's presidents, but instead, a controversial war and regional divisiveness overshadowed his successes.

Polk stated that he would serve only one term, and he kept his word. He had made the promise to unify political factions within his own Democratic party and to calm the nation as a whole. However, the hardworking president wasn't able to bridge differences among the party leaders, especially over the issue of slavery. He left office exhausted and discouraged, and he died just over three months into his retirement, at the age of fifty-three.

A Difficult Childhood

James Knox Polk was born in a log cabin at Pineville, North Carolina, on November 2, 1795, the eldest of ten children of Samuel and Jane Knox Polk. His father had been a prosperous farmer after 1806, when he moved his family to a rural area near the town of Columbia in Tennessee's Duck River Valley. James's grandfather

Eleventh president of the United States, 1845–1849

Full name: *James Knox Polk*
Born: *November 2, 1795, Pineville, North Carolina*
Died: *June 15, 1849, Nashville, Tennessee*
Burial site: *State Capitol Grounds, Nashville, Tennessee*
Parents: *Samuel and Jane Knox Polk*
Spouse: *Sarah Childress (1803–1891; m. 1824)*
Children: *None*
Religion: *Presbyterian; Methodist*
Education: *University of North Carolina (B.A., 1818)*
Occupation: *Lawyer*
Government positions: *Tennessee state representative and governor; U.S. representative from Tennessee; Speaker of the House*
Political party: *Democratic*
Dates as president: *March 4, 1845–March 4, 1849*
Age upon taking office: *49*

Ezekiel had settled there, too, and became a successful land speculator. Polk's mother, Jane, was a descendant of John Knox, the founder of the Presbyterian church of Scotland.

Polk was small and thin as a boy, and it was obvious that he wouldn't grow up with enough strength to become a farmer. Plagued with stomach ailments all his young life, when he was seventeen, Polk was diagnosed with gallstones, which were surgically removed by the noted physician Ephraim McDowell in Danville, Kentucky. At that time, there was no such thing as anesthesia, and the painful operation was performed while he was fully conscious, strapped to a table, and holding his father's hand. He survived the ordeal, and his health improved.

His formal education began the following year at a local church. He had barely learned to read and write before then, but he quickly excelled and moved on to a school in Murfreesboro, Tennessee. Devoting all of his time to learning, Polk became proficient in English, Greek, and Latin, and when he took an entrance examination at the University of North Carolina, he qualified to enter as a sophomore. He graduated in 1818, at the age of twenty-two, with first honors in mathematics and classics. But he fell ill once again, and didn't make the long trip home for several months. He spent the time studying law.

Timeline

1795: Born in North Carolina
1818: Graduates from the University of North Carolina
1823–25: Serves in the Tennessee House of Representatives
1825–39: Serves in the U.S. House of Representatives
1835–39: Serves as Speaker of the House
1839: Elected governor of Tennessee
1841: Fails to win reelection as governor and loses 1843 gubernatorial election as well
1844: Emerges during the Democratic national convention as the first "dark-horse" candidate for president; wins the election, primarily for his support of the annexation of Texas and expansionist sentiments
1845–49: Serves as eleventh U.S. president
1846–48: Mexican war
1849: Dies in Tennessee

A Branch Falls from the Family Tree

James Knox Polk's mother was a grandniece of John Knox, who founded the Presbyterian church in Scotland. When his parents took him to be baptized as a Presbyterian, the pastor refused to conduct the ceremony unless both parents professed their faith. Knox's father declined, and the boy went unbaptized. He went to his mother's church out of a sense of duty, and continued after marrying Sarah Childress, who was also a devout Presbyterian. At heart, though, James Knox Polk was a Methodist, following a decision he made at a revivalist camp meeting as a young man. When he was on his deathbed, his wife called for a Methodist bishop, who baptized him.

The Start of a Political Career

After returning home, Polk continued his law studies in the offices of local attorney Felix Grundy, and it was there that he was bitten by the political bug. Like his father and grandfather, he was a great admirer of the principles of Thomas Jefferson, especially Jefferson's agricultural policies and values. Polk was also inspired by fellow Tennessean and family friend Andrew Jackson, a war hero and politician with enormous support from the rural population.

"Politics had become [Polk's] whole life, aside from which he had no aspirations, intellectual interests, recreation, or even friendships."
—*Charles G. Sellers, Polk biographer*

Polk's political career began when Grundy recommended him for a job as clerk to the Tennessee General Assembly, the state congress. After he was admitted to the Tennessee bar in 1820, he established his own practice as a lawyer in Columbia. An economic depression that had begun the previous year and severely affected the South, strengthened his commitment to farmers and small tradesmen. He became more deeply involved in local politics and left his clerkship to run for the assembly. A powerful speaker, the young lawyer was playfully called the "Napoleon of the stump" because of his small stature and his commanding presence. The

popular and electoral votes than Adams, but he didn't have the required majority, and a constitutional mandate forced the election into Congress, which decided in favor of Adams as the president-elect.

Polk's enthusiastic support for Jackson's policies and his presidential bid made him a popular Tennessee politician, and he was elected to Congress in 1825. Bitterness over the controversial presidential election was quite strong, and John Quincy Adams's presidency was greatly weakened by a hostile Congress and by Jackson, who immediately began campaigning for the next election, still four years into the future.

Polk quickly emerged as a leader of the Jacksonian Democrat wing in Congress. He advocated limiting federal power in favor of states' rights. He reformed the banking system to curb the influence of financial establishments in the Northeast. He worked with other Democratic-Republicans to lower tariffs. He also introduced legislation to disband the Electoral College system in favor of the popular vote, but the bill was not successful. On the hugely divisive issue of slavery, Polk supported the right of individual states to decide for themselves whether to allow it.

Polk's political alliance paid off when Jackson won the presidency in 1828. As chairman of the powerful House Ways and Means Committee, which determines the costs and methods for enacting legislation, he led Jackson's opposition to renewing the charter of the Second Bank of the United States. The bank had a government charter to regulate the flow of currency, control credit, and perform essential banking services for the Department of the Treasury, and Jackson's people argued that while it had a powerful voice in national affairs, it wasn't responsive to the will of the people. They noted that of the bank's twenty-five directors, only five were appointed by the government, and some were even citizens of foreign counties. Polk's congressional stand against renewing the bank's charter helped make Jackson's veto of the eventual legislation a popular political move. The next presidential election centered around the bank issue, in fact, and Jackson easily won a second term.

assembly met in Murfreesboro, where Polk first met Sarah Childress, who came from a wealthy local family. They became engaged and were married on New Year's Day, 1824.

After Polk was elected to the Tennessee legislature in 1823, he aligned himself closely with Andrew Jackson, who was a candidate in the upcoming presidential election at the head of a strong faction of the Democratic-Republican Party, called the Jacksonian Democrats. The three previous presidents—Thomas Jefferson, James Madison, and James Monroe—had all been Democratic-Republicans, but the party had grown increasingly divided among the regional lines of North and South. The northern part of the country was mostly urban while the southern region was mostly rural. The North was represented by John Quincy Adams, and the South by Jackson. In the election of 1824, Jackson received more

Left: Polk and his running mate, George M. Dallas, on a Democratic campaign poster.

Right: The Whig candidate, Henry Clay, made his point with banners.

Polk's influence in Congress continued to grow during Jackson's second term. He was elected Speaker of the House in 1835, and was successful in broadening the Speaker's administrative powers. But the opposing Whig party's congressional delegation grew stronger following the elections of 1836. Martin Van Buren, Jackson's vice president and his chosen successor, won that year, but Whigs won many congressional seats, and part of that success can be traced to Jackson's banking policies, which upset the economy. As a Democrat—which had became the official name for the party following the 1832 convention that renominated Jackson—Polk faced increasing hostility over banking issues and slavery. He worked hard and was an effective administrator during a period of waning political fortunes for his party. Faced with growing opposition and an economic downturn called the Panic of 1837, he decided to go back into state politics.

Polk was elected governor of Tennessee in 1839. Campaigning vigorously throughout the state, he helped breathe life into the downtrodden Democratic Party and made a national impression, which lasted even though he was defeated for reelection as governor in 1841 and lost again in 1843.

Martin Van Buren was the expected nominee for president at the Democrats' 1844 national convention in Baltimore. However, he couldn't muster the necessary majority of delegates, largely because of their opposition to annexing the Republic of Texas. Lack of support by Southern delegates kept him from winning a majority through seven ballots, and James K. Polk was nominated on the eighth ballot as a compromise candidate supporting the annexation of Texas. Then Polk won unanimous approval on the convention's ninth ballot and became the nation's first "dark-horse" candidate—a term describing a little-known candidate showing marginal promise.

The Whig party nominated well-known politician Henry Clay and immediately seized on the dark-horse theme, presenting voters with the question, "Who is James K. Polk?" His Democratic supporters answered by calling Polk "Young Hickory," a reflection of Jackson's nickname, "Old Hickory." This new label was used

The Great Locofoco

Martin Van Buren lost his bid for the Democrats' nomination in 1844, but he still had the power to help the delegates decide who would get it. He wasn't too excited about the prospect that the nomination might go to James K. Polk until he found out that Polk was a Locofoco. It sounds like an insult, and it was to everybody but urban Democrats. The name, which means "self-moving fire," came from friction matches that had just been invented. They would burst into flame against any hard surface, and the image was perfect for an arm of the party made up of working-class people who supported labor unions and opposed big business. Van Buren was their champion, and Polk's credentials as a Locofoco sympathizer was all it took for Old Kinderhook to put his OK on the Polk candidacy.

to imply that Polk was carrying on Jackson's fighting spirit. The election centered on the issue of American expansionism—involving not only Texas but the Oregon Territory as well.

Polk came out firmly for annexing Texas, while Clay was less forceful. On the issue of the Oregon Territory, which the United States shared with Great Britain, Clay favored a diplomatic solution. But Polk took a more vigorous stance, suggesting that the United States would be willing to go to war with Britain over the Oregon Territory and beyond—including the modern-day Canadian province of British Columbia, all the way north to the Alaskan border, where Russian territory began. The popular slogan "54°40' or Fight!" that rallied Democrats on this issue referred to the latitude parallel at fifty-four degrees, forty minutes, that marks Alaska's southern border.

"James K. Polk [was] a great president. Said what he intended to do and did it."

—*former president Harry S Truman*

Polk's expansionist policies won him solid support of the South and West, except for Ohio and his home state of Tennessee. It was the state of New York, however, that proved most crucial. A third candidate from the state, James G. Birney of the antislavery Liberty party, siphoned off enough votes from Clay to make Polk the winner. Believing that it could help reduce divisive partisanship, Polk announced that he would not seek a second term if elected.

Polk presented four basic goals for his administration in his inaugural address: (*1*) reestablishing an independent treasury system, (*2*) lowering tariffs, (*3*) settling the Oregon issue with Great Britain, and (*4*) acquiring the California territory from Mexico. He succeeded on all four counts. He also reformed the executive branch's

Hail to the Chief

Whenever a president appears for a formal occasion, his presence is announced with a rendition of a tune called "Hail to the Chief." Apparently it was first played at a Boston party in 1815, marking what would have been George Washington's eighty-third birthday. President John Quincy Adams was serenaded with a version played by the Marine band at the groundbreaking for the Chesapeake and Ohio Canal in 1828, and Julia Tyler ordered it played when her husband, John Tyler, arrived at a formal reception. James Polk's wife, Sarah, requested it more often, possibly because her husband didn't stand out in a crowd. The custom took hold after that (except during the administration of Chester A. Arthur, who didn't like the tune), and it became an official requirement in 1954 when Dwight D. Eisenhower was president. It is an old Gaelic folk song, adapted in 1811 by Sir Henry Rowland Bishop for a production of "The Lady of the Lake" at London's Covent Garden Theater. Bishop also wrote words to go with the tune, which are rarely heard these days:

> *Hail to the Chief who in triumph advances!*
> *Honored and blessed by the ever-green pine!*
> *Long may the tree, in his banner that glances,*
> *Flourish the shelter and grace of our line.*

"Hail to the Chief" is always preceded by "ruffles and flourishes," a fanfare developed for military bands to use at honors ceremonies. The ruffles are played on the drums, and the flourishes on brass instruments. A president rates five of them, and the vice president four, all the way down to one for generals and admirals.

ENGLAND   AMERICA

Right: Polk threatened to go to war with Britain over territory in the Pacific Northwest.

1844 Election Results

Presidential / Vice Presidential Candidates	Popular Votes	Electoral Votes
James K. Polk / George M. Dallas (Democratic)	1,337,243	170
Henry Clay / Theodore Frelinghuysen (Whig)	1,299,062	105

A two-thirds majority was required by the Democrats to secure the nomination. Former president Martin Van Buren and former secretary of war Lewis Cass were the early leaders in the first seven ballots, but neither received two-thirds of the votes. Polk's name was introduced in the eighth ballot, and he won the nomination on the ninth ballot.

recordkeeping procedures to eliminate waste, and he was successful in invoking the Monroe Doctrine to stop what he regarded as an increasing French influence in Mexico, including the possibility that the Yucatán Peninsula might become a French protectorate. All of these successes should have made for a triumphant administration, but the success was overshadowed by a war with Mexico. This conflict was a lightning rod for political, popular, and journalistic disapproval, and the public's opinion of Polk soured.

His first two goals were accomplished without much difficulty. The Independent Treasury had been established in 1840 after Jackson vetoed the charter for the second national bank. The new entity consisted of several regional banks that stored the nation's money supply and regulated currency. The system was terminated by Whigs in Congress in 1841, but the party couldn't gather enough support for a replacement after vetoes by President John Tyler. Polk and the Democratic majority in Congress that emerged on his coattails reestablished the Independent Treasury System in 1846, and it would continue as the nation's banking system until 1913, when the Federal Reserve was established.

Polk was also successful in lowering tariffs. Many of the import duties in effect at the time protected northern manufacturing interests, so as a way of leveling the playing field, the administration enacted the Walker Tariff Act, which reduced all tariffs except for those on luxury items. The lower tariffs helped Western states sell excess grain abroad, which Polk had promised as an inducement for Western support of his policy.

Expansionism issues created the greatest controversy. Americans had been arriving and settling in droves in

The Polk Administration

Administration Dates: March 4, 1845–March 4, 1849
Vice President: George Mifflin Dallas (1845–49)
Cabinet:

Secretary of State	James Buchanan (1845–49)
Secretary of the Treasury	Robert J. Walker (1845–49)
Secretary of War	William L. Marcy (1845–49)
Attorney General	John Y. Mason (1845–46)
	Nathan Clifford (1846–48)
	Isaac Toucey (1848–49)
Secretary of the Navy	George Bancroft (1845–46)
	John Y. Mason (1846–49)
Postmaster General	Cave Johnson (1845–49)

the Oregon Territory since 1843, assuming that it would become an American possession. The territory had been claimed and administered both by the United States and by Great Britain, and Polk tried a diplomatic solution by staking the American claim as far north as the forty-ninth parallel, just above the Columbia River in what is now the state of Washington. Britain would continue to have possession of land between that boundary and Alaska. However, English trappers and merchants had important trading posts on the Columbia River and refused the offer.

Polk revived his "54° 40' or Fight" slogan, suggesting that the United States was prepared to go to war over the entire territory. Meanwhile, Great Britain was able to establish new trading posts north of the forty-ninth parallel, in the area around what is now Vancouver, British

Columbia, and agreed to set the boundary at that parallel. Facing pressure from the Senate, Polk went along with it. The settlement extended the northern border of the United States along the forty-ninth parallel from what is now Minnesota all the way to the Pacific Ocean.

The acquisition of California from Mexico proved to be more difficult and complex. Texas had been officially annexed during the final days of the administration of Polk's predecessor, John Tyler, but a border dispute still lingered there. The United States recognized the Rio Grande as the southern border of the former Texas Republic, while Mexico placed it at the more northerly Nueces River, but emissaries from both sides failed to negotiate a treaty. Polk's plan for financing the return to power of former Mexican dictator Antonio López de Santa Anna, who would negotiate such a treaty as a return favor, failed when Santa Anna seized control of Mexico's army. Tensions grew worse when John Slidell, the U.S. minister to Mexico, was expelled, and Polk ordered the forces of General Zachary Taylor to set up a camp along the Rio Grande.

An American patrol suffered casualties in April 1846, when it was attacked by forces of Mexican general Mariano Arista, and on May 11, the president spoke before Congress, demanding a declaration of war on the grounds that Mexico had invaded American territory and shed American blood.

The resulting war was hotly debated across the United States. It was popular in Western states, but northerners viewed it as a pretext for expanding areas for slavery. Senator and former secretary of state Daniel Webster criticized Polk strongly, claiming that the war was of his making. First-term Illinois congressman Abraham Lincoln even questioned the truth of the report of a Mexican attack, and challenged Polk to show him the spot where American blood had been spilled.

Nevertheless, the war moved quickly. General Taylor attacked from Texas straight through central Mexico, and General Winfield Scott invaded Mexico through the port of Veracruz, east of Mexico City. Meanwhile, by August of 1846, the New Mexico area was placed under the command of General Stephen Watts Kearn. California had been conquered from the sea by the forces of Commodore Robert Stockton, and overland by the forces of Captain John C. Frémont at the head of the Bear Flag army. Mexico City itself fell in September of 1847.

Polk carefully exercised his authority as commander in chief during the war as well as in the peace process. He was motivated in part to offset the growing heroics of Taylor, who was being actively courted as a presidential candidate by the Whigs. Polk approached all of the issues before him as president with the same careful attention.

"I suspect he is deeply conscious of being in the wrong—that he feels the blood of this war, like the blood of Abel, is crying to Heaven against him. … He is a bewildered, confounded, and miserably perplexed man."

—Congressman Abraham Lincoln

Stamp Collectors Take Note

Polk's postmaster general, fellow Tennessean Cave Johnson, was the first to authorize the use of postage stamps, which had somehow seemed an un-American idea previously, considering the fuss over England's Stamp Act that made so many colonists want to go to war.

Right: Polk authorized a war with Mexico to settle the Texas border dispute.

John C. Frémont

The first presidential candidate of the Republican Party, John Charles Frémont was an explorer, politician, and soldier. Born on January 31, 1813, in Savannah, Georgia, Frémont was the son of John Charles Frémon and Anne Whiting Pryor. (The family added a "t" to its last name after Frémon's death.) Raised in Charleston, South Carolina, Frémont showed early talent in mathematics and the natural sciences. After attending Charleston College for two years, he taught mathematics on a ship and sailed to South America in 1833. In 1836, he helped survey a railroad route between Charleston and Cincinnati, Ohio, and in 1836–37 he worked on a survey of Cherokee lands in Georgia.

In 1838, Frémont obtained a commission as second lieutenant in the Corps of Topographical Engineers of the U.S. Army. Assigned to an expedition that explored Minnesota and the Dakotas, he learned more about natural science and topographical engineering, as well as life on the frontier. He met Thomas Hart Benton, a powerful senator from Missouri, and fell in love with Benton's daughter Jessie. Benton secured an appointment for Frémont to explore the Des Moines River, which was accomplished in 1841. That fall, Frémont and Jessie Benton were married.

In 1842, Frémont was sent to explore the Wind River chain of the Rocky Mountains and to make a scientific exploration of the Oregon Trail. His report was filled with tales of adventure and contained an excellent map. Frémont was on his way to becoming a popular hero with a reputation as the "Great Pathfinder," but, in reality, he had been following trails already established by mountain men. In 1843, Frémont headed another expedition to Oregon territory and returned by way of Mexican California. Ten thousand copies of his report were printed just as James K. Polk became president, a time when hopes were high for American expansionism.

In 1845, Polk sent Frémont and soldiers to California, which was still a province of Mexico. Expelled from California by its governor, Frémont wintered in Oregon. After the Mexican War broke out in 1846, Frémont returned to California under Polk's orders and assumed command of the American settlers' Bear Flag Revolt. Aided by commodores J. D. Sloat and Robert F. Stockton, his forces were victorious, and he received the surrender of California on January 13, 1847. Frémont became embroiled immediately in a fight for the governorship of California with General Stephen W. Kearny, who had marched from Missouri. Frémont was arrested, taken to Washington, D.C., and tried for mutiny, insubordination, and conduct prejudicial to good order. Found guilty, he was dismissed from the army. Polk set aside the penalty, but Frémont resigned in anger.

Frémont moved to California, along the way conducting a private survey for a railroad route. In California, he acquired land in the Sierra foothills, formed the Mariposa estate, and grew wealthy from mining. He bought real estate in San Francisco and lived lavishly, winning election as a U.S. senator from California. In 1853–54, he conducted another private expedition surveying a railroad route. In 1856, the newly formed Republican Party named Frémont its first presidential candidate because of his strong stand on free soil (antislavery) in Kansas and his attitude against enforcement of the Fugitive Slave Law that returned escaped slaves to their slave owners. He lost the election to James Buchanan.

Early in the Civil War, Frémont performed disastrously as a major general in St. Louis and in western Virginia. In 1864, Radical Republicans approached Frémont about running for president in opposition to Abraham Lincoln; Frémont first accepted, then declined. After the war, he was involved in promoting the Kansas and Pacific Railroad and the Memphis and Little Rock Railroads. Both lines went bankrupt in 1870, leaving Frémont almost penniless as he approached the age of sixty. In 1878, he won an appointment as governor of the Arizona territory and held the position until 1881, when angry protests from that territory led to his removal.

Frémont's old age was filled with frustrating schemes to recoup his fortune. In 1890, he was pensioned at $6,000 per year as a major general, but he died shortly thereafter, on July 13, 1890, in New York.

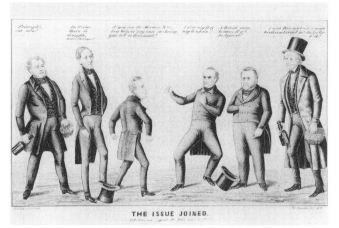

THE ISSUE JOINED.

Left: A newspaper cartoon highlighting the difference of opinion over the Mexican War.

The treaty negotiations dragged on for several months, until February of 1848. In the resulting Treaty of Guadalupe Hildago, Mexico gave up its claims to California, New Mexico, and Texas in return for a $15 million settlement. Additionally, all claims made by Americans for reparations against Mexico would become the responsibility of the U.S. government. Some Americans wanted to annex all of conquered Mexico, but Polk accepted the Rio Grande as the southern U.S. border of Texas. Acquisitions of Texas, New Mexico, California, and the Oregon Territory rounded out the Southwest and Pacific Northwest of the United States to nearly its present continental shape, except for parts of southern New Mexico and Arizona. The Treaty of Guadalupe Hidalgo, which ended the war, added more than half a million square miles to the United States, the largest annexation since the Louisiana Purchase. Mexico was reduced to about half its former size.

Triumphs Overshadowed

Polk had hoped that expansionism, the fulfillment of "Manifest Destiny"—a popular concept of the time describing America's right to claim and settle the western frontier—would unite the nation. However, expansionism only further fueled the most divisive of unresolved issues affecting the nation: slavery. In August 1846, Congressman

David Wilmot introduced the Wilmot Proviso, a bill that would bar slavery in all states acquired through war. It passed the House of Representatives twice, but was defeated both times in the Senate. Nevertheless, a strong abolitionist faction in the Northeast demanded that the new territories should be free states, and continued to press for an end to slavery everywhere.

Polk's attempt to deal with the issue was a frustrating failure. He himself was a slave owner and protective of the rights of states to determine their own laws, but he was not ardently proslavery. He opposed the abolitionists as well as proslavery apologists, but his solution—invoking the Missouri Compromise of 1820—was not acceptable to either Northern or Southern groups. The Missouri Compromise, which was repealed in 1854, designated areas that could enter the Union as free or slave states, using the Missouri state line as a boundary. By trying to remain neutral on the issue, Polk angered the Whigs and many members of his own Democratic party, who were splitting along regional lines. The Democrats' antislavery faction was led by former president Martin Van Buren. Polk had already lost a good deal of popular support over the Mexican conflict, which some called "Mr. Polk's War," and his administration ended with a deep sense of failure over the slavery issue. It was only later, through the Compromise of 1850, that the issue of slavery in the new territories was settled. Texas became a slave state, California would be a free state, and other states would decide individually by themselves. The issue of slavery

Right: The disputed territory in Oregon.

that had slowly but surely divided the nation since the very beginning had become far more complicated and divisive during Polk's term.

Keeping his word not to run again, Polk stepped aside from participating in the presidential election of 1848. By that time, the president was not very popular, even though he had accomplished his promised goals. He went back home to Tennessee a broken man, and was succeeded in office by Zachary Taylor.

"I predict that no President of the United States, of either party, will ever again be reelected. The reason is that the patronage of the government will destroy the popularity of any president, however well he may administer the government."

—James K. Polk

Polk was exhausted and in poor health. He had rarely vacationed during his term and had been extremely active in all issues. As he noted in an 1847 diary entry, "Though I occupy a very high position, I am the hardest working man in this country." He died at age fifty-three in August of 1848, and was buried in the garden of his Nashville home, Polk Place. His wife, Sarah, lived on until 1891, always keeping the doors of their estate open to visitors from the North or South, even during the days of the Civil War. Both Polk's body and that of his wife were moved to a tomb on the grounds of the Tennessee state capitol in 1893.

Legacy

James K. Polk was the last of the Jacksonian Democrats, who held the White House from 1828 to 1849 (except for the ineffective Harrison-Tyler administration of 1841–45). The legacy of Jacksonian Democrats lies in promoting states' rights over federal influence. His economic policies—centered on low tariffs and the reestablishment of the Independent Treasury—departed somewhat from Jacksonian ideals, but both policies were effective. The newly reestablished Independent Treasury survived into the twentieth century before being enlarged and reformed.

"No man and no administration was ever more assailed, and none ever achieved more. … The United States were never in a more proud, peaceful, and prosperous condition than at present."

—New York Sun

The United States expanded greatly during Polk's term, and fulfilled the concept of Manifest Destiny. California became a state just two years after he left office, and the areas of present-day Texas, New Mexico, and Arizona, as well as of Oregon and Washington, were all eventually added to the Union after being secured during Polk's administration.

This expansionism, however, brought slavery, the most divisive issue facing the Republic, to the forefront. Polk's attempt to stay neutral or to rely on past compromises on the issue made him the target of animosity from abolitionists as well as from those who favored slavery. Every president who followed him through the Civil War in 1861 would also be challenged and overshadowed by the same divisiveness.

Left: The Polk family.

Sarah Polk

Born September 4, 1803, Murfreesboro, Tennessee
Died August 14, 1891, Nashville, Tennessee

"It is only the hope that you can live through the campaign that gives me a prospect of enjoyment."

—*Sarah Polk to James Polk*

Most wives of politicians during the 1800s stayed out of the public eye, but not Sarah Polk. She was an independent woman who shared in her husband's political career publicly and was a key adviser, helping him with speeches and letters. She was an avid reader and made many friends in Washington, where her husband, James K. Polk, served for fourteen years in Congress and for four years as president. The respect she had earned for her intellect was reflected in the official visits politicians continually made to Polk Place, the couple's estate in Tennessee, which she managed for forty years following her husband's death five months after retiring from the presidency.

Sarah Childress was born to a wealthy family in Murfreesboro, Tennessee, on September 3, 1803. Her father, Captain Joel Childress, and her mother, Elizabeth, were planters and innkeepers. Sarah lived a life of elegance as a child and was also encouraged to be self-confident through good schooling. She was tutored at home and then sent to a private Nashville school for girls before being accepted at age thirteen to the Salem Female Academy in North Carolina, considered the finest school for girls in the area. It had been founded by Moravians, a Protestant religious sect that emphasizes missionary work. Sarah's sister also attended the school, but returned to Murfreesboro one year later, when their father died.

The family's wealth allowed Sarah to avoid menial chores, and she spent most of her time reading and studying the Bible. She became acquainted with James K. Polk when he went to Murfreesboro to serve as a clerk for the Tennessee legislature. Reportedly, their romance

was encouraged by Andrew Jackson, a war hero and politician familiar with both the Polk and the Childress families. James and Sarah were married on New Year's Day in 1824, shortly after he had been elected to the Tennessee legislature. He was twenty-eight and she was twenty.

Even at an early age, Polk was a strong supporter of Jackson, who lost the presidential election in 1824 to John Quincy Adams. Polk was elected to the House of Representatives in 1825 and quickly established himself as an influential congressman. Sarah Polk had remained in Tennessee during his first term in Congress, but she joined him two years later, helping him with his political career. His career blossomed when Jackson won the presidency in 1828 and served two terms.

Sarah helped her husband privately, reading up on issues of the day and discussing his speeches and political maneuvers with him. Publicly, she proved to be an excellent hostess and conversationalist, even as she refused—as a strict Presbyterian—to attend theaters or sporting events and forbade alcohol at gatherings she hosted. She freely expressed her opinions with a charm and good humor that won over critics who believed that the wives of politicians should be seen and not heard. Occasionally, she was accused of controlling her husband, but Polk freely sought her advice and assistance in spite of the wagging tongues.

Polk's health was frail throughout his life, but early in his political career, he kept late hours reading over documents. When Sarah asked him to cut down on his

Left: The fan Sarah used to keep cool at her husband's inauguration.

work for the sake of his health, he responded by suggesting that she read through some of the stack of papers. She did. Thus began a common practice between them. Sarah would go through her husband's political papers and mark the ones she felt most needed immediate attention.

During her time in Washington, Sarah Polk was admired by progressive thinkers, including Supreme Court justice Joseph Story, and such outspoken women as Marcia Van Ness, a social activist; Floride Calhoun, wife of Senator John C. Calhoun; and Josephine Seaton, a writer and newspaper editor. They did not share all of the Polks' political views, but they valued Sarah Polk for her own opinions and good judgment. Sarah's political involvement, although mostly private, was rarely seen in first ladies up until that time. The lone exception was Abigail Adams, with whom Sarah Polk has been favorably compared.

Polk left Congress in 1839 and was elected governor of Tennessee. He served one term, and then was defeated twice before emerging as the dark-horse Democratic presidential candidate in 1844. He won the election, and the Polks moved back to Washington, where Sarah received guidance from former first lady Dolley Madison, who helped her establish her own style. Sarah also continued to assist her husband in preparation and decision-making. He was not a particularly popular president, largely because of the war with Mexico, but he is viewed as having been successful in achieving the goals he set for his administration.

Sarah Polk was popular as first lady, even as a few critics continued to wonder about how great an influence she had on her husband and the nation's affairs. Nevertheless, after Polk left office in 1849, Sarah was cited by *Peterson's Magazine*, a national journal, as among the most admirable women and role models. Polk presidential historian Charles Sellers called her "increasingly indispensable" to her husband as secretary, political counselor, nurse, and emotional resource."

Even after her husband's death five months after he left office, Polk Place in Tennessee remained an important national site, visited by state legislators, national politicians, and the general public. Polk Place housed the collection of a local historical society during the Civil War for safekeeping, and it remained open as a neutral site during the Civil War. After her husband's death, Sarah Polk wore black for the rest of her life. She lived until 1891, and was buried next to her husband at Polk Place.

Right: The Polk homestead at Columbia, Tennessee.

Polk's Inaugural Address

Delivered on March 4, 1845

In his inaugural address, James K. Polk outlined four basic goals for his administration: (1) limit the power of the federal government in favor of states; (2) stabilize the economy by cutting the federal debt; (3) pursue expansion of U.S. territory; and (4) participate forcefully and diplomatically in international relations. Even as he generally accomplished all of those goals, he lost popular support, primarily over America's aggressive approach to Mexico and westward expansion.

Just before Polk took office, President John Tyler offered statehood to the Republic of Texas, which was opposed by people concerned that slavery would spread into new U.S. territories. Polk's election, however, was seen as a mandate by the majority of the people for annexing Texas. Polk also set his sights on acquiring the Oregon territory, which the United States controlled jointly with Great Britain at the time.

Polk's aggressive approach to expansion marked the beginning of a new era in American history. Previously, territorial expansion had been watched with worries over whether the country had any right to expand further and how its Constitutional form of government would work in a much larger nation. President Thomas Jefferson, for instance, debated on the Constitutionality and the wisdom of authorizing the Louisiana Purchase. During Polk's term, questions about U.S. expansion were overcome in the minds of many people by the belief that the United States had a right—indeed, a moral obligation—to spread the virtues of democracy and Christian values, a goal they called "Manifest Destiny." The views Polk put forward in his inaugural address reflect those ideals.

Excerpt from Polk's Inaugural Address

Fellow-Citizens:

The Republic of Texas has made known her desire to come into our Union, to form a part of our Confederacy and enjoy with us the blessings of liberty secured and guaranteed by our Constitution. Texas was once a part of our country—was unwisely ceded away to a foreign power—is now independent, and possesses an undoubted right to dispose of a part or the whole of her territory and to merge her sovereignty as a separate and independent state in ours. I congratulate my country that by an act of the late Congress of the United States the assent of this Government has been given to the reunion, and it only remains for the two countries to agree upon the terms to consummate an object so important to both.

I regard the question of annexation as belonging exclusively to the United States and Texas. They are independent powers competent to contract, and foreign nations have no right to interfere with them or to take exceptions to their reunion. Foreign powers do not seem to appreciate the true character of our Government. Our Union is a confederation of independent States, whose policy is peace with each other and all the world. To enlarge its limits is to extend the dominions of peace over additional territories and increasing millions. The world has nothing to fear from military ambition in our Government.

While the Chief Magistrate and the popular branch of Congress are elected for short terms by the suffrages of those millions who must in their own persons bear all the burdens and miseries of war, our Government can not be otherwise than pacific. Foreign powers should therefore look on the annexation of Texas to the United States not as the conquest of a nation seeking to extend her dominions by arms and violence, but as the peaceful acquisition of a territory once her own, by adding another member to our confederation, with the consent of that member, thereby diminishing the chances of war and opening to them new and ever-increasing markets for their products.

To Texas the reunion is important, because the strong protecting arm of our Government would be extended over her, and the vast resources of her fertile soil and genial climate would be speedily developed, while the safety of New Orleans and of our whole southwestern frontier against hostile aggression, as well as the interests of the whole Union, would be promoted by it.

In the earlier stages of our national existence the opinion prevailed with some that our system of confederated States could not operate successfully over an extended territory, and serious objections have at different times been made to the enlargement of our boundaries. These objections were earnestly urged when we acquired Louisiana. Experience has shown that they were not well founded.

The title of numerous Indian tribes to vast tracts of country has been extinguished; new States have been admitted into the Union; new Territories have been created and our jurisdiction and laws extended over them. As our population has expanded, the Union has been cemented and strengthened. As our boundaries have been enlarged and our agricultural population has been spread over a large surface, our federative system has acquired additional strength and security. It may well be doubted whether it would not be in greater danger of overthrow if our present population were confined to the comparatively narrow limits of the original thirteen States than it is now that they are sparsely settled over a more expanded territory. It is confidently believed that our system may be safely extended to the utmost bounds of our territorial limits, and that as it shall be extended the bonds of our Union, so far from being weakened, will become stronger.

None can fail to see the danger to our safety and future peace if Texas remains an independent state or becomes an ally or dependency of some foreign nation more powerful than herself. Is there one among our citizens who would not prefer perpetual peace with Texas to occasional wars, which so often occur between bordering independent nations? Is there one who would not prefer free intercourse with her to high duties on all our products and manufactures which enter her ports or cross her frontiers? Is there one who would not prefer an unrestricted communication with her citizens to the frontier obstructions which must occur if she remains out of the Union?

Whatever is good or evil in the local institutions of Texas will remain her own whether annexed to the United States or not. None of the present States will be responsible for them any more than they are for the local institutions of each other. They have confederated together for certain specified objects. Upon the same principle that they would refuse to form a perpetual union with Texas because of her local institutions our forefathers would have been prevented from forming our present Union.

Perceiving no valid objection to the measure and many reasons for its adoption vitally affecting the peace, the safety, and the prosperity of both countries, I shall on the broad principle which formed the basis and produced the adoption of our Constitution, and not in any narrow spirit of sectional policy, endeavor by all constitutional, honorable, and appropriate means to consummate the expressed will of the people and Government of the United States by the reannexation of Texas to our Union at the earliest practicable period.

Nor will it become in a less degree my duty to assert and maintain by all constitutional means the right of the United States to that portion of our territory which lies beyond the Rocky Mountains. Our title to the country of the Oregon is "clear and unquestionable," and already are our people preparing to perfect that title by occupying it with their wives and children. But eighty years ago our population was confined on the west by the ridge of the Alleghanies. Within that period—within the lifetime, I might say, of some of my hearers—our people, increasing to many millions, have filled the eastern valley of the Mississippi, adventurously ascended the Missouri to its headsprings, and are already engaged in establishing the blessings of self-government in valleys of which the rivers flow to the Pacific.

The world beholds the peaceful triumphs of the industry of our emigrants. To us belongs the duty of protecting them adequately wherever they may be upon our soil. The jurisdiction of our laws and the benefits of our republican institutions should be extended over them in the distant regions which they have selected for their homes. The increasing facilities of intercourse will easily bring the States, of which the formation in that part of our territory can not be long delayed, within the sphere of our federative Union. In the meantime every obligation imposed by treaty or conventional stipulations should be sacredly respected.

In the management of our foreign relations it will be my aim to observe a careful respect for the rights of other nations, while our own will be the subject of constant watchfulness. Equal and exact justice should characterize all our intercourse with foreign countries. All alliances having a tendency to jeopard the welfare and honor of our country or sacrifice any one of the national interests will be studiously avoided, and yet no opportunity will be lost to cultivate a favorable understanding with foreign governments by which our navigation and commerce may be extended and the ample products of our fertile soil, as well as the manufactures of our skillful artisans, find a ready market and remunerating prices in foreign countries.

What Happened Next

Texas was officially welcomed into the Union in 1845. However, a disagreement over its southern border led to skirmishes with Mexico the following year. This led the president to petition Congress for a declaration of war on Mexico, which was granted. Victory in the Mexican War established the Texas border at the Rio Grande River, and the United States acquired former Mexican territory encompassing much of present-day New Mexico, Arizona, and California. Meanwhile, the United States effectively pressured Britain to relinquish claims on the Oregon Territory, and redrew the map of the Pacific Northwest with the present-day border dividing the state of Washington and Canada. United States territory had spread to the Pacific Ocean during the Polk presidency.

Though the nation had expanded, the unpopular Mexican War and Texas annexation divided the country over slavery. Violence broke out during the 1850s and eventually led to the Civil War, with Texas leaving the Union to battle with it as one of the Confederate States of America. Expansionism had magnified internal problems within the United States.

Polk had pledged to serve only one term in office, but it probably wasn't very likely that he would have been reelected anyway. The hardworking president had fulfilled the goals of his administration, but he left office exhausted, and he died a few months later.

Zachary Taylor

"If elected, I would not be the mere president of a party—I would endeavor to act independent of party domination and should feel bound to administer the government untrammeled by party schemes."

—*Zachary Taylor*

Zachary Taylor was a national hero when he came the White House in 1849. His triumphs in the Mexican War had brought him acclaim after a forty-year career in the military. His nickname, Old Rough and Ready, suited him perfectly.

Taylor was elected as the candidate of the Whig Party, made of factions of the former Democratic-Republican Party to oppose the Democratic Party founded by Andrew Jackson, but he wasn't what anyone would call a party man. He was very independent-minded, far better suited to military command than to the political give and take of a president. Plain of dress and blunt in his speech, Old Rough and Ready went to Washington with strong ideas on how the United States should move forward. He stuck to his scruples to such an extent that he brought the country to the brink of civil war. His untimely death after little more than a year in office allowed for compromises on the slavery issue that postponed the Civil War for another decade.

The third of nine children born to Richard and Sarah Dabney Strother Taylor, Zachary Taylor was born in Montebello, Virginia, on November 24, 1784. His father, a lieutenant colonel under George Washington during the Revolutionary War, was given 6,000 acres of land in Kentucky as compensation for his service. As a result, the Taylors moved to a large plantation near Louisville when Zachary was less than a year old. Richard Taylor became

Twelfth president of the United States, 1849–1850

Full name: *Zachary Taylor*
Born: *November 24, 1784, Montebello, Virginia*
Died: *July 9, 1850, Washington, D.C.*
Burial site: *Congressional Cemetery, Washington, D.C.; moved to Zachary Taylor National Cemetery, Louisville, Kentucky*
Parents: *Richard and Sarah Dabney Strother Taylor*
Spouse: *Margaret "Peggy" Smith (1788–1852; m. 1810)*
Children: *Ann Margaret Mackall (1811–75); Sarah Knox (1814–35); Octavia Pannill (1816–20); Margaret Smith (1819–20); Mary Elizabeth (1824–1909); Richard (1826–79)*
Religion: *Episcopalian*
Education: *No formal education*
Occupations: *Farmer; soldier*
Government positions: *None*
Political party: *Whig*
Dates as president: *March 5, 1849–July 9, 1850*
Age upon taking office: *64*

a prominent citizen, a member of the state legislature, and customs collector for the port of Louisville.

Although Richard Taylor had a degree from William and Mary College, he showed little enthusiasm for educating his children. Zachary studied for a short time under a private tutor, but he spent far more time working with his father on the family's farm. Even after his great military success later in life, he always considered himself a farmer, and he enjoyed talking about raising crops, especially cotton, until the end of his life.

Drawn to the Military

Although young Taylor was groomed to run the family plantation, he joined the militia in 1806 and discovered that he liked military life even more. After his first unit was disbanded, he was awarded a first lieutenant's commission in the Seventh Infantry by his second cousin, Secretary of State James Madison, and he spent the next forty years in military service, mostly on the frontier in present-day Indiana, Wisconsin, Louisiana, Minnesota, and Florida. His wife, Margaret Taylor, followed him from post to post with their six children, two of whom died very young.

Taylor's first public notice came during the War of 1812, when his company of some fifty men held back an attack by four hundred Indians, led by the Shawnee Chief Tecumseh, on Fort Harrison in Indiana. He was given a battlefield promotion, but when the war was over, he was reduced back to the rank of captain. Furious over the demotion, he resigned his commission. But a short time later, President Madison restored his rank and reassigned him to the Third Infantry at Green Bay, Wisconsin.

Making Do

Even as commander of the army, General Taylor lived in a small tent with no more creature comforts than the lowliest foot soldier. He was well known for patching his clothes and wearing them until there was nothing to sew a patch onto. After he became a national hero, P. T. Barnum offered to buy his trousers to display in his American Museum, and Taylor was pleased to take his money. Chances are that he didn't use it to buy a new pair. As one of his soldiers said, "He always wears an old cap, dusty green coat, a frightful pair of trousers, and on horseback he looks like a toad."

Timeline

1784: Born in Virginia
1806: Joins the Virginia militia at age twenty-two
1810: Accepts a commission in the Seventh Infantry of the United States Army by his second cousin, Secretary of State James Madison
1812: Taylor's company of about fifty men holds back an attack by four hundred Native Americans led by famous warrior Tecumseh at Fort Harrison in Indiana
1832: At Fort Crawford (now Prairie du Chien, Wisconsin) during the Black Hawk War, Taylor supervises the surrender of Chief Black Hawk
1837: On Christmas Day, Taylor's forces defeat Seminoles in a battle at Lake Okeechobee in Florida
1846–48: Taylor's small army unit repulses a Mexican force three times as large at the Battle of Palo Alto during the Mexican War; victories in Mexico at Resaca de Palma, Monterrey, and Buena Vista bring national hero status to General Taylor
1849–50 Serves as twelfth U.S. president
1850: Dies in Washington, D.C., after falling ill during a Fourth of July celebration

The Taylor family moved frequently over the next sixteen years as he supervised the building of forts and the recruitment of soldiers, mostly in the Louisiana Territory. Then, in 1832, he was promoted to colonel and shipped to Fort Crawford (now Prairie du Chien, Wisconsin) to command a detachment of four hundred men during the Black Hawk War, where he forced the surrender of Chief Black Hawk during a battle with Sauk and Fox warriors.

In 1837, Colonel Taylor was sent with a force of eleven hundred men to the Florida Everglades, where the Seminole nation was forcibly resisting relocation to "Indian lands" in present-day Oklahoma. He defeated the Seminoles in a battle at Lake Okeechobee on Christmas Day, and was promoted to brigadier general. Five months later, he was given command of the entire Florida department, a post he held for two years, all the while fighting Seminoles and grumbling about the tropical climate. It was during his Florida years that his men nicknamed him Old Rough and Ready.

Hero of the Mexican War

Left: The hero of the Battle of Buena Vista.

Below: The Mexican War brought Taylor national attention and acclaim.

It was the Mexican War that brought Taylor to national attention after decades in relative obscurity. In March of 1845, the United States invited Texas to join the Union, although Mexico strongly objected, because the border between Mexico and Texas was in dispute. In anticipation of a shooting war, President James K. Polk dispatched Taylor to the contested territory between the Nueces River and the Rio Grande, where he raised an army of 4,000 regulars and volunteers.

The following January, Taylor was ordered to advance south to the Rio Grande, and his forces prepared to fight. The first major conflict took place on May 8, 1846, when Taylor's small army drove back a Mexican force three times their size at the Battle of Palo Alto.

This victory brought Taylor another promotion, this time to major general. Old Rough and Ready proved equal to the promotion in September when he led his men to another lopsided victory against the fortified city of Monterrey in northern Mexico. Braving devastating enemy gunfire, Taylor and his troops invaded the city and fought hand to hand in the streets against a superior force. The Mexican troops finally surrendered after Taylor agreed to an eight-week armistice and allowed the Mexican soldiers to retreat with their weapons.

His Victories at Palo Alto, Resaca de Palma, and Monterrey brought hero status to General Zachary Taylor, by then as famous for his scruffy clothing and his devotion to his horse, Old Whitey, as for his military skills. This level of success didn't sit well with President Polk, though, correctly perceiving that Taylor might have political ambitions for a rival party. Polk expressed outrage at the armistice agreement Taylor had drawn up

in Monterrey, and had the general not been so popular, the president probably have relieved him of his command. As it was, Polk ordered another popular general, Winfield Scott to advance on Mexico City—and to take Taylor's best soldiers to do it.

As his most dependable troops joined Scott, Taylor was ordered to stay where he was in Monterrey in a strictly defensive posture. Taylor ignored the order and started moving southward with what was left of his army. On February 23, 1847, his force of 5,000 met an army of 15,000 to 20,000 led by the famous Mexican general Antonio López de Santa Anna at Buena Vista Hacienda. The two-day battle that followed was another resounding victory for the Americans, accomplished in no small part because Taylor showed amazing personal valor. At the end of the battle, the American force reported 267 men killed and 456 wounded, compared to more than 2,000 fatalities for the Mexican army. The fighting in northern Mexico was effectively over, although Winfield Scott was still some months away from marching into Mexico City.

"Hurrah for Old Kentuck! That's the way to do it. Give 'em hell, damn 'em."

—General Taylor during the Battle of Buena Vista

President Polk's plan to minimize Taylor's heroism failed miserably. As news of the Battle of Buena Vista spread, Whig leaders across the country began to court the popular general and to draft him as their presidential candidate.

Landed Gentry

"You'll never get rich," the song says, "you're in the army now." But that wasn't the case with Zachary Taylor. After he retired from army service, he had owned three Louisiana plantations before settling down in a rose-covered cottage at Baton Rouge, and his net worth was estimated at $200,000, a tidy sum in the 1840s. At a time when slavery was such a burning issue, fewer than two thousand Southern planters owned more than a hundred slaves, and Zachary Taylor was one of them.

Right: A negative campaign poster shows the Whig candidate comfortably seated atop skulls of the war's victims.

AN AVAILABLE CANDIDATE.
THE ONE QUALIFICATION FOR A WHIG PRESIDENT.

Below: One the positive side, the Whigs presented their nominee as a peace candidate.

JUSTICE.   PEACE

UNION

Black Hawk

Black Hawk was born into the Thunder Clan in 1767 in the region of the Virginia Colony that is now Rock Island, Illinois. He developed into a brave warrior and married a woman named Assheweque ("Singing Bird"), with whom he had three children. The chain of events that would make Black Hawk a resistance leader began in 1804, when the leaders of the southern Sauk and Fox of the Missouri signed the Treaty of St. Louis, handing over all tribal lands east of the Mississippi River to the United States. Black Hawk claimed that these tribal leaders did not speak for or represent the northern Sauk and Fox of the Mississippi River area. He refused to move to Iowa from his territory in Illinois and Wisconsin.

Black Hawk became a supporter of Shawnee tribal leader Tecumseh, who proposed a native tribal confederacy, an alliance of tribes who would protect one another's interests. Like Tecumseh, Black Hawk sided with the British against America in the War of 1812 (1812–15), which was fought over international trading rights. The U.S. government began to hold discussions with Keokuk (1788–1848?), a younger rival chief of the Fox clan. In 1816, the U.S. Army built Fort Armstrong at Rock Island, Illinois, within Black Hawk's traditional homeland. Two years later, the Illinois Territory became the twenty-first state. During the 1820s, while the state still had a small population, Black Hawk strengthened his ties with the British Empire by making frequent trading trips back and forth to Canada.

Keokuk continued to negotiate with the U.S. government for Sauk and Fox land. In 1829, he advised peace to his people. In company with two other Sauk and Fox chiefs, Keokuk gave up the Rock River land area to the United States in exchange for land west of the Mississippi in what is now Iowa, and an annuity for the tribe. Black Hawk's band returned from their winter hunt in the spring of 1829 to Saukenuk, their Rock River village, to find their land and homes occupied by whites. Though enraged, Black Hawk and his followers nonetheless stayed and shared their village with the newcomers for the remainder of that summer and for the next two years.

In the summer of 1831, the U.S. government invaded Saukenuk to force the 2,000 dwellers of Black Hawk's village across the Mississippi River in accordance with Keokuk's agreement.

Warned in advance of the attempt, however, Black Hawk and his villagers had escaped the previous night into Iowa and remained there through the following March. Black Hawk received spiritual and political support for his resistance from the Winnebago prophet White Cloud, and counted more than 2,000 people, including 600 warriors, among his followers. However, Black Hawk received no aid in the struggle from the British. On April 5, 1832, Black Hawk's band of 1,000 crossed the Mississippi River back into Illinois and headed north, trying to win support from other tribes in the area. The Winnebago and Potawatomi, however, declared their neutrality and refused to support Black Hawk. Meanwhile, the U.S. Army and state militias were called up. Among the volunteers to fight were such future political notables as Zachary Taylor and Jefferson Davis. A month later, Black Hawk was ready to admit defeat and surrender.

On May 14, 1832, as his truce party approached the U.S. troops under a white flag, nervous soldiers fired on them. His warriors retaliated and won the battle, which became known as Stillman's Run, after the panicked flight of the troops of Major Isaiah Stillman. Happy in their victory, but cautious about reprisals, Black Hawk and White Cloud headed back north to Wisconsin. For the next two months, however, the combined U.S. forces kept Black Hawk's band on the run with minor skirmishes along the way. With no aid from other tribes, lacking food, and losing warriors to desertion, Black Hawk continued to press north into Wisconsin. On July 21, 1832, the U.S. Army and Wisconsin militia, aided by Winnebago informers, attacked Black Hawk in the Battle of Wisconsin Heights, near present-day Sauk City, northwest of Madison. Many natives were killed, but others escaped by raft across the Wisconsin River, pushing westward toward the Bad Axe River that flows into the Mississippi. On August 3, 1832, the U.S. Army attacked with cannon, artillery, and sharpshooters in what became known as the Massacre at Bad Axe River. Exhausted and demoralized, Black Hawk, White Cloud, and the remaining resistance fighters surrendered at Fort Crawford (present-day Prairie du Chien), Wisconsin, on August 27, 1832.

From Wisconsin, Black Hawk was taken to Jefferson Barracks, Missouri, and then held as a prisoner of war in Fort Monroe, Virginia. Black Hawk became something of a celebrity after his surrender. In 1833, he was taken to Washington, D.C., to meet President Andrew Jackson, and he later toured cities in the eastern United States. He died in Iowaville, Iowa, on October 3, 1838.

1848 Election Results

Presidential / Vice Presidential Candidates	Popular Votes	Electoral Votes
Zachary Taylor / Millard Fillmore (Whig)	1,360,099	163
Lewis Cass / William O. Butler (Democratic)	1,220,544	127
Martin Van Buren / Charles Francis Adams (Free Soil)	291,263	0

"Independent of Party Domination"

Although he owned a home in Louisiana and a cotton plantation with some 100 slaves in Mississippi, Zachary Taylor had never really lived at a fixed address. He had never voted in an election and had never even registered to vote. However, as his popularity swept the nation, these things seemed to be just minor details. Nor did it seem to matter much that no one knew where he stood on any of the domestic or foreign issues of the day.

In a letter he made public in April of 1848, Taylor admitted that he felt ignorant of many public issues. He further confused his supporters by declaring, "I am a Whig but not ultra Whig." He added that, "If elected, I would not be the mere president of a party—I would endeavor to act independent of party domination and should feel bound to administer the Government untrammeled by party schemes."

Taylor's election was helped immensely when antislavery Whigs defected from his platform and formed the Free Soil Party, with ex-president Martin Van Buren as its candidate. Although Van Buren finished a distant third in the popular vote, he drew enough voters away from the Democratic candidate, Lewis Cass, to give Taylor a key victory—and thirty-six electoral votes—from the state of New York. Taylor won the presidency without a majority of the popular vote (he received 1,360,099 votes to Cass's 1,220,544 and Van Buren's 291,263), but perhaps more importantly, he won without any trust within his own party.

Taylor was inaugurated on March 5, 1849, and immediately marked himself as a controversial president. The great debate in Congress at the time concerned the extension of slavery into regions of the Southwest

New Job Description

With the country bursting at the seams, the Taylor administration added a new cabinet post, secretary of the interior, who would oversee Indian affairs and public land, along with control of the patent office and supervision of the government pension system. The man chosen for the job, Thomas Ewing, had served as treasury secretary during the Harrison and Tyler administrations.

The Taylor Administration

Administration Dates: March 5, 1849–July 9, 1850
Vice President: Millard Fillmore (1849–50)
Cabinet:

Secretary of State	John M. Clayton (1849–50)
Secretary of the Treasury	William Morris Meredith (1849–50)
Secretary of War	George W. Crawford (1849–50)
Attorney General	Reverdy Johnson (1849–50)
Secretary of the Navy	William Ballard Preston (1849–50)
Postmaster General	Jacob Collamer (1849–50)
Secretary of the Interior	Thomas Ewing (1849–50)

that had been ceded to the United States after the Mexican War. A gold rush had begun in California, and that territory was expressing an interest in statehood. New Mexico and Utah had been free of slavery while in Mexican hands, but Southerners wanted to extend slavery into those areas, too.

A slave owner himself, Taylor might have been expected to support the extension of slavery. He did not. He felt that the institution of slavery was based on economics and should not be used in regions where cotton wasn't grown. He was also concerned that this one issue could tear the nation apart, and he worked hard to prevent this. For example, he invited California and

Dear Sir ...

When the Whigs nominated Taylor by acclamation after the fourth ballot at their Philadelphia convention, the general wasn't there to hear the cheering. He was at home in far-off Baton Rouge. A committee was formed to let him know of the great honor they had bestowed on him, but several weeks passed with no acknowledgment from him. They had chosen to send him a letter and dropped it in the mailbox without a stamp. When it arrived postage-due, Taylor didn't bother to pick it up at the post office because he'd had letters from political parties before, and he was sure the postage on this one would be just the first of many costs. The committee posted a second letter and just to make sure the message got through, they also sent him a telegram, which was delivered by steamboat from Memphis. There is no record of whether he gave the messenger a tip, but he did accept the party's offer.

Lewis Cass

Twice a presidential nominee, Lewis Cass served as secretary of war, minister to France, and secretary of state. Born on October 2, 1782, in New Hampshire, Cass was the son of a Revolutionary War veteran, Major Jonathan Cass, and Mary Gilman Cass. He studied at Phillips Exeter Academy. In 1800, the family moved to the Ohio frontier, where Cass studied law and began a practice in 1803. In 1806, he married Elizabeth Spencer and was elected to the legislature in Ohio.

During the War of 1812, Cass advanced from colonel of militia to brigadier general and fought with distinction at the Battle of the Thames in present-day Ontario. In 1813, he was appointed governor of the Michigan Territory. He made a fortune by buying land in Detroit and later selling it in city lots. Promoting universal education, the establishment of libraries, road-building, and surveying tracts for settlers, Cass sped up the American settlement of Michigan. As Indian commissioner, he conducted expeditions to the northwestern area of the territory, studied Native American languages, and supported scholarly work on Native American culture. Still, he persuaded Native Americans to cede their lands; as President Andrew Jackson's secretary of war from 1831 to 1836, he vigorously supported the forced removal of the Cherokee from the South.

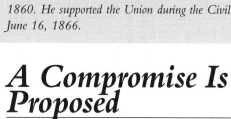

Appointed minister to France in 1836, Cass used his influence against British efforts to stop the international slave trade. In 1842, he sought the Democratic nomination for president, but lost to James K. Polk. Elected to the Senate in 1845, Cass urged war against Britain, if necessary, to obtain all of the Oregon Territory. He defended American involvement in the Mexican War above protests that it was an act of aggression, and he advocated the acquisition of Cuba.

With Southern support, Cass was the Democratic nominee for president in 1848, but he lost narrowly to General Zachary Taylor. Cass returned to the Senate and was a candidate for president in 1852, at age seventy, but the Democrats nominated Franklin Pierce. Cass supported the Compromise of 1850, including the Fugitive Slave Law, which forced return of runaway slaves to their slave owner. He supported the "popular sovereignty" doctrine of Stephen Douglas, whereby new territories could decide for themselves whether or not to permit slavery. In 1856, the Republican legislature in Michigan removed Cass from the Senate.

President James Buchanan made the aged Cass his secretary of state. As sectional conflicts dominated the American scene, Cass lost Southern friends by referring, in Michigan, to slavery as "a great social and political evil." He broke with Buchanan and his Southern advisers and resigned his office in 1860. He supported the Union during the Civil War. He died on June 16, 1866.

New Mexico to apply for statehood, with each state's own local legislatures deciding whether or not to allow slavery inside its borders. Both territories had let it be known that they did not want slavery, and it was generally understood that they would be admitted as free states.

Taylor's views were welcomed by antislavery politicians, but not surprisingly, the vast majority of Southern slaveholders denounced him and began hinting that they might secede from the Union. Taylor answered their threats with tough talk of his own, saying that he would send troops to police a disputed boundary between Texas and New Mexico, and that he would personally lead an army against any state that attempted to break away from the Union.

A Compromise Is Proposed

Moderate Whigs and Democrats were dismayed by Taylor's hard-line stand. In January of 1850, respected elder statesman Henry Clay offered a compromise bill that would address most of the points of dissent in a single piece of legislation. He proposed to have California admitted as a free state but would establish territorial governments for New Mexico and Utah, leaving the issue of slavery open in them. He also introduced a harsh Fugitive Slave Law that would give Southern slave owners federal assistance in recapturing runaway slaves.

Left: An official badge for the Taylor inauguration.

Right: Henry Clay proposed a compromise to help balance slave and free states.

In his speech defending the bill, Clay urged his fellow lawmakers to consider the legislation a compromise that could both save and strengthen the Union. The legislation became known as the Compromise of 1850.

Meanwhile, Taylor's secretary of state, John Clayton, signed a treaty with Great Britain, which was represented by diplomat Sir William Bulwer. The pact, which became known as the Clayton-Bulwer Treaty, concerned the proposed construction of a canal across the Isthmus of Panama, and declared that neither nation could "obtain or maintain for itself any exclusive control over the said ship-canal." It became obsolete in 1881 after Secretary of State James G. Blaine asserted that any canal built in Central America must be under the political control of the United States.

Debate on the Compromise of 1850 continued to rage in the Senate, but Taylor held to his own views and remained essentially aloof. He indicated that he would veto the legislation if it reached his desk, and this was is how matters stood when fate intervened and President Taylor met an untimely death.

Taylor attended a long ceremony celebrating the start of construction on the Washington Monument on July 4, 1850, spending hours in the hot sun listening to patriotic speeches, drank great quantities of cold water and ate cherries in iced milk. That night the sixty-five-year-old president fell desperately ill and was diagnosed with acute indigestion. He was dead just five days later. Following a state funeral, he was buried in Congressional Cemetery in the nation's capital, but later his body was moved to the family burial grounds in Louisville, Kentucky, which has became known as the Zachary Taylor National Cemetery.

Legacy

Zachary Taylor's successor, Millard Fillmore, was a moderate Whig who supported the Compromise of 1850 and signed it into law. However unpopular Taylor's stand on the Compromise had been, Fillmore's position was just as unpopular. Fillmore was the last Whig ever to serve as president. Many Whigs defected to the Republican Party that formed in 1854 and supported the abolition of slavery.

"Zachary Taylor is dead and in hell, and I am glad of it."
—*Brigham Young*

In the years following Taylor's sudden death, some historians have declared that Old Rough and Ready might have been poisoned in order to clear a path for the passage of the Compromise of 1850. They interpreted the descriptions of Taylor's final suffering as symptoms of arsenic poisoning. Finally, in 1991, Taylor's descendants agreed to have the distinguished general's corpse disinterred so that tissue samples could be taken to test for traces of the poison. They proved inconsistent with arsenic poisoning, and any arguments that Taylor had been secretly assassinated were put to an end.

"The presidency, even to the most experienced politicians, is no bed of roses, and General Taylor, like others, found thorns within it. It did not happen to General Taylor, once in his life, to fight a battle on equal terms, or on terms advantageous to himself, and yet he was never beaten and he never retreated."

—From Congressman Abraham Lincoln's eulogy

Untrained in the arts of political diplomacy, Taylor left behind a legacy not as an effective president but as a man of principle and plain speech. His threats of an armed response to any attempt at Southern secession may have helped to stop fighting in the territories won from Mexico. The Clayton-Bulwer Treaty signed during his presidency assured that no war would break out between America and Britain over lands in Central America by declaring that neither the United States nor Great Britain would be in control of the proposed Panama Canal. Seen by ordinary citizens as a "brave old feller," to quote one popular song of the day, Taylor was a legend in his own time, and he would have been even without his brief tenure as America's president.

Margaret Taylor

Born September 21, 1788, Calvert County, Maryland
Died August 14, 1852, East Pascagoula, Mississippi

"[My husband's] nomination is a plot to deprive me of his society and to shorten his life by unnecessary care and responsibility."

—Margaret Taylor

A popular legend held that Margaret Taylor, who had become a belle of Southern society, took a vow during the Mexican War pledging that if her husband Zachary Taylor should return safely, she would withdraw from every society. He did return safely. His heroism in the war made him a national figure, and he was elected president in 1848, but "Peggy" Taylor kept her vow. She undertook few duties as first lady, probably because her age was advanced and her health delicate after spending so many years as a military wife.

The Life of a Military Wife

Peggy Taylor was born in Calvert County, Maryland, the daughter of Revolutionary War veteran Walter Smith and his wife, Ann Mackall. She grew up in comfortable and genteel surroundings, and was educated in the manner of young ladies of her time. In 1809, the twenty-one-year-old Peggy traveled to Kentucky to visit her sister, and she met a handsome lieutenant named Zachary Taylor. After a brief courtship, they were married on June 21, 1810.

At the beginning of her marriage, she lived on the farm that her father-in-law had given the couple as a wedding gift. Her first daughter, Ann, was born there in 1811. It soon became clear, however, that Zachary Taylor's military career wouldn't allow him to be at home very much, and if she wanted to be with her husband, Peggy was going to have to travel with him from post to post, wherever his military superiors chose to send him. She embarked on a decades-long pilgrimage, following Zachary Taylor to a succession of remote outposts in the South and West.

She had to educate and raise her children in sometimes harsh surroundings. In 1820, the growing Taylor family was hit with a violent and communicable fever that killed two of the youngsters—Octavia and Margaret—and left her own health deteriorated. She recovered from the tragedy sufficiently to accompany her husband on his travels, and eventually Zachary and Peggy Taylor had two more children together, Mary Elizabeth and Richard.

When the surviving four Taylor children grew to adulthood, their father took a strong stand against his daughters marrying army men, because he knew that the life of a military wife was a hard one. The brunt of his hostility fell on his daughter Sarah Knox when she fell in love with a dashing young lieutenant named Jefferson Davis. Later in life, Davis would become president of the Confederate States of America, the Southern states that separated from the United States during the 1860s. Defying her father's wishes, Sarah Knox married Davis and went to live at his Southern plantation, only to

Above: Life in the field was as grueling for the general's wife as for the old soldier himself.

contract malaria and die three months later. The other two Taylor daughters, Ann and Mary Elizabeth, also married military men, becoming the wives of Robert C. Wood and William Bliss, respectively. Their father may not have been pleased, but it was probably to be expected of girls who grew up on military reservations and didn't often socialize with civilian men.

While her husband was away fighting in the Mexican War, Peggy Taylor lived in a mansion at Baton Rouge, Louisiana, that the couple had bought in 1840. She became a prominent member of Southern society, finding herself ever more popular as her husband's victories were reported. She wasn't terribly pleased to learn that his national fame might lead to a presidential nomination. At the age of sixty, she could hardly have been expected to be excited about moving to Washington. She did make the move, however, and during her husband's brief tenure as the twelfth president, she lived in the executive mansion by his side, even if she kept a low profile as first lady.

Peggy Taylor was a private first lady, rarely venturing out of her official home except to worship at St. John's Episcopal Church. Almost all of the first lady's official duties were relegated to Mary Elizabeth (Betty) Bliss, her lively and attractive daughter whose husband served as the president's secretary. Betty Bliss proved to be a capable official hostess, but her career as an assistant first lady was quite short. Soon after celebrating his first anniversary as chief executive, her father died suddenly of a gastric illness. The remaining members of his family quickly vacated the executive mansion when Millard Fillmore became president, and turned the hostess duties over to Fillmore's wife, Abigail.

Peggy Taylor lived only two more years after her husband's death. She died in 1852, survived by three of her children. Her son, Richard Taylor, served as an officer in the Confederacy during the Civil War. Her White House helper, Betty Bliss, survived into the twentieth century, before dying in 1909.

Taylor's Only Annual Address to Congress
Delivered on December 4, 1849

In 1848, the year Zachary Taylor was elected president, the Treaty of Guadalupe Hidalgo officially ended the Mexican War. In addition to settling the border of Texas, which had been annexed to the United States in 1844, the treaty gave the United States additional territory in the Southwest—areas of present-day New Mexico, Arizona, and California. This new land was in addition to the Oregon Territory, which forms the present-day states of Oregon, Washington, and Idaho, acquired during President Polk's administration.

Such a large increase in territory meant that new states would soon be entering the Union, a prospect that further inflamed debate over the nation's most divisive issue—slavery. There had been an equal number of free and slave states in the Union since the 1820 Missouri Compromise, and federal power was balanced between the North and the South. Abolitionists and even some of those who defended slavery, like Taylor, believed that it should not be extended to new territories.

In his first, and only, annual address to Congress, President Zachary Taylor insisted that he could end the long debate on slavery. He recognized the Constitutional right for existing states to decide on the issue, but he would not permit slavery to spread into new territories.

Excerpt from President Taylor's Only Annual Address to Congress

No civil government having been provided by Congress for California, the people of that Territory, impelled by the necessities of their political condition, recently met in convention for the purpose of forming a constitution and State government, which the latest advices give me reason to suppose has been accomplished; and it is believed they will shortly apply for the admission of California into the Union as a sovereign State. Should such be the case, and should their constitution be conformable to the requisitions of the Constitution of the United States, I recommend their application to the favorable consideration of Congress.

The people of New Mexico will also, it is believed, at no very distant period present themselves for admission into the Union. Preparatory to the admission of California and New Mexico the

people of each will have instituted for themselves a republican form of government, laying its foundation in such principles and organizing its powers in such form as to them shall seem most likely to effect their safety and happiness. By awaiting their action all causes of uneasiness may be avoided and confidence and kind feeling preserved. With a view of maintaining the harmony and tranquillity so dear to all, we should abstain from the introduction of those exciting topics of a sectional character which have hitherto produced painful apprehensions in the public mind; and I repeat the solemn warning of the first and most illustrious of my predecessors against furnishing "any ground for characterizing parties by geographical discriminations." [. . .]

Our Government is one of limited powers, and its successful administration eminently depends on the confinement of each of its coordinate branches within its own appropriate sphere. The first section of the Constitution ordains that—

> *All legislative powers herein granted shall be vested in a Congress of the United States, which shall consist of a Senate and House of Representatives.*

The Executive has authority to recommend (not to dictate) measures to Congress. Having performed that duty, the executive department of the Government can not rightfully control the decision of Congress on any subject of legislation until that decision shall have been officially submitted to the President for approval. The check provided by the Constitution in the clause conferring the qualified veto will never be exercised by me except in the cases contemplated by the fathers of the Republic. I view it as an extreme measure, to be resorted to only in extraordinary cases, as where it may become necessary to defend the executive against the encroachments of the legislative power or to prevent hasty and inconsiderate or unconstitutional legislation. By cautiously confining this remedy within the sphere prescribed to it in the contemporaneous expositions of the framers of the Constitution, the will of the people, legitimately expressed on all subjects of legislation through their constitutional organs, the Senators and Representatives of the United States, will have its full effect. As indispensable to the preservation of our system of self-government, the independence of the representatives of the States and the people is guaranteed by the Constitution, and they owe no responsibility to any human power but their constituents. By holding the representative responsible only to the people, and exempting him from all other influences, we elevate the character of the constituent and quicken his sense of responsibility to his country. It is under these circumstances only that the elector can feel that in the choice of the lawmaker he is himself truly a component part of the sovereign power of the nation. With equal care we should study to defend the rights of the executive and judicial departments. Our Government can only be preserved in its purity by the suppression and entire elimination of every claim or tendency of one coordinate branch to encroachment upon another. With the strict observance of this rule and the other injunctions of the Constitution, with [. . .] respect and love for the Union of the States which our fathers cherished and enjoined upon their children, and with the aid of that overruling Providence which has so long and so kindly guarded our liberties and institutions, we may reasonably expect to transmit them, with their innumerable blessings, to the remotest posterity.

But attachment to the Union of the States should be habitually fostered in every American heart. For more than half a century, during which kingdoms and empires have fallen, this Union has stood unshaken. The patriots who formed it have long since descended to the grave; yet still it remains, the proudest monument to their memory and the object of affection and admiration with everyone worthy to bear the American name. In my judgment its dissolution would be the greatest of calamities, and to avert that should be the study of every American.

Upon its preservation must depend our own happiness and that of countless generations to come. Whatever dangers may threaten it, I shall stand by it and maintain it in its integrity to the full extent of the obligations imposed and the powers conferred upon me by the Constitution.

What Happened Next

Insisting that slavery should be prohibited to expand beyond the Southern states into new territories, President Taylor threatened to veto legislation that would give the new territories the right to decide for themselves on whether to permit slavery. Nevertheless, Congress moved toward completing legislation that would grant that right to new states. Taylor died before the legislation was completed. Soon after, a series of bills, called the Compromise of 1850, was submitted to President Millard Fillmore who signed them into law. Among other things, the Compromise allowed new territories to decide for themselves on slavery.

The Compromise was thought by some as the final answer to the issue of slavery. It was not. The Fugitive Slave Law, where runaway slaves could be pursued into the North, prosecuted, and returned to their owners, further enflamed abolitionists. In 1856, a civil war raged in Kansas territory between pro- and antislavery forces. Taylor was followed by three presidents—Millard Fillmore, Franklin Pierce, and James Buchanan—who permitted slavery as a means for preserving the Union. They were followed by Abraham Lincoln, who began by taking the same position as Taylor had against the expansion of slavery. When Southern states resisted him by seceding from the Union, Lincoln gained more authority and issued an Emancipation Proclamation in 1863, which began the end of slavery.

Millard Fillmore

"An honorable defeat is better than a dishonorable victory."

—*Millard Fillmore*

Thirteenth president of the United States, 1850–1853

Full name: *Millard Fillmore*

Born: *January 7, 1800, Locke (now Summerhill), New York*

Died: *March 8, 1874, Buffalo, New York*

Burial site: *Forest Lawn Cemetery, Buffalo, New York*

Parents: *Nathaniel and Phoebe Millard Fillmore; Eunice Love (stepmother)*

Spouse: *Abigail Powers (1798–1853; m. 1826); Caroline Carmichael McIntosh (1813–1881; m. 1858)*

Children: *Millard Powers (1828–1889); Mary Abigail (1832–1854)*

Religion: *Unitarian*

Education: *No formal education*

Occupations: *Lawyer; educator*

Government positions: *New York state assemblyman; U.S. representative from New York; vice president under Zachary Taylor*

Political party: *Whig*

Dates as president: *July 9, 1850–March 4, 1853*

Age upon taking office: *50*

illard Fillmore's tenure as the thirteenth president of the United States was brief but significant. Taking over the presidency after the death of Zachary Taylor (in July of 1850), Fillmore signed into law a series of five bills that were known as known as the Compromise of 1850—legislation meant to resolve issues dividing the free and slave states. While he was a Northerner himself, and opposed slavery, Fillmore was also dedicated to preserving the Union. He was willing to accept measures that many abolitionists found repulsive in order to calm the Southern states. The result was that he narrowly avoided a sectional crisis between the Northern and the Southern States, and delayed the Civil War for another decade.

Below: The California Gold Rush was in full swing when Fillmore became president.

The nation was expanding at the time of Fillmore's presidency. New railroads were needed to move settlers into the West; a gold rush had begun in California, and it was admitted to the Union as a free state. New markets were needed for American goods, and the United States began a trade relationship with Japan, which had previously rejected American advances. All of these things—some of them controversial—were accomplished during the two and a half years Fillmore was president. He was the last of the Whig candidates to serve as a chief executive, and he was the second vice president to assume the office after the death of a sitting president.

A perfect example of the self-made man, Fillmore was an imposing figure, but with limited skills as a public speaker. He didn't particularly enjoy being president, but once the office was thrust on him, he proved quite capable of making executive decisions and standing by them through the toughest opposition. His support of the Compromise of 1850, including its most controversial provision, the Fugitive Slave Act, however, earned him a host of political enemies who did everything to make

Book Learning

Before he went to school, young Millard Fillmore learned to read by studying the family Bible. After a library opened nearby, he branched out to other books, but they were filled with unfamiliar words, so he bought a dictionary and read that during breaks in his job as an apprentice cloth maker. By the time he became president, his personal library contained more than 4,000 books, and apparently, he had read every one of them.

his life miserable, and to see to it that he would never be elected president on his own after serving out the rest of Taylor's term.

Ambitious and Self-Taught

The second child and oldest son in a family of nine, Millard Fillmore was born in Cayuga County, New York, on January 7, 1800. His ancestors had struggled in New England for several generations, and his father, Nathaniel, rented a farm in what was still frontier country in western New York in hopes that he would have better luck. Young Millard worked on the farm and was apprenticed to a textile mill in his teens. His only education came during breaks in the production schedule at the mill. He jumped at every opportunity to learn how to read and write and he succeeded thanks to a local schoolteacher named Abigail Powers At that time, there were no laws requiring that children had to go to school, but Fillmore went anyway, whenever he could. When the New Hope Academy opened, he enrolled there at the age of nineteen, and became a favorite of Miss Powers, his teacher, who was only two years older than he was. They were married seven years later.

Long before then, Fillmore had gone to work as a clerk and personal secretary for a Cayuga County attorney named Walter Wood, and began studying the law by reading the books in the lawyer's small personal library. When the Fillmore family moved on to East Aurora in Erie County, New York, he continued his legal studies and also worked as a schoolteacher.

Timeline

1800: Born in New York
1814: Begins attending school at age fourteen
1818: Begins studying law
1823: Passes New York bar
1828–31: Member of New York State Assembly
1833–35: Serves in U.S. House of Representatives as member of the Anti-Masonic Party
1836–42: Serves in U.S. House of Representatives as member of the Whig Party
1844: Fails in bid to be elected governor of New York
1849–50: Serves as vice president under Zachary Taylor
1850: Taylor dies; Fillmore becomes thirteenth president on July 10; signs Compromise of 1850
1852: Fillmore loses Whig nomination to General Winfield Scott, an antislavery advocate; Harriet Beecher Stowe's *Uncle Tom's Cabin* is published
1862: Named the first chancellor of the University of Buffalo (now State University of New York at Buffalo)
1874: Dies in New York

Tall, blonde, and handsome, with a pleasing personality and high moral standards, Fillmore slowly began to win his way in the world. He was admitted to the Erie County bar in 1823 and opened a law office in East Aurora. Three years later, he proposed marriage to Abigail Powers, and she accepted. The couple would have two children. In the meantime, he moved his family and his law practice to Buffalo, New York, and became active in local politics.

In 1828, Fillmore met newspaper publisher Thurlow Weed, an influential political boss. Weed had been instrumental in the formation of the Anti-Masonic Party, a new political organization that opposed secret fraternal organizations like the Masons, and he backed Fillmore as its candidate for the state legislature. He won the election easily, and served three terms, playing an important role in abolishing laws that confined debtors to prison. Fillmore's success in state politics—not to mention his friendship with Weed—started him on a roll toward bigger and better opportunities on the national scene.

To Congress and Beyond

Fillmore was elected to Congress in 1832 as an Anti-Masonic candidate. After serving one term, he switched to the Whig Party, a coalition that had been formed to oppose the Andrew Jackson administration. After refusing to run for reelection in 1834, he went back to Congress in 1836 and served three consecutive terms. Meanwhile, the Whig Party grew in prominence until it became the majority party in Congress after the 1840 election.

Immensely popular in Congress as well as back in his home state, Fillmore was given the prestigious chairmanship of the House Ways and Means Committee, which determines the costs and methods for enacting legislation. He used the high visibility it brought him to promote higher tariff rates, keeping with his belief that American businesses needed protection from foreign competition. He also used his influence to pass an appropriation bill that provided money to help Samuel F. B. Morse develop the telegraph.

At the height of his popularity in 1842, Fillmore announced that he wouldn't run for another term in Congress, but he wasn't interested in leaving politics, either. He had other offices in mind. He went back to New York and two years later he became the Whig candidate for governor, but the Party was losing its popularity, and he lost the election. He and others blamed the loss on abolitionists and Catholic foreigners. It was apparent, in any case, that the voters' rejection wasn't personal because the Whig's 1844 presidential candidate, Henry Clay, lost too. Still, Fillmore walked away from politics once again, and went back to his law practice.

Right: A Whig banner promoting Zachary Taylor and his running mate, Millard Fillmore, in the 1848 presidential election.

However, as before, his "retirement" was only temporary. He was elected state comptroller, the government's chief financial officer, with an impressive majority of the popular vote in 1847. He had barely completed a year in the job when another opportunity came up, a chance to run for vice president. He accepted the offer, even though his heart wasn't completely in it.

A Vice President with Integrity

At their 1848 presidential nominating convention, the Whigs named Zachary Taylor as their candidate, in spite of the fact that he was a Southern slave owner (though he was against the extension of slavery into new territories). The Whigs needed a Northerner to balance the ticket, and their first choice was Abbot Lawrence, a Massachusetts cotton manufacturer and former congressman. There was dissention, however; a powerful faction led by Henry Clay opposed Lawrence, objecting to having cotton-based moneymakers on both ends of the ticket, no matter what good might be accomplished by their regional differences. It was this group that successfully pressed for Fillmore to become Taylor's running mate.

The Taylor-Fillmore ticket won the presidential election in November of 1848, but the victory proved very hollow for Fillmore at first. His alliance with Thurlow Weed and the New York senator William H. Seward came to an end when Fillmore found out that the

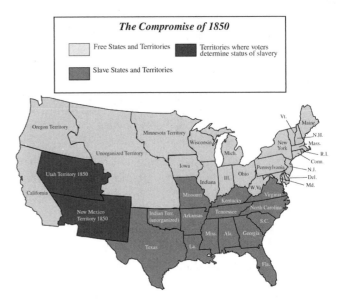

Above: The Compromise of 1850

two men were actively working to undermine his political influence. Unable to hand out patronage appointments, Fillmore found himself left with little more than the ceremonial vice presidential duty of presiding over the Senate. However, the duty became unusually important when Congress began a lengthy and heated debate on the bills collectively known as the Compromise of 1850.

This legislation—the bulk of which had been drafted by Henry Clay—was a desperate attempt to resolve the bitter sectional dispute that would eventually lead to the Civil War. At issue was the status of slavery in the lands acquired by the United States after the Mexican War. California was close to admission as a free state, but that would upset the balance between free states and slave states. Added to that, the slave state of Texas was claiming parts of what would become New Mexico and was threatening to extend slavery into that territory as well.

Although he was a Southerner and a slaveholder, Zachary Taylor objected to any expansion of slavery, and he threatened to send federal troops to enforce the Texas–New Mexico boundary. Furthermore, he announced an intention to veto any compromise that Congress might send to him if it included legislation that supported the expansion of slavery.

Powerless

Millard Fillmore had few enemies when he started out as vice president, but by the time he became president a year later, he had more enemies in the state of New York than he could count. The state's senator, William H. Seward, had made a deal with President Taylor that he, and not the vice president, should decide on patronage jobs for New Yorkers. It left Fillmore toothless; even his own law partner couldn't get a job in the administration. Naturally, the Whigs that Seward chose to pass over blamed the vice president, and it wasn't easy to explain why the number-two Whig in Washington didn't have any influence.

In his position as president of the Senate, Vice President Fillmore listened closely. He served several times as an arbiter when tempers got out of hand, although he generally kept his own opinions on the matter to himself. As a vote came close, he informed President Taylor that he intended to break any tie by voting in favor of the Compromise. This stand, Fillmore hastened to add, was not taken out of hostility toward the president, but instead, he felt he must vote out of his own deep conviction that the Compromise was the only way that the Union could be protected and a civil war averted.

For his part, President Taylor had promised to veto the Compromise bills, but he fell ill at an 1850 Independence Day celebration, and died on July 9. Fillmore was immediately sworn in as the thirteenth president the next day.

The Fillmore Administration

Administration Dates: July 9, 1850–March 4, 1853
Vice President: None
Cabinet:

Secretary of State	John M. Clayton (1850)
	Daniel Webster (1850–52)
	Edward Everett (1852–53)
Secretary of the Treasury	William M. Meredith (1850)
	Thomas Corwin (1850–53)
Secretary of War	George W. Crawford (1850)
	Charles M. Conrad (1850–53)
Attorney General	Reverdy Johnson (1850)
	John J. Crittenden (1850–53)
Secretary of the Navy	William B. Preston (1850)
	William A. Graham (1850–52)
	John P. Kennedy (1852–53)
Postmaster General	Jacob Collamer (1850)
	Nathan K. Hall (1850–52)
	Samuel D. Hubbard (1852–53)
Secretary of the Interior	Thomas Ewing (1850)
	Thomas M. T. McKennan (1850)
	Alexander H. H. Stuart (1850–53)

President Fillmore asked for and received the resignation of Taylor's entire cabinet as his first official act, and then he chose his own advisors, including Daniel Webster as secretary of state. Fillmore's new cabinet was made up of allies who favored the compromise measures still being debated in Congress. In a statement to both houses of Congress on August 6, 1850, the new president recommended that Texas be paid to abandon its claims to the disputed New Mexico territories—a key provision in the compromise legislation. Clearly, Fillmore was in favor of preserving the Union at any cost. Congress responded by quickly passing the series of bills that would come to be known as the Compromise of 1850.

A Bitter Compromise

The Compromise of 1850 contained five bills that produced these results: (*1*) California was admitted as a free state; (*2*) Texas was compensated for the loss of territory in the boundary dispute with New Mexico; (*3*) New Mexico was granted territorial status; (*4*) the slave trade—but not slavery itself—was abolished in the nation's capital; and (*5*) most controversially, the Fugitive Slave Law was enacted, allowing slave owners to pursue and recapture runaway slaves in free states. It even put federal troops at the disposal of the slaveholders. Not only did Fillmore sign the bill into law, but he supervised its enactment. He felt that the measure was necessary to placate the slave states, where prominent politicians were already seriously discussing the possibility leaving the Union of States.

Not surprisingly, the Fugitive Slave Law increased the already divisive tensions between proslavery and abolitionist groups. The antislavery movement grew more vocal following the 1852 publication of Harriet Beecher Stowe's *Uncle Tom's Cabin,* the most sympathetic work of antislavery sentiments in popular literature up until that time. The uneasy truce won by the Compromise of 1850 proved to be temporary and didn't add to Fillmore's popularity as president. When the Whig Party met to nominate its ticket for the 1852 election, he lost to an antislavery candidate, General Winfield Scott.

The conflict over slavery overwhelmed other important developments during the Fillmore presidency. Northern states were growing more prosperous by developing industries and investing in the expansion of the nation's railroads across the Great Plains and the far West. American trade with China had opened up during

Harriet Beecher Stowe

Harriet Beecher Stowe was born on June 14, 1811, in Litchfield, Connecticut. She was the seventh child of preacher Lyman Beecher and his first wife, Roxana Foote, who died when Stowe was four years old. In 1824, Stowe's older sister Catherine, with whom she was very close, started a school for teenaged girls in Hartford, Connecticut, and Stowe was one of the first pupils. She began writing poetry, but her sister dismissed that activity and put Stowe to work teaching girls her own age.

The Stowe family moved to the Cincinnati, Ohio, area in 1832 when Stowe's father became president of Lane Theological Seminary. Having read Shakespeare, Stowe soon joined a literary society called the Semi-Colon Club. A fellow member, future Supreme Court justice Salmon P. Chase, introduced her to the growing antislavery movement. In 1833, Stowe wrote an article about grammar and punctuation, for which she received fifty dollars. This led her to a career of writing. The same year, she crossed the Ohio River and saw a southern plantation for the first time, an experience that provided her with the setting for Uncle Tom's Cabin. Around the same time Stowe began caring for her deceased friend's widower, Calvin Stowe, fixing his meals and mending his clothes. In January 1836, they were married and she became known as Harriet Beecher Stowe. The couple had twin daughters in September 1837.

Stowe contributed short stories, essays, and articles to the Western Monthly magazine. But the Fugitive Slave Law of 1850 caused Stowe to begin writing seriously. She read everything available about slavery, but did not consider writing a book until a vision of an old slave filled her mind. Convinced that God had reached out to her, she wrote down what she had seen. The first episode of Uncle Tom's Cabin appeared in the National Era in March 1851, and other episodes followed weekly. Her stories were so popular that when they were collected in a book and published for the first time in 1852, Uncle Tom's Cabin became a huge success. Three million copies had been sold by the time the Civil War began in 1861. The book was translated into thirty-seven languages. The book helped inspire many readers to join in efforts to abolish slavery. Its impact on society is among the greatest of any novel ever published.

To answer attacks that her novel exaggerated the harshness of the lives of slaves, Stowe compiled A Key to Uncle Tom's Cabin, which contains case histories to verify the scenes in her book. During 1853 and 1854, Stowe wrote an average of one magazine article every two weeks.

When her husband retired in 1863, the family moved to Hartford, and it was there during the Civil War that Stowe wrote magazine articles advocating employment for the freed slaves and compassion toward the Confederacy once the seceded states had returned to the Union. With the coming of peace, Stowe rented a cotton plantation in Florida, installed her son, Fred, as manager, and hired former slaves to work for her. The Stowes had planned to spend their winters there, but the project proved to be unsuccessful. Stowe then bought an orange grove in Mandarin, Florida, and founded a school for former slaves. Her contributions to the state earned her the approval of General Robert E. Lee and the acceptance of the Southern people.

Stowe's seventieth birthday, in 1881, was a national event; newspapers published editorials about her, and the school children in Hartford were given a holiday in her honor. She died on July 1, 1896, at the age of eighty-five, and is buried in Andover, Massachusetts.

Image Problem

Shortly after he became president, Fillmore decided to buy a new carriage to reflect his new station in life. The best one he could find was a used one. When he asked the salesman if it would be appropriate for a president to ride around Washington in a second-hand carriage, the answer was, "Mr. Fillmore, you are a second-hand president."

Right: An editorial cartoon laments the choice of war hero candidates over qualified statesmen. The voters were unimpressed.

the mid-1840s, and Fillmore commissioned Commodore Matthew Perry to visit Japan—which had kept itself isolated since the seventeenth century—and open it up for trade as well. In the midst of crippling divisiveness, America was going through a period of exciting growth.

Postpresidential Accomplishments

Shortly after the end of his term, Fillmore went back to Buffalo as a grieving widower. Abigail Fillmore had died on March 30, 1853, just weeks after his successor was inaugurated. Fillmore never held political office again. He was nominated in 1856 as a candidate for the presidency by the American—or Know-Nothing—Party, a movement concerned with issues of national unity and curbing immigration. Fillmore believed that the American Party held the only hope of uniting the nation, which was still bitterly divided by the slavery issue, and he campaigned earnestly throughout both the South and the North, but on election day, he was soundly defeated by Democrat James Buchanan. Fillmore finished a distant third—behind Buchanan and Republican John C. Frémont—with only 22 percent of the vote. His defeat was a fatal blow to the American Party's influence as well as his own political life.

Fillmore became a leading citizen of Buffalo in his later years, serving as the first chancellor of the University of Buffalo (now the State University of New York at Buffalo), and he was one of the founders of the Buffalo Historical Society. He supported the Union during the Civil War, but he became increasingly concerned about the policies of President Abraham Lincoln, who he called a military despot, and he supported Lincoln's opponent, George B. McClellan, in his reelection campaign. After

THE RIGHT MAN FOR THE RIGHT PLACE.

Lincoln's assassination, Fillmore supported President Andrew Johnson's program for Reconstruction of the South.

Fillmore's second marriage, in 1858, to Albany heiress Caroline Carmichael McIntosh gave him the means to undertake many philanthropic activities, including the creation of Buffalo General Hospital. He died quietly at his home on March 8, 1874, after suffering a stroke. He is buried beneath an imposing monument at Forest Lawn Cemetery in Buffalo.

The Company He Keeps

Fillmore was on a tour of Europe when the American Party nominated him as their presidential candidate. Another former president, Martin Van Buren, was there at the same time, and they appeared together at the British House of Commons. He also had an audience with Pope Pius IV in Rome, but the anti-Catholic political party that nominated him chose to forgive him for it. Like his predecessor, Zachary Taylor, he was notified of their nomination by mail, accepted by return mail, and then sailed home, cutting his grand tour short.

Above: Caroline McIntosh, Fillmore's second wife.

Right: The treaty that resulted from Matthew Perry's mission to Japan.

Below: Japan as Commodore Perry found it.

Legacy

The most noteworthy event of Millard Fillmore's presidency was the compromise of 1850; his support ensured that it would be passed by Congress and become law. Although the compromise proved unpopular in both the North and the South, it helped delay the start of the Civil War for ten more years. During that decade, the North expanded its industrial activity immensely, giving it a distinct advantage when the war finally broke out in 1861.

"When he had carefully examined a question and had satisfied himself that he was right, no power on earth could induce him to swerve from what he believed to be the line of duty."
—Interior Secretary Alexander H. H. Stewart

The high points of Fillmore's administration also included the expansion of the nation's railroads across the Great Plains and in the far West. And he gave America one more important legacy. It was he who commissioned Commodore Matthew Perry to visit Japan and open it for trade. Perry's mission was successful, but its results weren't felt until after Fillmore had left office.

"It must always be regretted that such a man as Millard Fillmore has not a mind comprehensive enough to properly meet a great crisis.... It was, moreover, his misfortune to see in slavery a political and not a moral question. Upon this issue which, it is true, was one of transcendant importance, he was a politician and not a statesman."
—The New York Times

Abigail Fillmore

Born March 13, 1798, Stillwater, New York
Died March 30, 1853, Washington, D.C.

"I pursued much of my study with, and perhaps was unconsciously stimulated by, the companionship of a young lady whom I afterward married."

—*Millard Fillmore*

Abigail Fillmore was the first of the nation's first ladies to hold a job after her marriage, continuing her career as a schoolteacher. In fact, it was as a teacher that she first met future president Millard Fillmore, who was one of her students.

The daughter of Lemuel Powers, a respected Baptist minister, Abigail Powers was born in Saratoga County, New York, in 1798. Her father died while she was still young, and in order to conserve what little money she had, her mother moved west, into the sparsely populated New York frontier. Abigail was schooled at home there, using books that had belonged to her father.

Abigail began teaching school, in the village of New Hope, New York, when she was only sixteen years old. In those days, country schooling was somewhat informal. Students went to school when their farm chores were done, and youngsters of all ages crowded into one room. It wasn't terribly unusual for somebody like young mill worker Millard Fillmore to show up at the school, even though he was only two years younger than the teacher.

The pretty, red-haired Abigail was impressed by the young man's determination to get an education that could improve his life, and she devoted many extra hours to his schooling. It was possible, of course, that she was attracted to this handsome young man. As a matter of fact, no one was very surprised when they got invitations to Millard and Abigail's wedding.

Left: Fillmore's mansion in Buffalo, New York.

Abigail Powers taught school while Millard Fillmore studied law and completed his examinations. When he eventually passed the bar examination in Erie County, he opened a small law practice in East Aurora, New York, and he and Abigail were married in 1826, while Fillmore was still a struggling young attorney. As a newlywed, Abigail Fillmore went on teaching school for two more years while her husband's law practice grew. By the time their first child, Millard Powers Fillmore, was born, the family was prosperous and the elder Millard was getting involved in state politics.

In 1830, the family moved into a six-room house in Buffalo, New York, where their daughter, Mary Abigail, was born two years later, the same year Fillmore won his first Congressional election. Abigail had an active social life, and she was noted for her flower garden, but she still found time to read and to play music. Throughout her husband's political career, she quietly advised him, but her public role was only ceremonial—standing at his side at dinners and receptions, engaging in conversation with other political wives, and doing charitable work.

She moved to Washington in 1849 when her husband was elected vice president. However, by that time her health was not as robust as it had been, and she delegated some of her official responsibilities to her daughter, Abby, who had been given a formal education and was quite good at the job.

The sudden death of President Zachary Taylor in July of 1850 thrust the Fillmores into the presidential mansion, a place they found to be surprisingly primitive. While the new president ordered a cooking stove for the kitchen, where food was still being prepared over an open fire, Abigail took the more drastic step of petitioning Congress for money to begin a presidential library in the house. After she got the funds, she started buying books and shelving them in a charming oval-shaped room on the second floor. It was there that she spent much of her private time, reading, sometimes listening to musical concerts taking place in other parts of the house, and chatting with her closest friends. The room would much later become the president's working space, called the Oval Office.

A chronic sore ankle made many of Abigail Fillmore's official duties quite difficult. Often she had to stand at her husband's side shaking hands for hours at a time, and she was expected to plan and preside over an endless round of dinner parties and receptions. Abigail was an elegant dresser, and she loved to wear expensive, well-made clothes. Her wit and grace made her an able first lady whose sought-after presence was enhanced by her more vivacious daughter, who was usually at her side.

Millard Fillmore's tenure as president was brief, because he failed to secure the Whig nomination in the 1852 election. His wife was in poor health when his term ended, but she attended the inauguration of the new president, Franklin Pierce, braving snowy conditions and a chill wind. A cold she caught that day turned into pneumonia, and she died on March 30, 1853. Her body was returned to Buffalo for burial at Forest Lawn cemetery.

The Fillmores were sober and serious people, and they moved into the executive mansion during a period of mourning after the death of President Taylor. Therefore, their days as president and first lady were not marked by lavish entertainment. When a reception was scheduled, they banned smoking and drinking, to the chagrin of some of their guests. Abigail Fillmore's lasting contribution to the White House was not memories of lavish, spirited parties but rather a modest library of volumes that she knew would be useful to future holders of the nation's highest office.

Fillmore's First Annual Address to Congress

December 2, 1850

When Millard Fillmore assumed the office of president following the death of Zachary Taylor in July 1850, Congress and the nation both were bitterly divided over the issue of slavery. The new president intended to use his power to stop the spread of slavery to new territories, but he was willing to accept measures that would calm those who favored slavery. As a way of protecting the rights of Southern states, he supported the series of bills in Congress that became known as the Compromise of 1850, which President Taylor had promised to veto. After Fillmore became president, Congress quickly passed and signed the bills that formed the Compromise of 1850.

Among the terms of the Compromise, California was admitted into the Union as a free state, and New Mexico would be allowed to decide for itself whether it would be free or permit slavery within its borders. Its most controversial component was the Fugitive Slave Act that allowed federal authorities to be enlisted to help track, prosecute, and return slaves who had escape to the North. Anyone who assisted runaway slaves could be prosecuted and punished as well.

At the time of his first annual address, President Fillmore had been in office less than five full months. He used the occasion to give a speech similar to an inaugural address, in which a new president presents his vision for the years ahead. He discussed foreign policy as well as domestic issues and, on the home front, he asked the American people to be patient and allow time for the legislation of the Compromise of 1850 to reach its goal of promoting national unity.

Excerpt from Fillmore's First Annual Address to Congress

Nations, like individuals in a state of nature, are equal and independent, possessing certain rights and owing certain duties to each other, arising from their necessary and unavoidable relations; which rights and duties there is no common human authority to protect and enforce. Still, they are rights and duties, binding in morals, in conscience, and in honor, although there is no tribunal to which an injured party can appeal but the disinterested judgment of mankind, and ultimately the arbitrament of the sword.

Among the acknowledged rights of nations is that which each possesses of establishing that form of government which it may deem most conducive to the happiness and prosperity of its own citizens, of changing that form as circumstances may require, and of managing its internal affairs according to its own will. The people of the United States claim this right for themselves, and

they readily concede it to others. Hence it becomes an imperative duty not to interfere in the government or internal policy of other nations; and although we may sympathize with the unfortunate or the oppressed everywhere in their struggles for freedom, our principles forbid us from taking any part in such foreign contests. We make no wars to promote or to prevent successions to thrones, to maintain any theory of a balance of power, or to suppress the actual government which any country chooses to establish for itself. We instigate no revolutions, nor suffer any hostile military expeditions to be fitted out in the United States to invade the territory or provinces of a friendly nation. The great law of morality ought to have a national as well as personal and individual application. We should act toward other nations as we wish them to act toward us, and justice and conscience should force the rule of conduct between governments, instead of mere power, self-interest, or the desire of aggrandizement. To maintain a strict neutrality in foreign wars, to cultivate friendly relations, to reciprocate every noble and generous act, and to perform punctually and scrupulously every treaty obligation—these are the duties which we owe to other states, and by the performance of which we best entitle ourselves to like treatment from them; or, if that, in any case, be refused, we can enforce our own right with justice and a clear conscience.

In our domestic policy the Constitution will be my guide, and in questions of doubt I shall look for its interpretation to the judicial decisions of that tribunal which was established to expound it and to the usage of the Government, sanctioned by the acquiescence of the country. I regard all its provisions as equally binding. In all its parts it is the will of the people expressed in the most solemn form, and the constituted authorities are but agents to carry that will into effect. Every power which it has granted is to be exercised for the public good; but no pretense of utility, no honest conviction, even, of what might be expedient, can justify the assumption of any power not granted. The powers conferred upon the Government and their distribution to the several departments are as clearly expressed in that sacred instrument as the imperfection of human language will allow, and I deem it my first duty not to question its wisdom, add to its provisions, evade its requirements, or nullify its commands.

[. . .]

It was hardly to have been expected that the series of measures passed at your last session with the view of healing the sectional differences which had sprung from the slavery and territorial questions should at once have realized their beneficent purpose. All mutual concession in the nature of a compromise must necessarily be unwelcome to men of extreme opinions. And though without such concessions our Constitution could not have been formed, and can not be permanently sustained, yet we have seen them made the subject of bitter controversy in both sections of the Republic. It required many months of discussion and deliberation to secure the concurrence of a majority of Congress in their favor. It would be strange if they had been received with immediate approbation by people and States prejudiced and heated by the exciting controversies of their representatives. I believe those measures to have been required by the circumstances and condition of the country. I believe they were necessary to allay asperities and animosities that were rapidly alienating one section of the country from another and destroying those fraternal sentiments which are the strongest supports of the Constitution. They were adopted in the spirit of conciliation and for the purpose of conciliation. I believe that a great majority of our fellow-citizens sympathize in that spirit and that purpose, and in the main approve and are prepared in all respects to sustain these enactments. I can not doubt that the American people, bound together by kindred blood and common traditions, still cherish a paramount regard for the Union of their fathers, and that they are ready to rebuke any attempt to violate its integrity, to disturb the compromises on which it is based, or to resist the laws which have been enacted under its authority.

The series of measures to which I have alluded are regarded by me as a settlement in principle and substance—a final settlement of the dangerous and exciting subjects which they embraced. Most of these subjects, indeed, are beyond your reach, as the legislation which disposed of them was in its character final and irrevocable. It may be presumed from the opposition which they all encountered that none of those measures was free from imperfections, but in their mutual dependence and connection they formed a system of compromise the most conciliatory and best for the entire country that could be obtained from conflicting sectional interests and opinions.

For this reason I recommend your adherence to the adjustment established by those measures until time and experience shall demonstrate the necessity of further legislation to guard against evasion or abuse.

By that adjustment we have been rescued from the wide and boundless agitation that surrounded us, and have a firm, distinct, and legal ground to rest upon. And the occasion, I trust, will justify me in exhorting my countrymen to rally upon and maintain that ground as the best, if not the only, means of restoring peace and quiet to the country and maintaining inviolate the integrity of the Union.

What Happened Next

President Fillmore called the Compromise of 1850 "a final statement," but it did little to settle national divisiveness over slavery. Northern abolitionists only grew more determined to put an end to the institution following enforcement of the Fugitive Slave Law. Fillmore, himself, was in a bind: he didn't approve of slavery, but he believed that the Constitution allowed for it.

The divisiveness of the times was reflected in Fillmore's presidential career. He served only the remainder of Taylor's term and lost his nomination bid in 1852 to Winfield Scott, who eventually lost the election to Franklin Pierce. The Whig Party that Fillmore led as president dissolved over the issue of slavery; and its followers who favored abolition formed the Republican Party in 1854. In the meantime, the country grew more disunited through the 1850s after Fillmore left office. Like Fillmore, the next two presidents—Democrats Franklin Pierce and James Buchanan—were Northerners who supported the Constitutional right for individual states to decide on slavery. But they were even less effective as chief executives than Fillmore had been.

Franklin Pierce

"You have summoned me in my weakness. You must sustain me in your strength."

—*Franklin Pierce*

Fourteenth president of the United States, 1853–1857

Full name: *Franklin Pierce*

Born: *November 23, 1804, Hillsborough, New Hampshire*

Died: *October 8, 1869, Concord, New Hampshire*

Burial site: *Old North Cemetery, Concord, New Hampshire*

Parents: *Benjamin and Anna Kendrick Pierce*

Spouse: *Jane Means Appleton (1806–63; m. 1834)*

Children: *Franklin (1836–36); Frank Robert (1839–43); Benjamin (1841–53)*

Religion: *Episcopalian*

Education: *Bowdoin College, (B.A., 1824)*

Occupations: *Lawyer; general*

Government positions: *New Hampshire state legislator; U.S. representative and senator from New Hampshire*

Political party: *Democratic*

Dates as president: *March 4, 1853–March 4, 1857*

Age upon taking office: *48*

During the 1850s, the United States grew bitterly divided over the issue of slavery. An agreement on the issue that had been passed by Congress, the Compromise of 1850, was intended to offer a balanced approach that could be acceptable to both pro-slavery and abolitionist groups. But one of its provisions, the Fugitive Slave Law, may well have been the final insult that united the abolitionists. It allowed Southern slave owners to pursue slaves who had escaped into the North, often resulting in violent confrontations.

When Franklin Pierce began his duties as president of the United States in March of 1853, he firmly believed that the Compromise had settled all of the differences between North and South, but he was wrong. As the country grew more divided and frustrated over slavery, government became less and less effective. By the end of Pierce's term, conflicts over slavery had cost the United States an opportunity to acquire Cuba and had sparked bloody fighting in Kansas.

There were other factors that contributed to his dreary presidency. On the personal side, Pierce went to Washington a heartbroken man. His eleven-year-old son, Bennie, had died in a tragic accident just weeks before the inauguration, and although Pierce tended to his official duties with determination, the death haunted both him and his frail wife throughout his single term as president.

Timeline

1804: Born in New Hampshire
1829–33: Serves as New Hampshire state representative
1833–37: Serves as U.S. representative
1837–42: Serves in U.S. Senate
1846: Enlists to fight in the Mexican War (1846–48); rises to the rank of brigadier general
1852: Emerges as dark-horse candidate and wins nomination on forty-ninth ballot
1853–57: Serves as fourteenth U.S. president
1856: Loses Democratic presidential nomination to James Buchanan
1869: Dies in New Hampshire

On the political side, Pierce wasn't a good leader. He had always been more comfortable following others rather than inspiring them. Only forty-eight at the time of his election—the youngest man to serve as president up until that time—he seemed to be too eager to compromise for the good of his party. He was widely disliked by the time his term ended, especially in the North and in the new territories west of the Mississippi River.

Groomed for Politics

Franklin Pierce was born on November 23, 1804, in Hillsborough Lower Village, New Hampshire. His family roots stretched back in America to the 1630s, and his father, Benjamin Pierce, a decorated veteran of the Revolutionary War, was very active in New Hampshire politics. Young Franklin was educated at Hillsborough Center, Hancock Academy, and Bowdoin College, where he became a close friend of the poet Henry Wadsworth Longfellow, as well as the noted author Nathaniel Hawthorne, who wrote a short biography of Pierce used during his presidential campaign. After graduating with honors from Bowdoin, Pierce studied law and was admitted to the New Hampshire bar in 1827.

"He has in him many of the chief elements of a great ruler. His talents are administrative, he has a subtle, subtle facility of making affairs roll onward according to his will, and of influencing their course without showing any trace of his action. There are scores of men in this country that seem brighter than he is, but he has the directing mind, and will move them about like pawns on a chessboard, and turn all their abilities to better purpose than they themselves could do."

—Nathaniel Hawthorne

This view of Bowdoin College in Maine was painted in 1821, three years before Pierce graduated.

Left: Bowdoin College in Maine, Pierce's alma mater.

Left: Pierce's law office in New Hampshire.

"[He was] a small politician of low capacity and mean surroundings, proud to act as a servile tool of men worse than himself but also stronger and abler. He was ever ready to do any work the slavery leaders set him."

—*Theodore Roosevelt*

Pierce's real education came through his father, who served two terms as governor of New Hampshire, and had a lot to teach him about politics. He became skilled at speechmaking and consensus building, and his father's efforts began to pay off when Pierce was elected to the New Hampshire legislature in 1829. He became Speaker of the House, but he had other worlds to conquer. He was elected to Congress in 1833, at the age of twenty-nine.

He went back to Amherst, New Hampshire, the following year to marry Jane Means Appleton, a shy and deeply religious woman who he had been courting for nearly ten years. As a couple, the Pierces had opposite personalities: He was comfortable mingling with people and finding ways to put aside differences, but she was retiring and held fast to her beliefs.

Pierce's popularity as a politician led to his election, at thirty-three, to the U.S. Senate. As a Democrat, he had always been willing to support the party's policies. It had been organized to support states' rights during Andrew Jackson's presidency, and like the leaders of his party, Pierce was enthusiastically in favor of the rights of states to operate with limited interference by the federal government.

Pierce's career seemed poised for greatness, but then he abruptly quit the Senate because his wife found life in Washington intolerable. Jane Pierce was adamantly opposed to alcohol, but she was well aware that the lifestyle of politicians in the capital often included drinking and lively parties. Out of respect to his wife—and possibly with a bit of concern about his own drinking problem—Pierce resigned and went home to New Hampshire with Jane and their two sons.

The Mexican War

The family settled in Concord, the capital of New Hampshire, where Pierce opened what quickly became a highly successful law firm. He continued to have enormous political clout in the state, and he kept in touch with his allies in Washington.

When war broke out between the United States and Mexico in 1846, Pierce raised two companies of volunteers from New Hampshire and marched south with them. He made himself a private, but the following year he was appointed a brigadier general. After they arrived in Mexico, they marched through 150 miles of hostile country to join General Winfield Scott's army. During the Battle of Contreras in August, Pierce fell from

Right: Pierce saw service as a brigadier general in the Mexican War.

his horse and was injured in the leg and groin, leaving his men leaderless and panic-stricken to the point of widespread desertion. His injuries were serious enough to call for discharge, but Pierce rejected the order, and continued to travel with the army.

He returned to New Hampshire after the war and rejoined his wife, who was raising their surviving son (after having lost their firstborn in infancy, a second son had died at the age of four). Pierce quickly immersed himself in state politics and turned his attention to the national Democratic Party. The issue of slavery had so divided Democrats by that time that some abolitionists among them had left to form the Free-Soil Party, which nominated former president Martin Van Buren, one of the first of the Democrats, as its presidential candidate.

Pierce was greatly disturbed by these defections. He believed that slavery was officially approved by the U.S. Constitution, and he sided with people who wanted to let individual states decide whether they would permit slavery or not. Along with his Southern allies, Pierce felt that threats of federal interference by Northern abolitionists were dangerous to the Union. Pierce held to those views so firmly that he helped to defeat a New Hampshire Democratic gubernatorial candidate who had abolitionist sympathies.

Right: From war horse to dark horse, Pierce was as surprised as anyone when the Democrats made him their standard bearer.

Hero Without Honor

When the Battle of Vera Cruz started, General Pierce, untrained as a military man, did what any good lawyer would do. He mounted his horse, rode to the front of his men and made a speech. His horse bolted and he was thrown forward onto the pommel of his saddle, and then he fainted. There was no question that he was in pain, but word spread among his men that "the general is a damned coward." But as soon as he recovered consciousness, Pierce mounted another horse and retook command, becoming the only senior officer to stay with his men through the night. When General Scott ordered him out of the field, Pierce's lawyerly talents came to the fore again and he argued the general out of the decision. Then he fainted again from the pain he was suffering, but this time he refused offers of help and led his men on foot. Medals of Honor have been awarded for less, but none of Pierce's men, or his fellow officers, regarded him as a brave and heroic officer.

Pierce was strongly in favor of the Compromise of 1850, a series of laws that aimed to diffuse tensions between free and slave states, and his support of it made him popular in the South. They welcomed the support of a Northern leader, and quite suddenly he found himself back in the political limelight again.

Dark-Horse Candidate

Pierce didn't have any presidential ambitions going into the 1852 election. His Democratic Party had plenty of other qualified candidates, including Stephen A. Douglas, James Buchanan, and Lewis Cass, all of whom had strong possibilities of winning the general election. However, when the nominating convention began in June, the delegates were hopelessly deadlocked and they couldn't agree on a candidate after forty-eight rounds of balloting. After Pierce's name was put into the mix, he was chosen as a compromise candidate on the forty-ninth ballot—a "dark horse" from the North who was acceptable to the

Presidential / Vice Presidential Candidates	Popular Votes	Electoral Votes
Franklin Pierce / William Rufus King (Democratic)	1,601,474	254
Winfield Scott / William A. Graham (Whig)	1,386,578	42

Through fifty-two ballots, neither Scott nor incumbent president Millard Fillmore could secure enough votes to win the nomination of the Whig Party. Scott finally won on the fifty-third ballot. On the Democratic side, former secretary of state James Buchanan, Senator Lewis Cass of Michigan, Senator Stephen Douglas of Illinois, and former secretary of war William L. Marcy were early leaders, but none received a majority of electoral votes to win the nomination. Dark-horse candidate Pierce, a former senator from New Hampshire, emerged and, on the forty-ninth ballot, received a majority tally of 282 votes, securing the nomination.

Left: A cartoon shows General Winfield Scott pulling the presidential chair out from under Pierce, his opponent in the election.

Left: The Pierces' son Benjamin was killed in front of their eyes in a train wreck.

South. William Rufus King of Alabama was named the vice presidential candidate. Reluctantly accepting his party's wishes, Pierce ran as "Young Hickory from the Granite State," a nickname intended to link him to the popular president Andrew Jackson, of Tennessee, who was known "Old Hickory." It was a not-so-subtle way of telling Southerners that Pierce was on their side even if he was a New Englander. The Democrats supported him with the campaign slogan, "We Polked you in '44, and we'll Pierce you in '52." Pierce defeated Whig candidate General Winfield Scott, his former commanding officer, by a narrow margin of the popular vote, but he put together a large majority in the Electoral College, 254 votes to 42.

Tragedy struck as Pierce and his family traveled by train from New Hampshire to Washington and the train derailed. Neither Pierce nor his wife was injured, but their eleven-year-old son, Benjamin, was crushed to death before their eyes. The blow was particularly stunning to Jane Pierce, who never recovered enough to be able to take on most of her duties as first lady.

Franklin Pierce delivered his inaugural address completely from memory in a March snowstorm. He advocated territorial expansion, a bold foreign policy, and strict adherence to the Constitutional rights of individual states. His cabinet included men with diverse opinions, among them Secretary of War Jefferson Davis, who

Presidential Oath

"I do solemnly swear that I shall faithfully execute the office of President of the United States and will to the best of my ability, preserve, protect, and defend the Constitution of the United States."

Every president since George Washington has assumed the office with those words. But when he was inaugurated, Franklin Pierce changed one of them. He didn't solemnly swear, but rather, solemnly affirmed, an alternative allowed by the Constitution.

would later become president of the Confederate States of America during the Civil War. His vice president, William Rufus King, was sworn into office in a hospital bed in Havana, Cuba, where he was being treated for tuberculosis. King died one month into his term, and Pierce served the rest of his presidency without a vice president.

The Pierce Administration

Administration Dates: March 4, 1853–March 4, 1857
Vice President: William Rufus De Vane King (1853)
None (1853–57)

Cabinet:

Secretary of State	William L. Marcy (1853–57)
Secretary of the Treasury	James Guthrie (1853–57)
Secretary of War	Jefferson F. Davis (1853–57)
Attorney General	Caleb Cushing (1853–57)
Secretary of the Navy	James C. Dobbin (1853–57)
Postmaster General	James Campbell (1853–57)
Secretary of the Interior	Robert McClelland (1853–57)

A Rising Tide

The Compromise of 1850 had achieved some positive results. It allowed California to be admitted into the Union as a free state, for example. However, the bundle of legislation also included the Fugitive Slave Law, which empowered Southern slaveholders to pursue runaway slaves across state lines into the North. By the 1850s, white abolitionists and free African Americans as well as former slaves had formed the Underground Railroad, a series of routes that made it easier for runaway slaves to make their escape to the North, with help and safe havens along the way. They weren't safe until they reached Canada, and the way stations along the Underground Railroad were established to keep them hidden and safe until they could cross the border.

Pierce carefully enforced the Fugitive Slave Law, following the example of his predecessor, Millard Fillmore. Among the Northern abolitionists who showed contempt for the law with open hostility was Harriet Beecher Stowe, whose 1852 novel, *Uncle Tom's Cabin*, highlighted the plight of runaway slaves trying to save their children from a life of forced labor. The novel was an overnight sensation, becoming the best-selling book of its time. The book inspired its many readers to join a

Left: Franklin Pierce at the start of his presidency.

Matthew C. Perry

Matthew Calbraith Perry was born on April 10, 1794, in Newport, Rhode Island. Entering the navy as a midshipman in 1809, he was assigned to a vessel commanded by his elder brother, Oliver Hazard Perry. During the War of 1812 (1812–15), he served first on a large frigate, then on another warship, the United States, which was stranded in New London, Connecticut, during a blockade by the British Navy. Venturing to New York City on leave, he courted and married Jane Slidell in 1814.

Perry enjoyed a wide variety of activities in the navy: he transported freed American slaves to Liberia, a colony established for the return of illegally captured slaves (under a recently enacted law) to Africa; he helped police African shores to rid them of slave traders and pirates; and he transported the new American minister to Russia, where the Russian czar tried to entice him to join the Russian Navy. From 1833 to the early 1840s, Perry served shore duty in the New York Navy Yard, beginning as second officer and then becoming commander. His duty there was significant: he introduced technological and educational improvements, contributed to the development of the Naval Lyceum—a complex that includes a museum, study areas, and lecture halls—and helped start a naval magazine. For such efforts, Perry was nicknamed "chief educator of the navy."

Perry was also instrumental in transforming the U.S. Navy from sailing vessels to steam-powered vessels, taking advantage of the latest development in water transportation. The superiority of steam vessels in the U.S. and British Navies helped put an effective end to piracy. Perry helped design new hulls and engines and was given command of the first navy steam warship, the Fulton II.

During the 1840s, Perry hunted for slave traders as commander of the navy's African Squadron, led expeditions that captured several coastal cities during the Mexican War (1846–48), and—as commander of the gulf squadron—backed General Winfield Scott in taking the key Mexican port city of Veracruz during the war. When combat ceased, he supervised construction of ocean mail steamships. Meanwhile, American trade with China was expanding. Safe areas were needed for purchasing coal and supplies, and American whalers in the northern Pacific Ocean needed protection. Perry was authorized by President Millard Fillmore to open trade negotiations and diplomacy with Japan. He set out from Norfolk, Virginia, on

November 24, 1852, with four ships and arrived at Edo (modern Tokyo) on July 2, 1853. He had a letter requesting a treaty to present to the Japanese emperor, but upon landing in Edo he was told to go to Nagasaki, the only Japanese port open to foreigners. Perry refused, and when the Japanese saw his decks cleared for action, they relented. In an elaborate ceremony, Perry went ashore and delivered the letter to two princes representing the Emperor, promising to return in twelve months for the answer.

Perry journeyed to Hong Kong, then returned to Japan in February 1854. He received a warm welcome, especially since French and Russian naval operations in the Pacific were beginning to worry Japanese authorities. At Yokohama, representatives of the United States and Japan began negotiations; on March 31, 1854, they concluded a treaty that opened two Japanese ports, Hakodate and Shimoda, for trade and supplies and guaranteed fair treatment for shipwrecked American sailors. Japan, which had been closed to Western nations, was now a trading partner with the United States. Perry returned to New York in January 1855 as a hero. After being honored with many celebratory receptions around the country, Perry prepared an account of his expedition to Japan. He completed his writings in late December of 1857, and died on March 4, 1858.

growing movement for repeal of the Fugitive Slave Law, but Pierce was as immovable as New Hampshire granite. In fact, his administration made several fateful decisions that widened the rift between North and South.

His support of slavery became evident early in his presidency, and it contributed to a failed policy called the Ostend Manifesto. Pro-slavery forces believed that the Spanish colony of Cuba was about to free its slaves or be overrun by a slave revolt, and to prevent either such fearsome thing from happening, they encouraged Pierce to purchase the island for the United States. He authorized Pierre Soulé, his representative in Spain, to begin negotiations, and Soulé, along with James Buchanan, then minister to England, and John Y. Mason,

minister to France, drafted a document called the Ostend Manifesto. It offered to pay as much as $120,000 for Cuba, but it also threatened that the United States would seize Cuba by force if Spain freed the slaves there or allowed a slave revolution. When details of the plan were leaked to the public, it caused an international uproar. Pierce disclaimed it, but the damage was already done. Spain refused to even talk about selling Cuba.

Another muddled outcome for Pierce occurred during discussions of plans for a transcontinental railroad. A route through the southern portion of the United States to California was chosen, and then Pierce then authorized the Gadsden Purchase, a plan to buy land in what is now southern Arizona and southern New Mexico where the railroad would be built. But the influential senator Stephen A. Douglas had different plans. As a senator from Illinois, naturally he was in favor of starting the railway in Chicago and running it across the Great Plains. By supporting an opposing plan that favored the South, Pierce allowed the issue to become overwhelmed by debate within his own party.

In the meantime, Douglas introduced the Kansas-Nebraska Bill, which would create two territories between the Missouri River and the Continental Divide in the Rocky Mountains. Concerned that his bill wouldn't get Southern support, he added the condition that the status of any new territories—free or slave—could be settled by vote of their inhabitants. That provision opened land that had been closed to slavery by

the Missouri Compromise of 1820, an attempt to balance the number of slave states and free states. When the bill came up for a vote, Southern politicians demanded an outright repeal of the Missouri Compromise. Believing that federal restrictions on slavery were unconstitutional, Pierce agreed with them, and when the Kansas-Nebraska bill became law, the Missouri Compromise was repealed.

It created a hornet's nest of problems. Hoping to ensure that Kansas would be a slave state, proslavery people from Missouri flooded into the territory, obtained the right to vote, and organized a proslavery legislature at Lecompton, Kansas. Abolitionists moved in, too, and after organizing their own government in Topeka, they began to fight for free-state status. Pierce formally recognized the Lecompton government and ordered the one at Topeka disbanded. The difference of opinion had turned to violence by then. Known historically as "Bleeding Kansas," the open hostilities between residents and transients, slavery advocates and abolitionists, was the first indication that the issue of slavery was never going to be settled through diplomacy.

Pierce didn't fare much better in foreign policy. He tried to annex the territories of Hawaii and Alaska, but made no progress on either initiative. Following the efforts of President Fillmore, the Pierce administration was successful in opening up trade with Japan. The ceremonial visit to Japan in 1854 by Commodore Matthew C. Perry was the first great highlight in relations between the two nations.

Left: A prelude to Civil War: Bleeding Kansas.

LIBERTY. THE FAIR MAID OF KANSAS_IN THE HANDS OF THE "BORDER RUFFIANS".

Unhappy Ending

As the troubles in Kansas got bloodier, hostile political cartoonists characterized Pierce as a drunken devil trampling on liberty and encouraging slavery's worst abuses. The president hardly saw himself that way. He thought that he was a champion of the Constitution and the strict stance it took on state's rights. His views alienated some Northern Democrats and many of them defected and joined the Republican Party, which was founded in 1854 by former members of the Whig, Free-Soil, and Know-Nothing parties, along with the Northern Democrats who were unhappy with their party's support of slavery.

Unpopular·though he may have been, Pierce still hoped to be renominated for a second term in 1856. As it happened, he was replaced instead by James Buchanan, another Northern Democrat who supported the institution of slavery.

After he left office, Pierce and his wife embarked on a long tour of Europe. They went home to settle in Concord, New Hampshire, where Pierce became a strong critic of President Abraham Lincoln, although by that time he was so widely discredited that his views were frequently met with public scorn. After Jane Pierce's death in 1863, Franklin Pierce lived in near-seclusion until his own death on October 8, 1869. He was buried in a family plot in the Old North Cemetery at Concord, New Hampshire.

Left: A cartoon condemns the Pierce administration for turning Kansas into a battleground.

Legacy

Franklin Pierce was the second of three successive presidents from the North who supported the rights of states to determine whether or not to permit slavery. Like his predecessor, Millard Fillmore, and his successor, James Buchanan, he felt that legislation—specifically, the Compromise of 1850—had settled the slavery issue once and for all. Instead, all three of these presidents were overwhelmed by national divisiveness that undermined their effectiveness.

Abolitionist sentiments expanded quickly through the 1850s and led to the formation of the Republican Party in 1854 to champion the cause nationally. A civil war erupted in Kansas in 1856 during Pierce's final year in office. More compromises and more defenses of slavery were attempted by President Buchanan, but Northern states grew more solidly abolitionist, leading to the election of Republican Abraham Lincoln in 1860. The issue of slavery was finally settled during Lincoln's presidency through the Civil War.

Expansion of American territory and trade were the most positive developments during Pierce's presidency. The Gadsden Purchase expanded the territories of Arizona and New Mexico to their present-day southern borders, and the United States officially began trade relations with Japan, and enlarged the American presence in Asia. However, all of Franklin Pierce's accomplishments were shrouded by the specter of slavery.

Right: The ceremonial signing of the Gadsden Purchase.

Jane Pierce

Born March 12, 1806, Hampton, New Hampshire
Died December 2, 1863, Andover, Massachusetts

"I have known many of the [first] ladies … none more truly excellent than the afflicted wife of President Pierce. Her health was a bar to any great effort on her part to meet the expectations of the public in her high position but she was a refined, extremely religious and well educated lady."

—Mrs. Robert E. Lee

When she first heard that her husband, Franklin Pierce, had received his party's nomination for president, Jane Pierce fainted. Pious, retiring, and frail, Mrs. Pierce detested Washington, and she had spent much of her adult life trying to persuade her husband to retire from politics.

It is quite likely that no other American first lady was more reluctant to assume her duties than this minister's daughter. Her distaste for those official duties was made worse by the tragic death of her eleven-year-old son just weeks before her husband's inauguration.

Raised on Religion

Jane Means Appleton grew up in Brunswick, Maine, the daughter of noted Congregationalist minister Reverend Jesse Appleton, who was president of Bowdoin College during much of her youth. Jane was well educated and raised in a strict and deeply religious household. After her father's death in 1819, when she was thirteen, her mother moved the family to Amherst, New Hampshire, and it was there that she met Franklin Pierce, an ambitious Bowdoin graduate whose father was a high-ranking politician.

The courtship of Jane and Franklin Pierce went on for a long time. Jane's family didn't approve of politics as a career, which he was already following. Franklin was almost thirty years old and Jane twenty-eight when they were finally married in 1834. By that time, Pierce had been elected to Congress.

Their marriage wasn't particularly happy. Jane gave birth to three sons, one of whom died after only three days and another at the age of four from typhus. Their third son was healthy, but Jane Pierce did not relish the idea of bringing him up in Washington. She was appalled by the casual atmosphere and social drinking in the nation's capital, and she actively encouraged her husband to retire from national office. Although he had been elected to the Senate at the age of thirty-two and seemed to be headed for a promising career in national politics, he finally acceded to her wishes, and the family moved back to New Hampshire, where Pierce resumed his law practice.

War and Politics

The Pierce family might have lived quietly in New Hampshire for the rest of their lives, but Franklin Pierce volunteered for service in the Mexican War. When he came home again, he became active again in local Democratic politics in his home state. The news that he had been nominated as the party's candidate for president in 1852 came as a most unpleasant surprise to Jane and her third son, Benjamin, to whom she was deeply devoted. Neither mother nor son wanted to move back to Washington, but Franklin Pierce was able to persuade them that his success would help to improve Benjamin's prospects.

On January 6, 1853, the Pierce family was traveling by train between Concord, New Hampshire, and Boston, Massachusetts, when the train ran off the tracks. Although the future president and his wife escaped with only minor injuries, Benjamin Pierce was crushed to death before his horrified parents' eyes.

Jane Pierce didn't recover from the tragedy for the rest of her life. She regarded it as a sign from God that her husband was not to have any distractions from his family while running the nation. Retiring by nature, she became reclusive. A pall of sorrow lay over the executive mansion the whole time the Pierces lived there. The suddenness of the tragedy—coming so soon before his inauguration—affected Franklin Pierce's ability to discharge his duties. Even the inaugural ball was canceled, and social events were few and far between during his presidency.

Jane Pierce tried occasionally to serve as her husband's official hostess, but she just wasn't up to it. She relied heavily on a childhood friend, and her uncle's wife, Mrs. Abigail Kent Means, to handle the duties of a first lady. Mary Anna Lee—wife of Confederate general Robert E. Lee and a granddaughter of the first first lady, Martha Washington—wrote of her: "I have known many of the ladies of the White House, none more truly excellent than the afflicted wife of President Pierce." Mrs. Lee added, "Her health was a bar to any great effort on her part to meet the expectations of the public in her high position but she was a refined, extremely religious and well educated lady."

When Franklin Pierce's presidential term ended, the couple toured Europe in search of treatment for Jane's ailments. They returned to New Hampshire, and Jane Pierce died there on December 2, 1863. She was buried near her son Benjamin in a family plot in Old North Cemetery at Concord, New Hampshire.

Left: The Pierce homestead in Concord, New Hampshire.

Pierce's Inaugural Address

Delivered on March 4, 1853

Franklin Pierce took office in troubled times. Debate over the institution of slavery had grown fierce and was threatening to tear the Union apart. For Pierce, as well as for a majority of federal officials of the time, the moral crisis over slavery was of less important than the principle that individual states had the right to determine their own laws within the framework of the Constitution, which acknowledged the existence of slavery.

The widening divide between abolitionists and people who supported slavery defied a resolution. The Compromise of 1850 had been the most recent attempt to balance the opposing sides, to equalize Congressional power between the North and South, and to maintain the principle of states' rights. Pierce intended to enforce the Compromise, including the Fugitive Slave Law that was part of it. It gave Southern slaveholders the right to track runaway slaves across state lines into the North.

As a Northern Democrat who was against any federal attempt to undermine the rights of states to determine the legality of slavery for themselves, Pierce was a popular candidate to Southern voters as well as those in the North who didn't share the abolitionist cause. He made it clear in his inaugural address that he was going to continue to the principles endorsed by the voters who elected him.

Pierce's speech was divided into fourteen sections. He began by expressing his feeling of humility at taking on the office of president, and then he recalled that the United States itself had humble origins, gradually expanding to former frontier lands. Picking up themes of his own time, Pierce declared his support for further territorial expansion and a bold foreign policy. In the final five sections, from which the following excerpt is taken, he emphasized his commitment to strictly uphold the Constitutional rights of individual states. He concluded by stressing that if all Americans respected that approach, regional differences would disappear.

The great scheme of our constitutional liberty rests upon a proper distribution of power between the State and Federal authorities, and experience has shown that the harmony and happiness of our people must depend upon a just discrimination between the separate rights and responsibilities of the States and your common rights and obligations under the General Government; and here, in my opinion, are the considerations which should form the true basis of future concord in regard to the questions which have most seriously disturbed public tranquillity. If the Federal Government will confine itself to the exercise of powers clearly granted by the Constitution, it can hardly happen that its action upon any question should endanger the institutions of the States or interfere with their right to manage matters strictly domestic according to the will of their own people.

In expressing briefly my views upon an important subject which has recently agitated the nation to almost a fearful degree, I am moved by no other impulse than a most earnest desire for the perpetuation of that Union which has made us what we are, showering upon us blessings and conferring a power and influence which our fathers could hardly have anticipated, even with their most sanguine hopes directed to a far-off future. The sentiments I now announce were not unknown before the expression of the voice which called me here. My own position upon this subject was clear and unequivocal, upon the record of my words and my acts, and it is only recurred to at this time because silence might perhaps be misconstrued. With the Union my best and dearest earthly hopes are entwined. Without it what are we individually or collectively? What becomes of the noblest field ever opened for the advancement of our race in religion, in government, in the arts, and in all that dignifies and adorns mankind? From that radiant constellation which both illumines our own way and points out to struggling nations their course, let but a single star be lost, and, if these be not utter darkness, the luster of the whole is dimmed. Do my countrymen need any assurance that such a catastrophe is not to overtake them while I possess the power to stay it? It is with me an earnest and vital belief that as the Union has been the source, under Providence, of our prosperity to this time, so it is the surest pledge of a continuance of the blessings we have enjoyed, and which we are sacredly bound to transmit undiminished to our children. The field of calm and free discussion in our country is open, and will always be so, but never has been and never can be traversed for good in a spirit of sectionalism and uncharitableness. The founders of the Republic dealt with things as they were presented to them, in a spirit of self-sacrificing patriotism, and, as time has proved, with a comprehensive wisdom which it will always be safe for us to consult. Every measure tending to strengthen the fraternal feelings of all the members of our Union has had my heartfelt approbation. To every theory of society or government, whether the offspring of feverish ambition or of morbid enthusiasm, calculated to dissolve the bonds of law and affection which unite us, I shall interpose a ready and stern resistance. I believe that involuntary servitude, as it exists in different States of this Confederacy, is recognized by the Constitution. I believe that it stands like any other admitted right, and that the States where it exists are entitled to efficient remedies to enforce the constitutional provisions. I hold that the laws of 1850, commonly called the "compromise measures," are strictly constitutional and to be unhesitatingly carried into effect. I believe that the constituted authorities of this Republic are bound to regard the rights of the South in this respect as they would view any other legal and constitutional right, and that the laws to enforce them should be respected and obeyed, not with a reluctance encouraged by abstract opinions as to their propriety in a different state of society, but cheerfully and according to the decisions of the tribunal to which their exposition belongs. Such have been, and are, my convictions, and upon them I shall act. I fervently hope that the question is at rest, and that no sectional or ambitious or fanatical excitement may again threaten the durability of our institutions or obscure the light of our prosperity.

But let not the foundation of our hope rest upon man's wisdom. It will not be sufficient that sectional prejudices find no place in the public deliberations. It will not be sufficient that the rash counsels of human passion are rejected. It must be felt that there is no national security but in the nation's humble, acknowledged dependence upon God and His overruling providence.

We have been carried in safety through a perilous crisis. Wise counsels, like those which gave us the Constitution, prevailed to uphold it. Let the period be remembered as an admonition, and not as an encouragement, in any section of the Union, to make experiments where experiments are fraught with such fearful hazard. Let it be impressed upon all hearts that, beautiful as our fabric is, no earthly power or wisdom could ever reunite its broken fragments. Standing, as I do, almost within view of the green slopes of Monticello, and, as it were, within reach of the tomb of [George] Washington, with all the cherished memories of the past gathering around me like so many eloquent voices of exhortation from heaven, I can express no better hope for my country than that the kind Providence which smiled upon our fathers may enable their children to preserve the blessings they have inherited.

What Happened Next

Pierce's pleas for harmony were not enough to stop the growing gulf between the North and South. The Abolitionist movement was growing stronger, and it soon overwhelmed Northerners who had been supporting slavery as the right of self-determination of individual states.

The abolitionist movement gained strong momentum after the 1852 publication of *Uncle Tom's Cabin,* by Harriet Beecher Stowe, a best-selling book that dramatized the miserable lives of slaves who were often the victims of violence and family separations. The Fugitive Slave Law, which allowed Southern slave owners to recapture runaway slaves in the North, also rallied Northerners against the institution of slavery. The Slave Law was part of the Compromise of 1850 that Pierce mentioned in his speech. Like many politicians, he expected that the Compromise would end tensions over slavery by including some measures that would be popular in the North, and others that would find favor in the South.

As the abolitionists became a more powerful and united group, they began to drop away from the Whig and Democratic Parties, because each group included members who were more supportive of states' rights than the abolition of slavery. Most abolitionists joined the Republican Party that was formed in 1854 and grew quickly, with Abraham Lincoln elected the first Republican president in 1860.

In the meantime, tensions appeared to be getting out of hand. The Kansas-Nebraska Act of 1854 allowed those two territories to determine whether or not they would enter the Union as free or slave states, a civil war erupted in Kansas over the issue. Acts of violence continued on until 1861, when a full scale Civil War erupted. The Emancipation Proclamation, which led to the Thirteenth Amendment to the U.S. Constitution in 1865, was the beginning of the end of slavery.

James Buchanan

"My dear sir, if you are as happy on entering this house as I on leaving, you are a very happy man indeed."

—James Buchanan, to his successor, Abraham Lincoln

Fifteenth president of the United States, 1857–1861

Full name: *James Buchanan*
Born: *April 23, 1791, Cove Gap, Pennsylvania*
Died: *June 1, 1868, Lancaster, Pennsylvania*
Burial site: *Woodward Cemetery, Lancaster, Pennsylvania*
Parents: *James and Elizabeth Speer Buchanan*
Spouse: *None*
Children: *None*
Religion: *Presbyterian*
Education: *Dickinson College (B.A., 1809)*
Occupation: *Lawyer*
Government positions: *Pennsylvania state representative; U.S. representative and senator from Pennsylvania; minister to Russia and England; secretary of state under James K. Polk*
Political party: *Democratic*
Dates as president: *March 4, 1857–March 4, 1861*
Age upon taking office: *65*

An incident that occurred just a month before James Buchanan left office in early 1861 would influence a negative assessment of him for decades. On that day, a formal declaration of secession from the Union was presented to him by seven Southern pro-slavery states. Buchanan's enemies—Democrats and Republicans, Northerners and Southerners alike—would first blame him for action and then blame him for inaction that plunged the country into the secession crisis. It would be resolved only after American blood was spilled on American soil during the Civil War.

Buchanan was a highly skilled politician with forty years of experience in public service before he became the fifteenth president in 1857. He had a solid intellectual grasp of the issues behind the secession crisis: states' rights, regional economic power, and the ability to amend the U.S. Constitution. However, Buchanan was less politically adept on the issue of slavery.

Though he was a Northern Democrat, Buchanan was regarded as a Southerner in spirit. He believed that the American Constitution provided adequate means of resolving such disputes as the slavery issue. The insistence of Southern landowners on keeping their economic system and the determination of Southern politicians in Washington to allow slavery—which they often called their "peculiar institution"—to expand westward had already proved impossible to resolve in Congress and

JAMES BUCHANAN,
DEMOCRATIC CANDIDATE FOR PRESIDENT OF THE UNITED STATES.

Left: A Buchanan campaign poster.

Look Here

James Buchanan had a way of looking at people that could appear either flattering for what seemed to be attentiveness or off-putting by making it seem as though his mind was elsewhere. He had a problem with his neck that caused his head to be continually tilted to his left, but that was only part of it. He was nearsighted in one eye and farsighted in the other, and in conversation he usually closed the farsighted one, which, along with his cocked head, made it appear that he had eyes for no one else, which was exactly the case. If he needed to look across the room, though, he'd close the nearsighted eye so he could see into the distance. Some people mistook these actions as sly winks.

the courts for decades. Buchanan became one of many political leaders who found himself overwhelmed by the issue's divisiveness.

Pennsylvania Lawyer

Born on April 23, 1791, James Buchanan was the last president born in the eighteenth century. He was one of eleven children of emigrants from County Donegal, Ireland. His father, also named James Buchanan, became a storekeeper and real-estate investor in the area around Cove Gap, Pennsylvania. Young Buchanan attended school in nearby Mercersburg, and at the age of sixteen, he enrolled in Dickinson College in Carlisle, Pennsylvania. After graduating with honors two years later, he studied law with an attorney in Lancaster, Pennsylvania.

Buchanan was admitted to the Pennsylvania bar in 1813 and he began to practice law in Lancaster. He earned a reputation as an astute trial lawyer with an impressive mastery of the law's complexities, and his practice was profitable for many years. By the time he was thirty, in fact, he estimated his personal fortune at more than $300,000.

Buchanan's political career began when members of the local Federalist Party invited him to run for a seat in the Pennsylvania assembly in 1814. Six years later, he moved from there to Washington, D.C., when he was elected to the first of five terms in the U.S. House of Representatives.

Around that time, a tragedy in his personal life dimmed growing success. Buchanan was engaged to Anne Coleman, a young woman whose father was Pennsylvania's first millionaire, and whose family disapproved of him. She went along with the wishes of her family and broke off the engagement, but a short time later she died in what was rumored to have been a suicide. Buchanan never considered marriage to anyone else after that, and he became America's only bachelor president. (Grover Cleveland started his presidency as a single man, but he was married fifteen months later.)

Timeline

1791: Born in Pennsylvania
1813: Admitted to the bar of Pennsylvania and opens a law practice in Lancaster; elected to the Pennsylvania state legislature as a Federalist and reelected in 1815
1821–30: Serves in the U.S. House of Representatives
1831: Appointed U.S. minister to Russia
1834–45: Elected to U.S. Senate as Democrat from Pennsylvania
1845–49: Serves as secretary of state under President James K. Polk
1853–56: Serves as U.S. minister to Great Britain
1857–61: Serves as fifteenth U.S. president
1859: John Brown's raid on Harpers Ferry, Virginia, furthers tension among abolitionists and supporters of slavery
1868: Dies in Pennsylvania

Above: Buchanan's estate, Wheatland, near Lancaster, Pennsylvania.

Foreign Affairs Expert

With the disintegration of the Federalist Party in the early 1820s, Buchanan became a Jacksonian Democrat. The Democratic-Republican Party dominated the American political scene, holding the presidency from 1801 until 1829, but split into factions after the controversial 1824 presidential election. Jacksonian Democrats were one of those factions loyal to Andrew Jackson, who represented the common people and favored states' rights over federal influence; another of them rallied around John Quincy Adams, an aristocrat who favored a strong federal government. The Jackson wing dominated the party by the end of the 1820s, and it was transformed into the modern-day Democratic Party in 1832.

Jackson, elected president in 1828, appointed Buchanan minister to Russia in 1831. Three years later, Buchanan was elected to the U.S. Senate and served more than a decade there. President James K. Polk named Buchanan his secretary of state in 1845, and four years in Polk's cabinet earned Buchanan a reputation as a solid supporter of territorial expansion. He proposed and pursued the building of a canal in Central America, although it wouldn't be a reality for decades, and he directed negotiations that settled a border dispute between America and Great Britain.

The Oregon Territory, stretching from the northern border of present-day California to the southern border of present-day Alaska, was claimed at the time by both the United States and Britain. As the prospect for war seemed close at hand, a compromise was reached, and the territory was divided at the forty-ninth parallel latitude, the present-day northern border stretching from Minnesota to Washington state. In addition to helping put that agreement together, Buchanan also attempted to negotiate a peace with Mexico over a border dispute with the Republic of Texas. The dispute was resolved in the two-year Mexican War with an American victory.

In 1848, when the Whig Party candidate Zachary Taylor, a hero of the Mexican War, was elected president, Buchanan retired from politics at the age of fifty-seven and went home to Pennsylvania, where he bought a large estate near Lancaster; he called it Wheatland. This gave him an opportunity to enjoy the company of his large extended family, which included twenty-two nieces and nephews and half again as many of their children, and he enjoyed their company. Buchanan was the legal guardian of one of them, Harriet Lane, who had been orphaned at the age of eleven.

When Democrat Franklin Pierce won the presidential election of 1852, Buchanan was appointed minister to Great Britain, an interval in his career that was notable for his involvement in the Ostend Manifesto, the declaration by the United States that it could rightfully seize the enormous colony of Cuba by force if Spain refused to sell or relinquish the island. Pro-slavery forces were worried that the Spanish colony was about to free its slaves or be overrun by a slave revolt, and they encouraged President Pierce to buy the island and make it part of the United States—as a slave territory, of course. The Ostend Manifesto, intended to pressure Spain, was leaked by the press and caused such an uproar both at home and abroad that the United States quietly abandoned its attempt to make Cuba its own slave territory.

Above: A political cartoon portrays the 1856 presidential election campaign as a boxing match.

1856 Election Results

Presidential / Vice Presidential Candidates	Popular Votes	Electoral Votes
James Buchanan / John C. Breckinridge (Democratic)	1,838,169	174
John C. Frémont / William L. Dayton (Republican)	1,341,264	114
Millard Fillmore / Andrew Jackson Donelson (American [Know-Nothing])	874,534	8

Buchanan received the nomination on the seventeenth ballot; incumbent president Franklin Pierce was in second place for the first fourteen ballots, before U.S. senator Stephen Douglas of Illinois overtook him. Fillmore also ran as a Whig, the last election in which the Whig Party participated.

"Save the Union"

Pierce had steadily lost popularity throughout his term, and antislavery forces were uniting behind the new Republican Party that was founded in 1854. Buchanan, who appealed to both Northern and Southern voters, won the Democratic Party's nomination for president in 1856. His opponent was John C. Frémont, the Republican Party's first national candidate, who was running on an antislavery platform. The unpopular former president, Millard Fillmore ran as the last nominee of the Whig Party as well as the American (Know-Nothing) Party.

Some of Frémont's more radical supporters were calling for the North to secede from the Union on grounds of their opposition to slavery, which brought votes to Buchanan's campaign with its slogan, "Save the Union." Buchanan was personally opposed to slavery, but he believed that its presence in the Southern half of the United States was perfectly legal. He thought of the Northern abolitionists as an increasingly dangerous element in American politics.

Buchanan won the election with 1.8 million popular votes to Frémont's 1.3 million and winning nearly all of the Southern electoral votes. After assuming the office, he named moderates and conservatives from both the North and the South to his cabinet, but his position on the slavery issue was made clear in his inaugural address when he said that the question should be settled in the federal courts.

Above: Buchanan and his Cabinet.

Below: Republican candidate John C. Frémont campaigns as a Rocky Mountain explorer.

COL. FREMONT

> "I believe slavery to be a great political and great moral evil. I thank God my lot has been cast in a state where it does not exist."
>
> —James Buchanan

Just two days after his inauguration, the United States Supreme Court issued a fateful ruling on the matter in the *Dred Scott v. Sandford* case. Dred Scott was a slave who sued for his freedom when his slavemaster moved him into a state where slavery was illegal. The High Court decided in favor of the slave owner, arguing that slaves weren't American citizens and therefore had no right to sue in court. The ruling also negated the Missouri Compromise of 1820, which had been Congress's master plan for keeping peace by allowing one slave state to enter the Union for every free one.

The Buchanan Administration

Administration Dates: March 4, 1857– March 4, 1861
Vice President: John C. Breckinridge (1857–61)
Cabinet:

Secretary of State	Lewis Cass (1857–60)
	Jeremiah S. Black (1860–61)
Secretary of the Treasury	Howell Cobb (1857–60)
	Philip F. Thomas (1860–61)
	John A. Dix (1861)
Secretary of War	John B. Floyd (1857–60)
	Joseph Holt (1861)
Attorney General	Jeremiah S. Black (1857–60)
	Edwin M. Stanton (1860–61)
Secretary of the Navy	Isaac Toucey (1857–61)
Postmaster General	Aaron V. Brown (1857–59)
	Joseph Holt (1859–61)
	Horatio King (1861)
Secretary of the Interior	Jacob Thompson (1857–61)

> "With a Democrat elected by the unanimous vote of the slave states, there could be no pretext for secession for four years. … I therefore voted for James Buchanan for president."
>
> —Ulysses S. Grant

John Brown

A radical abolitionist who believed that he was chosen by God to destroy slavery in the United States, John Brown led a failed raid on a federal arsenal at Harpers Ferry, Virginia (now West Virginia). He became a martyr in the eyes of antislavery Northerners. Brown was born on May 9, 1800, one of sixteen children of Owen and Ruth Brown. Brown's father taught his children that slavery was evil, and John Brown became a lifelong opponent of slavery.

Brown's life was frequently marked by tragedy. His mother died when he was eight; his first wife died young; and seven of his twenty children from two marriages died in childhood. He worked as a cattle driver, leather tanner, stock grower, wool merchant, and farmer, but all of his ventures ended in failure. He was forced to declare bankruptcy in 1842 and failed in subsequent efforts to recover financially.

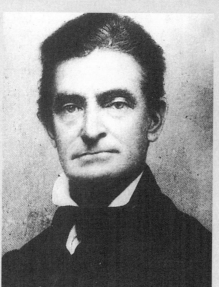

As he grew older, Brown became fanatical on the subject of slavery. He worked on the Underground Railroad, tried to integrate the Congregational Church he attended, and grew more extreme in his views on slavery and slave owners. He said he would be willing to die for the destruction of slavery. He told black abolitionist Frederick Douglass (1817–1895) that he planned to arm the slaves he led to freedom, because violent resistance would give them a sense of their own manhood. In 1851, he urged blacks to kill any official who tried to enforce the Fugitive Slave Act, which decreed that escaped slaves must be returned to their owners.

Brown was stirred to violence when Congress passed the Kansas-Nebraska Bill in 1854. This bill allowed citizens of new territories to legalize slavery, if they so desired, where it had previously been forbidden. Brown and other Northern abolitionists believed the legislation was a Southern conspiracy to introduce slavery to the territories. Five of Brown's sons joined hundreds of free-soil pioneers who set out for Kansas. They witnessed the invasion of Kansas in 1855 by Missourians who voted illegally during an election to establish Kansas as a slave state and promised to kill any abolitionist who attempted to settle in the territory. Brown's sons informed their father that a war in Kansas between freedom and slavery was imminent and implored him to join them and come armed. Brown collected an arsenal of guns and swords and hurried to Kansas.

Violence broke out in Kansas soon after Brown arrived. On the nights of May 24 and 25, 1856, Brown led four of his sons and three other men to Pottawatomie Creek, where they killed five pro-slavery settlers. These murders in addition to raids by pro-slavery Missourians helped spark an open civil war in Kansas. Brown's son Frederick was killed during the violence.

After federal forces and a new governor imposed an uneasy peace on Kansas, Brown traveled to the Northeast to try to raise funds in support of his antislavery campaign. Believing that slaves would rise up and wage war to win their freedom, Brown planned to invade Virginia and march into Tennessee and northern Alabama. His attack on Virginia was delayed when one of his men revealed Brown's plans to some politicians. Returning to Kansas, Brown led a bloody raid in Missouri, freeing a number of slaves, killing one slaveholder, almost inciting another outbreak of war, and provoking President James Buchanan to put a price of $250 on his head. (Brown responded by putting a price of $2.50 on the president's head.) As he had after the Pottawatomie massacre, Brown again eluded capture. He returned east and prepared for his attack on Harpers Ferry, Virginia, the site of the federal arsenal and armory. Brown rented a farm in Maryland, seven miles from Harpers Ferry, and gathered his weapons and recruits there. On the evening of October 16, 1859, Brown and his tiny army of sixteen whites and five blacks set out for Harpers Ferry.

By the next morning, the Harpers Ferry townspeople were firing at Brown's men. Virginia and Maryland militiamen soon joined in. During the afternoon fighting, eight of the raiders (including two of Brown's sons) and three townspeople were killed. Seven of Brown's men, two of whom were later caught, escaped. During the night, troops under the command of Robert E. Lee (1807–1870) and Jeb Stuart (1833–1864) arrived. In the morning, Stuart asked Brown to surrender. When Brown refused, Stuart jumped back and gave the signal to attack. The troops quickly captured Brown.

The raid on Harpers Ferry—over barely thirty-six hours after it had begun—ended in hopeless failure. No slaves had risen up anywhere in Virginia or Maryland because they had been given no advanced warning of Brown's plans. Brown and six of his men were captured, indicted, tried, and convicted of treason, murder, and inciting slave insurrection. All were sentenced to be hanged. Brown was executed on December 2, 1859.

The Gathering Storm

The *Dred Scott* decision ignited a storm of controversy and it created new popular support for the abolitionist cause. When the territory of Kansas applied to enter the Union, the issue of the expansion of slavery into the West aroused even stronger emotions across the country. The earlier Kansas-Nebraska Act allowed prospective states to decide for themselves whether to permit slavery or not. Buchanan's efforts to engineer an agreeable compromise didn't work out. The majority of settlers in the Kansas Territory were opposed to slavery, but a pro-slavery government had been made legitimate by the Kansas-Nebraska Act. When Kansas applied to join the Union as a slave state the petition was blocked in Congress, and Buchanan offered legislation as a temporary resolution. He suggested that Kansas be admitted as a slave state but with a greatly reduced federal land grant. Congress passed the bill, but during a cooling-off period, heated debate in Kansas resulted in its being admitted into the Union as a free state three years later.

Buchanan's faith that the Supreme Court ruling would answer critics of slavery was misguided. The issue had already flared into warfare during the 1850s, but Buchanan continued to believe that an acceptable solution was right around the corner. Meanwhile, the United States was going through a period of enormous change. Railroads were stretching across the land, the invention of the steamboat improved water transportation, the telegraph made nearly instant communication possible, and the United States was growing into an industrial power. Cultural changes were occurring as well: Advances in science challenged long-held religious beliefs, which led to a surge in religious revivalism. Buchanan had been a career politician who never ventured far into the land, and events were quickly moving beyond any influence he could possibly attempt.

He had come to office as a foreign policy expert, and he hoped to use his presidency as an opportunity for expanding America's influence abroad. Trade was growing, Latin American nations emerging from the crumbling Spanish empire were given recognition by the United States and offered protection as well, and Buchanan persuaded British officials to stop trying to control Central America. Still, divisiveness within the United States was reflected by a divided Congress. As Buchanan began losing support during the growing crisis over slavery, his ability to act decisively on any issue was compromised. He negotiated treaties with Mexico, to help protect its unstable government, and with Nicaragua, to help protect it from foreign intervention, but both treaties were rejected by the Senate.

Closet Abolitionist

Although Buchanan was opposed to slavery, he was viewed as a Southern sympathizer, and as if to prove it, he never joined the movement to abolish it. However, during his years in Congress and his service as a senator, he bought slaves in Washington on several different occasions and took them home to Pennsylvania, where he freed them.

Republicans won a plurality of seats in the House in the 1858 midterm elections, and during the final two years of Buchanan's term, all crucial legislation was deadlocked by the increasingly hostile political atmosphere. The controversial raid at Harpers Ferry, Virginia (now West Virginia), led by abolitionist John Brown in October of 1859, worsened the already critical sectional division of the country.

Abolitionist Brown had already killed five people in Kansas in an earlier skirmish, and then he escaped and showed up at Harpers Ferry with a plan to free the South's slave population—estimated at over 3.8 million— by seizing a federal arsenal and dividing the arms and ammunition among abolitionists and slaves. Brown and his forces were caught in the act, and he was executed by hanging six weeks later.

Buchanan had a bitter attitude toward men and women like Brown, whom he believed kept the slavery question from being discussed and resolved more rationally. He had close ties to many Southern Democrats, including Jefferson Davis, the Mississippi senator who would in a short time become president of the Confederacy.

As tensions grew between North and South, some members of Congress began to carry guns. The situation became desperate with the new year of 1860, and Buchanan was advised to send troops to southern ports to protect federal property. He refused on grounds that the action would only provoke Southerners to violence. The situation was so volatile that Buchanan's portrait was removed from the Capitol Building to keep his enemies from vandalizing it.

Another Country Heard From

After the Mormons established themselves in the place they called Deseret, the government moved in, called it Utah, and made it a territory of the United States. The Mormon leader, Brigham Young, was made its territorial governor, but the Mormons were interested in establishing their own kingdom out there by the Great Salt Lake. Their independent attitude, and suspicion of what was viewed as their odd ways, prompted Buchanan to appoint a new governor. But his intelligence apparatus indicated that the Mormons were planning to overthrow the U.S. government, and while the reports weren't true, he decided to send a company of U.S. troops to go to Salt Lake City with the new governor. The problem was, he forgot to inform Brigham Young that these soldiers were on a ceremonial, not hostile, mission. When they appeared on the horizon, the city was evacuated and the local militia mustered to head them off at the pass. The Utah War ended peacefully, but not until after two years of tense negotiations. And it all could have been avoided if James Buchanan had let Brigham Young in on his plans.

Buchanan believed that a president should be limited to one term, and he sat out the 1860 presidential campaign. His goal in the meantime was to keep some appearance of political order and to keep the Union intact—an impossible task. The Democratic Party was split into Northern and Southern factions by then, and there was agreement on neither a standard bearer nor a platform. When Abraham Lincoln, a former Illinois congressman and avowed enemy of slavery, became the Republican presidential nominee, some Southern states made it very clear that if he won the election, they would leave the Union.

Left: The Mormon Trek to Utah led to a war of misunderstanding by the Buchanan administration.

Crucial Last Weeks

A few weeks after Lincoln won the presidential election, South Carolina announced its secession from the Union. Buchanan responded by asserting that a state didn't have that right under the Constitution. However, the Constitution didn't offer him a way to remedy the situation. He held meetings with South Carolina leaders to talk them into reconsidering, but it was an exercise in futility. His only option was military force, but Buchanan refused to go that route even if it might keep the Union intact.

As he finished out the last weeks of his term, Buchanan was virtually powerless. Neither side in the slavery dispute could agree on a compromise that could ease the tense situation. Buchanan urged President-elect Lincoln to call a constitutional convention to resolve the crisis, believing that the action would isolate South Carolina's secession as an extreme measure, but Mr. Lincoln was not interested in a compromise.

Buchanan refused to use force even when federal forts were being threatened in the South. Similar threats and violence against government interests had been countered decisively by such presidents as George Washington, who had called out several state militias to stop the Whiskey Rebellion of 1794, and Andrew Jackson had threatened federal intervention if the state of South Carolina seceded from the Union during the nullification crisis of 1832. Buchanan did not want to provoke a regional war, but his inaction did nothing to stop the growing conflict.

Many members of Buchanan's cabinet had resigned by New Year's Eve. Northern politicians were enraged over his refusal to act decisively on the South Carolina matter, and Southerners wanted the president to affirm their right to secede. Buchanan moved quickly to appoint new Cabinet officials—this time choosing many Northerners, whom Lincoln would retain. He submitted a four-point plan to Congress that he hoped might save the Union. It included calling a constitutional convention and a promise to take no action likely to provoke a war. Congress refused to consider the bill. Part of the resistance was led by Republican forces who wanted Lincoln to act on the crisis when he took office in March, damaging the reputations of the Democrats in the bargain.

Seven Southern states formed the Confederate States of America in February 1861, and Lincoln's inaugural ceremonies a few weeks later were tense and disrupted by the strong presence of federal troops to discourage potential terrorists.

Buchanan retired to Wheatland after that, and he wrote a book, *Mr. Buchanan's Administration on the Eve of the Rebellion*, which received little attention when it was published in 1866. He died on June 1, 1868.

Legacy

The distractions of the slavery issue left James Buchanan with little time for other matters. His foreign policy goals might have succeeded if Congress had been able to agree on anything. Halfway through his presidency, the growing opposition in Congress refused to ratify treaties his administration had negotiated. In his inaugural speech, Buchanan had called for a national railroad linking the land from the Atlantic to the Pacific, but Congress couldn't decide whether tracks should run across the plains from the upper Midwest or through the Southwest. Buchanan persisted in his aims for implementing the Ostend Manifesto by annually requesting an appropriation from Congress in case Spain might decide to sell Cuba after all. The request was rejected each year. He was successful in opening and securing American ports on the West Coast, which improved the growing trade with Asian nations.

Buchanan's presidential character was often attacked during his term and for many years afterward. When he died, his *New York Times* obituary skipped over most of his presidential career. The exception was a notation that "he met the crisis of secession in a timid and vacillating spirit, temporizing with both parties, and studiously avoiding the adoption of a decided policy." In subsequent decades, Buchanan was ridiculed for his approach, and his weak leadership was viewed as a decisive factor in the outbreak of the Civil War.

More recent historical assessments have recognized that no single administration could have done anything to prevent the ugliest and deadliest political dispute in American history, but Buchanan is often credited for delaying full-scale armed conflict at a time when war appeared to be inevitable.

Harriet Lane

Born May 9, 1830, Mercersburg, Pennsylvania
Died July 3, 1903, Narragansett Pier, Rhode Island

"I receive so many evidences of kindnesses and good feelings and so many regrets at my leaving [the White House after her uncle's defeat] that it makes me feel very sad."

—Harriet Lane

James Buchanan's niece, Harriet Lane, served as the official hostess for America's only bachelor president. A well-educated, well-traveled young woman, she became a popular Washington social figure. The term "first lady" appeared for the first time in print in 1860, and it was used to describe her.

Together after Tragedies

Harriet Lane was born in 1830 in Mercersburg, Pennsylvania, and she grew up in the well-to-do family of Elliot Tole Lane and Jane Buchanan Lane. Her mother was James Buchanan's sister. Both her mother and father died by the time she was eleven, and her uncle James, who was a U.S. senator at the time, became her guardian. She was sent to a private school for girls in Lancaster, Pennsylvania, and then she moved to Buchanan's home in Washington, where he enrolled her in a convent school, Visitation Academy in Georgetown.

Buchanan's political career continued to prosper while she was growing up. He served as secretary of state for President James K. Polk, and he was named minister to Britain by his presidential predecessor, Franklin Pierce. Harriet, who was twenty-three years old at the time, went to England with him, and she was formally presented at court to Queen Victoria. Her lively personality and appreciation for the arts made her one of the queen's favorites, and she was given special court privileges.

Harriet went back to Washington with her uncle when he began his campaign for the presidency in 1856.

Buchanan had already begun to train her in the art of political socializing, including how to keep her ears open for potentially valuable clues about secret alliances, pending legislation, or clues to the kind of skullduggery that could make or break a political career. She was a very attractive young woman with blond hair and violet eyes. She was such a fashionable dresser that her favored style of low-cut gown, known as "the low-neck lace bertha," became a staple in the wardrobes of society women from Washington to New York. Many of those women also attempted to imitate her witty conversation and her spirit on the dance floor, but most came to the conclusion that they couldn't hold a candle to Harriet Lane.

When her uncle was elected president, Harriet went to work making the social events of his administration the only bright spots in an otherwise subdued time in the capital. She introduced some of the old-world customs that had impressed her in England. She wore elaborate white dresses, filled rooms with fragrant roses, and hired a formal catering staff that was almost entirely English. She was also skilled in the established official protocols of the American presidency. During her uncle's administration, the country was hopelessly divided by sectional differences, and she had to take special care in the seating arrangements for weekly dinners, making sure that political enemies were kept apart from one another without making it obvious.

With her often beleaguered uncle, whom she called "Nunc," Harriet followed a ritual of reading the day's newspapers every morning. She had a keen interest in politics and a capacity for understanding the complexities and subtleties of political rivalries. She became the first first lady in several years to officiate at a formal event when she christened a battleship that had been named in her honor. She began an unusually good relationship with the press almost as soon as her uncle was inaugurated, but her public approval decreased in direct proportion to Buchanan's increasing political woes.

Other Causes

When in England, Harriet had associated with notable aristocratic women who were involved in a host of social reform activities. Following their example as first lady, she gave her support to prison reform and public education issues as well as to improving health care for Native Americans, which made a particular favorite among them.

Her appreciation for art ranged from the works of the European masters to far more avant-garde objects from non-Western cultures. She became the first executive mansion hostess to invite artists to official dinners, and she also organized evenings of musical performances. The visit of Queen Victoria's son—the Prince of Wales and future king Edward VIII—to the United States in the fall of 1860 was a social highlight of the Buchanan administration, and Harriet served as Prince Edward's official escort in Washington.

It is likely that she was under great stress during the final months of the Buchanan administration, as was her uncle, who would later be blamed for a policy of inaction that led to the Civil War. Like the president, Harriet had a great fondness for Southern manners and customs, and some of her closest friends were women who would

leave Washington when slave-owning states began to secede from the Union in 1861. Buchanan reportedly sent his niece to ask his secretary of the treasury, Georgian Howell Cobb, and his wife Mary Ann, not to abandon the administration.

Ironically, the *Harriet Lane* became the first Union Navy vessel to fire a shot when Confederate forces attacked Fort Sumter in South Carolina. The ship was later captured off the coast of Galveston, Texas, and served the Southern war effort after 1863. A second vessel christened the *Harriet Lane* was used to stop smuggled liquor shipments during the Prohibition era in the 1920s. A third naval vessel called *Harriet Lane* was commissioned for service in 1984.

Later Life

After Abraham Lincoln was inaugurated in 1861, Harriet and her uncle went back to his Pennsylvania estate, Wheatland. She had rejected several marriage proposals over the years, but she married banker Henry Elliott Johnston on January 11, 1866, at the age of thirty-six. Johnston was from a well-established and honored Baltimore family, and she moved there with him and began a family with the birth of her first son, James Buchanan Johnston. Both he and his younger brother, Henry, died of rheumatic fever when they were in their early teens. After these tragedies, the Johnstons founded the Harriet Lane Home for Invalid Children in Baltimore. It became part of the pediatric-care facility at Johns Hopkins University Hospital in 1972.

Buchanan died in 1868 and left his Pennsylvania home, Wheatland, to Harriet, and she spent summers there. After her husband died from pneumonia sixteen years later, she moved back to Washington and began working to establish a national gallery of art. When she died in 1903, her impressive collection of paintings was donated to the Smithsonian Institution research and education center. She also left a large endowment for St. Albans, a private school in Washington, D.C.

Buchanan's Final Annual Address to Congress

Delivered on December 3, 1860

A Northerner who was against the abolition of slavery, President James Buchanan tried to keep peace in the United States during a period of increasing tension. He stuck to his belief that divisiveness over slavery could be resolved without abolishing it. But by the end of his presidency, Buchanan had little support from either Northerners or Southerners.

Abraham Lincoln had already been elected president when Buchanan made his last address to Congress. Southern states had threatened to secede from the Union if Lincoln, an avowed opponent of slavery, was elected. Buchanan used the occasion of his final annual address as a last-ditch effort to save the Union.

Buchanan is viewed by many historians as the least effective of all the presidents. Even as the nation became more divided, he still viewed the slavery issue in simplistic terms. He concluded his final annual address, for example, by proposing what he called an "Explanatory Amendment" to the Constitution. The proposed amendment, which would have recognized the legality of slavery once and for all, was never taken seriously by either side.

Excerpt from President Buchanan's Final Annual Address to Congress

Fellow-Citizens of the Senate and House of Representatives:

Throughout the year since our last meeting the country has been eminently prosperous in all its material interests. The general health has been excellent, our harvests have been abundant, and plenty smiles throughout the land. Our commerce and manufactures have been prosecuted with energy and industry, and have yielded fair and ample returns. In short, no nation in the tide of time has ever presented a spectacle of greater material prosperity than we have done until within a very recent period.

Why is it, then, that discontent now so extensively prevails, and the Union of the States, which is the source of all these blessings, is threatened with destruction?

The long-continued and intemperate interference of the Northern people with the question of slavery in the Southern States has at length produced its natural effects. The different sections of the Union are now arrayed against each other, and the time has arrived, so much dreaded by the Father of his Country, when hostile geographical parties have been formed.

I have long foreseen and often forewarned my countrymen of the now impending danger. This does not proceed solely from the claim on the part of Congress or the Territorial legislatures to exclude slavery from the Territories, nor from the efforts of different States to defeat the execution of the fugitive-slave law. All or any of these evils might have been endured by the South without danger to the Union (as others have been) in the hope that I have long foreseen and often forewarned my countrymen of the now impending danger. This does not proceed solely from the claim on the part of Congress or the Territorial legislatures to exclude slavery from the Territories, nor from the efforts of different States to defeat the execution of the fugitive-slave law. All or any of these evils might have been endured by the South without danger to the Union (as others have been) in the hope that time and reflection might apply the remedy. The immediate peril arises not so much from these causes as from the fact that the incessant and violent agitation of the slavery question throughout the North for the last quarter of a century has at length produced its malign influence on the slaves and inspired them with vague notions of freedom. Hence a sense of security no longer exists around the family altar. This feeling of peace at home has given place to apprehensions of servile insurrections. Many a matron throughout the South retires at night in dread of what may befall herself and children before the morning. Should this apprehension of domestic danger, whether real or imaginary, extend and intensify itself until it shall pervade the masses of the Southern people, then disunion will become inevitable. Self-preservation is the first law of nature, and has been implanted in the heart of man by his Creator for the wisest purpose; and no political union, however fraught with blessings and benefits in all other respects, can long continue if the necessary consequence be to render the homes and the firesides of nearly half the parties to it habitually and hopelessly insecure. Sooner or later the bonds of such a union must be severed. It is my conviction that this fatal period has not yet arrived, and my prayer to God is that He would preserve the Constitution and the Union throughout all generations.

But let us take warning in time and remove the cause of danger. It can not be denied that for five and twenty years the agitation at the North against slavery has been incessant. In 1835 pictorial handbills and inflammatory appeals were circulated extensively throughout the South of a character to excite the passions of the slaves, and, in the language of General [Andrew] Jackson, "to stimulate them to insurrection and produce all the horrors of a servile war." This agitation has ever since been continued by the public press, by the proceedings of State and county conventions and by abolition sermons and lectures. The time of Congress has been occupied in violent speeches on this never-ending subject, and appeals, in pamphlet and other forms, endorsed by distinguished names, have been sent forth from this central point and spreadbroadcast over the Union.

How easy would it be for the American people to settle the slavery question forever and to restore peace and harmony to this distracted country! They, and they alone, can do it. All that is necessary to accomplish the object, and all for which the slave States have ever contended, is to be let alone and permitted to manage their domestic institutions in their own way. As sovereign States, they, and they alone, are responsible before God and the world for the slavery existing among them. For this the people of the North are not more responsible and have no more right to interfere than with similar institutions in Russia or in Brazil.

[...]

[The] election of any one of our fellow citizens to the office of President does not of itself afford just cause for dissolving the Union. This is more especially true if his election has been effected by a mere plurality, and not a majority of the people, and thus resulted from transient and temporary causes, which may probably never again occur. In order to justify a resort to revolutionary resistance, the Federal Government must be guilty of a deliberate, palpable, and dangerous exercise of powers not granted by the Constitution. The late Presidential election, however, has been held in strict conformity with its express provisions. How, then, can the result justify a revolution to destroy this very Constitution? Reason, justice, a regard for the Constitution, all require that we shall wait for some overt and dangerous act on the part of the President elect before resorting to such a remedy. It is said, however, that the antecedents of the President elect have been sufficient to justify the fears of the South that he will attempt to invade their constitutional rights. But are such apprehensions of contingent danger in the future sufficient to justify the immediate destruction of the noblest system of government ever devised by mortals? From the very nature of his office and its high responsibilities he must necessarily be conservative. The stern duty of administering the vast and complicated concerns of this Government affords in itself a guarantee that he will not attempt any violation of a clear constitutional right. After all, he is no more than the chief executive officer of the Government. His province is not to make but to execute the laws. And it is a remarkable fact in our history that, notwithstanding the repeated efforts of the antislavery party, no single act has ever passed Congress, unless we may possibly except the Missouri compromise, impairing in the slightest degree the rights of the South to their property in slaves; and it may also be observed, judging from present indications, that no probability exists of the passage of such an act by a majority of both Houses, either in the present or the next Congress. Surely under these circumstances we ought to be restrained from present action by the precept of Him who spake as man never spoke, that sufficient unto the day is the evil thereof. The day of evil may never come unless we shall rashly bring it upon ourselves.

It is alleged as one cause for immediate secession that the Southern States are denied equal rights with the other States in the common Territories. But by what authority are these denied? Not by Congress, which has never passed, and I believe never will pass, any act to exclude slavery from these Territories; and certainly not by the Supreme Court, which has solemnly decided that slaves are property, and, like all other property, their owners have a right to take them into the common Territories and hold them there under the protection of the Constitution.

[...]

The most palpable violations of constitutional duty which have yet been committed consist in the acts of different State legislatures to defeat the execution of the fugitive-slave law. It ought to be remembered, however, that for these acts neither Congress nor any President can justly be held responsible. Having been passed in violation of the Federal Constitution, they are therefore null and void. All the courts, both State and national, before whom the question has arisen have from the beginning declared the fugitive-slave law to be constitutional. The single exception is that of a State court in Wisconsin, and this has not only been reversed by the proper appellate tribunal, but has met with such universal reprobation that there can be no danger from it as a precedent. The validity of this law has been established over and over again by the Supreme Court of the United States with perfect unanimity. It is founded upon an express provision of the Constitution, requiring that fugitive slaves who escape from service in one State to another shall be "delivered up" to their masters. Without this provision it is a well-known historical fact that the Constitution itself could never have been adopted by the Convention. In one form or other, under the acts of 1793 and 1850, both being substantially the same, the fugitive-slave law has been the law of the land from the days of Washington until the present moment. Here, then a clear case is presented in which it will be the duty of the next President, as it has been my own, to act with vigor in executing this supreme law against the conflicting enactments of State legislatures. Should he fail in the performance of this high duty, he will then have manifested a disregard of the Constitution and laws, to the great injury of the people of nearly one-half of the States of the Union. But are we to presume in advance that he will thus violate his duty? This would be at war with every principle of justice and of Christian charity. Let us wait for the overt act. The Fugitive Slave Law has been carried into execution in every contested case since the commencement of the present Administration, though often, it is to be regretted, with great loss and inconvenience to the master and with considerable expense to the Government. Let us trust that the State legislatures will repeal their unconstitutional and obnoxious enactments. Unless this shall be done without unnecessary delay, it is impossible for any human power to save the Union.

The Southern States, standing on the basis of the Constitution, have a right to demand this act of justice from the States of the North. Should it be refused, then the Constitution, to which all the States are parties, will have been willfully violated by one portion of them in a provision essential to the domestic security and happiness of the remainder. In that event the injured States, after having first used all peaceful and constitutional means to obtain redress, would be justified in revolutionary resistance to the Government of the Union.

[. . .]

But may I be permitted solemnly to invoke my countrymen to pause and deliberate before they determine to destroy this the grandest temple which has ever been dedicated to human freedom since the world began? It has been consecrated by the blood of our fathers, by the glories of the past, and by the hopes of the future. The Union has already made us the most prosperous, and ere long will, if preserved, render us the most powerful nation on the face of the earth. In every foreign region of the globe the title of American citizen is held in the highest respect, and when pronounced in a foreign land it causes the hearts of our countrymen to swell with honest pride. Surely when we reach the brim of the yawning abyss we shall recoil with horror from the last fatal plunge. [. . .]

Congress can contribute much to avert it by proposing and recommending to the legislatures of the several States the remedy for existing evils which the Constitution has itself provided for its own preservation. This has been tried at different critical periods of our history, and always with eminent success. It is to be found in the fifth article, providing for its own amendment. Under this article amendments have been proposed by two-thirds of both Houses of Congress, and have been "ratified by the legislatures of three-fourths of the several States" and have consequently become parts of the Constitution. To this process the country is indebted for the clause prohibiting Congress from passing any law respecting an establishment of religion or abridging the freedom of speech or of the press or of the right of petition. To this we are also indebted for the bill of rights which secures the people against any abuse of power by the Federal Government. Such were the apprehensions justly entertained by the friends of State rights at that period as to have rendered it extremely doubtful whether the Constitution could have long survived without those amendments.

[. . .]

This is the very course which I earnestly recommend in order to obtain an "explanatory amendment" of the Constitution on the subject of slavery. This might originate with Congress or the State legislatures, as may be deemed most advisable to attain the object. The explanatory amendment might be confined to the final settlement of the true construction of the Constitution on three special points:

An express recognition of the right of property in slaves in the States where it now exists or may hereafter exist.

The duty of protecting this right in all the common Territories throughout their Territorial existence, and until they shall be admitted as States into the Union, with or without slavery, as their constitutions may prescribe.

A like recognition of the right of the master to have his slave who has escaped from one State to another restored and delivered up to him, and of the validity of the fugitive-slave law enacted for this purpose, together with a declaration that all State laws impairing or defeating this right are violations of the Constitution, and are consequently null and void.

It may be objected that this construction of the Constitution has already been settled by the Supreme Court of the United States, and what more ought to be required? The answer is that a very large proportion of the people of the United States still contest the correctness of this decision, and never will cease from agitation and admit its binding force until clearly established by the people of the several States in their sovereign character. Such an explanatory amendment would, it is believed, forever terminate the existing dissensions, and restore peace and harmony among the States.

What Happened Next

There wasn't anything Buchanan—or anyone else, for that matter—could do to stop the chain of events that was leading to the Civil War. Three weeks after this speech, South Carolina seceded from the Union, and within three months the Confederate States of America was formed. Within five months, the country was at war with itself.

President Lincoln mobilized the Union army after the Confederate military fired on a federal fort (Fort Sumter) in Charleston, South Carolina. He used his power as president to bring about the end of slavery. Because Southern states had seceded from the Union, Lincoln and Congress faced little opposition in enacting legislation and executive orders. like the Emancipation Proclamation of 1863 freeing slaves in the South. But Lincoln's actions and the Civil War itself didn't bring about a society with equal rights for all citizens. They did, however, achieve what Buchanan and all of his predecessors had failed to accomplish: the issue of slavery was settled, once and for all, in all of the United States.

Abraham Lincoln

"'A house divided against itself cannot stand.' I believe this government cannot endure permanently half-slave and half-free."
—*Abraham Lincoln*

Sixteenth president of the United States, 1861–1865

Full name: *Abraham Lincoln*
Born: *February 12, 1809, Hodgenville, Kentucky*
Died: *April 15, 1865, Washington, D.C.*
Burial site: *Oak Ridge Cemetery, Springfield, Illinois*
Parents: *Thomas and Nancy Hanks Lincoln; Sarah Bush Johnston (stepmother)*
Spouse: *Mary Todd (1818–1882; m. 1842)*
Children: *Robert Todd (1843–1926); Edward Baker (1846–1850); William Wallace (1850–1862); Thomas "Tad" (1853–1871)*
Religion: *No formal affiliation*
Education: *No formal education*
Occupation: *Lawyer*
Government positions: *Illinois state legislator; U.S. representative from Illinois*
Political party: *Republican*
Dates as president: *March 4, 1861–March 4, 1865 (first term); March 4, 1865–April 15, 1865 (second term)*
Age upon taking office: *52*

When a president takes the oath of office, he swears to "preserve, protect and defend the Constitution." Based on that promise, Abraham Lincoln exerted more power than any president before him. He made full use of the broad Constitutional authority given to the president in case of a national uprising. He helped preserve the United States and brought about the end of slavery.

As a self-made man leading a self-governing nation, Lincoln became a folk hero. Tales continue to be told, from stories of his humble, backwoods upbringing to examples of his leadership during the Civil War, the country's greatest crisis. He is the president most often written about and studied.

Ambitious and willful, Lincoln was a skilled speaker and a clever politician. He always seemed to know exactly when it was best to be forceful and when he should wait for a better opportunity. For example, he moved more cautiously than most abolitionists who were demanding full freedom for slaves. Above all, he crafted his policies to preserve the Union. He established lenient terms of surrender when the American Civil War ended, and then he called for the restoration of friendship and harmony among all the states.

Famous Face

When someone accused Lincoln of being two-faced, he said, "If I had another, why do you think I'd be showing you this one?" His black hair was coarse, his cheekbones unusually prominent, and his left eye was slightly higher than his right one. He had a wart on his right cheek and a scar over his right eye. But his secretary, John Nicolay, said that it was a face no artist could paint. "…[it] moved through a thousand delicate gradations of line and contour, […] the sparkle of the eye and curve of the lip, in the long gamut of expression from grave to gay and back again, from the rolicking jollity of laughter to that far away look." Lincoln was also tall and gangly—at six feet, four inches, the tallest of all the presidents.

Below: Lincoln's log cabin birthplace in Kentucky.

Timeline

1809: Born in Kentucky
1835–36: Serves in Illinois state legislature
1847–49: Serves in to the U.S. House of Representatives
1855: Serves again in Illinois state legislature
1858: Loses Senate race to Stephen Douglas, but achieves national recognition for the Lincoln-Douglas debates
1861–65: Serves as sixteenth U.S. president
1861: Civil War begins
1864: Reelected president
1865: Civil War ends; Lincoln assassinated; Thirteenth Amendment to the U.S. Constitution—abolishing slavery—is ratified

President Lincoln was assassinated shortly after the war, and "Now he belongs to the ages," as his secretary of war, Edwin M. Stanton, put it. A funeral procession watched in silence by thousands and thousands of mourners traced back the route from Washington, D.C., to Springfield, Illinois, that he had followed in the other direction only fifty months earlier.

Humble Origins

Abraham Lincoln was born on February 12, 1809, in a one-room, dirt-floor log cabin by Nolin Creek, near present-day Hodgenville, Kentucky. His father, Thomas, was a skilled carpenter who was able to provide basic necessities for his family. Lincoln ancestors first arrived in Massachusetts from England in 1637, spreading to Pennsylvania and then to Virginia. Thomas Lincoln's father, Abraham, took his family to Kentucky, where he was killed by an Indian while he was clearing his farmland. Lincoln's mother, Nancy, who never learned to read, gave birth to a daughter, Sarah, two years before Abraham was born.

The family moved to a nearby farm on Knob Creek when the boy was two, and he began hunting, fishing, and doing farm chores as soon as he was old enough. The family crossed the Ohio River in 1816 and moved into a heavily forested area in southern Indiana. Another crude log cabin was built, and young Abe and his father began clearing land and establishing a farm near what is now Gentryville, Indiana.

Lincoln's mother died when he was nine years old, and the following year, his father married Sarah Bush Johnston, a widow with three children. The two families mixed well, although Tom Lincoln had to build an extension on the cabin, and with his stepmother's encouragement, young Abe learned to read and write and do arithmetic. He worked mostly on his own, and had only about one year's worth of formal schooling during his entire life.

Lincoln read the Bible, Aesop's Fables, histories, and biographies. He was especially impressed by a biography of George Washington, and he went on to enjoy reading the plays of William Shakespeare. However, most of his time was spent chopping down trees, plowing, planting,

Above: A typical 19th-century frontier farm.

Below: The New Salem, Illinois, general store where Lincoln worked.

Bookworm

Lincoln once said that "my best friend is the man who'll give me a book I ain't read." Unlike most boys raised on the frontier, he detested hunting, and he wasn't interested in sports popular at the time. Apart from an occasional game of chess and long hours swapping jokes with his cronies, Abe Lincoln's passion was reading. He was especially fond of Shakespeare's Macbeth and Hamlet, and could recite passages from them with all the skill of a trained actor. He also loved the works of Edgar Allan Poe, and the poetry of Oliver Wendell Holmes, Robert Burns, and Lord Byron.

and harvesting, just like every other youngster growing up on the frontier. He also found a job: He piloted a ferryboat carrying passengers and their baggage to riverboats docked along the Ohio River.

"Railsplitter"

Lincoln had reached his adult height of six feet, four inches by the time he was nineteen, the year he was hired by a local merchant to run a flatboat down the Ohio River to the Mississippi and then south to New Orleans. Not long after he got back, his family moved again to a wilderness area about ten miles west of present-day Decatur, Illinois. He kept on working with his father, but he also hired himself out to their neighbors as a handyman. His nickname, "Railsplitter," came from his skill in splitting long logs into rails for their fences.

He made a second trip down the Mississippi River to New Orleans in 1831, and while he was there that he saw a slave auction for the first time. He was disgusted by it, and he reportedly said, "If I ever get a chance to hit that thing, I'll hit it hard."

After he got back to Illinois, Abe was hired as a clerk at a general store in the town of New Salem. In those days, the general store was the center of the social life in towns like New Salem. In addition to chatting with his new neighbors, Lincoln had plenty of time to read—his favorite form of entertainment. But it was the chatting that influenced his immediate future. He became well liked enough among his customers that some of them asked him to run for a seat in the Illinois House of Representatives. That same summer he answered a call for volunteers to fight rebellious Indians led by the Sac Chief Black Hawk. He was elected captain of his company, but they didn't see any action during his three months of service. He returned to New Salem, lost the election, and decided to open a store with a friend. Neither he nor his friend had much of a head for business, and their store quickly went bankrupt. Abe spent most of his time reading law books, while his friend drank steadily and piled up debts. Abe moved on to salaried job as the town's postmaster.

Political Career Begins

Lincoln was elected to the Illinois legislature in 1834. As a member of the Whig Party, he supported a strong federal government and business-friendly legislation. Democrats dominated the national scene at the time, and they were in favor of limited federal influence over states and policies more favorable to small farmers than to urban businesses. Meanwhile, Lincoln continued to study law. He became a licensed attorney and joined a law firm in Springfield, Illinois, where the state capital had recently moved. As a leader of the Illinois legislature, he was in on the ground floor during the time of transition.

Lincoln supported the extension of voting rights to female taxpayers, but the idea wasn't approved by his fellow legislators. He was against the expansion of slavery into new U.S. territories, but he didn't support the immediate national abolishing of slavery, because he believed it would be illegal. He was afraid that supporting abolition would spark reactions among slave owners that would "increase its evil."

Lincoln had arrived in Springfield at age twenty-seven, so poor then that he'd had to borrow a horse to make the trip from New Salem. Everything he owned fit easily into two saddlebags. He continued to read and to serve in the Illinois State Congress while he wrestled with the idea of getting married. Over the years, historians have disagreed about whether Lincoln had fallen in love with a young woman named Ann Rutledge, whose tragic death plunged him into sadness and deep depression.

"Common-looking people are the best in the world: that is why the Lord makes so many of them."

—*Abraham Lincoln*

In 1840, he met Mary Todd, a well-educated and quite sensitive Kentucky woman who was staying with her married sister in Springfield. They became engaged, but Lincoln didn't show up for their wedding ceremony. After patching things up, the couple was married the following year. Despite both of their stormy personalities, and their grief over the deaths of two sons—Eddie died at age four, Willie when he was eleven—they remained devoted to each other. (After Lincoln's death, their youngest son, Tad, died at age eighteen.)

Lincoln began devoting most of his attention on his law practice about two years after he got married. He attended court in Springfield and spent six months of the year in a circuit court that served fifteen Illinois counties. In those days, opportunities for entertainment were limited, to say the least, and people found stimulation in listening to court cases. Lincoln's cases always filled the visitors' galleries to overflowing because of his reputation as a dynamic speaker. Many national politicians built their careers in this way, and Lincoln also used the

Below: The area near Lincoln's first law office in Springfield, Illinois.

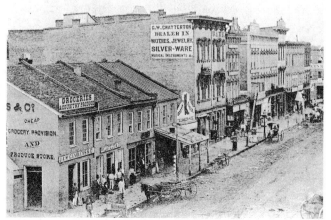

Below: Lincoln's home in Springfield.

circuit court to make contacts he knew would help his national political career—if he'd ever have one. He tried several times to snag the Whigs' nomination for national office and failed each time. When he finally did get their attention and won their nomination as a candidate for a U.S. congressional seat in 1846, he scored big in the general election.

Controversial Congressman

Lincoln faced the same challenge most first-term congressmen did. He couldn't get an opportunity to press issues he regarded as most important, and he was an unknown in Washington political and social circles. The Lincolns lived in a small boardinghouse with their two sons, and among their small group of friends was Georgia congressmen Alexander H. Stephens, who would later become vice president of the Confederate States of America during the Civil War.

"A horrid-looking wretch he is, sooty and scoundrelly in aspect, a cross between a nutmeg dealer, the horse-swapper, and the night-man. [...] He is a lank-sided Yankee of the uncomliest visage and of the dirtiest complexion. Faugh! After him, what white man would be president?"
—Charleston Mercury

Once he was able to get himself noticed, Lincoln made his mark in Congress in two areas. But it was a good news–bad news situation. The United States was involved in the Mexican War, which President James K. Polk had asked Congress to declare after Mexican soldiers had fired on American soldiers inside the U.S. territory of Texas. Lincoln claimed that the war was unconstitutional and he challenged Polk to show him the exact spot where the alleged attack had taken place. The Mexican War was generally unpopular, but not in Illinois, and Lincoln's opposition was widely denounced back home.

As the United States moved toward victory over Mexico, the expansion of slavery became a heated issue. The new territories of Texas and California would soon petition for statehood, and Lincoln supported the Wilmot Proviso, which Congressman David Wilmot had introduced to bar slavery in all states that would be acquired through the war. The bill was passed in the House of Representatives twice, but it was defeated both times in the Senate. Nevertheless, a strong abolitionist faction in the Northeast demanded that the new territories must be free states as they continued to press for an end to all slavery.

Lincoln proposed his own slavery policy : (*1*) all children born to slaves after January 1, 1850, would be free and apprenticed to learn a trade; (*2*) slaveholders could voluntarily free their slaves and receive federal compensation for them; and (*3*) voters in Washington, D.C., would be allowed to decide whether or not to abolish slavery in their district. His moderate approach to abolition never came up for discussion. His score as a congressman was 0 for 2.

His term in Congress came to an end in 1849. He had campaigned for Whig presidential candidate Zachary Taylor, who, although he won the 1848 election, didn't carry the state of Illinois largely because Lincoln had lost his vote-getting power for his stand against the Mexican War. After being turned down for any worthwhile government job from the Taylor administration, Abraham Lincoln gave up politics.

Back in Illinois, he picked up his law practice where he had left off and he quickly became a celebrated attorney. He argued cases in Chicago's federal court and in the state Supreme Court at Springfield. He also went back to the rounds of the circuit court and began listening more closely to the concerns of common people. In the meantime, he continued his reading and forming new ideas about government, even though he would tell anyone who asked that he had no intention of ever getting back into politics.

Political Comeback

But never is a long time. When the Kansas-Nebraska Bill became law in 1854, he was redrawn to the idea of public life. The bill, written by Illinois senator Stephen Douglas, allowed voters in the territories of Kansas and Nebraska to decide for themselves whether to permit slavery. In effect, it repealed the Missouri Compromise, which had set the southern border of Missouri as a

Left: A campaign portrait made during Lincoln's 1858 losing race for the U.S. Senate.

"I do the very best I know how, the very best I can; and I mean to keep on doing it to the end. If the end brings me out all right, what is said against me will not amount to anything. If the end brings me out all wrong, then a legion of angels swearing I was right will make no difference."

—*Abraham Lincoln*

dividing line between slave and free states to keep an equal balance between them.

Lincoln was worried that slavery would be expanded farther, and he campaigned vigorously for fellow Whig candidates for Congress. When Douglas went back to Illinois to make a speech defending the Kansas-Nebraska Bill, Lincoln announced that he would reply to it the following day. Lincoln's forceful rebuttal positioned the institution of slavery as a moral issue rather than a political one. At the same time, he distanced himself from abolitionists. He wanted slavery confronted as a national issue, rather than an action promoted by one part of the country at the expense of another. When Lincoln repeated his speech twelve days later in Peoria, Illinois, it was reported in newspapers, and became famous as the "Peoria speech." It made Mr. Lincoln famous, too, if notorious in some circles.

With his popularity expanding rapidly, Lincoln ran for the U.S. Senate in 1855, but he lost. In those days, senators were elected by state legislatures, and he couldn't persuade enough of his former colleagues to give him sufficient votes to win. He left the Whig Party after that and joined the recently established Republican Party, which was made up of former Whigs like himself as well as abolitionist ex-Democrats.

He lost in the balloting for a presidential candidate at the party's 1856 national convention and he campaigned vigorously for the man who took the nomination, John C. Frémont. Frémont lost to James Buchanan, a Northern politician who had no intention of forcefully challenging the institution of slavery.

The issue wasn't going to go away. A regional civil war broke out in Kansas between pro- and antislavery zealots, and the following year, in its decision on the *Dred Scott v. Sandford* case, the Supreme Court ruled that Congress didn't have the authority to restrict slavery in new territories. Then abolitionist John Brown led a raid on the federal arsenal at Harpers Ferry, Virginia. He was hoping to distribute weapons among abolitionists and slaves, but he and his forces were overwhelmingly defeated, and he was executed by hanging six weeks later.

In the midst of these developments, Lincoln was nominated by the Illinois Republican Party as its candidate against Douglas in the 1858 Senate race. His acceptance speech at the party's state convention was highlighted by his use of a biblical quotation—"a house divided against itself cannot stand"—to emphasize his dedication to preserving the Union. He argued that the Union could not continue to be half slave, half free, and must cease to be divided, he insisted, so that it would not dissolve.

During the campaign, Lincoln and Douglas engaged in a series of seven debates that are still considered among the most admirable examples of American politics in action. The debates were fierce, but always respectful. As many as 15,000 people assembled in outdoor meeting places to hear the speakers, whose discussions were reprinted by newspapers around the country, an usual thing for debates in a single state's election campaign.

Above: One of the seven Lincoln-Douglas debates.

"I am rather inclined to silence, and whether that be wise or not, it is at least more unusual nowadays to find a man who can hold his tongue than to find one who cannot."

—*Abraham Lincoln*

Lincoln edged Douglas in the popular election, but once again a Democratic majority in the state legislature passed over him and gave the office to Douglas, the candidate of their own party. Reacting to the bitter defeat, Lincoln displayed the kind of homespun humor that often appeared in his speeches. He compared himself to a boy who stubbed his toe. "It hurts too much to laugh," he said, "but I'm too old to cry."

In spite of his loss to Douglas, Lincoln's arguments in the debates made him a national figure. He was invited to speak throughout the Midwest, and in the East he greatly impressed New Yorkers with a speech on February 27, 1860. Remembered as the "Cooper Union Speech," it put forward a more moderate approach to outlawing slavery than the solution abolitionists were demanding. New York senator William H. Seward was one such abolitionist and a leading contender for the Republican presidential nomination in 1860. However, Seward couldn't gather enough support at the party's convention in Chicago, and Lincoln steadily gained ground as an alternative choice. He won the nomination on the fourth round of balloting.

Lincoln's Democratic challenger was expected to be Stephen Douglas, but Douglas had lost some of his national

Steamroller

When the Republicans met at Chicago to nominate a presidential candidate in 1860, the smart money was on former New York governor and senator William H. Seward. There were other contenders, too, but Lincoln had an edge: He was practically a hometown boy. Balloting was scheduled for the third day, and Lincoln's men secretly printed extra tickets to make sure the house would be packed. When his name was placed in nomination, a reporter said that their whooping and hollering "made soft vesper breathings of all that preceded. A thousand steam whistles, ten acres of hotel gongs, a tribe of Comanches headed by a choice vanguard from pandemonium might have mingled in the scene unnoticed."

support after his debates with Lincoln. He had stated that a territory could outlaw slavery before it became a state—but only if the people refused to support laws that would protect slave owners, an opinion that cost his support in the South. After he was nominated, Southern Democrats turned to two other candidates, incumbent vice president John Breckinridge of Kentucky and former U.S. senator John Bell of Tennessee. The division cost the Democrats the election. Although Lincoln won only 40 percent of the popular vote, he won all 18 free states for a total of 180 electoral votes. Breckinridge had 72 electoral votes; Bell had 39; and Douglas only 12. Together, his opponents outpolled him by more than a million popular votes.

The House Divides

Even before Lincoln took office, South Carolina seceded from the Union in December 1860. By the following February, when Lincoln left Springfield, Illinois, for his inauguration in Washington, seven more Southern states—South Carolina, Mississippi, Florida, Alabama, Georgia, Louisiana, and Texas—had banded together to form the Confederate States of America, separate from the United States. However, Lincoln turned his trip to Washington into a triumphal tour through twelve states. Because of concerns for his safety, he slipped into the capital quietly in the dead of night.

Lincoln's inauguration took place on March 4, 1861, under heavy military guard, although he offered peace

Election Results

1860

Presidential / Vice Presidential Candidates	Popular Votes	Electoral Votes
Abraham Lincoln / Hannibal Hamlin (Republican)	1,866,452	180
John C. Breckinridge / Joseph Lane (Democratic [Southern])	847,953	72
John Bell / Edward Everett (Constitutional Union [American])	590,631	39
Stephen A. Douglas / Herschel V. Johnson (Democratic [Northern])	1,375,157	12

The Democratic Party divided into three sectional factions, which helped Republican Lincoln win election.

1864

Presidential / Vice Presidential Candidates	Popular Votes	Electoral Votes
Abraham Lincoln / Andrew Johnson (Republican [National Union])	2,213,635	212
George B. McClellan / George H. Pendleton (Democratic)	1,805,237	21

The eleven Confederate states—comprising eighty electoral votes—did not vote in this election.

and not war in his inaugural address. He promised not to interfere with the rights of any state, pledged not to attack the South, and invited the South back into the Union. The Confederacy wasn't interested.

Confederate forces demanded the evacuation of Fort Sumter in Charleston, South Carolina, because it was within the CSA's territory, and represented a foreign presence there. When basic supplies within the fort started to run low, Lincoln announced to South Carolina's governor that new provisions were on the way by boat. Before the freight arrived, Jefferson Davis, who had been named president of the Confederacy, ordered that Fort Sumter be taken by force.

The attack began on April 12, 1861, and the fort was surrendered two days later. Under the authority of the Militia Act of 1796, President Lincoln declared that the action went against federal laws in a manner "too powerful to be suppressed by ordinary judicial proceedings" and he called for 76,000 militia volunteers. Virginia, North Carolina, Tennessee, and Arkansas responded by joining the Confederacy instead of sending soldiers to wage war on their former sister states. Many people in Kentucky, Maryland, and Missouri shared their position and went to fight alongside the Confederates, although these so-called "border states" didn't leave the Union.

Left: A recruit answers the call to do his part to save the Union.

Lincoln-Douglas Debates

Before the adoption of the Seventeenth Amendment to the U.S. Constitution in 1913, state legislatures elected U.S. senators. Candidates did not normally conduct a statewide campaign for the office. The times were not normal in 1858, however, when the Republicans in Illinois nominated Abraham Lincoln as their candidate for the senate seat held by Stephen Douglas. Lincoln, who had served only one term in Congress and had failed in his bid for the Senate in 1856, had nothing to lose by debating Douglas.

Speeches by the candidates and their seven debates attracted tens of thousands of listeners and received wide newspaper coverage. The debates started after Lincoln's "House Divided" speech in Springfield on June 16, 1858, at the Republican meeting endorsing him for the Senate. In that speech, Lincoln stated that the expansion of slavery into new territories had divided the nation. He used a quotation from the Bible—"A house divided against itself cannot stand"—to call for an end to the divisiveness. Douglas replied in Chicago on July 9, and Lincoln made another speech on July 10. The debates formally began in Ottawa, Illinois, on August 21, 1858. The contestants then journeyed to Freeport on August 27, Jonesboro on September 15, Charleston on September 18, Galesburg on October 7, Quincy on October 13, and Alton on October 15.

The strategy of both men was set before the first formal meeting. Lincoln concentrated on the Kansas-Nebraska Act, authored by Douglas. He charged that Douglas was merely a puppet of the slave-power conspiracy, that popular sovereignty had been buried by the Dred Scott decision, and that there was a national conspiracy to legitimatize slavery in the free states. Douglas criticized Lincoln for supporting black suffrage and charged him with attempted subversion

Above: Stephen Douglas.

of the Supreme Court. He accused Lincoln of opposing the Supreme Court's Dred Scott decision on the grounds that it denied citizenship to African Americans and that Lincoln would interfere with the domestic business of individual states.

Lincoln was embarrassed by Douglas' effort to associate him with abolitionism. While admitting his opposition to slavery, Lincoln acknowledged his inability to come up with a solution to the problem short of abolition. Like Douglas, Lincoln believed that blacks were basically inferior to whites; but Lincoln, unlike Douglas, held that slavery was an immoral system inconsistent with the principles and practices of democratic government. Lincoln insisted that slavery must be kept out of the new territories. Douglas countered by demanding that the decision was up to settlers of a territory. Lincoln pointed out that since the Dred Scott decision prohibited Congress from legislating about slavery in the territories, territorial legislatures were similarly prohibited because they had been created by Congress. Douglas, seeking to salvage popular sovereignty, suggested at Freeport that regardless of the Dred Scott decision, the people of a territory could lawfully exclude slavery prior to the formation of a state government, for slavery could not exist without the protection of a slave code enacted by the territorial legislature. Lincoln advocated that principles of equality as set forth in the Declaration of Independence should be applied to the new territories. Douglas concluded with his belief that the nation could endure forever half slave and half free.

In the November elections, the Republicans swept Northern states, but Douglas was reelected in Illinois. The Republican state ticket in Illinois won by over four thousand votes, but the Democrats retained a majority in the legislature. In the process of losing, however, Lincoln became a national figure.

Throughout the war, Lincoln made it clear that his main goal was to preserve the Union. He said that his actions had been taken to suppress a rebellion and to protect free national elections. As commander in chief, he ordered a naval blockade of Southern ports, expanded the military, and directed expenditures without waiting for Congress to authorize them. It was the first time in American history that any president had taken such strong actions. But by continually insisting that his motive was only to save the Union, Lincoln became a

symbol of towering moral strength and inspiration to the North—and the people rallied around him even when it became apparent to them that they were in for a long and bloody war.

It became evident quite early that the Civil War wasn't going to end quickly. The bad news began coming when. Union forces were defeated soundly as early as July at the Battle of Bull Run, also called the First Manassas, in Virginia not far from Washington.

The Lincoln Administration

Administration Dates: March 4, 1861–March 4, 1865
March 4, 1865–April 15, 1865

Vice President: Hannibal Hamlin (1861–65)
Andrew Johnson (1865)

Cabinet:

Secretary of State William H. Seward (1861–65)
Secretary of the Treasury Salmon P. Chase (1861–64)
William P. Fessenden (1864–65)
Hugh McCulloch (1865)
Secretary of War Simon Cameron (1861–62)
Edwin M. Stanton (1862–65)
Attorney General Edward Bates (1861–64)
James Speed (1864–65)
Secretary of the Navy Gideon Welles (1861–65)
Postmaster General Horatio King (1861)
Montgomery Blair (1861–64)
William Dennison Jr.
(1864–65)
Secretary of the Interior Caleb B. Smith (1861–62)
John P. Usher (1863–65)

Black Sheep

During the Republican Convention, Simon Cameron, the political boss of Pennsylvania, gave his support to Lincoln's candidacy in return for the promise of a cabinet post. Lincoln himself wasn't aware of the promise, but he made good on it by appointing Cameron secretary of war. Cameron jumped right in and began making sweetheart deals, awarding military contracts to his friends. An honest politician, he said, "is a man who, when he's bought, stays bought." Lincoln rewarded him for his loyalty by naming him minister to Russia, getting him as far from the trough as he could.

Below: The assault on Fort Sumter.

1862: Losses and Triumphs

In April of 1862, 13,000 Union soldiers died in the Battle of Shiloh in Virginia, and during the summer, Union forces were defeated again in two more Virginia encounters, the Seven Days' Battle and the Second Battle of Bull Run (Manassas). But they weren't the only problems Lincoln faced. A group of radical Republicans in Congress regarded the war as a holy crusade, and they were agitating for a more vigorous offensive against the South, punishment for leaders of the Confederacy, and immediate emancipation of slaves. Lincoln had already sidetracked his secretary of state, William H. Seward, who had begun enacting policies the radical Republicans supported without the president's permission, but they were scheming to undermine him and gain national control in time for the next presidential election. In a meeting involving Lincoln's entire Cabinet and all of the radical Republicans, Lincoln was able to assert his authority as president, and, reluctantly or not, they decided to back him. It cleared the air, and from then on the conduct of the war was firmly in Lincoln's hands as commander in chief.

Meanwhile, personal tragedy struck, and Lincoln was grieving over the death of his eleven-year-old son, Willie, the second of the four Lincoln boys to die in childhood.

Below: The First Battle of Bull Run, also called First Manassas, in Virginia.

Jefferson Davis

Jefferson Davis was born on June 3, 1808, in what is now Todd County, Kentucky. Raised in Mississippi, he attended Transylvania University for three years and then entered the U.S. Military Academy at West Point, from which he graduated in 1828. He served in the infantry for seven years. While stationed at Fort Crawford, Wisconsin, Davis fell in love with Sarah Knox Taylor, daughter of post commandant Zachary Taylor (a future U.S. president). Taylor disapproved of his daughter marrying a military man. Davis resigned his commission in 1835, married Sarah, and took her to Mississippi. However, within three months she died of malaria. Davis had also contracted a light case of the disease, and it permanently weakened his health. From 1835 to 1845, he lived in seclusion.

Davis spent much of his time reading and developed a fascination for politics. Elected to the House of Representatives in 1845, Davis took Varina Howell, his new bride, to Washington, D.C. War with Mexico interrupted Davis's congressional service. He resigned in 1846 to command a volunteer army regiment. Distinguished service by Davis's outfit at Monterey, Mexico, was followed by real heroism at Buena Vista. A wounded Davis returned to Mississippi a hero.

In 1847, Davis was elected to the U.S. Senate. In 1851, however, Mississippi Democrats called him back to run for governor, thinking that Davis's reputation might cover the party's shift from secessionist (pro-separation) to one of cooperation. However, Davis lost the election.

President Franklin Pierce appointed Davis secretary of war in 1853. Davis enlarged the army, modernized military procedures, and boosted soldiers' pay (and morale). He directed important Western land surveys for future railroad construction and masterminded the Gadsden Purchase (comprising present-day New Mexico and Arizona). Davis reentered the Senate after Pierce's presidency and became a major Southern spokesman. He worked to preserve the Compromise of 1850 as a means for maintaining peace; he argued that Congress had no power to limit slavery's extension. At the 1860 Democratic Convention, Davis cautioned against secession. However, he accepted Mississippi's decision to secede. On January 21, 1861, he announced his state's secession from the Union and his own resignation from the Senate.

Davis reluctantly accepted the presidency of the Confederate States of America. He quickly grasped his problems: 9 million citizens (including at least 3 million slaves) of sovereign Southern states pitted against 22 million Yankees; 9,000 miles of usable railroad track against the North's 22,000 miles; no large factories, warships, or shipyards; little money; and no manufacturing arsenals to replenish military supplies. Davis built an army out of state volunteers; supplies, arms and ammunition, clothes, and transportation came from often reluctant governors and citizens. When supplies dwindled, Davis began confiscating private property. When military manpower shrank, a draft was authorized.

Davis made excellent choices for army commanders. He devised a strategy based on hoarding supplies and repelling invaders. A series of battlefield successes led Davis to a general offensive in the summer and fall of 1862 designed to terrify Northerners not yet touched by war; to separate other, uncertain states from the Union; and to convince the outside world of Southern strength. Though it failed, the strategy had merit. Meanwhile, Virginia was secured, and in spring 1863 it looked as though Vicksburg, Mississippi, would remain a stronghold.

Unfortunately for the South, Union general Ulysses S. Grant had other plans. His continued pressure on Vicksburg forced Davis to a gamble that resulted in the Battle of Gettysburg. It failed. Vicksburg (at a cost of over 50,000 men) fell about the same time. Davis adopted the idea of a "theater of war" that would isolate areas into separate, large-scale operations. Undermanned, undersupplied, and underfunded, Confederate forces were fighting valiantly in a losing battle. As Confederate chances dwindled, Davis became increasingly demanding. He eventually won congressional support for most of his measures but at high personal cost. By the summer of 1864, most Southern newspapers were criticizing his administration, state governors were quarreling with him, and he had become the focus of Southern discontent. The South was losing; Davis's plan must be wrong, the rebels reasoned.

Peace sentiments arose in unaffected areas of several states, as did demands to negotiate with the enemy. Confederate money had severely declined in value. Soldiers deserted and invaders stalked the land with almost no opposition. General Robert E. Lee surrendered on April 9, 1865. Davis was captured on May 10.

Davis spent two years in prison and was treated harshly. Federal authorities decided not to try him for treason. He returned to Mississippi, wrote a book about his Confederate experiences, and died on December 6, 1889.

Lincoln was prepared to issue a proclamation during the summer of 1862 that would free all slaves in states that had seceded from the Union. Waiting for a moment of strength, he finally released his Emancipation Proclamation on September 22, 1862, on the heels of a show of Union strength in the Battle of Antietam.

The Proclamation was scheduled to go into effect on January 1, 1863, and in the meantime Slave states that had not seceded were encouraged, but not forced, to free slaves voluntarily. Lincoln also pressed Congress to pass a Constitutional amendment barring slavery throughout the country. It would have to be ratified by three-fourths of the states, and it took until late in 1865 for the Thirteenth Amendment to become part of the Constitution. States that had seceded were required to ratify it before they would be admitted back.

There were other positive developments in 1862. With many new immigrants entering the United States, Lincoln signed the Homestead Act, which gave settlers in western lands a 160-acre farm for a small fee, provided they stayed on the land for five years. Other new laws provided free federal land for states to help them establish agricultural and technical colleges. New railroads were being built to open up the West, and two new states—Nevada and West Virginia (a part of Virginia that hadn't seceded)—were welcomed into the Union during the Lincoln administration.

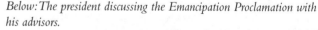

"My paramount object in this struggle is to save the Union, and it is not either to save or destroy slavery. If I could save the Union without freeing the slaves, I would do it, and if I could save it by freeing all the slaves, I would do it; and if I could save it by freeing some and leaving others alone I would also do that. What I do about slavery, and the colored race, I do because I believe it helps save the Union; and what I forbear, I forbear because I do not believe it would help save the Union. I shall do less whenever I shall believe what I am doing hurts the cause, and I shall do more whenever I shall believe doing more will help the cause."

—Abraham Lincoln

Left: Lincoln visiting the battlefield at Antietam.

Below: The president discussing the Emancipation Proclamation with his advisors.

Union Forces Rally

The Grand Army of the Republic, as the Union forces were called, continued to be battered into the spring of 1863. Then two pivotal events on July 4 changed the war's momentum dramatically. After several discouraging attempts, Union troops under General Ulysses S. Grant routed the Rebel defenders in the Battle of Vicksburg in Mississippi, which gave them control of the Mississippi River, not to mention possession of an important Confederate stronghold. Meanwhile, a steady advance into Pennsylvania by Confederate general Robert E. Lee was halted at Gettysburg. After an unusually bloody battle, Lee's forces retreated, but they were stopped by flooding of the Potomac River. Lincoln ordered General George Meade to attack them with force, but Meade responded too slowly, and Lee's men managed to escape back into Virginia.

Lincoln made one of his most moving speeches at the consecration of the Gettysburg battlefield on November 19, 1863. But the war still wasn't over. During that same month, General Grant's forces won a decisive battle at Chattanooga, Tennessee, and by the following spring, Lincoln had named him his supreme field commander. Lincoln had changed commanders several times up to that point. George McClellan had been replaced by

Left: The Battle of Gettysburg in Pennsylvania.

Ambrose Burnside in November 1862, and he in turn was succeeded by Joseph Hooker the following January. Hooker was replaced in June of 1863 by Meade, who lost Lincoln's favor by moving too slowly against the trapped Confederate army retreating from Gettysburg.

Grant ultimately led the Union forces to victory, but not without heavy losses. He began what was called the Wilderness Campaign against Lee's army, in May 1864, and close to 60,000 Union soldiers were killed during that spring alone. But Union troops advanced steadily through the following winter. General George H. Thomas crushed Confederate forces at Nashville, Tennessee, and General Philip H. Sheridan systematically swept through the Shenandoah Valley of Virginia while General William Tecumseh Sherman was marching through Georgia and South Carolina. Finally, on April 9, 1865, General Lee surrendered at Appomattox Court House, Virginia, and the Civil War was over.

"I'm like the man who was tarred and feathered and rode out of town on a rail. When they asked him how he felt about it, he said that if it weren't for the honor of the thing, he would rather have walked."
—Abraham Lincoln

Right: Crowds gathering for the dedication of the Gettysburg battlefield and to hear the president's address.

Reunification

Lincoln was reelected president the previous November by 400,000 votes out of about 4 million cast. The Thirteenth Amendment to the Constitution, barring slavery throughout the country, passed the House of Representatives in January of 1865, following Senate approval eight months earlier. His second inaugural address was given just weeks before the end of the war, and it concluded on a soothing note, and an expression of hope for lasting peace.

The terms of surrender for the Confederacy were generous. There were to be no punishing moves against Rebel soldiers once they pledged allegiance to the U.S. Constitution. The president proclaimed the end of war on April 11, and he expressed hope that the United States would be unified again as quickly as possible.

Three days later, on Good Friday, April 14, 1865, the president met with his cabinet to plan the policy of Reconstruction. Afterward, the president and Mrs. Lincoln left the White House for a carriage ride. That evening they went to see a play, *Our American Cousin*, at Ford's Theater in Washington. Their lives were finally getting back to normal.

At around ten o'clock, a pro-slavery extremist, actor John Wilkes Booth, entered the box where the Lincolns were seated and bolted the door behind him. He shot the president in the back of the head, stabbed one of the Lincolns' guests, and then leaped down to the stage, shouting "*Sic semper tyrannis*" (Latin for "Thus always to tyrants!"). Booth was tracked down later in a Virginia barn, which had been set on fire to force him out. He was found dead of a gunshot wound. Meanwhile, one of his accomplices stabbed Secretary of State William H. Seward in his bed, where he was recovering from a fall. Rumors began spreading throughout the capital that Lincoln's entire cabinet had been attacked. (In fact there had been a conspiracy to kill Lincoln, Johnson, Grant, and Seward in the hopes of destabilizing the Union, and for this four of Booth's coconspirators were later found guilty and hanged.) But ultimately Seward was the only other victim, and he survived. Lincoln died the following morning, April 15.

Lincoln's coffin was placed in the East Room of the executive mansion, where thousands of mourners came to pay respects. Beginning on April 19, Lincoln's body

Right: John Wilkes Booth

Above: After shooting the president, John Wilkes Booth made a dramatic stage exit and became a fugitive.

"Next to the destruction of the Confederacy, the death of Abraham Lincoln was the darkest day the South has ever known."
—Jefferson Davis

Below: Lincoln's funeral train retraced the slain president's original route to success from Washington, D.C., back to his Springfield, Illinois, home.

was put aboard a train that retraced his route between Springfield and Washington as president-elect as millions watched in stunned silence, not only in the cities and towns, but out along the right-of-ways as well. Lincoln's final journey ended on May 4 at Oak Ridge Cemetery in Springfield, Illinois, where he was buried.

Legacy

Using his office to address the issue of slavery, Lincoln held firmly to the proposition that the issue should be dealt with once and for all. He held fast to his conviction, and he moved gradually by focusing first on stopping the spread of slavery. He wanted to avoid a war, but when rebellion occurred, Lincoln acted with more authority than any previous president ever had. His defense was that he was preserving the Union, no matter what it might cost.

Lincoln's example of acting as the sole authority in a time of war was repeated successfully by other presidents, most notably Woodrow Wilson during World War I and Franklin D. Roosevelt during the World War II. Far more important than his conduct of war was Lincoln's struggle for peace. His forceful eloquence helped turn the institution of slavery from a political issue to a moral one. But at the same time, he insisted on gradual approach to emancipation. He wanted to make it less an imposition of one region upon another and more a course of action representing the highest ideals of liberty and equality that the United States stands for.

Lincoln had other successes during his presidency. The Homestead Act made it possible for poor people to buy land, provided they were willing to settle and work there for at least five years. The act helped open up the western frontier for settlement and encouraged business growth following the Civil War. But the war overshadowed everything else during his presidency. To

In the year 2000, Congressional television network C-SPAN surveyed fifty-eight presidential historians, asking them to rate presidents in ten different categories. Their overall ranking had Abraham Lincoln on top as the nation's greatest leader.

the end—in his second inaugural address, in the lenient surrender terms to the Confederacy, and in his plans for Reconstruction—the war was less important to him than preserving the Union and making it more perfect.

Left: The Homestead Act began the settling of the American West.

Mary Todd Lincoln

Born December 13, 1818, Lexington, Kentucky
Died July 16, 1882, Springfield, Illinois

"The change from this gloomy earth, to be forever united with my idolized husband and my darling Willie, would be happiness indeed."
—*Mary Lincoln*

Mary Lincoln was looking forward to life as the wife of the president as she began the journey to Washington from Springfield, Illinois. The Lincoln family—Abraham and Mary and their three sons—set off for the capital in February 1861. The inauguration of recently elected President Abraham Lincoln was scheduled for March 4. Lively and impulsive, witty and sarcastic, Mary imagined herself serving as hostess at lively parties, becoming a leader of washington society, and basking in her husband's importance.

However, events turned out to be quite different. She couldn't seem to please either politicians or the press. They considered her first few parties too extravagant, and then later they complained that there weren't enough of them. When she attempted to celebrate the progress of Union forces during the Civil War, she was branded as a traitor to her southern heritage. Her periods of mourning—over the death of her eleven-year-old son, Willie, her four brothers who died fighting for the Confederate cause, and then her husband's assassination—seemed to some to be excessive and insincere.

Emotional, energetic, and well-educated, Mary Lincoln became a misunderstood and tragic figure. After the death of her devoted husband—the one person who seemed able to moderate her rapidly changing moods—she suffered bouts of mental illness and poverty that had been brought on by her own extravagance.

Southern Belle

The daughter of Eliza Parker and Robert Smith Todd, Mary was born on December 13, 1818, in Lexington, Kentucky. Her parents, pioneer settlers of Kentucky, were local aristocrats, and while she was growing up, she enjoyed a spirited social life and a private education. She loved dancing, fine clothes, and riding horses. She came in contact with politicians at an early age. Her family was

well acquainted with Henry Clay, a famous American statesman who ran for president in 1832, when Mary was fourteen.

After she turned sixteen, Mary moved to Springfield, Illinois, to stay with her married sister, Ninian. Springfield became the state capital at about the same time, and it offered a lively social scene that she enjoyed. She also seemed to be husband-hunting, and she was courted by several suitors, including Stephen Douglas—the man her future husband, Abraham Lincoln, would later face in races for the senate and for the presidency.

Mary first met Abe Lincoln, a state senator and lawyer, at a dance in 1840. He approached her and said, "Miss Todd, I want to dance with you in the worst way." Considering that she was five feet, two inches tall, and he was six feet, four inches, she said that, indeed, he did dance in the worst way.

Lincoln later described himself as "a poor nobody" back then, and most members of the Todd family agreed. When they became engaged, some of the Todds felt Mary was marrying beneath her social level. It was Abe, though, who failed to show up for their wedding ceremony on January 1, 1841, but their stormy courtship was soon renewed. Although opposites in background, they were devoted to each other and they were finally married on November 4, 1842.

Robert Todd Lincoln, the first of the couple's four boys, was born the following year, after Lincoln had retired from the state senate and gone back to his law practice. A second son, Edward (Eddie), was born in 1846, the same year his father was elected to the U.S. House of Representatives. Eddie died in 1850, the same year the couple's third son, William (Willie) Wallace was born. Their fourth son, Thomas (Tad), was born in 1853.

The Road Back to D.C.

After Lincoln served one term as a congressman, the family went back to Springfield. While he worked as a lawyer and failed in two bids for the U.S. Senate, Mary raised the boys and became accustomed to a modest lifestyle. When Lincoln was elected president in 1860, she looked forward to being a leader in social circles. Journeying to Washington through twelve states, the Lincolns were greeted by noisy and high-spirited crowds at seemingly every stop, and Mary's spirits were primed for good times ahead. However, Southern states opposed to Lincoln's antislavery views (which Mary shared) had already begun seceding from the Union. The Lincolns' entrance into the capital—under tight security and under cover of darkness—was a forbidding omen of things to come.

Lincoln had always been a casual man. As a lawyer in Illinois, he occasionally ended a day in court by placing important documents inside his stovepipe hat for safekeeping. Mary had much more of a formal social sense, and it showed in her elaborate Washington parties. Her years as first lady were marked by shopping sprees (she once bought more than three hundred pairs of gloves in just four months, and she spent $27,000 on "trifles" during 1864 alone); visits to the war wounded in military hospitals; and problems with her temper, which occasionally brought on migraine headaches.

Mary was overwhelmed by deep grief when the couple's eleven-year-old son, Willie, died in 1862. Her grieving became so pronounced that Lincoln was afraid that he might have to have her hospitalized. She tried holding a séance in hopes of communicating with her dead son, but it brought her more ridicule than solace.

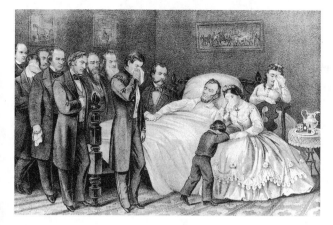

Left: Lincoln on his deathbed.

The couple's youngest son, Tad, was a source of joy and mischief that helped lighten their years of tragedy and the ever bloodier Civil War. Tad frequently sat on his father's knee during policy discussions, and he was fond of having his wagon pulled through the presidential mansion by a pair of goats. Perhaps after overhearing war talk, Tad once sentenced a doll to death for "insubordination," and after hearing about it, his father wrote a proclamation and handed it to his son. It was an executive order pardoning the doll for its crime.

More Tragedy

Mary never quite recovered from Willie's death. But shortly after Lincoln began his second term in March of 1865, the future seemed bright again after the Civil War finally ended in April. On Good Friday, April 14, 1865, the president met with his cabinet during the early afternoon, and afterward he and Mrs. Lincoln went for a carriage ride in the spring sunshine. It was time of rebirth and a time to look ahead, and no one appreciated it more than Abe and Mary Lincoln. That evening they attended a play—one of Mary's favorite pastimes. The president shared her love for theater and literature, often carrying a volume of Shakespeare's plays everywhere he went for casual reading when he found the time.

At around ten o'clock, while they were engrossed in the play, a proslavery extremist actor named John Wilkes Booth entered the box where they were seated and bolted the door behind him, and then shot the president in the back of the head. Mary screamed with horror and then fainted. Her husband died the following morning.

Her husband's assassination completely devastated the first lady. She was so distraught that she couldn't attend her husband's state funeral. She went back to Illinois, but still couldn't find any comfort for her grief and began having mental problems. She would spend lavishly and then feel miserably impoverished. She ran up debts she couldn't afford to repay while her husband's modest estate was being settled, and she suffered a long list of physical ailments.

She traveled with her son Tad to Europe in hopes of improving her health. And when Congress granted her a pension, she moved to Chicago, where she seemed to have found emotional balance. But Tad grew progressively ill in 1871 after having caught a cold. His shocking death at the age of eighteen was too much for Mary to bear, and she slipped into a world of illusion.

The Lincoln's remaining son, Robert, tried to help her, but he began to fear for her sanity. Mary Lincoln was admitted to a mental institution in 1875, and judged

Right: Robert Todd Lincoln.

mentally sound the following year. She took another trip to Europe after that, and returned to the United States in 1880 after suffering injuries from a fall. Both her physical and mental health deteriorated after that, and she died in 1882 at Springfield in the same home she had left on her wedding day forty years before.

Robert Todd Lincoln was the couple's only son to survive into adulthood. At the time of his mother's death, he was serving as secretary of war to President Chester A. Arthur, and had held that post for his predecessor,

James Garfield, who was assassinated. Robert had wanted to fight during the Civil War (he was eighteen when it began), but his mother held him back out of fear that he, too, would die young, like her other sons and her brothers, although he eventually served on General Grant's staff during the war. Later in life, he was minister to Great Britain in the Benjamin Harrison administration, and became president of the Pullman Company. He died in 1926, and his grandson, Abraham Lincoln's last direct descendant, died in 1985.

Lincoln's Emancipation Proclamation

Delivered on September 22, 1862

Abraham Lincoln favored gradual emancipation of slaves, a program that could keep the Union intact while moving toward ending the institution of slavery. When Southern states seceded from the Union and formed the Confederate States of America after his election, he was careful to focus his actions as president on preserving the Union. However, the Confederate states had united against what they felt were unfair policies of the federal government and the prospect that the expansion of slavery would be stopped and the institution itself ended. When the Confederate military fired on Fort Sumter in April of 1861, President Lincoln called for federal military force against what he considered to be an act of aggression. The Civil War began with these incidents.

While the war was being fought, Lincoln wanted to pursue his policy of gradual emancipation. When he met with opposition from Congress, he decided it was time for more forceful action. On July 22, 1862, he presented his plan to make an emancipation proclamation that would begin the process of abolishing slavery. His secretary of state, William Seward, suggested that he should wait for a more opportune time to issue it, since the Union still hadn't won momentum on the battlefield.

The opportunity came following the Battle of Antietam on September 17, 1862. The battle was a standoff, for the most part, but it was the most impressive Union army showing up until then. Lincoln issued the Emancipation Proclamation on September 22, 1862, and it was to go into effect one hundred days later, on January 1, 1863. Lincoln said, "I never in my life, felt more certain that I was doing right than I do in signing this paper."

By the President of the United States of America: A PROCLAMATION

Whereas on the 22nd day of September, A.D. 1862, a proclamation was issued by the President of the United States, containing, among other things, the following, to wit:

"That on the 1st day of January, A.D. 1863, all persons held as slaves within any State or designated part of a State the people whereof shall then be in rebellion against the United States shall be then, thenceforward, and forever free; and the executive government of the United States, including the military and naval authority thereof, will recognize and maintain the freedom of such persons and will do no act or acts to repress such persons, or any of them, in any efforts they may make for their actual freedom.

"That the executive will on the 1st day of January aforesaid, by proclamation, designate the States and parts of States, if any, in which the people thereof, respectively, shall then be in rebellion against the United States; and the fact that any State or the people thereof shall on that day be in good faith represented in the Congress of the United States by members chosen thereto at elections wherein a majority of the qualified voters of such States shall have participated shall, in the absence of strong countervailing testimony, be deemed conclusive evidence that such State and the people thereof are not then in rebellion against the United States."

Now, therefore, I, Abraham Lincoln, President of the United States, by virtue of the power in me vested as Commander-In-Chief of the Army and Navy of the United States in time of actual armed rebellion against the authority and government of the United States, and as a fit and necessary war measure for suppressing said rebellion, do, on this 1st day of January, A.D. 1863, and in accordance with my purpose so to do, publicly proclaimed for the full period of one hundred days from the first day above mentioned, order and designate as the States and parts of States wherein the people thereof, respectively, are this day in rebellion against the United States the following, to wit:

Arkansas, Texas, Louisiana (except the parishes of St. Bernard, Plaquemines, Jefferson, St. John, St. Charles, St. James, Ascension, Assumption, Terrebonne, Lafourche, St. Mary, St. Martin, and Orleans, including the city of New Orleans), Mississippi, Alabama, Florida, Georgia, South Carolina, North Carolina, and Virginia (except the forty-eight counties designated as West Virginia, and also the counties of Berkeley, Accomac, Northhampton, Elizabeth City, York, Princess Anne, and Norfolk, including the cities of Norfolk and Portsmouth), and which excepted parts are for the present left precisely as if this proclamation were not issued.

And by virtue of the power and for the purpose aforesaid, I do order and declare that all persons held as slaves within said designated States and parts of States are, and henceforward shall be, free; and that the Executive Government of the United States, including the military and naval authorities thereof, will recognize and maintain the freedom of said persons.

And I hereby enjoin upon the people so declared to be free to abstain from all violence, unless in necessary self-defence; and I recommend to them that, in all case when allowed, they labor faithfully for reasonable wages.

And I further declare and make known that such persons of suitable condition will be received into the armed service of the United States to garrison forts, positions, stations, and other places, and to man vessels of all sorts in said service.

And upon this act, sincerely believed to be an act of justice, warranted by the Constitution upon military necessity, I invoke the considerate judgment of mankind and the gracious favor of Almighty God.

What Happened Next

The Emancipation Proclamation is most significant as a symbolic gesture and part of a series of events that culminated with the Thirteenth Amendment to the U.S. Constitution. That amendment, ratified late in 1865—after Lincoln was assassinated—outlawed slavery. The Emancipation Proclamation reflects Lincoln's approach of gradually undermining the institution of slavery in order to forcefully bring it to an end. The Emancipation Proclamation did not apply to slaves in border states or any others still in the Union; and states in the Confederacy disregarded it, since they didn't consider themselves part of the Union.

Although the Southerners turned a deaf ear to the Emancipation Proclamation, it allowed Northern troops to free slaves they found in the South and recruit them into their army. During the previous years of the war, blacks hadn't been allowed to serve in the Union Army, but the rule had to be swept aside after emancipation. By the time the war ended, one in eight members of the federal army was African American.

The Proclamation is most significant for showing that the Civil War was being fought to end slavery. The tide of battle turned in the Union Army's favor in July of 1863. Still, the Civil War dragged on until April of 1865. The Thirteenth Amendment to the U.S. Constitution, outlawing slavery, was passed later that year. All of the former Confederate states had to ratify it in order to be readmitted into the Union.

Lincoln's Gettysburg Address

November 19, 1863

President Abraham Lincoln delivered the Gettysburg Address at the Civil War battlefield near Gettysburg, Pennsylvania, which was being dedicated as a national cemetery. The main speaker at the ceremony was Edward Everett, a famous American orator and statesman. who had served in the U.S. House of Representatives for ten years, as well as governor of Massachusetts, president of Harvard University, secretary of state, and U.S. senator.

Everett's speech lasted two hours and was widely reported in newspapers the following day. Lincoln's speech lasted less than two minutes and got far less attention at the time. (Indeed, many of the spectators did not even know the president had started speaking when he finished.) Not until after Lincoln's death was his Gettysburg Address acclaimed as an example of classic oratory for its powerful phrasing. This tribute to the dead challenged the living to continue the fight to achieve the ideals the soldiers had defended and for which they had died.

There were reports that Lincoln jotted down his speech on the back of an envelope on the way to the dedication. Historians generally agree, however, that he had prepared two drafts of the speech and made spontaneous changes while he was delivering it. The next day he wrote down his exact wording.

Four score and seven years ago our fathers brought forth upon this continent a new nation, conceived in Liberty, and dedicated to the proposition that all men are created equal.

Now we are engaged in a great civil war, testing whether that nation or any nation so conceived and so dedicated can long endure. We are met on a great battlefield of that war. We have come to dedicate a portion of that field as a final resting place for those who here gave their lives that that nation might live. It is altogether fitting and proper that we should do this.

But, in a larger sense, we cannot dedicate—we cannot consecrate—we cannot hallow—this ground. The brave men, living and dead, who struggled here have consecrated it, far above our poor power to add or detract. The world will little note nor long remember what we say here, but it can never forget what they did here. It is for us the living, rather, to be dedicated here to the unfinished work which they who fought here have thus far so nobly advanced. It is rather for us to be here dedicated to the great task remaining before us—that from these honored dead we take increased devotion to that cause for which they gave the last full measure of devotion—that we here highly resolve that these dead shall not have died in vain—that this nation, under God, shall have a new birth of freedom—and that government of the people, by the people, for the people, shall not perish from the earth.

Lincoln's Second Inaugural Address

Delivered on March 4, 1865

When Abraham Lincoln made his second inaugural address, the Union was close to total victory in the Civil War. In fact, the end of the war would come just over a month later. Thousands of spectators stood in thick mud at the Capitol to hear the president; Washington had been enduring weeks of wet spring weather.

Lincoln made many memorable speeches, but his second inaugural address ranks among his most significant for two reasons. The last sentence of the speech strikes a conciliatory and reverent tone in expressing hope for "a just and lasting peace," and the speech took on even greater poignancy in history when Lincoln was assassinated just over a month later, and just days after the end of the war.

Fellow-Countrymen:

At this second appearing to take the oath of the Presidential office there is less occasion for an extended address than there was at the first. Then a statement somewhat in detail of a course to be pursued seemed fitting and proper. Now, at the expiration of four years, during which public declarations have been constantly called forth on every point and phase of the great contest which still absorbs the attention and engrosses the energies of the nation, little that is new could be presented. The progress of our arms, upon which all else chiefly depends, is as well known to the public as to myself, and it is, I trust, reasonably satisfactory and encouraging to all. With high hope for the future, no prediction in regard to it is ventured.

On the occasion corresponding to this four years ago all thoughts were anxiously directed to an impending civil war. All dreaded it, all sought to avert it. While the inaugural address was being delivered from this place, devoted altogether to saving the Union without war, urgent agents were in the city seeking to destroy it without war—seeking to dissolve the Union and divide effects by negotiation. Both parties deprecated war, but one of them would make war rather than let the nation survive, and the other would accept war rather than let it perish, and the war came.

One-eighth of the whole population were colored slaves, not distributed generally over the Union, but localized in the southern part of it. These slaves constituted a peculiar and powerful interest. All knew that this interest was somehow the cause of the war. To strengthen, perpetuate, and extend this interest was the object for which the insurgents would rend the Union even by war, while the Government claimed no right to do more than to restrict the territorial enlargement of it. Neither party expected for the war the magnitude or the duration which it has already attained. Neither anticipated that the cause of the conflict might cease with or even before the conflict itself should cease. Each looked for an easier triumph, and a result less fundamental and astounding. Both read the same Bible and pray to the same God, and each invokes His aid against the other. It may seem strange that any men should dare to ask a just God's assistance in wringing their bread from the sweat of other men's faces, but let us judge not, that we be not judged. The prayers of both could not be answered. That of neither has been answered fully. The Almighty has His own purposes. "Woe unto the world because of offenses; for it must needs be that offenses come, but woe to that man by whom the offense cometh." If we shall suppose that American slavery is one of those offenses which, in the providence of God, must needs come, but which, having continued through His appointed time, He now wills to remove, and that He gives to both North and South this terrible war as the woe due to those by whom the offense came, shall we discern therein any departure from those divine attributes which the believers in a living God always ascribe to Him? Fondly do we hope, fervently do we pray, that this mighty scourge of war may speedily pass away. Yet, if God wills that it continue until all the wealth piled by the bondsman's two hundred and fifty years of unrequited toil shall be sunk, and until every drop of blood drawn with the lash shall be paid by another drawn with the sword, as was said three thousand years ago, so still it must be said "the judgments of the Lord are true and righteous altogether."

With malice toward none, with charity for all, with firmness in the right as God gives us to see the right, let us strive on to finish the work we are in, to bind up the nation's wounds, to care for him who shall have borne the battle and for his widow and his orphan, to do all which may achieve and cherish a just and lasting peace among ourselves and with all nations.

What Happened Next

The Civil War ended on April 9, 1865, when Confederate general Robert E. Lee surrendered at Appomattox Court House, Virginia. Five days later, on Good Friday, April 14, 1865, President Lincoln was assassinated by a proslavery extremist, actor John Wilkes Booth. By the end of 1865, the Thirteenth Amendment to the Constitution—abolishing slavery—was ratified.

In his second inaugural address, Lincoln spoke of a future "with malice toward none, with charity for all," an ideal that was too often compromised in the aftermath of the war. Freed slaves faced discrimination and intimidation, and by the end of the century a new form of racism—segregation—had become commonplace. Nearly one hundred years later, in 1964, civil-rights legislation was passed by Congress and signed into law by President Lyndon B. Johnson—a step that had become necessary because the concept of equality was still not in practice throughout the land.

Lincoln had outlined the means for reunifying the United States following the Civil War through a program called Reconstruction. Too often, however, powerful factions looking for political gain and a way to punish the Southern states failed to understand the ideal "with malice toward none, with charity for all." Each act of malice made it that much more difficult to "bind up the nation's wounds."

Andrew Johnson

"I have discharged all my official duties and discharged my pledges. And I say here tonight that if my predecessor Lincoln had lived... wrath would have been poured upon him."

—*Andrew Johnson*

Seventeenth president of the United States, 1865–1869

Full name: *Andrew Johnson*
Born: *December 29, 1808, Raleigh, North Carolina*
Died: *July 31, 1875, Carter's Station, Tennessee*
Burial site: *Andrew Johnson National Cemetery, Greeneville, Tennessee*
Parents: *Jacob and Mary McDonough Johnson*
Spouse: *Eliza McCardle (1810–1876; m. 1827)*
Children: *Martha (1828–1901); Charles (1830–1863); Mary (1832–1883); Robert (1834–1869); Andrew Jr. (1852–1879)*
Religion: *No formal affiliation*
Education: *No formal education*
Occupation: *Tailor*
Government positions: *Alderman and mayor of Greeneville, Tennessee; Tennessee state representative, senator, and governor; U.S. representative and senator from Tennessee; vice president under Abraham Lincoln*
Political party: *Democratic; National Union as vice president and president*
Dates as president: *April 15, 1865–March 4, 1869*
Age upon taking office: *56*

Vice President Andrew Johnson was sworn into the office of president on April 15, 1865, after the assassination of President Abraham Lincoln. The Civil War was over, and the seemingly impossible job of bringing the Northern and Southern states back together was ahead. Lincoln had selected Johnson as his vice president in 1864 partly as a symbolic gesture—Lincoln was a Northern Republican, Johnson a Southern Democrat. He also chose Johnson because of his outstanding political record.

Attempting to follow the course Lincoln had set for reunifying the country, Johnson was frustrated by the attitudes of Northern politicians and by discrimination against former slaves in the South. Unable to put together a strong core of support, Johnson was overwhelmed by congressmen intent on punishing the South over the war and expanding their own influence over national policies. His struggles against a mighty Congressional majority, known as the Radical Republicans, nearly forced him from office.

Johnson persevered, as he had through turmoil and personal hardships through his entire life. His failures as president must be understood in the context of larger problems. Congress took steps, later considered unconstitutional, in order to broaden its own power during his administration. Former slaves were free, but not free from local and state laws that had been passed to limit their freedom. Also, although the Civil War had ended, the long-standing political warfare between North and South went right on as though the shooting war had never happened.

A. Johnson, Tailor

Andrew Johnson, youngest of two sons of Jacob and Mary McDonough Johnson, was born in a small log house in Raleigh, North Carolina, on December 29, 1808. His father worked as a caretaker at a church and as a baggage porter. Already very poor, the family became completely destitute by Jacob's death when Andrew was three years old. Andrew Johnson never had any formal schooling, and he became an apprentice to a tailor when he was ten.

He moved to Greeneville, Tennessee, in his late teens. After suffering nothing but hardships his entire life, he stumbled on an opportunity at age eighteen when the best tailor left town. He set up a small shop of his own, "A. Johnson, Tailor," and began earning a living. Shortly before his twentieth birthday, Johnson married seventeen-year-old Eliza McCardle, and they had four children over the next seven years, bringing a fifth into the world eighteen years later.

Eliza helped her husband improve his very basic reading, writing, and math skills. Johnson had become interested in education when he was an apprentice tailor; while they performed their work, the apprentices often entertained one another by having one of them read aloud from a book. After he and his wife joined a local debating society, the shop of A. Johnson, Tailor, became a gathering place for their neighbors to discuss issues

Right: For Johnson, the road to the White House began in a Greenville, Tennessee, tailor shop.

Johnson is consistently ranked among the least effective of the American presidents. In 2000, fifty-eight presidential historians were asked to rate presidents in ten different categories by the Congressional cable television network, C-SPAN. Johnson finished next-to-last in their overall ranking, while his predecessor—Abraham Lincoln—ranked first.

Timeline

1808: Born in North Carolina
1827: Arrives in Greeneville, Tennessee, and sets up tailor shop
1828–35: Involved in Greeneville politics as alderman and mayor
1835–42: Serves in the Tennessee State Legislature as congressman and senator
1843–53 Serves in the U.S. House of Representatives
1853–56: Serves as governor of Tennessee
1857–62: Serves as U.S. senator
1862: Serves as military governor of Tennessee
1864: Elected as Abraham Lincoln's vice president
1865–69: Serves as seventeenth U.S. president following Lincoln's assassination
1868: Survives trial of impeachment by one vote
1875: Serves as U.S. senator for nearly four months before dying in Tennessee

of the day among one another. Johnson developed into a forceful speaker and a defender of small farmers and working people, and he became so well known that he was elected alderman of the Greeneville town council at age twenty and went on to become the town's mayor. A few years later he served in the Tennessee state legislature and later still as both a congressman and senator.

Jacksonian Democrat

The period from 1829 to 1848 is often called the Age of Jackson. Tennessean Andrew Jackson served as president from 1829 to 1837. Two of his key supporters served after him—Martin Van Buren from 1837 to 1841, and James K. Polk from 1845 to 1849. Like Jackson, Johnson was a Democrat whose policies favored workers and small farmers, and he became their champion as a congressman. During a ten-year tenure in Congress, Johnson fought for homestead laws that would offer free public land to settlers as a way of encouraging them to build homes. His proposals never passed, but in arguing for them, Johnson became known as an independent politician who was always well prepared with facts. He consistently opposed tariffs on imports because the higher prices they created hurt people who couldn't afford them.

Johnson lost his seat when the congressional district he represented was divided, but he turned right around and ran for and was elected governor of Tennessee. During his two terms in the office, he introduced taxes to support education, mandated equal pay for male and female teachers, and set standards for the teaching profession. He helped establish the state's first public library and its first agricultural fair. On one occasion, Johnson defended his policies toward the less advantaged by asking an assembled group of the state's wealthiest people, "Whose hands built your capitol? Whose toil, whose labor built your railroad and your ships? I say let the mechanic and the laborer make our laws, rather than the idle and vicious aristocrat."

The Summit of His Ambition

U.S. senators were elected by state legislatures in those days, and when the legislators gave him the nod and he was leaving to take his place in the U.S. Senate, he told them, "I have reached the summit of my ambition." Back in Washington, he began pushing for a homestead act, but

Right: Johnson's national career was kicked off with an appointment to the U.S. Senate.

Nest Egg

Johnson's tailoring business thrived even during the years he was away serving in Congress, and his wife, Eliza, took good care of their money. They had bought property in Greeneville, and were said to be worth about $50,000, a tidy sum back then. Andrew squeezed the value out of every nickel, and he was just as tight with the public purse. Given a check for $768 in back pay when he left Congress, he gave back $216 of it because it represented days he hadn't worked.

although the bill passed, it was vetoed by President James Buchanan. Two years later, it finally became law under President Abraham Lincoln, who knew very well where the credit belonged.

Johnson was so well respected by then that he was mentioned as a possible Democratic Party presidential candidate in 1860. The nomination went instead to Illinois senator Stephen Douglas, but he was not a popular choice in the South, and his nomination split the party.

The nation was deeply divided over the issue of slavery by 1860. Republican candidate Abraham Lincoln was seen by many as a leader who would take steps to abolish the institution of slavery, an action no previous president had dared to take. Past presidents who opposed slavery had always approached it as a political or legal issue to be decided by individual states or by an act of Congress. Lincoln presented it to voters as an issue that had divided the nation and threatened to tear apart the

Criticized for Slurred Speech

When the Union Army was able to win control of a seceded state, a military government faithful to the United States was quickly established there, and Johnson was appointed military governor of Tennessee in 1862, with a mandate to restore its constitutional government. Officials in the state government had to swear allegiance to the Constitution, and Johnson replaced the mayor of Nashville and the entire city council when they refused.

The Republican Party's presidential convention met in Baltimore, Maryland, in 1864, hoping to capitalize on the growing success of the Union Army in the Civil War. They called their meeting the National Union Convention and opened it to all Americans who were interested in preserving the Union. Republicans and War Democrats were united behind incumbent Republican president, Abraham Lincoln, and Johnson, the War Democrat. The party hoped that combination would demonstrate solidarity toward preserving the Union and to appeal to Southerners who were opposed to secession. When Lincoln and Johnson won, their success marked only the second time in history that the president and the vice president were from different political parties. (Lincoln and Johnson had agreed to join forces, but in 1796, Democrat-Republican Thomas Jefferson

Union. The prospect of his election so upset Southern political leaders that state officials began to threaten to secede from the Union, and South Carolina became the first state to make good on the threat shortly after Lincoln's election.

Johnson never took a strong stand against slavery. He generally viewed it as a states' rights issue, but he quickly denounced the idea of secession. When his Southern colleagues stood up and walked out of Congress, Johnson stayed in his seat and kept his ground. He became a leading spokesman for the "War Democrats," representing the handful of his party colleagues who stood by the Union after the Southern delegations left town. Johnson was branded a traitor in the South, and his family was turned out of their home in Tennessee. It didn't help their image in Nashville when one of Johnson's sons joined the Union Army.

"[The Union will be] divided into 33 petty governments, with a little prince in one, a little potentate in another, and republic someplace else …with quarrelling and warring amongst the little petty powers that will result in anarchy."

—Andrew Johnson

Iron Fist

Johnson held the rank of brigadier general when he was appointed military governor of Tennessee, and he didn't waste any time pulling rank. Along with firing officeholders who wouldn't swear allegiance to the United States, he shuttered anti-Union newspapers, arrested clergymen whose sermons were anti-Union, and he seized the railroads and imposed new taxes. He was also successful in getting President Lincoln to exempt Tennessee from the Emancipation Proclamation, the only Southern state to be excluded, because both men agreed that saving the Union was more important than freeing slaves, and that the gesture would stave off an open rebellion against his military government.

Above: Johnson's swearing-in as president after Lincoln's assassination.

became vice president under Federalist John Adams at a time when the second-place vote-getter became vice president, regardless of party affiliation.)

At the time of President Lincoln's second inaugural in early March of 1865, Andrew Johnson was weak with typhoid fever. Nevertheless, he joined the inaugural festivities at Lincoln's request to project a symbol of solidarity. During the festivities and speeches on a wet and windy day, Johnson sipped some brandy to help him stay alert, and when his time finally came to speak, he gave a rambling speech mumbling many words, which led many in the crowd to conclude that he must have been drunk. Rumors that he had a drinking problem spread quickly, and they would follow him the rest of his life. Historians generally agree, however, that Johnson almost never drank alcohol, but at the time many people were not willing to let the truth get in the way of a good rumor.

The Civil War ended with the surrender of the Confederacy on April 9, 1865, just over a month later. In another five days, President Lincoln was shot while he and his wife were watching a play at a Washington theater, and he died the next morning. Andrew Johnson was sworn into office later that same day. He was facing an explosively unstable situation. Lincoln's assassination by proslavery extremist John Wilkes Booth played into the plans of the Radical Republicans in Congress led by representative Thaddeus Stevens of Pennsylvania and Secretary of War Edwin M. Stanton. They had been calling for harsh punishment against the former Confederate states, but were kept under control by others, including moderate Republicans and almost all Democrats, who were in favor of the more conciliatory approach of Lincoln and Johnson. Over the next two decades, the Radical Republicans instituted actions that restricted the full participation of the former Confederate states in national affairs, and by doing so, they maintained their own substantial power base. Bitterness over the war remained in the South as well, and open hostilities broke out over issues related to the new status of emancipated slaves.

The Johnson Administration

Administration Dates:	April 15, 1865–March 4, 1869
Vice President:	None
Cabinet:	
Secretary of State	William H. Seward (1865–69)
Secretary of the Treasury	Hugh McCulloch (1865–69)
Secretary of War	Edwin M. Stanton (1865–68)
	Ulysses S. Grant (1867–68; interim)
	John M. Schofield (1868–69)
Attorney General	James Speed (1865–66)
	Henry Stanberry (1866–68)
	William M. Evarts (1868–69)
Secretary of the Navy	Gideon Welles (1865–69)
Postmaster General	William Dennison Jr. (1865–66)
	Alexander W. Randall (1866–69)
Secretary of the Interior	John P. Usher (1865)
	James Harlan (1865–66)
	Orville H. Browning (1866–69)

Foreign Policy Achievements

Johnson would become one of the most maligned and ineffective presidents, and his combative attitude only worsened his situation. His presidency was marked by losing battles with Congress, and he was nearly removed from office. Johnson's prolonged and losing battles

Left: William H. Seward, who, as secretary of state, negotiated the Alaska purchase.

over Reconstruction and the powers of the presidency dominated his tenure in office, and it overshadowed several foreign policy successes that would have greater impact in future years.

In 1867, Secretary of State William H. Seward negotiated the purchase of the Alaska territory from Russia for just over $7 million. The purchase of the vast area far north from the continental United States was widely ridiculed at the time as "Seward's Folly." He also negotiated the purchase of the Midway Islands in the Pacific, but nobody was too sure where they were, and they confined their jokes to Alaska.

During that same year, the Johnson administration invoked the Monroe Doctrine to stop France from setting up a European prince as co-emperor of Mexico. The doctrine, issued during the presidency of James Monroe, discouraged European intervention in North American affairs. The Johnson administration also demanded Civil War reparations from Great Britain for having built a battleship, the *Alabama*, for the Confederacy. The reparations were later secured by the administration of his successor, President Ulysses S. Grant.

Caught Between Extremes

While Congress was adjourned between April and December of 1865, Johnson began implementing his program of Reconstruction. He offered full membership in the Union to all seceded states, if they would meet certain conditions. Ten percent of their citizens had to swear an oath to uphold the constitution, and state conventions needed to ratify the Thirteenth Amendment to the Constitution outlawing slavery. Only then were they granted the power to elect national senators and representatives.

Johnson's Reconstruction policy made great headway in those early months. He recognized the new government of Virginia by May 9, and, by the end of the month, he offered amnesty to all Confederate veterans who swore allegiance to the Union. Southern states began repealing secession and ratifying the Thirteenth Amendment as quickly as they could, but several local

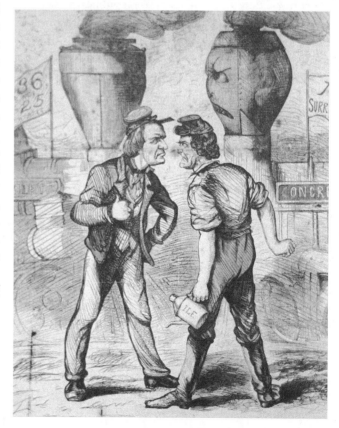

Right: Johnson's moderation on Reconstruction prompted Radical Republican Thaddeus Stevens to oppose him and call for his impeachment.

Left: Pennsylvania Congressman Thaddeus Stevens formed the Radical Republican Party to fight for the rights of freed slaves.

Right: Secretary of War Edwin Stanton, whose firing by the president led to impeachment hearings.

and state governments also began introducing "black codes," laws and provisions that limited civil rights and placed economic restrictions on African Americans.

Already angered by Johnson's conciliatory Reconstruction program, Radical Republicans seized on the issue of the black codes when Congress reconvened at the end of the year. Looking for a more punishment-oriented approach to the South, they created the Joint Committee on Reconstruction and made their leader, Thaddeus Stevens, its chairman. They were able to draw wider support from their Northern colleagues when the South reelected many of the same leaders who had originally supported secession. By adding a restrictive clause to the proposed Fourteenth Amendment to the Constitution, they moved to refuse to seat any congressman who had served in the Confederate Congress. Ironically, the amendment itself was intended to protect the rights of all citizens and not limit them.

Johnson's Reconstruction program emphasized working with states to bring about reunification of the nation, but Congress began imposing federal acts on the former Confederate states. Congress created the Freedmen's Bureau, an agency to get federal help for freed slaves, and successfully overrode Johnson's veto of it along with a civil-rights bill, marking the first time that a presidential veto was upset on such a major piece of legislation.

Sorry Spectacles

The 1866 midterm Congressional election brought more grief for Johnson. As a way of countering his opponents' formidable power, he tried to bring together supporters from both parties, by reconvening the National Union Convention—the assembly of Republicans and Democrats that had met in 1864 to bolster President Lincoln's reelection campaign and had nominated Johnson as vice president. However, Johnson's action came too close to election day to be effective. When he campaigned for candidates who supported his moderate policies, he was often challenged by hecklers, and his appearances did more harm than good.

Johnson was always well prepared as a speaker, but he was short-tempered and stubborn. During his campaign appearances, he often argued long and loud with hecklers, turning political rallies into sorry spectacles that resulted in scorn and ridicule. Opponents pointed to his often mean-spirited campaign appearances as proof of their false claim that Johnson drank too much.

Encouraged by midterm election victories of more Radical Republicans, Congress passed the Reconstruction Act of 1867, placing military governments over the Southern states until the Fourteenth Amendment could be ratified in 1868. Congress went even further and passed two acts intended to increase its authority over the executive branch. This so-called Tenure of Office

Act made it impossible for the president to remove an officeholder, including a cabinet member, without congressional approval. Their second new law, the Army Appropriations Act, limited the president's command of the military. Both acts were obviously unconstitutional, but Congress overrode Johnson's veto of the Tenure of Office Act. Meanwhile, because the appropriations bill included the annual appropriation for the military, Johnson had no choice but to sign it into law.

A politician's level of success or failure often depends on how he chooses to fight political battles. Johnson's response to the actions of Congress was not effective. He decided to test the Tenure of Office Act by suspending his secretary of war, Edwin M. Stanton, who was a Radical Republican sympathizer. Stanton responded by barricading himself in his office while Congress mounted vigorous criticism against the president. Johnson named Civil War hero Ulysses S. Grant as an interim secretary of war, and assigned him to a tour of the South to report on conditions there, after which he stepped down.

Johnson felt betrayed by Grant's action, but Grant replied that he had planned to serve only temporarily. His resignation certainly made him more appealing as a future presidential candidate to Republicans. When Johnson finally dislodged Stanton from his office, the Radical Republicans reacted with a vengeance. Because Johnson had violated their Tenure of Office Act, they opened impeachment hearings charging him with misconduct.

Johnson's trial began on March 30, 1868, and ended with the final impeachment votes on May 16.

Just Say Nay

"I almost literally looked down into my open grave," said first-term Kansas senator Edmund Ross as he rose to announce his vote on Johnson's future as president. "Friendships, position, fortune, everything that makes life desirable to an ambitious man were about to be swept away by the breath of my mouth, perhaps forever." Voting his conscience over his party, Ross voted not guilty, and it proved to be decisive when the conviction of President Johnson failed by that single vote. Radical Republicans made sure that Ross's national political career ended that day.

Johnson's presidency was saved, but it was an empty victory. He remained virtually powerless during the last few months of his administration. He continued to veto legislation, and Congress continued to override his vetoes. (Johnson's twenty-nine vetoes as president were the most ever by a president up to that time.) He found himself passed over for the Democrats' 1868 presidential nomination in favor of New York governor Horatio Seymour, and Ulysses S. Grant, the Republican nominee, won the election. A bitter Johnson left office criticizing Congressional Republicans in his final annual address and again in his farewell address.

The Impeachment of Andrew Johnson

President Andrew Johnson was impeached on charges of violating the recently enacted federal law, the Tenure of Office Act, and of defying the authority of Congress.

The impeachment process begins with a House committee that debates whether or not the president committed impeachable offenses. If the committee agrees that he has committed such actions, it drafts articles of impeachment—a list of items that note specific offenses in the accusation. Then the entire House of Representatives votes on whether to impeach the president on those charges. If two-thirds of the representatives vote for impeachment, the president is placed on trial in the Senate. A two-thirds majority vote is required there to remove the president from office. The following excerpt from the U.S. Constitution (Article I, Section 3) describes the rules of impeachment:

The Senate shall have the sole Power to try all Impeachments. When sitting for that Purpose, they shall be on Oath or Affirmation. When the President of the United States is tried, the Chief Justice shall preside: And no Person shall be convicted without the Concurrence of two thirds of the Members present.

Judgment in Cases of Impeachment shall not extend further than to removal from Office, and disqualification to hold and enjoy any Office of honor, Trust or Profit under the United States: but the Party convicted shall nevertheless be liable and subject to Indictment, Trial, Judgment and Punishment, according to law.

Radical Republicans dominated the House Committee that evaluated Johnson's actions. The committee voted for eleven articles of impeachment, ten of which were for violations of the Tenure of Office Act, and the eleventh cited the president for undermining Congress.

In preparing for an impeachment trial in the Senate, the House of Representatives appoints a number of its members to act as managers in prosecuting the case against the president before the Senate, and the president is defended by his lawyers.

Johnson's lawyers argued that the president had been testing the constitutionality of the Tenure of Office Act when he fired Secretary of War Edwin M. Stanton. They also noted that Stanton had been appointed to his position by President Lincoln; and since President Johnson had the right to appoint his own cabinet members, the Tenure of Office Act did not apply to his dismissal of Stanton.

After the arguments were completed, the Senate voted first to determine whether each of the eleven articles was, indeed, grounds for impeachment, and they voted against all but three of them. The next step—voting on the three remaining article—would determine whether the president would be removed from office.

Republican senators managed to delay the vote until they could be sure they had enough support to convict Johnson and have him removed from office. At the time, there were fifty-four senators; thirty-six of them had to vote guilty in order to achieve the two-thirds majority needed to remove Johnson from office. Forty-two senators were Republican at the time. At first, twelve of them were planning to vote "guilty," but during the delays, that number dwindled down to six. During the vote, however, a seventh Republican—Edmund Ross, a first-term senator from Kansas—voted not guilty. That made the vote 35–19; the Senate failed to remove the president from office by that single vote.

The Republicans postponed the next two votes, but after ten days, they still weren't able to change any minds, and the 35–19 tally was repeated when the other two articles came up for a vote.

Needless to say, Edmund Ross, like the other six Republicans who had voted against removing Johnson from office, wasn't reelected to the senate. He was shunned back home in Kansas, and eventually moved to New Mexico, where he switched his political allegiance to the Democratic Party. He was the publisher of several newspapers there over the next twenty years, and he served a four-year term as governor of the Territory of New Mexico. He ended up dying in poverty, but he was not forgotten.

During the 1998 impeachment trial of President Bill Clinton, stories about the Johnson impeachment trial were published to help provide the public with information about the history of such events, and Ross was frequently mentioned for his brave action. An article in Time magazine on December 21, 1998, noted that Ross had been "hunted like a fox" by factions on both sides of the impeachment debate to win his support.

In 1955, future president John F. Kennedy wrote of his admiration of Ross, and included him in his book Profiles in Courage, a Pulitzer Prize–winning best-seller that presented biographies of people Kennedy considered to be courageous Americans. Kennedy wrote that Ross's vote "may well have preserved for ourselves and posterity constitutional government in the United States."

Left: A cartoon showing Johnson crushed by the Constitution he was trying to uphold.

Belated Salute

Johnson went back to Tennessee after his presidency. He remained active politically and won back the respect he had enjoyed before his political problems began. Remarkably, he was elected U.S. senator from Tennessee in 1874, making him the only former president to have served in the senate. He received a standing ovation when he first walked onto the senate floor, and his desk there was covered with flowers. However, Johnson wasn't able to serve for long. He suffered a stroke that summer and died on July 31, 1875. He was buried in Greeneville, Tennessee, the town where he pulled himself up from poverty and where his early political career was launched.

Legacy

Andrew Johnson's tireless work for the Homestead Act, which provided land to settlers for a small fee, showed his true political spirit—fighting for the less advantaged. He showed courage in remaining in Congress to place the Union above the concerns of individual states. His presidential administration took some controversial stands that proved historically wise, such as his moderate approach to Reconstruction, and the purchase of Alaska.

In spite of these things, Johnson is generally regarded as one of the least effective presidents, not able to control a mean-spirited congress. Even if some of his stands proved wise, historically, he didn't have the political savvy to overcome his opponents. Johnson's actions contributed to the sorry political spectacle that surrounded his administration. Nevertheless, the failure to remove him from office following his impeachment trial may have saved the Constitution from being rewritten by Congress.

Beginning in the Johnson years, Congress dominated the national political scene through the early 1890s. A series of strong presidents—Grover Cleveland, William McKinley, and especially Theodore Roosevelt and Woodrow Wilson—helped restore the power and independence of the presidency decades later.

Above: Edmund G. Ross, whose single vote saved Johnson from being removed from office.

Eliza Johnson

Born October 4, 1810, Greeneville, Tennessee
Died January 15, 1876, Carter County, Tennessee

"I knew he'd be acquitted; I knew it."

—Eliza Johnson

When Andrew Johnson first came to Greeneville, Tennessee, at age seventeen, he caught the eye of fourteen-year-old Eliza McCardle. She must have seen something that others missed in that tired and disheveled young man. "There goes my beau," she confided to one of her friends.

Andrew had just crossed the mountains between North Carolina and Tennessee, and he was riding on a rickety wagon pulled by a rundown horse. Eliza helped him find a place to stay that day, and a short time later, Eliza and Andrew were married.

Although she was content with a humble life, Eliza was always looking for ways to improve herself. She helped improve Andrew Johnson, too, by tutoring him to expand on his meager reading, writing, and math skills. Andrew Johnson became a politician soon afterward, dedicated to improving the lives of poor and humble people, fighting for their cause locally, then across the state, and later from the center of power in Washington.

Home, Shop, and Meeting Place

Eliza was born on October 4, 1810, in Leesburg, Tennessee, the only child of Sarah and John McCardle, a shoemaker. Like Andrew Johnson's father, John died when his child was very young, and Eliza's mother supported the family by sewing quilts. Eliza had some schooling at the local Rhea Academy, but her future husband, the son of poverty-stricken parents, had none and was apprenticed to a tailor when he was only ten years old.

It was a lucky day when young Andrew moved to Greeneville, Tennessee. He not only met Eliza that day, but he was told that the town's only tailor had recently left town, which was his opportunity to open a new shop and go into business. He and Eliza lived in back of the shop building after they were married in 1827—when she was sixteen years old, the youngest bride of any first lady. Eliza helped teach Andrew to read and write and to do arithmetic while the shop of A. Johnson, Tailor, was becoming a favorite meeting place for neighbors who gathered to discuss politics. Johnson's views impressed them, and he was elected to the Greeneville town council at the age of twenty. By the time he was twenty-six, he had become the town's mayor.

Eliza, meanwhile, focused on raising their family. By 1834, the Johnsons were the parents of four children, two girls (Martha and Mary) and two boys (Charles and Robert). Johnson began serving in the Tennessee legislature in 1835, and from 1843 to 1853, he served in the U.S. House of Representatives. Eliza and the family stayed in Tennessee during most of this time, except for occasional visits to Washington.

After he had served four years as governor of Tennessee, Johnson went back to Washington as a senator. He was there at the start of the 1860s, a decade that would prove more difficult for the Johnsons than their struggles over poverty had been.

A Decade of Conflict

When Abraham Lincoln was elected president in 1860, Southern states began to secede from the Union even before his inauguration. The Civil War began the following April, but Johnson refused to follow his fellow Southern legislators when they walked out of Congress to join the Confederate States of America. He wanted to help preserve the United States.

He was appointed military governor of Tennessee in 1862, and sent to Nashville. The Greeneville area, where Eliza and the children stayed, was loyal to the Union, but all Northern sympathizers were eventually ordered out of the region by Confederate soldiers. Eliza was allowed to stay behind because of an illness, but she soon had to leave too, and she was allowed to cross Confederate lines with her ten-year-old son, Andrew, to join her husband. Although they had been guaranteed safe passage, she survived cold and hunger on the way, and ran a gantlet of insults from Confederate sympathizers.

Johnson became vice president in Lincoln's second term, but he assumed the office of president after Lincoln's assassination in April of 1865. Eliza had become an invalid by then, suffering from tuberculosis. In those days, remaining indoors was considered the best treatment for the disease, and Eliza chose a room on the second floor of the executive mansion as the center for family activities and rarely left it. She read, sewed, and spent time there with her children and grandchildren.

Andrew and Eliza Johnson shared their living quarters with their sons Robert and Andrew, their widowed daughter Mary and her two children, and their daughter Martha and her three children. The Johnson's son Charles had died fighting in the Civil War, as had Mary's husband, both serving on the side of the Union.

Eliza Johnson was seen publicly during only two presidential social functions. She attended a reception for Queen Emma of Hawaii in 1866, and two years later she served as hostess for a Children's Ball. The mansion was filled with children dancing and playing on that day, which happened to be her husband's sixtieth birthday.

The Johnson presidential years were a time of trial as he battled with Congress almost continuously, beginning in 1865 and not ending until his impeachment trial three years later. After Johnson survived his impeachment ordeal in mid-May of 1868, the gloomy atmosphere of the White House lightened somewhat. More receptions and parties were held during the last nine months of his term, with the Johnson's eldest daughter, Martha Johnson Patterson, the wife of Tennessee Senator David C. Patterson, serving as hostess.

Martha's other duties involved overseeing the restoration of the executive mansion. Many of its furnishings and even the walls themselves had been trashed by souvenir hunters after President Lincoln's assassination. Martha had visited the mansion in her late teens as a guest of President James K. Polk and his wife, Sarah, who, like the Johnsons, were from Tennessee.

A Better Life

Martha and her mother were both happy to leave Washington in 1869 for a quieter life in Tennessee. Unfortunately for Andrew and Eliza Johnson, the tough decade of the 1860s ended with another misfortune when their remaining son, Robert, died at the age of twenty-five.

The Johnsons returned to Tennessee in 1869. Their home, vandalized during the war, was restored, and Johnson gradually returned to politics. After the turmoil of his presidency, he won a measure of vindication by being elected to the U.S. Senate in 1874, and was given a warm welcome back to Washington. Unfortunately, his satisfaction was short-lived. Johnson died in July of 1875. Eliza moved in with her daughter Martha at the Patterson home, and she died there seven months after losing her husband.

Left: Daughter Martha Johnson Patterson served as her father's official White House hostess.

Johnson's Final Annual Address to Congress

Delivered on December 9, 1868

Andrew Johnson delivered his last annual message to Congress in December of 1868, just six months after he had survived an impeachment trial. His administration had been marked by bitter, losing struggles with Congress.

Johnson wanted a moderate approach to the Southern states that had seceded and fought against the Union in the Civil War, but Congress, under the domination of a powerful group of Republicans, wanted much harsher treatment toward the former Confederate states. The Congressional program won out.

Johnson took the opportunity of his final annual message to point out how congressional actions had only prolonged problems between the North and South and worsened an already dangerous situation. He covered several other subjects—the national debt, foreign relations, and topics he hoped Congress would address the following year—but his ringing denunciation of Congress's Reconstruction Plan stood out. It highlighted how testy the president's relationship with Congress actually was, and it reflected the divisive mood that still gripped the nation more than three years after the war had ended.

Excerpt from President Johnson's Final Annual Message to Congress

Fellow-Citizens of the Senate and House of Representatives:

Upon the reassembling of Congress it again becomes my duty to call your attention to the state of the Union and to its continued disorganized condition under the various laws which have been passed upon the subject of reconstruction.

It may be safely assumed as an axiom in the government of states that the greatest wrongs inflicted upon a people are caused by unjust and arbitrary legislation, or by the unrelenting decrees of despotic rulers, and that the timely revocation of injurious and oppressive measures is the greatest good that can be conferred upon a nation. The legislator or ruler who has the wisdom and magnanimity to retrace his steps when convinced of error will sooner or later be rewarded with the respect and gratitude of an intelligent and patriotic people.

Our own history, although embracing a period less than a century, affords abundant proof that most, if not all, of our domestic troubles are directly traceable to violations of the organic law and excessive legislation. The most striking illustrations of this fact are furnished by the enactments of the past three years upon the question of reconstruction. After a fair trial they have substantially failed and proved pernicious in their results, and there seems to be no good reason why they should longer remain upon the statute book. States to which the Constitution guarantees a republican form of government have been reduced to military dependencies, in each of which the people have

been made subject to the arbitrary will of the commanding general. Although the Constitution requires that each State shall be represented in Congress, Virginia, Mississippi, and Texas are yet excluded from the two Houses, and, contrary to the express provisions of that instrument, were denied participation in the recent election for a President and Vice-President of the United States. The attempt to place the white population under the domination of persons of color in the South has impaired, if not destroyed, the kindly relations that had previously existed between them; and mutual distrust has engendered a feeling of animosity which, leading in some instances to collision and bloodshed, has prevented that cooperation between the two races so essential to the success of industrial enterprise in the Southern States. Nor have the inhabitants of those States alone suffered from the disturbed condition of affairs growing out of these Congressional enactments. The entire Union has been agitated by grave apprehensions of troubles which might again involve the peace of the nation; its interests have been injuriously affected by the derangement of business and labor, and the consequent want of prosperity throughout that portion of the country.

The Federal Constitution—the Magna charta of American rights, under whose wise and salutary provisions we have successfully conducted all our domestic and foreign affairs, sustained ourselves in peace and in war, and become a great nation among the powers of the earth—must assuredly be now adequate to the settlement of questions growing out of the civil war, waged alone for its vindication. This great fact is made most manifest by the condition of the country when Congress assembled in the month of December 1865. Civil strife had ceased, the spirit of rebellion had spent its entire force, in the Southern States the people had warmed into national life, and throughout the whole country a healthy reaction in public sentiment had taken place. By the application of the simple yet effective provisions of the Constitution the executive department, with the voluntary aid of the States, had brought the work of restoration as near completion as was within the scope of its authority, and the nation was encouraged by the prospect of an early and satisfactory adjustment of all its difficulties. Congress, however, intervened, and, refusing to perfect the work so nearly consummated, declined to admit members from the unrepresented States, adopted a series of measures which arrested the progress of restoration, frustrated all that had been so successfully accomplished, and, after three years of agitation and strife, has left the country further from the attainment of union and fraternal feeling than at the inception of the Congressional plan of reconstruction. It needs no argument to show that legislation which has produced such baneful consequences should be abrogated, or else made to conform to the genuine principles of republican government.

Under the influence of party passion and sectional prejudice, other acts have been passed not warranted by the Constitution. Congress has already been made familiar with my views respecting the "tenure-of-office bill." Experience has proved that its repeal is demanded by the best interests of the country, and that while it remains in force the President can not enjoin that rigid accountability of public officers so essential to an honest and efficient execution of the laws. Its revocation would enable the executive department to exercise the power of appointment and removal in accordance with the original design of the Federal Constitution.

The act of March 2, 1867, making appropriations for the support of the Army for the year ending, June 30, 1868, and for other purposes, contains provisions which interfere with the President's constitutional functions as Commander in Chief of the Army and deny to States of the Union the right to protect themselves by means of their own militia. These provisions should be at once annulled; for while the first might, in times of great emergency, seriously embarrass the Executive in efforts to employ and direct the common strength of the nation for its protection and preservation, the other is contrary to the express declaration of the Constitution that "a well-regulated militia being necessary to the security of a free state, the right of the people to keep and bear arms shall not be infringed."

It is believed that the repeal of all such laws would be accepted by the American people as at least a partial return to the fundamental principles of the Government, and an indication that hereafter the Constitution is to be made the nation's safe and unerring guide. They can be productive of no permanent benefit to the country, and should not be permitted to stand as so many monuments of the deficient wisdom which has characterized our recent legislation.

[…]

I renew the recommendation contained in my communication to Congress dated the 18th July last—a copy of which accompanies this message—that the judgment of the people should be taken on the propriety of so amending the Federal Constitution that it shall provide—

> *First. For an election of President and Vice-President by a direct vote of the people, instead of through the agency of electors, and making them ineligible for reelection to a second term.*
>
> *Second. For a distinct designation of the person who shall discharge the duties of President in the event of a vacancy in that office by the death, resignation, or removal of both the President and Vice-president.*
>
> *Third. For the election of Senator of the United States directly by the people of the several States, instead of by the legislatures; and*
>
> *Fourth. For the limitation to a period of years of the terms of Federal judges.*

Profoundly impressed with the propriety of making these important modifications in the Constitution, I respectfully submit them for the early and mature consideration of Congress. We should, as far as possible, remove all pretext for violations of the organic law, by remedying such imperfections as time and experience may develop, ever remembering that "the constitution which at any time exists until changed by an explicit and authentic act of the whole people is sacredly obligatory upon all."

In the performance of a duty imposed upon me by the Constitution, I have thus communicated to Congress information of the state of the Union and recommended for their consideration such measures as have seemed to me necessary and expedient. If carried into effect, they will hasten the accomplishment of the great and beneficent purposes for which the Constitution was ordained, and which it comprehensively states were "to form a more perfect Union, establish justice, insure domestic tranquillity, provide for the common defense, promote the general welfare, and secure the blessings of liberty to ourselves and our posterity." In Congress are vested all legislative powers, and upon them devolves the responsibility as well for framing unwise and excessive laws as for neglecting to devise and adopt measures absolutely demanded by the wants of the country. Let us earnestly hope that before the expiration of our respective terms of service, now rapidly drawing to a close, an all-wise Providence will so guide our counsels as to strengthen and preserve the Federal Union, inspire reverence for the Constitution, restore prosperity and happiness to our whole people, and promote "on earth peace, good will toward men."

What Happened Next

At the time of the speech, Johnson was a lame duck president, finishing a term before his successor, Ulysses S. Grant, took over. Johnson went home to Tennessee after his failed presidency. However, he returned to Washington when he was elected to the U.S. Senate in 1874. He was greeted there with a standing ovation, but he died less than four months later.

The Congressional form of Reconstruction prevailed until it was disbanded in 1877. The program was largely a failure and accomplished little in either healing the wounds of the Civil War or reuniting the nation. Whether Johnson's program would have been more effective is debatable: There were hopeful signs that a peaceful reunification would occur shortly after the war, but such local and state legislation as the "black codes," which placed voting and economic restrictions on African Americans, showed that fundamental issues remained.

Ulysses S. Grant

"One of my superstitions has always been when I started to go anywhere, or to do anything, not to turn back or stop until the thing intended was accomplished."

—*Ulysses S. Grant*

Eighteenth president of the United States, 1869–1877

Full name: *Hiram Ulysses Simpson Grant*
Born: *April 27, 1822, Point Pleasant, Ohio*
Died: *July 23, 1885, Mount McGregor, New York*
Burial site: *Grant's Tomb, New York, New York*
Parents: *Jesse Root and Hannah Simpson Grant*
Spouse: *Julia Boggs Dent (1826–1902; m. 1848)*
Children: *Frederick Dent (1850–1912); Ulysses S. Jr. (1852–1929); Ellen "Nellie" Wrenshall (1855–1922); Jesse Root (1858–1934)*
Religion: *Methodist*
Education: *U.S. Military Academy, West Point (1843)*
Occupations: *Farmer; real estate agent; soldier*
Government positions: *Interim secretary of war (under Andrew Johnson)*
Political party: *Republican*
Dates as president: *March 4, 1869–March 4, 1873 (first term); March 4, 1873–March 4, 1877*
Age upon taking office: *46*

"Let us have peace," suggested Ulysses S. Grant in his letter accepting the Republican Party's nomination for president. The Civil War had ended four years earlier, and outgoing president Andrew Johnson had survived a vote of impeachment, in the first such trial in American history.

Johnson had initiated a policy of Reconstruction to rebuild the South after the war and to help bring the Southern states back into the Union. Some Republicans in Congress wanted to punish the South for having left the Union in the first place and for their part in the war. Grant's remark, "Let us have peace," was aimed at party members who had vengeance on their agenda. He believed it was time for all Americans to put the conflict behind them.

However, the years of Grant's presidency, 1869 through 1877, turned out to be very difficult. Two different financial panics left many people bankrupt. Newly freed former slaves faced hostility, threats of violence, and even death. International disputes nearly led the United States into war with Great Britain and Spain. The federal government was riddled with scandal and corruption.

Grant was the Civil War general who led the Union to victory. "One of my superstitions," he wrote after the crucial Battle of Vicksburg, "has always been when

Right: Grant painted this Indian scene during his student years. The U.S. Military Academy at West Point in the 1840s.

I started to go anywhere, or to do anything, not to turn back or stop until the thing intended was accomplished." Instead of retreating after twice failing to take the city, he found a way to win what became one of the most important battles of the war.

Grant pushed himself to succeed all through his life. Although he had been only a fair student, he graduated from the U.S. Military Academy at West Point, one of the country's toughest schools. He fought in the Mexican War—although he was opposed to it—out of a sense of duty to his country and was cited for bravery in several key battles. After failing as a farmer and then as a real estate agent, Grant began his Civil War service by recruiting a group of volunteers, training them, and then leading them to the first significant Union victory of the war.

Grant didn't fare as well as president, however. His selection of cabinet officials more often than not put friendship over ability. In war, he had commanded 500,000 men on the battlefield, but his presidency was jeopardized by a handful of men whom he had entrusted with power. He stood firm on financial policies even when they were proving to be ineffective while the economy was growing more and more unstable. A combination of growing violence against African Americans and pressure from political opportunists led him to take a more aggressive Reconstruction policy. The war had ended, the slaves had been freed, and business and industry were expanding—but the country was still not at peace.

From Hiram to U. S. Grant

The oldest of six children, Grant was originally named Hiram Ulysses, although he was usually called Ulysses when he was growing up. He was born in a two-room log cabin in Point Pleasant, Ohio, on April 27, 1822. His father, Jesse, owned a leather-tanning business and worked his own farm. His mother, Hannah Simpson Grant, was a devoutly religious woman, and was as hard-working as she was God-fearing. The family moved to a

Timeline

1822: Born in Ohio

1843: Graduates from the U.S. Military Academy at West Point, New York

1846–48 : Serves in the Mexican War; twice cited for bravery in combat

1854: Resigns from military

1861: Civil War begins; Grant rises from commander of a volunteer regiment to the rank of lieutenant general, which until then had been held only by George Washington

1865: Accepts surrender of Confederate general Robert E. Lee, effectively ending the Civil War

1869–77: Serves two terms as eighteenth U.S. president

1869: Financial crisis called Black Friday causes stock market to close on September 24

1872–73: Crédit Mobilier financial scandal hits Grant administration

1873: Another financial crisis—the Panic of 187—hits the United States

1877: Grant family tours the world, and Grant meets with the heads of state of many European, African, and Asian nations

1880: Grant tries for an unprecedented third term, but loses nomination to James A. Garfield

1885: Grant dies in New York, shortly after completing *Personal Memoirs of U. S. Grant,* which becomes a best-seller

Chapter 18 ★ Ulysses S. Grant ★ 287

Top: *The U.S. Military Academy at West Point in the 1840s.*

Bottom: *Fort Vancouver in the Oregon Territory was one of Grant's early military posts.*

Career Path

Grant worked in his father's leather shop as a teenager, but he couldn't stomach the idea of working with the skins of dead animals and made an early decision not to follow in his father's footsteps. The elder Grant had some political influence and wrangled a West Point appointment for his son, who considered it the lesser of two evils that would at least get him out of Ohio. Besides, he had always wanted to see New York, and this gave him the chance. But in describing his first trip east, Grant wrote, "I would have been glad for a steamboat or railway collision by which I might have received a temporary injury sufficient to make me ineligible." The academy authorities may have wished for the same thing. He was rated "unsoldierly," and consigned to the "Awkward Squad." But he stuck it out and finished twenty-first in a class of thirty-nine. (Thirty-seven didn't make it at all.)

farm in Georgetown, Ohio, the year after their first son was born, and working on the farm through his boyhood honed his special talent for training and taking care of horses.

Ulysses was enrolled at the Maysville Seminary in Kentucky when he was fourteen, and he went from there to the Presbyterian Academy in Ripley, Ohio, until he graduated at seventeen. He won an appointment to West Point in 1839. Grant had been signing his name Ulysses H. Grant by this time, but his sponsor, Congressman Thomas Hamer, mistakenly wrote it as Ulysses S. Grant on the documents he submitted to the military academy. Hamer, an old family friend, probably assumed that Grant's middle name was Simpson—his mother's maiden name and the middle name of his younger brother. Grant decided to keep the new name. He especially liked the initials U. S., which got him a lot of attention at the academy and led to his nickname, Uncle Sam, or just plain Sam.

He displayed excellent skills as a horseman at West Point, but except for a strong showing in mathematics, he was only an average student. He hoped to become a math teacher after he graduated in 1843, but first, like all academy graduates, he had a military obligation to take care of. He was commissioned as an officer and stationed near St. Louis, Missouri. His West Point roommate, Frederick T. Dent, was from the area, and Grant met Dent's sister, Julia, soon after he got there. The two began a romance that led to their engagement just before he was shipped to Louisiana a year later.

When the Mexican War broke out in another two years, Grant fought in it in spite of strong misgivings about a war he characterized as "one of the most unjust ever waged by a stronger nation against a weaker nation." He took part in almost all of its major battles and served under two distinguished commanders, Zachary Taylor and Winfield Scott. Grant quite likely learned a great deal about the art of war by observing these two generals in action. Both of them got along well with men of all ranks, fought valiantly and tenaciously, and had a healthy respect for the enemy. Grant was given a battlefield promotion to second lieutenant after the fall of Mexico City.

Following the war, he and Julia were married in St. Louis on August 22, 1848. She went with along with him to his new assignments: Sacketts Harbor, New York, in the fall, and then Detroit, Michigan, the following year. She was back in St. Louis in another year to give birth to their first child, Frederick. Grant, meanwhile, went back to Sacketts Harbor, and then he was transferred to Fort Vancouver in the Oregon Territory.

The trip to the Pacific Northwest required him to sail from New York to Panama, cross by land to the Pacific Ocean, and then sail north to Vancouver Island. Julia remained at home and gave birth to the couple's second son, Ulysses Jr. The elder Ulysses wasn't at all happy out there on the Oregon coast, and he ended up resigning from the army in April 1854. There is some speculation that he was drinking heavily at the time, and historians have debated whether Grant had an alcohol problem that continued during his service in the Civil War, but there isn't much solid evidence for them to come to any definite conclusion.

Hardscrabble Civilian Becomes Military Hero

If there is such a thing as seven-year strings of bad luck, Grant must certainly have believed that it was plaguing him after he left the army. He endured one failure after another for the next seven years. He built a house and cleared land for a farm, but he wasn't able to support Julia and his family, which had grown to four children, on this spread he called Hardscrabble, for its poor and rocky soil. He tried his hand at selling real estate, but he didn't have a knack for that, either. By the time the Civil War broke out, he was working for his brother in the family's Galena, Illinois, leather-goods store, where behind his back, they used his unflattering childhood nickname, Useless.

Grant rejoined the army and recruited a group of volunteers, earning an appointment as colonel of the 21st Illinois Regiment. Within a year he had emerged as a leader in the Union Army, although it didn't start out that way. In its first engagement, his regiment came face to face with a Confederate force at Belmont, Missouri, in November 1861. They forced a retreat, but then they retreated themselves.

Poor Showing

When Grant's volunteers marched off from Galena to join the state militia, Grant had drilled them into a presentable unit, but he was the least presentable of all of them and marched several paces behind them in his patched and threadbare clothes. He was made a drill master and did a good job of turning farm boys into soldiers, but he never managed to make himself look like anything but a farmer, and a poor one at that, because he couldn't afford to buy a uniform. He let junior officers lead his men in dress parades and skulked in the background because he couldn't afford a horse, either. Finally a local businessman came to the rescue, and when the unit moved on to Missouri, Colonel Grant was proudly riding ahead of them on a brand-new horse, wearing a brand-new uniform.

Below: Grant's early home in Galena, Ohio.

Bottom: The capture of Fort Donelson was Grant's first major Civil War victory.

Ulysses S. Grant Civil War Timeline

April 12, 1861: Fort Sumter, South Carolina, is attacked by Confederate troops. President Abraham Lincoln issues call for 75,000 volunteers.

April 23, 1861: Grant rejoins the army as a volunteer.

June 17, 1861: Grant is appointed colonel of the 21st Illinois Regiment of Volunteers.

September 1861: Grant establishes headquarters in Cairo, Illinois, in command of the District of Southern Illinois and Southeastern Missouri. He occupies Paducah, Kentucky, giving the Union a strong western foothold.

November 7, 1861: Grant confronts a Confederate force at Belmont, Missouri, scattering his opponents and then withdrawing.

February 1862: Grant captures Fort Henry on the Cumberland River. He leads forces that capture Fort Donelson on the Tennessee River—the first major Union victory of the war. His correspondence to Confederate general Simon Bolivar Buckner—"No terms except an unconditional and immediate surrender can be accepted"—earns him the nickname "Unconditional Surrender" Grant. He captures 13,000 Confederate troops and becomes a Union hero.

April 1862: After being pushed back by a surprise attack, Grant's forces regroup and hold their line in a major and bloody battle at Shiloh, in Virginia. Because of initial confusion under attack, Grant's preparedness for battle is questioned, but he is supported by President Lincoln.

Autumn 1862: Grant enjoys victories at Iuka and Corinth in Mississippi. He is named commander of the Department of Tennessee, October 25, 1862. He is charged with taking Vicksburg, Mississippi— the principal Confederate stronghold on the Mississippi River.

December 1862: Grant's troops are driven back several times by Confederate forces in an attempt to take Vicksburg; he decides to make another try rather than retreat and begin again.

April 1863: After moving his forces through back country to attack from behind Confederate lines, Grant takes Jackson, Mississippi, and assaults and lays siege on Vicksburg.

July 4, 1863: Grant accepts the surrender of Vicksburg (30,000 troops, 15 generals, and 172 cannons). On the same day, Union forces win a major battle at Gettysburg, Pennsylvania.

September 1863: Grant is sent to rescue the Union Army under siege at Chattanooga, Tennessee.

November 1863: Union forces under Grant win three significant battles to take control of Chattanooga, a major east-west railroad junction.

March 1864: Grant is commissioned lieutenant general. As supreme commander of the Union Armies, Grant begins coordinating Union Armies throughout the Confederacy. Previously in the war, armies acted independently in the western and eastern theaters. Grant uses Union economic advantage to win battles and dig in for long sieges.

May 1864: Grant faces Confederate general Robert E. Lee, commander of the Army of Northern Virginia in the Wilderness Campaign. The campaign results in severe losses on both sides (17,000 for the Union; 11,000 for the Confederates) and a stalemate. More heavy casualties occur at the Battle of the Bloody Angle. On the North Anna River, Grant's armies force Lee to withdraw to powerful entrenchments south of the river.

June 1864: Grant suffers heavy losses (5,000 to 7,000 men) at the Battle of Cold Harbor. Close to 60,000 Union soldiers are killed in battle during the spring of 1864. Grant moves over 100,000 troops south of the James River before Lee learns of the movement. Grant begins the Petersburg Campaign to cut supply lines between Richmond, Virginia, and the rest of the South. Long war of attrition follows.

Summer 1864/Winter 1865: Elsewhere, Union forces win many battles. General George H. Thomas crushes Confederate forces at Nashville, Tennessee; General Philip H. Sheridan systematically sweeps the Shenandoah Valley of Virginia; General William Tecumseh Sherman marches through Georgia and South Carolina.

April 1865: In the Battle of Five Forks, Grant forces Lee to abandon Petersburg. The Appomattox Campaign follows: Richmond, Virginia, is captured April 3; the Union takes Sayler's Creek; and Lee surrenders at Appomattox Court House, Virginia, April 9, effectively ending the Civil War.

Above: The United States as it was in 1861.

Below: General Grant in the field.

In February 1862, backed by gunboats, a force Grant was leading captured Fort Donelson on the Tennessee River—the first major Union victory of the war. When the smoke cleared, Grant wrote a letter to the fort's commander, Confederate general Simon Bolivar Buckner, informing him that, "No terms except an unconditional and immediate surrender can be accepted." Buckner's surrender on Grant's terms led to the capture of 13,000 Confederate troops, and he became an overnight hero throughout the Union states where he was being called "Unconditional Surrender Grant."

Grant was a persistent military leader, often following setbacks with clever strategies that gave him victory. In April 1862, when his forces were hit with a surprise attack at Shiloh, in Virginia, they regrouped and won a major, if bloody, battle. However, his preparedness was questioned because his men had nearly been overrun. Some military leaders suggested to President Abraham Lincoln that Grant should be removed from his leadership role, but Lincoln didn't agree: "I can't spare this man," he said. "He fights."

Grant had several other great accomplishments as a military leader. On July 4, 1863, after eight months of trying to take Vicksburg, Mississippi—the principal Confederate stronghold on the Mississippi River—he succeeded in capturing 30,000 troops, 15 generals, and 172 cannons. On that same day, Union forces won a major battle at Gettysburg, Pennsylvania. Grant was commissioned as a lieutenant general the following year, the first man to earn the rank since George Washington.

Beginning in May 1864, General Grant took on Confederate general Robert E. Lee, commander of the Army of Northern Virginia. Their two armies engaged one another for almost a year until the Battle of Five Forks the following April, when Grant's forces finally overcame Lee's. In the Appomattox Campaign that followed, Grant captured Richmond, the Confederate capital, on April 3, after which General Lee surrendered to Grant in the name of the Confederacy at Appomattox Court House on April 9, 1865.

"I have carefully searched the military records of both ancient and modern history, and have never found Grant's superior as a general."
—*General Robert E. Lee*

Robert E. Lee

Robert E. Lee was born into a famous Virginia family on January 19, 1807. Lee's father, Henry "Light-Horse Harry" Lee, was a war hero who fought under General George Washington during the American Revolution, then served in Congress and as governor of Virginia. Lee's mother, Ann Hill Carter, came from a respected family that had long held prominent positions in Virginia's government and society. Two of his father's cousins, Richard Henry Lee and Francis Lightfoot Lee, were among the fifty-six signers of the Declaration of Independence. After his formal education in Alexandria, Virginia, Lee entered the U.S. Military Academy at West Point in 1825. He excelled academically and militarily, and was commissioned into the army's famed Corps of Engineers after his graduation in 1829. Two years later, he married Mary Anne Randolph Custis, great-granddaughter of Martha Washington.

Lee first achieved military distinction in the Mexican War. Serving under army commander Winfield Scott, Lee made several scouting trips that helped lead to the capture of Mexico City. Wounded in battle, he showed extreme bravery and was promoted from captain to colonel by the war's end in 1848. Four years later, he received the distinguished assignment of superintendent of West Point. He held this post for three years before the War Department transferred him to a cavalry regiment in the Southwest. During the 1850s, violence broke out over the issue of slavery. In October 1859, fiery abolitionist John Brown and his antislavery followers seized a government arsenal at Harpers Ferry, Virginia. Lee was ordered to lead a military unit against this rebellion. After Brown refused to surrender, Lee's forces assaulted the building and in three minutes defeated Brown's tiny band.

Brown's raid and the election of Abraham Lincoln in 1860 contributed to outrage in the South that led several states to secede from the Union. In February 1861, these states formed the Confederate States of America; two months later, the Civil War began. Lee thought slavery was a moral evil and secession was unconstitutional, but he believed his first duty was to his home state of Virginia. He refused command of Union forces and resigned from the army on April 20, 1861, two days after Virginia seceded. Lee assumed command of Virginia's military and naval forces and accepted the position of general in the Confederate Army. After mixed success in 1861, Lee was called to the Confederate capital of Richmond, Virginia, on March 2, 1862, to help lead defense of the city against attack by Union general George B. McClellan. After assuming the overall command, Lee ended McClellan's threat in what came to be known as the Seven Days' Battles (June 26–July 2). McClellan then tried to transfer his men to the army of Major General John Pope. Before they had time to combine their forces, Lee attacked Pope at the second battle of Bull Run in Virginia on August 29–30. The Northerners were routed. To threaten Washington, D.C., Lee then marched his men into Maryland. McClellan learned of Lee's plans and met him at Antietam on September 17. The ensuing battle was a draw, but the Union army had succeeded in stopping the Confederate invasion.

Lee spent the next eight months blocking any Union advance on Richmond. After victories in Virginia in December 1862 in the Battle of Fredericksburg and the following May in the Battle of Chancellorsville, Lee took the offensive and moved into Pennsylvania. The Confederates lost to Union forces in a three-day battle at Gettysburg. Lee blamed the loss on himself and offered Confederate president Jefferson Davis his resignation, but Davis refused it. Lee did not take part in any major campaigns until he met Union general Ulysses S. Grant the following year at Petersburg, Virginia, just south of Richmond. From June 1864 to April 1865, Grant assaulted the area, but Lee's defenses held. Grant was able to replenish his army with men and supplies, while Lee could not. Eventually, the Confederate lines were too weak to hold off the Union forces. On April 2, 1865, they gave way, and Richmond had to be abandoned. Not wishing to see his men suffer anymore, Lee surrendered to Grant at Appomattox Courthouse on April 9.

After the war, Lee became president of Washington College (now Washington and Lee University) in Lexington, Virginia. He earned admirers in both the North and the South with his quiet dignity. He swore renewed allegiance to the United States, but Congress refused to restore his citizenship. Lee died in Lexington, Virginia, on October 12, 1870.

A Grateful Nation

General Grant was showered with gifts when he went home from the war. His neighbors in Galena, Illinois, took up a collection and gave him a $16,000 house furnished in the latest fashion. The citizens of Philadelphia gave him a house worth a whole lot more, and New York City gave him $100,000 in cash. Boston came up with $50,000 worth of books for his library, and he was more than pleased to accept what he may have considered the greatest gift of all: twenty prize horses. Gifts kept pouring in throughout his presidency, and a day never went by that he didn't receive a box—or on some days, dozens of boxes—of cigars. He gave most of these away, but once he claimed that he smoked twenty cigars a day. That's nearly one an hour, with no time out for eating and sleeping.

With President Lincoln's approval, Grant's surrender terms were respectful. Confederate troops were allowed to keep their sidearms and their horses, and they were given Union rations to deal with their hunger. None were taken prisoner, but all had to sign pledges that they would honor the conditions of their release. These parole documents stated they were "not to be disturbed by United States authority" as long as they observed the laws in force where they lived. Grant stopped the traditional firing of an artillery burst celebrating the occasion. "We did not want to exult in their surrender," he explained.

Grant Elected President

Following the war, Grant toured the South and reported on conditions there to President Andrew Johnson. Grant favored a moderate policy of Reconstruction that would help restore the war-ravaged South and protect the rights of the newly emancipated former slaves. President Johnson's attempt to remove his secretary of war, Edwin M. Stanton, created an uproar in Congress, which had just passed a bill making such a removal illegal without

the approval of Congress. The resulting furor forced Johnson to face a vote on impeachment.

Johnson had appointed Grant as the new secretary of war without approval by Congress, and after serving on an interim basis, Grant decided against continuing. Johnson thought that Grant betrayed him, but Grant insisted that he had never intended for it to be anything but temporary. Johnson had been hoping that Grant's immense popularity would rub off on his administration.

Republicans nominated Grant as their candidate for the 1868 presidential election, and he won it handily with 214 electoral votes to 80 for his opponent, New York governor Horatio Seymour.

Right: Ruins of the Confederate capital, Richmond, Virginia.

Election Results

1868

Presidential / Vice Presidential Candidates	Popular Votes	Electoral Votes
Ulysses S. Grant / Schuyler Colfax (Republican)	3,012,833	214
Horatio Seymour / Francis P. Blair Jr. (Democrat)	2,703,249	80

Incumbent president Andrew Johnson, severely weakened politically by his impeachment, received very little support for election at the Democratic convention. Seymour won the nomination on the twenty-second ballot.

1872

Presidential / Vice Presidential Candidates	Popular Votes	Electoral Votes
Ulysses S. Grant / Henry Wilson (Republican)	3,597,132	286
Horace Greeley / Benjamin G. Brown (Democratic)	2,834,079	—

Wilson defeated incumbent vice president Colfax for the Republican vice-presidential nomination. Democratic presidential nominee Greeley died less than one month after the election; his electoral votes were redistributed among four other men.

In his inaugural address, Grant called for an end to regional divisiveness, and strongly supported ratification of the Fifteenth Amendment to the Constitution, which states that no citizen can be denied the right to vote based upon race, color, or previous condition of servitude. He also pledged to work for reform of national policy toward Native Americans. He signed the Public Credit Act in one of his first presidential actions. It mandated that all government debts should be paid in gold.

"[Grant] has done more than any other president to degrade the character of Cabinet officers by choosing them on the model of the military staff, because of their pleasant personal relations with him and not because of their national reputation or the country's needs."
—Congressman James A. Garfield

It was an exciting time in the United States. The West was being settled, and railroads stretched from coast to coast. However, President Grant was discovering that the complexities of politics and finance were much harder to handle than fighting a war. He was not at all diplomatic as president, and he showed poor judgment by surrounding himself with friends who were as unsophisticated as he was when it came to politics. He faced financial crises and government scandals during both of his terms, and in the meantime, the end of the Civil War and abolition of slavery didn't bring an end to regional divisiveness and racial oppression.

Right: The building of the Union Pacific iron rails to the West.

The Grant Administration

Administration Dates: March 4, 1869–March 4, 1873
  March 4, 1873–March 4, 1877

Vice President: Schuyler Colfax (1869–73)
  Henry Wilson (1873–75)
  None (1875–77)

Cabinet:

Secretary of State:	Elihu B. Washburne (1869)
	Hamilton Fish (1869–77)
Secretary of the Treasury	Alexander T. Stewart (1869)
	George S. Boutwell (1869–73)
	William A. Richardson (1873–74)
	Benjamin H. Bristow (1874–76)
	Lot M. Morrill (1876–77)
Secretary of War	John A. Rawlins (1869)
	William T. Sherman (1869)
	William W. Belknap (1869–76)
	Alphonso Taft (1876)
	James D. Cameron (1876–77)
Attorney General	Ebenezer R. Hoar (1869–70)
	Amos T. Akerman (1870–71)
	George H. Williams (1871–75)
	Edwards Pierrepont (1875–76)
	Alphonso Taft (1876–77)
Secretary of the Navy	Adolph E. Borie (1869)
	George M. Robeson (1869–77)
Postmaster General	John A. J. Creswell (1869–74)
	James W. Marshall (1874)
	Marshall Jewell (1874–76)
	James N. Tyner (1876–77)
Secretary of the Interior	Jacob D. Cox (1869–70)
	Columbus Delano (1870–75)
	Zachariah Chandler (1875–77)

Above: President Grant and his Cabinet.

From Black Friday to Crédit Mobilier

Among Grant's more questionable cabinet appointments were Secretary of the Treasury Alexander T. Stewart, a New York department store tycoon; Secretary of the Navy Adolph E. Borie, a Philadelphia merchant; and Secretary of State Elihu B. Washburne, an old friend of Grant's who had no experience in diplomacy. Fortunately, Stewart was quickly replaced by an experienced Massachusetts politician, George S. Boutwell; Borie was replaced by New Jersey attorney general George Robeson; and Washburne by Hamilton Fish, an ex-governor and senator of New York who went on to help Grant win success in international affairs.

Financial matters proved most volatile. During the Civil War, the government had printed money called "greenbacks" to help farmers and workers pay for necessities. Unlike dollars and coins, these greenbacks weren't backed by gold reserves, so their value was never stable. Sometimes a greenback could be worth about the same as a dollar, but at other times it took two of them to equal one dollar.

Grant took his time addressing the greenback problem, and in the meantime two Wall Street speculators, Jay Gould and Jim Fisk, were buying up huge amounts of gold and pushing up its value. The value of greenbacks plunged in proportion to the gold-backed dollar, ruining many individuals and banks that were holding them. Gould and Fisk's attempt to corner the gold market blew up into a financial crisis called Black Friday on September 24, 1869, and the stock market was forced to close.

President Grant quickly authorized the government to sell some of its own gold reserves to help bring the price back down. Investors who had bought gold at higher prices lost money, but it helped settle the crisis in the financial markets. Nevertheless, the damage had already been done, and historians generally agree that it all could have been avoided if Grant had moved more quickly on the greenback problem.

Hamilton Fish

As secretary of state, Hamilton Fish distinguished himself in the otherwise scandal-ridden administration of President Ulysses S. Grant. Fish entered politics as a member of the Whig Party; he was elected to Congress in 1842, and governor of New York in 1848. His administration expanded the New York canal system and established a statewide framework for public education. In 1851, he was elected to the U.S. Senate. His father had been a member of a dying political party (the Federalists) and so too was Fish: After the Whig Party became hopelessly weak in the early 1850s, Fish joined the Republican Party, which was founded in 1854.

Fish was not known nationally when President Grant appointed him secretary of state in 1869 to replace the inept Elihu Washburne. Fish accepted reluctantly but found the job to his liking and remained for the rest of Grant's two terms. Fish's influence helped rescue Grant's presidency from total failure. Three major foreign policy problems confronted Fish during his tenure. The first was Grant's effort to annex Santo Domingo. Cool toward the project, Fish nevertheless set about loyally to carry out his superior's wishes. A treaty of annexation was concluded, but it was blocked in the Senate. Fish's efforts to settle the Alabama claims were more successful. The United States won its claims against Great Britain for having allowed Confederate cruisers, especially the Alabama, to be built and supplied in England, in violation of British neutrality. A commission with representatives from each nation met in Washington, D.C. With Fish leading the way, the commission negotiated the Treaty of Washington, which provided for the arbitration of the Alabama claims and of minor issues between the United States and Canada. The arbitration tribunal awarded the United States $15,500,000 in damages in the Alabama case.

An insurrection by Cubans against Spanish authority was in process when Fish took office. In 1873, the Virginius, a Cuban rebel–owned steamer illegally registered as American, was engaged in carrying arms. The ship was captured by the Spanish, and fifty-three crewmen and passengers, including several Americans, were executed as pirates. The incident could have led to war, but Fish negotiated a settlement, which included money for the families of dead Americans and a Spanish promise (never fulfilled) to punish the officer responsible for the executions. Fish retired from public life in 1877 and busied himself in civic and social affairs. He died in New York on September 6, 1893.

"It was my fortune, or misfortune, to be called to the office of chief executive without any previous political training....Mistakes have been made, as all can see, and I admit, but it seems to me oftener in the selections made of the assistants appointed to aid in carrying out the various duties of administering the government."

—Ulysses S. Grant

Left: Jim Fiske, a manipulator who sparked a financial recession.

Right: Fiske's partner, Jay Gould

Grant had intended to follow the moderate Republican Reconstruction program, but by 1870 he began supporting tougher measures. Upset by the lack of progress in race relations in the South, he issued a proclamation celebrating the ratification of the Fifteenth Amendment. It was followed by the Enforcement Act of May 1870, authorizing the use of federal troops to protect the voting rights of African Americans, who were facing intimidation in the South. Nevertheless, violence against former slaves increased, especially by the Ku Klux Klan, a white supremacist group. The Ku Klux Klan Act of April 1871 was intended to rid the region of such organized racial violence.

Radical Republicans, meanwhile, exploited the situation. The president was authorized to declare martial law in areas where violence erupted, and people arrested for violence would be prosecuted by federal authorities rather than by state officials. Makeshift courts and governments were set up in several Southern areas, and state powers were effectively limited. Northerners who traveled south to take advantage of federal authority were called "carpetbaggers" by resentful Southerners.

Grant signed the Indian Appropriation Act in March 1871. It allowed Native Americans to hold citizenship; it provided education and medical programs for them; and it began financial drives for food, clothing, and education. Grant's actions on behalf of African Americans and Native Americans represented honest attempts at reform and social improvement, but the nation as a whole wasn't ready to support racial equality.

There were some bright spots in Grant's first term. He signed a bill into law that made a Wyoming nature preserve called Yellowstone, the country's first national park. The Grant administration also successfully resolved a potential conflict with Great Britain. The United States demanded reparations for damage caused during the Civil War by the Confederate warship *Alabama*, which had been built in British shipyards. When negotiations for reparations came to a halt, many Americans began calling for war. They felt that Great Britain had tried to undermine the United States by interfering in the Civil War. Grant pressured Britain into accepting a neutral international tribunal to arbitrate the conflicting claims, and it defused the war threat. The court eventually awarded the United States more than $15 million in damages.

Another source of foreign difficulties came from the Dominican Republic and Haiti. Hispaniola, the island the two countries shared in the West Indies, had been bounced back and forth between Spanish and French rule before it became independent in the mid-eighteenth century, but a faction within the Dominican Republic was calling for a return to Spanish rule. Backed by Congress, the Grant administration promised to support the independent government there, but Grant wanted to take it a step further. He proposed annexing the

Left: The nightriders of the Ku Klux Klan.

Right: Yellowstone, the country's first national park, was established during Grant's administration.

Dominican Republic, and he sent his private secretary, Orville E. Babcock, to arrange it, although Congress and his own cabinet opposed it. The issue was politically dead by 1870, but Grant kept right on pushing for the annexation of the Dominican Republic through the end of his presidency.

As the presidential election of 1872 neared, the taint of scandal began sweeping through the federal government. Scandal, hard economic times, and continued racial and regional divisiveness would be commonplace through Grant's second term, but the Crédit Mobilier of America business scheme was one of the greatest financial and political disgraces of the entire century.

Several stockholders of the Union Pacific Railroad, including Massachusetts Congressman Oakes Ames, bought the Pennsylvania Fiscal Agency and changed its name to Crédit Mobilier of America, after Crédit Mobilier of France. The agency purchased the remaining Union Pacific stock and combined the ownership of the two corporations. The Union Pacific had been commissioned by the U.S. government with loans, subsidies, and land grants to build the railroad from the Midwest to the Pacific coast. The Union Pacific Railroad turned around and awarded the contract for the actual construction to Crédit Mobilier. In effect, Union Pacific awarded large amounts of government money to itself as owner of the company. Construction costs reported by Crédit Mobilier and paid to the company were often twice as much as the actual costs, and as a result its stockholders got rich beyond their wildest dreams.

When an investigation was suggested, Congressman Ames tried to stop it by distributing Crédit Mobilier stock among his colleagues in the House of Representatives, bribes that amounted to some $33 million. The scandal was exposed during the 1872 presidential campaign, and among those who were implicated was outgoing vice president Schuyler Colfax, and President Grant's own running mate, Henry Wilson. Many other prominent Republicans were also tainted by the scandal, which put the spotlight on the extent of widespread political corruption and unethical business practices. Though, apparently, the light wasn't bright enough—Grant won reelection in a landslide.

More Scandals

The Crédit Mobilier scandal spilled into 1873 and Grant's second term before Congress finished its investigation. Meanwhile, a fresh scandal—the Sanborn Contracts—began making headlines. That uproar implicated Secretary of the Treasury William A. Richardson in a tax fraud scheme, and the House Ways and Means Committee moved to declare "severe condemnation of Richardson." Grant fired him, but then promptly appointed him to a judgeship on the U.S. Court of Claims.

Richardson was replaced as secretary of the treasury by Benjamin H. Bristow, who landed running with an investigation of Internal Revenue Service officials for fraud involving the collection of taxes on whiskey. Known as the "Whiskey Ring," the conspiracy involved more than two hundred people, among them Grant's private secretary, Orville E. Babcock. Other scandals involved officials in the post office and the Department of the Interior, and Secretary of War William W. Belknap was discovered to have accepted kickbacks when the government sold off rights to set up trading posts on Indian land. Congress, meanwhile, didn't convict Belknap, reflecting its own problems with corruption. On the final day Congress was in session in 1873, it voted for a two-year retroactive pay raise for all of its members.

Meanwhile, the Grant administration faced yet another financial crisis, almost four years to the day after Black Friday of 1869. The Panic of 1873 began in September with the failure of a major New York banking firm, Jay Cooke & Company. Economic hard times began again and continued through the rest of Grant's second term. In January 1875, Grant signed the Specie Resumption Act, which helped stabilize the economy by reducing the number of greenbacks that were still in circulation, continuing to fluctuate in value, and leading to inflation and a loss of consumer spending power.

Left: The bank panic of 1869 might have been avoided if Grant had acted in time.

government agencies. As he had with Great Britain during his first term, Grant avoided calls for war against Spain in his second. The merchant ship *Virginius*, commanded by an American citizen and flying the U.S. flag, was captured by Spanish authorities. All aboard were executed by the Spanish, who claimed that the crew was providing aid to revolutionary Cubans attempting to liberate their island. It was proved later that the boat was owned by Cubans and was flying the American flag under false pretenses, and Grant secured an apology from the Spanish government.

The happiest day of the Grant presidency was May 21, 1874, when his daughter Nellie was married in an extravagant ceremony in the executive mansion.

World Tour

After he left office in 1877, Grant and his wife went on an extended world tour, the third time that a former president had traveled abroad following his administration. Foreign nations had been unsure how to greet the previous two ex-presidents—Martin Van Buren and Millard Fillmore—but the Grants received state welcomes wherever they went. During their travels through Europe, Africa, and Asia, they met with such dignitaries as Queen Victoria of England, the pope, and the emperor of Japan, Meiji. Many leaders consulted with Grant about situations in their country, as though he were still president.

The Grants settled in New York City after the tour ended. He was still a hugely popular figure, and was courted to make another run at the presidency in 1880. His successor, Rutherford B. Hayes, had promised to serve only one term, and he was unpopular at the end of his presidency anyway. Grant was the early favorite among delegates at the Republican National Convention, but he couldn't amass enough votes to win the nomination. When his opponent, Maine senator James G. Blaine, threw his support to Ohio congressman James A. Garfield, his fellow Ohioan walked away with the Republican nomination.

The policy of Reconstruction was failing too. Most Southerners resented the continued presence of federal troops in their region, but Grant stood firm. In his annual address to Congress in 1874, he affirmed that all the laws and provisions of the Constitution would be "enforced with rigor," and to counter complaints about federal interference, he said, "Treat the negro as a citizen and a voter, as he is and must remain," and added, "then we shall have no complaint of sectional interference." Later, he dispatched Federal troops to Vicksburg, Mississippi, after a mass murder of African Americans there.

Racial problems were especially apparent around voting time. White Southerners tended to support Democratic candidates, leading to an erosion of Republican power in the South. However, blacks tended to support Republicans, and many of them were intimidated from voting. The winner of the 1876 presidential election, Rutherford B. Hayes, had to be determined by a specially appointed electoral commission because of massive voter fraud. Grant hoped that the Civil Rights Act of 1875, which prohibited racial segregation in public housing and transportation, would help improve racial interaction. However, the act was declared unconstitutional in 1883.

There were a few positive developments during Grant's second term. Congress passed a bill calling for equal pay for women and men holding similar jobs in

In Ruins

Although virtually everyone around him managed to get rich during both of Grant's terms as president, he himself didn't leave office with much more than a small nest egg. After he moved to New York in 1881, his son Ulysses Jr. went into the investment banking business with Ferdinand Ward, and his father invested all of his money in it. He was so sure his money was safe that he borrowed from William H. Vanderbilt to up the ante on his investment. But he was wrong. The firm of Grand and Ward went bankrupt three years later, and Ward went to jail for his display of creativity with its books. The senior Grant was left with only $200 to his name. The showman P. T. Barnum offered him $100,000 plus a percentage of admissions to display his war souvenirs, but Grant turned him down, instead selling the stuff to repay Vanderbilt.

Grant remained active over the next few years. He served as president of the Mexican Southern Railroad Company beginning in 1881 and, after having supported increased trade between the United States and Mexico, helped negotiate a trade agreement between them. He was never lucky with finances, however. Grant went bankrupt after investing heavily in a New York investment banking firm that failed.

Deep in debt and and dying of throat cancer, Grant followed the advice of author Mark Twain to write his memoirs. He finished the book in June 1885 and died the following month, on July 23, at the age of sixty-three. *The Personal Memoirs of U. S. Grant* became a best-seller, providing the money to pay off the family's debts and give his widow, Julia, a comfortable retirement. The book is considered to be one of the finest military autobiographies ever written.

Grant is entombed in New York City's Riverside Park in a mausoleum bearing the inscription "Let us have peace." Julia Grant's body was placed next to his after she died in 1902.

Legacy

Ulysses S. Grant's presidency is not generally ranked among the more successful administrations in American history. Government scandals, economic hardships, and continuous regional divisiveness are often the most discussed topics of his presidential years.

Grant's efforts to improve the social situations of African Americans and Native Americans were commendable, but they were eventually obscured by later policies and social behavior.

Above: Grant's post-presidential tour spread his fame throughout the world.

Below: The dying former president rushed to complete his memoirs.

Left: Grant's Tomb overlooking the Hudson River in New York City.

His civil-rights legislation was overturned in 1883, and racial segregation became an unpleasant fact of American life.

Grant's successor, Rutherford B. Hayes, officially ended the period of Reconstruction in 1877, and shortly afterward political power in the South became concentrated among Democrats. Democratic congressmen often voted together on issues, forming a bloc called "the Solid South" that was influential well into the twentieth century.

Government scandals during the Grant administration helped fuel reform in the 1880s curtailing the patronage system. In such a system, government officials are appointed based on their support for an elected official rather than for their ability to handle the job. Had Grant been less inclined to surround himself with friends, it is likely that his administration would have been less scandalous.

Finally, the financial crises Grant faced were repeated during the next two decades. The cycle of boom and bust—prosperity and decline—characterized the American economy until a period of sustained prosperity kicked in at the end of the nineteenth century. A period of reform early in the twentieth century brought stability to the economy until the stock market crash of 1929 led to the Great Depression.

Final Tribute

After Grant died, some 90,000 ordinary people donated a total of $600,000 to build a marble tomb as his memorial. Twelve years after its dedication in 1897, Grant's Tomb became New York City's most popular tourist destination, on more "must-see" lists than even the Statue of Liberty. The flood of visitors began to slow down during World War I, when Americans had other things on their minds, but it still attracts thousands.

Julia Grant

Born February 16, 1826, St. Louis, Missouri
Died December 14, 1902, Washington, D.C.

"The light of [Grant's] flame still reaches out to me, falls upon me, and warms me."

—Julia Grant at the dedication of her husband's tomb

Julia Dent Grant foresaw great things for the man she called "Ulyss," and she kept that faith through the most difficult times. Their wedding was delayed for four years while Ulysses S. Grant fought in the Mexican War, and their early married life was spent in forts in New York and Michigan, far from the easy plantation life Julia had led as a girl. Their young children were fatherless while Grant was stationed in the Pacific Northwest—a remote outpost too dangerous for Julia and the children to join him. Then came seven years while Grant struggled, first as a farmer, then as a real estate agent, and then as a clerk in his family's leather-goods business and failed at all of them.

Grant was nearly forty when the Civil War broke out, but he assembled a group of volunteers, requested a commission, and went off to do some fighting. Great things followed. Grant became the famous, popular, and victorious general of the Civil War. He was elected president three years later, and after delivering his inaugural address, he turned to the woman who had always believed in him. "I hope you're satisfied," he said.

Plantation Upbringing

The daughter of Frederick and Ellen Dent, Julia was born in 1826 on a plantation near St. Louis, Missouri. She grew up in relative ease, attending a boarding school, mixing with the wealthy families of St. Louis, and enjoying a peaceful life.

After Grant graduated from the U.S. Military Academy at West Point, New York, in 1843, he became an officer and was stationed at a fort near St. Louis. He first met Julia when he paid a visit to the Dent family home, which was known locally as the "White House." Although the executive mansion in Washington wasn't called by that name until the administration of Theodore Roosevelt, it could be said that Julia was the only first lady to have lived in two White Houses. Julia's brother, Frederick T. Dent, had been Grant's roommate at West Point, which gave Grant an excuse to pay regular visits to the Dent plantation, but it was obvious that Julia was the reason behind it. During long afternoons of horseback riding, it was easy to see that they were in love.

One day he arrived in his horse and buggy just as the Dent family was about to leave for a wedding. They invited him to join them, and Julia rode in his buggy. When they came to a bridge that was nearly flooded over, Julia grabbed on to Grant's arm and clung to him as they made their way over the swaying structure. "I'll cling to you no matter what happens," Julia murmured, and once they had passed over safely and had gone a little farther down the road, he turned to her and said, "I wonder if you would cling to me all of my life." That was his proposal of marriage. Julia accepted.

Hardscrabble Life

Ulyss and Julia became engaged in 1844, but he was soon transferred to a fort in Louisiana, and then to another in Texas. At the time, relations between the United States and Mexico were tense over a border dispute involving Texas. War broke out and Grant served heroically. He didn't get home to Julia until the war was over, and they were married in St. Louis on August 22, 1848.

Julia accompanied her husband to his new assignment at Sacketts Harbor, New York, in the fall, and she moved with him when he was assigned to Detroit, Michigan, the following year. She went home to St. Louis in 1850, to give birth to their first child, Frederick. Grant was reassigned to Sacketts Harbor in 1851, and then transferred to Fort Vancouver in the Oregon Territory the following year.

The trip to that outpost on the Pacific coast required Grant to sail from New York to Panama, then overland to the Pacific Ocean, and then by boat north to Vancouver Island. The trip was too difficult for Julia and her baby, and she stayed at home where she gave birth to their second son. Grant, meanwhile, was miserable in the Northwest and he resigned from the army in April 1854.

Taking possession of land that Julia's father had given her, the Grants tried to make a living as farmers on a rough tract Grant called Hardscrabble. The farm was a dismal failure, and he tried his hand at selling real estate, quickly discovering that he didn't have a knack for that, either. They had four children by then, and the Grants decided to move on to Galena, Illinois, where Grant's younger brothers gave him a job in the family leather-goods business—work he wasn't cut out for, as things turned out. Still, it was all in the family, and it was a living.

Greatness Later in Life

Within two weeks after the Civil War began in April 1861, Grant had rounded up a group of volunteers and led them in a victorious battle a few months later. He rose rapidly through the Union military ranks, becoming commander of the Department of Tennessee by October 1862. He was ordered to capture Vicksburg, Mississippi, the main Confederate stronghold on the Mississippi River, but his troops were turned back several times in the attempt. He decided to make one more try rather than retreat and begin again, and his mission was gloriously accomplished, making him the most famous of all the Union officers.

Julia visited her husband several times during the war, whenever it was safe. When they met shortly before Grant was to make a final assault on the Confederate stronghold, she asked him, "Why do you not move on Vicksburg?" That simple question was all he needed.

Grant was the commander of all Union forces by the time the war ended in 1865, and he accepted the surrender of Confederate general Robert E. Lee. He was elected president three years later.

Julia thoroughly enjoyed her time as first lady. She was the hostess at many parties, nearly all of which could be described as lavish. Guests often included industrialists, bankers, military officers, and publishers. Weekly receptions were open to the general public, and it wasn't uncommon for everyday citizens to mingle with royalty. A high point of the Grants' social life was the wedding of their daughter in 1874 during his second term as president. Nellie Grant married Algernon Sartoris, the nephew of a famous actress, Fanny Kemble, and went to live with him in England for a time before they separated. Although their marriage didn't work out, he left her his considerable fortune when he died in 1890.

Left: The president and his family.

Julia was so happy in her role as first lady that she wanted her husband to run for a third term in 1876. But Grant had lost some popularity by then. His administrations were riddled with corruption, and he said, "I never wanted to get out of a place as much as I did to get out of the presidency."

World Tour and Memoirs

Shortly after leaving office, the Grants went on a world tour. They were honored guests wherever they went, treated to parades and banquets. They met with Queen Victoria of England and with royalty in Russia and Austria. They met with the pope in Rome, toured the Holy Lands of the Middle East, and were provided with a boat to explore the Nile River in Africa by the ruler of Egypt. Passing into Asia, they toured the Taj Mahal in India and enjoyed extravagant receptions in China. The emperor of Japan presented Julia with a set of dining room furniture that she had admired.

Upon returning home in 1880, Grant was courted by Republican supporters to seek the presidency again, and Julia urged him on. He was interested, but he refused to make an appearance at the Republican convention that year, even though it would likely have turned a close vote in his favor. Julia urged him to go, but he felt that his appearance would be an embarrassment. As it turned out, Grant's supporters couldn't get enough votes to nail down the nomination, and it went to James A. Garfield instead.

The Grants went back to New York and lived happily there for a few years. Suddenly, however, they were financially ruined when a brokerage firm they had invested in heavily failed.

Meanwhile, Grant had been contributing anecdotes about his Civil War experiences to *Century* magazine, and the famous American author Mark Twain suggested that he write his memoirs. He helped Grant get a profitable deal with Webster and Company, a publishing house Twain partly owned. Grant finished the book just a few weeks before his death from throat cancer in 1885. *The Personal Memoirs of U. S. Grant* was published the following year and became a tremendous best-seller. Profits from it paid off the family debts and allowed Julia to live the rest of her life with financial security. She died in New York in 1902.

Above: The wedding of the Grants' daughter, Nellie, was a social highlight of their Washington years.

Right: Author Mark Twain encouraged Grant to write his memoirs as a means of supporting Julia in her old age.

Grant's Recollection of the Confederate Surrender

Surrender occurred on April 9, 1865; recollections recorded in 1879

On April 9, 1865, Union general Ulysses S. Grant and Confederate general Robert E. Lee met at Appomattox Courthouse in Virginia to discuss the surrender of the Confederacy. Their armies had been engaged in fierce battles for months. The Confederacy was making its last stand against superior military power and economic support enjoyed by the Union Army. When the city of Richmond, Virginia, fell to the Union army, the Civil War was effectively over.

Though the war had been bitterly fought and divided the nation, many key figures were anxious for a respectable peace that would unify the nation. President Abraham Lincoln, General Grant, and General Lee were among them. The surrender terms demonstrated their shared respect. The following excerpt is from General Grant's own recollection of his meeting with General Lee to discuss the surrender. It provides a human side of a historical event, showing two men humbled by the great and tragic experience of war, rather than exulting in victory or being embittered by defeat.

Excerpt from Ulysses S. Grant's Recollection of the Confederate Surrender

On the night before Lee's surrender, I had a wretched headache—headaches to which I have been subject, nervous prostration, intense personal suffering. But, suffer or not, I had to keep moving. The object of my campaign was not Richmond, not the defeat of Lee in actual fight, but to remove him and his army out of the contest. You see the war was an enormous strain upon the country. Rich as we were I do not see how we could have

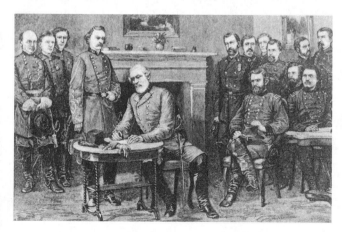

endured it another year, even from a financial point of view. So with these views I wrote Lee […] he does not appear well in that correspondence, not nearly so well as he did in our subsequent interviews, where his whole bearing was that of a patriotic and gallant soldier, concerned alone for the welfare of his army and his state.

I received word that Lee would meet me at a point within our lines near [Union commander Philip H.] Sheridan's headquarters. I had to ride quite a distance through a muddy area. I remember now that I was concerned with my personal appearance. I had an old suit on, without my sword, and without any distinguishing mark of rank except the shoulder straps of a Lieutenant-general on a woolen blouse. I was splashed with mud in my long ride. I was afraid Lee might think I meant to show him studied discourtesy by so coming—at least I thought so.

I went up to the house where Lee was waiting. I found him in a new, splendid uniform, which only recalled my anxiety as to my own clothes while on my way to meet him. I expressed my regret that I was compelled to meet him in so unceremonious a manner, and he replied that the only suit he had available was one which had been sent him by some admirers in Baltimore, and which he then wore for the first time. We spoke of old friends in the army. I remembered having seen Lee in Mexico. He was such much higher in rank than myself at the time that I supposed he had no recollection of me. But he said he remembered me very well. We talked about old times and exchanged inquiries about friends.

Lee then broached the subject of our meeting. I told him my terms, and Lee, listening attentively, asked me to write them down. I took out my manifold order book and pencil and wrote them down. General Lee put on his glasses and read them over. The conditions gave the officers their side-arms, private horses, and personal baggage. I said to Lee that I hoped and believed this would be the close of the war; that it was most important that the men should go home and go to work, and the government would not throw any obstacles in the way. Lee answered that it would have the most happy effect, and accepted the terms. I handed over my penciled memorandum to an aide to put into ink, and we resumed our conversation about old times and friends in the army. Various officers came in—[James] Longstreet, [John B.] Gordon, [George E.] Pickett, from the South; [Philip H.] Sheridan, [Edward O.] Ord and others from our side. Some were old friends—Longstreet and myself for instance, and we had a general talk. Lee no doubt

Left: General Grant signing the surrender papers at Appomatox.

expected me to ask for his sword but I did not want his sword. It would only have gone to the Patent Office to be worshipped by the Washington Rebels.

There was a pause, when General Lee said that most of the animals in his cavalry and artillery were owned by the privates, and he would like to know, under the terms, whether they would be regarded as private property or the property of the government. I said that under the terms of surrender they belonged to the government. General Lee read over the letters and said that was so. I then said to the General that I believed and hoped this was the last battle of the war; that I saw the wisdom of these men getting home and to work as soon as possible, and that I would give orders to allow any soldier or officer claiming a horse or mule to take it. General Lee showed some emotion at this—a feeling which I also shared—and said it would have a most happy effect.

The interview ended, and I gave orders for rationing his troops. The next day I met Lee on horseback and we had a long talk. In that conversation I urged upon him the wisdom of ending the war by the surrender of the other armies. I asked him to use his influence with the people of the South—an influence that was supreme—to bring the war to an end. General Lee said that his campaign in Virginia was the last organized resistance which the South was capable of making—that I might have to march a good deal and encounter isolated commands here and there, but there was no longer any army which could make a stand. I told Lee that this fact only made his responsibility greater, and any further war would be a crime.

I asked him to go among the Southern people and use his influence to have all men under arms surrender to the same terms given to the army of Northern Virginia. He replied that he could not do so without consultation with President [Jefferson] Davis. I was sorry. I saw that the Confederacy had gone beyond the reach of President Davis, and that there was nothing that could be done except what Lee could do to benefit the Southern people. I was anxious to get them home and have our armies go to their homes and fields. But Lee would not move without Davis, and as a matter of fact at that time, or soon after, Davis was a fugitive in the woods.

What Happened Next

The surrender at Appomattox effectively ended the Civil War. While the two generals had arranged a respectful surrender, many in the nation were not as forgiving. President Abraham Lincoln was assassinated within a week by a pro-Confederate extremist named John Wilkes Booth. A group of Northern politicians dominating Congress placed punitive measures on the South, and many former Confederate states were supervised by the federal military for another decade, even after they were readmitted to the Union. Meanwhile, the institution of slavery was abolished by the Thirteenth Amendment to the U.S. Constitution later in 1865. Other forms of institutionalized racism, including segregation, soon appeared.

General Lee continued to lead a distinguished life, but he was never given back his citizenship—a reflection of the continued bitterness over the war. General Grant was quickly courted as a presidential candidate, and he won the next election, in 1868. He was reelected in 1872 and was nearly nominated again in 1880.

Official Terms of Confederate Surrender

The following official terms of surrender were presented by Union general Ulysses S. Grant to Confederate general Robert E. Lee.

Head Quarters of the Armies of the United States
Appomattox C.H. Va. Apl 9th 1865
Gen. R. E. Lee
Comd'g C.S.A.

General,
In accordance with the substance of my letter to you of the 8th inst., I propose to receive the surrender of the Army of N. Va. on the following terms to wit;

Rolls of all the officers and men be made in duplicate, one copy to be given to an officer to be designated by me, the other to be retained by such officer or officers as you may designate. The officers to give their individual paroles not to take up arms against the Government of the United States until properly exchanged, and each company or regimental commander to sign a like parole for the men of their commands—

The arms, artillery and public property to be parked and stacked and turned over to the officer appointed by me to receive them. This will not embrace the side arms of the officers nor their private horses or baggage. This done each officer and man will be allowed to return to their homes, not to be disturbed by United States authority as long as they observe their parole and the laws in force where they may reside—

Very Respectfully
U. S. Grant
Lt. Gen

Rutherford B. Hayes

*"My task was to wipe out the color line, to abolish sectionalism...
I am forced to admit the experience was a failure."*

—*Rutherford B. Hayes*

Nineteenth president of the United States, 1877–1881

Full name: *Rutherford Birchard Hayes*
Born: *October 4, 1822, Delaware, Ohio*
Died: *January 16, 1893, Fremont, Ohio*
Burial site: *Spiegel Grove State Park, Fremont, Ohio*
Parents: *Rutherford and Sophia Birchard Hayes*
Spouse: *Lucy Ware Webb (1831–1889; m. 1852)*
Children: *Sardis Birchard Austin (1853–1926); James Webb Cook (1856–1935); Rutherford Platt (1858–1927); Joseph Thompson (1861–1863); George Crook (1864–1866); Frances (Fanny) (1867–1950); Scott Russell (1871–1923); Manning Force (1873–1874)*
Religion: *Methodist*
Education: *Kenyon College (1842); Harvard University Law School (1845)*
Occupations: *Lawyer; soldier*
Government positions: *U.S. representative from Ohio; Ohio governor*
Political party: *Republican*
Dates as president: *March 3, 1877–March 4, 1881*
Age upon taking office: *54*

The presidential achievements of Rutherford B. Hayes are overshadowed, historically, by accounts of the election of 1876—one of the most disputed presidential elections in American history. Hayes faced conflict throughout his term. Democrats in Congress were combative, and he gradually lost support within his own Republican Party as well. He had promised to serve only one term, but it wasn't likely that he would have been nominated for a second term, even if he wanted to.

Still, Hayes provided stability and moderate leadership to an American system that was rocked by serious problems. Government scandals, political partisanship, an unstable economy, and sectionalism had been plaguing the country since the end of the Civil War, a decade before. Hayes maintained conservative financial policies while many were calling for more radical approaches, but his methods helped revive what had been a sluggish economy. Finally, Hayes lobbied for the civil rights of minorities, particularly African Americans and Chinese Americans, at a time when many white men were fighting to maintain a base of power that was theirs alone.

Such political conflicts reflected the divisiveness that still dominated the country long after the Civil War had ended. The antagonism made it impossible for Hayes to have a successful administration, even though he proved to be trustworthy and he presided over a rebounding economy. "My task was to wipe out the color line, to abolish sectionalism…," Hayes said half-way through his term, "[but] I am forced to admit the experience was a failure."

Overcomes Childhood Illness

Rutherford Birchard Hayes was born in Delaware, Ohio, on October 4, 1822. His family had settled there after moving from Dummerston, Vermont, five years earlier. His father, also named Rutherford Hayes, decided to move from Vermont to what was then the American West to find new opportunities. He went there with his wife, Sophia, their two children, and Sophia's brother, Sardis Birchard.

Hayes's father did quite well in Ohio over the next few years. He bought land and built a large house, but he died during a malaria epidemic two months before the future president was born, leaving his widow with three children, a farm, and two houses. She rented out the farmland and one of the houses in the town of Delaware to give herself a steady income.

Hayes was a frail youngster, and his mother was very protective of him, even more so after the accidental drowning death of his brother Lorenzo when the younger boy was two years old. She kept him isolated and gradually taught him to read and write at home, although he began attending private schools by age nine, with tuition paid by his uncle Sardis.

Hayes went on to Kenyon College in Ohio, and graduated first in his class in 1842. Then he went on to Columbus, Ohio, to study law before entering Harvard Law School. He went back to Ohio after he got his degree, and was admitted to the bar, beginning a practice at East Sandusky with the help of his uncle, who had become a wealthy department store owner.

Above: Hayes's birthplace in Delaware, Ohio.

Timeline

1822: Born in Ohio
1842: Graduates from Kenyon College
1845: Graduates from Harvard Law School; establishes practice in Fremont (then called East Sandusky), Ohio
1849: Moves law practice to Cincinnati
1861: Begins fighting in Civil War; wounded four times through 1865
1865–67: Serves in U.S. House of Representatives
1868–72: Serves two terms as governor of Ohio
1876–77: Serves third term as governor of Ohio
1876: Trails Samuel J. Tilden in disputed presidential election
1877: Special electoral commission formed containing fifteen members (five representatives, five senators, five Supreme Court justices); disputed electoral votes awarded to Hayes, who is declared the victor on March 2, 1877, only days before the presidential inauguration
1877–81: Serves as nineteenth U.S. president
1881: Retires to Ohio
1893: Dies in Ohio

Career as Lawyer

Hayes spent at least as much time with his hobbies—literature and natural science—as he did lawyering with his partner, Ralph P. Buckland. He also enjoyed traveling and toured the United States and Canada. His most noteworthy accomplishment at the time was his work on

Religious Differences

Lucy Hayes was a Methodist to the core of her soul, but her husband had been baptized a Presbyterian and attended the Episcopal church most Sundays. After they were married, of course, he went to the Methodist church with his wife, but he never formally joined it. "I am not a subscriber to any creed," he said. "I try to be a Christian. Or rather I want to be a Christian and do Christian work." He gave money, as well as time, to many denominations. As president he instituted Sunday night hymn-singing to the executive mansion. However, throughout his political career, he campaigned often for the strict separation of church and state.

Left: The 23rd Ohio Infantry.

a successful campaign to change the name of the town from East Sandusky to Fremont.

Hayes became more ambitious with his career in 1849, when he moved to Cincinnati, Ohio, a thriving and important western town. He quickly made a reputation there as a lawyer by often presenting shrewd defenses in the most difficult cases. As soon as he arrived there, he made a call at the home of Lucy Webb. He had met and been impressed with Miss Webb several years earlier when she was a student in Delaware, Ohio. She had been fifteen back then—"too young to fall in love with," he would recall—and he was nine years older. By the time they were reunited in Cincinnati, Lucy was an educated and spirited eighteen-year-old woman who was strongly against drinking alcohol and slavery. They were married three years later.

Lucy Webb Hayes's strong abolitionist views influenced "Rud," as she called her husband, to begin defending runaway slaves who were being tracked into the North. Slave owners could claim their "property" and go back to the South with their recaptured slaves to the South under the terms of the Compromise of 1850, a group of bills that included allowing Texas to enter the Union as a slave state and California as a free state.

As Hayes became more politically active, he helped found the Ohio branch of the Republican Party, which had been established nationally in 1854 by attracting members of the former Whig Party as well as the short-lived Free-Soil and American parties. All these parties were opposed to the expansion of slavery into newly settled territories, a stand that also attracted Northern Democrats with abolitionist sentiments and were at odds with their Southern counterparts over slavery.

Meanwhile, Hayes continued to cultivate his interest in books by joining the local Literature Club of Cincinnati, where he met many of the city's powerful citizens. He was responsible for arranging guest lectures by notable writers, including American essayist Ralph Waldo Emerson.

He was chosen to fill the vacant city solicitor position by the City Council in 1858, and the next year, he was elected to the job. He strongly supported the candidacy of fellow Republican Abraham Lincoln in his successful election to the presidency in 1860.

Hayes had taken only a mild interest when Southern states began seceding from the Union following Lincoln's election. However, when Confederate troops attacked Fort Sumter in South Carolina in April 1861, he was galvanized into action, and organized about three dozen members of his fellow Literary Club members and led them in military drills. As the war spread, he was commissioned as major of the 23rd Ohio Infantry.

Civil War Hero

Rutherford Hayes proved to be an effective war leader and a brave soldier. Within a year, he showed his courage by leading nine companies of soldiers to safety after they were overwhelmed by a surprise attack by Confederate troops in Parisburg, Virginia. Later he commanded a regiment in the Battle of South Mountain that was attacked by Confederate forces led by General Robert E. Lee.

"Fighting battles is like courting girls; those who make the most pretensions and are boldest usually win."

—*Rutherford B. Hayes*

Hayes was severely wounded in that battle, and his wounds took several weeks to heal. When word of it reached his wife, Lucy, she traveled hundreds of miles to be with him, even though she didn't know his exact location. She was trained as a nurse and helped Union soldiers throughout the war, while her children were cared for by her mother. Grateful soldiers commonly referred to her as "Mother Lucy."

Hayes was wounded three more times during the war, but he was still fighting at the end. He was leading an expedition against Confederate troops in Lynchburg, Virginia, when the Civil War ended in 1865 with General Lee's surrender.

Meanwhile, Hayes's popularity back home grew with reports of his heroism on the battlefield. He was nominated as a Republican candidate for Congress in 1864, while he was still in uniform. Replying to a request to go home and campaign, he wrote, "I have other business just now. Any man who would leave the army at this time to electioneer for Congress ought to be scalped." But even without campaigning, he won the election easily in a mostly Democratic district.

His first term in Congress was relatively uneventful, but he became more active after his reelection to a second term. Hayes supported the Republican policy of Reconstruction and was chairman of a committee on the Library of Congress, the nation's library. He secured funds to expand its collection of books on science, putting together his two main interests in life: books and science.

He ran successfully for governor of Ohio in 1867 and served two terms, during which his state ratified the Fifteenth Amendment to the Constitution, addressing voting rights of former slaves. Ohio State University was also established during his tenure as governor.

Hayes wanted to retire from public life after his second term, but he was convinced by the Republicans to run again for Congress in 1872. He lost the election, but his presence on the Republican ticket helped the presidential candidate, Ulysses S. Grant, carry the state.

Then Hayes kept the promise he had made himself and retired from public life, and he and his family moved to Fremont to live with his uncle, Sardis Birchard. When Birchard died in 1874, he left his substantial wealth to the Hayes family, as well as his imposing mansion, Spiegel Grove.

Called to Serve, Again

Hayes's retirement turned out to be a short one. Even though he had lost the congressional race in 1872, the loyalty he showed to embattled President Grant made him a winner as far as the Republicans were concerned, and they talked him into running for governor again. The party was losing power in Ohio at the time, and its need for an appealing candidate was close to desperate. Hayes won the election for them, and his victory brought him more national attention among Republicans. He became their dark-horse candidate for president the following year.

Republicans had held the presidency since 1860, but the outgoing Grant administration had been mired in corruption. Maine senator James G. Blaine was the likely nominee when their convention began, but he had been involved in a scandal involving the illegal sales of stocks. After six ballots failed to achieve the necessary majority of delegates to nominate any of their proposed candidates, support turned to Hayes, who had a trustworthy reputation and was a war hero. Ohio also had a high number of electoral votes—nominating him would probably result in the Republicans carrying Ohio. Democrats nominated Samuel J. Tilden, a lawyer and

political leader from New York, which also had a large number of electoral votes to deliver.

Hayes immediately declared that if he were elected he wouldn't run for a second term, a stand that helped him promote a major campaign issue—restoring a nonpartisan civil service system. Many government workers had been pressed into giving financial support for the Grant administration by political bosses. Hayes took the position that reforming of the system "can best be accomplished by an Executive who is under no temptation to use the patronage of his office to promote his own re-election."

The statement reflected the integrity that Hayes intended to invest into his administration if he were elected president. He proved, indeed, to be a model of integrity. But his actions were greatly overshadowed by a tainted election and by deeply embedded partisan and sectional differences.

The Tainted Election

The political environment in the United States of the mid-1870s was ripe for controversy. Following the Civil War, federal troops remained stationed in the South to ensure that the laws of the land were carried out. The Republican Party had rallied under President Lincoln to abolish slavery in the 1860s, and after the Civil War, the federal policy of Reconstruction was intended to restore the relationship between the former Confederate states and the federal Union, to oversee the transition of the

Left: A Campaign banner for Republican candidates Rutherford B. Hayes and William A Wheeler in 1876.

Samuel J. Tilden

Samuel Jones Tilden was the Democratic candidate in the most controversial presidential election in American history. An attorney who rose to become governor of New York in the 1870s, Tilden established a reputation as an effective and dedicated reformer. He lost the 1876 presidency to Republican candidate Rutherford B. Hayes in a bitterly disputed election.

Born February 9, 1814, in New Lebanon, New York, Tilden became immersed in the world of politics at a relatively young age. A talented writer, he penned a number of political papers while in his twenties for his friend Martin Van Buren, president of the United States from 1837 to 1841. Around this same time, Tilden studied law at the University of the City of New York, and he passed the state bar exam to become a certified lawyer in 1841. He became counsel for the City of New York two years later, and in 1846 was elected to the New York state legislature.

By the early 1850s, Tilden was firmly entrenched as one of New York City's leading attorneys. He embraced the Democratic Party that his friend Van Buren had helped establish during the 1830s. After the conclusion of the Civil War in 1865, Tilden emerged as a key figure in the Democrats' reorganization efforts. Republicans had rallied behind Abraham Lincoln in the early 1860s, and Congressional Republicans emerged as the nation's strongest political force after Lincoln's assassination. Tilden's unblemished reputation was further enhanced in the late 1860s and early 1870s when he and fellow reformer Thomas Nast crusaded against William "Boss" Tweed and Tammany Hall, the corrupt Democratic political group that dominated New York City at that time. The notorious Tweed Ring had cheated the city out of millions of dollars over the years. Tilden, Nast, and other reformers were finally able to convict Tweed and send him to prison.

In 1874, Tilden was named the Democratic nominee for the governorship of New York. He won the election and made an immediate impact. One of his most notable achievements was the dismantling of the Canal Ring, a group of politicians and building contractors that had enriched themselves via fraudulent water canal repair agreements. A skilled administrator and determined reformer, Tilden was a popular governor. By the mid-1870s, meanwhile, the

Democratic Party had revitalized itself across much of the nation. In the years following the Civil War, Southern Democrats had banded to turn Republicans out of their public offices in the South, and by the mid-1870s only three Southern states were still in Republican hands. Northern Democrats, meanwhile, knew that the public was angry with the corruption-riddled administration of Ulysses S. Grant, a Republican president elected in 1868 and 1872. Tilden's reformer image and his popularity made the governor of New York an ideal choice to head the Democratic ticket in 1876.

On election night, Tilden won the popular vote and secured 184 uncontested electoral votes, one short of clinching the presidency. Nineteen additional electoral votes, however—from the Republican-held states of South Carolina, Louisiana, and Florida—were claimed by both the Republican and Democratic parties, and a tense standoff ensued as the two sides grappled for possession of the pivotal votes. A few days before the scheduled inauguration of America's new president, a specially appointed electoral commission finally announced an agreement. The Republicans would get the disputed Electoral College votes, thus pushing Hayes's total just over the number needed to claim victory. In return for handing Hayes the presidency, the Democrats secured promises that the South would receive significant funding for railroads and public works projects and appointment of a Southerner to the president's cabinet. In addition, Hayes promised to pull the last of the federal troops out of the South (a move that some historians believe would have taken place anyway).

Despite winning the popular vote, Tilden had been denied the presidency of the United States. Mindful of ongoing hostilities between the Southern and Northern regions of the nation, the governor tried to accept the results gracefully. "I can retire to private life with the consciousness that I shall receive from posterity the credit of having been elected to the highest position in the gift of the people, without any of the cares and responsibilities of the office," he said after the agreement was announced. Tilden returned to New York, where he resumed his law practice. A wealthy man at the time of his death in 1886, he left much of his $6 million fortune for the construction of a public library. Tilden's money was combined with the city's Astor and Lenox libraries to form the renowned New York Public Library in 1895.

1876 Election Results

Presidential / Vice Presidential Candidates	Popular Votes	Electoral Votes
Rutherford B. Hayes / William A. Wheeler (Republican)	4,036,298	185
Samuel J. Tilden / Thomas A. Hendricks (Democratic)	4,300,590	184

Hayes won the Republican nomination on the seventh ballot; U.S. senator James G. Blaine of Maine was the leader on the first six ballots. Despite having fewer popular votes than Democrat Tilden, Hayes won the election after a special electoral commission awarded the twenty disputed electoral votes of Florida, Louisiana, Oregon, and South Carolina to Hayes.

newly freed slaves into citizens, and to help convert the Southern economy from one based on slave labor to one based on paid labor.

During Reconstruction, an intense national struggle over the shape of government occurred in the postwar South. Republican leadership became increasingly seen as a federal intrusion, and conservative Southern Democrats united to form a political bloc that represented the traditional white, male power of the South. African Americans, who had the right to vote, sided with the Republican Party, helping it keep a foothold in the South. Troops stayed on to ensure that federal laws were followed.

The presidential election of 1876 became a dispute that challenged the very workings of the American political system. Vote counts in Florida and South Carolina were close and were tainted by claims of fraud and intimidation by the Democrats. The Florida State Canvassing Board, which counted the votes, was authorized to reject returns "that shall be shown, or shall appear to be so irregular, false, or fraudulent that the board shall be unable to determine the vote." The board exercised that power, as did a similar commission in South Carolina. Both revised counts resulted in a majority of votes for Republican candidate Hayes. The situation couldn't have been more controversial. There had indeed been voter intimidation for Democratic candidates, but the election boards were dominated by Republicans.

The clear majority of the vote was Democratic in Louisiana, but the results were questioned by the Republican-dominated State Returning Board, which had the power to dismiss votes that they believed resulted

Below: The Electoral Commission met by candelight in March 1877, toward the end of the election controversy.

Below: This engraving celebrates the universal male suffrage granted by the Fifteenth Amendment. Still, troops were stationed in the South to protect black voters from white adversaries.

from violence and fraud. Louisiana ended up sending two different vote counts to Washington. The original one proved that Tilden the winner, but the revised count showed a Republican victory.

The number of electoral votes needed for election was 185. Excluding those that had come under review in the South and West, Tilden had 184 electoral votes to Hayes's 165. Twenty electoral votes were still under dispute—eight from Louisiana, seven from South Carolina, four from Florida, and one from Oregon. Those disputed votes would determine who won the election. The new president was to take office in March of 1877, but no winner had yet been determined by the end of 1876.

In January, after several sessions, Congress established an electoral commission to resolve the issue. It was made up of fifteen members—seven Republicans, seven Democrats, and one independent from among five senators, five representatives, and five Supreme Court justices. However, the lone independent, Justice David Davis, was elected by the Illinois legislature to fill an open Congressional seat, and his replacement on the commission shifted the balance of power to the Republicans.

Naturally, a great deal of haggling followed, with the Republican majority following a strict party line and Democrats doing everything they could to disrupt the proceedings. The dispute wasn't settled until shortly before the date the new president was to be inaugurated, and it took a stormy eighteen-hour session to get it done. Probably not surprisingly, the twenty disputed electoral votes went to Hayes, which made him the winner in the Electoral College, 185 votes to 184. In a deal that is often called the Compromise of 1877, the Republican candidate was declared the winner, but Democrats were appeased too. They were assured that federal troops would be removed from the South, that a Southern Democrat would be selected to serve in Hayes's cabinet, and that legislation awarding a federal subsidy for the proposed Texas and Pacific railroad would be passed.

Most of the country came around to the inevitability of the decision, but a large number of newspapers couldn't resist calling the new president Ruther*fraud* B. Hayes.

During the proceedings of the electoral commission, Hayes waited quietly at home. When the declaration that

For a Price

During the vote recount after the 1876 election, it was revealed that a Republican member of the Electoral College from Oregon had been "bought" by the other side for $10,000, and it was hinted that other "outrageously villainous" manipulations had taken place in other states as well. The Democrats produced what they characterized as proof that the other side had been paid even more, and that both sides had been offered Louisiana's entire slate of electors for a million dollars. Neither side admitted that they had been paid anything, but one of the players pointed out that "the spirit of politics is different in Louisiana."

he had won was finally made on March 2, 1877, Hayes was already on the way to the capital—just in case his presence was required in time for the inauguration.

"Pacification"

The major themes of Hayes's inaugural address were "permanent pacification of the country," the return of self-government to the Southern states, and the need for civil service reform. He wasn't able to resolve political conflicts between Republicans and Democrats, but he was effective in ending Reconstruction, reforming the civil service, and strengthening the economy.

In disassembling Reconstruction, Hayes first turned to the situation in the states of South Carolina and Louisiana. Each of them had two state governments policed by federal troops. After meeting with the rival

Right: Hayes taking the oath of office as the nineteenth president.

Left: President Hayes meeting with his Cabinet.

governors of South Carolina, he withdrew the troops, and the state had a single government again.

Federal troops had also been stationed in Louisiana to preserve order, but the responsibility was turned back to the state, and troops were withdrawn from there, too. Reconstruction ended as the Southern states regained their independence from federal occupation.

"The policy of the president has turned out to be a give-away from the beginning. He has nulled suits, discontinued prosecutions, offered conciliations in the South, while they have spent their time in whetting their knives for any Republican they could find."
—*Congressman James A. Garfield*

The Hayes Administration

Administration Dates: March 4, 1877–March 4, 1881
Vice President: William Almon Wheeler (1877–81)

Cabinet:

Secretary of State	William M. Evarts (1877–81)
Secretary of the Treasury	John Sherman (1877–81)
Secretary of War	George W. McCrary (1877–79)
	Alexander Ramsey (1879–81)
Attorney General	Charles Devens (1877–81)
Secretary of the Navy	Richard W. Thompson (1877–80)
	Nathan Goff Jr. (1881)
Postmaster General	David M. Key (1877–80)
	Horace Maynard (1880–81)
Secretary of the Interior	Carl Schurz (1877–81)

Below: Hayes during his presidency.

Triumphal Entry

After having been declared president by a committee, Hayes began receiving death threats from disgruntled voters, and it was suggested that he go to Washington in secret. But he opted instead to ride into town in an open carriage. Six special government agents were enlisted to surround it, the first time that the "Secret Service" was assigned to protect a president. It turns out, however, that their service wasn't required, at least if an assassin wanted to block Hayes's inauguration—he had secretly taken the oath of office two days ahead of the scheduled date.

In June of 1877, Hayes began acting on civil service reform in June of 1877. He issued an order prohibiting government officials from taking part in "the management of political organizations, caucuses, conventions, or election campaigns." The order further stated: "Their right to vote and to express their views on public questions, either openly or through the press, is not denied, provided it does not interfere with the discharge of their official duties. No assessment for political purposes on officers or subordinates should be allowed." Those who went against this presidential order were immediately suspended. The most famous case of suspension occurred at the New York Customs House when the collector Chester A. Arthur, who would later become president, was stripped of his responsibilities for continuing political wheeling and dealing after the presidential order was issued.

President Hayes's financial policy helped bring the economy out of the doldrums associated with the Panic of 1873, and it also ensured economic stability. Hayes insisted on paying off the national debt. He favored the principle of "sound money," giving all paper currency a single value based on the country's gold reserves. During the Civil War, the government had printed bank notes promising money to the holder. The flood of these so-called greenbacks resulted in an increased money supply, which lessened the value of money and caused widespread inflation.

In spite of the sorry lesson of the greenbacks, which often weren't worth the paper they were printed on, Congress opposed Hayes's plan because the legislators wanted to make even more money available by coining silver as well as gold. Hayes managed to delay bills allowing the unlimited coinage of silver and refunding of the national debt, but Congress eventually succeeded in overriding his vetoes.

Congress had other headaches in store for Rutherford B. Hayes. A Democratic majority routinely included riders on basic appropriations bills, attempting to pass legislation that they knew the president would otherwise veto. One such rider prohibited the use of federal troops to "keep the peace at the polls." Hayes agreed that military interference with elections should be prevented, but he insisted that such power might be needed someday, and so he vetoed the bill. He also defended the supervision of national elections by national authority, as opposed to state authority, to guard against voter fraud and intimidation. He was motivated to maintain measures that could be used in an emergency when it appeared that black voters were being intimidated. Congress couldn't muster enough votes to override these vetoes, and the basic appropriations bills were finally passed with the riders removed.

Hayes was successful on other fronts. In 1880, he gained American approval for a French firm to begin construction of the Panama Canal. A basic policy statement called the Monroe Doctrine explained the position of the United States on the activities of European countries in the Western Hemisphere, and since its declaration, the United States had been consistently opposed to European presence in the Americas. But Hayes was able to convince Congress to back the building of the canal with the help of the French. The Panama Canal project, however, would take another two decades to get underway.

Hayes vetoed a bill restricting Chinese immigration. Railroad builders had encouraged Chinese immigration for years to help meet their labor needs, but many Americans wanted to stop the Chinese presence from growing any larger.

Right: A cartoon comparing Hayes to Cinderella when he refused to run for a second term.

Retirement in Ohio

As Hayes's term came to a quiet close, he was not considered a candidate for reelection. He intended to keep his promise of serving one term, but he had been drawn out of retirement before. Not this time, though. His public career ended with his retirement from the presidency, and he returned to Spiegel Grove in Fremont, Ohio. Over the next few years, he worked to improve veterans' organizations, and he served as a trustee of the Peabody Fund for the education of underprivileged children in the South.

After falling ill in Cleveland, Hayes went home once more to Fremont, where he died at Spiegel Grove on January 17, 1893. He was buried there next to his wife, Lucy, who had died four years before him.

Legacy

Rutherford B. Hayes effectively ended the era of Reconstruction, returning self-determination to the states of the South. His civil service reforms were continued by successors, including Chester A. Arthur, who had been suspended during the Hayes administration for continuing to use his government finance position for political purposes. Hayes's fiscal conservatism—balancing the federal budget and regulating the supply of money—proved to have stabilizing effects. His efforts to protect the civil rights of minorities were praiseworthy, but many battles were still waiting to be fought.

The end of Reconstruction and opposition to Republicans solidified Southern Democrats into a bloc that could wield great influence on legislation. The Solid South, as the bloc came to be called, was united and powerful through the mid-twentieth century.

Lucy Hayes

Born August 28, 1831, Chillicothe, Ohio
Died June 25, 1889, Fremont, Ohio

"Woman's mind is as strong as man's—equal in all things and his superior in some."

—*Lucy Hayes*

Lucy Webb Hayes was a spirited woman, but her political activism remained subdued—which was perhaps a sign of the times. Although her influence on her husband and her personal views on issues remained behind the scenes, she was a visible presence in the cause of education and public service.

As a teenager, Lucy Webb's intellect was so sharp that she was allowed to study in the all-male Wesleyan College in Ohio. Later, the fiercely abolitionist Lucy helped convince lawyer Rutherford Hayes to defend runaway slaves. She married Hayes, bore eight children, and often followed him to the battle sites of the Civil War. He commanded troops, and she served as a nurse. Later, as first lady, Lucy Hayes was an active supporter for improved schooling for the less advantaged. She promoted the National Deaf Mute College as well as education for Native Americans, Hispanics, and African Americans, and she continued to be involved with these causes throughout her life.

Well-Schooled

Lucy Webb was born in 1831 in Chillicothe, Ohio, the daughter of Dr. James Webb and Maria Cook Webb. Her father died when she was two, after traveling to Kentucky to free slaves he had recently inherited. He was infected during a cholera epidemic while there.

When Lucy was entering her teens, her mother relocated the family to Delaware, Ohio, so that her two older brothers could study at Wesleyan College. During a couple of visits to the school, Lucy greatly impressed professors there with her unusual intelligence, and they invited her to attend classes, even though it was an all-male college. Fifteen-year-old Lucy first met young Hayes at a popular swimming hole on the campus, but there was a nine-year age difference between them. He later recalled that he found her "bright-eyed, sunny-hearted, and not quite old enough to fall in love with."

After her brothers graduated, the Webb family relocated to Cincinnati, where the young men could go on to medical school. Lucy, meanwhile, finished her own education at nearby Wesleyan Female College, graduating at the age of eighteen.

At about that time in 1849, Rutherford Hayes had also relocated to Cincinnati. After having been an unremarkable lawyer for four years in Fremont, Ohio, he wanted greater opportunities, and he found them in Cincinnati, a thriving town of what was then the American West. He also took advantage of the opportunity to get reacquainted with Lucy Webb, who had become quite old enough to fall in love with.

Rutherford Hayes and Lucy Webb began a romance that summer. They attended a wedding together, and "Rud," as she called him, found a gold ring in his piece of wedding cake. It was a playful custom of the time that the wedding guest who found a ring in a piece of cake would be the next one to be married. Rud gave the ring to Lucy, and she returned the favor by putting it on his finger on their wedding day two years later. He wore the ring the rest of his life.

Right: Lucy and her husband at the White House.

Mother Lucy

The Hayeses were active in the causes of abolition of slavery and abstinence from alcohol. With Lucy's encouragement, Hayes soon began defending runaway slaves who fled to the free North and were tracked down by their owners.

Lucy Hayes gave birth to eight children over the next twenty years, five of whom survived into adulthood. Her mother helped her raise the children, allowing Lucy to

Right: Lucy and three of her children.

take occasional trips with her husband. He was a respected lawyer and an avid Republican. He campaigned actively for Abraham Lincoln in 1860, and the new president invited him to ride on part of his journey from Illinois to Washington to take office. The Hayeses rode with the Lincolns from Indianapolis to Cincinnati.

When the Civil War broke out in 1861, Hayes became a commander of the 23rd Ohio Volunteer Regiment. Lucy often joined her husband after battles while her mother cared for her children, and she also accompanied her brother Joe, a doctor, to battlefield hospitals where she helped him tend to the wounded. She was nicknamed "Mother Lucy" by grateful soldiers. She once undertook a journey of several hundred miles from the Hayes home in Ohio after learning that her husband was recuperating from severe wounds that he suffered in a battle in Virginia.

A Politician's Wife

Rutherford Hayes was elected to the House of Representatives in 1864 without even having to campaign—he was still fighting in the war. During his two terms in Congress, Lucy frequently sat in the gallery above the House floor wearing a checkered scarf so that Hayes could spot her. Hayes served two terms as governor of Ohio after that, and as first lady of Ohio, Lucy regularly visited with orphans and war veterans and was a force for improvement of schools, prisons, and mental asylums. She worked hard for state funding for an orphanage for children whose parents had been killed in the war.

Hayes planned to retire from politics when his term as governor ended in 1872. He and Lucy moved to Fremont to be with his uncle, Sardis Birchard, who died two years later and left them a substantial fortune, as well as a large estate called Spiegel Grove, which they both came to love. Hayes was nominated again for governor of Ohio in 1875. He won the election and made such an excellent impression that he became the Republican presidential nominee the following year.

The Hayeses served in Washington for one term, from 1877 to 1881. Lucy went to work to improve education for disadvantaged youngsters and pushed for completion of the Washington Monument after construction had been delayed for lack of funds. Presidential social occasions were lively and informal, although alcohol was banned from them. Apart from the fact that the president and first lady were teetotalers, he didn't want to offend supporters of temperance, many of whom were Republicans. Lucy Hayes supported the ban on alcohol out of respect for her Methodist upbringing. No matter what the reason, Washington society wasn't too pleased to find the bars closed, and Mrs. Hayes became know as "Lemonade Lucy." After one of her parties, a guest reported that "the water flowed like champagne."

Lucy Hayes stayed behind the scenes politically, even when her husband didn't support issues she favored—like women's suffrage. She was well known as a good singer, and her love of animals was almost legendary. The executive mansion became home to several dogs, birds, and cats, including a Siamese that is believed to have been the first ever brought into the United States. Among many social occasions, the Hayeses celebrated their twenty-fifth wedding anniversary with a lavish party, and Easter egg hunts on the presidential lawn became an annual event after Lucy staged the first one.

Home in Spiegel Grove

After the Hayes administration ended in 1881, Lucy and Rud went back to Fremont, Ohio. It was the second time they had retired from public life, but this time it was for good. They remained active in the cause of education, and Lucy continued in her role as president of the Methodist Woman's Home Missionary Society, which gave shelter to homeless women. She remained quite active in the cause of education and helping homeless women until her death in 1889. She was buried at Spiegel Grove. Her husband died four years later and was buried next to her.

Hayes's Speech on the End of Reconstruction

Delivered on September 24, 1877

President Rutherford B. Hayes toured the South even before he took office. He made many speeches announcing his plan to end the federal policy of Reconstruction that followed the end of the Civil War. He was hoping that Southerners would respond by protecting equal rights guaranteed to all American citizens by the Constitution.

Hayes was a well-reasoned gentleman. He believed that the rightness of his views on equality and fairness could prevail. He wanted to end the post–Civil War iniquities of the North dominating the South politically, and some Southern whites using violence and intimidation to deny the Constitutional rights of African Americans.

Hayes had won the controversial presidential election of 1876, in which vote tallies in several states were disputed: In some cases, African Americans had been denied their voting rights, and other vote tallies were influenced by the political party in power in a particular area. Hayes hoped to unite the nation by inspiring those were divided— Northerners and Southerners, Republicans and Democrats, blacks and whites—to begin respecting one another.

Excerpt from Hayes's Speech on the End of Reconstruction

I suppose that here, as everywhere else, I am in the presence of men of both great political parties. I am speaking, also, in the presence of citizens of both races. I am quite sure that there are before me very many of the brave men who fought in the Confederate army: some, doubtless, of the men who fought in the Union army. And here we are, Republicans, Democrats, colored people, white people, Confederate soldiers, and Union soldiers, all of one mind and one heart today! And why should we not be? What is there to separate us longer? Without any fault of yours or any fault of mine, or of any one of this great audience, slavery existed in this country. It was in the Constitution of the country.

The colored man was here, not by his voluntary action. It was the misfortune of his fathers that he was here. I think it is safe to say that it was by the crime of our fathers that he was here. He was here, however, and we of the two sections differed about what should be done with him. As Mr. [Abraham] Lincoln told us in the war, there were prayers on both sides for him. Both sides found in the Bible confirmation of their opinions, and both sides finally undertook to settle the question by that last final means of arbitration—force of arms. You here mainly joined the Confederate side, and fought bravely, risked your lives heroically in behalf of your convictions; and can I, can any true man anywhere, fail to respect the man who risks his life for his convictions? And as I accord that respect to you, and believe you to be equally liberal and generous and just, I feel that, as I stand before you as one who fought in the Union army for his convictions, I am entitled to your respect. Now that conflict is over, my friends.

[…]

Now, shall we quit fighting? I have been in the habit of telling an anecdote of General [Winfield] Scott and a statesman at Washington, in which the statesman said that as soon as the war was over and the combatants laid down their arms, we should have complete peace. "No," said General Scott, "it will take several years in which all the powers of the general government will be employed in keeping peace between the belligerent non-combatants!" Now, I think, we have got through with that and having peace between the soldiers and the noncombatants, that is an end of the war. Is there any reason, then, why we should not be at peace forevermore? We are embarked upon the same voyage, upon the same ship, under the same old flag. Good fortune or ill fortune affects you and your children as well as my people and my children.

Every interest you possess is to be promoted by peace. Here is this great city of Atlanta, gathering to itself from all parts of the country its wealth and business by its railroads; and I say to you that every description of industry and legitimate business needs peace. That is what capital wants. Discord, discontent, and dissatisfaction are the enemies of these enterprises. Then, all our interests are for peace. Are we not agreed about that? What do we want for the future? I believe it is the duty of the general government to regard equally and alike the interests and rights of all sections of this country. I am glad that you agree with me about that. I believe, further, that it is the duty of the government to regard alike and equally the rights and interests of all classes of citizens. That covers the whole matter. That wipes out in the future in our politics the section line forever. Let us wipe out in our politics the color line forever.

And let me say a word upon what has been done. I do not undertake to discuss or defend particular measures. I leave the people with their knowledge of the facts to examine, discuss, and decide for themselves as to them. I speak of general considerations and notions.

What troubles our people at the North, what has troubled them, was that they feared that these colored people, who had been made freemen by the war, would not be safe in their rights and interests in the South unless it was by the interference of the general government. Many good people had that idea. I had given that matter some consideration, and now, my colored friends, who have thought, or who have been told, that I was turning my back upon the men whom I fought for, now, listen! After thinking over it, I believed that your right and interests would be safer if this great mass of intelligent white men were let alone by the general government. And now, my colored friends, let me say another thing. We have been trying it for these six months, and, in my opinion in no six months since the war have there been so few outrages and invasions of your rights, nor you so secure in your rights, persons, and homes, as in the last six months.

Then, my friends, we are all together upon one proposition. We believe, and in this all those who are here agree, in the Union of our fathers, in the old flag of our fathers, the Constitution as it is with all its amendments, and are prepared to see it fully and fairly obeyed and enforced. Now, my friends, I see it stated occasionally that President Hayes has taken the course he has because he was compelled to it. Now, I was compelled to it. I was compelled to it by my sense of duty under my oath of office. What was done by us was done, not merely by force of special circumstances, but because it was just and right to do it.

Now let us come together. Let each man make up his mind to be a patriot in his own home and place. You may quarrel about the tariff, get up a sharp contest about the currency, about the removal of state capitals and where they shall go to, but upon the great question of the Union of the states and the rights of all the citizens, we shall agree forevermore.

What Happened Next

The end of Reconstruction was necessary in order for the nation to return to the normal relationship between individual states and the federal government. Unfortunately, the country was not yet ready. When federal supervision was removed, discrimination and segregation became rampant in most of the South. Republicans—the party of Abraham Lincoln—quickly lost power in the region. Democrats, many representing the concerns of whites only, won elections and formed a solid voting bloc that would persist into the mid-twentieth century.

Halfway through his term, Hayes admitted the failure of his noble pursuits. The president attempted to unite the nation and embrace the laws of the Constitution, but the nation as a whole wasn't ready to live up to those ideals.

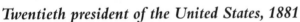

James A. Garfield

"I love agitation and investigation and glory in defending unpopular truth against popular error."

—*James A. Garfield*

Twentieth president of the United States, 1881

Full name: *James Abram Garfield*
Born: *November 19, 1831, Orange, Ohio*
Died: *September 19, 1881, Elberon, New Jersey*
Burial site: *Lake View Cemetery, Cleveland, Ohio*
Parents: *Abram and Eliza Ballou Garfield*
Spouse: *Lucretia Rudolph (1832–1918; m. 1858)*
Children: *Eliza Arabella (1860–1863); Harry Augustus (1863–1942); James Rudolph (1865–1950); Mary (Mollie); (1867–1947); Irvin McDowell (1870–1951); Abram (1872–1958); Edward Abram (1874–76)*
Religion: *Disciples of Christ*
Education: *Williams College (1856)*
Occupations: *Educator; soldier*
Government positions: *State senator and U.S. representative from Ohio*
Political party: *Republican*
Dates as president: *March 4, 1881–September 19, 1881*
Age upon taking office: *49*

James A. Garfield's presidency lasted only a little more than six months. On July 2, 1881, he was wounded several times by an assassin. Garfield lived for ten more weeks following the shooting, but he never recovered, and he died on September 19, 1881.

A supporter of a strong federal government, Garfield wanted to infuse a greater sense of independence and leadership in the presidency. The presidency had become overshadowed by Congress since the end of the Civil War. Garfield was also especially interested in reforming the civil service system, the jobs under the authority of the federal government, at a time when government appointments were dominated by patronage, with jobs going only to political activists and donors. Garfield's efforts in this area were carried on by his successor, Chester A. Arthur, who signed a civil service reform bill in 1883.

Garfield was an excellent speechmaker who projected a sense of dignity and friendliness at the same time. He served in Congress for seventeen years before being elected president, and a speech he made there is considered one of the most eloquent defenses of the right of the federal government to influence laws above the concerns of individual states. It was reprinted and used as campaign information during his run for the presidency.

Above: Garfield's birthplace in Orange, Ohio.

Timeline

1831: Born in Ohio
1857–61: Serves as president of Hiram College
1859: Serves in Ohio State Senate
1861–63: Serves as colonel in Civil War
1863–80: Serves in the U.S. House of Representatives
1877: Member of the fifteen-man electoral commission appointed by Congress to investigate the presidential election of 1876 and to declare a winner
1881: Inaugurated as president, March 4; shot several times by an assassin, July 2; dies in New Jersey on September 19

Garfield was a leader several times over. He was a college president; he commanded Civil War fighting units; he chaired Congressional committees; and he was elected president. Along the way, he managed to overcome a serious illness, battlefield dangers, and political scandals.

From a Log Cabin to the White House

James Abram Garfield was born to Abram and Eliza Garfield in a log cabin near the town of Orange, near Cleveland, Ohio, on November 19, 1831, the youngest of five children. His father died when James was two years old, and Eliza went to work to support her family. The children divided their time between working and attending school, and as they were growing up, the family became active in a religious group called the Disciples of Christ.

Garfield enjoyed hunting and reading, especially sea stories, which gave him the idea that he wanted to become a sailor. When he was a teenager, he traveled to Cleveland to sign aboard a cargo ship headed for the ocean. He decided against it, though, after being interviewed by a drunken sea captain, and instead began working on canal boats and piloting a tugboat. However, he gave it all up and went home after contracting what appeared to be malaria.

"The truth is, no man ever started so low that accomplished so much in all our history. Not Franklin or Lincoln, even."

—*Rutherford B. Hayes*

While he was recovering, his mother convinced him that getting an education might be a better idea, especially since he liked reading so much, and he enrolled at the nearby Western Reserve Eclectic Institute, a school founded by the Disciples of Christ. He went from there to Williams College in Massachusetts, where he earned

Right: The school young Garfield attended.

honors in Latin and literature and was known as a strong and excellent athlete. He also edited the school magazine and used his skills as a public speaker to take part in political debates, which he loved because, as he said, "I love agitation and investigation and glory in defending unpopular truth against popular error."

Garfield used his public-speaking skills to serve as a traveling preacher for the Disciples of Christ, routinely preaching from two pulpits every Sunday, and then he went back to the Western Reserve Eclectic Institute, which had been renamed Hiram College, as a teacher, another role he enjoyed.

Garfield was a very popular professor and the leader of a literary society. He was so well liked there, in fact, that he won election from his congregation to become the college's president when he was twenty-six years old.

Hiram College's new president immediately began introducing improvements to the school. Teachers were required to attend instruction workshops and to hold informal discussion groups with students in addition to regular class instruction. Classes Garfield taught himself were always overflowing with students.

The college presidency made Garfield a pillar of the local community, and he became involved in its political scene as a strong supporter of the antislavery movement. He established a local reputation with his speeches as well as his leadership, and he was elected to Ohio's state senate, where he became even more vocal about ending slavery. Although he had been a pacifist all of his life, Garfield became a staunch supporter of the pledge by newly elected president Abraham Lincoln to use federal force to preserve the Union. He had campaigned hard for Lincoln, making more than fifty speeches at gatherings in rural areas all over Ohio.

In the meantime, Garfield had married Lucretia Rudolph on November 11, 1858. "Crete," as he called her, was the daughter of a trustee of Hiram College, and they had known each other since childhood. They would have seven children, five of whom would survive into adulthood.

Garfield began studying law and was certified as an attorney in 1861. Then he turned his attention to reading books on military strategy and organization in anticipation of the war that he knew would surely come.

Disciples of Christ

The Disciples of Christ emerged in Kentucky in 1804 and in Pennsylvania five years later among evangelical Presbyterians. The religion was formally organized in 1832 in response to what was seen as a decline of faith among Protestants. Run by the authority of individual congregations, the Disciples reject any practices that weren't part of the original Christian church, sometimes even banning music, basing their belief on strict interpretation of the words of scripture. They are believers in social action and highly tolerant of other religions.

Right: Garfield became a major general in the Union Army.

Neat Trick

Among his other talents, James A. Garfield had a flair for languages. When asked, he could write in Greek with one hand and Latin with the other.

Book-Trained Soldier

When the Civil War broke out in 1861, Garfield volunteered for service and he was appointed to a position as colonel of the 42nd Ohio Volunteer Infantry. Many of the men were former students of his, and they were willing, even eager, to follow him into battle.

Garfield led his unit through a series of skirmishes in Kentucky, forcing retreats of Confederate soldiers in all of them, and he took part in several major battles, including Middle Creek and Shiloh. His heroism during the Battle of Chickamauga was widely and glowingly reported back home.

He was elected to the U.S. House of Representatives while he was still serving in the Union Army, thanks largely to his local reputation as a speaker and as a college president, not to mention his battlefield exploits. Voters in his highly Republican district were prompted to elect Garfield even though he didn't campaign for the job. Reportedly, President Lincoln encouraged him to accept the seat because he needed more support in Congress at the time than he did on the battlefield.

Skirting Disaster and Emerging as a Leader

Garfield began a distinguished seventeen-year career in Congress with that election. He served as chairman of the Military Affairs Committee and established the Reserve Officer Training Corps (ROTC) program on college campuses. He chaired the Banking and Currency Committee, giving his silver-tongued support to "hard money"—currency values based on the gold standard. He also chaired the Appropriations Committee, which authorized funds for projects. While he was on that committee, he lobbied against spending money on projects that would put the country in debt.

"A brave man is one who dares to look the Devil in the face and tell him he is a Devil."

—*James A. Garfield*

After the Democrats gained a majority in Congress in 1874, Garfield became the House minority leader. Along with his firm stand on backing currency with gold, he supported harsher elements of Reconstruction, the federal policy toward the former Confederate states. In particular, he was in favor of seizing property owned by people who had served the Confederacy, and he was a strong advocate for expanding and protecting the voting rights of blacks.

Garfield had managed to avoid disasters all his life. He survived malaria when he was young, during a time when the disease usually proved fatal; and in spite of not having had much military training, he fought in several bloody Civil War battles without ever being severely wounded. Likewise, as a politician, Garfield was touched by scandal but not ruined by it. He was connected with the Crédit Mobilier scandal of the Grant administration for having accepted stock as an insider in what proved to be an illegal business venture. He also accepted legal fees from a company that was bidding on a government contract for street repairs and improvements in Washington, D.C. In both of these cases, Garfield's participation is generally viewed as having been minor, and dismissed as little more than lapses in judgment, but many at the time believed that where there's smoke, there's fire. Still, it didn't do much harm to his reputation.

"Garfield has shown that he is not possessed of the backbone of an angle-worm."

—*Ulysses S. Grant*

Left: The future president became famous for his heroism at the Battle of Chickamaugua.

Rise in Prominence

Garfield distinguished himself on two occasions late in his Congressional career. He served on the electoral commission that was formed to decide the disputed presidential election of 1876. Many voters in the South had favored Democratic candidates, but election boards there were dominated by Republicans. Those boards determined the number of questionable votes they claimed had been cast after intimidation of individual voters and subtracted them from the final count, switching majorities in three states in favor of the Republican candidate. One hundred eighty-five electoral votes were needed for election, and Democrat Samuel J. Tilden had 184 of them to 165 for Republican Rutherford B. Hayes. Twenty other electoral votes were contested—eight from Louisiana, seven from South Carolina, four from Florida, and one from Oregon.

As a member of the electoral commission, Garfield plunged into investigative work. He interviewed many people from the areas involved, examined tally sheets that recorded totals from different areas, and visited polling places. The commission eventually agreed with the electoral boards of the disputed states and awarded the remaining twenty electoral votes to Hayes, who was named the winner. The verdict, made three days before the inauguration was set to take place, allowed the nation to proceed, but party bickering only increased. A majority of the commission was Republican, and Democrats felt that they had simply put partisanship above the will of the people.

The Hayes administration was seriously weakened by conflict in Congress. Democrats were hostile and unreceptive, and Republicans gradually abandoned Hayes for taking a middle ground instead of automatically supporting their pet causes. Garfield was one of the few Republicans who remained supportive of Hayes. When Democrats became the majority party in Congress following the elections of 1878, they began looking for ways to weaken the influence of the federal government in favor of states' rights, but as House minority leader, Garfield rose to make an eloquent defense of the powers of the federal government.

Above: Even Garfield himself was surprised when he took the Republican presidential nomination in 1880.

Dark Horse

When the Republicans met in 1880 to nominate a presidential candidate, the party was united on political issues but divided on the issue of patronage. One faction was headed by Roscoe Conkling, a senator from New York who wanted to ensure that all political appointees in his state were controlled by a group he headed called the Stalwarts. They supported the nomination of former president Ulysses S. Grant, but an opposing faction, nicknamed the "Half-Breeds," supported Maine legislator James G. Blaine. This group insisted that all political appointments should be made by the next administration.

Garfield was the campaign manager for a third candidate, John Sherman, Hayes's secretary of the treasury. Hayes, Sherman, and Garfield were all from Ohio, and Sherman inspired enough support at the convention to block both Grant and Blaine from getting the necessary number of votes for the nomination. Garfield helped as chairman of the convention's rules committee by introducing a rule that allowed all delegates to vote individually rather than in large state blocks. This rule stopped larger states like New York from dominating the voting for one candidate.

When Garfield nominated Sherman, he gave a rousing speech that received a long round of applause. However, he did not mention Sherman's name until fifteen minutes into it. Most of the applause was for Garfield himself.

The convention voted thirty-five times without any of the three candidates drawing enough support. Finally,

Presidential / Vice Presidential Candidates	Popular Votes	Electoral Votes
James A. Garfield / Chester A. Arthur (Republican)	4,454,416	214
Winfield Scott Hancock / William H. English (Democratic)	4,444,952	155

After having retired from politics for four years, former president Ulysses S. Grant ran for an unprecedented third term. On the first thirty-five ballots, he failed to receive enough votes to defeat Maine senator James G. Blaine and Secretary of the Treasury John Sherman for the Republican nomination; he lost when the supporters of Blaine and Sherman switched their allegiance to dark horse Garfield.

Sherman and Blaine dropped out in favor of Garfield, who won the nomination on the next ballot. To appease New Yorkers and the Stalwarts, Chester A. Arthur, a powerful political leader from New York, was selected as his running mate.

The general election was a close contest decided by states of the Northeast, where Garfield was favored because the Republican Party supported a high protective tariff, which would be good for the region. Garfield polled just ten thousand more popular votes than the Democratic nominee, Winfield Scott Hancock, but he won big in the Electoral College by taking the big eastern states and benefited when many voters in the West favored small-party candidates with regional interest.

" ... no president since the younger Adams has been so well prepared to get along with second-rate men as Mr. Garfield. He does not, like Lincoln or Grant or Hayes, need cabinet officers to 'keep him straight' on any point whatever."

—The Nation *magazine*

Brief Presidency

During his short time as president, Garfield faced two unpleasant issues, the first of which was the Star Route case. Western postal officials had secretly schemed with stagecoach operators to steal funds, such as tax collections, that were being delivered to Washington. Garfield quickly assembled a team of government prosecutors to try the case.

Left: A political cartoon published after Garfield became a presidential candidate.

Right: Garfield's inaugural parade.

The Garfield Administration

Administration Dates: March 4, 1881–September 19, 1881

Vice President: Chester A. Arthur (1881)

Cabinet:

Secretary of State	James G. Blaine (1881)
Secretary of the Treasury	William Windom (1881)
Secretary of War	Robert Todd Lincoln (1881)
Attorney General	Wayne MacVeagh (1881)
Secretary of the Navy	William H. Hunt (1881)
Postmaster General	Thomas L. James (1881)
Secretary of the Interior	Samuel J. Kirkwood (1881)

The second issue involved patronage, a problem that had seemed dead, but came back again as he took office. Garfield appointed James G. Blaine as his secretary of state, generally passing over men who had connections with the party's Stalwart faction. Congress had to approve his appointments, and Roscoe Conkling tried to block them. When he failed, Conkling resigned his position in protest.

Garfield pushed for legislation to reform the patronage system, but he wasn't able to follow through. While he was waiting in a Washington train station to begin a trip through New England on the morning of July 2, 1881, Garfield was shot several times by a crazed assassin, Charles J. Guiteau. A religious fanatic, Stalwart supporter, and former civil servant, Guiteau was angry at having been passed over for a government job, and he was determined to kill the president "to unite the Republican Party and save the Republic."

Right Place at the Wrong Time

Robert Todd Lincoln, son of President Lincoln and later Garfield's secretary of war, had been the first person called when his father was assassinated. He was also with James A. Garfield on the day he was shot, and he was nearby when President William McKinley was assassinated twenty years later.

The wounded president was taken back to the executive mansion, where surgeons removed bullets from his body. A metal detector—a recent invention by Alexander Graham Bell—was used to locate the bullets in Garfield's body, but one bullet remained undetected because of interference: Garfield was lying on a bed with metal springs, which disrupted the metal detector's readings.

An infection caused by that wayward bullet continued to spread, and Garfield was never strong enough to leave his bed. He was moved to Elberon, on the New Jersey Shore, away from the heat of Washington and hubbub of the executive mansion to be with his family. Garfield died on September 19, 1881, ten weeks after he was wounded.

In a eulogy for Garfield, Secretary of State Blaine recalled the president's own great speechmaking skills: "He was a preeminently fair and candid man in debate, took no petty advantage, stooped to no unworthy methods, avoided personal allusions, rarely appealed to prejudice, did not seek to inflame passion."

Below: Garfield was shot at the Baltimore and Potomac Railroad Depot on July 2, 1881.

Below: The wounded president was taken to the White House, where he died ten weeks later.

Alexander Graham Bell

Remembered as the inventor of the telephone, Alexander Graham Bell was also an outstanding teacher of the deaf, a prolific inventor of other devices, and a leading figure in the scientific community. He invented the graphophone—the first sound recorder—as well as the photophone, which transmitted speech by light rays. Among his other innovations were the audiometer, a device for the deaf; the induction balance, used to locate metallic objects in the human body; and disc and cylindrical wax recorders for phonographs. The prestigious journal Science, which became the official publication of the American Association for the Advancement of Science, was founded primarily through his efforts. Bell was also involved in establishing the National Geographic Society.

Bell was born in Edinburgh, Scotland, to a family of speech educators. His father, Alexander Melville Bell, had invented visible speech, a code of symbols for all spoken sounds that was used in teaching deaf people to speak. Young Bell began studying at Edinburgh University in 1864 and assisted his father at University College in London from 1868 to 1870. During these years, he became deeply interested in the study of sound and the mechanics of speech, which gave him the idea of telegraphing speech. After Bell's two brothers died of tuberculosis, his father took the family to the healthier climate of Canada in 1870. The following year, Bell journeyed to Boston, Massachusetts, to join the staff of the Boston School for the Deaf. In 1872, he opened his own school in Boston for training teachers of the deaf.

Bell's interest in speech and communication led him to research the transmission of sound over wires. In particular, he experimented with the development of the harmonic telegraph, a device that could send multiple messages simultaneously over a single wire. Bell also worked on the transmission of the human voice, experimenting with vibrating membranes and an actual human ear. He was backed financially in his investigations by Gardiner Hubbard and Thomas Sanders, fathers of two of his deaf pupils. Early in 1874, Bell met Thomas A. Watson, a young machinist at a Boston electrical shop. Watson became Bell's indispensable assistant, bringing technical expertise in electrical engineering to his experiments.

Together, Bell and Watson spent endless hours experimenting. On June 2, 1875, the critical breakthrough on the telephone accidentally came about while they were working on the telegraph. When a stuck reed on Watson's transmitter changed an intermittent current into a continuous one, Bell, who had extraordinarily sharp hearing, picked up the sound on his receiver in another room. This event confirmed what Bell had previously suspected: Only continuous, varying electrical current can transmit and reconvert continuously varying sound waves. On March 10, 1876, Bell tested a new transmitter. Watson, who was in an adjoining room with a receiver, clearly heard Bell's summons: "Mr. Watson, come here, I want you!" It was the first message transmitted by telephone. The new invention was exhibited at the Philadelphia Centennial Exposition the following June. Together with financial backers Hubbard and Sanders, Bell and Watson formed the Bell Telephone Company in 1877.

After marrying Mabel Hubbard, the daughter of his new partner, Bell sailed to England to promote the telephone. Bell Telephone grew rapidly, making Bell a wealthy man. Upon returning to the United States in 1879, he pursued other interests but also spent much of the next several years defending hundreds of lawsuits over his patents. (All of his patents were finally upheld by the U.S. Supreme Court in 1888.) Pursuing a wide range of interests, Bell worked on air conditioning, an improved strain of sheep (to bear multiple lambs), an early iron lung, and sonar detection of icebergs. In 1881, one of Bell's inventions, a metal detector, was used to locate bullets in President James Garfield's body.

After 1895, Bell turned his attention to aviation. He invented the tetrahedral kite, which is capable of carrying a human being. He helped found the Aerial Experiment Association in 1907. He also designed a hydrofoil boat that set the world water speed record in 1918. Bell, who became a U.S. citizen in 1882, died at his summer home on Cape Breton Island, Nova Scotia, in 1922.

Portrait of an Assassin

In 1872, a strange man, who in his checkered career had been a street-corner evangelist, a bill collector, a storefront lawyer, and a blackmailer, decided to try his hand at politics. He thought an ambassadorship would be nice and might even lead to the presidency.

Charles Julius Guiteau took the first step by writing a campaign speech supporting Horace Greeley in the 1872 election, and he delivered it every time he got the chance. When Greeley lost the election, Guiteau went back to preaching on street corners, but he believed that God had singled him out for greater things, and when Ulysses S. Grant emerged as a contender for the Republican presidential nomination in 1880, he changed a few words in his Greeley speech and got ready to take the hustings for Grant.

As it turned out, James A. Garfield got the nomination, but that was no problem for Guiteau. All it took was a new title and a new paragraph or two, and after sending his speech off to the printer, he sat back to wait for invitations to join the campaign. None came, but when Garfield was elected, Guiteau knew in his heart that his speech had done the trick.

He spent the next several months hanging around the lobby of the Fifth Avenue Hotel, the New York City headquarters of the Republican Party, and he developed a nodding acquaintance with all the politicians who rushed past him every day. He came to believe that they were his close friends, and he expected to get the red carpet treatment from the new administration in Washington.

To his credit, the new president didn't even smirk when the scruffy little man demanded an appointment as minister to Austria, or even when he said Paris would do after being told the job had been filled. Garfield turned the matter over to James G. Blaine, his secretary of state, and Guiteau was sure that the job was in the bag. After all, Blaine had often tipped his hat to him back in New York.

Of course, it wasn't, so Guiteau began haunting the State Department and the executive mansion, leaving behind notes he signed only with his initials. But after two months of daily visits, he began to get the message, and he decided that "if the president was out of the way, everything would go better." He didn't have much money, but he invested in an expensive handgun, convinced that it would one day be a museum piece. Then he started stalking Garfield, waiting for the right moment to act. Because Guiteau had worn out his welcome at the president's home, he couldn't gun down Garfield there, and since he didn't know how to handle a gun, Guiteau didn't want to shoot into a crowd, but he knew his opportunity would come.

It came a full month after he began stalking Garfield, and after he had come close to shooting on three separate occasions before losing his nerve each time. As Garfield was crossing the waiting room of Washington's Baltimore & Potomac Railroad Station, Guiteau fired two bullets, one into the president's back and the other into his arm, and then surrendered to the nearest police officer. He had already checked out the police station, and knew he'd be safe from a lynch mob there.

At his trial, he claimed that the Lord had made him do it, but he was sentenced to hang anyway. As he mounted the scaffold he said, "I am going to the Lordy. I am so glad."

Legacy

With James A. Garfield's death, political support for civil service reform gradually became more serious. After legislation was held up in Congress, his successor, Chester A. Arthur, helped push a bill through, and he signed the Pendleton Act two years later. It created the Civil Service Commission, an agency that reviews political appointments to ensure that they are based on merit rather than handed out as political favors.

A new era of political reform began, and the Republican Party was gradually transformed from a collection of political factions into a more united party by the 1890s. Although Garfield's term was much too short to evaluate, he was a forerunner of the more powerful presidents who were elected after him on through World War I.

Lucretia Garfield

Born April 19, 1832, Hiram, Ohio
Died March 13, 1918, South Pasadena, California

"[Lucretia] grows up to every new emergency with fine tact and faultless taste."

—James A. Garfield

It was fitting that Lucretia Rudolph and James A. Garfield first met as youngsters in school. They both loved reading and both later became teachers. Exchanging letters helped them through many separations when Garfield spent long periods away from home as a Civil War commander and as a politician. "Crete," as Garfield called his wife, stayed behind at home in Ohio raising their children. The family later maintained two homes: one in Washington, where Garfield served in Congress for seventeen years before becoming president, and the other in Ohio.

Three in One

Rutherford B. Hayes's term of office ended on March 3, 1881, and James A. Garfield became president. When he died in September, Chester A. Arthur took the oath of office, giving America three presidents in a single year. It had happened once before, in 1841, when Martin Van Buren left office on March 3, and was followed by William Henry Harrison, who died a month later, and John Tyler became the third president in a single year.

When she was a young schoolteacher, Lucretia challenged the system that automatically paid her less for similar work than her male counterparts, but the public never saw that independent-thinking side of her. During the nineteenth century wives of politicians were expected to keep their opinions to themselves, and Garfield agreed, but she preferred to stay out of the public eye anyway. The letters she exchanged with her husband reveal a progressive-minded woman who likely kept her own views to herself for the sake of appearances.

Lucretia was most widely known to the public for the grace she displayed during the difficult period after the assassination of her husband. She herself was ill at the time, but she nursed him while he tried to recover from the bullet wounds.

Raised on Religion and Learning

Lucretia Rudolph was born on April 19, 1832, in Hiram, Ohio. Her father, Zebulon, was a leading citizen of the town and in the Disciples of Christ religious group. She went to local schools and also had the benefit of a fine education at home. In her teens, she enrolled at the Western Reserve Eclectic Institute, a school of higher learning founded by the Disciples of Christ.

Lucretia first met James Garfield at school when they were children. He lived in a nearby town, but he left for Cleveland when he was a teenager. Inspired by sea stories, he attempted to become a crew member on a ship heading out for an ocean voyage. But after a disappointing interview with a drunken sea captain, he decided instead to work on canal boats. However, he contracted a case of malaria, and had to go back home to recover. His mother convinced him that he ought to finish school, and Garfield enrolled at the Western Reserve Eclectic Institute, where he rediscovered Lucretia Rudolph.

Both Garfield and Lucretia were excellent public speakers. Lucretia became a schoolteacher, and Garfield went off to college in Massachusetts. Although they corresponded frequently, he had fallen in love with another woman in Massachusetts. But he went back to Ohio to teach at the Institute, which had been renamed Hiram College, where he renewed his romance with Lucretia. They married in 1858.

Meanwhile, Garfield's career was blossoming. He was so popular as a professor at Hiram College that he was elected its president. When the Civil War began in 1861, he was made a colonel, heading a group of volunteers, many of whom had been his former students, and were enthusiastic about following him into battle.

By 1863, Garfield had become a war hero, and his exploits were widely known back home. He was already a popular speaker, having campaigned vigorously for Abraham Lincoln, who won the presidential election of 1860, and he was elected to the House of Representatives in 1863. Lucretia stayed in Ohio after he came home from the war and headed on to Washington, and the couple's relationship was strained when Garfield had an extramarital affair with a widow from New York. Then, after the Garfields drew close together again, they suffered the death of their three-year-old daughter.

When they relocated to Washington, the Garfields met regularly with a literary society, a group that met to discuss books they had read, and often hosted its gatherings in their home. Lucretia was fond of small dinners and conversation, a preference she maintained when her husband was elected president in 1880. Rather than having large-scale parties or formal dinners, the Garfields made a habit of having twice-weekly receptions where one could dine and talk with friends and politicians in a more intimate setting than large parties and lavish balls. The schedule of small receptions ended all too soon, however.

New Emergencies

Garfield had once observed that Lucretia "grows up to every new emergency with fine tact and faultless taste." He was commenting on how she had endured the deaths of two of their children, their marital problems, and everyday political pressures as he battled with his political opponents. A new series of emergencies began shortly after Garfield took on the office of president.

In May 1881, just weeks after Garfield's inauguration, Lucretia fell ill with symptoms of malaria and exhaustion, and she was taken to the seaside town of Long Branch, New Jersey, to restore her health and strength.

She was there on the morning of July 2, 1881, when Garfield waited for a train that would take him to New England, with a stopover to visit her. He never boarded the train. He was shot several times in the station, and rushed back to the executive mansion a few blocks away for emergency care. Although she was still frail and exhausted, Lucretia rushed back to Washington by special train. She was at her husband's side during the three months he fought for his life. An outpouring of sympathy and respect from all over the country helped her survive the long ordeal.

Garfield was moved to Elberon, New Jersey, so that his whole family could be with him in a more private setting. But the president never recovered. He died from his wounds on September 19, 1881, ten weeks after the shooting.

The images of Lucretia Garfield and her children at the funeral services were very moving. She was described as having coped during the difficult time with dignity and strength, in spite of her own weakened health. One of her daughters, Caroline, shed a long, slow tear during the service—an image that was widely described in newspaper reports throughout the country.

Following the funeral, the Garfield family went back to their farm in Ohio. Lucretia Garfield lived another thirty-six years, mostly in seclusion. She supervised the

Below: Pages from Lucretia's diary discussing her husband's election.

preservation of her husband's papers and correspondences—still among the largest of any president. Her correspondences and diaries are also part of the collection. They reveal a woman who had a strong sense of independence that she kept to herself for the sake of social propriety and her husband's career.

She lived to see her children grow up and become successful. Harry, the eldest, was a lawyer and a professor and later became president of Williams College, in Massachusetts, a school his father had attended. James was a lawyer and politician who served as secretary of the interior under President Theodore Roosevelt. Irwin was a lawyer; Abram was an architect; and the youngest, Mollie, married Joseph S. Brown, who had been her father's private secretary while he was president.

Lucretia Garfield died on March 13, 1918. She was buried in the tomb of the Garfield Monument in Cleveland, Ohio, next to her husband.

Garfield's "Revolution Against the Constitution" Speech

Delivered on March 29, 1879

Following the end of Reconstruction in 1877, Democrats made large gains in congressional elections in the South. Northern Republicans had been responsible for Reconstruction programs that undermined the powers of individual Southern states—partly to protect the rights of recently freed slaves, and partly to maintain its own influence over the national government. No Democrat was elected president from 1860 through 1884.

A Democratic majority gained control of the House of Representatives in 1878. They wanted to remove the last example of Reconstruction and return full constitutional power to the Southern states. Nevertheless, the federal government continued to supervise elections in the South because of widespread evidence that African-American voters were being intimidated from voting—through laws enacted to discriminate against them, and often through violence.

James A. Garfield, a Republican congressman from Ohio, had served on the special committee that investigated voter fraud during the 1876 presidential election, of which Rutherford B. Hayes had been declared the winner. Garfield had interviewed many people as part of his investigation, and found evidence supporting many examples of fraud. That led him to continue supporting federal supervision of elections in the South.

A Democratic majority in the House of Representatives in 1879 consistently added riders to basic appropriations bills—legislation that provided funding for government programs—that were their attempts to pass legislation that they knew the president would otherwise veto. One such rider prohibited the use of federal troops to supervise elections. Since that rider was attached to an important funding bill, Congress either had to pass the entire piece of legislation or deny important funding to government programs.

Garfield viewed this situation as unconstitutional. Usually a dignified speaker, he made an impassioned speech before Congress, declaring that Democrats supporting the rider were attempting to revolt against the federal government. He accused congressmen of "resolv[ing] to enter upon a revolution against the Constitution and government of the United States."

Excerpt from "Revolution Against the Constitution"

Mr. Chairman, I have no hope of being able to convey to the members of this House my own conviction of the very great gravity and solemnity of the crisis which this decision of the chair and of the Committee of the Whole has brought upon this country. I wish I could be proved a false prophet in reference to the result of this action. I wish I could be overwhelmed with the proof that I am utterly mistaken in my views. But no view I have ever taken has entered more deeply and more seriously into my conviction than this, that the House has today resolved to enter upon a revolution against the Constitution and government of the United States. I do not know that this intention exists in the minds of half the representatives who occupy the other side of this hall; I hope it does not; I am ready to believe it does not exist to any great extent; but I affirm that the consequence of the programme just adopted, if persisted in, will be nothing less than the total subversion of this government. Let me in the outset state, as carefully as I may, the precise situation.

At the last session, all our ordinary legislative work was done in accordance with the usages of the House of Senate, except the passage of two bills. Two of the twelve great appropriation bills for the support of the government were agreed to in both houses as to every matter of detail concerning the appropriations proper. We were assured by the committees of conference in both bodies that there would be no difficulty in adjusting all differences in reference to the amounts of money to be appropriated and the objects of their appropriation. But the House of Representatives proposed three measures of distinctly independent legislation; one upon the army appropriation bill, and two upon the legislative appropriation bill. The three grouped together are briefly these: first, the substantial modification of certain sections of the law relating to the use of the army; second, the repeal of the jurors' test oath; and third, the repeal of the laws regulating elections of members of Congress. These three propositions of legislation were insisted upon by the House, but the Senate refused to adopt them. So far it was an ordinary proceeding, one which occurs frequently in all legislative bodies. The Senate said to us through their conferees, "We are ready to pass the appropriation bills; but we are unwilling to pass as riders the three legislative measures you ask us to pass." Thereupon the House, through its conference committee, made the following declaration—and in order that I may do exact justice, I read from the speech [...] on the report of the second conference committee on the Legislative, Executive, and Judicial Appropriation Bill:

"The Democratic conferees on the part of the House seemed determined that unless those rights were secured to the people"—alluding to the three points I have named—"in the bills sent to the Senate, they would refuse, under their constitutional right, to make appropriations to carry on the government, if the dominant majority in the Senate insisted upon the maintenance of these laws and refused to consent to their repeal."

Then, after stating that, if the position they had taken compelled an extra session, the new Congress would offer the repealing bills separately, and forecasting what would happen when the new House should be under no necessity of coercing the Senate, he said:—

"If, however, the president of the United States, in the exercise of the power vested in him, should see fit to veto the bills thus presented to him, [...] then I have no doubt those same amendments will be again made part of the appropriation bills, and it will be for the president to determine whether he will block the wheels of government and refuse to accept necessary appropriations rather than allow the representatives of the people to repeal odious laws which they regard as subversive of their rights and privileges.... Whether that course is right or wrong, it will be adopted, and I have no doubt adhered to, no matter what happens with the appropriation bills."

That was the proposition made by the Democracy in Congress at the close of the Congress now dead.

Another distinguished senator, Mr. [Allen G.] Thurman, of Ohio—and I may properly refer to senators of a Congress not now in existence—reviewing the situation, declared in still more succinct terms: "We claim the right, which the House of Commons in England established after two centuries of contest, to say that we will not grant the money of the people unless there is a redress of grievances. [...]"

The question, Mr. Chairman, may be asked, Why make any special resistance to certain repealing clauses in this bill, which a good many gentlemen on this side declared at the last session that they cared but little about, and regarded as of very little practical importance, because for years there had been no actual use for any part of the laws proposed to be repealed, and they had no expectation there would be any? It may be asked, Why make any controversy on either side? So far as we are concerned, Mr. Chairman, I desire to say this. We recognize the other side as accomplished parliamentarians and strategists, who have adopted with skill and adroitness their plan of assault. You have placed in the front one of the least objectionable of your measures; but your whole programme has been announced, and we reply to your whole order of battle. The logic of your position compels us to meet you as promptly on the skirmish line as afterward when our intrenchments are assailed; and therefore, at the outset, we plant our case upon the general ground where we have chosen to defend it. [...]

Up to this hour our sovereign has never failed us. There had never been such a refusal to exercise those primary functions of sovereignty as either to endanger or cripple the government; nor have the majority of the representatives of that sovereign, in either house of Congress, ever before announced their purpose to use their voluntary powers for its destruction. And now, for the first time in our history—and I will add, for the first time for at least two centuries in the history of any English-speaking nation—it is suggested and threatened that these voluntary powers of Congress shall be used for the destruction of the government. I want it distinctly understood that the proposition which I read at the beginning of my remarks, and which is the programme announced to the American people today, is this: that if this House cannot have its own way in certain matters not connected with appropriations, it will so use or refrain from using its voluntary powers as to destroy the government.

Now, Mr. Chairman, it has been said on the other side, that, when a demand for the redress of grievances is made, the authority that runs the risk of stopping and destroying the government is the one that resists the redress. Not so. If gentlemen will do me the honor to follow my thought for a moment more, I trust I shall make this denial good.

Our theory of law is free consent. That is the granite foundation of our whole superstructure. Nothing in this republic can be law without consent—the free consent of the House, the free consent of the Senate, the free consent of the executive, or, if he refuse it, the free consent of two thirds of these bodies. Will any man deny that? Will any man challenge a letter of the statement that free consent is the foundation of all our institutions? And yet the programme announced two weeks ago was, that, if the Senate refused to consent to the demand of the House, the government should stop. And the proposition was then, and the proposition is now, that, although there is not a Senate to be coerced, there is still a third independent branch of the legislative power of the government whose consent is to be coerced at the peril of the destruction of this government; that is, if the president, in the discharge of his duty, shall exercise his plain constitutional right to refuse his consent to this proposed legislation, the Congress will so use its voluntary powers as to destroy the government. This is the proposition which we confront; and we denounced it as revolution.

It makes no difference, Mr. Chairman, what the issue is. If it were the simplest and most inoffensive proposition in the world, yet if you demand, as a measure of coercion, that it shall be adopted against the free consent prescribed in the Constitution, every fair-minded man in America is bound to resist you as much as though his own life depended upon his resistance. Let it be understood that I am not arguing the merits of any one of the three amendments. I am discussing the proposed method of legislation; and I declare that it is against the Constitution of our country. It is revolutionary to the core, and is destructive of the fundamental principle of American liberty, the free consent of all the powers that unite to make laws. In opening this debate, I challenge all comers to show a single instance in our history where this consent has been thus coerced. This is the great, the paramount issue, which dwarfs all others into insignificance.

I now turn aside from the line of my argument, for a moment, to say that it is not a little surprising that our friends on the other side should have gone into this great contest on so weak a cause as the one embraced in the pending amendment to this bill. [French novelist] Victor Hugo said, in his description of the battle of Waterloo, that the struggle of the two armies was like the wrestling of two giants, when a chip under the heel of either might determine the victory. It may be that this amendment is the chip under your heel, or it may be that it is the chip on our shoulder; as a chip, it is of small account to you or to us; but when it represents the integrity of the Constitution, and is assailed by revolution, we fight for it. […]

And now, Mr. Chairman, I ask the forbearance of gentlemen on the other side while I offer a suggestion, which I make with reluctance. They will bear me witness that I have, in many ways, shown my desire that the wounds of the war should be healed; that the grass which has grown green over the graves of the dead of both armies might symbolize the returning spring of friendship and peace between citizens who were lately in arms against each other. But I am compelled by the conduct of the other side to refer to a chapter of our recent history.

The last act of Democratic domination in this Capitol, eighteen years ago, was striking and dramatic, perhaps heroic. Then the Democratic Party said to the Republicans, "If you elect the man of your choice president of the United States, we will shoot your government to death"; but the People of this country, refusing to be coerced by threats or violence, voted as they pleased, and lawfully elected Abraham Lincoln president. Then your leaders, though holding a majority in the other branch of Congress, were heroic enough to withdraw from their seats and fling down the gage of mortal battle. We called it rebellion; but we recognized it as courageous and manly to avow your purpose, take all the risks, and fight it out in the open field. Notwithstanding your utmost efforts to destroy it, the government was saved. […] And now lawfully, in the exercise of our right as representatives, we take up the gage you have this day thrown down, and appeal again to our common sovereign to determine whether you shall be permitted to destroy the principle of free consent in legislation under the threat of starving the government to death.

We are ready to pass these bills for the support of the government at any hour when you will offer them in the ordinary way, by the methods prescribed by the Constitution. If you offer your other propositions as separate measures, we will meet you in the fraternal spirit of fair debate and will discuss their merits. Some of your measures many of us will vote for in separate bills. But you shall not coerce any independent branch of this government, even by the threat of starvation, to surrender its lawful powers until the question has been appealed to the sovereign and decided in your favor. On this ground we plant ourselves, and here we will stand to the end.

What Happened Next

Garfield's speech proved decisive, as he rallied all Republicans and some Democrats to back his position. The basic appropriations bills were finally passed without the riders. His impassioned speech helped him become the Republican candidate for the presidential election of 1880, and his speech before Congress was reprinted and distributed as part of his campaign literature during his successful run for the presidency.

Garfield showed promise as an independent and powerful president, but he was assassinated in 1881 after only a few months in office. Since the 1865 assassination of President Lincoln, Congress had come to dominate the federal government. Garfield might have become the first president to reassert the firm authority of the executive branch of the U.S. government. Instead, he helped restore the power of the presidency by setting in motion a trend of executive leadership that was broadened by presidents Grover Cleveland and William McKinley.

Chester A. Arthur

"All personal considerations and political views must be merged in the national sorrow. I am among millions grieving for their wounded chief [President James A. Garfield]."

—*Chester A. Arthur*

Twenty-first president of the United States, 1881–1885

Full name: *Chester Alan Arthur*

Born: *October 5, 1829, Fairfield, Vermont*

Died: *November 18, 1886, New York, New York*

Burial site: *Rural Cemetery, Albany, New York*

Parents: *William and Malvina Stone Arthur*

Spouse: *Ellen Lewis Herndon (1837–1880; m. 1859)*

Children: *William Lewis Herndon (1860–1863); Chester Alan Jr. (1864–1937); Ellen Herndon (1871–1915)*

Religion: *Episcopalian*

Education: *Union College (B.A., 1848; M.A., 1851)*

Occupations: *Educator; attorney*

Government positions: *Vice president under James A. Garfield*

Political party: *Republican*

Dates as president: *September 20, 1881–March 4, 1885*

Age upon taking office: *51*

A fancy dresser, an expert on fine food and wine, and a cheery conversationalist, Chester A. Arthur was nicknamed "the Elegant Arthur" and "the Gentleman Boss," although his friends called him "Chet." He had risen to become a powerful boss in the New York political machine known as the Stalwarts, which had unchallenged control of the state Republican Party and had a great deal of national influence as well, in the years after the Civil War.

Arthur, in fact, had been nominated as a vice presidential candidate in order to please the Stalwarts. Their candidate for the 1880 presidential election, former president Ulysses S. Grant, was passed over at the Republican convention in favor of James A. Garfield, who represented different party factions, and Arthur was chosen as his running mate to ensure that Stalwarts would unite behind the ticket and help the party win in the electoral-vote–rich eastern states. It was a politically brilliant strategy, and it worked.

Chester A. Arthur's career had greatly benefited from the patronage system, which afforded elected officials the opportunity to reward their supporters with government jobs. Garfield and Arthur were an odd combination,

1829: Born in Vermont
1844: Holds first political job, as a crier—a boy who stands on street corners and shouts out the name and qualifications of a candidate running for office
1848: Graduates from Union College
1854: Certified as a lawyer
1860–63: Named chief of the state military of New York, an honorary position that becomes important with the beginning of the Civil War
1868: Named collector of the New York Customs House
1877: Fired from Customs House position by President Rutherford B. Hayes
1880: Nominated as surprise vice-presidential candidate to James Garfield
1881: Assumes presidency following the assassination of Garfield
1881–85: Serves as twenty-first U.S. president
1886: Dies in New York

because Garfield wanted to reform civil service that was putting party loyalty above ability. Garfield's quest ended when he was assassinated just a few months after taking office, and when Arthur succeeded him, everyone expected that civil service reform would be a dead issue with the Gentleman Boss.

But Arthur surprised them all by pushing for and achieving an end to the patronage system. It cost him support from his party, but he managed to be a fairly effective president without much help from Congress. His small-scale victories were early signs that national political reform might be possible and that America could rise above divisive partisanship at last.

Country Boy

Chester Alan Arthur was born in Fairfield, Vermont, on October 5, 1829, the eldest of the seven children of William and Malvina Stone Arthur. His father was an Irish-born Baptist minister and schoolteacher who had a quick temper and difficulty keeping jobs in Baptist congregations. The family moved frequently among towns in Vermont and northern New York, which

prompted some of his political enemies to claim that he had been born further north, in Canada, and wasn't eligible to serve as president.

The family settled in New York's Saratoga County in 1839, and although Chet would grow up to be an unabashed city slicker, concerned with fashion and culture, he often slipped off to the country to do some fishing, a hobby cultivated as a boy. Salmon fishing was his idea of pure joy.

He got his first political job when he fifteen in 1844, working for pennies as a "crier," standing on street corners and shouting out the names and qualifications of candidates who paid him; in this case it was the Whig presidential candidate, Henry Clay.

Arthur graduated from Union College—then regarded as one of the finest schools in the East—at Schenectady, New York, in 1848. He was in the top third of his class and a member of Phi Beta Kappa. He taught school and studied law after that, and he was principal of North Pownal Academy in Bennington, Vermont, when James A. Garfield taught there for one semester. He moved to New York City to study in a law office and was certified as a lawyer in 1854.

He quickly established a reputation as one of the best attorneys in New York, a city that even then had more than its share of them. Involved in several civil-rights

Below: Fishing was among Arthur's many passions.

Arthur had a chubby round face framed by bushy side-whiskers. By the time he became president, the six-footer weighed more than 225 pounds, thanks to his enthusiasm for lavish dinner parties back in New York. He dressed expensively, and his wardrobe was said to have included eighty pairs of trousers. He changed his clothes several times a day to suit the occasion.

Above: Chester Arthur was a very dapper dresser.

cases, Arthur successfully represented Lizzie Jennings, an African-American woman who sued the city of New York for the right to ride on city streetcars. The suit was successful, and the color bar was dropped, at least in public transportation.

Arthur's interest in civil rights led him to get involved in politics. He lent his support to protests over the Kansas-Nebraska Act of 1854 that would allow those states to decide for themselves whether or not to permit slavery when they entered the Union. The Republican Party was formed around that time to oppose expansion of slave territory, and Arthur was active at the convention that established it in New York. He supported the candidacy of John Frémont, the Party's first presidential candidate, in 1856, and he also supported the successful election of Abraham Lincoln four years later.

Arthur left New York for a short time to try his luck with a law practice in Kansas, and shortly after he gave up on it, he began courting Ellen Lewis Herndon, the sister of a friend of his, who came from a wealthy family and shared his taste for high fashion and culture. They were married in 1859, and would have three children, two of whom grew to adulthood.

In 1860, New York governor Edwin D. Morgan appointed Arthur engineer in chief of the state military, which carried the rank of brigadier general. Though the job was an honorary one with no paycheck attached, it did put him in charge of supervising the state's military operations, which made it a very powerful post when the Civil War broke out. He was in charge of recruiting soldiers and making sure that that they were fully equipped for battle. By 1863, more than 200,000 New Yorkers had been outfitted for war.

Arthur was relieved from the position in 1863 when a Democrat became governor of New York. He had won and then lost the job because of patronage, and the system came back to help him again a short time later when Senator Roscoe Conkling of New York made a deal with him to build and run a state political machine.

Arthur organized voters and regularly recommended Conkling supporters for government jobs, and little by little, Conkling's machine became powerful enough by 1868 to become a factor in national Republican politics with its support of New York resident and Civil War general Ulysses S. Grant for the presidency.

Above: Roscoe Conkling.

The Arthur Administration

Administration Dates: September 20, 1881–March 4, 1885

Vice President: None (1881–85)

Cabinet:

Secretary of State	James G. Blaine (1881)
	Frederick T. Frelinghuysen (1881–85)
Secretary of the Treasury	William Windom (1881)
	Charles J. Folger (1881–84)
	Walter Q. Gresham (1884)
	Hugh McCulloch (1884–85)
Secretary of War	Robert Todd Lincoln (1881–85)
Attorney General	Wayne MacVeagh (1881)
	Benjamin H. Brewster (1882–85)
Secretary of the Navy	William H. Hunt (1881–82)
	William E. Chandler (1882–85)
Postmaster General	Thomas L. James (1881–82)
	Timothy O. Howe (1882–83)
	Walter Q. Gresham (1883–84)
	Frank Hatton (1884–85)
Secretary of the Interior	Samuel J. Kirkwood (1881–82)
	Henry M. Teller (1882–85)

Roscoe Conkling

Born on October 30, 1829, in Albany, New York, Roscoe Conkling attended Mount Washington Collegiate Institute and studied law. He became a lawyer and rose quickly to the position of district attorney of Albany. Becoming a powerful figure in the new Republican Party (founded in 1854), he moved to Utica, New York, and was elected the city's mayor. In 1858, he was elected to the House of Representatives, where he served from 1859 to 1863 and 1865 to 1867. A staunch supporter of Thaddeus Stevens and the Radical Republicans, Conkling sat on the committee that drafted the Radical program of Reconstruction meant to punish Southern states following the Civil War.

By 1867, Conkling controlled the New York State Republican organization. He was elected to the Senate and became a devoted follower of President Ulysses S. Grant, who served as chief executive from 1869 to 1877. Conkling was able to place supporters in the New York Customs House, which collected a majority of the nation's taxes on imported goods. Conkling used the operation to build a strong party organization called the "Stalwarts" that provided jobs and involved workers in donations of time and money to the Republican Party. President Grant offered to make him Chief Justice of the United States in 1873, and President Chester A. Arthur, one of Conkling's leading supporters, offered him a seat on the Court a decade later. Both times, he declined.

Conkling had a brilliant, quick mind in debate and saved his most scathing remarks for reformers who sought to eliminate political patronage through civil service reform. Conkling worked hard in 1880 to have Grant elected to the presidency for a third time, but Republicans nominated James A. Garfield of Ohio. Conkling battled with President Garfield over the patronage issue. In an attempt to rebuff him, Conkling resigned his Senate seat: He planned to be reelected to show up Garfield and demonstrate his personal power in New York. Unfortunately, Garfield was assassinated by a madman claiming to be a "Stalwart," and the shocked New York Legislature refused to elect Conkling back to the Senate seat he had vacated. Conkling retired to a lucrative legal practice and to fashionable New York City society. He died in New York City on April 18, 1888.

To the Victors Go the Spoils

As expected, Arthur was rewarded generously for delivering votes for Grant. He was named collector of the New York Customs House, a huge operation employing more than 1,000 workers responsible for collecting almost 70 percent of all taxes on imported goods. Everyone on

Opportunity

When Chester A. Arthur became the collector of customs in the Port of New York, it was the busiest port in the world, and the biggest source of revenue for the federal government. His salary was $50,000 a year, the same as the president's. Members of Congress and Supreme Court Justices were only paid $7,500 at the time. But Chet Arthur controlled an annual payroll of more than $2 million, which represented potential employee kickbacks of some $40,000 a year to the Republican Party, and he was the man who decided who got jobs and who kept them.

the staff, which included a great many more employees than were actually needed, were Republicans who spent a good portion of their work hours on party causes. As one of the party's most important patronage dispensers, Arthur became a significant leader of a Republican faction called the Stalwarts, who offered full support for all Republican policies and could also deliver thousands and thousands of votes.

The system Arthur established for the Customs House was not illegal at the time. Employees did not directly benefit financially, other than performing little work for good pay. Part of their wages was donated to the Republican Party—a legal maneuver at the time, but regarded as vaguely corrupt even then.

The patronage system was just one of many scandals that riddled the Grant administration. By the 1876 presidential election, scandal was so widespread that Republicans faced the real possibility of losing control of the presidency after having won the previous four national elections. Their nominee, Rutherford B. Hayes helped head off defeat in the controversial election of 1876 by promising to reform the civil service system.

Shortly after he took office, Hayes started taking action on his promise, first by setting his sites on the high-profile Customs House. Charging that Arthur had used his position inappropriately, Hayes bluntly asked him to quit. But Arthur had a powerful protector in the person of Senator Conkling who promised a Senate challenge to Hayes's action. But the president outsmarted him by waiting until the Senate adjourned for the summer and then fired Arthur.

Arthur returned to his law practice and managed to restore his reputation, and he was still a major power

broker when the next election came around. Hayes had promised to serve only one term, but by 1880 he wasn't popular enough to run for reelection anyway.

The Republican Stalwarts named former president Grant as their candidate, while another wing of the Party, the Half-Breeds, nominated Maine senator James G. Blaine. The Half-Breeds embraced a wider variety of positions on issues than the Stalwarts, and they based their center of power in Washington. A third candidate, Secretary of the Treasury John Sherman, was backed by the strong Ohio-based Republican Party led by Congressman James A. Garfield. Outgoing president Hayes was also from Ohio.

After thirty-five rounds of balloting at the Republican national convention, no candidate had gathered enough delegates to win the nomination, and Sherman and Blaine decided to drop out of the running in favor of James Garfield, an eight-term congressman who had served as Sherman's campaign manager and was well respected among all the factions. After Garfield won the nomination, the convention chose Arthur, who had never run for any office before, as his running mate to pacify the Stalwarts and to ensure that Republicans could win in eastern states. The ploy worked: Garfield won the election by fewer than ten thousand votes, but he won all of the important eastern states for a sure victory in the Electoral College.

Options

When President Hayes tried to fire Chet Arthur, he gave him the option of an ambassadorship so he could leave New York with his head held high, but Arthur preferred to take his chances and sit tight. The firing was the result of an investigation that concluded that the operation of the Customs House was overstaffed, inefficient, and corrupt. Few employees collected less than $500 a year in bribes, mostly to rush shipments through, and many admitted to taking twice as much. Arthur retorted that he was running a tight ship, but himself almost never showed up for work until after lunch, and he had to admit he couldn't vouch for his employees. Hayes finally got him four months later when a government investigator found a Customs House employee who had pocketed some $40,000 of Uncle Sam's money and then was promoted.

James G. Blaine

James Gillespie Blaine was among the most powerful American politicians of the second half of the nineteenth century. He served twice as secretary of state and was a presidential candidate on several occasions. He was born January 31, 1830, in West Brownsville, Pennsylvania. His father, Ephraim Lyon Blaine, was a lawyer and a county clerk. Blaine graduated from local Washington and Jefferson College in 1847. He took a teaching position at the Western Military Institute in Georgetown, Kentucky. While working there from 1848 to 1851, he courted Harriet Stanwood, a teacher at a nearby woman's seminary. They married on June 30, 1850, and would have seven children.

Blaine had a growing interest in politics, inspired by Whig Party leader Henry Clay, an influential senator from Kentucky. Leaving Kentucky in late 1851, Blaine taught at the Pennsylvania Institute for the Blind from 1852 to 1854. He also pursued legal studies while in Philadelphia. Through his wife's family connections and his own activism on behalf of the Whig Party, Blaine was asked in 1853 to fill a vacancy for an editor position of the Kennebec Journal, a Whig newspaper in Augusta, Maine. By November 1854, he was managing the paper.

The Whig Party dissolved around this time, and Blaine became active with the new Republican Party. He was elected to the Maine legislature in 1858 and was reelected three times. In 1862, he was elected to the U.S. House of Representatives. Known as "Blaine from Maine," he spent thirteen years in the House and served as its Speaker between 1869 and 1875. He was a moderate on Reconstruction, endorsed black suffrage, and favored protection of civil rights in the South, standing against more aggressive action toward the region favored by the powerful Congressional group called the Radical Republicans.

As a moderate, Blaine became a leader of a group nicknamed the "Half-Breeds." Republican "half-breeds" contrasted with Republican "Stalwarts," who formed a more united and unwavering loyalty to issues of interest to northern businessmen. Blaine and Roscoe Conkling, a representative from New York, often clashed on issues. Conkling helped undermine Blaine's presidential chances in 1876 and 1880. In 1876, Blaine moved to the Senate. He had been the leading candidate for the Republican presidential nomination that year, but a controversy arose over whether Blaine had acted corruptly in helping to save a land grant for an Arkansas railroad in 1869. The facts on the case were allegedly contained in a packet of documents known as the Mulligan Letters, named for the man who possessed them. The letters came into Blaine's hands, he read from them to the House, and his friends said that he had vindicated himself. Enemies charged that the papers proved his guilt. Republican delegates at the party's national convention that year decided that Blaine was too controversial to win the presidency, and they turned instead to Rutherford B. Hayes of Ohio.

After Hayes served a single term, the race to be the Republican nominee for president in 1880 was wide open. The Stalwart faction favored former president Ulysses S. Grant. Blaine led opposition to Grant. Congressman James A. Garfield of Ohio became the compromise nominee. After Garfield won narrowly in the national election, he asked Blaine to be his secretary of state. In his brief tenure at the State Department, Blaine pursued his concern for a canal across Central America, improved relations with South American nations, and expanded trade. Following Garfield's assassination in the summer of 1881, President Chester A. Arthur, a longtime Stalwart, received Blaine's resignation.

Blaine received the Republican nomination for president on the first ballot in 1884. He lost in a bitter campaign to Grover Cleveland, governor of New York. Over the next four years Blaine led opposition to Cleveland's policy of low tariff rates. Blaine stayed out of the presidential race of 1888 and strongly supported the Republican Party's nominee, Benjamin Harrison. After Harrison defeated Cleveland, Blaine was again named secretary of state.

As a member of the Harrison cabinet, Blaine faced quite a few important diplomatic issues, including a conflict with Great Britain over fishing rights and the fur trade along the Pacific coast. He convened the first Pan-American Conference, a meeting among nations of the Americas, in Washington in 1889; fought for annexation of Hawaii; and pushed for broader presidential power in trade agreements. Blaine resigned as secretary of state shortly before the Republican Convention of 1892. It is not clear whether Blaine was actually a candidate for the presidency, but the incumbent Harrison easily controlled the convention and was renominated on the first ballot. Blaine made one speech for the Republicans in the 1892 campaign, a race Harrison lost to Grover Cleveland, but he was ill with Bright's disease, a kidney ailment. He died on January 27, 1893, at the age of sixty-two.

Above: An 1880 campaign poster for the Republican candidates, Garfield and Arthur.

Below: Arthur was the first president, after Washington, to take his oath of office in New York City.

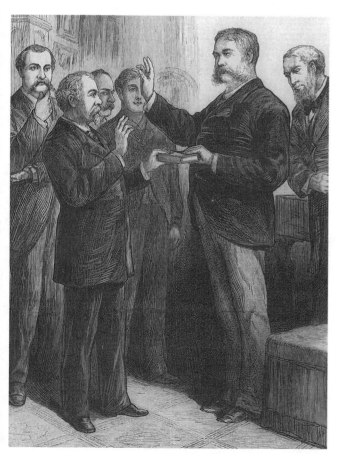

Succession

Chester Arthur was sworn in as president by New York Supreme Court Justice John R. Brady at his own home, 123 Lexington Avenue, in New York. There was no vice president by then, of course, but neither a president pro-tem of the Senate nor a Speaker of the House of Representatives had been appointed yet, which meant there was no constitutional line of succession in place. Arthur dealt with the problem by mailing a proclamation to himself calling the Senate into session, and when he got to Washington, he destroyed the letter and personally convened the Senate, where he took a second oath of office two days later.

Death amid Victory

Arthur's sudden rise to national prominence came at a time when he was in mourning. His wife Ellen caught a cold while she was waiting outside for a carriage on a snowy evening, and it quickly developed into pneumonia. She died on January 12, 1880, a few months before Arthur's national triumph.

At his inauguration in March 1881, President Garfield announced his intention to make good on his campaign pledge of reforming the civil service system. An earlier attempt at such reform had been started by his predecessor, Rutherford B. Hayes, but it had been stalled in Congress.

Garfield lost support for his efforts when his cabinet selections leaned heavily to Half-Breeds, as did the majority of his other political appointments. He was selecting the men he felt comfortable with, but Stalwart leader Roscoe Conkling and his fellow New Yorker Thomas Platt both resigned from the Senate in protest. As a show of strength, Conkling and Platt went before the New York State Legislature to have themselves reappointed to their seats—the point of their resignations having been made—and Arthur joined them.

While Arthur and the two ex-senators were in New York, President Garfield was planning a trip to New England, but while he was waiting for a train in a Washington station, he was shot twice by Charles Guiteau, a deranged Stalwart supporter who was upset over Garfield's brush-off of his job requests. Reportedly,

Guiteau had shouted, "I am a Stalwart and now Arthur is president!" before he shot Garfield.

Arthur hurried back to Washington as the president was taken to the executive mansion to have the bullets removed, but Garfield never did recover. After ten weeks, as the nation grimly read daily bulletins on his condition, he died on September 19, 1881. When word reached Chester A. Arthur that the president was dead, he wept openly, not for the dead president, but for the new one. "I hope…my God, I do hope it's a mistake."

There was no mistake, and he was sworn in as president the following day. Many expected that he would serve as a puppet with the Stalwarts pulling the strings, but they were wrong. He emerged as his own man instead. Meanwhile, the Stalwarts were beginning to lose support after the assassination, because the killer had shouted that he was one of them, giving rise to a major conspiracy theory, and Conkling and Platt were not reappointed to their Senate seats by the New York legislature. Chet Arthur had done some soul searching while Garfield lay dying, and he was determined to steer his own course.

Doing the Right Thing

Arthur had benefited as much as anybody from the spoils system, but he acted quickly to continue the reforms that had been promised by both Hayes and Garfield. He supported the trial against postal workers in the Star Route Fraud case that Garfield's administration had begun prosecuting, and he pushed for civil service reform legislation. The Star Route trial, which involved western postal officials who had conspired with stagecoach companies to steal money collected by the government, didn't produce any convictions, but revealing testimony helped bring about overwhelming public sentiment for cleaning up government corruption, which most people thought had been going on too long.

"I have but one annoyance with the administration of President Arthur, and that is, in contrast with it, the administration of Hayes becomes respectable, if not heroic."

—Roscoe Conkling

Above: Although every bit a city boy, President Arthur enjoyed days in the country.

Arthur pushed for civil service legislation in 1882, but he was ignored by Congress. He tried again the following year, this time with the public solidly behind him. Dorman B. Eaton, president of the grassroots National Civil Service Reform League, drafted legislation that was sponsored by Senator George H. Pendleton of Ohio. The Pendleton Civil Service Reform Act passed Congress, and President Arthur signed it into law in 1883. It established the Civil Service Commission, to oversee

Makeover

When Chester Arthur got his first look at the place where he was expected to live as president, he refused to move in. He personally inspected every room and put labels on everything he couldn't live with, which added up to twenty-four wagonloads of furniture and bric-a-brac hauled off to be sold at auction. Before the renovations that followed, the Army Corps of Engineers inspected the mansion and concluded that it would be an act of mercy to tear it down and start over. But thanks to public pressure and congressional disapproval, it was decided to fix up the old place instead, and the president hired Louis Comfort Tiffany, easily the best interior decorator of the day, to do the job. His most striking addition was a fifty-foot stained-glass screen that sparkled with red, white, and blue jewels intended to keep the wind from blowing through the north-facing front door.

federal appointments, administer competitive tests, and ensure that appointees to public jobs do not actively participate in partisan affairs while they hold those jobs. Eaton was named its first chairman.

In doing the right thing, Arthur lost support among some of his fellow Republicans. The Pendleton Act was the most noteworthy accomplishment of his administration, but unfortunately, it created a vacuum of support that stood in the way of his other efforts and ensured that the Republican Party would look elsewhere for a candidate for the 1884 presidential election.

"I am but one of 55 million; still, in the opinion of this one-fifty-five-millionth of the country's population, it would be hard indeed to better President Arthur's administration."

—*Mark Twain*

Arthur is not generally ranked among the most effective presidents. However, he proved stronger than even his supporters had expected. Intending to keep the government out of debt, for example, Arthur vetoed several appropriations bills, though his vetoes were overridden by Congress. He vetoed legislation that would limit Chinese immigration and deny citizenship to recent Chinese immigrants for twenty years. That veto was also overridden, but Arthur won a small victory by having the citizenship waiting period cut to ten years. He supported appropriations for building new naval ships, improving the U.S. Navy, which emerged a decade later as one of the world's most important naval forces.

"[Arthur's presidency] has unquestionably been more satisfactory than was expected."

—*The* New York Times

None of those measures won back support from his party, and Arthur quietly finished his term. Presidential receptions and other social occasions, meanwhile, were among the most festive and elegant Washington had seen in years. Arthur had taken a personal chef and a butler along with him when he went to Washington. He was the first president to have a valet, and he hired the famous interior designer Lewis Comfort Tiffany to completely redecorate the executive mansion. He had new plumbing, a new bathroom, and the first elevator installed in a house. Chet Arthur loved to entertain and hated to leave a party. Dinner guests would often stay well past midnight when he was their host.

In one of his final acts as president, Arthur dedicated the newly completed Washington Monument on February 27, 1885. Although ill with Bright's disease, a kidney ailment, when he left office in 1885, the former president reopened his New York law practice, but he never again enjoyed good health. He died of the kidney disease on November 18, 1886.

Legacy

Often overlooked in listings of the most effective presidents, Chester A. Arthur proved to be a more able and fairer administrator than his background suggested. The Pendleton Act, which he signed into law, reformed the civil service system and still remains in effect in the twenty-first century. Arthur's support of the legislation cost him the base of support that carried him to the presidency, but it brought much needed and lasting improvement to the American political system.

Arthur's support for fairer treatment of Chinese immigrants won a small measure of success, and it helped the United States maintain diplomatic relations with China. Like his earlier success in winning the rights for blacks to use New York streetcars, the small victory helped the cause of civil rights. Finally, Arthur's support for the appropriations bill that added new ships to the U.S. Navy was a significant early step toward the United States becoming a major naval power. Just over a decade later, the United States achieved a quick and decisive victory in the Spanish-American War thanks in large part to its strengthened navy.

Arthur presided over a dying era. The New York political machine, of which he had been a major player, lost its momentum while he was in office, and he helped bring about its downfall. The end of Stalwart influence was assured when Democrat Grover Cleveland was elected governor of New York during Arthur's term. Significantly, the reform-minded Cleveland followed Arthur as president and broke a Republican stranglehold on the office that had existed since 1860. In addition, Cleveland defeated a Half-Breed, James G. Blaine, in the 1884, effectively weakening that powerful wing of the Republican Party as well. The Republican Party would regroup and unify in the 1890s, but without the spoils system.

Ellen Arthur

Born August 30, 1837, Culpeper, Virginia
Died January 12, 1880, New York, New York

"Honors to me now are not what they once were."
—*Chester A. Arthur, upon his nomination of vice president*
soon after the death of his wife

Vice President Chester A. Arthur was a widower when he assumed the presidency after the assassination of James Garfield. His wife, Ellen Lewis Herndon Arthur, had died the previous year after contracting pneumonia.

The Arthurs had enjoyed an elegant lifestyle of dinner parties, shopping sprees, and cultural events in New York City, and as president, Arthur did his best to continue as much of it as he could. He took along his own chef and butler to Washington, and he hired the best designers to redecorate the executive mansion's rooms and grounds, to make them, he said, look less like "barracks." Each morning, he placed a fresh flower near a portrait of his beloved wife, whom he had affectionately called Nell.

Singer in the Church Choir

Nell was born Ellen Lewis Herndon on August 30, 1837, in Culpeper, Virginia, the only child of Elizabeth Hansbrough and William Lewis Herndon. The family could trace its roots back to the twelfth century and William I, king of Scotland. Ellen's father was a naval officer and moved his family to Washington when he was assigned to help his brother-in-law Lieutenant Matthew Fontaine Maury establish the Naval Observatory.

Young Ellen had a lovely contralto voice, and she joined the choir at St. John's Episcopal Church on Lafayette Square, where she sang for several years before the family moved to New York City when she was in her late teens.

In New York, she was introduced by her cousin, Dabney Herndon, to Chester Alan Arthur, a young lawyer who was beginning to make a name for himself as a defense attorney in civil-rights cases. He was also active in local and national politics as a member of the recently formed Republican Party. Chet and Nell began a romance, but tragedy struck the following year: Her father died at sea when caught in a storm off Cape Hatteras, North Carolina, and went down with his ship.

Chet helped Ellen through her period of mourning, and gradually they began attending social and cultural activities around New York City, and occasionally retreated to the countryside. He had been raised near Saratoga Springs in Upstate New York, and he liked to go back there to fish for salmon. The couple was married on October 25, 1859.

Arthur's career began to prosper shortly after marriage. In 1860, he was named to an honorary position as engineer in chief of the state military; he was in charge of recruiting soldiers and equipping them for battle. The post became essential when the Civil War broke out the following year. By 1863, the fighting force from New York reached more than 200,000 men. After the war, he became a major figure in the New York Republican Party, organizing support for Senator Roscoe Conkling, for which he was given the desirable assignment of collector at the New York Customs House in 1868.

Meanwhile, the Arthurs were raising a family. Their first child, a boy named after Ellen's father, died at the age of two. A second boy, Chester Jr., was born in 1864, and the couple had a daughter, Ellen, in 1871. The Arthurs bought a large townhouse in New York City and had it elegantly decorate. They were active in New York social circles, which were at their glittering height in these post–Civil War years.

Arthur lost his Customs House post in 1877 on charges of having used it to help support the Republican Party. He returned to his law practice but still remained an important force in the party as a leader of the Stalwarts, a powerful faction based in New York. When Ohioan James A. Garfield was the surprise nominee for president at the Republican convention in 1880, he chose Arthur as his running mate to ensure that the ticket would receive full support from the Stalwart faction. By then, Arthur was a widower.

On the evening of January 10, 1880, Ellen Arthur had attended a benefit concert and caught cold while she was waiting for her carriage to take her home, and it quickly deteriorated into pneumonia. Her husband, at the state capitol in Albany, rushed home to be at her side, but she was already unconscious by the time he arrived. When she died on January 12, 1880, she was only forty-two years old.

Tribute to a Singer

Chet Arthur had loved to hear Ellen sing. When he arrived in Washington, the town where she had been raised, to begin his term as vice president, he paid a visit to the church where Ellen used to sing in the choir, and presented a stained-glass window to the parish in her memory. The glass depicted angels of the Resurrection, the Christian concept of the rising of the dead for the Last Judgment. After becoming president, he requested that the window be placed in a location where he could see it at night from his bedroom with the lights of the church shining through.

Arthur paid other tributes to Ellen, including a daily practice of placing fresh flowers by her portrait. At official dinners, the place next to him was always left vacant in memory of his beloved Nell.

New Elegance

Arthur had the executive mansion completely redecorated, and he personally supervised the work in his spare time. Meanwhile, he asked his sister Mary McElroy to handle hostess duties for larger occasions. After having supported reform-minded ideas when she was young, Mary had become a more conservative mature woman. She had married a minister and focused on raising a family. In her early forties, when her brother became president, she temporarily left her family from fall to spring for the following four years to organize formal gatherings and to assist him with the details of entertaining.

Arthur's First Annual Address to Congress

Delivered on December 6, 1881

In his first annual address to Congress, President Chester A. Arthur acknowledged that the U.S. government's relations with Native Americans had been "a cause of trouble and embarrassment" since the beginning of the nation. At the time he spoke, Native Americans were seriously endangered as a people. War and disease had severely reduced their number. Land where the nomadic Plains tribes hunted was being rapidly settled by whites, who were defended by the U.S. military in a series of wars from Montana to Texas. These battles raged during much of the last half of the nineteenth century on the final area of frontier within the continental United States.

By the time the United States was founded with ratification of the Constitution in 1789, Americans were journeying beyond the thirteen states to settle in present-day Ohio, Kentucky, and Tennessee—areas where various Native American nations were still strong. A series of battles over the land concluded in 1795 with the Treaty of Greenville, which designated land as either "Indian Territory" or white settlement. During the administration of President Thomas Jefferson from 1801 to 1809, a program was developed to try integrating Native Americans into the larger society with the help of religious groups. While that program was failing to take hold, further land concessions were gained from Native Americans in Indiana and the Great Lakes region during the period that ended with the War of 1812. The Black Hawk War of 1832 effectively pushed Native Americans west of the Mississippi River in the present-day Midwest. The Indian Removal Act of 1830 empowered President Andrew Jackson to move Native Americans from Southern states across the Mississippi River to what was then "Indian Territory" in present-day Oklahoma.

As the government acquired more western territory to form the present-day continental United States during the late 1840s, Americans began crossing into the Plains and the Rocky Mountains in larger numbers. Railroads stretched to those areas after the Civil War, and during the administration of Ulysses S. Grant in the early 1870s, the U.S. government abandoned the practice of making treaties with Native American tribes because the treaties usually failed. Instead, Congress began to pass legislation that affected all Native Americans by making them dependent on Washington for their protection.

Excerpt from Arthur's First Annual Address to Congress

Prominent among the matters which challenge the attention of Congress at its present session is the management of our Indian affairs. While this question has been a cause of trouble and embarrassment from the infancy of the Government, it is but recently that any effort has been made for its solution at once serious, determined, consistent, and promising success.

It has been easier to resort to convenient makeshifts for tiding over temporary difficulties than to grapple with the great permanent problem, and accordingly the easier course has almost invariably been pursued.

It was natural, at a time when the national territory seemed almost illimitable and contained many millions of acres far outside the bounds of civilized settlements, that a policy should have been initiated which more than aught else has been the fruitful source of our Indian complications.

I refer, of course, to the policy of dealing with the various Indian tribes as separate nationalities, of relegating them by treaty stipulations to the occupancy of immense reservations in the West, and of encouraging them to live a savage life, undisturbed by any earnest and well-directed efforts to bring them under the influences of civilization.

The unsatisfactory results which have sprung from this policy are becoming apparent to all.

As the white settlements have crowded the borders of the reservations, the Indians, sometimes contentedly and sometimes against their will, have been transferred to other hunting grounds, from which they have again been dislodged whenever their new-found homes have been desired by the adventurous settlers.

These removals and the frontier collisions by which they have often been preceded have led to frequent and disastrous conflicts between the races.

It is profitless to discuss here which of them has been chiefly responsible for the disturbances whose recital occupies so large a space upon the pages of our history.

We have to deal with the appalling fact that though thousands of lives have been sacrificed and hundreds of millions of dollars expended in the attempt to solve the Indian problem, it has until within the past few years seemed scarcely nearer a solution than it was half a century ago. But the Government has of late been cautiously but steadily feeling its way to the adoption of a policy which has already produced gratifying results, and which, in my judgment, is likely, if Congress and the Executive accord in its support, to relieve us ere long from the difficulties which have hitherto beset us.

For the success of the efforts now making to introduce among the Indians the customs and pursuits of civilized life and gradually to absorb them into the mass of our citizens, sharing their rights and holden to their responsibilities, there is imperative need for legislative action.

My suggestions in that regard will be chiefly such as have been already called to the attention of Congress and have received to some extent its consideration.

First. I recommend the passage of an act making the laws of the various States and Territories applicable to the Indian reservations within their borders and extending the laws of the State of Arkansas to the portion of the Indian Territory not occupied by the Five Civilized Tribes.

The Indian should receive the protection of the law. He should be allowed to maintain in court his rights of person and property. He has repeatedly begged for this privilege. Its exercise would be very valuable to him in his progress toward civilization.

Second. Of even greater importance is a measure which has been frequently recommended by my predecessors in office, and in furtherance of which several bills have been from time to time introduced in both Houses of Congress. The enactment of a general law permitting the allotment in severalty, to such Indians, at least, as desire it, of a reasonable quantity of land secured to them by patent, and for their own protection made inalienable for twenty or twenty-five years, is demanded for their present welfare and their permanent advancement.

In return for such considerate action on the part of the Government, there is reason to believe that the Indians in large numbers would be persuaded to sever their tribal relations and to engage at once in agricultural pursuits. Many of them realize the fact that their hunting days are over and that it is now for their best interests to conform their manner of life to the new order of things. By no greater inducement than the assurance of permanent title to the soil can they be led to engage in the occupation of tilling it.

The well-attested reports of their increasing interest in husbandry justify the hope and belief that the enactment of such a statute as I recommend would be at once attended with gratifying results. A resort to the allotment system would have a direct and powerful influence in dissolving the tribal bond, which is so prominent a feature of savage life, and which tends so strongly to perpetuate it.

Third. I advise a liberal appropriation for the support of Indian schools, because of my confident belief that such a course is consistent with the wisest economy. [...]

What Happened Next

Arthur represented the concerns of Americans who wanted to take humanitarian actions on behalf of Native Americans, but not much progress on Indian affairs occurred during his term. His three-part policy based on land ownership, citizenship, and education provided a model for future action. Unfortunately, none of those actions helped. The lives of Native Americans worsened as the century progressed.

Congress introduced a plan to simultaneously protect Native Americans and undermine their tribal structures. Under the Dawes Act (or General Allotment Act), which went into effect in 1887, tribal-owned land was parceled in 160-acre allotments on an individual basis to Indian families. The remaining land was to be sold, with proceeds going to the tribe that owned it. The Dawes Act was a disaster. Native Americans lost their "surplus" land to white speculators and settlers, and many Indian families ended up losing their allotted land as well. The poorest of groups in North America just got poorer.

A majority of Native Americans continued to resist the idea of integrating into American culture. The slaughter of Sioux men, women, and children on December 29, 1890, at Wounded Knee, South Dakota, was the last major battle in a series of wars that had ranged on the Plains since the 1860s. Native Americans reached their lowest population numbers shortly after the turn of the twentieth century.

Grover Cleveland

"A public office is a public trust."

—*Grover Cleveland*

Twenty-second and twenty-fourth president of the United States, 1885–1889 and 1893–1897

Full name: *Stephen Grover Cleveland*
Born: *March 18, 1837, Caldwell, New Jersey*
Died: *June 24, 1908, Princeton, New Jersey*
Burial site: *Princeton Cemetery, Princeton, New Jersey*
Parents: *Richard and Anne Neal Cleveland*
Spouse: *Frances Folsom (1864–1947; m. 1886)*
Children: *Oscar Folsom (1874–?; Cleveland claimed paternal responsibility for this child, named after his law partner and future father-in-law; the mother later gave him up for adoption); Ruth (1891–1904); Esther (1893–1980); Marion (1895–1977); Richard Folsom (1897–1974); Francis Grover (1903–1995)*
Religion: *Presbyterian*
Education: *High school*
Occupation: *Lawyer*
Government positions: *Erie County, New York, sheriff; Buffalo, New York, mayor; New York governor*
Political party: *Democratic*
Dates as president: *March 4, 1885– March 4, 1889 (first term); March 4, 1893–March 4, 1897 (second term)*
Age upon taking office: *47*

Grover Cleveland is the only president to have served nonconsecutive terms. He was elected president in 1884, lost his bid for reelection in 1888, and won again in 1892. His shifting political fortunes reflected the state of the nation at the time. Americans were facing an unstable economy in spite of the continued growth of industry and railroads. Many businessmen were growing extremely wealthy, while farmers and laborers struggled against steadily increasing prices for such basic necessities as food and clothing. National politics had been dominated for years by patronage, partisanship, and scandals, and the country was becoming increasingly involved in international affairs and schemes.

Cleveland is admired not so much for what he did about these problems as for what he did not do. He followed conservative economic policies in spite of calls from many quarters for more radical programs. He fended off attempts to raise tariff rates and to increase the money supply. In foreign affairs, Cleveland countered attempts to expand American influence and the acquiring of territory beyond the limits of the continental United States. In Washington, he frustrated attempts by some members of his own Democratic Party to get important government jobs, insisting that job applicants should have skills and qualifications for the job rather than just political connections.

Cleveland's reputation is based on the integrity that he displayed as chief executive. He maintained those qualities even as his support was eroding because he refused to back down on his principles in favor of more popular policies. His actions reflected his statement that "A public office is a public trust." He is considered to have been a strong president for his independence and leadership.

Finding Success in Buffalo

Stephen Grover Cleveland was born in Caldwell, New Jersey, on March 18, 1837, the fifth of nine children of Richard and Anne Neal Cleveland. His father was a Presbyterian minister who moved his family to Fayetteville, New York, to become district secretary of the American Home Mission Society. Richard Cleveland died in 1853, when Grover was sixteen, and the family's financial resources were quickly drained. He abandoned his plans for college in favor of working to help support the family, and he taught at a school for the blind in New York City for a time before he headed west looking for something better.

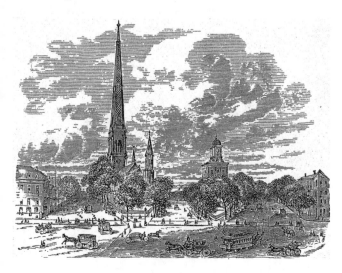

He stopped in Buffalo, New York, where his uncle, Lewis F. Allen, owned a cattle ranch, and it turned out to be a lucky break. He was hired to do bookkeeping for his uncle's ranch, and he had enough time left over to study law. He passed the bar in 1859 and set up a law practice that quickly prospered. It was during this time that he became active in politics as a Democrat.

When the Civil War broke out, Cleveland was caught in the military draft, but he hired another man to replace him, which was perfectly legal under the Federal Conscription Act because he was still supporting his family. His career was burgeoning too. He served for a brief period as assistant district attorney of Erie County, New York, and when he went back to his private practice, his law firm grew even more.

Cleveland was elected county sheriff in 1870, and was highly regarded as a crime fighter. He was so well respected, in fact, that he was elected mayor of Buffalo in 1881. He noticed that the lion's share of contracts the city awarded to local businesses were weighted heavily for the benefit of elected officials, and he began exposing the grafters. He was nicknamed the "veto mayor" for his refusal to approve contracts and bills that would benefit politicians at the expense of the taxpayers. He saved the City of Buffalo more than $1 million during his first year in office alone.

Left: Buffalo, New York, when Cleveland was its mayor.

Timeline

1837: Born in New Jersey

1870–73: Serves as sheriff of Erie County, New York

1881–82: Serves as mayor of Buffalo, New York

1883–85: Serves as governor of New York

1885–89: Serves as twenty-second U.S. president (first term)

1888: Loses bid for reelection to Benjamin Harrison

1893–97: Serves as twenty-fourth U.S. president (second term), becoming the first chief executive to serve nonconsecutive terms

1893: Financial crisis hits the United States

1908: Dies in New Jersey

Cleveland's reputation spread quickly during a time of growing public distaste for political patronage and scandal. New York politics had been under the influence of U.S. Senator Roscoe Conkling and future president Chester A. Arthur, who ran the senator's political machine, and they rewarded their supporters with government jobs. They in turn worked for Republican causes while they were on the government payroll. By the time Arthur became vice president of the United States, however, the political machine had begun to run out of steam, and when he became president after the assassination of James A. Garfield, he surprised everyone by continuing Garfield's plans for civil service reform, which ultimately led to the end of the New York Republican political machine he himself had built.

When the state machine fell apart, Cleveland became an attractive candidate for governor of New York, and with popular sentiment clearly favoring government reform, he easily won the 1882 election. He did what the voters expected of him and went right to work routing out corruption on the state level.

The Republicans chose James G. Blaine as their candidate for the 1884 presidential election. He was a powerful national figure, but he was the wrong kind of candidate for a public weary of government corruption. Blaine had been accused of involvement in a shady deal with railroad officials, and he was also head of a political machine operating out of Washington.

Cleveland and Reform.

GOV. GROVER CLEVELAND,
22ND. PRESIDENT OF THE UNITED STATES.

Above: A political poster squeezes in multiple reasons to vote for Cleveland.

Below: Caricatures of the 1884 presidential ticket (L-R) Republicans James G. Blaine and John A. Logan; Democrats Thomas A. Hendricks and Grover Cleveland.

DRINK TO YOUR FAVORITES.

When the Democrats met to name their candidate, Cleveland was the front-runner right from the start. He had a spotless record as a reformer and it looked like he could win New York, the state with the largest number of electoral votes. Those plusses and an anti-Blaine faction within the Republican ranks helped win the presidential election for Cleveland, but New York turned out to be more important than anyone had guessed: Cleveland accumulated thirty-seven more electoral votes than Blaine, and thirty-six of them came from his home state. It turned out a squeaker as Cleveland won New York by less than 1 percent—with about one thousand more votes than Blaine out of about one million votes cast.

The 1884 presidential campaign was, in a word, ugly. Blaine's ties with railroad interests and political machines were used against him, and when his campaign manager made a slur against Irish Catholics, it cost him thousands of votes. However, Blaine's shortcomings were overlooked when it was revealed that the bachelor Cleveland had fathered a child, and had also bought his way out of duty in the Civil War. Cleveland candidly acknowledged the truth of both charges. He noted that he helped support the child he had fathered, and he explained that his legitimate strategy for avoiding military service had allowed him to support his family. His honesty probably saved his candidacy. A honest politician was a bit of a novelty in those days.

Scandal

In the 1870s, a widow in Buffalo named Maria Halpin had "bestowed her favors" on several local men including Grover Cleveland. She became pregnant and claimed that the father of her son was the rising young lawyer, and Cleveland accepted the responsibility and arranged to support the boy. In the meantime, Maria turned to alcohol and suffered a mental breakdown and Cleveland arranged to have her institutionalized. Then he forgot about the whole thing until the day ten years later, in the midst of his presidential campaign, demonstrators appeared at his door shouting, "Ma, Ma, where's my Pa?" Another man, whose name was shrouded in secrecy because he was married, came forward and admitted that he was the boy's father, but that Cleveland, who was single, "did the right thing," and took the responsibility. When the Democratic Cleveland narrowly won the election, his supporters countered with: "Gone to the White House. Ha, ha, ha."

Incumbent president Harrison was defeated by Cleveland four years after Harrison defeated then-incumbent president Cleveland (see Harrison entry for 1888 election results). This marked the only time in U.S. history that a president served two nonconsecutive terms.

Election Results

1884

Presidential / Vice Presidential candidates	Popular Votes	Electoral Votes
Grover Cleveland / Thomas A. Hendricks (Democratic)	4,874,986	219
James G. Blaine / John A. Logan (Republican)	4,851,981	182

Incumbent president Chester A. Arthur finished second in the Republican nomination voting.

1892

Presidential / Vice Presidential candidates	Popular Votes	Electoral Votes
Grover Cleveland / Adlai E. Stevenson (Democratic)	5,556,918	277
Benjamin Harrison / Whitelaw Reid (Republican)	5,176,108	145
James B. Weaver / James G. Field (Populist)	1,041,028	22

Above: Cleveland managed to rise above scandal, including one portraying him as the father of an illegitimate child.

The Cleveland Administrations

Administration Dates:	March 4, 1885–March 4, 1889
	March 4, 1893–March 4, 1897
Vice President:	Thomas A. Hendricks (1885)
	None (1885–89)
	Adlai E. Stevenson (1893–97)
Cabinet:	
Secretary of State	Thomas F. Bayard Sr. (1885–89)
	Walter Q. Gresham (1893–95)
	Richard Olney (1895–97)
Secretary of the Treasury	Daniel Manning (1885–87)
	Charles S. Fairchild (1887–89)
	John G. Carlisle (1893–97)
Secretary of War	William C. Endicott (1885–89)
	Daniel S. Lamont (1893–97)
Attorney General	Augustus H. Garland (1885–89)
	Richard Olney (1893–95)
	Judson Harmon (1895–97)
Secretary of the Navy	William C. Whitney (1885–89)
	Hilary A. Herbert (1893–97)
Postmaster General	William F. Vilas (1885–88)
	Donald M. Dickinson (1888–89)
	Wilson S. Bissel (1893–95)
	William L. Wilson (1895–97)
Secretary of the Interior	Lucius Q. C. Lamar (1885–88)
	William F. Vilas (1888–89)
	Hoke Smith (1893–96)
	David R. Francis (1896–97)
Secretary of Agriculture	Norman J. Colman (1889)
	Julius S. Morton (1893–97)

Prevention Is the Best Medicine

As president, Cleveland delivered what he had promised during the campaign. His cabinet included businessmen who supported lower tariff rates—against the wishes of many Democrats. He included Southerners in his administration too. All of the previous presidents since the Civil War had been Northerners, and they rarely, if ever, offered positions to anyone who had supported the Confederacy during the war.

Cleveland began an all-out fight against corruption that extended even to government pensions. At the time, Civil War veterans who didn't qualify for some disability pensions could petition their local representative to introduce a special "pension bill" that would grant money to that particular veteran. Many had taken advantage of the process to make fraudulent claims, and Cleveland carefully examined each and every pension bill that came before him and ended up rejecting more than two hundred that he believed weren't necessary. Needless to say, that didn't do much for his popularity among Civil War veterans.

"The Hangman of Buffalo"

Grover Cleveland was the first Democrat to become president in twenty-four years, and there couldn't have been a more unlikely candidate. When he took the oath of office in Washington, it was the second time in his life that he had ever been to the capital. The audience he addressed was the biggest he had ever seen, and almost no one in the crowd had ever seen him before. The only elective offices he had ever held were mayor of Buffalo, New York, and governor of New York State, and he hadn't served a full term in either job. Yet there he was, all 280 pounds of him, with double chins hanging below a huge walrus mustache, looking for all the world like "the hangman of Buffalo," which was what the Republicans had called him in the recent campaign. The slur came from the fact that once, while Cleveland was a county sheriff, he stepped in to hang a man when the official executioner lost his nerve.

Susan B. Anthony

Born on February 5, 1820, in a New England farmhouse, Susan Brownell Anthony was the daughter of Lucy Read Anthony and Daniel Anthony, a cotton-mill owner. Her father instilled in his children the ideals of self-reliance and self-discipline. She was raised a Quaker, a religion founded on the belief that places of organized worship are not necessary for a person to experience God. They do not believe in armed conflict or slavery, and they were among the first groups to practice full equality between men and women. Other American women did not experience the freedom and respect Anthony did while she was growing up, and she worked to change that disparity by becoming a leader in the crusade for women's rights.

After having completed her schooling at the age of seventeen, she began teaching in schools in rural New York State. Teaching wages for men and women differed greatly in those days, and Anthony's weekly salary was equal to one-fifth of the wages of her male colleagues. When she protested the inequality, she lost her job. But she went on to secure a better position as principal of the Girls' Department at an academy in Rochester, New York. In 1849, after having taught for more than ten years, she found her spirit drained and her professional future bleak. She began focusing her energies on social improvements and joined the local temperance society. After she was denied a chance to speak at a Sons of Temperance meeting because she was a woman, she founded the Daughters of Temperance, the first women's temperance organization, and she began writing temperance articles for the Lily, the first woman-owned newspaper in the United States. Through the paper's editor, Amelia Bloomer, Anthony met women involved in the abolitionist movement and in the recently formed woman suffrage movement.

At a temperance meeting in 1851, she met women's rights leader Elizabeth Cady Stanton, and they formed a deep personal friendship and a political bond that would last for the rest of their lives. From this point on, Anthony worked tirelessly for the women's suffrage movement. She lectured on women's rights and organized a series of state and national conventions on the issue. She collected signatures

for a petition to grant women the right to vote and to own property. Her hard work helped. In 1860, the New York State legislature passed the Married Women's Property Act, which allowed women to enter into contracts and to control their own earnings and property. During the Civil War, Anthony and most other members of the women's movement worked toward the emancipation of the slaves. In 1863, she helped form the Women's Loyal League, which supported the policies of President Abraham Lincoln. After the war, Anthony and others tried to link women's suffrage with that of the freed slaves, but they were not successful.

Anthony and Stanton formed their own organization, the National Woman Suffrage Association. The Constitution's Fourteenth Amendment, adopted in 1868, had declared that all people born in the United States were citizens and that no legal privileges could be denied to any of them. Anthony decided to challenge this amendment. Pointing out that women were citizens and the amendment did not restrict the privilege of voting to men, she registered to vote in Rochester on November 1, 1872, and four days later, she and fifteen other women voted in the presidential election. All sixteen of the women were arrested three weeks later, but only Anthony was brought before a court. Her trial, United States v. Susan B. Anthony, began on June 17, 1873. The presiding judge opposed women's suffrage and wrote his decision before the trial even began. Refusing to let Anthony testify, he ordered the jury to find her guilty, and then sentenced her to pay a $100 fine. She refused, but no further action was taken against her.

Anthony continued to campaign for women's rights. Between 1881 and 1886, she and Stanton published three volumes of The History of Woman Suffrage, a collection of writings about the movement's struggle. In 1890, they strengthened the suffrage cause by forming the larger National American Woman Suffrage Association. Through Anthony's determined work, many professional fields became open to women by the end of the nineteenth century. Nevertheless, at the time of her death in Rochester, on March 13, 1906, only four states—Wyoming, Colorado, Idaho, and Utah—had given women the right to vote. Her crusade carried on after her, and in 1920, Congress adopted the Nineteenth Amendment, finally giving women throughout America the right to vote.

Above: A poster puts candidate Cleveland in the company of the previous chief executives.

Above: Grover Cleveland was determined to keep his campaign promises.

His political appointments, which he tried to base on merit rather than political influence, were continually questioned by Congress. The policy of executive privilege, which allows the president to keep certain papers private, became an integral part of administration policy during Cleveland's term when he repeatedly refused to let Congress have files concerning his appointments. He said that he wanted to protect his ability to make decisions without having the legislative branch constantly looking over his shoulder.

For the most part, Cleveland considered himself a "preventative president." Rather than aggressively enacting new policies, he tried to improve and protect the ones that were already in place. In his political appointments, for example, he used the recently enacted Pendleton Civil Service Reform Act as his guide, and

although he vetoed hundreds of pension requests, he supported the ones that were already in place.

The late 1880s was a time of dramatic change in American history. Big businesses were overpowering smaller ones, and railroads and industries grew prosperous while workers and farmers were struggling to survive. Responding to the need to monitor the pricing practices of the railroad companies, Cleveland supported the establishment of the Interstate Commerce Commission, which was authorized to make sure that railroad rates were reasonable and fair.

To protect the rights of Native Americans, Cleveland supported the Dawes Act of 1887, which encouraged Native Americans to move from a tribal culture and become private citizens by allowing individuals to buy lots on tribal lands. Almost 500,000 acres of tribal land had been offered for sale during the administration of Cleveland's predecessor, Chester A. Arthur, but much of that land was returned to the Native Americans under Cleveland.

He wasn't quite as forward-thinking on the issue of women's rights. He publicly disagreed with his sister, Rose Elizabeth "Libbie" Cleveland, who served as his official hostess during his first year in office, while he was still a bachelor, and was a strong supporter of equal rights between the sexes and for women's voting rights. Her views were shared by other women activists, including Susan B. Anthony and Elizabeth Cady Stanton, who together published three volumes of *The History of Woman Suffrage* between 1881 and 1886.

During Cleveland's first term, the federal government had large budget surpluses, and some politicians were eager to spend the excess money on projects that would benefit their home states and, thus, enhance their popularity. Cleveland recognized that the surpluses were a result of high tariff rates, and he thought lowering them made the most sense.

High tariffs were favored by manufacturers because the taxes on imports added to the cost of foreign goods and gave them a competitive edge. However, consumers— especially those in poorer sections of the country—were hurt by the added costs of basic necessities like clothing. Cleveland spent his entire annual address to Congress in 1887 arguing for tariff reduction, and when Congress failed to address the issue, tariffs became a major topic of the 1888 election between Cleveland and his Republican opponent, Benjamin Harrison.

Meanwhile, the Cleveland presidency was brightened when he became the first president to get married in the executive mansion. His bride, Frances Folsom, was the daughter of his former law partner, Oscar Folsom. Cleveland had looked after Folsom's widow, Emma, and their daughter, Frances, after Oscar died. When his future bride was born, Cleveland bought the family a baby carriage as a gift.

When Frances and Emma Folsom visited Washington, D.C., in the spring of 1885, Cleveland and "Frank," as he called her, became secretly engaged, and they were married the following June in the most glittering social event of the season.

Above: Cleveland was the first president to wed in the White House.

Changing Fortunes

Cleveland bet his 1888 reelection bid on the tariff issue, and Benjamin Harrison, his Republican opponent, took the opposing view, which made him popular in the business community. On top of that, Harrison was a Civil War hero, and he was sold to the public as less of an "Indian supporter" than Cleveland. Still, Cleveland received over 100,000 more popular votes than Harrison, although he lost in the Electoral College, 233 to 168.

Cleveland went back to his law practice in New York after he lost the election. He spent time fishing off Cape Cod, Massachusetts, and occasionally commenting on issues of the day. He came out strongly against bimetallism, a policy where two precious metals are used to give value to money. Gold was the basis for the value of legal tender in the United States, but there was a new movement to include silver as well. Its strongest supporters were generally farmers living in western and southern states, who argued that "free silver" would allow the government to print more money that people could earn and use to buy things like food and clothing that many of them couldn't afford. Those against including silver believed that increasing the money supply would only lead to inflation. Cleveland called it "a dangerous and reckless experiment."

J. P. Morgan

As an investment banker, railroad baron, and founder of U.S. Steel Corporation, the nation's first billion-dollar company, J. P. Morgan was deeply involved and influential during a period of aggressive economic growth and industrialism in the United States. He was born John Pierpont Morgan on April 17, 1837, in Hartford, Connecticut, to Junius and Sarah Morgan. His mother came from a preacher's family in Boston, Massachusetts. His father owned part of a large trading company, and eventually became partner and later successor to banker George Peabody, an American who made his career in London, England. Junius settled there in 1854 and lived there the rest of his life.

J. P. Morgan was educated in New England and Europe. Seriously ill as a teenager, he had a long and successful recovery in the Azores. He began his career as a clerk in a New York bank at the age of twenty, and two years later, while traveling in the Caribbean to study the sugar and cotton markets, he bought, without authorization, a cargo of unwanted coffee using his employer's money. The employer complained, but he accepted the profit of the several thousand dollars he earned by selling the coffee to New Orleans retailers. Morgan set up his own company in 1860 with plenty of business from his father in London, and he also took advantage of many opportunities to buy and sell in the booming commercial city of New York. In 1861, he married Amelia Sturges, who died of tuberculosis a year later.

Forming a business called J. P. Morgan and Company, Bankers, Morgan traded in gold and on one occasion bought obsolete arms from the federal government in the East and then sold them to General John Charles Frémont in the West at an enormous profit. By the age twenty-seven, Morgan was a leading financier in the nation's largest city. He helped raise money for the wounded and widowed during the Civil War, and he worked to establish and enlarge the Young Men's Christian Association (YMCA), an organization devoted to improving the lives of young men. In 1865, he married Frances Tracy, with whom he would have four children. In the summer of 1869, Morgan and his wife rode the new transcontinental railroad to Utah

and on to California, where they toured extensively by stagecoach and horseback. Returning east, he accepted a new partnership with the powerful Drexels of Philadelphia. He would be a full partner and would head their New York office doing business as Drexel, Morgan, and Company.

Morgan wanted to ensure that railroads were efficiently managed so that stockholders and bondholders would be properly rewarded for their investments. He helped establish the practice of bringing railroads into large, integrated systems, in which a single corporation controlled main lines and feeders and could operate without competition. He also brought in other major banking houses, both in the United States and abroad, to organize syndicates to help protect investments during times of financial crisis.

Morgan was involved in the finances of the federal government on four major occasions. With other leading bankers, he helped refinance the federal debt under President Ulysses S. Grant, and in the summer of 1877, he lent the U.S. Army money to pay its troops after Congress had adjourned without setting aside the funds. Since the army was not authorized to borrow, Morgan paid out more than $2 million at his own risk; Congress, however, repaid the banker. Much more effort was required to save the U.S. Treasury's gold reserve during the depression of 1893. A combination of laws had forced the treasury to sell gold until it was on the brink of bankruptcy, and the Panic of 1893 had generated a flight of gold to Europe. To save the situation, Morgan formed a syndicate of American and European bankers to lend gold to the government at acceptable rates and to stop the flow of gold out of the country.

Morgan's greatest triumphs and defeats came at the end of his life. In 1901, he formed the U.S. Steel Corporation, the world's first billion-dollar corporation. Then he turned to a merger of the Northern Pacific railroad with its regional rival, the Great Northern. President Theodore Roosevelt ordered an antitrust prosecution, contending that the combination of the two railroads would be too powerful and in violation of antitrust law. The government won the lawsuit in 1904, and the merger fell apart, but Morgan was called on again in 1907 to lead yet another syndicate of bankers to prevent a financial panic. He died in 1913.

The Harrison administration reversed several of Cleveland's policies. U.S. Senator William McKinley of Ohio sponsored the McKinley Tariff Act of 1890, which led to higher import taxes, and Harrison eagerly enacted new pension benefits for veterans and their widows and families. When a revolt in Hawaii led by private American citizens toppled the island's leader, Queen Liliuokalani, Harrison actively tried to annex the island, an action Cleveland strongly opposed.

As the presidential election of 1892 drew near, the nation seemed to be more divided than ever, and once again, the Democrats turned to Cleveland as their nominee. Because the McKinley Tariff had proven to be unpopular and Harrison was an uninspiring leader, they believed Cleveland could beat Harrison this time around.

The presidential campaign was somber that year. First Lady Caroline Harrison had fallen ill, and President Harrison refused to leave her side to campaign, and Cleveland showed his respect by refusing to campaign as well. Cleveland won the popular vote again, this time by more than 400,000 votes. More important, he won in the Electoral College this time, 277 to 145. James B. Weaver, a member of the Populist Party, which united the interests of farmers and laborers and favored bimetallism, siphoned off twenty-two electoral votes in western states.

"His Obstinacy"

Cleveland's second term was made difficult right from the beginning when the economy took a nosedive: Over five hundred banks failed in 1893, major railroads went bankrupt, millions of workers were thrown out of work, and thousands of others went on strike. Cleveland continued to show integrity with his decisions, but his actions, however well reasoned, often proved unpopular. He stuck to his principles, though, and was nicknamed "His Obstinacy," because he refused to bend.

The financial crisis that began right after he took office in 1893 didn't improve through much of his second term. Historians and economists often blame high tariff rates and overexpansion of the railroads for the problems. Still, Congress passed an even higher tariff rate during Cleveland's second term, and with businesses solidly behind the tariff, Cleveland faced the prospect of having his veto overridden. By neither signing nor vetoing the legislation, he allowed it to become law ten days after it reached his desk.

Overexpansion of railroads led to job losses and pay cuts, which had a ripple effect in other industries as well. When the workers who made Pullman train cars went on strike in 1894, the American Railway Union pulled its members off the job in sympathy, and as the railroads came to a stop, Cleveland sent in federal troops to break the strike.

Meanwhile, Cleveland had to confront foreign policy issues as well. He had been disturbed by the American-led revolt in Hawaii that overthrew the island's monarchy and established a civil government, and five days after taking office for his second term, he withdrew a treaty that would have led to annexation of the island, even though he officially recognized the Republic of Hawaii that had negotiated it. He saw the events in Hawaii as an example of American imperialism that he believed ought to be avoided.

Cleveland invoked the Monroe Doctrine twice to help Venezuela and Cuba, respectively, as they fought

Left: Cleveland took the unpopular stance of sending federal troops to break up a strike of railway-car builders.

Left: The Cleveland family in Grover's retirement years.

Right: The president and his dog.

against European colonizers. A border dispute between Venezuela and British Guiana was eventually settled, but during Cuba's struggle for independence from Spain, the islanders received only diplomatic support from the United States. Cleveland maintained American neutrality while Spanish forces overran the Cuban revolutionaries.

Finally, Cleveland resisted efforts by groups of people who favored printing more currency and adding silver to the nation's reserves. It would have made more cash available to consumers, but the flip side would almost certainly have been runaway inflation. When the country's gold reserves, which were used to back the value of money, became alarmingly low, Cleveland negotiated with wealthy industrialist J. P. Morgan to help rebuild them. The policy proved helpful, but it frustrated many Americans: Morgan got richer while many people were having problems making ends meet.

Cleveland was unpopular as his term came to a close. Democrats turned to William Jennings Bryan, who supported more radical approaches to fiscal policy, and made him their candidate in the 1896 election.

Back to Where He Began

When Cleveland retired from office in 1897, he took his wife and three children to New Jersey, where he had been born sixty years earlier. The Clevelands would have two more children. He remained politically active as a member of the Anti-Imperialism League, a group that opposed the United States maintaining the possessions—Cuba, Puerto Rico, and the Philippines—that it had acquired during the Spanish-American War in 1898. Some of his supporters wanted him to run for president again in 1904, but he had clearly had enough.

Cleveland lived until June 24, 1908, and by that time, he had won back respect for having been an honest and independent politician. During his last years, he was a trustee of Princeton University, where he established a relationship with its president, Woodrow Wilson, who would later become president of the United States. Cleveland's last words were fitting: "I have tried so hard to do right."

Legacy

Grover Cleveland's courageous stands against higher tariffs, American expansionism, and radical economic policies, as well as his uncommon honesty, helped provide stability to a troubled nation on the edge of the modern world. Electricity and skyscrapers were becoming commonplace. Power struggles between business and labor were often bitter. That Cleveland remained independent—trying hard to do right—instead of taking more popular stands, was his finest quality. After almost five decades with Congress dominating national policy, Cleveland was the first in a succession of strong presidents who reinstated forceful executive leadership to the nation.

Nevertheless, many of his policies were overturned by his successor, William McKinley, who reinstated high tariff rates before gradually easing them to lower levels in order to further international trade. Cleveland's antiexpansionist views were also overwhelmed during McKinley's presidency, which saw the fulfillment of American expansion and the idea of manifest destiny, the belief that American expansionism was meant to happen. McKinley reintroduced the annexation of Hawaii, and following victory in the Spanish-American War, the United States took possession of Cuba, Puerto Rico, and the Philippines.

Cleveland's fiscal policies were generally maintained by his successor. He, too, was against bimetallism, and the economy recovered early in his presidency. McKinley's popularity mushroomed as people went back to work and had more spending power. As chief executive, McKinley was the firm leader of the nation, enjoying the power and independence that Cleveland had brought back to the office of president.

Frances Cleveland

Born July 21, 1864, Buffalo, New York
Died October 29, 1947, Baltimore, Maryland

"I want you to take good care of all the furniture. I want to find everything just as it is now when we come back again."
—*Frances Cleveland, to a White House caretaker at the end of her husband's first term*

When bachelor president Grover Cleveland entertained widow Emma Folsom and her daughter, Frances, at the White House shortly after he became president, gossip swirled about a possible romance. Rumors continued even as the Folsoms left for a European vacation during that summer of 1885. Cleveland, meanwhile, grew impatient with the gossip: "I don't see why the papers keep marrying me to old ladies," the confirmed bachelor reportedly said to an aide.

When the Folsoms came home to the United States in May 1886, reporters were waiting for their ship, eager to follow up on the romance angle. Cleveland's White House secretary, meanwhile, chartered a boat and met the ship out in the harbor. The Folsoms were helped aboard, and the boat sped away to a pier safe from nosy reporters.

In the meantime, Cleveland had arrived in New York for the Memorial Day festivities. Inspired by news of a possible presidential romance, a marching band suddenly began playing a wedding march as the parade passed the presidential reviewing stand, and then it broke into a popular song, "He's Going to Marry Yum-Yum." The next morning, newspapers kept the beat going by running stories about Emma Folsom, who was rumored as the president's bride-to-be. Later that day, an official announcement came that the forty-nine-year-old president was indeed engaged. However, he wasn't going to marry the woman mentioned in all those rumors. Instead, he was marrying her daughter, twenty-two-year-old Frances Folsom, whom he affectionately called "Frank." They had become secretly engaged before the Folsoms' European vacation.

On June 2, 1886, President Cleveland became the first chief executive to be married in the White House. Outside the White House grounds, the group of reporters that had been waiting on New York docks was joined by a throng of their peers from all over the country. The mob of journalists followed the newlywed Clevelands on their Maryland honeymoon, where Cleveland complained that he couldn't get any freedom from the press. After the couple returned to Washington, he wrote a letter that was published in the New York *Evening Post*, referring to snooping reporters as "a colossal impertinence."

Carriage, Love, and Marriage

Cleveland had known Frances since she was born in 1864, and he had given her parents a carriage as a gift for their newborn baby. Cleveland and Oscar Folsom, Frances's father, were law partners in Buffalo, New York, and when Oscar died in a horse-and-buggy accident in 1875, Cleveland administered the Folsom estate. He helped ensure that Emma and Frances would live comfortably, and he helped support Frances's education.

Cleveland was elected mayor of Buffalo in 1881 and governor of New York in 1882, and he and Frances wrote letters to each other at that time. She had recently begun studying at Wells College in New York. When the couple married in 1886, Frances Cleveland became the youngest-ever first lady at the age of twenty-two.

Before the wedding, the president told his sister, Rose Elizabeth Cleveland, that "a good wife loves her husband and her country with no desire to run either," and during the wedding ceremony he had traditional vows altered to omit the word "obey." Cleveland's sister served as White House hostess during the period between his inauguration in 1885 and his wedding in 1886. Strongly independent, "Libbie" Cleveland was a proponent of equal rights between the sexes and for women's voting rights. She was a teacher at a girl's school and a respected writer of essays on literature.

Famous American composer John Philip Sousa conducted the U.S. Marine Band at the wedding reception. His fame would increase within the next dozen years after writing such well-known marches as "Semper Fidelis" and "The Stars and Stripes Forever," but the Cleveland wedding was a relatively small ceremony attended only by cabinet officials and a few close friends of the family. The train of the bride's wedding dress was nearly as long as the receiving line.

Popular First Lady

Vivacious and attractive, Frances Cleveland was a popular first lady. She was soon more popular than her husband. A flock of journalists followed the Clevelands, as much to report on events involving the first lady as to provide information on her husband's administration. There were rumors that the Clevelands were having marital difficulties during the presidential campaign of 1888, but the first lady emphatically denied such reports.

Cleveland lost the 1888 election, and as the couple was leaving the White House shortly before the inauguration of his successor, Benjamin Harrison, Frances told a caretaker: "I want you to take good care of all the

Below: Frances meeting with the Cabinet wives.

Left: The family's retirement home in Princeton, New Jersey.

furniture," and she added, "I want to find everything just as it is now when we come back again." The Clevelands were indeed back in the White House following the presidential election of 1892.

In her role as first lady, Frances Cleveland held two receptions each week. She made sure that one of them was open to the public and held on Saturday afternoon, when women with jobs were free to attend. At one reception, she personally greeted over eight thousand guests.

A Long and Happy Life

After the president's defeat in 1888, the Clevelands lived in New York City, where their first child, Ruth, was born. Frances, meanwhile, had remained so popular that she was often pictured with candidate Cleveland on his campaign posters for the 1892 election. Much of her time during the president's second term was spent caring for the couple's children, two of whom were born while the Clevelands were in the White House. Esther was born in 1893, and Marion in 1895. A son, Richard, was born shortly after the Clevelands left the White House in 1897. Their youngest child, Francis Grover, was born in 1903 in Princeton, New Jersey, where the couple had retired.

The Clevelands often entertained the faculty members and students of Princeton University. They became friends with Woodrow Wilson, president of Princeton at the time, who would be elected president of the United States in 1912. Cleveland occasionally wrote articles on political matters and was approached about running for president in 1904, an offer he declined. Cleveland's health began failing soon afterward, and he died in 1908 at the age of seventy-two. His widow, Frances, was forty-four.

Frances continued to live in Princeton and was involved in fundraising activities for several schools, including her alma mater, Wells College. In 1913, she married Thomas J. Preston Jr., an archaeology professor at Princeton. She lived a long and happy life, dying at age eighty-three in 1947. Shortly before her death, she attended a White House luncheon arranged by President Harry S Truman and was introduced to World War II hero Dwight D. Eisenhower, who would follow Truman as president. After learning that Frances had lived in Washington many years before, Eisenhower asked her where in town she had lived, and she responded, "In the White House."

Cleveland's Message to Congress Opposing the Annexation of Hawaii

Delivered on December 18, 1893

In 1892, the monarchy that ruled Hawaii was overthrown by a group led by American businessmen. This led to a new constitutional government which negotiated a treaty of annexation with the United States. President Benjamin Harrison presented the treaty to the U.S. Senate for ratification in February 1893.

President Harrison's term of office expired in March 1893 before the treaty could be approved. He was succeeded by Grover Cleveland, who opposed ratification. Cleveland was among those Americans who had warned against American imperialism—actions by a stronger nation to dominate a weaker one. The new president withdrew the treaty from the Senate and supported efforts to return Hawaii's deposed monarch, Queen Liliuokalani, to the throne. Cleveland officially described his reasons for withdrawing the treaty during his annual message to Congress in December 1893.

Excerpt from Cleveland's Message to Congress

When the present administration entered upon its duties, the Senate had under consideration a treaty providing for the annexation of the Hawaiian Islands to the territory of the United States. Surely under our Constitution and laws the enlargement of our limits is a manifestation of the highest attribute of sovereignty, and if entered upon as an executive act, all things relating to the transaction should be clear and free from suspicion. Additional importance attached to this particular treaty of annexation because it contemplated a departure from unbroken American tradition in providing for the addition to our territory of islands of the sea more than two thousand miles removed from our nearest coast. [...]

I conceived it to be my duty, therefore, to withdraw the treaty from the Senate for examination, and meanwhile to cause an accurate, full, and impartial investigation to be made of the facts attending the subversion of the constitutional government of Hawaii and the installment in its place of the Provisional Government. [...]

As I apprehend the situation, we are brought face to face with the following conditions:

The lawful government of Hawaii was overthrown without the drawing of a sword or the firing of a shot by a process every step of which, it may safely be asserted, is directly traceable to and dependent for its success upon the agency of the United States acting through its diplomatic and naval representatives.

But for the notorious predilections of the United States minister for annexation, the Committee of Safety, which should be called the Committee of Annexation, would never have existed.

But for the landing of the United States forces upon false pretexts respecting the danger to life and property, the committee would never have exposed themselves to the pains and penalties of treason by undertaking the subversion of the queen's government.

But for the presence of the United States forces in the immediate vicinity and in position to afford all needed protection and support, the committee would not have proclaimed the Provisional Government from the steps of the government building.

And, finally, but for the lawless occupation of Honolulu under false pretexts by the United States forces, and but for Minister [John L.] Stevens' [U.S. minister to the Hawaiian Islands in 1889] recognition of the Provisional Government when the United States forces were its sole support and constituted its only military strength, the queen and her government would never have yielded to the Provisional Government, even for a time and for the sole purpose of submitting her case to the enlightened justice of the United States.

Believing, therefore, that the United States could not, under the circumstances disclosed, annex the islands without justly incurring the imputation of acquiring them by unjustifiable methods, I shall not again submit the treaty of annexation to the Senate for its consideration, and in the instructions to Minister [Albert S.] Willis [U.S. minister to the Hawaiian Islands from 1893 to 1897], a copy of which accompanies this message, I have directed him to so inform the Provisional Government.

But in the present instance our duty does not, in my opinion, end with refusing to consummate this questionable transaction. It has been the boast of our government that it seeks to do justice in all things without regard to the strength or weakness of those with whom it deals. I mistake the American people if they favor the odious doctrine that there is no such thing as international morality; that there is one law for a strong nation and another for a weak one, and that even by indirection a strong power may with impunity despoil a weak one of its territory.

By an act of war, committed with the participation of a diplomatic representative of the United States and without authority of Congress, the government of a feeble but friendly and confiding people has been overthrown. A substantial wrong has thus been done which a due regard for our national character as well as the rights of the injured people requires we should endeavor to repair. The Provisional Government has not assumed a republican or other constitutional form, but has remained a mere executive council or oligarchy, set up without the assent of the people. It has not sought to find a permanent basis of popular support and has given no evidence of an intention to do so. Indeed, the representatives of that government assert that the people of Hawaii are unfit for popular government and frankly avow that they can be best ruled by arbitrary or despotic power.

The law of nations is founded upon reason and justice, and the rules of conduct governing individual relations between citizens or subjects of a civilized state are equally applicable as between enlightened nations. The considerations that international law is without a court for its enforcement and that obedience to its commands practically depends upon good faith instead of upon the mandate of a superior tribunal only give additional sanction to the law itself and brand any deliberate infraction of it not merely as a wrong but as a disgrace. A man of true honor protects the unwritten word which binds his conscience more scrupulously, if possible, than he does the bond a breach of which subjects him to legal liabilities, and the United States, in aiming to maintain itself as one of the most enlightened nations, would do its citizens gross injustice if it applied to its international relations any other than a high standard of honor and morality.

On that ground the United States cannot properly be put in the position of countenancing a wrong after its commission any more than in that of consenting to it in advance. On that ground it cannot allow itself to refuse to redress an injury inflicted through an abuse of power by officers clothed with its authority and wearing its uniform; and on the same ground, if a feeble but friendly state is in danger of being robbed of its independence and its sovereignty by a misuse of the name and power of the United States, the United States cannot fail to vindicate its honor and its sense of justice by an earnest effort to make all possible reparation.

These principles apply to the present case with irresistible force when the special conditions of the queen's surrender of her sovereignty are recalled. She surrendered, not to the Provisional Government but to the United States. She surrendered, not absolutely and permanently but temporarily and conditionally until such time as the facts could be considered by the United States. Furthermore, the Provisional Government acquiesced in her surrender in that manner and on those terms, not only by tacit consent but through the positive acts of some members of the government who urged her peaceable submission, not merely to avoid bloodshed but because she could place implicit reliance upon the justice of the United States and that the whole subject would be finally considered at Washington.

What Happened Next

By the time Cleveland withdrew the treaty, revolutionaries in Hawaii were firmly in power and refused to yield to Cleveland's pressures for a return to monarchy. Realizing that annexation was being delayed, the revolutionaries began to establish an independent republic. On May 30, 1894, they held a constitutional convention in Honolulu, and the constitution creating the new Republic of Hawaii took effect on July 4.

Cleveland was successful in making Americans consider whether the nation should continue to pursue foreign relations that bordered on imperialism. Many Americans, however, were more concerned about increasing and benefiting from international trade. The anti-imperialist views of Cleveland and his fellow Democrat William Jennings Bryan were not as well received as the more aggressive internationalist approach of Republican presidents Benjamin Harrison and William McKinley. McKinley succeeded Cleveland as president in March 1897, and a year later both houses of Congress approved a joint resolution to annex Hawaii. A joint resolution is different from a treaty because it requires only a majority vote in both houses of Congress, while a treaty needs two-thirds ratification by the Senate. President McKinley signed the resolution on July 7, 1898, and the formal transfer of Hawaiian sovereignty to the United States took place in Honolulu on August 12. Hawaii became a U.S. territory on June 14, 1900, making all its citizens U.S. citizens. The territory—which includes the islands of Hawaii, Kahoolawe, Kauai, Lanai, Maui, Molokai, Nihau, and Oahu—became a state in 1959.

Since the arrival of whites in Hawaii in the late eighteenth century, natives of the island lost their religion, their land, and their traditions; with the overthrow of the monarchy, they lost their independence as well. Cleveland had hoped to avoid that situation.

Benjamin Harrison

"The law, the will of the majority [of Americans]…is the only king to which we bow."

—*Benjamin Harrison*

Twenty-third president of the United States, 1889–1893

Full name: *Benjamin Harrison*
Born: *August 20, 1833, North Bend, Ohio*
Died: *March 13, 1901, Indianapolis, Indiana*
Burial site: *Crown Hill Cemetery, Indianapolis, Indiana*
Parents: *John and Elizabeth Irwin Harrison*
Spouse: *Caroline Lavinia Scott (1832–1892; m. 1853); Mary Scott Lord Dimmick (1858–1948; m. 1896)*
Children: *Russell Benjamin (1854–1936); Mary Scott (1858–1930); unnamed girl (died at birth in 1861); Elizabeth (1897–1955)*
Religion: *Presbyterian*
Education: *Miami (Ohio) University (B.A., 1852)*
Occupation: *Lawyer*
Government positions: *U.S. senator from Indiana*
Political party: *Republican*
Dates as president: *March 4, 1889–March 4, 1893*
Age upon taking office: *55*

Benjamin Harrison was a soft-spoken man who patiently went about his business as a lawyer and as a politician. There were no major events during his presidency, but he signed several important economic measures into law and worked to expand the Union. Montana, North Dakota, South Dakota, Washington, Idaho, and Wyoming all became states during his presidency, and he supported measures that helped several other territories—Utah, Oklahoma, and Hawaii—become states after he left office. At the beginning of Harrison's term in 1889, the number of states in the Union was thirty-eight; when he left office in 1891, it had grown to forty-four.

The most difficult challenges Harrison faced as president were in foreign relations. The governments of the United States and Great Britain argued over fishing rights in the Bering Straits around the Alaska Territory. Anti-Italian sentiments in New Orleans caused a major diplomatic crisis between the United States and Italy. The United States confronted Chile over the deaths of two American sailors there. After the monarchy of Queen Liliuokalani of Hawaii was overturned in a revolution that was led by Americans, Harrison attempted to annex the island.

Harrison was an effective president although not a powerful or an inspiring one. Like many administrations between 1865 and 1896, his was continually challenged by congressional actions, while the general public was more interested in regional issues. While Harrison received 100,000 fewer votes than his Democratic opponent, incumbent president Grover Cleveland, in the 1888 presidential election, he won in most of the large states for a sure victory in the Electoral College (233 to 168).

After he failed to win reelection in 1892, Harrison returned to his law practice and served as an attorney in important international trials. He also wrote the book *This Country of Ours,* which explains how the federal government operates.

Little Ben and the Family Tree

It isn't surprising that Benjamin Harrison became involved in politics. His grandfather, William Henry Harrison, was elected president in 1840, when young Ben was seven years old. His great-grandfather, also named Benjamin Harrison, was one of the signers of the Declaration of Independence and later served as governor of Virginia. Another Harrison ancestor, Thomas, served as an official under Oliver Cromwell, a leader of the English Revolution that overthrew the monarchy of King Charles I; he was ultimately beheaded for his involvement in the revolution, and his descendants fled to America. Ben's father, John, was elected to Congress in 1854, when his son was twenty-one years old.

Benjamin Harrison was born on his grandfather's farm in North Bend, Ohio, on August 20, 1833, the second of the six children of John and Elizabeth Harrison, his father being the only man to have been the son of one American president and the father of another. The boy was raised on his parents' six-hundred-acre farm nearby, where he performed farm chores as a youngster, attended school, and spent his spare time swimming and hunting. He moved on to Farmer's College near Cincinnati, and

Timeline

1776: Benjamin Harrison's great-grandfather, also named Benjamin Harrison, is one of the signers of the Declaration of Independence

1833: Benjamin Harrison is born in Ohio

1840: William Henry Harrison, Benjamin's grandfather, is elected president when young Ben is seven years old

1854: Benjamin Harrison opens law practice in Indianapolis

1862: Begins fighting in Civil War; finishes the war as brigadier general

1876: Loses Indiana governor's race

1881–87: Serves in U.S. Senate

1888: Defeats incumbent Grover Cleveland to become the "centennial president," elected to office one hundred years after George Washington became the first U.S. president

1889–93: Serves as twenty-third U.S. president

1892: Loses 1892 election to former president Cleveland

1901: Dies in Indiana

then he transferred to the University of Miami in Ohio, and graduated from there in 1852. He was an excellent student and participated in debates. He became deeply religious around this time and considered becoming a Presbyterian minister, but he eventually chose to study law instead.

He married Caroline Livinia Scott in 1853. They had been friends for several years and fell in love while they both attended school in Oxford, Ohio; he was a student at the University of Miami, and she was enrolled at the nearby Oxford Female Institute. Her father, a Presbyterian minister, presided over the wedding ceremony. The couple would have three children, one of whom died at birth.

Harrison was admitted to the bar in 1854, and he decided to open a law office in Indianapolis, Indiana. He and Caroline maintained a home there for the rest of their lives, fulfilling a promise he made to her that their lives would be filled with "quiet usefulness."

Harrison gradually developed a distinguished law practice, and was highly regarded for his careful, polite, and persistent cross-examinations of witnesses. He became involved in presidential politics as a Republican, campaigning locally for John C. Frémont in 1856, and for Abraham Lincoln four years later. He became city attorney for Indianapolis, and he was elected secretary of the Republican State Central Committee.

During the Civil War, Harrison was commissioned as a colonel in the army charged with recruiting and preparing soldiers to fight in the Seventieth Indiana Volunteer Infantry. Short and stocky, Harrison was nicknamed "Little Ben" by his soldiers, who respected his seriousness and determination. After fighting successfully in a few small battles in Kentucky, Harrison's group came under the leadership of General William Tecumseh Sherman, and he took part in the key battles of Atlanta and Peach Tree Creek. He was cited "for ability and manifest energy and gallantry in command of brigades," and by the end of the war in 1865, he had risen to the rank of brigadier general.

What's in a Nickname?

Benjamin Harrison is considered to have been one of the dullest presidents. His low-key demeanor did not exactly inspire lively nicknames: His Civil War troops called him "Little Ben" (he was only five feet, six inches tall), political opponents in Indiana called him "Kid Gloves" Harrison (for his mild nature), friends called him the "human iceberg" (for his stiffness and formality in public), and he was also known as the "centennial president" (for taking office one hundred years after George Washington).

On the other hand, Harrison's grandfather, William Henry Harrison, the nation's ninth president, was known as a more charismatic, vigorous individual. As a famous general, he defeated Chief Tecumseh and then ran for president with the famous nickname "Tippecanoe" for the battle. The public's fond memories of Grandfather Harrison often annoyed his grandson. According to The American President (Philip B. Kunhardt Jr., Philip B. Kunhardt III, and Peter W. Kunhardt, 1999), Benjamin Harrison sought to distance himself from his famous grandfather. "My ambition is for quietness rather than for publicity," he said. "I want it understood that I am the grandson of nobody."

Left: Harrison received national attention as head of the Mississippi River Commission.

"Kid Gloves" Harrison Overcomes Defeat

After the war ended, Harrison went back to Indianapolis and resumed his law practice as well as his involvement in Republican politics. He was selected as the defense lawyer in 1871 when the government was sued for $100,000 by Lambdin Milligan, a Southern civilian and a secret member of a Confederate group supporting the states that had separated from the Union. Accused by federal troops of inciting a rebellion, he was tried before a military tribunal, found guilty, and sentenced to death, but his case was eventually heard by the United States Supreme Court, which overturned the conviction. The Court ruled that the case should have been tried in a civil court rather than by a tribunal of federal forces occupying the South.

In the subsequent civil case, Harrison made the convincing argument that the tribunal had acted in good faith and was performing a normal procedure. The jury ruled in favor of Milligan, but his compensation for damages was set at only $5, although he had sued for $100,000.

Harrison's professional career prospered in the postwar years, and he became a more powerful force within the Republican Party, even though he kept losing when he ran for office. He tried but failed to win the Republican nomination for governor of Indiana in 1872, and four years later he lost the gubernatorial election to

James D. "Blue Jeans" Williams, a farmer who got his nickname for the plain clothes he wore.

In 1879, President Rutherford B. Hayes appointed him to head the Mississippi River Commission with responsibility for developing economic activity along the river, a position that gave him exposure in several states. At the 1880 Republican national convention, he was one of the early supporters of James A. Garfield, who emerged as the party's dark-horse nominee, even though he was not one of the three leading contenders when the convention began.

Harrison won his first election when the Indiana legislature voted him to the U.S. Senate in 1881. During his tenure, he supported many of the same causes that he later championed as president: statehood for the Dakota territory (the measure failed); creation of a civil government for the Alaska territory (a step toward statehood); support for civil rights (regulating the power of railroads to remove settlers and Indians from land adjacent to their rights-of-way); backing high

Sideline

Most men who came home from the Civil War were faced with mountains of debt that had accumulated while they were away. But Benjamin Harrison had a thriving law practice to come home to, and he managed to wrangle an appointment as Indiana's Supreme Court Reporter. In return for collecting and organizing all the decisions of the state's highest court, he was able to sell the resulting books to lawyers around the state and keep the profits for himself. He added a new wrinkle by offering to pay the postage on out-of-town shipments, and sold out the 1864 report in a couple of weeks. His profit was $1,500, far more than any of his predecessors ever even dreamed of earning.

Naturally, his windfall raised eyebrows down at the Internal Revenue office, but Harrison refused to pay a tax on his sideline income, noting that his book sale was official state business and therefore exempt from federal taxes. The tax man didn't see it that way, and when the case went to court, the judge ruled that taxes were due. The decision was reversed on appeal, and Harrison got his money back. Even as president, Harrison had little regard for tax collectors. He regarded them as a necessary evil, but an evil nonetheless.

tariffs to protect American businesses; and supporting the expansion of government pensions and providing additional benefits to Civil War veterans. In an 1886 speech on the Senate floor, he shamed Democrats by coming to the defense of a poor widow who had been fired from her post-office position in a small Illinois town and replaced by a Democratic Party supporter.

Harrison lost his bid for reelection to the Senate in 1887 when the Indiana legislature, which was responsible for electing the state's senators, favored his Democratic counterpart by a single vote. But he remained a nationally known figure because of his family background and the integrity he had displayed in Congress. He was popular with Civil War veterans and well respected in the key Electoral College states of the Midwest.

Republican official H. T. Michner began a quiet, behind-the-scenes campaign to have Harrison nominated as the Republican presidential candidate for the 1888 election. He won the nomination and campaigned effectively against his Democratic opponent, Grover Cleveland. His support for high tariffs and his appeal to Civil War veterans (Cleveland had not fought in the war) helped him carry large states of the East and Midwest. The result was an Electoral College victory (233 votes to 168), even though Cleveland had surpassed him by more than 100,000 popular votes.

1888 Election Results

Presidential/Vice Presidential Candidates	Popular Votes	Electoral Votes
Benjamin Harrison/ Levi P. Morton (Republican)	5,444,337	233
Grover Cleveland/ Allen G. Thurman (Democratic)	5,540,309	168

Former secretary of the treasury John Sherman was the early leader in the race for the Republican nomination. Harrison went from fifth place on the first ballot to his victory on the eighth ballot. On the Democratic side, former Ohio senator Thurman was selected as the incumbent president Cleveland's running mate. Cleveland's previous running mate, Thomas A. Hendricks, had died during his first year as vice president.

A "Legal Deal"

Harrison had promised a "legal deal" in his campaign for the presidency. It had been common for incoming presidents to reward their party supporters with government jobs, but Harrison proved to be more independent. Two future presidents, Theodore Roosevelt and William Howard Taft, held federal positions during Harrison's tenure, as did many lawyers. However, in bypassing some Republican supporters, Harrison lost support from his own party in Congress, and the situation grew worse when a Democratic majority was elected to the House of Representatives in 1890.

The Emergence of Populism

The concerns of farmers were largely ignored in the post–Civil War era as industry brought prosperity to America. Agricultural prices sagged during the 1870s and 1880s, and Eastern, urban-based trusts dominated distribution of farm products. The problem was especially critical in the South and West, where agriculture still remained the backbone of the economy, and a political movement emerged out of these frustrations to challenge the established Democratic and Republican parties. The People's Party, better known as the Populist Party, became powerful in those regions during the 1880s and 1890s as farmers and urban laborers joined up, both faced with minimum wages barely enough to buy basic necessities.

Populists wanted to increase the money supply, which they believed would circulate more money among farmers and laborers. Among programs that were later adopted, they called for an income tax that would shift the burden of taxation from land to income; an eight-hour workday for wage earners; and the popular election of U.S. senators, who had previously been elected by the state governments. The Populist movement gained enough strength to elect numerous candidates to statewide and national offices, and by 1892 the party mounted a presidential campaign with General James B. Weaver of Iowa as their leader.

The 1892 Populist platform called for free and unlimited coinage of silver and government ownership of the railroad and telegraph industries. Weaver polled over one million votes and carried four states, placing third behind the winner Grover Cleveland and President Benjamin Harrison. The campaign divided the working people along racial lines, with Southern blacks lining up with the Populists, while Western and Southern white farmers stuck with the Democratic Party, fearful of losing what little political clout they had. The solid black vote for the Populists and a continuing cycle of poverty in the South led to a backlash by whites, who enacted Jim Crow laws that placed voting restrictions on black citizens.

The Populist movement grew stronger during an economic depression between 1893 and 1896. When 1896 Democratic presidential candidate William Jennings Bryan embraced the unlimited coinage of silver in his famous "Cross of Gold" speech ("You shall not press down upon the brow of labor this crown of thorns, you shall not crucify mankind upon a cross of gold," he said to Republicans who supported a currency backed only by gold), Populists jumped on the Bryan bandwagon, and in a close race, Bryan, the champion of both Democrats and Populists, lost to Republican William McKinley. It was the last major effort of Populism and the end of the agrarian movement against industrialism.

The Harrison Administration

Administration Dates: March 4, 1889–March 4, 1893
Vice President: Levi P. Morton (1889–93)
Cabinet:

Secretary of State	James G. Blaine (1889–92)
	John W. Foster (1892–93)
Secretary of the Treasury	William Windom (1889–91)
	Charles Foster (1891–93)
Secretary of War	Redfield Proctor (1889–91)
	Stephen B. Elkins (1891–93)
Attorney General	William H. H. Miller (1889–93)
Secretary of the Navy	Benjamin F. Tracy (1889–93)
Postmaster General	John Wanamaker (1889–93)
Secretary of the Interior	John W. Noble (1889–93)
Secretary of Agriculture	Jeremiah M. Rusk (1889–93)

Still, Harrison was effective working with Congress in several areas. The McKinley Tariff, which placed high taxes on many imported goods, was signed into law. The Sherman Antitrust Act, which made it illegal for large corporations to force out competing, smaller businesses from a particular market, was also passed, and Harrison's continued support for Civil War veterans led to the authorization of government funds for disabled veterans even if their injuries occurred after the war.

Harrison faced a series of international disputes. A conflict with Great Britain over fishing rights in the Bering Sea was eventually settled in arbitration through a neutral third party. When American sailors were injured in an unprovoked attack in Chile, Harrison threatened to end diplomatic relations, and the dispute was quickly settled by an apology and reparations from the Chilean government. Harrison also faced a crisis with Italy after a case concerning Italian-based organized crime in New Orleans escalated into violence: A policeman was killed, and then eleven Italians were murdered by an angry mob. In an apologetic letter to the Italian government, Harrison denounced the lynchings and answered the Italian government's insistence that the federal government should prosecute the offenders by carefully explaining that the case was subject to state legal procedures, rather than federal jurisdiction, as mandated by the Constitution.

In Hawaii, meanwhile, Americans began a revolt against Queen Liliuokalani, the native leader who had taken measures against the growing American business influence in her kingdom. Hoping to extend American naval bases there, Harrison did nothing when a revolution overthrew the queen and resulted in an American-led civil government, which Harrison backed. He signed a treaty with them and proposed the annexation of the islands.

Harrison was generally viewed as an honest but dull politician, never quite able to rally great enthusiasm for his causes. The 1892 presidential election, which once again pitted Harrison against Cleveland, was somber: Harrison's wife, Caroline, was gravely ill, and he refused to campaign, choosing instead to remain at her side. Cleveland showed his respect by refusing to campaign as well. Caroline died shortly before the election.

The only real excitement of the campaign occurred in western states, where Populist candidate James B. Weaver was enthusiastically supported by farmers and settlers. Meanwhile, Harrison's chances were hurt by labor unrest—several strikes occurred throughout the country—and by predictions of an economic downturn. Cleveland had attracted over 100,000 more votes than Harrison in 1888; in 1892, the difference grew to more than 400,000 popular votes, and Cleveland won the election handily with 277 electoral votes to Harrison's 149. Weaver, the well-liked Populist of the West, captured 22 electoral votes.

Below: Queen Liliuokalani of Hawaii.

James B. Weaver

James Baird Weaver was born on June 12, 1833, in Dayton, Ohio. His family soon moved to Iowa, and he attended country schools there. He made his way to California at the age of twenty during the great gold rush years, but he went home empty-handed. After that, he entered and graduated from Cincinnati Law School in a single year, and then opened a law practice in Bloomfield, Iowa.

Weaver became involved in local politics as a Republican opposed to the expansion of slavery into new territories. During the Civil War, he volunteered as an officer and participated in the bloody battles at Fort Donelson, Shiloh, and Corinth, where he assumed field command when his superior officers were mortally wounded. He was soon promoted to major, and by the time he returned to Iowa in 1864, he had become a brevetted brigadier general and was known as "General" Weaver for the rest of his life.

He became a district attorney in 1866, and between then and 1873, while holding the appointive position of assessor of revenue for the federal government, he found himself at odds with the Republican leadership over currency policies and the subsidization of railroads. Weaver wanted the currency expanded to meet the needs of common people, and he joined the Greenback Party, which favored his views on monetary reform. He was elected to Congress in 1878, ran for president in 1880, lost the congressional election in 1882, but won two additional terms after 1884 as a third-party candidate.

Weaver joined a group called the Farmers' Alliance, which reflected his views on money matters, and played a major role in bringing it into the Populist Party. As the Populist candidate for president in 1892, he received more than a million popular votes and twenty-two votes in the Electoral College. Four years later, he brought about a merger with the Democrats behind William Jennings Bryan's unsuccessful presidential campaign. This terminated the Populist crusade, and Weaver's career as a national politician was over. He later served as mayor of Colfax, his Iowa hometown. Weaver died in Des Moines, Iowa, on February 6, 1912.

An Active Aftermath

Harrison mourned the death of his wife through the remainder of his term, eventually returning to the Indianapolis home that they had shared for almost forty years, but he was soon active again. He lectured on constitutional law at Stanford University and wrote the book *This Country of Ours*, which was published in 1897. Meanwhile, he remarried in 1896 and fathered a daughter the following year, at the age of sixty-five. His second wife, Mary Scott Lord Dimmick, a niece of Caroline Harrison, had been widowed in 1882, less than three months after she was married.

In 1899, former president Harrison helped represent the nation of Venezuela in a border dispute, and he was appointed to the international court of arbitration at The Hague the following year. After falling ill, Harrison went home again to Indianapolis, where he died on March 13, 1901.

Legacy

Benjamin Harrison's most noteworthy accomplishments rest in avoiding or settling several international disputes. After years of isolationism, the United States was finding itself increasingly involved in international conflicts, which continued after Harrison's presidency. Harrison foresaw the trend, and he supported appropriations bills to expand the navy's fleet. His interest in annexing Hawaii was at least partly due to its prime location for naval operations in the Pacific Ocean.

"The indiscriminate denunciation of the rich is mischievous. It perverts the mind, poisons the heart, and furnishes an excuse to crime. No poor man was ever made richer or happier by it. It is as illogical to despise a man because he is rich as because he is poor. Not what a man has, but what he is, settles his class. We cannot right matters by taking from one what he has honestly acquired to bestow upon another what he has not earned."

—*Benjamin Harrison*

Grover Cleveland, Harrison's successor, withdrew the annexation treaty from Congress, but William McKinley,

Right: Mary Harrison, the former president's second wife.

who followed him into the White House, reintroduced the measure and Hawaii officially became a U.S. territory in 1900. McKinley also presided during the Spanish-American War when America emerged as a major international naval power.

The economy took a downturn shortly after Harrison left office. Many blamed high tariff rates, excessive government spending, and a currency devaluation, all of which can be traced to policies Harrison supported. Still, the high tariff rate established in 1890 was established by William McKinley, and the tariff issue did not hurt him when he ran for president in 1896. A good portion of increased government spending under Harrison went for good causes—pensions and improvement of the U.S. Navy. The devaluation of the currency arose because of widespread public support for printing more money, backed by increased mining of silver.

Harrison is often referred to as the "centennial president" because he was elected one hundred years after the first U.S. president, George Washington. The country was in a period of transition while Harrison was in office. His family roots stretched back to the beginnings of the republic, and he was among the last leaders of that old order. A new century was close at hand, and the beginning of the modern presidency is often set by historians at 1896 with the administration of William McKinley.

Caroline Harrison

Born October 1, 1832, Oxford, Ohio
Died October 25, 1892, Washington, D.C.

"We have within ourselves the only element of destruction, our foes are from within, not from without. Our hope is in unity and self-sacrifice."

—Caroline Harrison

An accomplished pianist and painter, Caroline "Carrie" Harrison blended her interest in the arts with the growing sense of national history that accompanied her husband's presidential administration. Benjamin Harrison was called the "centennial president," having taken office one hundred years after the first American president, George Washington.

Carrie Harrison supported the founding of the Daughters of the American Revolution, a group that helps preserve items and places of historical significance, and she served as the group's first president. She applied its historical service to the White House: Among other accomplishments, she designed the china pattern used for place settings during her husband's presidency and she gathered examples of dinnerware from past administrations. The china collection she started has since grown into one of the more visually informative displays on exhibit at the White House.

The White House had undergone alternating periods of grandeur and neglect. It was described as "barracks" just ten years earlier by President Chester A. Arthur, who introduced many improvements. Under Carrie Harrison's direction, the executive mansion was transformed into its modern status as a stately manor filled with historically significant artifacts and artworks. As the nation moved into a second century of Constitutional government, an especially appropriate symbol of progress was introduced to the White House when Carrie Harrison supervised the installation of electricity.

Artistic Background

Caroline Lavinia Scott was born on October 1, 1832, in Oxford, Ohio, the second daughter of John W. Scott, a Presbyterian minister, and Mary Potts Neal Scott. Reverend Scott was founder of the Oxford Female Institute, where Carrie later studied, and where, after graduating, she briefly taught piano classes. Her father was a longtime professor at Miami University in Oxford. He was teaching there at the time of Caroline's birth and was still there eighteen years later, teaching the physical sciences, when Benjamin Harrison arrived.

Harrison was a junior, recently transferred from Farmer's College in Cincinnati, and he already knew Caroline. He was a serious young man who was becoming more deeply religious and who excelled in the study of Latin, Greek, and the natural sciences. Caroline was more lively and interested in the arts and dancing. They graduated from their respective schools in 1852, became engaged, and were married in 1853.

The Harrisons moved to Indianapolis the following year, and Harrison established a law practice. With a distinguished family that included grandfather William Henry Harrison, the ninth president of the United States, the Harrison name was well known in Indiana for his grandfather's exploits in leading troops that defeated Native Americans in the famous Battle of Tippecanoe in 1811. Benjamin and Caroline lived modestly as he established his law practice and became involved in politics as a supporter of Republican Party presidential candidates John C. Frémont in 1856 and Abraham Lincoln four years later.

Harrison served in the Civil War while Caroline raised their two children in Indianapolis. He returned there after the war and resumed his law practice, becoming a distinguished lawyer over the next decade and a leader in the Republican Party. Nevertheless, he twice failed in bids to be elected governor of Indiana. He was elected to the U.S. Senate in 1881 and served through 1887, when he lost a chance for reelection. But Harrison remained a nationally known figure because of his family background and the integrity he had displayed in Congress. He was nominated as the Republican presidential candidate for the 1888 election and won a close contest.

Above: The Harrison home in Indianapolis, Indiana.

Active First Lady

The Harrison White House was an extremely active place. The couple was joined by their son and daughter and their families. Benjamin Harrison was seven years old when his grandfather was elected president; now he was president himself and his grandchildren roamed the White House grounds. Caroline's father, her sister, and a niece also lived in the mansion, forming a large extended family that enlivened White House dinners and parties.

Carrie Harrison was active with local charities and with her public role as president of the Daughters of the American Revolution. She was involved in fund-raising, helping to gain financial support for a new medical school at Johns Hopkins University. She plunged into that cause after being assured that the school would accept female applicants.

In addition to painting china, designing dinnerware patterns, and establishing the White House china collection, Carrie Harrison was involved in White House improvements. She supervised the installation of electricity and also worked with an architect on plans to enlarge the mansion. Wanting to create more office space for the president and administration officials, as well as more living space, which had become cramped, she proposed building two wings that would give the building a U-shaped appearance. One wing would be devoted entirely to office space, while the other would be devoted to a museum. However, Congress never approved the plans, and before Carrie could pursue them further, she was struck down by a serious illness during the winter of 1891.

Carrie Harrison never recovered from what was diagnosed as tuberculosis. Her husband was nominated to run for a second term in 1892, but his thoughts and feelings were focused on his stricken wife, and he refused to leave her side to campaign. In respect toward his action and to honor the first lady, Harrison's opponent, Grover Cleveland, also refused to campaign. On October 25, 1892, shortly before election day, Caroline Harrison died. Mary Harrison McKee, her daughter, fulfilled hostess duties for the remainder of her father's term.

Harrison's Message to the Senate Supporting the Annexation of Hawaii

Delivered on February 15, 1893

During the latter part of the nineteenth century, American and European business leaders in Hawaii struggled against native royalty, King Kalakaua, who ruled from 1874 until his death in 1891, and his sister, Queen Liliuokalani, who succeeded him. By 1887, a group of American and other white business leaders had established an armed militia and were successful in creating a new constitution that limited royal powers. The so-called Bayonet Constitution based the right to vote on wealth, a provision that disenfranchised about three-quarters of the native Hawaiian voters. European and American males could vote, even if they were not Hawaiian citizens, but Asian immigrants were denied the right.

Queen Liliuokalani attempted to recover some of the power of the monarchy when she took the throne in 1891, and she opposed efforts of the white business community to have the islands annexed to the United States. When she attempted to impose a new constitution, powerful white leaders occupied the government office building in Honolulu and overthrew the monarchy. The rebels were helped by the official U.S. representative there who ordered troops from a U.S. warship to land in Honolulu to protect American lives and property. The rebels proclaimed a provisional government headed by Sanford B. Dole, the son of an American missionary.

Two days after taking over, the new government sent representatives to Washington to negotiate a treaty of annexation, which was signed in February 1893. On February 15, President Benjamin Harrison sent a message to the Senate and formally presented the treaty for ratification.

Excerpt from Harrison's Message to the Senate Supporting the Annexation of Hawaii

It has been the policy of the administration not only to respect but to encourage the continuance of an independent government in the Hawaiian Islands so long as it afforded suitable guarantees for the protection of life and property and maintained a stability and strength that gave adequate security against the domination of any other power. The moral support of this government has continually manifested itself in the most friendly diplomatic relations and in many acts of courtesy to the Hawaiian rulers.

The overthrow of the monarchy was not in any way promoted by this government, but had its origin in what seems to have been a reactionary and revolutionary policy on the part of Queen Liliuokalani, which put in serious peril not only the large and preponderating interests of the United States in the islands but all foreign interests, and, indeed, the decent administration of civil affairs and the peace of the islands. It is quite evident that the monarchy had become effete and the queen's government so weak and inadequate as to be the prey of designing and unscrupulous persons. The restoration of Queen Liliuokalani to her throne is undesirable, if not impossible, and unless actively supported by the United States would be accompanied by serious disaster and the disorganization of all business interests. The influence and interest of the United States in the islands must be increased and not diminished.

Only two courses are now open—one, the establishment of a protectorate by the United States, and the other annexation, full and complete. I think the latter course, which has been adopted

in the treaty, will be highly promotive of the best interests of the Hawaiian people and is the only one that will adequately secure the interests of the United States. These interests are not wholly selfish. It is essential that none of the other great powers shall secure these islands. Such a possession would not consist with our safety and with the peace of the world. This view of the situation is so apparent and conclusive that no protest has been heard from any government against proceedings looking to annexation. Every foreign representative at Honolulu promptly acknowledged the Provisional Government, and I think there is a general concurrence in the opinion that the deposed queen ought not to be restored.

What Happened Next

The issue of the annexation of Hawaii occurred very late in Harrison's presidency. In fact, by the time his administration had negotiated the treaty of annexation and transmitted it to the Senate, Harrison had already been defeated in a reelection bid. His presidential term expired three weeks after the treaty was sent to the Senate.

Grover Cleveland, Harrison's successor as president, withdrew the treaty of annexation. He wanted an investigation of the overthrow of the Hawaiian government to be conducted to ensure that the negotiated treaty was legal. Under the guidelines of the Constitution, the president is responsible for negotiating a treaty, and the Senate votes on whether to ratify it with a two-thirds majority. Cleveland never reintroduced the treaty to the Senate, but his successor, President William McKinley, supported annexation of Hawaii, as did a majority of the American people. It became official in July 1898 following a joint resolution of Congress. Hawaii became a U.S. territory two years later, and the fiftieth state in 1959.

William McKinley

"We have good money, we have ample revenues, we have unquestioned national credit, but what we want is new markets."
—William McKinley

Twenty-fifth president of the United States, 1897–1901

Full name: William McKinley Jr.
Born: January 29, 1843, Niles, Ohio
Died: September 14, 1901, Buffalo, New York
Burial site: McKinley National Memorial, Westlawn Cemetery, Canton, Ohio
Parents: William and Nancy Campbell Allison McKinley
Spouse: Ida Saxton (1847–1907; m. 1871)
Children: Katherine (1871–1876); Ida (1873–1873)
Religion: Methodist
Education: Attended Allegheny College
Occupations: Soldier; lawyer
Government positions: U.S. representative from Ohio; Ohio governor
Political party: Republican
Dates as president: March 4, 1897–March 4, 1901 (first term); March 4, 1901–September 14, 1901 (second term)
Age upon taking office: 54

William McKinley was a popular president. He led the nation during the emergence of the United States into its modern position as a global economic and military power.

Businesses did well during the McKinley administration, jobs were abundant, and the booming economy grew even stronger as the United States became more heavily involved in international trade. It was also during McKinley's presidency that the United States quickly and decisively won the Spanish-American War.

Debate continues, however, about his effectiveness as president. He intended to address several key issues during his second term. But his opportunity was cut short with his assassination in 1901.

Throughout his political career—as a congressman, as governor of Ohio, and as president—McKinley promoted business interests. Taking a cautious approach, he supported the protection of American business and industry by taxing imported goods to keep their prices high and stifle competition. He preferred to allow home businesses to manufacture and sell their goods without government controls.

Timeline

1843: Born in Ohio

1861: Civil War begins with firing on Fort Sumter; McKinley enlists in the Twenty-third Ohio Voluntary Regiment under the command of future president Rutherford B. Hayes

1865: Civil War ends; McKinley leaves the military, having been honored several times for bravery and having reached the rank of brevet major

1877–84, 1885–91: Serves in the U.S. House of Representatives

1890: Writes the McKinley Tariff Act; loses election and his seat in the U.S. House of Representatives

1893–97: Serves as Ohio governor

1897–1901: Serves as twenty-fifth U.S. president; seeks to revive a stagnant economy

1898: Economy booming; battleship *Maine* explodes in Havana Harbor, killing 266 Americans; McKinley asks for and receives from Congress a Declaration of War on Spain; Spanish-American War lasts four months, with the United States winning and gaining control of Cuba, Puerto Rico, and the Philippines

1900: McKinley's Open Door policy to China is threatened by the Boxers, a revolutionary group who want to drive all foreigners out of China; U.S. Marines join forces with other Western nations to end the Boxer Rebellion; McKinley is reelected

1901: McKinley undertakes an ill-fated cross-country tour following his second inauguration; first lady becomes ill while in California, and McKinley is assassinated in Buffalo, New York

As president, McKinley also urged a cautious and diplomatic approach in dealing with the increasing tensions between the United States and Spain over Cuba, which was still a Spanish colony during the 1890s. When Cubans began rebelling against Spanish rule over their island, Americans supported their cause. That support first emerged as a result of sometimes sensationalistic newspaper accounts of Spanish oppression in Cuba, and later by the suspicious and unexplained explosion of an American battleship in Havana harbor, which led McKinley to ask Congress to declare war on Spain in April 1898.

American forces won quick, decisive battles in Cuba and other Spanish colonies, including Puerto Rico and the Philippines, and the war lasted only four months. With victory, the United States took possession of land beyond the North American mainland for the first time in its history.

The success of the economy, the war, and American expansionism helped McKinley win reelection in 1900 against his Democratic opponent, William Jennings Bryan, whom he had also defeated in 1896. Shortly after his second inauguration, McKinley undertook a transcontinental tour to reach out to the American people, but it turned out to be tragic. First lady Ida McKinley fell ill in California at the start of the tour, and near the end, President McKinley was assassinated in Buffalo, New York. Many Americans paid their heartfelt respects as the train bearing the president's casket made its way from Buffalo to Washington and then on to Canton, Ohio, where he was buried.

Civil War Hero

William McKinley was born in Niles, Ohio, in 1843, the seventh of nine children. Both of his great-grandfathers fought in the Revolutionary War. His father's father settled in Niles and opened up an iron foundry. When the future president was nine, he and his younger siblings and their mother moved to Poland, Ohio, where

Left: William Jennings Bryan (center) campaigning against McKinley.

Above: McKinley's home in Niles, Ohio.

the schools were better, but his father, William, stayed behind in Niles to run the foundry.

While a student at the Poland Academy, the boy seemed unusually shy. With encouragement from his mother and his teachers, however, he overcame his shyness and even developed a great talent for public speaking. He took an active role in the school's debating club and became president of a local debating group.

McKinley was close to his mother, Nancy, who was a devout Methodist and hoped her son would become a minister. She believed that a life of virtue would lead to wealth and that vice led to poverty—views that influenced McKinley throughout his life. In his mid-teens, he decided against the ministry, however, choosing instead to study at Allegheny College in Pennsylvania, across the border from Ohio. Unfortunately, an illness and a lack of money interrupted his education plans. McKinley went home to Poland, Ohio, in 1860 and worked as a postal clerk and a part-time schoolteacher, saving money in hopes of going back to college.

When the Civil War broke out, the eighteen-year-old McKinley enlisted with the Twenty-Third Voluntary Ohio Regiment. This unit went to western Virginia to battle Confederate forces of the seceding Southern states and was led by Major Rutherford B. Hayes, who would

later become the nineteenth president of the United States.

McKinley quickly displayed his bravery in battle by delivering supplies and food to soldiers while under heavy fire. He quickly rose to the rank of second lieutenant on the battlefield and served as an officer on Hayes's staff. Near the end of the war, he distinguished himself in several battles, including Opequan, Cedar Creek, and Fisher's Hill.

After considering a career in the military when the war was over, McKinley chose to go back to Ohio and get on with his schooling. Major McKinley, as he liked to be called—based on his last military rank—studied law at the offices of Charles E. Glidden, a county judge in Youngstown, Ohio, and then at Albany College. He passed the bar exam in 1867 and opened a law office in Canton.

McKinley soon became active in politics, supporting his former commander, Rutherford B. Hayes, during his campaign for governor, which he won in 1867. As for Hayes, he was horrified that his former aide had developed an interest in politics, and he dashed off a letter to him advising him to get into railroading instead. "A man with half your wit ought to be independent at forty," he said. But William McKinley's mind was already made up. The following year he was involved on the local level, helping Republican Ulysses S. Grant carry Ohio in his election to the presidency. McKinley himself ran for the local office of prosecuting attorney two years later and was elected in spite of the fact that his corner of Ohio was a Democratic stronghold.

Right: McKinley fought in several Civil War battles as an aide to future president Rutherford B. Hayes.

Happiness and Grief

During this time, McKinley met Ida Saxton, the daughter of an influential Canton banker. She was full of life and very fashion-conscious, and had recently taken a job at her father's bank so that she could become a more responsible young woman. It was there that she and McKinley first became friends. They were married in 1871.

Everything was going well for the newlyweds, who had their first child, Katherine, the following year. But health problems and tragedy soon came into their lives.

Ida was ill during her pregnancy with the couple's second child, and the situation grew worse when her mother died, leaving her grief-stricken. In 1873, Baby Ida was born premature and died at four-and-a-half months. Then, two years later, daughter Katherine came down with typhoid fever and died within a few weeks. Ida never again fully recovered her physical or mental health. She suffered through occasional episodes of epileptic seizures and depression. In between, she made great efforts to be a spirited public figure during her husband's official appearances.

Saddened by the deaths of his daughters and the illnesses of his wife, McKinley plunged further into work to help him cope with those difficult times. His local reputation, based on his engaging speeches, spread wide enough for him to consider running for the U.S. Congress, and he was elected to the House of Representatives in 1876, the same year his fellow Ohioan Rutherford B. Hayes was elected president.

McKinley was reelected through 1890, except for one term when his district was gerrymandered. As a young congressman, he was immediately faced with two issues that would have a lasting effect on his political career—bimetallism and tariffs.

Defining Issues

Bimetallism is a policy of using two different precious metals to give value to legal tender. Gold was the single metal used as the basis for the value of money in the United States, but there were people during the

Above: As a congressman from Ohio, McKinley had almost no time to enjoy his family, but there were exceptions.

last half of the nineteenth century who wanted to include silver as well. The advocates of silver were generally farmers who lived in western and Southern states who argued that "free silver" would allow the United States to print more money that people could earn and use to buy much needed goods—like food and clothing—that many Americans couldn't afford. Those who were against including silver were generally bankers and industrialists in the eastern states. They believed that increasing the money supply would only lead to inflation, a decline in the value of money in relation to the goods and services it will buy.

Although his fellow Republicans and President Hayes were against bimetallism, McKinley noted that the people he represented in his Ohio congressional district generally favored including silver in the monetary standard, and he voted for a limited inclusion of silver. Then, after President Hayes vetoed the measure, McKinley voted with the Democratic majority to override his veto.

McKinley then turned to another major issue—tariffs, which allowed the government to keep the prices of imported goods as high as or higher than the same goods produced in America. For example, when more cheaply manufactured shoes from foreign lands were imported into the United States, a tariff ensured that they would be sold at a comparable price to those made in America. Since most consumers used price as the deciding factor for their purchases, this helped the domestic shoe business stay profitable and prevented worker layoffs.

McKinley consistently backed high tariffs as a congressman in order to protect American businesses. His long-standing support of tariffs reached its high point with the McKinley Tariff Act of 1890, which created new highs on imported goods except for a few isolated items. In order to win enough support from fellow congressmen for his bill, McKinley voted for increased but limited coinage of silver.

Defeat Leads to New Opportunities

The McKinley Tariff Act contributed to the loss of his congressional seat in the election of 1890. While higher prices on goods protected American businesses, they also meant that people had to pay more for many items. Angry consumers voted against congressional incumbents that year to protest the higher prices they were forced to pay.

McKinley didn't let the defeat stop him. With Ohio Republican Party bigwig and industrialist Mark Hanna in his corner, he ran for governor of Ohio the next year. His excellent speech-making skills and his pro-business platform in a lively and vigorous campaign won him the election, and McKinley was easily reelected two years later. His popularity increased as the country faced hardships and fell into an economic depression in 1893, and most officeholders were feeling the wrath of the voters.

He impressed his fellow Republicans at their 1892 convention, where many party members argued heatedly over whom the party should nominate for president, and he was even mentioned as a possible candidate. He always made it a point to reveal as little as possible about himself, and wouldn't say whether he'd accept a presidential nomination. President Harrison, who wanted a second term, thought McKinley would, and made him chairman of the convention so that he'd be too busy for politicking. The ploy worked, but it put McKinley in the spotlight, and when he adjourned the convention, he was carried out of the hall on the shoulders of admiring delegates who seemed intent on ignoring the man they

Above: McKinley's political mentor, Mark Hanna.

had just named their standard bearer. Then, four years later, McKinley was backed once again by Hanna, who had abandoned his business dealings and used his great financial resources and excellent organizational skills to run the McKinley presidential campaign.

McKinley won the Republican nomination. His opponent in the presidential election, William Jennings Bryan, had been nominated both by the Democratic Party and the People's Party, or the Populists. The Populists represented people of the west and the South who had been hit hard by the depression, people who were suspicious of powerful banking institutions of the East and supporters of bimetallism.

Below: McKinley's support for the gold standard was one factor in his success; the promise of prosperity turned the tide.

The two familiar issues—bimetallism and tariffs—helped energize the McKinley campaign. Bryan proposed several options to reform the economy, such as increasing the use of silver as a currency standard, which prompted McKinley to abruptly switch his position on bimetallism, announcing that he favored only the gold standard, which won him overwhelming support from the business community. Coupled with his continued strong stand on tariffs, McKinley was offering a cautious but clear message on how to regain prosperity for the nation. Bryan, meanwhile, was increasingly portrayed as a man with wild economic ideas that could further damage the economy. McKinley won a close election.

Presiding in Prosperity

Beginning with his inaugural address and his appointment of several successful businessmen to Cabinet posts, McKinley tackled issues relating to the economy. Helped by good timing—the economy was finally beginning to show signs of improvement—the president and a supportive Congress enacted a few carefully chosen tariffs to protect American industry. Many raw materials, such as iron ore, were not taxed with a tariff; manufacturers could buy them cheaply to help keep down their cost for producing goods. Meanwhile, the administration promoted a generous business climate, and

Election Results

1896

Presidential / Vice Presidential Candidates	Popular Votes	Electoral Votes
William McKinley / Garret A. Hobart (Republican)	7,104,779	271
William Jennings Bryan / Arthur Sewall (Democrat)	6,509,052	176

Bryan was also the People's [Populist] Party presidential nominee; that party's vice presidential nominee was Georgia politician Thomas E. Watson.

1900

Presidential / Vice Presidential Candidates	Popular Votes	Electoral Votes
William McKinley / Theodore Roosevelt (Republican)	7,207,923	292
William Jennings Bryan / Adlai E. Stevenson (Democratic)	6,358,138	155

Bryan was also the presidential nominee of the People's [Populist] and Imperialist parties. Roosevelt's selection as Republican vice presidential nominee was necessitated by the death of Hobart in 1899.

Above: The sinking of the battleship U.S.S. Maine *sent America to war with Spain.*

Left: McKinley delivering his inaugural address.

the Alaskan gold rush in the final years of the nineteenth century made more gold available, while also effectively killing the bimetallism issue. Prosperity returned, and McKinley's popularity grew with the good times.

McKinley favored a laissez-faire approach to the economy, in which the government does not intervene in business affairs. It helped stimulate growth and investment, but it also allowed for the proliferation of trusts—corporate monopolies formed to dominate a business sector and to control a certain section of business. Unwilling to disrupt the booming economy, McKinley hesitated to address this unfair, and later illegal, business practice.

Meanwhile, trouble had been brewing for several years just offshore. Cuba was still ruled as a colony by Spain, as it had been for centuries, but many Cubans wanted to establish their own government. A rebellion had failed in 1894, but tensions soon heated up again.

The McKinley Administration

Administration Dates:	March 4, 1897–March 4, 1901
	March 4, 1901–September 14, 1901
Vice President:	Garret A. Hobart (1897–99)
	None (1899–1901)
	Theodore Roosevelt (1901)

Cabinet:

Secretary of State	John Sherman (1897–98)
	William R. Day (1898)
	John M. Hay (1898–1901)
Secretary of the Treasury	Lyman J. Gage (1897–1901)
Secretary of War	Russell A. Alger (1897–99)
	Elihu Root (1899–1901)
Attorney General	Joseph McKenna (1897–98)
	John W. Griggs (1898–1901)
	Philander C. Knox (1901)
Secretary of the Navy	John D. Long (1897–1901)
Postmaster General	James A. Gary (1897–98)
	Charles E. Smith (1898–1901)
Secretary of the Interior	Cornelius N. Bliss (1897–99)
	Ethan A. Hitchcock (1899–1901)
Secretary of Agriculture	James Wilson (1897–1901)

William Jennings Bryan

Three-time presidential nominee William Jennings Bryan was a gifted speechmaker and an influential figure in America from the 1890s through the 1920s. His father was a school superintendent and a politician. The family lived on a five-hundred-acre farm near Salem, Illinois, where he was born on March 19, 1860. The entire family worked on the farm and was very religious.

In 1872, Bryan's father ran unsuccessfully for a seat in the U.S. Congress. Already a gifted speaker, his son campaigned for him. After graduating from high school, Bryan went to Whipple Academy to prepare for Illinois College. He was a good student and an active debater, using his powerful voice and well-researched speeches to establish positions he would fight for throughout his life. After graduating in 1881, he entered Chicago's Union College of Law, and two years later he joined a law firm in Jacksonville, Illinois. He married Mary Baird in 1884, and the couple would have two children. The Bryans eventually moved to Lincoln, Nebraska, where the Republican Party was dominant, but Bryan thought that Democrats had a chance in districts that included large cities. His theory proved accurate when he was elected to the U.S. Congress in 1890.

Bryan favored income tax changes and also spoke out against gold as the only standard for the country's money. He said he would support anything that would promote free citizens, just laws, and an economical government. When a depression hit in 1893, Bryan proposed to help the economy by taking U.S. currency off the gold standard. Many countries guaranteed the value of their money by keeping reserves of gold, while others kept reserves of both gold and silver to guarantee their paper money. With two different standards, some countries had a difficult time trading with others. Bryan argued that there was not enough gold in the world to support all the money of the world and that the United States should accept both gold and silver as guarantees. He was certain trade would improve and prosperity would return.

Bryan served two terms in the U.S. House, but he lost an 1894 bid for a U.S. Senate seat. He was nominated for president of the United States three times—in 1896, 1900, and 1908—and he was defeated each time. Although he never held elected office again, Bryan was still recognized as the leader of the Democratic Party.

His continued pleas for the average citizen and his battles against trusts and tariffs earned him the nickname the "Great Commoner." Bryan went on to serve as secretary of state in the Woodrow Wilson administration from 1913 to 1915.

As a lifelong Christian fundamentalist who believed the Bible to be completely accurate, Bryan often spoke out strongly against evolution, and in 1925, when the state of Tennessee arrested Dayton high-school teacher John T. Scopes for using a textbook in his classroom that described evolution, a violation of state law, prominent attorney Clarence Darrow was the defense lawyer and Bryan helped with the prosecution.

Bryan's opening presentation during the Scopes trial made it quite clear that he was on a crusade for fundamentalist Christianity. Darrow, on the other hand, was prepared to fight for freedom of speech and thought in schools. Bryan spoke out to the media as well as the court, and he used every opportunity to make headlines. He even offered $100 to any scientist who would admit to being a descendent of apes. When a scientist came forward and made the admission, Bryan paid up, but he used the occasion to ridicule both him and the theory of evolution.

Witnesses were summoned, scientists explained their theory of evolution, and ministers defended their religious positions. Then, on the trial's ninth day, Darrow called Bryan to the witness stand, and through careful questioning, he led him to admit that some Bible stories are illustrations rather than fact. About Jonah and the whale, for example, Darrow wondered whether Bryan really believed that a man could be swallowed by a big fish and live inside for three days. The prosecution lost ground. Bryan was scheduled to make his closing arguments on the eleventh day, and he was still capable of preaching and using wit, sarcasm, and false reasoning to persuade any audience, which is what he intended to do. Darrow expected that, though. He believed that he had already won his point on the right of teachers to present new and challenging ideas, so he rose to tell the court that his client was, in fact, guilty as charged and asked that the case be closed. The judge agreed. Scopes was found guilty of violating Tennessee's antievolution law and was fined $100. Bryan lost the opportunity to give his great closing, a speech that some estimated would have taken six hours. On July 25, 1925, five days after the trial ended, a weary Bryan died in his sleep.

Right: The Spanish-American War was followed by an insurrection in the Philippines.

American newspapers began running lurid stories about Spanish oppression, including reports that many Cubans were being herded into internment camps, and thousands were dying there from malnutrition and disease. Some of the news stories, however, were only sensationalistic and meant to sell newspapers. Yellow journalism was becoming more common. A bitter rivalry between newspaper magnates William Randolph Hearst and Joseph Pulitzer was raging, and there were no holds barred when it came to their coverage of the situation in Cuba.

Sentiment in America began to move toward military intervention in Cuba, but President McKinley urged caution and diplomacy. In retrospect, some historians have argued that he moved too cautiously. Then, two events in February 1898 led him to change course. The *New York Journal*, a newspaper owned by Hearst, reprinted a letter it claimed had been written by Spain's minister to Washington describing McKinley as weak. The following week, a mysterious explosion destroyed the U.S.S. *Maine*, killing all 266 sailors aboard. The battleship had been sent to Cuba and was anchored in Havana Harbor. McKinley continued to urge caution until results of an official investigation into the explosion were released, but popular sentiment continued to grow for intervention. McKinley responded in April by asking Congress to declare war on Spain.

The Spanish-American War lasted little more than four months, with the United States winning crucial naval battles in Spanish possessions, including Cuba, Puerto Rico, and the Philippines. The swiftness of the victory, as well as newspaper stories and images such as Theodore Roosevelt leading his group of "rough riders" up San Juan Hill in Cuba, increased McKinley's standing.

The victory over Spain created an unprecedented event: For the first time, the United States was in possession of lands that weren't part of the North America mainland. McKinley soon began supporting expansion as well in international trade. Among several initiatives, he introduced the Open Door Policy to extend trade and relations with China, opening up a vast new market.

This expansionism became an issue in the election of 1900, when William Jennings Bryan, again the Democratic nominee, portrayed McKinley as an imperialist, a person who believes in acquiring or dominating other lands. He also called McKinley a tool of big business, noting that many trusts had developed under his administration and that the nation's finances continued to be dominated by Eastern bankers and industrialists.

The new internationalism also created new problems. Rebels in the Philippines, no more interested in being ruled by America as they had been by Spain, began insurrections, and over the next several years, McKinley sent more than 70,000 troops to maintain order and protect American interests there, and battles raged in the Philippines through 1902, when the rebellion was finally put down. Meanwhile, as another example of the United States moving from isolationism to expansionism, McKinley agreed that the United States should annex Hawaii. In setting out his reasons, he used the popular term "Manifest Destiny"—a concept stressing that American expansionism is not only inevitable but "divinely ordained."

Joseph Pulitzer

Born in Budapest, Hungary, in April 1847, Joseph Pulitzer was the son of a successful grain trader. He came to America at the age of seventeen and enlisted in the Union cavalry near the end of the Civil War. After becoming a civilian again, he settled in a largely German area of St. Louis, Missouri, where he worked as a mule tender, waiter, and driver before landing a job as a reporter with a German-language newspaper. A short time later, the local Republicans nominated him for the state legislature, but his candidacy was considered a joke because he had been nominated in a Democratic district. However, Pulitzer ran seriously and surprised everyone by winning. As a legislator, he fought against corruption, and in one wild dispute shot an adversary in the leg. He escaped punishment with a fine, which was paid by friends.

Industrious and ambitious, he bought the St. Louis Post for about $3,000 in 1872, and then he bought a German-language newspaper that was connected with the large Associated Press syndicate and sold it for a large profit. Six years later, Pulitzer bought the decaying St. Louis Dispatch at an auction and combined it with the Post. Aided by his brilliant editor in chief, John A. Cockerill, he launched crusades against lotteries, gambling, and tax dodging, mounted drives for cleaning and repairing streets, and sought to make St. Louis more civic-minded. The Post-Dispatch became a success, *and in 1883, Pulitzer, then thirty-six, bought the New York World for $346,000 from financier Jay Gould, who had been losing $40,000 a year on it. Pulitzer made the down payment from Post-Dispatch profits and made all later payments out of profits from the World itself. His eyes began to fail during the 1880s, and he went blind before the decade ended. During his battle for supremacy over William Randolph Hearst, publisher of the New York Journal, Pulitzer had to rely on secretaries to serve as his eyes.*

In New York, he pledged the World would "expose all fraud and sham, fight all public evils and abuses" and "battle for the people with earnest sincerity." He concentrated on lively human-interest stories, scandal, and sensational material. Pulitzer's World was a strong supporter of common people and it was frequently pro-union during strikes in an era of labor unrest. In the early part of his career, Pulitzer was opposed to large headlines and other attention-grabbing graphics, but during the 1890s, in a circulation war between the Pulitzer and Hearst newspaper empires, the World switched to larger headline type and fantastic art, and it began indulging in sensationalism.

Pulitzer died aboard his yacht in the harbor at Charleston, South Carolina, on October 29, 1911. In his will, he provided $2 million for the establishment of a school of journalism at Columbia University, and also the prizes bearing his name that were first awarded in 1917 and have become journalism's most prestigious honor.

William Randolph Hearst

William Randolph Hearst was born April 29, 1863, in San Francisco, California. His father, George, was a wealthy mine owner. Hearst was energetic from an early age and enjoyed private tutoring and travel. In 1879, he attended a private preparatory school in Concord, New Hampshire. A disruptive student, he was asked to leave the school the following year. After returning home for more private tutoring, he was admitted to Harvard University, where he took charge of the school's fading newspaper, the Harvard Lampoon, serving as editor and writer, selling advertising, and soliciting subscriptions from students, and he made it profitable. His work on the Lampoon was his major achievement at Harvard before he was expelled from the university in 1885 for playing pranks.

Meanwhile, his millionaire father had become interested in politics, supporting Democratic Party candidates and the newspaper that supported them, the San Francisco Examiner. After the paper could not repay loans he had extended to its owners, George Hearst took it over in 1880.

Six years later, he was appointed to complete the term vacated by the death of U.S. senator John F. Miller, and then he was elected to his own six-year term. His son, William Randolph Hearst, had been working as a reporter for the New York World and soon returned to San Francisco to run the Examiner, where he quickly became its publisher. Hearst revived a dying newspaper by hiring top reporters, including noted author Ambrose Bierce. He expected the Examiner to be the first newspaper to report an event, and to report the event more sensationally than any other newspaper. His idea was that a newspaper should be exciting to read. Hearst personally took charge of a front page column, and the Examiner staff searched for sensational news items and wrote about them in articles as lively and recklessly as possible. The newspaper was soon accused of practicing yellow journalism, that is, of exaggerating and playing up violence and scandal stories to increase sales.

Hearst agreed to direct the Examiner to support Democratic candidates in return for a share of campaign money, and he used the Examiner and, later, other papers he acquired to champion Democratic candidates and to smear their opponents. His methods were so successful that the Examiner began to prosper, and Hearst thought of starting a similar paper in the East. He acquired the New

Above: William Randolph Hearst.

Below: The battlefields in Cuba were characterized as "The Splendid Little War."

York Morning Journal in 1895, and a year later added the New York Evening Journal. He relocated to New York after that, and devoted most of his time to these newspapers.

While Hearst was in New York, difficulties between the United States and Spain eventually erupted into war in 1898. He had campaigned for war through his newspapers and even engineered a daring rescue of a Cuban girl held in a Spanish prison. At the same time, a newspaper war with Joseph Pulitzer's New York World began after the World investigated the Journal's rescue story and reported that the conditions it described were a sham. But readers continued to read Hearst's Journal and to believe what they read.

In 1898, a battleship, the U.S.S. Maine, was sunk in Havana Harbor after a mysterious explosion that killed 260 American sailors. Investigators thought that the explosion had come from outside the ship, possibly from a mine or a bomb set off by the Spanish. "Remember the Maine!" became a battle cry, especially in the Hearst papers. President McKinley called for the Spanish to leave Cuba, but Spain responded by declaring war on the United States. Hearst's papers continued with their sensational reports, encouraged war with Spain, and even offered a $50,000 reward to solve the mystery of who was responsible for the explosion on the Maine.

Hearst was determined that his New York Journal reporters would be first to publish accounts of the battles of the Spanish-American War, and he gathered reporters, artists, writers, and a printing press, and sailed off to war with them. With Hearst as the key reporter, the team stayed close to the battle lines—so close that they were accused of drawing enemy artillery fire on American troops.

The Spanish-American War greatly increased Hearst's influence in the publishing industry. He built an empire of dozens of newspapers and magazines, including Cosmopolitan, Good Housekeeping, and Harper's Bazaar. In 1903, he was elected to the House of Representatives, where he served for four years. He ran later, unsuccessfully, for mayor of New York City and then for governor of New York.

Hearst opposed American involvement in both world wars; the New York Tribune portrayed him as a snake named Hearssssst. His newspapers eventually campaigned for an all-out effort to win World War II against the Japanese after the bombing of Pearl Harbor, but his previous antiwar stances had damaged his reputation. Hearst died on August 14, 1951.

Above: McKinley usually limited the campaign trail to the route from his bedroom to his front porch.

Above: McKinley did, however, campaign from the back of a train on occasion.

Triumph and Tragedy

While the economy continued to boom, unrest in foreign lands became a major concern for McKinley. The rebellions in the Philippines were followed by others in China, where McKinley's Open Door policy was threatened by the Boxer Rebellion. Diplomats and businessmen from the West—Europe and the Western Hemisphere—used the term Boxers to describe a group of Chinese nationalists who called themselves Righteous and Harmonious Fists. They were dedicated to ridding their country of foreign influences, and when they began a violent campaign against foreigners, U.S. Marines were sent in to fight alongside troops from other Western countries. The Boxers were overcome in August 1900, just a couple of months before the U.S. presidential election.

McKinley chose the popular Theodore Roosevelt, who was governor of New York at the time, as his running mate. Garret Hobart, his original vice president, had died shortly before the end of his first term. As Bryan stormed the country in search of votes, McKinley stayed in Canton, Ohio, where he met delegates from around the country on his front porch and promised continued prosperity—"a full dinner bucket" for everyone. Reelected by a large margin, McKinley planned to address several pressing issues during his second term: He wanted to further U.S. involvement in international trade after years of isolationism, and he was concerned about the growing influence of corporate monopolies.

Following his second inauguration, McKinley decided to take a transcontinental tour to meet and hear from Americans across the country. The scheduled six-week trip would turn tragic. It had barely begun in California when first lady Ida McKinley, who had been frail since the deaths of her daughters almost thirty years earlier, fell ill.

In September, McKinley made an address at the Pan-American Exposition in Buffalo, New York, and as an indication of the direction he planned for his second term, he announced in his speech that he planned to abandon the protectionism of high tariffs in favor of

Left: The face of the assassin Leon G. Czolgosz.

Right: McKinley was shot at the Pan American Exposition in Buffalo, New York.

Below, right: The body of the assassinated president was taken by train to Canton, Ohio. Thousands of mourners turned out to watch it pass.

free trade. He stressed the term "reciprocity," a trading balance achieved by nations by transacting items of equal value. For example, sugar was a popular import into the United States, and instead of regulating imported sugar through a tariff, the United States would export items of similar value in trade agreements with sugar-exporting countries.

The day following his speech at the Exposition, McKinley stood before a long line of people, greeting them, shaking hands, and speaking briefly with them. Leon Czolgosz, a mentally disturbed man and an admitted anarchist, was in the line that day with a gun hidden beneath a handkerchief that was wrapped around his hand. McKinley extended his hand to Czolgosz, and Czolgosz shot the president. A crowd immediately tackled and began beating him, but they were held back after the fallen president cried out, "Don't let them harm him."

The wounded president was rushed to the Exposition's emergency hospital and treated, and then he was moved to a private residence. He seemed to be recovering, but gangrene set in, and in the early morning hours of September 14, a week after the shooting, McKinley whispered his final words: "Good-bye all, good-bye. It is God's way. His will be done."

McKinley's body was placed in a casket and taken to Washington for a state funeral, then it was moved to Canton, Ohio, where he was laid to rest. Americans lined the entire route to say farewell to the popular president.

Legacy

William McKinley is often called the first modern president. Several policies and events occurred during his administration that came to characterize the United States of the twentieth century. For example, the country moved away from isolationism to become a world economic and military power. It began adopting free-trade policies, as opposed to the policies of isolationism and protective tariffs that had been common throughout most of the nineteenth century.

McKinley's interpretation of the powers of the presidency and his use of those powers were much more expansive than those of the presidents immediately before him. He called a special session of Congress to pass a tariff act early in his presidency. During the Spanish-American

War, he functioned as the nation's chief diplomat: First, he tried to avoid war through diplomacy; when that failed, he directed the war effort; and following American victory, he personally supervised negotiations for the peace treaty. These are all examples of power characteristic of the modern presidency.

Although McKinley's effort to increase business competition in the United States by identifying and breaking trusts and monopolies was cut short by his assassination, his intentions were vigorously followed by his vice president, Theodore Roosevelt, who became known as a "trust-buster" after he assumed the office of president in 1901 and was reelected in 1904. McKinley's support for the single gold standard, coupled with the Alaska Gold Rush, put an end to the bimetallism issue, although it won a small measure of support again during the Great Depression of the 1930s.

McKinley reacted cautiously to the changing business and social climate, and some historians argue that he didn't do much to influence the changes. The economy, they contend, was already improving when he became president, and big business took advantage of his policies by forming trusts that squeezed out smaller businesses. On the international front, tensions with Spain over Cuba had been brewing for years, and McKinley took decisive action only after the explosion on the *Maine*.

Nevertheless, a more modern United States began taking shape during McKinley's administration, partly through his changing positions on bimetallism and tariffs. International trade began flourishing, and the American military became a stronger international presence. During his first campaign for the presidency, McKinley promised a cautious approach that favored business growth, and he certainly delivered on that promise.

We all accept as an article of faith that George Washington was first in the hearts of his countrymen, but no American president—not even Washington—touched the hearts of people who knew him quite as warmly as William McKinley. While current times might make the population cynical about nice guys, McKinley remains beloved even in the glare of history. No other word suits the man quite as well.

Right: During the mourning period, Americans of all ages paid tribute to the president's memory.

Ida McKinley

Born June 8, 1847, Canton, Ohio
Died May 26, 1907, Canton, Ohio

"My wife—be careful . . . how you tell her—oh, be careful."
—*William McKinley, after being shot*

As a young woman, Ida McKinley was known as the Belle of Canton, Ohio, because of her lively attitude and her family's social position. Her fashionable appearance and attractiveness—tufts of reddish brown hair around her delicate facial features—contributed to the image. Active in local theater and community affairs, she was also independent-minded and self-reliant, taking a job in her father's bank at a time when it was rare for a woman to be in a public business position. But before she turned thirty, Ida McKinley suffered health problems and personal tragedies. She spent the rest of her life in a semi-invalid condition, occasionally able to appear in public but in need of constant care.

Vibrant Youth

Ida Saxton was born in Canton in 1847. Her father was a wealthy banker and community leader. The large house where the family lived is still in excellent condition over a century later and is part of the National First Ladies' Library complex in Canton.

Ida attended private school in Cleveland and later graduated from Miss Eastman's Seminary, a finishing school in Media, Pennsylvania, where she was reported to have been an excellent student. When she went back to Canton, she became involved in community affairs, including fundraising to build a new Presbyterian Church for her family's congregation there. She participated in local theater, including performances at Schaefer's Opera House in Canton, where she was voted the most popular actress.

At about this time, in 1868, Ida first encountered William McKinley, a young lawyer active in Republican politics. They were introduced by his sister, Anna, who was the principal of Canton's West Grammar School. The couple did not become friends right away because they moved in different social circles. Twenty-one-year-old Ida was part of Canton's social elite, the richer and more powerful members of the local society. She was regularly invited to exclusive masquerade parties and debutante balls, but the twenty-five-year-old McKinley, a decorated Civil War veteran who liked to be called "major" for the military rank he had attained, was a lawyer just getting started in his career, and hadn't yet been accepted into Canton society.

Later that year, Ida and her sister Mary traveled to Europe with a chaperone for an extended vacation of sightseeing and shopping, and when the sisters got back home, Ida took a job at her father's bank, starting as a teller interacting with the general public, but soon working her way up to cashier and handling larger business transactions. It was so rare for a woman to work in such a position in those days that many friends of the Saxtons thought that the family was going through financial difficulties. Not so, replied Ida's father, James Saxton. He and his daughter both wanted her to become self-reliant, and the job made that likely.

Ida continued to have a passing acquaintance with William McKinley—they passed each other several times on Sunday mornings as they walked to their respective churches. Ida was Presbyterian, and McKinley a Methodist who taught Sunday school classes. But he had an account at the Stark County Bank where Ida worked, and their relationship blossomed there. He seemed to be at the bank several times a day, at least in part because of his growing success as a lawyer. He was elected prosecuting attorney of Stark County, and he and Ida became engaged shortly after he took office early in 1869.

Losses

William and Ida McKinley were married in 1871 in an extravagant ceremony attended by more than a thousand people. It was the first to be performed in the new Presbyterian church that Ida had helped raise funds to build. Their happy life as newlyweds was made more joyous when their first child, Katherine, was born on Christmas Day in 1871. However, Ida began having health problems while she was pregnant with the couple's second child. She suffered from phlebitis, a painful swelling of a vein, and from epileptic seizures. Her frail health was further complicated when her mother died. Deeply grieving, Ida fell into depression. The couple's second child, Ida, was born prematurely in April 1873 and was never fully healthy, dying four months later. Then three years after that, young Katie came down with typhoid fever and died.

The ordeals left Ida McKinley both physically and emotionally drained. In constant need of attention for her health, she became semi-invalid, only occasionally able to attend social functions. She would never again regain full physical or mental health. Still, Ida made efforts at meeting the demands of a public figure, because her husband won election to Congress and then served as governor of Ohio before he was elected president in 1896. McKinley was always attentive to her needs and concerned for her health, and he was never far from her for more than a few days.

He spent all of his free time with his wife, often sitting through entire evenings in the dark because the light hurt her eyes. Though McKinley was completely attentive to Ida's needs, he never neglected his career, which was important to both of them. During the day, when he was taking care of business, she busied herself with handicrafts. It was said that she crocheted more than five thousand pairs of bedroom slippers, which were given as gifts to Washington's officials. She also enjoyed making satin neckties, which became a kind of presidential trademark, but she was never as happy as when her beloved William was at her side. As she was fond of saying, "He is a dear good man, and I love him." Whenever a well-meaning aide inquired about her health, the president invariably responded, "Improving."

Right: Even as he was running the country, the president took time out to nurture his fragile wife.

Below: The McKinley home in Canton, Ohio.

The press was respectful to Ida McKinley as first lady and remained quiet about her fainting spells. In fact, many details concerning her health were only revealed later, after McKinley was assassinated and his widow had returned home to Canton.

Coping in Public

Ida McKinley spent most days of her adult life confined to a rocking chair, where she passed the time by knitting, crocheting, and reading. For those official functions she could attend, she was always fashionably dressed and often met guests while seated in a velvet chair. To ease the strain of social interaction, she would occasionally hold a bouquet of flowers, which would discourage guests from attempting to shake her hand and possibly sap her strength and energy. At dinners she always sat next to her husband, who monitored her health and watched for signs of an oncoming seizure. The president carried a large handkerchief, which he could use to shield the first lady from sight if she should happen to suffer a seizure. The seating arrangement of having her by his side was maintained even when it went against official protocol.

Following his reelection in 1900, the president decided to take a transcontinental tour to promote new policies, including his tougher stand against business trusts that dominated some markets. During McKinley's campaign tours and political travels, his wife usually stayed at home, but for this transcontinental tour she made an effort to travel with him. However, she fell ill at one of their first stops in California and had to be rushed away from the scene for treatment.

She was not with her husband when he stopped in Buffalo, New York, later that year to speak at the Pan-American Exposition. The day after the speech, the president greeted a long line of people at the exposition. In that line, a man named Leon Czolgosz stood with a gun hidden beneath a handkerchief and shot the president after McKinley extended his hand in greeting. As the president fell and gasped for life, he was heard to say to his secretary, George B. Cortelyou, "My wife—be careful . . . how you tell her—oh, be careful."

McKinley never recovered from his wounds and died a week later. His body was taken by train to Washington for a state funeral, and then Ida McKinley accompanied her husband's casket on a train from Washington back home to Canton.

Mrs. McKinley lived the remainder of her life under the care of her sister. She died in 1907 and was entombed next to her husband and their two daughters in the McKinley Memorial Mausoleum in Canton.

McKinley's First Inaugural Address

Delivered on March 4, 1897

Tariffs have been an issue of contention since the earliest days of the United States, and were particularly controversial during the nineteenth century. Tariffs are used to raise tax revenue for the government and also to protect domestic businesses from foreign competition. Some countries can afford to manufacture products more cheaply than others, or have greater access to resources or raw materials. The products, resources, or materials sell at lower costs than those of other nations, and in such cases, a country like the United States imposes tariffs on lower-cost imported goods as a way of making them less attractive to consumers, who will then buy similar goods produced in their own country.

During the 1820s and 1830s, the government imposed tariffs to help protect emerging American industries, and those tariffs were generally beneficial to the more industrialized North. People living in rural areas, especially in the South and in new states outside of New England, had to pay higher prices for basic necessities because of them. During the administration of President Andrew Jackson, the state of South Carolina rebelled against the taxes, and attempted to nullify new tariffs while threatening to secede from the Union over the issue. President Jackson, otherwise a champion of states' rights, threatened military action if any state defied the laws of the land.

After steady growth through the 1840s and 1850s, American industry boomed even more after the Civil War. Tariffs were used to protect emerging industries, but they only benefited industrialized areas. In addition to facing a shifting population from rural to urban areas, farmers faced higher prices for goods they needed. Heated debate over tariffs was characteristic of the last few decades of the century. Those who were opposed to tariffs rallied successfully behind Grover Cleveland for president in the 1884 and 1892 elections. Benjamin Harrison and William McKinley, both supporters of tariffs, won in 1888 and 1896.

As a congressman, McKinley had written a sweeping tariff act (called the McKinley Tariff of 1890) that contributed to an economic downturn that plagued the United States in the early 1890s. Nevertheless, McKinley had the solid backing of businesses and urban areas, and he won the presidential election of 1896 over William Jennings Bryan, who was antitariff and supported the causes of rural voters.

Excerpt from McKinley's First Inaugural Address

The credit of the Government, the integrity of its currency, and the inviolability of its obligations must be preserved. This was the commanding verdict of the people, and it will not be unheeded.

Economy is demanded in every branch of the Government at all times, but especially in periods, like the present, of depression in business and distress among the people. The severest economy must be observed in all public expenditures, and extravagance stopped wherever it is found, and prevented wherever in the future it may be developed. If the revenues are to remain as now, the only relief that can come must be from decreased expenditures. But the present must not become the permanent condition of the Government. It has been our uniform practice to retire, not increase our outstanding obligations, and this policy must again be resumed and vigorously enforced. Our revenues should always be large enough to meet with ease and promptness not only our current needs and the principal and interest of the public debt, but to make proper and liberal provision for that most deserving body of public creditors, the soldiers and sailors and the widows and orphans who are the pensioners of the United States.

[...]

The best way for the Government to maintain its credit is to pay as it goes—not by resorting to loans, but by keeping out of debt—through an adequate income secured by a system of taxation, external or internal, or both. It is the settled policy of the Government, pursued from the beginning and practiced by all parties and Administrations, to raise the bulk of our revenue from taxes upon foreign productions entering the United States for sale and consumption, and avoiding, for the most part, every form of direct taxation, except in time of war. The country is clearly opposed to any needless additions to the subject of internal taxation, and is committed by its latest popular utterance to the system of tariff taxation. There can be no misunderstanding, either,

about the principle upon which this tariff taxation shall be levied. Nothing has ever been made plainer at a general election than that the controlling principle in the raising of revenue from duties on imports is zealous care for American interests and American labor. The people have declared that such legislation should be had as will give ample protection and encouragement to the industries and the development of our country. It is, therefore, earnestly hoped and expected that Congress will, at the earliest practicable moment, enact revenue legislation that shall be fair, reasonable, conservative, and just, and which, while supplying sufficient revenue for public purposes, will still be signally beneficial and helpful to every section and every enterprise of the people. To this policy we are all, of whatever party, firmly bound by the voice of the people—a power vastly more potential than the expression of any political platform. The paramount duty of Congress is to stop deficiencies by the restoration of that protective legislation which has always been the firmest prop of the Treasury. The passage of such a law or laws would strengthen the credit of the Government both at home and abroad, and go far toward stopping the drain upon the gold reserve held for the redemption of our currency, which has been heavy and well-nigh constant for several years.

In the revision of the tariff especial attention should be given to the re-enactment and extension of the reciprocity principle of the law of 1890, under which so great a stimulus was given to our foreign trade in new and advantageous markets for our surplus agricultural and manufactured products. The brief trial given this legislation amply justifies a further experiment and additional discretionary power in the making of commercial treaties, the end in view always to be the opening up of new markets for the products of our country, by granting concessions to the products of other lands that we need and cannot produce ourselves, and which do not involve any loss of labor to our own people, but tend to increase their employment.

The depression of the past four years has fallen with especial severity upon the great body of toilers of the country, and upon none more than the holders of small farms. Agriculture has languished and labor suffered. The revival of manufacturing will be a relief to both. No portion of our population is more devoted to the institution of free government nor more loyal in their support, while none bears more cheerfully or fully its proper share in the maintenance of the Government or is better entitled to its wise and liberal care and protection. Legislation helpful to producers is beneficial to all. The depressed condition of industry on the farm and in the mine and factory has lessened the ability of the people to meet the demands upon them, and they rightfully expect that not only a system of revenue shall be established that will secure the largest income with the least burden, but that every means will be taken to decrease, rather than increase, our public expenditures. Business conditions are not the most promising. It will take time to restore the prosperity of former years. If we cannot promptly attain it, we can resolutely turn our faces in that direction and aid its return by friendly legislation. However troublesome the situation may appear, Congress will not, I am sure, be found lacking in disposition or ability to relieve it as far as legislation can do so. The restoration of confidence and the revival of business, which men of all parties so much desire, depend more largely upon the prompt, energetic, and intelligent action of Congress than upon any other single agency affecting the situation.

It is inspiring, too, to remember that no great emergency in the one hundred and eight years of our eventful national life has ever arisen that has not been met with wisdom and courage by the American people, with fidelity to their best interests and highest destiny, and to the honor of the American name. These years of glorious history have exalted mankind and advanced the cause of freedom throughout the world, and immeasurably strengthened the precious free institutions which we enjoy. The people love and will sustain these institutions. The great essential to our happiness and prosperity is that we adhere to the principles upon which the Government was established and insist upon their faithful observance. Equality of rights must prevail, and our laws be always and everywhere respected and obeyed. We may have failed in the discharge of our full duty as citizens of the great Republic, but it is consoling and encouraging to realize that free speech, a free press, free thought, free schools, the free and unmolested right of religious liberty and worship, and free and fair elections are dearer and more universally enjoyed to-day than ever before. These guaranties must be sacredly preserved and wisely strengthened.

What Happened Next

The economy of the United States rebounded, and President McKinley's popularity soared. The following year, the United States emerged victorious in the Spanish-American War and took possession of former Spanish colonies in the Caribbean and the Pacific. American military strength had grown along with the surging economy, and the American public was beginning to feel confident about the country's future.

There were problems as well. Americans debated about whether they should maintain control over areas that had been won from Spain. At home, living conditions in many cities were bad in spite of the improved economy. Segregation and voter intimidation became more rampant in the South, and Native Americans were facing a crisis for survival, as their population dipped to an all-time low. Large businesses were dominating smaller ones. McKinley was prepared to address these problems when he won reelection in 1900. However, he was assassinated months into his second term. Vice President Theodore Roosevelt would become known as the "trust-buster" for leading the government to investigate and punish large corporations that engaged in unfair business practices.

During McKinley's administration, the United States was transformed into its modern identity as an economic, industrial, and military giant. How much McKinley's policies actually contributed to that transformation is debatable, but there is no question that he was influential. Beginning with his election in 1896, Republicans held the presidency for twenty-eight of the next thirty-six years, winning seven of nine presidential elections. The economic policies McKinley advocated were echoed by each of those later Republican presidents.

Theodore Roosevelt

"Get action. Do things ... take a place wherever you are and be somebody; get action."

—*Theodore Roosevelt*

Twenty-sixth president of the United States, 1901–1909

Full name: *Theodore Roosevelt*

Born: *October 27, 1858, New York, New York*

Died: *January 6, 1919, Oyster Bay, Long Island, New York*

Burial site: *Young's Memorial Cemetery, Oyster Bay, New York*

Parents: *Theodore and Martha Bulloch Roosevelt*

Spouse: *Alice Hathaway Lee (1861–1884; m. 1880); Edith Kermit Carow (1861–1948; m. 1886)*

Children: *Alice Lee (1884–1980); Theodore Jr. (1887–1944); Kermit (1889–1943); Ethel Carow (1891–1977); Archibald Bulloch (1894–1979); Quentin (1897–1918)*

Religion: *Dutch Reformed*

Education: *Harvard University (B.A., 1880)*

Occupations: *Rancher; soldier; author*

Government positions: *New York state assemblyman; New York City police commissioner; New York governor; assistant U.S. secretary of the navy and vice president under William McKinley*

Political party: *Republican*

Dates as president: *September 14, 1901–March 4, 1905 (first term); March 4, 1905–March 4, 1909 (second term)*

Age upon taking office: *42*

One of the most popular, controversial, and important of all the American presidents, Theodore Roosevelt was a hearty, dynamic leader. His administration introduced much-needed monitoring of business with an established set of guidelines. His foreign policy made the United States a more significant force in international affairs as well as the guardian of the Western Hemisphere.

Roosevelt was full of personal contradictions. Born into a wealthy family, he used the influence of elected office to protect the average citizen against powerful institutions. He was a sickly child who grew into a strong and vigorous man. He was the first president to confront problems associated with industrialization, while at the same time becoming highly regarded for his groundbreaking efforts at conserving natural resources. A fearless and heroic military leader, he also received the Nobel Peace Prize. Along with his love for physical activity and outdoor life, he was a man of impressive intellectual achievement and the author of more than thirty books.

Above: Young T.R. grew up in a New York City townhouse.

Timeline

1858: Born in New York

1877: *The Summer Birds of the Adirondacks in Franklin County, New York*, the first of over thirty books written by Roosevelt, is published privately; his first major publication, *The History of the Naval War of 1812*, is published in 1882

1882–84: Serves as New York state assemblyman

1884–86: Builds and lives on Elkhorn Ranch in the Dakota Territory

1889–95: Serves on U.S. Civil Service Commission

1895–97: Serves as a police commissioner of New York City

1897–98: Serves as assistant secretary of the navy

1898: Volunteers for service during the Spanish-American War; as a lieutenant colonel in the First U.S. Volunteer Cavalry, he forms a squadron called the "Rough Riders," whose exploits are well publicized by newspapers

1899–1900: Serves as New York governor

1901: Serves as vice president under William McKinley; assumes the presidency following McKinley's assassination

1901–09: Serves as twenty-sixth U.S. president

1909–10: Leads an African safari, collects more than five hundred different birds and animals, and writes *African Game Trails*; tours Europe

1912: Finishes second in the presidential election (to Woodrow Wilson) as a third-party candidate, outpolling incumbent president William Howard Taft

1919: Dies in New York

Force of Will

Born October 27, 1858, in New York City, he was the second of four children of Theodore Roosevelt Sr.—a merchant, banker, and philanthropist—and Martha Bulloch Roosevelt, who came from a prominent Georgia family. Her brothers had fought for the Confederacy during the Civil War, and later, as Roosevelt developed a fascination with military history, he took great pride in the wartime service of his Southern relatives, even though he and his father were staunch Unionists.

The Roosevelt children were educated at home by private tutors, and although he was nearsighted, Teedy (as his family called him) learned to read very early and developed keen interests in a wide variety of subjects, especially American history and literature. He also acquired a love of nature and became a self-taught expert on birds, flowers, and animals. By the time he was fifteen, he had traveled throughout Europe, Africa, and the Middle East, and during his teens he lived with a family in Dresden, Germany, where he learned the German language.

In addition to nearsightedness, Teedy suffered from asthma as a child and he was frequently ill. His father cautioned him that, although he was eagerly training his mind, the weakness of his body might hold him back in the future, and so he started a training program to improve his physical condition. He learned to ride and hunt, took up boxing and swimming, and played sports, as well as hiked and camped in the wilderness. With this tireless emphasis on physical activity, he developed robust good health and was in remarkable physical condition as an adult.

Roosevelt had already published two books on birds before he graduated from Harvard University in 1880, and he had begun the research for another book, a naval history of the War of 1812 between Great Britain and the United States. Published in 1882, the book drew little public interest, but it was a highly respected scholarly study that became required reading at the Naval War College. The U.S. Navy ordered that one copy be made available aboard every ship in its fleet.

Roosevelt met Alice Hathaway Lee in 1878 and fell in love with her. They were married several months after

Above: Roosevelt during his boxing days.

Left: Roosevelt's first wife, the former Alice Hathaway Lee.

Chips off the Old Block

"I can do one of two things," Theodore Roosevelt once said, "I can be president of the United States or I can control Alice. I cannot do both." His daughter, Alice, had inherited his spirit and in her later years (she lived to the age of ninety-six) was famous for her wit, which was usually turned against the Washington establishment. She married Congressman Nicholas Longworth in an elaborate White House ceremony, and after his death in 1931, she became known as "Washington's other monument."

The president's son, Theodore Roosevelt Jr. earned a Purple Heart, a Distinguished Service Medal, and the Distinguished Service Cross in action during World War I, after which he followed in his father's footsteps as a member of the New York State Legislature and as assistant secretary of the navy in the Harding administration. In World War II, he served as a brigadier general and commander of the Twenty-sixth Infantry in Africa, Italy, and France. He was part of the first wave ashore in the D-Day landing on the Normandy beach, and was posthumously awarded the Medal of Honor for his bravery and leadership.

Another of Roosevelt's sons, Kermit, who accompanied him on his post-presidential treks, served in the British army during the early years of World War I, and then as a major of artillery in the U.S. Army. He served in both armies again in World War II.

Archibald Roosevelt was awarded the French Croix de Guerre for his World War I service. He was discharged because of his severe wounds, but served again in World War II, where he was once again discharged with a battlefield disability.

The president's youngest son, Quentin, was shot down and killed during a World War I air battle with German fighters. And Ethel Carow Roosevelt was in Paris at the time, serving as a nurse at the American Ambulance Hospital.

his graduation from Harvard, honeymooned in England, and then settled in New York City.

Political Career Begins

Roosevelt enrolled in law classes at Columbia University in New York, but he didn't enjoy going to class as much as he did researching and writing. Feeling a sense of duty to his fellow citizens, he ran for public office, and he was elected to the New York state assembly in Albany at the age of twenty-three.

Roosevelt quickly won the respect of his fellow legislators. He revealed abuses of power by a corrupt judge,

and he supported laws that began regulating sweatshops that operated under horrible conditions—many of them employing child labor. After being named Republican minority leader, he developed a reputation for working effectively with members of both political parties.

Roosevelt was serving his third term in the state assembly when tragedy struck. Alice died of kidney failure on February 14, 1884, following the birth of the couple's daughter, who was named Alice in honor of her mother. And on that same day, his mother died of typhoid fever. Grief-stricken, he continued to work, while his older sister, Anna (known as "Bamie") took care of baby Alice.

Left: As a rancher in the Dakota, T.R. made it a point to look the part.

Right: The Rough Rider gets in shape for the role on the back of a moose.

Home on the Range

In 1883, Roosevelt traveled throughout the western United States, and inspired by the wide-open frontier, bountiful animal life, and freedom of the range, he used some of his family inheritance to buy land in the Dakota Territory, where he built the Elkhorn Ranch, which was his home on the range from 1884 until 1886, where he wrote western history and operated a cattle ranch. He enjoyed the western lifestyle, wearing buckskin shirts, sporting a gun belt with a pearl-handled revolver, and spending most of his time with his cowboy work crews. He hunted big game, observed local wildlife and plants, and worked on several books of natural history and biography.

Roosevelt went home to New York City for a visit during this period, and fell in love with Edith Kermit Carow, a woman he had known for most of his life. When they became engaged, he moved back east to Sagamore Hill, a home he had built at Oyster Bay, Long Island, and soon turned back to politics. He became the Republican candidate for mayor of New York City, but lost badly, finishing third in the election.

Discouraged by his poor showing, he and Edith took a trip to Europe, and they were married in London on December 2, 1886. When they returned to the United States, they established their residence at Sagamore Hill, which would be their family home for the rest of their lives. They raised five children there, in addition to Alice, Roosevelt's daughter from his first marriage.

Roosevelt supported Benjamin Harrison in the presidential election of 1888, and he was appointed to the U.S. Civil Service Commission in Washington after Harrison's victory. He used the position to fight against the patronage system that gave government jobs to supporters who had no other qualifications than party loyalty. He believed jobs should go to the most qualified individuals. He also aggressively weeded out fraud, rewrote Civil Service examinations to make them fairer, and opened more jobs to women. Roosevelt's actions were considered radical at the time, but he quickly earned a growing reputation as a reformer.

Reformer and Rough Rider

Roosevelt returned to New York City in 1895 to accept the job of one of its four police commissioners. Although there were three other men with the same job title, and none of them had any real power, he took charge in his usual fashion, allowing his colleagues high-sounding responsibilities but putting himself in charge of press relations. Before very long, he was courting the national press, too, and to this day, many Americans, including some historians, believe that Roosevelt was New York's one and only police commissioner—and a crusading one at that.

During this period, people were beginning to express frustration over abuses of power by politicians and the huge profits of corporations. People demanded more accountability from both government and business, and many farmers and laborers in rural areas of the West and South supported a political movement called populism that supported their interests, while those in urban areas who wanted social, economic, and government reform turned to progressivism. So began the era of the reformer.

In his job on the police board, Roosevelt exposed police corruption—particularly the actions of officers who accepted money to overlook criminal activities. He called the corruption "utterly demoralized . . . [and steeped in] venality and blackmail." He enforced laws that regulated establishments where alcoholic beverages were served and began prosecution of landlords who treated tenants unfairly. In the process, Roosevelt made enemies throughout the city government, but his press coverage made him well known across the country, and even in Europe, and he learned a great deal about issues that mattered to common people.

Roosevelt made no bones about wanting a career in national politics. Through his study and his writing, he had developed strong ideas on how the country should be run, and he was eager to get on with the job. He recognized most of all that military strength, especially a strong navy, was vital for national survival and the key to enforcing foreign policy, and when Ohio governor William McKinley was elected president in 1896, Roosevelt talked his Washington friends into pressuring the new president to appoint him assistant secretary of the navy. McKinley never hesitated.

As assistant naval secretary, Roosevelt began helping to prepare the navy for a possible war with Spain. For some time, Spain had been trying to suppress a movement for independence in Cuba, a Spanish colony in the Caribbean just south of Florida. Some Cubans

Above: Roosevelt was one of four New York City police commissioners serving together, but the press rarely reported on the other three.

had started a revolution in 1895, hoping to free their country, but Spanish authorities remained in power and established prison camps to hold revolutionaries. American journalists began exposing the terrible conditions of those camps, although some of their reports were exaggerated, reflecting the sensationalistic yellow journalism reporting style popular at the time.

In 1897, the United States sent the battleship *Maine* to the port of Havana, Cuba's capital, to protect American citizens and property there. On February 15, 1898, the ship sank after being ripped by a mysterious explosion that killed 260 American sailors. Although no cause for the explosion was determined, sabotage was suspected

Above: Roosevelt is dressed for war in a uniform custom-tailored by Brooks Brothers.

After the Rough Riders' charge, Roosevelt's commanding officer, Major General Leonard Wood, filed the following report to Washington:

> Colonel Roosevelt, accompanied by four or five men, led a very desperate and extremely gallant charge up San Juan Hill [sic], thereby setting a splendid example to the troops and encouraging them to pass over the open country intervening between their position and the trenches of the enemy. In leading this charge, he started off first, as he supposed, with quite a following of men, but soon discovered that he was alone. He then returned and gathered up a few men and led them to the charge…Everybody finally went up the hill in good style.… During the assault, Colonel Roosevelt was the first to reach the trenches in his part of the line, and killed one of the enemy with his own hand.

If that sounds like a recommendation for a Medal of Honor, it probably was. But the army brass refused to consider awarding it because of Roosevelt's earlier efforts on behalf of the navy. When his own request was rejected, the Rough Rider sniffed, "I never wanted the infernal medal anyway." But somehow nobody seemed to believe him.

and widely reported, and many Americans began calling for war. (Over seventy years later, in 1969, the U.S. Navy determined that the explosion had been caused by a defective boiler.)

Roosevelt was in charge that day while the secretary of the Navy was out of town, and responded by instructing Commodore George Dewey, the commander of the navy's Asian fleet, to sail for Hong Kong and prepare for action in the Spanish-controlled Philippines. Hoping to see the end of European influence in the Caribbean, Roosevelt was eager for war with Spain. In April 1898, President McKinley approved a congressional resolution calling for the immediate withdrawal of Spanish forces from Cuba. Several days later, the Spanish officially rejected his demand and declared war on the United States. The following day, Congress voted for its own declaration of war on Spain. Commodore Dewey attacked and quickly defeated the Spanish fleet at Manila Bay in the Philippines.

Roosevelt had served for three years in the National Guard, attaining the rank of captain, and he desperately wanted to get into combat. After war was declared, he resigned his position as assistant secretary of the navy to serve as a lieutenant colonel in the First U.S. Volunteer Cavalry, and he organized his own unit, the "Rough Riders," with volunteers from his circle of friends, New York socialites and Texas cowboys. In almost no time at all, the Rough Riders found themselves on their way to Cuba.

Top: The Rough Riders in Cuba with their fearless leader.

Middle: Roosevelt worked hard as New York's governor.

Bottom: Rarely did anyone forget a Roosevelt speech, especially on election day.

The unit performed heroically in the war, and since Cuba was so close to the United States, newspapers were able to report on developments with daily reports. Roosevelt, already well known nationally because of his various high-profile reform efforts, made a good story. Reporters began referring to him as "Teddy," and made sure his fearless leadership of the Rough Riders was well documented. Promoted to colonel, he led a wild charge up Kettle Hill (San Juan was the name for a group of hills, but it was Kettle Hill that Roosevelt took) in the battle for San Juan and became an instant hero across America. When the war ended with a Spanish surrender after three months, Roosevelt gained even more publicity and popularity for his efforts to get the soldiers home as quickly as possible. Although he was, and still is, often called "Teddy," he considered the name vulgar and called it "an outrageous impertinence" if anyone used the name in his presence. Most of his government colleagues usually referred to him simply as "T. R."

Pesky Governor Made Vice President

In the summer of 1898, Roosevelt accepted a Republican invitation to run for governor of New York, and campaigning tirelessly and taking every opportunity to remind voters of his recent war record, he won by a narrow margin. He hit the ground running in Albany, as was his style, and he quickly became a popular and respected governor: He dismantled a system gave civil servants jobs through the patronage system; he attacked large corporations that were charging excessive prices for goods and services; he supported pro-labor legislation, increased teachers' salaries, and spearheaded support for a bill that outlawed racial discrimination in public schools; and he pushed for preservation of state forests and wildlife.

Roosevelt's success as governor, his increasing popularity, and especially his tendency to attack powerful businesses and politicians of both major parties, began to annoy senior New York senator Thomas Collier Platt. "Boss" Platt, as he was known, wanted to get rid of the young governor, and he convinced Republican Party officials to support Roosevelt for vice president on the ticket with President McKinley in the 1900 election. The vice presidency had been vacant since the death of Garret Hobart, and Roosevelt seemed to be an ideal replacement.

Although he was at first reluctant to become vice president, a position that didn't have any real political power, Roosevelt campaigned with his typical enthusiasm and helped McKinley win reelection by a landslide. But only six months into his second term, McKinley was shot by an assassin in Buffalo, New York, on September 6, 1901, and died eight days later. Theodore Roosevelt was sworn in as the twenty-sixth president of the United States at the age of forty-two, the youngest man to become president. (No one younger has held the office since then, although John F. Kennedy, the first president born in the twentieth century, was forty-three when he was elected in 1960.)

"Trustbuster"

Roosevelt's approach to the presidency surprised no one who had been following his political career. After carefully building momentum and support during his first few months in office, he pursued his policies with the same aggressiveness he had demonstrated in his cavalry charges in Cuba. Viewing himself as the representative of the common people, he believed that it was time for the federal government to get involved in resolving disputes between forces of business and labor.

Pushing for reform of business practices that benefited a few wealthy individuals and corporations, Roosevelt brought more regulation to big business, and as a result, he earned a reputation as a "trustbuster." Some businesses that created similar products or provided similar services had joined together to form trusts—a business combination that reduces competition and controls prices. Since a trust dominates a particular

market sector, it doesn't face competition over the prices it can demand for goods and services, leaving small and new companies to wither.

Unlike some of the more radical reformers, Roosevelt didn't want to dissolve all big companies, just the ones that he thought were exploiting their financial power at the expense of the public good. He influenced Congress to pass several measures that helped the federal government enforce antitrust laws that were already on the books. During the term Roosevelt completed as successor to President McKinley and the next term when he was elected on his own, the Department of Justice launched forty-three lawsuits against trusts and won several important judicial decisions. Among the victories was a suit against the Northern Securities Company, a group of several railroad companies that were operated as though they were one company, an arrangement that allowed them to kill off competition and control shipping prices, which was reflected in price tags for everything shipped by rail.

In his first annual address to Congress in 1901, Roosevelt argued that since many trusts were involved in goods and services vital to public welfare, they ought to disclose their financial records and business practices to the public they served. He persuaded Congress to create the Bureau of Corporations, which was given the power to investigate big companies.

In 1902, Roosevelt forced the federal government to intervene in a coal strike, convincing both sides to accept the ruling of an independent committee he had appointed himself. This is considered to be the first significant pro-labor move by any American president. They were part of a program the president called the "Square Deal," intended to show that no one, rich or poor, could expect special treatment under his administration.

That same year, Roosevelt named Oliver Wendell Holmes to the U.S. Supreme Court, and Holmes went on to become one of the most significant justices in the history of the court. Roosevelt believed that he would support his efforts to break up large corporations, but Holmes insisted on judging each case by his own standards. Selecting Holmes to the court, where he served with distinction for more than two decades, was one of several outstanding legacies of Roosevelt's presidency.

Oliver Wendell Holmes Jr.

Oliver Wendell Holmes Jr. was born in Boston, Massachusetts, on March 8, 1841. At the age of sixteen, he began attending Harvard University, where he wrote articles for student publications and complained of the school's unwillingness to accept new ideas. One such idea was the theory of evolution, first published in 1859 by English naturalist Charles Darwin. Holmes was fascinated by the scientific reasoning Darwin had used to arrive at his idea that humans and other animals had evolved from earlier forms of life.

Holmes served in the Civil War for three years before enrolling at Harvard Law School in 1864. Two years later, he began his career as a lawyer and he also wrote and taught law. In 1881, he published The Common Law, arguing strongly that laws should not be unchanging rules simply passed on from generation to generation, but should change and develop along with the changing times. Holmes thus applied Darwin's ideas to the history of law.

In 1882, he was named to the Massachusetts Supreme Court in 1882, and served there for twenty years. In the late 1800s, the nation began facing increasing tensions between workers and their employers, resulting from growth brought about by the Industrial Revolution, as large corporations with thousands of employees sprang up for the first time. Following Holmes's theories in The Common Law, new laws had to be made and old laws had to be interpreted in new ways.

President Theodore Roosevelt named Holmes to the U.S. Supreme Court in 1902, believing that he would support his political goals. In particular, Roosevelt was "trust-busting"—trying to break up large corporations that held monopolies and were controlling important industries. In Massachusetts, some of Holmes's opinions seemed sympathetic to Roosevelt's aims. But in Holmes's first trust-busting case as a Supreme Court justice, he angered Roosevelt by disagreeing with him. Holmes insisted on judging each case by his own standards, rather than by anyone's political goals.

Holmes's independent views and his eloquent language led to his being called the "Great Dissenter." The fact was, though, that his dissents only amounted to about 3 percent of the cases he heard. But his elegant writing style and clear logic made his opinions stand out more than those of other justices. In Lochner v. New York (1905), for example, the Court declared unconstitutional a New York law

establishing a sixty-hour workweek for bakers, saying that it limited the economic freedom of bakery owners. Remaining true to his idea of a living law that changes to follow the needs of society, Holmes wrote that the Constitution is not intended to embody a particular economic theory but to defend the rights of people with widely differing views.

When the United States entered World War I in 1917, Congress passed laws to prevent antiwar activists from spreading their views, which were thought to be dangerous to the war effort. The Federal Espionage Act of 1917 established stiff penalties for interfering with recruiting efforts. An amendment to the act also set penalties for disloyal language about the government, the war effort, or such symbols as the flag or the Constitution. After the war ended, several such cases came before the Supreme Court, with freedom of speech as the main issue. The Court's decisions—and Holmes's contributions—influenced how the issue would be viewed for the rest of the century. During the war, Socialist Party secretary Charles Schenck had been arrested under the Espionage Act and was convicted of trying to cause insubordination in the army and interfering with the draft by sending leaflets to drafted men urging them to oppose conscription and the war. The Supreme Court unanimously upheld Schenck's conviction, and Holmes wrote that in ordinary times Schenck's leaflets would be protected under the First Amendment, which guarantees freedom of speech. Yet, as Holmes had written in The Common Law, the character of every act depends upon the circumstances in which it is done. War, Holmes wrote, changed the circumstances of Schenck's acts, giving the state the right to limit them. Said Holmes: "The most stringent protection of free speech would not protect a man in falsely shouting fire in a theater and causing a panic. [...] The question in every case is whether the words used are used in circumstances and are of such a nature as to create a clear and present danger that they will bring about the substantive evils which Congress has the right to prevent." Both the "fire in a theater" scenario and the phrase "clear and present danger" have become commonplace in considering how the law applies in certain cases.

After thirty years on the Supreme Court, Holmes retired in 1932. He died in Washington, D.C., on March 5, 1935, just three days short of his ninety-fourth birthday.

"To announce that there should be no criticism of the president, or that we are to stand by the president, right or wrong, is not only unpatriotic and servile, but is morally treasonable to the American public."
—*Theodore Roosevelt*

The Roosevelt Administration

Administration Dates:	September 14, 1901–March 4, 1905
	March 4, 1905–March 4, 1909
Vice President:	None (1901–5)
	Charles W. Fairbanks (1905–9)
Cabinet:	
Secretary of State	John M. Hay (1901–5)
	Elihu Root (1905–9)
	Robert Bacon (1909)
Secretary of the Treasury	Lyman J. Gage (1901–2)
	Leslie M. Shaw (1902–7)
	George B. Cortelyou (1907–9)
Secretary of War	Elihu Root (1901–4)
	William Howard Taft (1904–8)
	Luke E. Wright (1908–09)
Attorney General	Philander C. Knox (1901–4)
	William H. Moody (1904–6)
	Charles J. Bonaparte (1906–9)
Secretary of the Navy	John D. Long (1901–2)
	William H. Moody (1902–4)
	Paul Morton (1904–5)
	Charles J. Bonaparte (1905–6)
	Victor H. Metcalf (1906–8)
	Truman H. Newberry (1908–9)
Postmaster General	Charles E. Smith (1901–2)
	Henry C. Payne (1902–4)
	Robert J. Wynne (1904–5)
	George B. Cortelyou (1905–7)
	George V. Meyer (1907–9)
Secretary of the Interior	Ethan A. Hitchcock (1901–7)
	James R. Garfield (1907–9)
Secretary of Agriculture	James Wilson (1901–9)
Secretary of Commerce and Labor	
	George B. Cortelyou (1903–4)
	Victor H. Metcalf (1904–6)
	Oscar S. Straus (1906–9)

The "Big Stick" Foreign Policy

Roosevelt's military record had enhanced his national reputation, and he was known to favor expansion of American interests abroad. However, his foreign policy initiatives were surprisingly modest. He often said that in diplomatic efforts, it was wise to "speak softly and carry a big stick," meaning that one should attempt peaceful solutions while at the same time being prepared to back up the talk with action when it was necessary.

Unlike some of his contemporaries, Roosevelt didn't favor American domination of the Caribbean, and he strongly opposed annexing Cuba and other islands. Still, he wanted European powers to continue to cut back on their influence in Latin America, a policy that came to be known as the Roosevelt Corollary to the Monroe Doctrine. The Monroe Doctrine was a policy statement issued during the presidency of James Monroe explaining the position of the United States against involvement of the European powers in the affairs of Western Hemisphere countries. The Roosevelt Corollary declared that if any country in the Western Hemisphere acted irresponsibly and caused a European country to intervene in its affairs, the United States would consider it a threat to its own interests.

Roosevelt's most controversial stand as president involved the Central American country of Panama, a part of Colombia at the time. Recognizing Panama's strategic importance to the commerce of the Western Hemisphere, he was greatly interested in a French company's plans to build a canal across the isthmus it occupied, and early in 1903, Roosevelt arranged to buy out the French firm's rights to the canal scheme.

When the Colombian government rejected his offer to build the canal, Roosevelt encouraged anti-Colombian forces in Panama to start a revolution, and three days after it began, the government of the United States officially recognized Panama as an independent country. At the request of the new Panamanian government, U.S. naval vessels arrived to prevent Colombian armed forces from suppressing the revolution, and the new government of Panama granted the United States full control of a strip of land ten miles wide, all the way across the isthmus, to construct the Panama Canal. Although the canal wasn't finished during his presidency, Roosevelt took a strong personal interest in the construction project and visited Panama in 1906.

Second Term

Since Roosevelt assumed office after the McKinley assassination, he was eager to prove that he could get elected on his own. He won his party's nomination for president in 1904, and ran with U.S. senator Charles W. Fairbanks of Ohio as his running mate. They were pitted against Democratic presidential nominee Alton B. Parker, a conservative judge from New York, and Henry G. Davis, an eighty-year-old former U.S. senator from West Virginia. Roosevelt won with the greatest margin of popular votes up to that time—over 1.5 million—and he easily won in the Electoral College, 336 votes to 140.

He continued to pursue business reform and, attacking high prices for railroad freight, he supported the Hepburn Act of 1906, which gave the Interstate Commerce Commission the authority to set railroad freight rates. Another key piece of legislation he backed was the Pure Food and Drug Bill, which was also passed in 1906. The new law set health standards for food safety

Right: The building of the Panama Canal, one of T.R.'s most rewarding accomplishments.

Upton Sinclair and the Muckrakers

American novelist and journalist Upton Sinclair was best known for his book The Jungle, *which—while fictional—exposed the very real unsanitary conditions in American meat-packing plants in 1901. During the first decade of the twentieth century, Sinclair was associated with a circle of investigative reporters called "muckrakers," because they exposed the seamier side of American life. Muckrakers are considered to have been excellent reporters who thoroughly researched their stories and based their reports on provable facts. Nevertheless, President Roosevelt lumped them together with more sensationalistic journalists who wrote stories without presenting evidence to back their claims.*

The term "muckraker," was, in fact, coined by President Roosevelt in a colorful speech he gave on April 15, 1906. Quoting from Pilgrim's Progress *by John Bunyan, he labeled journalists who focused their reporting on the seamier side of American life as "the Man with the Muckrake, the man who could look no way but downward," and he referred to those who wanted radical changes in government and business as the "lunatic fringe." The socially committed writers—Sinclair, Lincoln Steffens, Ida M. Tarbell, and Ray Stannard Baker, among others—who based their reports on significant evidence, enthusiastically adopted Roosevelt's scornful description and are linked by literary historians with the muckraking movement of 1900 to 1912.*

1904 Election Results

Presidential / Vice Presidential Candidates	Popular Votes	Electoral Votes
Theodore Roosevelt / Charles W. Fairbanks (Republican)	7,623,486	336
Alton B. Parker / Henry G. Davis (Democratic)	5,077,911	140

and it regulated medicine. Roosevelt had begun lobbying for reform of the meat-packing industry as far back as 1899, when he criticized the badly processed meat that had been sent to his soldiers in Cuba. The American people became aware of unsanitary conditions in meat-packing plants with the publication of *The Jungle,* a book by the American novelist and journalist Upton Sinclair, which exposed those conditions in horrifying detail. Such legislation further enhanced Roosevelt's image as the moral voice of the people.

Meanwhile, he continued his "Big Stick" policy in foreign affairs. Warships were rapidly increasing both their speed and firepower and they were becoming much more important as instruments of foreign policy. When Japanese forces defeated Russia in a series of naval battles in 1904 and 1905, the president thought it best to help calm things down. Since Japan was not in a strong economic position at the time, Japanese authorities eagerly accepted his offer to have the United States negotiate a peace treaty. The resulting Treaty of Portsmouth ended the Russo-Japanese War. Considered one of Roosevelt's greatest foreign-policy achievements, it earned him the Nobel Peace Prize in 1906.

Conservation

One of the most significant themes of Roosevelt's presidency is the emphasis he placed on the conservation of the country's natural resources. At a time when most people believed that clean air, water, healthy forests, and abundant wildlife would be available forever, Roosevelt recognized how fragile the ecology was in the wake of ever-expanding industrialization.

One of Roosevelt's key advisors in this area, Gifford Pinchot, was a university-trained naturalist who believed in the scientific management of undeveloped land. Roosevelt used the 1891 Forest Reserve Act to increase federal-owned land from forty million acres when he took office to more than two hundred million acres by the time he left the presidency, and he appointed Pinchot to head the new U.S. Forest Service to administer those lands.

With the assistance of Pinchot and other conservationists, Roosevelt brought a host of irrigation and dam projects under government control, along with forests, seashores, and wilderness areas. For the first time, private companies—like utilities and the mining and lumber industries—were subjected to federal regulations in protected areas and needed special permission to operate in the protected areas.

By the end of his second term, Roosevelt had doubled the number of national parks, created fifty-one wildlife refuges, and proclaimed eighteen national monuments. Among the national treasures that would be forever safeguarded were Yellowstone National Park and the Grand Canyon National Monument, which eventually became a national park itself.

After the Presidency

Roosevelt had pledged not to run for reelection in 1908. He kept his promise reluctantly and left the White House in 1909 after the inauguration of William Howard Taft, a close friend and advisor who had served as secretary of war. Roosevelt was only fifty-one when his presidency ended, and he was determined to continue leading what he called "the strenuous life." Shortly after leaving office, he led an African safari sponsored by the Smithsonian Institution, and collected more than five hundred different bird and animal specimens. While he was in Africa, he wrote his first post-presidency book, *African Game Trails*. After the safari, Roosevelt and his family toured Europe, where he met with heads of state, reviewed troops, made speeches, and lectured at universities.

He came home from his travels in June 1910 still hugely popular with the public. When his ship landed in New York, he rode in triumph up Broadway in the very first ticker-tape parade, but he came home to disappointment. Disagreeing with some of the sweeping conservation laws that Roosevelt had passed, President Taft had not carried out his predecessor's programs as expected and had forced Gifford Pinchot to resign as head of the Forest Service. Taft angered many progressive Republicans by backing the party's old-line conservatives in Congress, and he angered the public by backing legislation that raised taxes. Progressive Republicans were soon pressuring Roosevelt to run for the presidency again in 1912.

Roosevelt was content to spend time with his family as well as to travel, study, and write. He did eventually enter the race against Taft and beat the president in several states that held primary elections. At the Republican Party's national convention in Chicago, however, Taft's supporters were able to win the battle for delegates. Outraged Roosevelt backers stormed out of the convention hall, and urged Roosevelt to consider running as a third-party candidate.

Six weeks after the convention, Roosevelt's supporters formed the Progressive "Bull Moose" Party and named him its candidate for the presidency. While he making a campaign speech in Milwaukee on October 14, 1912, Roosevelt was wounded in an assassination attempt. The bullet just missed his right lung, but it didn't slow him down. He insisted on finishing his speech before he was taken to the hospital.

Unfortunately for the Republicans, Roosevelt's Bull Moose candidacy split the party's support, and the Democratic candidate, New Jersey governor Woodrow Wilson won by a landslide, taking 435 electoral votes. Roosevelt won over Taft by more than 500,000 votes but in the end, he was still an ex-president.

Below: Soulmates T.R. and John Muir at Yosemite.

Below: Gifford Pinchot, a naturalist who advised the president on land development.

Following the defeat, Roosevelt left the country again. He led an expedition to explore an unmapped river in Brazil, called the River of Doubt (now called the Roosevelt River), and collected animal specimens for the American Museum of Natural History in New York. It proved to be a much more difficult journey than his recent African adventure, and Roosevelt contracted a malarial fever that at one point threatened his life. He recovered, though, and published one of his most popular books, *Through the Brazilian Wilderness*. However, the illness probably contributed to his death.

The outbreak of World War I gave him a new cause. The sinking of the British passenger ship *Lusitania* by a German submarine in 1915 convinced him that the United States should prepare to go to war again, but President Wilson didn't ask Congress for a declaration of war until two years later. Ever the man of action, Roosevelt requested an army command in Europe, but he was turned down by Wilson's secretary of war, Newton D. Baker. Roosevelt went right on making fire-breathing speeches in favor of a strong national defense and constant military preparedness, and after the armistice in 1918, he publicly ridiculed Wilson's programs for postwar Europe.

Meanwhile, recurring problems with the malaria he had contracted in South America, combined with the death of his youngest son, Quentin, in air combat in Europe, had sapped Roosevelt's strength. He was hospitalized for a time with rheumatism, and he had lost hearing in one ear. Roosevelt died in his sleep at home in Oyster Bay on January 6, 1919. He was buried unceremoniously, according to his wishes, with no eulogies or military honors, at Sagamore Hill, the home he had built in 1884. At the time of his death, Vice President Thomas R. Marshall said, "Death had to take him sleeping, for if Roosevelt had been awake, there would have been a fight."

Below: On safari in Africa, 1909.

Below: A cartoon version of the 1912 presidential campaign with Taft riding a Republican elephant, Wilson riding a Democratic donkey, and Roosevelt perched on a bull moose.

Left: The Roosevelt home at Oyster Bay, New York, perfectly captures his personality.

Legacy

Theodore Roosevelt is consistently listed among America's most effective presidents. He quickly and forcefully led the government to address problems of the time. Badly needed reforms attacked unfair business practices, unhealthy food processing, and questionable medicines. Recognizing that the great expansion of business and industry had far exceeded the commerce laws addressed by the Constitution, he broadened federal powers to oversee interstate commerce.

Roosevelt's leadership also proved to be fair and balanced. Ignoring radicals who called for more vigorous pursuit of business reform, he ensured that careful investigations were completed before the government pursued lawsuits against trusts. By being the first president to recognize the rights of labor in disputes with management, he helped instill a more balanced negotiating process for wages and benefits. Also, his conservation efforts were the first large-scale endeavor to preserve and protect natural resources.

Roosevelt's foreign policy placed the United States at the forefront of international diplomacy backed by a strong military. He achieved great success—winning the Nobel Peace Prize for helping end the Russo-Japanese War—but his aggressiveness in this area also created problems. The Roosevelt Corollary to the Monroe Doctrine further enhanced the role of the United States as the leader and protector of the Western Hemisphere, but U.S. relations with Latin America became strained after his intervention against Colombia to help create and defend the new nation of Panama, and United States relations with several Latin American countries were strained over the next few decades.

After Roosevelt, Republican leaders became less reform-minded toward business. William Howard Taft, Roosevelt's successor, proved to be more successful as a trustbuster, but he also set up a more pro-business administration. More reforms followed when Democrat Woodrow Wilson became president in 1912, and then the three Republican administrations of the 1920s followed the principle that government should intervene as little as possible in the affairs of business. Their cautious approach to government was the direct opposite of Roosevelt's, who once expressed his credo as "Get action, do things."

Roosevelt's charisma is still legendary. In his years of retirement at Sagamore Hill, he welcomed a steady stream of visitors, important and otherwise, always with the same word that had become his trademark during his White House years: "Dee-lighted," he would say, and no one ever got the idea that he didn't sincerely mean every rolling syllable.

Edith Roosevelt

Born August 6, 1861, Norwich, Connecticut
Died September 30, 1948, Oyster Bay, Long Island, New York

"[Edith Roosevelt was] one of the strongest-minded and strongest-willed presidential wives who ever lived in the White House."
—Life magazine

Edith Roosevelt presided over a very active household as first lady. She was determined to maintain as normal a life as possible for her children and did her best to shield them from public attention. At the same time, she was a charming first lady who enthusiastically took a leading position in Washington's social life. She was the first president's wife to employ a full-time social secretary of her own.

New York Society

The daughter of Charles and Gertrude Tyler Carow, Edith Kermit Carow was born in Norwich, Connecticut, in 1861. She grew up in New York City where she enjoyed a childhood of wealth and privilege. One of her

best friends, Corinne Roosevelt—the younger sister of Theodore—came from another wealthy family.

Edith and Theodore became friends early in their lives. They moved in the same social circles, corresponded with one another when he went to Europe with his family as a teenager, and there was speculation that their friendship might one day develop into a romance. However, they lost touch with each other when he left for Harvard University in 1876.

In his junior year at Harvard, Theodore met and fell in love with Alice Hathaway Lee, another young woman from a prominent family. They were married in 1880, honeymooned in England, and then set up residence in New York City, where he began studying law at Columbia University. He quickly tired of his law studies, and in 1881 he was elected to the New York state assembly.

Alice Roosevelt died in 1884, shortly after giving birth to a daughter, Alice Lee Roosevelt, who was named in her honor. Theodore Roosevelt, distraught after the death of both his wife and mother on the same day, went to live on a ranch in the Dakota Territory, but during a trip back to New York, he ran into Edith Carow at his sister's house. They began seeing each other again and were secretly engaged in November 1885.

Left: The Roosevelt family, outdoors, of course.

Homemaker

Edith and Theodore Roosevelt were married in London, England, on December 2, 1886, and they eventually settled at Sagamore Hill, the house Roosevelt had built at Oyster Bay on Long Island. Even though Edith had a reputation for being somewhat aloof, their marriage proved to be an extremely happy one. They would have five children—four boys and a girl—in addition to Alice, Roosevelt's daughter from his first marriage.

Since Theodore's life in politics consumed a great deal of his time, Edith ran the household, managing the finances, disciplining the children, and planning the couple's social life. She was not always comfortable with her husband's love of danger—his active duty as a Rough Rider during the Spanish-American War or his big-game hunting trips—but she accepted it as part of his nature and handled family matters efficiently during his absences.

First Lady

Theodore Roosevelt became president in September 1901 after William McKinley died from an assassin's bullet. The family moved into the White House, and Theodore began the busy duties of the presidency right away.

With six children, ranging in age from an infant to a teenager, as well as dozens of pets, the family turned the White House into a noisy family home, but Edith managed the most famous residence in the country with the same efficiency she had demonstrated at Sagamore Hill. She won the devotion of the household staff with her kindnesses, and she hosted many lavish dinner parties and receptions.

Edith read as much as she could, studying a variety of subjects, and preparing carefully for her role as first lady. She was able to hold her own in conversations on almost any topic, and she greatly impressed everyone who met her with her intelligence, grace, and wit. She hired a full-time social secretary to help her with meetings and state functions, but she never delegated her own sense of style. In 1906, she arranged the most regal wedding ever held

Above: The White House security detail and a couple of honorary members.

at the White House for Alice, who was then twenty-two years old. Two years later, Edith presided over an elaborate coming-out party for her seventeen-year-old daughter, Ethel.

In addition to arranging social events, Edith also took an active role in her husband's work. She handled mail, reviewed his speeches, and highlighted stories in newspapers that she thought he should read. Many people felt that Edith was instrumental in balancing her husband's impulsiveness, and were convinced that she often saved him from making embarrassing errors in public by using her caution and thoughtfulness to keep him in check.

Life after the White House

When Roosevelt left the White House in 1909, he was still a relatively young man and wasn't in any mood for retirement. He stayed involved in politics, even making another bid for the presidency in 1912. He took trips to the wilderness of Africa and South America, and when the United States entered World War I in 1917, he made headlines with his opinions on the war. Through it all, Edith remained the rock of the family: She ran the household, supported her husband even when she didn't agree with his direction, and guided him as best she could.

After her husband's death in 1919, Edith traveled through Europe and Asia for a while. Back home at Sagamore Hill, she did a great deal of work for her church and for charitable organizations, and she also was active in the Women's Republican Club. She became a popular spokesperson for the Republican Party, giving speeches supporting both local and national candidates. When

Franklin D. Roosevelt, a distant cousin of Theodore's, became president on the Democratic ticket, she soundly denounced him and became a vocal critic of his "New Deal" policies.

Edith Roosevelt died on September 30, 1948, at the age of eighty-seven. An editorial in *Life* magazine at the time called her "one of the strongest-minded and strongest-willed presidential wives who ever lived in the White House."

Roosevelt's First Annual Address to Congress

Delivered on December 3, 1901

During the second half of the nineteenth century, the United States emerged as a major industrial nation. Industrialization involves a population movement from rural to urban areas and a shift from producing goods in homes or in small shops to manufacturing them in factories. By the 1890s, these new industries were enjoying large profits and employing millions of people, but there were drawbacks as well. Cities grew overcrowded and dirty, and there was an ever-widening gap between wealthy industrialists and wage earners, as large businesses began overwhelming smaller ones.

Some businesses that created similar products or provided similar services joined together to form trusts, which reduced competition and controlled prices. Trusts dominated such commodities as oil and coal, beef and sugar, and such services as railroads. By 1900, there were over 200 trusts operating in the United States. Since a trust dominates a particular market sector, it does not face competition to the prices it demands for goods and services, and it was becoming extremely difficult for small and new companies to survive in the sectors that trusts dominated.

President William McKinley did a great deal to encourage business growth during his first term in office between 1897 and 1901. He was well aware of the ever-increasing power of trusts and planned to address the issue during his second term, which began in March 1901. However, McKinley was assassinated six months later. His successor, Vice President Theodore Roosevelt, took up the cudgel and became an active "trustbuster" as soon as he assumed the office of president.

Since Roosevelt was already well known as a reformer, people were anxious to see how far he would go. Most observers expected that

he would be more aggressive than President McKinley, who wanted businesses to be relatively free of government regulation. Others were calling for swift action against trusts. Their passions had been aroused in part by a form of journalism that arose near the turn of the century. From sensationalistic yellow journalism reporting to more carefully researched stories, journalists were regularly exposing corruption, unhealthy living and working conditions, and business dominance by the trusts.

Roosevelt addressed the issue of trusts as part of his first annual address to Congress in December 1901. He recognized that the business combinations were legal, but he wanted to ensure that they engaged in fair business practices. Since trusts controlled goods and services vital to public welfare—such as food, energy, and transportation—Roosevelt argued that they ought to disclose their financial records and business practices to the public they served. That principle helped start the momentum for trust-busting.

Roosevelt's First Annual Address to Congress

The tremendous and highly complex industrial development which went on with ever accelerated rapidity during the latter half of the nineteenth century brings us face to face, at the beginning of the twentieth, with very serious social problems. The old laws, and the old customs which had almost the binding force of law, were once quite sufficient to regulate the accumulation and distribution of wealth. Since the industrial changes which have so enormously increased the productive power of mankind, they are no longer sufficient.

The growth of cities has gone on beyond comparison faster than the growth of the country, and the upbuilding of the great industrial centers has meant a startling increase, not merely in the aggregate of wealth, but in the number of very large individual, and especially of very large corporate, fortunes. The creation of these great corporate fortunes has not been due to the tariff nor to any other governmental action, but to natural causes in the business world, operating in other countries as they operate in our own.

The process has aroused much antagonism, a great part of which is wholly without warrant. It is not true that as the rich have grown richer the poor have grown poorer. On the contrary, never before has the average man, the wage-worker, the farmer, the small trader, been so well off as in this country as at the present time. There have been abuses connected with the accumulation of wealth; yet it remains true that a fortune accumulated in legitimate business can be accumulated by the person specially benefitted only on condition of conferring immense incidental benefits upon others. Successful enterprise, of the type which benefits all mankind, can only exist if the conditions are such as to offer great prizes as the rewards of success.

The captains of industry who have driven the railway systems across this continent, who have built up our commerce, who have developed our manufactures, have on the whole done great good to our people. Without them the material development of which we are so justly proud could never have taken place. Moreover, we should recognize the immense importance to this material development of leaving as unhampered as is compatible with the public good the strong and forceful men upon whom the success of business operations inevitably rests.

[…]

America has only just begun to assume that commanding position in the international business world which we believe will more and more be hers. It is of the utmost importance that this position be not jeopardized, especially at a time when the overflowing abundance of our own natural resources and the skill, business energy, and mechanical aptitude of our people make foreign markets essential. Under such conditions it would be most unwise to cramp or to fetter the youthful strength of our nation.

Moreover, it cannot too often be pointed out that to strike with ignorant violence at the interest of one set of men almost inevitably endangers the interests of all. The fundamental rule in our national life—the rule which underlies all others—is that, on the whole, and in times of adversity some will suffer far more than others; but speaking generally, a period of good times means that all, share more or less in them, and in periods of hard times all feel the stress in them to a greater or lesser degree.

[…]

There is widespread conviction in the minds of the American people that the great corporations known as trusts are in certain of their features and tendencies hurtful to the general welfare. This springs from no spirit of envy or uncharitableness, nor lack of pride in the great industrial achievements that have placed this country at the head of the nations struggling for commercial supremacy. It does not rest upon a lack of intelligent appreciation of the necessity of meeting changing and changed conditions of trade with new methods, nor upon ignorance of the fact that combination of capital in the effort to accomplish great things is necessary when the world's progress demands that great things be done. It is based upon sincere conviction that combination and concentration should be, not prohibited, but supervised and within reasonable limits controlled; and in my judgment this conviction is right.

It is no limitation upon property rights or freedom of contract to require that when men receive from government the privilege of doing business under corporate form, which frees them from individual responsibility, and enables them to call into their enterprises the capital of the public, they shall do so upon absolutely truthful representations as to the value of the property in which the capital is to be invested. Corporations engaged in interstate commerce should be regulated if they are found to exercise a license working to the public injury. It should be as much the aim of those who seek for social betterment to rid the business world of crimes of cunning as to rid the entire body politic of crimes of violence. Great corporations exist only because they are created and safeguarded by our institutions; and it is therefore our right and our duty to see that they work in harmony with these institutions.

The first essential in determining how to deal with the great industrial combinations is knowledge of the facts—publicity. In the interest of the public, the government should have the right to inspect and examine the workings of the great corporations engaged in interstate business. Publicity is the only sure remedy which we can now invoke. What further remedies are needed in the way of governmental regulation, or taxation, can only be determined after publicity has been obtained, by process of law, and in the course of administration. The first requisite is knowledge, full and complete—knowledge which may be made public to the world.

Artificial bodies, such as corporations and joint stock or other associations, depending upon any statutory law for their existence or privileges, should be subject to proper governmental supervision, and full and accurate information as to their operations should be made public regularly at reasonable intervals.

The large corporations, commonly called trusts, though organized in one state, always do business in many states, often doing very little business in the state where they are incorporated. There is utter lack of uniformity in the state laws about them; and as no state has any exclusive interest in or power over their acts, it has in practice proved impossible to get adequate regulation through state action.

Therefore, in the interest of the whole people, the nation should, without interfering with the power of the states in the matter itself, also assume power of supervision and regulation over all corporations doing an interstate business. This is especially true where the corporation derives a portion of its wealth from the existence of some monopolistic element or tendency in its business. There would be no hardship in such supervision; banks are subject to it, and in their case it is now accepted as a simple matter of course. Indeed, it is probable that supervision of corporations by the national government need not go so far as is now the case with the supervision exercised over them by so conservative a state as Massachusetts, in order to produce excellent results.

When the Constitution was adopted, at the end of the eighteenth century, no human wisdom could foretell the sweeping changes, alike in industrial and political conditions, which were to take place by the beginning of the twentieth century. At that time it was accepted as a matter of course that the several states were the proper authorities to regulate, so far as was then necessary, the comparatively insignificant and strictly localized corporate bodies of the day. The conditions are now wholly different and wholly different action is called for. I believe that a law can be framed which will enable the national government to exercise control along the lines above indicated, profiting by the experience gained through the passage and administration of the Interstate Commerce Act. If, however, the judgment of the Congress is that it lacks the constitutional power to pass such an act, then a constitutional amendment should be submitted to confer the power.

What Happened Next

During Roosevelt's first term (as he was completing the term of President McKinley) he influenced Congress to pass several measures that helped the federal government enforce existing antitrust laws. The Department of Justice then proceeded to initiate some forty-three different lawsuits against trusts and won several important judicial decisions. For example, the Northern Securities Company was a group of several railroad companies that were run as though they were one company, an arrangement that allowed them to eliminate competition and control prices. The government sued Northern Securities for violating the Sherman Antitrust Act of 1890, which outlawed such mergers.

Roosevelt's trust-busting practices were carried on by his successor, William Howard Taft, who served as president from March 1909 to March 1913. Taft had served as Roosevelt's secretary of war and was his close friend. The Taft administration broke the Standard Oil Company's dominance of the energy industry.

In addition to trust-busting, Roosevelt's presidency was distinguished by other examples of reform led by the federal government. The Pure Food and Drug Act, for example, prohibited the manufacture of unsafe foods or drugs. In 1905, Roosevelt urged "government supervision and regulation of charges by the railroads," which led to the Hepburn Act authorizing the Interstate Commerce Commission to determine rates for rail transport.

Roosevelt's "The Man with the Muck Rake" Speech

Delivered on April 15, 1906

President Theodore Roosevelt had a reputation as a reformer. There were many reform crusades by individuals or groups at the turn of the century, and it was during this period when exposé journalism first became widely popular in the United States. During the 1890s, investigative reporting was used to draw readers to newspapers, which had begun flourishing on a national scale. From 1900 to World War I, magazines also became increasingly popular, partly by featuring investigative reports.

Some journalists engaged in sensationalism, or yellow journalism, based on rumor rather than fact, which aggressively highlighted scandals and showcased the worst kinds of behavior. Exaggerating the truth made a greater impact on readers and sold more papers. At the same time, responsible reporters were able to expose actual wrongdoing, backing their reports with facts and thorough research.

President Roosevelt took the opportunity of a speech he delivered on April 15, 1906, at the Gridiron Club in Washington to discuss journalists and reformers intent on exaggerating conditions in order to further their personal, financial, or political causes. He was using his authority to speak from the "bully pulpit," a term he used to describe situation when a president lectures on moral issues or general problems in the nation and tries to influence improvement.

To underscore the theme of his address, Roosevelt quoted a passage from Pilgrim's Progress, *a work by English writer John Bunyan, first published in 1678, a moral story that became the second most widely read work in the English language after the Bible in its day. Roosevelt likened sensational journalists and reformers to a character Bunyan had called "the Man with the Muck Rake"—someone interested only in pleasures of the body and who sees only the seamy and vile parts of life.*

Excerpt from "The Man with the Muck Rake" Speech

Over a century ago Washington laid the cornerstone of the Capitol in what was then little more than a tract of wooded wilderness here beside the Potomac. We now find it necessary to provide great additional buildings for the business of the government.

This growth in the need for the housing of the government is but a proof and example of the way in which the nation has grown and the sphere of action of the national government has grown. We now administer the affairs of a nation in which the extraordinary growth of population has been outstripped by the growth of wealth in complex interests. The material problems that face us today are not such as they were in Washington's time, but the underlying facts of human nature are the same now as they were then. Under altered external form we war with the same tendencies toward evil that were evident in Washington's time, and are helped by the same tendencies for good. It is about some of these that I wish to say a word today.

In Bunyan's *Pilgrim's Progress* you may recall the description of the Man with the Muck Rake, the man who could look no way but downward, with the muck rake in his hand; who was offered a celestial crown for his muck rake, but who would neither look up nor regard the crown he was offered, but continued to rake to himself the filth of the floor.

In *Pilgrim's Progress,* the Man with the Muck Rake is set forth as the example of him whose vision is fixed on carnal instead of spiritual things. Yet he also typifies the man who in this life consistently refuses to see aught that is lofty, and fixes his eyes with solemn intentness only on that which is vile and debasing.

Now, it is very necessary that we should not flinch from seeing what is vile and debasing. There is filth on the floor, and it must be scraped up with the muck rake; and there are times and places where this service is the most needed of all the services that can be performed. But the man who never does anything else, who never thinks or speaks or writes, save of his feats with the muck rake, speedily becomes, not a help but one of the most potent forces for evil.

There are in the body politic, economic and social, many and grave evils, and there is urgent necessity for the sternest war upon them. There should be relentless exposure of and attack upon every evil man, whether politician or business man, every evil practice, whether in politics, business, or social life. I hail as a benefactor every writer or speaker, every man who, on the platform or in a book, magazine, or newspaper, with merciless severity makes such attack, provided always that he in his turn remembers that the attack is of use only if it is absolutely truthful.

The liar is no whit better than the thief, and if his mendacity takes the form of slander he may be worse than most thieves. It puts a premium upon knavery untruthfully to attack an honest man, or even with hysterical exaggeration to assail a bad man with untruth.

An epidemic of indiscriminate assault upon character does no good, but very great harm. The soul of every scoundrel is gladdened whenever an honest man is assailed, or even when a scoundrel is untruthfully assailed.

Now, it is easy to twist out of shape what I have just said, easy to affect to misunderstand it, and if it is slurred over in repetition not difficult really to misunderstand it. Some persons are sincerely incapable of understanding that to denounce mud slinging does not mean the endorsement of whitewashing; and both the interested individuals who need whitewashing and those others who practice mud slinging like to encourage such confusion of ideas.

One of the chief counts against those who make indiscriminate assault upon men in business or men in public life is that they invite a reaction which is sure to tell powerfully in favor of the unscrupulous scoundrel who really ought to be attacked, who ought to be exposed, who ought, if possible, to be put in the penitentiary. If Aristides is praised overmuch as just, people get tired of hearing it; and overcensure of the unjust finally and from similar reasons results in their favor.

Any excess is almost sure to invite a reaction; and, unfortunately, the reactions instead of taking the form of punishment of those guilty of the excess, is apt to take the form either of punishment of the unoffending or of giving immunity, and even strength, to offenders. The effort to make financial or political profit out of the destruction of character can only result in public calamity. Gross and reckless assaults on character, whether on the stump or in newspaper, magazine, or book, create a morbid and vicious public sentiment, and at the same time act as a profound deterrent to able men of normal sensitiveness and tend to prevent them from entering the public service at any price.

As an instance in point, I may mention that one serious difficulty encountered in getting the right type of men to dig the Panama canal is the certainty that they will be exposed, both without, and, I am sorry to say, sometimes within, Congress, to utterly reckless assaults on their character and capacity.

At the risk of repetition let me say again that my plea is not for immunity to, but for the most unsparing exposure of, the politician who betrays his trust, of the big business man who makes or spends his fortune in illegitimate or corrupt ways. There should be a resolute effort to hunt every such man out of the position he has disgraced. Expose the crime, and hunt down the criminal; but remember that even in the case of crime, if it is attacked in sensational, lurid, and untruthful fashion, the attack may do more damage to the public mind than the crime itself.

It is because I feel that there should be no rest in the endless war against the forces of evil that I ask the war be conducted with sanity as well as with resolution. The men with the muck rakes are often indispensable to the well being of society; but only if they know when to stop raking the muck, and to look upward to the celestial crown above them, to the crown of worthy endeavor. There are beautiful things above and round about them; and if

they gradually grow to feel that the whole world is nothing but muck, their power of usefulness is gone.

[…]

The fool who has not sense to discriminate between what is good and what is bad is well nigh as dangerous as the man who does discriminate and yet chooses the bad. There is nothing more distressing to every good patriot, to every good American, than the hard, scoffing spirit which treats the allegation of dishonesty in a public man as a cause for laughter. Such laughter is worse than the crackling of thorns under a pot, for it denotes not merely the vacant mind, but the heart in which high emotions have been choked before they could grow to fruition. There is any amount of good in the world, and there never was a time when loftier and more disinterested work for the betterment of mankind was being done than now. The forces that tend for evil are great and terrible, but the forces of truth and love and courage and honesty and generosity and sympathy are also stronger than ever before. It is a foolish and timid, no less than a wicked thing, to blink the fact that the forces of evil are strong, but it is even worse to fail to take into account the strength of the forces that tell for good.

Hysterical sensationalism is the poorest weapon wherewith to fight for lasting righteousness. The men who with stern sobriety and truth assail the many evils of our time, whether in the public press, or in magazines, or in books, are the leaders and allies of all engaged in the work for social and political betterment. But if they give good reason for distrust of what they say, if they chill the ardor of those who demand truth as a primary virtue, they thereby betray the good cause and play into the hands of the very men against whom they are nominally at war.

[…]

We can no more and no less afford to condone evil in the man of capital than evil in the man of no capital. The wealthy man who exults because there is a failure of justice in the effort to bring some trust magnate to account for his misdeeds is as bad as, and no worse than, the so-called labor leader who clamorously strives to excite a foul class feeling on behalf of some other labor leader who is implicated in murder. One attitude is as bad as the other, and no worse; in each case the accused is entitled to exact justice; and in neither case is there need of action by others which can be construed into an expression of sympathy for crime.

It is a prime necessity that if the present unrest is to result in permanent good the emotion shall be translated into action, and that the action shall be marked by honesty, sanity, and self-restraint. There is mighty little good in a mere spasm of reform. The reform that counts is that which comes through steady, continuous growth; violent emotionalism leads to exhaustion.

It is important to this people to grapple with the problems connected with the amassing of enormous fortunes, and the use of those fortunes, both corporate and individual, in business. We should discriminate in the sharpest way between fortunes well won and fortunes ill won; between those gained as an incident to performing great services to the community as a whole and those gained in evil fashion by keeping just within the limits of mere law honesty. Of course, no amount of charity in spending such fortunes in any way compensates for misconduct in making them.

[…]

More important than aught else is the development of the broadest sympathy of man for man. The welfare of the wage worker, the welfare of the tiller of the soil, upon these depend the welfare of the entire country; their good is not to be sought in pulling down others; but their good must be the prime object of all our statesmanship.

Materially we must strive to secure a broader economic opportunity for all men, so that each shall have a better chance to show the stuff of which he is made. Spiritually and ethically we must strive to bring about clean living and right thinking. We appreciate that the things of the body are important; but we appreciate also that the things of the soul are immeasurably more important.

The foundation stone of national life is, and ever must be, the high individual character of the average citizen.

What Happened Next

Roosevelt's speech helped to start a backlash against sensational news stories. Such reporting continued but it gradually began to lose popularity. Roosevelt, on the other hand, remained enormously popular and earned a reputation as a reformer. His successor, William Howard Taft, is not remembered as a reformer, but his administration actually had more success than Roosevelt's in breaking up companies that dominated a certain market. Those companies were illegal trusts, and although Roosevelt is remembered as the "trustbuster," Taft had even greater success in breaking them. Woodrow Wilson, another reformer, defeated both Roosevelt and Taft in the election of 1912, and by 1914, when World War I broke out, Americans had become less interested in reform and more interested in staying out of the war, and then winning it once America joined it in 1917.

Ironically, the term "muckraking" became less negative than "yellow journalism," or sensationalism, when a group of responsible writers began calling themselves "muckrakers" after Roosevelt's speech. Those writers had begun thriving around 1900 and their influence continued for about a dozen years. They are considered a historically significant group in American literature and journalism. Basing their stories on thorough research and documentation, muckrakers presented conclusive evidence in stories about dishonest public officials, hazardous working conditions, social problems, worthless medicines, and dangerous foods.

William Howard Taft

"I am entirely content to serve in the ranks."

—*William Howard Taft*

Twenty-seventh president of the United States, 1909–1913

Full name: William Howard Taft

Born: September 15, 1857, Cincinnati, Ohio

Died: March 8, 1930, Washington, D.C.

Burial site: Arlington National Cemetery, Arlington, Virginia

Parents: Alphonso and Louisa Torrey Taft

Spouse: Helen Herron (1861–1943; m. 1886)

Children: Robert Alphonso (1889–1953);
    Helen Herron (1891–1987); Charles Phelps (1897–1983)

Religion: Unitarian

Education: Yale University (B.A., 1878); Cincinnati Law School
    (LL.B., 1880)

Occupations: Lawyer, law professor

Government positions: Judge; U.S. solicitor general; Philippines
    governor, secretary of war under Theodore Roosevelt; U.S.
    Supreme Court chief justice

Political party: Republican

Dates as president: March 4, 1909–March 4, 1913

Age upon taking office: 51

William Howard Taft had a long and distinguished career of public service. Four different presidents appointed him to judicial, diplomatic, or cabinet positions before he achieved his main ambition when he was named chief justice of the U.S. Supreme Court in 1921.

Taft was much less successful in his role as president. "I am entirely content to serve in the ranks," he wrote to a supporter who wanted him to run again for president in 1916, four years after he had been soundly beaten in his bid for reelection.

The United States was undergoing tremendous economic growth during the first decade of the twentieth century when Taft was president. An increasingly profitable group of manufacturing, financial, and transportation corporations dominated American business, and in response to such collection of wealth, a strong political trend called progressivism arose to promote legislation that would monitor business practices and improve social conditions for a growing urban population.

Taft considered himself a progressive, but was in reality a cautious leader. As president, he was quickly caught between social activists who wanted change and the powerful business sector that wanted to be left alone. Unable to please either side, Taft suffered greatly during his term as one of the most criticized presidents of his era.

"GOODNESS GRACIOUS! I MUST HAVE BEEN DOZING!"

Taft was positioned—in his ideas, in his approach to governing, and in history—between two powerful and accomplished leaders. His predecessor, the popular Theodore Roosevelt, vigorously promoted leadership in matters of business regulation and social improvement. His successor, the forward-thinking Democrat Woodrow Wilson, reformed financial practices and set the nation's agenda through speeches, news conferences, and the solid backing of a Democratic majority in Congress.

In comparison to Roosevelt and Wilson, who were able to rally support for their policies, Taft wasn't able to prevail against his opponents. He allied himself with the more cautious and less popular side of his Republican Party, and he didn't have the ability to inspire public support for his policies, nor did he show much willingness

Left: Theodore Roosevelt was a tough act for Taft to follow, and few thought he was up to the job, least of all the political cartoonists.

to deal with the press. He was uncomfortable in the Oval Office. Skilled as a lawyer, his highest ambition had always been an appointment to the U.S. Supreme Court.

Political Roots

William Howard Taft was born on September 15, 1857, in Cincinnati, Ohio. Both sides of his family had deep roots in New England. His paternal grandfather had been a Vermont judge, but William's father, Alphonso, set out on his own. First, he walked from Vermont to New Haven, Connecticut, when he was accepted at Yale University. Then, after graduation, he relocated west to Ohio as a young lawyer, and became a judge in Cincinnati and a leader in the Ohio Republican Party. Later, he served briefly as secretary of war and as attorney general for President Ulysses S. Grant, and in the 1880s, he served as a diplomat in Russia and Austria-Hungary under President Chester A. Arthur.

Taft was raised in a household that included two older half brothers from his father's first marriage. Their mother, Fanny, died in 1852, and Taft's mother, Louise, bore four children. Always overweight as a child and throughout his life, Taft was sometimes called "Big Bill" or "Big Lub."

Timeline

1857: Born in Ohio
1880: Admitted to Ohio bar and works as court reporter for the *Cincinnati Commercial* newspaper
1883: Works as a lawyer in private practice
1887–90: Serves in Ohio Superior Court
1890–92: Serves as U.S. solicitor general
1892–1900: Serves as judge in the U.S. Circuit Court
1901–4: Serves as civil governor of the Philippines
1904–8: Serves as secretary of war
1909–13: Serves as twenty-seventh U.S. president
1912: Loses presidential reelection bid to Woodrow Wilson
1921–30: Serves as chief justice of the U.S. Supreme Court
1930: Dies in Washington, D.C.

Right: The president's father, Alfonso, had a long and distinguished career in government.

Robert A. Taft and the Taft Family

Several generations of Tafts have been influential in American politics since the Civil War years. Alphonso Taft was a prominent Ohio attorney and a Republican who served as secretary of war and attorney general under President Ulysses S. Grant, and as minister to Austria-Hugary and then to Russia under President Chester A. Arthur. His son, William Howard Taft, served as president and as chief justice of the U.S. Supreme Court. His son, Robert Alphonso Taft, was born in 1889, shortly before Alphonso Taft died. He served in the U.S. Senate from 1939 until 1953. His son, Robert Alphonso Taft Jr., served in the House of Representatives during the 1960s, and one term as a U.S. Senator in the 1970s. In 1998, Bob Taft, the son of Robert Taft Jr., grandson of Robert Taft and great-grandson of William Howard Taft, was elected governor of Ohio.

All of the Tafts have been leading Ohio Republicans, but it was the president's son, Robert A. Taft, who earned the nickname "Mr. Republican." He was a graduate of Yale University and he graduated at the head of his class from Harvard Law School. He went back to Ohio in 1913, was certified as a lawyer, and established a law practice in Cincinnati. On October 17, 1914, he married Martha Wheaton Bowers, whose father had served as solicitor general in the Taft administration. Robert and Martha would have four sons.

During World War II, Taft served his country as an assistant counsel for the U.S. Food and Drug Administration. After the war, he was a legal advisor for the American Relief Administration, after which he went back to Cincinnati, where he established his own law firm with his brother, Charles Phelps Taft.

Robert Taft was elected to the Ohio House of representatives in 1920. He was reelected three times and became Speaker of the House in 1926. He also served in the Ohio Senate for a term before he was elected to the United States Senate, where he earned the nickname "Mr. Republican" for his opposition to much of President Franklin D. Roosevelt's New Deal program and his foreign policy. Determined to keep the United States out of World War II, he strongly opposed such measures as trading fifty destroyers with Britain for leases on naval and air bases, and the Selective Training and Service Act, the first peacetime program of compulsory military service in the country's history. Taft strongly believed that America should remain neutral, especially after the Soviet Union became involved in the war. "My whole idea of foreign policy is based largely on the position that America can successfully defend itself against the rest of the world," he said. He strongly supported the war effort, though, once America became militarily involved.

In 1945, the year World War II ended, Taft began his second term in the Senate. He opposed the trials of Nazi wartime leaders at Nuremberg, explaining that he had little sympathy with war criminals, but noting that the U.S. Constitution prohibits the passage of laws enacted after a crime has been committed. He perceived a "spirit of vengeance, but vengeance is seldom justice." John F. Kennedy would later include Taft in his Pulitzer Prize–winning book, Profiles in Courage, which included essays on senators who showed courage by sticking up for principles against popular opinion.

Taft showed similar principles during his second term in the senate. When, at the request of President Harry S Truman, the House of Representatives passed a measure allowing strikers in vital industries to be drafted into the military, Senator Taft lodged a strong protest. Convinced that such action was unfair and violated workers' civil liberties, he joined with progressive Democrats in opposing it. Taft led the opposition to several initiatives of the Truman administration, including contributions to the International Monetary Fund and the creation of an international bank. Taft was deeply concerned with balancing the Federal budget, and limiting the government's power and influence. In 1946, after Republicans took control of both houses of Congress, he set about trying to restore what he perceived as a better balance between management and labor. Out of this came the Taft-Hartley Act, which outlawed the so-called closed shop that had forced all workers to join a union, provided that a union could be sued for beach of contract, and require an eighty-day "cooling off period" if a strike might jeopardize national health and safety.

Even though Robert Taft was the undisputed leader of the Republican Party, he never won its presidential nomination. He died of cancer on July 31, 1953.

Taft excelled academically throughout his early life, first in Cincinnati's public schools, and then at Yale, which he entered in 1874. After graduating second in his class, he returned to Ohio and enrolled in Cincinnati Law School, where he earned his degree in 1880. He served for a time as assistant prosecuting attorney in Hamilton County, Ohio, and he maintained a private law practice in Cincinnati. In March of 1887, he was appointed to an open superior court judgeship, and the following year, he was elected to a five-year term for the same seat. It would be the only time he was elected to any public position before he won the presidency.

Meanwhile, Taft met Helen Herron, a progressive-minded young woman, and he and "Nellie," as he called her, were married in 1886. They would have three children.

When President Benjamin Harrison named Taft to the post of solicitor general of the United States in early 1890, the family moved to Washington. Taft worried at first about his lack of experience with federal laws, but he mastered them quickly. During his first year on the job, he argued eighteen cases before the Supreme Court and won fifteen of them. When the federal circuit court system was created by an 1891 act of Congress, Taft was named judge of the Sixth District, which encompassed Michigan, Ohio, Kentucky, and Tennessee, and he spent eight productive years on the federal bench.

Governor of the Philippine Islands

President William McKinley invited Taft to head the newly created Philippines Commission in 1900 after the United States took possession of the Philippine Islands, previously ruled by Spain, following victory in the Spanish-American War in 1898. Taft had his heart set on becoming a Supreme Court justice and believed that the appointment would sideline him. Nellie Taft, however, urged her husband to take the post.

He was confident that the Filipinos would eventually have their own self-government, but he knew that he had a lot to do before they could. Among those things was clipping the wings of the authoritarian military

Right: Taft and his wife in Manila, where he served four years as Governor of the Philippines.

government running things in the islands. The task didn't seem very daunting at first, but the governor, Arthur Douglas (father of future general Douglas MacArthur), had strong opinions about everything, especially the prospect of being replaced by an overweight former judge who smiled a lot and didn't seem to have what he considered proper respect for the military.

Taft kept right on smiling, even when Governor MacArthur refused to move out of the presidential place and relegated him to a rundown house in the Manila suburbs. He eventually wore the general down, and when he replaced MacArthur, the civilian commission went to work in earnest.

He proved to be an able administrator in the Philippines, and was made governor of the territory, with one of his main challenges involving bringing stability and economic growth to the islands. Great strides were made in education and other social programs during his governorship, and he enjoyed his time in the Philippines in spite of continuous fighting between U.S. Marines and rebels there who wanted independence for their homeland.

Among the problems he faced was the Catholic priests who had acquired vast estates under Spanish rule, but had lost their lands in the revolution that drove the Spanish out. With the Americans in control, the priests were agitating to have those estates restored. The Filipinos themselves were opposed to the idea because it had been the tyranny of the priests that was at the root of their revolution. There were larger political considerations, however, not the least of which was the attitude of Catholic voters back home. It was one of those problems that politicians bend over backwards to avoid, but William Howard Taft was a judge, not a politician. His solution was to buy the land the priests were claiming as theirs and then have them replaced by new clerics, preferably Americans.

Vice President Theodore Roosevelt succeeded to the presidency in 1901 after the McKinley assassination, and he twice offered Taft a Supreme Court seat, but Taft declined, saying that he wanted to complete his duty in the Philippines. By that time, he had come to enjoy being a political leader, and his wife, Nellie, who influenced all of his career decisions, strongly supported his political pursuits. When Roosevelt was reelected to the White House in 1904, he offered Taft the cabinet post of secretary of war, which Taft accepted, and he and his family returned to Washington.

He served as one of Roosevelt's closest advisors during the next four years, offering balance and caution to the president, who often looked for quick solutions to the nation's problems. Taft also coordinated several foreign policy efforts: He traveled to Central America to supervise the start of construction of the Panama Canal (Roosevelt had told him to "make the dirt fly"), and in 1906, he sailed to Cuba when a rebellion there was threatening stability in the Caribbean region, and he negotiated a settlement that avoided U.S. military intervention.

Presidential/ Vice Presidential Candidates	Popular Votes	Electoral Votes
William Howard Taft/ James S. Sherman (Republican)	7,678, 908	321
William Jennings Bryan/ John W. Kern (Democratic)	6,409,104	162

Bryan lost for the third time as the Democratic nominee. He had lost in 1896 and 1900 to William McKinley, and did not run in 1904.

Reluctant Candidate

Taft quickly emerged as a favorite when President Roosevelt announced early in his second term that he wouldn't seek reelection. With his wife's encouragement, Taft overcame his personal reluctance and agreed to run for the office. His highest ambition was still the Supreme Court, but all of his friends and his family strongly encouraged him to consider the presidency.

With New York senator James S. Sherman as his running mate, Taft ran a mild campaign. He didn't like stumping to gain votes, but Roosevelt's ringing endorsement helped him easily defeat Democratic nominee William Jennings Bryan. Taft had pledged to continue Roosevelt's aggressive policy of business regulation, but with his predecessor's approval, he surrounded himself with more moderate politicians.

His first order of business was tariff reform, siding with many Americans wanted reductions in the taxes to slow the rising prices of consumer goods. Taft called a special Congressional session to address tariff reform during his first weeks in office. The Payne-Aldrich Act of 1909 originated in the House of Representatives as legislation to lower or eliminate many of the import a taxes, but a number of complex attachments that were added in the Senate actually increased tariffs in many cases. Although there was widespread public disapproval of the bill, Taft felt compelled to support it, and he undertook a cross-country trip in late summer of 1909 to get support from the voters.

The Taft Administration

Administration Dates: March 4, 1909–March 4, 1913
Vice President: James S. Sherman (1909–12)
None (1912–13)

Cabinet:

Secretary of State	Philander C. Knox (1909–13)
Secretary of the Treasury	Frank MacVeagh (1909–13)
Secretary of War	Jacob M. Dickinson (1909–11)
	Henry L. Stimson (1911–13)
Attorney General	George W. Wickersham (1909–13)
Secretary of the Navy	George V. Meyer (1909–13)
Postmaster General	Frank H. Hitchcock (1909–13)
Secretary of the Interior	Richard A. Ballinger (1909–11)
	Walter L. Fisher (1911–13)
Secretary of Agriculture	James Wilson (1909–13)
Secretary of Commerce and Labor	Charles Nagel (1909–13)

Right: As the cartoonists saw it, Taft couldn't have been elected except on the Rough Rider's coattails.

The enthusiasm that Taft showed in endorsing the bill came back to haunt him when the Payne-Aldrich Act—as well as Taft himself—was ridiculed in the press. Always overweight, he was usually depicted in cartoons as excessively portly. Taft was not shrewd when it came to evaluating public opinion—a highly important skill for an elected politician. Teddy Roosevelt had used that skill to maintain his influence. Taft, on the other hand, was quickly overwhelmed and lost his effectiveness as a leader.

A Less-Heralded Trustbuster

An often overlooked feature of the Payne-Aldrich Act was its introduction of the first-ever corporate income tax, which was levied on all companies with revenue above $5,000 and became a significant source of new revenue for the government. Along with Taft's efforts to continue former President Roosevelt's trustbusting practices, he proved to be more of a business reformer than he was given credit for during his presidency.

In the late nineteenth century, many large companies had joined forces to overwhelm their competitors, and consumer activists blamed these industrial combinations—called trusts—for high prices of sugar, beef, and tobacco. Congress had enacted the Sherman Anti-Trust Law in 1890 specifically to abolish such entities, but the law was ineffective and was successfully challenged in the Supreme Court in 1895. Along with a growing popular press campaign against trusts, President Roosevelt had won great support by ordering the Justice Department to initiate a series of antitrust lawsuits against many dominant companies.

President Taft went after the largest trust of them all—the Standard Oil Company owned by John D. Rockefeller. Taft supported the efforts of Attorney General George W. Wickersham to break up the oil-refining conglomerate, which dominated the industry through a series of corporate mergers that undermined competitors. In 1911, Wickersham took his case to the Supreme Court, and in a historic decision, the court supported the government and ordered Standard Oil to disband. Rockefeller retired that same year, and began establishing philanthropic organizations to dispense with $500 million of his personal fortune.

Taft and Wickersham lost the support of big business over the Standard Oil case, but they moved on to another big target—the U.S. Steel Corporation. The decision to prosecute the giant steel manufacturer and its prominent president, John Pierpont (J. P.) Morgan, dated back to a Wall Street crisis of 1907.

Above: John D. Rockefeller had a tight grip on an entire industry through his Standard Oil Company. Taft led the fight to break it.

Below: The president's next target was the powerful J. P. Morgan and his United States Steel Corporation.

Morgan, the most powerful banker in the country, had created U.S. Steel in 1901 after acquiring and merging several companies to create the first billion-dollar corporation in history. During the economic crisis in 1907, Morgan was approached by the government to help head off a financial collapse, and the financier and his U.S. Steel company were allowed to buy several failing brokerage firms that owned stock in the Tennessee Coal and Iron Company, which allowed the company and the brokerage firms to avoid bankruptcy.

In October 1911, Wickersham announced that his office intended to bring charges against U.S. Steel under the Sherman Anti-Trust Act for its acquisition of Tennessee Coal and Iron under false pretenses. The threat of financial crisis, it was argued, had been a trick Morgan used to acquire another large energy company. The government's legal brief mentioned President Roosevelt—although it didn't hint of any executive misconduct—implying that the president had been hoodwinked by Morgan. The government's case failed, but incensed by what he felt was a betrayal by Taft, Roosevelt began campaigning for the 1912 presidential election, and the long friendship between the two men was over.

Dollar Diplomacy

In spite of his good intentions, Taft's foreign policy efforts didn't help his standing. When he took office, he appointed former corporation lawyer Philander C. Knox as secretary of state. Knox reorganized the Department of State geopolitically—Europe, the Far East, and Latin America each had its own division, a setup that was still in place nearly a century later. Knox also established a Division of Information to improve communication between department sections, and he instituted a merit-based system for the promotion of Foreign Service officers.

As a policy aim, Taft worked to stabilize troubled areas of Asia and Central America in order to protect and expand U.S. commercial interests, continuing policies that had been begun by his predecessors, William McKinley and Theodore Roosevelt. Because he was less politically clever, however, Taft saw his strategy referred to as "Dollar Diplomacy," which quickly became a negative term. The administration strategy combined financial aid or investment and increased trade to help stabilize the economy of a given country.

Nicaragua became the proving ground for this unsuccessful policy. Its leader, José Santos Zelaya, was seen as an obstruction by the American business community with interests in Nicaragua. When an insurgency movement to unseat him arose in late 1909, the United States provided the rebels with financial aid. But after two Americans fighting alongside the rebels were captured and executed by the Zelaya army, the United States severed diplomatic ties and sent in troops. In the summer of 1910 American forces captured Nicaragua's capital, Managua, and emerged victorious.

The Taft administration strongly urged the new Nicaraguan government to accept a large loan from a coalition of Wall Street banks, while U.S. military forces took control of Nicaragua's customs ports to back it. The situation still proved unstable: Two years later, another rebellion emerged and another force of marines was sent in to end it.

When similar unrest occurred in the Dominican Republic and then in Mexico, Taft acted more cautiously. His administration adopted a neutral position on Mexico's problems, recognizing strong anti-American sentiment there. Still, Taft sent troops as a precaution to protect U.S. business interests there. Internal strife increased considerably, and Mexico dissolved into relative anarchy. Oil firms with business in Mexico, politicians from the Southwest, and even former president Roosevelt called for intervention, but Taft waited. His term came to an end as the situation worsened.

A Republican Disaster

Taft faced several challengers more than a year before the 1912 election. His greatest political enemy in Congress was the country's most prominent Progressive politician, Robert La Follette of Wisconsin, who formed the National Progressive Republican League in early 1911 and began campaigning for the presidency. Meanwhile, the campaign of former president Roosevelt quickly gathered considerable momentum. Taft, however, still had impressive support among powerful figures within the Republican Party, and they helped assure that he would win the presidential nomination at the Republican national convention of 1912.

Overwhelmed by more powerful party leaders, Roosevelt claimed that the nomination had been stolen from him, and he took a number of reform-minded Republicans with him to form the Progressive "Bull Moose" Party.

The presidential campaign of 1912 was hotly contested among the split Republican factions and Democrat Woodrow Wilson, who had won national acclaim in his role as governor of New Jersey. Roosevelt's Bull Moose candidacy split the Republican Party's support and made Wilson an easy winner, with Roosevelt coming in second, and Taft third. Taft's Electoral College defeat was the worst in the twentieth century for an incumbent president: He received only 8 electoral votes, compared with 88 for Roosevelt and 435 for Wilson.

Back to the Bench

Taft was happy to leave Washington. He was appointed the Kent Professor of Constitutional Law at Yale University. During World War I, he served as joint chair of the National War Labor Board, and in 1921, another Ohio-born Republican president, Warren G. Harding, appointed him as chief justice of the U.S. Supreme Court, and Taft became the first former president to serve on the court in its history. He had hardly put on the silk robe when he informed the press that "In my present life I don't remember that I ever was president."

Taft instituted several reforms that reduced the Court's backlog of untried cases, and he lobbied heavily for the construction of a new Supreme Court building. His promotion of the new headquarters was commemorated by his successor when the cornerstone for the Court was laid in 1932, two years after Taft retired from the Court when his health declined. He died a few weeks later, on March 8, 1930.

Taft's son, Robert Alphonso Taft, became an influential Republican in Congress in the 1940s. He opposed the New Deal legislation of President Franklin D. Roosevelt, as well as the creation of the North Atlantic Treaty Organization (NATO). The younger Taft also coauthored the Taft-Hartley Labor Act of 1947, which restricted many labor union practices.

Legacy

William Howard Taft's defeat in 1912 ended a virtual Republican lock on the White House. Between 1860 and 1912, eleven of thirteen elected presidents were Republican. After Woodrow Wilson's two terms from 1913 to 1921, three more Republicans were elected in succession as president.

Though not often linked with progressive politicians like Roosevelt, Wilson, or La Follette, Taft is credited with guiding several important pieces of progressive legislation through Congress. The Mann-Elkins Act of 1910 regulated railroad commerce and strengthened the powers of the Interstate Commerce Commission; it also included a rider that established government regulation of the telegraph and telephone companies. Taft's Commission on Economy and Efficiency—forerunner of the modern-day Office of Management and Budget—was the result of his impatience with a wasteful process that complicated the process for government departments to obtain their annual funding through Congress.

In most assessments of presidents' effectiveness, Taft often pales in comparison with Roosevelt and Wilson. Still, Taft maintained the momentum of Roosevelt's trust-busting. Wilson's foreign policy efforts in Central America and Asia were more modestly successful, but he failed when he took a more aggressive policy than Taft had toward Mexico. Wilson's foreign policy plans were completely disrupted by the outbreak of World War I in Europe in 1914.

Helen Taft

Born June 2, 1861, Cincinnati, Ohio
Died May 22, 1943, Washington, D.C.

"My dearest and best critic [my wife]."

—*William Howard Taft*

When she was sixteen years old, Helen Herron visited the White House with her parents as private guests of President Rutherford B. Hayes. She said later that the visit made such an impact on her that she vowed to return some day for a longer stay.

Years later, Helen became the wife of William Howard Taft, and she is credited by presidential scholars for having the ambition and providing the support that most assuredly landed her husband in the White House. Without her, Taft was unlikely to have ever run for the office.

Few Future Prospects

Born on June 2, 1861, Helen Herron was one of eleven children of John and Harriet Herron of Cincinnati, Ohio. Her father, a former law partner of President Hayes, served in Congress and was influential in the Ohio Republican Party from which presidents Hayes and James A. Garfield emerged.

"Nellie," as Helen was called throughout her life, attended a private Cincinnati school for young women; she studied music and languages and became known as an independent thinker with an adventurous streak. She wanted more than what was expected of her, but there were few opportunities available for females other than being a wife and mother.

She earned a living for two years as a teacher before realizing that she wasn't suited for the job, and in 1883,

she and two friends founded a "salon" to serve as a Cincinnati meeting place for intellectual, political, and cultural discussions. One of those who regularly attended the salon was William Howard Taft, a young lawyer and a graduate of Yale University. "Will" Taft was impressed with Nellie's intelligence and her forthright opinions, and a courtship followed in which Nellie twice rejected his marriage proposals. She eventually agreed, however, and the two were married in June of 1886.

Nellie became a Cincinnati housewife and the mother of three Taft children. She also began working for various causes as her husband became more and more influential in state politics. Fond of classical music, Nellie

Right: Will and Helen with their two sons, Robert and Charles.

used her husband's political connections to help found the city's Orchestra Association, the forerunner of the Cincinnati Symphony Orchestra.

Will and Nellie in Manila

In 1890, Taft was named to the post of solicitor general of the United States, and the family moved to Washington. Ten years later, Taft was invited to lead a delegation to the Philippine Islands. The United States had taken possession of the islands following victory in the Spanish-American War. Taft was uncertain whether he ought to go to the faraway and politically unstable islands, but Nellie convinced him that it was a good opportunity.

The Tafts stayed in the Philippines for four years, and Nellie wrote extensively about that period in her autobiography. She clearly enjoyed her husband's prominent role, and she eagerly participated in discussions with him about his duties as the territory's governor. She also battled prejudice among white officials, who sometimes treated Filipinos with contempt, and the Tafts urged tolerance and equality in official social occasions.

During her time in the Philippines, Nellie tried to improve the quality of life of the country's poor. She met with Filipino women to persuade them to accept food and medical supplies sent from the United States, and she founded the Drop of Milk program, which instructed residents about methods of milk sterilization. Showing her adventurous spirit, Nellie became the first white female to tour the rugged and dangerous Luzon Mountain region.

The family returned to Washington in 1904 when Taft was named secretary of war by President Theodore Roosevelt. Nellie often traveled with her husband on his official duties, including a three-month world tour. Back in Washington, however, she disliked the social formalities of political life. She was not fond of the constant socializing that was expected of cabinet wives, and her husband was just as uncomfortable as a politician. He was more ideally suited for law. President Roosevelt twice offered him a seat on the Supreme Court, but Nellie convinced him to turn down the offers. On the second occasion, she met with Roosevelt to explain why her husband shouldn't accept the position. The Tafts, or Nellie at least, had their eyes on a higher political office.

A Bold Beginning and a Setback

Taft won the nomination as the Republican presidential candidate in 1908, and during his campaign tours, he wrote to his wife every day, as was their custom whenever they were separated. At his inaugural, Nellie became the first first lady to accompany her husband on the parade route back to the White House after the swearing-in ceremony. Traditionally, the outgoing president would ride with the newly inaugurated chief executive, but Roosevelt had already left the capital. Nellie endured some criticism for her bold action, but she said later that it had been the proudest moment of her life.

However, a setback struck the Tafts just two months after his inauguration. The first lady, at the age of forty-seven, suddenly became partially paralyzed and unable to speak. Severely restricting her public appearances, she was usually seen publicly only from a distance for several months. The White House never acknowledged the condition as a stroke, preferring to call it a "nervous disorder." After a year, the determined first lady had regained much of her strength.

Returning to an active role as first lady, Nellie Taft quickly set about decorating the White House in a manner similar to the Tafts' arrangements at Malacanang Palace in the Philippines. In the meantime, she continued to consult with the president, who asked her opinions on issues and invited her to his informal meetings with politicians. A 1909 *Ladies Home Journal* article mentioned the advisory role she played for her husband. She supported the women's suffrage movement, but she believed that women should not become office-seekers themselves.

The Tafts participated in a glittering round of social events. On their twenty-fifth wedding anniversary, the first couple invited several thousand guests to a White House garden party that featured the novelty of a large, electrically lit sign that read "1886–1911." The occasion received negative press for what was perceived as an unnecessary extravagance, as well as for the many gifts that were given to the Tafts—some of which came from people courting the political favor of the Taft administration.

Springtime Legacy

Nellie Taft enjoyed several successes as first lady. She personally interceded on behalf of an immigrant woman whose young son had been denied entry into the United States because of a speech disability. Mrs. Taft's efforts resulted in a reversal of the decision. On another occasion, she attended House committee hearings about dangerous workplace conditions facing young women in the nation's textile factories. Her presence, and her comments on the committee's findings, was noted in the press. It was rare at that time for a first lady to be quoted on political matters in newspapers and magazines.

Nellie Taft was also responsible for several civic improvement projects in the nation's capital. She pushed for the creation of West Potomac Park, preserving a natural setting along the Potomac River as it runs through Washington, and she successfully campaigned for the construction of a bandstand by the river. Free weekly concerts by the marine band were instituted during her husband's administration.

Mrs. Taft's most enduring effort came about as a result of her past travels in Japan, when her husband had been secretary of war. As first lady, she gathered support to bring Tokyo's famous cherry blossom trees to the capital. The mayor of Tokyo presented 3,000 of the trees as a gift to the first lady, which she then donated to the government. To this day, thousands of tourists plan trips to be in Washington when the trees' pale pink petals blossom in early April.

More Joyous Times

After Taft lost the 1912 presidential election, he happily retired from politics to teach law at Yale. He received his long-desired Supreme Court appointment in 1921, and he served as chief justice until 1930, the year he died.

Nellie Taft stayed in Washington for the rest of her life. She died on May 22, 1943, and was buried in Arlington National Cemetery, the first of two first ladies given that honor. (Jacqueline Kennedy is the other.) The Tafts' daughter, Helen Taft Manning, was able to fulfill some of the ambitions that had not been allowed to her mother: She earned a doctorate degree from Yale University and became a history professor. The two Taft sons entered politics. Charles Phelps Taft was a mayor of Cincinnati, and his brother, Robert Alphonso Taft, served in the U.S. Senate from 1939 to 1953, where he became the leader of the Republican Party's conservative wing and was known as "Mr. Republican."

Taft's Final Annual Address to Congress

Delivered on December 3, 1912

During the early years of the twentieth century, many developing countries in Central and Latin America had unstable economies and governments. The United States, meanwhile, had enjoyed sustained prosperity since the mid-1890s. It had benefited from increased trade with other nations, which in turn created new business opportunities and markets.

The administration of William Howard Taft followed a policy of using trade and economic opportunity as a means for offering stability to troubled countries. Instead of helping them maintain peace with military force, the United States hoped to improve the economies and the social welfare of developing countries through business investment and trade. A "developing country" refers to a nation that is only beginning to develop modern industries; a developed country, on the other hand, has already reached an advanced stage of industrial progress.

Taft described his policy as "substituting dollars for bullets." He meant that the United States was creating business opportunities and offering financial assistance to troubled nations instead of turning to military force to maintain law and order. By 1912, however, Taft's policies had only seen modest success. In reporting on Taft's policies, newspapers increasingly referred to the president's foreign policy as "dollar diplomacy," suggesting that the United States was attempting to buy friends.

Taft used the occasion of his final annual address to Congress to restate his foreign policy and to call attention to its successes. His address was delivered in December 1912, about one month after he had finished a distant third in the presidential election. In the speech, Taft emphasized his belief that the United States could be a world leader by investing in smaller nations. He concluded by discussing a series of examples of nations that had achieved peace and improved economic conditions during his presidency.

Excerpt from Taft's Final Annual Address to Congress

The diplomacy of the present administration has sought to respond to modern ideas of commercial intercourse. This policy has been characterized as substituting dollars for bullets. It is one that appeals alike to idealistic humanitarian sentiments, to the dictates of sound policy and strategy, and to legitimate commercial aims. It is an effort frankly directed to the increase of American trade upon the axiomatic principle that the government of the United States shall extend all proper support to every legitimate and beneficial American enterprise abroad.

How great have been the results of this diplomacy, coupled with the maximum and minimum provision of the Tariff Law, will be seen by some consideration of the wonderful increase in the export trade of the United States. Because modern diplomacy is commercial, there has been a disposition in some quarters to attribute to it none but materialistic aims. How strikingly erroneous is such an impression may be seen from a study of the results by which the diplomacy of the United States can be judged.

In the field of work toward the ideals of peace, this government negotiated, but to my regret was unable to consummate, two arbitration treaties which set the highest mark of the aspiration of nations toward the substitution of arbitration and reason for war in the settlement of international disputes. Through the efforts of American diplomacy, several wars have been prevented or ended. I refer to the successful tripartite mediation of the Argentine Republic, Brazil, and the United States between Peru and Ecuador; the bringing of the boundary dispute between Panama and Costa Rica to peaceful arbitration; the staying of warlike preparations when Haiti and the Dominican Republic were on the verge of hostilities; the stopping of a war in Nicaragua; the halting of internecine strife in Honduras.

The government of the United States was thanked for its influence toward the restoration of amicable relations between the Argentine Republic and Bolivia. The diplomacy of the United States is active in seeking to assuage the remaining ill feeling between this country and the Republic of Colombia. In the recent civil war in China, the United States successfully joined with the other interested powers in urging an early cessation of hostilities. An agreement has been reached between the governments of Chile and Peru.

[…]

In China the policy of encouraging financial investment to enable that country to help itself has had the result of giving new life and practical application to the open door policy. The consistent purpose of the present administration has been to encourage the use of American capital in the development of China by the promotion of those essential reforms to which China is pledged by treaties with the United States and other powers. The hypothecation to foreign bankers in connection with certain industrial enterprises, such as the Hukuang railways, of the national revenues upon which these reforms depended, led the Department of State, early in the administration, to demand for American citizens participation in such enterprises, in order that the United States might have equal rights and an equal voice in all questions pertaining to the disposition of the public revenues concerned.

The same policy of promoting international accord among the powers having similar treaty rights as ourselves in the matters of reform, which could not be put into practical effect without the common consent of all, was likewise adopted in the case of the loan desired by China for the reform of its currency. The principle of international cooperation in matters of common interest upon which our policy had already been based in all of the above instances has admittedly been a great factor in that concert of the powers which has been so happily conspicuous during the perilous period of transition through which the great Chinese nation has been passing.

In Central America the aim has been to help such countries as Nicaragua and Honduras to help themselves. They are the immediate beneficiaries. The national benefit to the United States is twofold. First, it is obvious that the Monroe Doctrine is more vital in the neighborhood of the Panama Canal and the zone of the Caribbean than anywhere else. There, too, the maintenance of that doctrine falls most heavily upon the United States. It is therefore essential that the countries within that sphere shall be removed from the jeopardy involved by heavy foreign debt and chaotic national finances and from the ever present danger of international complications due to disorder at home. Hence, the United States has been glad to encourage and support American bankers who were willing to lend a helping hand to the financial rehabilitation of such countries because this financial rehabilitation and the protection of their customhouses from being the prey of would-be dictators would remove at one stroke the menace of foreign creditors and the menace of revolutionary disorder.

The second advantage to the United States is one affecting chiefly all the Southern and Gulf ports and the business and industry of the South. The republics of Central America and the Caribbean possess great natural wealth. They need only a measure of stability and the means of financial regeneration to enter upon an era of peace and prosperity, bringing profit and happiness to themselves and at the same time creating conditions sure to lead to a flourishing interchange of trade with this country.

I wish to call your especial attention to the recent occurrences in Nicaragua, for I believe the terrible events recorded there during the revolution of the past summer—the useless loss of life, the devastation of property, the bombardment of defenseless cities, the killing and wounding of women and children, the torturing of noncombatants to exact contributions, and the suffering of thousands of human beings—might have been averted had the Department of State, through approval of the loan convention by the Senate, been permitted to carry out its now well-developed policy of encouraging the extending of financial aid to weak Central American states, with the primary objects of avoiding just such revolutions by assisting those republics to rehabilitate their finances, to establish their currency on a stable basis, to remove the customhouses from the danger of revolutions by arranging for their secure administration, and to establish reliable banks.

During this last revolution in Nicaragua, the government of that republic having admitted its inability to protect American life and property against acts of sheer lawlessness on the part of the malcontents, and having requested this government to assume that office, it became necessary to land over 2,000 Marines and Bluejackets in Nicaragua. Owing to their presence the constituted government of Nicaragua was free to devote its attention wholly to its internal troubles, and was thus enabled to stamp out the rebellion in a short space of time. When the Red Cross supplies sent to Granada had been exhausted, 8,000 persons having been given food in one day upon the arrival of the American forces, our men supplied other unfortunate, needy Nicaraguans from their own haversacks.

I wish to congratulate the officers and men of the United States Navy and Marine Corps who took part in reestablishing order in Nicaragua upon their splendid conduct, and to record with sorrow the death of seven American Marines and Bluejackets. Since the reestablishment of peace and order, elections have been held amid conditions of quiet and tranquillity. Nearly all the American Marines have now been withdrawn. The country should soon be on the road to recovery. The only apparent danger now threatening Nicaragua arises from the shortage of funds. Although American bankers have already rendered assistance, they may naturally be loath to advance a loan adequate to set the country upon its feet without the support of some such convention as that of June 1911, upon which the Senate has not yet acted.

[…]

It is not possible to make to the Congress a communication upon the present foreign relations of the United States so detailed as to convey an adequate impression of the enormous increase in the importance and activities of those relations. If this government is really to preserve to the American people that free opportunity in foreign markets which will soon be indispensable to our prosperity, even greater efforts must be made. Otherwise the American merchant, manufacturer, and exporter will find many a field in which American trade should logically predominate preempted through the more energetic efforts of other governments and other commercial nations.

There are many ways in which, through hearty cooperation, the legislative and executive branches of this government can do much. The absolute essential is the spirit of united effort and singleness of purpose. I will allude only to a very few specific examples of action which ought then to result.

America cannot take its proper place in the most important fields for its commercial activity and enterprise unless we have a Merchant Marine. American commerce and enterprise cannot be effectively fostered in those fields unless we have good American banks in the countries referred to. We need American newspapers in those countries and proper means for public information about them.

We need to assume the permanency of a trained foreign service. We need legislation enabling the members of the foreign service to be systematically brought in direct contact with the industrial, manufacturing, and exporting interests of this country in order that American businessmen may enter the foreign field with a clear perception of the exact conditions to be dealt with and the officers themselves may prosecute their work with a clear idea of what American industrial and manufacturing interests require.

Congress should fully realize the conditions which obtain in the world as we find ourselves at the threshold of our middle age as a nation. We have emerged full grown as a peer in the great concourse of nations. We have passed through various formative periods. We have been self-centered in the struggle to develop our domestic resources and deal with our domestic questions. The nation is now too mature to continue in its foreign relations those temporary expedients natural to a people to whom domestic affairs are the sole concern.

In the past, our diplomacy has often consisted, in normal times, in a mere assertion of the right to international existence. We are now in a larger relation with broader rights of our own and obligations to others than ourselves. A number of great guiding principles were laid down early in the history of this government. The recent task of our diplomacy has been to adjust those principles to the conditions of today, to develop their corollaries to find practical applications of the old principles expanded to meet new situations. Thus are being evolved bases upon which can rest the superstructure of policies which must grow with the destined progress of this nation.

The successful conduct of our foreign relations demands a broad and a modern view. We cannot meet new questions nor build for the future if we confine ourselves to outworn dogmas of the past and to the perspective appropriate at our emergence from colonial times and conditions. The opening of the Panama Canal will mark a new era in our international life and create new and worldwide conditions which, with their vast correlations and consequences, will obtain for hundreds of years to come. We must not wait for events to overtake us unawares. With continuity of purpose we must deal with the problems of our external relations by a diplomacy modern, resourceful, magnanimous, and fittingly expressive of the high ideals of a great nation.

What Happened Next

The instability of Central American and Asian nations that Taft tried to address during his presidency was a worldwide phenomenon. While the United States concerned itself with nations in the Western Hemisphere, European nations were at odds over boundaries and over their colonies in Africa. The instability in the Western Hemisphere led to increasing tension between the United States and its nearest neighbors, and the conflicts in Europe erupted into World War I, which began the year after Taft left office.

Like the mixed success of Taft's foreign policy in Latin America, the United States continued to have successes and failures in dealings with Latin American countries. At times, some of the nations believed the U.S. businesses were trying to dominate their economy. On the other hand, political instability was continuing in many of the countries. U.S. relations with Latin American countries gradually improved, in general, as the century progressed. Each president faced some crisis in a Latin American country, but Taft faced several in the increasingly unstable world that preceded the outbreak of World War I.

Woodrow Wilson

"It is not men that interest or disturb me primarily; it is ideas. Ideas live; men die."

—*Woodrow Wilson*

Twenty-eighth president of the United States, 1913–1921

Full name: Thomas Woodrow Wilson
Born: December 28, 1856, Staunton, Virginia
Died: February 3, 1924, Washington, D.C.
Burial site: National Cathedral, Washington, D.C.
Parents: Joseph and Jessie Woodrow Wilson
Spouse: Ellen Louise Axson (1860–1914; m. 1885); Edith
 Bolling Galt (1872–1961; m. 1915)
Children: Margaret Woodrow (1886–1944); Jessie Woodrow
 (1887–1933); Eleanor Randolph (1889–1967)
Religion: Presbyterian
Education: Princeton University (B.A., 1879; M.A., 1882);
 University of Virginia Law School (LL.B., 1881); Johns
 Hopkins University (Ph.D., 1886)
Occupations: Lawyer; Princeton University president; professor
Government positions: New Jersey governor
Political party: Democratic
Dates as president: March 4, 1913–March 4, 1917 (first term);
 March 4, 1917–March 4, 1921 (second term)
Age upon taking office: 56

Woodrow Wilson was widely admired as a writer, scholar, and educator more than two decades before he became president. His first book, *Congressional Government* (1885), criticized the influence of Congress and argued that the president—as the highest elected official of the land—had the authority to set the political agenda of the nation.

Wilson immediately began translating his theory into practice when he was elected president in 1912. He called a special joint session of Congress to spell out his agenda, which he called the New Freedom. He started by concentrating on reducing tariff rates, and when legislation on tariff reform began to slow down in Congress, he called what can be considered the first modern presidential press conference, and suggested to reporters that big business interests were unduly influencing congressmen against tariff reduction. The idea was widely reported in newspapers, which helped rally support for his program among the voters. A flood of mail from various congressmen's constituents and numerous pro-Wilson editorials led to swift passage of the Underwood Tariff Act and a major victory for the new administration.

Wilson's programs were quickly enacted, thanks to a Democratic majority in Congress that had been elected along with him. But this rousing early success was hampered by foreign conflicts, beginning with a series of failures in relations with Mexico and followed

Timeline

1856: Born in Virginia; family moves to Georgia the following year

1882: Opens law office in Atlanta, Georgia

1883: Enrolls at Johns Hopkins University to prepare for a career as an academic

1885: Publishes first book, *Congressional Government*; begins teaching at Bryn Mawr College

1888–89: Teaches at Wesleyan College; publishes second book, *The State*

1890: Takes academic position at Princeton University

1893: Publishes book about the Civil War, *Division and Reunion*

1902–10: Serves as president of Princeton

1911–13: Serves as governor of New Jersey

1912: Defeats incumbent president William Howard Taft and former president Theodore Roosevelt in three-party presidential race

1913–21: Serves as twenty-eighth U.S. president

1914: Archduke Franz Ferdinand of Austria-Hungary is assassinated, beginning a series of events that results in World War I; first lady Ellen Wilson dies

1915: United States remains neutral in the war despite the loss of more than one hundred Americans in the German torpedoing of British ocean liner Lusitania; Wilson marries Edith Bolling Galt

1916: Troops are sent to Mexico; Wilson wins close election to second term

1917: United States settles with Mexico; diplomatic relations with Germany are broken; United States enters World War I

1918: Wilson gives famous "Fourteen Points" speech, which includes reasons for American involvement in war, terms for peace, and his vision of a League of Nations; armistice signed in November

1919: Wilson helps negotiate Treaty of Versailles in Paris and undertakes grueling tour to win popular support for it; suffers a stroke

1921: Retires; stays in Washington

1924: Wilson dies in Washington

by a war in Europe. Wilson's domestic agenda gradually lost momentum as a result, but his skillful leadership during World War I and, especially, his efforts to win and maintain peace, make him generally considered one of the most successful of American presidents.

Slowly Finding His Way

Thomas Woodrow Wilson was born in Staunton, Virginia, on December 28, 1856. His father, Joseph, was a Presbyterian minister who shaped his lifelong values in faith and education. There is some evidence that Wilson suffered from dyslexia during his childhood, but he eventually overcame the problem. Other health problems recurred throughout his life, and although he grew up to be tall and dignified-looking, he had continual problems with his breathing and blood circulation. He left college two different times for extended periods to recover from illnesses, and he suffered a stroke that severely weakened him during the last year of his presidency.

While Woodrow was still an infant, his father accepted a call to the ministry in Augusta, Georgia, and the family settled there. One of his earliest recollections, Woodrow said later in his life, occurred when he was four and he overheard someone say that Abraham Lincoln had been elected president and there would be war. The Civil War did indeed break out soon afterward, and young Wilson was an eyewitness to some of the hardships and damage of armed conflict.

His father served the Confederacy as a chaplain, and after the war, he moved his family to Columbia, South Carolina, where he became a professor at Columbia

Right: Wilson's birthplace in Staunton, Virginia.

Theological Seminary. The ruins of the war were still evident there more than five years after the conflict had ended.

Wilson entered Davidson College in North Carolina in 1873, but illness forced him to leave school the following year. He recovered at the home of his parents, who were living in Wilmington, North Carolina, by then, and he continued his studies on his own there. The family's large library and his father's excellent teaching skills had always provided Woodrow with home learning to enrich his public education.

In 1875, Wilson entered Princeton University, which was then called the College of New Jersey, the same school that had educated his father. He focused his studies on literature and history and he participated in several political debates. That summer, his essay, "Cabinet Government in the United States," was published in the journal *International Review*. It addressed what Wilson saw as the extreme influence of congressional committees on creating and passing legislation.

Wilson moved on to law school at the University of Virginia, but he suffered a physical breakdown the following year and returned home again. After studying law on his own, he passed the Georgia bar exam and opened a law office in Atlanta in 1882. But he didn't prosper as a lawyer and he was unhappy with his work. He went back to school—Johns Hopkins University—in 1883 to prepare for a career as a teacher of history and political science.

Left: Wilson studied at Princeton University, which was called the College of New Jersey when he went there in 1875.

The mid-1880s were good years for Wilson. He published his first book, *Congressional Government,* in 1885. It was an expanded version of his earlier essay on congressional committees, extending his exploration of American politics to argue that ultimate political authority rested with the president, although during this period, Congress had become the most forceful branch of the federal government.

That same year, Wilson married Ellen Louise Axson. He and "Miss Ellie Lou," as she was called, first met when they were children and met again in 1883 when Wilson was a young lawyer in Atlanta. A professional visit to the Axsons' home in Rome, Georgia, turned into romance between them. Wilson landed a teaching position at Bryn Mawr College two years later, all the while continuing work on his doctorate, which he completed in 1886.

Wilson moved on to Wesleyan College in 1888, where he taught and he published his second book, *The State.* After turning down several offers from other colleges, he went back to Princeton in 1890, this time as a professor and an administrator. He was already well known as an academic, a speaker, and a writer. In addition to addressing political themes, as he had in his first two books, he began writing essays on literature (collected in *Mere Literature and Other Essays,* 1896) and history (*A History of the American People,* 1902).

University President and New Jersey Governor

Wilson became president of Princeton University in 1902 and quickly demonstrated a talent for strong and effective leadership. He hired young scholars to help form discussion groups, which created a more dynamic interaction between Princeton's professors and its students. He also changed the university's curriculum to emphasize certain basic courses that all students were required to take while still allowing individuals to choose their remaining courses. Those changes, along with others he implemented, brought noticeable improvement to Princeton's academic standards in the short space of four years.

Left: Wilson served as president of Princeton University for nearly eight years.

Wilson was president of Princeton for about the same length of time—roughly eight years—that he would later serve as president of the United States. His progress in both positions was also somewhat similar. He demonstrated firm leadership and won early success and solid support, but the ends of both terms were soured when his most ambitious plans were stalled by forceful opponents and by his own unwillingness to compromise.

Wilson's most ambitious plan for Princeton was to do away with a kind of class system in effect at the school, with students from wealthier families enjoying exclusive living arrangements. He proposed a series of buildings that would form four quadrangles, or "quads," square spaces enclosed by four buildings, which have since become a common feature on college campuses. Each building in Princeton's quads featured similar housing, dining, and study facilities. Wilson wanted to centralize all university activities, but a wealthy donor had provided a large sum of money for a graduate school to be constructed away from the main campus. Wilson fought for his centralized plan for the final two years of his time at Princeton, but without success.

In 1910, Wilson was approached by New Jersey's Democratic Party through Colonel George Harvey, the editor of *North American Review* and part of a powerful Democratic coalition in the state. He offered to support Wilson as a candidate for governor, and exhausted and disappointed with his efforts at Princeton, Wilson accepted Harvey's support. He won the nomination, owing at least in part to the support of political bosses.

After winning the nomination, Wilson abruptly announced a progressive platform that, among other things, challenged the influence of the bosses and rejected other forms of political and economic influence. He was elected in a landslide, and his ideas moved quickly into law: Public utilities came under state regulation; the state's school system was reorganized and improved; and antitrust legislation was enacted.

Wilson's resounding success made him a popular candidate for the Democratic presidential nomination just two years later in 1912. At the Democratic national convention in Baltimore that summer, he made a strong showing against Speaker of the House James B. "Champ" Clark, who maintained a small lead but didn't have enough delegates to win the nomination. Clark pulled further ahead by the tenth ballot, thanks to the support of New York City political bosses, but he still didn't have

Right: Wilson moved from academic to political life when he became governor of New Jersey.

enough votes to win, and Wilson gained momentum when the three-time presidential nominee William Jennings Bryan announced his support for him just before the sixteenth ballot. It took thirty more rounds of voting before Wilson became the party's presidential candidate.

The election of 1912 was a close battle between Wilson, incumbent president William Howard Taft, and third-party candidate Theodore Roosevelt, who had been president before Taft, and who overshadowed him. Roosevelt, who removed his supporters from the Republican national convention when Taft was nominated to run for a second term, ran as the Progressive (Bull Moose) Party candidate. Roosevelt conducted a characteristically vigorous campaign, calling for a New Nationalism that would fight economic domination by big business through federal regulation. Wilson campaigned on a platform known as the New Freedom, which also promised to strengthen antitrust laws, reorganize banking and credit systems, and reduce tariffs. Although the popular vote was close—he led with only 42 percent—Wilson was easily elected by winning 435 of the possible 531 electoral votes.

Above: Wilson's success as New Jersey's governor made him a contender for the Democratic presidential nomination in 1912.

Election Results

1912

Presidential / Vice Presidential Candidates	Popular Votes	Electoral Votes
Woodrow Wilson / Thomas R. Marshall (Democratic)	6,293,454	435
Theodore Roosevelt / Hiram W. Johnson (Progressive)	4,119,538	88
William Howard Taft / James S. Sherman (Republican)	3,484,980	8

Former president Roosevelt lost the Republican nomination to incumbent president Taft, so he ran as a third-party candidate. Wilson gained the Democratic nomination after defeating Speaker of the House James B. "Champ" Clark on the forty-sixth ballot.

1916

Presidential / Vice Presidential Candidates	Popular Votes	Electoral Votes
Woodrow Wilson / Thomas R. Marshall (Democratic)	9,129,606	277
Charles Evans Hughes / Charles W. Fairbanks (Republican)	8,538,221	254

Former president Roosevelt was again nominated as the Progressive Party candidate, but he declined. Hughes was then nominated, but the party dissolved before the election. Republican vice-presidential nominee Fairbanks was a second-time candidate; he had been vice president under Roosevelt.

Triumphant Beginning

Wilson's first year in office was successful from the very beginning. He was determined to assert his leadership according to his view of the presidency, as he had spelled out in *Congressional Government* and other writings. He began his term by immediately calling a special session of Congress and making his first speech before them. Though he had a broad domestic agenda for progressive reform, he focused on winning one battle at a time.

The first area of success for the New Freedom was tariff reform: Wilson wanted to reduce government-imposed taxes on imported goods. The special session and Wilson's speech were widely reported in newspapers and enthusiastically applauded by the voters. When legislation on tariff reform began to stall in Congress, Wilson called a spontaneous news conference—the first time a president used the press in that way—to make an appeal to the people through the media. He charged that special interests were pressuring congressmen to vote against lowering tariffs. The special interests—in this case, big business—sent lobbyists to visit congressmen. The news conference produced its intended effect, sparking a huge amount of mail to congressmen from voters in their districts. This influenced Congress to vote into law the Underwood Tariff Act, which drastically cut tariffs back to levels of seventy years earlier.

The Wilson Administration

Administration Dates:	March 4, 1913–March 4, 1917
	March 4, 1917–March 4, 1921
Vice President:	Thomas Riley Marshall (1913–21)
Cabinet:	
Secretary of State	William Jennings Bryan (1913–15)
	Robert Lansing (1915–20)
	Bainbridge Colby (1920–21)
Secretary of the Treasury	William G. McAdoo (1913–18)
	Carter Glass (1918–20)
	David F. Houston (1920–21)
Secretary of War	Lindley M. Garrison (1913–16)
	Newton D. Baker (1916–21)
Attorney General	James C. McReynolds (1913–14)
	Thomas W. Gregory (1914–19)
	Alexander M. Palmer (1919–21)
Secretary of the Navy	Josephus Daniels (1913–21)
Postmaster General	Albert S. Burleson (1913–21)
Secretary of the Interior	Franklin K. Lane (1913–20)
	John B. Payne (1920–21)
Secretary of Agriculture	David F. Houston (1913–20)
	Edwin Thomas Meredith (1920–21)
Secretary of Labor	William B. Wilson (1913–21)
Secretary of Commerce	William C. Redfield (1913–19)
	Joshua W. Alexander (1919–21)

During his first year in office, Wilson also introduced or supported several other measures that would be enacted during his first term. Among them was the creation of the Federal Reserve System, which improved and regulated banking by establishing twelve banking centers spread throughout the country. Wilson also introduced the graduated income tax, which bases levies on income level. His vigorous support for antitrust legislation led to the creation of the Federal Trade Commission, with the power to investigate and prosecute "unfair" trade practices. Other initiatives he pushed through Congress included a forty-hour–maximum week for railroad workers, a law making child labor illegal, a bill that provided funding for vocational and agricultural training outside of colleges, and the establishment of the federal highway system.

Left: Wilson's inauguration parade, March 4, 1913.

Rarely has a president been able to accomplish so much so quickly. Wilson was able to count on support from a Democratic majority in Congress that had been elected along with him in 1912. He also effectively used the press to publicize and explain his positions and goals. He had a persuasive speaking style, which combined a firm voice, use of colorful language, and progressive ideas.

Even as he was enjoying a series of successes on the domestic front, Wilson's attention was taken away from his New Freedom platform halfway through the second year of his first term, as tensions with Mexico burst out after simmering under the surface for quite some time. At about the same time, Ellen Wilson's health began to deteriorate, and then war broke out in Europe when Germany invaded France. The conflict would eventually embroil thirty-two countries and become known in history as World War I.

Failure in Mexico

A series of revolutions in Mexico had left the country unstable and under the thumb of a military dictator, Victoriano Huerta. Wilson supported Huerta's rivals, a faction called the Constitutionalists. Tensions escalated in April 1914 when American sailors were arrested in Mexico, and in the meantime, German ships were approaching Mexico, reportedly carrying munitions. Those two circumstances prompted Wilson to order a naval blockade to stop ships from entering or leaving Mexico. When American troops subsequently occupied the city of Veracruz, a battle erupted, leaving 500 Mexicans and Americans either dead or wounded.

Tensions were eased when the nations of Colombia and Argentina offered to mediate the dispute, but conflict eventually broke out again. Wilson had supported Huerta's rival, Venustiano Carranza, who had become Mexico's new leader, but when he rejected the peacemaking efforts, Wilson turned his support to the rebel leader and peasant favorite Francisco "Pancho" Villa. However, Carranza encouraged Villa to make bandit forays across the border into the United States, and after he sacked the town of Columbus, New Mexico, on March 9, 1916, Wilson took stronger action, dispatching General John J. "Black Jack" Pershing to lead an expedition into Mexico to capture and punish Pancho Villa. The expedition was largely a failure. Villa lured Pershing and his forces deep

Right: Pancho Villa, Wilson's ally turned enemy.

John J. "Black Jack" Pershing

John J. Pershing was born on September 13, 1860, in Laclede, Missouri, and he grew up to become a teacher in Laclede's school for African Americans. He enrolled in the Missouri State Normal School and won a competition for entrance into the United States Military Academy at West Point. He graduated in 1886 as a senior cadet captain and developed a reputation as a leader. After his graduation, he asked to be posted to the 6th Cavalry Regiment, which was then nearing the end of operations against the Apaches in the Southwest. After the capture of their leaders, the last independent Apaches were brought into the reservations later that same year.

In late 1890, Pershing and the Sixth Cavalry were called to the Dakotas to help in operations against the Sioux. Arriving after the massacre at Wounded Knee on December 29, the 6th stayed in the Dakotas until mid-1891. From late 1891 until 1898, Pershing served mostly as a military instructor, first at the University of Nebraska and then at West Point. In 1895 and '96 he commanded the 10th Cavalry, a black cavalry unit in Montana, before he went back to West Point to teach. Pershing's harsh personality made him unpopular, and his students nicknamed him Black Jack because of his association with the Montana command.

In 1898, the United States went to war with Spain over Cuba, and Pershing, still in command of the 10th Cavalry, struggled to organize his unprepared troops, their supplies, and their departure. Still, the 10th fought bravely, taking many casualties, and Pershing and his men helped Colonel Theodore Roosevelt and his Rough Riders in the famous battle for San Juan Hill. Pershing's courage resulted in his promotion to major, and his next assignment was in the Philippine Islands, part of the Spanish empire taken over by the United States after Spain's defeat. The Filipinos had fought hard against the Spanish and weren't willing to accept American authority. Pershing was promoted to captain in 1902, and he was given command of a small outpost in an area controlled by the Moro tribe. Though Pershing battled the Moros in war, he aided those among them who were struck by disease, and his fairness led them to make him an honorary chief.

In 1905, Pershing married Frances Warren, the daughter of a Wyoming senator, and they spent their honeymoon in Tokyo, where Pershing was assigned to the American embassy. For the next two years he acted as an official observer of Japan's war against Russia, which Russia lost. In 1906, President Theodore Roosevelt promoted him to general.

He was given command of Fort William McKinley at the Philippine capital of Manila after his promotion, and for the next four years, he fought several tough military campaigns against dissatisfied Moro groups, whose traditional love of independence had inspired them to resist American rule. Assigned in 1914 to command the 8th Brigade in San Francisco, California, Pershing was soon ordered to take the unit to Texas. While he was there, a fire at his San Francisco house killed his wife and three of his four children. Promoted again in 1916, to major general, a grieving Pershing said, "All the promotions in the world would make no difference now."

In March 1916, Mexican rebel leader Francisco "Pancho" Villa, angered by U.S. support for his enemies, killed eighteen Americans during a raid on Columbus, New Mexico. Immediately, President Woodrow Wilson ordered Pershing into Mexico, and for almost a year, he chased Villa deep into the Mexican desert. Although unable to capture Villa, Pershing did succeed in breaking up Villa's guerrilla army.

America entered World War I on April 6, 1917, shortly after Pershing's return from Mexico. At fifty-seven, he was young and energetic enough to take the stress of commanding American military forces, and he met with British and French leaders to plot strategy, although he refused to put his American soldiers under their command. The American Expeditionary Force stood at about 200,000 men, insignificant compared to the Allied and German forces. He decided that he needed 1 million men in France by the middle of 1918, with more to follow.

By the summer of 1918, Pershing had persuaded the Allies to give the Americans a section of the front, and by late August, his army had crushed a German offensive in only two days, taking 16,000 prisoners. Within two more weeks, Pershing moved 600,000 of his men to their new position at the Argonne Forest for the Allied offensive. It proved to be one of several key victories for Allied forces that brought Germany to surrender later that year.

Following the end of the war, Pershing was named general of the armies. He served as army chief of staff until 1924, and then retired. He died on July 15, 1948, and is buried at Arlington National Cemetery.

into his home territory, and American forces weren't able to capture him. When mediation was finally acceptable to both nations, Pershing was recalled in January 1917.

From the beginning of his administration, Wilson and his secretary of state, William Jennings Bryan, had undertaken an aggressive approach to improving American foreign relations, meeting with representatives from dozens of different countries and signing thirty treaties of cooperation. Unfortunately, many of these treaties obligated the United States to send troops to troubled areas, including Haiti, Nicaragua, and the Dominican Republic, through 1915 and 1916.

World War I

Meanwhile, tensions had been building throughout Europe for more than a decade. Political boundaries were in dispute, nationalism was running high, nations were building up their military arsenals, and conflicts over international expansionism, especially in Africa, were increasingly unfriendly. The more powerful nations generally divided into two factions, with England and France on one side, and Germany, Turkey, and Austria-Hungary on the other. Russia leaned to the side of England and France because of tense relations with Germany, which Italy supported because the two countries shared imperialist goals in Africa.

These larger nations dominated smaller countries and ethnic groups: For example, Austria-Hungary held political power over Serbians who longed to be independent. When a Serbian nationalist assassinated the archduke of Austria-Hungary, it set off a chain of events that erupted into World War I.

Archduke Franz Ferdinand, in line to become the head of the Austro-Hungarian Empire, was assassinated on July 28, 1914, and Austria-Hungary immediately declared war on Serbia. Russia moved to defend the Serbians by declaring war on Austria-Hungary, and then, on August 1, Germany declared war on Russia. The following day, a mobilized German force also began marching westward, intending to cross through neutral Belgium to invade France. France declared war on Germany as soon as its army crossed into Belgium, and England also declared war on Germany. All of these events occurred during the same week that Ellen Wilson became gravely ill before dying—on August 6—of a kidney ailment.

The grieving president buried himself in work and he confided only in his few close friends. His grief didn't ease until early the following year when he met Edith Bolling Galt, whom he married in December 1915.

America maintained a position of neutrality as the war quickly intensified abroad. Wilson formally stated that his government's position was to remain neutral; to protect American trade and the safety of Americans abroad; to increase the preparedness of its military in case the United States should become involved in the war; and to serve as mediator to help bring the fighting to an end. Although America was officially neutral, many of its policies favored the Allied countries (Great Britain, France, and Russia) over the Axis powers (Germany, Austria-Hungary, Italy, and Turkey). Among other things, President Wilson did not protest a British blockade of German ports, even though it damaged U.S. trade in a large and vital market.

Germany established military superiority on land, but Great Britain ruled the seas. Germany relied on submarines, called U-boats, to slip through the blockade and into open seas where they could attack British vessels, and as the British blockade continued, they began attacking nonmilitary vessels that were capable of carrying supplies or weapons to its enemies.

Left: The assassination of Archduke Franz Ferdinand of Austria-Hungary was the spark the plunged the world into flames in 1914.

American popular sentiment fell squarely on the side of the Allies when a U-boat torpedoed the British ocean liner *Lusitania,* killing over 1,000 passengers, including 128 Americans. Following international pressure over the incident and others involving merchant ships, Germany agreed to attack only military vessels. Meanwhile, Wilson and his envoys continued to mediate the conflict; asking each of the nations involved to list their respective terms for peace as a means of beginning negotiations.

Wilson's domestic triumphs were overshadowed by these foreign conflicts. In addition, his New Freedom program—intended to reform business and banking and to provide more safeguards for the working class—was strongly opposed by big business and the wealthy. At the Democratic convention in 1916, there was no doubt that Wilson would be nominated as the party's candidate, but there were strong concerns about his fading popularity. When he accepted the nomination, he addressed the concerns of many Americans about the war in Europe by stressing how well his administration had put the country into a state of preparedness. The enthusiastic reception to this part of his speech produced a campaign theme that would prove to have an ironic ring: "He kept us out of war." Wilson would ask Congress to declare war on Germany early in his second term.

He was reelected by a slim margin—so thin, in fact, that if 1,500 votes in California had instead gone to his opponent, Charles Evans Hughes, Hughes would have won enough electoral votes to become president.

Above: A cartoonist saw Germany as a rapacious pirate after the sinking of the ocean liner Lusitania.

A World Safe for Democracy

Wilson's hopes for peace slipped away shortly after his second term began. Germany had renewed its aggression at sea early in 1917, and attempted to move to an ultimate triumph, feeling that the United States was already involved with its enemies. Diplomatic relations between the United States and Germany were broken off in February 1917, and the president who had "kept us out of war" went to Congress in April to ask for a declaration of war. As usual, Wilson's eloquence helped to provide a clear understanding of his goals. He spoke of the need for

Below: Wilson's campaign for reelection in 1916 employed modern sound trucks to get the message out.

The League of Nations

The League of Nations was proposed by Woodrow Wilson in Article XIV of his Fourteen Points, forming the basis of the Covenant of the League of Nations that was part of the Treaty of Versailles. However, the treaty was never ratified by the U.S. Senate. Among the senators' concerns was Article X of the treaty, which required all members to preserve the territorial independence of all other members. Violations could be met with joint action among nations against aggressors, and a strong group of politicians and citizens objected to the U.S. military participating with those of other nations, preferring that the United States maintain independence and free decision-making in employing military forces.

Without treaty ratification, the United States never became an official member of the League, which existed from 1920 to 1946. American diplomats assisted in League activities and attended its meetings, but the lack of official American participation lessened the League's effectiveness. It rarely had the resources to support its innovative concept that defined "criminal" threats of war against which the collective security of its member nations could be marshaled. The League was successful in supervising and eventually granting independence to territories that had been colonies of Germany and Turkey before World War I, restricting international drug traffic, and helping refugees from World War I. Some other effective League activities, such as monitoring and improving international health and labor conditions, were continued through the formation of the United Nations (UN).

The League of Nations voted to dissolve itself in 1946, and much of its organization became part of the United Nations. The UN had more active participation from the major powers, including the United States, which made it a more effective peacekeeping organization while continuing the social work, and it benefited from both the successes and the failures of the League to form a stronger international alliance.

"disciplined might"—military power that would "make the world safe for democracy"—while he continued to hold out hope for diplomatic solutions.

His speech resulted in a standing ovation, which was a much rarer tribute then than it is today, and the startled president responded by saying, "My message today was a message of death for your young men. How strange it is to applaud that." He also made it a point throughout the war to refer to those young men in uniform as "boys," a term we still use, because it was how he remembered the young people who had been his students for so many years.

Wilson proceeded vigorously in his role as commander in chief. The American military expanded from 225,000 men (compared with 11 million Germans in service) to over 4 million. When some railroad authorities were slow to respond to government demands for service overriding their business interests, he led the government in assuming control of all industries that were needed to further the war effort. In addition, he appointed a professional soldier—General Pershing—to command the American forces in Europe.

Wilson sincerely believed that World War I could be, as some optimists were calling it, "the war to end all wars." As the war dragged on through 1917 into 1918, he released a document to Congress that clearly spelled out his idealistic mission, presented as fourteen points. Along with a call for diplomacy to secure peace, the speech called for the establishment of a League of Nations that could exert moral leadership and help nations avoid going to war in the future. Wilson's pursuit of peace based on the Fourteen Points made him an internationally respected statesman with a stature no previous American president had ever managed to build. His mediation efforts contributed greatly to the armistice that was signed in November 1918, and the following year he was awarded the Nobel Peace Prize in recognition of his efforts.

Right: World War I was fought in networks of trenches and was the first in which such weapons as tanks and machine guns were used.

Henry Cabot Lodge

Henry Cabot Lodge, the man who led the successful fight against President Woodrow Wilson's plan for American involvement in the League of Nations, was born on May 12, 1850, in Boston, Massachusetts. His father, John Ellerton Lodge, was a prosperous merchant who added greatly to his fortune when U.S. trade with China was expanded. Lodge's mother, Anna Cabot, was granddaughter of George Cabot, a leading Federalist during the early years of the nation. Lodge graduated with a bachelor's degree from Harvard University, then married his cousin, Anna Cabot Davis, the daughter of Rear Admiral Charles H. Davis.

From 1873 to 1876, Lodge was assistant editor of the North American Review, which published his doctoral thesis, "The Anglo-Saxon Land Law." After graduating from Harvard Law School in 1874, Lodge was admitted to the Massachusetts bar the following year. Meanwhile, he completed his work for the first doctorate in political science ever awarded at Harvard, and he also wrote several books, including three biographies in the "American Statesman" series on Alexander Hamilton, Daniel Webster, and George Washington.

Lodge was elected to the Massachusetts House of Representatives in 1879, and he was reelected to a second term, but he failed in a bid for the state senate as well as an attempt to secure the Republican nomination for Congress. After managing the successful Massachusetts gubernatorial campaign of George D. Robinson, Lodge was a delegate to the Republican National Convention in 1884, and two years later, he was elected to Congress by a narrow margin. In January 1893, the Massachusetts legislature elected him to the U.S. Senate (in those days, senators were elected by state legislators). In all, Lodge served as a congressman for six years and a senator for thirty.

As a congressman, Lodge was a consistent supporter of civil-service reform and the protective tariff during the administrations of Benjamin Harrison, Grover Cleveland, and William McKinley. Like his close friend, President Theodore Roosevelt, he supported several measures for government regulation of industry, including the Pure Food and Drug Act and the Hepburn Act in 1906, where he wrote a provision that put private oil lines under the supervision of the Interstate Commerce Commission. Along with McKinley and Roosevelt, Lodge believed that American expansion was necessary for economic progress, and he supported a strong navy, territorial acquisition, and power diplomacy—and he called for the annexation of Hawaii during the controversy in the 1890s. He was a leading advocate of war with Spain in 1898, urged annexation of the Philippines after the American victory in the Spanish-American War, and supported Theodore Roosevelt's aggressive Caribbean policy.

Lodge had several disagreements with President Woodrow Wilson. He didn't believe that Wilson was aggressive enough toward Mexico during conflicts between the two nations from 1913 to 1917. He challenged Wilson's neutrality policies and his reluctance to arm the nation during World War I. Most significantly, Lodge's leadership in the fight against the ratification of the Treaty of Versailles and the Covenant of the League of Nations made him a national figure. He favored heavy reparations against Germany after the war, and he was opposed to coupling the Versailles Treaty and the League of Nations. As chairman of the Senate Foreign Relations Committee, Lodge presented reservations against the treaty and the covenant. The two documents (with the reservations added) were rejected, chiefly by the votes of Democratic senators following the advice of President Wilson, who was firmly against adding any reservations or revisions. Neither side compromised, and Wilson lost when the treaty and U.S. participation in the League of Nations were rejected by the Senate on two different occasions.

The presidential election of 1920, where the issue of the entry of the United States into the League of Nations was an outstanding issue, was won by Republican Warren G. Harding. Lodge had been chiefly responsible for Harding's nomination, and with a Republican victory in the election, Lodge's influence in the field of foreign relations became even greater, but his triumphs were overshadowed by his failing health. He underwent two surgeries and never recovered. He died on November 9, 1924, at the age of seventy-four.

Loses the Battle at Home

But while he had won international admiration, Wilson's fortunes at home were much less solid. He actively campaigned for Democrats during the 1918 congressional elections, but the voters elected Republican majorities to both the Senate and the House for the first time since his presidency began. The following month Wilson traveled to Paris to personally attend the peace talks—the first time a sitting American president had left the country for an extended period—but he picked almost all Democrats for his delegation; this further offended Republicans, who held the majority in the legislative branch.

At the talks that eventually led to the Treaty of Versailles, Wilson argued successfully for fairness on many issues, but he had to compromise on two vital points: France and England insisted on huge war reparations against Germany; and Japan, which had joined the Allies late in the war, had been allowed to keep control of a province of China that it had invaded. Wilson deeply opposed both resolutions, but he was forced into a compromise in order to keep his vision for the League of Nations alive.

He had arrived in Europe triumphant in his role as peacemaker, but he went home to a disinterested public in the United States that was tired of war and foreign entanglements. The U.S. Senate, required by the Constitution to ratify all treaties by a two-thirds majority, began debating various aspects of the Treaty of Versailles and proposed amendments to it. Wilson had misjudged the country's political and popular sentiments. He insisted to the Senate that modifications to the treaty were unacceptable, and he fought hard for the establishment of a League of Nations in the face of lukewarm interest. When he met stern opposition from Republicans on the treaty, he tried to take his case directly to the people, as he had done successfully on domestic issues at the beginning of his presidency.

Right: The "Big Three" heads of state: (L-R) British Prime Minister David Lloyd George, French Prime Minister Georges Clemenceau, and U.S. President Woodrow Wilson.

Below: After the war, Wilson went to Paris to meet with other heads of state and promote his idea for a League of Nations.

Starting in Columbus, Ohio, on September 4, 1919, Wilson went on an exhausting cross-country tour, often making several speeches a day. Everywhere he went, he was greeted with enthusiastic crowds wanting to cheer the president who had led the country through the war, but he wasn't able to gather enough support to be able to pressure Congress to pass the treaty. He pressed on to the West Coast, and then turned back east, but the strain of the effort overcame him, and he collapsed after making a speech in Pueblo, Colorado, on September 25. He went back to Washington to recover, but he suffered a severe stroke on October 2.

Meanwhile, debate on the Versailles Treaty raged on in the Senate. Wilson was too ill to lobby senators to his cause, and Republicans, led by Senator Henry Cabot Lodge of Massachusetts, were registering strong doubts, not only on the treaty, but on America's participation in the League of Nations as well. Wilson kept insisting on ratification of the entire treaty as it stood and instructed Democratic leaders to vote against any modifications.

It came up for a vote on two different occasions—in November 1919 and again in March 1920—and failed to pass both times. Wilson responded to the second failed vote by announcing that the 1920 presidential election would serve as a referendum on the treaty and his vision of the League of Nations.

Battle Fatigue

Wilson's all-or-nothing approach on the treaty and his inability to inspire the people to rally behind him for its ratification cost him and his supporters more political capital than they could afford. If the 1920 election was indeed a referendum, it showed clearly that the American people were tired of war issues and progressive postwar domestic policies. Republican Warren G. Harding won the presidential election in a landslide over Democrat James M. Cox, and the new administration quickly made a separate peace with Germany. Harding also vowed that the United States would never be a part of the League of Nations, and he established a pro-business administration in perfect timing with a postwar economic boom that ushered in the Roaring Twenties.

Wilson remained debilitated from the stroke he had suffered in 1919, but the public was never fully informed about the severity of the stroke and his incapacitation. He retired quietly to a large mansion on S Street in Washington, and lived there for the rest of his life with his wife, Edith. She had been his closest companion during his final year in the White House, making decisions about which issues he would address and which advisors he would see. Wilson died on February 3, 1924, in many ways a forgotten man.

The former first lady continued to live in the house until she died in 1961. Her will turned it over to the National Trust for Historic Preservation, and it has served ever since as the Woodrow Wilson House Museum.

Left: Wilson toured the country in 1919, to get support for the League of Nations. He suffered a stroke not long afterward.

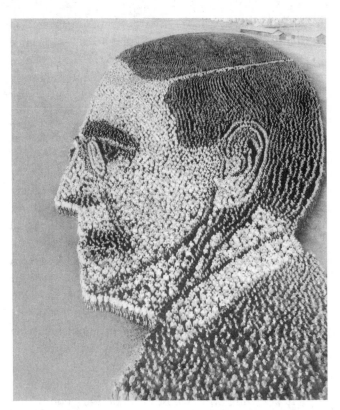

Legacy

Woodrow Wilson's lasting influence on the country is as strong as that of any president. Many of the early reforms of his New Freedom program, including the Federal Reserve System, the graduated income tax, and the Federal Trade Commission, were still intact at the end of the twentieth century. Other measures significantly reformed labor laws and changed banking practices.

His lasting importance is at least as strong internationally. The League of Nations failed, in general, but its successor, the United Nations, continued its positive work and became a more effective body through greater international cooperation, including the active participation of the United States.

Wilson's conduct as a president during wartime is still highly respected. He kept the country from entering the conflict and then ensured that the necessary resources were available to win once it did enter the war. Many of the same methods of preparedness on the home front were followed by President Franklin D. Roosevelt

during World War II. Roosevelt had served in the Wilson administration as assistant secretary of the navy.

Wilson's policies with Mexico and Latin America were not as fruitful, and his domestic program, the New Freedom, began to lose momentum in the latter part of his first term, perhaps reflected best in his slim margin of victory when he was elected to a second term.

Many of Wilson's failures, particularly the League of Nations, were noble causes. Had the Treaty of Versailles been more to his expectations, many argue, war reparations against Germany would not have been so severe. The high compensations that were demanded of Germany plunged it into a decade of economic hardship and resulted in a turn to fascism in the 1930s that led to World War II.

Wilson increased United States participation in world affairs more than any previous president, setting America on its course of becoming a world power. Many of his progressive domestic ideas that weren't fully realized during his term were revived and reformed by Roosevelt, contributing to the New Deal policies of the 1930s that helped the country survive the Great Depression.

Ellen Wilson

Born May 15, 1860, Savannah, Georgia
Died August 6, 1914, Washington, D.C.

"I am naturally the most unambitious of women and life in the White House has no attractions for me."

—Ellen Wilson

Ellen Wilson was a modest and artistic woman who preferred private, small dinners at the White House over large-scale parties and lavish balls. She had a studio room with a skylight built in the White House living quarters where she could practice her painting, although she didn't have much time to spend there, because she helped arrange White House weddings for two daughters and served as hostess for many private dinners. Her time for painting was also cut short when she was stricken by Bright's disease, a kidney ailment. She died on August 6, 1914, just a year and a half into her husband's presidency.

With her love of art and her gentle nature, Ellen was a good companion for Woodrow Wilson, who was studious and enjoyed literature, along with history, law, and political science. She would have been an especially valuable companion to him during the period surrounding her death, as a crisis in Europe occurred that quickly grew into World War I.

Ellen Louise Axson was born in Rome, Georgia, on May 15, 1860. Like Woodrow Wilson's, her father was a Presbyterian minister. Shortly after Ellen was born, the two ministers had a meeting. Joseph Wilson took along his son, Woodrow, who was four, and it was the first time that Woodrow and Ellen met. The next time was over twenty years later, in 1883, and they soon fell in love. At the time, "Miss Elly Lou," as she was called, was caring for her father, who was in despair over the death of her mother.

Ellen had graduated from Rome Female College in Georgia, showing talent as an artist and a teacher. Lack of funds stopped her from moving forward to develop those talents, and she went home to her family. Woodrow Wilson traveled there in April 1883 to take care of some Axson family legal matters. At the time, he was a lawyer with a practice in Atlanta, but he was unhappy with the profession and went back to college that fall, studying at Johns Hopkins University in Baltimore to become a teacher. He courted Miss Elly Lou during the summer of 1883, and asked her to marry him just before he left for school.

While Wilson was completing his education in Baltimore, Ellen continued to care for her father and her younger brother. Her father committed suicide in 1884, and Ellen and her brother moved to New York, where she enrolled in the Art Students League. She and Woodrow were married the following year after he had graduated from Johns Hopkins and accepted a teaching position at Bryn Mawr College in Pennsylvania. His career as an academic began to prosper when he took a position at Wesleyan College in Middletown, Connecticut, two years later. He also became a popular author during the 1880s and 1890s for works on American government, essays on literature, and a biography of George Washington. Ellen, who shared his passion for literature, helped review his writings.

Both Ellen and Woodrow were proud of their southern roots. They lived in the North, but when the time neared for her to deliver each of the couple's first two daughters, she traveled back home to Rome, so that their daughters—Margaret and Jessie—could be born Southerners. A third daughter, Eleanor, was born in Connecticut.

After Wilson had turned down several offers for teaching and administrative positions, he became a professor at Princeton University in 1890. While Ellen was raising her daughters during the 1890s, she was also able to develop her interest in painting. Already accomplished in doing crayon portraits, she practiced and became an expert landscape painter. She also took an interest in the American impressionist style when she joined an artist colony in Old Lyme, Connecticut. Her painting was so accomplished that Ellen Wilson began entering her artwork in juried competitions under pseudonyms. Her landscapes won awards in New York and Chicago art shows, and she sold several paintings to help raise funds for an art school in her native Rome, Georgia. After Wilson became president of Princeton in 1902, she redesigned the presidential grounds, and she was also active in helping to improve student living conditions, including the modernization of the college's infirmary.

Ellen was not outwardly politically active. Her influence on the president, then, was more subtle and behind-the-scenes. During Wilson's campaign to become the Democratic Party nominee for president in 1912, she convinced him to renew his acquaintance with William Jennings Bryan. The relationship between the two men had become strained after Wilson criticized Bryan's policies as a presidential candidate several years earlier. They settled their differences at Ellen's urging, and Bryan later proved essential to Wilson's successful Democratic nomination for the presidency.

Another behind-the-scenes triumph for Mrs. Wilson occurred early in Wilson's presidency when she arranged a small dinner with several congressmen who were wary of his plan to reduce tariffs. Over dinner, Wilson was able to convince the congressmen of the importance of tariff reform, and it helped lead to the first significant legislation to pass during his presidency.

Ellen Wilson's time in the White House was short—just a year and a half—but quite eventful. Her daughters Jessie and Eleanor each had White House weddings, and Ellen also presided over the first national celebration of Mother's Day, in May 1913. Shortly after her husband's election, she became active in promoting better living conditions for federal employees and for residents in the nation's capital. Astonished at the slums and alleyways of Washington, she led a delegation of congressmen on a tour of those areas, hoping to convince them that they should enact legislation to clean up the federal city.

In 1914, Ellen Wilson was slowed by Bright's disease—the most common form of nephritis, an inflammatory kidney disease. Following her death in August 1914, Congress enacted legislation in her honor for funding to improve living conditions among the economically disadvantaged of Washington.

Right: The white wedding of the Wilsons' middle daughter, Jessie Woodrow.

Edith Wilson

Born October 15, 1872, Wytheville, Virginia
Died December 28, 1961, Washington, D.C.

"Woodrow Wilson was first my beloved husband who I was trying to save, after that he was president of the United States."

—*Edith Wilson*

Edith Wilson grew up from a girl who never left her hometown until she was twelve to become a world traveler, a successful businesswoman, and an influential first lady. According to some sources, she virtually ran the country during the last year of her husband's administration, when Woodrow Wilson had become disabled by a stroke. It is more likely that during this period she simply expanded the role of confidante and advisor that she had always been with the president.

Mrs. Wilson was born Edith Bolling in Wytheville, Virginia, on October 15, 1872, the seventh of eleven children and fourth of five daughters in the family of Judge William Holcombe Bolling and his wife, Sallie. Edith's mother, born Sallie White, could trace her ancestry back seven generations to an original Virginia colonist, John Rolfe, the Englishman who married Native American princess Pocahontas.

During the Civil War, the Bolling family lost their property, including the family plantation and the slaves they owned. The large family lived in "genteel poverty," a term that describes people who do not have much money but who have social status and do not face desperate conditions. As the family gradually regained its financial standing, they lived simply, and Edith did not leave town until she was twelve years old, but at fifteen she was able to attend Martha Washington College, where she studied music. She also received a fine education at home while she was growing up and she helped raise four younger siblings.

In 1893, while she was visiting her sister in Washington, Edith met businessman Norman Galt, a senior partner in his family's jewelry business and a cousin to her sister's husband. After a courtship of several years, he and Edith were married in 1896. By that time, Galt had assumed full control of the family business, which included a jewelry store that was popular among the Washington elite. The couple traveled often, and they had a child born in 1903, but the baby died in infancy.

Norman Galt, who was quite a few years older than Edith, died in 1908, and she took control of her husband's business, promoting one of the firm's assistants, longtime employee Henry Christian Bergheimer, to manage it with her. They ran the business together successfully for many years while Edith continued to travel, making frequent trips to Europe and Asia. She also became the first woman in Washington to own and drive an electric car. She lived comfortably, and although she was well known in Washington society, she rarely dabbled in political activities and was not active in such issues as women's suffrage.

In 1915, Edith became acquainted with Cary T. Grayson, President Woodrow Wilson's personal physician, who introduced her to Wilson's cousin, Helen Woodrow Bones. Mrs. Bones had been serving in many of the social capacities of first lady since the death of the president's wife, Ellen Wilson. Edith and Helen became close friends.

One day during mid-March 1915, Edith and Helen went for a walk on the White House grounds, and on their return to the mansion they encountered the president and Grayson, who had just come back from playing a round of golf. Wilson, who had been in gloomy mourning since his wife's death, was enchanted with Edith, and he began writing notes and letters to her before actively courting her. They became engaged, but some of Wilson's advisors suggested that their relationship should be kept private, out of concern that the public might not accept a president marrying so soon after the death of his wife.

Nevertheless, the couple announced their engagement in October, and they were married in a private ceremony in December 1915. There was no public backlash over the event, and the White House staff noticed that the saddened president had perked up and the mansion became a festive place again.

As he had with Ellen, Wilson depended on his new wife for companionship. He read his speeches to her and usually followed her suggestions. They discussed policy matters, and she decoded messages from diplomat Edward House, who was trying to secure peace between Great Britain and Germany to end World War I. Edith accompanied Wilson on most major presidential trips, including the Paris peace talks after the 1918 armistice, which ended the fighting during World War I. She later accompanied him on tour across the United States when he attempted to rally the people to urge Congress to ratify the peace accord—the Treaty of Versailles—without modifications. Significantly, Edith tried to convince the president to compromise on a few points so that the treaty could pass the Senate and save his vision for a League of Nations. The president, however, resisted allowing any modifications, and the treaty was never ratified by the Senate.

Wilson's health had been fragile throughout his lifetime, and Edith saw to it that he maintained a healthy exercise routine, and she often golfed with him. In mid-September 1919, during the speaking tour when he tried to inspire public support for the Treaty of Versailles, the president collapsed in Colorado. Then, while he was recovering back in Washington, he suffered a stroke on October 2. The public was not made aware of the severity of the stroke, which left him bedridden, weak, and able to work only sparingly.

Edith took over routine duties, functioning as a sort of chief advisor. She decided which issues were most pressing for his attention, and she determined which staff members and officials the president would see. While Wilson continued to operate successfully, this "stewardship" on the part of the first lady proved to be controversial; some claim that Edith actually ran the country during the last year of the Wilson presidency. Most historians condemn this claim and confirm Edith Wilson's own description of her role, which she later spelled out in her book, *My Memoir*. She had always been the president's political confidante, more so than any previous first lady. Following his stroke and on the advice of the president's doctors, she managed his reduced schedule, which allowed the president to operate most effectively in short periods of activity to maintain his health. She did not initiate or make policy decisions and did not control the administration.

Edith and Woodrow Wilson retired to a large private home in Washington, in 1921, and she nursed him there until he died three years later. Edith remained active in Democratic politics and continued to operate her jewelry business, which she sold to her employees in 1934. She was active in foundations bearing the president's name and she helped establish the Woodrow Wilson School of Public and International Affairs at Princeton University, and at the age of eighty-eight, she took part in the inauguration of President John F. Kennedy. She died later that year, on December 28, 1961—what would have been Woodrow Wilson's 105th birthday.

Right: In 1961, Edith (far right) represented the Freedom from Hunger Campaign at the White House with (L-R) singer Marian Anderson; George McGovern, director of the Food for Peace program; President John F. Kennedy; and German chancellor Konrad Andenauer. The former first lady died a few weeks later.

Wilson's War Message to Congress

Delivered on April 2, 1917

Outlining the powers of the presidency, Article II of the Constitution states, "The President shall be Commander in Chief of the Army and Navy of the United States, and of the Militia of the several States, when called into the actual Service of the United States." The president, then, is the nation's chief commander during time of war. But the act of declaring war resides with Congress, as spelled out in the Constitution in Article I, Section 8. Therefore, the United States is never officially at war with another nation unless it is declared so by Congress. The ability to declare and lead in war is subject to the same checks and balances as other powers of the federal government. A president cannot go to war without the permission of Congress.

In 1916, President Woodrow Wilson pursued negotiations between nations involved in World War I, and in December, the German government informed the United States that it was prepared to participate in peace negotiations, but Great Britain refused because Germany had not announced any peace terms and its military alliance (called the Central Powers) had just conquered Romania and was in a favorable negotiating position. Wilson continued his efforts, but in January 1917, Germany announced that it would engage in full submarine warfare to stop shipping by or to Great Britain beginning on February 1; Germany hoped to defeat Great Britain in six months.

The United States had already expressed the view that unrestricted submarine warfare violated its rights as a neutral nation, and when Germany proceeded to renew unrestricted submarine warfare, the United States broke diplomatic relations with Germany for the first time on February 3, as did some Latin American nations. After several submarine attacks on American vessels, President Wilson asked Congress to declare war on Germany.

Excerpt from Wilson's War Message to Congress

I have called the Congress into extraordinary session because there are serious, very serious, choices of policy to be made, and made immediately, which it was neither right nor constitutionally permissible that I should assume the responsibility of making.

On the 3rd of February last, I officially laid before you the extraordinary announcement of the Imperial German government that on and after the 1st day of February it was its purpose to put aside all restraints of law or of humanity and use its submarines to sink every vessel that sought to approach either the ports of Great Britain and Ireland or the western coasts of Europe or any of the ports controlled by the enemies of Germany within the Mediterranean.

That had seemed to be the object of the German submarine warfare earlier in the war, but since April of last year the Imperial government had somewhat restrained the commanders of its undersea craft in conformity with its promise then given to us that passenger boats should not be sunk and that due warning would be given to all other vessels which its submarines might seek to destroy, when no resistance was offered or escape attempted, and care taken that their crews were given at least a fair chance to save their lives in their open boats. The precautions taken were meager and haphazard enough, as was proved in distressing instance after instance in the progress of the cruel and unmanly business, but a certain degree of restraint was observed.

The new policy has swept every restriction aside. Vessels of every kind, whatever their flag, their character, their cargo, their destination, their errand, have been ruthlessly sent to the bottom without warning and without thought of help or mercy for those on board, the vessels of friendly neutrals along with those of belligerents. Even hospital ships and ships carrying relief to the sorely bereaved and stricken people of Belgium, though the latter were provided with safe conduct through the proscribed areas by the German government itself and were distinguished by unmistakable marks of identity, have been sunk with the same reckless lack of compassion or of principle.

I was for a little while unable to believe that such things would in fact be done by any government that had hitherto subscribed to the humane practices of civilized nations. International law had its origin in the attempt to set up some law which would be respected and observed upon the seas, where no nation had right of dominion and where lay the free highways of the world. By painful stage after stage has that law been built up, with meager enough results, indeed, after all was accomplished that could be accomplished, but always with a clear view, at least, of what the heart and conscience of mankind demanded.

[…]

The present German submarine warfare against commerce is a warfare against mankind. It is a war against all nations. American ships have been sunk, American lives taken in ways which it has stirred us very deeply to learn of; but the ships and people of other neutral and friendly nations have been sunk and overwhelmed in the waters in the same way. There has been no discrimination. The challenge is to all mankind.

Each nation must decide for itself how it will meet it. The choice we make for ourselves must be made with a moderation of counsel and a temperateness of judgment befitting our character and our motives as a nation. We must put excited feeling away. Our motive will not be revenge or the victorious assertion of the physical might of the nation, but only the vindication of right, of human right, of which we are only a single champion.

When I addressed the Congress on the 26th of February last, I thought that it would suffice to assert our neutral rights with arms, our right to use the seas against unlawful interference, our right to keep our people safe against unlawful violence. But armed neutrality, it now appears, is impracticable. Because submarines are in effect outlaws when used as the German submarines have been used against merchant shipping, it is impossible to defend ships against their attacks as the law of nations has assumed that merchantmen would defend themselves against privateers or cruisers, visible craft giving chase upon the open sea.

[…]

Armed neutrality is ineffectual enough at best; in such circumstances and in the face of such pretensions it is worse than ineffectual: it is likely only to produce what it was meant to prevent; it is practically certain to draw us into the war without either the rights or the effectiveness of belligerents. There is one choice we cannot make, we are incapable of making: we will not choose the path of submission and suffer the most sacred rights of our nation and our people to be ignored or violated. The wrongs against which we now array ourselves are no common wrongs; they cut to the very roots of human life.

With a profound sense of the solemn and even tragical character of the step I am taking and of the grave responsibilities which it involves, but in unhesitating obedience to what I deem my constitutional duty, I advise that the Congress declare the recent course of the Imperial German government to be in fact nothing less than war against the government and people of the United States; that it formally accept the status of belligerent which has thus been thrust upon it; and that it take immediate steps, not only to put the country in a more thorough state of defense but also to exert all its power and employ all its resources to bring the government of the German Empire to terms and end the war.

What this will involve is clear. It will involve the utmost practicable cooperation in counsel and action with the governments now at war with Germany and, as incident to that, the extension to those governments of the most liberal financial credits, in order that our resources may so far as possible be added to theirs. It will involve the organization and mobilization of all the material resources of the country to supply the materials of war and serve the incidental needs of the nation in the most abundant and yet the most economical and efficient way possible. It will involve the immediate full equipment of the Navy in all respects but particularly in supplying it with the best means of dealing with the enemy's submarines. It will involve the immediate addition to the armed forces of the United States already provided for by law in case of war at least 500,000 men, who should, in my opinion, be chosen upon the principle of universal liability to service, and also the authorization of subsequent additional increments of equal force so soon as they may be needed and can be handled in training.

It will involve also, of course, the granting of adequate credits to the government, sustained, I hope, so far as they can equitably be sustained by the present generation, by well-conceived taxation. I say sustained so far as may be equitable by taxation because it seems to me that it would be most unwise to base the credits which will now be necessary entirely on money borrowed. It is our duty, I most respectfully urge, to protect our people so far as we may against the very serious hardships and evils which would be likely to arise out of the inflation which would be produced by vast loans.

In carrying out the measures by which these things are to be accomplished, we should keep constantly in mind the wisdom of interfering as little as possible in our own preparation and in the equipment of our own military forces with the duty—for it will be a very practical duty—of supplying the nations already at war with Germany with the materials which they can obtain only from us or by our assistance. They are in the field and we should help them in every way to be effective there.

I shall take the liberty of suggesting, through the several executive departments of the government, for the consideration of your committees, measures for the accomplishment of the several objects I have mentioned. I hope that it will be your pleasure to deal with them as having been framed after very careful thought by the branch of the government upon which the responsibility of conducting the war and safeguarding the nation will most directly fall.

[…]

We have no quarrel with the German people. We have no feeling toward them but one of sympathy and friendship. It was not upon their impulse that their government acted in entering this war. It was not with their previous knowledge or approval. It was a war determined upon as wars used to be determined upon in the old, unhappy days when peoples were nowhere consulted by their rulers and wars were provoked and waged in the interest of dynasties or of little groups of ambitious men who were accustomed to use their fellow men as pawns and tools.

What Happened Next

Congress declared war, and nearly 200,000 American troops were training in France within two months. By November 1918, the American Expeditionary Force (AEF), as the U.S. military fighting in World War I was called, numbered nearly 2 million troops. By spring of 1918, U.S. troops were playing a major role as the momentum of the war shifted to the side of the Allies— the nations, including the United States and Great Britain, who were at war with the Central Powers, led by Germany.

The German army was defeated by November 1918, and national and local governments in Germany were replaced by a democratic government, the Republic of Germany. That government signed an armistice with the Allied nations, acknowledging its acceptance of President Wilson's Fourteen Points, an outline of peace terms and postwar activities. Negotiations for a peace treaty were held at the Palace of Versailles, near Paris, beginning in 1919.

During the negotiations, the Allied Nations, except for the United States, sought revenge against the Central Powers—including payment for the cost of the war and control over lands Germany occupied during the war. Wilson opposed such stern measures, but he eventually relented in exchange for support for his proposed League of Nations, which was to be an international alliance of nations through which conflicts could be addressed. The Treaty of Versailles was completed with harsh surrender terms against Germany, and some historians believe that

it sowed the seeds for World War II, which began in 1939. The German nation suffered greatly during the 1920s, a circumstance preyed upon by Adolf Hitler, who became Germany's leader in the 1930s. Hitler soon had his army involved in armed aggression against neighboring nations of Germany.

The Treaty of Versailles was never ratified by the United States, where the executive branch negotiates treaties but the Senate has the power to accept or reject them (a two-thirds majority of senators must vote to ratify it). Rejection of the treaty was a stunning blow to Wilson's presidency, and his Democratic Party lost the presidential election of 1920. The United States eventually made a separate peace agreement with Germany and never joined the League of Nations. The League existed as a weak international body for more than two decades before it was replaced by the much stronger United Nations in 1946, with full participation by the United States.

Wilson's Fourteen Points

Delivered to Congress on January 8, 1918

The United States entered World War I in April 1917. A massive buildup of American troops followed, swelling the military ranks from around 500,000 combat-ready troops in 1917 to about 2 million by 1918. Vital industries at home were geared to the war effort, building the boats, vehicles, and supplies needed to fight the war.

In January 1918, as American troops were being prepared for a more massive involvement, President Wilson presented his Fourteen Points to Congress. They summarized the goals of the Allied Powers—those countries united in the war against the Central Powers of Germany, Austria-Hungary, and Turkey. Later in 1918, the Fourteen Points became the list of demands the Central Powers would have to meet in order to secure an armistice and begin serious peace negotiations.

Throughout the war, Wilson pursued various means to spur peace negotiations. Several key victories by Allied forces helped turn the momentum of the war against the Central Powers in 1918, and with defeat appearing to be imminent, the government of Germany was replaced and the nation was renamed the Republic of Germany. The new government met the terms outlined in the Fourteen Points and an armistice was called in the fall of 1918. Peace negotiations and an official end to the war followed in 1919.

It will be our wish and purpose that the processes of peace, when they are begun, shall be absolutely open and that they shall involve and permit henceforth no secret understandings of any kind.

The day of conquest and aggrandizement is gone by; so is also the day of secret covenants entered into in the interest of particular governments and likely at some unlooked-for moment to upset the peace of the world. It is this happy fact, now clear to the view of every public man whose thoughts do not still linger in an age that is dead and gone, which makes it possible for every nation whose purposes are consistent with justice and the peace of the world to avow nor or at any other time the objects it has in view.

We entered this war because violations of right had occurred which touched us to the quick and made the life of our own people impossible unless they were corrected and the world secure once for all against their recurrence. What we demand in this war, therefore, is nothing peculiar to ourselves. It is that the world be made fit and safe to live in; and particularly that it be made safe for every peace-loving nation which, like our own, wishes to live its own life, determine its own institutions, be assured of justice and fair dealing by the other peoples of the world as against force and selfish aggression. All the peoples of the world are in effect partners in this interest, and for our own part we see very clearly that unless justice be done to others it will not be done to us. The programme of the world's peace, therefore, is our programme; and that programme, the only possible programme, as we see it, is this:

I. Open covenants of peace, openly arrived at, after which there shall be no private international understandings of any kind but diplomacy shall proceed always frankly and in the public view.

II. Absolute freedom of navigation upon the seas, outside territorial waters, alike in peace and in war, except as the seas may be closed in whole or in part by international action for the enforcement of international covenants.

III. The removal, so far as possible, of all economic barriers and the establishment of an equality of trade conditions among all the nations consenting to the peace and associating themselves for its maintenance.

IV. Adequate guarantees given and taken that national armaments will be reduced to the lowest point consistent with domestic safety.

V. A free, open-minded, and absolutely impartial adjustment of all colonial claims, based upon a strict observance of the principle that in determining all such questions of sovereignty the interests of the populations concerned must have equal weight with the equitable claims of the government whose title is to be determined.

VI. The evacuation of all Russian territory and such a settlement of all questions affecting Russia as will secure the best and freest cooperation of the other nations of the world in obtaining for her an unhampered and unembarrassed opportunity for the independent determination of her own political development and national policy and assure her of a sincere welcome into the society of free nations under institutions of her own choosing; and, more than a welcome, assistance also of every kind that she may need and may herself desire. The treatment accorded Russia by her sister nations in the months to come will be the acid test of their good will, of their comprehension of her needs as distinguished from their own interests, and of their intelligent and unselfish sympathy.

VII. Belgium, the whole world will agree, must be evacuated and restored, without any attempt to limit the sovereignty which she enjoys in common with all other free nations. No other single act will serve as this will serve to restore confidence among the nations in the laws which they have themselves set and determined for the government of their relations with one another. Without this healing act the whole structure and validity of international law is forever impaired.

VIII. All French territory should be freed and the invaded portions restored, and the wrong done to France by Prussia in 1871 in the matter of Alsace-Lorraine, which has unsettled the peace of the world for nearly fifty years, should be righted, in order that peace may once more be made secure in the interest of all.

IX. A readjustment of the frontiers of Italy should be effected along clearly recognizable lines of nationality.

X. The peoples of Austria-Hungary, whose place among the nations we wish to see safeguarded and assured, should be accorded the freest opportunity to autonomous development.

XI. Rumania, Serbia, and Montenegro should be evacuated; occupied territories restored; Serbia accorded free and secure access to the sea; and the relations of the several Balkan states to one another determined by friendly counsel along historically established lines of allegiance and nationality; and international guarantees of the political and economic independence and territorial integrity of the several Balkan states should be entered into.

XII. The Turkish portion of the present Ottoman Empire should be assured a secure sovereignty, but the other nationalities which are now under Turkish rule should be assured an undoubted security of life and an absolutely unmolested opportunity of autonomous development, and the Dardanelles should be permanently opened as a free passage to the ships and commerce of all nations under international guarantees.

XIII. An independent Polish state should be erected which should include the territories inhabited by indisputably Polish populations, which should be assured a free and secure access to the sea, and whose political and economic independence and territorial integrity should be guaranteed by international covenant.

XIV. A general association of nations must be formed under specific covenants for the purpose of affording mutual guarantees of political independence and territorial integrity to great and small states alike.

In regard to these essential rectifications of wrong and assertions of right we feel ourselves to be intimate partners of all the governments and peoples associated together against the Imperialists. We cannot be separated in interest or divided in purpose. We stand together until the end.

For such arrangements and covenants we are willing to fight and to continue to fight until they are achieved; but only because we wish the right to prevail and desire a just and stable peace such as can be secured only by removing the chief provocations to war, which this programme does remove. We have no jealousy of German greatness, and there is nothing in this programme that impairs it. We grudge her no achievement or distinction of learning or of pacific enterprise such as have made her record very bright and very enviable. We do not wish to injure her or to block in any way her legitimate influence or power. We do not wish to fight her either with arms or with hostile arrangements of trade if she is willing to associate herself with us and the other peace-loving nations of the world in covenants of justice and law and fair dealing. We wish her only to accept a place of equality among the peoples of the world—the new world in which we now live—instead of a place of mastery.

What Happened Next

The Fourteen Points was important for clarifying the goals of the United States and the Allied Powers in World War I. As the momentum of the war shifted to the Allies in 1918, the Points became the demands the Central Powers had to satisfy in order to begin peace negotiations. In the fall of 1918, a new German government accepted the terms of the Fourteen Points and an armistice was declared. Peace talks began in 1919.

Peace negotiations resulted in the Treaty of Versailles, named for the French palace outside of Paris where the negotiations were held. President Wilson represented the United States during the Treaty negotiations. He was dismayed at the hard line against Germany demanded by the other Allied nations. Wilson's vision for an alliance of nations was only agreed upon after he had accepted the harsh surrender terms the other Allied nations wanted imposed on Germany.

The League of Nations was established during the 1920s, but it proved mostly ineffective over the next two decades. Despite the heroic stature as an international statesman that Wilson had attained—far above that of any previous president—he could not rally Congress or the American people to favor the Treaty of Versailles or to join the League of Nations. It was a crushing defeat that left Wilson exhausted and his administration weak after nearly two full terms of triumphs. Tired of war and foreign entanglements, Americans elected Republican Warren G. Harding president in 1920 over Democrat James M. Cox, who had pledged to continue President Wilson's policies, including pushing for American involvement in the League of Nations.

Warren G. Harding

"*I can take care of my enemies all right. But my friends … they're the ones that keep me walking the floors at night.*"

—*Warren G. Harding*

Twenty-ninth president of the United States, 1921–1923

Full name: *Warren Gamaliel Harding*

Born: *November 2, 1865, Blooming Grove, Ohio*

Died: *August 2, 1923, San Francisco, California*

Burial site: *Marion Cemetery, reinterred in Harding Memorial Tomb, Marion, Ohio*

Parents: *George Tryon and Phoebe Elizabeth Dickerson Harding*

Spouse: *Florence Mabel Kling (1860–1924; m. 1891)*

Children: *None legitimate; one or two rumored illegitimate*

Religion: *Baptist*

Education: *Attended Iberia College (later Ohio Central College)*

Occupations: *Teacher; insurance salesman; editor; publisher*

Government positions: *Ohio state senator and lieutenant governor; U.S. senator from Ohio*

Political party: *Republican*

Dates as president: *March 4, 1921–August 2, 1923*

Age upon taking office: *55*

When Warren G. Harding died about halfway through his term as president of the United States, he didn't know that several scandals would be remembered as the most remarkable events of his administration. After his death, the public learned that some of his appointees had defrauded the government of millions, taken illegal kickbacks from private industry, and sold public oil leases to line their own pockets.

A career politician, Harding rewarded his most loyal supporters with important government posts when he was elected president, but those friends took advantage of his trusting nature. Harding had his own personal scandals as well. Although his wife, Florence Harding, was the model of a modern, independent woman and an ambitious supporter of many of his plans, Harding indulged in extramarital affairs with at least two other women. One of them, Nan Britton, published a tell-all autobiography (*The President's Daughter*) four years after he died, claiming that Harding was the father of her child. The other was Carrie Phillips, whose fifteen-year on-again, off-again affair with him was uncovered in the 1960s with the publication of dozens of love letters written in his own unmistakable hand.

The news of scandal, both personal and political, served to make the president's achievements seem less important than they actually were, but Harding managed to bring America what he called a "return to normalcy."

Looking the Part

As he was rising through the ranks of Ohio Republicans, one of them once told Warren G. Harding, "You know, you'd make a dandy-looking president." Harding just smiled his best "aw shucks" smile and went back to the poker game, but the man was right. Six feet tall and barrel-chested, Harding had thick white hair and bushy black eyebrows, an almost perfect Roman nose and soft gray eyes. His complexion was rosy, his teeth even and pearly white. His voice was full and pleasant and never grating, and he had a sense of fashion remarkable for central Ohio. He acted like a president, too. People naturally liked him, and he liked them every bit as much. He once said in a speech that his father had told him, "Warren, it's a good thing you weren't born a gal because you'd be in a family way all the time. You just can't say no."

The World War was over, and people wanted to get on with their lives. Many of them wanted the United States to divorce itself from the affairs of foreign countries and let the rest of the world go its own way. The 1920s were beginning to roar during Harding's administration—business started to boom, and for most Americans the new prosperity made it an exciting time to be alive.

Ohio Farmer's Son

Warren G. Harding's family roots in America stretched back to an English Puritan, Richard Harding, who arrived in Massachusetts in 1623. As settlement expanded from the original thirteen colonies, various Harding descendants moved westward, first to the Wyoming Valley of Pennsylvania, and then later to Ohio. Warren Harding, the first president born after the Civil War, came into the world on November 2, 1865, in a farmhouse near Blooming Grove, Ohio. He was the oldest of eight children.

Harding's father, George, was what we'd call a renaissance man today. He was a farmer who turned his attention to the study of medicine and became a physician. He bought a local newspaper after arriving in Ohio, and Warren, not yet ten, worked with the paper's printer as an errand boy. By the time he reached his teens, young Harding had learned how to handle simple printing jobs and run a small printing press. Meanwhile, his early education came in one-room schools. In his later teens, he attended Ohio Central College and graduated in 1882, trained as a teacher for rural schools.

While Harding was finishing his studies, his parents moved to Marion, Ohio, a busy, fast-growing county seat. After deciding against a career as a teacher, Harding moved in with his parents and started looking for a more suitable line of work. He sold insurance for a time, and earned enough money to be able, along with two partners, to buy the struggling *Marion Star* newspaper for $300. Within a short time, Harding had the paper on its feet, and with subscriptions and advertising pouring in, he bought out his partners, and then went after the competition. The *Marion Star* became so popular that the two other newspapers in the area couldn't remain profitable and went out of business.

Timeline

1865: Born in Ohio
1884: Buys the *Marion Star* newspaper with the help of two partners
1891: Marries Florence Kling
1889–1903: Serves in the Ohio State Senate
1904–6: Serves as lieutenant governor of Ohio
1912: Makes speech for the renomination of President William Howard Taft at the 1912 Republican Party convention
1915–21: Serves in U.S. Senate
1921–23: Serves as twenty-ninth U.S. president
1923: Dies in California

Below: The Harding birthplace at Blooming Grove, Ohio.

BIRTH PLACE OF
WARREN G. HARDING

©C.E. COOMER
MARION, OHIO
1923

The success of the *Marion Star* helped to mold Harding's political philosophy. He beat his rivals by providing a newspaper that leaned in the direction of the strongly Republican views of the region, but he was also careful not to offend the Democrats among his readers. Whenever Republicans disagreed on issues and split into factions, which happened often, the *Star's* editorials called for compromise and party unity.

Still in his early twenties, Harding had become a newspaper publisher with a growing political influence. At about that time he met Florence Kling, an independent woman five years older than he was. Her father was a banker, not to mention the wealthiest man in Marion County. Florence had helped manage his business until their relationship became strained when she eloped at age nineteen. After giving birth to a son and being abandoned by her spouse, Florence divorced her husband and became a single mother. When she and Harding were married, he had found a spouse who supported his political and professional ambitions and went out of her way to advance his career.

Booster

As a newspaper publisher, it was only natural that Warren Harding would be a member of the Marion Chamber of Commerce, but he didn't stop there. He was a 33-degree Mason, an Elk, and a Rotarian, among other things. He played cornet in the town band and first base for its baseball team, which he also managed. If there was a hand to be shaken or a back to be slapped, Warren was always first in line. Fathers were usually pleased to see their sons in his company, and mothers were happy to see him out on the front porch with their daughters, even though they couldn't help worrying just a little.

From Ohio to Washington, D.C.

Florence Harding, called "Flossie" by everyone except Warren Harding (who called her "the Duchess"), began running the day-to-day operations of the *Marion Star* while her husband got involved in politics. He had been a delegate to the Ohio State Republican Party Convention in 1887 and was becoming quite well known for his efforts—both in print and in person—on behalf of the GOP, as the Republican Party is nicknamed. Handsome and well spoken, he projected a striking image of a small-town, self-made man, and after twelve years of campaigning for other Republicans and working for party unity, he was elected to the Ohio State Senate in 1900.

Harding spent two terms as a state senator. Loyal to Republican causes, he continued his role as a peacemaker and gained a number of influential friends. Among them was Harry M. Daugherty, a business lobbyist with political ambitions, who worked to increase Harding's influence in the hotbed of Ohio politics. Harding was elected lieutenant governor, but he went back to Marion and his newspaper work after serving a single term.

Although he spent the next few years out of public office, he was still a prominent member of the Republican Party. He ran for governor of Ohio in 1910, and although he lost the race, it gave him valuable national exposure. Just two years later, President William Howard Taft chose Harding to nominate him again as Republican presidential candidate at the party's national convention, and his political fortunes took off. Just four years later, he was elected to the U.S. Senate by a margin of more than 100,000 votes.

Harding spent six very undistinguished years in the Senate. He missed 40 percent of the roll-call votes and didn't introduce any important legislation. Unlike a majority of Americans, he supported steps that prepared the United States to fight in World War I, and he was openly critical of attempts of President Woodrow Wilson

to stay out of it. Otherwise, Harding voted in lock step with Republicans on matters that were good for business. He delivered the keynote address at the 1916 Republican National Convention.

When the United States entered World War I in 1917, Democrats and Republicans put their differences aside and worked together for the war effort. Prohibition of alcohol, and women's right to vote were two issues that Harding supported more for their political value than out of personal belief. As a social drinker, Harding didn't approve of the Prohibition Amendment himself, but he could see that most of his constituents were in favor of it. The same was true of giving women the right to vote. Harding voted in favor of universal suffrage, even though he privately didn't think it was an idea whose time had come. He later won the first presidential election in which women were allowed to vote.

After the war, the issue of America's support of the League of Nations was a much greater problem. In helping to negotiate the Treaty of Versailles that ended World War I, President Wilson pledged American involvement in an organization made up of various nations that could address international disputes and avoid another massive war.

Some Americans, particularly a majority of Republicans, were against a provision in the League of Nations charter that would commit the American government to provide military support for any other League member facing an aggressor. Republicans objected that this provision would lead to U.S. involvement in any European conflict, no matter how minor. They also wanted to change the Versailles Treaty, but President Wilson insisted that the treaty, which had to be ratified by the senate, must be approved as presented. Debate over the League of Nations quickly turned hostile and was defined by outgoing president Wilson as the major issue of the 1920 presidential election.

The "Smoke-Filled Room"

Harding's old friend Harry Daugherty convinced him to try for the presidential nomination in 1920, but Harding was a long shot: The Republicans had two popular frontrunners for the nomination—Frank O. Lowden and General Leonard Wood—and either one of them seemed like a shoo-in for election. Nevertheless, Harding allowed his name to be put into the field at the convention.

Harding needed 493 votes to win the nomination, and he polled only 65 on the first ballot, while the 2 frontrunners split the rest of the vote so evenly that a tie appeared possible. Subsequent rounds of voting didn't do much to change things, although Harding picked up a few more votes in each ballot.

While supporters for the leading candidates were debating each other on the convention floor, a private meeting was taking place in a nearby hotel room. Several

Immortal Words

Warren G. Harding believed that he had a way with words, but the fact is, he didn't. He did invent a few words during his career, such as "bloviating," which he used to describe his speaking style and defined as talking for extended periods without actually saying anything. He was fond of alliteration, which he pushed to the limits when he said, "Progression is not proclamation nor palaver. It is not pretense nor play on personal pronouns, not perennial pronouncement. It is not the perturbation of a people, passion-wrought, nor a promise proposed." What, then, is progression? Don't ask. The journalist H. L. Mencken described Harding's speaking style as "rumble and bumble, flap and doodle, balder and dash." One of his opponents called it the "big bow-wow style of oratory."

Left: Harding's old friend Harry Daugherty guided his political life from the beginning.

Right: Like other presidential candidates before him, Harding did most of his campaigning from his front porch—on a tree-lined street in Marion, Ohio.

influential Republicans discussed other possible candidates as alternatives to Wood and Lowden; Harding's name kept coming up. Although a consensus wasn't reached in that "smoke-filled room," the influence of the men meeting there was quite evident the next morning. Harding gained steadily in the next several rounds of balloting and clinched the nomination on the tenth ballot.

Harding didn't campaign actively for the presidency. Daugherty and his other advisors—in an early display of spin-doctoring—made sure that he campaigned without having to answer on-the-spot questions, out of fear that he might show his lack of understanding on major issues. He generally delivered carefully written statements from the front porch of his home in Marion, and rarely appeared

Just Relaxing

During his presidency, Harding found time to play golf twice a week, sometimes breaking the low nineties. He was an avid fan of boxing and baseball, too, but his first love was a night of poker. Once he bet a set of White House china on a single hand and lost.

anywhere else, while his opponent, Ohio governor James M. Cox, toured the country, covering more than two thousand miles, in an aggressive attempt to win votes.

---

*"We need another Lincoln
To do the country's thinkin'.
Mis-ter Har-ding,
You're the man for us."
— "Harding, You're the Man for Us," Al Jolson's campaign song*

Without leaving his front porch, Harding promised all Americans what he called a "return to normalcy" after eight years of Democratic rule, a world war, and an economic downturn. He hit the right note with that promise, and he won by a landslide, with a stunning 60 percent of the popular vote.

1920 Election Results

Presidential / Vice Presidential Candidates	Popular Votes	Electoral Votes
Warren G. Harding / Calvin Coolidge (Republican)	16,152,200	404
James M. Cox / Franklin D. Roosevelt (Democratic)	9,147,353	127

Cox won the Democratic nomination on the forty-fourth ballot; one of the early leaders was former U.S. secretary of the treasury William G. McAdoo, who was also the son-in-law of the outgoing president, Woodrow Wilson.

Betrayed by Friends

For his cabinet and other appointments, Harding picked some men on their merits and others on the basis of friendship. The cabinet members that he chose based on merit proved quite capable: Charles Evans Hughes as secretary of state, Herbert Hoover as secretary of commerce, and Andrew W. Mellon as secretary of the treasury. Among the cronies he appointed were Harry Daugherty as attorney general, Albert Fall as secretary of the interior, and Charles Forbes as director of the Veterans' Bureau. These three old and trusted friends would betray him.

The Harding Administration

Administration Dates: March 4, 1921–August 2, 1923
Vice President: Calvin Coolidge (1921–23)
Cabinet:

Secretary of State	Charles Evans Hughes (1921–23)
Secretary of the Treasury	Andrew W. Mellon (1921–23)
Secretary of War	John W. Weeks (1921–23)
Attorney General	Harry M. Daugherty (1921–23)
Secretary of the Navy	Edwin Denby (1921–23)
Postmaster General	William H. Hays (1921–22)
	Hubert Work (1922–23)
	Harry S. New (1923)
Secretary of the Interior	Albert B. Fall (1921–23)
	Hubert Work (1923)
Secretary of Agriculture	Henry C. Wallace (1921–23)
Secretary of Labor	James J. Davis (1921–23)
Secretary of Commerce	Herbert C. Hoover (1921–23)

Left: No, Lincoln didn't run in the 1920 election—Harding and Coolidge did, and they were hoping the Lincoln charisma might rub off on them.

Right: Secretary of the Treasury Andrew W. Mellon was the most influential member of both the Harding and Coolidge cabinets.

Charles Evans Hughes

During his distinguished career of governmental service, Charles Evans Hughes served as secretary of state and two different terms as a justice on the Supreme Court. He also lost a close presidential election in 1916 to Woodrow Wilson. Hughes was born in Glens Falls, New York, on April 14, 1862. He entered Madison University (now Colgate) at the age of fourteen, transferring later to Brown University. Hughes taught school for a year at Delaware Academy in Delhi, New York, and read law in his spare time. In 1882, he entered Cornell Law School, and he graduated in 1884. For the next twenty years, he practiced law, briefly interrupting his work to teach law at Cornell.

At the age of forty-three, Hughes was chosen by a legislative committee to investigate the gas and electric industry in New York. His success in exposing fraud led to other high-profile investigations, and in 1906 he was nominated as the state's Republican candidate for governor. He won in a bitter campaign against newspaper publisher William Randolph Hearst. The active governor won battles to regulate public utilities and to curtail racetrack gambling. He was also interested in conservation and in an employment compensation law. After a second term as governor, Hughes was appointed an associate justice of the Supreme Court by President William Howard Taft.

As a justice, Hughes supported national railroad rate regulation and wrote one of the most important decisions in this field. In a 1914 decision, he asserted in his majority opinion the supreme power of Congress over interstate commerce. In an era of government reform of business, Hughes defined the regulatory power of states and cities. In 1916, Hughes resigned from the Court to accept the Republican presidential nomination. He was narrowly beaten by Woodrow Wilson. Hughes had demanded bolder policies than Wilson against both Germany and Mexico and sterner measures of preparation for World War I. He could not challenge Wilson on business reform and ended up projecting a pro-business image that obscured his own reform credentials.

After returning to New York to practice law, Hughes reemerged as a critic of Wilson's plans for the League of Nations. During the presidential campaign of 1920, he joined thirty other distinguished Republicans in an appeal for Republican victory to ensure that American involvement in the League would not include making

the U.S. military available to help in foreign conflicts. Republican Warren Harding was elected president and named Hughes to the post of secretary of state. Overturning Wilson's work on the Treaty of Versailles that ended World War I, Hughes negotiated a separate peace with Germany.

Hughes favored cooperation on matters of international law. He was successful in arranging for American participation, without congressional interference, in the work of the League's Reparations Commission. In 1923, his suggestion that the commission invite American experts to help untangle Germany's postwar fiscal problems led to the adoption of the Dawes Plan, which—backed by Wall Street loans solicited by Hughes—brought momentary relief to the German economy.

At the Washington Conference (1921–22) on the worldwide buildup of naval forces, Hughes was able to win international cooperation to halt the naval arms race for a decade. In Latin America, Hughes moved American policy gradually away from the more aggressive stances of presidents Wilson and Theodore Roosevelt. Hughes's achievements won praise, but they did not last: Reparations agreements collapsed, as did the Washington Conference treaties. Hughes left office in 1925 to return to law practice, but President Herbert Hoover named him chief justice to the Supreme Court in 1930.

The early 1930s marked the worst economic crisis in American history. Hughes was prepared to adapt the language of the Constitution flexibly to the needs of the Great Depression. He differed more often than not with the Court's conservative justices appointed during twelve years of Republican presidential leadership. Nevertheless, he agreed when the Court found unconstitutional the National Industrial Recovery Act of Franklin D. Roosevelt. Hughes clashed with Roosevelt over the president's court-packing plan in February 1937, when the president wanted to appoint more justices in order to have more supporters on the court. On the other hand, Hughes helped inspire a momentous change of judicial attitude that proved favorable to Roosevelt. Believing that the Constitution was responsive to needs of a particular time, he helped expand government intervention in the economy. Throughout the 1930s, his decisions supported civil liberty and civil rights.

After his retirement from the Court in 1941, Hughes continued to live in Washington, D.C., where he died of heart failure at the age of eighty-six in 1948.

When he took office in 1921 with his own Republican Party in the majority in both houses of Congress, Harding thought he was going to have a smooth early presidency. However, members of both parties debated his proposals. He was able to push through some elements of the "America First" agenda that he had promised the voters: Tariffs on imported goods were raised, immigration was restricted, and he signed the Budget and Accounting Act, which called for stricter accounting practices in developing the annual federal budget and led to dramatic savings.

"I want to see the day come when black men will regard themselves as full participants in the benefits and responsibilities of American citizenship… . We cannot go on, as we have for more than half a century, with one great section of our population, numbering as many people as the entire population of some significant countries of Europe, set off from real contribution to national issues, because of a division on race lines."

—Warren G. Harding

After having pledged not to support the Treaty of Versailles, Harding was able to conclude peace treaties with Germany and Austria, finally putting a formal end to World War I without the United States having to join the League of Nations. Then he sent Charles Evans Hughes to an international conference that resulted in significant reductions in the navies of the United States, Japan, France, England, and Italy, ending an expensive arms race among them. One British naval officer said that he had "sunk more ships in thirty-five minutes than all the admirals of the world have sunk in centuries."

Those accomplishments didn't impress the average man in the street who expected more attention to their concerns. Harding refused to support legislation that

---

"I have just read the president's treaty message. I thought it was the best speech [Secretary of State Charles Evans] Hughes ever wrote."

—Will Rogers

Right: Harding's cabinet getting a much-needed breath of fresh air on the White House lawn.

Watchdog

Will Hayes, who served as Harding's postmaster general, quit the cabinet in 1922 to become president of the Motion Picture Producers and Distributors of America, establishing what became known as the "Hayes Office," which censored American films to keep them within his strict moral standards.

would give World War I soldiers a federal bonus, believing it would prove too costly to a nation paying off war debts. He supported measures aimed at helping distressed farmers, but most of the farmers themselves though, he didn't go far enough. When Harding proved himself to be ineffective and antiunion during a railroad workers' strike, his popularity fell so far that Democrats picked up a number of new seats in midterm elections.

By the fall of 1922, Harding was visibly tired and clearly overwhelmed by his job. When Mrs. Harding became ill and nearly died, it added to his burden. "It seems as though I have been president for twenty years," he admitted sadly. Then a bad thing began to get worse. Rumors of scandal were beginning to swirl around him.

Working behind the scenes through his position in the Justice Department, Harry Daugherty took bribes to grant immunity from prosecution to certain liquor dealers and sellers, and he also sold paroles to wealthy federal prisoners. At the same time, the normal business of the Justice Department was in confusion, and many Congressional leaders were calling for Daugherty's resignation.

First pictures of the Harding
Cabinet. Neg No 12565

Above: As at least one artist saw it, the Teapot Dome scandal rocked the Capitol to its rafters.

Below: When Harding became the first president to visit Alaska, he and the first lady bundled up against the cold, in contrast to Territorial Governor Scott C. Bone, who didn't bother to button up his overcoat.

Meanwhile, it was discovered that Veterans' Bureau chief Charles Forbes was illegally selling government medical supplies to private interests and taking kickbacks on contracts for new hospital buildings. When Harding confronted his old friend about the possibility that the charges might be true, Forbes quickly resigned and sailed for Europe. Later, when he came back to America, he was subjected to a thorough Senate investigation, convicted of defrauding the government, and sentenced to two years in jail.

However, this was just the tip of the iceberg. The worst of the scandals, which became known as the "Teapot Dome Conspiracy," was in large part the handiwork of Secretary of the Interior Albert B. Fall. Its full extent wouldn't be revealed until after Harding died.

Fall illegally leased federal oil deposits in Elk Hill, California, and Teapot Dome, Wyoming, to two oil-company executives, Harry Sinclair and Edward Doheny, in clear violation of an order by former President Wilson, who had the oil deposits set aside for the navy to use in an emergency. Fall had been paid an estimated $400,000 by the two oil barons for his "services." Evidence of the scandal had begun to show by the early months of 1923, and eventually, Fall was convicted of bribery and conspiracy to defraud the government. He was sentenced to a year in jail and was forced to pay a $100,000 fine. He served ten months and pocketed the rest of the bribe, which he called a loan, some $300,000.

As newspapers began to dig into the scandals, Harding and his wife left town for a national speaking tour, a trip that took them all the way to Alaska, making Harding the first chief executive ever to visit the territory. (Alaska became a state in 1959.) On their way home, the president suddenly became ill in Seattle. His personal physician called it food poisoning and refused to let other doctors examine him—even turning away army surgeons convinced that the president had suffered a heart attack. Harding continued the journey and died on August 2, 1923, in San Francisco.

As his flag-draped coffin traveled back across the country for the official ceremonies in Washington, D.C., hundreds of thousands of mourners gathered to watch the train pass. The entourage was greeted in Washington, by Harding's successor, former vice president Calvin Coolidge.

"[Warren Gamaliel Harding] was a very natural human being with the frailties mixed with the virtues of humanity."
—*The* New York Times

Legacy

When Calvin Coolidge succeeded Warren G. Harding, he faced two major challenges: to sustain the prosperity Americans had been enjoying in the years after World War I, and to restore faith in government. Coolidge, a much less active personality than Harding had been, succeeded on both counts.

Harding was successful in stopping two key aims of his predecessor, Woodrow Wilson. He reversed Wilson policies that had the federal government monitoring business practices, and he slowed American participation in international affairs by withdrawing the Treaty of Versailles. Wilson had won a Nobel Peace Prize in 1919 for his efforts in negotiating the treaty and conceptualizing the League of Nations, but Harding followed different policies. Meanwhile, the American economy was prospering, and Harding enjoyed the popularity that usually flows to a president in such times. He was undoubtedly one of America's most beloved presidents, at least during the first two years of his term. Although he was not directly linked to corruption, his reputation sank steadily beginning near the time of his death as the depth of scandal within his administration was gradually revealed.

Above: Harding's body was carried across the country from California to Washington on a funeral train, with thousands gathering to watch it pass. Few presidential deaths have caused as much genuine grief.

Below: Many American families still treasure the memorial souvenirs distributed as Harding's body passed through their towns.

Florence Harding

Born August 15, 1860, Marion, Ohio
Died November 21, 1924, Marion, Ohio

"If the career is the husband's, the wife can merge it with her own."
—*Florence Harding*

A new era for American women began in 1920. It was the first year that women were allowed to vote in a presidential election. In the 1920s, more females were holding professional jobs and living independently, and Florence Harding fit the image of the "new woman" perfectly. Strong-willed and ambitious, she was a forceful presence in her husband's administration. She created a whole new image for the first lady by holding her own press conferences, and expressing her own opinions, which were often unexpected. She helped humanize a president who was quickly losing popularity, and when her husband's administration became tainted with scandal, Florence did everything in her power to protect his name.

Early Independence

Born in Marion, Ohio, in 1860, Florence Kling grew up in a wealthy household. Her father, Amos Kling, was a banker and the richest man in town. Florence developed confidence and independence while she was growing up and working with her father, who taught her how to manage his business and how to communicate effectively with men and women, employees and customers.

The relationship between father and daughter became strained when, as a teenager, Florence became pregnant and left town with Henry De Wolfe, the baby's father. No legal records have ever turned up to show that he and Florence ever got married, but De Wolfe was a chronic alcoholic who couldn't earn a living. Florence was able to get a divorce, possibly based on the fact that they had lived together long enough to qualify as common-law man and wife.

As a single mother who needed to earn a living, Florence gave piano lessons, until she was able to patch things up with her father and go back to Marion.

She met Warren G. Harding after he became the owner of the *Marion Star* newspaper in the late 1880s. Harding made the newspaper popular and attracted a substantial political following. Handsome and respected in the community, Harding was considered Marion's most eligible bachelor. Florence captured him, and they were married in 1891.

Because Florence was five years older than her husband and an heiress to a fortune, there was some talk over backyard clotheslines that their relationship was a marriage of convenience, a business and political partnership. That view gained further support years later when evidence of Warren Harding's extramarital affairs was made public. Still, a wealth of stories and memoirs from their friends and neighbors shows that Florence Harding was deeply in love with her husband when she married him and deeply hurt when she discovered his infidelity.

Harding became more active in politics soon after they were married, and Florence took over the day-to-day operations of the *Marion Star*, supervising circulation and bookkeeping. The newspaper flourished, and Harding became an important political figure in the state of Ohio. As he advanced through Ohio politics and on to the U.S. Senate, hardworking Florence was always by his side. She expressed her opinion on issues and helped him deal with

Left: Florence was a strong-willed woman who was called "the duchess" by her husband.

negative press reports. She was so effective in keeping his extramarital affairs private that most people had no idea that he had been unfaithful until after he died. Meanwhile, she began suffering from chronic kidney problems, which would sideline her for a time.

Active First Lady

When Harding was nominated for president in 1920, Florence courted the newspapers and all different types of media, including news highlights that were shown in movie theaters, which were becoming common. She endeared herself to female voters by speaking out strongly on women's rights.

Both the White House and its grounds had been closed to the public while President Woodrow Wilson was seriously ill during the last year of his term. After Harding was elected, Florence reopened the place and again held garden parties on the White House lawn, many of them for veterans of World War I. The festivities were well covered by the media, and newspapers printed her remarks in favor of women competing in sports and running their own businesses. Behind the scenes, she encouraged her husband to speak more forcefully on the issue as well as on racial equality and religious tolerance.

Mrs. Harding encouraged the appointment of female federal employees, contributed her views to some of Harding's most important domestic and foreign accomplishments, and occasionally even gave speeches when her husband was ill or delayed. Editorial cartoons called her "Chief Executive" and praised her new style of leadership as first lady, but she wasn't flattered by the attention. More than almost anyone else, she knew that it was the changing times and not the force of her personality that was making the difference. The new opportunities open to women also changed the role of America's first lady.

Some of Florence Harding's contributions to her husband's presidency were not quite so praiseworthy. She mixed and served alcoholic beverages to White House guests, even though Prohibition, by constitutional amendment, had made alcohol illegal in the United States. She also strongly recommended the Hardings' friend Charles Forbes to head the newly created Veterans' Bureau, and he was eventually convicted and imprisoned for defrauding the bureau of millions of dollars. Mrs. Harding insisted that her husband's health be supervised by a personal physician she chose for him, and when he collapsed during a national tour, that same physician wouldn't allow any other doctors to examine him, insisting that it was a case of food poisoning and nothing more. Harding in fact was more likely suffering from heart problems, and he died slightly more than halfway through his presidency on August 2, 1923.

Right: The president's body leaving the White House en route to its final resting place back home in Marion, Ohio.

By that time, Mrs. Harding was aware that several massive scandals were about to undermine her husband's presidency. No one would have known that she was burdened by this information as she accompanied Harding's body back to Washington, D.C., on a train that was greeted by many thousands of mourners. In his biography of Mrs. Harding, *Florence Harding: The First Lady, the Jazz Age, and the Death of America's Most Scandalous President,* Carl Sferrazza Anthony asserts that the first lady quickly burned many of her husband's personal papers that might have involved him in the scandals.

Harding died before his administration became disgraced by scandals uncovered from 1923 through 1925. Florence Harding's health suffered, and she died on November 21, 1924, barely a year after her husband's demise, and she was buried along with him in the magnificent Harding burial plot in Marion, Ohio.

Harding's Speech to a Special Session of Congress

Delivered on April 12, 1921

Following the end of World War I, Americans were eager to return to normal life. The war had disrupted families, created shortages of many basic necessities, and filled the daily newspapers with stories from foreign locales. Nearly every aspect of life seemed geared to the war effort. Warren G. Harding rode the sentiment for normalcy to victory in the presidential election of 1920.

Harding campaigned against the views of outgoing president Woodrow Wilson and the Democratic Party candidate, James M. Cox. Both had wanted the United States to ratify the Treaty of Versailles, the pact that ended the war. However, Harding and many others were against ratification of the treaty because it called for U.S. involvement in the League of Nations. As a League member, the United States would be required to deploy military support for any other League member facing an aggressor. Republicans objected that this article would lead to U.S. involvement in all future European conflicts, no matter how petty.

Another area of disagreement between Harding and his Democratic counterparts concerned the relationship between government and business. President Wilson had supported regulations to ensure that business practices were fair. Harding planned to free business from all governmental controls.

Before a special session of Congress shortly after taking office in 1921, Harding spelled out the agenda for his administration. With support from a Republican majority in Congress, Harding wanted America to "put its own house in order"—to be concerned with problems at home instead of international affairs.

Excerpt from Harding's Speech to a Special Session of Congress

Under our political system the people of the United States have charged the new Congress and the new administration with the solution—the readjustments, reconstruction, and restoration which must follow in the wake of war. […]

First in mind must be the solution of our problems at home, even though some phases of them are inseparably linked with our foreign relations. The surest procedure in every government is to put its own house in order. I know of no more pressing problem at home than to restrict our national expenditures within the limits of our national income and at the same time measurably lift the burdens of war taxation from the shoulders of the American people. […]

The staggering load of war debt must be cared for in orderly funding and gradual liquidation. We shall hasten the solution and aid effectively in lifting the tax burdens if we strike resolutely at expenditure. It is far more easily said than done. In the fever of war our expenditures were so little questioned, the emergency was so impelling, appropriation was so unimpeded that we little noted millions and counted the Treasury inexhaustible. It will strengthen our resolution if we ever keep in mind that a continuation of such a course means inevitable disaster. […]

The most substantial relief from the tax burden must come for the present from the readjustment of internal taxes, and the revision or repeal of those taxes which have become unproductive and are so artificial and burdensome as to defeat their own purpose. A prompt and thoroughgoing revision of the internal tax laws, made with due regard to the protection of the revenues, is, in my judgment, a requisite to the revival of business activity in this country. It is earnestly hoped, therefore, that the Congress will be able to enact without delay a revision of the revenue laws and such emergency tariff measures as are necessary to protect American trade and industry.

It is of less concern whether internal taxation or tariff revision shall come first than has been popularly imagined because we must do both, but the practical course for earliest accomplishment will readily suggest itself to the Congress. We are committed to the repeal of the excess-profits tax and the abolition of inequities and unjustifiable exasperations in the present system.

The country does not expect and will not approve a shifting of burdens. It is more interested in wiping out the necessity for imposing them and eliminating confusion and cost in the collection.

The urgency for an instant tariff enactment, emergency in character and understood by our people that it is for emergency only, cannot be too much emphasized. I believe in the protection of American industry, and it is our purpose to prosper America first. The privileges of the American market to the foreign producer are offered too cheaply today, and the effect on much of our own productivity is the destruction of our self-reliance, which is the foundation of the independence and good fortune of our people. Moreover, imports should pay their fair share of our cost of government. […]

It is proper to invite your attention to the importance of the question of radio communication and cables. To meet strategic, commercial, and political needs, active encouragement should be given to the extension of American-owned and operated cable and radio services. Between the United States and its possessions there should be ample communication facilities providing direct services at reasonable rates. Between the United States and other countries, not only should there be adequate facilities but these should be, so far as practicable, direct and free from foreign intermediation. Friendly cooperation should be extended to international efforts aimed at encouraging improvement of international communication facilities and designed to further the exchange of messages. Private monopolies tending to prevent the development of needed facilities should be prohibited. Government-owned facilities, wherever possible without unduly interfering with private enterprise or government needs, should be made available for general uses.

Particularly desirable is the provision of ample cable and radio services at reasonable rates for the transmission of press matter, so that the American reader may receive a wide range of news and the foreign reader receive full accounts of American activities. The daily press of all countries may well be put in position to contribute to international understandings by the publication of interesting foreign news. […]

During the recent political canvass the proposal was made that a Department of Public Welfare should be created. It was endorsed and commended so strongly that I venture to call it to your attention and to suggest favorable legislative consideration.

Government's obligation affirmatively to encourage development of the highest and most efficient type of citizenship is modernly accepted, almost universally. Government rests upon the body of citizenship; it cannot maintain itself on a level that keeps it out of touch and understanding with the community it serves. Enlightened governments everywhere recognize this and are giving their recognition effect in policies and programs. Certainly no government is more desirous than our own to reflect the human attitude, the purpose of making better citizens—physically, intellectually, spiritually. To this end I am convinced that such a department in the government would be of real value. It could be made to crystallize much of rather vague generalization about social justice into solid accomplishment. Events of recent years have profoundly impressed thinking people with the need to recognize new social forces and evolutions, to equip our citizens for dealing rightly with problems of life and social order.

In the realms of education, public health, sanitation, conditions of workers in industry, child welfare, proper amusement and recreation, the elimination of social vice, and many other subjects, the government has already undertaken a considerable range of activities. […]

Somewhat related to the foregoing human problems is the race question. Congress ought to wipe the stain of barbaric lynching from the banners of a free and orderly, representative democracy. We face the fact that many millions of people of African descent are numbered among our population, and that in a number of states they constitute a very large proportion of the total population. It is unnecessary to recount the difficulties incident to this condition, nor to emphasize the fact that it is a condition which cannot be removed. There has been suggestion, however, that some of its difficulties might be ameliorated by a humane and enlightened consideration of it, a study of its many aspects, and an effort to formulate, if not a policy, at least a national attitude of mind calculated to bring about the most satisfaction possible adjustment of relations between the races, and of each race to the national life. One proposal is the creation of a commission embracing representatives of both races, to study and report on the entire subject. The proposal has real merit. I am convinced that in mutual tolerance, understanding, charity, recognition of the interdependence of the races, and the maintenance of the rights of citizenship lies the road to righteous adjustment. […]

Nearly two and a half years ago the World War came to an end, and yet we find ourselves today in the technical state of war, though actually at peace, while Europe is at technical peace, far from tranquillity and little progressed toward the hoped-for restoration. It ill becomes us to express impatience that the European belligerents are not yet in full agreement, when we ourselves have been unable to bring constituted authority into accord in our own relations to the formally proclaimed peace.

Little avails in reciting the causes of delay in Europe or our own failure to agree. But there is no longer excuse for uncertainties respecting some phases of our foreign relationship. In the existing League of Nations, world-governing with its superpowers, this republic will have no part. There can be no misinterpretation, and there will be no betrayal of the deliberate expression of the American people in the recent election; and, settled in our decision for ourselves, it is only fair to say to the world in general, and to our associates in war in particular, that the League Covenant can have no sanction by us. The aim to associate nations to prevent war, preserve peace, and promote civilization our people most cordially applauded. We yearned for this new instrument of justice, but we can have no part in a committal to an agency of force in unknown contingencies; we can recognize no super-authority.

Manifestly, the highest purpose of the League of Nations was defeated in linking it with the treaty of peace and making it the enforcing agency of the victors of the war. International association for permanent peace must be conceived solely as an instrumentality of justice, unassociated with the passions of yesterday, and not so constituted as to attempt the dual functions of a political instrument of the conquerors and of an agency of peace. There can be no prosperity for the fundamental purposes sought to be achieved by any such association so long as it is an organ of any particular treaty or committed to the attainment of the special aims of any nation or group of nations.

The American aspiration, indeed, the world aspiration, was an association of nations, based upon the application of justice and right, binding us in conference and cooperation for the prevention of war and pointing the way to a higher civilization and international fraternity in which all the world might share. In rejecting the League Covenant and uttering that rejection to our own people and to the world, we make no surrender of our hope and aim for an association to promote peace in which we would most heartily join. We wish it to be conceived in peace and dedicated to peace, and will relinquish no effort to bring the nations of the world into such fellowship, not in the surrender of national sovereignty but rejoicing in a nobler exercise of it in the advancement of human activities, amid the compensations of peaceful achievement. [...]

What Happened Next

Harding's economic policies were enacted and helped fuel a post–World War I boom called the Roaring Twenties. After Harding died in office in 1923, his successor, Calvin Coolidge, continued the policy of low taxation and minimal government interference in business. Economic prosperity continued through 1929, when a financial crisis led to the Great Depression, which lasted through the 1930s and into the early 1940s.

Government did become more involved in monitoring business in certain areas. The federal government took an active role in regulating development of promising new technologies to ensure that one company did not dominate an entire industry. Radio and commercial aviation are the two most noteworthy industries that made great strides during the 1920s with the assistance and supervision of the federal government.

Harding's proposed Department of Welfare and the commission on race relations proved insignificant. Only in 1939 did an executive-level agency arise that fulfilled the goals noted by Harding. While there were slight advances in relations between whites and African Americans, segregation was still widespread. It was during the 1920s, for example, that baseball became "America's pastime," but it was two decades later when the first African American played in a Major League Baseball game.

The United States never entered the League of Nations or ratified the Treaty of Versailles. The United States, unlike other Allied Nations that fought the Axis Powers (Germany and Austria) in World War I, made separate peace pacts with them. The United States never became an official member of the League, which existed from 1920 to 1946. American diplomats assisted League activities and attended meetings, but lack of official American participation lessened the effectiveness of the League. In 1946, the League of Nations voted to dissolve. Much of its organization was assumed by the United Nations (UN). The UN had more active participation from major powers, including the United States, making it a more effective peacekeeping organization while continuing the social work of the League to effect a stronger international alliance.

Calvin Coolidge

"… The chief business of the American people is business. They are profoundly concerned with producing, buying, selling, investing, and prospering in the world."

—*Calvin Coolidge*

Thirtieth president of the United States, 1923–1929

Full name: *John Calvin Coolidge*
Born: *July 4, 1872, Plymouth, Vermont*
Died: *January 5, 1933, Northampton, Massachusetts*
Burial site: *Plymouth Notch Cemetery, Plymouth, Vermont*
Parents: *John and Victoria Moor Coolidge*
Spouse: *Grace Anna Goodhue (1879–1957; m. 1905)*
Children: *John (1906–2000); Calvin Jr. (1908–1924)*
Religion: *Congregational*
Education: *Amherst College (B.A., 1895)*
Occupations: *Attorney*
Government positions: *Northampton, Massachusetts, councilman and mayor; Massachusetts state congressman, senator, lieutenant governor, and governor; vice president under Warren G. Harding*
Political party: *Republican*
Dates as president: *August 3, 1923–March 4, 1925 (first term); March 4, 1925–March 4, 1929 (second term)*
Age upon taking office: *51*

The Roaring Twenties is how the decade of the 1920s is usually remembered. American cities were expanding outward and upward, toward the sky; automobiles ruled the streets; a lively bull market on Wall Street was creating new millionaires almost by the hour; and Babe Ruth made baseball fans out of everyone when he smacked sixty home runs in 1927. That same year, Charles Lindbergh flew an airplane solo from New York to Paris, and even the 1919 constitutional amendment prohibiting the manufacture or sale of alcohol didn't slow anybody down. In fact, it only seemed to encourage revelers to party on in a time they were calling "the Jazz Age."

Calvin Coolidge, the man who presided over all this, was the direct opposite of the Roaring Twenties' image. A sober, reserved New England Republican without an ounce of charisma, "Silent Cal" simply went about his business as though nothing exciting were going on around him even though the country was giddily experiencing an economic boom bigger than any that had ever been seen before.

Coolidge's low-key image worked to his advantage as a politician. He was a reassuring figure to many Americans with terse and to-the-point public statements like "The chief business of America is business." Remarks like that summed up his ideas about his role as president. He

Timeline

1872: Born in Vermont

1895 Graduates from Amherst College

1897: Admitted to the Massachusetts bar; attorney in private practice in Northampton, Massachusetts, after 1898

1899–1901: Holds two elected positions in Northampton, Massachusetts

1907–8: Serves in Massachusetts state house

1910–11: Serves as mayor of Northampton, Massachusetts

1912–15: Serves in Massachusetts state senate

1916–18: Serves as Massachusetts lieutenant governor

1919–20: Serves as Massachusetts governor; gains national attention for firing striking police officers in Boston and using the state militia as temporary replacements

1921–23: Serves as U.S. vice president under Warren G. Harding

1923: Teapot Dome scandal rocks Harding administration

1923–29: Serves as thirtieth U.S. president, following death of Harding; fires all administration officials implicated in the Teapot Dome scandal

1929: After having declined to seek reelection, Coolidge retires to Northampton, Massachusetts; stock market crashes in October, beginning the Great Depression

1933: Dies in Massachusetts

Code of Silence

A guest at a White House party told Calvin Coolidge that she had made a bet that she could get him to say more than two words. "You lose," he said. He once told a reporter that he tried not to say much because, "If you don't say anything, no one can call on you to repeat it."

didn't call for forceful leadership. Having emerged from the horrors of World War I, people were ready to get back to work and to enjoy themselves, and Coolidge was happy to let them get on with their lives. Although his speeches were low-key and not always inspiring, he was the last president to write most of them himself, and he was the first to use the new medium of radio to deliver his words to a national audience.

Newspapers of the time usually portrayed Coolidge quite well. Good natured, he even allowed himself to be photographed in seemingly unpresidential situations, such as posing in an Indian war bonnet or working on his Vermont farm. Although he was drawn in political cartoons as a Gloomy Gus, he actually smiled quite often for the cameras and was known in private for his sharp wit.

believed that his job was to cut the cost of government and interfere as little as possible with the country's inner workings.

That approach has led some historians and political analysts to view Coolidge as a "do-nothing" executive who happily delegated the hard decisions to others, and that he was simply a tool of big business who didn't leave behind any truly noteworthy legislation or any personal stamp on the institution of the presidency.

Yet, by all accounts, Coolidge was a strictly honest politician, a candidate who won nearly every election he ever entered, and a family man whose White House years were saddened by the death of his teenage son. The tax cuts Coolidge championed during his term furthered economic growth, and he recognized that the times

Right: Calvin Coolidge was a man of the people, and didn't mind being seen doing things ordinary people do.

Early Years

John Calvin Coolidge was born on the Fourth of July 1872, and named after his father, an active business entrepreneur who held various public offices at both the local and state level. Coolidge grew up in Plymouth Notch, an isolated, rural Vermont town. The nearest railroad stop was about ten miles away in Ludlow, where his mother, Victoria Moor Coolidge, had attended a private academy. She was an avid reader who passed her love of books on to her children, Calvin and his sister Abigail. Victoria Coolidge was unfortunately plagued by poor health even as a young woman, and she died when her son was only twelve. The loss affected him deeply: He carried her portrait with him for the rest of his life, and it was in his breast pocket on the day he died.

As a youngster, Coolidge was a loner—a shy, frail boy who suffered from asthma. Six years after his mother died, tragedy visited the household again. When he was eighteen, his sister Abbie died at age fifteen from acute appendicitis. Both Calvin and his sister had been students at Black River Academy in Ludlow, where their mother had also gone to school.

"[The people I grew up among] were hard but wholesome. They suffered many privations and enjoyed many advantages without any clear realization of either one of them… . Their speech was clean and their lives were above reproach. They cherished the teachings of the Bible and sought to live in accordance with them."

—*Calvin Coolidge*

After he graduated from the academy, Coolidge enrolled at Amherst College in Northampton, Massachusetts. His fellow students remembered his four year there as altogether unremarkable; and none of them would have bet a nickel that he was destined for the White House, much less a career in politics; although he was a serious student, he wasn't what they would call sociable.

Coolidge stayed in Northampton after he graduated from Amherst, working as a clerk in a local law firm and studying law. The firm's partners were involved in local politics, and he began to help with their campaigns, although he was still painfully shy and had few friends. He made an effort to be more social, but still he never dated. After he passed the Massachusetts bar at the age of twenty-five, he opened his own law practice in Northampton and began to blossom on his own.

Coolidge won his first election in 1898 when he ran for a seat on the Northampton city council, and over the next decade, he made a name for himself as a dependable Republican and a local favorite of the state party bosses. After serving as city solicitor for Northampton, he was appointed court clerk for Hampshire County and given an impressive salary. At that same time, he met Grace Goodhue, a young woman from Burlington, Vermont, who had joined the staff of a school for the deaf in Northampton after graduating from the University of Vermont. Grace and Calvin were married in October 1905, and the first of their two sons, John Coolidge, was born a year later.

After working in the general court, or lower house, of the Massachusetts state legislature, Coolidge served two terms as mayor of Northampton, then was elected to a seat in the upper chamber of the state senate in Boston. He later served as the state's lieutenant governor and became governor of Massachusetts in 1918.

He won national recognition the following year for his decisive handling of a police strike in Boston by calling out the state militia to maintain order and firing all of the striking police officers. While he was being praised in conservative newspapers across the

Left: American Federation of Labor president Samuel Gompers tried to defend striking Boston policemen after Massachusetts governor Calvin Coolidge fired them. Coolidge informed him that, "There is no right to strike against the public safety by anybody, anywhere, any time."

Social Butterfly

Although Calvin Coolidge was almost painfully shy, when he and Grace went to Washington, D.C., after he became vice president, he suddenly began accepting any and all dinner party invitations. It was uncharacteristic of him and when Grace asked him what had changed him so suddenly, he said, "Gotta eat somewhere."

Coolidge and the new president were completely opposite in personality. Coolidge was modest and kept a low profile, while Harding was an outgoing backslapper and handshaker. However, Harding showed a disastrous inability to judge character and made several terrible choices in selecting his cabinet and White House staff, favoring men who had helped build his political career. Those men led the Harding administration into a political scandal that was front-page news in the early 1920s.

It was learned that some of Harding's cabinet officials profited from secret deals involving leases for land that contained emergency oil reserves used by U.S. Navy ships. The Teapot Dome scandal, as it came to be known for the name of one of the tracts in Wyoming, eventually resulted in a jail term for Harding's secretary of the interior, Albert Fall, and tainted his whole administration. Some believed that the strain of the Senate investigation

country as a hero of law and order, the nation's most famous labor leader—American Federation of Labor president Samuel Gompers—tried to intervene on behalf of the fired officers. Coolidge sent him a telegram with a short summary of his stand on the issue that was widely reprinted in newspapers across America: "There is no right to strike against the public safety by anybody, anywhere, any time."

As a result of this new fame, Republican enemies of organized labor began pushing for Coolidge as their candidate for president in 1920. However, Ohioan Warren G. Harding emerged as the surprise Republican frontrunner at their nominating convention and Coolidge was named as his running mate. Harding won the election, beginning what would be twelve straight years of Republican administrations.

Right: Coolidge's father, a justice of the peace, administered his son's oath of office at three in the morning, after which the new president went back to bed.

Left: The hit of the Roaring Twenties was a dance called the Charleston. It could be done anywhere, even in sight of the U.S. Capitol.

The Coolidge Administration

Administration Dates: August 3, 1923–March 4, 1925
March 4, 1925– March 4, 1929

Vice President: None (1923–1925)
Charles G. Dawes (1925–29)

Cabinet:

Secretary of State	Charles Evans Hughes (1923–25)
	Frank B. Kellogg (1925–29
Secretary of the Treasury	Andrew W. Mellon (1923–29)
Secretary of War	John W. Weeks (1923–25)
	Dwight F. Davis (1925–29)
Attorney General	Harry M. Daugherty (1923–24)
	Harlan F. Stone (1924–25)
	John G. Sargent (1925–29)
Secretary of the Navy	Edwin Denby (1923–24)
	Curtis D. Wilbur (1924–29)
Postmaster General	Harry S. New (1923–29)
Secretary of the Interior	Hubert Work (1923–28)
	Roy O. West (1928–29)
Secretary of Agriculture	Henry C. Wallace (1923–24)
	Howard M. Gore (1924–25)
	William M. Jardine (1925–29)
Secretary of Labor	James J. Davis (1923–29)
Secretary of Commerce	Herbert C. Hoover (1923–28)
	William F. Whiting (1928–29)

and public outcry over the scandal, which was only one of several, were too much for Harding, who was already suffering from heart problems. During a cross-country lecture tour—optimistically called "the Voyage of Understanding" and designed to restore confidence in his administration—Harding died on August 2, 1923, in San Francisco.

Coolidge and his family were vacationing at his father's home in Vermont at the time, and the vice president learned of Harding's death from a messenger who arrived in the middle of the night. His father's house didn't have a telephone. He was sworn into office by his father, a notary public, just before 3:00 A.M., after which, in Coolidge's characteristically laid-back style, he went right back to bed. When he got to Washington, however, the new president acted quickly to restore faith in the Republican administration as the full story of the Teapot Dome deals was still coming out. Coolidge immediately replaced Harding appointees who had been associated with scandal and named a special counsel to investigate the misconduct of government officials.

Right: Calvin Coolidge looked right at home in the Oval Office after he succeeded Warren G. Harding.

Campaign of 1924

After less than a year in office—a successful period during which Coolidge went a long way toward renewing public confidence—he was unanimously nominated as the Republican candidate in the 1924 presidential election. His running mate was banker and financier Charles Dawes. Their reelection slogan played up the sober, serene Coolidge style: "Keep Cool with Coolidge."

Tragedy struck the Coolidge family not long after the convention when, following a few tennis matches with his brother, sixteen-year-old Calvin Jr. developed a blister on one of his toes. It became infected and he soon developed blood poisoning, and he didn't tell anyone about it until it was too late. Even with the best medical treatment available, Calvin Coolidge Jr. died a few days later on July 7, 1924.

Overwhelmed by the loss, Coolidge was grief-stricken and he was never quite the same again. He barely participated in his own reelection campaign, leaving much of the actual campaigning to Dawes. Still, Coolidge easily beat his opponents, Progressive Party candidate Robert La Follette and West Virginia Democrat John W. Davis, by a landslide. The low voter turnout for the election showed the national political mood of those years of progress and prosperity. A new American middle class was growing rapidly, the result of steady economic growth since the end of World War I.

Coolidge maintained a pro-business atmosphere, keeping corporate taxes low and making sure that government regulation was almost nonexistent. The stock market was surging, and labor unions were struggling.

Right: "Hail to the Chief" took on a new significance after Henry Standing Bear made Coolidge a Sioux chief.

President Coolidge Being Made Sioux Indian Chief by Henry Standing Bear

Many of the comforts of modern life—electricity, telephones, cars, radios, refrigerators, and even the ability to buy a house on credit—were becoming within the reach of the average worker. The wages of the average worker were increasing, and the Revenue Acts of 1924 and 1926, which Coolidge signed into law, lowered tax burdens.

Privileges

The day after his father became president, Coolidge's son, Calvin Jr., started a job as a farm laborer. When one of his coworkers said, "If my father was president, I wouldn't be working here," Calvin Jr. shot back, "If your father were my father, you would."

1924 Election Results

Presidential / Vice Presidential Candidates	Popular Votes	Electoral Votes
Calvin Coolidge / Charles G. Dawes (Republican)	15,725,016	382
John W. Davis / Charles W. Bryan (Democratic)	8,386,503	136
Robert M. La Follette / Burton K. Wheeler (Progressive)	4,822,856	13

West Virginia politician Davis, a former ambassador to Great Britain, won the Democratic nomination on the 103rd ballot; former treasury secretary William G. McAdoo and New York governor Alfred E. Smith were early ballot leaders.

Above: President and Mrs. Coolidge with their sons, Calvin Jr. (far left) and John (far right), and a family friend. Calvin Jr. died of blood poisoning a month after this picture was taken.

Above: Prohibition agents disposed of the fruits of their raids by pouring whiskey down any handy sewer.

"The Chief Business of the American People Is Business"

In a January 17, 1925, speech before the American Society of Newspaper Editors, Coolidge spoke about the need for the American press to serve as a trustworthy source of information about business and financial matters. "It is probable that a press which maintains an intimate touch with the business currents of the nation, is likely to be more reliable than it would be if it were a stranger to these influences," Coolidge told the editors. "After all, the chief business of the American people is business. They are profoundly concerned with producing, buying, selling, investing, and prospering in the world."

Meanwhile, Prohibition, the constitutional ban on the manufacture and sale of alcoholic beverages, had widespread effects on the American public during the Coolidge years. Few Americans actually gave up the habit

of drinking—bootleg liquor was relatively easy to buy, and speakeasies were easy to find. (The term "bootleg" comes from the practice of smugglers of carrying bottles of liquor in the sides of their tall boots.) Even President Harding was known to keep a private supply at the White House, and although Coolidge rarely drank alcohol, he was privately opposed to the Prohibition Amendment. He saw the ban as an example of government interfering in people's lives, but he was compelled to publicly support it as the law of the land. He did make one telling statement

Media Attention

Although Coolidge was well known for keeping his thoughts to himself, unlike many who followed him into the Oval Office, he held press conferences often, and seemed to genuinely like the Washington press corps. It wasn't always a love fest, though. Many newspapers opposed him, but he was philosophical about it. "There is no cause for feeling disturbed about being misrepresented in the press," he said. "It would be only when they begin to say things detrimental to me which were true that I should feel alarm."

Left: When drinking became illegal under the Prohibition Amendment, it was a good idea to keep your booze hidden, and a garter could be a perfect hiding place.

about it in 1924: "Any law that inspires disrespect for other laws—the good laws—is a bad law."

Most Americans at the time were enjoying their prosperity, but there were some dark moments as well. The great Mississippi River flood of 1927 left large areas in the South devastated, with damage reaching into hundreds of millions of dollars. Coolidge opposed a congressional relief bill, arguing that the federal government should not favor one section of the country at the expense of another. But the legislation passed with a provision that gave the Army Corps of Engineers the job of taking measures to avoid such disasters in the

future. This act began an expansion of federal government responsibilities and obligations in an era when both the people and the politicians wanted individual states to take responsibility for the health and welfare of its citizens.

"You hear a lot of jokes every once in a while about 'Silent Cal Coolidge.' The joke is on the people who make the jokes. Look at his record. He cut taxes four times. We had probably the greatest growth and prosperity that we've ever known. I have taken heed of that because if he did that by doing nothing, maybe that's the answer."

—President Ronald Reagan

Foreign Policy

Coolidge's foreign policy mirrored his domestic administrative style: He favored nonintervention in foreign affairs except to protect American financial interests. He supported legislation that funded an expanded merchant marine fleet, believing that it would provide America with greater opportunities to prosper in international commerce, and he called for a joint venture with Canada for construction on the St. Lawrence Seaway to open the Great Lakes to European trade.

Conflicts erupted with Mexico in the mid-1920s when lands under lease to American oil companies were seized by the Mexican government. The conflict was later resolved through negotiation, but some Americans called for a military invasion, and Coolidge sent marines to land in Nicaragua in 1926 to put down a guerrilla war supported with Mexican arms, but again diplomats to the region resolved the situation. The only time in his life that Coolidge ever set foot outside American borders came when he attended the Sixth International Conference of American States in Havana, Cuba, in 1928.

The most notable foreign-policy event of the Coolidge years was the Kellogg-Briand Pact. His secretary of state, Frank Kellogg, was awarded the Nobel Peace Prize for engineering what was universally seen as an international law against war. Also named for Kellogg's French counterpart, Aristide Briand, the pact was response to the recent horrors of World War I, and

Left: The Jazz Age brought new attention to musicians of every stripe.

Frank B. Kellogg

President Calvin Coolidge was generally inclined to let the country run by itself, and his secretary of state, Frank B. Kellogg, pursued a similar course in international affairs. Yet Kellogg was instrumental in negotiating the Kellogg-Briand Pact, a stunning agreement intended to achieve international peace. The pact was eventually compromised, but it was a major achievement for an administration often accused of doing nothing to lead the country and of being disinterested in foreign affairs.

Frank Billings Kellogg was born in Potsdam, New York, on December 22, 1856. In 1867, the family joined many other Americans moving westward following the Civil War. The Kelloggs settled in Minnesota. Frank Kellogg worked on the family farm and had a very general education before moving to Rochester, Minnesota, to study law. He was admitted to the bar in 1877. Over the next ten years, he established a modest practice, and he married Clara M. Cook of Rochester in 1886. They did not have children. The following year, Minnesota's most prominent lawyer, former governor Cushman K. Davis, was so impressed with Kellogg that he invited him into his firm.

Kellogg's career took a sudden twist in the early 1900s as he became involved in suits against large companies. During the administration of Theodore Roosevelt, who governed from 1901 to 1909, Kellogg became involved in government antitrust suits. He was successful as the federal prosecutor in the government's case against General Paper Company, a monopolistic combination of newsprint manufacturers. That case ended in 1906, the same year he served as counsel to the Interstate Commerce Commission in its investigation of the activities of a railroad financier. At the same time, he was involved in the government's antitrust suit against Standard Oil. Kellogg pursued the case for several years, winning a favorable verdict in 1909 and in the appeal to the Supreme Court that resulted in a breakup of the trust. His success led to his election as president of the American Bar Association in 1912.

In 1916, Kellogg was elected to the U.S. Senate but was defeated for reelection in 1922. He served as ambassador to Great Britain from 1923 to 1925. In this post, he participated in the London and Paris conferences where the Dawes Plan for payment

of German reparations was negotiated, and he brought French and German leaders together.

In 1925, Kellogg was appointed secretary of state by President Calvin Coolidge. Kellogg regarded his negotiation of the Kellogg-Briand Pact for the maintenance of world peace as his most important State Department work. Taking advantage of a proposal by French foreign minister Aristide Briand for a pact binding France and the United States to refrain from war with each other, Kellogg proposed a much more ambitious policy—a general international agreement for the preservation of peace. Signed in August 1928 and ratified by most of the nations of the world, this pact bound the nations not "to resort to war as an instrument of national policy" but to settle all disputes by peaceful means. For his work on the pact, Kellogg received the Nobel Peace Prize in 1929 and was appointed a member of the Permanent Court of International Justice at The Hague, a post he held from 1930 to 1935. However, the pact proved ineffectual in preventing war because it did not address actions to be taken against an aggressor nation. For example, the pact had no effect when Nazi Germany invaded Czechoslovakia and Poland in 1939, actions that sparked World War II.

Kellogg died in 1937 in St. Paul, Minnesota, and was buried in the National Cathedral in Washington, D.C.

Left: Calvin Coolidge was a man of simple tastes, but he could get passionate about fishing.

the nations that signed it agreed not to use force to solve disputes. Coolidge signed the agreement for the United States on January 17, 1929, and sixty-one other countries also agreed to the terms.

Unparalleled Prosperity

The decade of the 1920s is often described as a "golden era" in America because of the prosperity and optimism that nearly everyone shared. In 1921, the country's gross national product was $69.9 billion. Three years later, that figure had soared to $93.1 billion. Unemployment fell rapidly, declining from 11.7 percent in 1921 to just 5 percent in the year of Coolidge's election. In 1927, the stock market's Dow Jones Industrial Average closed at an unheard of measurement at that time of 200 points. (By comparison, the number reached 11,000 points in 1999.)

That same year of 1927, the fourth of the Coolidge administration, New York Yankee slugger Babe Ruth set a new home-run record, and the first major motion picture to use sound, *The Jazz Singer,* ushered in Hollywood's own Golden Age. The first-ever solo airplane flight across the Atlantic was accomplished by a young, handsome pilot named Charles Lindbergh, and the arrival of his plane, the *Spirit of St. Louis,* in Paris, France, received massive international press coverage. On Coolidge's orders, Lindbergh was returned to America on board a navy cruiser.

"I was informed that while it wasn't an order to come back home," Lindbergh said about the president's gesture, "there'd be a battleship waiting for me."

Other Domestic Issues

Though generally a popular president, Coolidge was labeled in many parts of rural America as an enemy of the farmer. American farmers were going deeper into debt with each passing year, but Coolidge twice vetoed the McNary-Haugen Bill, first introduced in 1926, which had been intended to protect farmers from fluctuation in crop prices by allowing the federal government to purchase crop surpluses at a fixed price and to sell them abroad—sometimes at a loss. Coolidge opposed the bill on the principal of a free-market economy, believing that it would compel farmers to simply continue to produce more and more surpluses.

On the other hand, contemporary commercial aviation owes a great deal to Coolidge's foresight. He recognized that federal regulation could help assure American success in the new industry, and the Air Commerce Act of 1926 brought government regulation to commercial aviation and approval for the formation of the first two commercial airline routes.

Coolidge declined to run for reelection in 1928, although there was great public support for his candidacy. Characteristically, he refused to discuss his reasons for refusing to seek another term, but he made it clear that nothing could change his mind. When his term ended, he and Grace left Washington from Union Station aboard a train bound for Northampton. As they boarding, the ex-president made a typically succinct statement to the assembled press: "Good-bye. I have had a very enjoyable time in Washington."

Coolidge left office at the peak of American optimism and prosperity, but that era ended dramatically in October 1929 when stock prices on Wall Street fell hard. With the slide came an economic crisis, bank failures, and the loss of millions of jobs. Some Americans, longing for the Coolidge-era prosperity and optimism during the worst

Charles A. Lindbergh

Born in Detroit, Michigan, on February 4, 1902, Charles A. Lindbergh spent his childhood in Little Falls, Minnesota. He also lived in Washington, D.C., while his father served in the U.S. Congress. From 1920 to 1922, Lindbergh attended the University of Wisconsin, but he dropped out to go to an aviation school in Lincoln, Nebraska. After fewer than eight hours of instruction, he began flying with a stunt aviator and made his first parachute jump in June 1922. Lindbergh bought his first plane for $500 and made his first solo flight in April 1923. The following year he went through flight training in San Antonio, Texas, and in 1925 was commissioned in the U.S. Air Service Reserve. He began flying air mail service flights between Chicago and St. Louis on April 15, 1926.

Lindbergh soon learned of a $25,000 prize being offered to the first person to fly nonstop from New York to Paris. Thinking a successful flight would help promote St. Louis as a future site of aviation, some St. Louis businessmen agreed to fund Lindbergh's attempt. He traveled to San Diego, California, to oversee the construction of his airplane, which he named the Spirit of St. Louis. On May 10, 1927, he flew from San Diego to St. Louis and on to Long Island, New York, in 21 hours and 20 minutes, a new record.

Lindbergh began his New York to Paris flight at 7:52 A.M. on May 20, 1927. His flight plan took him up the coast of New England and Nova Scotia and then over the Gulf of St. Lawrence and the island of Newfoundland. He flew across the North Atlantic Ocean, eating only sandwiches. He dozed off several times and once awoke to find his plane skimming the ocean waves. Since his plane was without a radio, no one could track his flight. He also had to make all of his own navigational calculations with the chance that any error could push him off course. Lindbergh knew he was safe when he flew over the southern coast of Ireland in daylight on May 21, 1927. When Lindbergh reached the coast of Normandy, France, it was approaching nightfall. He found his way to Paris by following the Seine River upstream. Unknown to him, his progress was reported by telephone and radio by watchers who passed the news to Paris. As he approached the city, Parisians began heading for Le Bourget Field, where Lindbergh was to land. The first flight across the North Atlantic from New York to Paris covered 3,610 miles. Lindbergh completed it in 33 hours, 29 minutes, and 30 seconds.

Lindbergh instantly became a world hero. He was received by royalty, President Coolidge, and other heads of state. After arriving in New York City, Lindbergh was treated to a parade that was the largest ever to date in the United States. Afterward, Lindbergh traveled to Washington, D.C., where Coolidge gave a medal—the Distinguished Flying Cross—to Lindbergh, and the pilot dined at the White House. He made an air tour of the United States, traveling to seventy-five cities. At a reception at the American Embassy, he met Anne Morrow, the daughter of Dwight Morrow, U.S. ambassador to Mexico. Lindbergh married Anne on May 27, 1929; she became his copilot and navigator as they flew together to foreign countries.

Lindbergh was an intensely private person. After his marriage, he took a job as technical adviser to Transcontinental Air Transport and Pan American Airways, flying many of their new routes. The Lindberghs lived in a quiet estate in New Jersey. Their peace was shattered in 1932, when twenty-month-old Charles Augustus, the Lindbergh's only child, was kidnapped. The kidnapping soon became the world's biggest media event, labeled as the crime of the century. After several months, the boy's body was found, and an unemployed German immigrant, Bruno Richard Hauptmann, was charged, put on trial, and found guilty of the crime and executed. The Lindberghs soon moved to England.

In 1938 and 1939, Lindbergh traveled to Germany, was decorated by the Nazi government, and commented favorably on the state of the German Luftwaffe. When Lindbergh returned to the United States, he spoke out forcefully in favor of American neutrality when World War II began. These actions were unpopular with the public. Lindbergh was forced to resign his Air Corps Reserve commission.

Industrialist Henry Ford, who had several government war contracts, hired Lindbergh in 1943 to plan aircraft operations in the South Pacific during World War II. After the war, it was revealed that Lindbergh had worked as an unpaid consultant to the air force on secret projects from 1943 to 1945. This news helped regain some of Lindbergh's popularity. Lindbergh's book The Spirit of St. Louis won a Pulitzer Prize in 1953 and was made into a movie. President Dwight D. Eisenhower appointed Lindbergh a brigadier general in the air force in 1954. Lindbergh died on August 26, 1974.

Above: After Coolidge announced, "I do not choose to run," he spent the last summer of his presidency fishing in Wisconsin because "Choosin' to run isn't as restful as this."

Below: A smile calculated to deliver a million votes. The hat identifies Coolidge as a member of the Smoki Indian tribe in Arizona.

Listen Up

Coolidge went on a fishing trip to South Dakota in 1927, and he surprised not only the reporters who were following him around, but his wife as well, when he issued one of the strangest statements ever delivered by a president. He didn't actually say anything, but handed out little slips of paper to all of them, each containing the same simple message: "I do not choose to run in 1928." Typically, he didn't come right out and say that he wouldn't be a candidate, and other hopefuls had to tread softly to avoid getting in the way of an immensely popular incumbent. He kept them all guessing until the Republican national convention when he told the party leaders that, "We draw our presidents from the people. It is a wholesome thing for them to return to the people. I came from them. I wish to be one of them again."

days of the Great Depression that followed, suggested his name as the 1932 Republican presidential nominee, but Coolidge had made clear that he had retired from politics forever. He died at home after a heart attack on January 5, 1933. Congress adjourned the next day, and Coolidge's Republican successor, President Herbert Hoover, declared thirty days of national mourning.

Legacy

Two of the major achievements of the Coolidge era were later obscured by events of the 1930s. Some have blamed Calvin Coolidge's lack of government regulation of business for contributing to events that set off the Great Depression. A more balanced view recognizes that no single leader could have engineered the American prosperity of the 1920s nor could have foreseen the economic disaster that followed. The failure of the McNary-Haugen Bill continued the poor economic situation of many American farmers during the 1920s,

Safe at Home

When President Coolidge showed up for a baseball game between the Washington Senators and the New York Yankees, slugger Babe Ruth was the other star attraction and naturally they were both asked to say a few words over the public address system. The Babe proved to be Coolidge's match as a public speaker when all he said was, "Hot as hell, ain't it, prez."

and that worsened the effects of the Depression. Also, in light of the events of the 1930s, as fascist governments bullied their way to power in Europe, the celebrated Coolidge-era Kellogg-Briand Pact has been seen as an unrealistic and unenforceable agreement.

Noted newspaper editor and author H. L. Mencken once said of Coolidge that as a president, "he will be ranked among the vacuums." However, writing an obituary of the president in 1933, Mencken softened his view and said that Coolidge was perhaps a more complex man and politician than he first thought. "We suffer most when the White House bursts with ideas," he noted with his characteristic dry sense of humor. "His failings are forgotten; the country remembers only the grateful fact that he let it alone." Mencken went on to write, "Should the day ever dawn when…we reduce government to its

Home Again

After he retired, Calvin Coolidge lived a quiet life back home in Massachusetts, and he often went over to his father's house in Plymouth Notch. It didn't have a telephone when he was sworn in as president there, and it still did not, and that's one of the things he liked about it. He enjoyed sitting in a rocking chair on the front porch smoking cigars and taking a measure of the world. A friend who joined him there one day said that he must be proud to see so many cars cruising past for a look at the presidential birthplace. "Not as good as yesterday," he said. "There were sixty of 'em then."

simplest terms, it may very well happen that Calvin's bones now resting inconspicuously in the Vermont granite will come to be revered as those of a man who really did the nation some service."

Grace Coolidge

Born January 3, 1879, Burlington, Vermont
Died July 8, 1957, Northampton, Massachusetts

"I'm a simple, home-loving woman. I love best of all to gather my little family under my own roof and to stay there. We are just a plain New England family and we like, above all else, to live and do the things that simple New England families do."

—Grace Coolidge

Grace Coolidge seemed to be her husband's exact opposite both in personality and style. She was outgoing, lively, and spirited, in contrast to the president's reserved, almost gloomy personality. Nevertheless, the Coolidges enjoyed a solid union because they complemented each other's characters exceedingly well. "For almost a quarter of a century she was borne with my infirmities, and I have rejoiced in her graces," Calvin Coolidge said of his wife in his autobiography. Their otherwise happy years in the White House were marred by the tragedy of the death of their son, Calvin Jr., in 1924.

Vermont Native

Grace Coolidge, the first graduate of a public university to become a first lady, was born in Burlington, Vermont, in 1879. She was the only child of Andrew Goodhue, a mechanical engineer and steamboat inspector for the Lake Champlain Transportation Company, and Lemira B. Goodhue, a quiet, serious woman. Grace graduated from Burlington High School in 1897 and lived at home during her years as a student at the University of Vermont. She was a popular student, known for a high-spirited personality, and was a member of Pi Beta Phi, the first Greek sorority for women.

After she graduated in 1902, Grace convinced her parents to allow her to move to another state to begin a career; this was almost unheard of at the time, even a college graduate, since almost no females lived outside households that were headed by a father or a husband. The sister of one of her Burlington neighbors was head of the Clarke School for the Deaf in Northampton, Massachusetts, where the inventor of the telephone, Alexander Graham Bell, had once taught. Grace entered the school's teacher training program that fall.

Marriage and the Northampton Years

Grace met Calvin Coolidge in Northampton. A graduate of Amherst College, he was a young attorney who boarded at the home of Amherst's steward, Robert Weir. One day while passing on the street, Grace noticed a man standing in a window of the Weir house wearing a suit of long underwear and a hat, and shaving in front of a mirror. She asked Weir about this strange man, and he arranged an introduction. Coolidge explained to Grace that he wore a hat when he shaved because of a lock of hair that wouldn't stay in place.

The two began dating, although their personalities could not have been more unsuited to such a match. Grace was outgoing and enthusiastic, and Calvin was a man of very few words who often had a gloomy expression on his face. Weir offered the opinion that since Grace had been trained to teach the deaf to hear, possibly she could also teach a mute to speak.

Lemira Goodhue tried to discourage the relationship between her daughter and the lawyer who was seven years older, but Grace didn't take her advice. She and Calvin were married at her parents' home in Burlington on October 4, 1905. After they got back from a honeymoon

Right: The Coolidges loved to entertain, especially guests like actor John Drew (to the right of Grace) and entertainer Al Jolson (to the right of Calvin).

in Montreal, Coolidge presented his bride with fifty-two pairs of socks that he had been waiting to have mended; incredibly thrifty, he had been saving the socks with the hope that some day he'd find a wife who would repair them for him. The couple lived in half of a double house on Massasoit Street in Northampton, where their first son, John, was born in September 1906. A second son, Calvin Jr., arrived two years later.

Grace was often left alone with her sons in Northampton for long periods of time when her husband's new political career took him away. Although he was in Boston more than he was at home, he didn't want to spend the money to relocate his household to the far more expensive city. Coolidge became a Massachusetts legislator in 1907, and then went back to Northampton to serve four years as its mayor. He went to Boston again when elected to the state senate in 1912, but on weekends he went home, often spending Saturday nights watching the children so that Grace could visit with friends.

An Apolitical Wife

Grace was an active mother, often playing baseball with her boys. She noted in her autobiography that Coolidge never discussed topics of a political nature or even current events with her; and she usually learned of his decisions from newspapers, like everyone else. She believed that he considered her education inadequate.

Coolidge's stubbornness about maintaining a cheaper household for his family and having them live in Northampton during his term as governor caused some

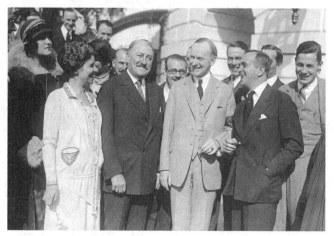

Above: Women were just beginning to take an interest in politics during the Coolidge years, and those of the Republican persuasion were welcomed at his White House.

head scratching among sophisticated Bostonians, but it enhanced his reputation as a cost-cutter, which was good for his political image. Curiously, his penny-pinching didn't extend to his wife's wardrobe. He liked to window-shop for her in Boston; sometimes he bought her extravagant hats, and it wasn't unusual to see him board the train for Northampton carrying an oversized hatbox.

When Coolidge became vice president after the victory of Warren G. Harding in the 1920 presidential election, Grace suddenly found herself the subject of a great deal of media attention, which she handled with characteristic style. The Coolidges moved to Washington, while their sons attended Mercersburg Academy, a school about a hundred miles away. The family spent their summer vacations at the Coolidge farmstead in Plymouth Notch, Vermont, where Calvin's father still lived. Grace was there with her husband in August 1923 when Harding became ill on the other side of the country; and a messenger arrived in the middle of the night with the news that he had died. Grace stood near as her husband took the oath of office, administered by his father, a notary public.

White House Tragedy

The Harding administration had been rocked by scandals, and as president, Coolidge was determined to restore faith in the Republican leadership. While he went about his official duties, Grace kept White House social events at a subdued level, appropriate for a mourning period following Harding's death and the scandals her husband was working to put to rest. Gradually, the

Coolidges began inviting celebrities to official dinners, beginning a practice that still continues.

The new first lady was seen as a positive attribute in her husband's political career. The press loved her sincerity and unaffectedness, as well as her photogenic qualities. Grace participated enthusiastically in her official duties and at such events as opening rest homes for veterans or ceremoniously laying cornerstones of new buildings.

In 1924, the younger Coolidge son, Calvin, died tragically during the same summer his father was nominated to run for a full term on the Republican presidential ticket. Not wearing socks with his sneakers during a tennis game, the youngster developed a blister on his foot and it became seriously infected. With an endurance for pain perhaps inherited from his father, Calvin Jr. didn't say anything about the wound for a few days and the infection went into his bloodstream. By the time blood poisoning was diagnosed, doctors told the Coolidges that the boy's condition was grave. The most modern medical treatments were attempted, but the infection still lingered, and after two days of severe illness, young Calvin died. His death shocked the country: Telegrams and letters of sympathy poured in to Washington from across the country and around the world.

The Coolidges buried their sixteen-year-old son in Plymouth Notch, took a small Vermont spruce tree back to Washington, and had it planted on the south grounds

Left: Grace Coolidge was an animal lover, and she was especially fond of her pet raccoon, Rebecca.

of the White House, near the tennis courts, where they placed a plaque commemorating the younger Coolidge's brief life. Grace Coolidge wrote a memorial poem to her son, "The Open Door," which was published in *Good Housekeeping* magazine in 1929.

Later Years

While she wasn't a political activist, Grace took advantage of a photographic opportunity staged on the White House lawn in 1925 that showed her filling out her absentee ballot for the upcoming elections. She firmly believed that American women weren't taking full advantage of their recently won right to vote.

After Coolidge declined to run for a second full term in 1928, he and Grace went home to Northampton, where they bought an estate called The Beeches. After a few happy years of retirement there, Coolidge died of a heart attack in January 1933, and Grace sold the house soon afterward, saying that it was too large for one person.

She stayed active in many ways over the next two decades, riding in an airplane for the first time and traveling to Europe in 1936. During World War II, she carried food and gifts to the train station for soldiers who were heading overseas. She also loved to listen to Boston Red Sox baseball games on the radio and to spend time with her son, John, his wife Florence, and their two daughters. When Northampton's Forbes Library created a Calvin Coolidge Memorial Room, Grace was invited to the dedication in September 1956. It would be her last public appearance. Grace Coolidge died on July 8, 1957.

Right: Grace Coolidge loved baseball almost as much as she loved Calvin, and she appeared at the 1949 World Series, even through it was between the New York Yankees and the Brooklyn Dodgers and her favorite team, the Boston Red Sox, was sitting it out.

Coolidge's Speech on Government and Business

Delivered on November 19, 1925

Calvin Coolidge presided during a period of economic prosperity called the "Roaring Twenties." His pro-business administration emphasized limiting government regulations on business activity. He lowered taxes, reasoning that the money individuals and businesses saved on paying taxes could be spent on investments to further encourage business growth.

Because Coolidge did not propose many government programs, some thought of him as a "do-nothing president," content to let the country run on its own. He believed that the same freedoms enjoyed by American citizens ought to be extended to business as well. Not known as a great speechmaker, he was famous instead for brief remarks, such as: "The chief business of the American people is business," a quote from a speech the president gave to the American Society of Newspaper Editors on January 17, 1925. Business and government was also the theme of this 1925 address to the New York State Chamber of Commerce.

Excerpt from Coolidge's Speech on Government

If a contest could be held to determine how much those who are really prominent in our government life know about business, and how much those who are really prominent in our business life know about government, it is my firm conviction that the prize would be awarded those who are in government life. This is as it ought to be, for those who have the greater authority ought to have the greater knowledge. But it is my even firmer conviction that the general welfare of our country could be very much advanced through a better knowledge by both of those parties of the multifold problems with which each has to deal. While our system gives an opportunity for great benefit by encouraging detachment and breadth of vision which ought not to be sacrificed, it does not have the advantages which could be secured if each had a better conception of their mutual requirements.

While I have spoken of what I believed would be the advantages of a more sympathetic understanding, I should put an even stronger emphasis on the desirability of the largest possible independence between government and business. Each ought to be sovereign in its own sphere. When government comes unduly under the influence of business, the tendency is to develop an administration which closes the door of opportunity; becomes narrow and selfish in its outlook; and results in an oligarchy. When government enters the field of business with its great resources, it has a tendency to extravagance and inefficiency, but, having

the power to crush all competitors, likewise closes the door of opportunity and results in monopoly. It is always a problem in a republic to maintain on the one side that efficiency which comes only from trained and skillful management without running into fossilization and autocracy, and to maintain on the other that equality of opportunity which is the result of political and economic liberty without running into dissolution and anarchy. The general results in our country, our freedom and prosperity, warrant the assertion that our system of institutions has been advancing in the right direction in the attempt to solve these problems. We have order, opportunity, wealth, and progress.

[…]

True business represents the mutual organized effort of society to minister to the economic requirements of civilization. It is an effort by which men provide for the material needs of each other. While it is not an end in itself, it is the important means for the attainment of a supreme end. It rests squarely on the law of service. It has for its main reliance truth and faith and justice. In its larger sense it is one of the greatest contributing forces to the moral and spiritual advancement of the race.

It is the important and righteous position that business holds in relation to life which gives warrant to the great interest which the National Government constantly exercises for the promotion of its success. This is not exercised as has been the autocratic practice abroad of directly supporting and financing different business projects, except in case of great emergency, but we have rather held to a democratic policy of cherishing the general structure of business while holding its avenues open to the widest competition, in order that its opportunities and its benefits might be given the broadest possible participation. While it is true that the Government ought not to be and is not committed to certain methods of acquisition which, while partaking of the nature of unfair practices try to masquerade under the guise of business, the Government is and ought to be thoroughly committed to every endeavor of production and distribution which is entitled to be designated as true business. Those who are so engaged, instead of regarding the Government as their opponent and enemy, ought to regard it as their vigilant supporter and friend.

It is only in exceptional instances that this means a change on the part of the national administration so much as it means a change on the part of trade. Except for the requirements of safety, health, and taxation, the law enters very little into the work of production. It is mostly when we come to the problems of distribution that we meet the more rigid exactions of legislation. The main reason why certain practices in this direction have been denounced is because they are a species of unfair competition on the one hand or tend to monopoly and restraint of trade on the other. The whole policy of the Government in its system of opposition to monopoly, and its public regulation of transportation and trade, has been animated by a desire to have business remain business. We are a politically free people and must be an economically free people.

[…]

[The] present generation of business almost universally throughout its responsible organization and management has shown every disposition to correct its own abuses with as little intervention of the Government as possible. This position is recognized by the public, and due to the appreciation of the needs which the country has for great units of production in time of war, and to the better understanding of the service which they perform in time of peace, resulting very largely from the discussion of our tax problems, a new attitude of the public mind is distinctly discernible toward great aggregations of capital. Their prosperity goes very far to insure the prosperity of all the country. The contending elements have each learned a most profitable lesson.

This development has left the Government free to advance from the problems of reform and repression to those of economy and construction. A very large progress is being made in these directions. Our country is in a state of unexampled and apparently sound and well distributed prosperity. It did not gain wealth, as some might hastily conclude, as a result of the war. Here and there individuals may have profited greatly, but the country as a whole was a heavy loser. Forty billions of the wealth of the Nation was directly exhausted, while the indirect expenditure and depreciation can not be estimated. The Government appreciated that the only method of regeneration lay in economy and production. It has followed a policy of economy in national expenditures. By an enormous reduction in taxation it has released great amounts of capital for use in productive effort. It has sought to stimulate domestic production by a moderate application of the system of protective tariff duties. The results of these efforts are known to all the world.

[…]

Great as the accomplishments have been, they are yet but partly completed. We need further improvement in transportation facilities by development of inland waterways; we need railroad consolidations; we need further improvement of our railway terminals for more economical distribution of commodities in the great congested centers; we need reorganization of Government departments; we need still larger extension of electrification; in general, we need still further effort against all the various categories of waste which the Department of Commerce has enumerated and so actively attacked, for in this direction lies not only increased economic progress but the maintenance of that progress against foreign competition. There is still plenty of work for business to do.

What Happened Next

America continued to prosper throughout President Coolidge's presidency. His policy of minimal government involvement in business encouraged further economic growth. Coolidge's similar approach to other areas of American life proved more frustrating to many Americans. Numerous farmers faced bankruptcy with the absence of federal assistance during times of drought or flooding. Improvements in civil rights were few, though some historians believe Coolidge's efforts on that issue were superior to those of his five predecessors.

Coolidge did not act against risky business practices that allowed investors to buy stocks on margin. Many stocks became overvalued because investors were continually buying, selling, and trading them at ever higher prices. Little more than six months after Coolidge left office, the prices of stock suddenly nosedived, and many people lost money. The collapse of the stock market was the start of the Great Depression, which lasted for more than a decade.

Coolidge did not have to face such a formidable challenge during his presidency. His pro-business approach and policy of limited government worked well enough during his administration in a time of peace and prosperity. Doing more to help expand prosperity and to protect against such events as the stock market collapse would have resulted in a different kind of presidency than Coolidge offered.

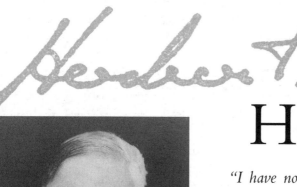

Herbert Hoover

"I have no fears for the future of the country. It is bright with hope."

—*Herbert Hoover*

Thirty-first president of the United States, 1929–1933

Full name: *Herbert Clark Hoover*

Born: *August 10, 1874, West Branch, Iowa*

Died: *October 20, 1964, New York, New York*

Burial site: *Herbert Hoover National Historic Site, West Branch, Iowa*

Parents: *Jesse Clark and Hulda Randall Minthorn Hoover*

Spouse: *Lou Henry (1875–1944; m. 1899)*

Children: *Herbert Charles (1903–1969); Allan Henry (1907–1993)*

Religion: *Society of Friends (Quaker)*

Education: *Stanford University (B.A., 1895)*

Occupation: *Mining engineer*

Government positions: *Public administrator; secretary of commerce under Warren G. Harding and Calvin Coolidge; food relief coordinator*

Political party: *Republican*

Dates as president: *March 4, 1929–March 4, 1933*

Age upon taking office: *54*

Herbert Hoover had a long and distinguished career in public service and private business. He was a self-made man, becoming a multimillionaire as a mining engineer. A world traveler by the time he was thirty, he had a narrow escape during the 1900 Boxer Rebellion in China when he was twenty-six. When World War I broke out, he used some of his own money to help Americans who were stranded in Europe. His public service with several war relief agencies earned him a place on a list of the ten greatest living Americans published by the *New York Times* shortly after the war.

After serving with distinction as secretary of commerce for presidents Warren G. Harding and Calvin Coolidge during the 1920s, Hoover was elected president in 1928. His earlier accomplishments with war relief agencies had earned him a great reputation for "crisis management," but no one could predict that during his first year as president, he would face the most serious economic crisis in American history: the stock market crash in October 1929 and the Great Depression that followed it.

Hoover believed that communities should unite together to help themselves during times of crisis, but the Great Depression seemed to defy any solution. None of the modest policies he supported made any real impact on a problem that seemed to only get worse. Predictably, Hoover's popularity had almost completely vanished by the time he left office in 1933. He was able to recover

Timeline

1874: Born in Iowa
1885: Left an orphan, Hoover travels by train from Iowa to Oregon to live with an uncle
1897: Hired by Bewick, Moreing, a London mining firm, and sent to Australia to search for gold
1900: While working in China, Hoover is trapped along with his wife and other Westerners in an uprising against foreigners called the Boxer Rebellion
1908: Forms his own mining and engineering consulting firm
1914: Organizes assistance and safe passages for Americans stranded in Europe at the beginning of World War I; also forms the Commission for the Relief of Belgium during the war
1915–19: Heads the U.S. Food Administration
1921–28: Serves as secretary of commerce under presidents Warren G. Harding and Calvin Coolidge
1929–33: Serves as thirty-first U.S. president
1929: Stock market crashes; Great Depression begins (ends in 1941)
1946: Named head of the international Famine Relief Commission by President Harry S Truman and visits twenty-five countries in less than two months to supervise relief measures
1964: Dies in New York

Below: Seven American presidents were born in log cabins, and Herbert Hoover came close when he first saw the light of day in this simple house in West Branch, Iowa.

some public respect through his efforts during World War II when he managed relief efforts for war victims once again, but his name still doesn't inspire the respect it deserves.

Quaker Heritage

Herbert Clark Hoover was born on August 10, 1874, in West Branch, Iowa, a Quaker community. The values of the Quakers he was raised among—hard work, community cooperation, spirituality, and nonviolence—deeply influenced him all of his life. Orphaned before he was ten years old, Hoover was sent to Oregon to live with his uncle, Henry Hinthorn, a physician and real-estate agent. Hinthorn planned to send him to a Quaker college, but instead Herbert enrolled in the newly established Stanford University in California to study mining and engineering. To support himself, he ran a laundry service and delivered newspapers. He spent summers working for the U.S. Geological Survey and worked for the agency full-time after he graduated from Stanford in 1895.

He was offered a job with British mining company Bewick, Moreing two years later and worked as a scout looking for mineral deposits in Western Australia. Then Hoover was promoted to become the company's representative in China. Before traveling there to begin

Right: Both Herbert and Lou Hoover were educated at California's Stanford University, and ranked among its most loyal alumni.

Left: In August 1900, American, British, and Japanese troops were brought in to put down the Boxer Rebellion in Peking, China. Here, Christian Chinese refugees assemble at the boat landing on the Pei-ho, Tientsin, China.

Insider

After Hoover became a partner in one of the world's biggest mining firms, it was revealed that one of the senior partners had embezzled a million dollars from it. Lawyers assured them that the other partners weren't liable for the loss, but Hoover believed they were and that they should all chip in to repay the money, which he said actually belonged to their clients. However, his share of the repayment was all the money he had saved in Australia and China. He was broke again, but wouldn't be for long.

Crisis Management

Not long after the birth of their second son, Allan Henry, Hoover started his own engineering consulting firm, with offices in several major cities across the United States and in Europe. When World War I broke out in 1914, thousands of Americans either living or traveling in Europe discovered that their money had lost its value and travel was restricted. The Hoovers were among those trapped in London, and when an angry mob of Americans descended on the American consulate, the U.S. ambassador called on Hoover for help. Backed by his personal assets of more than $10 million, he formed an organization with the long-winded, if not descriptive, name of "The Committee of American Residents in London for Assistance to American Travelers," which organized lodging and food for stranded Americans and arranged for safe passage home. Every stranded American traveler was safely back home in less than six weeks.

his new job, he went back to California to marry Louise "Lou" Henry, a geology student he had met at Stanford. After their wedding in February 1899, the newlyweds sailed to China to begin a life together that would take them to the four corners of the world.

Living in Beijing, China, the Hoovers soon found themselves in the midst of the dangerous, antiforeigner Boxer Rebellion. "Boxers" was the name Westerners gave to a group of Chinese nationalists, who called themselves "The Righteous and Harmonious Fists." Their goal was to drive foreigners out of their country by force, and the Hoovers were caught in the middle of it when the rebels surrounded the city of Tienjin, where Hoover was working, and kept it under siege for several weeks. After the troubles died down, Hoover continued working in China, and before long he was made a junior partner in Bewick, Moering, involved in strategic planning and decision-making. The Hoovers and their son, Herbert Charles, spent the next seven years traveling around the world while Herbert supervised company operations in Asia, Africa, and Europe.

Time Saver

During his business career Herbert Clark Hoover always signed his name with his middle initial. Then, when he took his first government job as food administrator in the Wilson administration, he dropped the C. forever. He figured that as a public official he would have to sign his name hundreds of times a day, and that by dropping the letter he might save as much as half an hour a week for more important things. In everything he did, Herbert (C.) Hoover was a model of efficiency.

Left: As head of the post-World War I American Relief Administration, Hoover oversaw the shipment of millions of tons of food to Europe.

Helping Hand

When the shooting started in World War I, officers of Hoover's company in Russia, Australia, Burma, and South Africa all sent urgent messages to him in London that banks were closing and payrolls couldn't be met, that their workers were being dragooned into the military. His mining empire was crashing around him, but then he found out that other people had problems, too. Thousand of Americans in Britain were being turned out of hotels that no longer accepted dollars, and the banks wouldn't exchange them, which left them out on the street even though they had money in their pockets. Hoover took all of the gold and currency from his office and set up shop, exchanging American dollars for British pounds. He knew that other American were also stranded in Europe, and galvanized his friends to help them get to London. Before the operation ended, in a record six weeks, more than 120,000 Americans managed to escape the war thanks to Herbert Hoover. He loaned them more than $1.5 million, and every penny was repaid.

His almost unbelievable accomplishment in London led to Hoover's appointment as head of the Committee for Relief of Belgium (CRB). Germany had invaded Belgium during the first weeks of the war, and the country, heavily dependent on food imports, was facing the threat of famine under foreign occupation. Hoover wasn't certain he could do the job, but he quickly found ways to set up a distribution system and thanks to him, the Belgians were saved from starvation.

The American press characterized Herbert Hoover as one of the great heroes of the European War, and their praise didn't go unnoticed in the White House. President Woodrow Wilson appointed him to head the U.S. Food Administration when America formally entered the war itself, and as the country's "food czar," Hoover created programs and rallied support to conserve food resources at home so that food supplies would be available for the men on the front lines. His program, which was called "Hooverizing," cut American food consumption by fifteen percent.

After the war ended in 1919, Hoover was offered several positions to oversee a host of charities feeding and clothing millions of European refugees. Hoover himself founded the American Relief Administration (ARA) to fight famine in Europe, and Congress gave him $100 million to finance it. It made him a hero all over again in Europe. At a ceremony in Poland, a parade of children greeted him with a banner that read "God Bless Herbert Hoover." At one point, a group of them scattered, and then rejoined the procession with a rabbit they caught and presented it to him.

Right: Less than a year after the hungry marched on Washington, veterans looking for relief appeared in their wake. They were received much less compassionately.

More Public Service

With the relief effort up and running, Hoover decided to the get back to his mining business and was looking forward to settling into his family's new house on a Palo Alto, California, hillside, but his plan was put on hold when Warren G. Harding was elected president and asked Hoover to serve in his cabinet as secretary of commerce.

Hoover took the assignment and landed running, reorganizing what had been a minor cabinet department. During the next eight years under Harding and his successor, Calvin Coolidge, he instituted a manufacturing code program that regulated manufacturing standards, and common products, like nuts and bolts, paper, automobile tires, and even milk bottles began being made in specific standard sizes for the first time. He also put together a set of municipal building codes that introduced standardization in the construction industry. These regulations, taken for granted today, simplified manufacturing processes and made it easier for consumers to know what they were buying and to find replacement parts when they needed them. Hoover oversaw the issuing of broadcast licenses as radios began appearing in American homes during the 1920s, and he worked to expand foreign markets for American products as well.

Hoover was selected by President Coolidge to supervise relief efforts during a particularly severe Mississippi River flood in 1927, and he convinced business and industry leaders to lend resources to help. He firmly believed in community cooperation in such situations, a reflection of his Quaker upbringing, and he preferred volunteer efforts over emergency laws and federal cash assistance. Some victims of the flooding claimed that the government wasn't doing enough to help them and, against the wishes of both Hoover and Coolidge, Congress passed relief legislation that included an expansion of government responsibilities and obligations to states in emergency situations. The crisis, and Hoover's response to it, would foreshadow events of his presidency.

Right: As commerce secretary, Herbert Hoover set laws in motion to regulate the radio broadcasting industry. In those days everyone listened to radio programs through earphones.

"Many years go I concluded that a few hair shirts were part of the mental wardrobe of every man. The president differs only from other men in that he has a more extensive wardrobe."

—Herbert Hoover

The Election of 1928

When Calvin Coolidge announced that he wouldn't run for another term, Hoover was urged by Republican Party leaders to run for office for the first time in his life. He accepted their nomination in 1928 with Kansas Senator Charles Curtis as his running mate. Democrat Alfred E. Smith, the progressive governor of New York, was the Democratic Party's choice to run against him.

The 1928 election was one of the uglier campaigns of the era, although both candidates maintained a sense of decency toward each other. Smith met with prejudice over his religion (he was the first Roman Catholic to run for president), and Hoover was opposed by poor people,

Above: Former New York governor Al Smith, the first Roman Catholic candidate for the presidency fueled by a major party, lost to Hoover in the 1928 election.

small farmers, and laborers—those who hadn't benefited from the economic prosperity of the 1920s. Not a comfortable public speaker, Hoover made only seven speeches during the campaign, but he won the election by a large margin, and Curtis became the most prominent government official with a Native American heritage.

Hoover's oath of office was administered by former President William Howard Taft, who had become chief justice of the Supreme Court. At the time of Hoover's inaugural, America's prosperity and its outlook for the future was at an all-time high. He reflected that optimism in his inaugural address when he said, "I have no fears for the future of our country. It is bright with hope."

The American economy had been robust throughout the 1920s, and almost everyone seemed better off, from businessmen to working-class Americans. There were some warning signs, however. Many Americans were borrowing money from banks, based more on confidence in the future than their current income, and others were all too eager to make investments in risky enterprises.

Right: In what many regarded as a bad omen, a blizzard hit Washington a week before Hoover's inauguration. It melted away before the big day, but it might have been a sign of bad days to come.

1928 Election Results

Presidential / Vice Presidential Candidates	Popular Votes	Electoral Votes
Herbert Hoover / Charles Curtis (Republican)	21,392,190	444
Alfred E. Smith / Joseph T. Robinson (Democratic)	15,016,443	87

Incumbent president Calvin Coolidge chose not to run for another term. He still received seventeen votes for the Republican nomination.

Right: The country was in an upbeat mood the day Herbert Hoover became president. His inaugural ball at the Washington Auditorium gave revelers enough standing room, but not much space for dancing.

The Hoover Administration

Administration Dates:	March 4, 1929–March 4, 1933
Vice President:	Charles Curtis (1929–33)
Cabinet:	
Secretary of State	Henry L. Stimson (1929–33)
Secretary of the Treasury	Andrew W. Mellon (1929–32)
	Ogden L. Mills (1932–33)
Secretary of War	James W. Good (1929)
	Patrick J. Hurley (1929–33)
Attorney General	William D. Mitchell (1929–33)
Secretary of the Navy	Charles F. Adams (1929–33)
Postmaster General	Walter F. Brown (1929–33)
Secretary of the Interior	Ray L. Wilbur (1929–33)
Secretary of Agriculture	Arthur M. Hyde (1929–33)
Secretary of Labor	James J. Davis (1929–30)
	William N. Doak (1930–33)
Secretary of Commerce	Robert P. Lamont (1929–32)
	Roy D. Chapin (1932–33)

During his first months in office, Hoover enacted a program of reform aimed at some policies that had been putting investors and debtors in financial jeopardy. The Agricultural Marketing Act of 1929, which was part of it, established the Federal Farm Board to ensure that crop prices stayed at stable rates and to provide loans to farmers who pooled their resources in agricultural cooperatives. While their neighbors in cities and towns were giddy with prosperity, many of America's farmers were on the brink of financial ruin.

The Crash of 1929

In October 1929, President Hoover took a trip to a museum complex built by automaker Henry Ford at Dearborn, Michigan. Hoover was there to celebrate the fiftieth anniversary of the invention of electric light in the company of inventor Thomas A. Edison—at the laboratory where electric light had been invented—which had been relocated to Ford's museum from Menlo Park, New Jersey.

As Hoover was returning to Washington on October 24, the value of stocks was beginning to fall, and crowds were gathering outside the New York Stock Exchange, where frantic trading was underway. Overnight, panic began to sweep the nation. Fortunes were lost, and banks were closing their doors. The president tried to reassure the nation by announcing that "the fundamental business of the country, that is, the production and distribution of commodities, is on a sound and prosperous basis."

Secretary of the Treasury Andrew W. Mellon was convinced that the stock market would balance itself out, and most leading economists agreed with him. Hoover wasn't quite so sure, though, and he called a series of meetings with top business leaders, convincing them to pledge that profits, and not wages, would be the first victims of an economic depression. He believed that common sacrifice was the only way to head off widespread misery.

He urged state and local governments to expand public works projects as a way of creating more jobs, and by early 1930, the stock market tumble seemed to have passed its worst stage, prompting Hoover to announce in February that the worst was over. Still, unemployment was still rising, and many banks were beginning to foreclose on mortgages, forcing people out of their homes. The situation went from bad to worse when a serious drought struck the Great Plains during the summer of 1930. Thousands of farmers went bankrupt, banks failed in every state, and 5 million people were out of work.

Hoover worked tirelessly to find a way out of the deep depression that had set in. He was out of bed before

Above: Soup kitchens sprung up in every part of the country during the Great Depression. This one, in Chicago, was financed by mobster Al Capone.

Backfire

When President Hoover urged business leaders not to cut wages, most kept their promise to keep wage rates stable for about a year. Henry Ford even raised his workers' pay to seven dollars an hour. But as the Depression got worse, many corporations began reducing payrolls as an alternative to cutting individual paychecks. The combined purchasing power of American consumers fell, and workers—worried that they might be laid off—stopped spending, which only made a bad situation worse. Only a few years earlier, these same people had been spending all of their current income and committing future income as well with installment buying.

dawn each day, held endless rounds of meetings, and cancelled all ceremonial public appearances. He urged state and local governments to involve themselves in relief efforts, but few could because their funding had dried up. After rejecting appeals to implement federal aid projects, Hoover became a public scapegoat for the nation's troubles.

Foreign Policy

By the summer of 1931, economic depression had reached Europe as well. Both Great Britain and France were experiencing difficulties in maintaining their World War I debt payments to the United States, and Hoover suspended the payments. While this move was necessary, it could only mean more economic trouble for the United States. Hardships were most difficult in Germany, which faced massive factory closings and widespread unemployment. Germany had tried parliamentary government after the war, but with limited success, and the German people were ready for a dramatic change. It seemed to be just around the corner when charismatic Adolf Hitler and his National Socialist Party gained a majority in the 1932 parliamentary elections. The following January, Hitler's fascist forces took over the government by forcing Germany's aging president, Paul von Hindenburg, to appoint Hitler as chancellor, the chief minister of the state.

Meanwhile, a crisis in Asia had begun in September 1931, when Japan invaded the resource-rich Chinese province of Manchuria. The major U.S. foreign policy initiative during Hoover's presidency came the following

Choice of Words

Modern presidents go to great lengths to use buzz words that put the right spin on what they're doing. Although the word "depression" had been used to describe economic downturns for years, it didn't have the same association with disaster as "crisis" or "panic," and Hoover made an early decision to call the 1929 tragedy a depression because it had a less ominous ring to it. He used the word early and often, until no one could think of any other to describe it.

Right: As the Hoover family was getting ready to celebrate its first Christmas in the White House, a raging fire destroyed most of the offices in the mansion.

year, when secretary of state Henry L. Stimson formulated what became known as the "Stimson Doctrine," which stated that nations whose governments were violently overthrown through rebellions would not enjoy formal diplomatic relations with the United States. Then the Hoover administration withdrew U.S. troops that had been sent to maintain peace in Nicaragua and Haiti.

Things Get Worse

Unemployment rose to over 8 million people in the United States by the summer of 1931. Thousands of homeless people began camping out in city parks like Chicago's Grant Park, when they couldn't find shelter anywhere else. Riots over scarce food supplies occurred in several cities.

Hoover's initiatives in 1932 intended to counteract the Depression only made him all the more unpopular. Early in the year, Congress passed a bill forming the Reconstruction Finance Corporation, which established a fund of $500 million to provide loans to banks, farmers, and major transportation companies to head off bankruptcies. Opponents claimed that it helped business

Brother, Can You Spare a Dime?

As the Depression grew grimmer, even former president "Silent Cal" Coolidge had to admit that "the country is not in good condition." A story that made the rounds was that Hoover asked a banker to loan him a nickel so he could call a friend. "Here's a dime. Call both of them," the banker responded.

leaders and their companies, but not the legions of poor and suffering people. By mid-1932, 12 million Americans were out of a job. Communities of cardboard huts sprang up across the country—in some cases near city garbage dumps, where it was easier to scavenge for food. These makeshift settlements were called "Hoovervilles." In some states, entire school systems were shut down because of lack of funds.

The worst public-relations move the Hoover administration made became known as the Bonus Army March. It had its roots back to 1925, when Congress authorized adjusted-compensation ("bonus") certificates to World War I veterans. During the Depression, unemployed veterans across the country began petitioning the government for early payoffs on those certificates, and Congress passed a bill that would allow them to be redeemed for $225 to $400 per veteran, but Hoover vetoed it in 1931.

A group of veterans united on the West Coast to begin a march on Washington, riding trains across the country toward the nation's capitol during the spring of 1932. By June, more than 20,000 of them were camped in Washington. Images of these down-and-out veterans begging the government for a few hundred dollars each and cooking skimpy meals over open fires became one of the starkest reflections of the Depression.

Many of the veterans eventually went home empty-handed, but about 2,000 stayed, quite possibly because they didn't have homes to go back to, which would help explain why they had their families with them. Fearing that the remaining veterans were being influenced by

Left: Lawyer Henry L. Stimson lent his negotiating talents to the Hoover administration in both Europe and Asia. He would serve Franklin D. Roosevelt as secretary of war, and supervised the development of the atomic bomb.

Right: Shack villages that sprung up in most cities during the Depression were called "Hoovervilles." The name association extended to everything they had, and an empty pocket turned inside out was called a "Hoover flag."

communists, Washington, D.C., police officers were called to remove some Bonus Marchers barricaded in a building. After shots were fired and one of the veterans was killed, the police backed off and U.S. Army general Douglas MacArthur was sent in with a military police squad to evict the Bonus Marchers from their encampment with orders for a restrained show of force. MacArthur called for a tear gas attack, however, and a civilian mob attacked the veterans and set fire to their cardboard huts. A baby was killed in the struggle.

Reelection Fails

When Democratic presidential candidate Franklin D. Roosevelt heard about the Washington riot, he said, "Well…this elects me," but he was already emerging as a popular alternative to Hoover among the voters. He fairly bubbled over with confidence and optimism, while Hoover was harassed and defensive. Several of Hoover's campaign stops were spoiled by crowds throwing eggs and tomatoes, and there were at least two attempts to sabotage railroad tracks ahead of his campaign train. Nearly 40 million people cast votes in the election of 1932, and 23 million of them voted for Roosevelt. Hoover received barely 40 percent of the popular vote.

After he left office, the former president established the Hoover Library on War, Revolution and Peace at Stanford University. He became an outspoken critic of President Roosevelt's New Deal program and gave serious consideration to running for the presidency again in 1936.

During World War II, Hoover headed the Polish Relief Commission, and his work was expanded in 1946 by President Harry S Truman, who named him to head the international Famine Relief Commission. The seventy-two-year-old Hoover visited twenty-five countries in less than two months to supervise relief measures. Truman also paid tribute to his engineering background by signing a Congressional resolution that officially named the Hoover Dam on the Colorado River in honor of the former president. It had been named the Hoover Dam while he was in office, but the Roosevelt administration referred to it as Boulder Dam.

"I outlived the bastards."

—*Herbert Hoover in his old age, explaining how he dealt with his critics*

As head of the Hoover Commission, organized to suggest improvements in federal government practices, Hoover made nearly 300 recommendations that were approved by Congress in 1947. Meanwhile, the former president also served as chairman of the Boys' Clubs of America for eight years. In 1962, on his eighty-eighth birthday, he was honored at the dedication ceremony of the Hoover Presidential Library in his birthplace of West Branch, Iowa. He died two years later, on October 20, 1964.

Legacy

Herbert Hoover's reluctance to have the federal government take charge during the early years of the Great Depression led voters to elect Franklin D. Roosevelt president in 1932, and Roosevelt's more aggressive federal action made him immensely popular: Voters reelected him president three more times, and he is generally viewed by historians as one of America's greatest presidents. Hoover, on the other hand, is typically ranked as one of the least effective. He was in charge when economic hard times hit the nation, and it is generally viewed that he didn't do enough to lift it from Depression.

Busy to the End

After he retired, Herbert Hoover moved into a $32,000-a-year suite on the thirty-first floor of New York's Waldorf Towers, where he lived for thirty years. He had four desks there, one for each of the books he was working on at any given time, and five secretaries who transcribed his penciled manuscripts. He personally answered more than 20,000 letters a month, because he thought that anyone thoughtful enough to write to him deserved an answer. Though a busy man, he indulged himself every afternoon at 5:00 with exactly one and a half Gibson cocktails, which he had invented himself years before, when he decided he didn't really like olives in his martinis and substituted little white onions instead.

"In many ways [Hoover] was superbly equipped for the presidency. If he had been president in 1921 or 1937, he might have ranked with the great presidents."

—former vice president John Nance Garner

Some economic reforms had been underway during Hoover's administration. In March 1932, he signed the Norris-LaGuardia Anti-Injunction Act, which stopped federal injunctions against strikes. The 1932 Revenue Act he signed increased taxes on corporations and large estates, and brought more money to the government for relief efforts. President Roosevelt's Works Projects Administration (WPA), praised for providing jobs for the unemployed, was a direct successor to the Emergency Relief and Construction Act; Hoover had signed that act into law in July 1932, authorizing $1.5 billion in funds for public works projects.

Hoover's other accomplishments include a major prison reform, which, along with some of his other actions, are often obscured by the universal miseries that were associated with the Great Depression.

Left: After World War II, Hoover took up where he had left before become president when President Harry S Truman made him head of the Famine Relief Commission.

Louise Hoover

Born March 29, 1874, Waterloo, Iowa
Died January 7, 1944, New York, New York

"[Lou was] a symbol of everything wholesome in American life."
—Herbert Hoover

The first woman in the United States to earn a degree in geology, Louise "Lou" Henry Hoover led an adventurous life. Whether globetrotting with her husband and two sons or serving actively in Washington as the wife of a politician, she had a wide range of hobbies and interests. Her husband once referred to her as "my good lady who already knows all about a thing or else finds out."

Lou and Bert Meet at Stanford

Like her future husband, Lou Hoover was a native of Iowa, born in the town of Waterloo in 1874. Her father, Charles D. Henry, was a banker who inspired in his daughter a love of the outdoors. When she was ten, her family moved west to California, hoping that a warmer climate would improve her mother, Florence's, weak health. Living in Monterey, Lou learned to hunt and fish with her father, and she also became an expert horseback rider as well as an avid hiker. During her hikes, she was fascinated by the colorful rocks and minerals she discovered in the hills of Northern California, and after attending a lecture on geology while she was still in high school, Lou abandoned her plans to become a teacher.

She enrolled in the geology program at Stanford University in Palo Alto, and it was where the tall, independent, first-year student first met Herbert Hoover in a laboratory on campus. A senior, he was a member of Stanford's first class when the university opened in 1891. After he graduated with a major in mining engineering, he left to work with mining companies, and within two years, he was earning a better-than-average salary as a mining engineer in Australia.

Lou and "Bert," as she called him, kept up a correspondence after he left school, and shortly after she left school herself, Bert was offered a job as a mining engineer in China. He sent her a letter telling her about it that also contained a marriage proposal.

They were married on February 10, 1899, and later that same day they boarded a boat bound for China. Lou began learning to speak Chinese, and she often accompanied her husband on mining expeditions. When a group of Chinese began a movement to halt the spread of foreign influences in their country, it turned into the violent Boxer Rebellion of 1900. Military forces from several countries arrived to protect their people and interests, but the Hoovers were trapped for two weeks in the town of Tienjin, during which time Lou Hoover carried a pistol for her own protection.

World Travelers

As Hoover's responsibilities with the mining company increased, he and his wife traveled together throughout Asia, Europe, and Africa inspecting or supervising various mining sites, and their two sons, Herbert Charles and Allan Henry, went everywhere with them.

Hoover started his own mining consulting firm in 1908, and the family was living in London, England, when World War I began seven years later. Lou worked closely with her husband in his work as head of a massive aid project to help tens of thousands of Americans stranded in Europe by the war. To distract these frightened Americans from their problems, Lou led them on tours of the English countryside, and during the war, she also assisted her husband with famine-relief effort. She had converted to her husband's Quaker faith shortly after their marriage, and performing these acts of charity was among the strong spiritual convictions they shared.

The Hoovers were both involved in several relief efforts during World War I, including the Committee for Relief of Belgium (CRB) and the U.S. Food Administration. After the war, he founded the American Relief Administration (ARA) to fight famine in Europe, and they were involved in other works as well. They found time to design their dream house in California, and they translated a 1556 text on metals, *De Re Metallica*, from the original Latin.

Twelve Years in Washington, D.C.

When Herbert Hoover was appointed secretary of commerce by President Warren G. Harding in 1921, the family moved to Washington, where Lou served for three years as president of the Girl Scouts of America, which stressed good citizenship, self-reliance, and outdoor activities for girls, exactly matching her own values. When her husband was elected president in 1928, Mrs. Hoover continued to work closely with the organization, which she had become involved with years before as a troop leader.

During the 1920s, Lou Hoover offered some daring public views for the time. She believed, for example, that a woman could have an active career after marrying and having children. She served in several organizations, including the National Amateur Athletic Federation (as the only woman officer), the National Women's Athletic Association, the American Association of University Women, and the National Geographic Society.

When scandal rocked the White House in the early 1920s over illegal financial deals involving several members of the Harding administration, Mrs. Hoover organized the national Women's Conference on Law Enforcement. Addressing over five hundred women from across the country at a meeting in Washington, she said that "women of the country are tired of seeing the laws of our land ignored." And she added: "We must arouse the whole country to an understanding of the dangerous significance of continued evasion of the law."

Lou Hoover took a similarly active position on the role of women in politics. In addition to urging women to vote, she encouraged them to become active in politics through community involvement and membership in the League of Women Voters, an organization dedicated to providing voters with information on issues and candidates.

Left: After her White House years, Lou Hoover stayed involved in a host of causes, including the Girl Scouts of America, an association she shared with First Lady Eleanor Roosevelt.

Right: Photography was among Lou Hoover's long list of avid interests, and she became a member of the White House News Photographers Association.

Right: The Hoovers were both animal lovers, and they had a small menagerie of pets that were mostly gifts from friends. But when an opossum wandered onto the White House Grounds, it became part of the gang.

Active First Lady

Mrs. Hoover softened some of her more strident, feminist statements after her husband's election to the presidency in 1928, but she continued to play an active role in causes she felt strongly about. She maintained her religious value of performing works of charity without expecting any recognition for them. Among topics she pursued publicly were health-related ones. For example, she encouraged women to stay active and to enjoy the outdoors during pregnancy, at a time when it was customary for them to stay indoors, and pregnancy was still being called "confinement."

When the United States faced a financial crisis in 1929 that began the Great Depression, the first lady delivered radio speeches urging Americans to share resources and help others in need. She usually spent full days in her office addressing pleas that arrived from struggling Americans, and hired a secretary to help answer her mail and to direct the needy to relief agencies. When no aid was available, Mrs. Hoover often sent some of her own money to help a family buy such necessities as shoes. Many people paid her back later, but she never cashed those checks, and her husband never knew of those personal acts of charity until after she died in 1944 and he found the checks hidden among her private papers.

In the White House, the Hoovers personally paid for their secretaries and staffs. Mrs. Hoover oversaw some White House renovations, including the restoration of a sitting room with furniture of the 1820s that was named the Monroe Room after the nation's fifth president, James Monroe. She also restored a room that had been used as a study by President Abraham Lincoln.

As the country faced deeper economic problems, the Hoovers received more bad press reports. Mrs. Hoover endured a controversy that was stirred in June 1930 when she hosted a tea for the wife of Oscar De Priest, an African-American congressman from Illinois. It was a bold move at the time, and the first lady was sternly condemned by southern newspapers that supported racial segregation.

The Hoovers remained deeply supportive of each other during their trying White House years. Whenever the president was away, Lou would send him a daily telegram offering her encouragement. When poverty-stricken veterans gathered in Washington in 1932, Mrs. Hoover arranged for food and beverages for them—the only gesture of help the veterans received from anyone in the government.

After Hoover lost his bid for reelection, he and his wife returned to Palo Alto, California, where Lou continued to work with the Girl Scouts and supported the Friends of Music at Stanford. The Hoovers moved to New York City a few years later and maintained an apartment at the Waldorf Towers, a part of the Waldorf-Astoria Hotel during the World War II years. The former first lady continued to assist her husband with relief efforts before she died of a heart attack in January 1944. She was buried in Palo Alto, but her body was later moved to West Branch, Iowa, where she was buried next to her husband, who died twenty years after her.

Hoover's "Rugged Individualism" Campaign Speech

Delivered on October 22, 1928

During the 1920s, the United States enjoyed a sustained period of economic prosperity. The Roaring Twenties was an exciting time: Cities were growing and the use of automobiles and airplanes becoming more widespread; there were new forms of popular media, like radio and movies, and new forms of music, like jazz; dance crazes swept through nightclubs, and sports like baseball and golf attracted many more fans. Business was booming, and people had jobs, usually well-paying ones.

The nation wasn't without difficulties during the Roaring Twenties, a period that generally dates from 1920 to 1928. Many rural areas did not enjoy economic prosperity, as farmers faced increasingly challenging market conditions that threatened their livelihood. Urban areas experienced sharp increases in crime. Prohibition—the ban on the manufacture and sale of alcohol—had been in effect since 1919, and criminals were finding ever more resourceful and violent ways to distribute and sell liquor. Many businesses and banks were enjoying large profits, while many citizens were borrowing money from banks to buy houses and land.

Some Americans wanted the government to be more active in addressing the nation's problems. Presidents in the first two decades of the century—Theodore Roosevelt, William Howard Taft, and Woodrow Wilson—had been successful in enacting policies that regulated business and improved social conditions.

Other Americans warned against increasing government power and influence. They pointed out that government involvement in business and social life in European countries had not been successful in achieving the kind of economic prosperity enjoyed in the United States. Some feared that the U.S. government would control certain industries or move toward socialism. Russia, for example, had already embraced socialism—an economic system where government controls the production and distribution of goods—and many Americans were appalled by the example.

Former U.S. secretary of commerce Herbert Hoover was the Republican presidential candidate in 1928. His insistence on limiting government involvement in American business and social affairs won out in the election that year. Americans expected that the good times of the Roaring Twenties would be sustained by Hoover, whose beliefs were similar to those of his predecessors, Warren G. Harding and Calvin Coolidge. Hoover was a self-made multimillionaire whose book American Individualism, published in 1922, praised the American system for encouraging individuals to succeed on their own, without any direction or assistance from government. That theme was prominent in his presidential campaign, where he extolled the value of "rugged individualism."

Excerpt from Hoover's "Rugged Individualism" Campaign Speech

During one hundred and fifty years we have built up a form of self government and a social system which is peculiarly our own. It differs essentially from all others in the world. It is the American system. [...] It is founded upon the conception that only through ordered liberty, freedom and equal opportunity to the individual will his initiative and enterprise spur on the march of progress. And in our insistence upon equality of opportunity has our system advanced beyond all the world.

[...]

When the war closed, the most vital of issues both in our own country and around the world was whether government should continue their wartime ownership and operation of many instrumentalities of production and distribution. We were challenged with a choice between the American system of rugged individualism and a European philosophy of diametrically opposed doctrines—doctrines of paternalism and state socialism. The acceptance of these ideas would have meant the destruction of self-government through centralization.

[...]

When the Republican Party came into full power it went at once resolutely back to our fundamental conception of the state and the rights and responsibility of the individual. Thereby it restored confidence and hope in the American people, it freed and stimulated enterprise, it restored the government to a position as an umpire instead of a player in the economic game. For these reasons the American people have gone forward in progress.

[...]

There is [in this election] ... submitted to the American people a question of fundamental principle. That is: shall we depart from the principles of our American political and economic system, upon which we have advanced beyond all the rest of the world.

[...]

When the Federal Government undertakes to go into commercial business it must at once set up the organization and administration of that business, and it immediately finds itself in a labyrinth. [...] Commercial business requires a concentration of responsibility. Our government to succeed in business would need to become in effect a despotism. There at once begins the destruction of self-government.

[...]

It is a false liberalism that interprets itself into the government operation of commercial business. Every step of bureaucratizing of the business of our country poisons the very roots of liberalism—that is political equality, free speech, free assembly, free press and equality of opportunity. It is not the road to more liberty, but to less liberty. Liberalism should not be striving to spread bureaucracy but striving to set bounds to it.

[...]

Liberalism is a force truly of the spirit, a force proceeding from the deep realization that economic freedom cannot be sacrificed if political freedom is to be preserved. [An expansion of the government's role in the business world] would cramp and cripple the mental and spiritual energies of our people. It would extinguish equality and opportunity. It would dry up the spirit of liberty and progress. [...] For a hundred and fifty years liberalism has found its true spirit in the American system, not in the European systems.

I do not wish to be misunderstood. [...] I am defining general policy. [...] I have already stated that where the government is engaged in public works for purposes of flood control, of navigation, of irrigation, of scientific research or national defense [...] it will at times necessarily produce power or commodities as a by-product.

Nor do I wish to be misinterpreted as believing that the United States is a free-for-all and devil-take-the-hindmost. The very essence of equality of opportunity and of American individualism is that there shall be no domination by any group or [monopoly] in this republic. [...] It is no system of laissez faire. [...]

I have witnessed not only at home but abroad the many failures of government in business. I have seen its tyrannies, its injustices, its destructions of self-government, its undermining of the very instincts which carry our people forward to progress. I have witnessed the lack of advance, the lowered standards of living, the depressed spirits of people working under such a system. [...]

And what has been the result of the American system? Our country has become the land of opportunity to those born without inheritance, not merely because of the wealth of its resources and industry but because of this freedom of initiative and enterprise. Russia has natural resources equal to ours. [...] But she has not had the blessings of one hundred and fifty years of our form of government and our social system.

By adherence to the principles of decentralized self-government, ordered liberty, equal opportunity, and freedom to the individual, our American experiment in human welfare has yielded a degree of well-being unparalleled in the world. It has come nearer to the abolition of poverty, to the abolition of fear of want, than humanity has ever reached before. Progress of the past seven years is proof of it.

[...]

The greatness of America has grown out of a political and social system and a method of [a lack of governmental] control of economic forces distinctly its own—our American system—which has carried this great experiment in human welfare farther than ever before in history. [...] And I again repeat that the departure from our American system [...] will jeopardize the very liberty and freedom of our people, and will destroy equality of opportunity not only to ourselves, but to our children.... .

What Happened Next

Hoover's 1928 speech, delivered just weeks before the presidential election, reflected the feeling of accomplishment and optimism that most Americans felt at the time. However, in October 1929—just over six months after Hoover took office—the United States was plunged into an economic crisis. Many people went bankrupt, banks failed, businesses closed, and people were out of work. The crisis soon turned into the Great Depression, in which more than ten million people were thrown out of their jobs.

Many factors contributed to the economic crisis, which grew worse during each year of Hoover's presidency. The situation was further complicated when foreign countries were unable to pay off debts they owed to the United States for assistance during World War I.

Reflecting his dislike of government interference in business affairs and the lives of people, Hoover tried to improve conditions through volunteer efforts. He wanted businesses to sacrifice profits to ensure that they could pay workers their rightful wages, and he urged states and local communities to actively seek ways to improve conditions.

Hoover lost public support as the Great Depression continued to worsen. His opponent in the 1932 presidential election, Franklin D. Roosevelt, appealed to voters by presenting plans that had the federal government taking an active role to improve social conditions and to stimulate the growth of employment opportunities. Roosevelt won the election and went on to become largely acknowledged as one of the greatest presidents.

Hoover bore the brunt of blame for the Great Depression, but later historical assessments are generally more positive. His values of individualism and minimal government interference in the affairs of business are still popular, especially in "normal" times when the nation isn't facing economic crises or at war.

Franklin D. Roosevelt

"When you get to the end of your rope, tie a knot and hang on."
—*Franklin D. Roosevelt*

Thirty-second president of the United States, 1933–1945

Full name: *Franklin Delano Roosevelt*
Born: *January 30, 1882, Hyde Park, New York*
Died: *April 12, 1945, Warm Springs, Georgia*
Burial site: *Family plot, Hyde Park, New York*
Parents: *James and Sara Delano Roosevelt*
Spouse: *Anna Eleanor Roosevelt (1884–1962; m. 1905)*
Children: *Anna Eleanor (1906–1975); James (1907–1991); Franklin Delano Jr. (1909–1909); Elliott (1910–1990); Franklin Delano Jr. (1914–1988); John Aspinwall (1916–1981)*
Religion: *Episcopalian*
Education: *Harvard University (B.A., 1903); attended Columbia Law School*
Occupations: *Lawyer; banker*
Government positions: *New York state senator and governor; assistant secretary of the navy under Woodrow Wilson*
Political party: *Democratic*
Dates as president: *March 4, 1933–January 20, 1937 (first term); January 20, 1937–January 20, 1941 (second term); January 20, 1941–January 20, 1945 (third term); January 20, 1945–April 12, 1945 (fourth term)*
Age upon taking office: *51*

Franklin D. Roosevelt was president during two of the most serious crises of the twentieth century—the Great Depression and World War II. During both of these ordeals, he was able to implement massive efforts and rally tremendous support from government and the American people. He was the only president elected more than twice, and he won each of his four presidential elections by wide margins.

Roosevelt was adept at building coalitions, often among competing political groups. He frequently favored experimentation and change when progress stalled. His social programs, together called the New Deal, offered relief and jobs to Americans struggling through the Depression, and it also reformed financial practices that had contributed to it. Roosevelt's administration instituted such acts as the Social Security program, which guaranteed financial support to retired Americans.

The Depression ended when the United States entered World War II in 1941. American industries were revived by manufacturing the materials needed to fight a global war, a large-scale effort that required supervision by many different agencies and military departments. As commander in chief, Roosevelt worked effectively with American military commanders and leaders of other nations to plan war strategies.

Old Money

FDR often described himself as a "Hudson River gentleman," and his father and grandfathers were squires of the Hyde Park estate they called Springwood since before the American Revolution. His great-great grandfather, Isaac Roosevelt, had secured the family fortune with a sugar-refining business, and his son, as future generations would do, married well and went into the banking business. The president's father, James, was a chip off the old block, with a successful coal business and a membership on the board of the Delaware and Hudson Railroad. He carefully avoided people he considered nouveaux riches, and once rejected a dinner invitation from the Vanderbilts because he didn't want to have to return the favor by inviting them to his house.

Roosevelt was the first physically challenged president: Stricken by polio at the age of thirty-nine, he couldn't walk without heavy leg braces and canes for the rest of his life. The public was largely unaware of how severe his illness had been, although polio was relatively common in those days, attacking skeletal muscles and the spinal cord, and frequently resulting in death. While polio took away Roosevelt's mobility, it didn't rob him of his enthusiasm or energy. Like his efforts against the Depression and American enemies during World War II, he was tireless and persistent, facing the challenges of living with a physical disability.

Below: After being crippled by polio, Franklin D. Roosevelt found relief in the mineral waters of Warm Springs, Georgia, where he established his "little White House."

Timeline

1882: Born in New York
1907: Passes bar exam
1910–13: Serves as New York state senator
1913–20: Serves as assistant secretary of the U.S. navy
1914–18: World War I
1914: Runs unsuccessfully as U.S. senate candidate
1920: Runs unsuccessfully as Democratic vice-presidential candidate
1921: Stricken with polio
1929–41: Great Depression
1929–33: Serves as New York governor
1933–45: Serves as thirty-second U.S. president
1933: New Deal programs begin in Congress
1939–45: World War II
1941: United States enters World War II after Japanese bomb Pearl Harbor
1945: Dies in Georgia; Japanese surrender, ending World War II

Value in Public Service

Franklin Delano Roosevelt was born January 30, 1882, at his family's Hudson River estate in Hyde Park, New York. His father, James Roosevelt, headed the family's successful coal and transportation business. He was a fifty-two-year-old widower of four years with a sixteen-year-old son when he married Sara Delano, who was twenty-six. She was from a wealthy New York family and had traveled widely by then.

Roosevelt's American ancestors stretched back to the 1640s, when Nicholas Roosevelt arrived from Holland, and eventually had two sons, Johannes and Jacobus. The family line from Johannes included Theodore Roosevelt, who was U.S. president from 1901 to 1909. Franklin D. Roosevelt came from the family line connected with Jacobus.

Roosevelt was raised in wealth on a large estate. He went to private schools and he had a governess until he was fourteen. He learned to speak French and German, enjoyed swimming, and became an expert sailor. He explored nature and collected stamps as a youngster, and he often spent summers traveling with his parents in Europe or staying at family summer homes along the east coast of the United States and Canada.

Above: Springwood, the Roosevelt estate at Hyde Park, New York.

Name Recognition

Roosevelt studied law at Columbia University but left without graduating after he passed the bar exam and found a good job with a corporate law firm. He grew restless, however, and an opportunity to run for the state senate excited him. His name recognition as a Roosevelt (Theodore Roosevelt had been a popular president and New York governor), his ability to use his own wealth to finance a campaign, and his interest in reform interested local Democratic leaders, and they handed him the nomination with pleasure.

Campaigning by car and listening to other people as much as making speeches, Roosevelt won as a Democrat in a mostly Republican district. As a state senator, he challenged legislation that was favored by powerful business interests, he supported women's suffrage, and he favored state control instead of private ownership of the energy industry. All of these things would prompt Establishment Republicans to characterize him a "traitor to his class," but that was only the beginning.

Roosevelt backed Democrat Woodrow Wilson for president in 1912 even though Theodore Roosevelt was running as a third-party candidate in the same election. Working closely with his friend Louis McHenry Howe,

He was sent to Groton, a prestigious preparatory school in Massachusetts, from 1896 to 1900 with students from other wealthy families, where they were drilled in the virtues of public service—a lesson that helped shape Roosevelt's outlook on life. He was only a fair student there and didn't get high grades when he went on to Harvard University, either. He became editor in chief of the *Harvard Crimson*, though, and even stayed an extra year just to keep the job, which he said prepared him for public service more than anything else he did.

While he was still in college, he fell in love with Anna Eleanor Roosevelt, a distant cousin—she was the daughter of Theodore Roosevelt's brother. Eleanor, as she preferred to be called, came from a troubled background. Her high-society mother didn't pay much attention to her, and her father was an alcoholic. She was orphaned at age ten.

At the Roosevelts' wedding ceremony on March 17, 1905, President Theodore Roosevelt escorted the bride up the aisle. The Roosevelts would have six children, one of whom died in infancy, and while their family life was prosperous and secure, it wasn't without problems; he had an affair with her personal secretary that went on for several years. Later, in 1921, when he was crippled by polio, Eleanor nursed him and helped him continue an active life.

Below: Following a tradition he began as a candidate for the New York State Senate, Roosevelt relied on his wife's presence in most of his campaign tours.

a former journalist, he had developed into a brilliant political strategist and an important asset to the Wilson campaign in the East. After Wilson won the election, Roosevelt accepted his offer for the job of assistant secretary of the navy and moved with his family to Washington. It was the same post that Theodore Roosevelt had held during President William McKinley's first term.

Stressing preparedness and expansion of the navy as World War I loomed, Roosevelt showed a rare talent for working with a variety of people—from admirals leading fleets of ships, to business tycoons negotiating for government contracts. Those people skills, however, didn't help him much when he failed to win the Democratic nomination for the U.S. Senate in 1914.

Right: Roosevelt made his debut on the national scene as assistant secretary of the navy in the Woodrow Wilson administration.

Hardships and Perseverance

After his distinguished service in the Wilson administration, Roosevelt was chosen in 1920 as the Democratic vice-presidential running mate of Ohio governor James M. Cox. Young, handsome, energetic, and a proven administrator, Roosevelt worked hard, but it was a losing cause. Cox and Roosevelt were associated with the policies of the Wilson administration, and Americans had turned away from them. Republican Warren G. Harding's call for a "return to normalcy" was more in tune with the mood of the times than the progressive idea the Democrats were selling, and Harding and his running mate, Calvin Coolidge, won in a landslide. After the election, Roosevelt became a partner in a New York law firm.

"If [Roosevelt] became convinced tomorrow that coming out for cannibalism would get him votes … he would be fattening up a missionary in the White House backyard come Wednesday."
—*H. L. Mencken*

Roosevelt was stricken by polio the following August, and just as he approached nearly every political challenge and social problem, he tried many ways to overcome the affliction that paralyzed his legs. He visited many doctors,

tried various medicines, exercised vigorously, and made frequent trips to Warm Springs, Georgia, in hopes that the warm waters there could help heal him. In spite of it all, he wasn't able to walk without leg braces and a cane, but he didn't let that slow him down.

Still a political force, Roosevelt nominated New York governor Alfred E. Smith for president at the Democratic convention in 1924, and although Smith wasn't chosen, Roosevelt helped rally a dispirited Democratic Party that had been losing ground to the Republicans. He encouraged the Democrats to become an aggressive alternative by saying that "progressivism with the brakes on" is preferable to "conservatism with a move on."

The New Deal

In 1928, he campaigned successfully for Smith's nomination and agreed to run for governor of New York to help him win that state's electoral votes. Smith carried New York, but he lost the national election to Herbert Hoover.

Roosevelt won the governor's race by appealing to a coalition of rural and urban groups. He was an active governor: Rural voters were rewarded by his support for reforestation of land ruined by overuse; workers benefited from his backing of state-financed pensions, unemployment insurance, and regulated working hours; and the public liked his program for state control of the

Left: Although Roosevelt never made a secret of his handicap, only two photographs exist showing him in a wheelchair, including this one taken the day fellow polio victim Ruthie Bie visited the president and his dog, Fala, at Hyde Park.

Relaxing

Roosevelt was a pack-a-day cigarette smoker, nearly always distancing himself from them with a long holder that became his trademark. He was also well known as a stamp collector, maintaining more than forty large albums with some 25,000 rare stamps. He was given the first sheet of every commemorative stamp issued during his White House years, and the foreign service was always on the lookout for foreign rarities. He ended each day with a martini, but once in a while switched to a drink he invented himself, a concoction of rum, orange juice, and brown sugar. Prohibition had been repealed in 1933, so he wasn't breaking any law.

energy industry.

Using the new medium of radio, Roosevelt began broadcasting "fireside chats" to keep New Yorkers informed about issues and policies in a relaxed format, and it helped him win reelection in 1930 by the largest margin in state history.

Roosevelt proved to be a dynamic and imaginative leader as the economic crisis that began in October 1929 worsened into the Great Depression. He met with distinguished academics and listened to the ideas of ordinary people as well as experts to form consistently bold policies to help "the forgotten man," as he called people who had lost their jobs. His character traits of persistence and experimentation in dealing with problems helped define him to party leaders as he looked for support for the Democratic nomination for president in 1932.

He led balloting at the Democratic convention during the first three rounds of voting but could not reach the majority he needed to win the nomination.

He offered the vice presidency to one of his rivals, Texas representative and Speaker of the House John Nance Garner, who freed delegates committed to him and threw his support to Roosevelt. It turned out to be shrewd move, because Garner appealed to rural voters and complemented Roosevelt's popularity among urban easterners

Unlike the incumbent Republican president, Herbert Hoover, who took a cautious approach to economic problems, Roosevelt promised the New Deal, an aggressive response to the nation's economic crisis. He vowed that he would spend federal funds for relief to the unemployed and to create jobs; that his farm policy would stop overproduction of some crops that lowered their value. He said that he wanted to conserve public resources and have the government control power utilities; and he promised pensions for workers and regulation of the stock exchange. He kept many of those promises by putting them into effect during his first one hundred days in office.

Election Results

1932

Presidential / Vice Presidential Candidates	Popular Votes	Electoral Votes
Franklin D. Roosevelt / John Nance Garner (Democratic)	22,821,857	472
Herbert Hoover / Charles Curtis (Republican)	15,761,845	59

Roosevelt won the Democratic nomination on the fourth ballot, defeating 1928 nominee Alfred E. Smith. Hoover won the Republican nomination on the first ballot.

1936

Presidential / Vice Presidential Candidates	Popular Votes	Electoral Votes
Franklin D. Roosevelt / John Nance Garner (Democratic)	27,476,673	523
Alfred M. Landon / Frank Knox (Republican)	16,679,583	8

1940

Presidential / Vice Presidential Candidates	Popular Votes	Electoral Votes
Franklin D. Roosevelt / Henry A. Wallace (Democratic)	27,243,466	449
Wendell L. Willkie / Charles L. McNary (Republican)	22,304,755	82

Roosevelt went against two-term tradition and sought a third term, frustrating such presidential hopefuls as incumbent vice president Garner; Roosevelt easily received the nomination on the first ballot. Newcomer Willkie defeated early ballot leaders Thomas E. Dewey and Robert A. Taft on the sixth ballot.

1944

Presidential / Vice Presidential Candidates	Popular Votes	Electoral Votes
Franklin D. Roosevelt / Harry S Truman (Democratic)	25,602,505	432
Thomas E. Dewey / John W. Bricker (Republican)	22,006,278	99

Amid World War II, voters opted to keep incumbent Roosevelt in office, despite his already having served an unprecedented three terms. Missouri senator Truman replaced Wallace as the vice-presidential nominee.

"I always voted for Franklin Roosevelt for president. My father before me always voted for Franklin Roosevelt for president."

—Bob Hope

The One Hundred Days

Franklin D. Roosevelt easily defeated President Hoover in the 1932 election, but when Roosevelt was inaugurated the following March, more than thirteen million people were out of work. One of them, Giuseppe Zangara, an unemployed bricklayer, attempted to assassinate Roosevelt one month before the inauguration, and although he failed, Chicago mayor Anton J. Cermak was killed. "Too many people are starving to death," he shouted wildly as he emptied his gun at the president-elect's open car.

"It is regrettable that Giuseppe Zangara hit the wrong man when he shot at Roosevelt in Miami. Roosevelt made many decisions in favor of the Soviet Union, beginning with his recognition of the Soviet government. Thereafter he permitted the whole bureaucracy to become infested with spies."

—Columnist Westbrook Pegler

Many of the unemployed were living as transients, moving from place to place, looking for work and a permanent home, rarely finding either. Others lived in makeshift camps they called "Hoovervilles." Banks had closed in thirty-eight states, and the economic collapse had spread around the world. Still, Roosevelt gave a spirited inaugural address, telling Americans that "the only thing we have to fear is fear itself." Then he called a special session of Congress and began to act.

Congress immediately passed the Emergency Banking Act to provide help to banks. Then, through the Economy Act, they made cuts in payments to federal workers, freeing up some $500 million that went to local and state agencies as relief grants. People were put to work through agencies that coordinated a range of programs, from large-scale construction projects to conservation efforts and cleanup work.

As confidence in the federal government was quickly being restored, Roosevelt set up agencies that reformed banking policies, helped guide negotiations between management and labor, and established minimum wage and maximum work hours. To help speed legislation, the administration sometimes wrote bills that were quickly debated and passed by Congress and signed by the president—sometimes all in a single day. An amazing amount of legislation was passed during his first one hundred days in office, followed by even more legislation in 1934 and 1935.

Roosevelt worked effectively with Congress, and he appointed several Republicans to key positions within his administration, among them Secretary of the Interior Harold Ickes. Many others were progressive Democrats, including Secretary of Labor Frances Perkins, the first woman to hold a cabinet position. Secretary of Agriculture Henry Wallace was originally a Republican, but by then he was a Democrat, and became Roosevelt's vice president from 1941 to 1945, and later a presidential candidate for the Progressive Party in 1948. Harry L. Hopkins, Roosevelt's closest advisor, had been director of the New York State Temporary Relief Administration, and he also headed the New Deal's Federal Emergency Relief Administration and the Works Progress Administration, and served as secretary of commerce from 1938 to 1940, later becoming an influential advisor during several World War II conferences.

Roosevelt made good use of his executive powers and he drummed up enthusiasm for his programs through regular press conferences, speeches, and fireside chats. In the chats, broadcast coast to coast over the radio, he often took time to carefully explain problems to the public.

Keep Seeking a Cure

Roosevelt became more progressive in 1935. He raised taxes on wealthy individuals and supported a measure that gave the federal banking system, the Federal Reserve, more influence on the economy than private businessmen. He helped establish the Social Security system that pays old-age pensions, provides unemployment compensation, and offers financial help to the needy and the handicapped.

The New Deal programs as a whole only made modest gains against the devastating effects of the Depression, but they brought Roosevelt tremendous support out of proportion to their effectiveness. "He understood," wrote historian Garry Wills, "the importance of psychology— that people have to have the courage to keep seeking a cure, no matter what the cure is." Roosevelt was reelected president in 1936 by a margin of eleven million votes over Republican nominee Alf M. Landon, the governor of Kansas. Roosevelt's landslide showed impressively in the Electoral College—46 states and 523 electoral votes to Landon's two states and eight electoral votes.

Right: Roosevelt had great compassion for what he called "the forgotten man." Among them was this impoverished man who watched hopelessly as his shack burned down, leaving him homeless.

Major Acts of the New Deal

New Deal legislation began in a special session of Congress in 1933. Through the Emergency Banking Act and the Economy Act, Congress authorized sweeping powers for the president to begin implementing New Deal programs after they were passed by Congress. More New Deal programs followed in 1934 and 1935.

- *Emergency Banking Act:* Introduced in Congress, passed, and signed by the president—all in one day—the act provided sweeping power to the federal government to confront the banking crisis. Roosevelt's first fireside chat described the importance of this act. Among other measures, the act greatly increased the authority of the Federal Reserve Board, the government agency that oversees banking activity.
- *The Economy Act:* Reduced government salaries and pensions to provide federal money that could be sent to states to provide relief for unemployed workers. Opposed by many Democratic representatives in Congress, the act passed with pressure from Roosevelt and support by most Republicans.

The vast scope of New Deal programs are typically organized under the "three R's"—relief, recovery, and reform measures. The following New Deal programs are identified and described in the "three R" arrangement.

Relief Measures

Government actions designed to provide immediate relief (in the form of money or work) during the worst period of the Great Depression in 1933 and 1934.

- *Federal Emergency Relief Administration (FERA):* Provided large amounts of money to states (much of it freed for use through the Economy Act). This agency expanded from the Reconstruction Finance Corporation (RFC), established under President Herbert Hoover, Roosevelt's predecessor. The RFC provided loans to financial institutions, railways, and public agencies. FERA reorganized the RFC, and simplified and greatly expanded that loan process.
- *Civil Works Administration (CWA):* A subdivision of FERA, it provided work to a large number of men during the winter of 1933 and 1934.

- *Works Progress Administration (WPA, later renamed the Work Projects Administration):* Replaced FERA in 1935, as the government moved from providing immediate economic relief to creating jobs. WPA projects included road repair and construction; building of schools, libraries, and other public structures; and programs to encourage artists, musicians, and writers.
- *Civilian Conservation Corps (CCC):* Provided work for more than 250,000 unemployed and unmarried young men, many of them from city slums. Workers received food, shelter, and pay, lived in camps under the management of army officers, and performed land improvement projects.
- *National Youth Administration (NYA):* Funded part-time jobs at schools for high school and college students and provided part-time employment for other young people.

Recovery Measures

Acts designed to revive businesses and provide jobs for the unemployed.

- *National Industrial Recovery Act (NIRA):* Passed by Congress in June 1933. Authorized the Public Works Administration and the National Recovery Association (described below).
- *Public Works Administration (PWA):* Greatly expanded a public works program begun by Hoover. Under the authority of Secretary of the Interior Harold L. Ickes, the PWA started slowly (Ickes was careful to avoid having congressmen claim money for projects in their particular state). After careful planning, a massive construction program of public buildings, large dams, and irrigation and flood-control projects began in 1937.
- *National Recovery Administration (NRA):* Designed to provide assistance to businesses by creating codes of fair competition. Suspended laws against combining large businesses in exchange for guarantees to workers (a minimum wage, limited hours, and the right to bargain as a group). By 1934, however, the codes and monitoring practices were excessively complicated. The NRA was unanimously declared unconstitutional by the Supreme Court in 1935.
- *Agricultural Adjustment Administration (AAA):* Established within the Department of Agriculture, the AAA addressed overproduction of crops. Financed by special taxes, the AAA purchased surplus crops and paid farmers to reduce production. These acts helped many farmers out of debt. The AAA was declared unconstitutional by the Supreme Court in 1936. A new and more modest AAA was created by Congress in 1938.

Reform Measures

Between 1933 and 1938, the administration and Congress passed the most sweeping reform program since the progressive period of 1901 to 1907.

- *Federal Deposit Insurance Corporation (FDIC):* Insured savings deposits in banks. As Roosevelt explained in his first fireside chat, banks invest money deposited by customers, rather than simply storing that money. As the Depression worsened from 1929 to 1933, customers began withdrawing their savings. Since much of the money had been invested and was lost when stock prices fell, the banks did not have the money available that customers wanted to withdraw. The FDIC ensured that such money would be available in the future.
- *Securities and Exchange Commission (SEC):* An independent agency empowered to monitor the sale of stocks and bonds to ensure that actions are carried out within legal limits.
- *Reciprocal Trade Agreements Act:* Authorized the president to negotiate agreements with other nations for a mutual lowering of import taxes (bypassing the normal process for import tax reduction that had to be approved by Congress). Created the most-favored-nation clause that offers the same import tax rates to all countries that sign a commercial treaty with the United States (if the United States lowers tariffs in a treaty with one nation, all tariffs for other countries with most-favored-nation status have to be reduced as well).
- *Home Owners' Loan Corporation (HOLC):* Assisted individuals with refinancing (changing the payment rates on) their home loans to avoid defaulting on payments and possibly losing their homes.
- *Federal Housing Administration (FHA):* Encouraged banks to continue making home loans by insuring loans up to 80 percent of the value of the property.
- *U.S. Housing Authority:* Helped to rebuild slums and encouraged low-cost housing construction—the first direct involvement of the federal government in building houses.
- *Tennessee Valley Authority (TVA):* An independent federal corporation that addressed conditions in an area that reached parts of seven states. The program was designed largely by progressive Republican senator George W. Norris of Nebraska, who shared Roosevelt's conviction that public utilities (like energy and water companies) should be owned by the government since the utilities provide public necessities. The TVA was responsible for dams that provided energy, flood control, and better transportation. Electricity was made available to some areas within the seven states for the first time. Opposed by the country's private power companies, the TVA was not expanded to other parts of the country, although dams and power plants were constructed with federal help in the western United States.
- *Social Security Act:* After a commission studied problems caused by unemployment, old age, and physical disability, it recommended changes that involved the federal government. Unemployment insurance was established (funded by a federal payroll tax paid in equal parts by employers and employees); an old-age pension system (Social Security) administered by the federal government was enacted and financed by taxes on both employers and employees; and federal money was provided to states to encourage them to care for dependent children and the blind. National health insurance was abandoned, however, when opponents threatened to block the entire Social Security Act legislation.
- *National Labor Relations Act:* Guaranteed workers the right to organize and bargain collectively without interference from employers.
- *National Labor Relations Board (NLRB):* An independent agency established through the National Labor Relations Act that monitors relations between employers and labor and contributed greatly to the rise of unions.
- *Fair Labor Standards Act:* Passed in 1938 as the last significant New Deal legislation, the act set a minimum wage and limited the number of working hours. Those measures were originally part of the National Recovery Administration that was unanimously declared unconstitutional by the Supreme Court in 1935.

Right: The Civilian Conservation Corps, a New Deal program to rescue the environment, brought many city people out into the wilderness. Some found surprises there, like the bear cubs who wandered into a West Virginia CCC camp.

Frances Perkins

Frances Perkins, President Franklin D. Roosevelt's only secretary of labor, drafted important New Deal legislation, including the Social Security Act and the Fair Labor Standards Act. She was born Fannie Coralie Perkins in 1880 in Boston, Massachusetts, to Susan Bean and Frederick W. Perkins. Her father owned a stationery business that also sold books and periodicals. He helped educate her. Fannie attended a largely male preparatory school, then went to Mt. Holyoke College in Massachusetts beginning in 1898. She switched her interest from chemistry and physics to social work after attending meetings of the National Consumers' League and hearing lectures by Florence Kelley, national secretary of the league. The group was dedicated to the elimination of child labor and of low-paying shops that exploited immigrant laborers. Not able to land a job in social work after she graduated from college, Perkins taught briefly in New England and then at a girls' school in Illinois.

Perkins began working with laborers in Chicago, helping them collect their pay from corrupt businessmen and assisting as a nurse. She changed her baptismal name of Fannie to Frances when converting her faith from Congregationalist to Episcopalian. In 1907, she became a professional social worker in Philadelphia, where she joined the Socialist Party and attended classes in economics and sociology at the University of Pennsylvania. Perkins moved to New York in 1909 for training at the New York School of Philanthropy. In 1910, she earned a master's degree in political science from Columbia University and became secretary of the New York City Consumers' League. Her responsibilities involved monitoring sanitary regulations for cellar bakeries, overseeing fire prevention in factories, and limiting the working hours for those under the age of eighteen.

After the 1911 Triangle Shirtwaist Fire in New York City that claimed the lives of 146 workers, mostly young girls, she was named executive secretary of the Committee on Safety of the City of New York. She worked with the Factory Investigating Commission that ordered new fire laws for the state.

In 1913, Perkins married Paul C. Wilson, a New York economist involved in city politics. In the spring of 1915, Perkins suffered a miscarriage; in December of the following year, her daughter Susanna Winslow was born. Perkins was named to the New York State Industrial Commission by New York governor Al Smith in 1919, making her the first woman to hold such a position in the state and the highest paid woman in any state government.

After Smith lost the 1920 election, Perkins served as executive secretary of the Council on Immigrant Education. At Smith's urging, Perkins joined the Democratic Party in 1920. Smith won election again in 1922 and appointed her to the Industrial Board, where she was named chairperson in 1926. In 1929, newly elected governor Franklin D. Roosevelt appointed her industrial commissioner of the state of New York, making her the first woman to serve in a governor's cabinet. She became the first woman to hold a federal cabinet post after newly elected president Roosevelt named her secretary of labor in 1933.

"I came to work for God, FDR, and the millions of forgotten, plain, common working men," said Perkins about her cabinet position. She reorganized the Labor Department to increase efficiency. In addition, Perkins advised Roosevelt on key appointments, including Harry Hopkins, who became head of the Federal Emergency Relief Administration.

Perkins played a major role in the government's response to the San Francisco general strike of 1934. Perkins opposed federal intervention in the strike, believing that it would be quickly resolved. Though it was, she was targeted by some anticommunists for not deporting a union leader suspected but not proved to be a communist. That incident helped fuel an attempt to impeach her in 1938 by the House Un-American Activities Committee (HUAC), formed in the spring of 1937. The impeachment proceedings were very painful for Perkins, and she received hate mail. In March 1938, the Judiciary Committee refused to recommend impeachment, but the HUAC continued to investigate her.

Meanwhile, Perkins aided in drafting legislation for the Social Security Act and the Fair Labor Standards Act. Those achievements, and her negotiating skills in disputes among automobile industry workers and management in the mid-1930s, were the high points of her career. During World War II, she fought for such labor rights as the forty-hour workweek and payment for overtime. She remained in the cabinet after Roosevelt's death. President Truman later asked her to resign and then appointed her to the Civil Service Commission.

When her husband died in 1952, Perkins began a new career as a college lecturer at the age of seventy-three. She served as a visiting professor at Cornell University until her death on May 14, 1965, at the age of eighty-five.

Losing Ground

As he began his second term in 1937, Roosevelt noted that there was still a lot of work to be done—that one third of Americans were still "ill-housed, ill-clad, ill-nourished." He suggested that Americans had a "rendezvous with destiny"—that there was a turning point ahead when better things would come. Roosevelt himself would face challenges with the Supreme Court and Congress, and he would deal with international tensions during his second term.

Some of his New Deal programs were declared unconstitutional by the U.S. Supreme Court, and he believed he was being held back by conservative justices who had been appointed by the previous three Republican presidents. His solution was to add as many as six new judges, but his attempt to "stack the court" in his favor met with hostile resistance, even among Democrats.

Meanwhile, a series of strikes by workers who were unhappy with their wages led some to accuse Roosevelt of having been too favorable to labor. On the other hand, the continued desperate economic conditions led others to promote more radical solutions to the nation's problems than the New Deal, and as a sign that they had some popular support, more than two hundred thousand Americans voted for socialist and communist candidates in the presidential elections of 1932 and 1936.

Inauguration Day Calendar Change

The Twentieth Amendment to the Constitution changed the presidential inauguration date from March 4 to January 20 in 1937. The change was made to shorten the length of time between the election and Inauguration Day, eliminating what was roughly a four-month lame-duck period for an outgoing president. The longer time frame had been necessary in earlier years when communication and transportation were slower.

The Roosevelt Administration

Administration Dates: March 4, 1933–January 20, 1937
January 20, 1937–January 20, 1941
January 20, 1941–January 20, 1945
January 20, 1945–April 12, 1945

Vice President: John Nance Garner (1933–41)
Henry A. Wallace (1941–45)
Harry S Truman (1945)

Cabinet:

Secretary of State	Cordell Hull (1933–44)
	Edward R. Stettinius Jr. (1944–45)
Secretary of the Treasury	William H. Woodin (1933–34)
	Henry Morgenthau Jr. (1934–45)
Secretary of War	George H. Dern (1933–36)
	Harry H. Woodring (1937–40)
	Henry L. Stimson (1940–45)
Attorney General	Homer S. Cummings (1933–39)
	Francis W. Murphy (1939–40)
	Robert H. Jackson (1940–41)
	Francis B. Biddle (1941–45)
Secretary of the Navy	Claude A. Swanson (1933–39)
	Charles Edison (1940)
	William F. Knox (1940–44)
	James V. Forrestal (1944–45)
Postmaster General	James A. Farley (1933–40)
	Frank C. Walker (1940–45)
Secretary of the Interior	Harold L. Ickes (1933–45)
Secretary of Agriculture	Henry A. Wallace (1933–40)
	Claude R. Wickard (1940–45)
Secretary of Commerce	Daniel C. Roper (1933–38)
	Harry Lloyd Hopkins (1938–40)
	Jesse H. Jones (1940–45)
	Henry A. Wallace (1945)
Secretary of Labor	Frances Perkins (1933–45)

Above: In order to get approval for his programs, FDR attempted to alter the political makeup of the Supreme Court by adding as many as six new justices.

"They didn't even treat us like humans. We were paid sixteen cents an hour and if you asked to get off on Sunday, the foreman would say, 'All right, you stay away on Sunday, and when you come back on Monday, someone else will have your job.'—No sir, I'll never forget what President Roosevelt done for us."

—*a Southern factory worker*

After a short period of improvement, the economy got worse in 1936, and forced drastic cuts in federal spending, and Roosevelt was only able to convince Congress to pass small-scale programs related to public housing, fair labor standards, and aid to tenant farmers. The 1938 midterm congressional elections changed the balance of power in Congress, bringing in enough Republicans to easily defeat any more legislation for urban welfare.

Right: Both FDR and his wife, Eleanor, were powerful individuals. Together, they were a force to be reckoned with.

Foreign Affairs

During his first two terms, Roosevelt tried to help stimulate the American economy by increasing foreign trade. He improved diplomatic relations with Russia, which was still struggling to modernize after heavy losses in World War I, and he instituted a "good neighbor" policy with Latin American countries based on reciprocal trade agreements intended to benefit both sides. He also pledged to end American intervention in Latin American countries that had occurred several times over the previous decades when American business interests were threatened. Meanwhile, the United States did not participate in international attempts to stabilize the world economic crisis because Roosevelt believed that such actions might hinder efforts at home.

Economic hard times led to increasing international tensions. Military dictatorships were established during the 1930s in Germany, Italy, Spain, and Japan, which invaded Manchuria the following year. Roosevelt

Winston Churchill

A celebrated statesman, historian, and Nobel laureate, Winston Churchill is best remembered for his leadership as Britain's prime minister during World War II. Born at Blenheim Palace in Oxfordshire, England, Churchill was the son of Lord Randolph Henry Spencer Churchill, a prominent parliamentarian, and Jennie Jerome Churchill, an American socialite. Churchill received his early education in private schools. An unexceptional student, he enrolled at the Royal Military Academy to prepare for a career as a military officer. Graduating with honors in 1894, he was appointed to the Fourth (Queen's Own) Hussars as a sublieutenant in 1895.

During the late 1890s, Churchill traveled to Cuba, India, and the Sudan to report on various military campaigns as a war correspondent for the London Daily Telegraph and the London Morning Post. His capture by Boer soldiers in 1899 and escape from a South African prison won him renown and helped secure his election to Parliament in 1900. He served continuously in Parliament for more than six decades in several high-ranking positions.

As first lord of admiralty during World War I, Churchill directed a failed campaign in Eastern Europe that resulted in heavy casualties and Churchill's demotion. He resigned his office in 1916 to go to the front as a lieutenant colonel in command of the Sixth Royal Fusiliers.

At the outbreak of World War II, Churchill was briefly reappointed first lord of admiralty. Then, after the resignation of Neville Chamberlain, Churchill became prime minister of Great Britain in 1940. Churchill founded the Atlantic Charter with the United States in 1941. The charter grew out of discussions he had with President Roosevelt aboard warships near Newfoundland, Canada. They formed a statement that supported the right of all people to choose their leaders, called for freedom on the seas, and denounced aggressors of war.

Churchill helped orchestrate the Allied victory over Germany with Roosevelt and Soviet leader Joseph Stalin. In 1943, Churchill and Roosevelt agreed that there would be no negotiated peace with the Axis powers. They decided on strategies for winning back Europe from Nazi forces; Allied forces would begin by invading Sicily and Italy in 1943 and then launch a major offensive from western France in 1944. The leaders also agreed to support the founding of the United Nations.

Churchill kept Stalin informed on Allied plans. Churchill, Roosevelt, and Stalin met at the Yalta Conference in 1945 to discuss postwar Europe (Germany's defeat was expected soon) and the war against Japan.

Churchill lost his position as prime minister in 1945 but regained it in 1951. He supported British involvement in international affairs, including the North Atlantic Treaty Organization (NATO) and the Council of Europe (CE). He resigned in 1955, turning over his office to Anthony Eden. He remained active in politics during the last decade of his life and continued to win praise as a writer.

His books revealed Churchill to be an intelligent observer of military campaigns and geopolitical affairs, and he was an excellent biographer and historian. In The World Crisis, Churchill provided comprehensive analysis of international affairs and military activities during World War I as a participant in the events he recorded. His later five-volume work, The Second World War, provided a general history of the war intermingled with Churchill's recollections and analysis of military and diplomatic events he personally witnessed and directly influenced.

Churchill's sense of the glory of England remained with him all his life. Four times in two centuries, he noted, England had saved Europe from tyrants: Louis XIV, Napoleon I, Kaiser Wilhelm II, and Adolf Hitler. As Churchill saw it, "this island race" was on the side not only of progress and enlightenment but of liberty and justice, as well. Churchill regarded history as a question of morality, a struggle between right and wrong, between freedom and tyranny. The purpose of history, according to Churchill, is to teach by example, especially by the examples of great leaders and of war.

maintained the strained diplomatic relations with Japan begun by the Hoover administration, but by 1940, he suspended a commercial treaty with the Japanese Empire. Italy, led by dictator Benito Mussolini, invaded the eastern African empire of Ethiopia, and Adolph Hitler's Nazi regime in Germany teamed with him to provide help for the overthrow of the Spanish monarchy. Meanwhile, in March 1938, Germany sent military troops to Austria, occupying and annexing it. Then at the end of August 1939, the Germans concluded a nonaggression pact with the Union of Soviet Socialist Republics (USSR), and when the Nazis invaded Poland a few weeks later, France and Britain declared war on Germany.

As a way of delaying American involvement in foreign conflicts, Congress had proclaimed American neutrality in 1934, and placed an embargo on shipping armaments to countries at war. The armaments embargo was repealed in 1939 to allow the sale of weapons to nations that could pay cash and transport the material on their own ships. However, as most of Europe fell under German domination by 1940 and Britain was being hit by Nazi warplanes with daily raids, President Roosevelt arranged a trade: Great Britain was given fifty American destroyers in exchange for leases on military bases in the Pacific. Criticism was as swift as it was harsh. Most Americans wanted to stay neutral, but Roosevelt favored

Below: "Tomorrow, the world," was Adolph Hitler's warning when his armies attacked Poland in 1939. Most Americans refused to believe him.

the efforts of Britain and France against Nazi Germany, and his agreement with England was seen as the first step down the road to war.

The United States had been getting into a state of military preparedness by the late 1930s, and the tremendous surge in defense spending created massive numbers of jobs as it promoted industrial expansion and began lifting the nation out of the Great Depression. In 1941, responding to pleas for aid from British prime minister Winston Churchill, Roosevelt asked Congress to authorize a Lend-Lease program. This plan, which was expanded to include the thirty-eight countries that formed the Allied powers fighting Germany, Italy, and Japan—the Axis powers—sidestepped laws that didn't allow the United States to sell arms on credit. Instead, the United States claimed that it was simply "lending" military hardware and expected it to be returned.

Meanwhile, Roosevelt ran for an unprecedented third term. Concern over the war in Europe and Asia made Americans cautious about changing leaders, even though Roosevelt's popularity had fallen. He was reelected by fewer than five million votes—a clear show of support but less than half the margin of his landslide election in 1936. Still, Roosevelt had a sure win over Republican Wendell Willkie in the Electoral College, 449 votes to 82.

A Day of Infamy

The United States moved closer to war in September 1941 when a German submarine fired a torpedo at an American destroyer, and American warships were authorized for the first time to shoot back. Roosevelt maintained a facade of neutrality, but by that time America was clearly offering assistance to Allied powers often beyond supplying them with weapons. American ships, for example, were providing information on German naval operations to Great Britain.

Meanwhile, the Roosevelt administration increased aid to China and placed an embargo on the export of iron and steel scrap to Japan. Then, on December 7, 1941, all doubt was lifted over whether the United States would enter World War II. The Japanese Air Force struck a major blow with a surprise attack on American naval

New Deal programs were canceled when America went to war, and issues that might have caused political deadlock were addressed quickly if they might affect the war effort. For example, President Roosevelt had delayed civil-rights legislation to assure that his other New Deal measures would be enacted without a long debate, but when a march on Washington to protest racial injustice was announced, he acted quickly to empower the Fair Employment Practices Committee (FEPC) to prevent any form of racial discrimination in defense plants.

"We look forward to a world founded on four essential human freedoms …freedom of speech and expression …freedom for every person to worship God in his own way …freedom from want …freedom from fear."

—*Franklin D. Roosevelt*

---

vessels stationed at Pearl Harbor, Hawaii. The action rallied American support against the Japanese, but some wondered about why American forces were open to such an attack in the first place. Historians generally agree that the attack was a well-executed military maneuver by Japanese forces against a nation they already regarded as an enemy and suspected would soon enter World War II, with or without the attack.

Eight American battleships and ten other naval vessels were sunk or badly damaged, almost two hundred American aircraft were destroyed, and about three thousand military personnel were killed or wounded in the Pearl Harbor attack, but the Japanese neither destroyed any aircraft carriers nor made any attempt to land troops in Hawaii.

Calling December 7 "a day which will live in infamy" in a radio broadcast to the nation, Roosevelt asked Congress to declare war on Japan, and when Germany and Italy backed their Japanese ally by declaring war on the United States, Congress declared war on them as well.

Right: The day after characterizing December 7, 1941, as "a date that will live in infamy," President Roosevelt signed the declaration of war against Japan.

Left: Plowshares into swords. American industry retooled virtually overnight to support the war effort. This assembly line that once produced Chrysler automobiles began turning out heavy tanks.

In 1942, the United States defeated the Japanese Navy at the Battle of Midway in the mid-Pacific and assisted in the Allied invasion of North Africa. Meanwhile, struggling Russian forces stopped a major German advance in the Battle of Stalingrad.

Roosevelt met with British Prime Minister Churchill in January 1943 at Casablanca, Morocco, to make further plans and to announce that they were insisting on the enemy's unconditional surrender. The president met with Churchill and Chinese leader Chiang Kai-shek at Cairo, Egypt, in November 1943, to prepare plans for the war against Japan. Roosevelt made further plans with Soviet leader Josef Stalin at Tehran, Iran, and agreed to an offensive against Germany that would begin with an invasion of Nazi-occupied France by Allied forces. That invasion—D-Day—began on June 6, 1944, and from there, the Allies moved inexorably toward Germany itself.

World War II

As commander in chief, Roosevelt decided on military strategy and oversaw the buildup of an enormous army and navy. By the end of the war, more than fifteen million people had served in the armed forces of the United States. At home, people went back to work: Unemployment dropped from 17 percent in 1939 to 1 percent in 1944, and personal income doubled. Large numbers of people relocated to urban areas where military-related items were manufactured.

Executive authority was broadened. An agency called the Selective Service Administration supervised a military draft, a program that required men to register for possible military service. Various agencies monitored industries supporting the war effort. Vital supplies, from tires and gasoline to foods and even nylon, were rationed and made available in limited supplies and purchased with special stamps at prices set by the government. As he had with his cabinet, Roosevelt surrounded himself with aggressive, hardworking administrators and advisors—Democrat and Republican alike. His secretary of the navy, Frank Knox, had been outspoken against the New Deal and he was the Republican vice-presidential candidate in 1936. Henry L. Stimson, who had served in the cabinets of three Republican presidents, was named secretary of war.

Above: Japanese-Americans were relegated to interment camps during World War II. This one in Idaho was originally a Civilian Conservation Corps camp, a legacy of the New Deal.

Final Weeks

Roosevelt was in frail health in the election year of 1944. He had rarely appeared in public during the war years, but he was still popular, and bolstered by American success in the war in Europe, he won election for an unprecedented fourth term. His margin of victory was the smallest of his four presidential wins—just over two and a half million popular votes, but he won by an overwhelming 432 to 99 votes in the Electoral College over the Republican candidate Thomas E. Dewey.

Victory over Nazi Germany was expected soon, and after his inauguration in January 1945, President Roosevelt traveled in February to attend the Yalta Conference, held in the Crimea region of the Soviet Union, where he discussed war strategies and the fate of postwar Europe with Churchill and Stalin, and secured Stalin's promise to enter the war against Japan once the Nazis were defeated. He also obtained Stalin's promise to ensure that free elections would be held in the East European nations that were occupied by the Soviet military as it pushed toward Germany. That promise was broken soon after the war.

After Roosevelt went back to Washington, he immediately left for his vacation home in Warm Springs, Georgia, and on April 12, 1945, he died there of a cerebral hemorrhage. He was buried in the rose garden in the family estate at Hyde Park, less than a month before the war with Germany was over.

Legacy

Franklin D. Roosevelt effectively used broad presidential authority to organize massive efforts to combat the Depression as well as the Axis powers. On the home front, his New Deal programs benefited millions of people and helped restore confidence in the American economic system. While the New Deal did not end the Depression, its progressive legislation brought about many needed changes. Several of the programs were still in place at the end of the twentieth century.

Traveling Companion

When FDR traveled out of the country, it was usually aboard ships of the U.S. Navy, and he nearly always had his little Scottie dog, Fala, with him. It was once reported that the dog was left behind after a stop in the Aleutian Islands, and the president sent a destroyer back on a rescue mission. He answered the charge during a campaign speech: "The Republicans have not been content with attacks on me, nor my wife, nor my sons. No not content with that, they now include my little dog, Fala. Well, of course, I do not resent attacks and my family doesn't resent attacks, but Fala does. You know, Fala is Scotch, and being a Scottie, as soon as he learned that the Republican fiction writers had concocted a story that I had left him behind on the Aleutian Islands and had sent a destroyer back for him—at a cost to the taxpayers of two or three, or eight or twenty million dollars—his Scotch soul was furious. I am accustomed to hearing malicious falsehoods about myself—such as that old worm-eaten chestnut that I have represented myself as indispensable. But I think I have the right to resent, to object to, libelous statements about my dog."

"If you had spent two years in bed trying to move your toes, you'd understand how easy the rest has been."

—*Franklin D. Roosevelt*

Below: The Big Three—Winston Churchill, Franklin D. Roosevelt and Josef Stalin—met at Yalta on the Crimean Peninsula in February 1945.

Left: Former British Prime Minister Winston Churchill, Roosevelt's comrade-in-arms, lays a wreath at the president's grave in Hyde Park during a visit to Eleanor Roosevelt.

Critics argue that Roosevelt could have been more aggressive in attacking the nation's economic woes, while others contend his powers were too broad, and the debate over the role of the federal government in the daily lives of citizens continues to this day. Many Americans strongly identify the modern-day Democratic Party with Roosevelt's belief in using the powers of government to address the country's problems.

Roosevelt's role as commander in chief has also been analyzed time and again. Some commentators suggest that aggressive U.S. actions toward Japan invited the attack on Pearl Harbor or that the United States was not prepared for the surprise assault. Others view the attack as a strategic, well-coordinated first strike by Japan. During the war, government agencies closely supervised American industries to direct work toward the war effort, although that domination of industry by government was quickly stopped once the war emergency ended.

Roosevelt's foreign policy clearly favored the Allied powers in dealing with events that lead up to America's involvement in World War II. After the war, the agreements Roosevelt and Stalin forged at the Yalta Conference became controversial when Russia's promise of free elections in the Eastern European countries it occupied was not kept. Those nations fell under Russian domination—behind an "iron curtain," as the boundary was called. Although they had been allies during the war, it wasn't long before the United States and the Soviet Union were engaged in what was called the "Cold War"—a tense period of strained diplomatic relations, military buildup, and the constant threat of war that lasted until the late 1980s.

The continuing debate about Roosevelt's policies is a reflection of the tremendous impact of his administrations on United States history. He is regularly ranked by presidential historians among the greatest presidents.

Right: Among the dreams President Roosevelt didn't live to see come true was the creation of the United Nations. Delegates to the first meeting of the General Assembly in San Francisco, less than a month after the president died, took time out to honor his vision.

Eleanor Roosevelt

Born October 11, 1884, New York, New York
Died November 7, 1962, New York, New York

"We cannot wait until tomorrow. Tomorrow is now."
—*Eleanor Roosevelt*

Eleanor Roosevelt was the most politically active of all the first ladies. She held weekly press conferences and wrote newspaper and magazine columns. She worked tirelessly on programs to help the less-advantaged; she was active in promoting civil rights; she lobbied for jobs, promotions, and equal pay for qualified women; and she had a strong influence on some of her husband's New Deal programs. After her husband, Franklin D. Roosevelt, died in 1945, she was part of the first U.S. delegation to the United Nations.

Her transformation from a timid child to a self-reliant, energetic, and outspoken woman gradually developed through several life crises. Eleanor Roosevelt was orphaned at ten, and she felt out of place, a kind of ugly duckling, as a teenager in her family's high-society life in New York. After she was married, she put up with a bossy mother-in-law who never hid her disapproval; she confronted her husband's unfaithfulness, but went on to help him deal with his physical handicap without losing his energy and enthusiasm for life.

Her outspokenness for humanitarian causes was sometimes ridiculed when she was first lady, at a time when most Americans—male Americans, anyway—believed that a woman's place was in the home. She got a lot of hate mail among the three hundred thousand letters that arrived at the White House addressed to her during her first year as first lady. But many others, including her husband, admired her incredible energy: "My missus," he said, "goes where she wants to, talks to everybody, and does she learn something!"

Born into Wealth

Anna Eleanor Roosevelt was born on October 11, 1884, in New York City. Her mother, also named Anna, was an attractive socialite, and her father, Elliott, was the wealthy and handsome brother of former president Theodore Roosevelt. Her mother, who died when Eleanor was eight, generally ignored her daughter and her two sons. Although an alcoholic, her father doted on Eleanor, but was often away, either on drinking binges or getting treatment for his addiction. He died when she was ten, and Eleanor and her brothers went to live with their grandmother, a strict disciplinarian.

Shy and self-conscious about her looks, feeling gangly and unattractive, Eleanor found enjoyment in solitude, riding horses, learning French, and writing. Her life changed for the better when she was sent to a finishing school in England when she was fifteen. The school's headmistress, Marie Souvestre, was impressed by her intelligence and encouraged her to come out of her shell. She took Eleanor with her on trips to the European continent, challenged her intellectually, and developed her practical skills with such assignments as having her make their travel arrangements.

As she approached her eighteenth birthday, Eleanor was back in New York. As was expected of girls from wealthy families like hers, she had a "coming out" party and was involved in a whirlwind of balls, teas, luncheons, dinners, and parties. It was in that social setting that she became reacquainted with Franklin Roosevelt, a Harvard student who was also making the society rounds. Distantly related, they had sometimes played together as children.

The following year, Franklin drove Eleanor to Groton, a preparatory school that he had attended and where Eleanor's younger brother was a student, and he proposed to her there. Franklin's mother was livid when she heard about the engagement; she booked a Caribbean vacation for him, in hopes that he would change his mind, but the engagement was officially announced in the fall of 1904 in spite of her. Meanwhile, Franklin began studying law at Columbia University, and Eleanor taught classes in a New York slum neighborhood. When they were married on March 17, 1905, her uncle, Theodore Roosevelt, who was President of the Unites States at the time, escorted the bride down the aisle.

Social Purpose

While they were in their teens and away at school, both Eleanor and Franklin had mentors who helped inspire them to work for social improvements. When Franklin first entered politics, in 1910, they were both fascinated by the idea of helping the less fortunate. As Franklin began writing speeches as a candidate for the state senate, Eleanor found herself agreeing with most of his progressive views. She became even more interested in politics after he was elected and they moved to the state capital at Albany, New York. The move also took her away from a life of privilege on the Roosevelt's Hudson River estate, where she felt dominated by her mother-in-law, who lived nearby, although managing a household and raising three children was liberating for her. Anna Eleanor was born in 1906, James was born in 1907, the first Franklin Jr. was born and died in 1909, and Elliott was born in 1910. She would later have two more children: the second Franklin Jr. was born in 1914, and John in 1916.

The family moved to Washington, D.C., in 1913, when Roosevelt was appointed to a position in the Woodrow Wilson administration, and in addition to hosting parties and socializing, Eleanor became active

with the Red Cross after the start of World War I. In 1918, however, her marriage was threatened when she discovered her husband had been involved with her social secretary. Roosevelt ended the affair, Eleanor forgave him, and the couple remained married, drawing on each other's strengths, but they were more a team than the usual concept of husband and wife.

Eleanor became more deeply involved in social causes during those years. She regularly visited wounded soldiers, attended meetings of the International Congress for Women Workers, took classes in typing and shorthand, and put together monthly reports on Congress for the League of Women Voters. She was easily the busiest woman in Washington, and she seemed to love every minute of it.

Great Suffering, Greater Sympathy

Franklin Roosevelt was stricken with polio, in August 1921. It left him partially paralyzed, and for the rest of his life, he couldn't walk without heavy leg braces and a cane, but Eleanor helped him continue to lead an active political life. After she became first lady, she was once challenged after a speech with the question of whether her husband's ailment had affected his mental capacity: "Yes," she replied. "Anyone who has gone through great suffering is bound to have a greater sympathy and understanding of the problems of mankind."

She frequently drove him to speeches and often drove voters to the polls to vote for him. Overcoming her own shyness, Eleanor occasionally substituted for him when he had a conflict in speech-making dates, and she began giving her own talks as well. As if she didn't have enough to do, she also worked as a teacher in private schools, served as editor of the *Women's Democratic News,* and served on the boards of several charitable foundations.

When Franklin Roosevelt was elected governor of New York in 1928, Eleanor became even more active in politics, and her role expanded further four years later when her husband ran for the presidency. She helped write biographical profiles of her candidate husband, worked with the women's division of the Democratic

Party, and went with her husband on campaign trips. He rarely made a speech that he hadn't read to her in advance, relying on her advice to make them more effective.

Above and Beyond

As first lady, Eleanor Roosevelt presided graciously over the usual festive occasions in the White House. She traveled extensively—more than 38,000 miles in 1933—and still more the following year. With the country in the grips of the Great Depression, she used her frequent trips to give the president firsthand reports on conditions across the country. She also became involved in several new causes: Her report on poor neighborhoods in Washington led Congress to appropriate money for social improvement in the nation's capital; she spoke out for equal pay for women and for consumer protection; and she became involved in projects connected with her husband's New Deal program.

Eleanor Roosevelt is credited with having expanded at least two New Deal projects: She lobbied successfully to have artists and entertainers included in appropriations for work through the Civil Works Administration; and she championed the National Youth Administration that funded part-time jobs at schools for high school and college students and part-time jobs for other young people. She promoted that program after becoming concerned that young people would become dispirited and restless over their future. She also lobbied to have noted educator Mary McLeod Bethune named to head of the program.

Her support for Bethune was among many examples of Eleanor Roosevelt's activism on the part of African Americans, who were regularly invited to dinners and policy discussions on a scale notably larger than any previous administration. For example, the National Association for the Advancement of Colored People (NAACP) was consulted often for its input into administration policies, and she resigned from the Daughters of the American Revolution when it

Right: Educator Mary McLeod Bethune, a valued advisor to both Franklin D. and Eleanor Roosevelt, was named head of the National Youth Administration, one of the New Deal programs.

refused to allow noted African-American singer Marian Anderson to perform at one of its functions. The first lady sponsored Anderson's use of the Lincoln Memorial on Easter Sunday, and more than 75,000 people attended the event. When Eleanor went to a lecture in Alabama and found that the seating was segregated, with whites on one side and blacks on the other, she picked up her chair and moved it to an open area in the middle.

Among her many humanitarian causes, Eleanor founded the homestead community of Arthurdale, West Virginia, after she visited and saw how horrible the poor miners' living conditions were. From impoverished regions in Appalachia to Japanese internment camps in the West to military bases in Europe and the Pacific, it seemed as though Eleanor Roosevelt was everywhere. A cartoon of the day showed a thick black box representing

a mine where a lone miner exclaims, "For gosh sakes, here comes Mrs. Roosevelt!"

Eleanor Roosevelt was also busy as a columnist, contributing *Mrs. Roosevelt's Column* regularly to *Woman's Home Companion* magazine, and *If You Ask Me* ran in a competing magazine, *Ladies' Home Journal,* and later in *McCalls* magazine. If that wasn't enough, she began writing a syndicated newspaper column, *My Day,* which ranged from general chatter to commentary on social issues. Her autobiography, *This Is My Story,* became a best seller in 1937. Three years later, she spoke out angrily when John Steinbeck's novel *The Grapes of Wrath* was banned in several cities.

Tomorrow Is Now

When Franklin D. Roosevelt died in April 1945, Eleanor broke the news to Vice President Harry S Truman, and she stayed active during his administration, especially in her strong support of the United Nations. She was part of the committee that drafted the UN Declaration of Human Rights and served as a delegate under presidents Truman and John F. Kennedy. Her other responsibilities during the Kennedy administration included serving on the board that developed the Peace Corps and on the President's Commission on the Status of Women. She was eventually slowed by a blood disease and died of it on November 7, 1962.

"The future is literally in our hands to mold as we like," she wrote in *Tomorrow Is Now,* a book that was published shortly after she died. "But we cannot wait until tomorrow. Tomorrow is now." It was the philosophy she had always lived by.

Roosevelt's First Inaugural Address

Delivered on March 4, 1933

When Franklin D. Roosevelt was sworn into office as president, the country was at the worst point in the Great Depression. More than thirteen million people were out of work, and just a month earlier, millions of people were so worried about the nation's economy and their own outlook for survival that they tried to pull their savings out of the bank, and by the time of the inauguration, banks had closed in thirty-eight states.

Roosevelt had a plan of action to combat the Depression. He called it the New Deal during the election campaign. He had already fought the effects of the Depression as governor of New York by consulting with business leaders, scholars, and ordinary citizens to take an aggressive approach to the woes of common people in New York. As president, he was planning an even more ambitious program.

President Roosevelt took the occasion of his inauguration to rally the people. He spoke candidly about problems, and inspirationally about the challenge ahead. "The only thing we have to fear is fear itself," he assured the nation.

Excerpt from Roosevelt's First Inaugural Address

I am certain that my fellow Americans expect that on my induction into the Presidency I will address them with a candor and a decision which the present situation of our Nation impels. This is preeminently the time to speak the truth, the whole truth, frankly and boldly. Nor need we shrink from honestly facing conditions in our country today. This great nation will endure as it has endured, will revive and will prosper. So, first of all, let me assert my firm belief that the only thing we have to fear is fear itself—nameless, unreasoning unjustified terror which paralyzes needed efforts to convert retreat into advance. In every dark hour of our national life a leadership of frankness and vigor has met with that understanding and support of the people themselves which is essential to victory. I am convinced that you will again give that support to leadership in these critical days.

In such a spirit on my part and on yours we face our common difficulties. They concern, thank God, only material things. Values have shrunken to fantastic levels; taxes have risen; our ability to pay has fallen; government of all kinds is faced by serious curtailment of income; the means of exchange are frozen in the currents of trade; the withered leaves of industrial enterprise lie on every side;

farmers find no markets for their produce; the savings of many years in thousands of families are gone.

More important, a host of unemployed citizens face the grim problem of existence, and an equally great number toil with little return. Only a foolish optimist can deny the dark realities of the moment.

Yet our distress comes from no failure of substance. We are stricken by no plague of locusts. Compared with the perils which our forefathers conquered because they believed and were not afraid, we have still much to be thankful for. Nature still offers her bounty and human efforts have multiplied it. Plenty is at our doorstep, but a generous use of it languishes in the very sight of the supply.

Primarily this is because the rulers of the exchange of mankind's goods have failed, through their own stubbornness and their own incompetence, have admitted their failure, and abdicated. Practices of the unscrupulous money changers stand indicted in the court of public opinion, rejected by the hearts and minds of men. True they have tried, but their efforts have been cast in the pattern of an outworn tradition. Faced by failure of credit they have proposed only the lending of more money. Stripped of the lure of profit by which to induce our people to follow their false leadership, they have resorted to exhortations, pleading tearfully for restored confidence. They know only the rules of a generation of self-seekers. They have no vision, and when there is no vision the people perish.

[…]

Our greatest primary task is to put people to work. This is no unsolvable problem if we face it wisely and courageously. It can be accomplished in part by direct recruiting by the Government itself, treating the task as we would treat the emergency of a war, but at the same time, through this employment, accomplishing greatly needed projects to stimulate and reorganize the use of our natural resources.

Hand in hand with this we must frankly recognize the overbalance of population in our industrial centers and, by engaging on a national scale in a redistribution, endeavor to provide a better use of the land for those best fitted for the land. The task can be helped by definite efforts to raise the values of agricultural products and with this the power to purchase the output of our cities. It can be helped by preventing realistically the tragedy of the growing loss through foreclosure of our small homes and our farms. It can be helped by insistence that the Federal, State, and local governments act forthwith on the demand that their cost be drastically reduced. It can be helped by the unifying of relief activities which to-day are often scattered, uneconomical, and unequal. It can be helped by national planning for and supervision of all forms of transportation and of communications and other utilities which have a definitely public character. There are many ways in which it can be helped, but it can never be helped merely by talking about it. We must act and act quickly.

Finally, in our progress toward a resumption of work we require two safeguards against a return of the evils of the old order; there must be a strict supervision of all banking and credits and investments; there must be an end to speculation with other people's money; and there must be provision for an adequate but sound currency.

There are the lines of attack. I shall presently urge upon a new Congress in special session detailed measures for their fulfillment, and I shall seek the immediate assistance of the several States.

Through this program of action we address ourselves to putting our own national house in order and making income balance outgo. Our international trade relations, though vastly important, are in point of time and necessity secondary to the establishment of a sound national economy. I favor as a practical policy the putting of first things first. I shall spare no effort to restore world trade by international economic readjustment, but the emergency at home can not wait on that accomplishment.

[…]

If I read the temper of our people correctly, we now realize as we have never realized before our interdependence on each other; that we can not merely take but we must give as well; that if we are to go forward, we must move as a trained and loyal army willing to sacrifice for the good of a common discipline, because without such discipline no progress is made, no leadership becomes effective. We are, I know, ready and willing to submit our lives and property to such discipline, because it makes possible a leadership which aims at a larger good. This I propose to offer, pledging that the larger purposes will bind upon us all as a sacred obligation with a unity of duty hitherto evoked only in time of armed strife.

With this pledge taken, I assume unhesitatingly the leadership of this great army of our people dedicated to a disciplined attack upon our common problems.

[…]

I am prepared under my constitutional duty to recommend the measures that a stricken nation in the midst of a stricken world may require. These measures, or such other measures as the Congress may build out of its experience and wisdom, I shall seek, within my constitutional authority, to bring to speedy adoption. But in the event that the Congress shall fail to take one of these two courses and in the event that the national emergency is still critical, I shall not evade the clear course of duty that will then confront me. I shall ask the Congress for the one remaining instrument to meet the crisis—broad Executive power to wage a war against the emergency, as great as the power that would be given to me if we were in fact invaded by a foreign foe.

For the trust reposed in me I will return the courage and the devotion that befit the time. I can do no less.

What Happened Next

President Roosevelt called a special session of Congress, which had been adjourned and wasn't scheduled to begin meeting again until December 1933. The legislators granted him special powers and helped him enact dozens of measures to provide relief by creating jobs and reforming financial systems. Through the end of June—a period called the First Hundred Days—Congress and the president worked closely together to bring the country out of the worst stage of the Depression.

Many people benefited from the programs that were enacted by the federal government. In general, the economy improved modestly until more problems emerged in 1936, but the worst was clearly over. The New Deal programs were dismantled by 1941, when the United States entered World War II and millions of people went to work again in jobs that helped the war effort.

Roosevelt's First Fireside Chat

Delivered on March 12, 1933

Radio first emerged as a major national medium during the 1920s, and Franklin D. Roosevelt was one of the first politicians to make use of it to broadcast messages to the general public. He began broadcasting Fireside Chats while he was governor of New York from 1928 to 1932, using common language to address issues of concern to citizens of New York, and he continued the practice on a national scale after he was elected president.

His first presidential Fireside Chat focused on the banking crisis, and he carefully explained the nature of the problem, urged people to be calm, and announced his intention to call a bank holiday—to close all banks while the government arranged for funds that would keep them in business.

Excerpt from Roosevelt's First Fireside Chat

I want to talk for a few minutes with the people of the United States about banking—with the comparatively few who understand the mechanics of banking but more particularly with the overwhelming majority who use banks for the making of deposits and the drawing of checks. I want to tell you what has been done in the last few days, why it was done, and what the next steps are going to be.

[...]

First of all, let me state the simple fact that when you deposit money in a bank the bank does not put the money into a safe deposit vault. It invests your money in many different forms of credit—bonds, commercial paper, mortgages and many other kinds of loans. In other words, the bank puts your money to work to keep the wheels of industry and of agriculture turning around. A comparatively small part of the money you put into the bank is kept in currency—an amount which in normal times is wholly sufficient to cover the cash needs of the average citizen. In other words, the total amount of all the currency in the country is only a small fraction of the total deposits in all of the banks.

What, then, happened during the last few days of February and the first few days of March? Because of undermined confidence on the part of the public, there was a general rush by a large portion of our population to turn bank deposits into currency or gold—a rush so great that the soundest banks could not get enough currency to meet the demand. The reason for this was that on the spur of the moment it was, of course, impossible to sell perfectly sound assets of a bank and convert them into cash except at panic prices far below their real value.

By the afternoon of March 3rd scarcely a bank in the country was open to do business. Proclamations temporarily closing them in whole or in part had been issued by the Governors in almost all the States. It was then that I issued the proclamation providing for the nationwide bank holiday, and this was the first step in the Government's reconstruction of our financial and economic fabric.

The second step was the legislation promptly and patriotically passed by the Congress confirming my proclamation and broadening my powers so that it became possible in view of the requirement of time to extend the holiday and lift the ban of that holiday gradually. This law also gave authority to develop a program of rehabilitation of our banking facilities. I want to tell our citizens in every part of the Nation that the national Congress—Republicans and Democrats alike—showed by this action a devotion to public welfare and a realization of the emergency and the necessity for speed that it is difficult to match in our history.

The third stage has been the series of regulations permitting the banks to continue their functions to take care of the distribution of food and household necessities and the payment of payrolls.

This bank holiday, while resulting in many cases in great inconvenience, is affording us the opportunity to supply the currency necessary to meet the situation. No sound bank is a dollar worse off than it was when it closed its doors last Monday.

[…]

We had a bad banking situation. Some of our bankers had shown themselves either incompetent or dishonest in their handling of the peoples funds. They had used the money entrusted to them in speculations and unwise loans. This was, of course, not true in the vast majority of our banks, but it was true in enough of them to shock the people for a time into a sense of insecurity and to put them into a frame of mind where they did not differentiate, but seemed to assume that the acts of a comparative few had tainted them all. It was the Government's job to straighten out this situation and do it as quickly as possible. And the job is being performed. I do not promise you that every bank will be reopened or that individual losses will not be suffered, but there will be no losses that possibly could be avoided; and there would have been more and greater losses had we continued to drift. I can even promise you salvation for some at least of the sorely pressed banks. We shall be engaged not merely in reopening sound banks but in the creation of sound banks through reorganization.

It has been wonderful to me to catch the note of confidence from all over the country. I can never be sufficiently grateful to the people for the loyal support they have given me in their acceptance of the judgment that has dictated our course, even though all our processes may not have seemed clear to them.

After all, there is an element in the readjustment of our financial system more important than currency, more important than gold, and that is the confidence of the people. Confidence and courage are the essentials of success in carrying out our plan. You people must have faith; you must not be stampeded by rumors or guesses. Let us unite in banishing fear. We have provided the machinery to restore our financial system; it is up to you to support and make it work.

It is your problem no less than it is mine. Together we cannot fail.

What Happened Next

The Emergency Banking Act passed by Congress (the second step Roosevelt noted to address the banking crisis) provided the funds necessary for banks to operate normally. Governors of some states had been closing banks beginning in late February, and the nationwide bank holiday began on Friday, March 10. Banks were beginning to open again for business on Monday, March 13.

Within a week, the federal government passed several more acts to confront the economic crisis: Federal workers had their pay cut by 15 percent, government pensions were reduced, and taxes on beer and wine went into effect. Those acts provided the government with money to help banks and provide funds for states to use in their own job programs.

The bank holiday, and President Roosevelt's New Deal program in general, marked the greatest government peacetime involvement in the American economy in history. The programs helped lift the morale of the nation and provided many Americans with temporary jobs. The Depression ended after the United States entered World War II and industries began massive production of war matériel.

Roosevelt's War Message to the American People

Delivered on December 8, 1941

World War II began in September 1939. The United States maintained neutrality, but in spite of the official policy, the U.S. government's actions were often openly supportive of the Allied nations—Great Britain, France, and the Soviet Union—in their struggle against Nazi Germany. Meanwhile, the United States had been going through a period of strained relations with Japan since 1931, when it invaded and occupied the Manchuria region of China, and those tensions grew worse when the Japanese army occupied several other countries. The United States announced a trade embargo against Japan in 1941.

The United States and Japan continued to make occasional attempts at negotiation, but it all ended on December 7, 1941, when the Japanese launched a surprise attack on the American naval base at Pearl Harbor, on the Hawaiian island of Oahu. In response to the attack, President Roosevelt asked for and received from Congress a declaration of war on Japan. He announced his request for the declaration to the American public in a nationally broadcast radio address on December 8, 1941.

Yesterday, December 7, 1941—a date which will live in infamy—the United States of America was suddenly and deliberately attacked by naval and air forces of the Empire of Japan.

The United States was at peace with that nation and, at the solicitation of Japan, was still in conversation with its government and its emperor looking toward the maintenance of peace in the Pacific. Indeed, one hour after Japanese air squadrons had commenced bombing Oahu, the Japanese Ambassador to the United States and his colleague delivered to the secretary of state a formal reply to a recent American message. While this reply stated that it seemed useless to continue the existing diplomatic negotiations, it contained no threat or hint of war or armed attack.

It will be recorded that the distance of Hawaii from Japan makes it obvious that the attack was deliberately planned many days or even weeks ago. During the intervening time, the Japanese Government has deliberately sought to deceive the United States by false statements and expressions of hope for continued peace.

The attack yesterday on the Hawaiian Islands has caused severe damage to American naval and military forces. Very many American lives have been lost. In addition, American ships have been reported torpedoed on the high seas between San Francisco and Honolulu.

Yesterday the Japanese Government also launched an attack against Malaya.

Last night Japanese forces attacked Hong Kong.

Last night Japanese forces attacked Guam.

Last night Japanese forces attacked the Philippine Islands.

Last night the Japanese attacked Wake Island.

This morning the Japanese attacked Midway Island.

Japan has, therefore, undertaken a surprise offensive extending throughout the Pacific area. The facts of yesterday speak for themselves. The people of the United States have already formed their opinions and well understand the implications to the very life and safety of our nation.

As commander-in-chief of the Army and Navy, I have directed that all measures be taken for our defense.

Always will we remember the character of the onslaught against us.

No matter how long it may take us to overcome this premeditated invasion, the American people in their righteous might will win through to absolute victory.

I believe I interpret the will of the Congress and of the people when I assert that we will not only defend ourselves to the uttermost but will make very certain that this form of treachery shall never endanger us again.

Hostilities exist. There is no blinking at the fact that our people, our territory and our interests are in grave danger.

With confidence in our armed forces—with the unbounding determination of our people—we will gain the inevitable triumph—so help us God.

I ask that the Congress declare that since the unprovoked and dastardly attack by Japan on Sunday, December 7, a state of war has existed between the United States and the Japanese Empire.

What Happened Next

Congress declared war on Japan the same day as Roosevelt's speech to the nation. After Germany, an ally of Japan, declared war on the United States, the United States declared war on Germany on December 11, 1941. Against Japan, the United States used a strategy of "island hopping," engaging Japanese forces in a series of isolated battles while the United States also fought Nazi forces in North Africa and Europe. There were many battles in the Pacific Ocean, including the famous battles of Midway and Okinawa, but the U.S. military did not give full attention to the war against Japan until after victory was assured in Europe, which occurred in June 1945, two months after President Roosevelt died.

American military experts were certain that the Japanese military would not surrender, and that five hundred thousand soldiers might die during a military invasion of Japan. Those factors weighed heavily on the decision by Roosevelt's successor as president, Harry S Truman, to use the atomic bomb on Japan to force a surrender. Nuclear bombs were dropped on the Japanese cities of Hiroshima and Nagasaki in August 1945, causing massive destruction and loss of life. The Japanese military officially surrendered a few days later.

Harry S Truman

"The buck stops here."

—*a sign on Harry S Truman's desk*

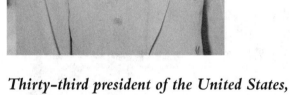

Thirty-third president of the United States, 1945–1953

Full name: *Harry S Truman*
Born: *May 8, 1884, Lamar, Missouri*
Died: *December 26, 1972, Kansas City, Missouri*
Burial site: *Courtyard of the Truman Presidential Library, Independence, Missouri*
Parents: *John Anderson and Martha Ellen Young Truman*
Spouse: *Elizabeth "Bess" Virginia Wallace (1885–1982; m. 1919)*
Children: *Mary Margaret (1924–2008)*
Religion: *Baptist*
Education: *Attended Kansas City School of Law*
Occupations: *Clerk; salesman, farmer; soldier*
Government positions: *Jackson County, Missouri, judge; U.S. senator from Missouri*
Political party: *Democratic*
Dates as president: *April 12, 1945–January 20, 1949 (first term); January 20, 1949–January 20, 1953 (second term)*
Age upon taking office: *60*

ecisive, blunt, fair-minded, and well-informed, Harry S Truman was the "common man" president. Where others had been supportive of average citizens, he was one of them. He had worked as a farmer, a clerk, and a salesman, among other jobs; he served in the military during World War I; and he became a straight-talking and honest politician who continually beat the odds to win elections.

As president, Truman had to face some of the most profound issues of the twentieth century. He was the first leader to authorize the use of the atomic bomb; he supported war crimes trials against Nazi leaders after World War II; and he fought aggressively, both through diplomacy and military action, to check the spread of Communism.

Dedicated to fairness at home, he proposed strict economic measures and wide-ranging civil rights legislation as part of his administration's "Fair Deal" program to help the nation make a smooth transition from war to peace.

Truman's sweeping foreign and domestic programs met hostile resistance from his opponents in Congress, and his tough measures lost him public support as well. When he ran for election in 1948, some members of his own Democratic Party formed a third party to oppose him. But persisting with determination and conviction, Truman scored a stunning upset victory in spite of them. His campaign theme was borrowed from a remark shouted by a supporter at one of his rallies: "Give 'em hell, Harry!" He would say later that, "Well, I never gave anybody hell—I just told the truth on those fellows and they thought it was hell."

Avid Reader

Born in Lamar, Missouri, on May 8, 1884, Harry S Truman was the oldest of three children of Martha Ellen Young Truman and John Anderson Truman. He had no middle name, but his parents added the initial "S" as a compromise between his grandfathers' names: "Shipp" for his father's father, Anderson Shipp Truman, and "Solomon" for his mother's father, Solomon Young. During the 1948 campaign, some opponents called him Harry "S stands for nothing" Truman, but they knew very well that politically he stood firmly for what he believed was right for the country.

The Truman family moved to Independence, Missouri, in 1890, and he was enrolled in the local public school. He enjoyed playing the piano, but his real passion was reading, although he wore glasses with thick lenses to correct extreme nearsightedness. He read an amazing number of biographies, histories, and accounts of great military battles, but he seemed interested in everything. The staff at the Independence Library swore that he had read every book on every subject in their collection.

After he graduated from high school, Truman didn't have enough money to go on to college, and his nearsightedness kept him from being accepted into the U.S. Military Academy at West Point Military, where he applied. He worked a series of odd jobs—clerking for the Santa Fe Railroad, for the *Kansas City Star* newspaper, and at a bank—before he went to work to help his parents run a farm they had inherited in Grandview, Missouri. While still doing farmwork, Truman trained with the national guard, and he joined a Kansas City Democratic

Right: As soon as young Harry learned to read, he devoured the local library's entire collection.

Timeline

1884: Born in Missouri
1906–16: Works on family farm in Grandview, Missouri
1918: Leads army units with distinction in France and Italy during World War I
1919–22: Works at a men's clothing store in Independence, Missouri
1923–33: Serves as judge in Jackson County Court, Missouri
1934–45: Serves as U.S. senator from Missouri
1939–45: World War II
1945: Serves as vice president under Franklin D. Roosevelt; assumes the office of president after Roosevelt dies; World War II ends
1945–53: Serves as thirty-third U.S. president
1950–54: Korean War
1953: Retires to Independence, Missouri
1972: Dies in Missouri

Above: Harry Truman was a proud Doughboy during World War I.

Political Career Begins

Truman was part owner of a men's clothing store in Kansas City, Missouri, through 1922, when he became the surprise winner of an election as supervisor of roads and buildings in Missouri's Jackson County. Even he was surprised because he had won without the backing of the powerful Pendergast machine, and not only that, but he had beaten a popular candidate supported by the local Ku Klux Klan. Not much authority came with the job, but he managed to improve the county roads and save money at the same time. In the meantime, he studied at the Kansas City Law School and continued drilling with the national guard. He was beaten for reelection by a Klan-supported candidate after he had refused to join the white supremacist group. After working at a job selling memberships to automobile clubs and in a bank, Truman went back to politics in 1926 with the blessings of the local political boss, Tom Pendergast.

Elected to a post with authority over county roads, buildings, and taxes, Truman greatly improved the local construction system, and fired officials, including members of the Pendergast organization, who were pocketing tax money. Nevertheless, Pendergast went

organization run by the politically powerful Pendergast family, which helped him get a job as Grandview's postmaster. When the United States entered World War I in 1917, his national guard unit was mobilized, and he was shipped to Fort Sill, Oklahoma, for training, after which he went back to Missouri as an army recruiter before being elected first lieutenant by the men of Missouri's Second Field Artillery.

Truman was promoted to captain by March 1918, and he commanded a unit that fought with distinction in several battles in France. By the time he was discharged and went back home the following spring, he had reached the rank of major. He married Elizabeth "Bess" Virginia that summer, a girl he had known since they were in fifth grade together. Their only child, Mary Margaret, was born in 1924.

Right: President Truman, First Lady Bess Truman, and their daughter, Margaret.

right on supporting him and he was reelected to a second four-year term. Although the Pendergast machine became associated with gangsters, Truman maintained his integrity as an honest politician, and based on his reputation, he was elected to the U.S. Senate in 1934.

As a senator, Truman was a solid supporter of Franklin D. Roosevelt's New Deal programs, and it enhanced his reputation with the administration. However, when federal investigators began looking into the criminal activities of the Pendergast machine, he found himself accused of being guilty by association. The investigation uncovered strong evidence of corruption and intimidation, and Tom Pendergast went to jail for income tax evasion, although Truman wasn't found to be connected with even a minor act of wrongdoing. But instead of turning his back on the organization, Truman told a reporter that, "Tom Pendergast has always been my friend, and I don't desert a sinking ship."

Meanwhile, Senator Truman was named to the Appropriations Committee, and the Interstate Commerce Committee. He cowrote the Truman-Austin bill, which created the Civil Aeronautics Board to supervise the airplane industry, and he was also a major force behind the Transportation Act of 1940, which brought much needed reform and regulation to the country's railroads.

Surprising Reelection

In spite of his outstanding record in the Senate, Truman was an underdog when he ran for reelection. He was opposed for the Democratic nomination by Missouri governor Lloyd Stark, who had President Roosevelt's backing for his work in bringing down the Pendergast machine. Running behind Stark and another popular candidate and having little money to campaign with, Truman drove around Missouri in his own car, making speeches in plain language concentrating on his record of public service.

Truman won the Democratic nomination by a slim thread, but he went on to defeat his Republican opponent, Manvel H. Davis, who based his campaign on Truman's early ties with Pendergast. Truman's surprising reelection showed that an honest and straightforward politician could win even with meager resources, and his

Painting the Town

During his investigations of government waste, Truman found a warehouse filled to the rafters with drums of olive drab paint left over from World War I. There was enough of it to paint, and repaint, every mailbox in the United States for the next thirty years.

senate colleagues gave him a standing ovation when he went back to Washington to begin his second term.

The United States was dealing with the prospect of entering World War II by then. After finding that military camps and defense plants in his home state were in a deteriorated condition and had padded payrolls, Truman drove around neighboring areas, where he discovered similarly overstaffed operations and poor-quality equipment—paid for with tax dollars. After he reported his findings on the Senate floor and demanded an inquiry, he was named the head of a Senate investigation that was later called the Truman Committee. Its detailed report, supported by many witnesses, uncovered widespread fraud and waste that had cost the taxpayers $400,000 in just three years. However, that was only the beginning. By the time its work was done, the Truman committee saved the country an estimated $15 billion, and he became an important national political figure.

As the 1944 presidential election was closing in, President Roosevelt was noticeably in poor health, and his outspoken vice president, Henry A. Wallace, was considered a political liability. No clear vice-presidential candidate emerged at the nominating convention, and Truman won it on the second round of balloting. He turned out to be an excellent campaigner while Roosevelt limited his appearances to protect his health and to focus on steering the country through the war. The United States had entered World War II three years earlier, and by 1944, the Allies were pushing across Europe toward Germany itself, and it was beginning to look as though victory might be close.

Truman was an active vice president, although he saw very little of Roosevelt. Right after the inauguration, the president went to Eastern Europe for the Yalta Conference where he discussed war strategies and ways the Allies would manage lands they reconquered. British prime minister Winston Churchill and Soviet leader Josef

Above: Harry S Truman takes the oath of office as president administered by Chief Justice Harlan Fiske, April 12, 1945.

Stalin signed the agreement that ended the conference, and Roosevelt went back to Washington, but he didn't share any information with Truman about what had been discussed at Yalta. All the vice president knew was what he read in the newspapers.

Roosevelt left for his vacation home at Warm Springs, Georgia, on March 30, and two weeks later, Truman was called to the White House for a meeting with Eleanor Roosevelt, the president's wife. As he walked into her office, she said, "Harry, the president is dead." Truman asked if there was anything he could do for her, and she answered, "Is there anything we can do for you? For you are the one in trouble now." Truman had been vice president of the United States for fewer than ninety days. He was sworn into the office of president on April 12, 1945.

"I don't know whether any of you fellows ever had a load of hay fall on you, but when they told me what had happened, I felt like the moon, the stars, and all the planets had fallen on me."
—Harry S Truman, to reporters at his swearing-in

A New Weapon

Truman met with Roosevelt's Cabinet and asked them all to stay in their positions. Secretary of War Henry L. Stimson stayed in the room after the others left, and he informed Truman about a new weapon that the United States had successfully tested—the atomic bomb. It was the first time Truman had heard that such a weapon was even on the drawing board. Meanwhile, the Nazi defeat became official on May 8, 1945—Truman's sixty-first birthday, which he proclaimed as Victory-in-Europe Day (V-E Day).

Below: All America mourned the passing of President Roosevelt, and many also wept in sympathy for his successor.

A Rocky Start

When President Roosevelt asked Harry Truman to run for vice president in 1944, he told him to go to hell. It took a great deal of arm-twisting and appeals to party loyalty to make him change his mind. But when he moved into the White House, the Democrats weren't too sure they had made such a smart move, and they spent the next three years plotting to dump Harry in the 1948 election. They were chagrined when he gave a speech stating, "There's going to be a Democrat in the White House in 1949, and you're lookin' at him." The general reaction was "over our dead bodies," and they decided to humiliate him at history's first televised political convention by arguing over platform issues deep into prime time, and not getting around to actually nominating him until two o'clock in the morning.

The Truman Administration

Administration Dates: April 12, 1945–January 20, 1949

January 20, 1949–January 20, 1953

Vice President: None (1945–49)

Alben W. Barkley (1949–53)

Cabinet:

Secretary of State	Edward R. Stettinius Jr. (1945)
	James F. Byrnes (1945–47)
	George C. Marshall (1947–49)
	Dean G. Acheson (1949–53)
Secretary of the Treasury	Henry Morgenthau Jr. (1945)
	Frederick M. Vinson (1945–46)
	John W. Snyder (1946–53)
Secretary of War	Henry L. Stimson (1945)
	Robert P. Patterson (1945–47)
	Kenneth C. Royall (1947)
Attorney General	Francis B. Biddle (1945)
	Thomas C. Clark (1945–49)
	James H. McGrath (1949–52)
	James P. McGranery (1952–53)
Secretary of Defense	James V. Forrestal (1947–49)
	Louis A. Johnson (1949–50)
	George C. Marshall (1950–51)
	Robert A. Lovett (1951–53)
Secretary of the Navy	James V. Forrestal (1945–47)
Secretary of the Interior	Harold L. Ickes (1945–46)
	Julius A. Krug (1946–49)
	Oscar L. Chapman (1949–53)
Secretary of Agriculture	Claude R. Wickard (1945)
	Clinton P. Anderson (1945–48)
	Charles F. Brannan (1948–53)
Secretary of Commerce	Henry A. Wallace (1945–46)
	William Averell Harriman (1946–48)
	Charles Sawyer (1948–53)
Secretary of Labor	Frances Perkins (1945)
	Lewis B. Schwellenbach (1945–48)
	Maurice J. Tobin (1948–53)

Above: British Prime Minister Winston Churchill, U.S. President Harry Truman, and Soviet Premier Josef Stalin in a lighter moment at Potsdam.

Foreign affairs issues took up nearly all of his time. In June, he addressed the final session of the founding conference of the United Nations (UN) in San Francisco, and then he presented the United Nations Charter to the Senate for ratification. From July 17 until August 2, he attended the Potsdam Conference in Germany. Meeting with Stalin, Churchill, and Clement Attlee, Churchill's successor, Truman proposed the establishment of an international council to settle issues related to World War II and to conduct trials against high-ranking Nazis for war crimes. He also secured Stalin's promise that the Soviet Union would declare war on Japan.

Truman issued the Potsdam Declaration calling for Japan's unconditional surrender on July 26, and in the meantime his administration convened a committee of distinguished citizens to debate moral and military issues surrounding the use of the atomic bomb. Military leaders reported that an invasion of the Japanese mainland would probably cost another 500,000 lives, and agreed that using the atom bomb could force a quick Japanese surrender.

When Japan didn't respond to the Potsdam surrender

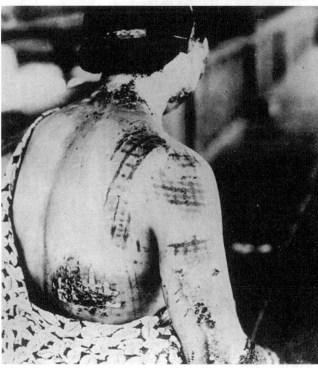

Left: On August 8, 1945, two days after the bombing of Hiroshima, a second atomic bomb was dropped on the city of Nagasaki.

ultimatum, Truman authorized use of the atomic bomb. Dropped on Hiroshima, Japan, on August 6, 1945, at 9:15 A.M. Tokyo time, the explosion virtually destroyed the city, and according to Supreme Allied Headquarters, almost 130,000 people were killed, injured, or missing, and another 175,000 were left homeless.

While Soviet forces invaded Japanese strongholds in Manchuria and Korea, a second nuclear bomb was dropped on the city of Nagasaki on August 9. One third of the city was destroyed and nearly 70,000 people were killed or injured. Five days later, on August 14, Japan asked for peace. The official Japanese surrender took place on September 2, 1945, aboard the battleship U.S.S. *Missouri* anchored in Tokyo Bay.

The Cold War Begins

The end of World War II was followed almost immediately by the beginning of a different kind of war, this time between the United States and the Soviet Union. The two nations never directly engaged in battle, but tense conflicts and failed diplomacy came to be known as the Cold War. The Soviet Army controlled much of Eastern Europe, and the Soviet government refused to hold free elections. When the Union of Soviet Socialist Republics (USSR) moved to "protect" naval stations in Turkey, and nearby Greece was embroiled in a civil war with Communist-dominated rebels, the president responded with the Truman Doctrine, which sent aid to anticommunist forces in both countries. Truman wanted to inspire American public sentiment for fighting the Cold War, and Congress backed his request for $250 million for Greece and $150 million for Turkey.

World War II had left much of Europe in ruin. Truman worked closely with his secretary of state, General George C. Marshall, to create the European Recovery Plan. Better known as the Marshall Plan, it helped rebuild

Left: Survivors of the atomic bomb suffered flash burns that corresponded to the patterns on the clothing they were wearing at the time.

European economies (while also benefiting U.S. trade) and strengthened democratic governments. Under the Marshall Plan, the United States spent more than $12.5 billion over four years, helping to promote a quick recovery throughout Western Europe, including West Germany. The Soviet Union called the Marshall Plan an "imperialist plot to enslave Europe."

Above right: Japan's leaders make the war's end official by signing surrender papers on the deck of the U.S.S. Missouri.

Above left: Among the Nazi leaders who stood trial for war crimes at Nuremberg was Herman Goering, who cheated the hangman by swallowing cyanide in his cell.

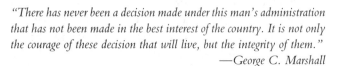

"There has never been a decision made under this man's administration that has not been made in the best interest of the country. It is not only the courage of these decision that will live, but the integrity of them."
—*George C. Marshall*

Below: No one who was in New York's Times Square on August 14, 1945, V-J Day, ever forgot the experience.

The USSR established its own plan for Eastern Europe, which was dominated by communist governments allied with it. The Soviets closed Allied access to the city of Berlin and helped create a communist state called East Germany around it. Truman countered by ordering continuous airlifts of essential supplies into Berlin—a program called the Berlin Airlift and unofficially called Operation Vitals, which lasted for nearly a year. War was distinctly possible, with each side waiting for the other to make the first military move. Truman's humanitarian gesture toward Berlin helped solidify anti-Soviet sentiments among noncommunist nations.

George C. Marshall

George Catlett Marshall Jr. was born on December 31, 1880, in Uniontown, Pennsylvania. Socially awkward and a poor student, he gradually developed a strong drive to succeed. His father had served in the Civil War, and Marshall decided to attend the Virginia Military Institute. He thrived in the disciplined environment, graduating as the top cadet in his class. He married Elizabeth Carter Coles shortly after he received a commission as a second lieutenant in the U.S. Army in 1902. After serving in the Philippines, he returned to the United States to attend an infantry training school and then the army's command and general staff school. He taught for two years at Fort Leavenworth, Kansas.

During World War I, Marshall was among the first members of the American Expeditionary Force sent to France in 1917 when the United States entered the war. He served as chief of operations at the American headquarters in France and earned the nickname "Wizard" for his ability to make plans with firm details for commanders. Winning the respect of General John J. Pershing, America's supreme commander in World War I, Marshall worked as Pershing's personal aide from 1919 to 1924. After a tour of duty in China, Marshall was left a widower when his wife died unexpectedly in 1927. In 1930, Marshall met and married Katherine Tupper Brown.

During the middle of the Great Depression in the 1930s, Marshall supervised Illinois National Guard units and Civilian Conservation Corps (CCC) camps. One of many New Deal government programs designed to combat the Depression, the CCC was run in military fashion and gave unemployed young men work on conservation projects. In 1938, Marshall was appointed to manage the War Plans Division of the army, then he became army chief of staff after World War II began in 1939. He is credited with helping the U.S. military rebound effectively from the Japanese attack at Pearl Harbor in December 1941.

As a trusted military advisor to President Franklin D. Roosevelt, Marshall participated in all major wartime policy-making conferences. Marshall was responsible for elevating General Dwight D. Eisenhower to command early military moves against Germany. Marshall was expected to command what became the Allied D-Day invasion of 1944, but Eisenhower headed the invasion instead;

Roosevelt said he "could not sleep well at night with Marshall out of Washington." Marshall became Time magazine's Man of the Year in 1944.

Marshall began a well-earned retirement after the war ended in 1945, but President Harry S Truman asked him to mediate an end to the long civil war in China. A firm and patient negotiator, Marshall accomplished more than previous American leaders had, but in the end his mission failed. Nevertheless, in 1947, Truman asked Marshall to become his secretary of state. With Europe still reeling from the destruction of World War II and a threat of communist expansion by the Soviet Union and China looming, Marshall developed a plan to help bolster European nations. What became known as the Marshall Plan succeeded grandly. The United States provided money and materials while noncommunist Europeans worked together to solve their problems. An economically healthy Western Europe defeated postwar hunger, resumed trade with the United States, and rejected communism. Marshall went on to win the Nobel Peace Prize for his efforts.

Marshall resigned as secretary of state early in 1949, but when North Korean communists invaded South Korea in June 1950, Truman convinced Marshall to take the recently created post of secretary of defense. The president thought that only Marshall had sufficient prestige to get Congress, Cabinet departments, and different branches of the military to cooperate in the United Nations effort to stop communist aggression in Korea.

When President Truman rejected General Douglas MacArthur's plan to expand the war to Communist China, MacArthur publicly criticized the president's policies, and Truman relieved him of command. MacArthur's supporters were outraged. Senator Joseph McCarthy of Wisconsin claimed that the U.S. government, as represented by Roosevelt, Truman, and Marshall, had allowed the Soviets to take over Eastern Europe and had "lost China" to communism as well. McCarthy published a book proving, he claimed, that Marshall was the leader of a communist conspiracy. However, in 1954, it was McCarthy, not Marshall, who was disgraced during nationally televised hearings concerning communist infiltration of the American military. McCarthy's accusations, many of them exaggerated and false, hurt the reputations of many respectable Americans, including Marshall. Marshall's reputation was quickly restored with McCarthy's downfall. Marshall died on October 16, 1959.

Problems at Home

At home, the end of the war was greeted with unbounded joy and celebration, but it took time for life to get back to normal again. From the beginning of the Great Depression in 1929, through the end of World War II in 1945, Americans had either lived through rough economic times or faced limited supplies and food rationing to help the war effort. Remembering the economic problems that plagued the country after World War I, Truman was determined to avoid a similar period of runaway inflation and high unemployment.

In an attempt to take decisive action, Truman proposed wage controls, price controls, and rent controls, and he also called for expanding public housing and extending old-age benefits. He supported a national health insurance program, a higher minimum wage, and a permanent Fair Employment Practices Commission to help minorities. These sweeping proposals met with quick opposition from Congress and were stalled. Without controls, prices started going up, and workers began striking for higher wages. Always a strong labor sympathizer, Truman nevertheless used executive orders and court injunctions to prevent or end strikes harmful to the national economy.

Truman's actions were widely criticized, even by members of his own party. With rising prices, strikes, and scarcities, the midterm elections of 1946 were a clear-cut victory for Republicans, who gained majorities in both houses of Congress for the first time since 1930. In 1947, the new Congress easily passed the Taft-Hartley Act, which outlawed union-only workplaces, prohibited certain union activities, forbade unions to contribute to political campaigns, established loyalty oaths for union leaders, and allowed court orders to stop strikes that could affect national health or safety. Truman vetoed the bill, but Congress overrode it. When Truman called for legislation to control rising prices, Congress instead voted a tax-cut bill that favored wealthy people. Several of his other measures were bottled up in Congress, including his fair employment and national health proposals.

One of Truman's more far-reaching accomplishments was the result of an executive order that didn't need congressional approval when he ordered desegregation

Extracurricular Activity

The Trumans' daughter, Margaret, was a trained coloratura soprano who performed in a national radio broadcast with the Detroit Symphony Orchestra and even appeared on Ed Sullivan's television show. When she sang at Washington's Constitution Hall, the Post's music critic said, among other unkind things, that "She is flat a good deal of the time." The president was furious, and he sat down and dashed off a letter: "I have just read your lousy review buried in the back pages. You sound like a frustrated old man who never made a success. […] I have never met you, but if I do you'll need a new nose and a supporter below." Then the president went back to the affairs of state.

Below: Harry Truman was an accomplished piano player. His most famous appearance in that role was at the National Press Club, where actress Lauren Bacall showed up to sing along.

of the armed forces. But when he called for an end to "Jim Crow" state laws that maintained racial segregation in the South, he lost support even within his own party. Southern Democrats abandoned their party when those policies were written into the 1948 presidential platform, and South Carolina governor J. Strom Thurmond formed a third party: the States' Rights Democrats, or Dixiecrats. Meanwhile, former vice president Henry Wallace broke away and formed yet another new organization, the Progressive Party.

With the Democratic Party in disarray, and Republicans enjoying increasing support, Truman's popularity was at an all-time low: Workers were angry at his interference in strikes; businesses bristled at his insistence on maintaining wartime controls on the economy; and his civil-rights policies alienated some white voters.

"Dewey Defeats Truman"

After he received the Democratic Party nomination, Truman pulled a master political stroke by calling Congress back into session on July 26 to give Republicans a chance to carry out their party's platform pledges. When the special session ended without any important legislation, Truman took off on an extensive cross-country whistle-stop tour, defending his record and blasting the "do-nothing" Republican Congress. When someone yelled, "Give 'em hell, Harry!" at a stop in Albuquerque, New Mexico, that became his campaign slogan.

Nearly everyone, from political pundits to lifelong Democrats, thought that the Republican candidate, New York governor Thomas E. Dewey, would win a walk, but Truman campaigned hard right up until the end. A few hours after the polls closed, the *Chicago Tribune* put out an early edition with the headline DEWEY DEFEATS TRUMAN, but as the image of a smiling Truman holding up a copy of the paper showed the next day, he had proved them wrong. His whistle-stop tour had energized small town, rural, and minority voters, and he was reelected.

The Gathering of Zion

At the end of World War II, the survivors of the Nazi Holocaust, who were called "displaced persons" began wandering across Europe in the direction of Palestine, their "Promised Land." It was under control of the British who closed the door to these would-be settlers, but there was strong support in the U.S. to open it. The matter was the subject of one of the earliest debates in the new United Nations Organizations, which finally decided to partition Palestine into separate Jewish and Arab states, though neither side accepted this. President Truman was a man on a tightrope. His Truman Doctrine pledging to stand in the way of Soviet expansion into Greece and Turkey meant that he needed Arab goodwill as a buffer in the region, and oil under their territory made it even more important. Harry Truman was a man who didn't mind making tough decisions, and he announced that it was time to forget about political answers and Palestine should come under a United Nations trusteeship. While the UN was debating that, the Jews took matters into their own hands and on May 14, 1948, they declared themselves an independent country and said its name would be Israel. They'd have to fight for it, of course, and they did. But it never could have happened without Harry Truman's support.

Below: Truman takes his message to the people from the back of a train.

1948 Election Results

Presidential / Vice presidential candidates	Popular Votes	Electoral Votes
Harry S Truman / Alben W. Barkley (Democratic)	24,105,695	303
Thomas E. Dewey / Earl Warren (Republican)	21,969,170	189
J. Strom Thurmond / Fielding L. Wright (States' Rights Democratic)	1,169,021	39

Incumbent president Truman upset Dewey, who had also lost in the 1944 presidential election. Two factions of the Democratic Party broke off: one, the States' Rights Democratic (Dixiecrat) Party, led by South Carolina governor Thurmond, won four states; the other, the Progressive Party, led by former vice president Henry A. Wallace, was less successful. Popular World War II general Dwight D. Eisenhower was wooed by both parties, but he declined to enter the race.

Left: After winning the 1948 election, President Truman couldn't help poking fun at the Chicago Tribune, *which reported that he had lost.*

Cold War Hits Home

A Democratic majority was elected to Congress in the 1948 election, but Truman still had only modest success with his domestic programs during his second term. Increased public housing, expanded Social Security coverage, increased minimum wages, and stronger farm price support bills were parts of his Fair Deal domestic program that passed Congress. However, his request for repeal of the Taft-Hartley Act, as well as plans for constructing public hydroelectric companies and proposals for civil-rights legislation were rejected. He managed to strengthen civil rights within the Justice Department, and he appointed a few African Americans to important government positions.

Meanwhile, the Cold War hit home in 1948. Writer and editor Whittaker Chambers testified before California representative Richard Nixon and the House Un-American Activities Committee that he had been a communist in the 1920s and 1930s. He testified that Alger Hiss, a member of the State Department, had given him classified documents to send to the Soviet Union. Hiss denied the charges, but microfilm copies of documents identified as classified and bearing Hiss's handwriting were uncovered, and Hiss was indicted for perjury. The jury failed to reach a verdict, but he was convicted after a second trial two years later.

In February 1950, Wisconsin senator Joseph R. McCarthy made a speech in Wheeling, West Virginia, charging that the State Department knowingly employed over two hundred communists. He consistently reduced the number over time, and an investigation revealed that all of his charges were false, but McCarthy went right on accusing government officials and private citizens of having communist sympathies. He held hearings that implicated hundreds of people, many of whom lost their jobs and were deprived of their rights. Not one spy was unearthed, and McCarthy was eventually discredited, but not until after he had damaged many lives, careers, and reputations. He was so powerful at one point that two senators who dared to challenge him lost their bids for reelection.

Also in 1950, Congress passed the Internal Security Act, known as the McCarran Act, over Truman's veto. It required all communist organizations to register with the government, allowed the government to jail communists

Left: Senator Joseph R. McCarthy (R.WI) with his investigations committee's chief counsel, Roy Cohn.

Whistle Stop

Harry Truman told his campaign advisors that most people out in the American heartland had never seen their local airport and probably didn't even know where it was. But, he said, everybody knew where the train station was, and that was the place to reach out to them. He traveled over 30,000 miles by train, and made more than 300 speeches to some 20 million people. He thought that meeting voters face-to-face was the only way to campaign. "When you get on television," he said, "you're wearing a lot of powder and paint that somebody else has put on your face. And you haven't even combed your own hair."

during national emergencies, prohibited communists from working in defense positions, and denied admission into the United States of anyone who was a member of any totalitarian organization.

When the White House underwent a major renovation during Truman's second term, the family lived at Blair House, a large house across the street. Work, entertaining, and Truman's brisk daily walks all proceeded as usual during the three years it took to rebuild the executive mansion. Truman escaped an assassination attempt at Blair House when two gunmen tried to kill him on November 1, 1950. A secret service agent and one of the gunmen were killed. The second gunman was found guilty of attempted murder and sentenced to execution,

but Truman commuted the sentence to life in prison. Twenty-nine years later, President Jimmy Carter commuted the life sentence, and the prisoner was set free.

The Korean War

In foreign affairs, Truman strongly supported the United Nations and continued the Marshall Plan. Seeking to establish a collective defense against communist aggression, he also supported the development of the North Atlantic Treaty Organization (NATO), a regional defense alliance. The Senate ratified the NATO treaty after extensive debate, and World War II hero Dwight D. Eisenhower was selected to command the organization.

Left: No president was more in love with the White House than Harry Truman, and none did more to preserve it for future generations.

Right: One of President Truman's most important decisions was his executive order ending segregation in the military. The policy had a dramatic effect during the war in Korea.

Douglas MacArthur

Douglas MacArthur was born on January 26, 1880, in Little Rock, Arkansas, where MacArthur's father, Arthur, was stationed. His father had fought in the Civil War, earned the Congressional Medal of Honor for heroism, and served as military governor of the Philippines. By then, Douglas MacArthur was beginning his own distinguished military career.

A 1903 graduate of West Point, MacArthur rose rapidly in the military, beginning in the Philippines as an aide to his father. Douglas MacArthur became a captain in 1911, was promoted to major in 1914, and was on the general staff of the army when the United States entered World War I in 1917. MacArthur backed a plan to enlist state national guard units to strengthen the small and inexperienced army, proposing to form a single battalion from volunteers of every state; he called it the Rainbow Battalion, and he argued that it was a practical military plan as well as a way to help unite the nation in the war effort. President Woodrow Wilson approved the idea, and MacArthur was elevated to the rank of colonel. He led the former guardsmen into battle as a brigadier general, and won medals for his bravery and leadership. One of his officers was future president Harry S Truman.

After the war, MacArthur served as superintendent of West Point, went on an assignment to the Philippines, and commanded several army posts. In 1930, he became chief of staff of the army. MacArthur had an unsuccessful marriage in the 1920s, but in 1937 he wed Jean Marie Faircloth and they had a son. General MacArthur retired from the U.S. Army in 1937. Philippines president Manuel Quezon asked him to serve as a military adviser. He became a field marshal in the Philippine army and had as his assistant a young major named Dwight D. Eisenhower.

The Philippines had been a U.S. territory since the Spanish-American War in 1898. It was about to become a free country when World War II began. In 1941, MacArthur was promoted to lieutenant general in charge of the U.S. forces in the Pacific. He believed that the Philippines was not threatened by the war even after Japanese airplanes struck Pearl Harbor on December 7, 1941. But ten hours later, the Japanese struck Clark Field in the Philippines, destroying most of MacArthur's planes. A huge Japanese invasion force hit the Philippines, and MacArthur's troops were penned up in jungles with little possibility of escape or reinforcement. MacArthur took personal command of his army's defenses and refused to leave the desperate situation until he was commanded to by President Franklin D. Roosevelt. MacArthur sent a last message to the Japanese and Filipinos: "I shall return." The army had recommended that his official pronouncement should be, "We shall return."

Two years after he left, and now in command of the army in the Pacific, MacArthur did return to the Philippines. MacArthur made his base on the island nation and directed the army in the final days of the war. As commander of the U.S. forces and of the Allied forces in the Pacific, General MacArthur accepted the Japanese surrender in 1945. He was then charged with helping the transformation of Japan from rule by an emperor to an elected government.

For five years after the war, General MacArthur held several positions—commander of the U.S. forces in the Pacific, commander of the Allied and then the UN forces, and military commander of Japan. An uprising in Korea in 1950 caught the general and the United States by surprise. The attack was so sudden by the communist North Korean military against the democratic South that within a few days the South Korean capital city of Seoul was threatened and U.S. forces were fleeing south. The American army, now joined by UN troops, established a defense line in the far south of the peninsula nation, but this was soon threatened.

MacArthur designed a counteroffensive that put North Korean forces in retreat. It appeared that the war would end quickly with a UN victory. The North Koreans, however, regrouped and were joined by thousands of volunteers from China; together they again pushed back South Korea's defenders. MacArthur carried out an excellent battle plan and repelled the invaders. He proposed to bombard China and help noncommunist Chinese to rebel. Such action would lead to war with China and perhaps the Soviet Union. President Truman, meanwhile, directed all military leaders to refrain from making any plans contrary to the specific police action in Korea. When MacArthur began to speak out against the president's policies, Truman found it harmful and fired his most famous and popular general.

MacArthur returned to Washington, D.C., where 20,000 admirers welcomed him. MacArthur died on April 5, 1964.

In China, the government of Chiang Kai-shek, which the United States supported, was overwhelmingly defeated by communist forces led by Mao Tse-tung in 1949 and was forced into exile on Taiwan, an island off the coast of Mainland China. The People's Republic of China was formed, with Mao as its chairman.

The nation of Korea was divided after World War II, with a communist regime in the north and an anticommunist government in the south, and civil strife in the South inspired North Korea's leader, Kim Il Sung, to try to reunite the country. The North Korean army, equipped mainly by the USSR, invaded South Korea in June 1950, and the United States immediately sent supplies to South Korea and sponsored a UN resolution for military sanctions against Kim Il Sung's government. Then President Truman ordered U.S. troops stationed in Japan to Korea. American and South Korean forces were joined by units from fifteen other nations under UN command, with U.S. general Douglas MacArthur at its head.

The Old Soldier

After President Truman fired General MacArthur for insubordination, the general went to Washington to make a speech before Congress. Truman had no comment, except to note that it was inappropriate for a five-star general to go to Washington and not report to the commander in chief. MacArthur followed-up his speech with a tour of the country drumming up support, many believed, for a run for the presidency. The sitting president predicted that everybody would forget MacArthur in six weeks or so, and he was right, as it turned out. The general himself had unwittingly predicted it when he told Congress, "Old soldiers never die, they just fade away."

Originally a policing effort to protect South Korea, the mission changed as the American and UN forces threw back a North Korean invasion, moved into North Korea, and began approaching the Chinese border. After several warnings, Chinese forces pushed the UN contingent back toward the South, and General MacArthur requested an extension of the war into Communist China, but the Truman administration returned to the original peacekeeping mission. When MacArthur publicly attacked his policy, Truman relieved him of his command in April 1951 and replaced him with Lieutenant General Matthew B. Ridgway.

MacArthur, a hero for his efforts during World War II, returned home to a rousing welcome. On the same day that MacArthur was given a ticker-tape parade in New York City, President Truman was heavily booed when he threw out the ceremonial first pitch of the 1951 baseball season in Washington.

Near the end of Truman's second term, he tried to head off a steel strike. Just hours before it was scheduled to begin, he announced to a nationwide radio audience that Secretary of Commerce Charles Sawyer had been directed to seize the mills to maintain production for the war effort. However, on June 2, 1952, the Supreme Court declared the seizure unconstitutional in *Youngstown Sheet & Tube Co. v. Sawyer*. Truman could have used the Taft-Hartley Act to delay the strike, but he hated the law too much to use it. By that time, Truman had declared that he wouldn't run for reelection.

Left: The war in Korea was undeclared, and was usually called a "police action." But it had all the earmarks of a war to the U.S. Marines.

Legacy

Harry S Truman assumed the office of president during World War II and left while the Korean War was still being fought. The Cold War occupied most of his time in between. Through his support for the United Nations and NATO, the United States became involved in international organizations that could respond to acts of aggression. Truman's attempts to contain communism were continued by his successors, as was reflected by the Vietnam War. His successor, Dwight D. Eisenhower, fulfilled his campaign pledge to end U.S. involvement in Korea.

Truman's success with promoting civil rights was mixed. Progress was made in desegregating the military after his executive order, but civil-rights legislation did not pass through Congress. His attempts to stabilize the postwar economy also met only modest success. A pro-labor president, Truman nevertheless took action against labor when strikes threatened to hurt the nation.

Discussion of Truman's presidency always considers his decision to use the atomic bomb. While it brought a quick end to the war and probably resulted in fewer deaths than in a prolonged conflict, the new weapon brought fears of mass destruction as well. Its influence on history has been immense.

Above: A testament to the power of the atomic bomb. Where a city once stood, all that remained of Nagasaki was a ruin of a Roman Catholic cathedral.

Truman retired to Independence, Missouri, where in 1957 he dedicated the Harry S. Truman Library. He published his memoirs, *Year of Decisions,* and *Years of Trial and Hope, 1946–1952,* and he recounted the events of his administration in a nationally televised series, *Decision: The Conflicts of Harry S. Truman.* Truman died in 1972 and is buried on the grounds of the Truman Library and Museum in his hometown, Independence, Missouri.

Bess Truman

Born February 13, 1885, Independence, Missouri
Died October 18, 1982, Independence, Missouri

"Three things can ruin a man—money, power, and women. I never had any money. I never wanted power. And the only woman in my life is up at the house right now."

—*Harry S Truman*

When Harry S Truman opened a men's store in Kansas City, Missouri, after World War I, his wife, Bess, helped behind the scenes, taking responsibility for advertising and for the store's inventory. She was content with a similar behind-the-scenes role during

her husband's political career in Washington, where he was a senator and eventually president. Bess handled his mail, did some research on issues, and advised him on his speeches.

Avoiding publicity and living quietly, Bess Truman was not comfortable in the role as first lady, which she assumed in 1945. She announced early that she would not speak out on issues or hold press conferences. "I am not the one who was elected," she said. "I have nothing to say to the people." She went to Washington as a small-town woman and never changed. She maintained her modest lifestyle throughout the nearly twenty years she spent in the capital, and then went back to her small town, where she lived for almost another thirty years.

Who's That Playing Third Base?

Harry and Bess first crossed paths at Sunday School in a Presbyterian church in 1890, when he was six and she was five. His family had recently moved to Independence, Missouri, where Bess was born Elizabeth Virginia Wallace to Margaret "Madge" and David Wallace on February 13, 1885. Harry immediately developed a crush on Bess, and he never changed his mind about his feelings for her.

They didn't become friends until they were both in fifth grade, but it was an odd friendship because they had almost nothing in common. Bess's family, who owned a flour mill, was wealthy and lived in a big house. Harry's family, on the other hand, was poor, and he worked in a drugstore as a boy to help make ends meet. Unusually short and very nearsighted, Harry preferred playing piano and reading, while Bess was active, riding horses or skating, and playing whatever sports were in season. Neighbors interviewed many years later by her daughter, Margaret, remembered her as "a marvelous athlete …the best third baseman in Independence …a superb tennis player …a tireless ice skater …and pretty besides."

Both families were struggling when Bess and Harry graduated from high school. Bess's father became distraught by business failures, and he killed himself in the family's bathroom. It deeply affected Bess, and she refused to ever talk about it again. Her daughter Margaret

would say later that Bess was always afraid that the suicide would be brought up as an issue in her husband's political campaigns. It never was, but she remained disturbed over the incident for the rest of her life.

Bess, her mother, and her three younger brothers moved to her grandparent's house when she was nineteen, and the following year her grandfather arranged for Bess to enroll in a nearby finishing school, where young women learned social graces, domestic tasks, and briefly continued their education. After she graduated, she settled into a quiet life, playing bridge, doing needlework, and riding horses.

A Persistent Suitor

Harry, meanwhile, had moved to Grandview, Missouri, where he worked on his family farm. He was visiting an aunt and cousins back in nearby Independence when an opportunity arose to renew his acquaintance with Bess. His aunt had borrowed a cake plate from Bess's mother, and Harry eagerly volunteered to return it, and he and Bess picked up where they had left off. Although he worked long hours on the farm, Harry found time to write letters to Bess, and he visited her as often as he could. One of his letters, written in 1911, included a marriage proposal. He admitted that he was struggling, but he told her, "I've always had a sneakin' notion I'd amount to something."

Bess turned down his proposal, but she didn't turn him away. "The best girl in the universe" and "an ordinary gink," as Truman referred to Bess and himself, gradually became closer. She hadn't planned to get married, but in 1917 she was ready. This time it was Truman who delayed; America was about to enter World War I, and his national-guard unit was ready for military service. He promised to come back and ask her again after the war was over.

Truman did return to Bess and Independence when the war ended, and the couple was married in June 1919. He opened his men's store that same year, and then he was elected to local office three years later. The couple's daughter, Margaret, was born in 1924. Truman's political reputation improved so much over the next ten years that he was elected to the U.S. Senate in 1934.

Life in the Capital

When the family moved to Washington, it was the first time that Bess had lived anywhere but Independence, and she spent most of her time sightseeing and shopping with her mother and her daughter. She also began working in Harry's senate office, helping with the mail and providing down-home advice. When the fact that she was on his payroll became a political issue, Truman quickly defended her: "She earns every cent I pay her."

Truman won reelection in 1940 by traveling around Missouri by car and making impromptu speeches wherever he could find a crowd. That same tactic was expanded in the presidential election of 1948 in a whistle-stop, cross-country train tour. Stopping in any small or large town that had a station, Truman spoke plainly to people who shared his experiences as a hardworking person from a small town who was just like them. He often ended his campaign talks by introducing his wife as "the Boss," and his daughter as "the Boss's Boss."

Truman had become vice president in 1944, and three months later, he was president after Franklin D. Roosevelt died. The Trumans took part in the ritual of White House social functions, and they entertained in simple and unassuming ways.

Bess Truman handled White House bookkeeping and she supervised the daily menu. She also advised her husband on reelection strategies and fulfilled her social obligations as first lady. When the White House was closed for a major renovation during Truman's second term, the family moved into nearby Blair House and kept their social life to a minimum.

Back Home Again

The Trumans retired to Independence after his presidency ended in 1953. Bess was happy to get back to a quiet life, but the streets of Independence were jammed with people celebrating their arrival. After things quieted down, she enjoyed reading and watching sports, and she helped arrange Margaret's wedding in 1956. Truman wrote his memoirs, and he occasionally spoke out on political issues. In 1957, the couple dedicated the Harry S. Truman Library in Independence, where he was buried after his death in 1972.

Bess Truman's last public appearance came four years later, when she joined President Gerald Ford to dedicate an expansion of the Harry S. Truman Library. After she died in 1982, at the age of ninety-seven, Bess was buried next to her husband on its grounds.

Left: Margaret Truman, the couple's only child, was the apple of her father's eye.

Right: Harry and Bess Truman.

Truman's Address to the Nation about the Bombing of Japan

Broadcast on radio and issued as a press release on August 6, 1945

From July 17 to August 2, 1945, American President Harry S Truman, British prime minister Winston Churchill, his successor, Clement Attlee, and Soviet premier Josef Stalin met in Potsdam, Germany, to discuss the future of Germany and to plan strategies against Japan. It was more than two months after Germany had surrendered, and the European war was over. Truman received a promise from Stalin that the Soviet Union (USSR) would enter the war against Japan.

Recently, the first atomic bomb had been tested at Alamogordo, New Mexico. Truman privately informed Churchill that the United States had successfully detonated the weapon and had built several more.

On July 26, the Allied Powers meeting at Potsdam issued an ultimatum to Japan demanding its unconditional surrender, and on July 29, the Japanese government decided not to comment on the ultimatum. The silence was interpreted as rejection. Two atomic bombs had been delivered to an American Air Force unit in the Pacific, and President Truman directed them to use one of them at the first opportunity if Japan did not surrender by August 3. On the morning of August 6, an atomic bomb was dropped on the city of Hiroshima, and sixteen hours later, President Truman informed the American people in a radio broadcast.

Sixteen hours ago an American airplane dropped one bomb on Hiroshima, an important Japanese Army base. That bomb had more power than 20,000 tons of TNT. It had more bomb power than two thousand times the blast power of the British "Grand Slam," which is the largest bomb ever yet used in the history of warfare.

The Japanese began the war from the air at Pearl Harbor. They have been repaid many fold. And the end is not yet. With this bomb we have now added a new and revolutionary increase in destruction to supplement the growing power of our armed forces. In their present form these bombs are now in production and even more powerful forms are in development.

It is an atomic bomb. It is a harnessing of the basic power of the universe. The force from which the sun draws its power has been loosed against those who brought war to the Far East.

Before 1939, it was the accepted belief of scientists that it was theoretically possible to release atomic energy. But no one knew any practical method of doing it. By 1942, however, we knew that the Germans were working feverishly to find a way to add atomic energy to the other engines of war with which they hoped to enslave the world. But they failed. We may be grateful to Providence that the Germans got the V-1's and V-2's late and in limited quantities and even more grateful that they did not get the atomic bomb at all.

The battle of the laboratories held fateful risks for us as well as the battles of the air, land and sea, and we have now won the battle of the laboratories as we have won the other battles.

Beginning in 1940, before Pearl Harbor, scientific knowledge useful in war was pooled between the United States and Great Britain, and many priceless helps to our victories have come from that arrangement. Under that general policy the research on the atomic bomb was begun. With American and British scientists working together we entered the race of discovery against the Germans.

The United States had available the large number of scientists of distinction in the many needed areas of knowledge. It had the tremendous industrial and financial resources necessary for the project and they could be devoted to it without undue impairment of other vital war work. In the United States the laboratory work and the production plants, on which a substantial start had already been made, would be out of reach of enemy bombing, while at that time Britain was exposed to constant air attack and was still threatened with the possibility of invasion. For these reasons Prime Minister Churchill and President Roosevelt agreed that it was wise to carry on the project here.

We now have two great plants and many lesser works devoted to the production of atomic power. Employment during peak construction numbered 125,000 and over 65,000 individuals are even now engaged in operating the plants. Many have worked there for two and a half years. Few know what they have been producing. They see great quantities of material going in and they see nothing coming out of these plants, for the physical size of the explosive charge is exceedingly small. We have spent two billion dollars on the greatest scientific gamble in history—and won.

But the greatest marvel is not the size of the enterprise, its secrecy, nor its cost, but the achievement of scientific brains in putting together infinitely complex pieces of knowledge held by many men in different fields of science into a workable plan. And hardly less marvelous has been the capacity of industry to design, and of labor to operate, the machines and methods to do things never done before so that the brain child of many minds came forth in physical shape and performed as it was supposed to do. Both science and industry worked under the direction of the

United States Army, which achieved a unique success in managing so diverse a problem in the advancement of knowledge in an amazingly short time. It is doubtful if such another combination could be got together in the world. What has been done is the greatest achievement of organized science in history. It was done under high pressure and without failure.

We are now prepared to obliterate more rapidly and completely every productive enterprise the Japanese have above ground in any city. We shall destroy their docks, their factories, and their communications. Let there be no mistake; we shall completely destroy Japan's power to make war.

It was to spare the Japanese people from utter destruction that the ultimatum of July 26 was issued at Potsdam. Their leaders promptly rejected that ultimatum. If they do not now accept our terms they may expect a rain of ruin from the air, the like of which has never been seen on this earth. Behind this air attack will follow sea and land forces in such numbers and power as they have not yet seen and with the fighting skill of which they are already well aware.

The Secretary of War [Henry L. Stimson], who has kept in personal touch with all phases of the project, will immediately make public a statement giving further details.

His statement will give facts concerning the sites at Oak Ridge near Knoxville, Tennessee, and at Richland near Pasco, Washington, and an installation near Santa Fe, New Mexico. Although the workers at the sites have been making materials to be used in producing the greatest destructive force in history they have not themselves been in danger beyond that of many other occupations, for the utmost care has been taken of their safety.

The fact that we can release atomic energy ushers in a new era in man's understanding of nature's forces. Atomic energy may in the future supplement the power that now comes from coal, oil, and falling water, but at present it cannot be produced on a basis to compete with them commercially. Before that comes there must be a long period of intensive research.

It has never been the habit of the scientists of this country or the policy of this Government to withhold from the world scientific knowledge. Normally, therefore, everything about the work with atomic energy would be made public.

But under present circumstances it is not intended to divulge the technical processes of production or all the military applications, pending further examination of possible methods of protecting us and the rest of the world from the danger of sudden destruction.

I shall recommend that the Congress of the United States consider promptly the establishment of an appropriate commission to control the production and use of atomic power within the United States. I shall give further consideration and make further recommendations to the Congress as to how atomic power can become a powerful and forceful influence towards the maintenance of world peace.

What Happened Next

A second atomic bomb was detonated over the Japanese city of Nagasaki on August 9. Meanwhile, the USSR had declared war on Japan on August 8 and invaded Japanese military strongholds in Manchuria the next day. On August 14, Japan announced its surrender, and the formal surrender took place on September 2 in Tokyo Bay aboard the battleship U.S.S. *Missouri*.

In the United States, President Truman transferred control and development of nuclear energy from the military to the civilian Atomic Energy Commission, and the authority to use the atomic bomb was placed solely with the president. When the Soviet Union announced that it had developed nuclear weapons, the threat of wide-ranging destruction became both possible and terrifying. That possibility remains; at the end of the twentieth century, at least six nations had successfully tested nuclear weapons, and the number appears to be growing.

Truman's Executive Order Banning Segregation in the Military

Issued on July 26, 1948

During all of American history, racial segregation was practiced in the military as well as in areas of the American South. African Americans trained in different facilities from whites, and many military units, especially combat units, were off-limits to non-whites. Calling segregation in the military "the most un-American activity in the whole government," President Harry S Truman issued Executive Order 9981 on July 26, 1948. To enforce desegregation of the military, he created the President's Committee on Equality of Treatment and Opportunity in the Armed Services to recommend a process that would ensure the executive order was carried out.

Excerpt from Truman's Executive Order

Establishing the President's Committee on Equality of Treatment and Opportunity In the Armed Forces.

WHEREAS it is essential that there be maintained in the armed services of the United States the highest standards of democracy, with equality of treatment and opportunity for all those who serve in our country's defense:

NOW THEREFORE, by virtue of the authority vested in me as President of the United States, by the Constitution and the statutes of the United States, and as Commander in Chief of the armed services, it is hereby ordered as follows:

1. It is hereby declared to be the policy of the President that there shall be equality of treatment and opportunity for all persons in the armed services without regard to race, color, religion or national origin. This policy shall be put into effect as rapidly as possible, having due regard to the time required to effectuate any necessary changes without impairing efficiency or morale.

2. There shall be created in the National Military Establishment an advisory committee to be known as the President's Committee on Equality of Treatment and Opportunity in the Armed Services, which shall be composed of seven members to be designated by the President.

3. The Committee is authorized on behalf of the President to examine into the rules, procedures and practices of the Armed Services in order to determine in what respect such rules, procedures and practices may be altered or improved with a view to carrying out the policy of this order. The Committee shall confer and advise the Secretary of Defense, the Secretary of the Army, the Secretary of the Navy, and the Secretary of the Air Force, and shall make such recommendations to the President and to said Secretaries as in the judgment of the Committee will effectuate the policy hereof.

4. All executive departments and agencies of the Federal Government are authorized and directed to cooperate with the Committee in its work, and to furnish the Committee such information or the services of such persons as the Committee may require in the performance of its duties.

5. When requested by the Committee to do so, persons in the armed services or in any of the executive departments and agencies of the Federal Government shall testify before the Committee and shall make available for use of the Committee such documents and other information as the Committee may require.

6. The Committee shall continue to exist until such time as the President shall terminate its existence by Executive order.

What Happened Next

Executive Order 9981 and Truman's support for civil-rights legislation were issues in the 1948 campaign, as much among members of his own party as it was for his opponents. Southern Democrats against Truman's civil rights policies defected from the party and supported South Carolina governor Strom Thurmond for president on the State's Rights Democratic (Dixiecrat) ticket.

Truman won the presidential election of 1948, but he wasn't able to pass any significant civil-rights legislation through Congress. The executive order banning segregation in the military, however, was a significant step in the growing civil-rights movement. During the 1950s, professional baseball was integrated, the Supreme Court (in *Brown v. Board of Education*) declared that any laws racially segregating public schools were unconstitutional, and acts of civil disobedience were staged against racist practices. The momentum developed further during the 1960s, culminating with the Civil Rights Act of 1964, which made it illegal to discriminate against people based on race, religion, and ethnic origin.

Dwight D. Eisenhower

"Dollars and guns are no substitute for brains and willpower."
—*Dwight D. Eisenhower*

Thirty-fourth president of the United States, 1953–1961

Full name: *Dwight David Eisenhower*

Born: *October 14, 1890, Denison, Texas*

Died: *March 28, 1969, Washington, D.C.*

Burial site: *Place of Meditation, on the grounds of the Eisenhower Presidential Center, Abilene, Kansas*

Parents: *David Jacob and Ida Elizabeth Stover Eisenhower*

Spouse: *Marie "Mamie" Geneva Doud (1896–1979; m. 1916)*

Children: *Doud Dwight (1917–1921); John Sheldon Doud (1923–)*

Religion: *Presbyterian*

Education: *U.S. Military Academy at West Point (B.S., 1915); graduate of several military colleges*

Occupations: *Soldier; general; Columbia University president*

Government positions: *None*

Political party: *Republican*

Dates as president: *January 20, 1953–January 20, 1957 (first term); January 20, 1957–January 20, 1961 (second term)*

Age upon taking office: *62*

After his heroic service in World War II, Dwight D. Eisenhower was so popular that he was courted as a presidential candidate by both the Democratic and the Republican parties. A brilliant military officer, he served as supreme commander of the Allied forces in Europe from 1942 until the end of the war. He also proved equal to the task of running the United States during the 1950s. The country enjoyed an extended period of prosperity during his two terms in office, and in spite of Cold War tensions between the United States and its allies and Communist governments in the Soviet Union and China and their allies, Eisenhower managed to keep the situation from boiling over into a hot war.

During his eight years in the White House, Eisenhower was sometimes criticized as an inactive leader who surrounded himself with a weighty bureaucracy and allowed his advisors to dictate policy. That view, which was widely held during the 1950s and 1960s, was reversed when his presidential papers were released for scholarly review in the 1970s. It wasn't until then that he began to be seen as a hands-on president. He had appeared to be effective during his tenure and projected a good-natured public image while the country seemed to be running on its own. Eisenhower was able to balance the political and the public demands of the office quite well as he was leading the nation into a new era of scientific and economic advances and concern for civil rights. An adoring electorate seemed to recognize his contributions

Timeline

1890: Born in Texas

1915: Graduates from West Point

1917: Supervises training of the Tank Corps at Fort Meade, Maryland, during World War I

1925: Attends the U.S. Army's Command and General Staff School, graduating first in his class

1930s: Serves as chief military aide to General Douglas MacArthur

1939–45: World War II

1943–45: Serves as supreme commander of Allied forces during the latter half of World War II

1944: Plans the successful invasions of German strongholds in North Africa and Italy; directs the D-Day invasion of France

1945: Commands the Battle of the Bulge, effectively ending Nazi aggression in Western Europe

1948–50: Serves as president of Columbia University

1950–52: Serves as commander of the NATO Forces in Europe

1953–61: Serves as thirty-fifth U.S. president

1954: Supreme Court calls for an end to racial segregation in schools in the *Brown v. Board of Education of Topeka* case, and Eisenhower orders regular army units to escort African-American students to class at Central High School in Little Rock, Arkansas

1955: Suffers a serious heart attack; recovers fully and is reelected in 1956

1969: Dies in Washington, D.C.

What's in a Name?

When Dwight D. Eisenhower was growing up, people usually called him David, which was his middle name, but at various times, he and all five of his brothers were known as Ike. He was usually called "Dwight" by his friends and "General" by his associates, but when it came time to run for president, someone resurrected the old nickname, which the guys in the foxholes called him among themselves (but never when he was within earshot) during the war. It had the right folksy ring to it for a candidate, and although it took him awhile to get used to it, he was known as Ike for the rest of his life.

and most Americans sincerely meant it when they repeated his campaign slogan, "I like Ike."

A Kansas Boyhood

Dwight David Eisenhower was born on October 14, 1890, in Denison, Texas, the third of seven sons born to David and Ida Stover Eisenhower. While he was still young, the family moved to Abilene, Kansas, where David Eisenhower supported them by working as a merchant. But the Eisenhowers were not wealthy: The seven brothers found themselves crowded together in a series of tiny houses where they were forced to share bedrooms and help with many chores that were at that time considered "woman's work," and young Dwight became a better-than-average cook, a talent he enjoyed for the rest of his life.

He was an above-average student who loved sports, especially football and baseball, and consistently earned high grades in mathematics and history. He was an avid reader of military histories, and was especially interested in the ancient battles of the Greeks and Romans. After he graduated from high school in 1909, he applied to the U.S. Naval Academy at Annapolis—only to discover that he was too old; an injury had forced him to repeat

Below: David Eisenhower and his wife, Ida Stover Eisenhower, at a 1926 family reunion with their sons (L-R) Arthur, Edgar, Dwight, Roy, Earl, and Milton.

Above: Young Ike made a name for himself as a football player during his years at West Point.

Below: Lieutenant Dwight Eisenhower and his future wife, Mamie Dowd, in San Antonio, Texas, 1916.

his freshman year of high school. He worked at the Belle Springs Creamery in Abilene for the next two years, but his life took a turn for the better when he landed an appointment to the U.S. Military Academy at West Point.

Never a brilliant student, Eisenhower found West Point demanding. He excelled in athletics, but he didn't like the academy's rules and regulations. When he graduated in 1915, he stood at about the middle of the class academically but in the bottom quarter for discipline. He was commissioned as second lieutenant in the infantry and was assigned to a post at Fort Sam Houston in Texas. It was during that tour that he met and married Denver socialite Mamie Doud.

On the Move

A career army officer can expect to move often and to pull a variety of assignments, and Lieutenant Eisenhower was no exception to the rule. He and Mamie moved almost a dozen times in the first seven years of his army career, serving in Texas, Georgia, Maryland, Pennsylvania, and New Jersey. He was promoted to captain in 1917, and was eager to go to Europe to fight in World War I. Instead, his orders were to supervise training of the Tank Corps in Fort Meade, Maryland. Although he was disappointed at the time, he learned a great deal about tanks and their deployment, which he put to good use during World War II. When he took part in a transcontinental convoy of tanks and trucks, watching their slow progress over bad roads, he became convinced that what this country needed was a good highway system.

Shortly after World War I ended, Eisenhower was promoted to major and made executive assistant to General Fox Conner in the Panama Canal Zone. Conner believed that the world was headed for another major war, and he urged Eisenhower to get himself ready for it. Taking the advice to heart, he enrolled in the army's Command and General Staff School, and graduated first in his class of 245. By 1929, he had finished courses at the Army War College and had been appointed executive officer to Assistant Secretary of War George Moseley. One of his more unusual assignments in that job was to visit France and write a guidebook on all the major battle sites of World War I.

Emerges as a Military Leader

During the Great Depression, Eisenhower served as chief military aide to General Douglas MacArthur, who was charged with preparing the Philippines for independence. Like so many of Eisenhower's superiors, MacArthur was impressed with him, and he wrote in one performance evaluation, "This is the best officer in the U.S. Army. When the next war comes, move him right to the top."

"Yes, I know [General MacArthur] well. Very well, indeed. I studied dramatics under him for years."

—*Dwight D. Eisenhower*

After serving with MacArthur in the Philippines until 1939, Eisenhower went back to the United States as a lieutenant colonel. By that time, Nazi Germany was at war with its European neighbors, and although he been planning to retire from the military, he stayed on as the

war broadened into a global conflict, and Japanese forces bombed the American naval station at Pearl Harbor, Hawaii, on December 7, 1941, bringing the United States into it.

Eisenhower was a colonel at the time of the Pearl Harbor attack. He had recently become chief of staff for the Third Army, and the top brass was impressed by how quickly and efficiently he could organize troops and look out for their welfare. He certainly couldn't have predicted the role he was about to play. Just five days after Pearl Harbor attack, he was ordered to Washington by Army chief of staff George C. Marshall, who put him in charge of the War Plans Division and ordered him to come up with a strategy for U.S. deployment in the two-front war.

Eisenhower recommended that the United States concentrate its forces in the African and European theaters, with the goal of defeating Germany and Italy first. His plan called for a defensive war against Japan in the Pacific theater until the Allies could reconquer Europe. Much to his surprise, he was placed in command of American troops. Based in England, he soon found himself debating strategy with President Franklin D. Roosevelt and British prime minister Winston Churchill. Both leaders were so impressed with Eisenhower that when battle plans were finally agreed upon, they named him supreme commander of all the Allied forces.

Right: British General Sir Bernard Montgomery served with Eisenhower through all of the march on Berlin that began in the deserts of North Africa.

Above: General Eisenhower was Commander of Allied Forces in North Africa, with the help of General Henri Giraud at the head of the French forces there.

A Victorious General

From the time the Allies invaded French North Africa in May 1942 until Germany formally surrendered on May 7, 1945, Eisenhower directed the entire Allied effort. He planned invasions of German strongholds in North Africa and Italy, and he was the chief planner of the D-Day (June 6, 1944) invasion of Normandy Beach in France, where Allied troops landed to push toward Germany, and he commanded the bloody Battle of the Bulge that effectively brought Nazi aggression in Western Europe to an end.

Eisenhower proved to be decisive and quick to act, with a great talent for moving large numbers of troops and their motorized backup of artillery and tanks. This was most important in the Battle of the Bulge, when he smashed a German counteroffensive by rushing armies to the front and overwhelming the Nazi's last-ditch efforts.

From the beginning of his time as supreme commander, Eisenhower realized that along with an enemy to conquer he had to keep peace among his various commanders and troops from Allied nations.

Right: Operation Overlord, the invasion of Normandy on D-Day, June 6, 1944, was the most massive undertaking in the history of warfare.

He devised the strategy of a "broad front" that did not allow any single Allied country or general to take credit for victories at the cost of other. As the Allied army was closing in on Berlin, which would be the most important victory of all, he ordered that Soviet forces closing in from the east would be allowed to occupy the German capital. The move seemed diplomatic and politically advantageous at the time, but many back home were distrustful of the Soviets and their communist agenda, and weren't too pleased that the biggest prize of the war should be handed over to them.

When Eisenhower cabled the news of victory in Europe to Chief of Staff Marshall in Washington, he received a reply praising his accomplishments in no small measure: "You have completed your mission with the greatest victory in the history of warfare. You have commanded with outstanding success the most powerful military force that has ever been assembled. [. . .] You have made history, great history for the good of mankind and you have stood for all we hope for and admire in an officer of the United States Army." And that was just the opening salvo. Eisenhower came home to a wildly enthusiastic hero's welcome.

The accomplishments that had made him one of the most famous men in the world did not make Eisenhower wealthy—nor was he lighthearted about a victory that had been enormously costly in terms of human suffering. He spent two postwar years as the army's chief of staff and then he retired from the military in 1948 as a five-star general—the U.S. military's highest rank.

Above: When it was over "over there," New York City gave credit where credit was due with a ticker-tape parade up Broadway honoring General Eisenhower.

Above right: Before the Eisenhowers moved into the White House, their home was the presidential mansion on the campus of Columbia University in New York.

Below: President Harry S Truman confers with General Eisenhower, the supreme commander of allied forces in Europe.

Road to the Presidency

After serving for two years as president of Columbia University, during which time Eisenhower published *Crusade in Europe,* a best-selling book about the war, he was called back into service by President Harry S Truman, who sent him to Europe as supreme commander of Allied forces. This time, his assignment was to organize a multinational army for the new North Atlantic Treaty Organization (NATO). While he was in Europe, he watched with dismay as the Soviet Union made advances in Eastern Europe.

By that time, both Democrats and Republicans were urging him to run for president even though he had never talked about his political views. He finally announced that he was a Republican and agreed to campaign for that party. Democrats had held the White House for the previous twenty years, but it hardly mattered. The Republicans knew that he was going to get it back for them, and they were quite right. With his thirty-nine-year-old running mate, Richard Nixon, Eisenhower

Reluctant Candidate

When reporters started questioning him about running for the presidency, Eisenhower told them, "I'm a soldier, and I'm positive no one thinks of me as a politician. In the strongest language you can command, you can state that I have no political ambitions at all." Then again, he hadn't planned to be a soldier, either. He didn't go to West Point until after he was turned down at the Naval Academy.

Left: Candidates Dwight Eisenhower and Richard Nixon get the 1952 presidential election off to a good start.

Right: In 1952, everybody, it seems, liked Ike. He won the 1952 presidential election in a landslide, and did even better in 1956.

easily defeated Democratic nominee Adlai Stevenson in the 1952 election.

During his campaign, Eisenhower promised to end the Korean War, which had ground on to a hopeless stalemate, and shortly after his inauguration as president on January 20, 1953, he began negotiating an armistice that was put in place in July. The former general began to draw down conventional military forces after that. He wanted to cut military costs to help balance the federal budget, but at the same time, mindful of the Cold War, he increased spending on nuclear weapons and missiles, starting an international arms race that would continue for decades.

The Cold War

Americans were generally experiencing a period of prosperity during the 1950s—New homes were being built in suburban areas, and jobs were plentiful—but even so, the Cold War was making most people vaguely uneasy. Concern about the spread of communist values had become more intense in the early postwar years, and Eisenhower responded by backing secret schemes by the Central Intelligence Agency (CIA) to discredit communist governments in the Middle East and Central America.

The Iron Curtain

A year after the end of World War II, a new term emerged that described the Eastern European nations dominated by the Soviet Union. Borders of those nations were sealed, travel and communication severely restricted, and the nations were subject to censorship. The term came into popular usage after former British prime minister Winston Churchill described post–World War II Eastern Europe in a speech in Fulton, Missouri, on March 5, 1946: "From Stettin in the Baltic to Trieste in the Adriatic, an iron curtain has descended across the continent."

Right: Celebrating their last Christmas before Ike took the oath of office, and one of their first with the whole family, the Eisenhowers shared the occasion with their grandchildren (L-R): Susan, eleven months, in Mamie's arms; David, four; and Barbara Anne, three, holding her doll. At left is Elvira Dowd, Mamie's mother, and at right, daughter-in-law Mrs. John Eisenhower.

Election Results

1952

Presidential / Vice presidential candidates	Popular Votes	Electoral Votes
Dwight D. Eisenhower / Richard M. Nixon (Republican)	33,778,964	442
Adlai E. Stevenson / John J. Sparkman (Democratic)	27,314,992	89

1956

Presidential / Vice presidential candidates	Popular Votes	Electoral Votes
Dwight D. Eisenhower / Richard M. Nixon (Republican)	35,581,003	457
Adlai E. Stevenson / C. Estes Kefauver (Democratic)	25,738,765	73

The Eisenhower Administration

Administration Dates: January 20, 1953–January 20, 1957
January 20, 1957–January 20, 1961

Vice President: Richard M. Nixon (1953–61)

Cabinet:

Secretary of State	John F. Dulles (1953–59)
	Christian A. Herter (1959–61)
Secretary of the Treasury	George M. Humphrey (1953–57)
	Robert B. Anderson (1957–61)
Attorney General	Herbert Brownell Jr. (1953–57)
	William P. Rogers (1957–61)
Postmaster General	Arthur E. Summerfield (1953–61)
Secretary of the Interior	Douglas McKay (1953–56)
	Frederick A. Seaton (1956–61)
Secretary of Agriculture	Ezra T. Benson (1953–61)
Secretary of Labor	Martin P. Durkin (1953)
	James P. Mitchell (1953–61)
Secretary of Commerce	C. Sinclair Weeks (1953–58)
	Frederick H. Mueller (1959–61)
Secretary of Defense	Charles E. Wilson (1953–57)
	Neil H. McElroy (1957–59)
	Thomas S. Gates Jr. (1959–61)
Secretary of Health, Education, and Welfare	Oveta Culp Hobby (1953–55)
	Marion B. Folsom (1955–58)
	Arthur S. Flemming (1958–61)

Playing off the fear of Communists, Wisconsin senator Joseph McCarthy began a heavily publicized investigation into communist activity in America, claiming that there was widespread communist infiltration into American cultural and political institutions. However, as America watched McCarthy's Senate hearings turn into mockeries of justice, filled with false accusations and wild conspiracy theories, Eisenhower finally emerged from behind the scenes to challenge him after McCarthy's committee started investigating the army.

As proliferation of nuclear weapons kept growing, Eisenhower took a public stand calling for peaceful applications of nuclear technology, and sponsored an "Atoms for Peace" campaign that educated the public about positive uses of atomic energy. He also called for serious diplomatic conferences with the Soviet Union to deal with the nuclear threat. The death of Soviet dictator Josef Stalin ushered in a slight thaw in relations between the U.S. and the USSR, and Eisenhower was able to arrange face-to-face meetings with Stalin's successor, Nikita Khrushchev. Nevertheless, there was deep distrust between the two countries, and there didn't seem to be a way to overcome it. Eisenhower initiated a secret program of high-altitude aerial surveillance of the Soviet Union, a program that would bring serious consequences during his second term.

Meanwhile, procommunist activity had spread to yet another country, the small southeast Asian nation of Vietnam. France had held Vietnam as a colony for decades, but their colonial overseers there were attacked

Adlai E. Stevenson

He lost two presidential elections to Dwight D. Eisenhower by wide margins, but Adlai Ewing Stevenson remained a popular and respected figure in American politics. Unlike Ike, Stevenson favored progressive politics of social programs and expansion of civil rights. Americans preferred their World War II hero, Eisenhower, and his more conservative policies. Had Stevenson won either election of 1952 or 1956, the course of American history would have been different. Instead, the more cautious approach of Eisenhower at home, and his tougher stance against communism abroad, won out and influenced the 1950s.

Born in Los Angeles, California, on February 5, 1900, to Lewis Green Stevenson, a former secretary of state for Illinois, and Helen Louise Davis Stevenson, Adlai was part of a prominent family in Bloomington, Illinois, where they returned to live after his birth. His grandfather, Adlai E. Stevenson, was vice president during the second term of Grover Cleveland, and a great-grandfather was a close friend and avid supporter of Abraham Lincoln. Graduating from the public schools, young Adlai Stevenson attended an eastern private school, graduated from Princeton University in 1922 (where he edited and wrote for the school newspaper), and earned a law degree from Northwestern University in 1926. Admitted that year to the Illinois bar, he began practicing law in Chicago.

Stevenson's interest in politics blossomed as he became familiar with the needs of farmers around Bloomington, and as he became active in the Chicago Council on Foreign Relations. On December 1, 1928, he married Ellen Borden. They had three sons, one of whom, Adlai E. Stevenson III (1930–), served as a U.S. senator from Illinois from 1970 to 1981. The Stevensons were divorced in 1949.

In 1933, Stevenson went to Washington, D.C., to work for President Franklin D. Roosevelt's Agricultural Adjustment Administration. In 1934, he rejoined his Chicago law firm, and the following year was elected president of the Chicago Council on Foreign Relations. He developed a reputation as a speechmaker and became involved in many causes, including protecting the rights of immigrants, minorities, and disadvantaged children. In 1940, he became chairman of the Chicago Chapter of the Committee to Defend America by Aiding the Allies, a group that pursued vigorous support for enemies of Nazi Germany during World War II, which the United States had

not yet entered. In June 1941, Secretary of the Navy Frank Knox appointed Stevenson as his agency's principal attorney.

Stevenson became a special assistant to Secretary of State Edward R. Stettinius Jr. under President Harry Truman. Stevenson was appointed senior adviser to the U.S. delegation for the first session of the General Assembly of the United Nations (UN) in 1946. In 1948, Stevenson was elected governor of Illinois. His administration was modestly successful, facing opposition from Republicans and a sharp division between rural and industrial regions of Illinois. Nevertheless, he attracted wide attention with speeches and articles. Early in January 1952, Stevenson announced that he would seek reelection as governor, but three weeks later President Truman asked him to seek the presidential nomination. Stevenson refused. As the Democratic Party's convention approached, some party leaders urged him to announce that he would accept the nomination if it were offered him. On the third ballot, Stevenson was drafted as the nominee because the convention wanted him and nobody else.

Stevenson conducted a high-spirited and dignified campaign: His speeches became best-selling books at home and abroad. Still, Stevenson was overwhelmed in the election by popular war hero Dwight D. Eisenhower. Stevenson then went on an international tour, wrote articles for Look magazine, and published Call to Greatness.

During his second presidential campaign in 1956, Stevenson supported a suspension of nuclear testing in the atmosphere; reduction of tensions with the Soviet Union; increased assistance to underdeveloped countries through the UN; and substantial federal assistance to education, the poor, and the elderly. After his second election defeat—again to Eisenhower—Stevenson helped found the Democratic Advisory Council to issue policy statements, traveled around the world, and formed his own law firm.

Stevenson was pressed again to run for president in 1960, but he refused. After John F. Kennedy's victory, Stevenson hoped to be appointed secretary of state; instead, Kennedy offered him the UN ambassadorship. He wanted the UN to be the center of U.S. foreign policy, but this concept was not accepted. During his time in the UN, Stevenson represented American interests during tense confrontations between the United States and the Soviet Union over events in Cuba, the near bankruptcy of the UN, and many other international crises. Stevenson died of a heart attack in 1965.

Left: Eisenhower generally ignored the investigations of Communists in government by Senator Joseph McCarthy, left, until McCarthy began looking into the activities of the military.

New Challenges

In the 1956 presidential election, Eisenhower defeated Adlai Stevenson a second time. Although it included passage of a huge public works bill to create America's first interstate highway program, his second term was more difficult than his first had been. In foreign affairs, he played a key role in the peaceful settlement of an international dispute centered on Egypt's Suez Canal, vital to shipping between the Mediterranean Ocean and the Red Sea. However, everything seemed to be mostly downhill from there.

Several serious domestic and foreign crises contributed further to Cold War tensions. An uprising against Soviet influence in Hungary was crushed by Soviet tanks and military power, after which the borders of Soviet-dominated nations were closed, and travel and means of communication, such as radio and newspapers, as well as free speech, severely restricted. The Soviet Union's domination of Eastern Europe came to be known as the Iron Curtain, after Sir Winston Churchill coined the phrase. When the Soviet Union launched the man-made satellite Sputnik into orbit around the

and routed by communist rebels. Eisenhower's advisors urged him to intervene on the theory that if Vietnam fell to the communists, other neighboring nations would also fall like so many dominoes. Eisenhower was not eager to involve American troops in another foreign war, especially for a French colony. Instead, he supported the partition of Vietnam into a communist-controlled North and an independent South. Meanwhile, he helped organize the South East Asia Treaty Organization (SEATO), dedicated to stopping the spread of communism in Asian and Pacific Island nations, which gave the United States expanded responsibilities in South Vietnam.

Shortly after meeting Soviet leaders at a conference in Geneva, Switzerland, in the summer of 1955, Eisenhower suffered a serious heart attack and was bedridden for three months. Republicans worried that their most popular candidate might not be well enough to run for a second term, but he had fully recovered by the spring of 1956, and announced that he was a candidate for reelection.

Below: Before Eisenhower pushed for the interstate highway program, it typically took two months for military convoys to travel from Washington, D.C., to San Francisco.

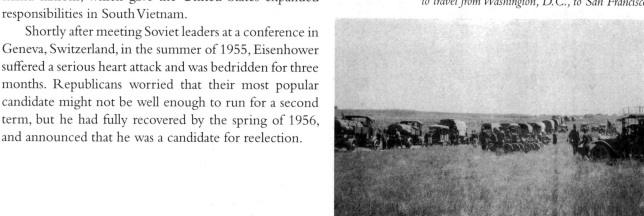

Above: The Soviets beat the Americans into space in 1957, by launching Sputnik, a 184-pound satellite that was an inch short of two feet in diameter.

Below: President Eisenhower sent federal troops to facilitate the integration of Central High School in Little Rock, Arkansas.

Earth, Democratic leaders claimed that Eisenhower had allowed a "missile gap" to open, and that the Soviets had gained superior strength in production of air weapons. The satellite launching led some Americans to argue that the nation's educational system had fallen dangerously behind in teaching science and mathematics.

Other issues concerning education developed as well. Although racial segregation had been eliminated in the military, it was still being practiced in schools, even those serving the children of the military. The Supreme Court's 1954 decision in the case of *Brown v. Board of Education of Topeka* called for an end to school segregation and led to a series of tense civil-rights confrontations. Though Eisenhower never made a distinct pronouncement either for or against segregation, he had helped to further the integration of the armed forces, even though, like all the military brass, he didn't have any enthusiasm for it. But when African-American students were refused admittance to Central High School in Little Rock, Arkansas, in 1957, he ordered regular army units to escort them to class, and sent a clear signal that court-ordered integration would not be compromised. Eisenhower also proposed and signed a civil-rights bill into law; however, it was so weakened by Senate amendments that its provisions were useless.

To strengthen education in America, Eisenhower launched the National Defense Education Act, which gave college scholarships to students specializing in mathematics and the sciences. He also created the first President's Science Advisory Committee and supervised the organization of the National Aeronautics and Space Agency (NASA), to which he gave the responsibility of catching up with the Soviets in the space race.

As for defense, Eisenhower was well aware that the "missile gap" theory was wrong. Informed by reports from high-altitude U-2 spy planes that regularly flew over the Soviet Union, he knew that the United States was well ahead of the Soviets in sophisticated military weaponry, but he couldn't make the information public without jeopardizing the U-2 flights, which were in violation of international law.

International Tour and Tension

During the last two years of his presidency, Eisenhower left the country on an international tour for peace. Using the new presidential jet, *Air Force One,* he visited several foreign countries and many parts of America, speaking to the public in a more personable manner than he had before. A summit meeting with Nikita Khrushchev was planned for Paris in the spring of 1960, but before it could take place, Eisenhower faced the biggest international scandal of his career.

Just prior to the Paris Summit, the Soviet military shot down one of the U-2 spy planes that had been supplying the Eisenhower administration with detailed information about enemy defenses. Although Eisenhower publicly denied the violation of Soviet air space, Soviet soldiers had recovered the plane, photographs of sensitive government installations, and a very frightened pilot, Francis Gary Powers. Faced with the hard evidence, Eisenhower said, "I goofed." Indeed he had. Khrushchev was furious, and he canceled the summit talks, which were to have included steps toward the first nuclear test ban treaty.

The cancellation of the Paris Summit was the biggest disappointment of Eisenhower's presidency. The Cold War just worsened, and it drew closer to home when communist rebel leader Fidel Castro took control of Cuba, less than a hundred miles off the coast of Florida.

A Gettysburg Address

Eisenhower finished his term in office on January 20, 1961, and two months later, President John F. Kennedy reinstated him as an army general, although he served in little more than an advisory capacity. Eisenhower and his wife, Mamie, were ready to settle down on a farm they had bought near Gettysburg, Pennsylvania—the only permanent home they had ever owned. From there, he was able to visit the nation's capital if he was needed, but he was in his seventies and eager to relax and work on improving his golf game. He once claimed that his happiest moment came in February 1968 when—at the age of seventy-seven—he shot his first and only hole in one.

A year later, the thirty-fourth president died of heart problems at Walter Reed Army Hospital in Washington. After lying in state at the White House, his body was flown to Abilene, Kansas, where he was buried in the Place of Meditation at the Eisenhower Center.

"I think that when the president stops being president, the best job we could give him in our country would be as director of a children's home. He would not harm children. But as head of a mighty state he is more dangerous and might do a lot of harm…. One shudders at the thought of what great force is in such hands."

—Soviet Premier Nikita Khruschev

Right: The Eisenhower farm at Gettysburg, Pennsylvania, overlooking the Civil War battlefield, was originally a log cabin but grew in sections before the Eisenhowers bought it in 1950.

Nikita Khrushchev

Nikita Khrushchev was born in Kalinovka, Russia, on April 17, 1894. After working as a coal miner, he received education and political training in schools for young workers set up by the Communist Party during the 1920s. He joined the Communist Party of the Ukraine, and from 1925 to 1953, he was connected with the political career of Joseph Stalin. In 1929, Khrushchev went to Moscow, the center of national power, and moved up the ranks of Moscow's party organization. In 1934, he became head of the Moscow branch of the Communist Party and was appointed to the Central Committee of the Soviet Communist Party, which consisted of the most powerful party figures.

Khrushchev helped strengthen Stalin's fierce dictatorship over Soviet society. From 1934 to 1938, Khrushchev oversaw construction of Moscow's subway system and helped Stalin purge political figures he found threatening. (Most of Khrushchev's Central Committee colleagues were executed.) In 1938, he became the leader of the Communist Party of the Ukraine, the nation's most important agricultural region and a center of resistance to Stalin's farm policy. Stalin had ordered all farm property to be nationalized to form a collective agricultural program supervised by the government. From 1938 to 1941, Khrushchev directed mass arrests and downgraded the Ukrainian language and culture in favor of Russian, a cultural policy used by Stalin to bring all regions of the Soviet Union under Moscow's control.

When Germany attacked the Ukraine during World War II, Khrushchev was a lieutenant general in the Soviet army. After the war, Khrushchev remained in the Ukraine to supervise reconstruction. He developed into a different kind of party leader, one who circulated among the population and who was interested in agriculture. As the powerful head of an important region, Khrushchev maintained as much of an independent position as anyone could in Stalin's dictatorial system.

In 1949, Khrushchev returned to lead the Communist Party in the Moscow region. A rivalry to succeed Stalin was underway. Stalin died in 1953, but it took Khrushchev about two years to solidify his power. This occurred in February 1956, when he called for "de-Stalinization." Khrushchev recounted Stalin's crimes against party members during the 1930s and condemned Stalin's mistakes during World War II. As a result, some Eastern Europe countries, under Soviet Union control since the end of World War II, sought changes in their own countries. Poles and Hungarians attempted to oust their ruling Communist governments. A settlement was made with Poland, but the Soviet Union army crushed a Hungarian rebellion in 1956 by killing thousands of rebels.

In October 1957, the Soviet Union launched Sputnik, the first space satellite, leading many foreign observers to view the Soviet Union as the world leader in advanced technology. The success of Sputnik spawned a space race against the much wealthier United States. Meanwhile, friction developed between the Soviet Union and the People's Republic of China. Faced with growing competition from both communist and non-communist countries, Khrushchev freed many of Stalin's victims from prison and ended a constant threat of police terror that had arisen in the 1930s. Americans continued to eye the Soviet Union suspiciously. Khrushchev's efforts to reduce political and military tensions were mixed with aggressive moves, such as threats made to the Western-controlled parts of Berlin in 1958 and 1961.

To boost his position at home, Khrushchev matched his political reforms with colorful promises of economic abundance. By the early 1960s, he spoke of Russia overtaking and surpassing the standard of living of the United States in the near future. However, his farm program did not produce results after an early, promising start.

Khrushchev had his own record of brutality, and he sometimes presented himself as a bully by threatening Berlin or angrily banging his shoe on a desk during a United Nations debate. In the fall of 1961, a military clash with the United States seemed likely when Khrushchev, reacting to the growing departure of East Germans to West Berlin, built the wall separating the communist and non-communist sectors of the city. The following fall brought about the most dangerous confrontation of the Cold War. The Soviet Union placed missiles in Cuba. The United States demanded that the missiles be removed. After a tense week in which the world stood on the edge of nuclear war, Khrushchev—unable or unwilling to risk a military clash with the United States—agreed to remove the missiles.

The aftermath of the missile crisis of 1962 brought a new wave of Soviet-American cooperation. The arms race was modified by a ban on nuclear testing in the atmosphere. The Soviet Union began to buy large quantities of food from the United States. Khrushchev's failures in agriculture and foreign policy, however, weakened his stature. He was removed from his position by party leaders in October 1964, and lived in Moscow until his death in 1971.

Legacy

The 1950s are often remembered as a time of calm, when not much happened to compare with the Great Depression of the 1930s, World War II during the 1940s, and the political idealism and civil strife of the 1960s. President Eisenhower, who was often content to delegate authority and did not initiate bold new plans, was a reflection of the times. Yet, he was able to maneuver successfully through a period marked by tense Cold War relations and the frightening prospect of nuclear war.

The nation enjoyed a general period of prosperity and growth, with a boom in housing and road construction, including a new interstate highway system. The U.S. space program was started on his watch, and programs like Social Security retirement benefits were expanded.

If the Eisenhower administration didn't initiate many bold programs, it didn't stand in the way of progress, either. In the area of civil rights, for example, the administration waited for the Supreme Court to make decisions, and after the 1954 *Brown v. Board of Education of Topeka* case ended segregation of schools, it backed the ruling, and even sent federal troops to Arkansas when officials there refused to allow integration of public schools to go forward.

Americans seemed to want firm leadership when it was needed, but more often to be left alone, without government interference in their lives. They liked Ike for those reasons, and he governed with the soft touch they seemed to want. He was anti-communist, but he did not support the excessive investigations of Senator Joseph McCarthy. He was a military man, but he preferred to use military power for diplomacy, rather than as a force, as was reflected in the subtitle of his White House memoirs: *Waging Peace.* Dwight D. Eisenhower was certainly not the most active president, but a majority of Americans seemed to like it that way.

Everybody Knows That

When someone asked Dwight Eisenhower's grandson what his name was, he piped up, "Dwight David Eisenhower."

The visitor pointed to the boy's grandfather who was also in the room, and said, "Well, then, who is he?"

"Oh," replied the boy, "that's Ike."

Mamie Eisenhower

Born November 14, 1896, Boone, Iowa
Died November 1, 1979, Washington, D.C.

"She's a career women. Her career is Ike."
—Headline in the Washington Post

Mamie Eisenhower's husband was one of America's most popular presidents, and she was a beloved and admired first lady. During the eight years she spent in the White House, Mrs. Eisenhower in many ways reflected conservative social values of the 1950s both in her appearance and behavior: A gracious hostess, she was always smartly dressed and ready to lend her name and time to charitable concerns. In matters of public policy, however, she was almost completely inactive. She did not play a significant part in the presidential administration of Dwight D. Eisenhower—other than her flawless performance at social functions. Even in that respect, she was a feminine ideal of her era.

Valentine Engagement

Born Mamie Doud on November 14, 1896, in Boone, Iowa, she was one of four daughters of a businessman who had made a fortune in the meatpacking business. When the family moved to Denver, Colorado, she was educated at public schools there. After her high-school graduation, she attended Miss Woolcott's, a private "finishing school" where young ladies learned social graces and foreign languages to prepare them for upper-class marriages.

The Doud family often spent the winters in San Antonio, Texas, where they kept a vacation home, and they were staying there when Mamie met Second Lieutenant Dwight Eisenhower at Fort Sam Houston. Both Dwight and Mamie recalled years later that the attraction was instant and mutual: She found him "just about the handsomest male I had ever seen," while he was dazzled by the "saucy look about her face and in her whole attitude." A courtship followed; on Valentine's Day 1916, Eisenhower presented Mamie with a miniature copy of his West Point class ring and proposed marriage.

The couple was married on July 1, at Mamie's family home in Denver, and after a short honeymoon, Mrs. Eisenhower moved into her husband's two-room apartment at Fort Sam Houston—the first of more than thirty temporary quarters they would share during his long career in the military. For a young society woman who had been raised in upper-class comfort, the transition was sometimes difficult for her, and "Ike" had

Left: Ike and Mamie became man and wife on July 1, 1916.

Right: Everybody liked Ike, and Ike made no secret about whom he liked himself.

to teach his bride how to cook and live on a budget. They went through frequent separations when he was ordered away on maneuvers, but their marriage proved to be a solid one. A son, Doud Dwight Eisenhower, was born on September 24, 1917.

The family faced tragedy when little Doud (nicknamed "Icky") died of scarlet fever in 1921. Mamie in particular grieved the loss of her child, her spirits lifting again only when she delivered a second son on August 3, 1922. Through this son, John Sheldon Doud Eisenhower, who himself would have a distinguished military and diplomatic career, the Eisenhowers would eventually have four grandchildren and eight great-grandchildren. One of the grandchildren, David, would marry Julie Nixon, the daughter of Eisenhower's vice president, Richard Nixon.

On the Move

The Eisenhower family moved frequently. Mamie and John followed Ike to the Panama Canal Zone, the Philippines, and France, as well as to numerous posts in America. The first lady once estimated that she packed up her household twenty-seven times in thirty-seven years. Throughout the 1920s and 1930s, as Dwight Eisenhower was advancing rapidly within the army ranks as a highly respected and efficient officer, Mrs. Eisenhower stayed out of the public eye, caring for her husband and son.

Soon after the Japanese attack on Pearl Harbor, Hawaii, in December 1941, Dwight Eisenhower was called to Washington to head the army's War Plans Division. Mrs. Eisenhower took an apartment at the Wardman Park Hotel, and she lived there throughout the rest of World War II while her husband served as supreme commander of the Allied forces in Europe. Separated for all but twelve days over three years, Mamie was anxious about her husband and her son. John was a student at West Point. Mrs. Eisenhower shunned the publicity that might have come to her as the wife of the nation's most famous general, preferring to volunteer hours with the

United Service Organization (USO) and the Red Cross. The USO, formed by a variety of agencies, is best known for providing entertainment for American armed services personnel, but the organization maintains hospitality centers and social and spiritual programs, as well, while the Red Cross is an international organization concerned with relieving suffering and improving health.

Victory in World War II didn't put an end to the couple's transient lifestyle. After serving as president of Columbia University for two years, the general was called back to Europe to supervise the creation of a North Atlantic Treaty Organization (NATO) military force. Although they had bought a farm near Gettysburg, Pennsylvania, in 1949, Ike and Mamie weren't able to call it home for eleven more years. Eight of those years were spent in the White House, the last of their many temporary residences.

First Lady

Like so many first ladies before her, Mamie Eisenhower was not thrilled by the loss of privacy that goes with being the president's wife. Especially embarrassing were questions about her use of alcohol.

Right: Mamie Eisenhower celebrated her 80th birthday with her son, his wife, and their children. Rear, left to right: Granddaughter Anne Echavarria; son David and his wife, the former Julie Nixon; General John Eisenhower; Susan Bradshaw and her husband, Alexander; Mary Millard and her husband, Jim. Front row: Mrs. John Eisenhower and Mamie Eisenhower.

Mrs. Eisenhower was afflicted with a disorder of the inner ear that sometimes caused her to stagger and stumble as though she had been drinking. She was content to say very little about her private life during the campaign and after beginning her two terms as first lady.

As the wife of the president, Mamie Eisenhower reflected the traditions of her times. She made a point of dressing elegantly, and she was a distinct influence on fashion during the 1950s. Equally elegant were the dinners and parties she presided over at the White House, events that mirrored the nation's prosperity and its place in world affairs. Only when President Eisenhower suffered a serious heart attack in 1955 did her duties become slightly more official, as she answered her husband's correspondence, supervised his recovery, and reassured the public about his condition.

When President Eisenhower had regained his health enough to run for a second term, Mrs. Eisenhower supported his decision. She was aware that her husband still needed to be active, and she had discovered that she actually enjoyed the role of first lady. However, the Eisenhowers' second term was not as lively with parties as the first term; the couple traveled frequently and was mindful of the president's ailing heart.

At the end of her eight years in the White House, Mrs. Eisenhower had neither given a press conference on a national issue nor contributed in any serious way to her husband's domestic or foreign policy decisions. Nevertheless, she was a celebrity in her own right, widely admired as a loving wife, mother, and grandmother, and nearly everything about her, from her clothing to her hairstyle, set the style for mature women of the 1950s.

When Eisenhower's presidency ended, he and Mamie retired to their farm at Gettysburg, where they lived quietly until he died in 1969. Mamie continued to live there through most of the next decade, continuing her work for charitable causes in her husband's name. She died on November 1, 1979, in Washington, and was buried next to her husband in a chapel—the Place of Meditation—at the Eisenhower Center in Abilene, Kansas.

Eisenhower's Farewell Address to the Nation

Delivered to Congress and broadcast on radio and television on January 17, 1961

During his eight years in the White House, President Dwight D. Eisenhower presided over an America that was experiencing a postwar economic boom. In the years following World War II, jobs were plentiful, many new homes and roads were constructed, and confidence in the American system was high. There were profound concerns as well: Americans were disturbed by communist values abroad and the threat of nuclear war. At home, racial inequalities continued to challenge American ideals.

President Eisenhower was a popular president who could have bid a fond farewell to the nation and rested on his high public rating. Instead, he used the occasion of his farewell address to discuss issues of concern. He urged Americans to be responsible with their economic, military, and technological power.

America is today the strongest, the most influential and most productive nation in the world. Understandably proud of this pre-eminence, we yet realize that America's leadership and prestige depend, not merely upon our unmatched material progress, riches and military strength, but on how we use our power in the interests of world peace and human betterment.

Throughout America's adventure in free government, such basic purposes have been to keep the peace; to foster progress in human achievement, and to enhance liberty, dignity and integrity among peoples and among nations.

To strive for less would be unworthy of a free and religious people.

Any failure traceable to arrogance or our lack of comprehension or readiness to sacrifice would inflict upon us a grievous hurt, both at home and abroad.

Progress toward these noble goals is persistently threatened by the conflict now engulfing the world. It commands our whole attention, absorbs our very beings. We face a hostile ideology global in scope, atheistic in character, ruthless in purpose, and insidious in method. Unhappily the danger it poses promises to be of indefinite duration. To meet it successfully, there is called for, not so much the emotional and transitory sacrifices of crisis, but rather those which enable us to carry forward steadily, surely, and without complaint the burdens of a prolonged and complex struggle—with liberty the stake. Only thus shall we remain, despite every provocation, on our charted course toward permanent peace and human betterment.

Crises there will continue to be. In meeting them, whether foreign or domestic, great or small, there is a recurring temptation to feel that some spectacular and costly action could become the miraculous solution to all current difficulties. A huge increase in the newer elements of our defenses; development of unrealistic programs to cure every ill in agriculture; a dramatic expansion in basic and applied research—these and many other possibilities, each possibly promising in itself, may be suggested as the only way to the road we wish to travel.

But each proposal must be weighed in light of a broader consideration; the need to maintain balance in and among national programs—balance between the private and the public economy, balance between the cost and hoped for advantages—balance between the clearly necessary and the comfortably desirable; balance between our essential requirements as a nation and the duties imposed by the nation upon the individual; balance between the actions of the moment and the national welfare of the future. Good judgment seeks balance and progress; lack of it eventually finds imbalance and frustration.

The record of many decades stands as proof that our people and their Government have, in the main, understood these truths and have responded to them well in the face of threat and stress.

But threats, new in kind or degree, constantly arise.

Of these, I mention two only.

A vital element in keeping the peace is our military establishment. Our arms must be mighty, ready for instant action, so that no potential aggressor may be tempted to risk his own destruction.

Our military organization today bears little relation to that known by any of my predecessors in peacetime, or indeed by the fighting men of World War II or Korea.

Until the latest of our world conflicts, the United States had no armaments industry. American makers of plowshares could, with time and as required, make swords as well. But now we can no longer risk emergency improvisation of national defense; we have been compelled to create a permanent armaments industry of vast proportions. Added to this, three and a half million men and women are directly engaged in the defense establishment. We annually spend on military security more than the net income of all United States corporations.

This conjunction of an immense military establishment and a large arms industry is new in the American experience. The total influence—economic, political, even spiritual—is felt in every city, every Statehouse, every office of the Federal government. We recognize the imperative need for this development. Yet we must not fail to comprehend its grave implications. Our toil, resources and livelihood are all involved; so is the very structure of our society.

In the councils of government, we must guard against the acquisition of unwarranted influence, whether sought or unsought, by the military-industrial complex. The potential for the disastrous rise of misplaced power exists and will persist.

We must never let the weight of this combination endanger our liberties or democratic processes. We should take nothing for granted. Only an alert and knowledgeable citizenry can compel the proper meshing of the huge industrial and military machinery of defense with our peaceful methods and goals, so that security and liberty may prosper together.

Akin to, and largely responsible for the sweeping changes in our industrial-military posture, has been the technological revolution during recent decades.

In this revolution, research has become central, it also becomes more formalized, complex, and costly. A steadily increasing share is conducted for, by, or at the direction of, the Federal government.

Today, the solitary inventor, tinkering in his shop, has been overshadowed by task forces of scientists in laboratories and testing fields. In the same fashion, the free university, historically the fountainhead of free ideas and scientific discovery, has experienced a revolution in the conduct of research. Partly because of the huge costs involved, a government contract becomes virtually a substitute for intellectual curiosity. For every old blackboard there are now hundreds of new electronic computers.

The prospect of domination of the nation's scholars by Federal employment, project allocations, and the power of money is ever present—and is gravely to be regarded.

Yet, in holding scientific research and discovery in respect, as we should, we must also be alert to the equal and opposite danger that public policy could itself become the captive of a scientific-technological elite.

It is the task of statesmanship to mold, to balance, and to integrate these and other forces, new and old, within the principles of our democratic system—ever aiming toward the supreme goals of our free society.

Another factor in maintaining balance involves the element of time. As we peer into society's future, we—you and I, and our government—must avoid the impulse to live only for today, plundering, for our own ease and convenience, the precious resources of tomorrow. We cannot mortgage the material assets of our grandchildren without asking the loss also of their political and spiritual heritage. We want democracy to survive for all generations to come, not to become the insolvent phantom of tomorrow.

Down the long lane of the history yet to be written America knows that this world of ours, ever growing smaller, must avoid becoming a community of dreadful fear and hate, and be, instead, a proud confederation of mutual trust and respect.

Such a confederation must be one of equals. The weakest must come to the conference table with the same confidence as do we, protected as we are by our moral, economic, and military strength. That table, though scarred by many past frustrations, cannot be abandoned for the certain agony of the battlefield.

Disarmament, with mutual honor and confidence, is a continuing imperative. Together we must learn how to compose differences, not with arms, but with intellect and decent purpose. Because this need is so sharp and apparent I confess that I lay down my official responsibilities in this field with a definite sense of disappointment. As one who has witnessed the horror and the lingering sadness of war—as one who knows that another war could utterly destroy this civilization which has been so slowly and painfully built over thousands of years—I wish I could say tonight that a lasting peace is in sight.

Happily, I can say that war has been avoided. Steady progress toward our ultimate goal has been made. But, so much remains to be done. As a private citizen, I shall never cease to do what little I can to help the world advance along that road.

So—in this my last good night to you as your President—I thank you for the many opportunities you have given me for public service in war and peace. I trust that in that service you find some things worthy; as for the rest of it, I know you will find ways to improve performance in the future.

You and I—my fellow citizens—need to be strong in our faith that all nations, under God, will reach the goal of peace with justice. May we be ever unswerving in devotion to principle, confident but humble with power, diligent in pursuit of the Nations' great goals.

To all the peoples of the world, I once more give expression to America's prayerful and continuing aspiration: We pray that peoples of all faiths, all races, all nations, may have their great human needs satisfied; that those now denied opportunity shall come to enjoy it to the full; that all who yearn for freedom may experience its spiritual blessings; that those who have freedom will understand, also, its heavy responsibilities; that all who are insensitive to the needs of others will learn charity; that the scourges of poverty, disease and ignorance will be made to disappear from the earth, and that, in the goodness of time, all peoples will come to live together in a peace guaranteed by the binding force of mutual respect and love.

What Happened Next

The American defense industry continued to grow, as the arms race between the Soviet Union and the United States dominated government spending in both nations through the 1980s. In an effort to stop the spread of communism, the United States became involved in several conflicts, including the Vietnam War.

Advances in science and technology were abundant through the end of the twentieth century. In general, those developments have been greatly beneficial to improving the quality of life. The potential for less desirable results remains, making Eisenhower's call for all Americans to remain informed and responsible continually relevant.

Eisenhower's call for more limited government was not heeded. The promise of a "new frontier," inspired by Eisenhower's successor, John F. Kennedy, faded by the mid-1960s with violence and social unrest: Kennedy was assassinated; America became deeply involved in an unpopular war in Vietnam; the civil-rights movement was ultimately successful, but racial tensions, violence, and inequality persisted; and government attempts to cure such social ills as poverty and urban decay did not produce lasting improvement.

John F. Kennedy

"A man must have goals. There is not sufficient time, even in two terms, to achieve those goals."

—*John F. Kennedy*

Thirty-fifth president of the United States, 1961–1963

Full name: *John Fitzgerald Kennedy*
Born: *May 29, 1917, Brookline, Massachusetts*
Died: *November 22, 1963, Dallas, Texas*
Burial site: *Arlington National Cemetery, Arlington, Virginia*
Parents: *Joseph Patrick and Rose Elizabeth Fitzgerald Kennedy*
Spouse: *Jacqueline Lee Bouvier (1929–94; m. 1953)*
Children: *Daughter (stillborn, 1956); Caroline Bouvier (1957–); John Fitzgerald Jr. (1960–99); Patrick Bouvier (1963–63)*
Religion: *Roman Catholic*
Education: *Harvard University (B.S., 1940); Stanford University Graduate School of Business Administration (1940)*
Occupations: *Navy ensign; author; journalist*
Government positions: *U.S. representative and senator from Massachusetts*
Political party: *Democratic*
Dates as president: *January 20, 1961–November 22, 1963*
Age upon taking office: *43*

Youthful and full of energy, President John F. Kennedy represented a generation of Americans looking for progressive social programs and improved interaction with other countries. Most of his administration's New Frontier programs, however, were barely underway when he was assassinated nearly three years into his presidency. The killing of the widely popular president in November 1963 shocked the nation and left people grieving, not only in America, but around the world.

Only forty-three when he took office in 1960, Kennedy was the youngest elected president. His administration developed strongly after early setbacks. Three months into it, he accepted responsibility for a failed military operation in Cuba, and the following year, he pressured the Soviet Union to remove nuclear missiles from there. Kennedy's reputation, both nationally and worldwide increased greatly over his handling of the Cuban missile crisis, and during the years that followed, he went on several triumphant tours abroad and made inspiring speeches in such places as France, West Germany, Ireland, and Mexico.

At home, Kennedy moved cautiously to develop his programs, after his close election. His cabinet included many younger men from the business world who were receptive to new ideas, and he was fairly bursting with them. Among his successful efforts were a large increase in the American space program and expanded trade with

Timeline

1917: Born in Massachusetts
1943: Awarded a U.S. Navy and Marine Corps medal for heroism in a noncombat situation
1947–53: Serves as U.S. representative from Massachusetts
1953–61: Serves as U.S. senator from Massachusetts
1957: Awarded Pulitzer Prize for Biography for his book *Profiles in Courage*
1961–63: Serves as thirty-fifth U.S. president
1961: Bay of Pigs invasion in Cuba fails
1962: Soviet Union and United States lock heads in Soviet missile crisis
1963: Assassinated in Dallas, Texas

democratic nations in Latin America and Europe. His initiatives for a sweeping civil-rights bill and a tax cut were facing delays in Congress at the time of his death, and his successor, Lyndon B. Johnson, fought successfully to get them passed in Kennedy's memory.

Overall, Kennedy's effectiveness is difficult to assess because his presidency ended early. Nevertheless, he remains among the most admired and discussed presidents, remembered for his ability to inspire young Americans and for the programs that he was pushing for when he died.

Happy Childhood

The second of nine children of Joseph and Rose Kennedy, John Fitzgerald Kennedy was born on May 29, 1917, in Brookline, Massachusetts. His father had been a bank president by the age of twenty-five, and expanded into shipbuilding, real estate, and other ventures. Joseph Kennedy was among the richest men in America by the time he was thirty, when his second son, John, was born. The boys' mother, Rose, was the daughter of Boston mayor John Francis "Honey Fitz" Fitzgerald, and her marriage to Joseph Patrick Kennedy united two of Boston's most powerful families.

During his happy childhood, John, often called Jack, became an excellent swimmer and sailor. A football injury to his back, however, would cause him pain all of his life. As the Kennedy family grew in size and wealth,

JFK and PT-109

In August 1943, John F. Kennedy was serving as commander of a PT (patrol torpedo) boat, a small craft called PT-109. The boat was cruising slowly and quietly on a dark night a few miles from a group of islands in the South Pacific Ocean. A fog was settling in. PT-109 was among fifteen PT boats scattered around the area on the lookout for Japanese boats rumored to be moving forces to prepare an attack. After midnight, other PT boats were returning to base. PT-109 went for one last patrol before turning back as well.

Suddenly, from out of a mist, PT-109 was rammed by a Japanese destroyer. The PT boat was split in half, spilling all twelve men aboard. Gas tanks exploded into fire, and the men struggled for safety from the flames and the wake of the destroyer.

After the destroyer passed, Kennedy discovered that two of his men were dead and a third was badly burned. The surviving men clung for hours to wreckage, waiting for help. After three hours, they decided to try and reach shore. Holding on to a large plank, they swam three miles before reaching an island. Kennedy towed along the burned sailor, who was unable to swim, by clenching his teeth on the cord of the man's life preserver and pulling him along through the water.

Over the next four days, Kennedy and another man swam under the cover of darkness to nearby islands they were familiar with from patrol duty. On one island, they found a stash of candy on a wrecked Japanese boat. The sweets helped the exhausted and hungry men survive. They were eventually found by a couple of island natives who worked with Allied forces. The natives carried a message Kennedy carved on a coconut to Allied agents, who helped rescue Kennedy and his crew. Kennedy was rewarded for his heroism with a U.S. Navy and Marine Corps medal, and the PT-109 incident was later recounted in a New Yorker article.

they moved to different homes around Boston and New York City before establishing their home base at Hyannis Port on Cape Cod, Massachusetts, in 1928. Jack was educated at private schools before he went on to study at the London School of Economics and then enroll briefly at Princeton University before entering Harvard University, majoring in political science and graduating cum laude in 1940.

His father, Joseph P. Kennedy, served as chairman of the Securities and Exchange Commission under President Franklin D. Roosevelt before being appointed ambassador to Great Britain. Young Kennedy joined him there in 1937 and in 1939, and he became acquainted

Patriarch

Jack Kennedy's father, Joseph P. Kennedy had a wealthy father himself, but enjoyed making money for its own sake, and was a millionaire in his own right before he was thirty-five. He built this fortune higher by investing in the stock market during the 1920s, and shrewdly sold all of his stocks a few months before the market crashed in 1929. He anticipated the end of Prohibition by investing $100,000 in a company that imported Scotch whiskey and gin from the British Isles, and when alcohol became legal again, he was ready to supply it months before American distillers could get up and running again. He eventually sold his interest in the company for $8 million. He had earned nearly as much as a movie producer by then, with another of his companies, RKO. He also invested heavily in real estate, and the family still owns the massive Merchandise Mart in Chicago.

Below: Jack Kennedy and his brother Joe Jr. spent a great deal of time in London with their father, Joseph P. Kennedy, when he was Ambassador to Great Britain.

with reporters, diplomats, and political leaders, including Winston Churchill, who became Britain's prime minister. On his travels through Europe, Jack was an eyewitness to the tensions that erupted into World War II, and after the war broke out in September 1939, he went to Scotland with his father to meet American survivors of a British ship, the *Athenia*, that had been torpedoed by a German U-boat.

Kennedy had transferred to Harvard University by then, and while there, he wrote a thesis on the Munich Pact, which Britain and France signed, accepting the demands of Nazi leader Adolf Hitler that the German-speaking Sudetenland, a part of Czechoslovakia, should be handed over to Germany. Hitler violated the agreement in a series of actions that started World War II. Kennedy's thesis, primarily on how Great Britain failed to challenge Hitler at the time, was later published as a book, *Why England Slept*. He donated the royalties it earned to the bombed-out town of Plymouth, England.

He entered the Stanford University Graduate School of Business in 1940, traveled in South America, and then volunteered for military duty in the spring of 1941. Because of his injured back, however, he was rejected from the service, but after a strenuous period of intense strengthening exercises, he was accepted by the Navy a few months later.

Success and Struggles

Kennedy set his sights on a U.S. Senate seat in 1952, and he started campaigning early by traveling around Massachusetts to get his message across. The Kennedy family and Jack's friends rallied around him and made the effort a success. It was a close race, but with the Kennedy money and the youthful enthusiasm of his supporters, he beat his Republican opponent, incumbent senator Henry Cabot Lodge Jr., in an election that swept Republicans into office in most other parts of the country on the coattails of presidential candidate Dwight D. Eisenhower.

"I don't have to worry about Jack Kennedy. I don't have to worry about the Kennedy money. But I do worry about that family of his. They're all over the state!"

—*Senator Henry Cabot Lodge Jr., defending his seat against Jack Kennedy*

The early part of Kennedy's Senate term was filled with both joy and pain. He helped forge a voting bloc among New England congressmen for legislation favorable to the region, and on September 12, 1953, he married Jacqueline Lee Bouvier, a photographer and journalist from a wealthy family.

Early Career

J.F.K.'s experience on the PT-109 (see box) further weakened his back, and he also contracted malaria during his South Pacific tour. He managed to recover, however, and went back to active duty, just as he learned that his older brother, Joseph Jr., had died in a flying mission over Suffolk, England.

After his discharge from the Navy, Kennedy worked as a reporter for the Hearst International News Service, which assigned him to San Francisco to cover the opening events of the newly established United Nations. However, he decided soon afterward to follow his late brother's political dreams and went home to Boston, where he set up a political organization staffed by family, friends, and navy buddies. Then he announced his candidacy for the congressional seat that was being vacated by longtime Boston politician James M. Curley.

Above: Naval Lieutenant John F. Kennedy in 1943.

Running a well-organized campaign during which he met face-to-face with the voters and highlighted his military service, Kennedy won the election and the next two as well. While in Washington, he backed legislation that could help his home state, and he supported most of the major policies of the Truman administration. But he revealed a streak of independence as well when he criticized Harry Truman, a fellow Democrat, for not giving enough support for China's leader, Chiang Kai-shek. Chiang had been ousted from power in a communist rebellion led by Mao Tse-tung, and had set up a new Chinese government on the island of Taiwan.

By the following year, though, Kennedy couldn't get around without crutches because of his back pain. He underwent a serious spinal operation that wasn't successful, and he was forced to go through the surgery a second time. This time it reduced the pain and helped make him mobile again. While he was recovering from those operations, he wrote a book, *Profiles in Courage*, a collection of essays on eight U.S. senators who risked their careers for important but unpopular causes. The book became a best seller, and it won the Pulitzer Prize for Biography in 1957.

Eligible Bachelor

Kennedy's personal life as a senator sometimes got more press attention than his public accomplishments. Life magazine ran a feature called "Life Goes Courting With a U.S. Senator," and the Saturday Evening Post ran a similar story that described him as "at once preoccupied, disorganized and utterly casual … [and] many women have hopefully concluded that he needs looking after. In their opinion, he is, as a young millionaire Senator, just about the most eligible bachelor in the United States, and the least justifiable one."

The Kennedys went through more hardships when Jackie suffered two miscarriages in 1955 and 1956, but their daughter Caroline was born in 1957, and son John Jr. three years later.

Jack Kennedy's national reputation began growing when he made the nominating speech for former Illinois governor Adlai Stevenson at the 1956 Democratic National Convention. Stevenson later surprised the convention by asking the delegates to select his running mate, and there was an immediate groundswell for Kennedy, who at the time was only thirty-nine years old, just four years above the age minimum to become president.

"The New Frontier of which I speak is not a set of promises—it is a set of challenges. It sums up not what I intend to offer the American people, but what I expect to ask of them."

—John F. Kennedy

He was edged out after three rounds of balloting, but the experience was extremely helpful to his political career. His excellent speech-making skills and his vibrant personality had been displayed on national television, and the opportunity to become vice president led journalists to regard him as an important Democrat. It also led them to reconsider the question of whether a Roman Catholic could someday be elected president. No Catholic had ever been elected to the presidency; and the only previous Catholic nominee, Alfred E. Smith, had met with some voter backlash over his religion in 1928. There was fear among some voters that a Catholic president would do whatever the pope—the leader of the Roman Catholic Church—told him to do.

Above: John F. Kennedy offers words of advice to his running mate, Lyndon B. Johnson, during the 1960 Democratic nominating convention.

Below: Jack Kennedy accepts his party's nomination for the presidency at Los Angeles in 1960. In the front row behind him are his mother, Rose, and his running mate, Lyndon B. Johnson.

DEMOCRATIC NATIONAL CONVENTION
1960

First Catholic President

Kennedy's standing in the Senate noticeably improved after that. He was active on the Foreign Relations Committee and the Senate Committee on Improper Activities in the Labor Management Field, which his brother, Robert F. Kennedy, served as counsel. Jack Kennedy was also among the Democrats assembled by Senate majority leader Lyndon B. Johnson who helped Congress pass civil-rights legislation that had been supported by President Dwight D. Eisenhower.

Kennedy was reelected in 1958 by the largest margin ever in a Massachusetts Senate race, and he began an early, well-organized bid for the 1960 presidential nomination. He was able to build momentum against far more experienced candidates as his campaign geared up for the primaries, the most decisive of which was in the predominantly Protestant state of West Virginia that indicated that his religion wouldn't stand in the way in a national election.

He earned enough support to win the nomination on the first ballot at the party convention, and Texan Lyndon B. Johnson accepted his invitation to run as vice president and help win in the Southwest. Kennedy launched his campaign with an acceptance speech that announced, "We stand today on the edge of a new frontier," running at a whirlwind pace from that moment on, while his opponent, Vice President Richard Nixon, campaigned against him with equal enthusiasm.

The close race was probably determined in a series of four televised debates—the first time television was used for such a forum. Kennedy proved through the debates that he was informed and experienced enough to handle the presidency. More important, his lively personality and good looks were contrasted, in the eyes of many, with Nixon's more serious comments and wooden appearance. Those debates made appearance a factor in all future presidential campaigns, and charisma became the most important presidential qualification of all. Kennedy ultimately won the election by just over one hundred thousand popular votes, with a margin of 303 to 219 votes in the Electoral College—almost too close for comfort.

1960 Election Results

Presidential / Vice Presidential Candidates	Popular Votes	Electoral Votes
John F. Kennedy / Lyndon B. Johnson (Democratic)	34,227,096	303
Richard M. Nixon / Henry Cabot Lodge Jr. (Republican)	34,107,647	219

Above: The first televised presidential election debates in 1960 put challenger Richard Nixon in an uncomfortable position against the Kennedy charisma.

Twentieth-Century Politics

Kennedy almost wrapped up enough delegates in the 1960 primaries to take the presidential nomination without a convention, and the old pros were impressed by how he did it. Kennedy had taught them how to use television and how to use polling, and even though he had nearly unlimited funds, he showed them how to get the most mileage out of their money. Things we take for granted in presidential elections today were developed and refined during Kennedy's primary push and in the national election that followed. He had taken politics into the twentieth century.

The Kennedy Administration

Administration Dates: January 20, 1961–November 22, 1963

Vice President: Lyndon Baines Johnson (1961–63)

Cabinet:

Secretary of State	Dean Rusk (1961–63)
Secretary of the Treasury	C. Douglas Dillon (1961–63)
Attorney General	Robert F. Kennedy (1961–63)
Postmaster General	J. Edward Day (1961–63)
	John A. Gronouski Jr. (1963)
Secretary of the Interior	Stewart L. Udall (1961–63)
Secretary of Agriculture	Orville L. Freeman (1961–63)
Secretary of Labor	Arthur J. Goldberg (1961–62)
	Willard Wirtz (1962–63)
Secretary of Commerce	Luther H. Hodges (1961–63)
Secretary of Defense	Robert S. McNamara (1961–63)
Secretary of Health, Education, and Welfare	Abraham A. Ribicoff (1961–62)
	Anthony J. Celebrezze (1962–63)

Above: Americans regarded the Kennedy family as their very own. Young Caroline and her little brother, John, took it all in stride.

The Kennedy presidency began with a stirring inaugural address and a festive atmosphere that hadn't been seen in Washington for years. The personalities of the president and first lady, their attractive young children, and their seemingly endless round of social events were constantly referred to in the media as "the Kennedy style." He bounced into the White House with a verve the country hadn't seen since Teddy Roosevelt lived there, and a cultured outlook that rivaled Thomas Jefferson's. Through the previous decade, people had taken to wearing celluloid buttons imprinted with smiling faces to remind them that they ought to be happy, but when the Kennedys arrived on the scene, the smiles shifted to their own faces.

The Lodge Connection

The 1952 U.S. Senate race between John F. Kennedy and Henry Cabot Lodge Jr. had an interesting parallel. In 1916, Henry Cabot Lodge Sr. defeated "Honey" Fitzgerald, Kennedy's maternal grandfather, for a Senate seat. Lodge Sr. went on to become a vocal opponent of President Woodrow Wilson's plans for American involvement in the League of Nations. Kennedy won in 1952 against Lodge Jr. and became a vocal proponent for further American involvement in international affairs. Kennedy and Lodge were involved in another election eight years later when Kennedy and his running mate, Lyndon B. Johnson, defeated Richard M. Nixon and his running mate, Lodge, in the presidential election of 1960.

Troubles off the Mainland

The establishment of the Peace Corps—a government-sponsored program that trains volunteers for social and humanitarian service in underdeveloped countries—in March 1961 was an early highlight of Kennedy's administration, and the New Frontier domestic program moved forward gradually. Although his foreign policy started off with a major setback, it followed with decisive actions that earned him a great deal of international attention.

When he became president, Kennedy inherited a plan from the Eisenhower administration supporting rebels in Cuba. A revolution there had placed Fidel Castro in power, and he quickly made his communist sympathies abundantly clear. Many U.S. companies that had been operating in Cuba were shut down and their property was nationalized. As Castro developed stronger ties with the Soviet Union, it drove another wedge into United States–Soviet relations, and increased Cold War tensions.

"There is always inequity in life. Some men are killed in a war and some men are wounded, and some men never leave the country ... life is unfair."

—*John F. Kennedy*

Left: The first wave of thousands of Peace Corps volunteers left Washington, D.C., in the summer of 1961, bound for teaching assignments in Ghana.

Right: President Kennedy (right) and his brother Robert were close confidants, especially during the buildup to the Cuban missile crisis.

Robert F. Kennedy

Born on November 20, 1925, in Brookline, Massachusetts, Robert Kennedy was the seventh of Joseph and Rose Kennedy's nine children. In 1946, he helped with his brother John's campaign for the U.S. House of Representatives, and two years later, he graduated from Harvard University and then earned his law degree from the University of Virginia.

In the early 1950s, Bobby Kennedy worked as a lawyer on the Senate investigations committee, a post he resigned in protest over the methods used by committee chairman Joseph R. McCarthy in his hunt for communists in the government. After McCarthy's spectacular downfall, Kennedy went back as the committee's chief counsel, and spent six years exposing organized crime's relationship with labor unions.

He managed his brother's successful bid for the presidency in 1960, and the new president chose his brother to serve as attorney general. It was the first time a president's close relative had been appointed to a cabinet post, and it drew some criticism.

The brothers decided against trying to push a civil-rights bill through Congress right away. Its passage would be difficult: Jack had won the presidency only narrowly, which weakened his influence in Congress. Instead, they focused first on enforcing existing civil-rights laws. As attorney general, Robert supported the Freedom Riders, a group of black and white activists who took a well-publicized bus trip through the South to dramatize the right of African Americans to sit anywhere on buses. The group was frequently threatened by white crowds as police stood by and just watched. Kennedy sent five hundred federal marshals to Montgomery, Alabama, where, reinforced by state troopers and the National Guard, they broke up a violent white crowd that had surrounded Dr. Martin Luther King Jr.'s Dexter Avenue Baptist Church.

Kennedy pushed for desegregation in schools and transportation but, like Dr. King, he thought that the most important job was protecting African Americans' right to vote. He promised support, but he wasn't sure of the government's legal right to act as a police force over local organizations, and his explanations about limits on federal powers didn't satisfy civil-rights leaders, and some began questioning the Kennedys' commitment to the cause.

In June 1963, President Kennedy sent a bill to Congress that would ban segregation in all public places, and Attorney General Kennedy took the lead in rallying support for it. African-American leaders organized the March on Washington, which brought out more than 250,000 people to demonstrate their support for the bill, and to hear Dr. King deliver his famous "I Have a Dream" speech. The demonstration notwithstanding, the bill was stalled in Congress by Southern senators, as the Kennedy brothers had feared it would. It wasn't until after John Kennedy's assassination in 1963 that Congress passed civil-rights legislation. Under President Lyndon B. Johnson, the Civil Rights Act of 1964 and the Voting Rights Act of 1965 were enacted.

In 1964, Robert Kennedy decided to run for one of New York's two senate seats, and he won easily, in spite of attacks against him for running in a state where he didn't live. He supported legislation for minorities and—hesitantly at first—he began to attack Johnson's escalation of the Vietnam War, which was gradually replacing civil rights as the dominant issue in American politics. In 1965 and 1966, Kennedy questioned whether the war was right, and by 1967, he was openly condemning it as wrong. In early 1968, the war's unpopularity was leading many to wonder if Kennedy would challenge Johnson for the Democratic presidential nomination.

Democratic senator Eugene McCarthy announced that he would enter the race against Johnson as an antiwar candidate, and after he scored surprisingly well against Johnson in the New Hampshire primary, Kennedy announced that he was a candidate too. McCarthy supporters were furious, charging that McCarthy had showed Johnson's weakness, and that Kennedy was using his famous name to take advantage of the situation. Two weeks later, Johnson surprised them all by withdrawing from the race. After winning primaries in Indiana, Nebraska, and the District of Columbia, Kennedy lost to McCarthy in Oregon, and the next primary, in California, was crucial.

Kennedy won in California, but shortly after giving his victory speech at Los Angeles's Ambassador Hotel, Robert Kennedy was shot, and he died twenty-five hours later, on June 6, 1968.

Many anti-Castro Cubans, who called themselves nationalists, emigrated to the United States, and a force of about a thousand of them was trained in military operations by the Central Intelligence Agency (CIA) as part of a plan to overthrow Castro by attacking the island and linking up with nationalists already there. The United States was going to back the effort with air support. Kennedy had approved this plan, which was called the Bay of Pigs invasion, for the beach area where the attack was to take place.

The operation turned out to be an embarrassing disaster. The anti-Castro forces inside Cuba never materialized, and Kennedy refused to approve American air support, which would have been considered an act of aggression. The invaders were easily defeated and many were taken prisoner. When Castro demanded money for their release, Kennedy refused, although eventually some $53 million in food and medical supplies was raised by businesses and private donors to free them. Kennedy took full responsibility for the failed invasion, and an anti-Kennedy faction grew more vocal against him, but his forthrightness helped rally support for him at the same time.

Other foreign policy initiatives proved to be more successful. Concerned about horrible economic conditions in the Caribbean and Latin America that might lead to revolutions, the Kennedy administration introduced a plan called the Alliance for Progress, which, like the Marshall Plan that helped rebuild post–World War II Europe, helped fund the economies of Latin American countries.

The program won back support for the United States in the region after many years of tension, and Kennedy made triumphant visits to Colombia and Argentina in 1961 and to Mexico in 1962. Just a few years earlier, Vice President Nixon had been threatened by hostile crowds in Venezuela, at a time when many South Americans felt that the United States regarded the region only for exploitation by American businesses and nothing more.

The Kennedys also made triumphant visits to France, England, Germany, and Ireland, among other nations, during his administration. So much attention was paid to first lady Jacqueline Kennedy in France that Kennedy told the press, "I am the man who accompanied Jacqueline Kennedy to Paris." Those high-spirited tours were balanced by more profoundly serious confrontations between Kennedy and Soviet premier Nikita Khrushchev and by a civil war in Southeast Asia.

Eyeball to Eyeball

When Kennedy and Khrushchev met in Vienna, Austria, in June 1961, Soviet tension with the United States was unusually high because of the U-2 incident, in which an American spy plane was shot down over the USSR the previous year, and because of the Bay of Pigs invasion. Khrushchev strongly believed that Kennedy was a weak leader, but Kennedy remained steadfast. "It's going to be a long, cold winter," he told reporters covering the meeting.

That summer, the Soviets began building a wall to separate their zone of influence within Berlin and the rest of East Germany from sectors occupied by the other Allied powers. Kennedy asked Congress for an increase in military spending to call up reserve troops, and fifteen hundred well-armed soldiers began a previously announced and legal mission through East Germany and

Left: President Kennedy meets Soviet Premier Nikita Khruschev (center) at the U.S. Ambassador's residence in Vienna. Secretary of State Dean Rusk is in the background.

Left: When President Kennedy went to Berlin in 1963, he told more than 300,000 enthusiastic listeners that he was one of them: "Ich bin ein Berliner."

into West Berlin. They were not challenged, although there were strong fears that they might have been. Right after that, Kennedy made another well-publicized trip abroad, this time to West Berlin. Declaring "Ich bin ein Berliner"—"I am a Berliner," in German—to a wildly enthusiastic crowd, he was able to show American support for a united, democratic Berlin. However, the city would remain divided for more than two more decades.

The Berlin trip took place after another serious setback in U.S.–Soviet relations, which came to be known as the Cuban missile crisis. On October 14, 1962, photographs taken from spy planes flying over Cuba revealed that nuclear missile facilities were being built there, apparently under Soviet supervision.

After Soviet leaders denied the accusation, Kennedy made a dramatic speech on national radio and television describing the situation, and noting that a nuclear attack

Right: The Cuban missile crisis compared to a wild west shootout between the white-hatted cowboy, J.F.K., and Soviet Premier Khruschev on a horse behind Fidel Castor on a mule.

from Cuba could be launched on any nation within the Western Hemisphere. He strongly demanded immediate removal of the missiles and declared a quarantine zone around Cuba, where every ship would be subject to U.S. inspection. He invoked the Monroe Doctrine, a policy established during the presidency of James Monroe to stand firm that against European intervention anywhere in the Americas. And he said dramatically, "It shall be the policy of this nation to regard any nuclear missile launched from Cuba against any nation in the Western Hemisphere as an attack by the Soviet Union on the United States, requiring a full retaliatory response upon the Soviet Union." U.S. military personnel were put on full alert, and America seemed to be on the brink of war, quite possibly a nuclear disaster.

After six tense days following Kennedy's address, the missiles were removed and Premier Khrushchev authorized American inspection of the sites. Cuba denied access to the inspectors, but spy planes watched over the dismantling of the launch sites. The two superpower nations had been at the brink of nuclear war, more than at any other time during the Cold War. As the tension began

Left: Among the many meetings held to defuse the Cuban missile crisis was this one with Soviet Ambassador Andrei Gromyko (second from left) and others. Kennedy sat in his trademark rocking chair, which helped relieve his almost constant back pain.

to ease, Secretary of State Dean Rusk told reporters that, "We're eyeball to eyeball, and I think the other fellow just blinked."

By August 1963, just a few months after the Missile Crisis, relations between United States and the Soviet Union started to get much more positive. A limited Nuclear Test Ban treaty between them and Great Britain outlawed the testing of atomic weapons in the air or on the water, but it allowed for underground testing. The United States also agreed to sell wheat to the Soviet Union, which was facing famine after a poor harvest.

Vietnam

Kennedy's concern about communist expansion became focused on Southeast Asia. The French abandoned their colony of Indochina following a communist uprising in 1954, and the area was partitioned into four nations: North and South Vietnam, Cambodia, and Laos. North Vietnam was controlled by communists, and the democratic government of South Vietnam was threatened by communist guerillas called the National Liberation Front, later known as the Vietcong.

A neutral government was established in Laos in 1962, but South Vietnam was threatened by unrest from communists as well as followers of the Buddhist religion who objected to the leadership of its president Ngo Dinh Diem. Ngo proved to be more interested in maintaining his base of power than in instituting reforms in his corrupt government, and he was killed in a rebellion in 1963.

After the French abandoned Indochina, President Eisenhower sent military advisors to help the South Vietnamese army fight the communist guerillas. Kennedy increased the number of advisors from 700 to 1,500 in 1961, and two years later there were more than 15,000 American military people in South Vietnam.

The question of whether Kennedy would have gone on to increase American involvement to combat and aerial bombing missions is impossible to determine. He was assassinated before U.S. troops and pilots became directly involved in the war in 1964. His most often quoted statement on the issue was that "in the final analysis it is their [South Vietnam's] war," seems to indicate that he might not have increased American involvement into what many believed was a useless war that divided American opinion.

The Kennedy Style

At home, the Kennedy administration became a model for America's popular culture. The White House was a center of glittering social activity and was often called Camelot, after the legendary kingdom of King Arthur. Writers, artists, and scientists were regularly invited to receptions and dinners, and Kennedy enjoyed good relations with the press. He spoke well and wittily during news conferences. In one instance, during a meeting with Soviet Premier Nikita Khrushchev, Kennedy inquired about a medal he was wearing. When the Russian leader identified it as a peace medal, Kennedy smiled and said, "I hope you get to keep it."

The New Frontier program proceeded slowly but steadily. In 1961, Kennedy won approval for a bill to improve urban housing and another to provide financial help to economically depressed areas. His attempts at providing government medical assistance to the elderly was denied by Congress, as were his attempts at civil-rights legislation. Kennedy's plan for creating a

cabinet-level Department of Urban Affairs was rejected, at least partly because he planned to name an African American, Robert C. Weaver, to head it. His tax-cut plans were also bottled up in Congress.

In 1962, Kennedy intervened in a threatened strike by steelworkers. An agreement that increased the workers' benefits but not their wages was, he believed, a solid compromise that would not lead to price increases and inflation. But when steel companies announced price increases anyway, Kennedy repealed them, which turned many business leaders against him.

"My father always told me that all businessmen were sons of bitches, but I never believed it until now."
—*John F. Kennedy, on the surprise steel price increase*

He was successful at increasing U.S. trade, arranging a financial deal that maintained the strength of the United Nations, and winning a billion-dollar appropriation for the National Aeronautics and Space Agency (NASA), calling on the agency to land a man on the moon by 1970.

Civil Rights

As his presidency gained momentum, Kennedy began more vigorous support for programs that would conserve and develop natural resources, provide aid for education, revise inefficient farm programs, and support civil rights. Calling racial tension "a moral crisis," he gave Attorney General Robert F. Kennedy the power to investigate cases of intimidation of African-American voters in the South. He also supported plans for a civil-rights march on Washington in August 1963, where Dr. Martin Luther King Jr. gave his famous "I Have a Dream" speech before more than 200,000 people.

Kennedy twice used his presidential authority to enforce existing civil-rights laws through the use of federal troops. In 1962, Mississippi governor Ross R. Barnett prevented the enrollment of an African-American student, James Meredith, to the University of

Left: Robert F. Kennedy announced his candidacy for the presidency in 1968, but he was assassinated after winning the California primary.

Left: Governor George C. Wallace challenges deputy attorney general Nicholas Katzenbach's right to enroll black students at the University of Alabama.

Mississippi, and when rioting broke out, Kennedy sent in federal troops. Meredith was admitted to the university with a well-armed military escort.

The following June, Alabama governor George Wallace resisted court-ordered desegregation of school districts in three major Alabama cities. By the time school opened in September, President Kennedy had federalized the state national guard to enforce the integration ruling.

Fateful Trip

With the 1964 presidential election a year away, Kennedy planned a trip to Texas, where his support was thin in spite of the role in his administration of Vice President Johnson, a beloved Texan. The period was a difficult one for the Kennedys, who had lost their newborn son, two-day-old Patrick, just a few weeks earlier.

The Texas trip in 1963 drew large, enthusiastic crowds. A motorcade was arranged to transport administration officials and Texas governor John C. Connally to a speech in Dallas on November 22. Just after the motorcade slowed to round a curve at around 12:30 that afternoon, shots rang out, and one of the bullets struck the president in the neck, and passed through, hitting Connally in

Right: President Kennedy arriving in Dallas on November 22, 1963. He would be shot a minute later. His wife, Jacqueline, is at his side; Texas Governor John Connally and his wife, Nellie, are in the front seat.

the front seat of the limousine. A second bullet struck Kennedy in the head, and after reeling back, he slumped forward into his wife's arms, and the car sped off to nearby Parkland Hospital.

The president was declared dead shortly after 1:00, and his body was placed in a casket that was put aboard Air Force One, where Mrs. Kennedy and Vice President Johnson were waiting for the return trip to Washington. Johnson was sworn in aboard the plane as the nation's thirty-sixth president.

The shots were identified as having come from a warehouse overlooking the highway, and an employee, Lee Harvey Oswald, was seen running away from the building at about the same time. He was accused of killing a police officer before he was arrested in a movie theater. Two days later, Oswald was shot by Dallas nightclub owner Jack Ruby in front of reporters and live television cameras while he was being moved from one jail to another, and he died in the same hospital where the president had.

On the day of the Oswald shooting, the president's flag-draped coffin was taken on a caisson, a two-wheeled horse-drawn gun carriage, from the White House to the

Left: Lee Harvey Oswald, the assumed killer of President Kennedy, was shot dead himself two days after Kennedy's assassination.

Capitol Rotunda. His state funeral the following day was attended by dignitaries from ninety-two countries, and an estimated one million people lined the route (and millions more watched on television) as the caisson took the coffin to Arlington National Cemetery. Among many tributes, Willy Brandt, mayor of West Berlin and a future leader of West Germany, remarked that "a flame went out for all those who had hoped for a just peace and a better life."

Legacy

Within a week after Lyndon B. Johnson assumed the presidency, he appointed a committee to investigate Kennedy's assassination. The Warren Commission, named for its chairman, Supreme Court Chief Justice Earl Warren, later delivered its findings: that a lone gunman—Oswald—acting on his own was responsible for killing the president.

Some people weren't satisfied with the investigations, believing that there had been a conspiracy behind the assassination. However, different groups supported different theories, and in the end, none of them seemed to be anything more than unfounded, and unproven, matters of opinion.

Unfortunately, those conspiracy theories have become part of the Kennedy legacy. A congressional panel was organized in 1977 and given the authority to examine evidence that had been overlooked by the Warren Commission. It concluded two years later that there was a "probable conspiracy" and recommended further investigation.

While he was president, Kennedy enhanced the status of the United States internationally with foreign policy initiatives that increased trade with developed nations and provided assistance for underdeveloped ones. In Berlin and Cuba, he challenged aggressive Soviet actions. Kennedy's Vietnam policy was unfinished at the time of his death: He was neither recalling American military advisors nor involving any more American combat forces.

Kennedy was extremely popular at home, but much of his domestic agenda was still being debated when he died. Civil-rights legislation was quickly enacted during the administration of his successor, Lyndon B. Johnson, who also increased American involvement in Vietnam. The latter half of the 1960s saw America divided over the war, with angry antiwar protests in the streets. In evaluating Kennedy's presidency, the question of how much he influenced America is often overwhelmed by how much the country changed after his assassination and speculation about how he might have reacted to that change.

Jacqueline Kennedy

Born July 28, 1929, Southampton, New York
Died May 19, 1994, New York, New York

"Can anyone understand how it is to have lived in the White House and then, suddenly, to be living alone as the president's widow?"
—Jacqueline Kennedy

In 1960, the year that John F. Kennedy was elected president, the most popular show on Broadway was a musical called *Camelot,* about the court and castle of the legendary King Arthur. It introduced several popular songs, including one with the lyric, "Don't let it be forgot / That once there was a spot / For one brief shining moment / That was known as Camelot."

The name Camelot was applied to the Kennedy White House. As well as being the center of power of a great land, it was transformed into a showcase of American history and a setting for an almost continuous round of festive occasions during the Kennedy years. The president and first lady staged elegant parties with guest lists that included foreign dignitaries, talented artists of all kinds, and accomplished scientists.

Most important, Jacqueline Kennedy restored the White House by recreating its historical past with antique pieces among more contemporary designs. She was also responsible for much of what was called the "Kennedy style." A popular and trendsetting first lady, her appearance and fashions were regularly featured in magazines, and she charmed fans around the world. Along with her attractive husband and their two young children, the first lady was photogenic, and she made for interesting news stories beyond the political headlines. If Jacqueline Kennedy radiated grace and charm as a public person, she also showed great dignity during the tragedy of her husband's assassination and her own misfortunes.

"Inquiring Camera Girl"

Jackie, as she was called, was born Jacqueline Lee Bouvier on July 28, 1929, at Southampton, on Eastern Long Island, into a wealthy but troubled household. Her father, John Vernou Bouvier III, was a handsome and outgoing stockbroker, and her mother, Janet Lee, was a stylish, if reserved, socialite. They quarreled often, usually over his drinking and her unfaithfulness, and they separated in 1936 and filed for divorce soon afterward.

While growing up, Jackie spent summers at the family estate in East Hampton, New York, and lived with her mother during the winter in a large Manhattan apartment. Her mother remarried in 1942 to Hugh D.

Left: Of all the memories of the Kennedy years, the fondest are images like this, in which 18-month-old John Jr. romps through the Oval Office.

Martin Luther King Jr.

Born on January 15, 1929, in Atlanta, Georgia, to Martin Luther and Alberta King, Martin Luther King Jr. was taught by his parents that he could overcome the humiliation of segregation. His father, who had grown up in poverty, rose to become a prominent Southern preacher. King grew up with racial segregation as a way of life. Blacks and whites had separate schools, hospital waiting rooms, and even drinking fountains. When both were allowed in the same room, lines were drawn on the floor to keep them divided.

Supported by his parents' teachings, King excelled at school, especially in public speaking. After completing high school early, King enrolled in Morehouse College in Atlanta in 1944. At this prestigious school for African American men, he majored in sociology and English and continued to participate in public-speaking contests. He had planned to attend medical or law school, but professors at Morehouse urged him to become a minister.

Upon his graduation in 1948, King went to Crozer Theological Seminary in Chester, Pennsylvania, to study religion. There he learned of the activities of Mohandas Gandhi, who used nonviolent means (such as boycotts and protests) to help free India from English rule. Gandhi's teachings greatly inspired King. After earning his degree from Crozer in 1951, King began doctoral studies at Boston University in philosophy and religion. He was awarded his doctorate in 1955. While at the university, he met and married Coretta Scott.

In 1954, King accepted the position of pastor at the Dexter Avenue Baptist Church in Montgomery, Alabama. That same year, the Supreme Court ruled in Brown v. Board of Education of Topeka that separate but equal schools for blacks and whites were unconstitutional. The racial climate in America soon changed as many African Americans began to challenge other segregation laws. The bus system in Montgomery operated under such a law: blacks and whites had separate seats. On December 1, 1955, seamstress Rosa Parks was arrested for refusing to give up her seat to a white man. In response, King and other African American leaders urged Montgomery's black community to boycott the city's buses on December 5.

After the boycott began successfully, King and the others formed the Montgomery Improvement Association to work for fairer laws. Chosen the group's president, King negotiated with city officials to change segregation in the bus system. When his demands were refused, the boycott continued for 382 days. Finally, on December 21, 1956, the Supreme Court ruled that the segregation of city buses was unconstitutional. This victory convinced King and the others to spread the movement for civil rights across the South. In 1957, they organized the Southern Christian Leadership Conference. As the group's leader, King toured the country over the next few years, giving speeches, attending rallies, and setting up protests.

In 1963, King traveled to Birmingham, Alabama, to organize a protest against segregation in downtown department stores. The Birmingham police moved against protesters with clubs and attack dogs. King was arrested and placed in solitary confinement. He spent the time writing his famous "Letter from Birmingham Jail," eloquently arguing for the moral right of his movement. Because of the protestors' efforts, Birmingham's white businessmen agreed to halt their racist practices.

On August 28, 1963, over two hundred thousand people marched on Washington, D.C. Organized by King, this rally sought to raise the nation's awareness of civil rights and to encourage Congress to pass the civil-rights bill submitted by President John F. Kennedy. At the end of the peaceful demonstration, King delivered his famous "I Have a Dream" speech.

For his leadership in the nonviolent fight for equality, King was awarded the Nobel Peace Prize in 1964, the youngest person ever to win the award at that time. Earlier that year, King had witnessed the signing of the Civil Rights Act of 1964. It forbade racial discrimination in public places such as restaurants and theaters.

While continuing his work for civil rights, King widened his concern to include human rights. In 1967, he spoke out against the Vietnam War. Later that same year, he began a campaign to fight poverty in America. He toured the country to recruit people for a new march on Washington to demand economic rights for everyone. During this tour, he went to Memphis, Tennessee, to speak on behalf of striking sanitation workers. On April 4, 1968, while standing on the balcony of the Lorraine Motel in Memphis, King was shot and killed by an assassin identified as James Earl Ray. Ray later claimed that he had been part of a larger conspiracy. As was suspected in the assassination of John F. Kennedy in 1963, evidence suggests that more than one individual was involved in the assassination.

Auchincloss, a wealthy Washington, D.C.-based lawyer with a large estate at Newport, Rhode Island. Jackie moved between the East Hampton and Rhode Island homes while developing into an excellent equestrienne. She also studied dance and ballet, and she loved to read and to write stories and poems. Through those years attending private schools, she was regarded as both curious and mischievous.

Jackie went to Vassar College to study art history, and she spent a year at the Sorbonne in Paris, where she majored in French language, art, and literature. In 1951, while she was a student at George Washington University in Washington, D.C., she won a contest sponsored by *Vogue* magazine from among a thousand entries. Contestants were required to submit a personal profile, an entire magazine layout with articles on high fashion, and a five-hundred-word essay on "People I Wish I Had Known." Among her selections of people were three artists whom she credited as having produced moments of beauty amid the transience of life. They were Serge Diaghilev, a force in Russian ballet; French poet Charles-Pierre Baudelaire; and English playwright Oscar Wilde.

The contest prize was a one-year job at *Vogue*—six months in New York and six in Paris. Jackie decided against taking the position, though, and instead, she took a job at the *Washington Times-Herald* newspaper. As the "Inquiring Camera Girl," she contributed photographs and interviews of people in Washington. Among her first subjects was Pat Nixon, the wife of Vice President Richard Nixon. Nixon himself was the subject of a later piece, as was a Massachusetts congressman, John Kennedy, whom most people called Jack.

Jack and Jackie

Jack and Jackie had met before. Earlier in 1951, they had both been invited to a dinner hosted by Washington newsman Charles Bartlett. He and his wife were playing matchmakers, and Jack and Jackie dated a few times but didn't develop a serious relationship. After Jackie received a marriage proposal from a stockbroker, though, Jack became more serious about her, calling her regularly and occasionally sending postcards when he was away from Washington, campaigning for the Senate. After he went

Above: Jack and Jackie announced their engagement on June 23, 1953.

back to Washington as a senator early in 1953, he took her to movies, met her for lunch, and escorted her to dinner parties.

Kennedy had a reputation as a womanizer, and he had to win Jackie's confidence. When she went to London in May 1953, to cover the coronation of Queen Elizabeth II, they kept in touch by phone and through letters, but they both recalled later that they each seemed to be doing well on their own. When Jackie went back to Washington, Jack was there to meet her at the airport, and she presented him with several gift books she had bought for him in London. They were engaged within twenty-four hours. The next day, the *Saturday Evening Post* ran a previously prepared article on Kennedy as the most eligible bachelor in Washington.

Their engagement was officially announced in late June of 1953, and the wedding took place on September 12, 1953, near Newport, Rhode Island. It was a huge social event, with more than six hundred guests at the ceremony and another seventeen hundred at the reception, which was held at Hammersmith Farm, Jackie's family's summer home.

Jackie helped broaden Kennedy's appreciation of the arts and fine dining. She was not politically minded, but she helped her husband by translating French reports on Indochina—the colony France vacated in 1954, part of which became North and South Vietnam.

Early Hardships

The Kennedys faced several hardships during first three years of their marriage. Jack had a painful back injury and couldn't walk without crutches. He went through two spinal operations, one of them so delicate that he was nearly given up for dead. During his recovery, Jackie read to him, and they played cards and board games. She arranged to have an acquaintance, actress Grace Kelly, dress as a nurse and announce to him that she would be his new caretaker; the joke fell on its face when Jack didn't recognize the famous celebrity.

As Kennedy recovered, he wrote a book, *Profiles in Courage,* about eight senators in American history who took courageous, but unpopular, stands. Jackie helped him with his research and made notes on the text. Kennedy credited her in the preface for providing the encouragement, assistance, and criticism for him to complete the book, which became a best seller and won the Pulitzer Prize for Biography in 1957.

Jackie, meanwhile, had hardships of her own. She suffered miscarriages in 1955 and 1956, and their marriage was strained by his extramarital affairs and her spending habits. The birth of their daughter, Caroline, in November 1957 helped bring them closer together.

Kennedy was campaigning for the presidency when Jackie was pregnant with their second surviving child, John Kennedy Jr. (also known as John-John), who was born shortly after his father was elected president. The two proved devoted parents, and images of the family charmed the public during their White House years.

The "Jackie Look"

Having little interest in the art of politics or much knowledge of it, Jackie wasn't expected to contribute much to Kennedy's presidential campaign except for photographic opportunities of the youthful, attractive, smartly dressed couple. However, the public soon found her to be witty, charming, and intelligent, and she began holding her own press conferences, attended fund-raising teas, and met with voters—from dairy farmers to shoppers at supermarkets to people in ethnic neighborhoods where she could speak to them in French, Spanish, or Italian. Kennedy once remarked, "I assure you that my wife can also speak English."

After moving into the White House, the Kennedys hosted parties that were informal and elegant, with opportunities for guests to mingle. Jackie's clothing choices were regularly reported by the fashion magazines—from her pillbox hat to her accessories to her gowns, the "Jackie look" became a style sensation. Her popularity spread worldwide, and she was watched with a great deal of interest during a visit to France, where crowds shouted, "Vive Jackie!" It prompted the president to jokingly introduce himself at a press conference as "the man who accompanied Jacqueline Kennedy to Paris." The first lady's subsequent trips to Pakistan and other Asian nations were also highly successful.

Jacqueline Kennedy's most enduring legacy as first lady was her restoration of the White House. She hired museum curators, historians, and art experts to help bring out the historical significance of the building. She decorated with things that she found squirreled away

Right: Jacqueline Kennedy escorts CBS reporter Charles Collingwood, and forty-eight million television viewers, through the newly restored White House in 1962.

in storage—a chair from the Jackson administration, for instance, and enough furnishings from the Monroe and Lincoln administrations to decorate entire bedrooms.

Her work prompted a book, *The Historic Guide to the White House,* and a television special in 1962, in which she served as guide for 48 million viewers.

That Terrible Year

A span of a few months in 1963 turned tragic for Jackie. Patrick Bouvier Kennedy, born in August 1963, died from an illness when he was two days old. It brought the Kennedys closer together again, and Jackie decided to go with her husband on a November campaign trip to Texas.

They were greeted with the usual fanfare of a presidential visit. But the president wasn't the whole show. A hotel manager in Houston brushed past Kennedy to greet his wife, and later that day, she stole the show in a meeting of Mexican Americans by speaking with them in Spanish. The next stop was Dallas, where there was vocal anti-Kennedy sentiment. As in other parts of the country, Kennedy had detractors who were angry at his unwillingness to back military action against Cuba, his support for civil rights, and his attempts to improve relations with the Soviet Union. A full-page ad with his picture in the form of a criminal with the words "Wanted For Treason" had appeared in a Dallas newspaper.

Nevertheless, the route of the Kennedy motorcade was lined with thousands of well-wishers, and Kennedy ordered the bulletproof "bubble" roof removed so they could enjoy the beautiful day. Jackie had been instructed to wave to people on her side of the car and the president to people on his side in order to double the number of potential voters they greeted.

Suddenly, a bullet struck the president, and as Jackie saw him crumple in pain and shouted, "He's been shot," a second bullet hit the president in the head and he slumped against her. The car sped away to a nearby hospital, where Jackie watched as doctors tried to save him, but Jack Kennedy died a half hour after he had been shot. Two hours later, still wearing the same blood-stained dress, Jacqueline Kennedy stood next to Vice President Lyndon Johnson as he took the oath of office as president.

Above: John Kennedy Jr. offers a salute as his father's funeral procession passes. Looking on are his sister, Caroline; his uncle Edward; his mother, Jacqueline; and his uncle Robert.

Back in Washington, Jackie herself made all the funeral arrangements and decisions. From an icon of youth and vitality, she became a symbol of strength and courage during the funeral. She met foreign dignitaries, thanked the general public on national television for their sympathy, and lit the eternal flame at her husband's grave at Arlington National Cemetery.

When she left the White House, Jackie left a card in the Lincoln bedroom, which she had restored and had shared with her husband. It read: "In this room lived John Fitzgerald Kennedy with his wife, Jacqueline, during the two years, ten months, and two days he was president of the United States."

In the News

Jackie Kennedy and her children stayed in the news after they left the White House. The former first lady worked hard to preserve her husband's legacy, requesting that Cape Canaveral—the site of American space launches—be renamed Cape Kennedy, and she also oversaw construction of the John F. Kennedy Library in Boston, Massachusetts. She supported her brother-in-law, Robert (Bobby) Kennedy in his campaign for the presidency in 1968, only to be shocked again when he, too, was assassinated.

In 1969, Jackie surprised many—and disappointed some—by marrying Aristotle Socrates Onassis, a wealthy Greek shipping businessman many years older than she was. She explained to friends that she loved Onassis and found relief from the constant reminders of the Kennedy legacy. After his death in 1975, Jackie said, "Aristotle Onassis saved me at a moment when my life was engulfed with shadows."

In 1975, Jacqueline Kennedy Onassis became a consulting editor with Viking Books and then moved to Doubleday Books three years later. She tried to avoid publicity all the while, but she and her children continued to be hounded by photographers and they were written about regularly. Daughter Caroline became an attorney,

Above: The family gathers for the dedication of the John F. Kennedy Library in 1989. (L-R) Senator Edward Kennedy, Caroline Kennedy Schlossberg, John F. Kennedy Jr., Jacqueline Kennedy Onassis.

married Ed Schlossberg in 1986, and had three children. Son John Jr. was admitted to the New York Bar in 1990, launched the political magazine *George* in 1995, and married Carolyn Bessette in 1996; he, his wife, and his sister-in-law died in a plane crash near Martha's Vineyard in 1999. The former first lady died of non-Hodgkin's lymphoma, a type of cancer, in 1994, and was buried next to President Kennedy at Arlington National Cemetery.

Kennedy's Inaugural Address

Delivered January 20, 1961

Following a night of heavy snow, a bitterly cold wind swept through the capital on the day John F. Kennedy was inaugurated as the nation's thirty-fifth president. The oath of office was administered by Supreme Court chief justice Earl Warren, who, close to three years later, would head a commission investigating the assassination of President Kennedy.

Among the most memorable of inaugural addresses, Kennedy's set the tone for his administration by placing the United States firmly in the position as a world leader pursuing the highest ideals. It is position that also assumes the burden of living up to those ideals, and to achieve that, Kennedy placed responsibility on each American citizen: "Ask not what your country can do for you," he implored, "ask what you can do for your country."

That phrase was among several memorable statements in Kennedy's speech. As a classic piece of oratory, the speech contained many bold statements followed by challenges to uphold the ideals expressed. In some places, Kennedy used repetitive phrases to create a rhythmic effect. Always, the phrases stressed an upbeat message.

Excerpt from Kennedy's Inaugural Address

[W]e observe today not a victory of party, but a celebration of freedom—symbolizing an end, as well as a beginning—signifying renewal, as well as change. For I have sworn before you and Almighty God the same solemn oath our forebears prescribed nearly a century and three quarters ago.

The world is very different now. For man holds in his mortal hands the power to abolish all forms of human poverty and all forms of human life. And yet the same revolutionary beliefs for which our forebears fought are still at issue around the globe—the belief that the rights of man come not from the generosity of the state, but from the hand of God.

We dare not forget today that we are the heirs of that first revolution. Let the word go forth from this time and place, to friend and foe alike, that the torch has been passed to a new generation of Americans—born in this century, tempered by war, disciplined by a hard and bitter peace, proud of our ancient heritage—and unwilling to witness or permit the slow undoing of those human rights to which this Nation has always been committed, and to which we are committed today at home and around the world.

Let every nation know, whether it wishes us well or ill, that we shall pay any price, bear any burden, meet any hardship, support any friend, oppose any foe, in order to assure the survival and the success of liberty.

This much we pledge—and more.

To those old allies whose cultural and spiritual origins we share, we pledge the loyalty of faithful friends. United, there is little we cannot do in a host of cooperative ventures.

Divided, there is little we can do—for we dare not meet a powerful challenge at odds and split asunder.

To those new States whom we welcome to the ranks of the free, we pledge our word that one form of colonial control shall not have passed away merely to be replaced by a far more iron tyranny. We shall not always expect to find them supporting our view. But we shall always hope to find them strongly supporting their own freedom—and to remember that, in the past, those who foolishly sought power by riding the back of the tiger ended up inside.

To those peoples in the huts and villages across the globe struggling to break the bonds of mass misery, we pledge our best efforts to help them help themselves, for whatever period is required—not because the Communists may be doing it, not because we seek their votes, but because it is right. If a free society cannot help the many who are poor, it cannot save the few who are rich.

To our sister republics south of our border, we offer a special pledge—to convert our good words into good deeds—in a new alliance for progress—to assist free men and free governments in casting off the chains of poverty. But this peaceful revolution of hope cannot become the prey of hostile powers. Let all our neighbors know that we shall join with them to oppose aggression or subversion anywhere in the Americas. And let every other power know that this Hemisphere intends to remain the master of its own house.

To that world assembly of sovereign states, the United Nations, our last best hope in an age where the instruments of war have far outpaced the instruments of peace, we renew our pledge of support—to prevent it from becoming merely a forum for invective—to strengthen its shield of the new and the weak—and to enlarge the area in which its writ may run.

Finally, to those nations who would make themselves our adversary, we offer not a pledge but a request: that both sides begin anew the quest for peace, before the dark powers of destruction unleashed by science engulf all humanity in planned or accidental self-destruction.

We dare not tempt them with weakness. For only when our arms are sufficient beyond doubt can we be certain beyond doubt that they will never be employed.

But neither can two great and powerful groups of nations take comfort from our present course—both sides overburdened by the cost of modern weapons, both rightly alarmed by the steady spread of the deadly atom, yet both racing to alter that uncertain balance of terror that stays the hand of mankind's final war.

So let us begin anew—remembering on both sides that civility is not a sign of weakness, and sincerity is always subject to proof. Let us never negotiate out of fear. But let us never fear to negotiate.

Let both sides explore what problems unite us instead of belaboring those problems which divide us.

Let both sides, for the first time, formulate serious and precise proposals for the inspection and control of arms—and bring the absolute power to destroy other nations under the absolute control of all nations.

Let both sides seek to invoke the wonders of science instead of its terrors. Together let us explore the stars, conquer the deserts, eradicate disease, tap the ocean depths, and encourage the arts and commerce.

Let both sides unite to heed in all corners of the earth the command of Isaiah—to "undo the heavy burdens …and to let the oppressed go free." […]

In the long history of the world, only a few generations have been granted the role of defending freedom in its hour of maximum danger. I do not shrink from this responsibility—I welcome it. I do not believe that any of us would exchange places with any other people or any other generation. The energy, the faith, the devotion which we bring to this endeavor will light our country and all who serve it—and the glow from that fire can truly light the world.

And so, my fellow Americans: ask not what your country can do for you—ask what you can do for your country.

My fellow citizens of the world: ask not what America will do for you, but what together we can do for the freedom of man.

Finally, whether you are citizens of America or citizens of the world, ask of us the same high standards of strength and sacrifice which we ask of you. With a good conscience our only sure reward, with history the final judge of our deeds, let us go forth to lead the land we love, asking His blessing and His help, but knowing that here on earth God's work must truly be our own.

What Happened Next

Kennedy was able to rally support for many of his policies. Establishing the Peace Corps was an example of idealism put into action. The struggle for human rights is a continuous one. Kennedy was able to initiate civil-rights legislation that eventually became law in 1964.

Kennedy's pledge to protect democracy abroad was acted on in several diplomatic confrontations with the Soviet Union and by sending military advisors to South Vietnam to help that country defend itself. The price for fighting the expansion of communism proved to be very high. Whether or not American involvement in Vietnam would have escalated under Kennedy remains unknown.

Kennedy's idealism, as expressed in his inaugural address, energized many Americans. They believed that, indeed, "the torch has been passed to a new generation of Americans." Those who believed that a new frontier had emerged were most dismayed at the Kennedy assassination. "We'll laugh again," said Kennedy's assistant secretary of labor, Daniel Patrick Moynihan, after the assassination. "It's just that we'll never be young again."

Lyndon B. Johnson

"Our institutions cannot be interrupted by an assassin's bullet."
—*Lyndon B. Johnson*

Thirty-sixth president of the United States, 1963–1969

Full name: *Lyndon Baines Johnson*

Born: *August 27, 1908, Stonewall, Texas*

Died: *January 22, 1973, Johnson City, Texas*

Burial site: *LBJ Ranch, near Johnson City, Texas*

Parents: *Samuel Ealy and Rebekah Baines Johnson*

Spouse: *Claudia Alta "Lady Bird" Taylor (1912–2007; m. 1934)*

Children: *Lynda Bird (1944–); Luci Baines (1947–)*

Religion: *Disciples of Christ*

Education: *Southwest Texas State College (B.S., 1930); attended Georgetown University Law School*

Occupations: *Teacher; rancher*

Government positions: *Congressional secretary; U.S. representative and senator from Texas; vice president under John F. Kennedy*

Political party: *Democratic*

Dates as president: *November 22, 1963–January 20, 1965 (first term); January 20, 1965–January 20, 1969 (second term)*

Age upon taking office: *55*

Lyndon B. Johnson's presidency was marked by his Great Society program—social legislation for civil rights, the "War on Poverty" to improve the living standards of disadvantaged Americans, and his escalation of the American military presence in the Vietnam War. Highlighting his impressive career as a persuasive political professional, his social programs put him high on the list of America's most active and effective presidents. The Vietnam War, however, hung like a cloud over his accomplishments, and he left office at the low point of a distinguished career.

Johnson assumed the presidency in the midst of a national tragedy. The assassination of the popular and idealistic President John F. Kennedy in 1963 left the nation reeling, and after Vice President Johnson was sworn in as president, he acted swiftly to restore stability to the grieving country. He was able to complete legislation Kennedy had put forward that was still stalled in Congress.

After winning a full term in 1964, the energetic Texan and his cabinet made tremendous gains in passing progressive social legislation much like that of President Franklin D. Roosevelt and his New Deal of the 1930s, which was enacted when Johnson first arrived in Washington, D.C.

Right: Johnson was twenty years old when he taught at the elementary school at Cotulla, Texas, in 1928. His colleagues included (L-R) Mrs. Elizabeth Johnson (no relation), Mrs. Jack Kerr, and Mrs. Mary Widenthal.

Timeline

1908: Born in Texas
1928–31: Teaches school in Texas
1931–35: Serves as aide to Texas congressman Richard Kleberg
1937–49: Serves as U.S. representative from Texas
1949–61: Serves as U.S. senator from Texas
1961–63: Serves as vice president under John F. Kennedy
1963–69: Serves as thirty-sixth U.S. president following assassination of Kennedy
1964: Gulf of Tonkin incident prompts heightened U.S. involvement in the Vietnam War
1973: Dies in Texas

Johnson increased the commitment of U.S. troops and military hardware in the battle against Southeast Asian communists with almost no positive results, and public debate over the Vietnam War grew increasingly tense. Demonstrations against the war and other issues were an almost daily occurrence, and in spite of his social programs and the restraint he had shown by refusing to involve the United States in other international confrontations, his chances for reelection in 1968 appeared to be impossible. When he dropped out of the race, he announced that he was going to devote all of his energies to ending the Vietnam War.

Life Lessons in the Texas Hill Country

Lyndon Baines Johnson was born on August 27, 1908, on a farm in central Texas near Johnson City. The Johnsons were a modest family, but they had strong political roots. An ancestor had served as governor of Kentucky, and his grandfather had served in the Texas state legislature. Lyndon's father, Sam Ealy Johnson Jr.,

the son of a veteran of the Confederate army in the Civil War, farmed the rough land of the Texas Hill Country, and also served in the state legislature.

Lyndon graduated from high school in Johnson City, first in his class of six, and his parents were firm about sending him to college, but he headed west to California instead. As a teenager, he worked at odd jobs like picking cotton and shining shoes, and he worked as a dishwasher in California before he went back home to work on a road-building crew. He soon got tired of the backbreaking work, and entered Southwest Texas State Teachers College in San Marcos.

During his time as a college student, he took a year off to teach school in Cotulla, Texas, in order to pay some of his growing personal debts. The school served the community's impoverished Mexican Americans, who not only lacked economic opportunities, but also faced long-standing racism. Johnson set high standards for

Smell of Power

When young Lyndon Johnson first arrived in Washington as a secretary to a congressman, he talked to anyone who seemed to have any kind of power, whether they wanted to listen to him or not. "There was that smell of power," he said. "It's got an odor, you know. Power, I mean." His boss, the congressman, didn't take his duties very seriously, and he let Johnson take care of the details, including filling patronage jobs. He put a new spin on that practice by requiring people he helped to help him around the office, both in the early morning and late into the evening. It quickly became the busiest Congressional office in Washington, and Johnson was able to devote his time to his own political education. None of the dragooned helpers seemed to mind the long hours. Johnson was enjoying himself, and his joy was contagious. They also owed their day jobs to him, and he never let them forget it.

his students, forcing them to speak English around the school, and when he discovered that many of them came from homes short on food, he helped establish a free school-lunch program for them. The struggle to survive in Cotulla and Johnson City greatly influenced Johnson's later political ideas.

Attracted to Politics

After he earned his teaching degree in 1930, Johnson taught for a year at a Houston high school, but a fascination for Democratic politics was leading his career in another direction. After campaigning for fellow Texan, Richard M. Kleberg, who won election to the U.S. House of Representatives, he was given a job as the new congressman's secretary in Washington. He became a staunch supporter of Franklin D. Roosevelt, who was elected president in 1932 and began a host of government programs to counter the devastating effects of the Great Depression that had left millions of people without jobs.

Left: Not every Texan is a cowboy, of course, and not every cowboy ropes and rides in a suit and tie, but L.B.J. was never exactly average.

Left: Johnson was the first member of Congress to volunteer for active duty in the early months of World War II. He served in the South Pacific as a naval lieutenant commander.

Sailor Boy

Johnson first met President Roosevelt aboard the presidential yacht in the Gulf of Mexico. Although he had spent his life in the Texas Hill Country, where there wasn't even a good-sized lake back then, he impressed the president with tales of his lifelong love for the sea, and Roosevelt recommended him for a spot on the House Committee on Naval Affairs. It was a juicy plum for a freshman congressman, and it marked Johnson as a Roosevelt insider, which paid off in delivering federal dollars to his district.

Johnson worked hard for Roosevelt's New Deal programs, and his enthusiasm landed him a job as the Texas director of the newly created National Youth Administration, a New Deal program that gave young people educational and job opportunities, including part-time jobs to helped recent high-school graduates afford to go on to college.

Meanwhile, Johnson had met and married University of Texas graduate Claudia Alta Taylor in 1934. "Lady Bird," as she was called, came from a wealthy family. Her father shared Johnson's aggressive personality traits and helped finance his son-in-law's successful 1936 campaign for a vacant seat as a U.S. representative from Texas.

Johnson's political standing in Texas mushroomed as he became a powerful congressman. As a member of the House Naval Affairs Committee, he sponsored legislation to build a naval training base in Corpus Christi, and he helped pass an appropriation for a program that brought electricity to Texas. When President Roosevelt toured the state in 1937, Lyndon Johnson was at his side.

He served six two-year terms in the House, interrupted only by World War II service, when he became a lieutenant commander in the navy. After an early assignment reporting on the morale of American servicemen, he made himself more useful by volunteering for flying missions, and he had a Silver Star to show for his service in the South Pacific.

Distinguished Congressman

Before his military service, Johnson had experienced both high and low points in his political career: In 1940, he headed a Congressional Campaign Committee that

Right: The Johnson family sold L.B.J.'s Broadcasting Company in Austin, Texas, in 2003 after more than fifty years of ownership.

Above: L.B.J.'s power base in Washington was unprecedented.
He was the Senate's majority leader, and his old mentor,
Sam Rayburn, was Speaker of the House.

Glad Hand

Johnson became the Senate Majority Leader in 1954, the youngest in history. He had already mastered the inner workings of the House of Representatives, but now he was in a position to dispense favors, and earn gratitude for them, from higher up in the power structure. He had a talent for it—and the will. No birthday went unmarked, no accomplishment unnoticed. He was a Dutch uncle to his colleagues, and Big Daddy to his staff, and his largesse extended all the way down to janitors in the Capitol Building. Everyone, it seemed, was indebted to Senator Johnson in one way or another. He was regarded as the most powerful man in Washington, and everyone agreed that the second most powerful wasn't the president, but Johnson's old mentor, Speaker of the House Sam Rayburn. Together, Johnson and Rayburn controlled both houses of Congress.

helped keep a Democratic majority in Congress, but he lost his own bid for the Senate the following year. After the loss, he began to limit his complete dedication for New Deal programs, which were beginning to lose their appeal as the Depression ended. By 1948, when Texans elected him to the U.S. Senate, Johnson had also cooled somewhat on civil-rights legislation and support of unions. He became a senate leader by focusing on military preparedness and elimination of inefficiency and waste.

Johnson had become the Senate majority leader by 1954, and he was in the national spotlight at the age of forty-six. His remarkable skill in personal persuasion

Sideline

Johnson never seemed to stop wheeling and dealing, but after a few years in Congress, it had become routine, and he used his spare time to get rich. He began by buying a bankrupt radio station in Austin, carefully putting it in his wife's name to avoid the appearance of profiting from a government-regulated business. Profits were slow in coming, only eighteen dollars the first year, but in less than twenty years, Lady Bird was earning a half-million dollars a year from the investment, and her husband was investing all of it in real estate, which made him one of the richest men ever to become president.

helped him form core support groups to ensure that legislation was passed. He even helped pass programs favored by President Dwight D. Eisenhower that were being slowed by the president's own Republican Party. Among other programs the Republicans opposed, his floor leadership eased passage of a bill that increased the minimum wage and expanded the range of workers who would qualify for it.

After being slowed down for six months after a heart attack in 1955, Johnson led the Senate in passing a civil-rights bill that Eisenhower supported. When the Soviet Union stunned the world by launching the first venture into space—the *Sputnik* satellite—Americans began questioning their own science and educational preparation. After leading a group that examined the possibility of an American space program, Johnson served as chairman of the congressional committee that formed the National Aeronautics and Space Administration (NASA), and Eisenhower chose him to make a speech before the United Nations on the need for international cooperation in space.

Supportive Role

As the 1960 presidential election approached, Johnson set his sights on the presidency, but he didn't campaign actively for the nomination, and he was left trailing behind Massachusetts senator John F. Kennedy, who

charmed the electorate with his youthful idealism and speech-making skills. Johnson finally spoke up for himself just before the Democratic National Convention, calling attention to his superior experience and qualifications over the forty-three-year-old Kennedy.

However, he was too late. Kennedy won the nomination on the first ballot. When he offered Johnson the opportunity to run for the vice presidency, the elder statesman surprised the party leadership by accepting. Even Kennedy was amazed that the ambitious and aggressive Johnson would accept second billing, and he may not have realized what a fortunate choice he had made. Johnson campaigned tirelessly, especially in the South where the Irish Catholic, Harvard-educated, and wealthy Kennedy was not expected to do at all well. Kennedy and Johnson won a narrow margin of popular votes (just over 100,000 out of 69 million votes cast) and a close edge in the Electoral College over Republican candidate Richard Nixon.

Like many other dynamic men, Johnson didn't like the job of vice president, and Kennedy understood. He gave him a number of responsibilities, and he made sure that Johnson stayed well informed about what the administration was doing. Johnson served as chairman of the Space Council as well as the Committee on Equal Employment Opportunity, and he traveled extensively. Johnson and his wife were following President and Mrs. Kennedy in an open-car motorcade through Dallas, Texas, on November 22, 1963, when sniper shots fired from a nearby building hit the president. Two cars behind, Johnson's vehicle followed the president's car to nearby Parkland Hospital, where Kennedy died from his wounds.

Johnson and Lady Bird accompanied Jacqueline Kennedy and the coffin of her murdered husband aboard Air Force One back to Washington, and ninety minutes after the president was declared dead, Johnson was sworn in as president on the plane. "Our institutions cannot be interrupted by an assassin's bullet," he said, and fear over the continued functioning of the government passed quickly as deep grieving set in.

Left: Johnson didn't find his role as vice president very challenging, but he had other interests, including his Texas ranch where the Hereford bulls were as challenging as recalcitrant Republicans.

Above: The bipartisan commission to investigate the Kennedy assassination included (L-R) Rep. Gerald Ford (R-Mich); Rep. Hale Boggs (D-La); Sen. Richard Russell (D-Ga); Chief Justice Earl Warren; Sen. John Sherman Cooper (R-Ky); banker John J. McCloy; Allen W. Dulles, former CIA Director; and J. Lee Rankin, general counsel.

Honoring Kennedy

"All I have I would have given gladly not to be standing here today," Johnson said in his first speech as president before a joint session of Congress, just five days after Kennedy's death. He moved quickly to set up an independent commission to investigate the assassination. Named the Warren Commission (after its chairman, Supreme Court Justice Earl Warren), the distinguished group concluded that the sniper arrested for the shooting, Lee Harvey Oswald, had acted alone. The killer himself was murdered during a jail transfer broadcast on live national television, two days after Kennedy's assassination, by Dallas nightclub owner Jack Ruby.

Johnson made it clear from the start that he planned to continue the Kennedy administration's goals and policies, and one of his first challenges was to see to it that Congress passed a sweeping Civil Rights Act, written in part by the late president's brother, Attorney General Robert F. Kennedy. "No memorial or eulogy," he said, "could more eloquently honor President Kennedy's memory than the earliest possible passage of the civil-rights bill for which he fought so long." The hotly contested bill is considered one of the most significant pieces of legislation in American history. It outlawed all forms of discrimination on the basis of race, religion, or ethnic origin, and it extended to employment, education, housing, and public accommodations, such as travel lodgings, food, and services, as well as space on buses, trains, and airplanes. Johnson pressured congressional leaders to make sure that all of the bill's measures were passed. He also fought for a tax-cut bill that had been in the works under Kennedy, based on the economic theories of John Maynard Keynes and intended to help increase consumer spending and stimulate the creation of more jobs to produce consumer goods.

The Great Society

Easily winning his party's nomination on the 1964 presidential ticket, Johnson scored a landslide reelection by about 15 million popular votes and a 486 to 52 margin in the Electoral College. But just before the November election, two significant events occurred that would shape the rest of the decade and would forever define Johnson's presidency. He announced plans for sweeping social legislation that he called the Great Society, and he began escalating American involvement in the Vietnam War.

The country was enjoying prosperity as a whole when Johnson announced in May 1964 that America's wealth should be used to erase poverty in the country

Below: Johnson worked with civil rights leaders such as (L-R) Roy Wilins, James Farmer, Dr. Martin Luther King Jr., and Whitney Young.

1964 Election Results

Presidential / Vice Presidential Candidates	Popular Votes	Electoral Votes
Lyndon B. Johnson / Hubert H. Humphrey (Democratic)	43,167,895	486
Barry M. Goldwater / William E. Miller (Republican)	27,175,770	52

once and for all, and he declared a "War on Poverty" as the Great Society's first order of business. "Even the greatest of all past civilizations existed on the exploitation of the misery of the many," he said. "This nation, this people, this generation, has man's first chance to create a Great Society: a society of success without squalor, beauty without barrenness, works of genius without the wretchedness of poverty."

The Johnson administration used the results and recommendations of fourteen separate task forces to begin sending bills to Congress. Always an excellent consensus builder, Johnson was able to bring together supporters of business and labor—from both parties—on many of the measures. Great Society legislation was far-reaching. The Economic Opportunity Act of 1964 established an Office of Economic Opportunity (OEO) to oversee many of the new programs.

"[Johnson] can be as gentle and solicitous as a nurse, but as ruthless and deceptive as a riverboat gambler."
—*Rowland Evans and Robert Novak*

In the area of education, Johnson's Great Society reformed public schools, which had become overcrowded as a result of a tremendous surge in the birthrate after World War II. His Elementary and Secondary Education

Contrast

While President Kennedy was an urbane Bostonian, Lyndon Johnson was a real "down-home" Texan: bold, brash, vulgar, and informal to a fault. He also had a passion for hard work, and he expected everyone around him to share it. If they didn't, he could be cruelly insulting. He explained his rationale to an aide he had just dressed down: "If I don't bawl you out every once in a while, you ain't part of the family."

The Johnson Administration

Administration Dates: November 22, 1963–January 20, 1965
January 20, 1965–January 20, 1969

Vice President: None (1963–65)
Hubert H. Humphrey (1965–69)

Cabinet:

Secretary of State	Dean Rusk (1963–69)
Secretary of the Treasury	C. Douglas Dillon (1963–65)
	Henry H. Fowler (1965–68)
	Joseph W. Barr (1968–69)
Attorney General	Robert F. Kennedy (1963–64)
	Nicholas D. Katzenbach (1965–67)
	William R. Clark (1967–69)
Postmaster General	John A. Gronouski Jr. (1963–65)
	Lawrence F. O'Brien (1965–68)
	William M. Watson (1968–69)
Secretary of the Interior	Stewart L. Udall (1963–69)
Secretary of Agriculture	Orville L. Freeman (1963–69)
Secretary of Labor	W. Willard Wirtz (1963–69)
Secretary of Commerce	Luther H. Hodges (1963–65)
	John T. Connor (1965–67)
	Alexander B. Trowbridge (1967–68)
	Cyrus R. Smith (1968–69)
Secretary of Defense	Robert S. McNamara (1963–68)
	Clark M. Clifford (1968–69)
Secretary of Health, Education, and Welfare	Anthony J. Celebrezze (1963–65)
	John W. Gardner (1965–68)
	Wilbur J. Cohen (1968–69)
Secretary of Housing and Urban Development	Robert C. Weaver (1966–68)
	Robert C. Wood (1969)
Secretary of Transportation	Alan S. Boyd (1967–69)

Act helped strengthen inadequate urban and rural schools, providing special education for the disabled, and remedial help for slower learners. Other education programs included Head Start, a preschool program in low-income communities, and the Higher Education Act, which provided funding to help colleges and universities expand to meet their growing enrollments.

The Higher Education Act also introduced scholarships, work-study programs, and student loan programs. Johnson signed it into law in the gymnasium of his alma mater, Southwest Texas State College, where he spoke of the Mexican children he had taught in Cotulla and of his own battle to put himself through college. "For them and for this entire land of ours, it is the most important door that will ever open—the door to education."

With Medicare—the first successful government program to provide health-care coverage for the growing elderly population—Johnson also helped people at the other end of the age spectrum. A related program, Medicaid, provided low-income Americans with similar access to health care. Meanwhile, the Voting Rights Act of 1965 ensured voting rights for all adults by authorizing federal authorities to intervene in cases where discriminatory practices are suspected.

The Fair Housing Act of 1968 barred landlords, sellers, or real estate agents from refusing to rent or to sell a property because of the buyer's race, ethnicity, or religion. The Model Cities Act provided federal funds for job training, community centers, medical clinics, and other social services in some of the country's most run-down urban areas. The programs often hired residents of those communities as staff and supervisors.

An existing government agency was reorganized into the cabinet-level Department of Housing and Urban Development in 1965 to better address the problems of urban decay. After World War II, a tremendous building boom transformed the outskirts of major American cities' suburban towns and villages. Meanwhile, houses and buildings within many large cities fell into neglect and decay.

The Fair Labor Standards Act raised the federal minimum wage, the lowest wage allowed by law. An immigration reform act erased a long-standing quota system for immigration into the United States, which for decades had favored western Europeans. Johnson also pushed through a bill authorizing the creation and funding of a National Foundation for the Arts and Humanities, which included the National Endowment for the Arts and the American Ballet Theater, among other notable institutions, and in 1967, he secured funding to create the Corporation for Public Broadcasting and National Public Radio. At about the same time, he also signed the Water Quality Act and Clean Air Act, the first major legislative efforts to lower the growing level of deadly toxins in the environment.

Left: Johnson signs the education bill at the side of Mrs. Chester Looney, the first grade teacher who taught him how to write his name. His wife, Lady Bird, and daughter Lynda Bird watch admiringly.

Right: L.B.J.'s record on human rights was remarkable, but animal rights activists were up in arms when he demonstrated picking up his pet beagles, Him and Her, by the ears.

Growing Troubles

Along with the president's announcement of the Great Society program in 1964, a second significant event occurred when he signed the Gulf of Tonkin Resolution, declaring that events in Southeast Asia were vital to international peace and security, and that the United States was prepared to "take all necessary steps, including the use of armed force," to deal with them. The resolution came after the U.S. destroyer *Maddox* was hit by torpedoes from North Vietnamese vessels in retaliation for increasing American involvement in the Vietnam War.

Johnson's Speech about the Gulf of Tonkin Incident

Delivered on August 4, 1964

The U.S. military presence in Vietnam increased regularly between 1960 and 1964. American combat troops weren't deployed, but military advisors were assisting South Vietnamese forces. In 1964, the North Vietnamese attacked U.S. vessels in the Gulf of Tonkin, an area of the South China Sea bordered on the west by Vietnam and on the north by China. Johnson asked Congress for a resolution to increase U.S. military involvement without a formal declaration of war. The measure was passed by both houses, and by February 1965, U.S. planes began regular bombing raids over North Vietnam. American marines landed at the South Vietnam port city of Da Nang on March 6, and by the end of the year, the United States had sent two hundred thousand combat troops to Vietnam. The following is the text of Johnson's broadcast report to the nation about the Gulf of Tonkin incident.

My fellow Americans:

As President and Commander in Chief, it is my duty to the American people to report that renewed hostile actions against United States ships on the high seas in the Gulf of Tonkin have today required me to order the military forces of the United States to take action in reply.

The initial attack on the destroyer *Maddox*, on August 2, was repeated today by a number of hostile vessels attacking two U.S. destroyers with torpedoes. The destroyers and supporting aircraft acted at once on the orders I gave after the initial act of aggression. We believe at least two of the attacking boats were sunk. There were no U.S. losses.

The performance of commanders and crews in this engagement is in the highest tradition of the United States Navy. But repeated acts of violence against the Armed Forces of the United States must be met not only with alert defense, but with positive reply. That reply is being given as I speak to you tonight. Air action is now in execution against gunboats and certain supporting facilities in North Vietnam which have been used in these hostile operations.

In the larger sense this new act of aggression, aimed directly at our own forces, again brings home to all of us in the United States the importance of the struggle for peace and security in Southeast Asia. Aggression by terror against the peaceful villagers of South Vietnam has now been joined by open aggression on the high seas against the United States of America.

The nations of North Vietnam and South Vietnam, as well as the bordering countries of Cambodia and Laos, had been formed in 1954 after French forces abandoned their colony of Indochina in the face of attacks by communist forces, and President Eisenhower sent military advisors to help the South Vietnamese people defend themselves from the communists in North Vietnam. About one thousand American advisors were there when Eisenhower left office in 1961, and during the Kennedy administration, the number swelled to twenty-five thousand. Historians debate whether or not Kennedy would have continued increasing American involvement, but one of his last policy statements was that "It's their [war] to win."

President Johnson increased American involvement. His Republican opponent for the presidency in 1964, Arizona senator Barry Goldwater, had promised an immediate, large-scale escalation, but Johnson moved more gradually. After a Vietcong (Vietnamese communists) attack on an American military base in February 1965, he ordered air strikes against North Vietnam, and by November, more than 165,000 American troops were on the ground in the South. The number swelled to over 460,000 by the following May, and Combat was fierce in the largely jungle environment. As the American death toll rose (in 1964, 146 …in 1965, 1,104 …in 1966, 5,008 …in 1967, 9,300), so, too, did the antiwar debate escalate at home.

Hawks in Congress demanded even more aggressive bombing, mining, and combat missions, even as the protest movement kept growing. At protest rallies, including a massive peace march on Washington in 1967, young men often burned their draft cards, symbolically refusing to serve in the military. The peace movement was increasingly met with armed federal resistance, and at the Washington march, the image of protesters stuffing flowers into the barrels of guns held by federal troops became a symbol of the conflict at home. Some members of Congress, including South Dakota senator George McGovern and New York senator Robert Kennedy, finally began speaking out against the war.

The determination of all Americans to carry out our full commitment to the people and to the government of South Vietnam will be redoubled by this outrage. Yet our response, for the present, will be limited and fitting. We Americans know, although others appear to forget, the risks of spreading conflict. We still seek no wider war. I have instructed the Secretary of State [Dean Rusk] to make this position totally clear to friends and to adversaries and, indeed, to all. I have instructed Ambassador [Adlai] Stevenson to raise this matter immediately and urgently before the Security Council of the United Nations. Finally, I have today met with the leaders of both parties in the Congress of the United States and I have informed them that I shall immediately request the Congress to pass a resolution making it clear that our Government is united in its determination to take all necessary measures in support of freedom and in defense of peace in Southeast Asia.

I have been given encouraging assurance by these leaders of both parties that such a resolution will be promptly introduced, freely and expeditiously debated, and passed with overwhelming support. And just a few minutes ago I was able to reach Senator [Barry] Goldwater [Johnson's opponent in the 1964 presidential election] and I am glad to say that he has expressed his support of the statement that I am making to you tonight.

It is a solemn responsibility to have to order even limited military action by forces whose overall strength is as vast and as awesome as those of the United States of America, but it is my considered conviction, shared throughout your Government, that firmness in the right is indispensable today for peace; that firmness will always be measured. Its mission is peace.

★

Thurgood Marshall

Thurgood Marshall was born on July 2, 1908, in Baltimore, Maryland. His mother was a teacher and his father a waiter and steward at a country club. Marshall graduated from Lincoln University and received his law degree from Howard University in 1933. While at Howard, he was influenced by a group of legal scholars who developed procedures for civil-rights litigation.

Marshall practiced law in Baltimore, Maryland, until 1938 and also served as counsel for the local branch of the National Association for the Advancement of Colored People (NAACP). In 1935, he successfully attacked segregation and discrimination in education, actions that helped lead to the desegregation of the University of Maryland Law School (where he had been denied admission because of race). Marshall became director of the NAACP's Legal Defense and Education Fund in 1939.

In 1938, Marshall was admitted to practice before the U.S. Supreme Court, the U.S. Circuit Court of Appeals, and the U.S. District Court for the Eastern District of Louisiana. Winning twenty-nine of the thirty-two civil-rights cases before the Supreme Court (and sometimes threatened with death as he argued cases in the lower courts of some Southern states), Marshall earned the reputation of one of America's most outstanding civil-rights lawyers. Several important cases he argued became landmarks in the destruction of segregation: Smith v. Allwright (1944) overruled practices that had denied the rights of African-Americans to vote in several Democratic primary elections; Morgan v. Virginia (1946) outlawed that state's segregation policy in interstate bus transportation; Shelley v. Kramer (1948) outlawed race restrictions in house selling; and Sweatt v. Painter (1950) required the admission of an African-American student to the University of Texas Law School. The most famous case involving Marshall was the Brown vs. the Board of Education (1954) decision that outlawed segregation in public schools and challenged all forms of legally sanctioned segregation.

The NAACP sent Marshall to Japan and Korea in 1951 to investigate complaints that African-American soldiers convicted by U.S. Army court-martials had not received fair trials. His appeal arguments reduced the sentences of twenty-two men. President John Kennedy nominated Marshall as judge of the Second Court of Appeals in 1961; he was confirmed by the Senate a year later after undergoing intense hearings. In 1965, Marshall accepted President Lyndon Johnson's appointment as solicitor general. In that post, Marshall defended civil-rights actions as an advocate for the American people instead of (as in his NAACP days) as a counsel strictly for African Americans; however, he personally did not argue cases in which he had previously been involved.

In 1967, President Johnson nominated Marshall as associate justice to the U.S. Supreme Court. Marshall's nomination was strongly opposed by several southern senators on the Judiciary Committee, but he was confirmed by a vote of 69 to 11. When he took his seat on October 2, 1967, he was the first African-American justice to sit on the U.S. Supreme Court.

During his nearly quarter century on the Supreme Court, Marshall remained a strong advocate of individual rights and never wavered in his devotion to ending discrimination. He formed a key part of the Court's progressive majority that voted to uphold a woman's right to abortion. His majority opinions covered such areas as ecology and the right of appeal for persons convicted of narcotic charges, failure to report into the U.S. Armed Forces, and obscenity. After suffering several ailments, Marshall vacated his seat in 1991. He died in 1993 at the age of eighty-four.

1968: That Violent Year

Social unrest was widespread, protest marches became commonplace, and demonstrations against the war expanded to forums for women's rights and environmental quality. Race riots had also occurred in several major cities: Thirty-five people died during rioting in the Watts area of Los Angeles in 1965, and over forty more in Detroit two years later. In spite of the new civil-rights laws, civil-rights legislation, and some notable events, such as Johnson's appointment of well-known civil-rights advocate Thurgood Marshall to the U.S. Supreme Court, racism was still all too common across the country.

Civil rights leader Dr. Martin Luther King Jr. was murdered in Memphis, Tennessee, in April 1968, and two months later, Robert F. Kennedy, who was emerging as the leading Democratic presidential candidate, was assassinated after a rally in Los Angeles.

Meanwhile, 15,000 American soldiers had died in Vietnam by November 1967; and the number would go up to 57,000 by early 1973, when the last American troops went home, with most of the deaths occurring in 1968 and 1969. The Vietnam War persistently bedeviled the Johnson administration, as the public began to believe that the government had misrepresented the situation— that Pentagon officials had known the situation was far more complicated than Americans had been told. A "credibility gap" clouded the already volatile situation when more Americans began asking hard questions of their leaders.

Feelings against the war became interchangeable with Johnson himself, and were highlighted when Wisconsin senator Eugene McCarthy finished nearly even with him in the New Hampshire presidential primary—the first test on the road to the Democratic presidential nomination. Johnson could see the handwriting on the wall and, bowing to increasing public pressure to stop the war that Congress had never officially declared, he ordered an end to the bombing of North Vietnam in an attempt to begin peace negotiations. At the end of the month, he shocked the country and even his closest aides with the televised announcement of his decision not to run for reelection. "With America's sons in the fields far away, with America's future under challenge right here at home, with our hopes and the world's hopes in the

Below: A day before he was assassinated on this spot in 1968, Dr. Martin Luther King Jr. (second from right) met with civil rights leaders (L-R) Hosea Williams, Jesse Jackson, and Ralph Abernathy.

Below: After winning the California presidential primary, Robert F. Kennedy, seen here with his wife, Ethel, and campaign manager Jesse Unruh, was assassinated as he was leaving the Ambassador Hotel in Los Angeles.

Hubert Humphrey

Born in Wallace, South Dakota, Hubert Humphrey was influenced by the experiences of his family and neighbors in his home state. By the age of twenty-five, he had witnessed hardships from drought, bank failures, farm failures, and other depressed economic situations.

His father was a pharmacist and owner of several different drugstores in South Dakota. One of his drugstores became the first of the widespread Walgreen chain in the United States. In 1927, however, Humphrey's father was forced to sell their home to pay off business debts. The same situation happened in 1932, and Humphrey withdrew from the University of Minnesota to help support his family.

Humphrey enrolled at Capitol College of Pharmacy in Denver, Colorado. He graduated from this intensive program in six months and returned to work for his father. In Humphrey's words, "The drugstore was my life and it seemed then it might always be." He remained a druggist from 1933 to 1937. He married Muriel Buck in 1936.

Humphrey returned to the University of Minnesota in 1937 and received his bachelor of arts degree in 1939. A year later, he received his master's degree in political science at Louisiana State University. He and his family returned to Minneapolis, Minnesota, where Humphrey performed further graduate work at the University of Minnesota. From 1941 to 1945, Humphrey held various public service jobs, including state director of war production training and assistant director of the War Manpower Commission. Humphrey's first attempt at elected public office occurred in 1943 when he ran for mayor of Minneapolis. He was narrowly defeated, but he learned from his loss. In 1945, he was elected mayor of Minneapolis and won reelection in 1947.

As mayor, Humphrey successfully passed a law supporting fair employment practices. In 1948, Humphrey had an opportunity to address civil rights at the Democratic National Convention. As a member of the committee responsible for the party's platform, Humphrey challenged the leadership of the party on its weak stance on civil rights. In a speech before the convention, Humphrey stated, "There are those who say: This issue of civil rights is an infringement on State's rights. The time has arrived for the Democratic Party to get out of the shadow of State's rights and walk forth-rightfully into the bright sunshine of human rights." Some delegates were so excited at Humphrey's statements that they paraded around the convention floor and voted in favor of the stronger civil-rights position. However, several conservative Southern Democrats walked out of that convention and established a splinter party, the Dixiecrats. Democratic candidate Harry S Truman had to face Republican Thomas Dewey and Dixiecrat J. Strom Thurmond.

Democrats were unable to pass civil-rights legislation. The first modern civil-rights law was adopted in 1957 under a Republican president, Dwight Eisenhower. Senate majority leader Lyndon B. Johnson, a Democrat, helped pass the bill through Congress. He worked with Humphrey, who served in the Senate from 1949 to 1965, when he became Johnson's vice president. As a senator, Humphrey supported the Peace Corps, the creation of a Food for Peace program (increasing agricultural trade), and legislation favoring labor unions, farmers, and the unemployed.

Humphrey ran for the presidency in 1960. His grass-roots campaign relied on bus transportation as opposed to the better financed campaign of John F. Kennedy. Humphrey withdrew from the race after losing to Kennedy in the West Virginia presidential primary. Later, as vice president under Johnson, who was elected president in 1964, he supported administration policies, including the increasing military involvement in the war in Vietnam. Johnson became unpopular because of the war and soon bowed out as a presidential candidate in 1968. Wisconsin senator Eugene McCarthy and New York senator Robert F. Kennedy emerged as favorites, with Humphrey lagging behind because of his support for the Vietnam War, even after he promised to end the conflict. Kennedy's effort ended in June when he was assassinated, but his supporters were reluctant to join Humphrey.

Humphrey became the Democratic candidate for the presidency in 1968 at the national convention in Chicago, where the streets were filled with antiwar rioters. When Humphrey campaigned on college campuses and in major American cities, he was heckled by antiwar activists. He lost the election to Richard Nixon. Disappointed, Humphrey returned to Minnesota and served as a professor of public affairs at the University of Minnesota. In 1970 and again in 1976, Humphrey was reelected to the U.S. Senate. He died of cancer on January 14, 1978.

Speechmaker

Few men in public life ever had as much experience as a public speaker as Lyndon Johnson. He once said that there are only two kinds of political speeches: the Mother Hubbard, which covers everything but reveals nothing, and the bikini, which covers only the essential points.

balance every day, I do not believe that I should devote an hour or a day of my time to any personal partisan causes or to any duties other than the awesome duties of this office," Johnson told the nation.

Vice President Hubert Humphrey became the leading contender for the nomination among older Democrats, while young people turned first to McCarthy and then to Robert F. Kennedy, and after Robert Kennedy's assassination, the party settled on Vice President Humphrey. Another image reflective of the unsteady state of the nation occurred during the Democratic convention that summer in Chicago where protesters and police officers clashed violently.

Johnson and his wife, Lady Bird, retired to their ranch in the Pedernales Mountains of Texas in 1969, and they lived quietly there for the next three years. Johnson died of a heart attack on January 22, 1973, just nine days after the final and lasting cease-fire in Vietnam was formalized. Lady Bird died July 11, 2007, in Austin, Texas.

Below: The Johnson Ranch in the Texas Hill Country near Johnson City.

Legacy

Like Franklin D. Roosevelt's presidency, Lyndon B. Johnson's began with an incredible number of new social programs intended to improve life in America, and many key pieces of legislation from both administrations were still in place as the country entered the new century. Among Johnson's programs, the Clean Air Act forced automakers for the first time to meet federal emissions-control standards to limit the amount of toxic materials cars can release in their exhaust gases. The immigration reform law brought about a large upsurge in Asian immigration during the 1960s and 1970s, with the result that Asian Americans play increasing economic, cultural, and political roles in the country. Latino immigration also benefited from the Immigration Act, and Head Start still serves underprivileged communities in both urban and rural areas.

The Vietnam War, and Johnson's escalation of America's role in it, profoundly influenced the political landscape of the country. Historians note that the war literally divided the country as few issues ever have, and even Johnson's own cabinet argued strongly against U.S. policy. Along with university students, coalitions of respected academics and clergy also spoke out against the war. During the Johnson years, the perception that the government was deceiving the public came to be called the "credibility gap."

Men who ran for president a generation later still had to confront questions about their own military service, or lack of it, during these years. Vietnam veterans came home to a nation indifferent and even hostile to them; and many of them suffered psychological problems from what was eventually identified as posttraumatic stress disorder.

The events of the Johnson presidency remain central in the country's political debate in two important areas: the conduct of military actions, and the role the federal government can and should play in improving society. His swift assumption of confident leadership after the Kennedy assassination, his support of civil rights, and the successes of his sweeping social programs leave a more unquestionably positive legacy.

Lady Bird Johnson

Born December 22, 1912, Karnack, Texas
Died July 11, 2007, Austin, Texas

"For Bird, a lovely girl with ideals, principles, intelligence and refinement."

—*An inscription written by Lyndon B. Johnson*

Claudia Alta Taylor Johnson—known all her life as "Lady Bird"—entered the White House under especially trying circumstances. While struggling with her husband, Lyndon B. Johnson, to establish a sense of stability and continuity for the grieving nation after the assassination of President John F. Kennedy, she followed one of the most beloved first ladies in history, Jacqueline Kennedy. During her husband's administration, Lady Bird devoted her energies to helping her husband cope with the strains of his presidency, while also traveling extensively to speak in support of his Great Society program.

Shy Girl

Claudia Alta Taylor was born on December 22, 1912, in Karnack, a town in East Texas. The Taylor family was relatively wealthy and had several servants; and it was a nursemaid of the infant girl who gave her the unusual and lasting nickname Lady Bird. Her father, Thomas Taylor, was a prosperous storekeeper and farmer. Her mother, Minnie, died when Lady Bird was only five.

Attending local schools, Lady Bird excelled academically, although she was painfully shy. After high school, she attended a private junior college for women in Dallas until a friend talked her into transferring to the University of Texas at Austin, where she studied journalism and earned a teaching certificate.

Soon after her graduation in 1934, she was introduced to Lyndon B. Johnson by a college friend. He asked her for a date the next day and soon afterward proposed marriage. Lady Bird was both enchanted and intimidated by Johnson's tough personality, which contrasted sharply to hers. True to form, Johnson was a persistent admirer, but all her friends advised her to wait. Her father, however, whose personality was very much like Johnson's, tipped the balance by encouraging her to go ahead and marry the guy, the sooner the better.

Financed First Campaign

They were married in November 1934, just three months after they first met, and moved into an apartment in Washington, D.C., where he was working as secretary to a Texas congressman. Not yet twenty-two, Lady Bird didn't even know how to cook. When a chance came for her husband to run for a suddenly vacant seat in the U.S. House of Representatives, Lady Bird found out that it would cost at least $10,000 to mount a campaign, and she knew that Lyndon didn't have much money. (The wedding ring he bought for her had only cost $2.50.) She telephoned her father and asked for an advance on her inheritance, which he wired the next day. After her husband won the election, Lady Bird carried the deposit slip for the $10,000 in her purse as a good-luck charm.

Lady Bird knew that she had married an ambitious and confident man, but she wasn't unaware of his bouts of depression. Johnson was first treated for it shortly before

Left: The Johnson family visiting John F. Kennedy. Next to Johnson is his wife, Lady Bird, and their daughters, Lynda Bird and Lucy Baines.

the birth of the first of their two daughters, Lynda Bird, in 1944. Their second daughter, Lucy (Luci) Baines, was born three years later.

After he was elected to the Senate in 1948, Johnson quickly became a leading Southern Democrat on Capitol Hill, but his schedule affected him physically, as well. He had a heart attack in 1955 and spent five weeks in the hospital, while his wife slept in the room next to his and used it as a substitute congressional office to help him go on with his work.

When her husband was chosen as the running mate with John F. Kennedy on the 1960 Democratic presidential slate, Lady Bird campaigned tirelessly for them. Democratic Party leaders began calling her the "Secret Weapon" because of her charm and popularity.

She spent nearly three years as the wife of the nation's vice president, and she was with him in the motorcade on November 22, 1963, in Dallas, Texas, when a gunman killed Kennedy. She and her husband were just two cars behind.

Difficult Transition

Lady Bird became first lady during a time of tremendous national grief. Her husband went to work continuing the Kennedy legacy while at the same time making the presidency his own. She became especially active as a helpmate in his War on Poverty, touring poorer parts of the country, such as towns in the Pennsylvania coal regions and inner-city neighborhoods in major cities, to call attention to the grim conditions there.

When her husband announced his bid for his own presidential term in 1964, Lady Bird campaigned for him across the Deep South, becoming the first wife of a presidential candidate to make political speeches on her own. Because of the Johnsons' support for sweeping civil-rights legislation that would end much

Left: Lady Bird became the first first lady to campaign for her husband when she rode the "Lady Bird Special" through the South.

Right: Among other things, Lady Bird was passionate about beautifying America, and she didn't mind getting her hands and knees dirty planting flowers.

of the generations-old segregation in the South, many politicians there were hostile to him, and his advisors decided that it was too risky for him to travel there. Lady Bird hired a speech coach to help her conquer her natural shyness, and then, using her genuine charm and her deep belief in her husband's policies, she convinced many state and local politicians to campaign with her on a whistle-stop tour across the Southern states.

Head Start and the Nation's Highways

One of the more enduring legacies of the Johnson era and its Great Society legislation was the Head Start preschool program, and Lady Bird was said to have been influential in convincing her husband to push for it. Studies had shown that when they started school, five- and six-year-olds from poorer households were far less prepared socially and intellectually than were their more well-off counterparts. Head Start was designed to address that problem. The first lady announced it at a tea in February 1965, and the program was in place that summer.

She would be linked by name with the Highway Beautification Act of 1965, which was introduced as "Lady Bird's Bill." She had announced in the beginning that as first lady, her specific project would be "The Beauty of America," and in her speeches, she connected it with her husband's War on Poverty and Great Society, asserting that crime was rooted in a sense of hopelessness that could be lessened somewhat by improving the physical environment.

After making numerous tours in her duties as first lady and viewing the increase of billboards and junkyards with disgust, she suggested a bill that would provide for the planting of trees and wildflowers along the nation's sprawling highway system. The legislation faced serious obstacles in Congress, but the president told his staff on more than one occasion, "You know, I love that woman and she wants that highway bill. By God, we're going to get it for her."

That attitude was typical of the Johnsons' relationship. On one hand, the president was a demanding, bossy spouse; but on the other, he was clearly devoted to Lady Bird, and he valued her opinion on policy and political matters. His tongue-lashing lectures against his staff were legendary, and often Lady Bird was on hand when he erupted, but simply walked out of the room without a word. When he noticed that she was gone, Johnson would leave to find her, and usually returned in much better spirits.

Drawn into Antiwar Protests

During their White House years, the Johnsons entertained extensively, sometimes offering their guests Texas hospitality with an occasional barbecue or hoedown. In all, they entertained more than two hundred thousand guests, but not all of them behaved like guests. Singer Eartha Kitt, who had been invited to one of the first lady's "Women Doers" luncheons, waited until the president made what was supposed to be a brief appearance, and used her speaking time to scold the administration for attempting to improve life in the inner cities while at the same time continuing a war that sent so many eighteen-year-old men of color to the jungles of Vietnam. Lady Bird responded, her voice shaking, that the continuing crisis in Southeast Asia "doesn't give us a free ticket not to try to work for better things" at home, such as crime prevention, improvements in education, and better health care.

Mrs. Johnson was an active, engaged first lady—realizing rather unexpectedly, like many of her predecessors, that she was well suited to the responsibilities and pace of the job. A sign on her office door read MRS. JOHNSON AT WORK in forbidding capital letters. Nevertheless, she was relieved when her husband announced that he wasn't going to run for another term. Daughter Luci supported the decision as well, in view of a noticeable decline in her father's health, but her sister, Lynda, who had married Marine captain (and, later, Virginia governor and senator) Charles Robb at an extravagant White House wedding in December 1967, felt that her father was giving up the reins of leadership too quickly. She believed that another Johnson administration would bring a quicker end to the war.

Back Home in Texas

The Johnsons retired to their ranch near the Pedernales River in Texas, just a mile away from the home where the former president was born. He died there, after a third and fatal heart attack on the afternoon of January 22, 1973. Lady Bird was in a car near the recently dedicated Lyndon B. Johnson Presidential Library in Austin when she was told of her husband's collapse. He was flown to a San Antonio hospital, and she met the plane there by helicopter, but he had already died.

At the close of the twentieth century, Lady Bird Johnson was the oldest surviving presidential spouse. She spent the years after her husband's death continuing her involvement with nature and conservation programs, and she also served on the board of regents of her alma mater, the University of Texas. Even in her late eighties, Lady Bird still swam every day, even though she was legally blind and suffered from arthritis. Her son-in-law, Virginia senator Charles Robb, credited her with doing a great deal to publicize conservation and other ecology issues during her term as first lady. "She made the environmental movement popular," Robb told *People* magazine in 2000.

Johnson's "Great Society" Speech
Delivered on May 22, 1964

Lyndon B. Johnson became president in November 1963 following the assassination of President John F. Kennedy. A strong consensus builder in Congress for over twenty years before he became vice president, Johnson rallied Congress as president to enact two pieces of legislation dear to Kennedy—a civil-rights act and a tax cut.

Meanwhile, Johnson began laying plans for a sweeping domestic program as the presidential election of 1964 drew near, and he occasionally used the expression "Great Society" to describe his vision. On May 22, 1964, in a commencement speech at the University of Michigan, he emphasized the term as the overall title and goal of his program. He wanted legislation that would improve the nation's cities, environment, education, and quality of life. The speech was given weeks before the Democratic National Convention, where Johnson would be officially nominated for president.

I have come today from the turmoil of your Capital to the tranquility of your campus to speak about the future of your country.

The purpose of protecting the life of our Nation and preserving the liberty of our citizens is to pursue the happiness of our people. Our success in that pursuit is the test of our success as a Nation.

For a century we labored to settle and to subdue a continent. For half a century we called upon unbounded invention and untiring industry to create an order of plenty for all of our people.

The challenge of the next half century is whether we have the wisdom to use that wealth to enrich and elevate our national life, and to advance the quality of our American civilization.

Your imagination, your initiative, and your indignation will determine whether we build a society where progress is the servant of our needs, or a society where old values and new visions are buried under unbridled growth. For in your time we have the opportunity to move not only toward the rich society and the powerful society, but upward to the Great Society.

The Great Society rests on abundance and liberty for all. It demands an end to poverty and racial injustice, to which we are totally committed in our time. But that is just the beginning.

The Great Society is a place where every child can find knowledge to enrich his mind and to enlarge his talents. It is a place where leisure is a welcome chance to build and reflect, not a feared cause of boredom and restlessness. It is a place where the city of man serves not only the needs of the body and the demands of commerce but the desire for beauty and the hunger for community.

It is a place where man can renew contact with nature. It is a place which honors creation for its own sake and for what it adds to the understanding of the race. It is a place where men are more concerned with the quality of their goals than the quantity of their goods.

But most of all, the Great Society is not a safe harbor, a resting place, a final objective, a finished work. It is a challenge constantly renewed, beckoning us toward a destiny where the meaning of our lives matches the marvelous products of our labor.

So I want to talk to you today about three places where we begin to build the Great Society—in our cities, in our countryside, and in our classrooms.

Many of you will live to see the day, perhaps 50 years from now, when there will be 400 million Americans—four-fifths of them in urban areas. In the remainder of this century urban population will double, city land will double, and we will have to build homes, highways, and facilities equal to all those built since this country was first settled. So in the next 40 years we must rebuild the entire urban United States.

Aristotle said: "Men come together in cities in order to live, but they remain together in order to live the good life." It is harder and harder to live the good life in American cities today.

The catalog of ills is long: there is the decay of the centers and the despoiling of the suburbs. There is not enough housing for our people or transportation for our traffic. Open land is vanishing and old landmarks are violated. Worst of all, expansion is eroding the precious and time honored values of community with neighbors and communion with nature. The loss of these values breeds loneliness and boredom and indifference.

Our society will never be great until our cities are great. Today the frontier of imagination and innovation is inside those cities and not beyond their borders. New experiments are already going on. It will be the task of your generation to make the American city a place where future generations will come, not only to live but to live the good life.

I understand that if I stayed here tonight I would see that Michigan students are really doing their best to live the good life.

This is the place where the Peace Corps was started. It is inspiring to see how all of you, while you are in this country, are trying so hard to live at the level of the people.

A second place where we begin to build the Great Society is in our countryside. We have always prided ourselves on being not only America the strong and America the free, but America the beautiful. Today that beauty is in danger. The water we drink, the food we eat, the very air that we breathe, are threatened with pollution. Our parks are overcrowded, our seashores overburdened. Green fields and dense forests are disappearing.

A few years ago we were greatly concerned about the "Ugly American." Today we must act to prevent an ugly America.

For once the battle is lost, once our natural splendor is destroyed, it can never be recaptured. And once man can no longer walk with beauty or wonder at nature his spirit will wither and his sustenance be wasted.

A third place to build the Great Society is in the classrooms of America. There your children's lives will be shaped. Our society will not be great until every young mind is set free to scan the farthest reaches of thought and imagination. We are still far from that goal.

Today, eight million adult Americans, more than the entire population of Michigan, have not finished five years of school. Nearly 20 million have not finished eight years of school. Nearly 54 million—more than one-quarter of all America—have not even finished high school.

Each year more than 100,000 high school graduates, with proved ability, do not enter college because they cannot afford it. And if we cannot educate today's youth, what will we do in 1970 when elementary school enrollment will be five million greater than 1960? And high school enrollment will rise by five million. College enrollment will increase by more than three million.

In many places, classrooms are overcrowded and curricula are outdated. Most of our qualified teachers are underpaid, and many of our paid teachers are unqualified. So we must give every child a place to sit and a teacher to learn from. Poverty must not be a bar to learning, and learning must offer an escape from poverty.

But more classrooms and more teachers are not enough. We must seek an educational system which grows in excellence as it grows in size. This means better training for our teachers. It means preparing youth to enjoy their hours of leisure as well as their hours of labor. It means exploring new techniques of teaching, to find new ways to stimulate the love of learning and the capacity for creation.

These are three of the central issues of the Great Society. While our Government has many programs directed at those issues, I do not pretend that we have the full answer to those problems.

But I do promise this: We are going to assemble the best thought and the broadest knowledge from all over the world to find those answers for America. I intend to establish working groups to prepare a series of White House conferences and meetings—on the cities, on natural beauty, on the quality of education, and on other emerging challenges. And from these meetings and from this inspiration and from these studies we will begin to set our course toward the Great Society.

The solution to these problems does not rest on a massive program in Washington, nor can it rely solely on the strained resources of local authority. They require us to create new concepts of cooperation, a creative federalism, between the National Capital and the leaders of local communities.

Woodrow Wilson once wrote: "Every man sent out from his university should be a man of his Nation as well as a man of his time."

Within your lifetime powerful forces, already loosed, will take us toward a way of life beyond the realm of our experience, almost beyond the bounds of our imagination.

For better or for worse, your generation has been appointed by history to deal with those problems and to lead America toward a new age. You have the chance never before afforded to any people in any age. You can help build a society where the demands of morality, and the needs of the spirit, can be realized in the life of the Nation.

So, will you join in the battle to give every citizen the full equality which God enjoins and the law requires, whatever his belief, or race, or the color of his skin? Will you join in the battle to give every citizen an escape from the crushing weight of poverty?

Will you join in the battle to make it possible for all nations to live in enduring peace—as neighbors and not as mortal enemies?

Will you join in the battle to build the Great Society, to prove that our material progress is only the foundation on which we will build a richer life of mind and spirit?

There are those timid souls who say this battle cannot be won; that we are condemned to a soulless wealth. I do not agree. We have the power to shape the civilization that we want. But we need your will, your labor, your hearts, if we are to build that kind of society.

Those who came to this land sought to build more than just a new country.

They sought a new world. So I have come here today to your campus to say that you can make their vision our reality. So let us from this moment begin our work so that in the future men will look back and say: It was then, after a long and weary way, that man turned the exploits of his genius to the full enrichment of his life.

Thank you. Goodbye.

What Happened Next

Soon after the address, fourteen separate task forces began studying nearly every major aspect of U.S. society. The average membership of a task force was nine, and each task force was assigned a particular subject: cooperation among government agencies in dealing with financial questions; making the federal government more efficient and less costly; developing policies to prevent economic recessions; developing policies on economic issues related to other countries; and determining how best to help individuals maintain their income. Many specific proposals were included in Johnson's State of the Union address delivered on January 7, 1965.

Johnson stated in the address that the government did not have answers for all the problems facing the United States. However, opponents to government social programs labeled the Great Society an overly costly attempt to solve all the nation's problems. The amount of money to be spent by the federal government on social programs became a source for debate in all subsequent presidential elections. Meanwhile, Johnson's programs arising from the task forces met with mixed results. Growing social debate over government programs and the war in Vietnam eclipsed his dream of a united effort to improve American society.

Richard M. Nixon

"That the way I tried to deal with Watergate was the wrong way is a burden I shall bear for every day of the life that is left to me."
—*Richard M. Nixon*

Thirty-seventh president of the United States, 1969–1974

Full name: *Richard Milhous Nixon*
Born: *January 9, 1913, Yorba Linda, California*
Died: *April 22, 1994, New York, New York*
Burial site: *Nixon Library Grounds, Yorba Linda, California*
Parents: *Francis Anthony and Hannah Milhous Nixon*
Spouse: *Thelma Catherine "Pat" Ryan (1912–1993; m. 1940)*
Children: *Patricia "Tricia" (1946–); Julie (1948–)*
Religion: *Quaker*
Education: *Whittier College (B.A., 1934);*
Duke University Law School (LL.B., 1937)
Occupations: *Lawyer; naval officer*
Government positions: *U.S. Office of Emergency Management attorney; U.S. representative and senator from California; vice president under Dwight D. Eisenhower*
Political party: *Republican*
Dates as president: *January 20, 1969–January 20, 1973 (first term); January 20, 1973–August 9, 1974 (second term)*
Age upon taking office: *56*

*R*ichard Nixon is the only president to resign as the nation's chief executive. Facing charges of misconduct in office for his involvement in the Watergate scandal, he chose to resign rather than go through a lengthy impeachment trial. The scandal broke out after the June 1972 break-in of the Democratic Party's national headquarters at the Watergate apartment and office complex in Washington, when it was revealed that the burglars were closely connected to members of Nixon's inner circle.

The scandal brought a shocking downfall to a man who had represented his political party on the national ballot five different times—twice as vice president under Dwight D. Eisenhower, and three times as the Republican presidential nominee. The scandal also overshadowed his accomplishments in foreign relations, as well as his efforts to end the Vietnam War and to improve a poor American economy.

Trying to preserve his day-to-day conduct in dealing with world issues for history, President Nixon recorded audiotapes of his discussions with cabinet officials and others. He had hoped that the tapes would provide a legacy of his achievements and insight into his accomplishments, but instead, they became the focus of a prolonged legal battle: There was a widespread suspicion that the tapes would reveal the extent of Nixon's participation in illegal activities, such as the Watergate break-in, and when they did, it hastened his downfall.

Timeline

Below: In his student days at Whittier College, young Dick Nixon was a football star.

Quaker Upbringing

Richard "Dick" Milhous Nixon was born on January 9, 1913, at Yorba Linda, California, the second of five sons of Francis Anthony and Hannah Milhous Nixon. The family was part of the Quaker religious sect, also known as the Society of Friends.

Nixon worked hard as a young man, including putting in long hours at the family-owned combination gas station and grocery store. After he graduated from high school in Whittier, California, he enrolled at Whittier College, a Quaker school. He stayed close to home to help his family, which was facing financial troubles, and one of his brothers was ill. He majored in history and won a scholarship to Duke University in North Carolina, and graduated from its highly regarded law school in 1937.

He went back to California to work in a well-established law firm, and he met Thelma Ryan soon afterward. "Pat" (her father's nickname for her) and Dick were married on June 21, 1940, and they would have two daughters, Tricia and Julie.

After America entered World War II in 1941, Nixon worked with a government agency, the Office of Emergency Management, and then he joined the U.S. Navy. He earned the rank of lieutenant and spent the war on a Pacific Island with the Naval Air Transport Command.

Left: Lieutenant Commander Richard Nixon saw World War II service in the Solomon Islands.

Challenge

Fresh out of the navy, former lieutenant commander Richard M. Nixon was approached by businessmen in his home town who had two questions for him: "Are you a Republican?" and "Would you like to run for Congress?" The answer to the first question was easy, but the second took some thought. His opponent in the election would be Jerry Voorhis of California's Twelfth Congressional District, who the Washington press corps had voted the "Best congressman from west of the Mississippi." But Nixon answered yes to both questions and the young lawyer with a good war record and a pregnant wife entered the world of politics as a candidate for Congress. He beat Voorhis by more than 15,500 votes by hinting, but never actually saying, that the congressman was supported by communists. He ran for his second term unopposed.

Aggressive Campaigner

After the war ended, Nixon went to Baltimore, Maryland, to wait for his discharge. He was contacted by a California Republican official and asked to run for the House of Representatives in 1946, he accepted the offer, and returned to California to begin his political career. Although he was reserved and awkward in crowds, he became an effective campaigner by making speeches and attacking the views of his rivals with all the tenacity of a bull terrier.

Following the war, the United States and the Soviet Union engaged in tense political conflicts, a situation that came to be known as the Cold War. The United States was especially sensitive to the spread of communism, and Nixon made anti-communism his signature. In his very first campaign, Nixon accused his opponent of being "soft on communism," and he frequently brought up the issue in debates. He won the election handily, and the issue was at the forefront of every Nixon campaign after that.

"Nixon lied to gain love, to shore up his grandiose fantasies, to bolster his ever-wavering sense of identity. He lied in attack, hoping to win. . . . And always he lied, and this most aggressively, to deny that he lied."
—Historian Fawn McKay Brodie

Right: Nixon's accusations that Alger Hiss was a Communist propelled him into the national spotlight.

Rapid Rise in Washington, D.C.

New congressmen generally take a while to learn the ropes, but Nixon was a fast learner. He quickly became involved in high-profile projects, including the drafting of the Taft-Hartley Act of 1947, which put restrictions on union activities and required loyalty oaths for union leaders. Nixon was also a member of a special committee that influenced many elements of the Marshall Plan, a program of financial support to help rebuild European economies devastated by World War II.

Nixon was a member of the House Un-American Activities Committee, which investigated individuals and organizations that might conspire against the U.S. government. In that capacity, he initiated the investigation of Alger Hiss, a high-ranking official in the State Department. Writer Whittaker Chambers testified before the Committee that he had been a member of the Communist Party in the 1920s and 1930s, and charged that Hiss had given him secret documents to send to

Left: Congressman Nixon arrives at New York's Federal Courthouse with a briefcase full of microfilm and documents to make his case against subversives in the government.

Getting the Message

When the New York Post *revealed that Nixon had a secret slush fund of money donated by California businessmen, he responded by saying that the contributions actually saved the taxpayers money, but when that argument didn't work, he volunteered to take his case to the people after presidential candidate Dwight D. Eisenhower challenged his running mate to prove that he was "clean as a hound's tooth." The suspense built up his television audience to more than 38 million. The speech itself was the stuff of soap opera, and even Nixon himself characterized it as a "flop." But then the telegrams started coming, more than 300,000 of them, calling on Eisenhower to keep Nixon on the ticket. The general was impressed. "I'd rather have one courageous honest man," he said, "than a whole boxcar full of pussyfooters."*

the Soviet Union. Hiss denied the charges, but when microfilm copies of documents in his own handwriting and identified as classified were found, he was indicted for perjury. The jury wasn't able to reach a verdict, but Hiss was convicted after a second trial in 1950.

The Hiss case, which occurred during Nixon's second term in Congress, brought him national recognition. He ran successfully for a senate seat in 1950, and again, he was able to undermine his opponent on charges of being soft on communism. Fear and suspicion of Communist Party sympathizers was so great during that period that the House Un-American Activities Committee and a

Tricky Dick

When Nixon challenged Representative Helen Gahagan Douglas for the Senate, he defeated her by calling her "the pink lady," and printed anti-Douglas handbills on pink paper. A local newspaper reported that "Tricky Dick Nixon is falsely accusing her of being a communist," and for years after the campaign was relegated to history and the name of Helen Gahagan Douglas forgotten, the name "Tricky Dick" was still with him.

senate committee began to misuse the situation. Many Americans who were accused of being communists by Congress simply held different views or led different lifestyles than did the politicians who investigated them.

Nixon, meanwhile, was concentrating his attention on running for higher office, and he became the running mate of Republican presidential nominee Dwight D. Eisenhower in 1952. However, newspapers revealed that Nixon had established a secret fund as a senator with money donated by California businessmen expecting political favors. Eisenhower was advised to drop him from the ticket, but instead, Nixon responded with an impassioned, nationally televised speech fully disclosing his personal finances. He said that his wife didn't own a mink coat, but wore a "respectable Republican cloth coat." He denied accepting any political gifts, but acknowledged that he did receive a gift: "a little cocker spaniel dog,...black-and-white, spotted, and our little girl Tricia, the six-year-old, named it Checkers." The address, which came to be known as the "Checkers speech," saved Nixon's place on the ticket.

Eisenhower was a calm and laid-back campaigner, but Nixon was much more aggressive. He accused the

Left: Nixon's famous "Checkers" speech saved his vice-presidential candidacy.

Bottom, left: When Vice President Nixon went to Venezuela on a goodwill tour in 1958, his motorcade was stoned by violent demonstrators with ill will on their minds.

Bottom, right: Nixon debated Soviet Premier Nikita Khruschev on the merits of capitalism versus communism in a tour of a Moscow trade exhibit. Khruschev's deputy, Leonid Brezhnev, is standing to the left of Nixon in this famous picture of the so-called kitchen debate.

Democratic nominee, Illinois governor Adlai Stevenson, of being soft on communism. Eisenhower won the election and became a popular president. He suffered a serious heart attack in 1955, and Nixon presided over administration meetings while Eisenhower was out of active service for three months. Republicans worried that their most popular candidate might not be well enough to run for a second term, but by the early spring of 1956, he had fully recovered, and announced that he intended to run. Some of his advisors wanted him to choose a new vice president, but Eisenhower ignored their advice and asked Nixon to run with him a second time.

Nixon was quite active as vice president. He traveled frequently, spreading American goodwill through Asia, Africa, and Europe during Eisenhower's second term, but he didn't fare as well in South America, where rocks were thrown at his motorcade. Nixon toured the Soviet Union in 1959, and he and Soviet premier Nikita Khrushchev were followed by television cameras as they visited a display of modern American households, and engaged in a heated debate about their respective forms of government and society in a model kitchen. The exchange became known as the "kitchen debate," although it had little to do with kitchens.

Changing Fortunes

Nixon quickly emerged as the frontrunner for the 1960 presidential election. He swept through the primaries and locked up the Republican nomination early. His opponent, Massachusetts senator John F. Kennedy, faced a stiffer fight before locking up the Democratic nomination. Always a vigorous campaigner, Nixon crisscrossed the country and established a strong lead in the polls. However, the lead dropped dramatically after a series of four nationally televised debates. They marked the first time that a presidential-campaign debate was broadcast on television, which had only recently reached a majority of American households.

Kennedy projected himself as relaxed in the debates, lively, and youthful, showing a sense of humor along with obvious idealism. Nixon seemed tired, stiff, and in need of a shave (he refused to wear makeup), and outlined a program with almost no fresh ideas. He couldn't very well accuse the millionaire Kennedy of being soft on communism. Neither candidate was stronger than the other in the quality of their remarks, nor did either say anything politically damaging. Some commentators, in fact, believed that Nixon had been the more effective debater. Nevertheless, momentum swung to Kennedy during the last few weeks of the campaign, and he squeezed out a victory. Kennedy won handily in the Electoral College, 303 to 220, but he edged Nixon in the popular vote by less than 1 percent.

Above: After losing the race for the California governorship in 1962, Nixon blamed the press, but promised them that they wouldn't have him to kick around anymore.

Disappointed, Nixon went back to California and turned his attention to the office of governor. He was not yet fifty years old. Once again, he waged an aggressive campaign in the 1962 California gubernatorial election, but his time-tested tactic of asserting that his opponent was soft on crime and communism didn't work this time. Democrat Edmund G. Brown Sr. defeated him. Believing he had received unfair cool treatment from the California press during the campaign, Nixon addressed his postelection comments directly to them, and in a postelection press conference, he told them that "You won't have Nixon to kick around anymore."

The Nixons moved to New York after that, and the former vice president quickly reestablished himself as a lawyer. He slowly reinstated his support within his party and was invited to campaign for Republicans all over the country, and as the campaign for the 1968 presidential nomination approached, he was well in the midst of a surprise comeback. As a more moderate politician than

Left: Nixon sold his California home and moved to New York in 1979. After being rejected twice in attempts to buy an apartment, he bought this townhouse on the Upper East Side. Among his neighbors on the block was Chase-Manhattan Bank President David Rockefeller.

the other hopefuls, including recently elected California governor Ronald Reagan and New York governor Nelson Rockefeller, Nixon enjoyed a smooth ride to the nomination at the party's 1968 convention in Miami.

There had been a few confrontations outside the convention hall in Miami. Demonstrations in protest of the Vietnam War and for various other social causes were met with resistance by local law enforcement, but they reflected great unrest throughout the nation: People disagreed passionately about the war and civil rights, among other issues, and widespread protests at the Democratic Convention in Chicago later that summer were met with even greater force by Chicago police.

The year 1968 was a violent one. Civil rights leader Dr. Martin Luther King Jr. was murdered in April. New York senator and former U.S. attorney general Robert F. Kennedy, emerging as the potential Democratic presidential nominee, was assassinated in June.

Vice President Hubert Humphrey became the Democratic nominee after overcoming tough primary challenges by Kennedy and Minnesota senator Eugene McCarthy, both of whom had pledged to end the war and had appealed strongly to youthful idealism. Nixon based his campaign on law and order, and appealed to what he called the "forgotten Americans," people who worked hard and weren't publicly protesting against their government. Alabama governor George C. Wallace, who had a clear history of resisting racial desegregation, ran on a third-party ticket, and won more than 13 percent of the popular vote and carried five Southern states in the Electoral College. Nixon and Humphrey each won about 43 percent of the popular vote, but Nixon won a sure victory in the Electoral College.

Foreign Policy Successes

Rather than fading, domestic unrest increased by the time Nixon took office in January 1969. Well-organized protests against the Vietnam War, for greater protection of the natural environment, and for improved civil rights for minorities and women had become almost daily occurrences. President Nixon supported the development of the Environmental Protection Agency, an executive-level agency responsible for maintaining environmental quality. On all the other issues, however, his administration carried out conservative policies. Civil-rights legislation was stalled, and he nominated four Supreme Court justices with decidedly conservative backgrounds. While defense spending increased, funds for education, urban renewal, and antipoverty programs were slashed in an effort to reduce government spending.

Election Results

1968

Presidential / Vice Presidential Candidates	Popular Votes	Electoral Votes
Richard M. Nixon / Spiro T. Agnew (Republican)	31,710,470	301
Hubert H. Humphrey / Edmund S. Muskie (Democratic)	31,209,677	191
George C. Wallace / Curtis E. LeMay (American Independent)	9,893,952	46

Democratic vice presidential incumbent Humphrey became presidential nominee only after incumbent president Lyndon B. Johnson dropped out of the race and New York senator Robert F. Kennedy was assassinated. Republican Nixon won the nomination on the second ballot.

1972

Presidential / Vice Presidential Candidates	Popular Votes	Electoral Votes
Richard M. Nixon / Spiro T. Agnew (Republican)	47,168,710	520
George S. McGovern / R. Sargent Shriver (Democratic)	29,084,726	17

Democrat McGovern won the nomination on the second ballot; Alabama governor George C. Wallace, an early Democratic challenger for the nomination, lost ground after being wounded in an assassination attempt on May 15, 1972.

Above: The 1968 Democratic National Convention in Chicago was the scene of one of the largest antiwar demonstrations of the era.

Below: The 1968 Republican Convention in Miami Beach nominated Nixon as the candidate on the fourth day.
He went on to defeat Hubert Humphrey, the Democratic nominee.

The Nixon Administration

Administration Dates: January 20, 1969–January 20, 1973

January 20, 1973–August 9, 1974

Vice President: Spiro T. Agnew (1969–73)

None (1973)

Gerald R. Ford (1973–74)

Cabinet:

Secretary of State	William P. Rogers (1969–73)
	Henry A. Kissinger (1973–74)
Secretary of the Treasury	David M. Kennedy (1969–71)
	John B. Connally (1971–72)
	George P. Shultz (1972–74)
	William E. Simon (1974)
Attorney General	John N. Mitchell (1969–72)
	Richard G. Kleindienst (1972–73)
	Elliot L. Richardson (1973–74)
	William B. Saxbe (1974)
Postmaster General	Winton M. Blount (1969–71)
Secretary of Interior	Walter J. Hickel (1969–70)
	Rogers C. B. Morton (1971–74)
Secretary of Agriculture	Clifford M. Hardin (1969–71)
	Earl L. Butz (1971–74)
Secretary of Labor	George P. Shultz (1969–70)
	James D. Hodgson (1970–73)
	Peter J. Brennan (1973–74)
Secretary of Commerce	Maurice H. Stans (1969–72)
	Peter G. Peterson (1972–73)
	Frederick B. Dent (1973–74)
Secretary of Defense	Melvin R. Laird (1969–73)
	Elliot L. Richardson (1973)
	James R. Schlesinger (1973–74)
Secretary of Health, Education, and Welfare	Robert H. Finch (1969–70)
	Elliot L. Richardson (1970–73)
	Caspar W. Weinberger (1973–74)
Secretary of Housing and Urban Development	George W. Romney (1969–73)
	James T. Lynn (1973–74)
Secretary of Transportation	John A. Volpe (1969–73)
	Claude S. Brinegar (1973–74)

Nixon faced an economy weakened by inflation, and he favored programs that increased U.S. exports and lowered imports. He imposed wage and price controls, following the economic theory that if the cost of goods held steady, workers wouldn't need to have pay increases, and the momentum of inflation would be broken. Inflation slowed by 1972, but it picked up again the following year, and Nixon responded by devaluing the dollar, hoping that it would slow inflation after his others ideas seem to have failed.

Nixon delegated domestic issues to his closest aides, chief of staff H. R. Haldeman and campaign advisor John Ehrlichman while he himself focused most of his direct attention on foreign policy. Working closely with his secretary of state, Henry Kissinger, he planned new foreign-policy initiatives, setting a new pattern for the presidency, which traditionally had simply reacted to foreign events.

President Nixon made two historic trips in 1972. The former anti-communist champion visited the People's Republic of China in February and signed a trade agreement. It was the first high-level contact between the two countries in more than twenty years. He visited the Soviet Union in May, and initiated the policy

Above: President Nixon exchanges copies of the Strategic Arms Limitation Treaty with Communist Party Chief Leonid Brezhnev as Soviet President Nikolai V. Podgorny looks on approvingly.

of détente—a relaxing of tensions between rival nations, with increased diplomatic, commercial, and cultural contacts. Along with signing a new trade agreement with the Soviets, Nixon initiated a missile reduction program called the Strategic Arms Limitation Treaty (SALT), and he also authorized the Soviets to buy massive amounts of American wheat to help overcome their failed agricultural programs.

Nixon defeated South Dakota senator George S. McGovern for a landslide reelection in 1972. The economy had steadied by that point; peace talks between the United States and North Vietnam showed promise of bringing the Vietnam War to an end; and Nixon had brought about a thaw in relations with two longtime enemies of the United States. When a cease-fire in Vietnam was announced in January 1973, Nixon was at the height of his popularity. However, his policies during the war had been further inflamed antiwar sentiments in 1970 after four young protesters were killed by National Guard troops at Kent State University in Ohio. Nixon made his disgust for protest demonstrations quite clear, while praising "average" Americans he called "the silent majority."

Left: Although he was a visitor himself, President Nixon guided American and Chinese officials on a tour of the Great Wall of China.

Henry Kissinger

Heinz Alfred Kissinger was born on May 27, 1923, in Furth, Germany. His father, a teacher, lost his job during the 1930s when the Nazi government persecuted Jews in Germany. The family, which included his younger brother, Walter Bernhard, left Germany in 1938, moving first to England and then several months later to the United States. They settled in New York City, where Heinz became "Henry," and attended high school for a year before switching to night school so that he could work during the day in a factory.

Kissinger served with U.S. Army Intelligence during World War II, and after the war, he was a civilian instructor at the European Command Intelligence School in Oberammergau, Germany. He went back to the United States to study at Harvard University, where he earned a bachelor's degree in 1950, a master's degree in 1952, and his Ph.D. in 1954, and then began teaching there in the government department. He wrote an acclaimed book, Nuclear Weapons and Foreign Policy, which influenced a flexible U.S. foreign policy, and he occasionally advised presidents Dwight D. Eisenhower, John F. Kennedy, and Lyndon B. Johnson. During summers from 1952 to 1969, he directed the Harvard International Seminar, which was attended by many international figures whom he would later deal with as a foreign affairs official.

Kissinger supported New York governor Nelson Rockefeller's unsuccessful bid for the Republican nomination for the presidency in 1968, and after his defeat by Richard Nixon, Rockefeller urged Nixon to appoint Kissinger to head the National Security Council. Taking on special assignments, Kissinger began pursuing secret negotiations to establish frameworks that were followed up with public diplomacy, including agreements on arms limitations with the Soviet Union, the reopening of relations with the People's Republic of China, and "shuttle diplomacy" that had him traveling back and forth between Middle Eastern countries to establish peace

in the region. Other behind-the-scenes developments were not as well received, including the Nixon administration's secret bombing of Cambodia and military operations there during the Vietnam War. Those actions were halted by Congress, but because war had not been officially declared against North Vietnam (and never was), the president needed congressional approval to undertake such missions. A high point in Kissinger's career came when he shared the Nobel Peace Prize with Le Duc Tho, a North Vietnamese negotiator with whom he had worked to bring an end to American military involvement in Vietnam.

The Strategic Arms Limitations Treaty (SALT) with the Soviet Union followed negotiations that lasted for nearly three years. Kissinger accompanied Nixon to Moscow, where the president and Soviet Communist Party chief Leonid Brezhnev signed the agreement. Another of Kissinger's successes that began in secret was his organizing of Nixon's reinstatement of relations with China. Working through Pakistani president Agha Muhammad Yahya Khan, Kissinger flew to China and arranged for an invitation for Nixon to make an official state visit. The Shanghai Communiqué of 1972 that resulted provided guidelines for the establishment of U.S.–China relations. During his eight years in the National Security Council and State Department, Kissinger flew to China a total of nine times.

After becoming secretary of state—the first to be foreign-born—in 1973, Kissinger conducted what became known as "shuttle diplomacy," where he facilitated negotiations to restore peace among Middle Eastern countries. He often flew from Egypt to Israel to Syria or other Middle Eastern nations to develop agreements to secure peace among officials who didn't want to meet face to face. After his departure from office following the 1976 defeat of President Gerald Ford, Kissinger became the director of his own consulting firm dealing with international political assessments. In addition to advising a wide variety of clients, he wrote several memoirs to help explain how history evolved while he was in office. Kissinger joined the faculty of Georgetown University in 1977.

Right: President Nixon and Communist Party Leader Leonid Brezhnev share a champagne toast to their 1974 summit meeting.

Above: On May 4, 1970, four antiwar demonstrators were killed by National Guardsmen at Kent State University in Ohio.

Vietnam

During the early 1950s, an uprising in a French colony in southeast Asia led the French to abandon the area. Formerly called French Indochina, it was divided into four nations—Cambodia, Laos, and North and South Vietnam—based on historical boundaries. Communists controlled North Vietnam, and South Vietnam was a democracy. In the late 1950s, North Vietnamese communist soldiers called the Vietcong invaded South Vietnam to overthrow the government and replace it with a communist system. Under presidents Eisenhower and Kennedy, America sent increasingly larger shipments of supplies and authorized military advisors to help the South Vietnamese. Under President Lyndon B. Johnson, aircraft bombing missions against the Vietcong began early in 1965, and American combat troops began arriving by the end of the year. By 1968, around 500,000 American servicemen were on the ground in Vietnam. When American involvement in the war ended in 1974, more than 55,000 American soldiers had been killed, and more than 150,000 were wounded.

When he took office in 1969, President Nixon defined his goal of achieving "peace with honor" in Vietnam, and began a program of withdrawing American troops. By August, 25,000 Americans had left Vietnam, and by December, another 65,000 were shipped home. American casualty rates dropped noticeably as the policy of Vietnamization—training and equipping South Vietnamese soldiers to fight—went into effect.

However, in spite of all that, the war was still expanding. In 1970, American air and ground forces crossed the border into Cambodia to destroy Vietcong strongholds, and the following year, American bombers started hitting targets in Laos, where the Vietcong had established supply lines. After a Vietcong offensive in March 1972, American planes began bombing North Vietnam for the first time since the Johnson administration, and later that year, mines were placed in northern harbors. When peace talks broke down late in 1972, the United States launched the largest aerial bombing in history of warfare against the North Vietnamese.

A cease-fire in January 1973 was generally welcomed, but it hardly seemed to be an appropriate time for rejoicing. Lost planes, American soldiers missing in action or taken prisoner, and the ever increasing protests at home had proven to be both exhausting and dispiriting. All American personnel were finally evacuated from Vietnam in 1974.

Below: Thousands converged on Washington for a peace rally in November 1969.

Above: The democratic National Committee had its offices in the Washington complex known as Watergate.

Above: Among the convicted Watergate conspirators was John D. Ehrlichman, the White House special assistant on domestic affairs.

Watergate

In 1973, the Vietnam War was replaced as front-page news by the Watergate scandal. It had actually begun on June 17, 1972, when five men were caught burglarizing the offices of the Democratic National Committee in the Watergate apartment and office complex in Washington. Investigations, primarily by newspapers following the lead of the *Washington Post,* uncovered connections between the burglars and members of the Nixon administration.

While the exact nature of the relationship between the burglars and the administration was still unclear, investigative reporters—such as Bob Woodward and Carl Bernstein, working with their source, "Deep Throat"— soon discovered other illegal activities connected with the White House. A group called the "plumbers" had been organized to stop "leaks," and it was involved in a 1971 burglary of a psychiatrist's office to find information against a patient, Daniel Ellsberg, who had leaked classified documents (the "Pentagon Papers") about bombing missions in Vietnam that the Nixon administration wanted kept secret. A grand jury indicted John Ehrlichman, the White House special assistant on domestic affairs, along with White House special counsel Charles Colson, and others for organizing the office break-in.

Meanwhile, reporters also discovered that the Committee to Re-Elect the President (CREEP) had solicited illegal campaign contributions that were used to finance spying on political opponents, and they found evidence that more than a half-million dollars of those funds had been paid to the Watergate burglars. Nixon's former attorney general, John Mitchell, White House counsel John Dean, and White House chief of staff H. R. Haldeman, as well as Ehrlichman, were implicated in political spying efforts.

Haldeman, Ehrlichman, and Attorney General Richard Kleindienst all resigned on April 30, 1973, and Dean was dismissed. The new attorney general, Elliot Richardson, appointed Harvard Law School professor

Below: Former attorney general John Mitchell was the head of the Committee to Re-Elect the President. In previous years he had been Nixon's law partner.

Above: Former White House Counsel John Dean broke down the stone wall the Watergate conspirators had built around the president in his testimony before the Senate investigating committee.

Archibald Cox as a special prosecutor to investigate the Watergate break-in, and a few days later, the Senate Select Committee on Presidential Activities opened hearings to look into it. These nationally televised hearings turned out to be riveting: John Dean testified that John Mitchell had ordered the Watergate break-in, and he added that a major cover-up was underway. Dean insisted that the president had authorized payments to the burglars to keep them quiet, but Nixon fiercely denied his accusations.

The investigation became bogged down in accusations and rebuttals, and there was no clear sequence of events emerging that could directly implicate the president. But then, on July 16, 1973, an incredible revelation changed everything. Testifying before the Senate committee, White House aide Alexander Butterfield said that Nixon had installed an audiotaping system in the White House

to record conversations so that future historians would have a better understanding of the day-to-day workings of the presidency. Special Prosecutor Cox immediately authorized a subpoena for eight of the tapes, homing in on the days and times when John Dean claimed the president had authorized illegal payments. When Nixon refused to release the tapes, claiming they were vital to the national security, U.S. District Court judge John Sirica, who had presided over the original case involving the Watergate burglars, ruled that Nixon had to honor the subpoena, and an appeals court upheld his decision.

Instead, on Saturday, October 20, 1973, Nixon ordered Attorney General Richardson to fire special prosecutor Cox, but Richardson immediately resigned, and so did Deputy Attorney General William Ruckelshaus, after which Solicitor General Robert Bork stepped in to discharge Cox. Called the "Saturday Night Massacre," Nixon's actions drew widespread public scorn, and to hold back the tide of criticism, Nixon appointed another special prosecutor, Texas lawyer Leon Jaworski, and gave the subpoenaed tapes to Judge Sirica. However, some conversations were obviously missing from them, and one tape had a mysterious eighteen minutes of silence, which experts determined was the result of erasing portions of the tape.

The Watergate scandal dragged on into 1974, sorely testing America's faith in their leaders. By that time, Gerald R. Ford had replaced Spiro T. Agnew as Nixon's vice president after Agnew had been implicated in a

No Contest

Before he became vide president in the Nixon administration, Spiro T. Agnew had served as Baltimore County Executive and Governor of Maryland. It was he who called the press "nattering nabobs of negativism," and intellectuals, "an effete corps of impudent snobs." In 1973, federal prosecutors charged that he had a long career of trading kickbacks for contracts back in Maryland, and added that he was still up to his old tricks as vice president. After a long negotiation with his accusers, Agnew agreed to resign from his office and to plead "no contest" to the charges that dated back more then ten years. He was convicted of income-tax evasion, and placed on three years' probation after paying a $10,000 fine. He became a business consultant after that.

Above: Nixon's refusal to make his secret Oval Office audiotapes public entangled him in a web that ultimately brought him down.

separate personal scandal involving income-tax evasion.

A grand jury indicted Mitchell, Haldeman, Ehrlichman, and four other White House officials in the Watergate cover-up, and Nixon himself was named as an "unindicted co-conspirator." With public sentiment clearly against Nixon, the administration slowed its defensive tactic of "stonewalling," as they themselves called the policy of obstruction and delay, in hopes that a more cooperative effort might have a positive effect on public opinion.

In April, Nixon complied with Jaworski's request for written transcripts of forty-two tapes: They clearly showed that the president had been looking for ways to punish his political opponents and to stonewall the Watergate investigation. Nixon refused to submit another sixty-four tapes the following month, claiming executive privilege, but on July 24, the Supreme Court voted eight to zero that he had to turn them over.

Meanwhile, impeachment hearings were already underway in the House Judiciary Committee, and by the end of July, it had approved three articles of impeachment: They charged Nixon with misusing his power in order to violate the constitutional rights of U.S. citizens, obstructing justice in the Watergate affair, and defying Judiciary Committee subpoenas. Nixon's last

attempts to rally support against a vote of impeachment, which would lead to a Senate trial, were futile. Three tapes he released on August 5, 1974, proved that he had ordered the Federal Bureau of Investigation (FBI) to stop investigating the Watergate break-in. The tapes showed without any doubt that Nixon had helped direct the cover-up.

Facing certain impeachment and subsequent removal from office, Nixon resigned on August 9, becoming the first president to step down voluntarily. His successor, Gerald R. Ford, pardoned him for all crimes that he might have committed in office, making Nixon immune from federal prosecution. When he took office, Ford proclaimed that "our national nightmare is over," and that the "American system worked." He meant that in spite of the disruption of the Watergate scandal and Nixon's resignation, the American government continued to operate effectively.

Richard and Pat Nixon went into seclusion at their home in San Clemente, California, after leaving Washington. The former president was disbarred in New York after a state court found that he had obstructed justice in connection with Watergate and the Pentagon Papers, and several more court rulings went against him. In 1977, the U.S. Supreme Court upheld a 1974 law giving the government control over Nixon's presidential papers and tape recordings.

Although he wrote several books and traveled abroad on personal diplomatic missions, Nixon was never able to fully regain respect as a politician or a statesman. The shadow of Watergate remained over his head. He died in New York City on April 22, 1994.

Articles of Impeachment

In July 1974, the House Judiciary Committee, chaired by Representative Peter Rodino, approved three articles of impeachment against President Nixon: (1) Obstruction of justice, making false or misleading statements to investigators, condoning or counseling perjury. (2) Abuse of power, misusing the FBI, the IRS, and the Secret Service, and maintaining an unlawful secret investigative unit (the Plumber). (3) Failure to comply with congressional subpoenas.

Nixon responded by resigning, saying that he was only guilt of errors in judgment, but "to continue the fight . . . for my personal vindication, would almost totally absorb the total attention of the president and Congress."

Legacy

There were plenty of achievements during Richard Nixon's administration, including détente with the Soviet Union and the reestablishment of relations with China. At home, his administration wrestled with an unstable economy and managed to slow inflation. Government spending was generally lowered, and the founding of the Environmental Protection Agency addressed an area that was of great concern to many Americans.

The unstable social atmosphere of the Nixon years challenged all national figures. President Nixon achieved a long-desired cease-fire in the Vietnam War. His authorization for bombing campaigns and expansion of the war into neighboring countries, however, increased the outspokenness of the antiwar movement.

Nixon had always taken aggressive approaches to overcoming his opponents. When his administration took that philosophy beyond legal limits, the country was faced with the lawbreaking activities of the executive who was responsible for carrying out the laws of the land. After a long investigation, the federal system, under the guidelines of the Constitution, followed the process

Above: Five presidents and first ladies attended Nixon's funeral in 1994: (L-R) Bill and Hillary Clinton, George and Barbara Bush, Ronald and Nancy Reagan, Jimmy and Rosalynn Carter, and Gerald and Betty Ford.

for expelling a chief executive for "high crimes and misdemeanors." Nixon's historic resignation occurred before the official removal of a president could take place, but when the Watergate affair was finally over, relieved Americans could say, "The system worked."

Born March 16, 1912, Ely, Nevada
Died June 22, 1993, Park Ridge, New Jersey

"It takes heart to be in political life."

—*Pat Nixon*

Pat Nixon was never comfortable in the public spotlight. She had grown accustomed to it as her husband, Richard Nixon, was serving two terms in Congress and then became a U.S. senator in 1950, and two years later, she was warming to her public position as the wife of the vice-presidential candidate. But when the Nixons had to reveal their personal finances to counter charges that he had received secret illegal funds, she strongly disliked the invasion of her family's privacy and made herself less accessible to the media.

Pat Nixon gradually became a more public figure as first lady. She traveled to Peru after an earthquake there to help with relief efforts; she made trips to Africa and South America as the personal representative of the president; and she traveled around the United States to meet with volunteer organizations for various causes. After the Watergate scandal began dominating the news in 1973, Pat Nixon once again shied away from the glare of publicity. She had always acted with grace and dignity, but she retreated when the political life became a media circus.

"St. Patrick's Babe"

Thelma Catherine Ryan was born on March 16, 1912, and was nicknamed Pat by her father. Actually, he called her "St. Patrick's babe in the morn," because she had been born on the eve of St. Patrick's Day, an important day to an Irish-American family like the Ryans. Her parents, William and Kate Halberstadt Bender Ryan, lived in Ely, Nevada, where her father worked as a miner.

The family moved to California not long after Pat was born and operated a small farm, where she worked regularly as soon as she was old enough, picking tomatoes, potatoes, and peppers. She learned to drive a wagon with a team of horses to help gather the crops and take them to market. When her mother died, Pat became the female head of the family at the age of thirteen, taking care of her father and two brothers. She nursed her father through his painful illness of silicosis, and he died when Pat was seventeen.

Pat looked after her brothers and attended school at Fullerton Junior College. When she was nineteen, Pat drove an elderly couple cross-country to New York City, where she lived for three years, working as a stenographer and then as an X-ray technician while taking classes at Columbia University. She went back to California in 1934 and enrolled at the University of Southern California in Los Angeles.

She was an excellent student, and she worked at several jobs to help support her education and herself. At various times, she was a store clerk, a dental assistant, an actress for walk-on scenes, and a telephone operator. One teacher claimed to have seen her in class in the morning, working behind a cafeteria counter at lunchtime, studying in a library in the afternoon, and working at a clothing store in the evening—all during the same day.

No Future in It

In the 1980s, after the smoke cleared, Nixon became something of an elder statesman, speaking out on behalf of Republican candidates, and that led to the ultimate question, Would he consider running for president again? His answer to that was: "I am the only native American citizen over the age of thirty-five who can't run for the presidency."

The World's a Stage

After she graduated, Pat became a teacher at Whittier High School in Whittier, California, and in addition to teaching typing, she coached the cheerleading team and arranged performances of plays. In 1938, she tried out for a part in a drama produced by the Whittier Community Players where she met another aspiring amateur actor, a young lawyer named Richard Nixon. He was attracted to her and asked her for a date, but she said, "Oh, I'm too busy," to which he replied, "You shouldn't say that, because someday I'm going to marry you."

Pat enjoyed being single and kept her persistent admirer at arm's length. Nixon tried sending her flowers and poems, but he and Pat remained just friends for a while. Gradually he won her over, and he knew he was succeeding when Pat began helping his mother at the Nixon family store. They were married in Riverside, California, on June 16, 1940. After a honeymoon in Mexico, they went back to Whittier, where Nixon was a rising young lawyer and Pat had a job teaching school.

After America entered World War II, Dick and Pat each took jobs with the Office of Price Administration (OPA), a government agency that helped oversee rationing programs, and worked in Washington for six months. When he enlisted in the navy and was sent to the Pacific, Pat went back to California, where she worked in an OPA branch office in San Francisco.

Political Life Begins

Nixon went to Baltimore, Maryland, after the war ended in 1945, and while he was waiting for his discharge from the navy, he was contacted by a Republican Party official back in Whittier, who asked him to run for Congress. Pat didn't like the fishbowl life of a politician, but she helped her husband at his campaign headquarters and often went with him when he traveled around the district making speeches.

Their first daughter, Tricia, was born in 1946, the same year they moved to Washington, after Nixon's victory in the congressional election. Two years later, another daughter, Julie, was born, and Nixon was reelected to a second term in Congress. He was elected to the Senate in 1950, and two years after that, he was chosen as the Republican vice-presidential candidate on the ticket headed by Dwight D. Eisenhower. Just three months before election day, the *New York Post* and other newspapers reported that Nixon had a secret fund built with contributions from businessmen as down payments on future political favors. While Nixon denied the accusations, Eisenhower was advised to drop him from the ticket, out of fear that the scandal might cost Republicans the election.

Although she resented the invasion of their privacy, Pat Nixon stood behind her husband's decision to save his spot in the ticket by making their family finances public and going on national television to protect his reputation. The speech helped to lessen the scandal, and Eisenhower coasted to election as president. Pat traveled extensively with her husband during his time as vice president, visiting Asia, Europe, Africa, and the Soviet Union. At home, Pat maintained a full schedule of meetings with women's groups across the country.

She was disappointed when her husband lost his bid for the presidency in 1960, but she was pleased to be able to return home to California and a quiet life. She resisted her husband's plan to run for governor of California in 1962, but after seeing how much he wanted to do it, she gave in. After her husband lost a tense and often bitter campaign to Democrat Edmund G. Brown Sr., they moved to New York with their two daughters.

Above: Vice-presidential candidate Nixon sings with his daughters, Tricia (L) and Julie (R), and wife, Pat, in 1952.

Back to Washington

Nixon maintained a visible role in Republican politics, and in 1968, he emerged as the leading contender for the party's presidential nomination, which led to winning a close election. He had always been somewhat reserved and awkward in crowds, but Pat helped him show his warmer side as a family man.

In her role as first lady, Pat Nixon served as hostess for formal dinner parties involving American and foreign officials. She also arranged informal affairs with more humble people, often inviting groups of senior citizens or physically challenged people to the White House. Though she preferred not to make public statements or to take on great causes, she supported volunteerism and she traveled around the country to call attention to the efforts of volunteer groups. She also traveled with her husband to such faraway places as China and the Soviet

Union, and she traveled to Peru on her own to help with relief efforts after an earthquake there, and to Africa and South America in the position of personal representative of the president.

She also grew more at ease with the press during the 1972 campaign, and even began expressing political opinions, including her hope that her husband would appoint a woman to the Supreme Court. Her interaction with the press stopped shortly after her husband began his second term, though, because coverage of the Watergate scandal included so much rumor and speculation as the facts were gradually discovered.

Last Years

After the Watergate scandal led to her husband's resignation in 1974, the Nixons went back to California. Pat had supported her husband through the ordeal, and she helped nurse him when he suffered from a life-threatening blood disorder. She enjoyed spending quiet time reading, gardening, and listening to music, but she suffered a stroke that left her partially paralyzed two years into her "retirement."

The Nixons moved to New York in 1980 and later bought an estate in New Jersey, where they could be nearer to their children and their families. Pat Nixon died of lung cancer in June 1993, and her husband died the following year. Both are buried on the grounds of the Richard Nixon Library and Birthplace in Yorba Linda, California.

Nixon's "Silent Majority" Speech

Delivered on November 3, 1969

During Richard Nixon's first year as president, the prospects for ending American involvement in the Vietnam War hadn't improved. The U.S. military had been engaged in combat in Southeast Asia since 1965, and more than 500,000 troops were stationed there when Nixon took office in January 1969. Protest demonstrations against the war in the streets of American cities and on college campuses had become commonplace and were growing larger and more widespread with every passing month.

In early November 1969, President Nixon made an address to the nation on the war in Vietnam. He wanted to ensure that Americans understood the situation there, the progress of peace talks, and the prospects for the withdrawal of American troops; he also wanted to address the growing unrest at home as reflected in antiwar protests. Americans were intensely divided over the war: Some wanted an immediate withdrawal of American troops, while others believed that the United States could still prevail in Vietnam and saw withdrawal as a cowardly act of surrender and defeat.

President Nixon's speech to the nation on November 3, 1969, roughly consisted of four parts: He reviewed the history of American involvement in Vietnam; he reviewed options for peace and the efforts of his administration to negotiate with North Vietnamese officials; and he presented his plan of "Vietnamization"—where troops would be withdrawn gradually while American military personnel trained and prepared South Vietnamese soldiers to continue defending their own

land. He concluded by addressing social unrest in the United States over the Vietnam War.

The speech became famous for President Nixon's use of the term "silent majority" to characterize those Americans who were not demonstrating in the streets against the war. In contrast, he called antiwar demonstrators "a vocal minority." "However fervent their cause," Nixon declared bluntly, if that minority "prevails over reason and the will of the majority, this Nation has no future as a free society."

My fellow Americans, I am sure you can recognize from what I have said that we really only have two choices open to us if we want to end this war.

I can order an immediate, precipitate withdrawal of all Americans from Vietnam without regard to the effects of that action.

Or we can persist in our search for a just peace through a negotiated settlement if possible, or through continued implementation of our plan for Vietnamization if necessary—a plan in which we will withdraw all of our forces from Vietnam on a schedule in accordance with our program, as the South Vietnamese become strong enough to defend their own freedom.

I have chosen this second course.

It is not the easy way.

It is the right way.

It is a plan which will end the war and serve the cause of peace—not just in Vietnam but in the Pacific and in the world.

In speaking of the consequences of a precipitate withdrawal, I mentioned that our allies would lose confidence in America.

Far more dangerous, we would lose confidence in ourselves. Oh, the immediate reaction would be a sense of relief that our men were coming home. But as we saw the consequences of what we had done, inevitable remorse and divisive recrimination would scar our spirit as a people.

We have faced other crises in our history and have become stronger by rejecting the easy way out and taking the right way in meeting our challenges. Our greatness as a nation has been our capacity to do what had to be done when we knew our course was right.

I recognize that some of my fellow citizens disagree with the plan for peace I have chosen. Honest and patriotic Americans have reached different conclusions as to how peace should be achieved.

In San Francisco a few weeks ago, I saw demonstrators carrying signs reading: "Lose in Vietnam, bring the boys home."

Well, one of the strengths of our free society is that any American has a right to reach that conclusion and to advocate that point of view. But as President of the United States, I would be untrue to my oath of office if I allowed the policy of this Nation to be dictated by the minority who hold that point of view and who try to impose it on the Nation by mounting demonstrations in the street.

For almost 200 years, the policy of this Nation has been made under our Constitution by those leaders in the Congress and the White House elected by all of the people. If a vocal minority, however fervent its cause, prevails over reason and the will of the majority, this Nation has no future as a free society.

And now I would like to address a word, if I may, to the young people of this Nation who are particularly concerned, and I understand why they are concerned, about this war.

I respect your idealism.

I share your concern for peace.

I want peace as much as you do.

There are powerful personal reasons I want to end this war. This week I will have to sign eighty-three letters to mothers, fathers, wives, and loved ones of men who have given their lives for America in Vietnam. It is very little satisfaction to me that this is only one-third as many letters as I signed the first week in office. There is nothing I want more than to see the day come when I do not have to write any of those letters.

I want to end the war to save the lives of those brave young men in Vietnam.

But I want to end it in a way which will increase the chance that their younger brothers and their sons will not have to fight in some future Vietnam someplace in the world.

And I want to end the war for another reason. I want to end it so that the energy and dedication of you, our young people, now too often directed into bitter hatred against those responsible for the war, can be turned to the great challenges of peace, a better life for all Americans, a better life for all people on this earth.

I have chosen a plan for peace. I believe it will succeed.

If it does succeed, what the critics say now won't matter. If it does not succeed, anything I say then won't matter.

I know it may not be fashionable to speak of patriotism or national destiny these days.

But I feel it is appropriate to do so on this occasion.

Two hundred years ago this Nation was weak and poor. But even then, America was the hope of millions in the world. Today we have become the strongest and richest nation in the world. And the wheel of destiny has turned so that any hope the world has for the survival of peace and freedom will be determined by whether the American people have the moral stamina and the courage to meet the challenge of free world leadership.

Let historians not record that when America was the most powerful nation in the world we passed on the other side of the road and allowed the last hopes for peace and freedom of millions of people to be suffocated by the forces of totalitarianism.

And so tonight—to you, the great silent majority of my fellow Americans—I ask for your support.

I pledged in my campaign for the Presidency to end the war in a way that we could win the peace. I have initiated a plan of action which will enable me to keep that pledge.

The more support I can have from the American people, the sooner that pledge can be redeemed; for the more divided we are at home, the less likely the enemy is to negotiate at Paris.

Let us be united for peace. Let us also be united against defeat. Because let us understand: North Vietnam cannot defeat or humiliate the United States. Only Americans can do that.

Fifty years ago, in this room and at this very desk, President Woodrow Wilson spoke words which caught the imagination of a war-weary world. He said: "This is the war to end war." His dream for peace after World War I was shattered on the hard realities of great power politics and Woodrow Wilson died a broken man.

Tonight I do not tell you that the war in Vietnam is the war to end wars. But I do say this: I have initiated a plan which will end this war in a way that will bring us closer to that great goal to which Woodrow Wilson and every American President in our history has been dedicated—the goal of a just and lasting peace.

As President I hold the responsibility for choosing the best path to that goal and then leading the Nation along it.

I pledge to you tonight that I shall meet this responsibility with all of the strength and wisdom I can command in accordance with your hopes, mindful of your concerns, sustained by your prayers.

Thank you and goodnight.

What Happened Next

About 90,000 American troops were withdrawn from Vietnam in 1969. The policy of Vietnamization—training and equipping South Vietnamese soldiers to fight—was instituted. In an earlier part of Nixon's speech, he vowed that the American withdrawal would stop and fighting would intensify if the North Vietnamese tried to take quick advantage of the declining American military presence.

To assist the Vietnamization effort, American forces attempted to wipe out North Vietnamese supply lines and military strongholds in South Vietnam. In 1970, that pursuit led to American air and ground forces entering neighboring Cambodia; the following year, American bombers began hitting targets in Laos, a country adjacent to North Vietnam, after a North Vietnamese offensive in the South. American planes began bombing North Vietnam for the first time in more than five years; then, late in 1972, the U.S. military hit North Vietnam with the largest-ever aerial bombing in history.

A cease-fire and treaty was agreed to between the United States and North Vietnam in January 1973, and all remaining American troops were withdrawn in March. Hostilities between North and South Vietnam began again the following year, however, and in 1975 South Vietnam fell under Communist control.

Meanwhile, antiwar demonstrations intensified from 1970 through 1972. In 1970, four demonstrators were shot and killed by national guardsmen at Kent State University in Ohio More demonstrations followed the 1971 publication of the "Pentagon Papers"—secret American military documents that were leaked to and published by the *New York Times*—revealing that the U.S. military had been aware that the situation in Vietnam was far bleaker long before the American people had been told. News of U.S. bombing missions also led to more angry antiwar protests.

The scars of the Vietnam War are still deep. Whenever the possibility arises that U.S. military forces might engage in combat, there is an inevitable exclamation: "Let's make sure we don't get involved in another Vietnam." Vietnam veterans didn't come home to parades or celebrations. Only by the mid-1990s, with the opening of the Vietnam Veterans War Memorial in Washington, did the nation begin to come to terms with a war that caused so many great losses and such deep dissension.

Gerald R. Ford

"My fellow Americans, our long national nightmare is over."
—Gerald R. Ford, on becoming president

Thirty-eighth president of the United States, 1974–1977

Full name: *Gerald Rudolph Ford; born Leslie Lynch King Jr.*

Born: *July 14, 1913, Omaha, Nebraska*

Died: *December 26, 2006, Rancho Mirage, California*

Parents: *Leslie Lynch King and Dorothy Gardner King Ford; Gerald Rudolf Ford (stepfather)*

Spouse: *Elizabeth (Betty) Ann Bloomer Warren (1918–2011; m. 1948)*

Children: *Michael Gerald (1950–); John (Jack) Gardner (1952–); Steven Meigs (1956–); Susan Elizabeth (1957–)*

Religion: *Episcopalian*

Education: *University of Michigan (B.A., 1935); Yale University Law School (LL.B., 1941)*

Occupation: *Attorney*

Government positions: *U.S. representative from Michigan; vice president under Richard Nixon*

Political party: *Republican*

Dates as president: *August 9, 1974–January 20, 1977*

Age upon taking office: *61*

erald R. Ford was the first vice president to assume the office of chief executive following the resignation of a president. He had served President Richard Nixon as vice president for only eight months. A quiet veteran of the national political scene and a former House minority leader, Ford was not in any way involved in the scandal that drove Nixon from office. He was also unique among the presidents for never having run in a national election. His only campaign experience was in Michigan's Fifth Congressional District, where he ran for his seat twelve different times, never once getting less than 60 percent of the vote.

Sworn in as president in a swift White House ceremony on August 9, 1974, Ford quickly proved himself up to the job. Although he endured a great deal of criticism for granting a full presidential pardon to Nixon just a month after he took office, Ford restored honesty and dignity to the nation's highest office after the scandal-ridden Nixon administration.

Adopted Son

Gerald Ford was born on July 14, 1913, in Omaha, Nebraska, and named Leslie Lynch King Jr. His father proved to be a jealous, difficult husband for Ford's mother, Dorothy Gardner King, and by 1915, she had divorced

Left: Grand Rapids paint manufacturer Gerald R. Ford Sr., seen here with his sister, Mrs. William Sheets, adopted Leslie Lynch King Jr. and gave him his name.

hundred-dollar-per-year scholarship to the University of Michigan, where he worked in a hospital to meet his college living expenses. He played center on Michigan's football team, and he was offered contracts to play in the National Football League when he graduated in 1935. Instead, he accepted a coaching job at Yale University, hoping to continue his education there. At first, administrators at the Ivy League school allowed him to enroll in their highly regarded law school, but only on a part-time basis. Nevertheless, Ford graduated in the top third of his class, and went back to Grand Rapids, where he began a private law practice with a college friend.

Long Tenure in Congress

When World War II erupted, Ford enlisted in the navy and served aboard an aircraft carrier in the Pacific theater. When he got back home after the war, he joined a prestigious Grand Rapids law firm, and with the support of his stepfather, who was the county Republican chairman, he decided to make a bid for a seat in the U.S. House of Representatives. He won the nomination over prominent archconservative Republican Bartel J. Jonkman, who had represented the Grand Rapids area for nine years.

him and gone home with her child to her family in Grand Rapids, Michigan. She married Gerald R. Ford, the owner of a local paint-and-varnish business, the following year, and her boy's name was legally changed to Gerald Rudolph Ford Jr. He assumed that his stepfather was his biological parent until he was told otherwise at the age of seventeen.

Ford worked in the family business with his three younger brothers when he was a teenager. A standout athlete at Grand Rapids South High School, he won a

Timeline

1913: Born in Nebraska
1935: Graduates from the University of Michigan
1942–46: Serves in U.S. Navy during World War II
1948–73: Serves as U.S. representative from Michigan
1965–73: Serves as U.S. House minority leader
1973: Appointed vice president by Richard Nixon
1974–77: Serves as thirty-eighth U.S. president following resignation of Richard Nixon
1976: Loses presidential election to Jimmy Carter

Right: Ford was a star center for the University of Michigan Wolverines in the 1930s.

War Record

Ford joined the navy four months after Pearl Harbor and, as might have been predicted, he was assigned to a flight school as a fitness instructor. He requested a transfer and was assigned to sea duty about the U.S.S. Monterey, a light aircraft carrier, as gunnery officer, and later became assistant navigator. His ship took part in nearly every major battle in the South Pacific, including Wake Island, Okinawa, and the Philippines, and he picked up ten battle stars.

Joining him on the campaign trail was his new wife, the former Betty Bloomer Warren. They had dated for just a few months before Ford proposed, and their wedding was delayed for several months because of his campaign. He and Betty were married a few weeks before the election, on October 18, 1948, and they went to a University of Michigan football game the next day as part of their honeymoon trip, which also involved several campaign stops. Ford won the November election by a large margin. He and Betty would have four children, three boys and a girl.

Ford went on to spend the next twenty-four years in the House of Representatives. In Washington, he quickly learned the art of political deal-making, and he won the respect of his colleagues as an honest politician. He joined a number of young House Republicans who called themselves the "Chowder and Marching Society," and it was in that dinner discussion group that Ford first came to know Richard M. Nixon, a congressman from California.

Above: Congressman Ford accepts the "Veteran of the Year" award from fellow Michigan Congressman Charles Potter.

Below left: Ford's mother, Dorothy, visited him often when he was in Congress.

Below: After his election to Congress, Jerry Ford became one of the hardest-working people in the House of Representatives.

Ford served on a number of influential committees during his years in the House, and among them was his appointment by President Lyndon B. Johnson to the Warren Commission, the official government inquiry into the 1963 assassination of President John F. Kennedy. Two years later, his colleagues elected him House minority leader. He had become one of the country's most respected and experienced politicians when a political scandal of destructive proportions arose involving the Nixon administration.

Nixon had wanted him as his running mate in the 1968 presidential election, but Ford turned down the offer, hoping instead that the Republicans would win a majority of seats in Congress, which would have made him Speaker of the House, a job he coveted. As it happened, the Republicans didn't win a majority, and he had to put his dream aside.

Watergate

In June 1972, several burglars were arrested after they broke into Democratic Party headquarters inside the Watergate apartment and office complex in Washington. A sustained investigation by news agencies, particularly the *Washington Post*, exposed evidence of a widespread conspiracy that included political espionage and abuse of power within the Nixon administration.

As the scandal unfolded, a number of illegal operations were uncovered—many of which were intended to harm the reputations of Nixon's political and personal enemies—that had been carried out by men in Nixon's inner circle and been paid for with campaign funds. The Watergate burglars were associated with the Committee to Re-Elect the President (CREEP).

A high-profile nationally televised congressional investigation was launched, and it revealed that Nixon had directed the Federal Bureau of Investigation (FBI) to cover up the matter. Based on the committee's findings, Nixon's attorney general and members of his staff were facing indictments.

Meanwhile, in a scandal not related to Watergate, Nixon's vice president, Spiro T. Agnew, was charged with income-tax evasion, and he was forced to resign on October 10, 1973. Under the terms of the Twenty-fifth Amendment to the Constitution, Nixon was allowed to appoint a successor, with congressional confirmation, and Ford emerged as his colleagues' choice for the job.

He was sworn in as Nixon's vice president on December 6, 1973, and at first he defended the president as more revelations of illegal activities surfaced in the Watergate scandal. Then, however, he began to distrust the men Nixon had appointed—and seemed to rely on— even as accusations swirled around them. Ford had been a team player throughout his political career, but he made

Left: Among Ford's close associates in Congress was Representative Donald Rumsfeld of Illinois.

an exception in this instance. In early 1974, he told an audience, "Never again must America allow an arrogant, elite guard of political adolescents like the Committee to Re-Elect the President to bypass the regular party system and dictate the terms of a national election."

Later that summer, the House Judiciary Committee adopted three articles of impeachment against Nixon, and the House of Representatives appeared likely to approve them, which would then be followed by a trial in the Senate. Shock, dismay, and disillusionment with the entire political system rocked the country. A leading Democratic senator told Ford, "You're all we've got now, and I mean the country, not the party."

"Our Long National Nightmare Is Over"

For a time, it seemed that Nixon might survive an impeachment vote in the House. However, three audiotapes that were released on August 5, 1974, showed clearly that Nixon had helped direct the cover-up. On August 8—more than two years after the Watergate break-in, which he had dismissed as a "third-rate burglary attempt"—the president informed his second-in-command that he was going to resign the next day. Nixon said, "Jerry, I know you'll do a good job." Ford took the oath of office the next day in the East Room of the White House and delivered a hastily written speech

before the assembled crowd and a national television audience. "My fellow Americans," he said, "our long national nightmare is over." The new president concluded by asking the nation to pray for Nixon and his family.

Ford immediately proved himself to be an upright and relaxed chief executive who did a great deal to restore America's faith in the presidency. He was vigorous and healthy, and he had an energetic wife, Betty, and four college-aged children. Ford also had a sense of humor. Among his endearing quirks: He stepped outside to pick up the morning newspapers from the doorstep every morning, and he asked that the Marine Band play the University of Michigan fight song instead of the traditional presidential tune "Hail to the Chief" when he appeared on formal public occasions.

"The trouble with Jerry Ford is that he can't walk and chew gum at the same time."

—*Lyndon B. Johnson*

Meanwhile, Nixon was still facing charges by a grand jury, and just a month after he took office, Ford surprised the country by issuing "Proclamation 4311, Granting a Pardon to Richard M. Nixon." As he noted in a statement to the nation, at least a year would pass before a Nixon trial would begin. "Someone must write the end," he said, to "an American tragedy." He added: "In the meantime, the tranquility to which this nation has been restored

Left: Ford takes the oath of office in the East Room of the White House ten months after being appointed vice president.

The Ford Administration

Administration Dates: August 9, 1974–January 20, 1977

Vice President: None (1974)
Nelson A. Rockefeller (1974–77)

Cabinet:

Secretary of State	Henry A. Kissinger (1974–77)
Secretary of the Treasury	William E. Simon (1974–77)
Attorney General	William B. Saxbe (1974–75)
	Edward H. Levi (1975–77)
Secretary of the Interior	Rogers C. B. Morton (1974–75)
	Stanley K. Hathaway (1975)
	Thomas S. Kleppe (1975–77)
Secretary of Agriculture	Earl L. Butz (1974–76)
	John A. Knebel (1976–77)
Secretary of Labor	Peter J. Brennan (1974–75)
	John T. Dunlop (1975–76)
	William J. Usery Jr. (1976–77)
Secretary of Commerce	Frederick B. Dent (1974–75)
	Rogers C. B. Morton (1975)
	Elliot L. Richardson (1976–77)
Secretary of Defense	James R. Schlesinger (1974–75)
	Donald H. Rumsfeld (1975–77)
Secretary of Health, Education and Welfare	Caspar W. Weinberger (1974–75)
	F. David Mathews (1975–77)
Secretary of Housing and Urban Development	James T. Lynn (1974–75)
	Carla A. Hills (1975–77)
Secretary of Transportation	Claude S. Brinegar (1974–75)
	William T. Coleman Jr. (1975–77)

by the events of recent weeks could be irreparably lost by the prospects of bringing to trial a former president of the United States. The prospects of such trial will cause prolonged and divisive debate over the propriety of exposing to further punishment and degradation a man who has already paid the unprecedented penalty of relinquishing the highest elective office of the United States."

Backlash

Ford's approval rating nosedived. The Gallup Poll, which had previously given him a rating of 71 percent, dropped to 49 in less than a week. Public opinion and media pundits charged that a Republican "deal" had been made to allow him to step up to the presidency in return for an assurance to absolve Nixon of any wrongdoing.

"There was no deal, period, under no circumstances."
—*Gerald Ford, before the House Judiciary Committee*

Ford had always been an honorable politician. He never risked his integrity—his honesty and his standards of behavior—for political gain. Nevertheless, after the pardon, he suffered from a negative press and took the full force of the Watergate backlash. Americans were beginning to say that perhaps the office of the president held too much power. Two pieces of significant legislation had already been passed by Congress just before Ford assumed office: The 1973 War Powers Act that forced a

Left: Ford fit comfortably into the day-to-day routine of the Oval Office.

Dad, I'd Like You to Meet . . .

Celebrity visitors to the White House are not considered at all unusual, but one that still stands out, even more so than England's Queen Elizabeth II, is Beatle George Harrison, who came to dinner at the invitation of the president's son Jack, a fan of rock music in general and the Beatles in particular. His father's own favorite entertainer was Pearl Bailey, who also headed Richard Nixon's list.

Left: One month after "Tricky Dick" Nixon resigned and left the White House, Ford pardoned him.

president to secure congressional approval before sending troops into battle; and a 1974 reform bill that limited presidential control over federal spending.

With the midterm elections of 1974, a new group of relatively young Democratic legislators, who came to be known as the Watergate babies, were elected to Congress, and new battle lines were drawn between the president and Capitol Hill. Those partisan divides continued through the end of the century, as the opposition party frequently stalled the agenda of the sitting president. At one point, Ford was even called before Congress to testify and defend himself over the Nixon pardon.

Distancing Himself from Nixon

Not long after he took office, Ford announced his Vietnam Era Reconciliation Program, a controversial clemency plan for draft-dodgers that appeared to have been influenced partly by the fact that he had draft-aged sons. Intended to help heal the division of national opinion influenced by the Vietnam War, the program also distanced Ford from the harsher policies of the Nixon era. However, only about 20 percent of the young men who were eligible applied for clemency. Thousands had

Twist of Fate

The economy was tanking when the new Congress convened in 1975 with the boast that it was strong enough to call itself "veto-proof." Then things got worse. The cost of imported oil was skyrocketing, and production of all forms of domestic energy dropped just as dramatically. Ford asked Congress for a $16 billion tax cut to help the economy, as well as higher taxes on oil and gas to cut consumption, and for cuts in government spending. Calling the proposals "misguided," congressional leaders bottled up the requests and no other action was taken. Ford, who had always been proud of being called a "congressman's congressman," clearly wasn't a congressman's president.

Left: Ford kept most of Nixon's Cabinet in place, including Secretary of State Henry Kissinger.

Nelson Rockefeller

Nelson Aldrich Rockefeller was born in Bar Harbor, Maine, on July 8, 1908, the third of six children of John D. Rockefeller Jr. and Abby Greene Aldrich. His grandfathers were John D. Rockefeller Sr., founder of the Standard Oil Company, and U.S. senator Nelson Aldrich of Rhode Island. Rockefeller attended Dartmouth University, where he majored in economics, taught a Sunday-school class, and occasionally worked in the school cafeteria to earn spending money. In 1930, he married Mary Todhunter Clark, a Philadelphia socialite. They had five children.

At the age of thirty, he was president of New York's Rockefeller Center. Several trips to Latin America in the late 1930s convinced him of the region's importance to national security, which led him to accept his first major governmental position at the head of the Office of Inter-American Affairs. His effectiveness earned him the government of Chile's Order of Merit; Brazil made him a member of its National Order of the Southern Cross; and Mexico enrolled him in the Order of the Aztec Eagle.

In 1950, he was appointed chairman of the International Development Advisory Board by President Harry S Truman. The agency encouraged economic growth in depressed areas in underdeveloped nations. Two years later, President Dwight D. Eisenhower made him chairman of the Advisory Committee on Government Organization. He also organized a new agency, the Department of Health, Education, and Welfare, and became its first undersecretary. Then, as a special assistant to President Eisenhower, Rockefeller helped develop the Atoms-for-Peace Plan that publicized and organized safe uses for nuclear power around the world.

He was elected governor of New York in 1958. Three years later, he divorced his wife, and in 1963 he married Margaretta Fitler "Happy" Murphy, who was nineteen years younger than her new husband. Five weeks before marrying Rockefeller, she had divorced her husband and gave him custody of their children. The remarriage caused so much public disapproval with Rockefeller that he lost the frontrunner status among the 1964 Republican presidential hopefuls.

He won four gubernatorial elections in New York, but at the same time he lost three attempts for the presidency. On December 11, 1973, more than a year before his fourth term expired, Rockefeller resigned as governor in order to head the National Committee on Critical Choices for Americans and the Commission on Water Quality. He denied that he had resigned in order to plan a fourth presidential attempt. On August 20, 1974, President Gerald Ford nominated him to fill the office of vice president that was left vacant after Ford became president.

After his two years as vice president, Rockefeller went back to his interest in art. In 1930, he had become a trustee of the Metropolitan Museum of Art; in 1939, he had served as president of the Museum of Modern Art; he founded the Museum of Primitive Art in 1957; and he assembled extensive collections of modern paintings, sculpture, and all types of primitive art. In 1978, he compiled Masterpieces of Primitive Art, a book about his personal collection. He was contracted to do four more books before he died on January 27, 1979.

refused to register for the draft during the unpopular Vietnam War, while thousands of others were being sent into the fight.

Ford selected former New York governor Nelson Rockefeller as his vice president and kept Nixon's cabinet in place. But during his 865-day term, he eventually replaced several officials who had been appointed in the Nixon era. He fired Secretary of Defense James Schlesinger and Central Intelligence Agency (CIA) chief William Colby. Schlesinger was replaced by Donald H. Rumsfeld, the youngest defense secretary in history, and Colby was replaced by future president George H. W. Bush. The shake-up came to be known as the Sunday Morning Massacre.

Ford was not particularly comfortable as a public speaker, but he communicated sincerity in spite of his hesitant delivery. Lyndon B. Johnson, president from 1963 to 1969, had once joked that perhaps Ford had played football too long without a helmet. The press picked up on the comment and began homing

in on Ford's mishaps. He was caricatured in political cartoons as unlucky, sometimes with a bandage on his forehead. One network newscast replayed footage of him stumbling down airplane steps—eleven times in a single broadcast. Ford was angered by the negative press, but he reacted graciously. Unlike Nixon, he granted the White House correspondents a great deal of access. He held monthly press conferences, and gave many one-on-one interviews.

Ford was one of the most athletic, physically fit presidents. The former college football star enjoyed swimming and skiing; he spent much of his vacation time at a residence in Vail, Colorado, which came to be known as the Winter White House. He narrowly avoided two

Left: Before he became president, Ford bought a condominium at Vail, the Colorado ski resort, which served as his winter White House.

assassination attempts in California in the fall of 1975—one by Lynette "Squeaky" Fromme in Sacramento, and the other by Sara Jane Moore in San Francisco.

Domestic Woes

The Ford years were plagued by economic troubles. Inflation increased rapidly in the second half of 1974 and, combined with a jump in unemployment and a slowdown in other economic indicators, the nation's economy grew steadily worse. Ford called inflation "domestic enemy number one" in his first presidential speech before Congress.

Two months later, he announced an anti-inflation program that included a reduction in federal spending and a national volunteer organization with the task of finding ways to keep prices down. The entire program was called "Whip Inflation Now," or WIN, and Ford wore a WIN button when he detailed the program to a joint session of Congress. It was seen by media pundits as an ineffective public-relations stunt, and Ford was once again ridiculed in the press. To his credit, however, he held his ground with Congress to hold back government spending, and he vetoed more than three dozen appropriations bills.

Below: After shots were fired at President Ford outside the St. Francis Hotel in San Francisco, Secret Service agents whisked him to the airport where his plane was waiting to take him back to Washington.

Below: After two assassination attempts, Ford's Secret Service detail became more alert than the job usually required.

In foreign affairs, Ford presided over the official end of the Vietnam War and the end of a divisive era. Some of his decisions angered his secretary of state, Henry Kissinger, who had guided American foreign policy since 1969. American ground troops had officially withdrawn from Vietnam after a 1973 cease-fire, but as a result both South Vietnam and Cambodia fell to communists within two years. When North Vietnamese communist forces closed in on Saigon, the capital of South Vietnam, Ford gave the order to begin evacuating of all American personnel. A massive effort, involving helicopters taking off day and night from the roof of the American embassy, helped fourteen hundred Americans and fifty-six hundred Vietnamese get away safely.

Ford also approved several million dollars in aid for a war in Angola, a former Portuguese colony in Africa where Cuban communist guerrillas were fighting against local and South African forces. The guerrillas were attempting to establish a Marxist government, and both China and the Soviet Union were providing generous help to opposing factions in what had turned out to be an unmanageable civil war.

Would-be Assassin

Ford sent a proposal to Congress for strong handgun legislation, and then went on a speaking tour to drum up support for other crime legislation in September 1975. As he was leaving a Sacramento hotel, a woman in a red dress approached him with her hand extended, and the president, assuming that she wanted to shake his hand, reached out to her. However, she had a gun in her hand and most assuredly no warm thoughts in her head. The would-be assassin was Lynette Alice "Squeaky" Fromme, a follower of the infamous Charles Manson, and it was assumed this was just an isolated incident. Two weeks later, on another California trip, shots rang out from across the street as he was leaving his hotel, and bullets missed him only by a few feet. The perpetrator this time was a radical named Sara Jane Moore. The president refused to change his public schedule, saying that, "I think it's important that we as a people don't capitulate to the wrong element." Both women were sentenced to life imprisonment, the sentence mandated by a 1965 law making a federal crime to attempt to assassinate a president.

Left: Lynette "Squeaky" Fromme had to be carried in and out of the courtroom during her trial on assassination charges, and requested that President Ford should appear as a defense witness. Her request was denied.

Right: Operation Freedom Wind was the biggest helicopter evacuation in history. Marine choppers logged 1,054 flight hours and 682 sorties to carry evacuees from the U.S. Embassy in Saigon to aircraft carriers in the South China Sea.

The Ford era included an overhaul of foreign intelligence operations within the CIA. Some of its agents had been contacted by Nixon administration officials to help cover up Watergate; and an internal investigation led by Vice President Rockefeller revealed other abuses of power, including illegal activities against foreign government officials. The CIA had been created in 1947 with a charter that gave it authority to conduct foreign espionage, but its involvement with Watergate and disclosures that the agency had been conducting domestic spying activities against American anti–Vietnam War protesters revealed that it had overstepped its mandate. Furthermore, the agency had been involved in unsuccessful assassination attempts of foreign leaders, including Cuba's Fidel Castro, during prior administrations.

Early in 1976, Ford issued the first executive order concerning intelligence services. It stated that the agency's goals should originate inside the president's National Security Council, and it also established several boards and committees to keep an eye on the CIA, restricted some forms of surveillance, and, for the record, restated that involvement in political assassination attempts on foreign leaders was prohibited.

Elsewhere in his foreign-policy strategy, Ford approved aid to both Israel and Egypt. The somewhat controversial measure helped convince leaders of the warring nations to agree to interim peace proposals that eventually led to the historic 1978 Camp David Agreement. The Ford administration also negotiated an arms-reduction agreement with the Soviet Union. President Ford authorized a dramatic and successful military response to the seizing of an American merchant ship, the *Mayaguez*, by Cambodian Khmer Rouge forces in the Gulf of Siam in May 1975.

Right: An attack on the merchant ship Mayaguez *by Cambodian rebels prompted Ford to retaliate with force.*

"Drop Dead"

The New York Daily News, *which has had more than its share of memorable front-page headlines, outdid itself in 1975 with one that read: "Ford to City: Drop Dead." The city, which was on the verge of bankruptcy, had appealed to Washington for help, but the Ford administration turned down the request. But Ford never said, "Drop dead." What he told the mayor and his minions was that New York needed to clean up its own act and help itself. They took his advice, and after the wheels were in motion, the president authorized $2.3 billion in short-term loans to keep New York City from going into default.*

Bid for a Full Term

The 1976 presidential campaign was well underway when the nation celebrated the two hundredth anniversary of the signing of the Declaration of Independence with a massive outpouring of national sentiment known as the Bicentennial Celebration, which peaked on July 4. Americans hoped it signaled an end to an era marred by a disastrous war, economic and energy woes, an unprecedented presidential scandal, and political assassinations.

Ford was opposed for the Republican presidential nomination by former California governor Ronald Reagan, representing the party's conservative wing. Reagan found strong support for his criticism of Ford's moderate politics and positioned himself as the genuine inheritor to Republican conservatism, as well as an outsider who would clean up Washington.

Reagan came close to taking the nomination from Ford at the national convention in August 1976, partly because of a split in the Republican Party over Nelson Rockefeller. Ford was urged to drop his vice president from the ticket, and when he did—in favor

Right: American's biggest birthday party on July 4, 1976, came to a glorious end with a massive show of fireworks and laser beams.

Below: President Ford met Soviet Communist Party Chief Leonid Brezhnev at Vladivostok in 1974.

Birthday Party

"Never in my wildest dreams had I imagined that I would be President of the United States on its 200th birthday," wrote Jerry Ford. And on the Fourth of July in 1976, he was a kid again, celebrating what had always been his favorite holiday. The celebration that year lasted for five days, and President Ford was at its center all the way. He was in New York on the glorious day itself and reviewed the parade of tall ships that thirty countries had sent to say "Happy Birthday, America." Of the hundreds of thousands of people who gathered in the shadow of the Statue of Liberty that day, perhaps not one of them was happier than Gerald R. Ford.

of Kansas senator Bob Dole—it was widely seen as an act of disloyalty. Meanwhile, the Democrats nominated plain-speaking Georgia governor Jimmy Carter, who campaigned with the promise, "I will never lie to you." Ford lost ground in a televised debate on foreign policy when he mistakenly downplayed the Soviet Union's dominance of Eastern Europe.

The 1976 election was notable for the lowest voter turnout since 1948. Ford lost to Carter by a narrow margin, and then retired from politics. He was considered for vice president by Ronald Reagan in 1980, but Reagan eventually dropped the idea, which included a plan to broaden the role of the vice president. Ford has spent his post-presidential years in good health, making many speeches and taking pride in his presidential library established in Grand Rapids, Michigan. He suffered a mild stroke during the Republican National Convention in 2000, but, typically, he emerged from the challenge with good spirits and optimism.

Legacy

In his inauguration speech in January 1977, Jimmy Carter opened with the words, "For myself and for our Nation, I want to thank my predecessor for all he has done to heal our land," and he reached over to shake Gerald Ford's hand. The thirty-eighth president has suffered from historical and political analysis that views him an interim president with little leadership ability. Yet Ford acted decisively at several critical moments, such as the *Mayaguez* incident, and he offered significant legislation that helped shape American politics during an era of change. His handling of the CIA, for instance, established far more congressional authority over the agency.

Ford's use of his deal-making abilities—a talent that had earned him respect in Washington years before he became vice president—meant that he was willing to pardon Nixon and build agreements with foreign powers like the Soviet Union. He faced considerable opposition, however, from the Democratic-controlled Congress, and he lost support among some Republicans as well for failing to apply stronger conservative values in domestic policy. The more conservative members of his Republican Party became energized and gradually asserted a more aggressive form of Republican politics, which Ronald Reagan came to represent. Reagan narrowly lost the Republican nomination for president to Ford in 1976, but he won the nomination and the presidency in 1980 and again in 1984.

Ford led the country through a transitional period where Congress gained more control over public policy and lawmaking than it had previously enjoyed. That change endured through the rest of the century, with the opposing party in Congress continually frustrating the sitting president. A certain national affection remained for the Midwestern ordinariness that Ford personified. Ford told biographer John Robert Greene that, "I want to be remembered as a . . . nice person, who worked at the job, and who left the White House in better shape than when I took over."

Betty Ford

Born April 8, 1918, Chicago, Illinois
Died July 8, 2011, Rancho Mirage, California

"Maybe if I as first lady could talk about [breast cancer] candidly and without embarrassment, many other people would be able to as well."
—*Betty Ford*

Betty Ford became one of the most admired American women of her time. After many years in Washington as the wife of a congressman, she landed rather suddenly in the public eye in 1973, when her husband, Gerald R. Ford, was appointed vice president, and she found herself in the full glare of the spotlight when they moved into the White House the following year after President Richard Nixon resigned from office.

The Fords worked hard to bring a refreshing air of normality to the White House. A former dancer and fashion model with a graceful bearing and forthright manner, Betty Ford was an immediately popular first lady known for her candidness and her sense of humor. Her battle with breast cancer and her later admission of a substance-abuse problem further endeared her to the public.

Dancer

Born Elizabeth Ann Bloomer on April 8, 1918, in Chicago, Illinois, "Betty" moved to Grand Rapids, Michigan, with her family as a very young child. Her father, William Bloomer, was a sales representative whose work took him away from home for long periods of time; as a very young girl, Betty swore that she would never marry a man whose job would make him an absent husband and father. Enrolled in a dance school by the age of eight, Betty subsequently studied many varieties of dance, and by the time she was in her teens, she was teaching dance to younger students.

When she graduated from Grand Rapids Central High School in 1936, Betty planned to move to New York City to pursue a career in dance. Her recently widowed mother objected, but they reached a compromise: Betty spent two summers at Bennington College, a progressive liberal arts school in Vermont that offered special sessions with Martha Graham, one of the most celebrated figures in modern dance. She moved to New York City in 1939, took more classes, and won a place in Graham's auxiliary concert troupe. She also worked as a model and enjoyed the fast-paced life of the city.

By her own admission, Betty didn't have either the discipline or the dedication to become a successful dancer, and after a time, she moved back to Grand Rapids, where she established her own dance troupe. In 1942, she married William G. Warren, a man she had

Right: As a young woman, Betty Ford was greatly influenced by the avant-garde dancer and choreographer Martha Graham, right, and danced in one of the master's troupes.

Right: When Ford campaigned for the presidency in 1976, it was the first time he ran for public office outside his congressional district in Michigan. His wife, Betty, and daughter, Susan, helped him get in the groove.

known for several years, but the marriage turned out to be a bad decision. "My friends were getting married, and I thought I ought to get married too," she later wrote in *The Times of My Life.* She and Warren were divorced after five years of marriage.

An Engaging Campaign

After her divorce, Betty became the fashion coordinator at a Grand Rapids department store. Through some mutual friends, she met Gerald Ford, a handsome Grand Rapids lawyer, World War II veteran, and former University of Michigan football star. They dated for just a few months before Ford proposed.

Their wedding was delayed for several months while Ford campaigned for a seat in Congress. Betty didn't know much about politics and she didn't think her fiancé had a chance of winning, but still she was energetic during his campaign. After he won the Republican nomination, the couple married on October 18, 1948, a few weeks before election day.

Ford won the election, and several more after that—making him the often-absent partner Betty had once vowed to avoid. During his two and a half decades representing Michigan's Fifth Congressional District in the House of Representatives, Betty Ford raised four children—Michael, John, Steven, and Susan, born between 1950 and 1957—at their home in Alexandria, Virginia. She was also active in a number of organizations, ranging from the Cub Scouts to the National Federation of Republican Women.

The demands of her active life eventually caught up with her; by the time her husband was elected House minority leader in 1965, she had begun to suffer from a number of physical problems. She also experienced a minor mental breakdown that led to visits with a psychotherapist. The therapy helped, but the pain medication her other doctors had prescribed did not. For the next several years, Betty Ford became increasingly dependent on a variety of tranquilizers and sedatives, whose effects were dangerously heightened by her social drinking habits.

Delayed Retirement

The Fords had planned to retire to Michigan at the end of Gerald's term in 1976, and they looked forward to enjoying a calmer life. Instead, they were suddenly pushed into the national spotlight in the fall of 1973, when Ford was appointed vice president after the resignation of Spiro T. Agnew.

Betty found that she liked the responsibilities of her new role. Much more was required of her than during her rather uneventful years as a congressional wife and suburban mother, and she rose to the challenge. Like her husband, she traveled extensively during his eight-month term, overcoming her fear of public speaking to address large crowds who were charmed by her warm, forthright style.

When President Nixon resigned and her husband was sworn in as president on August 9, 1974, Betty Ford held the Bible his hand rested on. Afterward, he said in a speech that, "I am indebted to no man and only to one woman— my dear wife." Ford and his family were instant celebrities, extremely well liked by the news media. Their family seemed very much like any other American one, with three college-age sons and a long-haired, blue jeans–wearing daughter in her final year of high school. Betty was a tremendous hit as the new first lady. "She seems to have just what it takes to make people feel at home in the world again," media observer Marshall McLuhan told the *New York Times Magazine.* "Something about her makes us feel rooted and secure—a feeling we haven't had in a while."

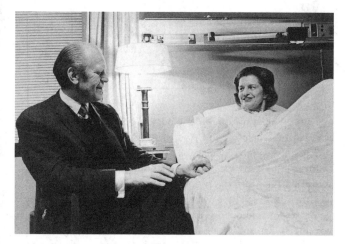

Left: Betty Ford's public bout with breast cancer raised awareness amongst American women about a condition that was traditionally kept hidden.

White House press secretary Ron Nessen dryly noted that "the President has long since ceased to be perturbed or surprised by his wife's remarks." Betty told Jane Howard in a 1974 interview for the *New York Times Magazine*, "I don't feel that because I'm First Lady I'm any different from what I was before. It can happen to anyone. After all, it has happened to *anyone*."

She conveyed a personal warmth, sincerity, and ordinariness that regularly landed her the top of "Most Admired Women" polls and other honors and tributes.

Early Advocate for Breast Cancer Awareness

Several weeks after her husband took office, Betty Ford underwent a radical mastectomy, which is the surgical removal of the breasts, after she had suddenly been diagnosed with breast cancer. News of the surgery shocked the country. Breast cancer was still somewhat of an unmentionable subject during that time. Thousands of letters of support poured in to the White House wishing the first lady well; many women recounted their own breast-cancer scares and thanked Betty for speaking so openly about her condition, and the publicity compelled many women to visit their doctors for a checkup.

After a speedy recovery, Betty was back at her White House desk and on the road with her husband within weeks of her ordeal. One of the most public presidential wives in American history, she gave an extraordinary number of interviews and was not a bit shy about publicly offering her opinion on issues of the day. She affirmed her support for the Equal Rights Amendment (ERA) to the Constitution, a proposal that would have prohibited discrimination on the basis of gender and was in the ratification process at the state level, although it was eventually defeated. The first lady also called the 1973 Supreme Court decision to legalize abortion "the best thing in the world . . . a great, great decision."

Such attitudes were quite in tune with the changing times, but for a first lady to support them was a dramatic break with the past. When reporters asked about the president's reaction to his wife's well-publicized opinions,

A Legacy of Help

Betty Ford campaigned intensely on behalf of her husband when he made his bid for the presidency in 1976. She was bitter about her husband's election loss, and after the couple officially retired to Palm Springs, California, her problems with drugs and alcohol worsened. After her family sat her down and told her how worried they were about her behavior, she checked herself into the Long Beach Naval Hospital Alcohol and Drug Rehabilitation Service for a detoxification program to free herself from dependence on addictive substances.

Once again, Betty Ford's public admission of a problem that had been considered a secretive affliction resulted in massive amounts of support mail. Inspired by many heartbreaking stories and pleas for help, Betty dedicated herself to a new, dual role, raising awareness of substance-abuse problems and improving the availability of treatment. In 1982, the Betty Ford Center, an inpatient clinic for drug and alcohol dependency was opened in association with a Palm Springs hospital. She served as its chairperson for many years and continued to be closely associated until the end of her life. Now known as the Hazelden Betty Ford Foundation, it hails their founder as "the First Lady of Recovery Advocacy."

In July 2011, Betty Ford died at the Eisenhower Medical Center in Rancho Mirage, California. She was 93 years old. In a tribute, fellow former First Lady Nancy Reagan said, "She was Jerry Ford's strength through some very difficult days in our country's history, and I admired her courage in facing and sharing her personal struggles with all of us."

Ford's Comments Regarding the Pardon of Richard Nixon

Delivered September 8, 1974

President Gerald R. Ford was in office for slightly less than a month when he granted a pardon to former president Richard Nixon. The pardon protected Nixon against prosecution for any crimes he committed during his presidency. Ford intended the gesture to help the nation move ahead following the Watergate scandal that had led to the first resignation by a president in office in the nation's history.

After taking the oath of office a month earlier, Ford proclaimed that "our national nightmare is over" and "the Constitution worked," meaning that a peaceful transfer of power from one president to another had taken place. The pardon a month later was welcomed by many as an end to the scandal—a view shared as well by many historians.

At the time, however, the pardon was extremely controversial. Some believed that a corrupt bargain had been struck between Nixon and Ford—that Ford had been nominated as vice president by Nixon in exchange for future protection. Others believed that the pardon indicated that some Americans are above the law; they argued that the former president Nixon should face the same form of justice that any other American would encounter.

Ladies and gentlemen: I have come to a decision which I felt I should tell you and all of my fellow American citizens, as soon as I was certain in my own mind and in my own conscience that it is the right thing to do. I have learned already in this office that the difficult decisions always come to this desk. I must admit that many of them do not look at all the same as the hypothetical questions that I have answered freely and perhaps too fast on previous occasions. My customary policy is to try and get all the facts and to consider the opinions of my countrymen and to take counsel with my most valued friends. But these seldom agree, and in the end, the decision is mine.

To procrastinate, to agonize, and to wait for a more favorable turn of events that may never come or more compelling external pressures that may as well be wrong as right, is itself a decision of sorts and a weak and potentially dangerous course for a President to follow.

I have promised to uphold the Constitution, to do what is right as God gives me to see the right, and to do the very best that I can for America. I have asked your help and your prayers, not only when I became President but many times since. The Constitution is the supreme law of our land and it governs our actions as citizens. Only the laws of God, which govern our consciences, are superior to it.

As we are a nation under God, so I am sworn to uphold our laws with the help of God. And I have sought such guidance and searched my own conscience with special diligence to determine the right thing for me to do with respect to my predecessor in this place, Richard Nixon, and his loyal wife and family. Theirs is an American tragedy in which we all have played a part. It could go on and on and on, or someone must write the end to it. I have concluded that only I can do that, and if I can, I must.

There are no historic or legal precedents to which I can turn in this matter, none that precisely fit the circumstances of a private citizen who has resigned the Presidency of the United States. But it is common knowledge that serious allegations and accusations hang like a sword over our former President's head, threatening his health as he tries to reshape his life, a great part of which was spent in the service of this country and by the mandate of its people. After years of bitter controversy and divisive national debate, I have been advised, and I am compelled to conclude that many months and perhaps more years will have to pass before Richard Nixon could obtain a fair trial by jury in any jurisdiction of the United States under governing decisions of the Supreme Court.

I deeply believe in equal justice for all Americans, whatever their station or former station. The law, whether human or divine, is no respecter of persons; but the law is a respecter of reality. The facts, as I see them, are that a former President of the United States, instead of enjoying equal treatment with any other citizen accused of violating the law, would be cruelly and excessively penalized either in preserving the presumption of his innocence or in obtaining a speedy determination of his guilt in order to repay a legal debt to society.

During this long period of delay and potential litigation, ugly passions would again be aroused. And our people would again be polarized in their opinions. And the credibility of our free institutions of government would again be challenged at home and abroad. In the end, the courts might well hold that Richard Nixon had been denied due process, and the verdict of history would even more be inconclusive with respect to those charges arising out of the period of his Presidency, of which I am presently aware.

But it is not the ultimate fate of Richard Nixon that most concerns me, though surely it deeply troubles every decent and every compassionate person. My concern is the immediate future of this great country. In this, I dare not depend upon my personal sympathy as a long-time friend of the former President, nor my professional judgment as a lawyer, and I do not.

As President, my primary concern must always be the greatest good of all the people of the United States whose servant I am. As a man, my first consideration is to be true to my own convictions and my own conscience.

My conscience tells me clearly and certainly that I cannot prolong the bad dreams that continue to reopen a chapter that is closed. My conscience tells me that only I, as President, have the constitutional power to firmly shut and seal this book. My conscience tells me it is my duty, not merely to proclaim domestic tranquility but to use every means that I have to insure it.

I do believe that the buck stops here, that I cannot rely upon public opinion polls to tell me what is right.

I do believe that right makes might and that if I am wrong, ten angels swearing I was right would make no difference.

I do believe, with all my heart and mind and spirit, that I, not as President but as a humble servant of God, will receive justice without mercy if I fail to show mercy.

Finally, I feel that Richard Nixon and his loved ones have suffered enough and will continue to suffer, no matter what I do, no matter what we, as a great and good nation, can do together to make his goal of peace come true.

[At this point, Ford began reading from the proclamation granting the pardon.] "Now, therefore, I, Gerald R. Ford, President of the United States, pursuant to the pardon power conferred upon me by Article II, Section 2, of the Constitution, have granted and by these presents do grant a full, free, and absolute pardon unto Richard Nixon for all offenses against the United States which he, Richard Nixon, has committed or may have committed or taken part in during the period from [January] 20, 1969 through August 9, 1974."

[President Ford signed the proclamation and then resumed reading.] "In witness whereof, I have hereunto set my hand this eighth day of September, in the year of our Lord nineteen hundred and seventy-four, and of the Independence of the United States of America the one hundred and ninety-ninth."

What Happened Next

Although many people welcomed the pardon as an act that could help the nation address other problems that had been overwhelmed by attention to Watergate, Ford's action drew a fierce public backlash. The response affected Ford's ability to carry out his administration's agenda. He had to appear before the House Committee on the Judiciary to explain that there were no deals connected with the pardon. Meanwhile, politicians increasingly found themselves having to promise not to lie to or mislead the public. The outcry gradually died down, but Americans' faith and confidence in their political leaders suffered.

A long legal battle over the public release of tapes of Nixon's White House conversations continued into the 1990s. Had the pardon not been issued, the case against former president Nixon would have been at least as time-consuming and complicated. The tapes, meanwhile, confirmed that public opinion against Nixon had been correct. There was no question that he had been personally involved in the Watergate scandal.

Jimmy Carter

"Our American values are not luxuries, but necessities—not the salt in our bread, but the bread itself."

—*Jimmy Carter*

Thirty-ninth president of the United States, 1977–1981

Full name: *James Earl Carter Jr.*
Born: *October 1, 1924, Plains, Georgia*
Parents: *James Earl and Lillian Gordy Carter*
Spouse: *Eleanor Rosalynn Smith (1928– ; m. 1946)*
Children: *John William (Jack) (1947–); James Earl (Chip) III (1950–); Donnel Jeffrey (1952–); Amy Lynn (1967–)*
Religion: *Southern Baptist*
Education: *U.S. Naval Academy (B.S., 1947)*
Occupations: *Farmer; warehouseman; navy lieutenant*
Government positions: *Georgia state senator and governor*
Political party: *Democratic*
Dates as president: *January 20, 1977–January 20, 1981*
Age upon taking office: *52*

When Jimmy Carter was elected the thirty-ninth president in 1976, public faith in elected officials was practically nonexistent. The long Vietnam War and the Watergate scandal that resulted in President Richard Nixon's resignation had left many Americans suspicious of their leaders. Inflation and fuel prices were on the rise; American industries faced increasingly stronger international competition and seemed to be responding too slowly. Also the expensive Cold War military buildup and the constant threat of real war between the United States and the Soviet Union was raging. Many people had come to distrust "Washington insiders," and Carter, a soft-spoken peanut farmer and former state legislator from Georgia, offered voters a refreshing alternative to the federal power brokers in the capital.

"Finally we have a president without an accent."
—*attributed to Loretta Lynn, commenting on the election of Jimmy Carter*

Over a remarkable two-year period beginning in 1974, Carter emerged from a political virtual unknown to become a candidate for president. He campaigned as an outsider, vowing to make the government "competent and compassionate" again. As it turned out, however, he wasn't able to stimulate the sagging economy, and his foreign policy successes—most notably in the Middle East, China, and Panama—were offset by the Soviet Union's invasion of Afghanistan and troubles with Iran. A revolution there in 1977 against a leader who was supported by the United States brought out anti-American sentiments that culminated with fifty-two Americans held hostage for 444 days, from November 1979 until January 1981.

Although compassionate and principled, Carter wasn't able to win the people's confidence, and he served only one term as president. The very quality that voters found appealing in Carter—his outsider status in Washington—weighed heavily against him when he tried to push his agenda through Congress. Both the Senate and the House had Democratic majorities during his administration, but he still found himself fighting for most of his legislation, and he was forced to accept compromises that weakened his policies. By the third year of his presidency, Carter had some of the lowest approval ratings of any twentieth-century president.

Carter became much more popular and more widely respected after he left the White House. He embarked on a career as an international human-rights mediator; a founder of and spokesman for Habitat for Humanity, an organization that helps build homes for poor families; and a founder of the Atlanta-based Carter Center, which brings attention to international problems. He was among the most active ex-presidents.

Boyhood on a Farm

James Earl Carter Jr. was born on October 1, 1924, in Plains, Georgia. His father, James Earl, was a farmer and the proprietor of a small store in Archery, three miles west of Plains. His mother, known as "Miss Lillian," was a registered nurse. Jimmy grew up with plenty to do on his father's farm. He "mopped" the family's cotton crop with a mixture of poisonous arsenic, molasses, and water to drive off boll weevils, and he helped pick the cotton when

Timeline

1924: Born in Georgia

1946: Graduates from U.S. Naval Academy

1953: Leaves the navy nuclear-powered submarine program to take over the family peanut farm

1963–67: Serves as Georgia state senator

1971–75: Serves as Georgia governor

1977–81: Serves as thirty-ninth U.S. president

1979: Iran takes fifty-two American embassy officials hostage; Soviet Union invades Afghanistan (United States responds by boycotting 1980 Olympics in Moscow)

1980: Loses presidential election to Ronald Reagan

1982: Founds the Carter Center, a nonprofit organization that promotes human rights, improved public health, and advances in agriculture

it ripened. He picked peanuts, too, boiling them and then selling bags of them in Plains and earning himself about a dollar a day, a money-making venture that earned him the nickname "Hot," short for "Hotshot." It was an apt nickname. When he was a teenager, Jimmy expanded his little business and saved enough to buy four rental houses, which he eventually sold to buy an engagement ring for Rosalynn Smith.

Right: Billy Carter, who ran a gas station and meeting spot in Plains, Georgia, sometimes embarrassed his brother the president, especially when he signed on as a lobbyist for the Libyan government.

Eventually, the Carter family would include two daughters, Gloria and Ruth, and another son, Billy, who was thirteen years younger than Jimmy. Their mother encouraged all of them to do their best in school and to prepare themselves for college. At his segregated public school, Jimmy was singled out by a teacher, Julia Coleman, who encouraged him to take on tough assignments. He was equally captivated by an uncle, Tom Gordy, who was in the navy. To a young boy who was getting out of bed before dawn to handle tiring farm chores, navy life—with travel to exotic ports—seemed like a perfect career choice. Not surprisingly, Jimmy set his sights on the U.S. Naval Academy at a very early age, writing to Annapolis for information while he was still in elementary school.

When it became clear that he would be the valedictorian of his high school class, Jimmy wrote to his congressman for the required recommendation to get into the Academy. He was accepted, but he didn't go to Annapolis right out of high school. Worried that he wasn't prepared academically for the rigorous science and mathematics there, he attended Southwestern Junior College for a year and Georgia Tech University for another, sharpening his skills in math and physics. He entered the U.S. Naval Academy in 1943.

Submarine Specialist

The extra preparation in science paid off quite well for Carter. He was an outstanding student at Annapolis, graduating in the top 10 percent of his class. One month later, he married Rosalynn Smith—another Plains native—and the newlyweds moved to Norfolk, Virginia, where he became a systems tester on two experimental gunnery ships, the *Wyoming* and the *Mississippi*.

Carter loved to be challenged. Shortly after his first son was born, in July 1947, he decided to transfer into the navy's submarine branch. More schooling followed, and after he finished his studies in December 1948, he was assigned to the U.S.S. *Pomfret*, based in Pearl Harbor, Hawaii. He hadn't been on the ship very long when it encountered bad weather while he was standing watch on the bridge, and he was swept overboard. As he struggled against the storm surge, another wave tossed

First Mother

In 1966, when her son, Jimmy, was serving in the Georgia state senate, his mother, known as "Miss Lillian," joined the Peace Corps at the age of sixty-eight. After a crash course in languages at the University of Chicago, she spent the next two years in India teaching birth-control methods. She was back in time to be an honored guest at her son's presidential inaugural.

him onto the submarine and he was able to crawl along a gun barrel and back onto the deck, narrowly escaping drowning.

When the Korean War began, Carter was reassigned to the experimental submarine U.S.S. *K-1*, which was still under construction. First in San Diego, California,

Below: Two years after his graduation from the Naval Academy, Jimmy Carter was a Lieutenant Commander aboard a nuclear submarine.

Above: Lieutenant Jimmy Carter keeps track of instrument readings aboard the experimental submarine U.S.S. K-1 in 1952.

and then in New London, Connecticut, he supervised engineering of quiet diving-and-surfacing mechanisms and techniques, and he was aboard the *K-1* when she made her maiden voyage.

Then another challenge presented itself. The navy was beginning to build nuclear-powered submarines under the supervision of Admiral Hyman Rickover, and Carter applied to him to be part of the program. Assigned to the new atomic submarine U.S.S. *Seawolf* as a senior officer, he spent long days helping to design the ship and train its crew. In the meantime, he continued his own graduate studies in nuclear physics at New York's Union College. The young lieutenant seemed destined for the highest ranks in the U.S. Navy.

Businessman

When Jimmy and Rosalynn went back to Plains, they not only ran the family farms, but sold seed and fertilizer to other farmers and bought their crops—mostly peanuts. It was a business that depended on the weather, and after a major drought during their first year back home, they netted just $200 for a whole year of backbreaking fifteen-hour days. But the following year more than made up for it and before long, the Carter holdings expanded to some 3,000 acres of farm and timberland with an annual gross income of more than $2.5 million.

A Return to Plains

When Carter's father died of cancer in 1953, Jimmy made a decision that shocked not only his superiors in the navy but his wife as well: He chose to move back to Plains and take over the family business. He felt that he wouldn't be able to spend enough time with Rosalynn and their three sons if he stayed in the navy, and he was also concerned about his mother's well-being. Although the idea of entering politics didn't factor into his decision at first, it eventually became another important reason for returning to his roots.

When they got back to Plains, Jimmy and Rosalynn discovered that the peanut warehouse and other family interests were in deep financial trouble. By combining hard work with more scientific farming methods, they were able to reverse the losses and make the farm and warehouse profitable again. Jimmy also followed his father's example of civic service: He was elected to the county board of education and served as president of the Georgia Planning Association. A move into state politics was the next logical step, and in 1962, he ran for a seat in the Georgia state senate.

He narrowly lost the primary election, but he was able to prove that his opponent was guilty of voter fraud, and the election was overturned. There was a great deal of ill will toward him after that, and the Carter family even

Right: Carter shovels peanuts in a warehouse at the family farm in Plains, Georgia.

Above: Carter attracted national attention during his years as governor of Georgia.

received death threats, but Jimmy Carter won the general election with an impressive majority and went on to reelection two years later. He took the job very seriously, reading every word of every one of the hundreds of bills that he was required to vote for or against, and he was particularly dedicated to improving public education in Georgia.

By 1966, Carter had decided to run for governor, even though he still wasn't well known, and finished third against well-established Democratic opponents, including the winner, Lester Maddox. The Carter family had traveled tirelessly throughout the state during the campaign, and losing left him disappointed and depressed. He found peace and hope after he moved back to Plains, and became deeply immersed in his religious faith. After that, Carter always referred to himself as a "born-again" Christian, and his deep respect for Christian principles became an important part of his life.

He ran again for Georgia governor in 1970, and this time, he won. His opponent was a moderate and although Carter was a moderate himself, he ran a conservative campaign, even to the point of inviting George Wallace, the archconservative governor of Alabama, to campaign for him. However, once he was in the governor's

mansion, Carter became what was called a "New South" leader, calling for an end to racial segregation. He made it clear that he supported the civil-rights movement, and expressed hope that race relations would improve not only in Georgia but all over the South.

After his single term as Georgia's governor, Carter decided to run in the 1976 election for president. He had already made a name for himself among the leaders of the national Democratic party, but he was still relatively unknown among voters outside Georgia. He appeared on the television program *What's My Line?* in 1974, after he had already announced his availability for the presidential nomination, and almost stumped the panel trying to guess who he was. He corrected that by meeting people in streets, diners, and town meetings, with the greeting, "Hello, I'm Jimmy Carter, and I'm going to be your next president." Often wearing blue jeans and work shirts, and staying in private homes rather than in hotels when he traveled, he projected a refreshingly populist image and, one at a time, potential voters came to know him and to like him.

Below: Jimmy, Rosalynn, and Amy took time out from campaigning to check out the White House, just like any other house-hunters.

Jimmy and Rosalynn campaigned vigorously together for the Democratic nomination. He emphasized the need to bring a more people-oriented, more virtuous government back to Washington. He was still a virtual unknown, and he couldn't match the financial resources of some of the better-known candidates, but during a time of political scandal, he wasn't tainted by accusations of corruption, nor had he ever held a previous position in the national government. That "outsider" status turned out to be his secret weapon in the campaign.

By promising a new style of government, Carter emerged on top in a large field of Democratic hopefuls, and he scored a narrow victory in the 1976 general election over his Republican opponent, incumbent president Gerald R. Ford. The negative fallout from Ford's pardon of former President Richard Nixon following the Watergate scandal contributed in no small part to the Carter victory.

Above: Carter's presidential campaign was based on his status as an "outsider," and he projected an image of sincerity and honesty.

1976 Election Results

Presidential / Vice Presidential Candidates	Popular Votes	Electoral Votes
Jimmy Carter / Walter Mondale (Democratic)	40,977,147	297
Gerald R. Ford / Robert Dole (Republican)	39,422,671	240

Incumbent president Ford narrowly defeated former California governor Ronald Reagan on the first ballot, 1,187 to 1,070. An interesting footnote in the election occurred when two former Georgia governors were on the national ballot: Jimmy Carter, as the Democratic nominee, and Lester G. Maddox, as the obscure American Independent Party nominee. Maddox had also served as Carter's lieutenant governor.

Right: Jimmy and Rosalynn Carter and daughter, Amy, walked from his inauguration at the Capitol back to the White House rather than riding, which had become a presidential tradition.

Challenges of the Presidency

At his inauguration on January 20, 1977, Carter made a symbolic point by walking to the Capitol with his wife and family to deliver his inaugural address. The message was clear: Jimmy Carter intended to restore confidence in government by proving himself to be one of the people, an ordinary Christian farmer who just happened to be running the nation.

Carter was both intelligent and ambitious. Realizing that his experience in national affairs was limited, he filled his cabinet with competent political veterans, prominent businesspeople, and academics, and he relied on his vice president, Walter Mondale, who had a long and distinguished record as a U.S. senator from Minnesota. African American voters had supported Carter overwhelmingly, and he recognized their confidence in him by recruiting two African American women for his cabinet and by naming Andrew Young as ambassador to the United Nations.

Carter's initial "honeymoon" period as president turned out to be very brief. His appointee to head the Office of Management and Budget, Georgia banker Bert Lance, came under close observation for his former banking practices, which seemed less than honest to many. Seizing on the Lance issue as proof that Carter was no different from his presidential predecessors, journalists and politicians demanded that he fire Lance, but Carter stood by his friend until Lance himself resigned in the early autumn of 1977. He was later acquitted of all the charges that had been filed against him, but the Lance affair—as well as continuing troubles with inflation and high gas and oil prices—cut deeply into Carter's approval rating within a matter of just a few months.

He also lost effectiveness by not making strong allies in Congress, believing that he could rally people and through them inspire Congress to action. When he made an impressive nationally televised speech on the need for an energy policy to counter high costs and dwindling supplies, legislation wasn't forthcoming from Congress, and the eventual energy policy that emerged was only modestly successful.

The Carter Administration

Administration Dates:	January 20, 1977–January 20, 1981
Vice President:	Walter F. Mondale (1977–81)
Cabinet:	
Secretary of State	Cyrus R. Vance (1977–80)
	Edmund S. Muskie (1980–81)
Secretary of the Treasury	W. Michael Blumenthal (1977–79)
	G. William Miller (1979–81)
Attorney General	Griffin B. Bell (1977–79)
	Benjamin R. Civiletti (1979–81)
Secretary of the Interior	Cecil D. Andrus (1977–81)
Secretary of Agriculture	Robert S. Bergland (1977–81)
Secretary of Labor	F. Ray Marshall (1977–81)
Secretary of Commerce	Juanita M. Kreps (1977–79)
	Philip M. Klutznick (1980–81)
Secretary of Defense	Harold Brown (1977–81)
Secretary of Health, Education and Welfare	Joseph A. Califano Jr. (1977–79)
	Patricia R. Harris (1979–80)
Secretary of Housing and Urban Development	Patricia R. Harris (1977–79)
	Maurice E. "Moon" Landrieu (1979–81)
Secretary of Transportation	Brockman "Brock" Adams (1977–79)
	Neil E. Goldschmidt (1979–81)
Secretary of Energy	James R. Schlesinger (1977–79)
	Charles W. Duncan Jr. (1979–81)
Secretary of Health and Human Services	Patricia R. Harris (1980–81)
Secretary of Education	Shirley M. Hufstedler (1979–81)

Right: Bert Lance, the head of the Office of Management and Budget, helped to tarnish Carter's image as an honest outsider when Lance's dealings as a former banker were called into question.

Camp David Principals: Anwar Sadat and Menachem Begin

When Jimmy Carter invited Egyptian president Anwar el-Sadat and Israel's Prime Minister Menachem Begin to try to settle their differences on the neutral ground of Camp David, the presidential retreat in Maryland, he predicted that they would be secluded there for "one week at the most." For his part, Sadat said he thought that the talks would break down "after a few days," and Begin told the world that he was free to walk away at any time. The meetings lasted for thirteen days, and they all left together. They announced an agreement on September 17, 1978, and the two Middle East leaders signed the Camp David Accords the following March 26.

Anwar el-Sadat was born on December 25, 1918, in a village near Cairo. He graduated from a military academy in 1938 and was stationed in Upper Egypt. He was jailed twice for contacts with Germans in World War II and was later tried and acquitted on charges of conspiring to assassinate a pro-British politician in 1946.

Sadat took part in the takeover of the Egyptian government in 1952 after Gamal Abdel Nasser overthrew Egypt's King Faruk, and after holding several government posts, Sadat served as vice president from 1964 to 1966 and again from 1969 to 1970, and he was elected president in 1970 after Nasser died. In a show of strength, he looked for revenge for Egypt's humiliating defeat by Israel in the Six-Day War of 1967 by launching the so-called Yom Kippur War, timed to begin during the Jewish high holy days. Egyptian forces advanced toward the heart of Israel, but a cease-fire agreement was negotiated before full-scale battles could begin.

Menachem Begin was born on August 16, 1913, in Brest Litovsk, Poland (now Belarus), and studied law at the University of Warsaw. He was active in Zionism, an international movement that began late in the nineteenth century to create a Jewish community in Palestine. When the Nazis invaded Poland in 1939, he fled to Lithuania, where he was arrested the following year by Soviet authorities for Zionist activity and sentenced to eight years of hard labor. He was held in Siberia in 1940 and 1941.

Begin arrived in Palestine in 1942 when Polish army units joined Allied forces in the Middle East and North Africa, and he soon became commander of a terrorist guerrilla group trying to drive the British occupiers from the Holy Land. After Israel became independent, Begin founded the Herut (Freedom) Party and represented it in Israel's parliament beginning in 1949. He served as the party's leader for more than thirty years, and he became Israel's prime minister in 1977.

Begin was the first Israeli prime minister to meet officially and publicly with an Arab head of state when he welcomed Egyptian president Sadat to Jerusalem in November 1977, and Sadat's surprise visit to Israel was the first for an Arab leader. President Carter brought the two together at Camp David, Maryland, in September 1978. They signed two agreements: One called for an Israeli-Egyptian peace treaty within three months, and the other began a five-year transition toward self-government for Palestinians, the Arabs who had been displaced when the nation of Israel was established. Begin and Sadat shared the Nobel Peace Prize for 1978, and they signed the final treaty in March 1979. The Palestinian part of the agreement, however, was still in negotiation stages more than twenty years later.

The Camp David Accords were rejected by other Arab nations, along with Sadat's program for modernizing Egypt, the president lost support within his own country. Sadat's economic policies created a new class of entrepreneurs who made quick fortunes, and his "open-door" policy encouraged foreign business, especially from Egypt's oil-rich neighboring Arab countries, but there was little investment in productive industries. Riots broke out in January 1977 when the government cut food subsidies for the average Egyptian.

During Sadat's last years, many Islamic religious groups began speaking out against the Westernization and corruption in Egypt, and especially the treaty with Israel. Violence between Christians and Muslims broke out, and in September 1981, Sadat struck back by arresting hundreds of politicians, banning journals, and expelling the Soviet ambassador. On October 6, Muslim religious radicals shot him to death as he reviewed a military parade. The shocked West paid tribute to Sadat, and three former U.S. presidents (Nixon, Ford, and Carter), as well as Israeli prime minister Begin, went to Cairo for his funeral. Egyptians and Arabs reacted differently. The streets of Cairo, which millions of mourners had jammed when Nasser died, remained eerily silent. Sudan's president was the only Arab head of state to attend the funeral.

After the Camp David Accords, Begin won a new term in office, and in 1982 he authorized an Israeli invasion of southern Lebanon. However, the following September, Begin suddenly resigned as prime minister, apparently believing that he could no longer perform his duties satisfactorily. He seemed to have been severely affected by the death of his wife the previous year and by the continuing casualties suffered by Israelis in Lebanon. Begin spent most of his remaining years in seclusion before he died in 1992.

Foreign Policy Successes

Carter had strong beliefs about human rights, and he wasn't afraid to criticize foreign governments that violated the rights of their citizens, although he didn't press the issue when his criticisms led to tension in foreign policy. However, several important events occurred during his administration that have had a lasting impact on world history. In spite of stiff opposition from Congress, Carter pushed for ratification of a treaty that would turn the Panama Canal over to the Panamanian government on December 31, 1999, and it was subsequently implemented without incident. Carter's administration also formally recognized the People's Republic as the sole government of China, which led to the establishment of normal diplomatic relations with Communist China.

The president's successful attempt to bring peace to the warring nations of Israel and Egypt was the single most important achievement of his administration. After meeting separately with Israeli prime minister Menachem Begin and Egyptian president Anwar el-Sadat, Carter invited both men to the presidential retreat at Camp David, Maryland, and urged them to negotiate a treaty. Very significant issues divided the two governments, but over a period of thirteen days in September 1978, Carter was able to help them bridge differences, and a peace treaty (the Camp David Accords) was drafted and signed in Washington on March 26, 1979.

Above: Egyptian president Anwar Sadat, President Jimmy Carter, and Israeli prime minister Menachim Begin at Camp David.

Deeply concerned about the destructive potential of nuclear weapons, Carter attempted to negotiate a strategic arms limitation treaty (SALT-II) with the Soviet Union. Months of talks between U.S. and Soviet diplomats produced a treaty, but some members of Congress felt that it threatened American defense. When the Soviet Union invaded Afghanistan in December 1979, all talk of ratifying the treaty was put aside, and the following year, Carter withdrew American participation in the Summer Olympics being held in Moscow.

Troubles at Home and Abroad

In spite of his efforts to stimulate the economy, Carter wasn't able to hold back the twin tides of domestic inflation and unemployment. In fact, by the end of his term, high interest rates were severely depressing the home-mortgage market and discouraging economic expansion. A severe energy crisis attributed to an increase in prices by the oil-producing nations of the Middle East created high costs—as well as shortages—of gasoline and fuel oil, and images of long lines of cars outside gas stations became frustratingly commonplace. Carter campaigned hard for conservation of fuel and use of alternative energy sources, including nuclear power plants, calling America's

Below: Tensions in the Middle East grew in 1977, when Israeli troops staged clandestine raids across the Lebanese border.

Left: A severe energy crisis in 1974 had Americans forming long lines at gas stations, which were sometimes found dry. Many citizens blamed the Carter administration directly for making joyriding impossible.

Right: An accident at the Three-Mile Island nuclear power plant in Pennsylvania all but eliminated the hope that atomic power might help solve the energy crisis.

need to conserve energy and to find alternative sources "the moral equivalent of war."

His administration created the Department of Energy, but Carter's attempts to encourage the use of alternate sources of fuel were dealt blows, first by a coal miners' strike and then by a reactor accident at the Three Mile Island nuclear power plant near Harrisburg, Pennsylvania. Conservation proved to be unpopular with voters who needed their cars to commute to work, as well as to heat their homes with oil or natural gas.

The final blow to the Carter administration came on November 4, 1979. An Islamic revolution had occurred in oil-rich Iran, and the American-supported shah, Mohammad Reza Pahlavi, was forced to leave the country. Gravely ill with cancer, he was admitted to a New York hospital for treatment and, as far as the Iranians were concerned, his presence in America suggested that he would use the United States as a base to reclaim his throne, with American backing. Shortly after the shah was hospitalized, an angry mob advanced

Below: Jimmy Carter welcomes the exiled Shah of Iran to the United States.

Below: Some of the hostages in Iran were blindfolded and handcuffed by supporters of Ayatollah Ruhollah Khomeini.

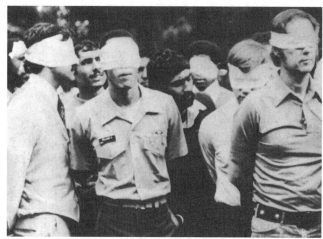

on the American embassy in Tehran and took the staff as hostages, demanding the shah's return for trial as ransom.

The hostage crisis was Carter's greatest test as president. As the days turned into months, the image of Americans being held captive seemed to be a symbol of his ineffectiveness as a leader. Diplomatic efforts to free the hostages proved to be useless, even after Carter froze all Iranian financial assets in the United States. Then, to make matters even worse, a military rescue operation failed: Almost half of the helicopters involved developed mechanical problems, and another crashed into a transport plane, killing eight American soldiers.

The Carter administration eventually secured the release of the American hostages. However, that didn't happen until after the 1980 presidential election. The level of public disappointment with Carter was clearly evident at election time, and although he had secured the Democratic nomination for a second term, he was soundly defeated by Republican Ronald Reagan, who won 489 electoral votes to Carter's 49. In a final insult directed at the outgoing U.S. president, the Iranians did not give the American hostages their freedom—after 444 days of captivity—until after Reagan had been sworn in as president on January 20, 1981, making it appear that it was he, and not Carter, who had brought an end to the hostage crisis.

Above: Carter's concession of the election to Ronald Reagan was one of the saddest moments of his career. On hand were Rosalynn and Amy, and Carter's grandson, Jason.

Life After the Presidency

Still in his fifties when he left office, Carter realized that he had many more productive years ahead of him. Free to pursue his interest in human rights, he became a private citizen with international stature. He served as an arbitrator in international disputes, supervised elections in other countries, and formed coalitions to find private solutions to social problems. In 1982, he and Rosalynn

Below: While other former presidents have established presidential libraries, Jimmy Carter built the Carter Center, which has become one of the most successful nonprofit agencies in the world, helping poor countries with health care, agricultural aid, and conflict negotiation.

Below: Among their charitable activities, Jimmy and Rosalynn donated long hours to building houses for the poor through Habitat for Humanity.

The Iran Hostage Crisis

What became known as the Iran hostage crisis began on November 4, 1979, when anti-American demonstrators in Tehran, the capital of Iran, stormed the American embassy, trapped fifty-two American workers there, and held them hostage for 444 days.

President Carter was a symbol of hatred for revolutionary Iranians because his administration had shown support for their ruler, Shah Mohammad Reza Pahlavi. The conflict between the shah and Islamic fundamentalists in Iran dated back to the 1950s. He had ruled since 1941, when he was twenty-one years old, and with help from the United States, he modernized the country after World War II and accumulated personal wealth by exporting oil.

The disparity in wealth between a small minority of Iranian—many with close connections to the shah—and a far larger, poorer class led to social tension. The shah continued to have the support of the United States as he instituted reforms during the 1960s and '70s, but many Iranians believed that the reforms were just a sham and they began distrusting the United States. The shah's special military forces cracked down on his opponents, but the effect was like pouring gasoline on a fire.

Ayatollah Ruhollah Khomeini was one of the shah's most vocal opponents, because he believed that traditional Islamic values were being lost as Iran modernized. The Ayatollah attracted a growing number of followers through the 1950s, and he was exiled from Iran in 1963 after publicly criticizing the shah.

An economic downturn in the country in the mid-1970s increased public outcries against the shah, and crackdowns against his opponents became more widespread. Anti-American sentiment spread along with them. As the shah's forces and revolutionaries clashed in a series of violent and bloody demonstrations, the Carter administration's continued support for the shah made "death to America" a rallying cry among the Islamic revolutionaries. The shah eventually left the country in 1979, and the revolutionaries were further incensed against the United States when he was allowed refuge in New York. He was receiving medical treatment for cancer there, but the rebels believed that he was courting American sympathy to help him return to power. Meanwhile, the Ayatollah Khomeini returned triumphantly to Iran in February 1979. He became the nation's leader and proclaimed Iran an Islamic Republic.

The Ayatollah highly praised the embassy takeover and the holding of hostages, and as anti-American sentiment crystallized, he became more powerful as the ultimate authority in a government based on the religious laws of Islam and run by Islamic clergy. He called for religious revolutions in surrounding countries, too, always opposing the culture of the United States.

After being held in the embassy for twenty days, the hostages were bound, blindfolded, covered with blankets, and shuttled around to a series of makeshift prisons. The Ayatollah had ordered the release of the women and blacks among the hostages by then, but fifty-two remained as pawns in a war of nerves. During seemingly endless interrogations, they were beaten and humiliated by their jailers. An hour of running in place each morning was the only exercise they were permitted. After three months, the hostages were locked in small cells and not allowed to communicate. Any hostages who violated the rules were locked in cold, dark cubicles for as long as three days. Toward the end of their confinement, they were forced to stand before mock firing squads.

The taking of the hostages immediately received worldwide attention, and most of the nations of the world joined the United States in condemning the actions of the Iranian revolutionaries. However, the Iranians' success in using hostages to humiliate a superpower inspired terrorists in other places to try similar tactics. Meanwhile, militants pieced together shredded documents they found in the embassy to try to prove that the building had been a "nest of spies." They produced documents that they claimed proved that the United States and the Soviet Union had joined forces to oppose the Iranian revolution.

The hostage crisis was humiliating for the United States, and it harmed the Carter administration, which had underestimated the growing Islamic revival in Iran. A rescue mission in April 1980, known as Eagle Claw, failed when helicopters broke down during a desert sandstorm. The mission was abandoned, but eight men died when a helicopter collided with a plane during the retreat. The failure of the operation further angered military and civilian leaders in the United States.

Economic sanctions by President Carter against Iran caused hardships for the Iranian people, but increased the determination of the hostage takers. President Carter's unflagging support of the shah and his inability to free the hostages contributed greatly to his landslide defeat by Ronald Reagan in 1980. The hostages' long ordeal finally ended after they had spent 444 days in captivity, with their release was timed for January 20, 1981—the day Ronald Reagan became president, creating the impression that Reagan had engineered the settlement, although the release had been completely arranged by the Carter administration with Algerian diplomats as go-betweens.

founded the Carter Center in Atlanta, a nonprofit organization that promotes human rights, democracy, improved public health, and advances in agriculture. Two years later, they also became involved with Habitat for Humanity International, a nonprofit organization dedicated to building new homes for the poor. Carter became a respected elder statesman frequently honored for his tireless work on behalf of humanity.

In October 2000, the former president announced that he was splitting from the Southern Baptist Convention because of its "increasingly rigid views that run against the basic premises of my Christian faith." Carter pointed to the Baptists' opposition to women as pastors and its call for wives to be submissive to their husbands as key factors in his decision.

Legacy

Jimmy Carter's administration was never able to establish momentum. He moved cautiously and supported moderate programs that rallied only a few Democrats in Congress and were generally opposed by Republicans, and a steadily worsening economy and problems overseas drained his attempts to build support. He had appealed to voters as a Washington outsider, but once he was inside Washington, Carter couldn't build the support he needed. Opinion polls showed that the public liked Carter as a person, but he consistently lost their favor for his perceived lack of leadership abilities.

Below: After her family left the White House, Amy Carter became a political activist, protesting CIA recruiting on the campus of the University of Massachusetts.

Above: Jimmy Carter has become one of the most active former presidents in American history.

Among his successes, Carter substantially increased the percentage of minorities and women in high-level political and judicial positions. He confronted the energy shortage by establishing a national energy policy. He created the Department of Education to improve public schools. In foreign affairs, the Camp David Accords in 1978 formally ended hostilities between Israel and Egypt. Carter fortified positive relations with China in 1979 when the United States formally recognized the Chinese communist government. Carter condemned the Soviet Union's invasion of Afghanistan and promoted human rights as a policy.

A weak economy and a setback in foreign affairs would have undermined any president. High inflation and high unemployment occurring at the same time, and the long, demoralizing hostage crisis in Iran were in the daily news as Carter ran for reelection in 1980, and Americans turned away from him when they went to the polls. But in spite of his resounding election defeat, Carter quickly reemerged as an independent statesman, showing that he had not lost the people's trust and respect during the difficult years of his presidency.

In 2002, Carter was awarded the Nobel Peace Prize for his decades of work seeking peaceful solutions and promoting political and social justice.

Rosalynn Carter

Born August 18, 1927, Plains, Georgia

"I had already learned from more than a decade of public life that I was going to be criticized no matter what I did so I might as well be criticized for something I wanted to do, attending cabinet meetings. If I had spent all day 'pouring tea,' I would have been criticized for that, too."

—Rosalynn Carter

Attractive and poised, Rosalynn Carter was a serious contributor to her husband's political campaigns, and an extremely busy and highly respected first lady. She had no reservations about traveling alone as a representative of the Carter administration, she attended cabinet meetings, and kept a full schedule of her own activities. Through her work as honorary chairman of the President's Commission on Mental Health, she helped raise national consciousness about the treatment and rights of mental health patients. Also, as she had been for almost all of her adult life, Mrs. Carter was a strong partner for her husband and a significant spokesperson for the causes she believed in.

Her Best Friend's Older Brother

Eleanor Rosalynn Carter was born in Plains, Georgia, on August 18, 1927, the oldest of four children of Wilburn Edgar and Allethea Murray Smith. Her father, a farmer and a mechanic, died of leukemia when she was thirteen, and her mother worked as a seamstress—and later in the local post office—to support the family, although she always struggled just to make ends meet. Rosalynn helped her with sewing, housework, and taking care of the other Smith children, while she worked in the local beauty parlor, and maintained an enviable record in school. What little spare time she had was spent with her best friend, Ruth Carter, Jimmy Carter's younger sister.

Rosalynn was three years younger than Jimmy; they didn't socialize during their high school years. They began to date after her freshman year at Georgia Southwestern College, while he was a midshipman at the U.S. Naval Academy. After a six-month courtship, carried on mostly through letter-writing, Jimmy proposed marriage, but she turned him down because she wanted to finish college. When he asked her a second time, through, she accepted, and they were married a month after he graduated from Annapolis in 1946.

Navy Wife

Having spent her entire life in Georgia—nearly all of it in Plains—Rosalynn welcomed the opportunity to be a navy wife and to see a bit more of the world. Her three sons were each born in different states: John William in Virginia, James Earl III in Hawaii, and Donnel Jeffrey in Connecticut. The Carters also lived at times in California and New York. Rosalynn enjoyed the independence she had found living away from home, and she was stunned when Jimmy told her that he wanted to move back to Plains and run his late father's business. In her autobiography, *First Lady from Plains,* she recalled, "I argued. I cried. I even screamed at him." She didn't want to go back there because the town with filled with memories of tough times.

Above: When Amy Carter was born in 1967, the youngest of her three brothers was fifteen years old, making her a kind of second family for Jimmy and Rosalynn. She was nine when this picture was taken, and had an itchy nose at the time.

Above: Amy married computer consultant Jim Wentzel in 1996.

She finally agreed to her husband's plan, and after they went back home, Rosalynn took over the accounting work for the Carter family's peanut warehouse while she supervised other family interests. She supported her husband completely when he became involved in state politics, and she spent many long hours campaigning for him as he ran for state senator—and then for governor—of Georgia. During his presidential campaign, she traveled by herself to forty-one states to give speeches on his behalf, and her enthusiasm greatly contributed to his election with a narrow defeat of President Gerald R. Ford in 1976.

Active First Lady

Once she became established as first lady, Rosalynn worked even harder to back her husband's policies, while at the same time emerging as a woman with missions of her own. She was a tireless supporter of the Equal Rights Amendment (ERA), a proposed Constitutional amendment to recognize the rights of women. It wasn't ratified, but not because the first lady didn't argue earnestly for it. She was a proponent of patients' rights for the mentally ill, and a supporter of the performing arts. She represented her husband on formal occasions and traveled to Latin America as his personal representative. She handled all of these things while she was also raising her daughter Amy, who was only nine years old when they moved into the White House.

By her own admission, Rosalynn Carter was quite bitter when her husband wasn't reelected in 1980. She felt betrayed by the press, which had attacked President Carter for the hostage situation in Iran, the continuing energy crisis, and runaway inflation. She felt strongly that her husband would have had a more successful second term, and she also frankly admitted that she expected to have trouble readjusting to a quiet life in Plains after having been so busy in the public eye for four years. Her bitterness faded quickly, though, when she realized that the American people still valued her opinions and were still watching her with admiration.

Above: Both Jimmy and Rosalynn have a busy schedule in their work for the Carter Center.

Respected Private Citizen

As a private citizen, Rosalynn Carter worked with her husband to promote international human rights through the Carter Center, which they established in Atlanta. She worked side-by-side with him to increase public awareness of Habitat for Humanity, a private program that builds homes for needy Americans. She also continued her work on behalf of the mentally ill, and in 1991, she cofounded a program called Every Child by Two, with the goal of early childhood immunization against diseases. Her humanitarian work has earned her numerous honors, awards, and citations, including several honorary degrees.

In her autobiography, Mrs. Carter wrote, "I would be out there campaigning right now if Jimmy would run again. I miss the world of politics." It reflected how she felt after she left the White House, before she discovered that she and her husband could continue to make a serious impact on international affairs. Although Rosalynn Carter stayed out of the limelight, she didn't slow down in her effort to improve the quality of life around the world, nor did she lose the independent spirit that had endeared her to so many during her years as first lady.

Carter's "Human Rights and Foreign Policy" Speech

In his speeches, President Jimmy Carter frequently invoked the ideals of American democracy as guides to explaining his policies. He had difficulty during his presidency, however, in translating those principles into action. He succeeded in restoring faith and trust in the presidency—as reflected in consistently high ratings in polls for his trustworthiness—but his effectiveness as a leader usually rated much lower. He wasn't able to rally support in Congress or among voters for many of his programs.

Carter's approach to American foreign policy was based on his belief that political actions should reflect the country's highest moral ideals. This standard emphasized human rights—that all individuals should be free and equal. His most profound statement of that belief was made at a commencement address at the University of Notre Dame in South Bend, Indiana, in June 1977—less than six months after he took office.

Excerpt from Carter's "Human Rights and Foreign Policy" Speech

I want to speak to you today about the strands that connect our actions overseas with our essential character as a nation. I believe we can have a foreign policy that is democratic, that is based on fundamental values, and that uses power and influence, which we have, for humane purposes. We can also have a foreign policy that the American people both support and, for a change, know about and understand.

I have a quiet confidence in our own political system. Because we know that democracy works, we can reject the arguments of those rulers who deny human rights to their people.

We are confident that democracy's example will be compelling, and so we seek to bring that example closer to those from whom in the past few years we have been separated and who are not yet convinced about the advantages of our kind of life.

We are confident that the democratic methods are the most effective, and so we are not tempted to employ improper tactics here at home or abroad.

We are confident of our own strength, so we can seek substantial mutual reductions in the nuclear arms race.

And we are confident of the good sense of American people, and so we let them share in the process of making foreign policy decisions. We can thus speak with the voices of 215 million, and not just of an isolated handful. [...]

For too many years, we've been willing to adopt the flawed and erroneous principles and tactics of our adversaries, sometimes abandoning our own values for theirs. We've fought fire with fire, never thinking that fire is better quenched with water. This approach failed, with Vietnam the best example of its intellectual and moral poverty. But through failure we have now found our way back to our own principles and values, and we have regained our lost confidence.

By the measure of history, our Nation's 200 years are very brief, and our rise to world eminence is briefer still. It dates from 1945, when Europe and the old international order lay in ruins. Before then, America was largely on the periphery of world affairs. But since then, we have inescapably been at the center of world affairs.

Our policy during this period was guided by two principles: a belief that Soviet expansion was almost inevitable but that it must be contained, and the corresponding belief in the importance of an almost exclusive alliance among non-Communist nations on both sides of the Atlantic. That system could not last forever unchanged. Historical trends have weakened its foundation. The unifying threat of conflict with the Soviet Union has become less intensive, even though the competition has become more extensive.

The Vietnamese war produced a profound moral crisis, sapping worldwide faith in our own policy and our system of life, a crisis of confidence made even more grave by the covert pessimism of some of our leaders.

In less than a generation, we've seen the world change dramatically. The daily lives and aspirations of most human beings have been transformed. Colonialism is nearly gone. A new sense of national identity now exists in almost 100 new countries that have been formed in the last generation. Knowledge has become more widespread. Aspirations are higher. As more people have been freed from traditional constraints, more have been determined to achieve, for the first time in their lives, social justice.

The world is still divided by ideological disputes, dominated by regional conflicts, and threatened by danger that we will not resolve the differences of race and wealth without violence or without drawing into combat the major military powers. We can no longer separate the traditional issues of war and peace from the new global questions of justice, equity, and human rights.

It is a new world, but America should not fear it. It is a new world, and we should help to shape it. It is a new world that calls for a new American foreign policy—a policy based on constant decency in its values and on optimism in our historical vision. [...]

Our policy must reflect our belief that the world can hope for more than simple survival and our belief that dignity and freedom are fundamental spiritual requirements. Our policy must shape an international system that will last longer than secret deals.

We cannot make this kind of policy by manipulation. Our policy must be open; it must be candid; it must be one of constructive global involvement, resting on five cardinal principles.

I've tried to make these premises clear to the American people since last January. Let me review what we have been doing and discuss what we intend to do.

First, we have reaffirmed America's commitment to human rights as a fundamental tenet of our foreign policy. In ancestry, religion, color, place of origin, and cultural background, we Americans are as diverse a nation as the world has even seen. No common mystique of blood or soil unites us. What draws us together, perhaps more than anything else, is a belief in human freedom. We want the world to know that our Nation stands for more than financial prosperity. [...]

Throughout the world today, in free nations and in totalitarian countries as well, there is a preoccupation with the subject of human freedom, human rights. And I believe it is incumbent on us in this country to keep that discussion, that debate, that contention alive. No other country is as well-qualified as we to set an example. We have our own shortcomings and faults, and we should strive constantly and with courage to make sure that we are legitimately proud of what we have.

Second, we've moved deliberately to reinforce the bonds among our democracies. In our recent meetings in London, we agreed to widen our economic cooperation, to promote free trade, to strengthen the world's monetary system, to seek ways of avoiding nuclear proliferation. We prepared constructive proposals for the forthcoming meetings on North-South problems of poverty, development, and global well-being. And we agreed on joint efforts to reinforce and to modernize our common defense. [...]

Third, we've moved to engage the Soviet Union in a joint effort to halt the strategic arms race. This race is not only dangerous, it's morally deplorable. We must put an end to it. I know it will not be easy to reach agreements. Our goal is to be fair to both sides, to produce reciprocal stability, parity, and security. We desire a freeze on further modernization and production of weapons and a continuing, substantial reduction of strategic nuclear weapons as well. We want a comprehensive ban on all nuclear testing, a prohibition against all chemical warfare, no attack capability against space satellites, and arms limitations in the Indian Ocean. We hope that we can take joint steps with all nations toward a final agreement eliminating nuclear weapons completely from our arsenals of death. We will persist in this effort.

Now, I believe in détente with the Soviet Union. To me it means progress toward peace. But the effects of détente should not be limited to our own two countries alone. We hope to persuade the Soviet Union that one country cannot impose its system of society upon another, either through direct military intervention or through the use of a client state's military force, as was the case with Cuban intervention in Angola.

Cooperation also implies obligation. We hope that the Soviet Union will join with us and other nations in playing a larger role in aiding the developing world, for common aid efforts will help us build a bridge of mutual confidence in one another.

Fourth, we are taking deliberate steps to improve the chances of lasting peace in the Middle East. Through wide-ranging consultation with leaders of the countries involved —Israel, Syria, Jordan, and Egypt—we have found some areas of agreement and some movement toward consensus. The negotiations must continue. [...]

And fifth, we are attempting, even at the risk of some friction with our friends, to reduce the danger of nuclear proliferation and the worldwide spread of conventional weapons. [...]

Let me conclude by summarizing: Our policy is based on an historical vision of America's role. Our policy is derived from a larger view of global change. Our policy is rooted in our moral values, which never change. Our policy is reinforced by our material wealth and by our military power. Our policy is designed to serve mankind. And it is a policy that I hope will make you proud to be Americans.

What Happened Next

The Carter administration had mixed results with its foreign policy. In 1977, the United States agreed to treaties that gave Panama sovereignty over the Panama Canal Zone (beginning on December 31, 1999). Some Americans objected to relinquishing power over such an important area. In 1978, Carter helped bring the nations of Israel and Egypt into a peace agreement called the Camp David Accords. In 1979, he formally recognized the government of communist China, helping to ease world tensions among large and powerful nations.

However, the 1979 Soviet invasion of Afghanistan led to renewed tensions between the two nations. A pact reducing nuclear weapons was delayed, and among actions that the Carter administration took against the Soviet Union was a boycott of American participation in the Summer Olympic Games that were held in Moscow in 1980. The Soviet Union and its allies responded by boycotting the Summer Olympics in Los Angeles the following year. And in 1979, a revolution toppled the leadership of the shah of Iran, Mohammad Reza Pahlavi, who had been backed by the American government. After the United States allowed the shah to enter a New York hospital for cancer treatment, fifty-two Americans were captured in Iran and held hostage for over a year.

After his presidency, Jimmy Carter became a more successful and respected international statesman in his pursuit of human rights. In addition to publicizing human rights through an organization called the Carter Center that he founded, he helped negotiate treaties and agreements among foreign countries and he supervised free elections in nations that only recently embraced democracy.

In 2002, Carter was awarded the Nobel Peace Prize for his decades of work seeking peaceful solutions and promoting political and social justice.

Ronald Reagan

"Government is not the solution to our problem, government is the problem."

—*Ronald Reagan*

Fortieth president of the United States, 1981–1989

Full name: *Ronald Wilson Reagan*

Born: *February 6, 1911, Tampico, Illinois*

Died: *June 5, 2004, Los Angeles, California*

Burial site: *Reagan Presidential Library Grounds, Simi Valley, California*

Parents: *John Edward and Nelle Wilson Reagan*

Spouses: *Jane Wyman (1914–2007; m. 1940, divorced, 1948); Nancy Davis (1921–2016; m. 1952)*

Children: *Maureen Elizabeth (1941–2001); Christina (1947–1947); Michael Edward (adopted; 1945–); Patricia Ann (1952–); Ronald Prescott (1958–)*

Religion: *Disciples of Christ*

Education: *Eureka College (B.A., 1932)*

Occupations: *Rancher; army captain; radio sports commentator; actor*

Government positions: *California governor*

Political party: *Republican*

Dates as president: *January 20, 1981–January 20, 1985 (first term); January 20, 1985–January 20, 1989 (second term)*

Age upon taking office: *69*

From the time American colonists first began to consider breaking away from England to form their own system of government, lively discussion has almost never stopped over the extent of the powers that government should have. When ratification of the Constitution was being debated in the late 1780s, some notable patriots argued that the federal government it described would have too much authority over individual states, and "states' rights" versus federal power has been a heated issue ever since.

In the twentieth century, federal powers expanded in such areas as government regulation of business and banking and in the enactment of social welfare programs. Franklin D. Roosevelt's New Deal in the 1930s, Harry S Truman's Fair Deal during the 1940s, and the Great Society of Lyndon B. Johnson during the 1960s were all designed to confront social and economic problems at the federal level.

In 1980, Ronald Reagan campaigned on the theme "Government is not the solution to our problem, government is the problem." By cutting taxes, ending several social welfare programs, and reducing government regulations on business, he reversed the political trends of the twentieth century, and his policies helped revive a sluggish American economy.

Timeline

1911: Born in Illinois
1938: Appears in first motion picture
1947–52, 1959: Serves as president of the Screen Actors Guild
1954: Becomes television spokesman for the General Electric Company and makes speeches around the country promoting the American way
1967–75: Serves as California governor
1976: Falls eighty ballots shy of becoming the Republican nominee for president
1981–89: Serves as fortieth U.S. president
1981: Wounded in assassination attempt
1985: The first of several summits with Soviet leader Mikhail Gorbachev takes place
1986: Iran-Contra scandal breaks
1994: Announces he has Alzheimer's disease
2004: Dies in California

Right: Reagan's name was misspelled "Donald" in the 1928 edition of the Dixon, Illinois, high school yearbook. The quote "Life is just one grand sweet song, so start the music" was his guiding philosophy through the ninety-three years of his life.

Reagan's policies and his speech-making skills inspired tremendous enthusiasm from his supporters, and resulted in two landslide election victories. His opponents, meanwhile, called attention to enormous federal budget deficits that grew out of control during his administration, and they also provided examples of business and administration officials who engaged in unlawful practices in the absence of federal supervision. Nevertheless, the nation's oldest president emerged vigorous and still popular after two terms. "I am the same man I was when I came to Washington," he said when he left the White House. "I believe the same things I believed when I came to Washington."

By the time Reagan went to Eureka College near Peoria, Illinois, his leadership skills, athletic ability, and interest in acting were already well developed. While majoring in economics, he served as president of the student body, he was captain of the swimming team, he played football, and he acted in the school's theater productions. He became a local radio sportscaster after he graduated in 1932 and moved on to a larger station, WHO, in Des Moines, Iowa, four years later. One of his jobs there was to "describe" Chicago Cubs baseball games and Big Ten football matchups, recreating the action from running wire service reports and making the broadcast sound as if it was coming live from the game.

Below: Although Reagan never smoked, one of his sponsors as a radio sports broadcaster was Kentucky Club tobacco, and he obliged the company by being photographed with an unlit pipe.

Multimedia Man

Ronald Wilson Reagan was born on February 6, 1911, at Tampico, Illinois, the younger of two sons of Nelle and John Reagan. His father took one look at the ten-pound baby and called his a "fat little Dutchman," and family and friends called him "Dutch" ever since. His father, who owned the local shoe store, fell on hard times during the Great Depression and became an alcoholic. Reagan's mother provided a stable home life and taught her sons to read at their home in Dixon, Illinois, where they lived from the time Ronnie was nine.

Above: Most critics agree that Reagan's most impressive film role was in King's Row, where he shared the screen with Ann Sheridan.

Right:Reagan played Notre Dame football star George Gipp in the movie Knute Rockne: All American, and was known as "The Gipper" ever since.

Below: Hollywood gossip columnist Louella Parsons could make or break any actor's Hollywood career, even Gary Cooper's. She took a special interest in young Ronald Reagan because they were both from Dixon, Illinois.

He eventually graduated from giving studio recreations to actually sitting in stadium press boxes, and while he was covering baseball spring training in California, Reagan took a screen test and was signed to an acting contract. He went on to appear in over fifty movies—from *Love Is on the Air* (1937) to *The Killers* (1964). His films included *King's Row* (1942), several westerns, and a series with a chimpanzee named Bonzo as his costar (including *Bedtime for Bonzo* in 1951). Possibly his best known screen role was his 1940 portrayal of Notre Dame football star George Gipp in *Knute Rockne: All American,* which earned him the nickname "the Gipper."

Reagan married actress Jane Wyman in 1941, and they had three children—Maureen, Michael, who was adopted, and Christina, who died when she was three days old—before their divorce in 1949. He served in the army during World War II and rose to the rank of captain. Based in California, he narrated training films, and he also appeared in the film version of Irving Berlin's *This Is the Army*.

He married actress Nancy Davis in 1952, and they would have two children. They appeared together in a movie, *Hellcats of the Navy* (1957), which was her last feature film, although they appeared together again in teleplay that was broadcast on the *General Electric Theater*. Reagan's acting career was on the back burner by then. He had served six one-year terms as president of the Screen Actors Guild from 1947 to 1952, and he was asked to serve again in 1959 to lead the union through a strike and negotiate with the major movie companies. The experience gave him a taste of the world beyond Hollywood when he went to Washington to testify as the Guild's president before the House Un-American Activities Committee, which was investigating possible communist activities within the movie industry.

Above: Reagan first appeared on the Washington stage with testimony before the House Un-American Activities Committee, which was investigating Communist activities in Hollywood.

Reagan accepted a position as spokesman for the General Electric Company in 1954. In addition to acting as host for a weekly television series, he traveled around the country as a guest speaker promoting the virtues of the American social and political system. He averaged fourteen twenty-minute speeches a day for eight years. Reagan was officially a Democrat through the 1950s, but his political views were much more in line with conservative Republicans. Their pro-business agenda, support for increased military spending, and obsession with limiting federal programs would resurface in the 1980s—when Reagan was serving as president.

"Freedom is never more than a generation away from extinction. We didn't pass it along to our children in the bloodstream. It must be fought for, protected, and handed on to them to do the same, or one day we will spend our sunset years telling our children and our children's children what it once was like in the United States when men were free."

—Ronald Reagan, in his General Electric-sponsored speeches

Political Action

Reagan became an active Republican in 1962. A relaxed and persuasive speaker before the cameras, he made a spirited televised campaign speech for Republican presidential nominee Barry Goldwater in 1964. His performance and obvious belief in the conservative Republican cause led a group of California businessmen to suggest that Reagan ought to run for office and make speeches like that on his own behalf.

Reagan won impressively when he ran for governor of California in the 1966 election against Edmund G. "Pat" Brown Sr., a fairly popular incumbent. His plurality of nearly one million votes was at that time the largest ever over an incumbent governor in the history of the United States.

California had become a haven for counterculture—young people who were rejecting the values of their parents' generation—while Reagan was governor, and it had also become a hotbed of protest over American involvement in the Vietnam War. Reagan made it clear that he was disgusted by such activities, finding them especially improper on college campuses. He appealed to a broad spectrum of voters, from wealthy Republicans to working-class Democrats—an impressive feat of coalition building that he would duplicate time and again during his presidential election campaigns.

Dealing with a state legislature that had a Democratic majority, Reagan acted gradually on his campaign promises to slow the growth of state government and to lower property taxes. He tied those initiatives to balancing the state budget, and some taxes were raised in order to provide the state with more money that could accomplish it. At the same time, government programs were reduced, and the state dispensed a large percentage of the tax money it collected to local communities, which took control of programs that had been previously administered by the state, with enough money left over to allow cities and towns to lower property taxes.

Above: During a protest over his proposed cuts in education funds, California governor Ronald Reagan responded by shutting his eyes and pursing his lips in a "see no evil, speak no evil" attitude.

Riding a Wave

Reagan was appealing to conservative Republicans, who believed that their party should take stands on social issues as well as limit government programs, and were annoyed that America had become a much more permissive society after the 1960s. Increasingly, conservative religious groups were gaining political strength. They wanted to contest Supreme Court rulings that didn't allow prayer in public schools and the 1973 *Roe v. Wade* ruling that overturned most state laws banning abortion. They found their champion in Reagan, who entered the race for president in 1976.

Reagan challenged the sitting president, Gerald R. Ford, who had assumed office following the resignation of President Richard Nixon in 1974. Ford had battled a Democrat-controlled Congress over cuts he wanted in social programs and taxes, and Reagan promised that he was a better man to get the job done. Ford was more moderate on social issues as well, and during a closely fought campaign for the Republican nomination, Reagan won support in several Southern and western states where conservative feeling ran high, but he lost the nomination to Ford by just eighty ballots at the convention. When Ford failed to win the presidential election of 1976, Reagan emerged as the man to beat for the nomination four years down the road.

Reagan prevailed in the 1980 Republican presidential primaries. His main opponents were George Bush, who eventually agreed to be his running mate, and John Anderson, who went on to run as an independent in the general election. Incumbent president Jimmy Carter was mired in difficulties and low approval ratings. The U.S. economy was stagnant, people were upset over continued high fuel costs, and an October 1979 raid on the American embassy in Iran had resulted in fifty-two Americans being taken hostage—an action supported by the Iranian government. Negotiations failed to win their release, as did a risky rescue mission, and as election day approached, the hostages were still being held captive. It all added up to a slam dunk for Ronald Reagan and the Republicans.

Continuing to challenge protests on college campuses, he reduced funding for the University of California system, and then restored it after the demonstrations cooled down, making it quite clear why he had cut off funds in the first place. Reagan's stance against the protest movement and his conservative values were drawing attention around the country, and he was mentioned as a possible presidential candidate in 1968. However, former vice president and candidate Richard Nixon began campaigning early and aggressively, and he locked up the party's nomination before Reagan had a chance.

After he was reelected governor of California in 1970, Reagan confronted welfare, another area of government spending that many politicians considered untouchable at the time. Claiming that there was uncontrolled cheating in the system, he introduced a program that dramatically reduced the number of people who qualified for welfare, but allowed increased financial assistance over a limited period of time for people who still did qualify. Reagan cut taxes even more than he had in his first term, and he put a curb on the state government's power to regulate business.

Election Results

1980

Presidential / Vice Presidential Candidates	Popular Votes	Electoral Votes
Ronald Reagan / George H. W. Bush (Republican)	43,904,153	483
Jimmy Carter / Walter Mondale (Democratic)	35,483,883	49
John Anderson / VP nominee was not chosen (National Unity)	5,720,060	0

Incumbent president Carter shook off a challenge by Massachusetts senator Edward Kennedy to win the Democratic nomination; Republican Reagan's main competition was from former CIA director and ambassador to China, George Bush (whom Reagan chose as his running mate) and Illinois congressman John Anderson (who ran in the general election as an independent).

1984

Presidential / Vice Presidential Candidates	Popular Votes	Electoral Votes
Ronald Reagan / George Bush (Republican)	54,455,075	525
Walter Mondale / Geraldine Ferraro (Democratic)	37,577,185	13

This election was most notable for former vice president Mondale's selection of New York representative Ferraro as his running mate, the first female from a major party to run on a national ticket.

Reagan promised to stimulate the economy with across-the-boards tax cuts. He planned to downsize government programs and, at the same time, greatly increase military spending. During televised debates between the two candidates, Reagan appeared polished and relaxed while dismissing Carter's policies (often saying, "There you go again") on conserving natural resources, reducing energy consumption, and pursuing détente with the Soviets. When Reagan proposed adopting a hard-line foreign policy, reducing regulations on business, and dismantling "wasteful" government-sponsored programs, he was able to inspire the voters. Along with the coalition he had developed of big-business and religious conservative supporters, he also attracted a fair number of working-class Democrats, and he won 51 percent of the popular vote as well as a landslide (489 to 49 votes) in the Electoral College. Riding along his wave of popularity, Republicans gained a majority in the Senate for the first time since 1954.

Right: President Reagan delivers his 1986 State of the Union Address with Vice President George Bush (L) and House Speaker Tip O'Neill in the background.

The Reagan Administration

Administration Dates: January 20, 1981–January 20, 1985

January 20, 1985–January 20, 1989

Vice President: George Bush (1981–89)

Cabinet:

Secretary of State	Alexander M. Haig Jr. (1981–82)
	George P. Shultz (1982–89)
Secretary of the Treasury	Donald T. Regan (1981–85)
	James A. Baker III (1985–88)
	Nicholas F. Brady (1988–89)
Attorney General	William F. Smith (1981–85)
	Edwin Meese III (1985–88)
	Richard L. Thornburgh (1988–89)
Secretary of the Interior	James G. Watt (1981–83)
	William P. Clark (1983–85)
	Donald P. Hodel (1985–89)
Secretary of Agriculture	John R. Block (1981–86)
	Richard E. Lyng (1986–89)
Secretary of Labor	Raymond J. Donovan (1981–85)
	William E. Brock III (1985–87)
	Ann Dore McLaughlin (1987–89)
Secretary of Commerce	Malcolm Baldrige (1981–87)
	C. William Verity (1987–89)
Secretary of Defense	Caspar W. Weinberger (1981–87)
	Frank G. Carlucci (1987–89)
Secretary of Housing and Urban Development	Samuel R. Pierce Jr. (1981–89)
Secretary of Transportation	Andrew L. Lewis Jr. (1981–83)
	Elizabeth H. Dole (1983–87)
	James H. Burnley IV (1987–89)
Secretary of Energy	James B. Edwards (1981–82)
	Donald P. Hodel (1982–85)
	John S. Herrington (1985–89)
Secretary of Health and Human Services	Richard S. Schweiker (1981–83)
	Margaret M. Heckler (1983–85)
	Otis R. Bowen (1985–89)
Secretary of Education	Terrel H. Bell (1981–85)
	William J. Bennett (1985–88)
	Lauro F. Cavazos (1988–89)

Above: Reagan waves to the crowd moments before being shot on March 30, 1981. Also wounded were Washington police officer Thomas Delahanty (first from right), Secret Service agent Timothy McCarthy (far right), and press secretary James Brady (behind, to the president's left).

Reaganomics

In his inaugural address, Reagan announced "an era of national renewal." The release of American hostages by Iran occurred on that day, raised national spirits, and his speech was well-received. Just two months into office, however, Reagan was shot by John Hinckley Jr., who was later judged insane. Concern for the president soon turned to relief as Reagan made limited public appearances and displayed his usual cheery nature during a recovery period that lasted several weeks. (Ever the humorist, he was quoted as saying to his wife, "Honey, I forgot to duck." And just before being treated, he reportedly said to a doctor, "I hope you are a Republican.")

National economic recovery took much longer. It was at a low point in October 1982, when 11 percent of Americans were out of work. Battling with a Democrat-controlled House of Representatives to begin cutting government social programs, Reagan was able to push through the Economic Recovery Tax Act of 1981, and along with lowering taxes, he cut federal spending for a variety of programs ranging from job training to college student loans to Medicare coverage. Many government restrictions on business were eased or eliminated, while organized labor was dealt a blow when he fired 11,800

Assassination Attempt

Early in the afternoon of March 31, 1981, John Hinckley, a twenty-five-year-old drifter from Colorado, was waiting outside the Washington Hilton Hotel when President Reagan and his entourage came out through a side door, and he fired six rounds from his revolver. One bullet ricocheted off the limousine and went into the president's left side, bounced off a rib, punctured a lung and stopped an inch from his heart. Another bullet hit press secretary James Brady in the head, leaving him paralyzed. Police officer Thomas Delehanty and Secret Service agent Timothy McCarthy were also severely wounded. At the first sound of gunfire, Secret Service agent Jerry Parr slammed the president into the limousine and then threw himself in as a human shield. Neither of them realized that Reagan had been harmed until he began coughing up blood. Agent Parr ordered the driver to get them to George Washington University Hospital on the double and when they got there, Reagan was able to walk up to the door unassisted. But he failed quickly—he had lost three pints of blood by then—and doctors who treated him said that he probably would have died if he had reached them as little as five minutes later. Less than two weeks later, the seventy-year-old Reagan was back at his desk in the Oval Office.

Below: Although he had been an active union supporter in his years as president of the Screen Actor's Guild, during his administration Reagan surprised the labor establishment by firing striking air traffic controllers.

air-traffic controllers who had gone out on strike. Calling the walkout illegal because it endangered public safety, Reagan took away the strikers' union certification, and very few of them ever went back to their old jobs.

Government deregulation of business placed fewer restrictions on business expansion, and many large companies began merging with one another or were bought by larger corporations, which helped bring about a surge in the stock market, and investors were rewarded when their stocks went up in value.

The president's pro-business policies, known as "Reaganomics," were based on "supply-side" theories that had been developed by economists like Milton Friedman. According to Reaganomics, tax cuts gave consumers more money to spend, and businesses would step up production of things for them to buy. While the American economy was perceived as recovered by 1983 and continued to grow for the next six years, there were some difficulties. Less economically advantaged people generally missed out on the growing prosperity, because they didn't have money to invest. At the same time, fewer restrictions on investments led some stockbrokers to take risky gambles or to take advantage of relaxed government monitoring of their activities. As investors consistently bought and sold stocks at ever-increasing prices, many of them became overvalued, a reality that struck hard on October 19, 1987, when the stock market plummeted.

As a whole, stocks lost a whopping 36 percent in value during that month alone. Although many people lost money, the downturn soon balanced out as stocks returned to more realistic values, and the economy continued to grow through 1988, Reagan's final full year in office.

Peace Through Strength

Military spending increased dramatically during the Reagan years. While that spending helped encourage the expansion of military-based industries, it also contributed to an increase in the national debt. Tax cuts, a widening trade deficit, and military spending all combined to put the government deeper in debt. The Reagan administration responded by cutting more federal social programs.

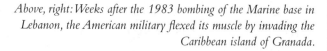

Above: In April 1983, a car bomb destroyed the American Embassy in Beirut, Lebanon. Six month later, 300 U.S. Marines were killed when another bomb destroyed their Beirut Operations Center.

Above, right: Weeks after the 1983 bombing of the Marine base in Lebanon, the American military flexed its muscle by invading the Caribbean island of Granada.

Right: Reagan's staunchest supporter on the internal scene was British Prime Minister Margaret Thatcher.

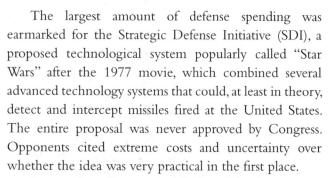

The largest amount of defense spending was earmarked for the Strategic Defense Initiative (SDI), a proposed technological system popularly called "Star Wars" after the 1977 movie, which combined several advanced technology systems that could, at least in theory, detect and intercept missiles fired at the United States. The entire proposal was never approved by Congress. Opponents cited extreme costs and uncertainty over whether the idea was very practical in the first place.

Increased military spending reflected Reagan's foreign policy approach of "peace through strength"—the belief that superior military power would make America's enemies (defined as those who undermined freedom) reluctant to try to expand their power over their own people or other nations. Reagan was specifically targeting the Soviet Union, which he called an "evil empire" in speeches during 1982 and 1983 before small groups and the British Parliament. He moved the United States away from the policy of détente with the Soviet Union, to be consistent in its demands that the Soviet Union extend freedom to people it dominated. A series of summit meetings between the Reagan administration and Soviet leaders eventually resulted in a 1987 treaty to scale back the production of nuclear weapons.

"Let us above all thank President Reagan for ending the West's retreat from world responsibility, for restoring the pride and leadership of the United States and for giving the West back its confidence. He has left America stronger, prouder, greater than ever before and we thank him for it."

—*Prime Minister Margaret Thatcher of Great Britain*

Above: Mikhail Gorbachev and Ronald Reagan in December 1987.

Mikhail Gorbachev

Mikhail Gorbachev was born on March 2, 1931, in the tiny Russian farm village of Privolnoe. He was two years old when Communist dictator Joseph Stalin ordered all private farms seized and placed under government control. Peasant farmers, including many members of Gorbachev's family, were forced to work on collective farms where the government dictated how much of what crops would be grown and what the farmers would be paid.

Gorbachev entered the distinguished Moscow State University in 1950, and he received a broad education there. While he was in school, he met and married a philosophy student, Raisa Maksimovna Titorenko. He also joined the Communist Party, and after he graduated, he went to the city of Stavropol to work for the Party. He rose through the leadership ranks over the next fifteen years, and he become the party leader in Stavropol in 1970. At the same time, he was elected to the Supreme Soviet, the highest legislative body in the Soviet Union.

Yuri Andropov, head of the KGB (secret police), had grown up in Stavropol, and he took Gorbachev under his wing, naming him agricultural secretary of the Communist Party in 1978. Just two years later, Gorbachev joined the Politburo—the Party's ruling body—which was considered unusual because of his age. While most Party leaders were in their seventies, Gorbachev was under fifty. Andropov became the Party's general secretary in 1982 following the death of Leonid Brezhnev, and as his key assistant, Gorbachev took control of running the economy.

When Andropov died in 1984, Konstantin Chernenko was chosen over Gorbachev to become the new leader. But after Chernenko died the following year, Gorbachev was finally appointed general secretary of the Communist Party, making him the leader of his country.

He immediately began a campaign of reforms that forced many conservative Communist leaders out of government and replaced them with younger members who shared Gorbachev's views. He instituted new policies called perestroika ("restructuring") and glasnost ("openness") that took away government controls over the economy and allowed the Soviet people to speak out openly about the problems their country was facing.

Looking for peace abroad and at home, Gorbachev and the American president Ronald Reagan signed a treaty in 1987 that limited the number of nuclear weapons each country could have. Gorbachev decided to end the draining war in Afghanistan, which had pitted anticommunist Afghans against their government and the Soviet Union since 1978, and by 1989, all Soviet troops were removed. For all of his peace efforts, Gorbachev was awarded the Nobel Peace Prize in 1990.

Gorbachev's most important change in the Soviet Union came in 1989 when he allowed other political parties to run against the Communists in general elections. Communists had controlled the Soviet Union since the Russian Revolution in 1917, but they lost their power in the 1989 elections, and Gorbachev separated himself from them by taking the position of Soviet president. The Communist dictatorship had come to an end.

With the weakening of communism in Eastern Europe, many countries and ethnic groups began calling for their own independence. In 1989, East and West Germany were reunited, and the following

Below: Reagan and Gorbachev met in New York, along with Vice President George Bush, and posed triumphantly in the shadow of the World Trade Center.

year, Lithuania became the first of the Baltic states to declare its independence from the Soviet Union. Ethnic wars broke out in the Soviet-controlled republics of Armenia and Georgia, which Gorbachev had hoped to maintain some control over, and his own position at home was in trouble. His plan to gradually release government control of farms and industry wasn't happening fast enough for the Soviet people. Because they had suffered in poverty for many years, they wanted quicker reforms. Boris Yeltsin, a chief critic of Gorbachev, was elected president of the Russian Republic in June 1991.

Conservative Politburo members thought that Gorbachev was giving away too much power, and they kidnapped him in August 1991, hoping to regain government control. However, the intended coup failed after four days when Yeltsin rallied the Russian people against the Communist leaders. Gorbachev went back to Moscow, although Yeltsin had the support of the majority of people, and he dissolved the Communist Party, admitting later that the defeat of communism was a victory for common sense, reason, democracy, and common human values.

Gorbachev granted independence to the remaining republics that had been controlled by the Soviet Union, forming a new economic federation—the Commonwealth of Independent States. Then he resigned the office of president, and became a private citizen. At midnight on December 31, 1991, the red Communist flag with its gold hammer and sickle was lowered in Moscow and the Union of Soviet Socialist Republics no longer existed.

Meanwhile, the Soviet Union's grip on its satellite nation was beginning to weaken. Tired of Soviet domination, groups of people within such countries as Poland, Czechoslovakia, and East Germany were calling on their countrymen to start demanding more democratic systems. The Soviet Union itself was also becoming more reform-minded through its leader, Mikhail Gorbachev. Between 1985 and 1990, he introduced perestroika ("restructuring") of the economy and glasnost ("openness") in political and cultural matters. By the end of the decade, communist states allied with the Soviet Union began transforming into independent democracies.

Meanwhile, the United States was involved in a series of military actions. A 1979 revolution in the Central American nation of Nicaragua had brought a Marxist regime into power. Reagan cut off American aid to Nicaragua and began supporting a group called Contras, who were fighting a similar rebellion against a group called the Sandinistas in the neighboring country of El Salvador. He also sent U.S. marines into the Middle East nation of Lebanon to stem the tide of international terrorist activities there, and more than two hundred of them were killed in a terrorist attack. Days later, Reagan ordered more marines to the Caribbean island of Grenada to restore the government there after it had been overthrown by rebels.

The north African nation of Libya was accused of encouraging terrorist activities that included a takeover of an Italian ocean liner in 1985 in which an American was killed; hijacking an airplane, redirecting it to Beirut, Lebanon, and holding hostages there for thirty-nine days; as well as bombings at airports in Rome and Vienna that killed several people, including five American tourists, and a bomb that exploded in a German dance club frequented by American servicemen. The Reagan administration responded to these provocations by ordering retaliatory bombing of several sites within Libya itself.

Left: In 1990, former President Reagan went to Germany to symbolically take part in tearing down the Berlin Wall.

Above: The Great Communicator never let his audiences down.

"The Great Communicator"

Reagan's popularity remained steadily high following his inauguration. Opponents were concerned with the loss of social programs that had helped those less fortunate, with the easing of government regulations that protected the environment, and with the continued buildup of the military. Reagan was increasingly seen as a spokesperson for powerful conservative groups.

His conservatism was demonstrated in his selection of judges to fill vacancies across the country. He influenced federal court decisions by appointing three conservative Supreme Court justices—Sandra Day O'Connor, the first female to serve on the court; Antonin Scalia; and William Rehnquist, as chief justice, in 1986. Scalia was chosen after two previous appointments had been rejected by Congress.

The growth of the economy, firm support by his backers, continued appeal to working-class Americans, and Reagan's upbeat speeches (he was nicknamed "the Great Communicator") were reflected in the 1984 presidential election, when Reagan was reelected with the largest total of electoral votes ever, 525. He won forty-nine states, losing only in Massachusetts and the District of Columbia, both of which went for the Democratic candidate, former vice president Walter Mondale, who won only thirteen electoral votes.

A highlight of Reagan's second term was the passage in 1986 of a sweeping tax law in 1976 that, among other effects, allowed millions of low-income families to stop paying taxes. Another came in 1987, when Reagan and Soviet president Mikhail Gorbachev signed a treaty limiting the number of nuclear weapons each country could have in its arsenal.

Still, opponents of Reagan's policies were becoming increasingly vocal. The 1986 midterm elections brought more Democrats into the House, and the party recaptured the majority of seats in the Senate. The new Congress hampered many of the president's attempts at further legislation, with a result of often bitter, ill will between the nation's two major parties that continued on through the end of the century.

In 1986, newspapers began reporting that the Reagan's administration had made illegal sales of weapons to Iran. Further stories traced money from those sales to secret funds to the Contras in the civil war in Nicaragua. Reagan angrily denied both charges, but a congressional investigation in 1987 revealed that administration officials had, indeed, arranged arms sales to Iran. Since 1979, when Americans were taken hostage there, Congress had prohibited all diplomatic and trade efforts with the Iranians. It was discovered that the sale had been made to help influence a political group based in Iran that had ties with another group that was holding more Americans hostage in Lebanon. Providing funds to Contra leaders constituted another illegal act, since Congress had to authorize such foreign aid.

Right: Sandra Day O'Connor, the first woman appointed to the United States Supreme Court.

Above: Marine Lieutenant Colonel Oliver North was found guilty of lying to Congress about his involvement in the Iran-Contra affair, but avoided a jail sentence. Soon afterward, he ran for the Senate and lost, but became a popular radio commentator and public speaker.

The Iran-Contra Scandal

President Reagan agreed to sell arms to the Iranians in exchange for the release of American hostages, even as he was pressuring the rest of the world to have nothing to do with them. A few hostages were set fee, but more were taken. When the arms sale was revealed in a Lebanese newspaper, the administration denied it, but then said the goal was to build trust among Iranian moderates.

It was soon revealed that the profits from the sales had been diverted to the Contras, the anti-Sandinista rebels in Nicaragua, and that White House officials had shredded documents related to the affair. In a televised congressional hearing, National Security Adviser John Poindexter admitted that he had approved the scheme, but didn't tell the president so that he could have "plausible deniability" if the plan should be revealed. He also admitted destroying documents to spare Reagan political embarrassment. Lieutenant Colonel Oliver North, a White House military attaché, also admitted to lying and falsifying documents, and revealed that the late CIA director, William Casey, had authorized him to establish a secret "stand alone" unit that could conduct similar covert actions without congressional approval. Special prosecutor Lawrence Walsh secured indictments against both North and Poindexter for conspiracy, fraud and theft of government funds. The charges against North were dropped when the administration refused to release classified documents in the case.

The nationally televised Iran-Contra hearings revealed an administration where many officials were acting without supervision. In spite of his claims that he didn't remember participating in the events, evidence suggested that Reagan had, in fact, personally authorized the arms sales. Even if he didn't know about the diversion of the funds, opponents charged, the president had either been misinformed or was unaware about events taking place in his own administration. Two Reagan officials were found guilty of illegal activities. Reagan, the committee concluded, "clearly failed to take care that the laws be faithfully executed."

Reagan's last year in office was comparatively unremarkable. His administration weathered the stock market crash of 1987 and the Iran-Contra scandal, and his support remained steady, even as Americans grew increasingly frustrated with partisanship in Congress. Reagan, meanwhile, left office after two terms as, he later noted, "the same man I was when I came to Washington." During the years between, the United States had regained its economic strength. His vice president, George Bush, was elected president in 1988.

Reagan published his autobiography, *An American Life*, in 1990, and he opened the Ronald Reagan Presidential Library in Simi Valley, California, a year later. It wasn't until 1994 that he began to slow down. He was discovered to be suffering from Alzheimer's disease, a degenerative affliction that affects the brain, and the Reagans immediately helped found the Ronald and Nancy Reagan Research Institute as part of the National Alzheimer's Association. In 2000, the House of Representatives voted to award the Congressional Gold Medal to Reagan and his wife. Reagan died at home in Los Angeles, California, on June 5, 2004.

Legacy

During Ronald Reagan's administration, fifty years of progressive social legislation that had begun with Franklin Roosevelt's New Deal was overturned. Government spending—except for defense—was sharply reduced, and taxes were cut. The deregulation of business encouraged a rush of corporate mergers and buyouts

Above: Long after both men had retired, the friendship between Ronald Reagan and Mikhail Gorbachev grew warmer with each passing year.

century and trade was vastly increased, the national debt finally began to go down. Some of the more harmful effects of deregulation—those that had fueled the stock market crash of 1987 (and another in 1989)—were eventually addressed.

During the Reagan years, the Cold War, which had dominated American foreign policy since the end of World War II, began to wind down. Supporters credit Reagan's hard-line approach with the Soviet Union and his support for American military buildup as major factors. A more general historical assessment emphasizes actions and events within the Soviet Union itself and in the surrounding nations it had dominated as key reasons for the thawing of the Cold War.

The nagging issue of how much influence the federal government should have continued to be a major source of debate in subsequent presidential elections. The Reagan administration clearly pursued policies that deemphasized the role of the federal government, and Republican presidential candidates in the next four elections campaigned on that theme with only slight variations.

that continued through the end of the century. Having selected one third of the Supreme Court justices in place when he left office, Reagan ensured that his conservative views would probably prevail for a long time to come.

Large increases in military spending and widening trade imbalances created a huge national debt that became an issue in both the 1988 and 1992 presidential elections. As the country prospered at the end of the

"What I'd really like to do is go down in history as the president who made Americans believe in themselves again."

—*Ronald Reagan*

Nancy Reagan

Born July 6, 1921, New York, New York
Died March 6, 2016, Los Angeles, California

"My life really began when I married my husband."

—*Nancy Reagan*

Nancy Reagan's eight years as first lady passed through three distinct stages: an initial period of serving as hostess at elegant parties, refurbishing the White House living quarters, and expanding the White House fine dinnerware collection; a second phase in which she became more active in social causes, such as the "Just Say No!" antidrug campaign; and a final phase when

Above: When they arrived back in California at the end of his presidency, Ronald Reagan donned a USC Trojan helmet to mark the couple's new beginning.

she became fiercely protective of her husband, Ronald Reagan, during the controversies surrounding the Iran-Contra investigation.

A devoted couple, the Reagans helped each other through the best and worst of times. Nancy helped arouse her husband's fighting spirit when he was recovering from a gunshot wound in 1981 following a failed assassination attempt, and she was at his side as he recovered from surgeries in July 1985 and January 1987.

At the end of his presidency, the two former actors went home to their California ranch, and, after finally riding off together into the sunset, the Reagans enjoyed a peaceful retirement. Their time together was made difficult as the former president was diagnosed with Alzheimer's disease, a degenerative affliction of the brain. The Reagans immediately helped found the Ronald and Nancy Reagan Research Institute in 1994 as part of the National Alzheimer's Association.

The Theater Life

Nancy Reagan was born Anne Frances Robbins in New York City on July 6, 1921 (although she officially gives the date as 1923). She was nicknamed Nancy by her mother, Edith Luckett, a theatrical actress, who was separated from her husband when her daughter was two.

Nancy saw little of her father, Kenneth Robbins, a New Jersey automobile dealer, while she was growing up. Her mother frequently toured the country with acting companies, and Nancy stayed with an aunt and uncle who lived in Bethesda, Maryland.

Edith Luckett visited her daughter as often as she could, especially when she was appearing in plays on Broadway and they could be together for extended periods in New York. As a child, Nancy enjoyed dressing in costumes and pretending that she was an actress, but not until after she learned an important lesson about the illusion of theater. She went to a play and watched in horror when the character her mother was playing died. She began sobbing in the audience, and her mother waved to her from the stage to show that she was just pretending.

Edith eventually married Loyal Davis, a neurosurgeon and chairman of the Department of Surgery at Northwestern University near Chicago, and she gave up acting. Nancy acquired the name Davis when she was adopted by her stepfather, and she acquired a new life, too, living with her parents in a large Chicago apartment on Lake Shore Drive.

Growing up in wealthy surroundings, Nancy learned to like fine clothes and dining out with her parents, often joined by socialites and theater people. She attended a private school, where she was president of the drama club, and she went on to Smith College in Northampton, Massachusetts, where she majored in drama.

While her stepfather served in the army medical corps during World War II, Nancy worked for a time with her mother as a nurse's aide. She moved to New York when she was hired for a small part in a play called *Ramshackle Inn*, which opened on Broadway in the mid-1940s.

The play ran for six months, and Nancy stayed in New York, picking up small acting jobs, working as a model, and socializing with her mother's friends, a circle that included actor Clark Gable. When she was invited to California for a screen test in 1949, another of her mother's friends, actor Spencer Tracy arranged to have a well-respected, professional director, George Cukor, work with her. Nancy did well with the test and went on to act in eleven films.

Nancy and Ronnie

The Reagans first met in 1949 when Nancy discovered that her name was on mailing lists of left-wing organizations. When she complained, she was referred to Reagan, who, as president of the Screen Actors' Guild was able to straighten it out. Apparently she had been confused with a different Nancy Davis, and he invited her to dinner so that he could explain.

Their romance developed gradually. Reagan was still upset over his recent divorce from Jane Wyman, but he found Nancy a comforting shoulder to lean on. He was extremely talkative and she was a good listener. They became engaged in February 1952, and, after postponing their wedding twice because of work conflicts, were married on March 4, 1952, with actor William Holden serving as best man. Later that year, their first child, Patricia Ann ("Patti"), was born. A son, Ronald Prescott, was born in 1958. Reagan had also had three children during his first marriage (one was adopted and one died in infancy).

Nancy and Ronald's film careers were both winding down during the 1950s. Reagan took a position as spokesman for the General Electric Company. He hosted a popular television program the company sponsored, and he traveled around the country making speeches promoting business and the American way. The Reagans bought a ranch and began moving among a wealthy circle of friends in southern California. They appeared together in a movie called *Hellcats of the Navy* in 1957. It was Nancy's last film work, and her husband had all but abandoned movies for television. After his eight-year stint as host of the *General Electric Theater,* he signed on as host of *Death Valley Days* in 1962.

Reagan became more politically active during the 1960s. His last film, *The Killers,* was released in 1964, the same year he made a televised campaign speech for Republican presidential candidate Barry Goldwater. Goldwater lost the election, but Reagan impressed California Republicans enough to become their candidate for governor in 1966. He won the election.

Governor's Wife

Nancy had never been very interested in politics, but she traveled with her husband to his campaign appearances and speeches, and her adoring gaze as he spoke was often noticed by political commentators. Reagan's advisors asked her to tone it down.

As California's first lady, Nancy Reagan oversaw the renovation of the state capitol in Sacramento, and she visited state hospitals, particularly as wounded servicemen were returning from the Vietnam War. She wrote a syndicated newspaper column during the Vietnam era, and donated her fees to the National League of Families of American Prisoners and Missing in Action in Southeast Asia.

After observing participants in the Foster Grandparent Program, which brought together senior citizens and handicapped children, she became a spokesperson for the cause, and later, as first lady of the United States, Mrs. Reagan helped expand the program on a national level.

She provided advice to the governor on the people he selected for his staff and she helped arrange his schedule. The Reagans acted as hosts for scores of festive events in Sacramento in the north and in the Los Angeles area of southern California.

In Washington, D.C.

After her husband won the presidential election in 1980, Nancy arranged glittering social occasions where men wore tuxedos and women donned glamorous floor-length gowns. Her expensive tastes in parties, White House dinnerware, designer gowns, jewelry, and furnishings met with some criticism by people who pointed out that while President Reagan was trimming the federal budget, White House social spending was growing almost out of control. Nancy Reagan handled the criticism by pointing out that her gowns were only on loan from designers and were donated to museums after she wore them. Early press troubles over her extravagance weren't helped by her autobiography, *Nancy,* which was published before she became first lady and which revealed a woman with decidedly champagne tastes.

Above: Nancy Reagan took her "Just Say No" anti-drug initiative to inner-city youngsters.

Those initial concerns soon passed, though. Her involvement with the Foster Grandparent Program and her fight against drug abuse revealed a more serious and caring first lady. She became a spokesperson for the "Just Say No!" campaign that advised young people to resist trying drugs, and she supported private efforts, rather than government programs, to help combat drug abuse. Mrs. Reagan expanded her drug awareness campaign to an international level by inviting first ladies from around the world to talks on drug abuse, and during the fortieth anniversary of the United Nations in 1985, she was host of a second international drug conference.

Tough Times

Nancy Reagan also helped her husband recover from some serious medical problems: He was wounded in an assassination attempt in 1981, he had colon surgery four years later, and prostate surgery in 1987, the same year Nancy herself had surgery to treat breast cancer.

She became increasingly involved in helping direct her husband's administration during his second term. Particularly after his hospitalization, she preferred a more relaxed schedule for him so that he could concentrate on the most significant issues needing his attention. As the Iran-Contra scandal entangled the Reagan administration, she became angry with staff members she felt hadn't helped prepare him for answering tough questions from the press.

Nancy Reagan enjoyed being first lady, but she welcomed retirement after the end of her husband's second term in 1989. She almost immediately established the Nancy Reagan Foundation to continue her campaign to educate people about the dangers of substance abuse, and in 1994, the Foundation joined forces with the BEST Foundation for a Drug-Free Tomorrow. Together they developed the Nancy Reagan Afterschool Program to promote drug prevention for young people.

The Reagans returned to their California ranch, where the former president remained active before beginning to deal with the effects of Alzheimer's disease. The couple remained devoted to each other as he began suffering more profound effects of the disease, and they founded the Ronald and Nancy Reagan Research Institute as part of the National Alzheimer's Association. Before her husband's death in 2004, Nancy was a tireless, devoted caregiver. President Obama said of her, ". . . in her long goodbye with President Reagan, she became a voice on behalf of millions of families going through the depleting, aching reality of Alzheimer's, and took on a new role, as advocate, on behalf of treatments that hold the potential and the promise to improve and save lives."

In March 2016, Nancy Reagan died in her Los Angles home of congestive heart failure. She was 94 years old. She had been a trusted advisor and fierce guardian of her husband throughout his career. Michael K. Deaver, a close, long-time friend of the Reagans said, "Without Nancy, there would have been no Governor Reagan, no President Reagan."

Below: Ronnie and Nancy spent their happiest moments at their California ranch, El Rancho del Cielo.

Reagan's First Inaugural Address

Delivered on January 18, 1981

The inauguration of Ronald Reagan in 1981 promised a new start for the nation. The 1970s had begun with U.S. soldiers fighting in the Vietnam War and ended with American hostages being held in Iran for more than four hundred days. The resignation of President Richard Nixon, soaring fuel prices, and diminishing international prestige were other problems of the 1970s that Americans were anxious to put behind them.

Reagan had capitalized on that sense of discontent during his campaign for the presidency. Always speaking with optimism, he declared that the federal government had grown too large and too intrusive in the lives of its citizens. Promising to scale back government programs to promote only those that created opportunity, Reagan hoped to begin a period of national renewal.

There was a sense of freshness surrounding his inaugural. For the first time, an inauguration ceremony was held on the terrace of the West Front of the Capitol. And on that same day, the American hostages held by the revolutionary government of Iran were finally released.

Excerpt from Reagan's First Inaugural Address

The business of our nation goes forward. These United States are confronted with an economic affliction of great proportions. We suffer from the longest and one of the worst sustained inflations in our national history. It distorts our economic decisions, penalizes thrift, and crushes the struggling young and the fixed-income elderly alike. It threatens to shatter the lives of millions of our people.

Idle industries have cast workers into unemployment, causing human misery and personal indignity. Those who do work are denied a fair return for their labor by a tax system which penalizes successful achievement and keeps us from maintaining full productivity.

But great as our tax burden is, it has not kept pace with public spending. For decades, we have piled deficit upon deficit, mortgaging our future and our children's future for the temporary convenience of the present. To continue this long trend is to guarantee tremendous social, cultural, political, and economic upheavals.

You and I, as individuals, can, by borrowing, live beyond our means, but for only a limited period of time. Why, then, should we think that collectively, as a nation, we are not bound by that same limitation?

We must act today in order to preserve tomorrow. And let there be no misunderstanding—we are going to begin to act, beginning today.

The economic ills we suffer have come upon us over several decades. They will not go away in days, weeks, or months, but they will go away. They will go away because we, as Americans, have the capacity now, as we have had in the past, to do whatever needs to be done to preserve this last and greatest bastion of freedom.

In this present crisis, government is not the solution to our problem.

From time to time, we have been tempted to believe that society has become too complex to be managed by self-rule, that government by an elite group is superior to government for, by, and of the people. But if no one among us is capable of governing himself, then who among us has the capacity to govern someone else? All of us together, in and out of government, must bear the burden. The solutions we seek must be equitable, with no one group singled out to pay a higher price.

We hear much of special interest groups. Our concern must be for a special interest group that has been too long neglected. It knows no sectional boundaries or ethnic and racial divisions, and it crosses political party lines. It is made up of men and women who raise our food, patrol our streets, man our mines and our factories, teach our children, keep our homes, and heal us when we are sick—professionals, industrialists, shopkeepers, clerks, cabbies, and truck drivers. They are, in short, "We the people," this breed called Americans.

Well, this administration's objective will be a healthy, vigorous, growing economy that provides equal opportunity for all Americans, with no barriers born of bigotry or discrimination. Putting America back to work means putting all Americans back to work. Ending inflation means freeing all Americans from the terror of runaway living costs. All must share in the productive work of this "new beginning" and all must share in the bounty of a revived economy. With the idealism and fair play which are the core of our system and our strength, we can have a strong and prosperous America at peace with itself and the world.

So, as we begin, let us take inventory. We are a nation that has a government—not the other way around. And this makes us special among the nations of the Earth. Our Government has no power except that granted it by the people. It is time to check and reverse the growth of government which shows signs of having grown beyond the consent of the governed.

It is my intention to curb the size and influence of the Federal establishment and to demand recognition of the distinction between the powers granted to the Federal Government and those reserved to the States or to the people. All of us need to be reminded that the Federal Government did not create the States; the States created the Federal Government.

Now, so there will be no misunderstanding, it is not my intention to do away with government. It is, rather, to make it work—work with us, not over us; to stand by our side, not ride on our back. Government can and must provide opportunity, not smother it; foster productivity, not stifle it.

If we look to the answer as to why, for so many years, we achieved so much, prospered as no other people on Earth, it was because here, in this land, we unleashed the energy and individual genius of man to a greater extent than has ever been done before. Freedom and the dignity of the individual have been more available and assured here than in any other place on Earth. The price for this freedom at times has been high, but we have never been unwilling to pay that price.

It is no coincidence that our present troubles parallel and are proportionate to the intervention and intrusion in our lives that result from unnecessary and excessive growth of government. It is time for us to realize that we are too great a nation to limit ourselves to small dreams. We are not, as some would have us believe, doomed to an inevitable decline. I do not believe in a fate that will fall on us no matter what we do. I do believe in a fate that will fall on us if we do nothing. So, with all the creative energy at our command, let us begin an era of national renewal. Let us renew our determination, our courage, and our strength. And let us renew our faith and our hope.

We have every right to dream heroic dreams. Those who say that we are in a time when there are no heroes just don't know where to look. You can see heroes every day going in and out of factory gates. Others, a handful in number, produce enough food to feed all of us and then the world beyond. You meet heroes across a counter—and they are on both sides of that counter. There are entrepreneurs with faith in themselves and faith in an idea who create new jobs, new wealth and opportunity. They are individuals and families whose taxes support the Government and whose voluntary gifts support church, charity, culture, art, and education. Their patriotism is quiet but deep. Their values sustain our national life.

[…]

In the days ahead I will propose removing the roadblocks that have slowed our economy and reduced productivity. Steps will be taken aimed at restoring the balance between the various levels of government. Progress may be slow—measured in inches and feet, not miles—but we will progress. It is time to reawaken this industrial giant, to get government back within its means, and to lighten our punitive tax burden. And these will be our first priorities, and on these principles, there will be no compromise. [...]

And as we renew ourselves here in our own land, we will be seen as having greater strength throughout the world. We will again be the exemplar of freedom and a beacon of hope for those who do not now have freedom.

[…]

This is the first time in history that this ceremony has been held, as you have been told, on this West Front of the Capitol. Standing here, one faces a magnificent vista, opening up on this city's special beauty and history. At the end of this open mall are those shrines to the giants on whose shoulders we stand.

[…]

Beyond those monuments to heroism is the Potomac River, and on the far shore the sloping hills of Arlington National Cemetery with its row on row of simple white markers bearing crosses or Stars of David. They add up to only a tiny fraction of the price that has been paid for our freedom.

[…]

Under one such marker lies a young man—Martin Treptow—who left his job in a small town barber shop in 1917 to go to France with the famed Rainbow Division. There, on the western front, he was killed trying to carry a message between battalions under heavy artillery fire.

We are told that on his body was found a diary. On the flyleaf under the heading, "My Pledge," he had written these words: "America must win this war. Therefore, I will work, I will save, I will sacrifice, I will endure, I will fight cheerfully and do my utmost, as if the issue of the whole struggle depended on me alone."

The crisis we are facing today does not require of us the kind of sacrifice that Martin Treptow and so many thousands of others were called upon to make. It does require, however, our best effort, and our willingness to believe in ourselves and to believe in our capacity to perform great deeds; to believe that together, with God's help, we can and will resolve the problems which now confront us.

And, after all, why shouldn't we believe that? We are Americans. God bless you, and thank you.

What Happened Next

In his speech, Reagan observed that "progress may be slow—measured in inches and feet, not miles—but we will progress." Small progress in overcoming the economic crisis he identified in the address was made during the first two years of his presidency. Beginning in 1983, the American economy improved and expanded consistently over the next six years—through the end of Reagan's second term.

Tax reduction acts passed in 1981 and 1986 helped relieve the tax burden that Reagan blamed for having stifled growth. Government programs, which Reagan identified as another form of burden, were cut back during his administration with mixed results. Businesses were able to act with less restraint, but some took advantage of reduced government supervision. The government deficit that Reagan targeted for reduction in his inaugural address actually grew during his presidency, partly from increased military spending and a trade imbalance where imports far outbalanced exports and partly from resistance by Congress to authorize further cuts in government programs.

The economy improved, and some government regulations were enacted later to help maintain order and stability in business. One of the results of the Reagan presidency has been the more careful consideration and debate, as well as resistance, that greets each potential new regulation. To his supporters, that reality is an example of what they call "the Reagan Revolution"—an administration that turned away from a fifty-year trend of large government social programs and brought renewed emphasis to the question of just how powerful Americans want their government to be.

George H. W. Bush

"A government that remembers that the people are its master is a good and needed thing."

—*George H. W. Bush*

Forty-first president of the United States, 1989–1993

Full name: *George Herbert Walker Bush*
Born: *June 12, 1924, Milton, Massachusetts*
Parents: *Prescott Sheldon and Dorothy Walker Bush*
Spouse: *Barbara Pierce (1925– ; m. 1945)*
Children: *George Walker (1946–);*
Pauline Robinson (Robin) (1949–1953);
John (Jeb) Ellis (1953–); Neil Mallon (1955–);
Marvin Pierce (1956–); Dorothy Walker (1959–)
Religion: *Methodist*
Education: *Yale University (B.A., 1948)*
Occupations: *Oilman*
Government positions: *U.S. representative from Texas;*
U.S. ambassador to the United Nations; CIA director;
vice president under Ronald Reagan
Political party: *Republican*
Dates as president: *January 20, 1989–January 20, 1993*
Age upon taking office: *64*

*K*nown as a team player, George Bush was skilled at establishing defined goals and then rallying support for them. That talent was displayed during his presidency in his international leadership during the Gulf War. Leading at home, in Washington's highly partisan political environment, proved to be more difficult.

Bush's presidency was challenged on two fronts—a Democrat-controlled Congress and an increasingly hostile conservative group within his own Republican Party. He came to office with a distinguished record of public service. After serving as vice president in the popular Ronald Reagan administration, Bush became the first sitting vice president to be elected to the presidency in 150 years. Conservative Republicans wanted him to continue Reagan's policies of tax cuts, increased military spending, and reduction of all other government spending. When Bush concentrated instead on reducing the huge federal budget deficit, supporting business reforms, and restoring education and environmental programs, he faced resentment within his own party. Democrats, on the other hand, claimed that his policies were too modest.

Bush was more effective with his foreign policy. He was president during a period of remarkable international developments. The Soviet Union's dominance over Eastern Europe had ended, and former republics in the

Timeline

Union of Soviet Socialist Republics (USSR), including Russia, itself, became independent. The Cold War that had exerted tremendous influence on American life and politics for forty years was over.

In 1991, an international coalition spearheaded by the Bush administration swiftly expelled the invading military of Iraq from the nation of Kuwait in the Gulf War. Bush's popularity soared over his handling of the war as well as his other accomplishments abroad, but the support wore away quickly the following year when the nation's economy gradually worsened, and he wasn't reelected in 1992.

Early Accomplishments

George Herbert Walker Bush was born on June 12, 1924, in Milton, Massachusetts, and grew up with his three brothers and a sister, primarily in Greenwich, Connecticut. His father, Prescott Bush, was a wealthy investment banker who also served as a Republican senator from Connecticut from 1952 to 1963. A moderate, Prescott supported the policies of President Dwight D. Eisenhower and distanced himself from more stridently conservative Republicans, and his son George would follow the same political principles.

Bush's mother, Dorothy, was from the wealthy family of a leading Missouri industrialist. She is credited with establishing a sense of humbleness in her children, a trait later seen in Bush's interest in team-building over individual accomplishment. After graduating from the private Phillips Academy in Massachusetts, Bush enlisted in the U.S. Navy during World War II, and became an ensign and the navy's youngest pilot. He flew fifty-eight combat missions in the Pacific theater during the war, and during one of them, his plane was shot down over the ocean, killing two of his crew. Bush clung to wreckage until he was rescued by a submarine, and he was awarded the Distinguished Flying Cross for bravery in action.

After he got back home, he married Barbara Pierce, the daughter of a New York magazine publisher. They would have six children; two of them—George W. Bush,

Left: Bush's father, Prescott Bush, was a wealthy investment banker. He was the father of the forty-first president and grandfather of the forty-third.

Right: In 1953, Senator Prescott Bush presents Senator Richard Nixon with a straw hat made in his home state of Connecticut.

Alter Ego

George Herbert Walker Bush was named for his grandfather, investment banker George Herbert Walker, and because his mother's father was known as "Pop," he was called "Little Pop." The name stuck with him and when he went off to collage, it was shortened to "Poppy," which has trailed him ever since.

the forty-third president of the United States, and John, known as Jeb, who later became governor of Florida—would follow their father into politics. A daughter, Robin, died of leukemia at the age of three.

Bush enrolled at Yale University and graduated in 1948, after a three-year accelerated program that had been put in place for returning GIs like him. He majored in economics, captained the school's baseball team, and was a member of Yale's most exclusive group, the Skull and Bones Society. After graduation, he moved his family to Texas, where he took an administrative job at an oil-field supply company. In 1953, he and a friend co-founded the Zapata Petroleum Company (named for the Marlon Brando film *Viva Zapata*) and the following year, he became president of a subsidiary called the Zapata Off-Shore Company. By the mid-1960s, Bush sold his stake in the company, and he became a self-made millionaire at the age of forty-one.

Young Hero

George Bush was eighteen years old when he joined the navy and got his pilot's wings. He was not only the youngest flier, but the youngest-looking officer in "This Man's Navy," and to make matters worse, his girlfriend, Barbara Pierce, was even younger. He asked her to lie about her age. On September 24, 1944, three months after his twentieth birthday, he was flying a TBM Avenger, a three-man dive bomber over the Japanese communications center on the island of Chichi Jima, part of the island chain that includes Iwo Jima, when he was hit by intense anti-aircraft fire. His cockpit filled with smoke and flames licked the edged of the plane's wings, but Bush kept on diving. As soon as he dropped all four of his 500-pound bombs and destroyed the target, he turned for the open sea and after his crew bailed out, he jumped, too. He was slightly injured on the way down, but he was still intact when he hit the water, where he floundered in an open life raft without a paddle, drifting slowly in the direction of the enemy-held island. Finally, an American submarine broke the surface, Bush was rescued, and the ordeal was over. The only bad news that day was that his two crewmates were lost at sea. He was awarded a Distinguished Flying Cross for his efforts to rescue them.

Below, left: George Bush has been known as "Poppy" since his childhood. The nickname was used in his prep school yearbook instead of his real first name.

Below, center: George Bush at Yale University, Class of 1948.

Below, right: Bush's official Naval service portrait.

CAPTAIN POPPY BUSH
It was worth staying an extra year

GEORGE HERBERT WALKER BUSH

Service Branch:
USN

Rank / Rate:
LT

Service Dates:
1942 to 1945

Born:
MILTON, MA
06/12/24

Photo: USS SAN JACINTO 1942

Above: While George was a student at Yale, he and Barbara lived in this New Haven house where their son George W. spent some of his childhood.

Enters Politics

George soon became active in Republican politics, helping to organize local and state groups. He won the Republican nomination for a U.S. Senate seat in 1964, but he lost to Ralph W. Yarborough during a landslide election year for the Democrats. Bush made a comeback two years later when he was elected to the House of Representatives, becoming the first Republican ever to represent the Houston area in Congress. Former vice president and 1960 presidential candidate Richard Nixon campaigned on Bush's behalf.

During his two terms in the House, Bush was a practical, business-oriented legislator. After Nixon was elected president in 1968, Bush supported the administration's policy of gradual troop reduction during the Vietnam War, and in 1970, he ran again for the Senate, but was defeated by Lloyd Bentsen, a moderate Democrat whose views were almost interchangeable with his own: Both represented the more business-oriented agenda of the changing South that would be labeled the "New

Right: During his term as U.S. Ambassador to the United Nations, Bush, who had been the U.S. representative to China, proposed UN membership for the People's Republic of China.

South." Later, in 1988, Bentsen and Bush would compete against each other once again when Bush was the Republican presidential candidate and Bentsen ran as the Democratic vice-presidential candidate.

Although he had lost the 1970 election, Bush wasn't out of political work for long. President Nixon nominated him to be U.S. representative to the United Nations, and in spite of concerns over Bush's lack of foreign-policy experience, his appointment was confirmed by the Senate. Bush's strong administrative and communication skills helped him in efforts to establish a peacekeeping force in the Middle East and to reduce U.S. financial support for the United Nations, which the conservative wing of Congress was demanding.

Bush became chairman of the Republican National Committee in 1973 at the strong urging of President Nixon. In that position, Bush directed the party's national activities, and within weeks he found himself mired in the Watergate scandal, which centered on a 1972 burglary of Democratic National Headquarters, and involved high-level members of the Nixon administration. Bush managed to hold his party together during the scandal, even as it forced the resignation of President Nixon in August 1974. Bush remained supportive of the president until the evidence left no doubt showed that Nixon was

involved, but then he sent him a letter recommending his resignation shortly before the president officially stepped down.

Nixon's successor, Gerald R. Ford, offered Bush an open opportunity to choose any position in his administration, and Bush opted to become envoy to China. President Nixon had reestablished U.S. relations with China two years earlier after a twenty-year period without any diplomatic contact, and Bush helped to reestablish diplomatic activities.

He was called back home in 1975 to become director of the Central Intelligence Agency (CIA), the department charged with collecting information about other countries. The agency had been wracked by investigations that had uncovered abuses of power and illegal, covert operations, and Bush succeeded in lifting the morale of its personnel through his professionalism in carrying out a presidential executive order that forced the agency to work within its defined, legal mission.

Following Ford's defeat in the 1976 presidential election, Bush went back to private life, taking care of his personal businesses and serving as chairman of a Houston bank, all the while quietly gathering support for a run at the White House.

Below: CIA Director George Bush briefs President Gerald R. Ford and members of the National Security Council in 1976.

Team Player

Bush's major opponent for the 1980 Republican presidential nomination was former California governor Ronald Reagan, who had very nearly clinched the nomination in 1976. Reagan had a strong appeal to religious conservatives who favored prayer in public schools and a ban on abortion, and added to that, he announced plans for a program of tax cuts, reduced government spending on social programs, and vastly increased military spending. Through tax cuts, Reagan reasoned, consumers would have more spending power and would be enough to turn the sluggish economy around. During his campaign for the nomination, Bush called the Reagan program "voodoo economics"—a magic plan that didn't have a chance of working.

Bush won the early Iowa caucuses, but he lost to Reagan in the New Hampshire presidential primary, and in spite of a few more primary victories, he was far behind Reagan, who gathered enough support to win the nomination. At first, Reagan offered the vice presidential slot to Gerald Ford, but when he realized that the former president had a kind of co-presidency in mind, he decided against it and asked Bush instead. Bush became a team player, supporting Reagan's economic policies while at the same time appealing to the more moderate voters who were his natural constituency, and bringing foreign-policy experience to the ticket as well.

Above: During his time at the United Nations, Bush earned foreign policy experience working with such leaders as Israeli Foreign Minister Abba Eban (L) and Ambassador Joseph Tekoah.

The Republicans won convincingly, defeating President Jimmy Carter and Vice President Walter Mondale.

Bush's foreign-policy experience was put to good use as vice president. He traveled to sixty countries over the next eight years, often in ceremonial roles, but also making valuable contacts and representing administration policies. At home, he headed task forces on crime, terrorism, and drug smuggling. Bush was a reassuring presence following an assassination attempt on the president after less than three months in office. He helped run the country while Reagan recovered from a gunshot wound, and in a more official capacity, he served as acting president for eight hours in 1985. President Reagan had arranged for the formal transfer of power when he was hospitalized for cancer surgery. The event, which ran from 11:30 A.M. to 7:30 P.M. on July 13, 1985, was the first such temporary transfer of power in the nation's history.

From Landslide to Scandal

Reagan was reelected in a landslide in 1984, this time defeating former vice president Walter Mondale, and he remained incredibly popular through all of his second term, in spite of a controversy involving the illegal sale of arms to Iran known as the Iran-Contra affair. Since the scandal involved some members of the president's National Security Council, and Bush was a member himself, the vice president was indirectly implicated as well.

The Iran-Contra scandal uncovered careless supervision within the Reagan White House, where some officials had been making illegal deals both with and without the president's knowledge. Bush denied any involvement in the illegal activities and, like Reagan, he was never officially charged with any wrongdoing, although the president eventually conceded that he had authorized illegal contact with members of the Iranian government.

A Kinder, Gentler Nation

Bush had to field questions about the Iran-Contra scandal when he ran for president in 1988, and Reagan's popularity among conservatives was another issue as well. Reaganomics, the fiscal policies that Bush had once called "voodoo economics," had revived the American economy, and conservatives wanted Bush to maintain Reagan's policies. But Bush recognized the need to confront a growing budget deficit, prosperity that primarily benefited the wealthiest people, and problems that grew out of Reagan's deep cuts in government programs, all of which was regularly attacked by Democrats. Calling for a "kinder, gentler nation," Bush proposed a more moderate approach as well as cuts in military spending that would not compromise the nation's military capabilities.

"I'm a conservative, but I'm not a nut about it."
—*George H. W. Bush*

In an effort to help satisfy conservative concerns, Bush made a pledge early in his campaign—"Read my lips: No new taxes"—which he would later come to regret. He ran a hard-hitting campaign against Democratic candidate Michael Dukakis, making accusations that the Massachusetts governor was weak on crime and environmental issues. However, except for promise of "no new taxes," which he couldn't keep, neither Bush nor Dukakis had much to say about the economy, even

Left: George Bush almost never ducked press conferences, even when the resulting headlines weren't to his liking.

though it was easily the most important political issue of the era. With the support of the popular, outgoing president, Bush won a clear victory, taking 53 percent of the popular vote and winning forty states in the Electoral College for a 426- to 111-vote victory.

Politics back in Washington, however, were neither kind nor gentle. Long nasty battles with Congress over the annual budget broke out, as Democrats pushed to increase Bush's proposed spending plans and Republicans called for deeper spending. Budgets need to be authorized by Congress and the president in order for federal workers to be paid, and the budget impasse came close to resulting in payless paydays for them. To help complete the budget process, Bush compromised with Democrats

on a federal deficit reduction plan that included tax increases. Conservatives were outraged and blocked the compromise, but a different version that included higher taxes, as well as Bush's tax reform ideas, passed.

Conservatives Began to Abandon Bush

Bush supported several other actions that went against the policies of the Reagan administration. He introduced regulations on unfair business and financial practices, as well as a social- and civil-rights program. The Americans with Disabilities Act, which lowered legal and physical obstacles to the physically challenged, was approved in 1990, additional money was targeted for the improvement of education and the nation's highways; and the Clean Air Act set new antipollution standards for fuel burning.

Meanwhile, the economy had stopped growing, and a recession hit. In spite of the financial growth of the 1980s, more than 14 percent of Americans were still living in poverty. In his battles with Congress, Bush vetoed thirty-five pieces of legislation, and the nation began viewing Washington as a place where nothing was being accomplished because of the nasty struggles between the two political parties.

Bush appointed two Supreme Court Justices during his term in office. His nomination of David Souter passed in Congress, but an uproar developed over Bush's nomination of Clarence Thomas. Anita Hill, a

1988 Election Results

Presidential / Vice Presidential Candidates	Popular Votes	Electoral Votes
George Bush / Dan Quayle (Republican)	48,886,097	426
Michael Dukakis / Lloyd Bentsen (Democratic)	41,809,074	111

Massachusetts governor Dukakis won the Democratic nomination by easily defeating Rev. Jesse Jackson of Illinois on the first ballot; Dukakis had outlasted such other prominent candidates as Missouri congressman Richard Gephardt, Tennessee senator Al Gore, and Illinois senator Paul Simon. Vice President Bush easily defeated his closest competitors: Kansas senator Bob Dole and television evangelist Pat Robertson.

former member of Thomas's staff, accused him of sexual harassment, resulting in a tense Senate confirmation hearing that was nationally televised. Thomas was eventually approved by the Senate by a narrow, 52-to-48 vote, mostly along partisan lines—a predictable reflection of the times.

Meanwhile, the Bush White House brought a refreshing sense of calm to the country. He held regular frequent press conferences, went jogging around Washington, and held more informal White House gatherings. First Lady Barbara Bush was a soothing, grandmotherlike presence.

The Bush Administration

Administration Dates:	January 20, 1989–January 20, 1993
Vice President:	Dan Quayle (1989–93)
Cabinet:	
Secretary of State	James A. Baker III (1989–92)
	Lawrence S. Eagleburger (1992–93)
Secretary of the Treasury	Nicholas F. Brady (1988–93)
Attorney General	Richard L. Thornburgh (1989–91)
	William P. Barr (1991–93)
Secretary of the Interior	Manuel Luján Jr. (1989–93)
Secretary of Agriculture	Clayton Yeutter (1989–91)
	Edward Madigan (1991–93)
Secretary of Labor	Elizabeth H. Dole (1989–90)
	Lynn Morley Martin (1991–93)
Secretary of Commerce	Robert A. Mosbacher (1989–92)
	Barbara H. Franklin (1992–93)
Secretary of Defense	Richard Cheney (1989–93)
Secretary of Housing and Urban Development	Jack Kemp (1989–93)
Secretary of Transportation	Samuel K. Skinner (1989–91)
	Andrew H. Card Jr. (1992–93)
Secretary of Energy	James Watkins (1989–93)
Secretary of Health and Human Services	Louis Sullivan (1989–93)
Secretary of Education	Lauro F. Cavazos (1989–90)
	Lamar Alexander (1991–93)
Secretary of Veterans Affairs	Edward J. Derwinski (1989–92)
	Anthony J. Principi (1992–93)

Above: Bush takes a presidential jog with his Secret Service detail, Congressman Larry Hopkins, and Brit Hume of ABC television. As they pass a pair of sunbathers, Bush calls out, "Smile, you're on national television."

World of Change

Bush's foreign policy experience proved to be his greatest strength. Through his support of sanctions against the government of the Republic of South Africa, he helped pressure reform that put an end to apartheid, South Africa's policy of legalizing racial segregation. In December of 1989, Bush authorized an American invasion of Panama to bring about the fall and arrest of the nation's leader, General Manuel Noriega, who had nullified a national election that he was clearly losing and was supporting the international drug trade. Twenty-four hundred American troops assisted Panamanian rebels to overthrow his government, and Noriega was taken to the United States to face trial for drug trafficking. He was later convicted. Twenty-three Americans died in the fighting in Panama.

Meanwhile, Eastern European nations (including Poland, Czechoslovakia, and East Germany) were beginning to free themselves from years of communist domination by the Soviet Union. During this time, Soviet president Mikhail Gorbachev introduced reforms in his own nation that weakened the exclusive power of the Soviet communist party. His reforms speeded up the collapse of the Soviet Union and freed the other former Soviet states to become independent nations.

Above: A U.S. military helicopter flies over a burning high-rise building in Panama City during the 1989 American invasion.

Bush and Gorbachev met and signed a strategic arms reduction pact in August 1991, and shortly afterward Gorbachev faced a coup back home. He was saved through the efforts of Boris Yeltsin, who was elected the new president of Russia the following year.

Bush encouraged the fall of the communist state in the Soviet Union, and he was quick to recognize the resulting governments of the new nations that

Left: During the invasion of Panama, Manuel Noriega, the principal target, took refuge in the Vatican Embassy. Tanks surrounded the embassy and broadcast loud rock music around the clock in the hopes of flushing Noriega out.

were formerly Soviet republics, and quickly established rapprochement with the new Yeltsin government. Another missile reduction pact between the United States and Russia was signed within a few months.

"Terrorism attempts to erode the legitimacy of democratic institutions. Its real and lasting effects cannot be measured in body counts or property damage but rather by its long-term psychological impact and the subsequent political results. The terrorists' cry is: Don't trust your government, your democratic institutions, your principles of law. None of these pillars of an open society can protect you. ... Terrorism is a kind of violent graffiti, and simply by capturing headlines and television time, the terrorist partially succeeds."

—George H. W. Bush

Operation Desert Storm

In August 1990, the small, oil-rich nation of Kuwait was attacked by its Middle East neighbor, Iraq, which also positioned armies near the borders of Saudi Arabia and Iran, threatening to dominate the world's oil supply (at the time, Kuwait held 10 percent of the world's oil reserves, Iran also held 10 percent, and Saudi Arabia held 25 percent).

President Bush helped forge a broad international coalition against Iraq that included support from most

United Nations (UN) members, including Arab nations that had often been reluctant to challenge their neighbors. Citing Iraq's unprovoked attack and its threat to the world's oil reserves, Bush ordered the largest deployment of American forces (425,000 troops) since the Vietnam War, calling it Operation Desert Shield. In January 1991, he secured congressional authority to use all necessary means to expel Iraqi forces from Kuwait. Operation Desert Storm, as the mission to liberate Kuwait was being called, was launched on January 17, 1991, with nine different nations participating in massive bombing missions on strategic sites within Iraq.

While Bush was achieving his goals of minimizing U.S. casualties and returning control of Kuwait to its government, Iraqi leader Saddam Hussein ordered a missile attack on Israel, hoping to draw it into the

Right: Iraqi leader Saddam Hussein, who ordered an invasion of Kuwait that sparked the Gulf War.

Right: A burned-out Iraqi tank against a backdrop of oil-well fires set by Saddam's army.

conflict, and inspire other Middle Eastern countries to withdraw. Bush managed to keep the Israeli government from retaliating, and offered military protection.

As Iraqi forces were being overwhelmed, Saddam offered to withdraw from part of Kuwait, but Bush, supported by UN resolutions against Iraq, remained firm on complete withdrawal. In February 1991, ground forces pushed the Iraqis out of Kuwait in less than 100 hours, and the short Gulf War was over in less than 2 months; in the process, 149 Americans died in action and at least 10,000 Iraqi soldiers were killed.

Bush's popularity skyrocketed with his handling of the Gulf War, although he was criticized in some quarters for not having gone on to remove Saddam Hussein from power. The defined mission, sanctioned by the UN, had been accomplished. When the Iraqi leader began putting down revolts within his own country, Bush helped establish a "no-fly" zone patrolled by the U.S. Air Force, where Iraqi aircraft were prohibited as a way of protecting ethnic regions from being assaulted.

Two more noteworthy foreign policy events took place during the Bush presidency. To help support Middle East peace talks, he convinced Israel to stop building new settlements on land outside its borders that had been occupied by its military. To help encourage international trade, closer to home, Bush aides began negotiating the North American Free Trade Agreement (NAFTA) with Canada and Mexico, which eliminated almost all trade barriers among the three nations, was later ratified in November 1993, after Bush left office.

Dramatic Fade

With the triumph in the Gulf War, and Bush's soaring popularity in 1991, his chances for reelection the following year seemed like a sure thing. But the continued sluggishness of the American economy cut into his support. He was attacked by conservatives within his own party over taxes and government spending. and at the 1992 Republican convention, outspoken conservatives were able to influence the party's platform away from Bush's more moderate beliefs.

Bush hadn't been able to break through in his struggles with Congress, and his attacks on Bill Clinton, his Democratic opponent, on issues of trust and character didn't have much effect. A relaxed and polished speaker, Clinton had become a master of a new type of presidential debate—the town meeting—a setting that frees a candidate to stroll around a stage, instead of standing behind a lectern, and to take questions directly from the audience.

Meanwhile, Bush's appeal to moderate conservatives was affected by the emergence of a third-party candidate, H. Ross Perot, a Texas billionaire, who drew support for his stand on two key issues: He wanted a more aggressive approach to attacking the federal budget deficit; and, as an outsider not associated with either of the major parties, he claimed that he could break through stalemates between the parties that were slowing down legislation in Washington for much too long.

Left: Bush's point men in the Gulf War were (L-R) General Colin Powell, Chairman of the Joint Chiefs of Staff; Defense Secretary Dick Cheney; and General Norman Schwarzkopf.

H. Ross Perot

Henry Ross Perot was born on June 27, 1930, in Texarkana, Texas. He grew up there and spent one year at the local junior college before going on to the U.S. Naval Academy, graduating as class president in 1953. He spent the next four years at sea.

Perot got a basic education in engineering at the Academy, and although he had no special training in electronics or computing, his personal qualities impressed a representative from International Business Machines, a leading company in the relatively new computer industry, and when he left the navy, IBM hired him to sell computers in Dallas. In 1962, after trying unsuccessfully to convince the company that it could make money by leasing unused computer time to clients who needed it, Perot started his own business, Electronic Data Systems (EDS). In the years that followed, EDS expanded to run entire data-processing departments for insurance companies, banks, and state and national governments. By the end of the 1960s, Perot sold a small portion of his shares in the business for $5 million.

As he grew extremely wealthy in the 1970s and 1980s, Perot became known for his international and philanthropic concerns. During the Vietnam War, he tried to improve the treatment of American prisoners of war in North Vietnam. In December 1969, Perot sent two planeloads of food, gifts, and medical supplies to them, but the North Vietnamese refused to accept delivery of the goods. The publicity surrounding the episode, however, may have led to improved conditions in prison camps.

In the early 1970s, EDS attempted to improve data processing on Wall Street by purchasing a subsidiary of a stock brokerage firm. Unfortunately, the firm was in serious financial difficulties, and Perot wound up losing $60 million. A few years later, EDS expanded internationally when it obtained contracts in Saudi Arabia and Iran. In 1978, after a financial dispute with the Iranian government, two leading EDS officers were arrested and imprisoned. Perot set out to win their release, even paying a quiet visit to Iran himself. An EDS rescue team was formed and trained but did not penetrate the prison where the men were held. Reportedly at the urging of an Iranian employee of EDS, an Iranian mob broke into the prison and released the prisoners. The EDS officials escaped and, with the rescue team, fled the country on foot. This episode was later recounted in a bestselling novel On the Wings of Eagles.

General Motors (GM) bought EDS in 1984, hoping to unify the data processing systems in its diverse operations. For the 45 percent of EDS stock that Perot owned, he received nearly $1 billion in cash and 5.5 million shares of stock in a new company called GME. Tensions between EDS and GM mounted, however, and Perot criticized GM's way of doing business. In the fall of 1986, GM bought out Perot's GME shares, ending his connection with EDS. Perot agreed not to open a new profit-making data-processing business for three years. By 1989, GM and Perot were in court over the question of whether Perot had held to this agreement in forming a new company, Perot Systems.

Perot's career switched gears in 1992, when he spearheaded a campaign to have himself elected president of the United States under the banner of the Independent Party. Perot appeared on the Larry King Live television show and said he would run for president if a grassroots effort was successful in placing his name on the ballot in all fifty states. Public reaction was phenomenal. Perot sounded like a candidate eager to be elected, and his supporters saw in him the country's economic and social salvation. "If [elected], we'll be working night and day to fix all these problems," he said in May 1992, on the People's Radio Network. He told the New York Times that he favored a congressional act to limit federal spending and claimed he could cut waste in the federal budget, and he vowed to balance the federal budget and erase the deficit. He also said he would finance his own presidential campaign instead of relying on donations.

As the summer unfolded, Perot began running into criticisms. He was increasingly painted as an arrogant, paranoid man unwilling to take a stand on any given issue. In the face of negative charges on every side, Perot abruptly dropped out of the race on July 19. As presidential candidates George Bush and Bill Clinton began scrambling to lure the abandoned Perot supporters to their sides, the media sought to expose the Texas billionaire as just another quitter. Perot proved them wrong. He reentered the race, performed fairly well in presidential debates, and ultimately won 18 percent of the popular vote.

Perot ran again in 1996, on the Reform Party ticket, and polled 8 percent of the vote. After the 1996 election, Perot continued to dabble in business and politics. His Reform Party, however, became deeply divided over candidates for the 2000 election, and didn't enter the race. The leading third-party candidate in that election was Ralph Nader, the Green Party candidate, who won about 3 percent of the vote. Although his campaign had drawn a lot of grassroots support, Perot abruptly dropped out of the race in August, but then he made a comeback just as suddenly in October. Meanwhile, Bush's support kept fading, and he eventually received only 37 percent of the popular vote to Clinton's 43 percent. Perot ran a strong third with 19 percent.

Above: Part of the Bush family at the White House in 1989. From left to right are son Jeb Bush; son Neil Bush with grandson Pierce, 2; daughter-in-law Margaret Bush holding grandson Marshall, 2; daughter-in-law Sharon Bush with granddaughters Lauren, 4, and Noelle, 11; granddaughters Barbara and Jenna, 7; the president; son George W. Bush; and daughter Dorothy LeBlond holding granddaughter Ellie, 2.

Above: George Bush celebrated his 75th birthday by parachuting from an airplane over his presidential library at College Station, Texas. He dedicated the jump to his two WWII crewmates who hadn't survived an emergency bail-out.

Legacy

Governing was frustrating in the highly partisan environment that had come to distinguish the nation's capital during the late twentieth century. That continuing struggle and Bush's limited-government approach during weak economic times contributed to his dramatic downfall. Ronald Reagan had won reelection in 1984 by asking Americans whether they were better off after his first term than they had been four years earlier, but Bush couldn't ask that same question with any confidence in 1992. Still, Bush's limited government policies and his careful reductions in military spending were carried forward by his successor, Bill Clinton, as the economy surged in the mid-1990s.

Moderates and conservatives within Bush's own party continued to struggle. In 1994, the conservatives won surprisingly large election victories that helped the Republicans take both houses of Congress, but two years later, they saw their presidential candidate, Bob Dole, lose the election and their congressional majorities slip away in the process.

Bush's handling of the Gulf War was regarded as easily his finest accomplishment: His goals were well defined, support was carefully assembled, and the results were swift. His leadership and diplomacy in the changing world of the 1990s set an example for future presidents to follow.

Barbara Bush

Born June 8, 1925, Rye, New York

Sometimes called "everybody's grandmother," first lady Barbara Bush projected a friendly, unassuming, and witty presence. With five grown children and more than twice as many grandchildren, she was the center of a large extended family, and that family rootedness shined through in her work for family literacy—the idea of involving the whole family to help both parents and children learn to read and write. She became a public spokesperson for the cause after her husband, George Bush, became vice president in 1981, and during her years as first lady, she established the Barbara Bush Foundation for Family Literacy. In 2001, she became only the second woman—and the first since Abigail Adams—who was both the wife and the mother of U.S. presidents.

"The home is the child's first school, the parent is the child's first teacher, and reading is the child's first subject," she said. "Parents who lack basic literacy skills cannot experience the pleasure of reading a story to their children. The children, in turn, will not reap the educational benefits of being read to. And, according to the experts, reading to children early and often is the single most important thing parents can do to prepare them to start school ready to learn. If no one intervenes, this pattern is repeated in each new generation."

Barbara Bush was a person who intervened. More appropriately, she volunteered. The social responsibility and satisfaction of this kind volunteer work was the centerpiece of her life, and her whole family joined in.

Young Love

Born Barbara Pierce on June 8, 1925, she was the daughter of Pauline and Marvin Pierce. Her father was a magazine publisher (and president of *McCall's*, one of the leading magazines of the time). Pauline was the daughter of an Ohio state supreme court justice. Barbara enjoyed a happy childhood in Rye, a suburb of New York City, and in her teens she went to Ashley Hall, a boarding school in South Carolina. She met George Bush at a dance during the 1941 Christmas vacation. She was sixteen and he was seventeen, but they were engaged within six months, just in time for her seventeenth birthday. Four days later, George celebrated his eighteenth by joining the navy.

He became a pilot and flew bombing missions in the Pacific theater during World War II. He was shot down on one of those missions, and his two crew members died when the plane plunged into the ocean, but he was rescued by a submarine. When he got his first leave, George and Barbara married on January 6, 1945.

After the war, Bush enrolled at Yale University and graduated in 1948 after a three-year accelerated program. Then he and Barbara and their young son, George, drove to Texas, where he took a job in the oil industry. The Bushes would have five more children. A daughter, Robin, died at age three of leukemia. Barbara later remarked, "Because of Robin, I love every living human more."

Bush became quite wealthy during the 1950s, and he turned to politics in the 1960s. He was elected twice to represent the Houston area in the U.S. Congress, and beginning in 1970, he held a variety of important government jobs, crowning his political career with the vice presidency in 1981 and the presidency in 1989. All the while, Barbara focused on raising her children and establishing homes. From 1945, when they were married, to 1993, when the Bushes retired to Houston, Barbara moved her family twenty-nine times.

Family Literacy

Barbara Bush first became a national spokesperson for family literacy while her husband was vice president. She consistently expanded on the role during the 1980s and during her time as first lady from 1989 to 1993. She was the host of a weekly radio program called *Mrs. Bush's Story Time*, where she read stories aloud and promoted the idea of family reading. She wrote a best-selling children's story, *Millie's Book,* based on the Bush family dog, and donated the profits to literacy programs. She organized the Barbara Bush Foundation for Family Literacy in 1989 and served as its honorary chairperson. The foundation supports family literacy programs and promotes the value of reading. Her spirit of volunteerism was also evident in her work on programs for the elderly and patients suffering from the AIDS virus. She supported school-volunteer programs as well.

As first lady, Barbara Bush selected her causes carefully and maintained a low political profile. Yet, she influenced President Bush's priorities and his appointments in the areas of health, housing, and drug enforcement. She raised money for the United Negro College Fund, assisted with a major fund-raising campaign for the Morehouse College School of Medicine, and she worked on behalf of Sloan-Kettering and other hospitals, nursing homes, and hospices.

Mrs. Bush was one of the most popular presidential wives. In her 1994 bestseller, *Barbara Bush: A Memoir,* she described a conversation she had with Raisa Gorbachev, the wife of the Russian leader, explaining her appeal: "I told [Raisa], as honestly as I could, that I felt it was because I threatened no one—I was old, white-headed and large. I also told her that I stayed out of my husband's affairs." Her admirers, though, found Barbara Bush "intense, irreverent, funny, and a whole lot tougher and more combative than her public image suggests," as Bill Minutaglio put it in his book *First Son: George W. Bush and the Bush Family Dynasty.*

Above: Barbara Bush's promotion of literacy including reading stories to children.

Active Retirement

Barbara Bush remained active after she and her husband retired to Houston in 1993. She served as official hostess for many events at the George Bush Library at Texas A&M University, and she still occasionally gave speeches on her favorite causes. She continued to be involved with health-improvement programs and the Barbara Bush Foundation, and she also has worked on behalf of both the Leukemia Society of America and the Boys & Girls Clubs of America.

Mostly, though, the former first lady focused her time on family matters, including the fourteen grandchildren who regularly joined their grandparents at their Kennebunkport, Maine, vacation home. Twelve grandchildren joined them there after the 2000 Republican National Convention, where her son, George W. Bush, had been nominated to run for president. His mother generally kept a low profile during the campaign, but the selective stops she made to support her son were always well attended. When George W. Bush was inaugurated in 2001 as the forty-third president, Barbara Bush became only the second woman to be both the wife and the mother of U.S. presidents.

Bush's Address to Congress on the Crisis in Kuwait

Delivered on September 11, 1990

On August 2, 1990, the army of Iraq invaded the neighboring nation of Kuwait, and also established a stronghold near the border of Saudi Arabia. Those actions were condemned through a series of resolutions passed by the United Nations (UN). But the resolutions and subsequent diplomatic efforts on the part of the United States and other nations failed to convince Iraqi leader Saddam Hussein to relinquish control of Kuwait.

President George Bush was solidly supported as he mobilized the American military and exerted diplomatic pressure on Iraq. A month after the invasion, he spoke before a joint session of Congress and a national audience to reinforce support and to demonstrate American resolve to the Iraqis.

While carefully defining America's stand on Iraqi aggression against Kuwait, Bush discussed—the new world order—the beginning of a profoundly different relationship among nations since the fall of the Soviet Union, which began disintegrating in 1989. That new world order was exemplified by the cooperation among countries through the UN in its condemnation of Iraqi aggression.

At the same time these events were taking place, Congress and the president were locked in a serious budget dispute. Turning to that budget problem in the address, Bush called for cooperation that could overcome the profoundly serious economic and political problems within the United States.

Excerpt from Bush's Address to Congress on the Crisis in Kuwait

We gather tonight, witness to events in the Persian Gulf as significant as they are tragic. In the early morning hours of August 2nd, following negotiations and promises by Iraq's dictator, Saddam Hussein, not to use force, a powerful Iraqi army invaded its trusting and much weaker neighbor, Kuwait. Within three days, 120,000 Iraqi troops with 850 tanks had poured into Kuwait, and moved south to threaten Saudi Arabia. It was then I decided to check that aggression.

At this moment, our brave servicemen and women stand watch in that distant desert and on distant seas, side by side with the forces of more than 20 other nations. [...]

So if ever there was a time to put country before self and patriotism before party, that time is now. Let me thank all Americans, especially those in this chamber, for your support for our forces and their mission. That support will be even more important in the days to come. So tonight, I want to talk to you about what is at stake—what we must do together to defend civilized values around the world, and maintain our economic strength at home.

Our objectives in the Persian Gulf are clear, our goals defined and familiar: Iraq must withdraw from Kuwait completely, immediately and without condition. Kuwait's legitimate government must be restored. The security and stability of the Persian Gulf must be assured. Americans citizens abroad must be protected. These goals are not ours alone. They have been endorsed by the UN Security Council five times in as many weeks. Most countries share our concern for principle. And many have a stake in the stability of the Persian Gulf. This is not, as Saddam Hussein would have it, the United States against Iraq. It is Iraq against the world.

[...]

We stand today at a unique and extraordinary moment. The crisis in the Persian Gulf, as grave as it is, also offers a rare opportunity to move toward an historic period of cooperation. Out of these troubled times, our fifth objective—a new world order—can emerge: a new era, freer from the threat of terror, stronger in the pursuit of justice, and more secure in the quest for peace. An era in which the nations of the world, east and west, north and south, can prosper and live in harmony. A hundred generations have searched for this elusive path to peace, while a thousand wars raged across the span of human endeavor. Today that new world is struggling to be born. A world quite different from the one we've known. A world where the rule of law supplants the rule of the jungle. A world in which nations recognize the shared responsibility for freedom and justice. A world where the strong respect the rights of the weak. This is the vision I shared with President Gorbachev in Helsinki. He, and other leaders from Europe, the gulf, and around the world, understand that how we manage this crisis today could shape the future for generations to come.

The test we face is great—and so are the stakes. This is the first assault on the new world we seek, the first test of our mettle. Had we not responded to this first provocation with clarity of purpose; if we do not continue to demonstrate our determination; it would be a signal to actual and potential despots around the world. America and the world must defend common vital interests—and we will. America and the world must support the rule of law—and we will. America and the world must stand up to aggression—and we will. And one thing more: In pursuit of these goals America will not be intimidated.

Vital issues of principle are at stake. Saddam Hussein is literally trying to wipe a country off the face of the Earth. We do not exaggerate. Nor do we exaggerate when we say: Saddam Hussein will fail. Vital economic interests are at risk as well. Iraq itself controls some 10 percent of the world's proven oil reserves. Iraq plus Kuwait controls twice that. An Iraq permitted to swallow Kuwait would have the economic and military power, as well as the arrogance, to intimidate and coerce its neighbors—neighbors who control the lion's share of the world's remaining oil reserves. We cannot permit a resource so vital to be dominated by one so ruthless. And we won't.

Recent events have surely proven that there is no substitute for American leadership. In the face of tyranny, let no one doubt American credibility and reliability. Let no one doubt our staying power. We will stand by our friends. One way or another, the leader of Iraq must learn this fundamental truth. From the outset, acting hand in hand with others, we've sought to fashion the broadest possible international response to Iraq's aggression. The level of world cooperation and condemnation of Iraq is unprecedented.

Armed forces from countries spanning four continents are there at the request of King Fahd of Saudi Arabia to deter and if need be to defend against attack. Muslims and non-Muslims, Arabs and non-Arabs, soldiers from many nations, stand shoulder to shoulder, resolute against Saddam Hussein's ambitions.

We can now point to five United Nations Security Council resolutions that condemn Iraq's aggression. They call for Iraq's immediate and unconditional withdrawal, the restoration of Kuwait's legitimate Government, and categorically reject Iraq's cynical and self-serving attempt to annex Kuwait. [...]

We are now in sight of a United Nations that performs as envisioned by its founders. We owe much to the outstanding leadership of Secretary General Perez de Cuellar. The UN is backing up its words with action. The Security Council has imposed mandatory economic sanctions on Iraq, designed to force Iraq to relinquish the spoils of its illegal conquest. The Security Council has also taken the decisive step of authorizing the use of all means necessary to ensure compliance with these sanctions. Together with our friends and allies, ships of the United States Navy are today patrolling Mideast waters. They have already intercepted more than 700 ships to enforce the sanctions. Three regional leaders I spoke with just yesterday told me that these sanctions are working. Iraq is feeling the heat. We continue to hope that Iraq's leaders will recalculate just what their aggression has cost them. They are cut off from world trade, unable to sell their oil. And only a tiny fraction of goods gets through.

The communiqué with President Gorbachev makes mention of what happens when the embargo is so effective that the children of Iraq literally need milk or the sick truly need medicine. Then, under strict international supervision that guarantees the proper destination, food will be permitted.

At home, the material cost of our leadership can be steep. That's why Secretary of State [James A.] Baker and Treasury Secretary [Nicholas F.] Brady have met with many world leaders to underscore that the burden of this collective effort must be shared. We are prepared to do our share and more to help carry that load; we insist others do their share as well.

[...]

I cannot predict just how long it will take to convince Iraq to withdraw from Kuwait. Sanctions will take time to have their full intended effect. We will continue to review all options with our allies, but let it be clear: We will not let this aggression stand.

Our interest, our involvement in the gulf, is not transitory. It predated Saddam Hussein's aggression and will survive it. Long after all our troops come home, and we all hope it's soon, there will be a lasting role for the United States in assisting the nations of the Persian Gulf. Our role, with others, is to deter future aggression. Our role is to help our friends in their own self-defense. And something else: to curb the proliferation of chemical, biological, ballistic missile, and above all, nuclear technologies.

Let me also make clear that the United States has no quarrel with the Iraqi people. Our quarrel is with Iraq's dictator, and with his aggression. Iraq will not be permitted to annex Kuwait. That's not a threat, or a boast, that's just the way it's going to be.

Our ability to function effectively as a great power abroad depends on how we conduct ourselves here at home. Our economy, our armed forces, our energy dependence, and our cohesion all determine whether we can help our friends and stand up to our foes. For America to lead, America must remain strong and vital. Our world leadership and domestic strength are mutual and reinforcing; a woven piece, as strongly bound as Old Glory. To revitalize our leadership capacity, we must address our budget deficit—not after Election Day, or next year, but now.

Higher oil prices slow our growth, and higher defense costs would only make our fiscal deficit problem worse. That deficit was already greater than it should have been—a projected $232 billion for the coming year. It must—it will—be reduced.

To my friends in Congress, together we must act this very month, before the next fiscal year begins October 1, to get America's economic house in order. The Gulf situation helps us realize we are more economically vulnerable than we ever should be. Americans must never again enter any crisis, economic or military, with an excessive dependence on foreign oil and an excessive burden of Federal debt.

Most Americans are sick and tired of endless battles in the Congress and between the branches over budget matters. It is high time we pulled together, and get the job done right. It is up to us to straighten this out. [...]

What Happened Next

When Iraq failed to honor the United Nations resolutions, the UN decided on a final date (January 15, 1991) for Iraqi forces to abandon Kuwait. When that date passed with no Iraqi action, several nations launched massive, coordinated air strikes on strategic targets in Iraq. They were followed a month later by land forces that quickly forced the Iraqi occupiers into retreat and liberated Kuwait within 100 hours.

When the clearly defined mission of removing the Iraqi army from Kuwait was accomplished, the Gulf War was over. There were still some Americans who thought that U.S. forces should have gone on fighting until Saddam Hussein was eliminated, but that would have been illegal under international law. Saddam continued to be a threat over the next decade, but his powers for aggression were closely checked.

The new world order that Bush had described continued to act through the United Nations against aggression in the world's trouble spots. The United States was successful in getting other countries to cooperate for the common good, although such alliances are frequently fragile. Other nations face the same concerns Americans have about the danger and human cost of sending young men and women to patrol foreign lands and to stand against aggression.

The speech summed up the Bush presidency in many ways. He was successful in rallying America and its allies to support the UN effort against Iraqi aggression. It was diplomatic masterstroke, and it earned him immense popularity both at home and abroad. However, he wasn't as successful in convincing Congress to go along with a legislative package that would cut the federal deficit and stimulate the sluggish economy. It was largely because of that failure that Bush wasn't reelected in 1992.

Bill Clinton (signature)

Bill Clinton

"I like the job of president. . . . The bad days are part of it. I didn't run to have a pleasant time. I ran to have a chance to change the country and if the bad days come with it, that's part of life, and it's humbling and educational. It keeps you in your place."

—**Bill Clinton**

Forty-second president of the United States, 1993–2001

Full name: _William Jefferson Clinton; born William Jefferson Blythe IV_

Born: _August 19, 1946, Hope, Arkansas_

Parents: _William Jefferson Blythe III and Virginia Dell Cassidy Blythe Clinton Dwire Kelley; Roger Clinton (stepfather)_

Spouse: _Hillary Diane Rodham (1947– ; m. 1975)_

Children: _Chelsea Victoria (1980–)_

Religion: _Baptist_

Education: _Georgetown University (B.S., 1968); attended Oxford University; Yale Law School (J.D., 1973)_

Occupations: _Attorney; law professor_

Government positions: _Arkansas attorney general and governor_

Political party: _Democratic_

Dates as president: _January 20, 1993–January 20, 1997 (first term); January 20, 1997–January 20, 2001 (second term)_

Age upon taking office: _46_

ill Clinton experienced heights and depths as president: He presided during the longest-ever sustained growth of the American economy, and he faced an impeachment trial that nearly resulted in his removal from office. The American public gave the clearest assessment of his presidency: Low marks for his personal conduct, and increasing support for his performance as president.

Clinton took office in 1993 during an unstable period: The American economy was weak because of a huge federal budget deficit; war and strained relations threatened several parts of the world; and the partisanship that had plagued the federal government for twenty years had grown worse. Having achieved only mixed success during his first two years in office, the Democratic president faced greater challenges when Republicans made large gains in Congress during the 1994 midterm elections. Midterm elections sometimes dramatically change the balance of power, and the 1994 elections did just that: Republicans had majorities in both houses of Congress for the first time in forty years, and they arrived in Washington ready to fight.

Timeline

1946: Born in Arkansas
1963: Meets President John F. Kennedy as part of the American Legion Boys Nation government study program
1977–79: Serves as Arkansas attorney general
1979–81, 1983–93: Serves as Arkansas governor
1993–2001: Serves as forty-second U.S. president
1998: Impeached on two counts in the U.S. House of Representatives
1999: Remains in office after a Senate trial does not result in the two-thirds majority needed to remove him from office

Clinton seemed to thrive after the setbacks, as he had during his entire political career. While continuing to increase American trade, he pushed for more moderate economic policies at home, and the economy began booming. In the meantime, he enjoyed foreign policy successes when he helped bring together warring factions in Europe and in the Middle East.

In 1999, Clinton faced a trial of impeachment in the U.S. Senate following improper relations with a White House intern as well as evidence of perjury and obstruction of justice. While the public debated whether his misdeeds added up to the "high crimes and misdemeanors" that the Constitution cites as impeachable offenses, Congress pushed ahead on the impeachment process. True to the partisan spirit of the times, its votes almost strictly followed party lines, and Clinton was impeached on two

counts in the House of Representatives, but a follow-up Senate trial did not result in the two-thirds majority vote that is required to remove the president. After the trial, Americans were at least reassured that the Constitutional process had worked. The entire episode reinforced the public's general opinion: They agreed that the president's personal conduct was shameful, but they generally approved of his performance as president.

Overcomes Troubled Home Life

Bill Clinton was born William Jefferson Blythe IV on August 19, 1946, in Hope, Arkansas. His father, William Jefferson Blythe III, a traveling salesman, died in an automobile accident three months before his son was born. Only much later in life did Clinton learn that his father had been married to two other women prior to his mother, Virginia; and he also discovered that he had relatives—a half-brother and a half-sister—from those other marriages. When he was two years old, Clinton was left in the care of his maternal grandparents, and his mother went to New Orleans, Louisiana, to study nursing. She married Roger Clinton there and went home to Hope, Arkansas, when Bill was four.

The family settled in Hot Springs, Arkansas, when he was seven, and he began attending school there. Clinton was a strong student even though he grew up in a troubled household. His stepfather was an alcoholic and a gambler who physically abused the family. At age fourteen, Clinton stood up to him to defend his mother, and the family became close enough again as a result that Bill was adopted by his stepfather at the age of sixteen and took his family name.

Clinton learned to play saxophone and was especially interested in studying government, and when he was sixteen he was selected to take part in the Boys Nation Program, a government study series sponsored by the American Legion. He traveled with other members

Left: Clinton has played the saxophone since he was a boy, and played an impressive rendition of "Heartbreak Hotel" on Arsenio Hall's television show in 1992.

Above: Bill Clinton got his first taste of politics as a teenager when he met President John F. Kennedy in 1963.

Above: Modern presidential politics involves endless discussions of candidates' military records. Clinton never served, but he managed this photo op at an Arkansas National Guard training camp in 1983.

of the program to Washington, D.C., where they met President John F. Kennedy, and Clinton was inspired to become a politician.

He went on to study international affairs at Georgetown University in Washington, and while a student, he served as an intern for Arkansas senator J. William Fulbright. He was active in public demonstrations for civil rights and against the Vietnam War. After he graduated from the university in 1968, he won a Rhodes scholarship, a competitive program that funds study for two or three years at Oxford University in England.

During that period, Clinton was subject to the lottery system that selected young men to be drafted into the army. He signed a letter of intent to join the Reserve Army Training Corps at the University of Arkansas, but he didn't follow through after his lottery number made

it extremely unlikely that he would be drafted. This was perceived as an action to avoid military service, and his political opponents used it in attempts to discredit him and challenge his patriotism.

After finishing his studies in England, Clinton moved on to the law school at Yale University, and after he graduated in 1973, he went home to teach at the University of Arkansas law school.

Learning from Defeat

Clinton was already politically active by then. He had worked in the 1972 presidential campaign of South Dakota senator George McGovern, serving as the campaign's coordinator in Texas. Hillary Rodham,

Left: Clinton worked as a volunteer for Democratic presidential candidate George McGovern. Here McGovern arrives at Little Rock, where the candidate was met by Arkansas Democratic leader Joe Purcell.

a fellow Yale law student he had fallen in love with, also worked for the McGovern campaign. She went on to teach at the University of Arkansas two years later after having served as a legal assistant to the U.S. House of Representatives committee that weighed impeachment charges against President Richard Nixon. Clinton and Rodham were married on October 11, 1975. Their daughter, Chelsea, was born on February 27, 1980.

Clinton ran for the U.S. House of Representatives in 1974, and lost the election to the popular Republican incumbent, John Paul Hammerschmidt. He did, however, gain valuable recognition and experience from his strong showing, and two years later, he was elected attorney general of Arkansas. In that position, he worked on behalf of consumers and the environment against large utility companies.

He was elected the state's governor in 1978 at the age of thirty-two. Backed by a group of young and idealistic supporters, he took an aggressive approach to improving the state's education system and its roads, but suffered a public-relations backlash when he raised driver's license fees to help pay for his program. In addition, he angered the state's powerful timber, poultry, and energy industries by challenging their pricing practices and land use. The result was his defeat in 1980 by Republican Frank White.

The loss transformed Clinton into a more cautious politician. He learned to build support and estimate public opinion rather than attempt to lead by the force of his authority. He won the governorship again in 1982 and was reelected to four consecutive two-year terms. He was reelected to a four-year term in 1990, after the state law on term length was changed.

Clinton was successful in tackling the state's education problems. Following a study coordinated by Hillary Rodham Clinton, he instituted a program that raised teacher salaries and set up testing programs for both teachers and students. Students had to pass a basic skills exam in order to move on to high school, and by 1992, Arkansas had the best high-school graduation rate in the country. Clinton also improved health care in the state and initiated a job-training program that was mandatory for all welfare recipients. His programs attracted businesses to the state that, in turn, led to the creation of more than two hundred thousand new jobs.

Right: Governor Bill Clinton attending a 1984 National Governors' Conference at the White House.

Above: Clinton was given an opportunity to make a nationally televised speech at the 1980 Democratic Convention in New York.

National Reputation

Clinton's national reputation grew with these successes and other innovations. In 1985 and 1986, he was chairman of the Southern Growth Policies Board, which recommended new areas for economic development for the region, and in 1988, he gave the nominating speech for the Democratic presidential candidate, Massachusetts governor Michael Dukakis, at the party's national convention. The national exposure was a mixed blessing: Often, the person giving the nominating speech is being presented to the public as someone to watch for in future elections; but many believed that Clinton overstayed his welcome by making an overly long speech.

In 1990, Clinton was named chairman of the Democratic Leadership Council, and used the position to convince party officials to take more moderate stands on policies than the party's New England faction was doing to push for large government programs to address the nation's problems. Working with other southern leaders, including Al Gore, a U.S. senator from Tennessee, Clinton forged a group called the New Democrats, promoting a more business-oriented approach to issues than their party colleagues did. In 1991, Clinton was voted the country's most effective governor by his peers in a poll conducted by *Newsweek* magazine.

"It's the Economy, Stupid"

That same year, Clinton announced his candidacy for president. Most leading Democrats were reluctant to enter the race at that point because Republican president George Bush was enormously popular. Bush's support gradually eroded, however, as the American economy weakened. Clinton's early start helped him stay ahead of leading Democratic challengers as they began entering the race. He recovered quickly from setbacks and was widely visible in town meetings and television talk shows. He proposed programs to improve the economy, create jobs, provide national health insurance, and reduce the federal budget deficit.

During the campaign, Clinton was confronted with several public revelations about his behavior—from avoidance of the draft to marital infidelities. By early summer of 1992, he trailed not only President George Bush, but a third-party candidate, Texas businessman H. Ross Perot, as well, although Perot's main campaign issue—reducing the federal deficit—was high on Clinton's agenda, too. Perot quit the race for personal reasons on the same day that Clinton was officially nominated as the Democratic candidate for president.

Right: Clinton's daughter, Chelsea, was his most admiring supporter when he won the 1992 presidential nomination.

Election Results

1992

Presidential / Vice Presidential Candidates	Popular Votes	Electoral Votes
Bill Clinton / Al Gore (Democratic)	44,908,233	370
George Bush / Dan Quayle (Republican)	39,102,282	168
H. Ross Perot / James B. Stockdale (Independent Ticket)	19,221,433	0

Texas businessman Perot's strong third-party presence in the race resulted in the first time in history that a presidential candidate (Clinton) won with less than half of the popular vote.

1996

Presidential / Vice Presidential Candidates	Popular Votes	Electoral Votes
Bill Clinton / Al Gore (Democratic)	45,590,703	379
Robert Dole / Jack Kemp (Republican)	37,816,307	159
H. Ross Perot / Pat Choate (Reform)	7,866,284	0

Clinton's vice-presidential selection of Tennessee senator Al Gore, an experienced Washington politician, gave energy to the campaign. The two idealistic and moderate Democrats formed the youngest-ever presidential ticket in combined years of age.

Campaigning on the theme that government should take a more active role in improving the economy, Clinton generated wide support over Bush's policy of limited government. The Clinton campaign staff was inspired by a slogan that they used among themselves, "It's the economy, stupid," to constantly remind them that the economy was what voters cared most about. Publicly, Clinton spoke for "the forgotten middle class"—working Americans who were most harmed by the effects of budget deficits and the sluggish economy.

Clinton took the lead in polls and maintained it when the Republican national convention became bogged down in debate among religious conservatives and the more moderate faction that Bush represented. When Perot suddenly jumped back into the race a few weeks before election day, none of the three candidates was able to draw any more support. Clinton won a sound victory in the Electoral College—370 votes to 168—over Bush, but he won only 43 percent of the popular vote. Bush won 37 percent, and Perot, in the best third-party

showing since former president Theodore Roosevelt placed second in 1912, won 19 percent.

Slow Start

President Clinton had very mixed success during his first two years in office. He appointed a record number of women and minorities to government positions, but several of his choices were not approved by Congress. He moved quickly on a controversial issue—whether or not homosexuals should be allowed in the military—before Congress, the military, and the general public had a chance to debate the issue. He promoted the Don't Ask, Don't Tell policy, meaning that military officials are discouraged from questioning new military recruits about their sexual preference, and military personnel are not required to answer questions about it. The policy was generally considered a failure, and it didn't resolve debates concerning sexual orientation and the military.

Meanwhile, the president changed his mind on a campaign pledge to restrict trade with China because of its human-rights violations. He decided that open trade might encourage China to establish a more democratic form of government.

Al Gore

After having been among the most active and influential vice presidents in American history, Al Gore narrowly lost the presidential election of 2000 to George W. Bush. Gore became the third Democratic Party candidate to win the popular vote but lose in the Electoral College. The other two were Samuel J. Tilden in 1876 and Grover Cleveland in 1888. When Gore left office as vice president in 2001, it was the first time in twenty-five years that he did not hold an elected position in Washington, D.C.

Born in 1948 in Carthage, Tennessee, Albert Gore Jr. spent part of his childhood living on the family farm and in Washington while his father served in the U.S. Senate. While his parents made the rounds of speeches and meetings, young Al was left in the care of Alota and William Thompson, tenant farmers who ran the Gore family farm. Al's father, Albert Gore Sr., was a three-term senator from Tennessee. His mother, Pauline, was among the first women to graduate from Vanderbilt University's law school.

After graduating from Harvard University in 1969, Al served in the U.S. Army as a reporter during the Vietnam War. Like his father, who lost reelection in 1970 in part for his opposition to the war, Gore did not support continued American military involvement in Vietnam. He remarked that his father's experience through the Vietnam era taught him the importance of standing up for one's beliefs. Following his military service, Gore worked as a reporter for a Nashville newspaper while he was a student at Vanderbilt's law school. He married his longtime sweetheart, Mary Elizabeth (Tipper) Aitcheson, and they would eventually have four children.

Covering local government as a reporter reawakened Gore's interest in politics. He ran for Congress in 1976 and won the election. During a distinguished congressional career, he served four terms in the House and was elected to two terms in the Senate. Gore became known for his intense attention to research and detail—a result of his days as an investigative reporter. In 1980, he was assigned to the House Intelligence Committee studying nuclear arms. Committing himself to eight hours a week of study on the subject, Gore eventually published a comprehensive security plan in the February 1982 issue of the Congressional Quarterly. Three weeks later, a group of American diplomats visiting Moscow to talk with Soviet arms-control experts first learned of the "Gore Plan" from the Soviets' copies of his article.

Gore announced his presidential candidacy in 1988, and he won presidential primaries in five southern states, although Massachusetts governor Michael Dukakis won his party's nomination. The following year, Gore experienced a life-changing moment. While leaving a baseball stadium with his six-year-old son, Albert III, he watched helplessly as the boy darted away from him and was hit by a car. The child was dragged a total of fifty feet, and he showed no sign of life by the time his father reached him. He was rushed to Johns Hopkins Hospital in Baltimore, Maryland, and he made a full recovery after surgery and months of rehabilitation. The trauma, though, changed Gore's outlook on life. During this time, he began writing Earth in the Balance, an examination of how mismanagement of the environment leaves children with what he characterized as a degraded Earth and a diminished future.

In 1992, Democratic presidential nominee Bill Clinton selected Gore as his running mate. Although both were southerners who shared many of the same views, Gore balanced the ticket in two important ways: He had served in Vietnam and he had experience in foreign relations. With unemployment high and issues such as health care prominent, Clinton and Gore were effective in campaigning on improving the economy. They won the election, and Gore became one of the most active, high-profile vice presidents in history. During the following eight years, he supervised fourteen major policy areas, including the environment, telecommunications, urban policy, government efficiency, and technology.

The Clinton-Gore team were reelected in 1996, and Gore remained loyal to Clinton while the president faced an impeachment trial. In 2000, Gore took on a new challenge, attempting to become only the second sitting vice president in 150 years to be elected president. In one of the closest and most dramatic elections in U.S. history, Gore won the popular vote but fell short in electoral votes to George W. Bush, the son of the former president.

The Clinton Administration

Administration Dates: January 20, 1993–January 20, 1997

January 20, 1997–January 20, 2001

Vice President: Al Gore (1993–2001)

Cabinet:

Secretary of State	Warren M. Christopher (1993–97)
	Madeleine Albright (1997–2001)
Secretary of the Treasury	Lloyd M. Bentsen (1993–94)
	Robert E. Rubin (1995–99)
	Lawrence H. Summers (1999–2001)
Secretary of Defense	Les Aspin (1993–94)
	William J. Perry (1994–97)
	William S. Cohen (1997–2001)
Attorney General	Janet Reno (1993–2001)
Secretary of the Interior	Bruce Babbitt (1993–2001)
Secretary of Agriculture	Mike Espy (1993–94)
	Daniel Glickman (1994–2001)
Secretary of Commerce	Ronald H. Brown (1993–96)
	Mickey Kantor (1996–97)
	William M. Daley (1997–2000)
	Norman Y. Mineta (2000–2001)
Secretary of Labor	Robert B. Reich (1993–97)
	Alexis M. Herman (1997–2001)
Secretary of Health and Human Services	Donna E. Shalala (1993–2001)
Secretary of Housing and Urban Development	Henry G. Cisneros (1993–97)
	Andrew M. Cuomo (1997–2001)
Secretary of Transportation	Federico Peña (1993–97)
	Rodney Slater (1997–2001)
Secretary of Energy	Hazel R. O'Leary (1993–97)
	Federico Peña (1997–98)
	Bill Richardson (1998–2001)
Secretary of Education	Richard W. Riley (1993–2001)
Secretary of Veteran Affairs	Jesse Brown (1993–97)
	Togo D. West Jr. (1997–2000)
	Hershel W. Gober (2000–2001)

Clinton experienced his biggest policy failure in his administration's pursuit of a national health insurance program. He appointed his wife, Hillary, to investigate various options and make proposals. She had handled a similar assignment on education issues when her husband was governor of Arkansas. The Clinton health plan faced resistance from the massive health insurance industry, which mounted an intensive public relations campaign against it. Many in Congress and among the general public found the program Clinton eventually proposed too complicated, and it was generally believed that too much government supervision was going to be required.

Clinton enjoyed several successes amidst the early setbacks. The Family and Medical Leave Act of 1993 allowed parents of newborns and people with medical problems to take up to twelve weeks of unpaid leave from their jobs. He also helped push through Congress the North American Free Trade Agreement (NAFTA), which the Bush administration had negotiated with Canada and Mexico, lifting virtually all restrictions in trade between the three nations. The more sweeping General Agreement on Tariffs and Trade (GATT) followed, and it further strengthened international trade. Another agreement opened up more American trade with Asian nations on the Pacific Rim.

Through the efforts of Vice President Gore, the Clinton administration was able to reduce the number of federal employees and make the government more

Below: Clinton's first major defeat was rejection of his plan for better health care and lower-cost health insurance.

efficient. A sweeping crime bill in 1994 provided federal money to states to hire an additional one hundred thousand police officers nationwide.

Clinton's early troubles, however, and a well-organized Republican national campaign, led to large gains by Republicans in midterm congressional elections of 1994. Republicans rallied around a "Contract with America," a promise by its candidates to move quickly on a wide variety of legislative programs within one hundred days. After Republicans won majorities in both houses of Congress, they were able to fulfill the contract. A sweeping welfare reform package was quickly passed as part of the contract, and President Clinton signed it into law. Both sides claimed credit for the program. For President Clinton to support and then sign a bill reforming and reducing government involvement in a major social program was a significant break from his Democratic presidential predecessors.

A stalemate over the president's budget in 1995, however, proved disastrous for congressional Republicans. They wanted to cut many of Clinton's proposed expenditures in order to fund a tax break, but Clinton refused to allow it. The federal budget must be approved in order for the government to pay federal workers and

Below: House Speaker Newt Gingrich (R-Ga) pushed the "Contract with America," intended to end a stalemate in Congress. Although successful at first, it eventually resulted in a shutdown of the federal government.

fund programs, and when the Republicans refused to enact temporary funding measures, the government literally shut down. National parks and museums, as well as many government agencies, were closed. The public backlash over this costly political showdown hurt Republicans more than the president, and Clinton gained further public support by defending such programs as Social Security and Medicare.

By the election year of 1996, momentum was clearly on the president's side. Clinton was helped by a booming economy. Increases in jobs and wages led to increased tax revenue, and the huge federal deficit was cut in half. Crime was down as well.

Clinton remained ahead of his rivals during the presidential campaign of 1996. Winning 6 percent more of the popular vote than he had in 1992, his 49 percent easily outdistanced Republican nominee Robert Dole, who won 37 percent of the vote, and third-party candidate H. Ross Perot, who polled 8 percent of the vote.

Assertive Militarism

Internationally, the world had changed in the early 1990s. After World War II, many nations allied either with the United States or with the Soviet Union. With the collapse of the Soviet Union in 1991, the United States began working more closely with the United Nations for international cooperation against acts of aggression by one nation or one ethnic group against another. For the important post of U.S. ambassador to the United Nations, he chose Madeleine Albright, who had previously advised several Democratic leaders on international affairs.

The first test faced by the United States and other nations occurred in the African country of Somalia, where a civil war had left thousands suffering from starvation and abuse. The United States sent a military force to protect food and medical supplies, but the mission proved unpopular at home when American military personnel came under fire. The American force was withdrawn and replaced by UN troops.

In other trouble spots, the United States worked through such organizations as the North Atlantic Treaty Organization (NATO), an alliance of nations that had

Left: The Clinton administration sent troops to Somalia as part of a UN initiative to end a civil war there.

been created by the North Atlantic Treaty in 1949. Fighting between ethnic groups in the nation of Bosnia was fierce, but West European countries were reluctant to enter the dangerous situation. (Bosnia and Herzegovina, which together became one of five nations formed after the dissolution of Yugoslavia, is often referred to simply as Bosnia.) American air strikes against Bosnian Serbs, a group that was engaged in the genocidal practice of "ethnic cleansing," helped begin peace negotiations. A multi-ethnic government was formed in 1995, and a NATO peacekeeping force that included twenty thousand U.S. soldiers enforced the ceasefire.

When the Kosovo region of Serbia attempted to gain its independence, Serbian president Slobodan Milosevic launched a brutal ethnic-cleansing campaign against citizens of Albanian descent in Kosovo. His army entered Kosovo early in 1999, and NATO began bombing raids in the spring. A peace agreement that granted self-rule for Kosovo was approved by the Serbian parliament, and the air strikes ended in June. Milosevic was voted out of power in Serbia in 2000. Meanwhile, beginning in late 1998, the United States and Great Britain launched air strikes against Iraq after that nation violated the terms of its surrender in the Gulf War of 1991.

This strategy of "assertive militarism," as Madeleine Albright called it, was a new form of international cooperation against acts of aggression. The United

Nations, often influenced by forceful leadership from the United States, became a stronger body able to form international coalitions to police troubled areas.

President Clinton faced difficulties with the communist nations of Cuba and North Korea. He ordered sanctions against Cuba when its government encouraged thousands of refugees, many emptied out of Cuban prisons, to flee to the United States. Meanwhile, evidence mounted that North Korea was building a nuclear weapons program, and after pressuring North Korea, the Clinton administration agreed to help it develop safe forms of nuclear energy; in exchange, North Korea agreed to shut down factories suspected of nuclear weapons research. In 2000, Madeleine Albright became the highest-ranking American official ever to visit North Korea. The United States established more normal relations with Communist China and the independent nation of Russia, as well, opening up trade while applying pressure privately for those nations to embrace democratic reform.

President Clinton's most successful foreign policy initiative involved Mexico. After it fell dangerously close to economic collapse in 1994. Clinton offered over $12 billion in loans over the objections of Congress. In return, he demanded that Mexico follow strict economic policies that would invite foreign investment. The plan worked, and Mexico paid off a majority of the loans ahead of schedule.

Right: U.S. troops joined with NATO to restore peace to Bosnia. The conflict left 250,000 dead and 2.5 million refugees, including this boy who was hustled aboard a bus, leaving his family behind in Kosovo.

Madeleine Albright

When Madeleine Albright was named U.S. ambassador to the United Nations in 1993, she completed a circle of family involvement with the organization. Her father, Josef Korbel, had been a Czechoslovakian diplomat and became chairman of a special UN commission shortly after World War II. When he completed his work, he asked the U.S. government for political asylum following a communist takeover of his country.

Born Maria Jana Korbel in 1937 in Prague, Czechoslovakia, Albright was rechristened Madeleine when her family settled in America. Describing her early life to the Los Angeles Times, she said she was "the little blond girl in the newsreels who would be handing flowers to arriving diplomats." After her family was granted political asylum in the United States, her father became a professor at the University of Denver.

Albright graduated with honors from Wellesley College in 1959, and three days later, she married Joseph Albright, a descendent of a family of newspaper publishers. Albright worked with the Rolla Daily News in Missouri before moving to Chicago with her husband, and she and her family moved to Washington in the mid-1970s. While she was raising her three young children, she earned a doctorate by commuting to Columbia University in New York. She became a legislative assistant to U.S. senator Edmund S. Muskie of Maine in 1976, and two years later she served on the national security staff of President Jimmy Carter as a legislative liaison for her former Columbia University professor, national security advisor Zbigniew Brzezinski.

Albright joined the faculty of Georgetown University in 1982 and served as an advisor to two Democratic presidential candidates, Walter F. Mondale in 1984, and Michael Dukakis in 1988. After Dukakis's defeat, she became president of the Center for National Policy, a Democratic think tank. Specializing in Eastern Europe and the Soviet Union, Albright consistently advocated a more active U.S. role in promoting democracy in those countries. Upon her appointment to the United Nations by President Clinton in 1993, she was thrust immediately into pressing issues, including the administration's response to the civil war in the former nation of Yugoslavia, which had divided into five independent nations. During the next four years, she supported policies involving economic sanctions against Iraq that were initially put in place after the conclusion of the Persian Gulf War. She backed relief efforts for the African nations of Somalia and Rwanda, and the movement toward democracy in the Caribbean country of Haiti.

Following President Clinton's reelection in 1996, several changes were made to his cabinet, including the resignation of the secretary of state, Warren Christopher. Clinton nominated Albright to succeed him as the country's first female secretary of state, and the senate quickly confirmed her nomination, and she took office at the beginning of 1997. Albright had numerous issues and conflicts to confront. She helped convince Clinton to keep U.S. troops stationed in Bosnia (one of the five nations formed from Yugoslavia) past a June 1998 deadline in order to protect a peace agreement. She was a forceful advocate for the improvement of the human-rights situation in China, and she helped ease Russian opposition to an expansion of the North Atlantic Treaty Organization (NATO) to include nations formerly dominated by the Soviet Union. Perhaps her most important mission as secretary of state was helping further Israeli-Palestinian peace negotiations.

According to U.S. News & World Report, Albright believed that there were some advantages to being a female secretary of state. "I can maybe be less formal or can sit down with children or hold a baby or something like that." She added, "It doesn't matter what gender the secretary of state of the United States is. The most important advantage is that I am representing the United States."

Left: Israeli prime minister Yitzhak Rabin (L) and PLO Chairman
Yasser Arafat join President Clinton in signing a 1993 peace accord.

The Clinton administration encouraged notable but fragile achievements in peace talks between Great Britain and Northern Ireland, and with Israel and its Middle East neighbors. Both of those areas, long in conflict, had the framework for peaceful coexistence and needed to find ways to make it work. In 1993, Clinton helped arrange a peace accord between Israeli prime minister Yitzhak Rabin and Palestine Liberation Organization (PLO) chairman Yasser Arafat. Rabin was later assassinated by an Israeli extremist upset with the agreement. Further cooperation between Israel and Palestine led to the 1998 Wye River Accord (named for the negotiation site in Maryland), but that sense of cooperation remained fragile. In the autumn of 2000, daily violence erupted in areas where Israelis and Palestinians share neighborhoods.

Economic Heights

At home, the economy continued to boom. In 1997, the level of unemployment in the nation reached a thirty-year low, and a year later the federal budget showed a surplus. By 2000, the nation continued the longest sustained economic growth in its history. The economic conditions were closely monitored by Federal Reserve Chairman Alan Greenspan.

Clinton had campaigned in 1992 on behalf of the "forgotten middle class" and had promised tax relief for middle-income Americans, but Greenspan impressed him with the need to concentrate instead on reducing the federal deficit. Clinton's 1993 deficit reduction plan included tax increases of $250 billion, largely gathered from the nation's wealthiest individuals and through a tax on gasoline. Greenspan, meanwhile, used his power as Federal Reserve chairman to encourage investment and spending, which helped fuel a return to prosperity. In addition, the Clinton administration's energetic expansion of international trade opened new markets for American products in the global economy.

As his presidency drew to a close, Clinton began introducing social, environmental, and education programs. He called for an end to the "digital divide"—an expression that describes how wealthier school districts have better access to the Internet than poorer ones.

Clinton's presidency began with questions about how best to attack the nation's economic problems, and it ended with the question of how best to use the government surplus. Clinton, however, was fortunate to still be in the Oval Office at the end of the century. In 1999, he became the second president ever to face an impeachment trial in the Senate. Andrew Johnson was the first, and he had escaped removal from office by the slimmest of margins: one vote.

Below: First Lady Hillary Rodham Clinton welcomes the 2000 Kennedy Center honorees to the White House. (L-R) Dancer Mikhail Baryshnikov, musician Chuck Berry, tenor Placido Domingo, actor Clint Eastwood, and actress Angela Lansbury are seated with the president.

Alan Greenspan

Born in New York City on March 6, 1926, Alan Greenspan was the only child of Herman H. and Rose G. Greenspan. He attended public schools in New York City and then enrolled in the famous Juilliard School of Music, which he left after a year to play tenor saxophone and clarinet in a swing band. In the meantime, he earned bachelor's and master's degrees in economics at New York University in 1948 and 1950.

In the early 1950s, Greenspan came under the intellectual influence of novelist Ayn Rand. According to U.S. News & World Report, he said that Rand made "me see that capitalism is not only efficient and practical, but also moral." Greenspan virtually invented the business of providing economic analyses specifically for senior business executives. He and bond trader William Townsend founded an economic consulting firm that provided industrial and financial institutions with forecasts and other business-related services. The firm was immediately successful, making Greenspan a wealthy man. He was named to the boards of such prestigious companies as Alcoa, Capital Cities/ABC, J. P. Morgan & Co., and Mobil Corporation, and he was also elected chairman of the Conference of Business Economists, president of the National Association of Business Economists, and director of the National Economists Club.

Greenspan's career in the private sector was interrupted by calls to public service, and he served as chairman of the Council of Economic Advisors, as chairman of the Commission on Social Security Reform, and as a consultant to the Congressional Budget Office. He assumed his most important public position on August 11, 1987, when he replaced Paul A. Volcker as chairman of the Board of Governors of the Federal Reserve System (the Fed). The Fed controls the creation of money and influences key interest rates, thereby controlling fluctuations in prices of financial market assets, such as stocks and bonds. The Fed also provides temporary loans to banks and other financial institutions in times of need. This "lender of last resort" function was the primary reason the Fed was created by Congress in 1913. It was intended to combat a trend that when an individual bank failed, it often affected other banks and led to a general financial market collapse.

Less than two months after assuming office, Greenspan was faced with just such a financial market crisis. On "Black Monday," October 19, 1987, the stock market collapsed as terrified sellers dumped millions of shares. Falling stock prices automatically triggered millions of additional sale orders, and buyers who had previously bought stocks "on margin"—borrowing portions of the purchase price—were forced to provide additional collateral when these stock prices fell, and the financial system faced collapse from a lack of ready cash. Acting quickly, Greenspan met with top Fed officials and mapped a strategy for easing the cash crunch, using the Fed's financial power to strengthen the troubled financial institutions. Before the market opened on Tuesday, October 20, Greenspan announced the Fed's "readiness to serve." With the full force and power of the Fed backing, the fear of a general collapse receded and stocks soon rebounded.

Greenspan's worries, however, were far from over. The federal budget deficit had swollen to $221 billion by 1986, and it was exerting a powerful inflationary effect on the economy. Having weathered the financial market panic of 1987, Greenspan decided to send a clear signal that the fight against inflation had become his top priority. His four-year term as chairman expired in 1991, but President Bush reappointed him, and President Clinton reappointed him again to additional four-year terms in 1996 and 2000.

Greenspan calmed uncertain domestic and global economic markets. From 1989 to 1992, he tightened lending practices, and he refused to inflate the money supply in reaction to a temporary worldwide spike in the price of oil. By 1992, the economy was on an upward trend, and In 1994, Greenspan raised interest rates several times in a successful effort to thwart possible inflation. Over the next few years, the Fed gradually decreased the prime lending rate, and as a result, the economy boomed at an historic pace, the federal budget was balanced, and the nation's inflation rate fell below two percent.

In 1998, a Louis Harris survey of 400 senior executives gave Greenspan a favorable rating of 97 percent. Greenspan, who married his second wife—television reporter Andrea Mitchell—in 1997, has sometimes been described as the second most powerful person in the world, after the American president. The 1990s, as a period marked by peace and prosperity in the United States, could easily be called the Age of Greenspan.

First Hint of Scandal

What became known as the Whitewater scandal began with a 1978 real-estate deal involving Bill and Hillary Clinton while he was governor of Arkansas. The Clintons' partner in the deal used profits to open up a bank that later failed and was bailed out by the federal government. Improprieties in the deal and the question of whether Clinton had misused his authority as governor became the focus of an investigation that began in 1994. An independent counsel was assigned to examine the evidence following the authority granted to an investigative lawyer, a government position established during the 1970s to investigate federal officials accused of crimes in a nonpartisan manner.

During the investigation, questions arose about several possibly related actions during Clinton's presidency, including misuse of Federal Bureau of Investigation (FBI) files, the firing of officials in the White House travel office, and campaign fund-raising activities. The taint of scandal seemed to be everywhere. However, after a five-year, $50 million investigation, the president was not charged with any wrongdoing when the Whitewater investigation ended in 2000.

Above: With the First Lady looking on, Clinton denied that he had had sexual relations with White House intern Monica Lewinsky. Seven months later, he admitted that he did.

Meanwhile, the president had been sued for sexual harassment by Paula Jones, a former Arkansas state government employee. She asserted that then-Governor Clinton had made sexual advances and, when rebuffed, had created a hostile work environment for her. Other claims of extramarital affairs involving Clinton had already surfaced. The Jones sexual harassment case was eventually dismissed in federal court in 1998, but the president was forced to testify during the proceedings after a historic Supreme Court ruling determined that a sitting president could be called to testify in a civil court case. Meanwhile, the Whitewater special prosecutor, Kenneth Starr, received permission from Attorney General Janet Reno to examine claims that some of the president's testimony in the Jones case was false and that he might be guilty of perjury.

The perjury charge came to light when it was discovered that the president had had an inappropriate relationship with a young White House intern, Monica Lewinsky, in 1997. Clinton denied the relationship, but taped phone conversations by a coworker of Lewinsky's, Linda Tripp, revealed her talking candidly about the relationship. Other evidence was uncovered to involve the president, and in August 1998, after months of denial, Clinton admitted to an "improper relationship" with the intern.

Left: Newspaper headlines following the impeachment of President Clinton by the House of Representatives on December 19, 1998.

Janet Reno

The seventy-eighth attorney general of the United States and the first woman to hold the position, Janet Reno had a high profile and an often controversial tenure. Born on July 21, 1938, in Miami, Florida, she was the eldest of the four children of journalists Henry and Jane Reno. Her father, a Danish immigrant, was a police reporter for the Miami Herald, and her mother was an investigative reporter for the now-defunct Miami News.

After graduating from local public schools, Janet attended Cornell University and graduated with a degree in chemistry in 1960, and then she entered the Harvard University Law School, graduating in 1963. In 1962, she had been denied a summer job by a prominent Miami law firm because she was a woman, but later, in the mid-1970s, she became a partner of that same firm. She worked with private law firms from 1963 to 1971, then began serving as a lawyer for the state of Florida. Working with the Florida House of Representatives during 1971 and 1972, she helped revise the state constitution to allow for a reorganization of its court system. She held other important positions with the state before returning to private practice in 1976. She was appointed the top prosecutor for Dade County, Florida, two years later, and she held the position until 1993.

After some early setbacks, Reno won a strong reputation as a tough prosecutor. Her successes in prosecuting violent crimes won approval from opponents, and she received praise from some minority communities for her efforts to use the prosecutor's office to tackle social problems affecting society. She tried alternatives to the incarceration of youth, stressing the link between a nurturing childhood and the prevention of crime. She also aggressively prosecuted child-abuse cases, pursued delinquent fathers for child support, and established a domestic-crime unit. By 1993, when she was nominated as attorney general by President Bill Clinton, her reputation was such that she was confirmed unanimously by the Senate after smooth hearings.

She barely had time to settle into the job when controversy erupted. The Branch Davidians, a religious cult with ties to private militia movements opposed to taxes and gun control, refused to allow government law officials into its compound near Waco, Texas, to investigate charges of illegal activities, including stockpiling weapons

and abusing children. Four federal agents died in an attempted raid in March 1993 when cult members barricaded themselves in the compound. After six weeks, federal agents stormed the compound, using tear gas. A raging fire ensued, and eighty of eighty-nine members of the cult were killed in the blaze. Arguments over the cause of the fire eventually led to a trial in 2000 to determine whether government officials had been responsible, and a five-person jury advised the judge of the case that the fire was likely started by cult members, and the judge cleared the government of wrongdoing.

Scandals involving President Clinton and members of his administration also brought controversy to Reno's office. She had to rule whether or not there was sufficient grounds to pursue several cases, and in the partisan atmosphere of Washington, D.C., Reno faced criticism whether she approved or denied such investigations. She did allow a special prosecutor of the Whitewater scandal to broaden his case, which eventually led to the impeachment trial of President Clinton.

In 2000, Reno's department became involved in an international affair surrounding Elian Gonzalez, a six-year-old boy who was part of a group of ten people fleeing Cuba. The boat carrying the ten refugees sank off the coast of Florida, and only the boy survived a rescue attempt. His relatives in Florida fought against judicial orders that he be returned to his father in Cuba. The event dragged on for several months before the boy was forcibly removed from the custody of relatives during a government raid and returned to his father. Outrage followed on the part of those who wanted Gonzales to stay in the United States. Some congressional Republicans called for an investigation, but the action was quickly halted when it became obvious that most Americans agreed that the court rulings should be upheld and the boy should be reunited with his father.

Reno weathered such controversies and sustained criticism by political opponents to become the longest-serving U.S. attorney general. She disclosed in 1995 that she was suffering from early stages of Parkinson's disease, a degenerative nerve disorder, which cut down on her ability to pursue her hobbies of hiking and canoeing, but she still remained dedicated to public service. She died on November 7, 2016.

Far left: Rep. Barney Frank (D-Mass) debates during the House Judiciary Committee in December 1998.

Left: Independent Counsel Kenneth Starr beginning his testimony at the House Judiciary Committee's impeachment hearing.

Independent Counsel Kenneth Starr released a long and detailed report in September 1998 that accused the president of having committed perjury and obstruction of justice. In November 1998, the House Judiciary committee began debate on whether the charges were grounds for impeachment. Voting strictly on party lines, the Republican-led majority of the committee voted on four articles of impeachment. The entire House of Representatives then voted by majority to impeach the president on two of the articles.

The Senate trial began on January 7, 1999, and it ended on February 6. Little changed in either the accusations or the evidence to convince the necessary two-thirds majority in the Senate to vote for impeachment. The president, meanwhile, was shamed before his family and the nation. However, the Constitutional process worked its course, and the president was able to govern effectively again.

When the impeachment trial ended, Senate leaders of the two parties shook hands—a hopeful sign that partisanship might be easing. Despite President Clinton's many confrontations with the Republican Congress, the two groups had managed to pass bills that helped to improve the economy and to reform welfare. While the impeachment of Andrew Johnson in 1868 had resulted in a weakened presidency, no significant change in power resulted from Clinton's impeachment. Meanwhile, the

High Crimes and Misdemeanors

Article II, section 4, of the U.S. Constitution states: "The President, Vice President, and all civil Officers of the United States, shall be removed from Office on Impeachment for, and Conviction of, Treason, Bribery, or other high Crimes and Misdemeanors."

The Framers of the Constitution deliberately used, but did not define, "high crimes and misdemeanors." Congress was left to decide the definition, and, as a result, impeachment is a matter of political judgment. When the Constitution was being written, George Mason and James Madison argued that there were other "great and dangerous offenses" than treason and bribery, and Mason proposed adding "high crimes and misdemeanors." In eighteenth-century English, a "misdemeanor" meant bad behavior (corruption, for example), and "high crimes" was similar to "great and dangerous offenses." Politicians, lawyers, and historians have been arguing about the exact meaning of "high crimes and misdemeanors" ever since.

That debate was prominent during the impeachment trial of President Bill Clinton. Most Americans and U.S. senators agreed that Clinton had committed personal offenses, and some argued that those wrongs had compromised the office of the president. However, many agreed that those acts did not jeopardize the nation as "great and dangerous offenses," and the president survived the Senate impeachment trial based primarily on that view.

The Impeachment of Bill Clinton

The House Judiciary Committee originally drew up four articles of impeachment against President Clinton, but the House of Representatives approved only two of them: Article I charged the president with having committed perjury; and Article II charged him with obstruction of justice. Several incidents led to the Clinton impeachment trial:

- **The Whitewater investigation:** President Clinton had been accused of illegal activities involving a real estate deal dating back to 1978 in Arkansas. In January 1994, after continuous pressure by his opponents, the Clinton administration appointed a special prosecutor to investigate the accusations. Formed during the 1970s Watergate scandal, the office of special prosecutor is a temporary position convened by the U.S. attorney general to conduct an independent investigation of officials in the Executive branch who are accused of wrongdoing. Kenneth Starr assumed the position of special prosecutor in August 1994, after the original appointee resigned.

- **The Paula Jones sexual harassment case:** In May 1994, former Arkansas state worker Paula Jones filed suit claiming sexual harassment by Bill Clinton while he was governor of Arkansas. The question of whether a sitting president can be the subject of a civil suit was argued in several courts until May 1997, when the Supreme Court made a historic ruling that Jones's lawsuit could continue while Clinton was serving as president.

- **Improper conduct by the president:** Clinton and White House intern Monica Lewinsky engaged in an improper sexual relationship during the winter of 1995–96, and the affair was brought to the attention of Kenneth Starr, who obtained proof by having Lewinsky's friend, Linda Tripp, audiotape conversations she had with the intern during January 1998. Lewinsky had denied the affair just a few days earlier while testifying in writing under oath in the Jones lawsuit. Tripp first began recording audiotapes of her conversations with Lewinsky during the summer of 1997, an action that was later declared illegal. The taping in January 1998, on the other hand, was a legal act since it was part of a criminal investigation.

KEY DATES, FROM 1998 THROUGH 2000

January 1998:

January 7—As part of the Paula Jones case, Monica Lewinsky signs an affidavit denying her affair with Clinton.

January 16—Lewinsky is privately confronted with evidence of the affair by Starr.

January 17—Clinton gives a deposition in the Jones suit, denying an affair with Lewinsky.

January 19—Rumors spread over the Internet about an article being planned by Newsweek magazine that would publicly expose the Clinton-Lewinsky affair for the first time; the magazine had planned to delay the article until more evidence was presented.

January 22 and 26—Clinton emphatically denies having had an affair with Lewinsky to television reporters; the denials are broadcast repeatedly on news shows.

February 1998: Starr is accused of pressuring Lewinsky to make false statements, and the Clinton administration files a complaint over leaks of information from Starr's team. Meanwhile, Clinton is accused of having coached and influenced aides to testify in his favor before Starr's grand jury. Clinton and several of his friends are accused of trying to help Lewinsky land a job in return for denying the affair.

Spring 1998:

April 1—A U.S. district judge in Arkansas dismisses the Jones lawsuit against Clinton for lack of evidence.

May 4—A U.S. district court in Washington, D.C., denies Clinton's claim of executive privilege to limit grand jury questioning of him and his aides.

Summer 1998:

July 17—A judge refuses an attempt by the Clinton administration to shield secret service agents from testifying. Clinton is subpoenaed to testify before the grand jury.

August 17—Clinton testifies for four hours before the grand jury. He admits to having had an inappropriate relationship with Lewinsky.

September 3—Senator Joseph Lieberman of Connecticut becomes the first Democrat in Congress to publicly rebuke the President. (Lieberman would later become the Democratic vice-presidential candidate in 2000).

September 11—Clinton publicly apologizes to Lewinsky and her family for the first time.

Fall 1998:

September 21—The Starr Report, which includes all of Lewinsky's grand jury testimony, is released to the public.

October 8—The U.S. House votes to conduct an inquiry on Starr's allegations that Clinton was guilty of perjury and obstruction of justice.

November 3—Despite the scandal, Democrats make gains in national elections; over 65 percent of voters polled do not want Clinton impeached.

November 13—Clinton and Jones settle the lawsuit for $850,000, but with no apology or admission of guilt.

November 20—The House judiciary committee begins an inquiry into whether to impeach Clinton.

December 11—The judiciary committee, voting strictly on partisan lines, approves four articles of impeachment against President Clinton.

December 19—The House votes to impeach Clinton on two of the articles.

1999:

January 7—Impeachment trial begins in the Senate.

February 12—Impeachment trial ends. A two-thirds majority (67 of 100 votes) was necessary to convict the president and remove him from office. The vote on Article I (perjury) was 54 not guilty, and 45 guilty. The vote on Article II (obstruction of justice) was 50 not guilty, 50 guilty.

Fall 2000: Independent Prosecutor Act is not renewed by Congress. Whitewater investigation concludes with no official charges of wrongdoing on the part of President or Mrs. Clinton.

legislation that created the office of the independent counsel came up for renewal before Congress in 1999, and it was allowed to expire.

Americans turned their attention to the question of what to do with the budget surpluses that were being generated by the booming economy. Some favored returning the money to the people through tax cuts. Others, like President Clinton, wanted to use the money to support Social Security, because many more Americans would be retiring in the near future. That debate, and the continuing concern over America's involvement in foreign peace-keeping missions, were significant issues to ponder as America entered the twenty-first century.

Legacy

During the presidential election of 2000, President Bill Clinton made only a few appearances on behalf of the Democratic nominee, Vice President Al Gore. The president's personal conduct had remained an issue, and there was concern that voters might react against Gore for his association with Clinton. On the other hand, Clinton remained very popular among groups of Americans who had prospered during his presidency and who believed that the federal government should take an active role in addressing the nation's problems. His rousing campaign appearances on behalf of his wife, Hillary, who was elected U.S. senator from New York in 2000, reflected his continued popularity among a large core group of supporters.

Clinton's approach to government was more moderate than previous Democratic presidents of the twentieth century. He demonstrated more concern for business growth, pursued trade policies that increased the role of American business in the global economy, and had success in reforming or restructuring some government programs. The economy boomed, trade increased, and waste in government spending was reduced, all of which helped fuel the longest sustained economic growth in American history.

Above: After his presidency, Clinton was welcomed to Harlem in New York City where he established his new office.

Sustained success in foreign policy proved more elusive. The Clinton administration worked hard in peace efforts between Israel and Palestinian officials, including two important agreements for cooperation. Those agreements did not lead to treaties, however, and daily violence erupted between the sides again in 2000. The president's continual pursuit of expanded trade helped improve U.S. relations with many countries.

Clinton proved adept at rebounding from setbacks and personal scandals. His problems and a general climate of partisan politics, however, clouded a time of relative peace and sustained prosperity. The accomplishments of the Clinton administration, especially the president's handling of the economy and his leadership in reforming or expanding government programs, reflected a more moderate approach to government than his Democratic predecessors.

My Life

Former presidents customarily publish a memoir or autobiography shortly after leaving office. In 2004, Clinton's autobiography, *My Life,* was released by the publisher Alfred A. Knopf. Weighing in at a daunting 957 pages, it sold approximately 400,000 copies its first day in the bookstores.

Presidential memoirs are almost uniformly dull, and Clinton's was no exception. *New York Times* book critic Michiko Kakutani described it as "sloppy, self-indulgent and often eye-crossingly dull—the sound of one man prattling away, not for the reader, but for himself and some distant recording angel of history." In spite of such reviews, *My Life* sold more than 2.25 million copies, earning back Clinton's record $15 million advance.

The 2008 & 2012 Presidential Elections

In January 2007, Senator Hillary Rodham Clinton announced her candidacy as the Democrats' nominee for president of the United States. "I'm in," she declared. "And I'm in to win." Bill Clinton became very active in his wife's campaign, where he was considered an important asset: As an ex-president, his popularity rating was high—a 2006 Gallup poll found that Clinton's approval rating among the American public stood at 66 percent, the highest of any former president in U.S. history. Furthermore, he had a loyal following among African-American voters, a key constituency in a primary race in which Hillary Clinton would be going up against Senator Barack Obama of Illinois.

The Clintons put up a tough fight, but Obama won more primaries and caucuses. On June 7, 2008, Hillary Clinton withdrew from the campaign and urged her supporters to throw their support behind Barack Obama. As for Bill Clinton, the potshots he taken at Obama, citing the candidate's inexperience as a leader stopped the moment Hillary bowed out of the race. At the Democrats' National Convention in 2008, Clinton took to the podium to declare, "Barack Obama is ready to lead America and to restore American leadership in the world. . . . Barack Obama is ready to be president of the United States." He was just as effective in 2012, saying "If you want a country of shared prosperity and shared responsibility—a we're-all-in-this-together society—you should vote for Barack Obama and Joe Biden."

The Washington Post has described the Clinton/Obama relationship as "complex and often strained." Nonetheless, in 2013, President Obama awarded former President Clinton the Presidential Medal of Freedom, the nation's highest civilian honor.

Humanitarian Work

Since leaving the White House, Clinton has been active in humanitarian projects, often teaming up with his predecessor, President George H. W. Bush. In the wake of natural disasters, Presidents Bush and Clinton have proven to be extremely effective fund-raisers. In 2005, the Bush Clinton Katrina Fund raised $1 million for those affected within the first six hours of its existence, and a final tally of contributions reached $130 million. The Bush Clinton Tsunami Relief Fund raised more than $1 billion from private individuals for victims in Thailand, India, Sri Lanka, and Indonesia. They had similar success for the people of Haiti after the earthquake in 2010, raising more than $50 million.

Bill set up the Clinton Foundation, which is made up of eleven nonprofit groups that work on four major issues: global health and wellness, climate change, economic development, and improving opportunities for girls and women.

The Foundation operates through a variety of in-house operations. One example is the Clinton Global Initiative (CGI), which fosters cooperation among nations, professional organizations, and individuals to address some of the world's most pressing problems. Since 2005, the CGI has provided access to schools for 10 million children and access to better health care for 48 million people. It has taught job skills to 650,000 people, and helped 3 million microentrepreneurs start their own small businesses.

In response to the growing crisis of overweight and obese children and teens—more than 25 million in the

Above: Haiti's President Rene Preval, to the right of Clinton, former President George W. Bush, second from right, and former President and U.N. special envoy for Haiti Bill Clinton, left, arrive at the earthquake damaged Presidential Palace in Port-au-Prince on March. 22, 2010.

United States alone—the Clinton Foundation joined with the American Heart Association (AHA) to get information about the problem into schools and doctors' offices as well as private homes. The Clinton Foundation and AHA estimate that they have helped 2.2 million children and teens commit to eating better and exercising more.

One of the most effective operations is Clinton Health Access Initiative (CHAI), which has helped negotiate HIV/AIDS therapy price cuts as high as 90%, which they claim ensures access to these treatments for more than 11.5 million people across more than 70 countries.

Through 2016, *The Washington Post* claimed the Foundation had raised an estimated $2 billion from U.S. corporations, foreign governments and corporations, political donors, and various other groups and individuals. Foreign donations to the Foundation while Hillary was secretary of state became a concern during the 2016 election. However, no correlation was found between donations and government policy. Charity Watch gave the Clinton Foundation an A grade, while GuideStar gave it a platinum rating.

Mission to North Korea

In August 2009, Clinton traveled to Pyongyang, the capital of North Korea, in hopes of persuading North Korean leader Kim Jong-il, to release from prison two American journalists, Laura Ling and Euna Lee. Ling and Lee, both reporters for Current TV, were filming a story about North Korean refugees who had fled to China. On March 17, 2009, they were arrested by North Korean border guards. At their trial, Ling and Lee were convicted of "hostile acts" against North Korea and illegally entering the country. Approximately three weeks before Bill Clinton's mission to Pyongyang, Secretary of State Hillary Clinton called on the North Korean government to grant amnesty to Ling and Lee.

Clinton's journey was described as a purely private mission, independent of the Obama administration. But a North Korean news agency reported that Clinton had brought a private message from President Obama to Kim Jong-il. Hours after Clinton's meeting with the North Korean leader, Kim Jong-il issued a pardon to Ling and Lee. They returned to the United States with Clinton aboard an unmarked plane.

Health Concerns

In September 2004, Clinton underwent emergency heart bypass surgery for four major blocked blood vessels. In February 2010, surgeons implanted two stents in one of Clinton's coronary arteries to help the blood flow smoothly. His heart health had since improved with his loss of 30 pounds and becoming a vegan. He told *The New York Times,* "It changed me . . . I'm a lot more laid back and a lot more relaxed and a lot more healthy."

The 2016 Presidential Campaign

Bill Clinton is respected as a savvy analyst for the Democrats. But he doesn't always have the Midas touch: in spite of campaigning for John Kerry in 2004 and his wife, Hillary Clinton, in 2008, neither candidate won the White House. When Hillary announced that she was running for president in 2016, Bill once again went out on the campaign trail, urging people to register to vote, to vote for Hillary, and to submit their ballots early. At the Democratic National Convention he reminded his audience of Hillary's commitment to public service which he said he first encountered when they met in law school.

There were a few stumbles along the way. At a rally, Bill got into a heated argument with a Black Lives Matter protester who attacked a crime bill President Clinton signed in 1994. And a little more than a month before Election Day, Bill characterized the Affordable Care Act, aka Obamacare, as "this crazy system" where some of the insured have seen "their premiums double and their coverage cut in half."

Despite the gaffes, Bill continues to be one of the most skillful politicians of our time.

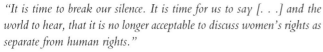

Hillary Rodham Clinton

Born October 26, 1947, Chicago, Illinois

"It is time to break our silence. It is time for us to say [. . .] and the world to hear, that it is no longer acceptable to discuss women's rights as separate from human rights."

—Hillary Rodham Clinton

The most politically active first lady since Eleanor Roosevelt, Hillary Rodham Clinton spoke out effectively on issues relating to education and children. Before coming to the White House, she chaired an Arkansas state commission on education, served on dozens of corporate and civic boards, and built a career as one of America's leading attorneys. She was named one of the nation's top 100 lawyers by the National Law Review in both 1988 and 1991. In 2000, as the first first lady to run for public office on her own, she defeated her opponent in the U.S. senate race in New York.

Social Work

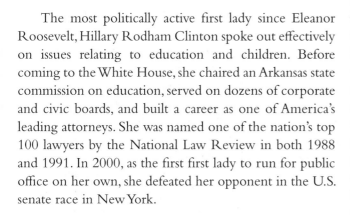

The oldest of three children of Hugh and Dorothy Rodham, Hillary was born on October 26, 1947. Her father owned a fabric store, and her mother was a homemaker. Hillary grew up in the Chicago suburb of Park Ridge, Illinois, where she was active in ballet, swimming, tennis, the Girl Scouts, and a church group. Led by Reverend Don Jones, the group served as babysitters for working parents, and also raised funds through sporting events and a small circus for poverty-stricken children in urban areas.

Hillary was her high-school class president and a member of the student council as well as the debate team,

and she was also active as a student at Wellesley College in Massachusetts. The 1968 assassination in of civil-rights leader Martin Luther King Jr., whom she had once met through Jones after hearing King preach, further increased her interest in social justice. She graduated from Wellesley with honors and became the college's first student commencement speaker, an honor usually reserved for a distinguished professional. She polled her classmates on what she should say and solicited poems and ideas from them with a goal to communicate the turmoil of America at a time of an unpopular war, political assassinations, and rioting in cities. Her speech was discussed in an article in *Life* magazine, giving Hillary her first national media exposure.

She went on to Yale Law School, where she wrote what became a well-known paper on the rights of children. Hillary worked with impoverished youths at the Yale–New Haven Hospital. At Yale, she met Marian Wright Edelman, the founder of the Children's Defense Fund (CDF), a Washington-based lobbying group, and she would later work for the group as a staff lawyer and board chairperson.

Hillary also met Bill Clinton at Yale. Their paths had already crossed briefly when she met him again while they were registering for classes. He talked with her for an hour as the registration line moved slowly forward, and when they reached the front of the line, an official cried out, "Bill, what are you doing here? You already registered."

Busy Professional Career

After graduation in 1973, Bill Clinton went home to Arkansas to teach, and Hillary went to Cambridge, Massachusetts, to work at CDF. Soon afterward, she went to Washington to serve as a legal assistant to the congressional committee that was considering whether or not to recommend the impeachment of President Richard Nixon. After it was shown that the president was involved in the Watergate scandal, Nixon chose to resign rather than face an impeachment trial.

Hillary joined Bill Clinton in Arkansas when she took a teaching position at the University of Arkansas Law School, and they were married in 1975. Hillary continued to teach and headed the legal aid clinic at the school until three years later when she joined the Rose Law Firm in Little Rock, Arkansas.

Bill Clinton was elected governor of Arkansas in 1978, but he lost his bid for reelection two years later, the same year the couple's daughter, Chelsea, was born. Clinton was reelected in 1982, and at the same time Hillary Rodham Clinton became chairperson of the Arkansas Education Standards Committee, an unpaid public position. Traveling throughout the state, she held meetings and visited schools as part of her preparation to recommend improvements in education to state legislators. She supervised a study that led to new standards for public schools, including teacher testing and smaller class sizes. Many of her recommendations became law, and the Arkansas education system showed measurable improvement over the next decade.

Below: The Clinton family in 1997.

Throughout her husband's twelve years as governor, Hillary continued her efforts to help children. She initiated the Home Instruction Program for Preschool Youth and became a board member of the state's Children's Hospital. She also served on the Southern Governors' Association Task Force on Infant Mortality.

Going National

At the onset of the 1992 presidential campaign, many Democratic presidential hopefuls believed that President George Bush was unbeatable because of his popularity after the Gulf War. Clinton began campaigning early for the nomination, and he established himself as a strong candidate. However, the campaign turned nasty as critics tried to discredit both of the Clintons. After charges of infidelity were made against her husband, Hillary felt obligated to defend her marriage on the television program *60 Minutes.*

Hillary Rodham Clinton's outspokenness sometimes made her a campaign issue. She was often quoted as saying, "If you vote for him, you get me." When asked by the press if her career as a lawyer conflicted with the responsibilities of first lady, she replied, "I suppose I could have stayed home and baked cookies and had teas, but what I decided to do is fulfill my profession." The media zeroed in on the cookie comment, fueling a new controversy. The press also focused attention on her legal writings, some of them twenty years old and dating from law school. She had once written that the rights of children are often ignored by courts and that at one time in history women, like slaves, had no rights. As a result, her critics accused her of encouraging children to sue their parents over trivial matters and equating marriage with slavery.

Soon after President Clinton's inauguration, he announced that his wife would take the unpaid position as chairperson of a task force charged with producing a health-care reform plan. No first lady had ever been given such an important assignment. The goal of the task force was to produce a health-care system that would insure all Americans, but the plan was not accepted by Congress, after strong opposition by health-care insurers who mounted a massive media blitz to convince the public that universal health care was not in the country's best interest.

In the spring of 1995, Hillary Rodham Clinton,

accompanied by her daughter, Chelsea, completed a twelve-day goodwill tour of southern Asia, where they met with heads of state and everyday citizens. In September 1995, she served as honorary chairperson of the American delegation to the United Nations Fourth World Conference on Women, held in Beijing, China. At the conference, the first lady delivered an impassioned speech in which, according to *Time* magazine reporter Karen Tumulty, she unleashed the most stinging human-rights rebuke ever made by a prominent American government representative on Chinese soil. To great cheers, Clinton declared, "It is time to break our silence. It is time for us to say here in Beijing, and the world to hear, that it is no longer acceptable to discuss women's rights as separate from human rights."

Around the same time, Hillary Rodham Clinton was in the process of writing *It Takes a Village: And Other Lessons Children Teach Us,* which was published in 1996. The book, which became a best seller, is based on an African proverb: "It takes a village to raise a child."

From Supporter to Senator

During her husband's scandal-plagued second term in office, Hillary Rodham Clinton continued to travel around the world, in the process becoming the most traveled First Lady in history. She often met with women who ran clinics and small businesses, and she delivered her usual strong message for better schooling, health care, and empowerment of women. In late 1997, she chaired a White House conference on the issue of child care.

She defended her husband during the impeachment proceedings of late 1998 and early 1999. Even in the 1990s, many in the general public did not know what to make of such an independent and politically active First Lady. She won a measure of sympathy after revelations concerning her husband's infidelities became public, but she kept her own feelings about them private.

In February 2000, after months of speculation, Hillary Rodham Clinton officially announced her candidacy for the U.S. senate seat in New York that was about to be vacated by the retiring Daniel Patrick Moynihan. She won the Democratic primary on September 13, and on November 7, she defeated her Republican opponent Rick Lazio to become New York's first female U.S. senator.

As a senator, Hillary Clinton has championed issues that were already dear to her heart while First Lady: universal health care, global prevention and cure of HIV/AIDS, and tax reforms and government programs to aid the poor and middle class and bring about equality for those still facing discrimination in housing and the workplace. She has served on five Senate committees and is the first New York senator ever to be a member of the Committee on Armed Services.

Clinton originally voted yes on proposed U.S. military actions in Afghanistan and Iraq. As the war in Iraq continued, however, and some of the original military intelligence was discredited, she voted for redeployment of troops to areas other than Iraq.

White House Dreams

In January 2007, Hillary Clinton announced her historic candidacy for president. (While she was not the first woman ever to do so, she was the first of a major U.S. political party.) The primaries were a close and rocky race against Illinois senator Barack Obama, who didn't definitively take the lead until the final primary, securing enough delegate pledges with an edge of a mere 2.4 percent. Hillary actually won the popular vote, with roughly 18 million supporters. There was hope in some quarters that

Left: Hillary Rodham Clinton kicks off her Senate campaign at Purchase, New York, near her new home.

Above: U.S. Secretary of State Hillary Rodham Clinton addresses a news conference with Adm. Mike Mullen, the chairman of the U.S. Joint Chiefs of Staff at U. S. embassy in Pakistan in May 2011 after the killing of Osama bin Laden.

she'd be tapped as Obama's vice-presidential running mate, but he put the idea to rest when he declined even to review her for the position, opting to team with Senator Joe Biden of Vermont. Hillary conceded with grace, and in a rousing speech at the 2008 Democratic Convention, she urged her loyal followers to join her in making sure that the Obama-Biden ticket would soar to victory.

Secretary of State

Hillary Clinton's 2008 bid for the Democratic presidential nomination was unsuccessful, but in November of that year, President-elect Barak Obama asked her to be secretary of state. Hillary accepted. In her acceptance speech, she mentioned various crises around the world, including the increasing nuclear threat from Iran and North Korea. "America cannot solve these crises without the world," she said, "and the world cannot solve them without America."

During Hillary's tenure, she spent time strengthening ties with allies while also engaging adversaries. To help repair America's on again/off again relationship with Pakistan, she traveled extensively in that country in October 2009, holding town hall meetings with ordinary Pakistani citizens

and giving countless interviews to Pakistani media outlets. She was the principal author of the tough sanctions on Iran in 2010 that helped bring them to the negotiating table regarding discontinuing nuclear weapons.

On May 1, 2011, Hillary was with President Obama and his national security staff as they watched via satellite the Navy SEALs raid Osama bin Laden's compound in Pakistan, in which the mastermind of the September 11, 2001, terrorist attacks on the United States was shot and killed. She was also a key player in normalizing U.S.–Pakistan relations after the raid.

On September 11, 2012, a mob affiliated with an al-Qaeda faction, attacked the U.S. consulate in Benghazi, Libya, killing four Americans—Ambassador Christopher Stevens, foreign service officer Sean Smith, and CIA contractors Glen Doherty and Tyrone Woods. By not initially calling it a terrorist attack, the Obama administration opened themselves up to charges of a cover up of a failure to properly react to the threat of attack. The Benghazi tragedy became a political debacle for Secretary Clinton as she took ultimate responsibility for the security of the compound. This led to a two-year-long costly investigation by the U.S. House Select Committee for Benghazi, resulting in an 800-page report on the attack and its aftermath. While the report did not find any professional misconduct by Hillary, it also uncovered that she used a private email server during her four years as secretary of state.

After traveling to 112 countries during her tenure, stumping continually along the way for women's rights, Hillary indicated that she would not be interested in a second term as secretary of state. In her farewell address to the State Department, she said, "I know what it's like when that blue and white airplane emblazoned with the words "United States of America" touches down in some far-off capital and I get to feel the great honor and responsibility it is to represent the world's indispensable nation. I'm confident that my successor and his successors and all who serve in the position that I've been so privileged to hold will continue to lead in this century just as we did in the last—smartly, tirelessly, courageously—to make the world more peaceful, more safe, more prosperous, more free. And for that, I am very grateful." After leaving office, Hillary wrote another volume of her memoirs, *Hard Choices*. At the time, some political commentators speculated that her extensive book tour was a prelude to a run for president in 2016. Their speculation proved to be prophetic.

Clinton's Final State of the Union Address

Delivered on January 27, 2000

When President Bill Clinton delivered his final State of the Union address on January 27, 2000, the United States was enjoying its longest-ever period of sustained economic growth. Accordingly, his speech was upbeat about the state of the nation, and optimistic on its future prospects.

The speech came less than a year after he survived an impeachment trial. That the president could speak boldly of the nation's well-being, and that he proposed more aggressive government programs, showed that the presidency had not been weakened by the impeachment ordeal. However, his speech did not inspire or rally Congress into swift action, either.

Clinton's final State of the Union address was important as a reflection of optimism expressed during a time of prosperity. He envisioned great achievements to come. That view contrasted with the state of the nation at the time he took office in 1992, when America was beset by a sluggish economy. His call in 2000 for increases in government investment in social and educational programs contrasted with his exclamation three years earlier that "the era of big government is over." His optimism contrasted as well with the image a year earlier of a beleaguered leader fighting to save his presidency.

Excerpt from Clinton's Final State of the Union Address

We are fortunate to be alive at this moment in history. Never before has our nation enjoyed, at once, so much prosperity and social progress with so little internal crisis and so few external threats. Never before have we had such a blessed opportunity—and, therefore, such a profound obligation—to build the more perfect union of our founders' dreams.

We begin the new century with over 20 million new jobs; the fastest economic growth in more than 30 years; the lowest unemployment rates in 30 years; the lowest poverty rates in 20 years; the lowest African American and Hispanic unemployment rates on record; the first back-to-back budget surpluses in 42 years. And next month, America will achieve the longest period of economic growth in our entire history.

We have built a new economy.

And our economic revolution has been matched by a revival of the American spirit: crime down by 20 percent, to its lowest level in 25 years; teen births down seven years in a row; adoptions up by 30 percent; welfare rolls cut in half to their lowest levels in 30 years.

My fellow Americans, the state of our union is the strongest it has ever been.

As always, the real credit belongs to the American people. My gratitude also goes to those of you in this chamber who have worked with us to put progress over partisanship.

Eight years ago, it was not so clear to most Americans there would be much to celebrate in the year 2000. Then our nation was gripped by economic distress, social decline, political gridlock.

The title of a best-selling book asked: *America: What Went Wrong?*

[. . .]

In 1992, we just had a road map; today, we have results.

But even more important, America again has the confidence to dream big dreams. But we must not let this confidence drift into complacency. For we, all of us, will be judged by the dreams and deeds we pass on to our children. And on that score, we will be held to a high standard, indeed, because our chance to do good is so great.

My fellow Americans, we have crossed the bridge we built to the 21st century. Now, we must shape a 21st century American revolution—of opportunity, responsibility and community. We must be now, as we were in the beginning, a new nation.

At the dawn of the last century, Theodore Roosevelt said, "the one characteristic more essential than any other is foresight . . . it should be the growing nation with a future that takes the long look ahead." So, tonight, let us take our long look ahead—and set great goals for our nation.

To 21st century America, let us pledge these things: Every child will begin school ready to learn and graduate ready to succeed. Every family will be able to succeed at home and at work, and no child will be raised in poverty. We will meet the challenge of the aging of America. We will assure quality, affordable health care, at last, for all Americans.

We will make America the safest big country on Earth. We will pay off our national debt for the first time since 1835. We will bring prosperity to every American community. We will reverse the course of climate change and leave a safer, cleaner planet. America will lead the world toward shared peace and prosperity, and the far frontiers of science and technology. And we will become at last what our founders pledged us to be so long ago—one nation, under God, indivisible, with liberty and justice for all.

[. . .]

[T]wo years ago, as we reached across party lines to reach our first balanced budget, I asked that we meet our responsibility to the next generation by maintaining our fiscal discipline. Because we refused to stray from that path, we are doing something that would have seemed unimaginable seven years ago. We are actually paying down the national debt.

[. . .]

Beyond paying off the debt, we must ensure that the benefits of debt reduction go to preserving two of the most important guarantees we make to every American—Social Security and Medicare. Tonight, I ask you to work with me to make a bipartisan down payment on Social Security reform by crediting the interest savings from debt reduction to the Social Security Trust Fund so that it will be strong and sound for the next 50 years.

But this is just the start of our journey. We must also take the right steps toward reaching our great goals. First and foremost, we need a 21st century revolution in education, guided by our faith that every single child can learn. Because education is more important than ever, more than ever the key to our children's future, we must make sure all our children have that key. That means quality preschool and after-school, the best trained teachers in the classroom, and college opportunities for all our children.

For seven years now, we've worked hard to improve our schools, with opportunity and responsibility—investing more, but demanding more in turn. Reading, math, college entrance scores are up. Some of the most impressive gains are in schools in very poor neighborhoods.

But all successful schools have followed the same proven formula: higher standards, more accountability, and extra help so children who need it can get it to reach those standards. I have sent Congress a reform plan based on that formula. It holds states and school districts accountable for progress, and rewards them for results. Each year, our national government invests more than $15 billion in our schools. It is time to support what works and stop supporting what doesn't.

Now, as we demand more from our schools, we should also invest more in our schools. Let's double our investment to help states and districts turn around their worst-performing schools, or shut them down. Let's double our investments in after-school and summer school programs, which boost achievement and keep people off the streets and out of trouble. If we do this, we can give every single child in every failing school in America—everyone—the chance to meet high standards.

Since 1993, we've nearly doubled our investment in Head Start and improved its quality. Tonight, I ask you for another $1 billion for Head Start, the largest increase in the history of the program.

We know that children learn best in smaller classes with good teachers. For two years in a row, Congress has supported my plan to hire 100,000 new qualified teachers to lower class size in the early grades. I thank you for that, and I ask you to make it three in a row. And to make sure all teachers know the subjects they teach, tonight I propose a new teacher quality initiative—to recruit more talented people into the classroom, reward good teachers for staying there, and give all teachers the training they need.

We know charter schools provide real public school choice. When I became President, there was just one independent public charter school in all America. Today, thanks to you, there are 1,700. I ask you now to help us meet our goal of 3,000 charter schools by next year.

We know we must connect all our classrooms to the Internet, and we're getting there. In 1994, only 3 percent of our classrooms were connected. Today, with the help of the Vice President's E-rate program, more than half of them are. And 90 percent of our schools have at least one Internet connection.

But we cannot finish the job when a third of all our schools are in serious disrepair. Many of them have walls and wires so old, they're too old for the Internet. So tonight, I propose to help 5,000 schools a year make immediate and urgent repairs; and again, to help build or modernize 6,000 more, to get students out of trailers and into high-tech classrooms. [. . .]

What Happened Next

Most of the items proposed in President Clinton's State of the Union address were approved by Congress as part of the annual budget. Since 2000 was a presidential election year and economic prosperity was continuing, many in Congress did not feel obliged to move swiftly to enact new programs proposed by the president. The two legislative branches continued to struggle in many battles to gain hard-won settlements.

President Clinton's speech began a new decade with a bold vision. What happened next would be determined by new leaders, and a new generation coming of age.

George W. Bush

"It seemed to me that elite central planners were determining the course of our nation. I wanted to do something about it."

—*George W. Bush*

Forty-third president of the United States, 2001–2009

Full name: *George Walker Bush*
Born: *July 6, 1946, New Haven, Connecticut*
Parents: *George Herbert Walker and Barbara Pierce Bush*
Spouse: *Laura Welch (1946– ; m. 1977)*
Children: *Jenna Welch (1981–); Barbara Pierce (1981–)*
Religion: *Methodist*
Education: *Yale University (B.A., 1968); Harvard University (M.B.A., 1975)*
Occupations: *Pilot; oilman; owner, Texas Rangers baseball team*
Government positions: *Texas governor*
Political party: *Republican*
Dates as president: *January 20, 2001–January 20, 2005 (first term); January 20, 2005-January 20, 2009 (second term)*
Age upon taking office: *54*

*F*ive weeks after the presidential election of 2000, George W. Bush could finally be assured that he had won one of the closest of presidential contests in one of the most contested of presidential elections. Bush polled a slim Electoral College majority over his Democratic challenger, Vice President Al Gore, 271 to 266. The historic 2000 election marked the first time that the U.S. Supreme Court made a ruling on a presidential election. In a divided judgment (with five justices supporting, and four dissenting), the Court's ruling stopped a recount of ballots in Florida, and ended weeks of dramatic twists and turns of legal wrangling.

Bush became the fourth president to win in the Electoral College but not carry the popular vote. He was also the second president's son to be elected president of the United States. His father, George H. W. Bush, served as president from 1989 to 1993 (the other father-son combination was John Adams and John Quincy Adams).

Taking office at a time of prosperity, Bush hoped to introduce several bold policies and to de-emphasize federal government programs. His first major task was helping to unite the nation and political factions deeply divided over the election. The popular and electoral votes had been very close; Democrats and Republicans each had fifty U.S. senators, and Republicans had only a small majority in the House; and the election controversies had led many to doubt the impartiality of courts as well as some election officials.

The focal point of the 2000 election was the state of Florida, whose twenty-five electoral votes were in dispute. Bush's brother Jeb was the governor of the state, and the winner there would win the presidency. Less than one thousand votes separated Bush and Gore, but thousands of votes in question: Some were not tabulated by vote-counting machines, while others had been validated by questionable practices that were allowed by some voting officials. Some voters claimed that they had been denied the opportunity to vote by officials who were using incomplete information, and future reform of voting practices might well prove to be the legacy of the 2000 election.

After a U.S. Supreme Court ruling on Tuesday, December 12, ended Gore's attempts to have disputed Florida votes recounted by people, rather than machines, Bush became the president-elect. Both candidates made efforts toward harmony in speeches to the nation on December 13, and Bush pledged to follow the same kind of consensus-building he had pursued as governor of Texas.

Below: The 2000 Republican presidential ticket: (L-R) Laura Bush, George W. Bush, Dick Cheney, and Lynne Cheney.

Timeline

1946: Born in Connecticut
1968: Graduates from Yale University
1978: Loses in bid for U.S. congressional seat; founds Bush Exploration oil company
1989: Is part of a group that purchases the Texas Rangers baseball team
1994–2000: Serves as governor of Texas
2000: Elected forty-third U.S. president

Bush had an opportunity to maintain an unprecedented period of prosperity in America and to use the abundance of wealth to further improve the country. He hoped to establish a more limited role for the federal government, and he intended to focus on legislation for tax relief, education, and retirement benefits. All of those initiatives, however, were dependent on his ability to lead effectively after a hotly contested election; politicians of both parties would have to put aside the partisanship that had been especially prominent in Washington during the last three decades of the twentieth century; and American voters would have to feel confident in the voting process.

Follows Family Traditions

George Walker Bush was born on July 6, 1946, in New Haven, Connecticut, where his father, George H.W. Bush, was a student at Yale University after having served in World War II. After his father graduated in 1948, he moved his family to Texas, and took an administrative position at a company that sold supplies for oil drilling. They lived in Midland, Texas, and then in Houston as the business thrived. When he was in seventh grade, George W. Bush attended the same junior high school in Midland as Laura Welch, although they didn't meet then. Years later, they would become husband and wife.

Like his father, Bush attended Phillips Academy in Andover, Massachusetts, and then went on to Yale University, where he was an average student, president of his fraternity, and a member of an exclusive group, the Skull and Bones Society. While he was still at Yale, his father was elected as a U.S. representative from Texas, continuing a family tradition of public service; George W. Bush's grandfather, Prescott Bush, had been a Republican U.S. senator from Connecticut from 1952 to 1963. After serving in Congress, his father went on to serve positions in the administrations of Richard Nixon and Gerald R. Ford during the 1970s, before he was elected vice president and then president in the 1980s.

George W. Bush went back to Texas after graduation from Yale in 1968 with a degree in history, and he became involved in the oil business. Restless in his mid-twenties, he completed a fifty-three-week program with the Texas Air National Guard, learning to fly fighter planes and earning the rank of lieutenant. (There is some controversy over Bush's military record, however. During his stint

Below: Bush was a fighter pilot in the Texas Air National Guard in the Vietnam era; he has been dogged ever since by accusations that he received special treatment that kept him out of the war.

with the National Guard, Bush took a six-month leave of absence to campaign in Alabama for Winton M. Blount, a friend of his father. He also left the reserve early to go to business school at Harvard.) At the time, he lived in the same Houston apartment complex as Laura Welch, but, again, their paths didn't cross. When his unit was not called to fight in the Vietnam War, Bush worked at several jobs, including a program called Pull for Youth for underprivileged children.

Bush continued to be restless, spending most of his time driving sports cars and enjoying an active social life. "I wasn't interested in taking root," he told *Time* magazine in 1994 about his early adulthood. "I was having fun."

He went back east to attend the Harvard Business School, and graduated with a master's degree in business administration (an M.B.A.) in 1975. Then, he went back to Texas again to become an oilman. In 1977, at an outdoor barbecue party in Midland, he finally met Laura Welch officially. A whirlwind romance followed, and they were married within three months. Their twin daughters, Jenna and Barbara, were born in 1981.

Successful Oilman

Bush ran for a seat in Congress from Texas in 1978. He explained years later in his autobiography, *A Charge to Keep*, why he wanted to get involved in politics. He was angered by federal legislation that put price controls on gas that was drilled and processed in the United States as well as by government monitoring that determined which industries could use natural gas, and he wrote, "It seemed to me that elite central planners were determining the course of our nation. I wanted to do something about it."

After losing the election to Democrat Kent R. Hance, Bush focused on his small, thriving company called Bush Exploration, which specialized in finding and evaluating new areas to drill for oil. In 1983, he merged his outfit with Spectrum 7; and three years later, it was bought by a large company, Harken Energy. Bush received $600,000 worth of Harken stock and was given a lucrative consulting contract. In 1990, he sold two-thirds of his Harken stake for nearly $850,000.

Meanwhile, his father served two terms as vice

president under Ronald Reagan and won the Republican nomination for president in 1988. George W. helped manage his father's presidential campaign, moving with his wife and twin daughters to Washington. He earned the respect from campaign insiders and Republicans in general by rallying the team through the ups and downs of a tight race that eventually turned into a solid victory for his father.

Back in Texas after the election, Bush served from 1990 to 1994 as head of Hearts and Hammers, a volunteer group dedicated to repairing homes. He also organized a group of wealthy investors to buy the Texas Rangers, a Major League Baseball team; took on a role as managing partner; and helped the team build a fan-friendly new stadium called The Ballpark in Arlington. Riding a wave of popularity from his success with the Rangers, Bush decided it was an ideal time for him to make another try for elected office.

"I Might Run for Governor"

"I vividly remember the night I first thought I might run for governor," Bush recalled years later in his autobiography. On May 1, 1993, Texas voters turned down a proposal for redistributing school funds, a program favored by Governor Ann Richards, and

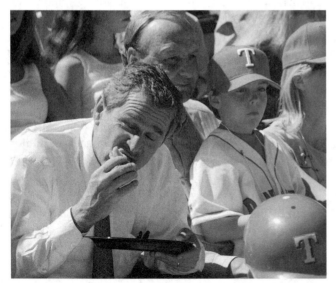

Above: The Arlington, Texas, home of the Texas Rangers baseball team was built largely at public expense thanks to the efforts of managing partner George W. Bush.

Bush watched a press conference where a disappointed Richards challenged voters to come forward if they had a better idea for the school finance system. Bush turned to his wife, Laura, and said, "I have a suggestion. I might run for governor."

Bush ran in 1994 against Ann Richards, the popular Democratic incumbent. Drawing on deep support among Republicans (including Kent Hance, the man who defeated him in 1978, and had switched to the Republican Party), and calling on experienced organizers, including some from his father's national campaigns, Bush ran a positive, issue-oriented race. Focusing on welfare reform, a crackdown on crime, and autonomy for local school districts, Bush, to the surprise of many, won with 53.5 percent of the vote. Twenty thousand people attended his inauguration in Austin, including famous evangelist Billy Graham, legendary baseball pitcher and former Texas Ranger Nolan Ryan, and, of course, George's parents, George and Barbara Bush, who were then in retirement.

After only a year in office, Bush was hailed as the most popular big-state governor in the country. He earned a

Left: Bush sold his interest in the Texas rangers after he became governor, but he still enjoyed the hot dogs and the company of new managing partner Tom Hicks and Hicks's son William.

reputation as a "compassionate conservative"—someone who believes in the principles of limited government and local control but also supports public education and some social programs. He worked to improve public schools, cut taxes, put welfare recipients to work, and he encouraged new business and job growth. Bush won reelection in 1998 with 68 percent of the vote.

That whopping triumph brought him more national attention, but even before then he had finished first in a 1997 poll among Republicans on preferences for possible candidates in the 2000 presidential election. On the day of his inaugural for his second term, he attended a church service that he described in his autobiography as one of his life-defining moments. The pastor of the First United Methodist Church in Austin said that America was starved for honest leaders with "ethical and moral courage." After the service, Bush's mother, Barbara, turned to him and said, "He was talking to you."

With his family's backing, Bush began gathering support and raising funds for a run for the presidency. Even before he officially announced an exploratory committee to examine his chances and organize support, groups of legislators from several states visited Austin to encourage him to run. By January 2000, before states begin holding caucuses or primaries to choose their presidential candidates, Bush was the frontrunner in a large field of Republican candidates. He established clear momentum early, and all of the other candidates gradually dropped from the race. By March 2000, he was endorsed by 41 U.S. senators, 175 U.S. representatives,

Above: Bush's mother, Barbara, who knew a thing or two about politics, encouraged him to get into the game.

and 27 governors. He secured enough delegate support to be the Republican nominee long before the party's summer national convention.

As Bush became more widely known, he was often called by the nicknames "W" or "Dubya" to distinguish him from his father and to show his more personable side. Questions persisted among the press and voters, however, about his grasp of national issues and foreign affairs. His first major decision as the likely nominee was selecting Dick Cheney as his running mate. Cheney had a long and

Far left: In his years as Texas governor, Bush adopted a three-finger "W" sign for his middle initial and nickname.

Left: "Dubya" Bush on the campaign trail.

Dick Cheney

When he became vice president under George W. Bush, Dick Cheney was serving his fourth Republican president, in addition to having been a strong congressional ally of President Ronald Reagan during the 1980s. Born Richard Bruce Cheney on January 30, 1941, in Lincoln, Nebraska, he grew up in Casper, Wyoming, where his father, Richard, worked for the U.S. Department of Agriculture. Cheney enjoyed hunting and fishing, captained his high school football team, and excelled academically. He did not fare so well when he went to college at Yale University. Feeling uncomfortable in New England, he left during his sophomore year and returned home.

Cheney worked for two years as a lineman for an electrical company before going back to college in 1963, this time at the University of Wyoming. He was partly motivated to return to school to keep up with his sweetheart, Lynne Vincent, who was showing great promise as a student writer. They were married in 1964. Lynne subsequently distinguished herself as an author, as editor of the Washingtonian magazine, as a university professor, and as head of the National Endowment for the Arts. The Cheneys raised two daughters, Mary and Elizabeth.

Cheney graduated from the University of Wyoming with a bachelor's degree in political science in 1965 and a master's degree the following year. Meanwhile, he served internships in the state legislature and the governor's office. He began coursework at the University of Wisconsin in 1967, but left for Washington to be an assistant for a Wisconsin senator. He moved on in 1969 to a position as special assistant to the director of the Office of Opportunity, a program initiated by newly inaugurated president Richard Nixon. Over the next few years, Cheney rose steadily to more prominent positions, including deputy White House counsel and assistant director of the Cost of Living Council. He left Washington in 1973 to become an investment advisor in Wyoming while the nation was in turmoil over the Watergate scandal.

In August 1974, after President Nixon resigned from office, Cheney was asked to join President Gerald Ford's transition staff, and he was soon promoted to assistant to the president and then to chief of staff. He advised the president on political matters, scheduled

meetings for him, and supervised the White House staff. After Ford was defeated by Jimmy Carter in the 1976 election, Cheney went back to Wyoming again, and worked with a banking firm. Two years later, he won the Republican nomination for the state's single seat in the House of Representatives. Despite having suffered a heart attack during the campaign, he went on to easily beat his Democratic rival, and was reelected to Congress five more times.

Cheney served as chairman of the Republican House Policy Committee and he strongly supported the policies of the administration of Ronald Reagan. In April 1989, after new president George Bush failed to win the approval of John Tower as his first choice as secretary of defense, he nominated Cheney for the post, and the Senate quickly confirmed it. Cheney had no military experience, but he had excellent organizational skills that were needed during a time of change and international turmoil. After the fall of the Soviet Union in 1989, the United States began cutting back on military spending—an area supervised by Cheney.

Cheney helped organize American military operations. Troops were sent to Panama to arrest the country's military dictator, Manuel Noriega, who had nullified a national election he was losing and was wanted on international drug charges. When the Iraqi army invaded Kuwait in August 1990, Cheney oversaw the massive troops, supply, and ship movements to the Persian Gulf. He helped direct the Gulf War, which began on January 16, 1991. The war was over by the end of February with the primary goal—pushing the Iraqi army out of Kuwait—quickly accomplished.

Following the war, Cheney resumed his role in cutting military costs, closing unnecessary military bases, and helping build American peacekeeping forces. His Cabinet stint ended when Bill Clinton was inaugurated president in January 1993.

In 1995, Cheney became chief executive at the Halliburton Company, the largest oil drilling and construction-services provider in the world. He left the firm five years later when George W. Bush asked him to be his vice-presidential running mate. Cheney's vast experience in Washington, his forthrightness, and his calm, assured manner were excellent compliments to the more lively, yet less-experienced, Bush. Following the Bush-Cheney victory in the controversial 2000 election, Cheney became vice president on Inauguration Day 2001.

distinguished political career and had the kind of federal government experience that Bush himself lacked.

Bush's pledge to build a team approach to his prospective presidential administration, his selection of Cheney, and his solid performances in debates and speeches reassured voters that he could handle the job of being president. His plans for large cuts in taxes and allowing young workers to invest part of their Social Security taxes in the booming stock market sounded promising. His policies that promised more individual and local control in the areas of medical insurance and education also struck the right chord among voters.

He solidified his support with a strong, nationally televised speech when he accepted the Republican nomination for president. Mixing a folksy approach ("Our founders first defined [the purpose of the federal government] here in Philadelphia. . . . Ben Franklin was here. Thomas Jefferson. And, of course, George Washington—or, as his friends called him, "George W.") with clearly defined policy measures, Bush took the lead in voter polls during the summer of 2000, maintaining a slight lead in most of them, but by election day most news agencies declared the presidential race "too close to call." Indeed, Election Day 2000 proved to be a great drama, and the saga went on for several weeks.

Right: Candidate Bush and his wife, Laura, accept the Republican presidential nomination at the 2000 convention in Philadelphia.

Tally Hassle, Florida

The 2000 election was the third time in American history that the winner had a majority of electoral votes, but fewer popular votes. In 1888, Benjamin Harrison lost the popular vote, but he had a clear majority in the Electoral College, and the outcome wasn't contested. In 1876, on the other hand, electoral votes were disputed in four states, and they proved to be decisive for Rutherford B. Hayes, who had lost in the popular tally. A similar situation developed in 2000 over the twenty-five electoral votes of one state, Florida, which would make the winner of the state the new president.

Election Results

2000	Presidential / Vice Presidential Candidates	Popular Votes	Electoral Votes
	George W. Bush / Richard Cheney (Republican)	50,456,167	271
	Albert Gore / Joseph Lieberman (Democratic)	50,996,064	266
2004	Presidential / Vice Presidential Candidates	Popular Votes	Electoral Votes
	George W. Bush / Richard Cheney (Republican)	62,040,610	286
	John F. Kerry / John Edwards (Democratic)	59,028,444	251

On election day (Tuesday, November 7, 2000), most news agencies predicted a close vote that would hinge on Pennsylvania, Michigan, and Florida, three key states with large numbers of electoral votes. Shortly after 8:00 P.M., they began projecting, based on their exit polls, that the Democratic challenger Al Gore had won the vote in all three states and was apparently headed for an Electoral College victory.

When actual vote tallies from Florida showed different trends, however, the agencies took back their projection at around 10:00 P.M., and started referring to Florida as "too close to call." The race was so close that at 1:30 A.M., both candidates, based on actual vote counts, had secured 242 electoral votes, with 54 still to be decided (270 were needed to win). Then, at 2:15 A.M., news agencies projected that Bush would win Florida, and since tallies in most other states also favored Bush, some of them declared him the winner.

At 2:30 A.M., Gore phoned Bush to congratulate him, and at 3:15 A.M., he was in a limousine on the way to make a concession speech before his supporters at the Nashville War Memorial. But along the way, he received word about voting irregularities in Florida. The car turned around, and Gore went back home where, at 3:45 A.M., he called Bush to retract his concession: "As you may have noticed," he said, "things have changed," pointing to reports from Florida. The two had a tense exchange.

When daylight came on Wednesday morning, there was still no new president-elect. NBC news anchorman Tom Brokaw noted that news agencies had confused the voters with their projections: "We don't just have egg on our face," he said. "We have omelet all over our suits." Florida vote tallies completed later in the day showed that Bush had edged Gore there by 1,784 votes. Under Florida law, such a close vote total automatically generates a recount.

Meanwhile, voting problems in the state were widely publicized. Some voters in Palm Beach County complained about a confusing ballot; more than nineteen thousand votes were disqualified there under a system where voters use a stylus to punch a hole in a card next to the name of the candidate of their choice. The cards have perforations, and when they are punched with a stylus, the perforation is supposed to fall away (the punched perforation, called a "chad," became a new part of the national vocabulary). The nineteen thousand ballots that had been disqualified had more than one candidate selected, or the chads were still attached to the perforations, and vote-counting machines couldn't tabulate them. To add to the confusion, a candidate who wasn't expected to attract many votes in that county—Reform Party nominee Pat Buchanan—was credited with 3,407 ballots. Voters (and Buchanan himself) agreed that the count had to have been a mistake. In nearby Broward County, another 6,686 ballots were disqualified, and similar problems were reported in adjacent Dade County. Gore requested manual recounts in the three counties as well as in Volusia County, where similar problems had also been found. All four counties had larger numbers of registered Democrats than Republicans.

How the Electoral College Works

The election of 2000 renewed debate over whether the Electoral College should be abolished in favor of using just the popular vote to determine who becomes president.

When the U.S. Constitution was being drafted, delegates devised the Electoral College as a way to give the responsibility to the people for electing presidents. They agreed that an election based on the popular vote could easily be influenced by partisan politics, and that voters in one state might not be well informed about a candidate from another state, considering the state of communications in their day.

Since 1961, the total of state and District of Columbia electors has been set at 538, and a simple majority of 270 is needed for election. The presidential candidate who receives the most votes in a particular state wins all of that state's electoral votes (except for Maine and Nebraska, where they are awarded on the basis of winning individual congressional districts). The number of electors in each state is equal to the total number of senators and representatives it sends to Congress.

Presidential electors are designated by each state legislature. Following a general election on the first Tuesday of November every four years, the electors meet to officially record the state's electoral votes. They meet simultaneously in all the states on the first Monday after the second Wednesday in December of presidential election years. Their votes are formally counted in the presence of both houses of Congress on January 6.

The Electoral College Through the Years

The Constitution (ratified in 1789): *Article II, Section 1, carefully defines the voting procedure to be followed by electors. Originally, the electors were to vote for the two most qualified persons without noting which of them was selected as president or vice president. The candidate receiving the greatest number of electoral votes, provided that the votes of a majority of the electors were received, would be president, and the candidate winning the second largest number of votes would be vice president.*

1796: *The first flaw in the system occurred when John Adams and Thomas Jefferson were elected president and vice president, respectively. Political parties had not been established back then, but the candidates still had decidedly opposing viewpoints.*

1800: *A majority of electors voted for both Jefferson, the head of the Democratic-Republican Party, and Aaron Burr, his running mate. The result was a tie because the electors voted for the two most qualified persons without noting which of them was selected as president or vice president. The election was referred to the House of Representatives, as mandated by the Constitution. and Jefferson's opponents tried various ways to have Burr elected. However, Jefferson was chosen president and Burr vice president after thirty-six rounds of balloting.*

1804: *Congress enacted, and the states ratified, the Constitution's Twelfth Amendment, providing for separate electoral votes for president and vice president.*

1820: *James Monroe technically won the electoral votes in every state, but one elector voted against him as a symbolic gesture to ensure that George Washington would remain the only president to have won all of the electoral votes in an election.*

1824: *None of four candidates received the necessary number of electoral votes to become president. In such a case, the House of Representatives decides the outcome. A bitterly divided Congress selected John Quincy Adams over Andrew Jackson, even though Jackson had won more electoral and popular votes.*

1836: *The Whig Party nominated three regional candidates for president, hoping to create a situation where neither candidate, including Democrat Martin Van Buren, would win enough electoral votes to become president. In such a case, the election would be decided by the House of Representatives, where the Whigs were the dominant party. The strategy failed when Van Buren won the general election and accumulated enough electoral votes.*

1876: *A dispute over the voting results in four states left crucial electoral votes in doubt. Under existing law, it was the duty of Congress to resolve the dispute, but it soon became deadlocked. The Electoral Commission of 1877, authorized by Congress, finally resolved the issue in favor of Republican Rutherford B. Hayes.*

1887: *Congress enacted a law authorizing states to resolve all controversies over the selection of presidential electors. Congress may intervene to settle a dispute over the election of the presidential electors only when a state isn't able to do so.*

1888: *Incumbent president Grover Cleveland outpolled Benjamin Harrison 5,540,309 to 5,444,337 in the popular vote, but received only 168 electoral votes to Harrison's 233 because Harrison had won more of the larger states.*

1960: *John F. Kennedy defeated Richard Nixon in the popular vote by less than one percent, and the scenario was repeated in 1968, when Nixon defeated Hubert Humphrey.*

1961: *The Twenty-third Amendment to the Constitution allowed the District of Columbia to vote for three electors.*

1969: *A challenge to the "winner-take-all" system of awarding electoral votes was rejected by the U.S. Supreme Court.*

2000: *Al Gore received more popular votes than George W. Bush, but he was narrowly defeated in the Electoral College in one of the most hotly contested presidential elections in American history. Bush did not become the clear winner until December 13—a little more than five weeks after election day—when Gore conceded the election following weeks of legal struggles and the involvement of Florida courts and the U.S. Supreme Court.*

Above: Palm Beach County election officials painstakingly inspect questionable ballots during the recount.

Under Florida law, recounts must be made within seven days, but the problems with disqualified votes—and the inability of machine counters to register them—led to legal proceedings over whether to count the cards manually, a more time-consuming process. Since recounts were due within a week, large counties couldn't accomplish manual recounts in time, and added to that, the legality of manual recounts had been challenged in court. On November 13, a federal judge in Miami rejected a request by Bush's lawyers to stop the hand recounts. Meanwhile, Florida's secretary of state, Katherine Harris, also called for an end to them, citing her legal authority over election results. Her power was upheld in a Leon County court on November 14 (which includes Florida's capital, Tallahassee). Harris stated that the machine recount already made would be final, and that only overseas absentee ballots that weren't counted

yet would be added to the final total. She was scheduled to certify the results on Saturday, November 18.

The machine recounts were finished on Wednesday, November 15, and they confirmed Bush as the winner, although his margin had shrunk to 327 votes. Meanwhile, officials in Palm Beach, Broward, and Dade counties decided to conduct another recount, this time manually. Harris attempted to block them, but the ruling that had supported her power was appealed by Gore's lawyers to the Florida Supreme Court.

Charges of partisan politics contributed to the controversy. Although Bush's brother, Jeb Bush, the state's governor, chose to recuse himself from the entire recount process, Harris, a Republican, had campaigned actively for Bush. The counties conducting the manual recount, on the other hand, were heavily Democratic, and Republicans were accused of wanting to hurry the process, even if some voters were disenfranchised because of mistakes. Democrats were accused of trying to find more votes. Most Americans simply wanted to be assured of the integrity of the voting process.

On Friday, November 17, the Florida Supreme Court agreed to hear arguments from lawyers representing the candidates, the secretary of state, and local officials about the certification and manual recount issues, setting Monday, November 20, as the court date and instructing Harris not to certify the results before then. The counting of absentee ballots added another 603 votes to Bush's lead, giving him an official advantage of 930 votes. Some ballots cast by U.S. servicemen that weren't properly postmarked were thrown out on Saturday, adding more fuel to the controversy. Manual recounts of the original vote, which had started and stopped several times, continued in both Palm Beach and Broward counties.

On Monday, November 20, lawyers for both Bush and Gore presented arguments to the Florida Supreme Court in a nationally televised hearing. The justices interrupted speeches by the lawyers to focus on specific issues. They were concerned that the vote counting could drag on toward the December 18 date when all electors are supposed to convene in the respective states to officially record electoral votes. If the recounts weren't finished in time, Florida might not be able to certify its electors, and all the votes from the state would be lost. On the other hand, the justices were reluctant to discontinue manual recounts because it might be the only way to count votes that weren't tabulated by computers.

The Court ruled unanimously (7–0) on Monday, November 21, that manual recounts could continue, and that the Florida secretary of state did not have the right to impose the November 18 date after local election officials had determined manual recounts were necessary. The court ruled that the manual recounts had to be completed by Sunday, November 26, at 5:00 P.M., or 9:00 A.M. the next day if the secretary of state's office was not open that day. Bush's lawyers appealed the ruling to the U.S. Supreme Court.

Meanwhile, Dade County officials stopped their manual recount for lack of time, and controversies erupted in Broward and Palm Beach counties over whether or not to count "dimpled chads" that indicate that a stylus made an impression on a ballot, but the chad didn't separate from the ballot, and, therefore, had not been recognized by the machines. The question of whether a voter's intent had been compromised by the process of counting votes, or whether the legal standard for voting should prevail, was argued by lawyers representing the two candidates before the U.S. Supreme Court on Friday, December 1.

The results certified on Sunday, November 26, gave Bush 2,912,790 votes to Gore's 2,912,253—a margin of just 537. Under that certification, Bush gained Florida's 25 electoral votes for a total of 271—one more than he needed to win the presidency. However, officials in Palm Beach County—who had missed the 5:00 deadline—continued counting until they finished just over two hours later. Because Harris would neither accept a partial manual recount nor extend the deadline, a previous machine recount had to serve as the final tally for Palm Beach County.

On that Sunday evening, Bush made a brief speech announcing that his transition team was moving forward, but more legal challenges were pending, and Gore addressed the nation on Monday, asking for patience. The next day, a Tallahassee circuit court judge rejected a Gore plea for a smaller recount, specifically of fourteen thousand ballots from Broward and Dade counties that clearly showed a vote but were not included in the machine counts.

On Friday, December 1, the U.S. Supreme Court heard arguments by lawyers representing Bush and Gore about the legality of the Florida manual recounts. The case had been initiated by Bush's lawyers after the ruling by the Florida Supreme Court for continuing manual recounts. On the following Monday (December 4), the Supreme Court returned the case to Florida's high court, ordering it to clarify its earlier judgment. Meanwhile, on that same Monday, a Florida circuit court judge ruled that there was no basis for continuing manual recounts.

The topsy-turvy, dramatic events continued on Friday, December 8, when two judges ruled against Democrats in separate cases brought by private citizens of Florida over the applications of several thousand absentee ballots that had missing information, but had been corrected (and made legal) by Republican officials. Democrats wanted those ballots thrown out, which would have tipped the election to Gore, but with courts ruling against them—by halting manual recounts and refusing to throw out the absentee ballots—the vice president's chances appeared to be dead. However, later that day, the Florida Supreme Court overturned the lower court's ruling against manual recounts and ordered them to proceed again.

Recounts began again on Saturday, December 9, only to be halted by order of the U.S. Supreme Court later in the day. The Court scheduled an appeal by the Bush legal team against the Florida Supreme Court's ruling, and in the hearing on Monday, December 11, the justices expressed concern about whether manual recounts were constitutional after all. Since state legislatures are authorized by the U.S. Constitution to make election laws, the Court feared that the Florida Supreme Court had overstepped its bounds by ordering the manual recounts. Lawyers for Gore argued that the state court had acted correctly, having fulfilled its role of interpreting laws.

The Supreme Court justices were also concerned about different standards used in different Florida counties to judge whether previously untallied votes should be counted. Finally, they were concerned that time was running out, a worry that was shared by the solidly Republican Florida state legislature, which moved to formally recognize electors for Bush based on the election results that had been certified by Florida's secretary of state.

On Tuesday, December 12, just before 10 P.M., the U.S. Supreme Court announced its official ruling: A bitterly divided court ruled 5-4 that the recounts were unconstitutional, and ordered a halt to all further recounts. The following evening, at 9:00, Vice President Gore conceded the election in a nationally televised address that called for the nation to unite behind the new president-elect. Bush followed with his own address an hour later.

"Work Together"

"After a difficult election, we must put politics behind us and work together to make the promise of America available for every one of our citizens," Bush stated in his first address to the nation as president-elect on December 13, 2000. Striking the right tone, according to most political observers, in an attempt to unite the country and ease partisanship, he continued, "I am optimistic that we can change the tone in Washington, D.C." He also said, "I believe things happen for a reason, and I hope the long wait of the last five weeks will heighten a desire to move beyond the bitterness and partisanship of the recent past."

In that speech, Bush made references to two other presidents who had taken office at a time of great national divisions. Abraham Lincoln had said, "A house divided cannot stand," in speaking of the dissolving Union near

Above: When all the votes were counted and the smoke of controversy cleared, George W. Bush became America's 43rd president on January 20, 2001.

the outbreak of the Civil War. Bush said, "Our nation must rise above a house divided. Americans share hopes and goals and values far more important than any political disagreements." Thomas Jefferson, when he took office in 1801 under the first transition of power from one party (the Federalists) to another (the Democratic-Republicans), offered unity by saying, "We are all Federalists. We are all Republicans." Bush offered, "Republicans want the best for our nation," then he paused, dramatically, before continuing, "and so do Democrats. Our votes may differ, but not our hopes."

However, Bush took office under ominous conditions after the disputed election. History has shown that presidents who win controversial elections usually face formidable opposition. John Quincy Adams in 1824 and Rutherford B. Hayes in 1876 each became one-term presidents who could not govern effectively because of constant challenges by their opponents. Most politicians

Left: On the day before his presidential inauguration, Bush and his wife, Laura, rode in triumph through the streets of Austin, Texas. The state Capitol in the background bears a remarkable resemblance to the national Capitol, where they would appear a day later.

spoke of a spirit of cooperation once the presidential election of 2000 was finally over, but the American people were watching to see whether or not those words would become political action.

Changing the Economy

By the time Bush moved into the White House, a combination of tax increases and budget cuts by the Clinton administration had allowed the treasury to collect half a trillion dollars more than it spent between 1998 and 2000, and the Congressional Budget Office projected that the gap would grow to $5.6 trillion in ten years if nothing else changed.

George W. Bush went to work to bring about some change. The Democrats were determined to use the surplus to create or expand social programs, but the Republicans believed that it should be returned to the taxpayers. Although the close election had left the choice up in the air, Bush acted quickly and decisively. He signed his plan for a massive tax cut into law on June 7, 2001, just eleven weeks after his inauguration. It was the greatest domestic achievement of his young presidency, but it would turn out to be a controversial one. It was charged that the cut had been weighted too heavily in favor of high-income taxpayers, even though the Congressional Joint Economic Committee reported in 2000 that the richest 2 percent of the country's taxpayers, who earned about 21 percent of the total income, were paying 27.5 percent of all federal income taxes.

After Bush's tax-cut legislation was passed, the business of governing on the domestic front seemed to be all downhill. His energy proposals were viewed with suspicion since it was believed that he was in the hip pockets of the big oil interests, and his environmental program enraged the people he called the "green, green lima beans," who were horrified at what they considered his cavalier attitude.

Bush scored a big success through his relationship with Mexican president Vicente Fox that hugely enhanced relations between the two countries and, not coincidentally, scored points among Mexican-Americans who traditionally voted for Democrats.

He was less successful when he traveled to Slovenia to

Right: The twin Bush daughters, Barbara and Jenna, stayed out of the limelight during their father's presidency, but they emerged in 2004 to help him campaign for a second term.

meet with Russian president Vladimir Putin. After a two-hour face-to-face meeting, Bush announced in a press conference that he had been able to get a sense of Putin's soul, and found him straightforward and trustworthy. The press, which had been recording the Russian leader's career since he was a key KGB operative, jumped all over him. The *Washington Post* pronounced him "naive," and MSNBC reporter Chris Matthews wrote, "Such powers of observation deserve our attention. George Reeves, the first Superman, could see whether a bad guy was hiding a gun under his coat. George W. Bush can see clear into a Russian ex-spymaster's soul."

But their carping was premature. Maybe Bush hadn't seen into Putin's soul, but he did acquire a staunch ally, and he had reoriented America's Grand Strategy toward Russia. His own Grand Plan for governing America ran into trouble in the summer of 2001, though. First he ran into stiff opposition over his energy plan, and then the makeup of the Senate turned against him when Senator James Jeffords of Vermont switched parties, putting the Democrats in the majority. Worse, Jeffords's chairmanship of the Labor and Education Committee went to Senator Ted Kennedy, who began challenging the president on education reform. There were other challenges, too. By the middle of July, Bush found himself blocked on every item in his first-year agenda, from judgeships to modernization

The Bush Administration

Administration Dates: January 20, 2001–
January 20, 2009

Vice President: Richard B. Cheney (2001–2009)

Cabinet:

Secretary of State	Colin Powell (2001–2005)
	Condoleezza Rice (2005–2009)
Secretary of the Treasury	Paul H. O'Neill (2001–2002)
	John Snow (2003–2006)
	Henry M. Paulson Jr. (2006–2009)
Secretary of Defense	Donald H. Rumsfeld (2001–2006)
	Robert M. Gates (2006–2009)
Attorney General	John Ashcroft (2001–2005)
	Alberto Gonzales (2005–2007)
	Michael Mukasey (2007–2009)
Secretary of the Interior	Gale A. Norton (2001–2006)
	Dick Kempthorne (2006–2009)
Secretary of Agriculture	Ann M. Veneman (2001–2005)
	Mike Johanns (2005–2007)
	Ed Schafer (2008–2009)
Secretary of Commerce	Donald Evans (2001–2005)
	Carlos Gutierrez (2005–2009)
Secretary of Labor	Elaine Chao (2001–2009)
Secretary of Health and Human Services	Tommy G. Thompson (2001–2005)
	Michael O. Leavitt (2005–2009)
Secretary of Housing and Urban Development	Melquides "Mel" Rafael Martinez (2001–2003)
	Alphonso Jackson (2003–2008)
	Steve Preston (2008–2009)
Secretary of Transportation	Norman Yoshio Mineta (2001–2006)
	Mary E. Peters (2006–2009)
Secretary of Energy	Spencer Abraham (2001–2005)
	Samuel W. Bodman (2005–2009)
Secretary of Education	Roderick Paige (2001–2005)
	Margaret Spellings (2005–2009)
Secretary of Veteran Affairs	Anthony J. Principi (2001–2005)
	Jim Nicholson (2005–2007)
	Dr. James Peake (2007–2009)
Secretary of Homeland Security	Tom Ridge (2003–2005)
	Michael Chertoff (2005–2009)

of the military to Social Security "reform." The Senate even torpedoed his plan for oil exploration in Alaska (choosing the environment over business interests), and his cherished faith-based initiative to involve religious institutions in dealing with social problems seemed in clear danger of never being enacted.

By August, most political commentators had concluded that the Bush administration was in such disarray that it would take a miracle to get him elected to a second term. Bush responded by taking a month-long vacation at his ranch in Crawford, Texas, but it turned out to be a working vacation, and a month of fence-mending within a variety of voting blocs, from the working poor to the middle class. He emerged from it with better poll numbers, but it was still clear that his political future was in trouble.

9/11

The world turned upside down and everything changed on the morning of September 11, 2001 when a hijacked airliner crashed into the North Tower of the World Trade Center in New York. It was quickly followed by another jet that was hurled into the South Tower. A third hijacked commercial jet hit a section of the Pentagon, and a fourth crashed in Pennsylvania when passengers apparently fought against the hijackers. That plane, it is believed, was on a course to crash into the White House.

President Bush was not at the White House at the time. He was in Sarasota, Florida, reading to a second-grade class at the Emma H. Booker Elementary School. His chief of staff, Andrew Card, whispered in his ear that it was confirmed that the plane crashes were terrorist attacks, but Bush went right on reading to the children. When he finished, he went to the microphones and solemnly promised that terrorism against the United States "will not stand."

He ordered the presidential aircraft, *Air Force One*, to get back to Washington right away, but as the plane approached the capital, the Secret Service received a report, later proved false, that the plane was a terrorist target, and a rerouting to Barksdale Air Force Base in

Louisiana was ordered. It was there Bush made his first formal statement, at 12:40 P.M. "The resolve of our great nation is being tested," he said, "but make no mistake. We will show the world that we will pass this test."

He flew on to Strategic Air Command headquarters at Offutt Air Base in Nebraska, but arrived back in Washington to make a nationally televised speech from the Oval Office that same evening.

For a lot of reasons, it wasn't George W. Bush's finest hour, but he recovered and began asserting his leadership during a memorial service for victims of the attacks on September 14, and a speech to a joint session of Congress six days later. In every case during those weeks in September, he worked to project an attitude of calm and restraint, but little by little, he added anger and resolve.

The "New Bush" emerged during a memorial service at Washington National Cathedral, and a visit to Ground Zero in New York later the same day. He was at home among the police officers, firefighters and construction workers in the still-smoldering pit, and he knew from their reaction that average Americans were behind him. He assured them that he would conduct a war on terrorism and it would be fought decisively. He wanted the killers "dead or alive," he said. His poll ratings soared.

Top, left: The world, and President Bush's life, changed forever on September 11, 2001, when hijacked airliners crashed into the twin towers of New York's World Trade Center.

Top, right: The President learned of the 9/11 attacks from his chief of staff, Andy Card, during a visit to the Emma E. Booker Elementary School in Sarasota, Florida.

Bottom: Bush promised to rally against terrorism during a memorial service at Ground Zero, where he appeared with dignitaries including UN Secretary General Kofi Annan.

It was quickly established that the terror attacks had been the work of Osama bin Laden and his organization, al-Qaeda, which was thriving under the protection of the Taliban, the extremist Muslim rulers of Afghanistan. The mountainous terrain there had earned Afghanistan the title of "the graveyard of empires," because it had stymied every attacker from Alexander the Great to the Soviet Union, but the Bush administration made the decision to take the fight to the enemy. With less than a month of preparation, U.S. troops and aircraft, along with allied forces, charged into the country, overthrew its government, and destroyed its terrorist strongholds, losing only fifteen troops to enemy resistance. Although bin Laden and most of his henchmen escaped, their ability to do damage was decreased dramatically, and the message was sent that the Bush administration was willing to give much more than lip service to the war on terrorism.

The Axis of Evil

For his 2002 State of the Union Address, Bush decided to make new policies for the Middle East his main emphasis. For more than half a century, the United States had opted for "stability" there, but that policy, he believed, had brought death and destruction to both New York and Washington, and the time had come to do something about it. Still harboring great hostility toward Saddam Hussein, Bush believed most strongly that the place to start was Iraq.

It seemed to his speech writers that Saddam, along with other governments that sheltered terrorists, had a great deal in common with the Axis powers—Germany, Japan, and Italy—of World War II. They all deeply resented Western democracy and its power. For its part, Iran had become a haven for terrorists and was hostile to the United States; and North Korea was blatantly developing a nuclear arsenal. The three countries, Bush warned in his speech, were an "Axis of Evil."

"These regimes pose a grave and growing danger," he said. "We'll be deliberate, yet time is not on our side. I will not wait on events, while dangers gather. I will not stand by as peril draws closer and closer. The United States will not permit the world's most dangerous regimes to threaten us with the world's most destructive weapons."

Left: It was generally agreed that the mastermind of the 9/11 attacks was exiled Saudi dissident Osama bin Laden and his organization, al-Qaeda.

Top, left: The bombardment of Baghdad in March 2003 marked the beginning of the end for the Saddam Hussein regime in Iraq.

Top, right: Secretary of Defense Donald Rumsfeld took on the role of the administration's spokesman on the conduct of the war in Iraq.

Right: Although the administration had been confident that the Iraqi people would welcome the Americans as liberators, the reality turned out to be a long, hard standoff between local rebels and U.S. troops.

He had delivered fighting words that night, and the reaction around the country and around the world was more negative than positive. In addition, much of the United Nations vehemently opposed war. However, Bush didn't take back a single word as he began building a case for overthrowing Saddam Hussein, who was first among equals in the "Axis of Evil."

Through much of 2002, the Bush administration presented dozens of arguments for going to war. Iraq's dismal disregard for human rights was among them, as was the need for democratic reform in the region. Bush mentioned Saddam's attempt to assassinate his father in Kuwait, and noted that the Iraqis had fired on American planes in the no-fly zone and had violated the sanctions that were put in place after the Gulf War. He charged that Iraq was harboring and arming terrorist groups, and that led to the most often repeated charge of all, that Saddam was developing weapons of mass destruction, including the capability for germ warfare and a program for assembling nuclear weapons.

After nearly a year of debate, Congress approved going to war against Iraq on October 2, 2002, despite the immense disapproval of numerous UN member nations. The first smart bombs and cruise missiles began falling on Baghdad in what was called "Operation Shock and Awe" on March 20, 2003. Ground forces took control of Saddam International Airport on April 3, and Baghdad itself fell six days later. On that same day, a huge iron statue of Saddam was pulled down, symbolically ending his reign of terror. Saddam's hometown, Tikrit, was captured with little resistance on April 13, 2003, and two days later the coalition partners declared the war effectively over; however, they spoke too soon.

Before long, the Iraqi people began to rebel against the occupiers, and coalition troops, as well as contractors sent to rebuild the country, were systematically killed or taken hostage. As the last year of his first term began, Bush faced more and more angry opposition to his plan, or perhaps his lack of one, while at the same time he was facing a downturn in the economy with record numbers of unemployed people. He vowed to "stay the course."

The 9-11 Commission

On November 27, 2002, the National Commission on Terrorist Attacks upon the United States (called more casually as the "9-11 Commission") was created by President Bush. Its mandate: to give a "full and complete accounting" of the events of September 11, 2001. Beginning in March 2003 and ending in June 2004, the commission held a series of twelve public hearings, grilling numerous public officials as well as listening to family members and surviving victims of the attacks. On April 29, 2004, President Bush met privately with the commission for two hours for what he called a "wide-ranging, important, good discussion." He and Vice President Cheney presented a united front at that meeting, refusing to testify under oath. (Then national security advisor Condoleezza Rice appeared at one of the public hearings but also declined to take the oath before doing so.)

The bipartisan panel of ten, chaired by Thomas H. Kean, fulfilled its obligation on July 21, 2004, issuing a 585-page report containing its analysis of what had led to the terrorist attacks, as well as specific suggestions regarding strengthening the security of the United States against future attack.

Believing the terrorist activities of September 2001 could and should have been prevented, the commission scolded the American government: "The 9/11 attacks were a shock, but they should not have come as a surprise." To support that contention, the report detailed numerous instances of prior, recent terrorism by al Qaeda against United States targets around the world as well as against other nations. Yet in spite of those events, it continued, America's "most important failure was one of imagination. We do not believe leaders understood the gravity of the threat. The terrorist danger from Bin Ladin [sic] and al Qaeda was not a major topic for policy debate among the public, the media, or in the Congress. Indeed, it barely came up during the 2000 presidential campaign." The commission also cited a lack of coordination among the nation's government agencies and officials as another serious weakness: At more senior levels, communication was poor. Senior military and FAA leaders had no effective communication with each other. The chain of command did not function well. The President could not reach some senior officials. The Secretary of Defense did not enter the chain of command until the morning's key events were over. Air National Guard units with different rules of engagement were scrambled without the knowledge of the President, NORAD, or the National Military Command Center.

The commission recommended the following steps be taken, among others:

- To find and deal with terrorist sanctuaries.
- To strengthen the country's friendly relationships with Afghanistan and Pakistan.
- To make the crux of the United States' relationship with Saudi Arabia less dependent on oil.
- To be a positive moral example for Muslim countries.
- To increase America's defense, along it borders, in the skies, and from within.
- To better coordinate emergency response in a twenty-first-century world.

The report was published in book form in August 2006. Because it is a public document, its text is available in its entirety for free download at www.gpoaccess.gov/911/.

The War on Terror

In his January 28, 2003, State of the Union Address, President Bush pressed for war with Iraq, uttering what came to be called the "Sixteen Words" that would come back to haunt his administration: "The British government has learned that Saddam Hussein recently sought significant quantities of uranium from Africa." The International Atomic Energy Agency later determined that the reports U.S. intelligence officials had obtained from the British, detailing sales of yellowcake from Niger, had been forged.

Even without genuine evidence of weapons of mass destruction (WMDs), the war continued. On May 1, 2003, the president made a surprise appearance—uniformed and laden with gear—on the USS *Abraham Lincoln*, then located off the coast of San Diego, to give what has become known as his "Mission Accomplished" speech—although he did not quite claim victory; he merely announced an end to major combat operations without committing to a time frame for American withdrawal from Iraq.

Saddam Hussein was captured in Ad Dahr, Iraq, on December, 13, 2003, brought to trial, and executed by hanging on December 30, 2006. Meanwhile, in June 2004, an Iraqi interim government was set up to succeed the authority of the Coalition Provisional Authority (CPA). In January 2005, free elections were held in Iraq for the first time in more than half a century, followed in April by that nation's election of Jalal Talabani, a Kurd, as the country's president and by Iraq's adoption of a new constitution on October 15.

The war against insurgents raged on. Although members of the Taliban regrouped in Afghanistan—Bush would send 3,500 additional troops to that country in March 2007—U.S. forces continued to pour instead into Iraq. Over 140,000 members of the American military have been deployed as part of the Multi-Nation Force in Iraq (MFI-I) coalition that replaced the CPA—composing over 90 percent of MFI-I's total troops—as of September 2008.

> President Bush survived an assassination attempt on May 10, 2005, while speaking in Tbilisi, in the Republic of Georgia. The grenade thrown by Vladimir Arutyunian failed to detonate.

Although opposed by Congress, in January 2007 Bush ordered a troop surge in Iraq of five more American brigades and, five months later, used his veto power to reject a bill that set a deadline for withdrawal of American troops from that country. However, in September 2008, General David Petraeus, leader of the surge forces, noted that military force alone would not solve the problems of that region. Speaking of Afghanistan as well as Iraq, he said, "Political, economic, and diplomatic activity is [sic] critical to capitalize on gains in the security arena." In 2008, Bush signed provisions stating that the United States government would fund the wars in Iraq and Afghanistan until his presidency ended in January 20, 2009, bringing total spending to over $650 billion on Iraq and almost $200 billion on Afghanistan.

President Bush (center) meets at the White House with Afghanistan president Hamid Karzai (left) and Secretary of Defense Robert Gates. The occasion was a 2008 video conference with U.S. Provincial Reconstruction team leaders, National Guard Agriculture Development team representatives, and Afghani governors.

Hurricane Katrina

In 2005, the most destructive storm ever to strike the United States wreaked havoc in the Gulf Coast from Florida to Texas, overpowering the levee system of New Orleans. Katrina is estimated to have caused $81.2 billion in damage and more than 1,800 fatalities, displacing roughly 1 million people and destroying 200,000 homes.

On August 26, Governor Kathleen Blanco declared a state of emergency in Louisiana; the next day, Governor Haley Barbour did so in Mississippi. The storm became a Category Five hurricane on August 28 and, that evening, the residents of New Orleans were asked to evacuate. Later that night, water rose above the levees; on the next day, the levee was breached, placing 80 percent of the city under water. During that time, Bush, who had been on vacation in Crawford, visited Arizona and California to press his pending Medicare reforms with public officials. The evening of August 29, Governor Blanco appealed to Bush: "Mr. President, we need your help. We need everything you've got." Michael Chertoff, secretary of the Department of Homeland Security, said that he only learned about the breach on August 30; at that point Chertoff designated the head of the Federal Emergency Management Agency (FEMA), Michael D. Brown, to take charge. Bush returned to Crawford to continue his vacation.

On August 30, National Guard Troops were finally ordered into Alabama, Florida, Louisiana, and Mississippi; and Bush stated his intention to "fly to Washington to begin work . . . with a task force that will coordinate the work of fourteen federal agencies involved in the relief effort." On August 31, a public health emergency was declared for the entire Gulf Coast. Chertoff stated, "We are extremely pleased with the response that every element of the federal government, all of our federal partners, have made to this terrible tragedy." On September 2, a week after the storm's approach, Bush's own aides asked the president to watch a compilation of newscasts showing the extent of the damage of Katrina. That evening, he and the Coast Guard went on television to assert that they were in control of the situation. Despite Bush's initial praise of Michael Brown, he was replaced as leader of the rescue effort eight days after his appointment to the mission.

Although a concerted effort was made to restore the areas of New Orleans considered to be attractive to tourists, as of September 15, 2008, more than 65,000 homes there remained vacant or abandoned and only 50 percent of the proposed FEMA Public Assistance Grants had been paid.

Above: President Bush meets New Orleans mayor C. Ray Nagin at the New Orleans airport on September 2, 2005. Bush toured the Gulf Coast communities battered by Hurricane Katrina, hoping to boost the spirits of increasingly desperate storm victims and exhausted rescuers.

High Finance

On May 30, 2002, President Bush signed the third-largest tax cut in U.S. history, amounting to $350 billion. Almost a year later to the day, he passed the Jobs and Growth Tax Relief Reconciliation Act of 2003. The $170 billion Economic Stimulus Act of 2008 gave most taxpayers rebates of $600, although low-income individuals received half that.

He approved of the Republican-sponsored Medicare Act of 2003, endorsed by AARP, which newly provided coverage for pharmaceutical drugs needed by the elderly. In his State of the Union Address of 2005, he suggested partially privatizing Social Security, though Democrats' opposition succeeded in shelving his proposed reforms. In 2006, feeling it was too much like socialized health care, which he opposed, Bush vetoed the State Children's Health Insurance Program (SCHIP) that Democrats had attached to a bill funding the war in Iraq.

Farewells and New Faces

Bush's cabinet underwent considerable overhaul during his second term, not the least being the loss of Attorney General Alberto Gonzales, who resigned in 2005 after months of strenuous investigation into his involvement in the unfair firing of seven U.S. attorneys.

Other major departures from the cabinet were those of Donald Rumsfeld, Tom Ridge, and Colin Powell. An especially notable appointment was that of former national security adviser Condoleezza Rice as Powell's replacement—the first black woman, second woman, and second African American to serve as secretary of state. Karl Rove, the president's chief of staff, resigned in August 2007 in the wake of various investigations and scandals.

After the death of Chief Justice William Rehnquist in 2005, Bush nominated Chief Justice John Roberts to the Supreme Court. Also in that year, Justice Sandra Day O'Connor announced her retirement. On the suggestion of Laura Bush, the president sought another woman to replace her on the bench and selected Harriet Miers, but Miers ultimately withdrew in the face of opposition by Congress. Bush's next choice, Samuel Alito, was approved and joined the other justices in 2006.

Cold War Redux

On August 8, 2008, war broke out between the Republic of Georgia and Russia, over the Russian occupation of South Ossetia, which, beginning in 1991, lobbied for separation from Georgia following skirmishes between their militias. America was caught up in the conflict.

In his Saturday radio address following the invasion, the president said, "The world has watched with alarm as Russia invaded a sovereign neighboring state and threatened a democratic government elected by its people. This act is completely unacceptable to the free nations of the world." Said President Bush on August 13, as the Russian tanks continued to roll, "The United States of America stands with the democratically elected government of Georgia. We insist that the sovereignty and territorial integrity of Georgia be respected. . . . This mission will be vigorous and ongoing."

Bearing a letter from French president Nicolas Sarkosy (whom she caught up with in Paris) to Georgian president Mikheil Saakashvili, Secretary of State Condoleezza Rice was dispatched to Tbilisi, where she called for a cease-fire. The military action ended and, on August 28, Russia recognized South Ossetia as an independent state.

"If America shows weakness and uncertainty, the world will drift toward tragedy. That will not happen on my watch."
—*George W. Bush*

Legacy

George W. Bush's eight years in national office constituted one of the most troubled presidential administrations in United States history. Both candidates for his seat, Democrat Barack Obama and Republican John McCain, pointedly sought to differentiate themselves from Bush during their campaign, promising great changes to the way America runs its government. Although the president had a high approval rating, hovering at near 90 percent, immediately following the 9/11 attacks, that rating subsequently plummeted and remained below 50 percent from December 2004 until the end of his second term.

At various times during Bush's presidency, there were outcries for his impeachment. On June 9, 2008, Representative Dennis Kucinich (D-Ohio) introduced thirty-five articles of impeachment on the floor of the House of Representatives, but the issue was removed from discussion by Speaker Nancy Pelosi.

Bush entered office as a peacetime president and left it in a state of war. He also left the country in debt: the Congressional Budget Office estimated that the Obama administration inherited a deficit of some $438 billion, exceeding the record of $413 billion set in 2004, largely due to the expenses of the War on Terror and the tax cuts Bush had imposed. (Just ten years earlier, President

Clinton announced a $70 million budget surplus, the first since 1969.)

Bush left office with no timetable for troop withdrawal from Iraq, and it was revealed in September 2008 that over the previous summer the president had secretly authorized military raids over the Afghanistan border into tribal areas of Pakistan, to the distress of just-elected Pakistan president Asif Ali Zardari.

On the positive side, he signed into law the first-ever Medicare bill to provide prescription drug benefits to senior citizens. His No Child Left Behind Act demonstrably helped raise children's test scores in math and reading and made schools more accountable to parents. Bush's three tax cuts put real money in the pockets of financially strapped members of the lower and middle classes: in 2003 alone, 24 million families received tax relief totaling $14 billion.

Going Home

President Bush and First Lady Laura Bush attended the inauguration of Barack Obama, then were driven to Andrews Air Force Base for the flight home to Texas. A Welcome Home party awaited them in Midland, Texas, then they went to their ranch in Crawford. Soon thereafter the Bushes bought a house in the Preston Hollows neighborhood of Dallas, which has become their primary residence.

Since leaving the White House, Bush has kept a low profile, steadfastly refusing to comment on President Obama's policies (in contrast to Bush's former vice president, Dick Cheney, who has been an outspoken critic of the Obama administration). In March 2009, before a crowd of approximately two thousand Canadian businesspeople in Calgary, Alberta, Bush declined to pass judgment on President Obama. "I'm not going to spend my time criticizing him," he said. "There are plenty of critics in the arena. He deserves my silence." Unlike conservative radio talk-show host Rush Limbaugh, who said he hoped Obama would fail as president, Bush stated that he hoped Obama would enjoy a successful presidency. He explained that he wished Obama well because "I love my country a lot more than I love politics."

He elaborated on his low-profile policy in February 2010, during a reunion of Bush and Cheney staffers. "I have no desire to see myself on television," Bush said. "I don't want to be [among] a panel of formers instructing the currents on what to do. . . . I'm trying to regain a sense of anonymity. I didn't like it when a certain former president—and it wasn't 41 [George H. W. Bush] or 42 [Bill Clinton]—made my life miserable." Bush was referring to Jimmy Carter, who was a frequent, outspoken critic of Bush and his administration while the forty-third president was in office.

Several weeks later, Bush threw out the first pitch at a Texas Rangers game (he once owned the team). At the game, Bush gave a brief speech, thanking the people of Dallas for making him and Laura feel welcome; the crowd responded with a standing ovation.

Fort Hood and Haiti

In November 2009 Army Major Nidal Malik Hasan allegedly fired on soldiers and civilians at the Foot Hood army base in Fort Hood, Texas, killing thirteen and wounding thirty-eight. The Bushes made a private, unannounced visit to the wounded and their families. Afterward, the Bushes explained that they had kept their trip to Fort Hood secret because they did not want a personal condolence call disrupted by the media.

In January 2010 a catastrophic earthquake struck Haiti, killing more than 300,000, injuring another 300,000, and leaving more than 1 million people homeless. Food, water, and medicine were all in short supply, and the country's infrastructure was in ruins. As President Obama mobilized the American military and relief organizations to bring aid to the devastated nation, he asked former presidents Clinton and Bush 43 to jointly chair the Haiti Fund, an organization dedicated to assisting the relief effort by raising funds from corporations, charitable foundations, and individuals. To discuss the Haiti Fund's mission, the three presidents met at the White House—it was the first time Bush had returned since he left the president's residence on Inauguration Day 2009. In a televised news conference, Bush addressed Americans who wanted to send food, or tents, or water to the Haiti Fund. "Just send your cash," he said.

In addition to purchasing necessities for the Haitian people, Bush and Clinton's organization also funded long-term recovery plans that built new housing, created jobs, established vocational schools, and opened new economic opportunities for the Haitian people. As of May 2011, the Clinton Bush Haiti Fund had collected $53.8 million to rebuild the lives of the Haitian people. The fund will continue to collect donations and channel funds to Haiti until 2013.

Decision Points

Almost immediately after leaving the White House, Bush began writing a book, with the assistance of Christopher Michel, who had served as deputy director of speechwriting to the president during Bush's second term. Each of the book's fourteen chapters focuses on a key moment in Bush's personal or political life, from his decision to stop drinking and become a committed Christian to his decision to invade Iraq. The consensus among book critics was that *Decision Points* is a lifeless book. Jonathan Yardley, reviewing the book for the *Washington Post*, described it as "competent, readable and flat." But he added that the memoirs of all the twentieth-century presidents—with the exception of Harry Truman—have been uniformly dull. Nonetheless, the book became a best seller—selling nearly 2 million copies in two months. By contrast, it took six years before Bill Clinton's memoir sold 2 million copies.

Osama bin Laden

The evening of May 1, 2011, Bush, his wife, Laura, and two friends were dining at their favorite French restaurant in Dallas when the former president was informed that he had a phone call. Bush left the table to take the call in private. It was President Obama, phoning with the news that Osama bin Laden, the mastermind of the attacks of September 11, 2001, and many other acts of terrorism, had been killed by U.S. Navy SEALs.

Obama explained the mission, as well as the planning that led up to it, and his decision to order the raid that killed bin Laden. Bush told Obama, "Good call."

Laura Bush

Born November 4, 1946, Midland, Texas

"[George and I] wanted to teach our children what our parents taught us—that reading is entertaining and important and fun"
—Laura Bush

When Laura Bush came onstage to make the first major speech of the 2000 Republican National Convention, she was greeted with the wild cheering typical of such party gatherings. After pausing for a moment, she asked for quiet and then she said, "Okay, that's enough." She probably felt like an elementary school teacher ready to begin class, which was only natural: She had been a public school teacher and a librarian for a decade.

Laura and her husband have complementary personalities and are well-balanced opposites. George W. Bush is more comfortable before large crowds, and is more talkative and energetic. His wife, Laura, is reserved and quietly persuasive. While he tackles big issues as a politician, she concentrates on programs related to education, libraries, and literacy. Before her husband was elected, she told the *New York Times* that if she became first lady, she would focus on "areas I'm already interested in. Literacy, libraries and early childhood." In that respect, she is following in the footsteps of another first lady, her mother-in-law, Barbara Bush.

Influenced by a Teacher

Born Laura Welch in Midland, Texas, on November 4, 1946, she was an only child. Her father owned a home-building business, and her mother worked for him as a bookkeeper. Laura had a happy, quiet childhood. Her second-grade elementary teacher made such a great impression on her that Laura decided early in her life that she wanted to be a teacher when she grew up.

When she was in seventh grade, Laura Welch and George W. Bush attended the same junior high school in Midland, but they never met. She wore glasses and was studious; he was mostly sarcastic (according to his mother) and dreamed of being a baseball star.

Laura's happy youth was marred by a tragedy during her teen years. She was involved at the age of seventeen in an automobile accident which killed a friend of hers.

Reading Teacher

Laura studied at Southern Methodist University, where she earned her education degree in 1968. She taught reading in public schools in Dallas and then in Houston, where she had another near-encounter with George W. Bush. They lived in the same apartment complex, but she was in a quieter part of it; Laura concentrated on her teaching job, and spent her evenings reading books. Bush preferred a more active lifestyle that he has called his "young and irresponsible" era. He flew planes with the Texas Air National Guard, drove a sports car, and enjoyed an endless round of parties.

Laura moved to Austin, Texas, where she studied and earned a master's degree in library science from the University of Texas. After she graduated in 1973, she became a librarian for the local public school system. On a visit back to Midland, during the summer of 1977, she was invited to an outdoor barbecue party where mutual friends introduced her to George W. Bush, who owned an oil business at the time. He began a whirlwind romance, including a first date for a round of miniature golf. They were married just three months later, in November 1977.

Bush's father, George H. W. Bush, who had served as a U.S. representative from Texas and in several positions in the administrations of presidents Richard Nixon and Gerald Ford, was already planning to run in the 1980 presidential election, and at the time of their engagement, Laura agreed to marry George W. after he promised that she would never have to make a political speech.

The following year, though, she did make a speech during her husband's unsuccessful bid for a seat in the U.S. Congress. After having spent their first year of marriage campaigning, they settled in Midland, where George concentrated on his oil business. The couple's twin daughters were born in 1981 after illness complicated

Right: On her travels with the president, Laura Bush often read stories to children in foreign countries, as she did in Tokyo.

Laura's pregnancy. They were born five weeks premature, but they gradually grew healthy. They were named Jenna and Barbara after their grandmothers.

Laura lived quietly as a homemaker while Bush built his oil business in Midland. During that period in the mid-1980s, she convinced her husband that his occasional social drinking had become alarmingly regular, and he gave up alcohol.

Promotes Literacy and Libraries

The Bush family moved to Washington in 1987, as George W. Bush worked on his father's presidential campaign. The elder Bush had served since 1981 as vice president to Ronald Reagan, who had defeated him, among others, for the Republican nomination for president in 1980. After her father-in-law was elected president in 1988, Laura and her family went back to Texas, where her husband became the managing general partner of the Texas Rangers baseball team. His association with the Rangers, which ended in 1994, brought him to larger public attention in Texas. The team was beginning to enjoy success on the field, and an impressive new stadium, The Ballpark in Arlington, was built.

After her father-in-law's difficult and unsuccessful reelection bid in 1992, Laura wasn't thrilled when her husband told her he wanted to run for governor of Texas against the popular incumbent Ann Richards. "I just wanted George to think about it, make sure it was really what he wanted," she later told the *New York Times*. Bush won the election and quickly gained national attention as a prominent governor. He was easily reelected in 1998, which helped him build a base for his successful run for the presidency two years later.

Laura Bush was active as first lady of Texas. She organized a luncheon at the University of Texas for talks by seven prominent Texas writers. The success of the event encouraged her to establish the Texas Book Festival, an annual celebration of books and authors that raises funds

for public libraries in the state. In 1998, she spearheaded the Early Childhood Development Initiative, a program that prepares children to learn to read before they enter school. She was involved with women's health issues through the National Governor's Association and worked on several programs to bring attention to the arts, and she encouraged artworks by Texans to be exhibited regularly at the state capitol.

Following George W. Bush's election as president in 2000, literacy and education remained important pursuits for his wife as she took on her role as the nation's first lady.

In 2001, Laura launched the now annual National Book Fair at the Library of Congress; she was also involved with such projects as Helping America's Youth, Teach for America, the New Teacher Project, and Troops to Teachers, in addition to serving as honorary ambassador for the UNESCO's Literacy Decade. Laura traveled the world to promote education, particularly as it relates to the advancement of women, visiting war-torn Afghanistan three times as well as cities and towns in Asia and Africa. Here at home, immediately following Hurricane Katrina, she established the Laura Bush Foundation for America's Libraries Gulf Coast Library Recovery Initiative Grant to benefit schools whose libraries had been decimated by the storm.

Bush's Presidential Nomination Acceptance Speech

Delivered on August 3, 2000

Texas governor George W. Bush was well organized and well financed early in his bid for the Republican nomination for president. He quickly emerged as the frontrunner among a large field of candidates and steadily gained strength while the other candidates gradually dropped from the race. He participated in some debates and gave many speeches, but he was still not widely known to the nation when delegates convened at the Republican National Convention in Philadelphia in August 2000 to officially nominate the party's presidential candidate. Bush's acceptance speech for the nomination, then, was considered extremely important. The speech outlined the themes he planned to follow if he was elected president.

Excerpt from Bush's Presidential Nomination Acceptance Speech

This is a remarkable moment in the life of our nation. Never has the promise of prosperity been so vivid. But times of plenty, like times of crisis, are tests of American character.

Prosperity can be a tool in our hands—used to build and better our country. Or it can be a drug in our system—dulling our sense of urgency, of empathy, of duty. Our opportunities are too great, our lives too short, to waste this moment.

So tonight we vow to our nation. . . . We will seize this moment of American promise. We will use these good times for great goals. We will confront the hard issues—threats to our national security, threats to our health and retirement security—before the challenges of our time become crises for our children. And we will extend the promise of prosperity to every forgotten corner of this country.

To every man and woman, a chance to succeed. To every child, a chance to learn. To every family, a chance to live with dignity and hope.

[. . .]

[T]his is a time for new beginnings. The rising generations of this country have our own appointment with greatness. It does not rise or fall with the stock market. It cannot be bought with our wealth. Greatness is found when American character and American courage overcome American challenges.

When Lewis Morris of New York was about to sign the Declaration of Independence, his brother advised against it, warning he would lose all his property. Morris, a plain-spoken Founder, responded . . . "Damn the consequences, give me the pen." That is the eloquence of American action.

We heard it during World War II, when General [Dwight D.] Eisenhower told paratroopers on D-Day morning not to worry—and one replied, "We're not worried, General. . . . It's Hitler's turn to worry now."

We heard it in the civil rights movement, when brave men and women did not say, "We shall cope," or "We shall see." They said, "We shall overcome."

An American president must call upon that character.

Tonight, in this hall, we resolve to be, not the party of repose, but the party of reform. We will write, not footnotes, but chapters in the American story. We will add the work of our hands to the inheritance of our fathers and mothers—and leave this nation greater than we found it. We know the tests of leadership. The issues are joined.

We will strengthen Social Security and Medicare for the greatest generation, and for generations to come. Medicare does more than meet the needs of our elderly, it reflects the values of our society. We will set it on firm financial ground, and make prescription drugs available and affordable for every senior who needs them.

Social Security has been called the "third rail of American politics"—the one you're not supposed to touch because it shocks you. But, if you don't touch it, you can't fix it. And I intend to fix it. To seniors in this country . . . You earned your benefits, you made your plans, and President George W. Bush will keep the promise of Social Security . . . no changes, no reductions, no way.

Our opponents will say otherwise. This is their last, parting ploy, and don't believe a word of it. Now is the time for Republicans and Democrats to end the politics of fear and save Social Security, together.

For younger workers, we will give you the option—your choice—to put a part of your payroll taxes into sound, responsible investments. This will mean a higher return on your money, and, over 30 or 40 years, a nest egg to help your retirement, or pass along to your children. When this money is in your name, in your account, it's not just a program, it's your property.

Now is the time to give American workers security and independence that no politician can ever take away.

On education . . . too many American children are segregated into schools without standards, shuffled from grade to grade because of their age, regardless of their knowledge. This is discrimination, pure and simple—the soft bigotry of low expectations. And our nation should treat it like other forms of discrimination. . . .

We should end it.

One size does not fit all when it comes to educating our children, so local people should control local schools. And those who spend your tax dollars must be held accountable. When a school district receives federal funds to teach poor children, we expect them to learn. And if they don't, parents should get the money to make a different choice.

Now is the time to make Head Start an early learning program, teach all our children to read, and renew the promise of America's public schools.

Another test of leadership is tax relief. The last time taxes were this high as a percentage of our economy, there was a good reason. . . . We were fighting World War II. Today, our high taxes fund a surplus. Some say that growing federal surplus means Washington has more money to spend. But they've got it backwards. The surplus is not the government's money. The surplus is the people's money.

I will use this moment of opportunity to bring common sense and fairness to the tax code. And I will act on principle. On principle . . . every family, every farmer and small businessperson, should be free to pass on their life's work to those they love. So we will abolish the death tax.

On principle . . . no one in America should have to pay more than a third of their income to the federal government. So we will reduce tax rates for everyone, in every bracket.

On principle . . . those in the greatest need should receive the greatest help. So we will lower the bottom rate from 15 percent to 10 percent and double the child tax credit.

Now is the time to reform the tax code and share some of the surplus with the people who pay the bills.

The world needs America's strength and leadership, and America's armed forces need better equipment, better training, and better pay. We will give our military the means to keep the peace, and we will give it one thing more . . . a commander-in-chief who respects our men and women in uniform, and a commander-in-chief who earns their respect.

A generation shaped by Vietnam must remember the lessons of Vietnam. When America uses force in the world, the cause must be just, the goal must be clear, and the victory must be overwhelming.

I will work to reduce nuclear weapons and nuclear tension in the world—to turn these years of affluence into decades of peace. And, at the earliest possible date, my administration will deploy missile defenses to guard against attack and blackmail. . . .

In Midland, Texas, where I grew up, the town motto was "the sky is the limit" . . . and we believed it. There was a restless energy, a basic conviction that, with hard work, anybody could succeed, and everybody deserved a chance. Our sense of community was just as strong as that sense of promise. Neighbors helped each other. There were dry wells and sandstorms to keep you humble, and lifelong friends to take your side, and churches to remind us that every soul is equal in value and equal in need. This background leaves more than an accent, it leaves an outlook.

Optimistic. Impatient with pretense. Confident that people can chart their own course. That background may lack the polish of Washington. Then again, I don't have a lot of things that come with Washington.

I don't have enemies to fight. And I have no stake in the bitter arguments of the last few years. I want to change the tone of Washington to one of civility and respect.

The largest lesson I learned in Midland still guides me as governor. . . . Everyone, from immigrant to entrepreneur, has an equal claim on this country's promise.

So we improved our schools, dramatically, for children of every accent, of every background. We moved people from welfare to work. We strengthened our juvenile justice laws. Our budgets have been balanced, with surpluses, and we cut taxes not only once, but twice.

We accomplished a lot. I don't deserve all the credit, and don't attempt to take it. I worked with Republicans and Democrats to get things done. . . .

[W]hen problems aren't confronted, it builds a wall within our nation. On one side are wealth and technology, education and ambition. On the other side of the wall are poverty and prison, addiction and despair. And, my fellow Americans, we must tear down that wall.

Big government is not the answer. But the alternative to bureaucracy is not indifference. It is to put conservative values and conservative ideas into the thick of the fight for justice and opportunity.

This is what I mean by compassionate conservatism. And on this ground we will govern our nation.

What Happened Next

Bush's speech was well received: He communicated his ideas forcefully, and his support in polls rose dramatically after the convention. His lead in the polls over challenger Al Gore was reduced following Gore's acceptance speech for the Democratic nomination for president three weeks later. The race remained close following three debates by the candidates and on to election day. It was so close in fact, that the election was not over after the votes were in. Bush lost the popular vote to Gore, but he won in the Electoral College, 271 to 266. The twenty-five electoral votes from the state of Florida proved decisive. After having won the original count as well as a recount, Bush had to endure several court challenges before he was finally awarded Florida's electoral votes and the presidency.

Barack Obama

"I know that my satisfaction is not to be found in the glare of television cameras or the applause of the crowd. Instead, it seems to come more often now from knowing that in some demonstrable way I've been able to help people live their lives with some measure of dignity."

—*Barack Obama*, **The Audacity of Hope**

Forty-fourth president of the United States, 2009–2017

Full name: Barack Hussein Obama

Born: August 4, 1961, Honolulu, Hawaii

Parents: Barack Obama and Stanley Ann Dunham Obama Soetoro

Spouse: Michelle LaVaughn Robinson Obama (1964–; m. 1992)

Children: Malia Ann (1998–) and Natasha "Sasha" (2001–)

Religion: Congregationalist (Protestant)

Education: Occidental College, Los Angeles (1979–81);
   Columbia University, New York (B.A., 1983);
   Harvard Law School (J.D. magna cum laude, 1991)

Occupations: Consultant, community organizer, civil rights lawyer

Government positions: State senator, U.S. senator from Illinois

Political party: Democrat

Dates as president: January 20, 2009–January 20, 2017

Age upon taking office: 47

As the 2008 Democratic presidential candidate, Barack Obama inspired in the American people a wave of hope and a new belief in change, evoking many comparisons to the youth and idealism of John F. Kennedy. The country's first African-American president, Obama was born on the very cusp of change: during JFK's administration, on August 4, 1961, in Hawaii, which had joined the country as its fiftieth state less than two years earlier. His parents—a white mother from Kansas and a black father from Kenya—had daringly married in 1960, when "miscegenation" was a felony in more than half the country. Obama's pursuit of the Democratic nomination was another first, pitting him against former first lady Hillary Clinton. For many Americans, this historic race—and its nail-biting outcome, with Clinton snagging a slim majority of the popular vote but Obama prevailing on delegate count—felt like a dream. Just a few years earlier, it would have been difficult to imagine either an African American or a woman in the Oval Office within our lifetime. Today, that dream is a reality.

Exotic Beginnings

Barack Obama's mother, Stanley Ann Dunham (known by her middle name), was born in Kansas and reared in Texas by parents Stanley and Madelyn Dunham. Obama's American grandparents had eloped in the face of opposition from their parents, who found Stanley a bit wild for their straitlaced Methodist daughter Madelyn. Growing disenchanted with the racial discrimination they encountered on the mainland, the Dunhams moved to Hawaii in 1959, when Ann was a teenager.

At nineteen, Ann tested her own parents' values by bringing home to dinner Barack Obama, of the Kenyan Luo tribe, who had won scholarships first to attend college in Nairobi and then to study economics at the University of Hawaii, as its first African student. Ann had met him in Russian-language class. They fell in love and her parents, if not altogether happy about the match, gave their consent. The couple was married in a civil ceremony and produced a son, also named Barack—which means "blessed"—the following year. As a child, he was known as Barry.

Timeline

1961: Born in Hawaii
1983: Graduates from Columbia University
1991: Graduates from Harvard Law School
1997–2004: Serves as Illinois state senator
2000: Loses his challenge to unseat Representative Bobby Rush
2004–2008: Serves as U.S. senator from Illinois
2008: Elected forty-fourth president of the United States

Obama Sr. graduated from the University of Hawaii in just three years and had his choice of two scholarships to pursue his master's degree: to the New School, in New York City, or to Harvard University. According to Obama's mother, the New School would have been willing to support the family of three, but Obama Sr. decided on Harvard, whose scholarship covered only his tuition. He couldn't afford to take his new family with him, so Ann and their son remained with her parents in Hawaii. The couple divorced when Obama was two; post-Harvard, Obama Sr. returned to Kenya.

Left: Kenyan-born Barack Obama Sr., father of President Obama.

In Hawaii, Barack Jr. learned to surf and swim, pleasures he continues to enjoy, and blended right in with the ethnic smorgasbord of his neighbors. His grandfather would amuse himself by telling unsuspecting tourists that the boy was the great-grandson of Hawaii's first king, Kamehameha. When he was six, Ann married again, this time to an Indonesian student, Lolo Soetoro. The family moved to Indonesia, near Jakarta, where Obama went to school with native Indonesians and learned their language; Ann also enrolled him in English-language correspondence courses to try to keep his education up to American grade levels. Ann worked there as a cultural anthropologist. A half sister, Maya Kassandra, was born in 1970.

Lolo was a good stepfather, introducing Barack to a variety of adventures and experiences well beyond the usual upbringing of a homegrown American boy, from eating snake meat and grasshoppers to flying fighting kites

Below: Nine-year-old Barack (right) with his mother, Ann Dunham; his Indonesian stepfather, Lolo Soetoro; and his infant half sister, Maya Soetoro, in Jakarta, Indonesia.

and boxing. But, during his Indonesian years, Barack was largely unaware of the political underpinnings of Lolo's work as a geologist for his country's army during the corrupt regime of the nation's first president, Sukarno. To Ann, Lolo had become private and mysterious ever since his forced return to his country following Sukarno's coup; he wouldn't answer his wife's questions about rumored massacres and shakedowns, and Ann began to fear for her child's welfare. Also troubling her was the severe poverty of those who lived just outside the gated homes of the Indonesian wealthy. Her own values finally won out. In 1971, she and Lolo split up and mother and children moved back to her parents' home in Hawaii.

That year, Barack Obama Sr. visited Hawaii from Kenya for a month, offering to take Ann back to Kenya with him (she refused). Barack Jr. never saw his father again. In 1988, he traveled to Kenya to meet his paternal family, but his father had died six years earlier in a car accident. He did, however, meet his paternal grandmother, Sarah Hussein Obama, and would revisit Kenya several times after that.

In Hawaii, Obama and his sister attended the Punahou School, a private college preparatory school that provides continuous education from kindergarten through the twelfth grade. He entered as a fifth-grader and graduated in 1979. During that period, Ann returned to Indonesia to resume her work as an anthropologist, leaving her parents to raise her two children.

Above: Barack Obama and his father, who left the family to study at Harvard when his son was just two, returning only once. Obama wrote poignantly about this visit in his memoir, remembering the basketball his father gave him, the African records they danced to, and the Dave Brubeck concert they attended. Barry, then ten, never saw his father again.

Above: Barack Obama, in 1979, during his high school graduation in Hawaii with his maternal grandparents, Stanley and Madelyn Dunham.

Identity and Ideals

It was not until he was in high school, where his fellow students were predominantly white, that Obama began to wonder just where he fit in. Was he biracial? Was he black? Because of his mixed-race parentage and early upbringing in Indonesia, he was not accepted by his African-American peers, and he quit the tennis team after a coach uttered a racial slur against him. He loved playing basketball (although his coach often benched him), and experimented with pot, alcohol, and cocaine along with his fellow students.

It was during these high school years that Obama began to read such black authors as W. E. B. DuBois and Langston Hughes, and found himself impressed by the self-determinism of Malcolm X. He began to wear his hair in an Afro. In college, he dropped the name Barry in favor of his given name.

By the time he graduated from high school, Obama had had enough of feeling isolated from the mainstream culture of the United States mainland. He won a scholarship to attend the small, L.A. suburban liberal arts institution Occidental College in 1979. Though most of his fellow students came from middle- to upper-class backgrounds, he sought out campus activists and became uncomfortable with the university's investments in then apartheid South Africa. He began to participate in student protests against

Youthful-looking Barack Obama is not America's youngest president—Teddy Roosevelt had that honor, sworn in at age 42 after the assassination of William McKinley. At 43, John F. Kennedy was the country's youngest elected president. Bill Clinton and Ulysses S. Grant were both sworn in at age 46. Had John McCain won the 2008 election, he would have been the oldest elected president, at 72.

that policy, and he realized his own power as a public speaker during campus rallies.

Taking advantage of a reciprocal program with New York's Columbia University, Obama graduated from there in 1983 with a bachelor's degree in political science and marked interests in activism and reading, reading, reading.

In 1984, Obama hit the streets, taking a job as a community organizer at the Harlem campus of City College of the City University of New York. Then president Reagan had proposed cutting student aid, and the young graduate worked with student leaders of various ethnic groups, "almost all of them the first in their families to attend college," to collect signatures on petitions and hand-deliver them to the congressional representatives from New York down in Washington, D.C.

Obama joined the global consulting firm Business International Corporation in New York City as an editor and research assistant. But then, in 1985, idealism again reared its head. He moved to Chicago and—for just $13,000 a year—became a community organizer for the Developing Communities Project, which focused its efforts on improving conditions for the city's inner-city poor. Living on the South Side, among those he was committed to helping, placed him in the middle of the densest black community in the entire country. During his three years with the organization, he managed to increase its budget by more than 500 percent and its staff from just one to more than a dozen workers. It was also during this time that he became acquainted with the charismatic preacher Jeremiah A. Wright Jr. of the Trinity United Church of Christ, who became something of a mentor for the earnest young man. It was from a sermon of Wright's that Obama would adopt as his own the term "the audacity of hope."

Chicago's first black mayor, Harold Washington, had been elected in 1984 and spent his first two years in office battling white members of the city council to

Above: Barack Obama and his bride, Michelle Robinson, on their wedding day, October 18, 1992, in Chicago.

push through his agenda to redistrict council wards and otherwise give greater political and social opportunities to minorities; it would take a special election two years later to finally elect members who shared his views. But just one year after that, in November 1987, Washington died suddenly of a heart attack. Obama was struck by how small his successes as a neighborhood organizer had been compared with Washington's victories citywide. At age twenty-seven, he decided to go back to school and carve out a new path for himself.

Nairobi and Cambridge

Nineteen eighty-eight was a banner year for Barack Obama. First, he flew to Africa to meet his father's extended family in Kenya, where he was struck by the citizens' generally poor standard of living and lack of governmental services. As he wrote in *Dreams from My Father*, "Almost all the family's younger members were unemployed, including the two or three who had managed, against stiff competition, to graduate from one of Kenya's universities. If [the working relatives] ever fell ill, if their companies ever closed or laid them off, there was no government safety net. There was only family, next of kin; people burdened by similar hardship." The identity problems he had tried so hard to resolve in Chicago's inner city bubbled up once more within him—what use is personal success if one's fellow man is still struggling? "Without power for the group, a group larger, even, than an extended family, our success always threatened to leave others behind. And perhaps it was that fact that left me so unsettled—the fact that even here, in Africa, the same maddening patterns still held sway."

When Obama returned to the United States in 1988, it was to enter Harvard Law School to study civil rights law, thinking that perhaps he might someday follow in Washington's footsteps as mayor. He excelled in his studies, graduating magna cum laude, and became the first African American to serve as president of the school's prestigious *Harvard Law Review*. His election gave him an early taste of criticisms he would encounter later in government: that he did not use his position to appoint other African Americans or minorities. Obama took a broader view, appointing even several conservatives to the *Law Review*'s masthead.

It was just after his first year at Harvard that Obama met his future wife, Harvard graduate Michelle Robinson, while working as a summer intern in a Chicago law office, Sidley & Austin (now Sidley Austin Brown & Wood), where she was already a lawyer. At first, she balked at becoming involved with him, believing his charisma to be only surface deep. She also felt self-conscious about their being the only two people of color at their law firm. They settled into a long-distance, gradual relationship once he returned to Harvard; he received his law degree in 1991 and they married the following year, moving into a walk-up condominium in Chicago's Hyde Park.

Second Wind in the Windy City

An important project of Obama's post-Harvard Chicago years was his participation in Project Vote for the election year of 1992, during which he and fellow organizers oversaw a team of seven hundred volunteers who helped register some 150,000 previously unregistered voters throughout the state of Illinois. For this work, he was lauded as one of *Crain's Business Chicago*'s forty young movers of 1993. After the November election—which culminated in the victory of Illinois's first black senator (and, to date, its only female African-American senator) Carol Moseley Braun—he accepted a position at the law firm of Miner, Barnhill & Galland, which took on the civil rights cases he sought. Obama was not a trial lawyer, but he worked behind the scenes, writing briefs and working up contracts.

His professional involvement with a case that succeeded in blocking the gerrymandering of a city ward inspired Obama to want to "join 'em rather than beat 'em"—to become a part of the local government and effect changes from within. An opportunity came his way in 1995, when African-American state senator Alice J. Palmer changed gears to run for U.S. Congress, creating an opening in the thirteenth district, Chicago's South Side. As the story

Above: This undated photo shows Barack Obama teaching at the University of Chicago Law School.

goes, she was eager for Obama to succeed her, even if she lost her bid for Congress. Indeed, she lost that election, to Jesse Jackson Jr. . . . and filed to run against Obama in the March 2006 primary for her old seat! Obama used his knowledge of voter politics to defeat her, exposing the fact that she had filed more signatures supporting her bid than she could possibly have collected legally. Other would-be candidates' petitions were also called into question. Palmer withdrew and Obama won the primary unopposed.

Being a Democrat within a largely Republican state senate had its frustrations for Obama, but at least he was representing a Democratic district. He served as co chairman of the state's bipartisan Joint Committee on Administrative Rules, and worked to push through tax credits for the poor, health-care reforms, and childcare subsidies. He was reelected state senator in 1998 and 2002, though, in 2000, he was roundly defeated in his attempt to depose black incumbent Illinois congressman Bobby L. Rush. He began to think about running for the Senate and achieved the backing of a number of influential Democrats. An unexpected opponent was Carol Moseley Braun, who had lost the 1998 senatorial election to Peter Fitzgerald but was thinking of running again. However, she pulled out to run for president in

the 2000 Democratic primaries, leaving him to regroup and gain supporters. In 2002, he delivered a spectacular speech responding to critics of his opposition to the American invasion of Iraq. In 2003, he was made head of the Health and Human Services Committee and went on to sponsor more than seven hundred bills in Chicago, about two-thirds of which were signed into law by Chicago's new Democratic governor, Rod Blagojevich. In 2003, he filed petitions to be allowed on the Democratic primary ballot for U.S. senator and publicly announced his campaign; he won the primary with 52 percent of the vote. For the Senate seat, he was opposed initially by Jack Ryan, until Ryan withdrew in the midst of a sex scandal and was replaced by African-American Republican Alan Keyes, who taunted that even "Jesus would not vote for Barack Obama."

Jesus' political affiliations notwithstanding, on January 4, 2005, Obama was sworn in as a member of the 109th Congress, America's third African-American senator since Reconstruction, having been elected with 70 percent of the vote.

A Progressive Senator

Obama steadfastly pursued the same kinds of health and housing issues that had concerned him within Illinois's state government, including his championing the Bernardin amendment, which would have constitutionally guaranteed health insurance to all his constituents; unfortunately, that measure fell through. He was successful, however, in his co-sponsorship of a bill that would give donors a tax credit if their funds were used to create or repair affordable housing. He worked in many areas of reform, from limiting candidates' personal use of campaign funds to demanding that local governments tape closed-door meetings, to bringing welfare reform to his state. He sought to end racial profiling and worked on death penalty reform. He cosponsored a reintroduction of the Equal Rights Amendment and advocated the Equal Pay Act, and has vowed to reform the Child and Dependent Care Tax Credit to give a credit of up to 50 percent to low-income families who need child care to be able to go to work. Although he is pro–*Roe v. Wade*, he has taken numerous

Above: Obama (left) files a petition with the State Board of Elections to get on the March primary ballot as the Democratic candidate for the U.S. Senate on Monday, December 8, 2003, in Springfield, Illinois.

Left: Then Senate candidate Obama speaks to delegates during the Democratic National Convention in Boston on July 27, 2004. Some have called it, "The Speech," a seventeen-minute star-making turn as keynote speaker that may have led to his eventual candidacy for president.

Obama has always been mindful of putting a stop to all forms of discrimination. In 2006, he voted no on a constitutional ban on same-sex marriage. On September 6, 2007, at a primary debate at Dartmouth College, the senator was asked whether he was comfortable with gay issues' inclusion in elementary school materials. He responded, "My nine-year-old and my six-year-old are already aware that there are same-sex couples. . . . one of the things I want to communicate to my children is not to be afraid of people who are different, and because there have been times in our history where I was considered different. And one of the things I think the next president has to do is to stop fanning people's fears."

Obama spoke out in 2002 against the United States' involvement in Iraq and later against the troop surge led by General David Petraeus. He had voted to fund the war but ultimately came out against providing a blank check toward the effort. Rather than continuing to pour American military power into Iraq, he advocated troop withdrawal and redeployment elsewhere, particularly to Afghanistan, where bin Laden was rumored to be rebuilding the Taliban. In 2007, he voted yes on a measure, stands to reduce the need for abortions: in 2005, he voted yes on using $100 million to reduce teen pregnancy by education and contraceptives and, the following year, sponsored a bill that would provide contraceptives for low-income women.

As a senator, Barack Obama served as chairman of the Senate's Subcommittee on European Affairs and on its committees for Foreign Relations, Environment, and Public Works; Veterans Affairs; and Homeland Security and Governmental Affairs, among others.

In 2004, an election year fraught with divisiveness between "red" and "blue" states, Obama was a keynote speaker at the Democratic National Convention, in support of candidate John Kerry. He has almost always voted along party lines, but on that evening, he underscored his longstanding commitment to reach across the aisle: "There is not a liberal America and a conservative America; there's the United States of America."

Above: Barack Obama poses with the Reverend Jeremiah Wright of Chicago's Trinity United Church of Christ on March 10, 2005. The senator's affiliation with the outspoken Wright provoked concerns about his character during the fierce 2008 presidential campaign, leading Obama to make a landmark speech about race in America that helped him secure the presidency.

The Audacity of Hope

Barack Obama's July 27, 2004, keynote address to the Democratic National Convention, in support of presidential candidate John Kerry, outlined the ideals brought by Obama to his own candidacy four years later. In it, he quoted from the Declaration of Independence, in his own declaration of how the United States is unique for its "inalienable rights, that among these are life, liberty, and the pursuit of happiness." He continued:

That is the true genius of America—a faith in simple dreams, an insistence on small miracles. That we can tuck in our children at night and know that they are fed and clothed and safe from harm. That we can say what we think, write what we think, without hearing a sudden knock on the door. That we can have an idea and start our own business without paying a bribe. That we can participate in the political process without a fear of retribution, and that our votes will be counted—at least, most of the time. . . .

I'm not talking about blind optimism here—the almost willful ignorance that thinks unemployment will go away if we just don't think about it, or the health care crisis will solve itself if we just ignore it. I'm talking about something more substantial. It's the hope of slaves sitting around a fire singing freedom songs. The hope of immigrants setting out for distant shores. The hope of a young naval lieutenant bravely patrolling the Mekong Delta. The hope of a millworker's son who dares to defy the odds. The hope of a skinny kid with a funny name who believes that America has a place for him, too.

Hope in the face of difficulty. Hope in the face of uncertainty.

The audacity of hope! In the end, that is God's greatest gift to us, the bedrock of this nation. A belief in things not seen. A belief that there are better days ahead.

which President Bush ultimately vetoed, that would have provided a timetable for the withdrawal of troops and improved health care for troops and veterans. After he learned about the poor conditions at Walter Reed Army Medical Center, Obama introduced the Dignity for Wounded Warriors Act. He proposed that the Iraqi war budget be made part of the U.S. defense budget, rather than continue to be treated as a separate emergency fund that, during the war, failed to adequately outfit the troops with protective gear and equipment. This measure passed in the Senate 98–0. In 2007, he called it a "disgrace" that President Bush refused to meet with foreign leaders of such nations as North Korea or Cuba. In numerous speeches, he vowed to refocus America's effort on ridding Afghanistan of the Taliban and capturing bin Laden, as well as to pursue what he deemed "high-value terrorists" in Pakistan if its government would not. In 2007, he told *New York Times* reporters that he would "engage in aggressive personal diplomacy" with Iran to try to defuse its perceived nuclear aggressiveness and cooperation with terrorists. Opponents labeled these positions liberal, naive, and even dangerous to America's security.

On the homefront, in early 2008, Obama proposed the creation of an expanded national service program to give Americans civilian educational and employment alternatives to joining the military. He envisioned that the program could include not only an enlarged Peace Corps and AmeriCorps, but also a Classroom Corps, a Health Corps, a Clean Energy Corps, a Veterans Corps, and a Homeland Security Corps; and suggested giving each participant in such a program $4,000 to put toward college.

Making History

The 2008 Democratic primary was one for the record books, when the first woman of a major party and the first African American of a major party ran neck-to-neck toward the presidential nomination. White males Joe Biden, John Edwards, Chris Dodd, Mike Gravel, Dennis Kucinich, and Hispanic-American Bill Richardson would drop out of the race. Senator Hillary Rodham Clinton (D–New York) garnered an estimated 18,046,007 popular votes to Obama's 17,869,542. Obama won the nomination by virtue of his 2,201 (he'd needed 2,118) pledges by delegates and superdelegates versus Clinton's 1,896 (41.8 percent to 39.4 percent)—a loss for her but a victory nonetheless for women. At the Democratic National Convention (DNC), Michelle Obama and other speakers would repeatedly refer to this former count as "18 million cracks in the glass ceiling."

The official count was skewed by a mix-up over whether several caucuses could be counted. The Democratic National Committee, in 2006, permitted only Iowa, New Hampshire, and South Carolina to hold their primaries earlier than February 5, 2008. However, Florida jumped the gun, scheduling its primary for January 28. When Michigan decided to go ahead with a primary on January 15, Obama, as well as several other male candidates, withdrew their names from the state's ballot but Clinton did not. None of the candidates campaigned in Florida or Michigan. Clinton won a majority of delegate pledges in both maverick states but the DNC refused to count them or to seat those delegates at the August convention.

Although the DNC would declare Obama the victor, competition between the two contenders would continue from the primary right up until the convention, fired up yet again after Obama announced that he'd selected Vermont senator Joe Biden as his vice-presidential running mate without serious consideration of Clinton. Nevertheless, Clinton gave a rousing speech on the second day of the convention, in which she strongly urged her supporters to follow her lead and support Obama actively and wholeheartedly, and to keep their minds on the bigger picture ("I want you to ask yourselves: Were you in this campaign just for me?").

Above: Senator Hillary Rodham Clinton speaks with Senator Barack Obama on July 19, 2006, during the annual convention of the National Association for the Advancement of Colored People in Washington, D.C.—prior to their heated race for the Democratic presidential nomination.

The Americanization of Barry

The emphasis of the 2008 Democratic National Convention was on family and the American Dream. Although Barack Obama was not whitewashed in any racial sense—indeed, there were numerous references to his advancing the ideals of black notables from Harriet Tubman to Martin Luther King Jr.—nearly all mention of his foreign roots was prominently absent from the four-night event. His half sister Maya spoke on the opening night (she attended the convention with her Chinese-Canadian husband Konrad Ng, visibly seated if rarely identified, just behind Michelle Obama and the children on August 28), but their mother's marriage to Lolo Soetoro went undiscussed—Barack Obama was repeatedly described as being the product of a "single mother" who had had a "brief union" with his Kenyan father—wording that also carefully sidestepped the fact that, by American law, Obama senior had been a bigamist at the time of Barack's birth.

The candidate's maternal uncle, Charles T. Payne, who had served with Patton during World War II, was saluted from the audience by Senator John Kerry in the audience on the third night of the convention; in the video presentation leading up to Obama's acceptance speech, the delegates and world audiences alike saw photographs of the candidate's mother and American grandparents. Nowhere in evidence during the convention—in discussion, in image, in the flesh—were Obama's many African blood relatives—his half siblings, grandmother, aunts, and uncles—about whom he had written so warmly and at length in Dreams from My Father.

The ultimate message: This convention was all about family . . . but not about all family. (Obama would subsequently mention his father, however, toward the end of his first presidential debate.)

The hatchet was further buried within the hour by her husband, former president Bill Clinton, as he forthrightly ordered those who voted for Hillary to join him and his family in their support of Obama ("Everything I learned in my eight years as president and in the work I've done since, in America and across the globe, has convinced me that Barack Obama is the man for *this* job. . . . The long, hard primary tested and strengthened him. And in his first presidential decision, the selection of a running mate, he hit it out of the park. . . . Barack Obama is ready to lead America and restore American leadership in the world."). As for

Obama's youth and brief years in the Senate, President Clinton reminded his listeners to recall another U.S. president, elected not so long ago: "Together, we prevailed in a campaign in which the Republicans said I was too young and too inexperienced to be commander in chief. Sound familiar? It didn't work in 1992, because we were on the right side of history. And it won't work in 2008, because Barack Obama is on the right side of history."

Aptly scheduled on the forty-fifth anniversary of the Reverend Dr. Martin Luther King Jr.'s legendary "I Have a Dream" speech, Obama's August 28 acceptance speech at the fifty-yard line at the open-air Invesco Field in Denver, Colorado, attended by almost eighty thousand people, reminded all Americans that in the coming election they needed to look beyond him and deep into themselves, to put an end to the bitter national divisiveness trickled down from the Bush administration:

"America, our work will not be easy. The challenges we face require tough choices, and Democrats as well as Republicans will need to cast off the worn-out ideas and politics of the past. For part of what has been lost these past eight years can't just be measured by lost wages or bigger trade deficits. What has also been lost is our sense of common purpose—our sense of higher purpose. And that's what we have to restore.

We may not agree on abortion, but surely we can agree on reducing the number of unwanted pregnancies in this country. The reality of gun ownership may be different for hunters in rural Ohio than for those plagued by gang violence in Cleveland, but don't tell me we can't uphold the Second Amendment while keeping AK-47s out of the hands of criminals. I know there are differences on same-sex marriage, but surely we can agree that our gay and lesbian brothers and sisters deserve to visit the person they love in the hospital and to live lives free of discrimination. Passions fly on immigration, but I don't know anyone who benefits when a mother is separated from her infant child or an employer undercuts American wages by hiring illegal workers. This, too, is part of America's promise —the promise of a democracy where we can find the strength and grace to bridge divides and unite in common effort.

I stand before you tonight because all across America something is stirring. What the nay sayers don't understand is that this election has never been about me. It's been about you."

★ ★ ★

The 2008 and 2012 Elections

In 2008, Republicans nominated Senator John McCain of Arizona for the presidency. McCain had made a run for his party's nomination in 2000, but his bid had been unsuccessful. In 2008 he had to walk a fine line between distancing himself from the unpopular George W. Bush, and thereby appealing to independents, while not moving too far away from Bush's policies, which would alienate the Republican base of dyed-in-the-wool conservatives. His other problem was his opponent, Senator Barack Obama of Illinois. The darling of the mainstream media, Obama had star power. In an effort to capture the attention of voters and the press, McCain chose as his running mate Governor Sarah Palin of Alaska.

Palin was young—forty-four, while McCain was seventy-two. She was attractive, with a reputation in Alaska as a reformer. On social issues like abortion she was a true conservative, which would appeal to the Republican base. And because she was the first female vice presidential candidate to appear on the Republican ticket, McCain hoped to solidify his support among Republican women, attract women independents, and perhaps—and this was a long shot—win the votes of Hillary Clinton supporters who were unhappy with the Obama candidacy. But Palin proved to be a polarizing figure, and the media that cheered for Obama frequently savaged her, often with unfair personal attacks. Palin added to her woes by making a number of gaffes, such as remarking that she did have some foreign policy experience since she could see Russia from her porch. As Palin's missteps accumulated, the *Anchorage Daily News* observed that on the campaign trail the governor seemed to be "unprepared or over her head."

Above: President Barack Obama and New Jersey Governor Chris Christie surveying storm damage in Brigantine, N.J., on October 31, 2012.

McCain's effort to woo voters failed. As Election Day approached, talking heads projected that McCain would get 200 electoral college votes, while Obama would receive 338. In fact, the totals were even more skewed: 365 Obama, 173 McCain.

In the 2012 election, Obama's opponent was Mitt Romney, former governor of Massachusetts. His campaign focused on an issue that worried so many Americans in 2011—the sluggish economy. Romney presented himself as a businessman who could turn the economy around and create jobs; as a Republican who had won the governorship of a state—Massachusetts—that the Democrats all but owned and so had learned how to be bipartisan; and as a Washington outsider who had never been associated with any political or personal scandal. He appealed to the base of the Republican Party of social conservatives, fiscal conservatives, evangelical Christians, and civil libertarians and had cultivated a substantial list of donors who helped the campaign amass a considerable war chest. Drawing on his own personal fortune as well, the former Massachusetts governor would mount a $1 billion campaign for the presidency.

Using social media to get out his message, Obama appealed to groups who had been essential to his victory in 2008—young people, women, African-Americans, Latinos, and members of the LGBT community. His campaign stressed that Osama bin Laden had been found and taken out on President Obama's watch. The economy was still battered, but Obama could say that his policies kept the U.S. auto industry alive—an argument that went over well in Ohio, a significant battleground state, where one in eight jobs depended on the auto industry. And then, just a few days before Election Day, came the devastating Hurricane Sandy, which gave Obama an opportunity to show leadership shortly before voters went to the polls. Even Governor Chris Christie of New Jersey—a Republican and a Romney supporter—praised the president for his swift reaction to the disaster.

In the days leading up to the election, polls offered conflicting data regarding which candidate the voters favored. A Gallup poll published on November 1, 2012 showed Romney ahead of the president, 62 percent to 55 percent. On Election Eve, Gallup pollsters reported that Romney was still ahead, but by only one percentage point—49 percent to Obama's 48 percent.

It didn't turn out that way. On Election Night, Obama walked away with 332 electoral votes and 51 percent of the popular vote, while Romney garnered 206 electoral votes and 47 percent of the popular vote.

Election Results 2008

Presidential/Vice Presidential Candidates	Popular Votes	Electoral Votes
Barack Obama/Joseph R. Biden Jr. (Democratic)	66,882,230	365
John S. McCain/Sarah Palin (Republican)	58,343,671	173

In a historic election, Barack Obama was elected the 44th President of the United States on November 4, 2008. The first-term senator from Illinois easily defeated John McCain (R–AZ), winning a larger share of the popular vote than any Democrat since Lyndon Johnson in 1964.

Election Results 2012

Presidential/Vice Presidential Candidates	Popular Votes	Electoral Votes
Barack Obama/Joseph R. Biden Jr. (Democratic)	65,455,010	332
Mitt Romney/Paul Ryan (Republican)	60,771,703	206

Barack Obama won a decisive victory over Romney, becoming the eleventh president to win a majority of the popular vote more than once.

Above: President-elect Barack Obama and his wife, Michelle, left, and Vice President-elect Joe Biden and his wife, Jill, wave to the crowd after Obama's acceptance speech at his election night party at Grant Park in Chicago on November 4, 2008.

> *"As commander in chief, I will never hesitate to defend this nation, but I will only send our troops into harm's way with a clear mission and a sacred commitment to give them the equipment they need in battle and the care and benefits they deserve when they come home."*
>
> —Barack Obama, August 28, 2008, acceptance speech
> at the Democratic National Convention

The Economy

Dominating all other issues, from the time Barack Obama took office in January 2009, was the economy. In February 2009, Congress passed an $800 billion economic stimulus package intended to save jobs and create new ones through tax credits and by funneling money to cash-strapped state and local governments for infrastructure projects and to help them bridge their own budget gaps. Called the American Recovery and Reinvestment Act, the stimulus was designed to create 3 million new jobs; how many jobs actually were created or saved became a point of dispute between the Obama administration and its critics.

Not subject to dispute were the stubborn unemployment statistics. In spite of the stimulus package, unemployment continued to climb, peaking at 10.1 percent in October 2009. In the first quarter of 2010, unemployment dipped to 9.7 percent, but in all of 2010 it never fell below 9.6 percent. In the 2010 midterm elections, voters demonstrated their discontent with the Democrats by giving the Republicans control of the House of Representatives, and sending five new Republicans to the Senate. Of the thirty-seven races for state governor, twenty-three went to Republicans.

On July 21, 2010, Obama signed the Dodd-Frank Wall Street Reform and Consumer Protection Act to re-regulate the financial sector in response to the recession. The bill was designed to improve acountability and transparency in the financial system. However implementing the 2,300-page, broadly written legislation has been difficult, as the process has been more complex than regulators anticipated.

Ironically, economic growth slowed in 2012 largely because of the presidential race. President Obama and Governor Mitt Romney had strongly divergent views on how to stimulate economic growth. As a result, many business owners did little or nothing to grow their businesses as they waited to see who would capture the White House and implement his economic policy.

In December 2013, a study of the Bush and Obama administrations' $80 billion bail out of the auto industry reported that the controversial move saved 1.5 million U.S. jobs. It also preserved $105.3 billion in unemployment benefit payments and personal and social insurance tax collection.

In 2013, consumers' faith in the economy's growth swung wildly from month to month, but at the end of the year confidence had improved, although the numbers were still negative: Gallup's U.S. Economic Confidence Index averaged −16 for 2013, which was not great news, but it was an improvement over 2012 when the confidence index stood at −21. In other good news, daily consumer spending was up from $72 in 2012 to $88 in 2013. And Gallup's Job Creation Index for all workers found a slight uptick, from 18 in 2012 to 20 in 2013.

Unemployment dropped to 6.1 percent in 2014, but job creation was uneven: dismally low in January, it spiked upward in February; saw a modest drop-off in March, but then soared to 304,000 in April; in May it dropped to 224,000, but in June employers added 288,000 to their payroll. There were other signs of confidence among consumers, who were beginning to return to the marketplace.

The Nobel Peace Prize

On October 9, 2009, the Nobel Committee announced that it had awarded the Nobel Peace Prize to Barack Obama "for his extraordinary efforts to strengthen international diplomacy and cooperation between peoples."

The crowd of reporters gathered for the announcement gasped in surprise. At home, perhaps hoping to defuse critics who wondered what the president had done to win such an honor, Obama declared that he considered the prize less an award recognizing his achievements than "a call to action." He committed himself to pressing for nuclear nonproliferation and finding a resolution to the Arab-Israeli conflict.

Health Care Reform

Obama's wide-ranging reform of health care in the United States will be remembered as the standout piece of legislation. After a year of debate, the bill passed in 2010. Under this new law:

- The government's Medicaid program for the poor was expanded so more people could participate.
- To make health insurance more affordable for the uninsured, the states and the federal government will set up "exchanges" through which private insurance

companies offer coverage to individuals and small businesses.

- People who do not have health insurance will be required to buy it.
- Companies that do not offer their employees health insurance will be required to do so or pay a fine, unless they receive a waiver from the federal government.
- Health insurance companies no longer will be able to deny coverage to individuals with preexisting medical conditions.

Critics argued that Obamacare, as the new program came to be known, will cost $2.5 trillion in its first ten years and introduces new taxes on prescription drugs and medical devices. They asserted that companies offering some health insurance to their employees will opt out, because paying the fine is cheaper than paying the insurance premiums. In this situation, at least some employees of those companies will turn to Medicare for coverage, placing an additional financial burden on the state and federal governments.

Finally, critics said that, given the weak U.S. economy, the budget shortfalls among the states, and the staggering debt incurred by the federal government through the stimulus package, Obamacare was underfunded and likely to become a new fiscal burden.

The Republican-controlled House of Representatives voted six times to repeal Obamacare but were unsuccessful.

In 2011 twenty-six states and the National Federation of Independent Business brought suit in federal court challenging the individual mandate and the Medicaid expansion. In 2012, the U.S. Supreme Court heard the case and upheld the major provisions of the Affordable Care Act.

Obamacare was scheduled to roll out on October 1, 2013. It was an unmitigated disaster. That day, Healthcare.gov processed just one enrollment. The next day, the system failed to register 48 percent of applications. For weeks, would-be purchasers of health insurance were thrown off the system or sent endless error messages. And when they called the Healthcare customer service center, they found that that part of the system did not work, either. Adding to consumers' troubles was sticker shock: many of the state health exchanges were offering coverage at higher rates than what those with medical coverage were paying their insurance company; in some cases, the increase was 25, 50, even 100 percent more. And then there was the revelation that Obama's promise that had become the Obamacare mantra—"If you like your doctor, you can keep your doctor"—in many cases simply was not true.

Nonetheless, as the IT guys sorted out the registration system's bugs and glitches, more people were able eventually to get health care coverage. *Forbes* found that by January 1, 2014, the number of uninsured adults in the United States had dropped from 17.1 percent to 15.9 percent, a statistic that represents about 3–4 million Americans who now have health insurance. By 2016, the rate of uninsured Americans was at an all-time low of 8.6%, covering more than 20 million people since it went into effect. Also health care prices have risen at the lowest rate in 50 years.

Above: President Barack Obama signs the health care bill on March 23, 2010. He is flanked by Marcelas Owens of Seattle, Vice President Joe Biden, Vicki Kennedy, widow of Sen. Ted Kennedy, House Speaker Nancy Pelosi and Senate Majority Leader Harry Reid.

The Birth Certificate Controversy

During the 2008 presidential campaign there was a rumor that candidate Barack Obama refused to produce his birth certificate because it would show that he had been born in Africa and therefore was not eligible to run for president. (The U.S. Constitution restricts the office of president to native-born American citizens.)

To quell the rumors, the Obama campaign released his Certificate of Live Birth, which showed that Barack Obama had been born in Honolulu, Hawaii. Nonetheless, skeptics claimed the document was a forgery. The birth certificate controversy dogged Obama even after he moved into the White House.

In 2011, billionaire real estate developer Donald Trump flirted with the idea of running for the presidency as a Republican. In spite of criticism from Republicans and Democrats alike, Trump called on the president to prove definitively that he was a native-born American citizen. In April 2011, the White House released the Long Form Certificate of Live Birth, which showed that Obama had been born in Honolulu. "We're not going to be able to solve our problems if we get distracted by sideshows and carnival barkers," Obama said after its release. "We've got some enormous challenges out there. There are a lot of folks out there still looking for work. . . . We do not have time for this kind of silliness."

The Military

In December 2009, during a speech at the U.S. Military Academy at West Point, Obama announced that he was sending an additional 30,000 U.S. troops to Afghanistan as a counterinsurgency measure. Eighteen months later, shortly after the killing of Osama bin Laden, the president addressed the nation, saying that he had ordered 10,000 U.S. troops to be withdrawn from Afghanistan by the end of 2011, with an additional 23,000 withdrawn by the end of summer 2012. Saying that Afghanistan was no longer a haven for al-Qaeda, that the Taliban was in no position to overthrow the Afghan government, and that Afghan security forces were ready to police their own country, Obama asserted that it was time to bring American troops home.

A year earlier, in 2010, Obama had withdrawn 50,000 U.S. troops from Iraq, citing the stability of the Iraqi government and the decreased threat from al-Qaeda. All but 9,800 of the troops will be withdrawn by the end of 2014, with the balance pulled out by the end of 2016.

In December 2010, Obama signed legislation that repealed the "Don't ask, don't tell" military policy. "Don't ask, don't tell" had been a compromise between the Clinton administration and the U.S. military, which permitted gay men and lesbians to serve in the military as long as they kept their sexuality secret. At the signing ceremony Obama said, "No longer will tens of thousands of Americans in uniform be asked to live a lie or look over their shoulder."

Beginning in 2013, the Obama adminstration began withdrawing troops from Afghanistan. In 2011 the American presence in the country had peaked at 100,000; by the end of 2015 American troops in the country will be down to 9,800, and in 2016 all those troops will be withdrawn. With the Taliban clearly not destroyed and limited confidence in the Afghan army and security forces' ability to keep the peace, supporters and critics of the administration have questioned the wisdom of the withdrawal.

The year 2014 was a rocky one for the Obama administration's relationship with the U.S. military. In the spring a whistle-blower revealed that hundreds of veterans were waiting months for treatment, or never received any treatment at all, at Veterans Administration hospitals. Furthermore, at the Phoenix veterans hospital, between thirty-five and forty veterans had died while waiting for care. Then it was revealed that schedulers at the hospitals were pressured by their superiors to create secret wait lists of veterans and doctor's appointment lists to "prove" that the wait times were not excessive. On June 11, 2014, the FBI launched a criminal investigation of the VA.

The budget Obama sent to Capitol Hill in March 2014 called for such dramatic cuts to the size of the armed forces that tens of thousands of servicemen and -women would be forced out of the military. This increased the number of job hunters in the civilian workforce at a time when the job market was still shaky and only beginning to show signs of recovery.

Obama at a rally for American troops at the Bagram Airfield in Bagram, Afghanistan on May 25, 2014.

The Arab World

Early in 2011, a popular uprising in Tunisia overthrew the oppressive regime of Zine Ben Ali. Zine's brutal crushing of all dissent, his corrupt government, and the high unemployment rate in Tunisia combined to bring crowds of ordinary men and women into the streets, determined to expel Zine from power. Government forces fired on the crowds, killing hundreds; yet in spite of a media crackdown in the country, protesters got the word out via Facebook, uploading photos and videos of demonstrators being shot and killed.

Ultimately Zine fled the country. In the meantime uprisings flared up in Egypt, Bahrain, Syria, Libya, and Yemen. The insurgencies took the Obama administration—and the rest of the world—by surprise. But the Egyptian revolution put the U.S. government in an awkward position: Egyptian strongman Hosni Mubarak had been a staunch U.S. ally and supporter of Israel. So, when antigovernment protesters demanded Mubarak's resignation, Obama and his secretary of state, Hillary Clinton, initially seemed uncertain as to how to respond. When Obama called for "an orderly transition" from dictatorship to democracy in Egypt, Benjamin Netanyahu, prime minister of Israel, expressed his loyalty and gratitude to Mubarak, saying, "I don't say everything that he did was right, but he did one thing which all of us are thankful to him for: He kept the peace in the Middle East." After eighteen days of unrest, Mubarak resigned as president of Egypt.

In Libya, dictator Muammar Gaddafi unleashed his military against protesters, promising they would be shown no mercy. Obama responded by working with America's NATO allies to create a coalition force to give the rebels air cover and attack Libyan military and government installations—including Gaddafi's residence. Obama declared that no American ground troops would land in Libya, and he let NATO assume command of the operation. As for violence against demonstrators elsewhere in the Arab world, the Obama administration condemned it, but did not commit itself to opposing those governments with force.

Killing of Osama Bin Laden

On Sunday evening, May 1, 2011, the president appeared on television unexpectedly to announce to the nation and the world that Osama bin Laden, the mastermind of the September 11 attacks, and many other terrorist attacks around the world, had been found and killed. U.S. intelligence tracked bin Laden to a compound in the city of Abbottabad, Pakistan, where he had been living for several years. Declarations by Pakistani government officials that they had no idea bin Laden had been living in their country were met with disbelief in the United States and elsewhere.

Navy SEALs and CIA paramilitary forces entered the bin Laden compound, where they shot and killed him. The operation took about forty minutes. Bin Laden's guards fired on the U.S. commandos, but none of them were wounded or killed. After identifying bin Laden's body, the SEALs carried it away with them for burial at sea.

"Justice has been done," President Obama said in his televised address. Meanwhile, across the United States, spontaneous celebrations erupted in the streets of Washington, D.C., New York, and elsewhere. Jubilant crowds gathered at the site of the World Trade Center, waving flags and singing "The Star Spangled Banner."

The day before bin Laden was killed, Obama's job approval rating among the American public stood at 46 percent; afterwards his approval rating rose eleven points, to 57 percent. It soon returned to 46 percent again.

Obama and Vice President Biden, along with members of the national security team, watching live feed from drones operating over Osama bin Laden's complex in the Situation Room of the White House on May 1, 2011.

Gun Control and Gay Rights

On December 14, 2012, a disturbed young man shot his way into the Sandy Hook Elementary School in Newtown, Connecticut and opened fire on the children and staff. Minutes later, twenty children, all of them six or seven years old, and six staff members, including the school's principal, lay dead. Several weeks later, during his State of the Union address, Obama invoked the Newtown victims and called on Congress to pass stricter gun control legislation. The bill was amended time and again by supporters of easier access to firearms, but ultimately even the final watered-down version of the bill failed to pass. Nonetheless, Obama has continued to call for a revision of existing gun laws, although it appears that this is a call Congress will ignore.

In May 2012, six months before the presidential election, Obama announced during an interview with ABC News that he supported gay marriage. "I've been going through an evolution on this issue. I've always been adamant that gay and lesbian Americans should be treated fairly and equally," he said. "At a certain point I've just concluded that, for me personally, it is important for me to go ahead and affirm that I think same-sex couples should be able to get married."

The Obama Administration

Administration Dates:	January 20, 2009– January 20, 2017
Vice President:	Joseph R. Biden (2009-2017)
Cabinet:	
Secretary of State	Hillary Clinton (2009-2013)
	John Kerry (2013-2017)
Secretary of the Treasury	Timothy Geithner (2009-2013)
	Jack Lew (2013-2017)
Secretary of Defense	Robert Gates (2006-2011)
	Leon Panetta (2011-2013)
	Chuck Hagel (2013-2015)
	Ash Carter (2015-2017)
Attorney General	Eric H. Holder, Jr. (2009-2015)
	Loretta Lynch (2015-2017)
Secretary of the Interior	Ken Salazar (2009-2013)
	Sally Jewell (2013-2017)
Secretary of Agriculture	Thomas J. Vilsack (2009-2017)
Secretary of Commerce	Gary Locke (2009-2011)
	John Bryson (2011-2012)
	Penny Pritzker (2013-2017)
Secretary of Labor	Hilda Solis (2009-2013)
	Thomas E. Perez (2013-2017)
Secretary of Health and Human Services	Kathleen Sebelius (2009-2013)
	Sylvia Mathews Burwell (2013-2017)
Secretary of Housing and Urban Development	Shaun Donovan (2009-2014)
	Julián Castro (2014-2017)
Secretary of Transportation	Ray LaHood (2009-2013)
	Anthony Foxx (2013-2017)
Secretary of Energy	Steven Shu (2009-2013)
	Ernest Moniz (2013-2017)
Secretary of Education	Arne Duncan (2009-2016)
	John King (2016-2017)
Secretary of Veteran Affairs	Eric Shinseki (2009-2014)
	Sloan Gibson (2014)
	Robert McDonald (2014-2017)
Secretary of Homeland Security	Janet Napolitano (2009-2013)
	Jeh Johnson (2013-2017)

Immigration Reform

Immigration reform has been an elusive goal for Democrats and Republicans. The question has always been what to do with the estimated 11 million illegal immigrants in the United States. Obama described the lack of reform as his "biggest failure." However, during his years in office, he continued to strengthen border security, held businesses accountable for knowingly hiring illegal workers, and looked for legal ways that undocumented immigrants to earn citizenship.

The ISIL Threat

When an Islamic terrorist organization Islamic State in Iraq and the Levant, or ISIL, emerged in the Middle East, President Obama initially dismissed them as "a JV team." Since then, ISIL has become one of the greatest threats to the stability of the Middle East, particularly in Iraq and Syria. The group has become notorious for brutal slayings of soldiers and civilians, mass killings of religious minorities, sexual slavery, and the destruction of non-Islamic sacred and cultural sites. ISIL sympathizers have been responsible for deadly attacks in Europe and the United States.

In response, the Obama administration has built a global coalition to defeat ISIL and requested funding to train and equip Iraqis to fight them and conduct a range of military operations against them in the Middle East region. These include more than 12,000 targeted airstrikes against them since Operation Inherent Resolve started on August 8, 2014, destroying more than 31,000 targets, including tanks and staging areas. Obama also asked Congress in 2015 to formally authorize military force against the terrorist group. However, ISIL continues to be a threat.

International Climate Change Agreement

In a speech in 2013, Obama said "Someday, our children, and our children's children, will look at us in the eye and they'll ask us, did we do all that we could when we had the chance to deal with this problem and leave them a cleaner, safe, more stable world?" In response, he outlined his Climate Action Plan, which outlined the steps his administration would take to cut carbon pollution and work at home and internationally to address global climate change.

Negotiated in December, 2015, the Paris Agreement would reduce carbon emissions and increase carbon trading for the 195 countries participating, with 55 needed to ratify the agreement before it can go into effect. In 2016, the United States and China, the two largest emitters of greenhouse gasses, agreed to ratify the agreement. Obama was instrumental in the creation of this agreement, as well as enacting the Clean Power Plan in 2015, that would reduce carbon dioxide emissions of the country's power plants by 2030.

Employment Figures

According the Bureau of Labor Statistics, when Barack Obama took the oath of office in January 2009, unemployment stood at 7.8 percent. The recession hung on throughout the president's first term of office, and employment hovered above 9 percent for three years, reaching a high of 10 percent in October 2009. However, since then the economy has added 10 million jobs, unemployment hovers around 5%, and the deficit has fallen by about three quarters.

The Cuban Thaw

The restoration of diplomatic relations between the United States and Cuba—known as the Cuban Thaw—came about in July 2015, 54 years after outgoing president Dwight D. Eisenhower closed the American embassy in Havana and withdrew U.S. recognition of the government of Fidel Castro.

Under the new agreement, Cuba has an embassy in Washington, D.C., and America has an embassy in Havana. Travel restrictions between the two countries have been lifted. Obama also removed Cuba from the list of state sponsors of terrorism. In addition, American and Cuban firms have access to each other's markets. One thing that did not change is the status of the naval base at Guantanamo Bay—it remains in U.S. hands.

Michelle Obama

Born January 17, 1964, Chicago, Illinois

"What struck me when I first met Barack was that even though he had this funny name, even though he'd grown up all the way across the continent in Hawaii, his family was so much like mine." —Michelle Obama

Michelle and Barack Obama are partners in the truest sense of the word: tall, elegant graduates of Harvard Law School, they hit the streets of Chicago together to bring reform and improvements to the city's primarily black South Side. Parallel to Obama's rise in first the State Senate and then the U.S. Senate, Michelle forged her own career in community affairs. As America's first African-American First Couple, they stand together as the ultimate success story, of how intelligence, education, diligence, commitment to the community, and strong family values can bring a husband and wife with working-class backgrounds and a desire for change all the way to the White House.

Michelle Obama's favorite singer, Stevie Wonder, whose "You and I" had been sung at the Obamas' wedding by a friend, performed "Signed, Sealed, Delivered I'm Yours" at the final night of the Democratic National Convention.

Chicago, Chicago

Michelle LaVaughn Robinson is the younger child of Fraser and Marian Shields Robinson of Chicago. Like her older brother, Craig, she skipped second grade, and she entered Princeton two years after her brother did, majoring in sociology as he had. While still in college, she took an interest in community service, creating a daycare center for the children of the university's own maintenance and cafeteria staff. Graduating cum laude from Princeton in 1985, she entered Harvard Law School and graduated with a J.D. and joined the law firm of Sidley & Austin, where Barack Obama would work as a summer intern.

Michelle wasn't interested in dating Obama, but he pursued her undeterred. Finally the breakthrough came after a company picnic, when Obama offered to buy Michelle an ice-cream cone at a Baskin-Robbins. The ice cream was cold, but the ice between them melted. She agreed to date him. The stability of Michelle's home life made a tremendous impression on Obama. Once they were engaged, Obama shared with Michelle the more exotic aspects of his upbringing, taking her to Kenya to meet his late father's relatives.

On October 18, 1992, three-plus years after they first met, Michelle and Barack were married at Chicago's Trinity United Church of Christ by the Reverend Jeremiah A. Wright Jr. Their wedding plans had proceeded in the face of the loss of several close relatives: Michelle's father, who had long been ill with multiple sclerosis, and Obama's grandfather in Hawaii. But the occasion also brought family and friends together: Barack's half brother Abongo served as best man, dressed in an African gown and cap. Michelle's friend Santita Jackson, daughter of the Reverend Jesse Jackson Sr., sang. The couple settled in Chicago to pursue what they thought of as their life's work.

Community Service

Michelle left the law firm to work as deputy chief of staff for Chicago's then mayor Richard Daley, and then, from 1993 through 1996, worked as executive director of the Chicago branch she founded of Public Allies, as part of President Bill Clinton's AmeriCorps project, which placed young Americans in nonprofit businesses. In 1996, she became associate dean of students and director of the University of Chicago's Community Service Center, which placed young adults in internships.

Six years later, Michelle became University of Chicago Hospitals's executive director of community affairs. In 2005, she was promoted to vice president of external affairs and community relations. When Obama entered the race to become the Democratic candidate for president, Michelle stepped down to join him on the campaign trail. Her mother, Marian, pitched in to help with the kids—Malia Ann, born in 1998, and Natasha "Sasha," born in 2001.

First Mom

Although she has been selected by *Vanity Fair* for its best-dressed list, and *Ebony* has voted the pair one of America's hottest couples, Michelle has her feet on the ground. Likewise, the First Daughters behave totally

Above: Obama hugs Michelle after giving his acceptance speech at the Democratic National Convention. The open-air setting, at Invesco Field in Denver, heightened the drama of the moment.

naturally in the public eye, unabashedly outspoken in their adoration of their father. They may have traded a more private life in Chicago for the White House, but within the Obama household, affection, not affectation, is the name of the game. Unlike his own father, Obama is determined to be a husband and father that Michelle and his daughters can count on, and admires how his helpmate juggles the girls' activities "with a general's efficiency."

In May 2006, *Essence* magazine listed Michelle as one of "25 of the World's Most Inspiring Women." Now, constantly in the spotlight both as a mother and as First Lady, Michelle Obama continues to offer hope and promise globally.

During the campaign, Obama-watchers who suspected that Michelle was stuck in a casual T-shirt-and-cardigan rut were pleasantly surprised when the new First Lady appeared at her husband's inauguration in a yellow wool lace dress-and-coat ensemble created for her by Isabel Toledo, a Cuban American designer. That night, Michelle wore to the Inaugural Ball a white, one-shouldered gown by Jason Wu, a twenty-six-year-old designer who immigrated to the United States from Taiwan. People noticed—not least the editors at *Maxim*, who named Michelle to the magazine's "100 Hottest Women in the World." Michelle is the first First Lady to make the cut, coming in at number 93.

An Advocate for Children

To address the crisis of childhood obesity, Michelle made healthy eating and exercise for kids a priority. She invited Washington, D.C., grammar school pupils to the White House to help her plant an organic vegetable garden. A few weeks later, the kids returned to harvest and sample the produce, which included lettuce, peas, raspberries, and even the dreaded spinach and broccoli.

"Let's Move" is another Michelle initiative for kids. To set the example of getting off the couch and getting some exercise, Michelle visited the Alice Deal Middle School in Washington to dance with 450 students to a revised, kid-friendly version of Beyoncé's hit, "Get Me Bodied."

To encourage kids, especially girls, to dream big, Michelle celebrated Women's History Month by assembling twenty-one outstandingly successful women—including actress Alfre Woodard; singer Sheryl Crowe; WNBA star Lisa Leslie; Ann Dunwoody, America's first female four-star general; and Mae Jemison, the first African-American astronaut to travel to outer space—and sent them to Washington schools where they told their stories to the schoolkids. That night the all-stars returned to the White House for dinner with Michelle and 110 high school girls. Addressing her young guests, Michelle said, "Tonight we just want to say, 'Go for it!' Don't hesitate. Don't act with fear. Just go for it."

Of course, the children most important to Michelle are her two daughters, Malia and Sasha. Each week she juggles her calendar so she can meet her obligations as First Lady and still attend activities at the First Daughters' school.

During her husband's second term, Michelle expanded her Let's Move initiative. In 2013 and 2014 she invited kid chefs to submit recipes for the Epicurious Healthy Lunchtime Challenge. The fifty-four winners, from across the country, were invited to the White House for a state dinner with the First Lady. She also met with school nutritionists and educators to discuss strategies and hear stories of schools that have succeeded in getting kids to eat healthy meals in school.

In 2012, Michelle followed up her successful kitchen garden, located on the White House's South Lawn, with a book—her first ever—titled *American Grown*. The book encourages families to introduce more fruit and vegetables into their diet, to try the unfamiliar, and to shop for food that is seasonal and produced locally. The book also chronicles the story of the White House garden, and it includes one-of-a-kind recipes created by the White House chefs for produce freshly picked from Michelle's garden.

Above: President Barack Obama joins First Lady Michelle Obama at the Kids' State Dinner in the East Room of the White House on July 18, 2014.

The Social Scene

When the Obamas moved into the White House, Washington society saw a First Family the likes of which they had not seen since the Kennedy administration. The socialites expected that the Obamas would entertain in the elegant style of Jack and Jackie Kennedy. And the Obamas do entertain, but their guests are wounded veterans and their families, successful black women, old friends from Chicago, and community leaders from across the country. An Obama-style Camelot never materialized. Washington hostess Sally Quinn summarized the disappointment among Washington society, saying the First Lady is interested in "community outreach, not social outreach."

Above: First lady Michelle Obama, left center, poses with elementary school children after their harvest from the White House garden.

Obama's "A More Perfect Union" Speech

The following is an excerpt of the remarks of Democratic Illinois senator Barack Obama, delivered March 18, 2008, in Philadelphia, PA, at the Constitution Center. In it, Obama addresses the role race has played in the presidential campaign.

"We the people, in order to form a more perfect union...."

Two hundred and twenty one years ago, in a hall that still stands across the street, a group of men gathered and, with these simple words, launched America's improbable experiment in democracy. The document they produced was eventually signed but ultimately unfinished. It was stained by this nation's original sin of slavery, a question that divided the colonies and brought the convention to a stalemate until the founders chose to allow the slave trade to continue for at least twenty more years, and to leave any final resolution to future generations.

Of course, the answer to the slavery question was already embedded within our Constitution—a Constitution that had at its very core the ideal of equal citizenship under the law; a Constitution that promised its people liberty, and justice, and a union that could be and should be perfected over time. And yet words on a parchment would not be enough to deliver slaves from bondage, or provide men and women of every color and creed their full rights and obligations as citizens of the United States.

What would be needed were Americans in successive generations who were willing to do their part—through protests and struggle, on the streets and in the courts, through a civil war and civil disobedience and always at great risk—to narrow that gap between the promise of our ideals and the reality of their time.

This was one of the tasks we set forth at the beginning of this campaign—to continue the long march of those who came before us, a march for a more just, more equal, more free, more caring, and more prosperous America.

I chose to run for the presidency at this moment in history because I believe deeply that we cannot solve the challenges of our time unless we solve them together—unless we perfect our union by understanding that we may have different stories, but we hold common hopes; that we may not look the same and we may not have come from the same place, but we all want to move in the same direction—toward a better future for our children and our grandchildren.

This belief comes from my unyielding faith in the decency and generosity of the American people. But it also comes from my own American story.

I am the son of a black man from Kenya and a white woman from Kansas. I was raised with the help of a white grandfather who survived a Depression to serve in Patton's army during World War II and a white grandmother who worked on a bomber assembly line at Fort Leavenworth while he was overseas.

I've gone to some of the best schools in America and lived in one of the world's poorest nations. I am married to a black American who carries within her the blood of slaves and slaveowners—an inheritance we pass on to our two precious daughters.

I have brothers, sisters, nieces, nephews, uncles, and cousins, of every race and every hue, scattered across three continents, and for as long as I live, I will never forget that in no other country on Earth is my story even possible.

It's a story that hasn't made me the most conventional candidate. But it is a story that has seared into my genetic makeup the idea that this nation is more than the sum of its parts—that out of many, we are truly one.

Throughout the first year of this campaign, against all predictions to the contrary, we saw how hungry the American people were for this message of unity.

This is not to say that race has not been an issue in the campaign. At various stages in the campaign, some commentators have deemed me either "too black" or "not black enough."

We saw racial tensions bubble to the surface during the week before the South Carolina primary. The press has scoured every exit poll for the latest evidence of racial polarization, not just in terms of white and black, but black and brown as well.

And yet, it has only been in the last couple of weeks that the discussion of race in this campaign has taken a particularly divisive turn.

On one end of the spectrum, we've heard the implication that my candidacy is somehow an exercise in affirmative action, that it's based solely on the desire of wide-eyed liberals to purchase racial reconciliation on the cheap.

On the other end, we've heard my former pastor, Reverend Jeremiah Wright, use incendiary language to express views that have the potential not only to widen the racial divide, but views that denigrate both the greatness and the goodness of our nation—that rightly offend white and black alike....The remarks that have caused this recent firestorm weren't simply controversial. They weren't simply a religious leader's effort to speak out against perceived injustice.

Instead, they expressed a profoundly distorted view of this country—a view that sees white racism as endemic, and that elevates what is wrong with America above all that we know is right with America, a view that sees the conflicts in the Middle East as rooted primarily in the actions of stalwart allies like Israel, instead of emanating from the perverse and hateful ideologies of radical Islam.

[...]

Some will see this as an attempt to justify or excuse comments that are simply inexcusable. I can assure you it is not. I suppose the politically safe thing would be to move on from this episode and just hope that it fades into the woodwork.

But race is an issue that I believe this nation cannot afford to ignore right now. We would be making the same mistake that Reverend Wright made in his offending sermons about America—to simplify and stereotype and amplify the negative to the point that it distorts reality.

The fact is that the comments that have been made and the issues that have surfaced over the last few weeks reflect the complexities of race in this country that we've never really worked through—a part of our union that we have yet to perfect.

And if we walk away now, if we simply retreat into our respective corners, we will never be able to come together and solve challenges like health care, or education, or the need to find good jobs for every American.

[…]

That anger [over racial inequality] may not get expressed in public, in front of white co-workers or white friends. But it does find voice in the barbershop or around the kitchen table. At times, that anger is exploited by politicians, to gin up votes along racial lines, or to make up for a politician's own failings.

And occasionally it finds voice in the church on Sunday morning, in the pulpit and in the pews. The fact that so many people are surprised to hear that anger in some of Reverend Wright's sermons simply reminds us of the old truism that the most segregated hour in American life occurs on Sunday morning.

That anger is not always productive; indeed, all too often it distracts attention from solving real problems; it keeps us from squarely facing our own complicity in our condition, and prevents the African American community from forging the alliances it needs to bring about real change. But the anger is real; it is powerful; and to simply wish it away, to condemn it without understanding its roots, only serves to widen the chasm of misunderstanding that exists between the races.

In fact, a similar anger exists within segments of the white community. Most working- and middle-class white Americans don't feel that they have been particularly privileged by their race. Their experience is the immigrant experience—as far as they're concerned, no one's handed them anything; they've built it from scratch. They've worked hard all their lives, many times only to see their jobs shipped overseas or their pension dumped after a lifetime of labor.

So when they are told to bus their children to a school across town; when they hear that an African American is getting an advantage in landing a good job or a spot in a good college because of an injustice that they themselves never committed; when they're told that their fears about crime in urban neighborhoods are somehow prejudiced, resentment builds over time.

Like the anger within the black community, these resentments aren't always expressed in polite company. But they have helped shape the political landscape for at least a generation.

[…]

This is where we are right now. It's a racial stalemate we've been stuck in for years. Contrary to the claims of some of my critics, black and white, I have never been so naive as to believe that we can get beyond our racial divisions in a single election cycle, or with a single candidacy—particularly a candidacy as imperfect as my own.

But I have asserted a firm conviction—a conviction rooted in my faith in God and my faith in the American people—that working together we can move beyond some of our old racial wounds, and

that in fact we have no choice if we are to continue on the path of a more perfect union.

For the African American community, that path means embracing the burdens of our past without becoming victims of our past. It means continuing to insist on a full measure of justice in every aspect of American life. But it also means binding our particular grievances—for better health care, and better schools, and better jobs—to the larger aspirations of all Americans. And it means taking full responsibility for own lives—by demanding more from our fathers, and spending more time with our children, and reading to them, and teaching them that while they may face challenges and discrimination in their own lives, they must never succumb to despair or cynicism; they must always believe that they can write their own destiny.

What we know—what we have seen—is that America can change. That is the true genius of this nation. What we have already achieved gives us hope—the audacity to hope—for what we can and must achieve tomorrow.

In the white community, the path to a more perfect union means acknowledging that…the legacy of discrimination—and current incidents of discrimination, while less overt than in the past—are real and must be addressed. Not just with words, but with deeds—by investing in our schools and our communities; by enforcing our civil rights laws and ensuring fairness in our criminal justice system; by providing this generation with ladders of opportunity that were unavailable for previous generations.

It requires all Americans to realize that your dreams do not have to come at the expense of my dreams; that investing in the health, welfare, and education of black and brown and white children will ultimately help all of America prosper.

[…]

I would not be running for president if I didn't believe with all my heart that this is what the vast majority of Americans want for this country. This union may never be perfect, but generation after generation has shown that it can always be perfected.

And today, whenever I find myself feeling doubtful or cynical about this possibility, what gives me the most hope is the next generation—the young people whose attitudes and beliefs and openness to change have already made history in this election.

[…]

[This] is where we start. It is where our union grows stronger. And as so many generations have come to realize over the course of the two hundred and twenty-one years since a band of patriots signed that document in Philadelphia, that is where the perfection begins.

Donald J. Trump

"My whole life is about winning. I don't lose often. I almost never lose."

—*Donald J. Trump*

Forty-fifth president of the United States
2017–2021

Full Name: *Donald John Trump*

Born: *June 14, 1946, Jamaica Estates, Queens, New York*

Parents: *Fred and Mary Anne Trump*

Spouse: *Ivana Zelnickova (1949– ; m. 1977, divorced 1992), Marla Maples (1963– ; m. 1993, divorced 1999), Melania Knauss (1970– ; m. 2005)*

Children: *Donald (1977–); Ivanka (1981–); Eric (1984–); Tiffany (1993–); Barron (2006–)*

Religion: *Presbyterian*

Education: *Fordham University (1964–1966); Wharton School of Finance and Commerce at the University of Pennsylvania (B.S., 1966–1968)*

Occupations: *Real estate developer, reality television star*

Government positions: *None*

Political party: *Republican*

Dates as president: *January 20, 2017–January 20, 2021*

Age upon taking office: *70*

On Election Day 2016, Donald Trump defeated Hillary Clinton and made history. For the first time ever, American voters chose a man who has never held any public office or served in the military. They wanted an outsider who, they hoped, would smash government gridlock in Washington and find fresh solutions to lingering problems—flat incomes, the rising cost of medical insurance, immigration policy, terrorism, and trade deals that were disadvantageous to Americans. And their enthusiasm swept in a business magnate who promised to do just that.

Donald began his career in real estate development business thanks to a loan of $1 million from his father, Fred, who was in many ways his model. His father had charm, people liked him. But Fred was also ambitious—he wanted to be very wealthy and he wanted to cultivate powerful friends. That desire for power led him, of course, to get involved in politics. Fred had a tremendous work ethic. He often took his kids out in the field with him so they could learn how properties were developed, from the ground up—and Donald learned the lessons well.

Timeline

1946: Born in Queens, New York
1968: Graduates from the Wharton School of Business
1971: Given control of family real estate development company
1977: Marries Ivana Zelnickova Winklmayr. Son Donald Jr. is born
1980: Opens Grand Hyatt
1981: Daughter Ivanka is born
1982: Opens Trump Tower
1984: Opens first casino in Atlantic City. Son Eric is born
1987: *The Art of the Deal* published
1988: Buys the Plaza Hotel for $407 million
1992: Divorces Ivana
1993: Marla Maples gives birth to a daughter, Tiffany; Donald and Marla marry
1999: Divorces Marla
2004: *The Apprentice* airs
2005: Marries Melania Knauss; starts Trump University
2006: Son Barron is born
2015: Announces that he is running for the Republican nomination for president
2016: Elected forty-fifth president of the United States

Above: Donald Trump is shown in the 1964 Shrapnel yearbook at the New York Military Academy in Cornwall-on-Hudson, N.Y.

Military School

When Donald was 13 years old, his parents sent him to a military academy near West Point, about 60 miles from the family home. It was an austere place where the boys were expected to acquire discipline. At the academy, Donald's mentor was a veteran of World War II, a man who took no nonsense from the boys and was not above slugging one who was disrespectful, lazy, or in any other way fell short of what was expected from him at the school. It was here, according to Trump biographer Michael D'Antonio, that Donald acquired the quality of being single-minded in his pursuit of his goals. He also learned how to promote himself to his teachers and fellow cadets, and later how to get attention from the newspapers to build his name recognition.

Donald's father, Fred, made a fortune building middle-class housing in Queens, Brooklyn, and Staten Island—the areas Manhattanites refer to derisively as "the Outer Boroughs." They also include the Bronx in this put-down. After graduating from the Wharton School of Business with a degree in economics, Donald joined his father in the family business, and persuaded him to borrow against the equity in their housing developments to finance even more development projects.

Donald Takes Over

In 1971, Donald's father handed over control of the family business to him; Donald renamed it the Trump Organization. He moved to Manhattan where he expected to earn higher profits by developing larger, more affluent properties, especially in commercial real estate. In 1974 he bought the Commodore Hotel, which stood right beside Grand Central Station. Trump entered into a partnership with the Hyatt Hotel Corporation, renovated the hotel, covered its façade with reflective glass, and renamed the hotel the Grand Hyatt. It was a tremendous success, and established Trump as one of the most innovative developers in Manhattan.

One of Donald's most flamboyant projects at the time was the Trump Tower on Fifth Avenue. The lobby atrium

Above: Donald Trump, a real estate mogul, in his New York City offices where he managed the construction of his buildings.

soars up six stories, its walls are covered with pink marble. The focal point is an 80-foot-high waterfall. High-end retail stores fill the commercial space, and a stream of celebrities lived in the Tower's luxury apartments.

More projects kept coming. When voters in New Jersey approved casino gambling for financially ailing Atlantic City, Donald began building casinos: the Trump Plaza Hotel and Casino, Trump's Castle, and the Trump Taj Mahal. But the casinos did not thrive. To fund the

Left: Donald Trump, 33-year-old golden boy of New York real estate, holds a model of the Fifth Avenue tower that opened in 1983. One of the apartments sold for $12 million.

casinos, Trump borrowed money at such high interest rates that the casinos could never attract enough gamblers to repay the loans. Nonetheless, according to an article that ran in *The New York Times* in June 2016, Trump employed thousands of workers at his casinos, and paid tens of millions of dollars in tax revenue. All the Trump casinos have closed, the last being the Taj Mahal, which went out of business in 2016.

Family and Business

There was a downside to his fame, of course, and that came in the 1990s when Donald began an affair with an actress, Marla Maples, and he and his wife Ivana— the mother of his three eldest children—went through a nasty divorce that was covered very closely by the New York tabloids. In 1993 Donald and Marla had a daughter together, then married. They divorced in 1999.

Donald remains close with his children, all of whom work for him. They were almost inseparable from him during the 2016 campaign, as was his wife Melania whom he married in 2005.

Trump kept taking on high-profile projects: purchasing New York City's Plaza Hotel for $407 million, lavishing an additional $50 million to refurbish the property; buying the Eastern Air Lines Shuttle for $365 million and renaming

Below: Savannah Guthrie and Matt Lauer interview 2016 Republican presidential candidate Donald Trump, wife Melania, son Donald Jr., daughter Ivanka, son Eric, and daughter Tiffany during NBC's Today Trump Town Hall on April 21, 2016.

it the Trump Shuttle (the shuttle failed to be profitable); and at West Palm Beach, Florida, where he built a luxury condominium complex.

As early as 1999, Trump showed some interest in entering politics, but after a failed bid in the 2000 California presidential primary, Trump decided to withdraw from the race.

The Apprentice

The year 2004 saw the premiere of *The Apprentice,* a reality TV show in which contestants competed for a job working for the Trump Organization. Trump's signature line to unsuccessful contestants was "You're fired." *The Apprentice* became one of the most popular programs on television and gave Donald, already a celebrity, an even higher profile.

The Campaign

During his campaign, Trump never tried to cover up his flaws, like any practiced politician would do. He owned them. He said what was on his mind—and in a year when the electorate was fed up with career politicians, Trump was anything but a Washingtonian.

Above: Donald Jr., Donald Trump, and Ivanka during the filming of The Apprentice *Season 6 finale.*

One of his most famous campaign promises was that, to keep illegal immigrants out of the country, he'd build a wall along the southern border of the U.S., and he'd get the government of Mexico to pay for it.

Given the runaway costs of the Affordable Care Act (aka Obamacare), Trump declared he would repeal Obamacare and replace it with a new healthcare plan

Right: Real estate mogul Donald Trump announces his bid for the presidency in the 2016 presidential race during an event at the Trump Tower on Fifth Avenue in New York City on June 16, 2015.

that would be affordable and permit people who signed up for it to keep their doctors and their private insurer.

With his daughter Ivanka at his side, Donald proposed a plan that would let working parents deduct childcare expenses from their income taxes, and grant incentives to business owners to provide childcare in the workplace.

Donald claimed he would create 25 million new jobs over the next decade, and renegotiate trade deals that he said had undermined the American economy and been especially unfair to American workers.

On the subject of abortion, Trump was pro-choice for most of his life but became pro-life when he moved into politics. It became a cornerstone of his platform.

His foreign policy was founded on the principle of peace through strength, by rebuilding the military and improving intelligence-gathering.

Trump also promised to eliminate the red tape, waiting lists, and backlogs that veterans have experienced when they needed medical care. He said he would fire incompetent VA officials who have gotten in the way of doctors and provide nurses who are ready to give veterans the best medical care available.

Overcoming a Bombshell

The release of a tape from a 2005 interview with Billy Bush of *Access Hollywood* revealed Trump bragging about being able to kiss and fondle any woman he wanted, whether she consented or not, because he was a TV star. Eventually eleven women came forward, claiming that they were victims of these unwanted attentions. At the third debate, Donald declared, "I don't know these people. . . . I didn't do anything."

However, nothing could shake the avid support of his supporters, whose enthusiasm for the tell-it-like-it-is candidate propelled him to victory.

Trump Win

In a tight race that surprised many, Trump won 302 electoral votes to Clinton's 232 (a candidate needs 270 electoral votes to win). He swept the battleground states of Florida, Ohio, and North Carolina, and won in Michigan, Pennsylvania, and Wisconsin, states which have long been considered reliably Democratic. In Congressional races, Republicans held on to their control of the Senate 51 to 47, and in the House 236 to 193.

It was a stunning upset—on Election Day, most pundits and news outlets reported that Clinton had a slight lead over Trump and was expected to win the presidency. But Trump's supporters took the country and the world by surprise, handing him the White House and repudiating not only Hillary Clinton and the D.C. establishment, but also President Obama's policies and initiatives, from Obamacare to the Iran nuclear treaty.

Supporters of Hillary Clinton had gathered at the Jacob K. Javits Convention Center in Manhattan, expecting a victory and waiting to hear from their candidate. But as the returns came in, the large crowd grew silent. Some wept. At 2:30 in the morning, Hillary called Donald to concede and said in her concession speech the next day that she hoped he "will be a successful president to all Americans." President Obama called Donald soon thereafter to offer his congratulations and invited him to the White House to discuss the transition of power.

Meanwhile, at the New York Hilton Midtown, also in Manhattan, Trump supporters were jubilant. In an address to his supporters, Trump appealed to all Americans to come together. "Now it's time for America to bind the wounds of division," he said, and he was gracious to Hillary, saying the people of the United States owed her "a major debt of gratitude for her service to our country." His uplifting speech proclaimed that "Working together, we will begin the urgent task of rebuilding the nation and renewing the American dream."

Trump firing up the crowd at an election-day rally in Grand Rapids, Michigan.

2016 Election Results

Presidential Candidates	Popular Votes	Electoral Votes
Donald J. Trump	62,984,825	302
Hillary Clinton	65,853,516	232

Russian Interference

After Trump's surprising win, an investigation was launched, led by special counsel Robert Mueller. After months of study, his report concluded that Russia had interfered with the 2016 election. Their goals were to boost Trump's chances by damaging the Clinton campaign and to undermine trust in American democracy.

A wide-ranging group of Russian operatives hacked the sites of the Democratic National Committee, the Democratic Congressional Campaign Committee, and Hillary Clinton's campaign. They also attempted to do the same to the Republican National Committee and the campaign of Senator Marco Rubio but were unsuccessful. They accessed voter registration systems in at least twenty-one states, stealing the personal information of hundreds of thousands of voters. Politically damaging information and propaganda was spread on the Internet, including Twitter, Facebook, YouTube, and Instagram. Posing as grassroots activists, the operatives were even able to set up rallies in the swing states of Florida and Pennsylvania.

Special counsel Robert Mueller speaking at the Department of Justice in 2019 about the Russia investigation.

President Donald Trump signs a plaque on a new section of border wall along the Mexican–American border as acting DHS secretary Chad Wolf and Arizona governor Doug Ducey look on, June 23, 2020, in San Luis, Arizona.

In the months leading up to the election, members of the Trump campaign, including future attorney general Jeff Sessions, Trump's son-in-law Jared Kushner, and lawyer Michael Cohen, met with the Russians. At these meetings, the operatives offered damaging information on the Clinton campaign and discussed the possibility of developing a Trump-branded and -run skyscraper in Moscow with the Trump Organization. While Mueller's investigation could not prove that Donald Trump colluded with the Russians, his report did conclude that they had an undue influence on the president.

"Build the Wall"

A strong immigration policy was a cornerstone of Trump's campaign and his presidency. Just days after taking office, he began plans to construct "a beautiful, gorgeous, big wall" along the southern border of the U.S. The wall was not funded by Mexico but by the American taxpayer, and it fell far short of the two thousand miles originally promised. The U.S. constructed a total of 438 miles of border wall system during his term, the majority of which replaced dilapidated fencing in New Mexico, Arizona, and California.

Trump also vowed to tighten controls on the country's immigration system. Under the guise of protecting the lives and jobs of U.S. citizens from criminal aliens and foreign workers, he imposed a travel ban that targeted seven largely Muslim countries, which increased to thirteen countries in 2020.

Trump also imposed a "zero tolerance" policy for immigrants crossing the border illegally. This led U.S. Immigration and Customs Enforcement to separate children from their parents, with the adults jailed while awaiting a hearing and the children placed in shelters overseen by the Department of Health and Human Services. Thousands of children were taken. In the wake of national outcry and protests, the policy was suspended. Due to poor record keeping, reuniting families was a difficult and lengthy process. While families entering the country illegally thereafter were able to stay together while their fate was determined, the Trump administration ended the 1997 Flores Agreement, which said that migrant children could be detained only for twenty days and in the least restrictive setting possible. It was replaced with a policy that allowed them to be detained indefinitely.

In 2017, Trump attempted to cancel President Obama's Deferred Action for Childhood Arrivals executive order, which allowed the children of undocumented parents to work legally. This action was thwarted by the courts.

In 2018, a bipartisan group met in the Oval Office to discuss proposed changes to the visa lottery system from several countries, which included Haiti and African countries. Trump asked why America would want immigrants from "these shithole countries" instead of places like Norway. This led UN human rights office spokesman Robert Colville to condemn the comments as "shocking and shameful" and "racist."

While not all of his efforts to curb immigration were successful, Trump's administration pushed through changes that have lengthened the citizenship test, denied visas to immigrants, and limited grants of asylum claims. During his term, he reduced legal immigration by 49 percent.

Twitter War

When Donald Trump took office, he inherited Barack Obama's tens of millions of Twitter followers on @POTUS and @whitehouse. Those accounts, combined with his personal account, @realDonaldTrump, enabled him to reach more than 100 million people with his tweets, circumventing what he called the "lamestream media." He used the platform to directly reach his base with his thoughts, no matter how polarizing or untrue.

Because he was a world leader, his Twitter account did not have the same restrictions as the average citizen's, such as being blocked from the platform for promoting violence or spreading inaccurate information. However, Twitter began attaching fact-checking claims to his tweets in 2019, including flagging more than 200 tweets that falsely claimed voter fraud after Election Day.

Claims of Racism

Throughout his term in office, Trump was dogged by repeated accusations of racism against people who are not white. These claims were often due to his lack of condemnation of racial violence by his supporters.

One of the most telling incidents occurred in August 2017 in reaction to events in Charlottesville, Virginia. Pro-Confederacy and white nationalists clashed with counterprotesters, including members of Black Lives Matter. When a white nationalist drove into the crowd, killing one counterprotester and injuring others, Trump criticized both sides for the violence. He then defended the white nationalists, tweeting that many were "fine people."

Racial justice protests erupted after the death of George Floyd, a Black man killed in Minneapolis police custody in May 2020. Trump took to Twitter to say that he would send the National Guard to put down protests in the city. He then began conflating the demonstrations with violence and riots, tweeting "when the looting starts, the shooting starts," which harkened back to language used in the 1960s to quell the civil rights movement.

Trump's controversial comments also included telling congresswomen of color to go back to where they come from, calling Mexican immigrants "rapists," and his callout during a presidential debate to the Proud Boys, the thuggish, far-right movement whose members have attacked government protesters, telling them to "stand back and stand by."

Trump also attempted to tie the Black Lives Matter movement to anti-fascist activists, Marxists, and anti-government groups he claimed were trying to undermine his presidency.

Foreign Policy

Trump's "America First" anti-interventionist foreign policy deviated from his predecessors' approach to create international alliances. His administration disregarded international consensus, recognizing Jerusalem as the capital of Israel and escalating a trade war with China.

Trump reversed policy in key areas, such as withdrawing from several treaties, agreements, and organizations, including the Trans-Pacific Partnership, the Paris climate accord, the Joint Comprehensive Plan of Action with Iran, and the UN Human Rights Council. He also called for a withdrawal of troops from Afghanistan, Germany, and Syria.

Throughout his presidency, Trump fanned discord with tweets both goading and supporting autocratic rulers around the world, including Russia's Vladimir Putin and North Korea's Kim Jong-un. In 2019, the U.S. House of Representatives impeached Trump over allegations that he withheld military aid to Ukraine to pressure it to investigate Democratic presidential candidate Joe Biden.

Trump's Administration

Administration Dates: January 20, 2017–January 20, 2021

Vice President: Michael R. Pence (2017–2021)

Secretary of State: Mike Pompeo (2018–2021)
    Rex Tillerson (2017–2018)

Secretary of the Treasury: Steven Mnuchin (2017–2021)

Secretary of Defense: Mark Esper (2019–2020)
    Jim Mattis (2017–2019)

Attorney General: William Barr (2019–2020)
    Jeff Sessions (2017–2018)

Secretary of the Interior: David Bernhardt (2019–2021)
    Ryan Zinke (2017–2019)

Secretary of Agriculture: Sonny Perdue (2017–2021)

Secretary of Commerce: Wilbur Ross (2017–2021)

Secretary of Labor: Eugene Scalia (2019–2021)
    Alex Acosta (2017–2019)

Secretary of Health and Human Services: Alex Azar
    (2018–2021)
    Tom Price (2017)

Secretary of Housing and Urban Development: Ben
    Carson (2017–2021)

Secretary of Transportation: Elaine Chao (2017–2021)

Secretary of Energy: Dan Brouillette (2019–2021)
    Rick Perry (2017–2019)

Secretary of Education: Betsy DeVos (2017–2021)

Secretary of Veteran Affairs: Robert Wilkie (2018–2021)
    David Shulkin (2017–2018)

Secretary of Homeland Security: Kirstjen Nielsen (2017–
    2019)
    John F. Kelly (2017)

Criminal Charges

During Trump's term, seven of his advisors were criminally prosecuted. Six of his aides were charged as a result of special counsel Robert Mueller's investigation into Russia's interference in the 2016 election. These included his former national security advisor Michael Flynn, his former foreign policy advisor George Papadopoulos, and advisor Roger Stone.

The seventh aide, former White House chief strategist Steve Bannon, was charged through a federal investigation into a private organization created to solicit donations to fund the border wall. Bannon was indicted with three others on wire fraud and money laundering conspiracy charges for using hundreds of thousands of crowdsourced dollars for personal expenses.

In the last days of his presidency, Trump pardoned seventy-four people and commuted the sentences of seventy more. These included Bannon, Flynn, Papadopoulos, and Stone, as well as his top fundraiser, Elliott Broidy.

Trump's Triumphs

One area where President Trump was successful is the federal judiciary. With the support of Republicans led by Senate majority leader Mitch McConnell, he was able to appoint three Supreme Court justices—Neil Gorsuch, Brett Kavanaugh, and Amy Coney Barrett—giving conservatives a 6 to 3 majority.

He also appointed fifty-four appeals court judges, 174 district court judges, and three judges to the Court of International Trade. The influence of these appointments will be felt for years after his presidency, especially in the nation's regional circuit courts, where most federal appeals are decided.

In December 2017, Trump's administration enacted the Tax Cuts and Jobs Act, the first sweeping overhaul

President Donald Trump and Brett Kavanaugh at the swearing in of Kavanaugh as an associate justice of the Supreme Court in 2018.

of the tax code in thirty years. The reform simplified the process of paying taxes and lowered the rates on individuals and businesses, including decreasing the corporate tax rate from 35 percent to 21 percent.

Coronavirus Response

On January 23, 2020, China issued a lockdown for millions of people due to an outbreak of the coronavirus COVID-19. Four days later, the first confirmed cases appeared in the United States. On February 1, President Trump issued a ban on foreign travelers from China. By the end of February, there were outbreaks in multiple countries, including a spike in cases in Italy and Iran. The Centers for Disease Control and Prevention (CDC) warned Americans to begin preparing for the virus.

Although death tolls were rising throughout the world, President Trump downplayed the threat as well as the severity of the outbreak in the United States. In weekly press conferences, he told the American public that the disease was only as dangerous as the flu, although he had been briefed repeatedly that it was airborne and deadly. He claimed later that this was a strategy so that the public wouldn't panic. However, on March 13, he declared a national emergency to free up $50 billion in federal aid, and on March 25, a $2 trillion coronavirus aid package was approved by Congress.

President Donald J. Trump taking off his mask on the Truman Balcony at the White House on Monday, October 5, 2020, following several days at Walter Reed National Military Medical Center for treatment for COVID-19.

The administration's lack of urgency in the initial months meant that testing and contact tracing were delayed. With no federal intervention, states competed against each other to get protective and medical equipment to frontline workers in hospitals. Trump touted unproven remedies, ignored the advice of medical professionals and recommendations from the CDC, and sidelined experts, including Anthony Fauci, the head of the National Institute of Allergy and Infectious Diseases. On April 14, Trump halted funding to the World Health Organization (WHO) over its handling of the pandemic, which drew worldwide condemnation.

On May 5, 2020, with the U.S. leading the world in deaths from COVID-19 with seventy thousand, he said, "there'll be more death, that the virus will pass, with or without a vaccine. And I think we're doing very well on the vaccines but, with or without a vaccine, it's going to pass, and we're going to be back to normal." A few days later, it was reported that the U.S. economy lost 20.5 million jobs in April, the most since the Great Depression.

On May 29, Trump terminated the U.S.'s relationship with the WHO. He continued to refuse to wear a mask in public until the middle of July, politicizing a proven strategy for slowing the spread of the virus. He mocked people who did wear masks, including Joe Biden, and held large rallies with unmasked supporters, some of which became super-spreader events. When states began mandating stay-at-home orders, Trump tweeted support to protesters who claimed these orders infringed on their civil rights.

By the end of September, the U.S. had more than 7 million COVID-19 cases. On October 2, both Donald and Melania Trump tested positive for COVID-19, along with more than a dozen White House staff and aides. A team of doctors provided the president the best remedies, many not available to the general public, and he recovered. By that time more than 200,000 Americans had died from the disease.

In the run-up to the November election, Trump claimed that the pandemic was on the wane but the Democrats were using the disease to hurt him politically. He tweeted on October 26: "We have made tremendous progress with the China Virus, but the Fake News refuses to talk about it this close to the Election. COVID, COVID,

COVID is being used by them, in total coordination, in order to change our great early election numbers. Should be an election law violation!"

By the end of 2020, there was no national evidence-based plan in place to combat the disease. More than 400,000 Americans had died of the disease, and one out of every thirteen had tested positive. New strains of the coronavirus began to spread, with Colorado reporting the first U.S. case of the variant strain that originated in the United Kingdom.

2020 Presidential Election

Unlike any previous president, Trump began his reelection campaign within weeks of his inauguration. As part of this "permanent campaign," he held numerous rallies and fundraisers throughout his presidency, including during his impeachment. On the campaign trail he repeatedly claimed that the only way he would lose the election was if it was rigged.

Due to the pandemic, as many as 100 million votes were cast by mail. This meant it took longer than normal for votes to be counted, especially in swing states. However, by November 7, Biden had crossed the winning threshold of 270 Electoral College votes, and major news outlets declared him the winner. In an election with the highest voter turnout since 1900, Trump became the first U.S. president since 1992 to lose a bid for a second term.

Without evidence, Trump's team claimed widespread voter fraud, suggesting that voting machines changed votes from Trump to Biden and that dead people were on the voter rolls. They went to court in six states but lost more than fifty legal challenges, including at the Supreme Court.

However, Trump refused to concede the race, even when the results were affirmed by the Electoral College. He called officials in swing states, pressuring them to overturn results. His administration also refused to work with Biden's transition team, making it difficult to access information about federal agencies. This was especially damaging amid the devastating health and economic crises plaguing the nation.

Washington Capitol Riots

On January 6, 2021, Vice President Pence arrived at Congress to certify the Electoral College results of the 2020 presidential election. While this is a largely ceremonial process, Pence had to resist Trump's request to upend the results.

While the count was taking place, Trump held a rally near the White House in protest. During a speech to his supporters, which included members of far-right groups such as the Proud Boys, Trump called for them to march on the Capitol, saying, "You have to show strength." As the crowd made its way there, pipe bombs were reported at both the Republican and the Democratic National Committee headquarters.

When thousands of protestors reached the barricades around the Capitol Building, they began to clash with the U.S. Capitol Police. As the crowd swelled, the police were overcome and the barricades were breached. Calls for support by the National Guard went unanswered, and rioters broke into the building at 2:00 p.m. As police clashed with the mob, Pence and members of Congress, who had just taken a recess, either evacuated or had to shelter in place. The mob outside the building grew more violent, attacking police, who responded with pepper spray and tear gas.

Supporters of President Donald J. Trump breach Capitol Hill during the certification of the Electoral College's vote on January 6, 2021.

Watching the news from the White House, Trump tweeted his support of the rioters while also calling Pence a traitor for certifying the election, which he continued to insist was stolen. After the D.C. National Guard arrived and order was restored, Trump tweeted, "These are the things and events that happen when a sacred landslide election victory is so unceremoniously & viciously stripped away from great patriots who have been badly & unfairly treated for so long." During the rampage, five people died, including a member of the Capitol Police force. That evening, Congress reconvened to complete the count.

To mitigate the chance he could incite further violence, Trump was banned from Twitter, as well as other social media platforms such as Facebook and Snapchat. Calls immediately began for Trump's second impeachment. On January 13, the House of Representatives approved one article of impeachment, charging him with inciting an insurrection. "Trump gravely endangered the security of the United States and its institutions of Government," the article of impeachment reads. "He threatened the integrity of the democratic system, interfered with the peaceful transition of power, and imperiled a coequal branch of Government. He thereby betrayed his trust as President, to the manifest injury of the people of the United States."

Refusing to stay for the inauguration, Trump left the White House the morning of January 20. His impeachment trial in the Senate for inciting an insurrection began after he left office. On February 13, 2021, the Senate voted 57–43 to convict Trump. However, they needed a two-thirds majority, so for the second time in thirteen months, Trump was acquitted.

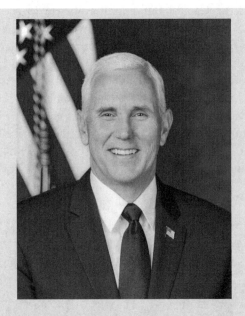

Michael R. Pence

"Mike is intensely loyal. That's a virtue. He has never uttered to me one syllable of disagreement with the president. And frankly, I admire him for that."

—former U.S. senator Jeff Flake

Vice President Mike Pence has repeatedly described himself as "a Christian, a conservative, and a Republican, in that order." This philosophy has shaped his entire career. From the time he became a born-again evangelical Christian at Hanover College, Pence has remained true to his faith and his belief in the Constitution.

Born in Columbus, Indiana, into a tight-knit Catholic family of six kids, Pence grew up a Democrat, even voting for Jimmy Carter in the 1980 presidential election. This changed when Ronald Reagan became president. "His ideals inspired me to leave the party of my youth and become a Republican like he did," Pence said at a speech at the Ronald Reagan Presidential Library. "His broad-shouldered leadership inspired my life."

After graduating from Indiana University McKinney School of Law in 1986, he went into private practice. In 1991, he joined the conservative-libertarian Indiana Policy Review Foundation and unsuccessfully ran twice for U.S. Congress. He then began a political talk radio show, which helped him tune in to the concerns of his potential constituents.

In 2000, Pence ran for Congress again at age forty and won. Known for his hardline conservative stance, he opposed the Bush administration's No Child Left Behind Act and the creation of Medicare Part D. He served as chairman of the House Republican Study Committee and as House Republican Conference chairman and focused on making government smaller and more effective while reducing spending. He led the government to the brink of a shutdown in 2011 in an attempt to defund Planned Parenthood. After being reelected five times, he decided in 2011 to run for governor of Indiana.

Focusing on tax cuts and job growth, Pence was elected in 2012. During his term as governor, his successes including signing into law a $1.1 billion tax cut and the state's first pre-K funding program. He also invested more than $800 million in new money for roads and bridges throughout the state known as the "Crossroads of America." His reputation took a hit when he signed the Religious Freedom Restoration Act, which allowed businesses to refuse service to same-sex couples. He also supported a controversial bill that prohibited abortions when the fetus had a disability, which was eventually ruled unconstitutional.

While Pence had initially supported Ted Cruz in the 2016 presidential election, he was clear about his support of Donald Trump when picked to be his running mate. "I think he is going to be a great president," Pence told reporters in Indianapolis in 2016. "I think he is someone who has connected with everyday Americans like no one since Ronald Reagan. I think he has spoken into the frustration and the longings of the American people as no one since the 40th president, and I think you're going to continue to see him do that."

While temperamentally different, Trump and Pence agreed on many key issues, including border security and enforcement of laws against undocumented immigrants, a strong national defense, opposing abortion, and the right to bear arms. At an address to the National Rifle Association in 2018, he said, "The best way to stop a bad guy with a gun is a good guy with a gun."

After their win, Pence moved to Washington, D.C., with his wife, Karen; their three children, Michael, Charlotte, and Audrey; two cats; and a rabbit named Marlon Bundo, which was the subject of a bestselling children's book.

During his time as vice president, Pence led the White House's response to the coronavirus pandemic, played a key role in staffing the federal government, and took the lead in rebuilding the nation's space program, including the creation of the Space Force, an extraplanetary military unit. Throughout Trump's rocky term, Pence remained stalwart and loyal, rarely breaking with the president's stance on issues, no matter how controversial.

This changed when Trump asked Pence to overturn the official confirmation of Joe Biden's electoral victory, which he refused to do. However, Pence also refused to invoke the 25th Amendment to remove Trump from power in the wake of the riots, causing Congress to seek impeachment instead.

President Donald Trump and Vice President Mike Pence during a campaign rally December 10, 2019, at Giant Center in Hershey, Pennsylvania.

Melania Trump

Melania Trump meets with students in the Kennedy Garden at the White House at her Be Best policy initiative rollout on May 7, 2018.

Born in 1970 in Novo Mesto, Slovenia, Melania Trump is the only first lady in nearly two hundred years to be born outside of the U.S. and the only one born in a communist country. She is also the first to be a naturalized U.S. citizen and to have English not be her first language.

After being signed at age eighteen to a Milan modeling agency, she began appearing in a number of high-profile ad campaigns. Melania's career as an international model took her all over the world, enabling her to be fluent in multiple languages. She met Donald Trump at New York Fashion Week in 1998, and seven years later, she became his third wife. Among the hundreds of guests at the reception at Mar-a-Lago were Bill and Hillary Clinton. The Trumps' son, Barron, was born in 2006, the same year Melania became a U.S. citizen.

Unlike her husband, Melania doesn't express her views often. This may be due in part to the press's reaction to her speech at the Republican National Convention. Several sentences were pulled from Michelle Obama's speech at the Democratic National Convention in 2008. The ensuing uproar was public and embarrassing, with her speechwriter saying the error was hers.

The press sought her views as an immigrant of her husband's strict immigration policies. She said they are focused on illegal immigrants. "It never crossed my mind to stay here without papers," she told *Harper's Bazaar*. "You follow the rules. You follow the law. Every few months you need to fly back to Europe and stamp your visa." In August 2018, Melania's parents, Viktor and Amalija Knavs, were granted U.S. citizenship.

In 2017, Melania unveiled her platform, "Be Best," which focused on children's well-being, fighting opioid abuse, and anti-bullying on social media. "As a mother and as first lady, it concerns me that in today's fast-paced and ever-connected world, children can be less prepared to express or manage their emotions and oftentimes turn to forms of destructive or addictive behavior such as bullying, drug addiction or even suicide," she said. "I feel strongly that as adults we can and should be best at educating our children about the importance of a healthy and balanced life."

In support of the initiative, Melania visited many schools and hospitals and undertook a multi-country tour of Africa. She also actively supports the Red Cross and Toys for Tots.

German chancellor Angela Merkel with Ivanka Trump during a roundtable discussion with business leaders in the Cabinet Room of the White House in Washington, D.C., on March 17, 2017.

Ivanka Trump

While many presidents have had family as unofficial advisors, few were government employees. Not true with Ivanka, Donald Trump's oldest daughter with his first wife, Ivana.

Not only did she serve as a quasi first lady when Melania chose to stay in New York until their son Barron finished the school year, but Ivanka was also officially hired as "First Daughter and Advisor to the President" in 2017. She was also made the head of the Office of Economic Initiatives and Entrepreneurship.

Since graduating from the Wharton School of Business at the University of Pennsylvania, Ivanka has spent most of her career in her father's orbit, including appearing as a judge on his shows *The Apprentice* and *Celebrity Apprentice*. As a vice president of the Trump Organization, she worked on several high-profile buildings and resorts, and she has launched her own jewelry, shoe, and apparel lines. Her business book *The Trump Card* was a *New York Times* bestseller. Her second book, *Women Who Work*, came out in 2017. When her father won the election, she separated from the business to be part of the administration.

During her father's administration, Ivanka worked with the president on the education and economic empowerment of women. She traveled the world to advance the White House's Women's Global Development and Prosperity Initiative and met with world leaders on various topics. As a mother of three, she was dismayed by the "zero tolerance" immigration policy, stating in 2018, "I am very vehemently against family separation and the separation of parents and children." She was a consistent supporter of family issues, including a child tax credit and paid family leave.

Ivanka's husband, Jared Kushner, also worked for the administration as a senior White House advisor. While neither was a registered Republican until March 2020, they were key components of the president's success.

President Donald Trump with his family and Vice President Mike Pence addressing his supporters after his stunning upset.

Against all odds, Donald Trump won the presidential election on November 9, 2016, beating out a stacked Republican primary field and a formidable opponent in Hillary Clinton. After an extremely close finish, Trump made the following speech at 3:00 AM in midtown Manhattan.

Excerpt from Trump's Victory Speech

[. . .]

Now it is time for America to bind the wounds of division, have to get together. To all Republicans and Democrats and independents across this nation, I say it is time for us to come together as one united people. It is time.

I pledge to every citizen of our land that I will be president for all Americans, and this is so important to me. For those who have chosen not to support me in the past, of which there were a few people, I'm reaching out to you for your guidance and your help so that we can work together and unify our great country.

As I've said from the beginning, ours was not a campaign but rather an incredible and great movement, made up of millions of hardworking men and women who love their country and want a better, brighter future for themselves and for their family. It is a movement comprised of Americans from all races, religions, backgrounds, and beliefs, who want and expect our government to serve the people, and serve the people it will.

Working together, we will begin the urgent task of rebuilding our nation and renewing the American dream. I've spent my entire life in business, looking at the untapped potential in projects and in people all over the world. That is now what I want to do for our country. Tremendous potential. I've gotten to know our country so well. Tremendous potential. It is going to be a beautiful thing. Every single American will have the opportunity to realize his or her fullest potential. The forgotten men and women of our country will be forgotten no longer.

We are going to fix our inner cities and rebuild our highways, bridges, tunnels, airports, schools, hospitals. We're going to rebuild our infrastructure, which will become, by the way, second to none, and we will put millions of our people to work as we rebuild it. We will also finally take care of our great veterans who have been so loyal, and I've gotten to know so many over this 18-month journey. The time I've spent with them during this campaign has been among my greatest honors. Our veterans are incredible people.

We will embark upon a project of national growth and renewal. I will harness the creative talents of our people, and we will call upon the best and brightest to leverage their tremendous talent for the benefit of all. It is going to happen. We have a great economic plan. We will double our growth and have the strongest economy anywhere in the world. At the same time, we will get along with all other nations willing to get along with us. . . . We will have great relationships. We expect to have great, great relationships. No dream is too big, no challenge is too great. Nothing we want for our future is beyond our reach.

America will no longer settle for anything less than the best. We must reclaim our country's destiny and dream big and bold and daring. We have to do that. We're going to dream of things for our country, and beautiful things and successful things once again.

I want to tell the world community that while we will always put America's interests first, we will deal fairly with everyone, with everyone. All people and all other nations. We will seek common ground, not hostility; partnership, not conflict.

[. . .]

And I can only say that while the campaign is over, our work on this movement is now really just beginning. We're going to get to work immediately for the American people, and we're going to be doing a job that hopefully [will make] you be so proud of your president. You will be so proud.

Again, it's my honor. It's an amazing evening. It's been an amazing two-year period, and I love this country. Thank you.

Joseph R. Biden Jr.

"He has brought change to Washington, but Washington hasn't changed him."

—*Barack Obama, August 2008, upon his selection of Joe Biden as his vice presidential running mate*

Forty-sixth president of the United States
2021–

Full name: *Joseph Robinette Biden Jr.*

Born: *November 20, 1942*

Parents: *Joseph Robinette Biden Sr. and Catherine Eugenia Biden (née Finnegan)*

Spouse: *Neilia Hunter Biden (July 28, 1942–December 18, 1972; m. August 27, 1966)*
Jill Tracy Biden (June 3, 1951– ; m. June 17, 1977)

Children: *Joseph R. [Beau] (1969–2015), Robert Hunter (1970–), Naomi Christina (1971–1972), Ashley Blazer (1981–)*

Religion: *Roman Catholic*

Education: *University of Delaware (B.A., 1965)*
Syracuse University, Syracuse, New York (J.D., 1968)

Occupations: *Lawyer, public defender, professor*

Government positions: *U.S. senator from Delaware, vice president of the United States*

Political party: *Democrat*

Dates as president: *January 20, 2021–*

Age upon taking office: *78*

The third time's the charm: After two unsuccessful presidential bids in 1988 and 2008, Joe Biden was finally the right man at the right time. Running on a ticket of decency, experience, and dignity, he was elected with more than 80 million votes, the most in presidential history. In January 2021, he returned to the White House, where he already spent eight years as vice president, and began to work with Congress, where he spent thirty-six years as a senator under eight presidents.

By his side was Kamala Harris, a running mate who balanced his experience the same way Biden did for President Obama. While they are of different generations, genders, and races and were raised on opposite coasts, both Biden and Harris had already spent decades in government fighting for the rights of all people.

Early Accomplishments

Joe Biden's road to the presidency ended in Pennsylvania, where his life also began. Joseph Robinette Biden Jr. was born November 20, 1942, in Scranton, into an Irish Catholic family, and grew up in a working-class neighborhood.

When he was in third grade, his family moved to

Wilmington, Delaware, where his father sold cars. Teased by classmates for his stutter, Biden practiced talking by holding pebbles in his mouth and planning out conversations. In high school, he played football and was elected class president.

Biden worked as an attorney at a firm in Wilmington, Delaware, before entering politics, after graduating with a J.D. from Syracuse University College of Law (following a B.A. from the University of Delaware). He was drafted for the Vietnam War but failed the physical because he had asthma.

Joe Biden in 1965 in the University of Delaware yearbook.

Timeline

1942: Born in Scranton, Pennsylvania
1965: Graduates from University of Delaware
1968: Graduates from Syracuse University
1973–2009: Serves as U.S. senator from Delaware
2009–2017: Serves as vice president of the United States
2020: Elected forty-sixth president of the United States

Politics and Tragedy

Biden's entrance into government came as a councilman in New Castle County, Delaware, from 1970 to 1972. He then ran for senator at the young age of twenty-nine against an incumbent Republican. In a campaign managed by his sister, Valerie Biden Owen, and staffed by his family and friends, Biden used his youth and energy to pull off a major political upset to defeat a veteran politician. He was one of the youngest people ever elected to the U.S. Senate.

Just one month after his election to the Senate, Biden's wife, Neilia Hunter, and thirteen-month-old daughter, Naomi, died in a collision with a tractor-trailer. The distraught father was sworn in at the Wilmington hospital bedsides of his two young sons, Beau and Hunter, who were also injured in the accident.

A young Beau, Ashley, and Hunter Biden.

As a widower with small children, he commuted daily by Amtrak between his home in Wilmington and downtown Washington, D.C. "I did it because I wanted to be able to kiss them goodnight and kiss them in the morning the next day," he later told a crowd at Yale. "But looking back on it, the truth be told, the real reason I went home every night was that I needed my children more than they needed me."

Joe Biden met Jill Jacobs on a blind date in 1975, and they wed two years later.

Together, they have one daughter, Ashley.

Decades in the Senate

Senator Joseph Biden, then chairman of the U.S. Senate Judiciary Committee, and Senator Ted Kennedy during hearings for Supreme Court nominee Clarence Thomas, 1991.

Biden's Senate career continued uninterrupted, with reelections in 1978, 1984, 1990, 1996, and 2002, even while he pursued the nomination for president in 1988. Throughout, he was known for working with senators across the aisle. "Joe has a good heart," said former Republican senator John Danforth. "He's got the temperament and the background to reach out and to work with all kinds of people."

During his tenure, Biden was chairman or ranking member of the Senate Judiciary Committee for sixteen years. He opposed the 1991 Gulf War and voted against the use of force to drive Iraq out of Kuwait. In 2002, he worked with Republican senator Richard G. Lugar to create a bipartisan bill to remove the purported weapons of mass destruction from Iraq without deposing its president, Saddam Hussein, but it failed to win the approval of the White House. Biden subsequently voted in favor of the invasion of Iraq, but later became one of Congress's harshest critics of the Bush administration's policies. He told Politico, "I regret my vote. The president did not level with us."

In 1994 he co-sponsored the Violence Against Women Act with Republican senator Orrin Hatch. The law provided $1.6 billion to investigate and prosecute violent crimes against women and allowed victims to sue their attackers in civil court.

During his twelve years on the Senate Foreign Relations Committee, he played a key role in the country's foreign policy, including in the areas of terrorism, post–Cold War Europe, and ending apartheid.

On the home front, Biden was strongly supportive of labor unions, civil rights leaders, and women's groups. He has been a champion of numerous crime and civil rights bills, and although he is Catholic, he supports a woman's right to choose.

Vice Presidency

Democratic presidential candidate Barack Obama joins his running mate, vice presidential candidate Joe Biden, following Biden's acceptance speech at the Democratic National Convention in Denver, Colorado, in 2008.

Biden's 2008 attempt to obtain the presidential nomination fizzled out early. After he finished fifth in the Iowa caucus, he returned to his work in the Senate. However, he soon found himself on Democratic nominee Barack Obama's shortlist for a running mate.

While other potential vice presidential nominees were chomping at the bit to learn their political fate in August 2008, Biden's mind was on the conflict between Russia and Georgia. Just days before his nomination was confirmed by Barack Obama, Biden was in Tbilisi,

Georgia, meeting with its president, Mikheil Saakashvili, to try to bring about a cease-fire.

By selecting Biden as his running mate, Barack Obama balanced his own qualifications with a veteran congressional insider. To any criticism of Obama's age, there was Biden's twenty-year seniority; of Obama's lack of experience, Biden's thirty-six years in the Senate as well as his strengths in foreign policy making. The two men also shared numerous positions, including a deep concern for civil rights and global AIDS prevention.

A few weeks before his inauguration, Biden appeared on *Larry King Live*, where he described his role as Barack Obama's vice president. When Obama offered him the vice presidency, Biden said, "I want to be there when you make every critical decision you make. I want to be in the room. Because I have a significant amount of experience. I'd like to be able to give my input. You're president. If you conclude my judgment is not the right judgment, I'll abide by that, but I want an opportunity to have an input."

On Inauguration Day 2009, Joe Biden became the first vice president of the United States to hail from Delaware and the first Roman Catholic to serve as VP. He was sworn in surrounded by his extended family and lifelong colleagues.

Obama and Biden immediately went to work on the financial crisis that faced the nation, implementing the president's Recovery Act. Biden helped oversee the massive plan, which had the goal of creating and saving millions of jobs, especially in the area of clean energy. It ended up being the most efficient government program in the country's history, with less than 1 percent in waste or fraud. This plan kicked off seventy-five uninterrupted months of job growth in the country.

Biden was also Obama's point man for U.S. diplomacy throughout the Western Hemisphere. He traveled repeatedly to Iraq, meeting with government officials and other leaders of the Iraqi people to monitor the country's progress and to offer assurances that the United States remained committed to helping Iraq become a stable, prosperous democracy. He also led the effort to bring home 150,000 troops from that country.

Biden's Gaffes

Biden had a reputation in the West Wing, as well as among the press and late-night comics, for loose talk—saying the wrong thing at the wrong time. As President Obama was signing the Affordable Care Act, which enabled more than 20 million people to get healthcare, a microphone caught Biden saying to the president, "This is a big f★★★★★★ deal." The gaffe was met more with laughter than with scowls. Senator Lindsey Graham said of the faux pas, "If there were no gaffes, there'd be no Joe."

But if Biden was gaffe-prone, he was also an effective advocate in the Oval Office. He was credited with persuading Obama to support gay marriage publicly. At a meeting of ProgressNow in Detroit, Arshad Hasan, the organization's executive director, introduced Biden, saying, "Those of us who hold marriage equality near and dear to our hearts and our homes, we know Joe Biden spoke first. I give Joe Biden credit for changing the dialogue in the White House."

Biden's Relationship with Obama

Biden with Obama before a campaign rally on September 7, 2012, in Portsmouth, New Hampshire.

When Biden was tapped to be Obama's running mate, they didn't have much of a relationship. "About six months in," Joe recalled, "the president looks at me and says, 'You know, Joe, you know what surprised me? That we've become such good friends.'" It surprised Biden as well. After eight years together in the White House, they were family.

In 2017, Obama surprised Biden with the Presidential Medal of Freedom, for his "faith in your fellow Americans, for your love of country, and for your lifetime of service that will endure through the generations." He went on to say, "To know Joe Biden is to know love without pretense, service without self-regard, and to live life fully."

Another Tragedy

In May 2015, Joe's family suffered another loss when Beau Biden lost his battle with brain cancer at age forty-six. The elder son and potential political heir to Joe, Beau was Delaware's attorney general and preparing for a run for governor when his health began to decline. In a statement released at Beau's death, Joe wrote: "Beau Biden was, quite simply, the finest man any of us have ever known." At the funeral, President Obama gave a moving eulogy, saying, "Joe, you are my brother."

While he spent the summer grieving, Biden also had to consider whether or not he would run for president in 2016. In September 2015, he appeared on *The Late Show with Stephen Colbert*, saying, "I don't think any man or woman should run for president unless, number one, they know exactly why they would want to be president, and, two, they can look at the folks out there and say, 'I promise you, you have my whole heart, my whole soul, my energy, and my passion to do this.' And I'd be lying if I said that I knew that I was there."

In October 2015, Biden made a formal decision not to run for president in 2016. He instead threw his support behind Hillary Clinton, who described him in a tweet as "a good friend and a great man. Today and always, inspired by his optimism and commitment to change the world for the better." While the polls predicted Clinton would win, she lost the presidential race to Donald Trump.

One More Run

Trump and Biden exchanging points during the first 2020 presidential debate in Cleveland, Ohio, on Tuesday, September 29, 2020.

On April 25, 2019, Biden announced his candidacy for president of the United States. In a video he released with the announcement, he cited Trump's comment that there were "very fine people on both sides" at the white supremacist rally in Charlottesville as the impetus, saying, "in that moment, I knew the threat to this nation was unlike any I had ever seen in my lifetime." He framed the 2020 election as a battle for the soul of this nation.

Biden's candidacy also focused on the need to rebuild the country's middle class and a call for unity. This message gained resonance in 2020 as the country confronted the pandemic, an economic crisis, urgent calls for racial justice, and the threat of climate change.

While he had high name recognition, Biden was not a front-runner until a victory in the South Carolina primary. By April 2020, he had pulled ahead of Senator Bernie Sanders to become the presumptive Democratic presidential nominee. In August, it became official, and he announced that Senator Kamala Harris would be his vice presidential nominee.

During the contentious debates with President Trump, they sparred about coronavirus, healthcare, a $15 federal minimum wage, and Trump's suspect personal finances, with Biden saying, "I released all my tax returns—22 years, go look at them. You have not released

President-elect Joe Biden with his wife, Jill Biden, wave to supporters on Saturday, November 7, 2020, at the Chase Center in Wilmington, Delaware, after he defeated Donald Trump to become 46th president of the United States.

a single solitary year of your tax return. What are you hiding? Why are you unwilling?"

Polls in the days leading up to the election had Biden leading by a comfortable margin. However, the polls had been wrong in the 2016 election. Early returns showed Trump leading in several key states. But as mail-in ballots trickled in and were counted, Biden pulled ahead in key states, including Pennsylvania, whose twenty electoral college votes put Biden above the 270 he needed to become president. While states were still certifying the results, a number of news agencies called the race for Biden.

On December 14, the Electoral College declared Biden the winner. However, Trump still refused to concede and filed more than sixty lawsuits challenging election results, almost all of which were dismissed or dropped. This includes losing twice at the Supreme Court level.

A handful of agencies, such as the Department of Defense and the Office of Management and Budget, refused to work with Biden's transition team. So the team figured out ways to move ahead without help from the Trump administration, including interviewing more than 7,500 people to fill necessary positions during the middle of a massive health crisis.

Insurrection, Impeachment, Inauguration

Like the rest of the nation, Joe Biden watched helplessly on January 6 as Trump incited his followers to attack the Capitol Building, his workplace for thirty-six years. Biden addressed the nation that day from Wilmington, Delaware. Calling it an "unprecedented assault on our democracy," Biden said the Trump-flag-toting rioters "weren't protesters. Don't dare call them protesters. They were a riotous mob, insurrectionists, domestic terrorists. It's that basic. It's that simple," Biden said.

While Congress began Trump's impeachment process in the wake of the siege, Biden's team began readying for his inauguration. With restrictions caused by both the threat of violence and the pandemic, there were few crowds outside of the tens of thousands National Guard called in to keep peace during the transition of power. In place of people, the National Mall was filled with flags that snapped in the stiff breeze. The audience heard songs, speeches, and a reading by National Youth Poet Laureate Amanda Gorman, whose stunning poem "The Hill We Climb" is a tribute to the nation's possibility: "We close the divide because we know, to put our future first, we must first put our differences aside."

Biden signing one of the seventeen executive orders he signed on Inauguration Day, Wednesday, January 20, 2021, in the Oval Office of the White House.

Biden's Presidential Victory Speech

Excerpt from Biden's Victory Speech

On the steps of the Capitol, where two weeks before rioters had clashed with police, Kamala Harris was sworn in by Supreme Court Justice Sonia Sotomayor as the forty-ninth vice president of the United States. Minutes later, Biden was sworn in as the forty-sixth president of the United States. He used his inaugural address to recognize the damage caused by the riots and as a call the nation to recognize the magnitude of the pandemic, to fight racial injustice, to renew focus on environmental issues, and to fight extremism.

President Biden's Inaugural Address

[...]

To overcome these challenges—to restore the soul and to secure the future of America—requires more than words.

It requires that most elusive of things in a democracy:

Unity.

Unity.

In another January in Washington, on New Year's Day 1863, Abraham Lincoln signed the Emancipation Proclamation.

When he put pen to paper, the president said, "If my name ever goes down into history it will be for this act and my whole soul is in it."

My whole soul is in it.

Today, on this January day, my whole soul is in this:

Bringing America together.

Uniting our people.

And uniting our nation.

I ask every American to join me in this cause.

Uniting to fight the common foes we face:

Anger, resentment, hatred.

Extremism, lawlessness, violence.

Disease, joblessness, hopelessness.

With unity we can do great things. Important things.

We can right wrongs.

We can put people to work in good jobs.

We can teach our children in safe schools.

We can overcome this deadly virus.

We can reward work, rebuild the middle class, and make health care secure for all.

We can deliver racial justice.

We can make America, once again, the leading force for good in the world.

I know speaking of unity can sound to some like a foolish fantasy.

I know the forces that divide us are deep and they are real.

But I also know they are not new.

Our history has been a constant struggle between the American ideal that we are all created equal and the harsh, ugly reality that racism, nativism, fear, and demonization have long torn us apart.

The battle is perennial.

Victory is never assured.

Through the Civil War, the Great Depression, World War, 9/11, through struggle, sacrifice, and setbacks, our "better angels" have always prevailed.

In each of these moments, enough of us came together to carry all of us forward.

And, we can do so now.

History, faith, and reason show the way, the way of unity.

We can see each other not as adversaries but as neighbors.

We can treat each other with dignity and respect.

We can join forces, stop the shouting, and lower the temperature.

For without unity, there is no peace, only bitterness and fury.

No progress, only exhausting outrage.

No nation, only a state of chaos.

This is our historic moment of crisis and challenge, and unity is the path forward.

And, we must meet this moment as the United States of America.

If we do that, I guarantee you, we will not fail.

We have never, ever, ever failed in America when we have acted together.

And so today, at this time and in this place, let us start afresh.

All of us.

Let us listen to one another.

Hear one another.

See one another.

Show respect to one another.

Politics need not be a raging fire destroying everything in its path.

Every disagreement doesn't have to be a cause for total war.

And, we must reject a culture in which facts themselves are manipulated and even manufactured.

My fellow Americans, we have to be different than this.

America has to be better than this.

And, I believe America is better than this.

Just look around.

Here we stand, in the shadow of a Capitol dome that was completed amid the Civil War, when the Union itself hung in the balance.

Yet we endured and we prevailed.

Here we stand looking out to the great Mall where Dr. King spoke of his dream.

Here we stand, where 108 years ago at another inaugural, thousands of protestors tried to block brave women from marching for the right to vote.

Today, we mark the swearing-in of the first woman in American history elected to national office—Vice President Kamala Harris.

Don't tell me things can't change.

Here we stand across the Potomac from Arlington National Cemetery, where heroes who gave the last full measure of devotion rest in eternal peace.

And here we stand, just days after a riotous mob thought they could use violence to silence the will of the people, to stop the work of our democracy, and to drive us from this sacred ground.

That did not happen.

It will never happen.

Not today.

Not tomorrow.

Not ever.

To all those who supported our campaign I am humbled by the faith you have placed in us.

To all those who did not support us, let me say this: Hear me out as we move forward. Take a measure of me and my heart.

And if you still disagree, so be it.

That's democracy. That's America. The right to dissent peaceably, within the guardrails of our Republic, is perhaps our nation's greatest strength.

Yet hear me clearly: Disagreement must not lead to disunion.

And I pledge this to you: I will be a president for all Americans.

I will fight as hard for those who did not support me as for those who did.

Many centuries ago, Saint Augustine, a saint of my church, wrote that a people was a multitude defined by the common objects of their love.

What are the common objects we love that define us as Americans?

I think I know.

Opportunity.

Security.

Liberty.

Dignity.

Respect.

Honor.

And, yes, the truth.

Recent weeks and months have taught us a painful lesson.

There is truth and there are lies.

Lies told for power and for profit.

And each of us has a duty and responsibility, as citizens, as Americans, and especially as leaders—leaders who have pledged to honor our Constitution and protect our nation—to defend the truth and to defeat the lies.

I understand that many Americans view the future with some fear and trepidation.

I understand they worry about their jobs, about taking care of their families, about what comes next.

I get it.

But the answer is not to turn inward, to retreat into competing factions, distrusting those who don't look like you do, or worship the way you do, or don't get their news from the same sources you do.

We must end this uncivil war that pits red against blue, rural versus urban, conservative versus liberal.

We can do this if we open our souls instead of hardening our hearts.

If we show a little tolerance and humility.

If we're willing to stand in the other person's shoes just for a moment.

Because here is the thing about life: There is no accounting for what fate will deal you.

There are some days when we need a hand.

There are other days when we're called on to lend one.

That is how we must be with one another.

And, if we are this way, our country will be stronger, more prosperous, more ready for the future.

My fellow Americans, in the work ahead of us, we will need each other.

We will need all our strength to persevere through this dark winter.

We are entering what may well be the toughest and deadliest period of the virus.

We must set aside the politics and finally face this pandemic as one nation.

I promise you this: as the Bible says weeping may endure for a night but joy cometh in the morning.

We will get through this, together.

The world is watching today.

So here is my message to those beyond our borders: America has been tested and we have come out stronger for it.

We will repair our alliances and engage with the world once again.

Not to meet yesterday's challenges, but today's and tomorrow's.

We will lead not merely by the example of our power but by the power of our example.

We will be a strong and trusted partner for peace, progress, and security.

We have been through so much in this nation.

And, in my first act as president, I would like to ask you to join me in a moment of silent prayer to remember all those we lost this past year to the pandemic.

To those 400,000 fellow Americans—mothers and fathers, husbands and wives, sons and daughters, friends, neighbors, and co-workers.

We will honor them by becoming the people and nation we know we can and should be.

Let us say a silent prayer for those who lost their lives, for those they left behind, and for our country.

Amen.

This is a time of testing.

We face an attack on democracy and on truth.

A raging virus.

Growing inequity.

The sting of systemic racism.

A climate in crisis.

America's role in the world.

Any one of these would be enough to challenge us in profound ways.

But the fact is we face them all at once, presenting this nation with the gravest of responsibilities.

Now we must step up.

All of us.

It is a time for boldness, for there is so much to do.

And, this is certain.

We will be judged, you and I, for how we resolve the cascading crises of our era.

Will we rise to the occasion?

Will we master this rare and difficult hour?

Will we meet our obligations and pass along a new and better world for our children?

I believe we must and I believe we will.

[. . .]

Election Results 2020

Presidential/Vice Presidential Candidates	Popular Votes	Electoral Votes
Joe Biden/Kamala Harris	81,283,485	306
Donald Trump/Mike Pence	74,223,744	232

More than 158 million votes were cast, with Biden winning more than 80 million votes, both historical highs.

"I pledge to be a president who seeks not to divide but unify, who doesn't see red states and blue states, only sees the United States. And who will work with all my heart to win the confidence of the whole people. For that is what America is about: the people."

—*Joe Biden victory speech*

Kamala D. Harris

Kamala Harris's life was filled with firsts. After completing two terms as the district attorney of San Francisco, she was the first Black person and the first woman to serve as California's attorney general. In 2017, she was sworn in as the first South Asian American senator in history. And she is the first woman, Black person, and South Asian American to become vice president. Even her husband, Doug Emhoff, has a few firsts, as the US's first second gentleman as well as first Jewish second spouse.

While she might not have imagined the vice presidency, Harris grew up aware of the importance of breaking new ground. "My mother would look at me and she'd say, 'Kamala, you may be the first to do many things, but make sure you are not the last,'" Harris said during a talk at Spelman College. "That's why breaking those barriers is worth it. As much as anything else, it is also to create that path for those who will come after us."

Growing up in Oakland, California, Harris learned from her mom, Shyamala, how to advocate for herself and those less fortunate. Her mom immigrated from India to receive her doctorate in nutrition and endocrinology at the University of California, Berkeley, and then became a breast cancer researcher. At a protest, she met Donald Harris, an immigrant from Jamaica, whom she married. After their divorce in the early 1970s, she continued to bring Kamala and her sister, Maya, to rallies for racial equality.

At the 2020 Democratic National Convention, Harris noted how her mother's moral code shaped her. "My parents would bring me to protests strapped tightly in my stroller, and my mother, Shyamala, raised my sister, Maya, and me to believe that it was up to us and every generation of Americans to keep on marching," Harris said. "She'd tell us 'Don't sit around and complain about things; do something.' So I did something. I devoted my life to making real the words carved in the United States Supreme Court: Equal justice under law."

This upbringing was evidenced in Harris's choice, after getting her undergraduate degree from Howard University and a law degree from the University of California, Hastings, to begin her career in the Alameda County District Attorney's office. Her rise from district attorney of San Francisco to California's attorney general to U.S. senator included working to protect those hit by the foreclosure crisis, fighting for marriage equality and increased wages for working people, addressing the substance abuse epidemic, and working to reform the criminal justice system. As a senator, she served on the Select Committee on Intelligence, the Homeland Security and Government Affairs Committee, and the Senate Judiciary Committee. She made a run for the presidency in 2020 before dropping out.

"At every step of the way, I've been guided by the words I spoke from the first time I stood in a courtroom: Kamala Harris, for the people," she said during her acceptance speech to become Joe Biden's vice president. "I've fought for children and survivors of sexual assault. I've fought against transnational gangs. I took on the biggest banks and helped take down one of the biggest for-profit colleges. I know a predator when I see one."

Harris's role as vice president has yet to be defined, but she and Biden have both discussed a hands-on model, as the "first and last person in the room" during any major decision.

Vice President Harris at the Pride Parade in San Francisco, California.

A

Photography Credits

The photographs on the following pages are courtesy of AP/Wide World Photos: pp. 475–479; 511; 513; 522, bottom right; 537, bottom right; 539; 540, top left, bottom right; 545, bottom left, bottom right; 547; 548, top left; 555, bottom right; 556; 557, bottom right; 558; 559, top left, top right; 563, bottom right; 564–565; 567; 575; 577, top, bottom; 579, top, bottom; 580–581; 582, top; 583; 584, top; 585, top, bottom; 587, bottom; 589–590; 596–599; 600, bottom; 601, top; 603–604; 607; 609; 611; 617–621; 623; 625, bottom; 626, bottom; 627; 637, top; 638–640; 642; 644–646; 647, top; 649, bottom; 650; 655; 657, top; 658–660; 662, bottom; 663, top left, top right; 664, top right, bottom left; 666; 668–669; 673; 674, left, bottom right; 675–676; 679–680; 681, bottom right; 683, top; 684; 685, top; 686; 693; 694, right, center; 695; 696, top; 697–700; 701, top; 702, bottom; 703; 711; 712, right; 713–714; 717–719; 721, bottom; 725; 727; 730; 735–736; 737, bottom left, top; 739; 744–749; 751–752; 756; 759–772. The photographs on the following pages are courtesy of Alamy: 793–800, 805–809. All other photographs are courtesy of the Gale Group, www.whitehouse.gov, and the editor's personal collection.